Was Ireland Conquered?

Was Ireland Conquered?

International Law and the Irish Question

Anthony Carty

LONDON • CHICAGO, ILLINOIS

First published 1996 by Pluto Press
345 Archway Road, London N6 5AA
and 1436 West Randolph, Chicago, Illinois 60607, USA

British Library Cataloguing in Publication Data
A catalogue record for this book is available from the British Library

ISBN 0 7453 0325 0 hbk

Library of Congress Cataloging in Publication Data
Carty, Anthony.
Was Ireland conquered? / Anthony Carty.
p. cm.
Includes bibliographical references and index.
ISBN 0–7453–0325–0
1. Conquest, Right of. 2. Self-determination, National—Ireland—History. 3. Territory, National—Ireland—History. 4. Ireland—History—Autonomy and independence movements. I. Title.
JX4093.C37 1996
320.9415—dc20 96–26360
CIP

Designed and produced for Pluto Press by
Chase Production Services
Typeset from disk by Stanford DTP Services
Printed in the EC by J.W. Arrowsmith Ltd, Bristol

Contents

Preface

I was born in Belfast and after living my early childhood in Dublin I went to Queen's University Belfast to read law. After my undergraduate studies I left Ireland to make a career as an international lawyer, studying in England, France and Germany, before returning to Scotland. I have lived most of my professional life in Scotland. While I cultivate very close European ties, especially with France and Germany, I have very little contact with Ireland, either North or South. I am not and never have been a member of any Irish or Northern Irish political association and I have a minimum of contact with the country.

Despite the distance of my ties with Ireland, I have felt increasingly, since the end of the 1980s, that the continuing tragedy of Northern Ireland needed a systematic treatment from an international law perspective. While I come from within what is in some circles known as the 'Minority Community' in Northern Ireland, I have spent much more of my life in Scotland and this has probably influenced my own perspective, particularly in Chapter 5 of this book.

I see the methodology of the book as firmly within the context of numerous other writings of my own on international law since the mid-1980s. I believe that international law is a law of peoples and not simply a law of states. The international lawyer must look directly to the people affected by political processes and not regard them as pawns to be played with by states and their officials operating behind closed doors. Legal obligation is based upon consent and consent is not a matter of 'signing a sheet of paper', but rather, of having one's identity respected.

While I cultivate close ties with the French and German Societies of International Law, this book is a solitary undertaking. The subject of Northern Ireland is unpalatable to very many people and I am conscious that in undertaking to address it, I cannot expect support and sympathy from the profession. There are no acknowledgements in this Preface. I have not consulted anyone. At the same time the work is written in what I regard as the proper spirit of the *academic* international lawyer. I am not whispering paid advice in the ears of my clients. I am expressing independent and unsolicited opinions which are not intended to please anyone.

Anthony Carty
University of Derby
April 1996

CHAPTER 1

The General International Law Framework and its Applicability to Ireland

The Classical Law of Conquest

Classical international law is assumed to operate with concepts of statehood, territorial sovereignty and effectiveness and, especially, the key concept of conquest. The latter concept is so central because statehood simply means the capacity to exercise effective control over a specific population and territory. The traditional image of a population is that it submits to effective, not necessarily democratic, government control. It is assumed that at some time or other (preferably in a time immemorial), a political authority has established itself, which has subsequently become unquestioned.[1] Hence the standard English-American text on international law until at least the 1920s, Wheaton's *Elements of International Law*, speaks of the identity of the state in terms of the continued habitual obedience of its members.[2] This is supposedly the case for every major European power. Spain reconquered Granada, England was taken by the Normans, Russia arose out of the struggles of Moscovy, and so on.[3]

A further feature of international legal society which appears to reinforce the above argument is that there is no world sovereign capable of conclusively resolving conflicts of legal opinion in international society. Hence where two or more parties are unable to agree with each other, the final recourse is still only the use of force and the international community is unable to undo the will of whoever succeeds in imposing their will. The notion that states or other parties cannot be compelled to submit their disputes to an international tribunal has as its corollary the acceptance of the outcome of an armed conflict over the matter, that is, in effect, a conquest.

Notwithstanding this, there has never been an historical consensus accepting that conquest is a source of definitive legal title to territory in international law. The standard classical study demonstrates that from the Middle Ages and into early modern times, the doctrine of the just war, put forward by the canonists, maintained that the use of force could only be for good cause, and, quite obviously, force could be used to resist force which was not employed for a good cause. This did not solve the problem: who decides what is a good cause? Despite the loss of authority of the canonist tradition after the Reformation, and the increased acceptance of the dimension of subjectivity in international conflicts, there was not a consensus of states' international law traditions accepting the language of a right of conquest. This did enjoy a certain acceptance in Britain, Prussia (later Germany) and the United States, but the notion that force could only be used in a just cause continued to be prevalent in many juridical traditions, particularly France. There it was strengthed by the ethos of the French Revoution which called for governments based upon the consent of populations.[4]

The first leading writer to accept the place for conquest in international law had been Vattel, a Swiss author, coming to exercise influence after the middle of the eighteenth century. He was especially taken up by English and American writers in the course of the nineteenth century.[5] However, this apparent consolidation of the right of conquest by the author, taken to have definitively disposed of the traditional canonist tradition of the just war (that is, Vattel), was accompanied immediately by an, as it were, modern doctrine of just war arising out of the French Revolution. MacMahon quotes the Abbé de Malby:

> arms, of themselves, give no title; they suppose an anterior one, and it is to try this contested right that war is waged ... if conquests by their nature form a legitimate right of possession to the conqueror, it is indifferent whether the war be undertaken on just or unjust grounds.[6]

So the arguments on both sides have a logical force. If conquest alone is an adequate title to territory, it can be no more than an invitation for the defeated to reconquer the same territory. Title to territory by conquest therefore signifies no more than a truce, in which the defeated and exhausted party bides its time until it has recovered its strength. At the same time, it does not help very much, in the anarchic state of international society, to invoke concepts of just conflict. When each party considers itself in the right, the outcome is left to be resolved through the use of force. So, one comes, either way, full circle.

The uncertainty surrounding the status of conquest has increased in the twentieth century, indicating the reversal of apparently well-established historical precedents. Wheaton could confidently conclude his comment on the place of conquest with the remarks:

> the general consent of mankind has established the principle, that long and uninterrupted possession by one nation excludes the claim of every other. Whether this general consent be

> considered as an implied contract, or as positive law, all nations are equally bound by it; since all are parties to it; since none can safely disregard it without impugning its own title to its possessions; and since it is founded upon mutual utility, and tends to promote the general welfare of mankind.[7]

It is precisely this point which the standard modern treatise on conquest disputed. Following a quotation of a part of the above text, McMahon notes, in turn: 'Within the present generation the principle of conquest as a legal mode of acquisition of territory or sovereignty has been repudiated in at least two leading instances, namely the re-emergence of the Polish nation and the establishment of the free and independent state of Eire.'[8]

This is not to argue a Whig view of the progressive development of international law. It appears to be marked at present not so much by tidy logical circles but by vicious circles where the subjectivity of international legal relations leads to paralysis. In his study *The Paralysis of International Institutions*, Istvan Bibo referred in 1976 to the increasing number of unresolved international disputes.[9] The subjectivity does not simply extend to differences of opinion between two parties in individual cases, but is rather systemic and covers the very foundations of the so-called international legal order. The principle of the self-determination of peoples is readily asserted but it is not supposed to contravene the principle of the inviolability of the territorial integrity of states.[10] So it is correct of Bibo to complain that

> [I]t is not possible to give definite answers in deciding what are the desirable conditions or the right directions for nation-forming, or which of the conflicting aspirations are the right ones; whether a large, comprehensive unit is better than a smaller, more homogeneous one; whether historical claims are more desirable than ethnic or linguistic ones.[11]

It is common, notes Bibo, writing in the 1970s, for discussions of these problems to be 'conducted within the rigid limits of declared power politics, unconditional demands, moral admonitions'. Modern diplomatic negotiations are characterised by an icy politeness alternating with outbursts of appalling discourtesy.[12] However difficult it may be to make generalisations about the quality of international negotiations, it remains the case that international law has not developed any conceptual framework to bring it beyond the statement of completely contradictory positions on the questions of self-determination of peoples and the territorial sovereignty of existing states.[13]

Democracy and International Law

At the same time there has developed an uncertain rhetoric about the importance of democracy in international legal relations. Taken in absolute terms, a principle of democracy would mean that no population could be transferred from one jurisdiction to another without its consent. Indeed, no population could continue to be held within a territorial boundary without its consent. Democracy should entail an unlimited right of unspecified numbers of people to move between national jurisdictions. Stated in these terms it can safely be said that the principle has no influence on the conduct of international relations. However, in a much more modified form the principle can mean that no population or section thereof may be transferred from the jurisdiction of one state to that of another without its consent. The application of this principle is very uneven, but it has been advocated since the French Revolution. It was applied by France and Sardinia/Italy to determine aspects of their common frontier in 1860 (but not by Prussia with respect to its border with France in 1871), and by the Allies to determine Germany's boundaries with Poland after 1918.

The concept of consent is not in any form, modified or otherwise, an agreed and effectively implemented norm of international law. This is because it does not mean anything in the absence of a definite subject which might exercise democratic rights. Majorities contain minorities at whatever level one wishes to look at them. The principle of the consent of the majority can only be made operational when one adds to it an ethnic or historical principle which allows a determination of the level of focus. The people of Ireland are a minority within the British Isles; the British and Irish are a minority within the European Union; the Northern Irish Protestants are a minority within Ireland, and, finally, the Catholics are a minority within Northern Ireland.

International law has no conventional, that is, international treaty, rules on the rights of minorities; the drafts which do exist significantly fail to define the concept of minority. The so-called evolving international law on the rights of minorities merely purports to attach certain rights and duties to *minorities as such*. That is to say it accepts the existing state structures and assumes that, within these, certain groups with particular characteristics find themselves as minorities. The law then endeavours to protect these.[14] While this enterprise is constructive it does nothing to resolve disputes where groups prefer to consider themselves as misplaced parts of majority groups.

The rhetoric of democracy in international law does nothing to inform the observer as to when democracy will be effectively applied by states *as a matter of legal conviction*. The conceptual framework of international law supposes that its main source is general customary law, that is, a consistent practice of a general nature which states follow because they consider that they are required to do so.[15] It will prove a decisive objection to the existence of a rule of law, that the practice of states with respect to the application of a principle has been inconsistent, or, simply, that the same practice has been too sparse. Whether one thinks of the democratic drawing of boundaries, rights of secession, or, as is most usually the case, a so-called democratic right of governance,[16] the principle of democracy will yield nothing in the event of a border dispute in which there are 'minorities' on either or both sides. However, the analyst, whether lawyer or political scientist, has to be alert to the use to which the rhetoric of democracy is being put in a particular case.

Colonialism and International Law

A very major deficiency in the doctrinal analysis of international law is that no systematic undertaking is usually offered of the influence of colonialism in the development of the basic conceptual framework of the subject. This criticism applies, above all, to the so-called topic of *methods of acquisition of territory*. The centrality of colonialism could not be clearer in the sweeping statement, now quoted several times in part, by Wheaton on the place of conquest:

> their claim [that is of the European powers] to the possessions held by them in the New World, discovered by Columbus and other adventurers, and to the territories which they have acquired on the continents of Africa and Asia, was originally derived from discovery, or conquest and colonization, and has since been confirmed in the same manner, by positive compact.[17]

Most of even the modern legal discussion and jurisprudence concerning the acquisition of territory has to do with territory which was regarded as marginal, remote territory, that is, outside Europe.[18]

What is not specifically highlighted in British international law doctrine is the *historical specificity* of the so-called law of conquest as taken from the last unabashed British imperial enterprise, the Boer War between Great Britain and the Orange Free State and the Transvaal. The *West Rand Central Gold Mining Co. Ltd* v. *Rex*[19] is a 'leading case' on the legal effects of conquest, in this case taken as an example of an international legal institution or concept, in English municipal law.[20] However no question is asked, at the time of the war or now, as to whether such cases belong in the contemporary repertoire of the international lawyer. In the United

States the role of conquest in constituting state-identity is probably even more fundamental – hence making it even less surprising, if that is possible, that its place is not questioned. Quite apart from the colonial escapades against Mexico and Spain in the course of the nineteenth century, there is the question of the very existence of the United States. McMahon suggests the deep-rooted place of conquest in the American concept of international law in considering the reflections of the nineteenth-century English international lawyer Lord Phillimore. The fact of conquest loomed so large in the decisions of the Supreme Court of the United States. After pointing out the quasi-international parallel between the States of the Union and the family of nations, Phillimore indicated that a cardinal maxim of the jurisprudence of 'the system under which the United States were settled has been that of converting the *discovery* of the country into *conquest*; and the property of the great mass of the community originates in this principle'.[21]

What is really needed for an understanding of the normative aspects of territorial conflicts which are a left-over of colonial territorial expansion, is a focus on how legal relations between the colonising power and the so-called *natives* were understood, particularly in the terms of the colonisers and their attitude to the colonists. How did they justify their conduct to themselves and to one another? (Assuming that they tried to.)

There is a considerable academic literature on this subject, but it is not to be found within the remit of international law scholarship. It is remarkable that, in the sixteenth and seventeenth centuries, international law doctrine did not provide support for the seizure of so-called native lands by Western colonial powers. Nor was it thought to have done so. In a leading review of the law of colonial expansion, written in the 1920s when expansion was at its peak but also on the verge of decline, the position is presented very distinctly. Grotius, the greatest seventeenth-century international lawyer, often seen as the founder of the discipline, supported his greatest sixteenth-century predecessor, Vitoria, in maintaining that the Spaniards had no right to take the Indians' territory.[22] In discussing the so-called concept of occupation as a means of acquiring territory, Pufendorf maintained, writing in 1672, that 'since every man is, by nature, equal to every man, and consequently not subject to the dominion of others, therefore this bare seizing by force is not enough to found a lawful sovereignty over men, but must be attended with some other title'.[23]

This is a reaffirmation of the supremacy of a just war doctrine over an unrestricted right of conquest. Indeed, even at the end of the eighteenth and begining of the nineteenth century, leading legal authorities continued to maintain that 'No nation is authorized by its qualities, whatever they are, notably not by a higher degree of culture, to take from another nation its property, even from savages and nomads.'[24] The argument continued to be, especially in the French tradition, that any other position was merely an affirmation that might was right.[25]

Once again, as with the concepts of just war and conquest, the Anglo-American approaches have been different. Their view, understandably, was simply to regard the Spanish acquisitions in what is now Latin America as conquests.[26] Blackstone, the greatest English constitutionalist of the eighteenth century, considered that American plantations were acquired either by right of conquest or cession.[27] Indeed, in the nineteenth century the argument was put more strongly by Westlake, Hall, Lawrence and Oppenheim, that any land occupied by entities below the level of organisation of the civilised state, could simply be occupied, without even having recourse to the concept of conquest.[28]

Here, despite the scarcity of evidence in Anglo-American legal doctrine justifying the former institution of conquest, it is possible to decipher or delineate what were underlying ideological justifications for their approach, justifications which it is possible to bring back to the practice of conquest. Underlying the approach is a rejection of the principle of the universality of mankind, a denial of human equality and a conviction of the hierarchy of the races. This does not find its way into orthodox, mainstream international law texts, but this is precisely because colonial relations were seen as beyond the law except in so far as other European powers were concerned. Indeed, the Anglo-American practice was to consider so-called 'natives' as not worthy of *conquest*: they thought it more appropriate to speak of *occupancy* of lands where the presence of these 'natives' was not worthy of mention. The following remarks of Justice Story, in the nineteenth century, were intended by him as a global explanation of the colonial experience, but they apply directly to the English practice beginning with Elizabeth I:

> The title of the Indians was not treated as a right of property and dominion, but as a right of mere occupancy. As infidels, heathens and savages, they were not allowed to possess the prerogatives belonging to absolute, sovereign, and independent nations. The territory over which they wandered, and which they used for their temporary and fugitive purposes, was, in respect to Christians, deemed as if it were inhabited only by brute animals. There is not a single grant from the British crown, from the earliest of Elizabeth down to the latest of George the Second, that affects to look to any title except that founded on discovery. Conquest or cession is not once alluded to.[29]

Lindley is determined to argue that the Anglo-American practice and the opinion informing it were not so nihilistic concerning the rights or even existence of 'natives'. There are many passages where writers appear to recognise that the trouble has to be taken to repress and conquer recalcitrant natives. However, he concludes this argument with a further citation of another American judge and jurist as prominent as Story, which serves to show that the fundamental point concerns not conceptual differences between different types of positive international institutions for acquiring territory, but rather the fact of the supreme superiority of one racial group over another, resulting in the latter's complete rightlessness. As Chancellor Kent wrote, 'The Indians have only a right of occupancy and the United States possess the legal title, subject to that occupancy, and with an absolute and exclusive right to extinguish the Indian title of occupancy, whether by conquest or purchase.'[30]

The conclusions to be drawn from this analysis of colonialism and international law are several. There is a considerable difficulty for the international lawyer to assess the significance of legal doctrine alongside the actual practice of states. However, it seems clear that there was never a consensus which allowed that it was justified, or, alternatively, that it did not require justification to seize the lands of so-called uncivilised or otherwise politically underdeveloped peoples. The ethos of a common humanity found expression in doctrines of just war which were to be applied just as much to non-European people as to those of European origin. If this principle was not applied in practice, the derogation was no more justified for that. There was no consensus that somehow international law accepted completed conquests as legal. This is not to say that conquests were not frequent, widespread and militarily decisive. However, Western legal conscience never found anything approaching a unanimous agreement that what had occurred could be given a clear legal justification. In this sense it was part of Western history which remained in a form of legal limbo.

At the same time, it is possible to find clearly stated in the Anglo-American constitutional tradition an explicit doctrine of racial supremacy which puts quite simply at jeopardy the very existence of so-called native or Indian peoples. It is significant that one speaks here of constitutional and not international law tradition. The statement of position is not even intended to serve an ideological function because there is no common humanity to whom an argument needs to be addressed. The specifically English and American constitutional traditions regard it as evident that the racially inferior will be accorded such rights as regarded as appropriate within the absolute sovereign discretion of the Anglo-

American polities. International law arguments need only be directed to fellow civilised peoples.

Ireland and International Law: A Case of Racial Supremacy

The Context

There is a well-known framework for the arguments, if they can be so grandly described, about the conquest of Ireland, which is just about within the parameters of the discipline of international law. It is not to be found within the traditional discussion of methods for the acquisition of territory. Instead, it comes within the general debate about the rights or lack of rights of Indians and other so-called native peoples. This is not to say that any professional international law literature has developed with respect to the subject. Rather, the more general remark can be made that the surplanting of the Irish population in Ireland by English and Scottish settlers could be justified in terms of the superior civilisation of the latter. Indeed, the difference of civilisation was seen to be so qualitatively large that the Irish could not be accorded any so-called natural rights to property or political authority.

It is possible and illuminating to compare the arguments used with respect to Ireland with those which accompanied the Spanish seizure of Mexico and Peru in the sixteenth century. What this will reveal is that at least one part of the debate took place in the Irish case. There were many arguments advanced concerning the superiority of English, and then British civilisation. Given the absence of the Catholic natural law tradition in post-Reformation England/Britain there was no response in terms of the common humanity of peoples such as was offered in Spain by Vitoria and Las Casas.[31] In the Irish case the record will show that the arguments are, none the less, inextricably bound up with arguments about the inferiority of some peoples in relation to others, which precedes the Reformation and, indeed, brings to bear the authority of the Roman Catholic Church itself against the Irish people.[32]

So there will be seen to be a continuity between the arguments which surround English/Norman justifications for the intrusions into Ireland in the twelfth century and the justifications which accompanied and followed the Elizabethan conquest of the turn of the sixteenth and seventeenth centuries. It is possible to find some arguments of a similar nature accompanying the Cromwellian campaign in Ireland, but it will be assumed that the conquest was completed by the close of the reign of Elizabeth. This had the perhaps odd consequence that the so-called Battle of the Boyne is of no significance in international law. At the end of the seventeenth century Ireland was undisputedly part of the Three Kingdoms of the British Crown and the conflicts of 1689–91 were civil wars.

The Material Sources

The primary source of international law, at present, is supposed to be the practice of states which they regard as evidence of a general custom binding upon them as law.[33] Ireland was not a state in the modern sense even during the sixteenth century, while England had already the marks of a state, at the latest with the consolidation of central power by the Tudor Dynasty. To which material sources does one look for the law at the time of the conquests? It is also recognised that the opinions of the most highly qualified publicists may also be used as subsidiary evidence of general international law.[34] This directive is easy to apply to the English/Norman/British side. It allows one to consider the major chronicle of the Norman Invasion, which does set out verbatim justifications actually used by officials[35] as well as the most systematic justification of the Elizabethan Conquest, which was written by the senior legal officer responsible for consolidating the conquest.[36]

However, it is necessary, even on the English/British side to go further, to consider more general historical and literary justifications for the conquests. In particular Edmund Spenser, as an official of the English administration in Ireland, provided a further justification for the conquest.[37] Far from offering an official justification in a narrower sense, his study was denied publication during the reign of Elizabeth, possibly because of his dismissal of the common law as an instrument for reform in Ireland.[38] None the less, he was an influential actor in the colonisation process, and the ground for English opposition to his work did not prevent its eventual appearance in 1633. It would not be argued by many that the application of the common law in Ireland was entirely impartial and hence his work is essential, if one is to understand the variety of opinions amoung the conquerors.

This brings us to a fundamental stage in the justification of the presentation of the sources to be used for this work. The study is not intended to be yet one more history of the Irish question. Instead, it is hoped to provide a systematic account of the normative justifications of the British, generally, and counter-objections of the Irish, generally, concerning the conquest. Inevitably, Irish objections can hardly be official, since Ireland was not a state. Indeed the defeat of the Irish means that whatever normative response they afford for their experience will be even more diffuse or dispersed. This leads to a conclusion which is quite radical from the point of view of the English sense of the polity, but not at all from the Irish experience. There is not in the nature of the Irish experience a real possibility that a single voice is going to emerge on any topic. The country was never united into a centralised state. Irish opinions will be individual. The task of an international lawyer trying to understand the mentality of the communities crushed by English/British domination will be to look – if at all, since the task has never been systematically undertaken – to the more reflective, or self-conscious sectors of Irish society. This will mean historians and even poets.[39]

Such an approach leads into the heartland of the debate concerning the Irish conquest – the fact that it is to the fore of contemporary Irish consciousness, and that its character is hotly disputed both by Irish and by British scholars, albeit the debate is almost entirely conducted outside the field of legal study in that of history and, less explicitly, but equally importantly in literature, both prose and poetry.[40] Precisely because this debate is not conducted in the legal chancelleries of the Irish and British states, but among the intellectuals of the two states the necessity directly presents itself to consider the status or significance of such writings for the international lawyer.

It is the unresolved quality of the British–Irish conflict which is represented by the disputed land of the six counties of Northern Ireland/Ulster, which makes it inevitable that one goes beyond the parameters of meaning generated by the state to consider the mentalities of the peoples who spread as divided communities beyond the boundaries of the Irish and British states. However, what further, as it were, unbounded (that is, by disciplinary constraints) research into the arguments advanced about the character of the conquest reveals is how little seems to be clearly accepted with respect to the history. Whether and how Ireland was conquered still remains a hotly disputed question.[41] Its implications for Irish identity are central, since the status of a victim of conquest will be a central feature of the self-esteem of Irish society. It is equally central to the questions both of the division of the country and its separation from Britain. If the country was not conquered, or if it might be said, in some modified sense, that the country was not 'really conquered', or not 'all that conquered', this would have serious implications for the quality of the association between Ireland and Britain and between Ireland and Northern Ireland. Simply, a country which has not been conquered does not require liberation.

Historical and Literary Paradigms of Conquest in Ireland

Hence it is not surprising that particularly the disciplines of history and literature debate hotly the question of the conquest at present. These are taken, in this study, as reflective but, at the same time, as representative reworkings of social consciousness of the experience of conquest or its absence, the pathway to the mentalities of the informal societies which cross one another in the no man's land of the North of Ireland. There are least three positions which are entertained. The first is that Ireland was definitely conquered, albeit in two stages (Norman and Elizabethan), but still quite categorically.[42] This is the primary English/ British perspective on what happened. It will be the main task of the first part of the study to demonstrate that such is how the British understood their arrival and continued presence in Ireland. This material will be treated in a separate section which will include and end with an analysis of how the British understood the negotiations of the Treaty of December 1921 concluded with the leaders of Sinn Fein.

There is a second perspective, which is the Irish response to the conquest as it happened. What were the terms in which it was resisted during the Norman and Elizabethan times?[43] It is intended to link this response to Irish arguments for autonomy in the nineteenth century and eventual independence in 1922. This is perhaps a most difficult part of the study. What were the quasi-official historical interpretations of the nature of the British presence at the time of the final break for independence? The place of Eoin MacNeill is taken as central, a leading academic historian and Sinn Fein figure.[44] The final part of this section will be to consider Irish arguments about the alleged incomplete or unsatisfactory character of the 1921 Treaty and the question of an Irish claim to the 'six counties'. Here the most complex questions of the epistemology of nationalism are implicated. A very commonly held view, especially in unionist and 'revisionist' nationalist circles is that the Irish political entity is a construction of cultural nationalism. This view implies that an otherwise 'grey matter' of the Irish landscape was somehow endowed with a Gaelic-Catholic idealist mantle, which had then the energy and the good fortune to assert itself enough to attain independence. Instead, in this study the ambition will be to show a consensus of historians concerning what both sides, Irish and British, saw as being at stake in the negotiation of the Treaty and immediately subsequently, until 1937–38.[45] It is essential to try to draw out of this analysis whether and how far the Irish considered that an original Irish entity had been extinguished by the conquest and on what basis Ireland as a political entity once again came into existence. The vital question is, was a conquest undone, or did, simply, one political community determine, by a clearly expressed wish – even although it used force to give effect to this wish – to separate itself from another, because, for whatever reason, it had decided upon a parting of the ways. The latter alternative would have different implications for the 'six counties' than the former. A mere freely exercised choice of a part of the population of the island need have no implications for the rest of the population.

There is at least one more perspective, maybe two. It is that Ireland was not conquered. There was, with the Norman 'arrival', a measure of acquiescence in the English/Norman presence. From this point onwards the English treated resistance to them as treason. Conflict always had the character of civil unrest, at worst, civil war. Assimilation was the primary mode of social development. There did not exist a distinctive, developed prior Irish political society. Hence Ireland, as it is known today, is a creation of British administration. This was set in place during the reign of James I in terms of the counties which are now dividied into the 'six' and the 'twenty-six'. The Union of Parliaments which might be taken to extinguish Irish independence in 1801 involved an Irish Parliament set up in the medieval period on an English model. Since 1691 it was the subject of an intellectual tradition which asserted autonomy, but much as, and following the model of, the British dominions.[46] The most extensive contemporary version of the implications of this argument was given by William Molyneux in 1698.[47] It was some version of this 'organic' development which the British may have attempted to save in the negotiations of the 1921 Treaty with Sinn Fein. In this case it is the attempt to break the continuity of British political tradition with the 'construction' of a cultural nationalist state which has created the chasm between North and South in Ireland. The present Irish state, a reconstructed Gaelic, Catholic entity, is a completely artificial body, which is by its nature, given its romantic search for origins, a reactionary body. If there was a measure of conquest at various early stages in the development of Ireland, the process of assimilation is so deep that the conquest cannot have been reversed. At its strongest this argument, very much alive in Ireland's (the island's) historical and literary production, represents an unwillingness to accept the final character of the Irish state and a hope that it be somehow unravelled. Perhaps the most sharply focused and bitter conflict of identities at present concerning the fact of conquest can be observed in Edna Longely's literary criticism of Seamus Heaney's book-poem *North*.[48]

Much of this perspective will be taken as shared by the present Ulster Protestant community, although its origin is in the so-called Anglo-Irish tradition of the island as a whole. However, there are possible variants of the tradition within Ulster. The latter sometimes prefer to stress a consciousness of a successful planter/settler society, following on the Elizabethan Conquest. Here the function of history in this study is directly as a guide to contemporary consciousness.[49] A further variant of the theme of conquest, which has international law implications, is that the conquest has never,

Sir John Davies notwithstanding, been completely carried through.[50] The crisis of Ulster has its roots as much here as in the construction of an artifical political entity in the South. This perspective has the very radical consequence, in legal terms, that the conquest is continuing, presumably being resisted, until today, by the IRA. It also means that no claim is made as to a completed process of assimilation, which leaves, in turn, the possibility that an argument is constructed for a quite separate political identity on the island of Ireland. It is arguable that the logical conclusion of this perspective is either that a finally completed conquest leads to the construction of an entirely separate political identity in the North East of Ireland, or that an abandonment of the attempted conquest leads to abandonment of the island entirely.[51]

These (eventually four) possibilities are presented, in some measure, as a cross between historically presented arguments and social paradigms. Not every aspect of any position is held entirely by any party. A considerable feature of the Irish tragedy is not merely the measure of confused identity, but also that of mistaken identity. None the less, it is possible to argue that there are four parties, the British, the Irish, the Anglo-Irish and the Ulster Protestants. While it might have been thought that the first had largely lost interest in the matter, it will appear, on closer examination, that, when the British party turns its attention to the matter, it still shares to a considerable degree the perceptions of the Anglo-Irish. The 1921 Treaty was not necessary, and as well – or, hence – the aspirations of the Ulster Protestants to remain British are reasonable. The Irish still largely hold the paradigm attributed to them, but they also betray a hankering for the Anglo-Irish paradigm, a wish not to see themselves as conquered and a hope that, through a vision of an ecumenical, even if republican in a civic sense, polity, Ireland can be united. The Anglo-Irish would have appeared to have been firmly defeated by the time of the 1937 Irish Constitution. However, the raising of the question of the status of the border has facilitated increasing challenges to the legitimacy of the Irish state, in terms of the cogency of its cultural and ideological foundations. This has given added power to a very articulate Anglo-Irish minority.

There is a crucial relationship between the place of conquest as an institution within the system of international law and the concept of objectivity in historical science. In law it does not matter whether one of the above perspectives is true. If it is subjectively firmly held and cannot be defeated, then it continues to hold validity, in the absence of a compulsory adjudication or total annihilation. At the same time, historical science can serve to chip at the edges of arguments used, as long as it is remembered that what is at stake for each party is its continued identity in its present form.[52] These deliberations raise the simple, crucial question: what is the point of this investigation?

The advantage of the introduction of the international law paradigm is its heuristic quality. The outcome will be to focus attention on the tragic dimension of Irish history as being the most fundamental. There was a conquest. It was complete and devastating. What is left of Irish Ireland is an artifically constructed entity, not because of the validity of the assimilationist argument, but because of the failure and abandonment of the assimilationist project. This Irish identity is a fragmented one which it hardly appears possible, at present, to piece together again.[53] At the same time, the increased questioning of the 'artificial entity' in the face of demands for and prospects of a United Ireland only serves to expose all the more acutely the rawness of the Ulster Protestant identity as a misplaced conqueror-settler society.[54] To talk of forgetting the past is pious sentimentality.

CHAPTER 2

Legal Title by Conquest: Norman, English and British Perspectives

The Anglo-Norman Beginning?

Opposing Retrospective Historical-Legal Arguments

The question whether Ireland existed in the twelfth century has to be answered as part of the question of whether or not the country was conquered. It is a problem common to colonial situations, and indeed to any historically extended territorial dispute. Did the entity alleged to have been wronged actually exist at the time? It has not been the rule to see post-colonial liberation movements as restoring the autonomy of the previously existing political entity. Yet the Irish revolutionary movement did make such a claim. In a pamphlet, 'The Sovereign People', published in March 1916, the movement's most influential leader, Padraic Pearse, wished to demonstrate that Gaelic Ireland 'from the landing of the Normans in 1169, to the defeat of O'Neill and O'Donnell at Kinsale in 1601, was separatist'.[1]

The word 'separatist' was itself crucial as it indicated an international law rather than a constitutional law perspective on the Irish question. An independent nation had been deprived of its legal right to be separate and was reasserting that right. It was not a matter of changing the political status of the Irish, however defined, within the UK by means of the latter's political process. None the less the essential element of the argument had to be that a continuity of identity could be demonstrated. If it could not, it would be quite unproblematic for those in Ireland who did not constitute part of the 'alleged' Irish nation to assert some variation of the argument that they were no more newcomers to the island than their neighbours and political opponents, and that their presence did not contravene any previously acquired right.

One possible way to attempt to approach this question is to consider the different perspectives of two antagonistic, authoritative historians, J.C. Beckett and Eoin MacNeill. How these writers might be used is extremely problematic both from an historical and from a legal point of view. I believe that they help to illuminate the nature of the conflict in so far as they elaborate detailed perspectives on the nature of the disagreement which exists with respect to the Irish problem. Their analyses allow one to see more clearly what questions can usefully be addressed to the historically available materials, to see whether, perchance, the latter can afford answers. The perspectives can only be drawn from the more articulate members of the two communities.

For instance, Beckett cannot be taken to be either an official spokesman of the province of Northern Ireland, which is not in any case a state in international law, or a representative of the Anglo-Irish community, which does not exist as a legal entity in any sense. However, the notion of general customary law, of binding legal obligation, or of a claim of legal right, has to be given a broader interpretation than an examination of the acts of state officials. For instance it is generally recognised that, at least in some circumstances, peoples have a right to self-determination. This means, above all, that they are entitled to some form of firm political organisation of their choice. It does not have to be an independent state. In this sense there is no doubt that the people of Northern Ireland are recognised by the UK as having a right to self-determination. They will not be transferred to the Irish Republic without their consent. In order to ascertain their views it is appropriate to have resort to a leading sympathetic historian. The system of international law has resort to the writings of leading and outstanding publicists in order to find evidence of the current legal consciousness of peoples as well as states. Of course it is democratically obviously appropriate to have resort to politicians for their views, but their opinions will not usually have the same measure of compelling logic and justice (see further, Chapter 5). Therefore it is helpful, even for an international lawyer, to look to Beckett as a leading publicist able and willing to present an elaborate interpretation of significant historical events.

In his introduction to his short study, *The Anglo-Irish Tradition*, Beckett, a Belfast, Queen's University, and Protestant historian lays a claim to be both Protestant and Irish. He wishes to establish that the very identity of Ireland has been shaped by the English presence since the twelfth century, so that it is not possible simply to talk of a country which was conquered and which has in the twentieth century attempted to break away. A major part of his argument is that the Ireland which has engaged in armed struggle has existed as a cultural force only since the course of the nineteenth century. It is in an important sense an invention and not an ancient historical reality (which could give rise to an historical title). So it is in an historical work by the leading Ulster academic on Irish history, published in 1976, after the present 'troubles' had started, that one finds a full statement of an essentially international law argument that in the twelfth century there was no such place as Ireland:

> In the 12th century, Ireland lay on the very fringe of Europe ... It can hardly be said to have formed any part of the European political system: a European ruler, counting upon possible friends or enemies, felt no need to include Ireland in his calculations. Ireland was unregarded because it lacked any political machinery through which it could take corporate action. No king, no council, no assembly could negotiate on Ireland's behalf with a foreign power, make a treaty binding on the whole country, or assemble and direct a national army. Yet no country in Europe had had a fairer opportunity of finding its own way to political unity. During the century and a half before the coming of the Normans Ireland had been free from external attack. It was a period during which other countries were achieving some measure of national solidarity and building up institutions ... through which an effective central administration could gradually develop. But Irishmen, living apart in a world of their own, made no attempt to follow this pattern; and Ireland remained, as it had been for centuries, no more than a congeries of independent kingdoms, often at war with one another, under a High King, whose authority when he could assert it at all stretched no further than a right to collect tribute. A common language and a common cultural tradition provided the basis for a sense of national distinctiveness; but there was no tradition of common action, nor any machinery for organising it. Ireland, in fact, was not a state in the contemporary European sense. Had Irishmen possessed the same degree of national solidarity as the Scots had attained, the Norman settlers would have been absorbed or expelled; and Henry's lordship, had he established it at all, would have proved as transient as his suzerainty over Scotland.[2]

How does one begin to engage in rational debate with the presuppositions of the text? Clearly it is a twentieth-century interpretation of a twelfth-century event. Does this have an impact on Beckett's approach? For instance, what is one to make of his view of the nature of the historical process? It appears to contain an evolutionist argument, that somehow Ireland was a backward political society, if one at all; that if it had been able to keep abreast of general European, and in particular Scottish political developments, it would not have suffered the political intrusion which it actually experienced. The invasion would not have happened. Underlying this type of argument one may find the view that the law recognises facts, the inevitable, etc. Europe was progressing towards politically centralised state organisations; Ireland was out of step with this process, so that its absorption in a politically more developed neighbour represents a progress which cannot, as well as should not, be undone.

To oppose Beckett one might consider Eoin MacNeill's *Phases of Irish History*, first published in 1919 by the Professor of Ancient Irish History in the National University of Ireland. Pearse was his disciple. Cronin is very critical of him but records that he was, besides being very prominent in the Irish Republican Brotherhood and the Irish Volunteers, the first Minister of Education of the Irish Free State, which was permeated by his ideas.[3] He is particularly reputed for having a cultural view of what he called 'nationality', derived from a blending of Christianity and Gaeldom in the fifth and sixth centuries.[4] Cronin himself criticises MacNeill as one who saw Celtic civilisation through a romantic haze, distinct from Wolfe Tone republicanism, stressing the fact of a different tradition rather than the modern statism one associates with nationalist theory.

MacNeill is careful to distinguish language from race. The Celts are no more a race than the Anglo-Saxons, etc. The term is indicative of the language which the Irish and Britons spoke.[5] He stresses that the Celtic form of government in historical times was that of a patrician republic, and makes an evaluation different from Beckett, although speaking generally of Celtic civilisation and not of Ireland in particular:

> The Celtic people were divided into a large number of small states without any organised superior power. From time to time, however, one or other of these states might acquire a degree of political pre-eminence over a group of neighbouring states, forming a loose federation in which it took chief direction of the common affairs. We find the same tendency amoung the states of ancient Greece.[6]

MacNeill insists that 'No trace has been discovered of any language other than Gaelic continuing to be spoken in any part of Ireland within the traditional memory of the people. From this it will appear that the Gaelic language had become universal throughout Ireland some centuries before Irish history and traditions began to be written.'[7] At the same time MacNeill objects that the invading Gaelic-speaking people did not exterminate the existing inhabitants.[8] Indeed he objects in general terms to histories which speak of successive populations exterminating one another. He prefers the ethnologist's lesson that 'races' such as the English are largely composed of descendants of so-called primitive inhabitants. In this sense no one 'race' is more 'primitive' than another.[9] So MacNeill concludes the first part of his argument by claiming that the ancient population of Ireland was both Celtic and pre-Celtic. He then proceeds to state that they were united in ancestry and thus symbolise an effective national unity. This he bases most directly on the Book of Invasions of which a convenient summary is given by Keating. There follows a statement which I believe is of incalculable importance:

> The land of Ireland is the unifying principle, and all the children of the land are joined into one genealogical tree. Some recent writer, I think it is Mr. George Moore, has remarked how Irish people, apparently quite naturally and unconsciously, speak and think of their country as a person. This they have been accustomed to do through all the ages of their literature. The first words spoken by a Gael on Irish soil, in the ancient legend, were an invocation addressed to Ireland herself by the druid Amorgen: 'I entreat the land of Eire' and the land itself, under its three names Eire, Fodla, and Banbha, when the Gaels arrived, was reigning as queen over the Men of Ireland. Thus we find the clearly formed idea of one nation, composed of diverse peoples, but made one by their affiliation to the land that bore them – the clearest and most concrete conception of nationality to be found in all antiquity.[10]

In his chapter 'Ireland's Golden Age' MacNeill elaborates a justification of nationality as something perennial in history. It means simply that in a people, such as the Greeks, 'resides the elemental power of transformation ... In every intense and distinctive development of a nation, there dwells the actuality of a potentiality of some great gift to the common good of mankind'.[11] He is contemptuous of the 'organisational genius' of feudalism, a culture which, with its charters, statutes, registers and inquisitions has not in four centuries (presumably contemporaneous with Ireland's Golden Age) left one school of note and no literature except 'the melancholy records of anti-national statecraft'. Indeed MacNeill elaborates a more general criticism of official learning for 'whatever learning there was was for the most part suborned to the purposes of a dominating officialdom'.[12]

There is also a development of the notion of the land of Ireland in the ideas of its nationality. He is distrustful of those who say that the Irish were instead attached only to the territory of the tribe, with no sentiment of a country more extended. If other European countries were feudalised at the time, to what extent could such a statement not also be true in England, France, Germany, etc.? Why is it made? To what end? It is not peculiarly or especially true of Ireland at the time. Indeed Ireland had the strongest sense of a country and people:

> Beginning with the 6th century chronicle, every Irish history is a history of Ireland – there is not one history of a tribal territory or of any grouping of tribal territories. Every Irish law-book is

> a book of the laws of Ireland – there are no territorial laws and no provincial laws. The whole literature is pervaded by the notion of one country common to all Irishmen.

His protagonist, a Mr Orpen, is correct that in Ireland, as in all other countries, there had not developed a fully modern sentiment of political nationality. Yet MacNeill will not be intimidated by Orpen's contrast between the centralised monarchies of Europe and Irish localism. These did not express any sentiment of country in the popular mind or in the ruler. Such a sentiment might sometimes be found in a delimitation of centralised power:

> but the sentiments which found expression in centralised power were those of fear on the one side and domination on the other; and students who study medieval history with a map will quickly apprehend that these two sentiments, fear and domination, shaped the boundaries of country in defiance of the sentiments connected with country, race, language, nationality. In Ireland, on the other hand, we find the clear development of the national consciousness, associated with the country to a degree that is not found elsewhere.[13]

Questions of Twelfth-Century Standards

RELIGIOUS ARGUMENTS

There is some contemporaneous support to be had for Beckett's apparent view that the conquest was justified or inevitable, although it does not follow him exactly. Beckett assumes that in the twelfth century Europe was converging towards a state system. This is definitely not accurate. The notion of authority and legitimacy was not clearly defined in purely state terms. Most especially, and this is a matter of enormous importance for the future history of Ireland, the Roman Catholic Church paid no importance to the notion that there was any state or other political organisation which could stand in the way of what it saw as being necessary to the welfare of the people of Ireland. In other words there was a very prevalent view that the world was one common community which should be governed by a single moral/religious standard. So, inevitably, it was not thought that the rights of any political organisation could be allowed to stand in the way of a more fundamental human welfare.

In 'Medieval Ireland', Martin shows how the ground was prepared for a remarkable papal grant of authority of Ireland to the English King Henry II. There were features of Gaelic society going back to pre-Christian times, concerning marriage, celibacy of the clergy, baptism and the sacramental system and control of church lands, which made Irish church leaders convinced of the incompatibility of the Gregorian church reforms with the Gaelic social system. This induced the bishops, abbots and other church prelates at the Synod of Cashel (1171–72) to accept Henry II as their temporal overlord.[14] Bernard of Clairvaux in his *Life of Malachy* had prepared for the Western Church a picture of the Irish as beasts, not men; Christians in name, but in fact pagans.

There was a total disregard of the fact that Ireland had retained a culture of its own, outside the Roman and Latin.[15] The Anglo-Norman theologian, John of Salisbury, was able to exploit this 'atmosphere' in papal circles to persuade Pope Adrian IV to grant Ireland to Henry II, speaking to him of the barbaric and impious people of Ireland.[16] The foundation for the promulgation of the Papal Bull, *Laudabiliter,* was the clear assumption that the Irish were not fit to govern themselves. Such a way of thinking has to be seen in the wider context of the papacy's assumption of a certain identification with the former Roman Empire. In particular there is the assumption that the Emperor Constantine had once made a gift to the Pope of all the islands surrounding Europe. John of Salisbury refers to this 'donation of Constantine' as the long-established right by which the Pope granted Ireland to Henry II.[17] However, much more important is the direct link which Adrian makes between this papal power and the extension of civilisation. So he decreed:

> That Ireland, and indeed all islands on which Christ, the sun of justice, has shed his rays, and which have received the teachings of the Christian faith, belong to the jurisdiction of the blessed Peter and the holy Roman church is a fact beyond doubt, and one which your Majesty recognises ... [W]e regard it as pleasing and acceptable to us that you should enter that island for the purpose of enlarging the boundaries of the church ... and that the people of that land receive you honourably and respect you as their lord.[18]

The same point is made much more forcefully by Alexander III in confirming the donation of dominium over the Kingdom of Ireland in 1172: 'In order that, once vile practices of that land have been stamped out, this barbarous nation, Christian only in name, by your [Henry's] diligent efforts ... may in future really earn the name of Christian which they now profess.'[19] However remote this may all appear to modern international law, it is central to the development of the subject. It is to the contemporary canonist Gratian that we owe the introduction of the concept of the just war into international jurisprudence. Around 1140 he put together a compilation of canon law known as *Concordia Discordantium Canonum*. In the vital Causa 23, on the question of war, he set out a justification of war simply to correct heresy.[20] This rested on an Augustinian theory that love of enemies did not go so far as tolerating sinning with impunity;[21] the physical punishment of sin, even by waging war, was not incompatible with Christian patience.[22] This goes back to imperial Roman times when Augustine had held to the right of the ecclesiastical hierarchy to insist upon imperial coercion of heretics as heretics.[23] With Gregory the Great the persecution of barbarians and heretics went together.[24]

One of the foremost exponents of these ideas was Bernard of Clairvaux, who had prepared the ground for an anti-Irish action. He was an exponent of the secular authority, as the Emperor, fulfilling its duty as the defender of the Church by combating schism and heresy.[25] Indeed Alexander III's own persecution of the Cathars was taken as evidence for actual clerical participation, although the distinction was usually drawn beween exhortation and execution.[26] The underlying assumption was simply that there was one single world political-religious authority, with the notion of Pax Romana sliding into a Pax Christiana. While church was definitely not conterminous with temporal power, the latter was definitely dependent upon the former for its order and stability. So it was, for example, extremely difficult to pose the question of coexistence with non-Christian, or supposedly barbarian or pagan powers. The whole modern legal framework of sovereignty, independence and freedom from intervention will eventually struggle to free itself from this unified conception of political authority. With Gratian there had already been developed the notion of Christians, as God's newly chosen people (following upon the Old Testament model) who were justified to wage war against God's enemies, that is, as necessary to defend the faith.[27]

The leading Decretist, Huguccio, tried to argue against this using a text of Justinian forbidding the harassing of peaceful pagans. He asked why Christians should not peacefully coexist with infidels, but still came to the conclusion that the allegedly peaceful conduct of pagans was no reason for not waging war against them, unless they gave up the rights they were holding. His subject was the question of the Saracens in the Holy Lands.[28] However, he was practically alone in taking the view that the main Saracen wrong was not disbelief but holding on to territory. This prohibited by implication wars of conquest, conversion and extermination against infidels simply on account of their beliefs.[29] However, this was not a majority view, and, as can be seen from the Bull of Alexander III, it did not apply to Ireland, as that case, supposedly, concerned Christians who had fallen away from their faith.

Geraldus, virtually the only complete recorder of the 'Conquest' mentions Henry II as very firmly attached to the title granted to him by the Popes.[30] As will be seen later, Henry VIII relies upon them in his declaration of kingship over Ireland in 1541. None the less both MacNeill and Flanagan throw great doubt on the conclusivess of any papal authority for the Anglo-Norman presence in Ireland. MacNeill does not dispute the authenticity of the *Laudabiliter* of Adrian, but puts a radically different interpretation on it. The sentiments which Adrian expresses, in response to a proposal made by Henry '... are merely an echo in brief of such words as those in which St Bernard describes the reforms already effected by St Malachy'. MacNeill has already quoted references to propagation of the faith, extirpation of vice, and a desire '... to reduce the people to obedience unto laws'. So MacNeill asks how far these 'war aims' of Henry's were carried out.[31] The decrees of the Synod of Cashel were confirmed by Henry. They relate, in eight subjects, to improvements in moral and religious practices, in particular the adoption of the ritual of the Church in England. 'That is all' concludes MacNeil.[32] He adds, for good measure, that the Norman barons and the King himself were not remarkable for orderliness or freedom from vice.[33]

Indeed, Flanagan makes the same general points. She says that there is no evidence of what Henry thought of the *Laudabiliter* either in 1155–56 or in 1171–72. There is no evidence that he exploited it during his expedition to Ireland, and this is, in Flanagan's view, not surprising as he had just murdered the prelate Beckett. The Irish bishops were favourably disposed towards him because of his role with Rome in the reform of the Church. This may have encouraged him to think of an appeal for a crown for his son John in 1177. He did send letters from the Irish bishops and asked Alexander III to confirm the *Laudabiliter*. However, Flanagan insists that the Pope's letter of confirmation is a forgery. The petition of 1177 for a crown was unsuccessful.[34]

A TITLE TO IRELAND BASED ON CESSION OR SUBMISSION

None of this is to say that the possible papal grants were the only grounds of title that Henry would try to use. The more secular dimension of his intrusion has to be considered. This is however an experience equally relevant to a refutation of one aspect of Beckett's argument, that Ireland should have been, for some reason or other, a state. The alleged motive – that Henry came to Ireland to foreclose the setting up of an independent Anglo-Norman state under one of his knights, Strongbow – is not relevant to a legal analysis of his conduct. Nor need it be decisive for the importance of his papal titles, that he did not use them to secure the submission of the Irish lords. Instead it is necessary to return to how the Irish conceived of themselves.

There is a remarkable recurrence in colonial history that those who seem to be 'destined' to be colonised accept their fate without question. Martin remarks that a succession of Irish kings and princes came to make submission and to swear fealty:

> They seem to have no hesitation about bowing to a foreign king and nationalism played no part in their thinking. The Irish had always recognised the Roman emperor as 'king of the world', and it is significant that Henry II was known to them as 'fitz Empress' (his mother's first marriage had been to the Emperor Henry V). It is not clear from the evidence if they did homage, as well as swearing fealty, but the balance seems to be in favour of fealty only. In any case, the very important feudal distinction between homage and fealty would mean little to the Irish.[35]

At least two points appear to arise out of these remarks. First Henry would not have had the intention to conquer Ireland. If there was no question of an intention to conquer, the very minimum required to enjoy any such title to territory would not be present. He did not bring an army of conquest. The second point concerns misunderstanding about the exact significance of the Irish submissions. If we treat the second point first, it has to be noted, for later discussions of the possible repeal of the Act of Union of 1801, that some unionist argument will see the origins of its position in these submissions. They appear to mark the fountainhead for the growth of a parliamentary tradition of an Irish kingdom, governed by the common law and the will of the King in Parliament. While the King might frequently have treated Ireland disadvantageously it might still be possible, in this view, for his Irish subjects to plead with him that he has broken his 'contract' with them. Such a perspective leads into what I would call a constitutionalist perspective on the Irish problem.

It continues today in exactly these terms in so far as the conflict in Northern Ireland is seen as resoluble with guarantees for the civil and political rights of the 'minority', even where such rights include group political representation. If such rights are to be obtained within the political process constituted by the successors to Henry this is grist to the mill of the unionist argument. Even MacNeill is troubled by the apparent submissions of Irish lords/kings. He notes that there was one feature of the coming of the Norman kings which is difficult to categorise, whether it comes from 'systematic bad faith or merely from incapacity to act according to ordered notions of law'. Irish kings, outside Ulster, generally made formal submission to Henry as their liege lord, supposedly to be received into his protection. This was a solemn contract of vassalage but:

> In not a single instance was this contract observed for a moment longer than the opportunity to violate it was delayed. The rights and possessions of the Irish vassal kings were straightaway granted

> afresh to one or another of the new adventurers – and the new grants were not preceded or accompanied by the pretence of any escheatment or invalidation of the existing contract – so little importance was attached by Henry and John and their filibustering captains even to the outward appearances of law and order.[36]

This is a remarkable statement because it reveals how, from the start of the Anglo-Irish tragedy, the issue is not clearly drawn between an Irish claim to absolute independence and a claim to the redress of unjust government. As a key figure in the years 1916–22, MacNeill does not draw clear conclusions from his statement. Its quality does not appear to be disputable if one follows what is reputed to be the only reliable witness of the time. The contemporary chronicle of Geraldus Cambrensis, a Welsh-Norman monk writing around 1188, very shortly after the Anglo-Norman intervention, allows us what is regarded as virtually the only complete record of the events described.

Geraldus was a successful law professor in Paris, a humanist of the twelfth-century Renaissance, who stood closer to John of Salisbury than to Abelard.[37] Although he preferred the Old Testament view that the good should be rewarded in this life and the wicked suffer, he also firmly believed in human free will and the unpredictability of historical developments.[38] It appears to be accepted that without his work we would be largely in the dark about the events.[39]

He concludes his book with an examination as to why no full and complete conquest had occurred.[40] He sees it as a missed opportunity in terms of inefficient, inconsistent use of military resources, and, above all, incompetent and unjust administrators. He confers great praise on the pacification policy of Hugh de Lacy[41] who followed a policy of restoring Irish cultivators to their lands, and deplores those who, around Prince John, actually dispossessed those who had been loyal allies. He stresses the refusal of Irish lords to renew allegiance to Prince John and his entourage as dangerous incompetents.[42] Geraldus makes the remarkable judgement that the Irish cannot have so provoked the wrath of God, if the conquest has been so unsuccessful. For this judgement he relies upon the Old Testament.[43] So 'the English [in this Old Testament standard] have not as yet won the right to obtain the full submission and placid obedience of a race that is already partly conquered and ready to serve them'. Neither side seems completely to have won God's favour or to have lost it.[44]

In her magisterial and very recent study of the Irish submissions, Flanagan categorises what MacNeill refers to as solemn contracts hopelessly disregarded. The submissions of the Irish kings, whether in Irish or in Angevian style, were understood as diplomatic and political in character. They depended on whatever future levels of pressure existed and had to be seen, in Irish historical terms, as an interruption of the concentration of power by the Irish lord-kingship. The Treaty of Windsor encapsulated the ambiguity. It established a purely liege, not vassal relationship between the Irish High-King Rory O'Connor and Henry 'to hold his land as fully and as peacefully as he held it before the King of England entered Ireland'. Such arrangements had been negotiated in pre-Norman Ireland between more powerful kings. They did not necessarily give the superior any right of disposition over the lands of subordinates or successors; nor were such arrangements stated to be binding upon heirs. Rory was to have lands outside Connacht: 'to have all the rest of the land and its inhabitants under him'. Rory's authority was thus defined only in relation to Henry, and not to the Irish inhabitants. Flanagan insists that the whole arrangement had a diplomatic, political context rather than a legal, constitutional one. The Irish kings still held their authority under Rory who was described by the annalist as the King of Ireland, although no longer as the overlord of Leinster, Mide and Dublin.[45]

Under the Normans there was a general policy of dividing Ireland into two different spheres of lordships, under the common overall lordship of Henry. Within the Irish section the practice was one of individual submissions to the overlordship of Henry. The submissions of individual Gaelic lords from the fourteenth century were ones of simple fealty, to abide by the King's peace and to pay a modest tribute. They did not enter into hereditary, tenurial relationships and this was not claimed by subsequent English kings.[46]

A TITLE TO IRELAND BY RIGHT OF CONQUEST?

Since these arguments, whether religious or secular, appear to be inconclusive of the question of English/Norman authority in Ireland in terms of nominal titles, it might be better to ask whether and how far the newcomers attempted to exercise effective jurisdiction and control within Ireland. To pursue this goal I intend to draw most fully on Geraldus, who entitled his work *The Conquest of Ireland*. This set out with remarkable frankness and clarity the thesis that the Anglo-Normans did see themselves as engaged in a military operation which had the character of an attempted conquest, even if no significant part of this operation took place during Henry's sojourn in Ireland.

This perspective is clearly rooted in a view of the Irish as subordinate, not worthy of equal and reciprocal treatment, as, in some not fully articulated sense, outside the pale of the law. In my view one sees at once a characteristic English view of Ireland as a colony to be conquered with title resting upon a right of conquest. At once Geraldus perceives that the undertaking is fraught with difficulties, that the conquest risks never being fully accomplished.

What is remarkable and worth stressing is that Geraldus did in a certain sense consider that a conquest had taken place, and that it was none the less unsatisfactory and incomplete. Henry's visit was only part of a Norman penetration into Ireland, which was at every stage immensely violent. He came to nip in the bud the possibility that Strongbow, the Norman leader already in the country, would set up an independent Norman kingdom. The latter had come to Ireland at the invitation of the Irish King of Leinster to assist him against his own vassals, who had expelled him. That king had promised him, contrary to Irish law, the succession to his title. Geraldus was firmly of the view that, from the beginning, a conquest was taking place. He speaks of 'the story of the subjugation of the Irish people, and of the taming of the ferocity of a very barbarous nation in these our own times'.[47] He constantly speaks of Ireland as a united entity. So he describes Ruaidri, Prince of Connacht as the supreme ruler of all Ireland.[48] He describes Robert Fitzstephen as 'the first to break through the defences of Ireland by force of arms'.[49]

Geraldus supposes that the alliance of Fitzstephen and Diarmait of Leinster was seen by 'the whole of Ireland' as a threat. Ruaidri is credited with seeing here a threat to the country as a whole from the arrival of the foreigners.[50] Ruaidri is supposed to have tried to persuade Fitzstephen to leave the country in which he could claim for himself no right of jurisdiction. In Geraldus's reconstruction of the speeches before the first major conflict, Ruaidri is supposed to speak of an unjust ruler, rightfully overthrown by his people, who brings in foreigners to redress the balance, the way, historically, that countries are usually conquered if one considers Roman history.[51] To confirm this analysis Fitzstephen says that the outcome may be that the five divisions of the island are reduced to one 'and the sovereignty over the whole kingdom will devolve upon our race for the future'.[52]

At a later battle of Waterford the legal status of the conflict is described in terms of conquest. It is argued that it is unwise to release prisoners in a war which is not completed. The curious 'twelfth-century Renaissance' perspective applies. Clemency is not the way Julius and Alexander of Macedon made all nations subject to themselves. Those nations did not converge from all parts as a result of being shown clemency, but 'rather bowed their necks in submission under the compulson of armed might and terror bred of cruel treatment'. The whole population of Ireland has joined in plotting 'our' destruction and not without good reason. The decisive argument against clemency is that to come to subdue a people and show clemency before subjugation is complete is inconsistent.[53]

At any rate the decisive submission to Henry II concerns his own Norman lords who have already conquered the Irish. The Earl Fitzstephen acknowledged that he had a bond of obedience to the King of England, and 'he surrendered to the king the chief town in the kingdom, Dublin, along with the adjacent centres, and also the coastal cities and all castles. As for the rest of the land he had conquered, he and his heirs were to acknowledge that it was held of the king and his heirs.'[54] Geraldus then refers to Henry as the conqueror of the Irish.[55] It is in this context that one must see the submission of so many Irish 'princes'. Each 'likewise obtained the English king's peace, became dependent for the tenure of his kingdom on the king as overlord, and bound himself in alliance with the king by the strongest ties of fealty and submission'.[56]

The concluding and decisive theme for Geraldus was that the conquest was not in fact completed. The Irish, as a fickle and unstable race,[57] rose in rebellion. Once again the entire population of Ireland rose with one consent against the English.[58] It is after this, in the chronology of events, that Geraldus mentions Henry putting himself in communication with the papacy and receiving confirmation of the privileges which the Pope granted him. He relied upon abuses in Irish church practice which Irish churchmen had provided at the Synod of Cashel. He then obtained Alexander III's declaration that he had authority to rule over the Irish, and this was read out with approval at an episcopal synod at Waterford.[59] Geraldus further refers to Vivian who as papal legate called an episcopal synod in Dublin and publicly proclaimed the rights of the King of England over Ireland and the Pope's confirmation of this. Martin refers to the Alexandrian letters as authentic,[60] while Flanagan considers them forgeries. In any case Geraldus stated that any going back on this authority was a rebellion, a going back on allegiance to the King, meriting excommunication.[61]

Geraldus finishes by stressing two points. First, Ireland is not conquered. It is dangerous to go out of the city walls. All roads were impassible.[62] Second, Ireland is the lawful possession of the kings of Britain, for the reasons already given.[63] So the remaining question is how the title is to be effectively exercised. It is hard to imagine a more consequent statement of a colonial mentality than is found in the following:

> So long as the Irish continue to obey the laws and do not refuse to serve us, we should win them over by making a firm treaty with them, and anticipate their demands by showing them respect. But when they presume to break the peace, thus revealing their innate fickleness, then we must dissemble any

> feelings of compassion we may have, and punishment must follow hard on the heels of the crime.[64]

It is remarkable how Geraldus goes on to complain that actual English administration appears to be motivated by the opposite policy, for instance by treating rebels with respect and plundering peaceful subjects.[65] It does appear that the English have, at least in this case, no particular talents as masters. It is very difficult to draw legal conclusions from these historical events, except to stress, once again, that from the very start, it is difficult to decipher whether Irish and English complaints against one another are to be characterised in constitutional or international law terms. The Irish are torn between attempting to throw off English control, while at the same time, trying to make it consistent with its own stated ideals or ideology. The English are torn between regarding Ireland as a no man's land which they can absorb as they please, and resenting what they take to be the unlawful rebelliousness and treachery/treason of the Irish. It may not be possible to demonstrate that Ireland was a political state in the twelfth century. Yet it can be shown that notions of personality were very fluid at the time and that Irish political identity was sufficiently developed for the Anglo-Norman intrusion to appear as very disruptive of the development of the country. What I would prefer to insist is that no legitimate English claim to Ireland, whether by modern or contemporaneous standards, was established. This is for two reasons. The Anglo-Normans did not effectively conquer the country. Nor did they enter into stable, reciprocal relations with the Irish.

The Elizabethan Conquest and its Jacobean Confirmation

The natural successor to Geraldus as a legal text can be taken to be Sir John Davies' *A Discovery of the True Causes Why Ireland Was Never Entirely Subdued*. In his recent critical edition of the work Myers stresses how it shares a number of characteristics with many Elizabethan and Jacobean writings on Ireland. They were written by those who had experience of Ireland as colonists, administrators or soldiers and 'express an ethnocentric, arrogant rejection of Irish culture, even as they paradoxically exhibit a fascination with their subject'. They focus primarily on the failure, over 400 years to secure effective control over Ireland.[66] Davies was the chief legal officer of James I and Speaker of his Irish Parliament and is taken to be in a large degree the guiding spirit of the Irish administration in these years.[67] Undoubtedly it was James I who was sovereign and the tract which Davies addresses to him was not requested. Nor does there seem to have been any royal response.[68] He identifies himself as His Majesty's Attorney

General for Ireland and it is reasonable, therefore, to interpret his work as a professional undertaking.

The heuristic mode of the international law method has to be stressed again at this point. The view of Ireland as conquered is not acceptable to the Anglo-Irish consciousness. Such a view threatens the very foundation of Anglo-Irish identity. One strategy which a historian in this tradition will use to neutralise the effect of a work such as Davies', is to treat it as a historical document 'which has to be understood in terms of its own times, etc.'. One of the most articulate representatives of this tradition at present is Roy Foster. I use the expression 'representative' deliberately, because the concept of historical paradigm, of which I say there are three to four in our study, is essential to an understanding of the opposing, and indeed irreconcilable legal perspectives on Irish history. Foster is Carroll Professor of Irish History at Oxford University. He relativises the significance of Davies, and indeed Geraldus in a paper which first appeared in the *Transactions of the Royal Historical Society* in 1988.

The question which Foster is posing is bewildering for the international lawyer and hence the justification for the length of the following citation:

> But when did the writing of Irish history come to have an effective political function in public discourse? The background is not to be found in the series of explanatory histories from the time of Geraldus Cambrensis, and including Elizabethan-Jacobean apologists like Fynes Moryson, Edmund Spenser, Edmund Campion, Sir John Davies and company. The didactic nature of their work was self-confessed and obvious to contemporaries; their function can only be understood in terms of their time. In some quarters, much emphasis is put on the fact that these works represent English manipulation of early Irish history in order to excuse the Conquest. So indeed they do; but to expect otherwise is to require a detached historical sense exercised on behalf of Irish history, at a time when it was not applied to English history, or to any other. The more sophisticated tradition which concerns us begins with antiquarian explorations in the late eighteenth century, compounded with the various senses of nationalism – colonial, Gaelic and revolutionary – stirring in Ireland at the time.[69]

This is a declaration of faith which it is useless to try to contradict by reference to such ideological controversy which did occur within societies such as Spain. Foster's perspective has to be pieced together as a whole and accepted as one which will not, in the foreseeable future, be moved. Indeed, any attempt to introduce the quality of the Spanish debates will immediately be faced with the general scepticism in which they are held by British scholarship.[70] At the very least, the international lawyer, as lawyer, can assume that people are responsible for their actions, and that they can be taken to mean what they say, and can give him or herself the task of trying to understand what they have said *within the tradition of the profession which they have* – in this case not merely the law but a legal tradition which stretches back from Davies to Geraldus.

Davies ask himself the question: *What is a Perfect Conquest?* [71] He means to ask himself whether Ireland was conquered in the time of Henry II. His intention is very uncomfortable from an Anglo-Irish perspective. He will argue that the country was not effectively taken in charge until the end of the sixteenth century and that the apparent development of the legal institutions of Ireland until then was without value. In particular England's title to Ireland could not be based upon peaceful submissions of the Irish. They were untrustworthy and unreliable. Only a breaking into submission of the inhabitants would suffice and this had happened only recently. The only healthy legal institutions which Ireland could have would have to be developed by the Conqueror as part of his conquest. They were, indeed, essential to it, and without their successful implantation, there could still not be said to be a completed conquest – a hostage to fortune, as Davies was merely proposing that English laws and institutions should, in the future, be applied in Ireland, *an assimilationist proposal.*

So Davies discounts the 'arrangements' which Henry II arrived at with the Irish lords in terms which appear technically sound in terms of one legal theory of his time:

> For the Irish lords did only promise to become tributaries to King Henry II. And such as pay only tribute, though they be placed by Bodin in the first degree of subjection, are not properly subjects but sovereigns ... And therefore, though King Henry II had the title of 'Sovereign Lord' over the Irish, yet he did not put those things in execution which are the true marks and differences of sovereignty.[72]

There follows a very close international law definition of the true marks of sovereignty.To give laws, enforce a criminal law, and, to have sole authority of making war and peace are the true marks of sovereignty which Henry II did not possess. The Irish applied their brehon laws and 'they made war and peace with another without controlment – and this they did not only during the reign of King Henry II, but afterwards in all times, even until the reign of Queen Elisabeth'.[73]

The remedy for Davies, to achieve the goal of effective kingship, had to be conquest. Submissions from the Irish were not simply worthless because they were fickle – which was indeed the case – but also because, in terms of their own traditions, no lord could bind his successor and no one could alienate his authority. An Irishman could never forfeit his land.[74] Whether Ireland was a state, or a series of statelets, civilised or barbaric did not matter for the purposes of conquest. The image which England/Britain was to have of itself was the expanding Roman Empire. Trial of military strength alone was enough to provide good title to territory. Davies could note that barbarous statelets, the case of Ireland, would simply require more imperial exertion: 'For a barbarous country is not so easily conquered as a civil ... And, again, a country possessed with many petty lords and states is not so soon brought under entirely as an entire kingdom governed by one prince or monarch ...'[75] This is within the context that Davies has decided: 'For the husbandman must first break the land before it be made capable of good seed ... so a barbarous country must first be broken by a war before it will be capable of good government.' The outcome of the suppression of Tyrone's Rebellion (1592–1601) was 'in the end an universal and absolute conquest of all the Irishry'.[76] Davies relied further on an argument that the Irish lords owed their own positions to wars which they had won over one another and not by sacrament, hereditary title or any succession of property, 'but with force over time each obtained his own kingdom. And therefore, they had no just cause to complain when a stronger king than themselves became a king and lord over them.'[77]

Davies sees an effective conquest as the first stage in the achievement of his goal of assimilation of the Irish to English rule – the alternative, which he expressly excludes, being an open policy of explusion and extermination. So the first outcome of a conquest is that then and only then will the Irish be, as it were, in the proper frame of mind and spirit, to absorb English legal traditions. An essential feature of this argument is that Davies is treating the broad sweep of the 'Irishry' as the object of his interest and is not somehow focusing only on the already present English settlers, the so-called 'Old English', as central to the development of an English Ireland. Hence, he cuts off any foundation for Irish identity which could be based upon a consensual relationship with England and ignores any distinction between colonial settlers and natives. The outcome of the defeat of Tyrone could be understood as follows:

> Whereupon the multitude, who ever loved to be followers of such as could master and defend them, admiring the power of the Crown of England, being brayed, as it were, in a mortar with the sword, famine and pestilence altogether, submitted themselves to the English government, received the laws and magistrates, and most gladly embraced the king's pardon and

> peace in all parts of the realm with demonstrations of joy and comfort; which made, indeed, an entire, perfect, and final conquest of Ireland.[78]

Davies' ambition for Ireland is inclusive and reformatory. The effect of a most crushing defeat , an utter breaking and destroying is to 'produce a general obedience and reformation of all the Irishry, which ever before had been disobedient and unreformed'.[79] It is a discriminatory policy, followed in the medieval period, which marked the very incompleteness of the conquest before.[80] The reason is the inevitable unrest which a discriminatory policy must cause. Its only logical outcome would be extermination. So Davies explains further:

> Whereby it is manifest that such as had the government of Ireland under the crown of England did intend to make a perpetual separation and enmity between the English and the Irish, pretending, no doubt, that the English should in the end root out the Irish; which the English not being able to do did cause a perpetual war between the nations.[81]

Davies ties the outcome of a successful conquest to a system of non-discriminatory inclusive laws for all the inhabitants of the island: 'For the conquest is never perfect till the war be at an end; and the war is not at an end till there be peace and unity; and there can never be unity and concord in any one kingdom but where there is but one king, one allegiance, and one law.'[82] Here, Davies cites in support the crucial cultural types which are determinative, for him, of English/British behaviour. The Romans, as conquerors, never hestitated to communicate their laws 'to the rude and barbarous people whom they had conquered'. Likewise 'our Norman Conqueror' did not distinguish between English and Normans.[83]

The assimilation of the Irish would not follow automatically from the application of English laws. The Irish were definitely uncivilised, although long Christianised. They had no efficient habit of husbandry. Nor could they construct dwellings appropriate for city-dwelling, inevitably essential to civilisation. They were, because of their unstable laws, lazy and unreliable. Furthermore, their sexual manners were undisciplined, repudiating their wives and neglecting their children. They were, generally, uncouth. Indeed, they were marked by 'their contempt and scorn of all things necessary for the civil life of man'.[84] An, as it were, 'holistic' approach had to be taken to the function of English law and institutions. Their educative, assimilationist role was paramount. So Davies hoped that

> we may conceive an hope that the next generation will in tongue and heart, and every way else, become English ... For heretofore,

> the neglect of the law made the English degenerate and become Irish; and now, on the other side, the execution of the law doth make the Irish grow civil and become English.[85]

A further vital constitutional and international law consequence followed from Davies' definition of the Irish problem. Only the English/British state could be entrusted to undertake the civilising and assimilating mission. There was no need for and no place for the development of independent Irish institutions. This is how he interpreted the institutional developments since the beginning of the Tudor times. The reformation undertaken by Sir Edward Poynings, – crucial to the Anglo-Irish struggle of 'Grattan's Parliament' – was to ensure a form of government in Ireland conformable to that of England. To this end Poynings passed an Act of Parliament (the 10th of Henry VII, cap. 22) whereby all the statutes made in England before that time were enacted, established and made force in Ireland. Another law, the celebrated 'Poynings' Act' of 1495, ensured that no Act should be propounded in any parliament of Ireland, but as such should first be transmitted into England and approved by the King and council there as good and expedient. The object was to obviate the typical and recurrent hazard of colonial regimes, that the colonisers in the land exploit it to their own advantage with exclusive policies not of benefit to the country as a whole. Hence, there must be preserved a full power of metropolitan intervention. So Davies remarks, of Poynings' Act:

> This moved them to refer all laws that were to be passed in Ireland to be considered, corrected, and allowed, first by the state of England, which had always been tender and careful of the good of this people and had long since made them a civil, rich and happy nation, if their own lords and governors there had not sent bad intelligence into England.[86]

The Significance of the Conquest for Later British Legal Policy Towards Ireland

It is difficult to continue to expound upon British legal perspectives on Britain's place in Ireland without encroaching upon the place for an exposition of the Anglo-Irish and certain Irish nationalist, constitutionalist views about the, as it were, organic development of independent Irish constitutional traditions. None the less, it seems clear that, even in the nineteenth century and the years leading up to the 1916–21 conflict and negotiation of the Treaty, the British perspective was that there was no independent Irish political or constitutional identity. Ireland went from its status as a conquered country to one of complete legal, political and military subordination. Subordination is a concept opposed to integration. There was no confusion in British legal and political minds that Ireland was an original part of the British Commonwealth. It was brought in forcibly and kept there through a British willingness, where necessary, to continue to apply force.

Until the Union of Parliaments in 1801 the question of British supremacy was posed in the context of the power of the British Parliament to legislate for Ireland. After 1801 it is difficult to see how the question can be posed legally, and one is left to speculate about what the British rulers thought to be the true foundation of their presence in Ireland. For the period before 1801 it is summarised effectively by Swift MacNeill in his *Constitutional and Parliamentary History of Ireland Until the Union*:

> The question whether the power of the English Kings was established by right of conquest, as English writers have chosen to assert, or, as Irish writers have said, by the voluntary submission of some Irish Chiefs, which would now be regarded as of an interest purely academic, was in times past a subject of the fiercest controversy in connection with the assertion of authority by the English Parliament to make laws binding on Ireland.[87]

It is a well-known fact that an authoritative *obiter dictum* of Lord Coke stated, in *Calvin's Case* that 'albeit Ireland was a distinct dominion, yet the title thereof being by conquest, Ireland might by express words be bound by the Acts of the Parliament of England'.[88] Swift MacNeill quotes Sir John Davies with approval concerning his claims as to the authority, effectively exercised, of the English Parliament to pass laws with respect to Ireland until 1613. He describes Davies as eminent in law and literature and remarks he had just been appointed Lord Chief Justice at the time of his death in 1626. Lord Coke is cited again to the same effect.[89] The practice is not entirely consistent, but there are innumerable instances until 1613 of English parliamentary jurisdiction being exercised. In 1641 a Judges Conference responded to the English House of Commons: 'That the subjects of His Majesty's Kingdom of Ireland are a free people, and to be governed only according to the Common Law of England and Statutes made and established by Parliaments in Ireland, and according to the lawful customs of the same.'[90] However, the English Parliament soon after passed an *Adventurer's Act* to dispose of the land of disloyal Irish and provide for its division among those who would provide for the quelling of rebellion.[91] After 1660 the Irish Parliament was formally responsible for the division of forfeited lands, but the work was in the hands of an English Lord Chancellor, and it was clear that the claim to legislate was merely not being exercised in this case, but was applied in others.[92] After 1690 the English Parliament passed the legislation excluding Catholics from the Irish Parliament. It was responsible, on this occasion, for key transfers of forfeited land and even prohibited the export of wool from Ireland. This last measure provoked Molyneux's *Case of Ireland Stated*,[93] which will be taken as the centrepiece for Chapter 4 on Anglo-Irish views of Ireland's status. In this context the response of the English Parliament is of particular note. It resolved that the treatise of Molyneux should be burnt by the common hangman. It affirmed that Ireland was subordinate to and dependent upon England, 'as being united *and annexed* to the Imperial Crown of that realm' (emphasis added).[94]

The decisive final step in the English/British assertion of supremacy concerned conflicts of appelate (court) jurisdiction between Irish and the English Houses of Lords which led to the devastatingly categorical Irish Declaratory Act of 1720 ('the Sixth of George I', 6 Geo. I, ch. 5). In an extensive study of this particular issue Flaherty demonstrates how complex the issue of an independent Irish Parliament is in terms of British imperial constitutional law. In particular one could suppose that Ireland was conquered and still plead for the autonomy of its Parliament. This could be taken to follow from a Royal grant of the common law to Ireland, then to be developed by its own representative institutions under the Royal authority, for which argument they also relied upon Lord Coke.[95] However, this argument could be taken to depend upon the continuing authority of the Crown *vis-à-vis* Parliament. Following the so-called Glorious Revolution, and particularly the Hanoverian Succession, the authority of Parliament in eighteenth-century England was supreme. The new legal authorities, Blackstone and Mansfield, also

> articulating the consensus view of conquest doctrine in Britain, ... contended that whenever the King acquired new territory and granted it the common law, the supreme power in the dominions, as in the realm of Great Britain, was the King-in-Parliament, leaving no doubt that they meant the *British* Parliament.[96]

The final response was that King George I backed the Lords of Great Britain by granting the Royal Assent to the Irish Declaratory Act. In its Preamble, this Act treated the struggle between the two Houses of Lords as 'attempts ... to shake off the subjection of Ireland upon the Imperial crown of this Realm, which will be of dangerous consequence to Great Britain and Ireland'. It is further stated, once again, that Ireland is 'inseparably *annexed* and united' to Great Britain, and that the British Parliament has full powers to make laws which bind the people and kingdom of Ireland (italics added).

Of course, once again, the word *annex* is used, a word which belongs to the language of conquest.

Given the predominance of Blackstone as the major English constitutional law commentarist of the eighteenth century it is appropriate to consider directly his views. Concerning the issue whether and how Ireland was bound by English statutes, he has the following to say:*

> The Act of 10 Henry VII made all English Acts till then binding, after which none binds unless expressly stated. So where there is mention, Ireland is bound.
>
> For this follows from the very nature and constitution of a dependent state: dependence being very little else, but an obligation to conform to the will or law of that superior person or state upon which the inferior depends. The original and true ground of this superiority is the right of conquest: a right allowed by the law of nations, if not by that of nature; and founded upon a compact either expressly or tacitly made between the conqueror and the conquered, that if they will acknowledge the victor for their master, he will treat them for the future as subjects and not as enemies.

In Blackstone's view the Declaratory Act was intended to reassert these forgotten facts. Ireland's dependence upon the Imperial Crown of Great Britain and its inseparable unification with it were once again stated.

From any historical perspective it would seem strange to speak of the Irish Declaratory Act without going on to describe the so-called Constitution of 1782 and the circumstances of the passing of the Act of Union. While the abolition of the Irish Parliament is partially a function of how the British saw the Anglo-Irish, it is primarily relevant to how the Anglo-Irish saw themselves, since the years 1782–1801 marked a high-water point of their institutional identity. So, the issue will be treated separately. It makes more sense, following the heuristic function of international law analysis, to present this historical material as part of a systematic Anglo-Irish case for a definition of legal-political Irishness. To conclude this chapter it is merely intended to outline how the British themselves understood their place in Ireland during the last 120 years before withdrawal. This should be seen in the context of the refusal of Home Rule to the Irish until 1914.

The stark argument presented here is that the approach to Ireland quite simply continued to be colonial until the end. This

At p. 101 of *Commentaries on the Laws of England* vol. I a Facsimile of the 1st edition of 1765 with an introduction by Stanley Katz, The University of Chicago Press, Chicago, London, 1979.

is seen most starkly in the resistance to Home Rule within the British Parliament. Once it is remembered that the original ideological justification for the conquest was a superiority of culture, it is quite logical to refuse to establish independent Irish political authority on the ground of the immaturity of the people. So, as Curtis documents:

> What both the (Home Rule) debates of 1886 and 1893–4 proved was that a majority of Englishmen, and especially those with education, property and position in society, refused to change their minds about the ingredients of Irish national character. What really killed Home Rule in 1886 was the Anglo-Saxon stereotype of the Irish Celt.[97]

The popular English conception of the Irish as a backward race played a role comparable to the Gramscian concept of hegemony or Foucault's notion of the ironclad disciplining function of 'discourse'.[98] Curtis demonstrates this by numerous citations of racial prejudice from virtually every significant sector of nineteenth and early twentieth-century British society. In particular, Lord Salisbury led the opposition to Gladstone's first Home Rule Bill in 1886 and dominated the Conservative governments of Britain for the next twenty years. He said, during the debates in Parliament in 1886: 'You would not confide free representative institutions to the Hottentots for instance.'[99] Disraeli remarked that the Irish 'hate our free and fertile isle ... Their history describes an unbroken circle of bigotry and blood.'[100] Furthermore, this view, echoed in the sentiments of the ideological founders of Fabian Socialism, the London School of Economics and the Labour Party, Sidney and Beatrice Webb. During a visit to Dublin in 1892 at the time of the second Home Rule Bill defeated in the House of Lords, the Webbs remarked of the Irish, 'The people are charming but we detest them, as we should the Hottentots – for their very virtues. Home Rule is an absolute necessity *in order to depopulate the country of this detestable race* [original emphasis].'[101]

It was a major argument of Home Rulers and some Anglo-Irish that Union and a strong British military presence were not historically necessary to put down the Insurrection of 1798 and to maintain Ireland firmly within the British Empire.[102] At the same time Lecky, who is cited to support the last arguments, (along with O'Connell), is also cited accepted that the fact that the Irish loyalists called for troops to assist them provided the British with the occasion to press for a surrender of their Parliament.[103] A specifically military history of the Union period remarks that the lesson which the British drew from the 1798 Insurrection was that Britain's means of control in Ireland must remain tangible and visible. Lord Redesdale, sent over to Ireland as Lord Chancellor in 1802, remarked 'I have said that this country must be kept for some time as a garrisoned country. I meant a Protestant garrison.'[104] In 1885, as the first Home Rule debate began, Joseph Chamberlain, who led the Liberal Unionist revolt against Gladstone, could say in a speech in Holloway, that: 'The [English] system in Ireland is founded on the bayonets of 30,000 soldiers, encamped permanently in a hostile country.' The atmosphere in late nineteenth-century Ireland has been described in terms of the 'Indian complex': 'It was not the English civilians who kept India. They only administered it. Without the Army there could not be strength – and the Indians, like the Irish, understood and admired strength ... Home Rule was the invention of disloyal fanatics or of paid agitators who only wanted to pull the Empire down.'[105] The conviction that the country would rebel if there was not the implied threat of military force[106] was matched by the confidence that the immature, mercurial Irish temper would respond well to firm military discipline and direction.[107] None of this is discounted by proof of a readiness of the Irish to serve. When war broke out in 1914 it is notorious that the Home Rule leader, Redmond offered his Irish National Volunteers to Kitchener, the War Minister, who refused proposals for an Irish Division or any place for commissions. No trust would be placed in the defence of Ireland by such Irish Volunteers, despite Redmond's appeal to the analogy of the Anglo-Irish Volunteers in 1782 at the time of the American War of Independence. The Irish were not to be trusted.[108]

The so-called conflict of cultures or mentalities remains an essential feature of British–Irish relations. Foster, as the doyen of Anglo-Irish historians, notes how the divergence goes back at least to the seventeenth century. In Gaelic Ireland two 'syndromes' were established by 1600 that would last: the practice of studying for the priesthood abroad and the prevalence of peripatetic Catholic primary school teachers. Alternative educational processes produced alternative patterns of thought. They drove a wedge between English and Irish perceptions. Foster continues, 'Language was a vehicle for this: exaggerations, strange uses of words, deliberate pleasure in paradox ... that awkward English-Irish inter-action that the novelist Elisabeth Bowen would describe as "a mixture of showing-off and suspicion, worse than sex".'[109]

CHAPTER 3

Irish Perspectives on the Conquest and the Foundation of the Irish Claim to Self-Determination

Introduction

A study of the English/British conquest from an Irish perspective is so complex because the significance of past events is inevitably a function of the importance which is attached to them, either at present or at key periods in the history of Irish independence: the founding of O'Connell's Repeal Campaign, the Home Rule Movement, and, above all, the Sinn Fein struggles from 1916 until independence. It is the international law perspective which treats the Elizabethan Conquest as the most significant, since it is from 1603 that Ireland was regarded by England and the international community as belonging to it. Yet that conquest may not occupy a decisive significance in Irish consciousness.

What is a search of the history supposed to yield? A lawyer will look for evidence of whether military defeats were regarded as decisive, as meriting an acceptance of the conquering power *de jure*. For a lawyer it will be very significant if it can be shown that at any point in time the *Irish* did accept the conquest and come to look upon the British monarchy as their own sovereign. A return to a claim to independence will not be possible by virtue of the illegality or illegitimacy of the conquest. It will have to be couched in the language of revolt against a system of government which is in breach of certain basic rights or which has otherwise so conducted itself as to cause a radical, new alienation of the Irish people from the British monarchy.

Obviously the examination of these issues is immensely complicated by the absence of representative, or otherwise authoritative Irish institutions whose standpoint can be analysed. However, this *must not* be allowed to constitute a fundamental obstacle in the view presented here, because the difficulty is itself a function of the conquest itself, the latter being the one – from the British perspective – uncontested fact. A complete destruction of the cultural-political structures of a society must not be allowed, of itself, to constitute evidence of acquiescence in their destruction. That is to say, the absence of an effective framework for the voicing of protest, even for several hundred years, need not mark an extinction of the rights of a people. This would allow for the hiatus represented by the space between the Battle of Kinsale (1601) and O'Connell's Repeal Campaign of the 1830s.

However, there is a more serious difficulty with the argument for the continuity of historical rights, which is the one that will be represented here. Where a conquest has a genocidal intent, and is very largely successful in the execution of that intent, the construction of *national rights* on the basis of historic continuity is bound to have a relatively spurious quality, which will be picked up sharply by the beneficiaries of the conquest. Appeals can be made , in forms of words or proclamations, to pre-conquest national entities or identities. These appeals may be resolutely defended by certain sections of Irish society at particular points in time, and indeed, with great, but *temporary* political and military success. None the less, the rhetoric will not be sustained and the consequences of what was a genocidal conquest will return to haunt the apparently successful revolutionaries.

This perspective is the one which will be used to situate several fundamental features of the Irish political predicament which otherwise appear confusing. The first is that the Gaelic society which was defeated by the Elizabethan Conquest saw itself, as a consequence, as doomed to extinction. The few traces there are of a reaction to the conquest do not look to a resurrection in the future. They saw themselves as experiencing a holocaust. The second feature, which follows as a logical consequence from the first, is that the political life of seventeenth-century Ireland is marked as one which is integral to the rest of the British Isles. The Irish, if they can be so spoken of, took part in British civil wars, on the losing side. The only issue which mattered to them was confessional and the outcome was as disastrous for the Catholic faith as the sixteenth-century conflict had been for the Gaelic Order. However, the Catholic issue was not connected to a matter of Irish independence.

The third and crucial feature of the, as it were, Irish political question, is that the eventual resurrection of the underclass of the Gaelic Order in the nineteenth century was undertaken within the terms of reference of the Anglo-Irish political tradition by O'Connell and, later, the Home Rulers. The crucial feature of this tradition was the relative independence of the so-called Grattan's Parliament. It is this which has led to a permanent reliving of the tragedy of the late sixteenth-century genocide. Above all, this was a House which the Irish wished to enter at a time when the Anglo-Irish no longer wanted any part of it. The acutely pathetic quality of this Irish direction is that it longed for an identity which was itself based upon a denial of the very existence of the Irish people at the time of a conquest, the fact of which could itself, *in consequence*, be denied.[1]

It was the frustration which some Irish felt at their attempt to appropriate to themselves essential features of the Anglo-Irish tradition which can be said to have stimulated others to attempt, in an atmosphere of intense division, to reconstruct rather than resurrect the concept of a Gaelic Order, which could only be in contradistinction to the Anglo-Irish political tradition. This reconstruction took place within the framework of a continental tradition of romantic political culture – a so-called return to origins. As an undertaking of an intellectual-military caste, it could hardly hope to do more than attempt a reversal of almost three hundred years of Irish history (viz. from the 1590s to the 1890s). The so-called cult of violence which accompanies this tradition has to be seen in the light of its attachment to the last remnants of an already virtually extinct Gaelic culture. Literature, in particular the work of Synge, can serve to illustrate the poignancy of an identity which attached itself to scattered Gaelic communities in the west of the country. At the same time the only alternative for the would-be modernising Irish was occupancy of a House, which had been deserted by its Anglo-Irish owners, and which was not considered by the British to give any rights. Home Rule was not for an Irish polity, if it was to mean equal political authority and respect within a British polity.

The would-be resurrected Irish political nation combined a claim of cultural self-determination, a product of nineteenth and twentieth-century international law, with an historical claim simply to restore the Gaelic Order preceding the Elizabethan Conquest. This claim was rejected by Britain in the treaty negotiations of the autumn of 1921, where Britain finally offered a compromise of an Anglo-Irish Grattan-style Parliament. Although the British were largely successful in the treaty negotiations themselves, it was at the price of further accentuating the divisions within Irish society in a civil war which replayed the Gaelic/Anglo-Irish paradigms of identity, both by now pure phantoms. The Gaelic paradigm was eventually enshrined in the Constitution of 1937, except for the partition of the country.

Ireland exists as a state, but has no *raison d'être* in international law. There is a consensus that the project of Irish cultural nationalism has failed. It is obvious that it excludes Protestant, British settlers. However, it is quite disingenuous for anyone to treat this fact as politically significant. The separateness of those inhabitants of Ireland who are of British origin rests in their own consciousness of themselves in terms of their origins, in their own anxiety not to allow their identity to be confused with that of the *natives*, however the latter may care to understand themselves. Such a perspective need not necessarily exclude, as a matter of logic, the *natives* from a revamped Anglo-Irish political culture. In the present context, as a matter of practical politics – since no one speaks of a reincorporation of Ireland into the United Kingdom – this could mean a Northern Irish Assembly as the main focus of political expression for the Catholic or nationalist minority in Northern Ireland.

The conclusion of this analysis is that there can be no legal solution to the Irish problem. It is laden with an immense amount of unfinished business. It will be the function of later chapters to demonstrate the inadequacy of Anglo-Irish and Ulster perceptions of the present crisis. The specific tragedy of the Irish, or the so-called 'mere Irishry' or natives of the island is that their Gaelic Order was exterminated with the conquest. The possibility of an alternative development into an Anglo-Irish political culture was closed to them on racial grounds and, in my view, remains closed to them. Their own project of a resurrected Irish/Gaelic identity has proved vacuous, and, with it, any legal foundation for the Irish state in terms of a right to cultural self-determination, the primary foundation actually asserted by Sinn Fein in 1916, 1918–19 and 1937.

The logic of this argument is the inappropriateness of any solution to the Irish problem which ignores the very seriously damaged nature of Irish political society. It will have to remain to the chapters on the Anglo-Irish and the Ulster Protestant communities to demonstrate that their own views of Irish history preclude them from any positive dialogue with the *natives*. At best what could be on offer would be a participation in a miniature form of an Anglo-Irish identity, which simply denies either the fact or the significance of the conquest. More likely, the assumption will be made, on the British side, that, under no circumstances, could the Ulster Protestant community be expected to associate with the 'mere Irishry' in their so-called Gaelic-Catholic state. This is the true meaning of the calls for the reform of the 1937 Constitution and the abandonment of the supposed exclusiveness of the Gaelic-Catholic project. It might conceivably be seen as common ground that that project be seen as, or be formally, abandoned. However, the problems this will present for the mere Irishry are not the problems of the Ulster Protestant community. Given that the right to cultural self-determination is the primary foundation for state legitimacy in present international law, this means there is no sound argument for an association between the two communities in Ireland. It also means, however, no assured place for the British in Ireland.

Early Seventeenth-Century Gaelic and Old-English Responses to the Conquest

A wide measure of agreement has arisen in Irish historiography that it is possible to use certain Gaelic sources as the most reliable material for an understanding of Irish responses to the Conquest. The two distinctive sources are taken to be the writings of the Gaelic bards and histories of Ireland, in particular that of Geoffrey Keating. Given the controversy, coming from England, which surrounds the quality of Irish historical writing at this time, it might be thought that the distinction between history and literature, which these two sources appear to have found, is a distinction without a difference. So Foster refers to Keating's history as taking 'its place with the outpouring of contemporary Irish hagiographies and annals as "a monument to a doomed civilisation"'.[2] In fact he cites Canny as his source and Canny treats Keating's *History*, in the passage cited, separately from the work done on the compilation of the lives of Irish saints. Indeed, he compares Keating's work, instead, to Sir John Davies's *A Discovery*. The implicit criticism of Foster is hardly worth attempting to resolve, not simply because he represents an irreconcilable Anglo-Irish perspective, but primarily because the general thesis of this study is to follow the radical subjectivisation of history with literature which the New Historicism favours. In particular Stephen Greenblatt explains the role of both as representations of 'the Other'. The discourses of colonialism do the work of colonialism (viz. Sir John Davies). The Gaelic responses are competing discourses.[3] As such both sets of discourses mark not merely problems of verification, but fundamental strangeness,[4] which, it is argued here, have still not been overcome. It is the inevitable subjectivity of the parties engaged which serves to conflate supposedly distinct disciplines. As Hadfield and Maley say in their introduction to *Representing Ireland,*

> every representation is a presentation and a production. The range of the discursive manifestations of Ireland cuts across genres and disciplines from print to painting, from manuscript to folio, from poetry to politics. The essays in this volume deal with literary and historical representation, legal documents, map-making, portraiture, reformation sermons and polemics.[5]

In any case, Canny remarks at the end of his study of the formation of the Irish mentalities after 1580, that the attention he has devoted to poetry is justified because this is the closest one finds in Gaelic literature to the political texts and treatises that would normally provide source material for the historian of political thought. He continues to attach himself to a history of mentalites, indeed, perhaps even to a Hegelian philosophy of mind, when he elaborates further: 'That it is valid to analyse this literature as one would a political text is made clear by the fact that writers who were widely dispersed throughout the country expounded political views that were almost identical, and they also evinced common responses to similar problems.'[6]

The methodological aspects of the uses of poetry are elaborated further by O'Riordan, in *The Gaelic Mind and the Collapse of the Gaelic World.*[7] She insists on making a break with all scholars up till then, who chose to regard the Gaelic poetry as dominated by an awareness of the Conquest.[8] This is to violate the basic hermeneutic rule that Gaelic literature has to be interpreted in its own terms. Such a course is, in her view, open to the charge that the poetry is being looked at through the eyes of nineteenth and twentieth-century nationalist and post-colonial historiography. Her position could be elaborated to mean that Gaelic poetry should not be read to show a consciousness of the implementation of a legal institution drawn from Roman imperial experience and imitated by new would-be Roman Empires. Concretely, this Gaelic perspective will reveal itself in a failure to differentiate extra-insular incursions into the endemic warfare of the Gaelic world.[9] It meant

> the Tudor encroachments were for the most part considered as further military incidents in the careers of the individual lords involved. So, individual Gaelic chiefs came to terms with the Tudor reconquest in a manner which was dictated by their own traditional perceptions of war and military or non-military political objectives.[10]

This is precisely the line of argument which leads to the conclusion that O'Riordan is considering a society which became extinct – hence the celebrated contrived quality of Gaelic-Catholic Ireland today.

However, it is to be doubted whether looking directly to the poetry as evidence of response to the conquest leads to such different results. Canny makes the same general point that the bards did not seem to distinguish conflicts with the English Crown from the internecine conflicts of centuries.[11] The crucial distinction is whether the Gaelic bards could be read as providing evidence that the Gaelic concept of dynasty or lordship, which was local, was being replaced as a primary focus of loyalty by the nation.[12] The consensus still appears to be that in traditional Irish political society unity was not always highly valued, and local autonomy remained central to native concepts of political and social organisation.[13] For the argument of this study – that an entire society was effectively extinguished by an English Conquest, and not that the Irish *responses* to the English Conquest somehow problematised it, it is more effective to be able to point to the incomprehension with which Gaelic society treated the English incursion. As Cunningham puts it, the self-sufficiency of native Irish explanations of contemporary events was an outcome of a society being so introspective that no explanation – that is, of catastrophe – could be afforded other than a supernatural one.[14]

Consistently with 'both' views of the uses to which Gaelic poetry can be put, O'Riordan demonstrates that a pre-conquest Gaelic bardic practice had been to treat as one of unquestioned acceptance the foreigners' rights through victory: 'no different in its perceptions of power and valid claims to that put forward by the poets on behalf of Gaelic lords'.[15] She stresses that whatever the fulminations of the bards against foreigners, they must always be understood as subject to the evident power and aspirations of the individual addressed. Respect for the *de facto* political situation is central to perceptions of the changing world.[16] At the same time O'Riordan considers that the evidence of responses to intrusions since Anglo-Norman times supports a Gaelic willingness to accommodate extraneous elements in their world.[17] Once a lord is settled and effectively wields his authority the only requirement of him is that he fulfil the social obligations expected of a Gaelic lord, notably support of the literati.[18] The dissonance arises where, as in the seventeenth century, the foreigners prove to be unsympathetic.[19]

The concepts of cultural and spiritual unity of Ireland preceeded the Elizabethan Conquest, but were never understood to have a political significance, with the vital consequence that resistance to outside interference could not be seen as having a realistic political dimension. Hence there could be no uniting in the face of foreign encroachments. Nor could foreigners be excluded either for their foreignness or for the threat they might constitute to Gaelic lords.[20] There was no questioning of the right of individual chiefs to make contracts of peace and declarations of war, the true enemy of unity of effort.

However, the English concept of consolidation of victory was opposed to the bards' acceptance of short-term success and hence was entirely foreign to their concept of warfare.[21] O'Riordan allows the inference that the Gaelic mentality could not have understood the English-Roman concept of conquest. From the poetry, it can be seen how the 'stark celebration of the use of force, of the excitement of battle, the glory of frenetic plundering regardless of the wider implications' show

> [T]he Gaelic Irish had little use for the concept of the consolidation of victory or of influence. The 'social lubricant' nature of the warfare in the Gaelic mentality reduced the significance of any one battle in general, but conversely, made it quite important at a particular and local level.[22]

At the same time, continual warfare (forays against the Saxon) was seen as the only guarantee of both protection against them and peace with them. Such familiarity with continual warfare fed a complacency with its vicissitudes and an indifference to the signing of treaties with the Crown and with the receipt of royal pardons.[23]

Acceptance of the right of conquest by force of battle, where land is subjugated to whoever is strongest[24] is none the less decisively limited by the expectation that these will not disturb the status and lifestyle of the Gaelic polity. Uncertainty about what was happening to them led the Gaelic bards to call, inconsistently, for united anti-English efforts and for accommodation, although the attitudes pre-date the conquest by two centuries. They are not prompted by 'awareness' of the eventual fate of the Gaelic system.[25]

At the same time the relative flexibility and compromise implicated in such perpetual vicissitudes of wars *within* the Gaelic polity was made possible, contends O'Riordan, by the cultural homogeneity of the polity. The loser would receive some measure of compensation and the conflict would eventually be taken up again. The key feature of the defeats was the possibility of acculturation of the victor and vanquished.[26] The terms of treaties and submissions were binding only in so far as their desired effect or objective was manifest: 'Victory is a swift and transitory experience – to be exulted in while it lasts.'[27] A royal pardon was an immediate benefit, just as a scrambling to emerge on the victorious side.[28]

Given the Gaelic attitude to the act of conquest, the question remains how they understood its consequences. Again, O'Riordan is anxious to stress that their approach to the defeat of Kinsale, regarded by historians as decisive, was not appreciated as a distinct event by the Gaelic bards.[29] The personalised role of the chiefs meant that an event such as the famous Flight of the Earls took Ireland's life with them. There was an equation of the life of the chief with the life of his lordship and with the sovereignty of his territory. Ireland without its leaders is without its life.[30] Loss is valued not in terms, for instance, of the intensity of anti-English activity, nor in terms of performance in the 'Nine Years War' leading to Kinsale, but simply in terms of the loss of power as such, in the sense of presence:[31] 'Ruin follows the death of the patron, the departure of a chief from his territory. The fertility of the area, the prosperity of the poets, the soul of the country, attach themselves to the person of the chief.'[32]

O'Riordan stresses repeatedly that the Gaels accept success from whatever quarter, and thereby, it can be inferred, they are not quick to appreciate the gradual erosion of their world. She writes:

> The willingness of the Gaelic chiefs to accept favourable terms from a strong adversary is part of the fabric of Gaelic history.

> Gaelic chiefs rarely allowed difference of race to interfere with their individual efforts to stay on the winning side or to blunt the consequences of having chosen the losing side.[33]

Indeed so personalised was the view of the bards that they could only see a defeat engineered by a Gaelic lord on behalf of the Crown as a triumph of the lord himself. This particularly concerns Ormond's identity as an arm of an ever-strengthening central administration.[34]

The conclusion is that Gaelic political civilisation could only be annihilated by the English/British penetration. It was not capable of the dynamic political development which marked its opponent. All it could muster was individual adaptation, the attempt to adjust in individual cases, as best as possible, to maintain one's own status and style. This could only appear, with hindsight and in the long term, as opportunistic and short-sighted. The Gaelic poets recognised the authority, in the sense of victorious power, of James I and assisted, where they were allowed, in the implementation of the Plantation of Ulster. Ireland became a single administrative unit for the first time during his reign. The older polity, which depended upon the power of the chiefs, was defeated by a rival civilisation and disappeared.[35] The objective of the English/British conquest was achieved in terms whereby its victims never understood what was happening to them.

It is almost as a postscript that one considers Keating's *History of Ireland*. The disputes between so-called revisionist and so-called nationalist historians will enter into the use which might be made of this work. Perhaps inconsistently with the heavy reliance which has just been placed on O'Riordan, who may be regarded, at the very least, as exceptionally anxious not to appear in the slightest degree xenophobic, it is now intended to place reliance upon the interpretations of Bradshaw who has provided the most closely argued historian's attack upon revisionism.[36] In fact the use which will be made of Bradshaw is to confirm what is regarded as the central feature of O'Riordan's argument. The significance of Keating in this study will not be that he provided an alternative and convincing political identity for the seventeenth-century new Irish Catholic nation. To satisfy O'Riordan, Keating would have had to provide a framework of political organisation alternative to that of the British. Writing in the 1630s he had clearly no significant impact upon the so-called Confederacy years, whose poetic reflections suffer, in O'Riordan's eyes, the same defects as earlier poetry, Keating's included.[37] However, it is quite another matter whether Keating marks the beginning of the construction of modern Irish Catholic identity. A judgement about this matter is not simply one of assessing whether he reflected accurately the consciousness of his immediate contemporaries. It is also a matter of noting whether and how his ideas were taken up after him. This claim is made by Bradshaw referring to the exceptional quantity of manuscript copies of his work which survive from the early modern period.[38]

Keating does develop a theory of origins connected with geographical identity which has considerable explanatory power when one comes to consider the place of Anglo-Irish and Ulster Protestant communities alongside Irish Catholic, as well as resurrected Gaelic nationalism from the mid-nineteenth century onwards. Ireland is seen as a island repeatedly subject to invasions throughout its history. O'Riordan has already been seen to stress that the exclusion of foreigners, a concept treated to inverted commas in her work, was a concept alien to Irish culture. Hence, even in her terms, the Irish could be said to have a distinctive political culture. It accepted the inevitability of invasions and prided itself on the genius with which it would both absorb invaders and adapt to them, without Ireland as such ceasing to exist.[39]

A crucial feature of such adaptation was the acceptance of the so-called 'Old English' by the 'Old Irish'. This is not surprising since Keating was 'Old English'. As Cunningham points out, the timescale of his history – until the establishment of the Norman Conquest – precludes Keating coming to terms with the New English (or Ulster Protestants). The New English are portrayed merely as alien commentators on Old English and Old Irish society. They are not recognised at all as co-habitants of the same territory.[40] At the heart of this argument is a point which touches the very centre of the English/British justifications of their conquest, the supposedly uncivilised quality of Irish society. The portrayal of the Old Irish as a civilised people is, for Cunningham, a core element of Keating's Catholic-reformation argument that adherence to the true faith had never lapsed in Ireland. This is in contrast to the views of Protestant writers that the Church had lapsed in the medieval period as Rome became corrupt, and that, consequently the Old Irish were barbarous and dependent upon New English Protestant reforming influences to civilise them.[41]

Canny builds upon the argument to provide a more speculative conclusion. Davies and the New English had been aware of the theme of the invasions of Ireland, referring to the *Book of the Taking*. However, they proclaimed that the Elizabethan Conquest had finally brought this process to an end. Keating argued that the conquest of Ireland by the Milesians or Gaelic Irish had been the final one. By doing so Keating was implying that the recent English conquerors of Ireland, like the Scandinavian invaders of earlier times, would, in due course, be expelled by the Milesians.[42]

Bradshaw insists that Keating's *History* is, in effect, a text which well deserves to be counterposed to Davies's *A Discovery*. It is not simply that Keating himself so intended. He says that his ambition is to refute the charges of barbarism made against the 'old foreigners' and the 'native Irish' by Davies, Spenser and others.[43] More significantly, recent scholarship demonstrates that Keating's work belongs squarely in the world of Old English Tridentine Catholicism and, more particularly, a Counter-Reformation historical scholarship and antiquarianism. It insisted upon the authority of ancient sources and on philological competence in expounding them. However, above all, the received opinion is now that Keating's work cannot be taken merely as a desire to record the experience of a doomed civilisation. His aim, as was that of other humanist antiquarians throughout Europe, was to mould the lore relating to the early history of Ireland into an origin-legend tailored to the needs of its seventeenth-century community.[44]

In effect, Bradshaw traces the crucial ethnic and sectarian antagonism of Ireland to Keating's seminal text, although the former does not put it in these terms. Keating redefined Irish identity. Bradshaw recognises and characterises Keating's work as having a crucial rhetorical dimension, which was, as already noted, eventually successful. The key passage in his argument should be quoted at length. Keating wishes to modify the pejorative connotations of the term *Gaill* as applied to the descendants of the twelfth-century colonists:

> This was achieved by means of the interchangeable prefixes *Sean* (Old) and *Fionn* (Fair), applied to the collective noun, the one signifying the antiquity of the medieval settlement, the other the benevolent dispositions of the settlers towards the Gaelic natives. Conversely, a new category of *Nua Ghaill* (New English) was also devised to describe the colonists brought in by the Tudor Conquest and who now constituted a common threat to the two older communities ... The full significance of the ideological shift here implied becomes clear in the light of a third new usage. This was the use of the collective *Éireannaigh* (Irish) – which rarely features in the medieval period – to designate the ancient stocks of Gaelic natives and Old English over and against the New English parvenus, stigmatised accordingly, as 'foreign intruders'.[45]

Bradshaw demonstrates that it was Keating's rhetorical purpose to so construe and present Irish history that it would emerge how the Ireland of the time of Elizabeth was a Catholic kingdom, a fief of the Crown of England, but not to support a myth that the Irish had submitted in time immemorial to an original British Empire.[46] Three essential features of his complex and abstruse argument need to be highlighted. Ireland remained Christian from the time of Patrick and could never lay itself open to a charge of barbarism which might somehow place itself outside the law of nations. Secondly, the transition from an independent kingdom to a fiefdom of England's Crown had been voluntary, not a conquest, and, thereby, accorded and preserved rights and privileges for the Irish Kingdom. Thirdly, there was a dimension of the Norman intrusion which itself could be better characterised as pagan and which was repeating itself with the incursion of the New English. This dimension meant that the new incursions could not be accounted Christian and would not become an integral part of Ireland, hence the expression 'foreign intruder'.

First, Ireland was not an uncivilised, semi-pagan society which had to be reformed by a Christian English monarch acting as an agent for the Pope. The latter had sent Patrick to convert the Irish, and so successful was this enterprise, that 'steadfastness in the Catholic faith' became an attribute of the Irish among the nations of Europe. More deliberately manipulative was Keating's argument, in addition, that the organisation of the Irish Church was not that of monastic Celtic federalism, but an episcopacy which established the bishops as members of the ruling elite. They joined 'the traditionally privileged estates of the laity – the nobility and the *literati* – in deliberating upon the nation's affairs at the triennial parliaments held at Tara and also in the crucial task of electing local kings and the national monarch'.[47] This was, as Bradshaw remarks, an appropriation of the early Irish Christianity for the Counter-Reformation Catholicism.

Secondly, Keating wished to incorporate the late twelfth-century Anglo-Norman Settlement within the framework of his origin-legend, to ensure that the ancient kingdom would survive and that the Anglo-Norman colonists, from whom the Old English were descendant, would be a common patrimony with the natives. The solution was a standard device of early modern origin-legends, the *translatio imperii*. Keating made a virtue of necessity with respect to Pope Adrian's Bull *Laudabiliter*. Keating situated this Bull in the context of an earlier episode. In 1092, Donough O'Brien, the high-king 'with opposition', acting in union with the native nobility, entrusted the sovereign authority to the Pope of the time, Urban II. The way was open to Adrian. He made a grave error in speaking of the state of faith and morals in Ireland, as native ecclesiastics and lay leaders had undertaken these reforms, so far as they were necessary. The crucial dimension of the Bull was its qualified terms 'to maintain and protect the privileges and liberties (termain) of the country'.[48] While a conquest would have established a constitutional *tabula rasa*, reasons Bradshaw, this last clause guaranteed the island's constitutional status as a kingdom. The constitutional basis upon which the Irish clergy accepted Henry II was 'on consideration of the conditions laid down in the [Pope's] letter'.[49] Bradshaw distinguishes the bonds of Gaelic clientship and the bands of Anglo-Norman fealty, but considers the end effect intended by Keating was that the native chiefs acknowledged the overlordship of Henry and were recognised as his vassals. This secured the assimilation of the island's political structure into the feudal conglomerate over which Henry presided.[50]

Thirdly, there was a shadow side to the Anglo-Norman incursion, a practice of plunder, murder etc. which Keating is able to compare to the character of the New English at the beginning of the seventeenth century. This leads him to make a distinction between a Christian conquest and a pagan conquest. In the latter, 'the natives are forcibly expelled, their language is suppressed and the territory is repopulated by colonists from the metropolis'. The former

> is achieved by moderation and is characterised by benevolence towards the native inhabitants: nothing more is required of them than to acknowledge the sovereignty of the conqueror and to accept colonists from the metropolis to settle among them. In a Christian conquest ... the colonists manifest their beneficent dispositions by accommodating themselves to native society, in particular by adopting the native language.[51]

This brings Bradshaw to what he sees as the central message of Keating, which is equally central to the argument of this study. While the work may be regarded as fanciful in its description of an ancient Irish polity,[52] it is very clear in its opposition to the project of Anglicisation of the Irish community, as being uncivilised in its present form. Keating is assuming that the desire to suppress the language implies a desire to extirpate those who speak it.[53] He insists upon an alternative process of inculturation whereby the colonists transformed themselves from aliens to naturalised denizens. In the twelfth century the military allies of the renegade Irish chief MacMurrough practised a violence which deserved the hatred of the natives. They became extinct, and it was a more beneficent Old English who assimilated with the natives. It is precisely this tendency which the notorious tract by Edmund Spenser, *A View of the Present State of Ireland*, deplores. So Keating establishes in the eyes of the Old Irish ('mere Irishry') a respectable genealogy for the Old English, who, as naturalised denizens, were joint legatees with the native Gaels, of the ancient Kingdom of Ireland. The crucial final stage in the argument is to compare the allies of MacMurrough with the New English. The latter have the pretension to be engaging in reforms, particularly cultural Anglicisation, religious penal law, land seizures through plantation, etc. These all are done in the name of reforming the inhabitants of the island. However, their violence and greed will eventually suffer the same fate as that of MacMurrough's buccaneering allies. So, Bradshaw concludes, 'Those now struggling to maintain the liberties and privileges of the historic Irish nation could be assured that God would crown their struggle with victory.'[54]

Such a vital conclusion requires a little further analysis. As O'Buachalla stresses in his Forward to the 1987 reprint of the *History*: 'The Elizabethan intellectual rationalisation for both Reformation and conquest in Ireland rested on one simple premise: the Irish were primitive barbarians, bereft of either civility or religion.'[55] In so far as the task of the study is to reconstruct the Irish justification for resisting a British claim to Ireland, it has to be seen, from the early seventeenth century quite simply in terms of resistance to a British project which is seen, and experienced as genocidal. The forging of a common Irish identity against the English/British, where none was there before, is definitely a construction of identity *in opposition,* but the process appears to have had a real foundation.

Sir John Davies gives, in *A Discovery*, an account of medieval Irish history which is similar to Keating's in accepting the rogue dimension to the English penetration and the advantage which English settlers expected to gain from the Irish being treated as outlaws. He commends that this practice should be firmly put into the past. The Irish should be entitled to the protection of the common law, albeit at the price that they should accept Anglicisation. Whether and how this policy was adopted became the crucial issue for debate in the course of the seventeenth century, as can be seen from a final look at Keating's *History* which needs, once again, to be placed in context. It is the threat and experience of genocide, based upon an openly articulated policy, itself founded on racial contempt, which forges an Irish political identity which need have no more content than to be rid of impossible masters. The claim of an Irish Catholic nation for independence is no more than a wish to be separated from a polity which they consider cannot accept them.

Hence, some further exploration of the paradox which has continued to plague British–Irish relations since the Elizabethan Conquest, at the latest, is necessary. What was the meaning of the charge of incivility against the Irish? What ideological purpose did it serve? To what extent were the Irish simply interested in an equality of rights within a British polity and what conditions favoured a decision to attempt to attain such an equality outside the British polity? This problematic does not place an Irish claim to statehood firmly in terms of a claim to separate idenity, nor to a restoration of prior rights, but simply expresses an exasperation with the continuance of an unviable polity. What follows will be an attempt to explore the nature of a racial antagonism from an Irish Catholic perspective by looking more closely at how Keating thought he was responding to his English racial critics. This is the starting point for the foundation of the Irish Catholic nation by Daniel O'Connell in the first half of the nineteenth century. The terms of his criticism of the functioning of the United Kingdom, and the need for a repeal of the Act of Union are, in fact, set by the controversies between such as Keating and his opponents.

The Racial Nature of the British–Irish Antagonism and the Foundation of the Modern Irish Catholic Nation

A crucial division within English/British opinion at the time of the conquest was whether to aim to integrate the Irish into a common British legal order or to marginalise them as at least semi-outlaws. It had been, at least ostensibly, the intention of Sir John Davies to insist upon an equality of treatment, accompanied by a policy of Anglicisation. However, a firmly opposed view had been Edmund Spenser's, which also added the spice that the Old English were particularly reprehensible because they had degenerated into the ways of the 'mere Irishry'. An importance of this perspective is its sustained character, which has attracted immense scholarly attention in post-colonial Ireland. However, the reason for looking more closely at it now is to throw some light on what may be called modern Catholic nationalism's (after O'Connell) main objection to the British state, namely, the inequality of its operation.

The details of Spenser's argument are not as important as the context in which it could be presented. There was a definite conflict between the style of Gaelic organisation and English law, particularly in terms of the rules of primogeniture, excluding the 'rest of the relatives' and any transformation from warlordship to subjection to monarchy, disenabling military retainers.[56] However, there was a standard colonial dimension to the extension of English law to Ireland, in that it need not limit the possibilities of plunder for the New English colonial administrators. 'The recovery of alleged concealed crown titles in both Gaelic and Anglo-Irish territories and the recovery of leases on which ancient conditions had apparently been violated' were the means whereby 'a larger administrative group … had decided to regard the use of English law in Ireland not as a means of reform, but simply as an aid towards personal advancement'.[57] The combination of these two factors favoured the view that English law could not triumph of itself. Coercion was needed. Yet to use coercion would be to abandon the idea of the English kingship of Ireland. Spenser appeared to ignore this ideological function of the law in arguing that conquest alone was the way to bring order to Ireland. However, once the conquest had been completed, Davies could argue *post facto* that it had been the only way forward, *and then give English law pride of place as the means to consolidate the conquest.* Then, Spenser's arguments could be reintegrated into Britain's ideological position and the ban on the publication of his work could be lifted.[58] Davies did not criticise the failure of English law as such, but the function which it now played was integrative with, not in opposition to, the assumption which underlay Spenser's analysis of Irish society. O'Connell was to return to this aspect of Davies's thought.

Hence the relevance of Spenser's conviction that the common law could not simply be applied to the exotic character of Irish political culture: the latter had to be extirpated. Only when this had been achieved through the reduction of the Irish, through mass starvation and full military repression, to a society without culture could the English law be applied.[59] So the reasons given for this view of Irish society provide an essential ideological background to the apparently continued tendency not to apply English law equally to the Irish. Spenser is taken as affording a defence of Lord Grey who was briefly Governor of Ireland from 1580 till 1582.[60] The irony of the 'cult of civility' of which the Irish were doomed to be the victims is that it was always a part of a so-called humanist homage to power: 'They plumped for the ruling classes, empires and luminaries of past civil times.'[61]

In this context Spenser demonstrates that the Irish are of barbarous Scythian descent and therefore peculiarly in need of the education which alone a conqueror could provide.[62] McCabe notes how, according to Grey, the Irish were addicted to treachery and breach of fidelity, itself attributable to a defective religion which dispenses with political oaths for advantage. Spenser is seen to go further in suggesting that the Catholicism of the 'mere' Irish springs less from spiritual conviction than from political defiance.[63] McCabe stresses that Spenser supported Grey long after he could expect any advantage because he shared the latter's politics. There was need for a 'thorough' policy in the face of the extent of the corruption of Ireland:

> for all those evils must first be cut away by a strong hand before any good can be planted like as the corrupt branches and unwholesome boughs are first to be pruned and the foul moss cleansed and scraped away before the tree can bring forth any good fruit.[64]

McCabe sees this spirit as distinctive of what Ireland had to expect through the seventeenth century. The 'thoroughness' of a policy was supposed to eliminate compromise. It was taken to arouse the fear of the natives, as mentioned in Elizabeth's commission to Grey, that 'we have a determination as it were to roote them out', which McCabe describes as a Cromwellian dream a century before

Cromwell.[65] He comments that such a policy could be taken 'to involve the extermination of large sections of the indigenous population. This, in effect, is what happened in Munster and was now being suggested for Ulster as well.'[66] The conception, in Spenser's words, was of the need to destroy 'all that rebellious rout of loose *people* which either do now stand out in open arms or in wandering companies do keep the woods spoiling and infesting the good subject.'[67,68] The final intention is suggested by the words 'The end I can assure me will be very short. The proof whereof I saw sufficiently ensampled in those late wars in Munster ... in short space there were none almost left and a most populous and plentiful country suddenly left devoid of man or beast.'[69] The civilisation of the Renaissance stimulated comparison between the English and the Irish following the differences between the Greeks and the Scythians.[70]

The fullest contemporary statement, in the 1630s, in opposition to Spenser-like arguments comes from Keating and they mark an easy starting point for the arguments of the Irish Catholic nation. The focus of his defence is 'the unfairness which continues to be practised on her inhabitants, alike the old foreigners who are in possession more than four hundred years from the Norman invasion down, as well as the native Irish who have had possession during almost three thousand years'.[71] He accuses so-called new foreigners, including Spenser and Sir John Davies, specifically of racism. They write of Ireland and the Irish – there being no difficulty on either side in identifying the object of abuse and defence, respectively – according to the fashion of the bettle.

> For it is the fashion of the bettle, when it lifts its head in the summertime, to go about fluttering, and not to stoop towards any delicate flower that may be in the field, or any blossem in the garden, though they be all roses or lilies, but it keeps bustling about until it meets with dung of horse or cow, and proceeds to roll itself therein. Thus it is with the set above-named; they have displayed no inclination to treat of the virtues or the good qualities of the nobles amoung the old foreigners and the native Irish who then dwelt in Ireland; such as to write on their valour and on their piety, on the number of abbeys they had founded, and what land and endowments for worship they had bestowed on them; on the privileges they had granted to the learned professors of Ireland, and all the reverence they manifested towards churchmen and prelates: on every immunity they secured for their sages ... However, nothing of all of this is described in the works of the present-day foreigners, but they take notice of the ways of inferiors and wretched little hags, ignoring the worthy actions of the gentry.[72]

The standard feature of racism is in this charge – a blanket rejection of a people by virtue of an undifferentiated judgement.

For instance, 'it is a lie to say that the Irish are a people who eat human flesh'.[73] Keating detects a genocidal intention in the criticism of Irish culture as such. He notes Stanihurst's criticism of the Old English that they were not firm enough in their resistance to Gaelic. He says that 'however excellent the Gaelic language may be, that whoever smacks thereof, would likewise savour of the ill-manners of the folk whose language it is'. He goes on to distinguish a Christian conquest from a pagan conquest as one in which it is sufficient to obtain a submission and fidelity from the people who have been subdued, rather than bringing destruction on the people who inhabit the land, so as to send new people from oneself to inhabit the country which has been taken by force. The conclusion of Keating's argument is that 'it is not possible to banish the language without banishing the folk whose language it is'.[74] The critics of Ireland and the Irish have not understood, since they were illiterate in the Irish language, that 'it was thus Ireland was (being) a kingdom apart by herself, like a little world, and that the nobles and the learned who were there long ago arranged to have jurisprudence, medicine, poetry, and music established in Ireland with appropriate regulations'.[75]

The criticism which Keating makes is simply that, in bad faith, English writers give a partial picture of all aspects of Irish life, leaving out anything that might be of advantage to the Irish.[76] As Greenblatt puts it with respect to European travel anecdotes in the Americas: 'The authors of the anecdotes with which this book concerns itself were liars – few of them *steady* liars ... but frequent and cunning liars nonetheless, whose position virtually required the strategic manipulation and distortion and outright suppression of the truth.' This is not to say that a clear picture will emerge, a truth behind the misrepresentation. Greenblatt continues: 'Instead we find ourselves groping uneasily amoung the mass of textual traces, instances of bad faith jostling homely (and often misleading) attempts to tell the truth.'[77] This is also the sense of Keating's charge of racism: 'In a like manner, if there are evil customs among part of the unfree clans of Ireland, all Irishmen are not to be reviled because of them, and whoever would do so, I do not think the credit of a historian should be given him.' This applies to the criticism of sexual laxity among Irish clergy – there is some evidence of it; equally, for the sexual manners of the lay population, in some cases there are lapses: 'the inhabitants of an entire country should not be censured because of these'.[78]

Sir John Davies was particularly abusive of the legal institutions of tanistry and gavelkind, which he characterised as 'evil'. He says of them that they mark laws which differ from 'the Laws and Customs of All Civil Nations'. The elections and partitions caused by these customs 'hath been the true cause of such desolation and barbarism in this land, as the like was never seen in any country that professed the name of Christ'.[79] Davies insists that people who use such customs 'must of necessity be rebels to all good government, destroy the commonwealth wherein they live, and bring barbarism and desolation upon the richest and most fruitful land of the world'.[80] Keating does not have any particular attachment to these customs. Each land develops and changes its laws according to its circumstances. In Ireland, given a widespread measure of violence, it seemed sound to have as a leader, not simply the son of the previous leader, who could turn out to be too young or otherwise unfit, but a person elected as the most effective. So much for the 'tanist'. It made sense to divide up inherited land among all of the sons, instead of going for primogeniture, because this created a partnership in the land and made it easier to defend it militarily than trying to raise a defence from the rent on the land, which would usually have been inadequate.[81] Davies's opinion has to be characterised for what it is: 'Whereof, it is not honest in John Davies to find fault with the native jurisprudence.'[82]

Clearly the object of Davies's writing, as O'Connell returns to the matter, is simply to find a pretext to dispossess the barbarians of their land. It was very much part of Davies's argument to accept the critique of Spenser and others that there was a need for a drastic response to the Irish problem because one could not speak of any organic development of the Kingdom since the Anglo-Norman conquest, as Keating wished to argue. Instead, the Anglo-Normans had themselves reverted to Irish ways and must therefore be considered as degenerate as the latter.[83]

As has already been noted, in the study of Bradshaw, Keating did not dispute an English kingship in Ireland. It had been accepted by the Irish, and particularly by the clergy, through a submission and transfer of the Pope. However, it had been subject to conditions, that the English King 'should maintain and protect every privilege and every term on land that was in the country'.[84] After this point Keating outlines the misbehaviour and misrule of the Anglo-Normans in Ireland. He concludes

> that it was owing to tyranny and wrong and the want of fulfilling their own law on the part of the Norman leaders in Ireland that there was so much resistance on the part of the Gaels to the Norman yoke. For I do not think there is a race in Europe who would be more obedient to law than the Irish if the law were justly administered to them. And this is the testimony which John Davies gives of them.[85]

O'Connell and the Rights of the Irish Nation

The construction of Irish rights which O'Connell presented between the 1820s and the 1840s is so important because he advocated not only Catholic emancipation, but also the coming together of an Irish Catholic political society for the first time since the defeat of James II at the Battle of the Boyne and the failure of the Treaty of Limerick of 1691. He is generally reputed to have been politically sectarian and to have contributed decisively to splitting Ireland into unionist/Protestant and nationalist/Catholic.[86] Whether or not O'Connell was himself sectarian, he chose to construct his legal grievances against the British state in a manner which took the debate back to the conquests of the sixteenth and seventeenth century. The central feature of this decision was that the very presence of the New English in Ireland could only come into dispute. Two hundred years, say from the 1620s to the 1820s would not be enough to establish a permanent place for that community in Ireland, particularly as it did not have an integrative project. Any Catholic intellectual construction which returned to this period would also bring to recollection that the Old English invasion had been taken to be the last which was acceptable.

The least which can be said for O'Connell is that his opponents, in the case of Catholic emancipation, saw the conflict in these terms. Sir Robert Peel assumed that emancipation would not resolve a Catholic sense of grievance and he gave way to it eventually without any recourse to principle, simply facing the unavoidable force of O'Connell's mass political movement. What would follow could only be a continued rearguard action, as the struggle went forth to recover the confiscated land and to remove the Protestant Ascendancy from all influence in the administration of the Irish state – a goal which could be most easily achieved through the Repeal of the Union and the re-establishment of an Irish Parliament.[87]

There may be liberal Catholics and liberal Protestants, but the struggle was about who controlled the political and economic resources of the country. It was seen by a significant proportion of Protestant, that is, New English, eyes that they owed their position to confiscations which they had to be able to maintain, hence Peel's 'unprincipled' resistance to both Catholic Emancipation and the Repeal Movement.[88] On the Catholic side there was equally 'a popular awareness of great historical injustice and a vague desire to recover lost rights and privileges stemming from events in the seventeenth and eighteenth centuries'.[89] As a populist politician it was inevitable that O'Connell would direct his scholarly and legal attention back to the very period of Davies and Keating.

O'Connell begins his work with a citation of legislation of James I, of 1612, which abolished all distinctions of race between English and Irish, with the intent that 'they may grow into one nation'.[90] This policy never was and still is not implemented. Instead the English government supported newly arrived English and Scottish Protestants against the native Irish and those of English descent who rejected the Reformation. There was a systematic confiscation of Irish lands through a 'Commission to Enquire into Defective Titles'. The Treaty of Limerick of 1691 was one final attempt to restore the unity and allegiance of the Kingdom on the basis of the equal protection of person and property, in particular with a freedom to exercise one's religion.[91] This was also dishonoured with the infamous Penal Laws.

A crucial interpretation of constitutional history concerns the republican movement of the 1790s, the '98 Rebellion. The Catholics were conciliated and kept away from the discontent: 'That which would otherwise have been a revolution, became only an unsuccessful rebellion. The intelligent and leading Catholics were conciliated and Ireland was once again, by the wise policy of concession and conciliation, saved to the British crown.'[92] There followed the Union, with once again the programme of equality of treatment, with the badge of religion having no significance, but emancipation came only after a struggle: 'At length a change came over the spirit of our proceedings. The people of Ireland ceased to court patronage ... They became "friends to themselves".'[93] If Ireland had retained its Parliament, the popular majority would have been able, by now, to have passed all the necessary salutary measures. Without the Union, Ireland would be, among the Dominions the country in which the greatest progress had been made in civil and religious liberties. With a Parliament, there could be a genuine allegiance to the British throne, but with a vindication of a title to constitutional freedom for the Irish people: 'She has vainly sought EQUALITY-IDENTITY. She has been refused. Her last demand is free from any alternative – IT IS THE REPEAL.'[94]

O'Connell sees this failure not as a matter of high state policy, but a matter of racial antipathy and religious bigotry which involves the English people in guilt with their Government.[95] In the first instance O'Connell relies upon Sir John Davies himself for evidence of the racial abuse to which the Irish were subject at least until the time of Elizabeth, meaning, quite simply, a refusal to apply the law equally and a practice of treating the Irish as outside the law.[96] He relies heavily upon Spenser to illustrate how the Elizabethan Conquest was executed – a genocidal project, which had, through devastation of the country, the object to starve the population to cannibalism and extinction.[97] O'Connell insists upon quoting what he calls a 'distinguished Protestant clergyman named Leland' to pinpoint the object of the English enterprise:

> The true cause which for a long time fatally opposed the gradual coalition of the Irish and English race, under one form of government, was, that the great English settlers found it more for their immediate interest, that a free course should be left to their oppressions; *that many of those* WHOSE LANDS THEY COVETED *should be considered as* ALIENS; that they should be furnished for their petty wars by arbitrary exactions; *and in their rapines and* MASSACRES, be freed from the terrors of a rigidly impartial and severe tribunal – *Leland etc.*[98]

Such argument by O'Connell is in no way dependent upon the construction, fictive or otherwise, of an Irish identity. On the contrary, the Irish had no sense of political union, or centralisation, being totally divided among themselves. Particular chieftains could easily be corrupted to make alliances with the British.[99] However, O'Connell does not base claims to Irish independence upon arguments about identity. In fact the issue of identity is, as a problem, solved for the Irish by the apparent ease with which their English and Scottish oppressors identify, for their part, whom they are going to exploit and murder. The Irish are, in his view, the passive recipients of a murderous racial loathing. There is instead 'an active anti-Irish spirit – the national antipathy to and jealousy of this country'.[100] Following on the distinction between Christian and pagan conquest, reminiscent of Keating, O'Connell observes that the style of the Elizabethan Conquest would have aroused compassion if it had been related with respect to the remotest and obscure barbarians and infidels: 'But let it be recollected that these are authentic and unimpeachable narratives of crimes which Christian Englishmen committed upon Christian Irish.'[101] The question is how to be rid of such a style of government. O'Connell finishes his treatment of the Elizabethan Conquest with a final quotation from Sir John Davies, using his metaphor about the Irish people being 'brayed as in a mortar with a sword'.[102] This remains the leading principle of British government of Ireland.[103] The only rational title which Britain could have to Ireland would be one of compact, which gave the people of Ireland a right to the benefit of British laws, 'a right which is a dead letter even unto the present day'.[104]

It is proposed to conclude the account of O'Connell's argument with his comments on the Plantation of Ulster and his description of the project which he saw as bound up with the Cromwellian conquest. Throughout, he assumes that Ireland is properly an integral part of the domains of the British monarchy. His only argument against the Plantation of Ulster is that it is, once again, part of a pattern of unjust administration and application of laws. The earls, particularly, Tyrone, are threatened and instigated to flight. There follows purely fabricated charges of conspiracy and treason. These are used as a pretext for a confiscation of estates. Even here there is an inconsistency in practice. The tenants are admitted to hold an interest in the lands which goes beyond that of the chieftains. So the legal arguments against the latter should not be decisive.[105] In fact, such arguments are not determining. Rather, decisive for James I and his administration are spurious arguments about the 'incivility' of the Irish and the need to implant their 'civil' elements of population. These were employed specifically by Sir John Davies before the Parliament of 1613 to justify the legislation which was to provide a legal foundation for the Ulster Plantation. It had to be directed against the tenants of the earls, whose estates were in perpetuities. As the tenants themselves had to be removed it was necessary to calumnise them. This is where the racial arguments of Geraldus, Spenser and others proved decisive. The importance of this argument of Davies merits its citation at length:

> And as these men had no certain estates of inheritance, so did they never till now claim any such estates, nor conceive that their lawful heirs should inherit the land which they possessed: which is manifest by two arguments:
>
> 1. They never esteemed lawful matrimony, to the end they might have lawful heirs!
> 2. They never did build any houses, nor plant orchards or gardens, nor take any care of their posterities.
>
> If these men had no estates in law, either in their main chiefries or in their inferior tenancies, it followeth, that if his Majesty, who is undoubted Lord Paramount, do seize and dispose of these lands, they can make no title against his Majesty or his patentees ... The only scruple which remains, consists in this point; whether the King may, in conscience or honour remove the ancient tenants, and bring in strangers amoung them. Truely his majesty may not only take this course lawfully, but he is bound in conscience so to do.
>
> For, ... his Majesty is bound in conscience to use all lawful and just courses to reduce his people from barbarism to civility ... Now, civility cannot possibly be planted among them but by this mixed plantation of civil men, which likewise could not be without removal and transplantation of some of the natives, and settling of their possessions in a course of common law; for if themselves were suffered to possess the whole country, as their septs have done – for many hundreds of years past, they would never to the end of the world build houses, make townships or villages, or manure or improve the land as it ought to be.[106]

For O'Connell the Cromwellian confiscations mark the virtual completion of the disinheriting of the Irish population, whether Old English or 'mere Irishry'. Although the Irish Catholics fought on the side of the Crown in the Civil Wars of the 1640s, they were not restored in their interests after 1660. The confiscations of Stafford, under Charles I were very severe,[107] but the intervention of Cromwell was on a different scale. O'Connell quotes from Leland, Warner, Clarendon, Carte's Ormond and others, to demonstrate that the stated objective of Cromwell's epoch was genocide. The object of seizing and settling the land of Ireland could, in any case, only be achieved if its population was removed completely from the land. The favourite word employed is 'Extirpation'.[108] Spenser appears again, with his remedy that the Irish be so starved that they be induced to eat one another.[109] Of course, particular stress is played on the massacres following the siege of Drogheda.[110] However, O'Connell cites from the reports of an English army officer charged with the clearing of Ireland on the success of his efforts: 'About the year 1652 and 1653, the plague and famine had so swept away whole counties, that a man might travel twenty or thirty miles and not see a living creature, either man, beast or bird; they being either all dead, or had quit those desolate places.'[111]

O'Connell's aim in describing this particular history is to confirm his general argument for Irish independence. Religious bigotry inflamed the national hostility of England to Ireland. Cromwell felt compelled to root out papists.[112] If it is said that it was not the people of England but the Government who were guilty of attempts to exterminate the Irish nation, this observation is absurd, in O'Connell's view:

> The Government had at all times in their slaughter of the Irish the approbation of the English people. Even the present administration is popular in England in the precise proportion of the hatred they exhibit to the Irish people; and *this* is the proposition of historic and perpetual truth, but to the Cromwellian wars, the distinction between the people and the Government could never apply. These were the wars, emphatically, of the English people. They were emphatically the most cruel and murderous wars the Irish ever sustained.[113]

By way of conclusion, it might be worth noting how far O'Connell discounted purely legal English arguments for sovereignty over Ireland as themselves a mark of English racism. They were so 'flippant' as to create the impression that it was not felt worth the trouble on their part to construct serious legal arguments. He considers Davies, as James I's Attorney-General, the best source to understand 'the nature of the English *acquisition* of Ireland, and the mode in which the supposed conquerors disposed of the country'. For O'Connell, the 'first specimen of the flippancy with which the English disposed or Ireland' was a grant of all of Ireland to ten of the English nation, though they had not gained possession of one-third part of the kingdom, thereby leaving nothing to be granted to the natives. On the basis of a precarious possession of a part of the land, the population were, somehow, to be bereft.[114] O'Connell concludes the treatment of the final conquest by reference to a statute of Elizabeth (1669, sess. 3 chap. 1). This speaks of legends of the Kings of Briton, myths of wanderings from out of the Bay of Biscay, and homages of numerous Irish kings to Henry II. This is regarded by O'Connell as 'ludicrous'. Such is the context in which he prefers, instead, to insist that the only rational ground of title to Ireland, *one which he does not dispute,* is a compact which gives the people of Ireland a right to the benefit of British laws, a right which is a dead letter.[115]

The Irish claim to independence, coming out of the Irish Catholic tradition which culminates in O'Connell is an *ex post facto* argument for human rights, rationalistically based on a claim to an equality and identity with English and Scottish people. It does not require to refute English legal claims to Ireland, if only because there is no claim that Ireland had any political identity preceding the various conquests. It is, however, based on the assumption that the English or British do not regard the Irish as part of their polity.

CHAPTER 4

The Anglo-Irish Perspective: Was Ireland Really Conquered?

The question whether Ireland was really conquered is likely to be posed by those who, quite simply, do not think that it needed liberating in the period 1916–22. There was not a decisive coercive element to the British presence in Ireland. This proposition has several vital elements. The relationship between Ireland and Britain rested upon consent. While the history of relations between the two countries was troubled, there was no principled racial hostility which divided Ireland from Britain. Injustices may have arisen. They could be addressed and overcome through reforms which the political system was perfectly capable of assuring.

To say that the relationship rested on consent is also to make an important statement about identity. It has been common ground that the intellectual presentation of the Irish Catholic nation involved an acceptance of the place of the Crown in Ireland through Henry II to James I. However, a crucial feature of the Anglo-Irish argument might be that there was no separation of Irish and British except on religious grounds, and these grounds were necessary for the security of the confessional states which dominated Europe as a whole until after the French Revolution. Britain, indeed, abandoned the essentials of its identity as a confessional Anglican state in 1829 to accommodate its Irish subjects. Continued disadvantage was of a class character and so of a kind common to the United Kingdom as a whole, even if especially accentuated in Ireland. The Irish were not 'the other' for British society and have never been treated legally as aliens.

The issue of common identity is taken to have serious implications for the formation of legal identity, indeed for the idea of Ireland as a political entity and as a state. Ireland's rights as a nation and a state can only be and should be formulated in language which is an integral part of Ireland's political development within an association with the Crown. These rights can be expressed in terms of the Irish Parliament: its original rights; its struggle for autonomy in the eighteenth century; possible irregularities in its dissolution; the subsequent struggle to have these rights restored; the quite unnecessary resort to force by persons motivated by a peculiarly intellectual construction of Gaelic mysticism, which was quite temporary and never succeeded in obtaining a hold on the Irish national imagination; a peace settlement in 1921 which entailed an acceptance by the Irish 'revolutionaries' of the main tenets of British imperial constitutional law; and a symbolic aberration brought about by de Valera's republicans in the 1930s, with the Constitution of 1937. The final stage in an uneven but, none the less, unbroken history, is to remove certain offensive symbols of the Constitution and leave the Irish state as British, with Irish name-tags, albeit in possession of a constitution which is rather more modern and European than its British original.

This is the fullest possible statement of the argument that Ireland was not conquered. It effectively reduces all legal questions, for virtually all of the history of the country, to constitutional rather than international law questions. It is not necessarily a refutation of this perspective that violence was used successfully to disrupt the natural, organic development of this constitutional history, since Ireland is not now in an uncontested constitutional environment. It may be that certain of such forced developments need to be reversed. In particular it has to be recognised that the Gaelic-nationalist construction of a right to cultural/political self-determination was a spurious, and indeed largely Anglo-Irish contrivance, which is anachronistic, not simply in the context of general British political culture, but also in terms of the true grievances of the Irish Catholic nation.

The intention is to test the above presentation as far as possible in the light of expositions by Anglo-Irish writers or by those who so understand themselves, primarily historians but also a number of constitutional theorists. No criticisms of the perspective will be taken into account unless they come from within this tradition. It may, however, be stated that the argument, even in its most unqualified form, is not incompatible with even the most unqualified Gaelic-Irish perspective. It is a perfectly coherent outcome of the successful political and cultural genocide of a people that the only language in which it is able to express itself is that of its conquerors. The crucial difference from the Anglo-Irish perspective is that this exercise should be understood not as genocide but as a successful modernisation and assimilation.

The Irish Parliament and the Irish Nation: The Seventeenth and Eighteenth Centuries

An argument that Ireland was not a colony could be regarded as quite close to the contention that the Irish should not be treated as if they were a colony. In other words Anglo-Irish arguments about their constitutional position might be found which could serve very well for Irish Catholics who were to claim that they were unjustly treated, even if the original Anglo-Irish argument was not intended to apply to them. Irish Protestants claimed that they did not live in a colony by relying on historical and legal considerations. The key figure in this picture is well known to be William Molyneux.[1]

Controversy in the historical literature tends to look directly to the question of whether Molyneux's arguments can be taken to have reflected accurately the conditions of Irish political life, above all, in the eighteenth century. Ireland's status as an independent Kingdom depended on the claim that the connection between the two Kingdoms rested in the person of the monarch. If this had some truth in the seventeenth century, the triumph of parliamentary government in the eighteenth century was to mean subordination of the Irish to the English Parliament.[2]

At the same time Molyneux's argument is taken to have claimed that not only had those who presently inhabit Ireland accepted English constitutional government, but also the Gaelic dimension of Irish life was no longer significant. The great body of the present inhabitants were descended from settlers. This is taken to be an appeal to common roots with English blood which came to have less and less appeal the more it was appreciated that it was not politically effective in persuading the English/British to treat their Anglo-Irish 'kith and kin' as equal.[3] Nor was it historically fair. This might seem an oddly evaluative argument for a historian to employ, but it responded to the factual enquiry whether the Irish Parliament could be said to speak for the Irish nation: 'If there had been an ancient contract between the English Crown and the Irish nation, it was a nation that Molyneux's own ancestors had subsequently deprived of its property and civil rights.' Molyneux's account of this is described as 'barefaced'. The supposition that there remained only a thousand or so 'ancient Irish' amounted to an identification of the Protestant Ascendancy as the only true Irish 'nation'.[4] This could be taken as a breaking-point for the whole attempt to construct the right of the Irish nation around the rights of its Parliament. This Parliament had never been willing to integrate the Irish Catholic nation into its life and this was the stumbling block in the way of it being the basis of Irish legal identity.[5] Hence, for Repealists, such as O'Connell, to campaign for a restoration of the Irish Parliament was not politically realistic, as such a parliament could not have the same significance to Protestant Irish people after they had lost their political ascendancy through Catholic emancipation.

However the object of the present analysis is quite different. It is to explore whether Molyneux's arguments can be taken to have shaped decisively all or virtually all of Irish independence discourse by whomever employed. He chose to construct his argument around the international law concept of *conquest* which confirms the centrality of the concept for an understanding of Ireland's legal position.

The Conquest and Molyneux's Case of Ireland Stated

Molyneux's tract is constructed on the same historical model as Davies's *A Discovery*. He defines conquest as an *'Acquisition of a Kingdom by Force of Arms, to which, Force likewise has been Opposed.'* He responds that Henry II received not the slightest opposition: 'all came in Peaceably, and had large Concessions made them of the like Laws and Liberties with the People of *England*, which they gladly Accepted'.[6]

Molyneux understands himself to be concerned with a question of international law, since he distinguishes the effect of conquest from that of rebellion – some interpretative framework must be given for the violence of Irish history. If Ireland had been conquered, this would give the English Parliament jurisdiction over Ireland. It is because Ireland was not conquered by Henry II, but was legally a part with England *from this time*, a position which Molyneux shares with Keating, that all subsequent rebellions cannot be regarded as conquests. Therefore, implicitly, none of the military victories of the sixteenth or seventeenth centuries can be taken to constitute a conquest of Ireland. And so, the Protestant Ascendancy may rest on the successful use of force, but this force does not constitute conquest: 'If every Suppression of a Rebellion may be called a *Conquest* I know not what Country will be exempt.'[7]

In fact, Molyneux's statement about the 'Antient *Irish*' is part of a hypothetical argument. Suppose that Henry II had a right to invade, and had been opposed by the inhabitants, such could not affect the issue:

> the *English* and *Britains*, that came over and conquered with him, retain'd all the Freedoms and Immunities of *free-born* Subjects; they nor their Descendants could not in reason lose these ... Now 'tis manifest that the great Body of the present People of *Ireland*, are the Progeny of the *English* and *Britains*, that from time to time have come over into this Kingdom; and there remains but a meer handful of the Antient *Irish* at this day; I may say, not one in a thousand.[8]

This statement is the very antithesis of an 'origin myth'. It is close to Keating, because it very clearly includes the so-called 'Old English' but, perhaps, can be said to try to rely upon the same *myth of invasions* as Keating, merely endeavouring to take the decisive further step, which is to include the 'New English' within the myth. This is, in any case, within an argument which starts from the same premise as Keating, that Ireland is not to be treated as a conquered country, because it was incorporated peacefully under the crown by Henry II.

Covering the same sweep of history as Davies, Molyneux considers, throughout his entire tract, that there is virtually no deviation from the practice which stems from the time of Henry II: that the people of Ireland can only be bound by laws which have been passed by their Parliament. The object of this argument is to deny the attempts which have been made by the English Parliament in the years immediately preceding his tract, and which provide his reason for writing it.[9] Molyneux consistently relies upon the peaceful submissions made over five hundred years previously and continuing to be effective. The Irish people are bound by, and happily so, decisions which were taken by their ancestors. There is no problem of identity or continuity in this picture: 'so the Act of a Publick Society of Men, done five hundred Years sithence, standeth as theirs who presently are of the same Societies, because Corporations are Immortal; we were then alive in our Predecessors, and they in their Successors do still live'.[10]

How does Molyneux explain the extreme violence of the sixteenth and seventeenth centuries? The framework has already been set. It can only be described as rebellion. Of the Elizabethan period and the Jacobean sequel, there is no specific mention at all, except to set out the innumerable statutes which may have followed the English exactly, but which were still regarded as necessary. The exceptions occur during the sequel to the rebellion of 1641 and at the time of the disturbances of 1688–91. Molyneux's solution to this legislation is that possibly, it can be said to have been passed in a state of emergency for the interest of the people of Ireland. In particular, the Statute of Adventurers of 1642 was to finance the suppression of rebellion by the confiscation of Irish land. It is true that compensation should be found in Ireland for the endeavours of the English made on behalf of the Irish. None the less, there is no need to make any concession of constitutional principle to achieve this. The English expenditure should be seen as a purchase by the Irish Parliament which may confirm the expenditure. It is possible that no great injustice is inflicted on persons when actions are done on their behalf and they appear to give their consent by acquiescence. None the less, the more correct course is for the Irish Parliament to confirm the actions, and this is what has usually been done.[11]

The substance of Molyneux's argument is very clearly based on the notion that no person should be bound by legislation unless he has had representatives in the Parliament which passed the legislation. This is a basic principle of English constitutional practice. However, as such, it is no more than an application of the principle of the law of nature, which should prevail throughout the whole world, of being governed only by such laws as the English have consented to in their own Parliament.[12] The abstraction of this argument indicates how far the doctrine of Irish parliamentarianism is, for Molyneux, equally compatible with a union of Parliaments. The reason is that for him the fundamental principle is simply representation in parliament. Hence Molyneux speaks almost wistfully of Irish representation in Westminster as a virtually unattainable ideal.[13] Indeed, he mentions individual cases where such representation was, exceptionally, made possible.[14]

How little independence from England as such is Molyneux's objective is clear from the fact that he has no difficulty with Poynings' Law. This merely demonstrates all the more that no act could be passed with respect to Ireland without the consent of her representatives. Why, otherwise, take such care to supervise the type of legislation which would be submitted to an Irish Parliament?[15]

At the same time, for as long as the English Parliament has only English representatives, any attempt to bind the Irish is contrary to both the law of nature and the law of nations. All men are equal by nature and equal in respect of jurisdiction and dominion. It is not necessary to search into the detail of the Law of Nations: '[T]he strength and vertue of that Law is such, that no particular Nation can lawfully prejudice the same by any their several laws and ordinances, more than a man by his Private resolutions the law of the whole Commonwealth or State wherein he liveth.'[16]

What, if anything, does Molyneux have to say about 'the enemy' – the papists? It appears that 'the People of Ireland' do not include the papists. Writing of the wars between William of Orange and James II, Molyneux declares that 'if we consider the Wars of *Ireland*, we shall perceive they do not ressemble the common Case of Wars between two Foreign Enemies; Ours are rather Rebellions, or *Intestine Commotions*; that is, *The Irish Papists* rising against the *King* and *Protestants* of *Ireland*'.[17] Earlier, he explained that during the heat of the same 'Bloody War' '... it was impossible to Secure our Estates and Properties by a Regular Parliament of our own'. The Protestants had then to rely upon the English Parliament. However, this guarantee took the Protestants a great way in securing that similar measures would be passed also in Ireland 'whenever it should please God to re-establish us in our own Country'.[18] Molyneux is not even directly interested to consider the status of the papists. His argument is concerned to demonstrate that the Irish Protestants are entitled to have their own legislation passed in their own Parliament. The Irish are simply absent. Molyneux's objective is to show '*the several steps by which the English form of Government, and the* English Statute Laws *were received in this Kingdom*; and that this was wholly by the *Peoples [sic] consent in Parliament*, to which we have had a very *antient* Right'.[19] He identifies the Protestant Irish with the People of Ireland, from the time of Henry II, but this People does not include the papists.

The Mentality of Eighteenth-Century Protestant Ireland

In his study of Protestant Ireland from 1660 to 1760 Connolly argues, from the perspective of a history of mentalities, that 'beliefs and attitudes that were shared by all or most of the members of a particular society cannot, by definition, have been either stupid or immoral'.[20] The question which is not resolved by Molyneux's *Case* is whether this mentality saw itself as accommodated better by incorporation within a British Parliament or whether it required an independent Irish Parliament. What does a history of mentalities suggest? It might appear that the answer to the ambiguity left by Molyneux would depend upon the maintenance of a religious solidarity with Britain. The Anglo-Irish now meant not those of ethnic English origin, but those, of whatever origin, who were of the Protestant religion. *It was this which afforded a common British-Irish identity.*[21]

This is to characterise Irish Protestant political culture as derivative of a general British commitment to Protestantism, which is not to say that the former has to be seen as colonial, in the sense of dependent or subordinate, except in so far as the part is always less than the whole. The high point of British Protestantism was from the Scottish Act of Union (1707) until the Battle of Waterloo (1815), a time when the main enemy of Britain was Catholic, absolutist France.[22] Protestant 'pluralism' was at the same time aggressive and intolerant, based upon a fear of Catholicism which was regarded as 'outlandish' in the sense that Catholics were strangers, out of bounds, not belonging. It was an intolerant Protestantism which was cementing the British nation (English, Scots, Welsh) in the eighteenth century.[23] The association of the Catholic Stuart dynasty with the French monarchy was opposed by an apocalyptic view of history in which Britain stood for Israel and its opponents, for Satan's accomplices. In this view, the Catholics of Spain, and then of France, were 'wasteful, indolent and oppressive, if powerful, poor and exploited if not'.[24]

Colley is describing a mentality, drawing upon the French historian Georges Duby, so that 'the attitudes of individuals and groups of individuals to their own situation in society and the conduct those attitudes dictate are determined not so much by actual economic conditions as by the image in the minds of the individuals and groups'.[25] The Protestant idea of liberty has therefore to be understood as an expression of mentality, rather than in purely institutional, legal terms. The Protestant British regarded themselves as utterly different from and far more privileged that the rest of

Europeans – what Colley calls 'a complacent exceptionality'. The enormously enhanced access to the printing press was accompanied by a very predominantly religious printing production. Whatever their level of society the British regarded themselves as having direct access to the word of God in a way that Catholics did not, and, in this sense, were free men. Catholics, dependent on priests, were unfree.[26]

This same Protestant conviction was required as a profession of the monarch when accepting the throne and, although Molyneux does not make this clear, as Colley puts it, 'a religious foundation of monarchy and the idea of a contract between ruler and ruled were thus, at least in theory, satisfactorily squared'.[27] So a Catholic was disloyal. There was a widespread conviction that the expulsion of the Catholic dynasty of the Stuarts and the uniting of the island under a Protestant dynasty, had transformed Britain's place in Europe and the world, from being a small, marginal island, to being a major player. At the same time this increase in power was due to the aggressive nature of a Protestant tradition which was channelled regularly into war and imperial expansion abroad.[28]

The Protestant Irish perception of their situation was a function of this more general perspective. Connolly's look at eighteenth-century England and Scotland also leads him to remark that 'a perception of Catholicism as a powerful and insidious menace may be seen less as a neurosis specific to Irish Protestants than as part of the common political culture of the three British kingdoms'. The expectation was that in Ireland, Catholics, who made up three-quarters of the population, remained loyal to the Stuarts and expected, for some time after the Treaty of Limerick of 1691, that there could be a reversal of the Stuarts' fortunes, provided there was assistance from the continent, and especially from France.[29] Over the next half-century the views of the small elite of politicians and administrators remained constant that Catholics were hostile and potentially mutinous. However, in a pre-democratic age, the three-to-one majority could be contained, given the attrition of the Catholic leadership class.[30] Notwithstanding this, the political strategy of the Catholic elites from the 1760s, through the Union (1801) until the 1820s and O'Connell's Emancipation, was 'deferential petitioning for the removal of legal disabilities combined with unqualified declarations of loyalty to crown and government'.[31]

Within the Protestant mentality there is a place for the characterisation of the 'Ascendancy Mind'. The exclusivity of Anglicanism combined with defensiveness and oversensitivity to produce an uneasy arrogance and a fear of 'destructive' British measures which would be against the interest of 'the country' for which they, the Ascendancy, could speak.[32] A feeling of dependency was accompanied by a restlessness born of resentment at enforced provincialism.[33] Characteristic of the 'Ascendancy caste' is, for Foster 'a certain savagery of mind, amplified by a subconscious recognition of the fundamental insecurity of their political and social position'.[34] It would be common for the elite, the aristocratic landowner to spend at least three-quarters of his time in England, 'in a life of restless movement'; careers in the army, administration or politics provided further reasons.[35]

While there was a transition from the impression that Ireland consisted of English and conquered Irish to a sense of being Irish with English civil rights, the Ascendancy still considered themselves exclusive. Railing against Poynings' Law and the Declaratory Act was on behalf of an exclusive quarter of the population.[36] The repeal of the two offending Acts in 1782 made little difference to the balance of compromise and political dealing between the English government and the Protestant Ascendancy. What was more decisive was that, with the ascendancy of Pitt in British politics, the advantage in Ireland went to the hard men who emphasised the profitability of the British connection.[37] For Foster a classic expression of their mentality comes from Fitzgibbon at the time of the Regency crisis of 1789, where there was an Irish tendency to support the Regency. He reminded:

> the gentlemen of Ireland that the only security by which they hold their property ... is the connexion of the Irish Crown with, and its dependence upon, the Crown of England ... [W]hen we speak of the people of Ireland, it is a melancholy truth that we do not speak of the great body of the people ... Sir, the ancient nobility of this country have hardly been treated. The Act by which most of us hold our estates was an Act of violence – an Act subverting the first principles of the Common Law in England and Ireland. I speak of the Act of Settlement.[38]

The irony of a deconstructionist critique that the language of 'Grattan's Parliament' does not belong, historically, in the pantheon of Irish nationalism is that, by expressing one historical truth it ignores another. The Parliament in Dublin in 1782 did enjoy legislative independence, to which appeal could be made by nationalists in the nineteenth century. At the same time those who were historically represented by that Parliament clung, after 1800, to the Union to protect their way of life. This allows the scrupulous historian to argue against any meaningful political continuity in Irish traditions of independence which could see even the Home Rule Movement of the latter quarter of the century until 1916 as an attempt to restore 'Grattan's Parliament'. This style of pseudo-constitutional continuity is seen as worth resisting in so far as it obfuscates the fundamental differences of political culture underlying different types of Irishness.[39]

So, Foster objects firmly that while throughout the nineteenth century 'the old house at College Green' was represented as the home of an ideal of national independence, the political elite of the eighteenth century, many of whom fought hard to maintain the independence of the Irish Parliament, accepted the Union, and with the coming of Catholic democracy, would cling to it as the guarantee of their privileges and survival.

However, such an analysis is perfectly compatible with the conclusion that English/British constitutional concepts of identity triumphed in an Ireland where the Gaelic political nation had been exterminated. The language of legal-political debate, whether nationalist or unionist was the same language: that of representative government, political liberties and national identity centreed around a parliamentary life. The claim to an Irish identity, given the constitutional language in which it was expressed, could be nothing more than a claim to an equality of the law, all that O'Connell purported to demand, and best to be achieved outwith the Union. At the same time the claims of unionism were, also, merely a demand for an equality of treatment, best to be maintained within the Union. The real divide was not over the abstract rights of a nation or state to independence, but the unspoken divide of racial difference, real or imagined.

Some Arguments for the Maintenance and Repeal of the Union

At the same time, the primary concern of Protestant Irish for equality of treatment with the English led them, when *The Case* was first published, to regard Union with England, rather than independence, as their best tactic to achieve equality. This is one reputed reason why *The Case* had, at the time of its publication, no champions in Ireland. The manifest power of the English Parliament and the anger which it had expressed at the book[40] led the leaders of Protestant opinion in Ireland to consider that their best hope of obtaining redress of their grievances at the English practice of legislating for Ireland was to work for a union which would give them representation at Westminster. Thus they would be freed of the trade restrictions which were the substance of their complaints.[41] It was the refusal of union with Ireland, such as Scotland had obtained, which reawakened interest in Molyneux's work and led to a reprint in 1706. The Declaratory Act provoked yet another edition in 1720. The criticism of England which Swift was to echo and the Americans, in particular, were to take up, was of government without the consent of the governed. When the Declaratory Act was repealed in 1782 another edition omitted reference to the alternative which Molyneux had recommended (viz. Union), but this independence was, obviously, short-lived.[42]

It is in this spirit of concern for equality that it was thought possible for one firm proponent of the maintenance of the Union in the 1880s to quote Adam Smith's arguments for a union of Irish and English Parliaments in the middle of the eighteenth century, to match the advantage of the union of the Scottish and English Parliaments. The latter union freed middling and inferior ranks of Scots from the power of an oppressive aristocracy. In Ireland a similar measure would free all ranks of a much worse oppression, distinctions based upon religious and political prejudice which are guaranteed to

> animate both the insolence of the oppressors and the hatred and indignation of the oppressed, and which commonly render the inhabitants of the same country more hostile to one another than those of different countries ever are. Without an union with Great Britain the inhabitants of Ireland are not likely for many ages to consider themselves as one people.[43]

The division of the Irish into two nations, a Catholic and a Protestant, gave a more specific twist to Smith's point. The desire of the Protestants to maintain the British connection, even with an independent Parliament was paramount, and yet its prospect was not clear if one thought Catholic emancipation to be inevitably a matter of time.[44]

For the Protestant Irish, equality of treatment with the English was not compatible with equality of treatment for the Catholics *within an Irish Parliament*. The Penal Laws, to subordinate the Catholics, were introduced after the Protestants despaired of a Union. They were motivated not by religious animosity but by fear that the Catholics might again, as they had tried in 1689, undertake to root out the Protestant community in Ireland. Laws disqualifying Catholics from political power were essential to the safety of Protestants.[45] The crucial turn of phrase which Ingram uses shows what underlay these concerns: 'After ... a union the demands of the Catholics might be safely conceded, but in a separate Ireland there was nothing to look forward to but national dissension, and perhaps a bloody convulsion followed by a reconquest.'[46]

At the same time Protestant Irish identity was fixated with the idea that the security of the Empire, especially in time of war – which, after 1793, was the case – required that the Empire speak with one voice. This was not guaranteed simply by the fact of there being one Executive. Two legislatures meant there could be two voices. Grattan is reported to have said that dissent of the Irish Parliament on the question of war was highly improbable. In Ingram's view, this was not enough: 'By the word "improbable" he admits the possibility; and possibilities of dissent should be excluded from that unity of operation which the needs of an Empire demand.'[47] Pitt was taken to stress the danger to safety and security which the existence of two voices represented.[48]

This question of security is, unfortunately, clearly identified by Ingram as connected with the apparent willingness of the Irish Parliament in 1793 to take steps which could lead to the political emancipation of the Catholics. Ingram believes that the pressure would eventually have built up for Catholic representation in Parliament. Given the entrenched Protestant nature of the Executive, attached to the Protestant Monarchy, this Catholic progress could only lead to Dissension. The Irish Parliament should have appreciated that the Catholic question was common to all parts of the Kingdom. The 1793 Act in Ireland, enfranchising Catholics, threatened the connection with England. Once again establishment of Religion and the history of the land question went together. Politically emancipated Catholics 'might, and probably would, have demanded the repeal of the Act of Settlement *and the restoration of the forfeited lands*'(my italics).[49] Clearly Ingram identified Britishness and Empire with Protestantism, as Colley has said it must be. The Catholicism which concerned him was political in the sense that it threatened the core of the British Empire, the British Isles.

Ingram recognises that, quite naturally, the Catholics would have preferred emancipation to take place without Union. With a majority in an 'unbounded field' they would have attacked the Protestant Establishment, the Act of Settlement and, finally, the confiscations: 'These questions alone would have led to civil war, perhaps to a separation and a fresh conquest by England.'[50] None the less, the Catholics submitted to the Union as a means of obtaining the emancipation which was politically virtually inconceivable without Union. He argues that as the representatives of the Catholic electorate in Parliament supported the Union this binds the Catholic Irish *and their successors.*[51]

In a wider sense there could be no constitutional impropriety in the Union by virtue of British promises implied in the repeal of the Declaratory Act. Britain continued to respect the right of the Irish Parliament to be the only body to bind the Irish people. The Union proposal was, instead, a treaty whereby one independent nation made a proposal to another. When the latter accepted the proposal the effect was that the Parliaments of the two countries were intermingled. By virtue of this fact the right of the Imperial Parliament to legislate for Ireland has been conferred on it by the Irish Parliament. One can also say that the Imperial Parliament is a mixture of the Parliaments of Ireland and Great Britain. On this basis the Imperial Parliament can pass laws which bind the inhabitants of Ireland.[52]

Ingram's retrospective on the Union comes from Dublin in 1887. The final major defence comes from Unionists in Dublin, Belfast and London in 1912. The arguments are presented before the Liberal Government has actually published its legislative proposals and they are simply against the very idea of any degree of political autonomy for Ireland.[53] There is as yet no attempt to distinguish the Ulster Protestant community as having a distinctive character which should be given institutional expression apart from that guaranteed by being an integral part of the United Kingdom.[54]

At this stage the Land Reforms of Liberal and Conservative administrations from 1881 till 1909 have been carried through. There is no longer a clear focus on the issue of land as a mark of conquest which an Irish Assembly would at once try to undo. Instead the arguments are made, that Home Rule would never have been effectively launched as a political issue if Parnell had not been able to tie it to the Land Question. Now, with the latter matter virtually resolved, Nationalist politicians are anxious to somehow keep the issue alive as virtually the only way of fomenting support for their cause.[55]

This leads to a new development in arguments about national identity. Ireland is denied any distinctive identity in the then common usage of racial origin. It is insisted that the Irish are, as much as the English, a mixture of different races, above all Anglo-Saxons, Celts, Normans, Norse, Danes and Vikings. There is, therefore, no clear difference of race between the English and the Irish. Each part of the British Isles is more or less as homogeneous or as distinctive as the other.[56] Nor is there any geographical sense in which Ireland can be regarded as more marginal than areas of Scotland. Compared to the islands of New Zealand, the British Isles are relatively compact.[57]

What were the arguments to address the wish of the majority of Irish MPs for political autonomy? There are a series of arguments which concern the institutional feasibility of an Irish Assembly. They affect all possible options except that of devolved government, where it is recognised that the reservation of unqualified sovereignty at the centre would allow the necessary power of central intervention in an emergency.[58] The concern is that the government of the British Isles must be with a single voice, that there is no way that power can be divided without friction becoming inevitable. Reference is made to the usual examples, Grattan's Parliament's support for the Prince of Wales during the Regency Crisis and the refusal of the Irish Parliament to agree to quite reasonable terms for free trade in 1785. These arguments are not distinguishable from the concerns about the Scottish threat to choose a different monarch in the last years of the reign of Queen Anne. Such disagreements between Parliaments are supposed to have convinced the English in their approach to a unitary rather than federal parliamentary system for the British Isles. To respond to arguments about the institutional overburdening of the Imperial Parliament by creating an Irish Parliament is to resolve minor difficulties by creating major ones.[59]

There is a firm rejection of the theory that a so-called Irish Parliamentary tradition should be restored. In particular, after the Conservative administrations had decided to complete the transfer of Irish land from absentee landlords to the sitting tenants, it is remarkable how the stress is placed upon the corrupt quality of the unreformed Parliament of pre-Union days. This Parliament is presented as serving the financial and other material interests of a small clique of individuals who acted against the well-being of the greater part of the population. They were, of course, the landowners whom the Conservative administrations have just removed. This Irish Parliament was not the basis of an authentic parliamentary tradition.[60] It was an institution which had to be abolished if there was to be a progressive reform of Irish society to the benefit of all. The reason for this is partially the tendency of the Protestant Ascendancy to act selfishly in its own exclusive interest.

However, a more fundamental difficulty is the unreasonable nature of the religious antagonism which separated the Irish. This was an accident of history. It was attributable to the fact that, unlike the English, most of the Irish did not accept the Reformation. This made it inevitable that the ferocity of religious division which separated Europeans through the sixteenth and seventeenth centuries should also be introduced into English–Irish relations. All the marks of religious wars of Germany and France were reproduced in Ireland. The bitterness remained, albeit the effects of the Penal Laws and, particularly, the Land Confiscations, had been completely removed.[61] However, given the tensions between the religious traditions the only way that they could be expected to coexist comfortably would be under the impartial external authority of the Imperial Parliament.[62]

The Ulster Protestants should not be presented as bigoted, antagonistic, otherwise alien elements in Ireland. The country was peaceful at the end of the sixteenth century until there occurred yet another rebellion in the province of Ulster. The Ulster Protestants were then brought over to Ireland, to 'show the way' in terms of land management, industry and general application. This they have done, making the counties they are engaged in among the most prosperous in the British Isles. They are entitled to have their rights of citizenship continually guaranteed in what is best described as the equivalent of Lanarkshire or Lancashire. Their function is not to be present as conquerors, but to offer an example of how the island should best develop. They have flourished under the Union, demonstrating that all the nationalist arguments about the damaging consequences of the Union for Ireland are not empirically demonstrated.[63]

While there is no Irish nation which could warrant a claim for political autonomy, and there is also no inferior element to the Irish people which would justify them receiving less than equal treatment with the other inhabitants of the British Isles, there are signs of disaffection about them which would make granting them political autonomy all the more problematic.[64] The Irish nationalists do not pin down how much autonomy they want, simply calling for Home Rule, or a restoration of the Irish Parliament. This might appear very convenient[65] and indicate that once they have a representative Executive they will use it to declare an Irish disengagement from a whole series of matters affecting British national security, regardless of whether the matters come, to any degree at all, within the remit of the Irish Parliament.[66] Ireland continues to be a central part of Britain's military and naval security at a time when the European situation is becoming more and more unstable. Historically, albeit often because of the force of religion, the Irish have frequently sided with Britain's enemies.[67]

Britain is here occasionally explicitly mentioned to include the Scots. They have shown themselves, under their Union with England, much more willing to take up their share of the burden of governing the Isles than the Irish.[68] However, the text most usually contrasts the Irish and the English, and more reference is made to the expression – concerning military security – that England's difficulty is Ireland's opportunity.[69] England's conduct towards Ireland has, on occasion, been unjust and, more particularly, ill-advised and even stupid.[70] However, its policy has been marked above all by hestitancy and confusion. It has often only been the threat of foreign invasion which has focused England's mind on the need for decisive action.[71] The Union of Parliaments had occurred at a time when conservative forces dominated in England as a response to the very serious threat of Napoleonic imperialism. This conservatism in England, in a time of mortal danger, explains the unfortunate fact that Catholic Emancipation was not carried out immediately after the Union, as the Catholics had been promised and had a right to expect. However, this measure was eventually carried through with effect for the whole of the British Isles, because it reflected the wishes of progressive opinion in both islands. The same cannot be said for the subsequent attempts to introduce Home Rule.[72]

One very firm reservation has to be drawn concerning the Irish situation. This concerns not the Irish people as such but the nature of the Roman Catholic religion.[73] Relations between Catholic and Protestant Christians in Ireland can be and usually are perfectly cordial. However, the Catholic religion has an institutional aspect which is not compatible with the British tradition of political liberties. Catholics are placed in a special position of subordination to priests and bishops wherever they find themselves. These clerical elements are required by their Church to claim extensive political power in states where they find themselves in a majority. This is required by the papacy and the Vatican itself. It is a power which extends to education and family matters: the questions of divorce, education of children in the parent's Christian faith. It may even amount to the officers of the Church claiming a special status outside the ordinary courts of law of the jurisdiction.[74]

Ireland is marked, for a country with a very substantial Catholic population, with a more than usual number of priests and bishops. One can hardly expect, therefore, that they will behave any differently than in other 'Catholic' countries. And how is that? In France and Portugal there has been a fierce struggle between the Church and anti-clerical forces which has been damaging and has led to the extreme secularisation of these societies. It might be expected that the same would happen in Ireland.[75] Eventually the dominance of the Catholic Church would be of limited duration. However, in the meantime, there would be great harm done to the quality of Christian life, to the nature of inter-denominational relations, and, last but not least, to the civic rights of Catholic Irish citizens. For all these reasons it is desirable that the Catholic Church in Ireland remain under the political jurisdiction of an Imperial Parliament which it has no possibility of controlling.[76] In this way the legitimate civic rights of Roman Catholics can be guaranteed – and no more!

The volume just analysed represents the considered views of the leaders of the Conservative and Unionist Party which played a decisive and determining role in the development of Irish–British political relations from 1912 until the conclusion of the Anglo-Irish Treaty of December 1921. It is remarked that they represented a type of unionist 'fundamentalism', an opposition to any form of Home Rule, against the express wishes of four-fifths of the Irish electorate. Fundamentalism meant an unwillingness to resort to the pragmatism which changing political realities might require. This was for a variety of reasons, but mainly it concerned a denial of Irish nationality and a determination, without particular respect to Ireland, to maintain the integrity of the British Empire. It was not the only model for development offered by the British political system. Liberal Imperialism favoured timely concession and enlistment of indigenous opinion. Indeed, Redmond, the Irish Parliamentary leader, also hoped to follow the model of a South

African prime minister. However, it was not Liberal administrations which controlled Britain, and so Liberal Home Rule policies did not count. In the end, 'Unionist fundamentalism, leading countenance to threats and preparations for armed resistance in Ulster to Home Rule in the years before the first world war, bore a heavy – possibly a decisive – responsibility for creating a situation in which a violent resolution of the Irish question became probable.'[77]

The question of comparison of Ireland with the dominions in the years from 1886 to 1922 is confused. The Irish did not regard themselves as settlers, but as a European people. It may be true that they did not define precisely what they wanted in the way of institutions. However, across the entire political spectrum – from Redmond, the most modest, through Parnell, as more demanding, to Sinn Fein, with Arthur Griffith – they all called for a restoration of Irish rights. Parnell wanted a restoration of the Irish Parliament, with adequate political and fiscal authority, including a right to levy tariffs. Redmond was willing, with the 1912 Home Rule Bill, to accept something much closer to devolution. Griffith was revolutionary because he rejected the authority of the British Parliament, but this was because it was held to have usurped the Irish Parliament without legal foundation in 1800. There was a common Irish ground for a restoration of the Irish Parliamentary tradition, whether or not it was an English import.[78]

Griffith's position was that by the 1783 Renunciation Act the British Parliament had renounced, for all time, authority to legislate for Ireland. As the Act was still on the Statute Book, the Irish Parliament had as much legal existence now as in 1783. This is what provided the framework for the policy of abstentionism from Westminister. Elected Irish representatives should remain in Ireland and ignore the passing of British laws with respect to Ireland.[79] Hence, it is possible to see even in the Sinn Fein negotiation of the 1921 Treaty a certain continuity with the wider Irish Parliamentary tradition rather than to stress the break with the much more modest Liberal Administration offers of Home Rule. Ireland was never offered dominion status until the summer of 1921 after three further years of warfare in Ireland.[80] However, when this happened, it was Griffith who was the leader of the Irish delegation to the treaty negotiations.

After 1916 the Sinn Fein movement went further than Griffith's Austro-Hungarian-style dual monarchy in claiming a completely unqualified independence, in republican form, expressed simply in terms of the democratically expressed will of the sovereign Irish people, an appeal, in effect, to the Wolf Tone republicanism of 1798, with its accompanying violence. This was decided at the 1917 Conference of Sinn Fein and was the basis for the successful 1918 election.[81] However, Britain was only willing to offer dominion status to Ireland and was prepared to return to the use of force if this was not accepted.[82] Davis remarks that, in such a context, in an uncanny way Griffith found himself rewinning ground lost since 1916. The differences between the upholders of the 1782 Constitution, as understood by Griffith, and the so-called 'physical force' tradition which wanted an outright Republic based only on the sovereignty of the Irish people, laid the ground for the Civil War which followed the signing of the Treaty by Griffith's delegation and Griffith's subsequent success against de Valera in the Dail Treaty debate: 'Griffith, negotiating with England for something like the 1782 Constitution, was opposed by de Valera, apparently prepared to use more force to win a republic.'[83]

Griffith's commitment to the 1782 Constitution was very profound. Wolf Tone's language of the natural rights of nations – which led to de Valera-style republicanism – was of the eighteenth-century Enlightenment. However, according to Davis, nineteenth-century European nationalists did not discard the eighteenth-century natural rights philosophy but injected into this right an historical content. They claimed this right for the living individual peoples which they claimed to find in history. So, for Griffith, Ireland had to be ransacked to produce an implicit constitution. In 1909 *The Irish Yearbook*, issued by the National Council of Sinn Fein, published an article most probably by Griffith, which argued that there had been five English (maybe one Scottish) rightful kings of Ireland in Irish history, acknowledged by the Irish Parliament, including Charles I, James II and George III, 'acknowledged king of Ireland by the Constitution of 1782–1800'. Even if the Irish Parliament denied Catholics full rights, it must be distinguished from the Irish Constitution, which made Ireland a sovereign state.[84] Obviously for this Constitution a fully autonomous Irish Parliament, particularly with power to impose tariffs to follow Griffith's aggressive economic nationalism, would be provided.

The fact that the legitimacy of this Parliament would be traced back to an English or British Act of Parliament, the Act of Renunciation of 1783, and that the Parliament existed within a framework of a common personal union in the British monarch, would not present ideological difficulties for Griffith, and with him many pro-Treaty figures, precisely because all of this accorded with Griffith's adherence to the doctrine of the historical Irish nation. Indeed, this argument also met the difficulty that the Irish, in a pre-'invasion' time, may not have existed as a nation-state in the sense which that is understood at the present time. This did not matter to Griffith because he wished to found Irish constitutional and national identity upon a process of historical accretion.[85]

The historical-constitutional argument was also much stronger in relation to Ulster than a more abstract appeal to a natural right of a district, community or nation to be the owner of himself/itself and never bound to submit to be governed by another people – as expounded by Finton Lalor. Griffith foresaw that this argument could be used to assure an unlimited application of the right to self-determination. Ulster Unionists could argue that the British Isles could claim to be a natural community with a small number of Irish 'discontents'. Or, alternatively the North-East of Ulster could claim to be a community which had the right to resist inclusion in an independent Ireland. Concludes Davis:

> Griffith's constitutionalism ... placed unionists in a less impregnable argumentative position unless they were prepared to deny they were Irish. Lalor's theory, taken to its logical conclusions, has helped to bring about the partition of peoples who with a modicum of tolerance might have been able to live peacefully together.[86]

There were arguably contradictions on both sides of the negotiating table, accentuated by distrust in 1921. On the British side Bonar Law argued that the application of the dominion status to the Irish situation, especially in the context that the Irish were mandated to negotiation for a republic, based on natural rights arguments of Irish popular sovereignty, could not be expected to provide a lasting solution. For the other dominions, the argument was for a commonwealth of British nations, based on a voluntary association of settler communities with the 'mother country', on the assumption not only that they could leave if they wished to, but that they would not so wish. These facts were quite inapplicable to Ireland.[87] At the same time the threat of force was used during the negotiation of the Treaty to ensure that the Irish delegation accepted the option of dominion status against that of a republic. It was pointed out by a leading pro-Treaty Irish government figure, Kevin O'Higgins, that the supposedly voluntary association of a commonwealth of nations included Ireland by an act of coercion. He said:

> It has been called a league of free nations. I admit in practice it is so; but it is unwise and unstatesmanlike to attempt to bind any such league by any ties other than pure voluntary ties ... I quite admit in the case of Ireland the tie is not voluntary ... the status is not equal.[88]

As Mansergh notes, in conclusion, Ireland was forced into a free association.

CHAPTER 5

The Question of the Legitimacy of the 'Protestant' Presence in Ulster/Northern Ireland

The Original Construction of the Ulster-Scots Identity

In *The Narrow Ground* Stewart ponders the possibility of natural boundaries in very striking terms:

> Nor can we even think in terms of natural boundaries determined by the sea. We have accepted those boundaries as natural for so long that we can easily forget that mountains, forests and marshes were at one time greater obstacles to man than the open sea. The Dutch geographer, Professor Heslinga, argues that from prehistoric times the Irish Sea had been the *centre*, not the frontier, of a vast cultural province.[1]

In other words a natural contiguity between at least the West of Scotland and the North-East of Ireland favoured the development of a distinctive culture. This Ulster-Scottish culture was isolated from the rest of Irish Catholic and Gaelic culture. Stewart's argument is that it would appear to have been created:

> not by the specific and artificial plantation of the early 17th century, but by the continous natural influx of Scottish settlers both before and after that episode: in particular, the heavy immigration which took place in the *later* 17th century [which] seems to have laid the foundations of the Ulster colony.[2]

The deliberate plantations, undertaken for strategic reasons have been unsuccessful and they have not prevented Ireland achieving political independence from England. However, the immigration from Scotland has been continuous for centuries before 1609 and is a fact of geography rather than a fact of history. So the Scots took advantage of the Stuarts to expand their immigration, taking over unexploited land and making it productive.

Although the Scots also expanded their immigration into Londonderry, the major part of their influx was into what were the unplanted counties of Antrim and Down. In the eastern counties there was never any true confrontation of planter and Gael. The West of the Plantation is, in this view, another matter. There 'the

Protestants are sparely settled in areas which have a largely Catholic population'.[3]

While Stewart appears anxious not to tie agrarian violence to the fact of the Plantation itself, he sees a continuity in both objects and methods of violence from the sixteenth century up to the contemporary activities of the Provisional IRA.[4] This is not to speak of a continuous struggle by a national liberation movement but rather, quoting a southern Irish historian 'a limited pragmatic programme' of resisting what they regarded as unjust dispossession.[5]

A not dissimilar argument is constructed by Perceval-Maxwell in *The Scottish Migration to Ulster in the Reign of James I*. This study is presented by the Duke of Abercorn, President of the Ulster-Scot Historical Foundation, as 'ideally suited to present this account of settlement in 17th century Ulster'.[6] The argument, again, is that 'in the north, where English authority was weak, Islander Scots and Highlanders had established themselves in considerable strength by the time Elizabeth died'.[7] Indeed by the middle of the sixteenth century Scots had consolidated their hold on parts of Antrim and parts of Down under Irish and Scots.[8] So it is said that from the 1570s, 'the MacDonnells remained in practical if not legal possession of Antrim', which is not to say that what was at issue was land-grabbing from the Irish, that is, the McQuillins, a process which accelerated with the rebellion of the Earl of Tyrone.[9]

He sees this as little more than a portent, which cannot be regarded as the vanguard of what came in the first quarter of the seventeenth century. Instead Percevel-Maxwell appears to stress the idea of occupation of underpopulated lands, conditions in Ulster being particularly favourable to settlement.[10] There is none the less considerable ambiguity in his expression that, with the union of the Crowns the migration of Scots to Ulster became something to be encouraged rather than restrained.[11] There is here a stress that all three nations accepted allegiance to the one Crown and that after 1603 greater movement was only to be expected.

None the less Percevel-Maxwell identifies clearly a colonial intention, where Ireland and Virgina were treated in parallel. The former was governed by customs regarded as regressive and, so to 'the Scot and Englishman alike ... Ireland appeared as a land rich in resources and populated by men unworthy of their opportunities'.[12] He stresses as well the level of underpopulation, following the war: 'there can be no question that the reduction in population encouraged the idea of plantation'.[13] Whatever the level of devastation, which cannot be exactly measured, the English view was that the land could support a far larger population. Percevel-Maxwell does not distinguish East from West, although he is speaking of the latter: 'In the six counties escheated for the main plantation ... the other two-thirds would be able to support

40,000 persons.'[14] Indeed Percevel-Maxwell persists in this theme with a striking remark about the necessity of Scots accumulating capital before they came to Ulster: 'This had little significance for Scots going to already functioning societies such as England, Sweden or Poland, but for those going to Ireland it was crucial. Here Scots had to create the means of production with which to support their settlement and develop the wilderness of Ulster.'[15]

This general argument finds favour in the description of population movements to Antrim and Down. In the grant of lands made to the MacDonnells, in Antrim, in 1586 to 1590 it is mentioned that the local Irish chieftain had insufficient people to inhabit the territory.[16] Equally, as to the Great Ards Peninsula, the records remark that here was a vast region, fertile etc., yet 'depopulated and wasted' in the words of the instructions to the new owners.[17] These statements converge with the thesis made by Stewart. They allow favour for a style of argument which is that no systematic attempt was made to displace the Irish, who received a full 20 per cent of the land as grantees and were left everywhere in place as labourers and tenants in a land structure which remained very largely the same.[18]

The heart of the Plantation concerned other matters. England had a strategic interest in Ireland, just as Spain had in the Netherlands. The extension of England's power could equally cover both territories. The King himself thought that, even if reasons of state did not compel the Plantation, he believed in 'the settling of religion, the introduction of civility, order and government amongst a barbarous and subdued people'.[19] In this spirit the Irish Attorney-General, Sir John Davies, warned 'that the Irish would "quickly overgrow" the British planters "as weeds overgrow the good corn" unless "civil" planters outnumbered the Irish from the beginning'.[20]

Chichester, James's Lord Deputy, objected that the large-scale displacement of the Irish and the importation of the Scots would be more trouble and less profit than if the Irish were left in possession.[21] Perceval-Maxwell emphasises that the Irish 'deprived of the land they loved and had defended for so long ... deeply resented the intrusion of the newcomers'. He remarks how the Scots in particular lived in constant jeopardy because 'although they were often willing to rent land back to the former owners and intermarry with them, the Irish hated them more deeply than the English'.[22] Chichester blamed the danger on the Scottish undertakers who continued to harbour the Irish on their land rather than clearing them completely, as required by their royal instructions. This is why they remained vulnerable to massacre in the event of an Irish rebellion.[23]

Perceval-Maxwell concludes with a statement of Scots-Irish identity which can be an effective starting point for further analysis. The original Plantation and subsequent migration gave the Scots

> a numerical as well as a political dominance in certain parts of Ulster, *while the repeated need to defend the territory they had acquired under the auspices of English strategic policy gave them a sense of identity* which was strongly reinforced by their dissenting Protestant views. The result has been that they have stood apart from the rest of Ireland ... James I sent his countrymen to Ireland in order to bind his three kingdoms more closely together; the efforts of his policy are still at work over 350 years later. He might well be satisfied (emphasis added).[24]

In my view these two historians deserve to be taken as authoritative contemporary spokesmen for the Ulster-Scots view of their origins in Northern Ireland. While they do not correspond exactly they allow for some converging general remarks.[25] There has been some measure of 'natural' migration of Scots to Ulster and, to a certain degree, it has been sufficiently complete to be uncontested in practice in certain parts of eastern Ulster. However, both leading historians are agreed that such is not the case for substantial parts of Ulster, where the 'native' Irish have remained, frequently in a majority, and always intermittently resisting the intrusion of Scots. Whether the identity of the Ulster-Scots owes anything to a pattern of natural migration appears difficult to assess.

In *Modern Ireland*, Foster argues, from the halting and contentious nature of the government-planned colonisation, that it adds weight to the argument that the 'real' Ulster plantation was that carried out 'invisibly' by the Scots, before and after. He continues, that Unionists would use this argument to show

> that Ulster's different nature is immemorial and uncontrollable, and stems from something more basic than English governmental policy. None the less, what must be grasped from the early seventeenth century is the importance of the plantation idea, with its emphasis on segregation and on native unreliability ... Ulster people believed they lived permanently on the edge of persecution; they gloried in covenanting against 'tyranny'; and they were committed to a democracy that extended to the elect alone.[26]

The Construction of Ulster Origins/Identity at the Time of the Home Rule Crisis

Ulster Unionists, as other Irish Unionists, raised objections to the merits of the repeal of the Act of Union in order to combat the Home

Rule Bills. However, they also made a much more specific criticism of any attempt to place them, as they saw would inevitably happen, outside the jurisdiction of the Crown. This aspect of unionism is seen as a betrayal of their primary political identity as subjects of the Crown. It does not specifically regard the nature of Irish nationalism or the character of a future Irish state. Instead, it affirms the roots of the political identity of Ulster Protestants. This seems to be firmly in terms of their political origins. So, in his contribution to Rosenbaum's authoritative collective work of Unionist politicians and lawyers *Against Home Rule, The Case for the Union*, Sinclair gives a statement of the position of Ulster in terms of the Plantation, that is, to secure Ireland as attached to the King's dominions. The greater number of Ulster Unionists who inhabit the province today are descendants of these settlers,[27] as trustees of the English and the Scots, 'having had committed to us, through their and our forefathers, the development of the material resources of Ulster, the preservation of its loyalty, and the discharge of its share of Imperial obligations'.[28]

This argument from definite historical identity leads to the argument that there is a covenant or bond between Britain and Ulster which cannot, apparently under any circumstances, be broken. Sinclair insists:

> Ulster Unionists, therefore ... constituting as they do a community intensely loyal to the British connection, believe that they present a case for the unimpaired maintenance of that connection which is impregnable on the grounds of racial sentiment, inherent justice, and the continued security of the United Kingdom and of the Empire.[29]

So for some Ulster Unionists a significant part of anti-Home Rule opposition was rooted in a conviction that it was yet another attempt to undermine the Protestant Ascendancy and to drive Protestants out of the country; as yet another of the attempts which had been made in the past to rid Ulster of the British element in its population and to regain possession of confiscated land.[30] Hamilton equated Home Rule with previous attempts by the 'native element' to dispossess the Protestant settlers, 'not ... by methods of open violence' but by more characteristic methods, such as electoral rigging, agrarian outrages and tammany methods.[31] Hamilton pushed this argument further. There may have been injustices in the Plantation, but the responsibility was a matter to resolve between the native proprietors and the English government and

> was no concern of Ulster Protestants, who, oblivious to laws relating to the possession of stolen property, were conscious of

> having done no man wrong. Their lands had been honestly come by, either by direct dealings with the English government or with those holding office under the English government. If the title of the government was faulty, then, ... the immorality of the transfer lies at the door of the government, not of the unhappy transferees.[32]

The fundamental danger, in the 'Ulster mind', is that what happened before – the massacres of 1641 and 1798 – could happen again. Their cause, the real grievance of the native Irish, is the existence on Irish soil of one-and-a-quarter million British colonists. To the English they may be Irish loyalists, Orangemen, etc., but 'to the native Irish mind they simply represent the one unspeakable evil, the British Usurper'.[33] Whatever the religious doctrinal differences, the Protestants recognise in the Catholics 'an inveterate foe nursing a deathless grievance'.[34] Catholics oppose Protestants not because of their hostility to the Vatican 'but because their Protestantism stamps them as usurping British colonists who have rested from them the best of their lands. This is the Ulster question.'[35]

Hamilton sees an irresolvable conflict of values in this crisis. The question is whether colonisation is seen as an act of piracy or as a necessary part of the gradual reclamation of the world.[36] For the native Irish the answer is clear: 'It matters nothing that the lands, when originally granted, were waste, and that the industry of the colonists has made them rich. It matters nothing that Ulster was then a sink of murder, misery and vice, and that now it is a land of smiling prosperity.'[37]

How are questions of responsibility to be allocated over centuries,[38] a universal question which affects the Americas and Africa at present? Even if the original Plantation was an injustice, the displacement of the planters after 310 years of exemplary occupation would be even more unjust. The deportation was not of their own doing, but an act of state policy.[39]

The reason for the intensity and duration of the colonial conflict in Ulster is to the credit of the colonists, as Perceval-Maxwell has already suggested. The colonists did not drive the natives out. There was not an effective clearance. As Hamilton puts it, 'When an expanding race encroaches upon the lands of weaker nationalities ... there is a tendency on the part of the invaded races to disappear.' For example, the native populations have almost vanished from North America and Australasia: 'In Ireland the reverse has been the case.'[40] Although on two historic occasions the natives have attempted the extermination of the settlers, the latter have never made a corresponding attempt. Whatever the military may have undertaken in Ireland in the sixteenth and seventeenth centuries, a 'settler is a farmer, or a trader, and his ways are for peace'.[41]

The settlers did no one a wrong: the vexed question of right and wrong rests between the native proprietors and the English Government. The natives are unjustified in equating the two, in treating the Protestant, colonial settlers as agents, if they are not principals. In Ireland the two can expect to suffer the same fate.[42]

Whether Unionists Claim a Right to Self-Determination in Subjective or Objective Terms

The question whether Unionists have a legal veto on the unification of Ireland is treated in the Irish constitutional jurisprudence as a matter of policy or a *de facto* acknowledgement without prejudice to a claim of right. What conditions of identity would the Unionists have to satisfy to be entitled to exercise such a veto as a matter of international law? One way to approach this question is simply to ask how the Unionists themselves understand this claim. It is not simply a matter of testing the possible nationalist arguments that the Unionists are mere planters/colonists, etc. It may be possible for the Unionists to argue that their ancestors were merely moving from one part of the jurisdiction to the other. Nationalists may respond that Ireland was a conquered country. To this Unionists might reply that there was no Irish state in the seventeenth century to which sovereignty could now revert.[43] My own approach to Unionist self-definition is much more subjective. It is possible that there is nothing to be said of them but that the settler–native dichotomy remains as deep as ever 'reproduced by a variety of mechanisms of which endogamy is perhaps the most important'.[44] However, the question still remains, in precisely what terms do Unionists wish to justify their claims to political organisation?[45]

Do the Unionists have a defensible political culture? It would not be enough to demonstrate that they do not have an independent or autonomous political identity, if they, for their part, wish to affirm precisely that they are an integral part of British political culture. Such a perspective raises the huge question of the character of the Union of 1801 between Ireland and England. Were the two countries so much joined together in the manner of imperial metropolis to colony that there could be no argument that there was in any respect a free Union? If the answer is negative it can surely follow that some part of the island of Ireland can state that it would prefer to continue the Union. Such an approach allows the Unionists to avoid arguments based on the possession of a particular political identity. Such arguments then only become relevant to defeat nationalist arguments that there is one political culture which embraces the entire island's population. Where a right to self-determination is based primarily on a cultural-nationalist notion of political identity, such an objection should prove decisive.

The most distinctive features of Unionist political culture have to be seen as a particular view of British constitutional theory. The text of the 1912 Covenant includes the following:

> Being convinced in our consciences that home rule would be disastrous to the material well-being of Ulster as well as the whole of Ireland, subversive of our civil and religious freedom, destructive of our citizenship, and perilous to the unity of the empire, we ... loyal subjects of His Gracious Majesty, ... do hereby pledge ourselves in solemn covenant ... to stand by one another in defending for ourselves and our children our cherished position of equal citizenship in the United Kingdom, and in using all means which may be found necessary to defeat the present conspiracy to set up a home rule parliament in Ireland. And in the event of such a parliament being forced upon us we further solemnly and mutually pledge ourselves to refuse to recognise its authority.[46]

It is important to see that this statement is not an objection to being made to leave the United Kingdom and form part of an independent Ireland. This was not on the political agenda in 1912. It is an insistence that the United Kingdom has a constitution which cannot be altered in significant respects without the consent of those subject to it.

The question arises whether the Ulster Protestant Unionists belong within the wider Irish Unionist view of Irish political identity. I believe that they do in so far as they are claiming that their political rights rest upon a theory of *their* consent to the manner in which they are governed. This raises once again directly the question whether Ireland was conquered. In *The Queen's Rebels*, Miller appears unsympathetic to the view that there was any question of consent to being governed by England. He shows the perhaps ironic congruence between the separatist Irish nationalist view of the history of the relations between the two countries and the dominant English view of the matter. So when Molyneux, an Irish Whig, tried to construct a theory that the Irish Parliament was entitled to powers established by a contract of government between king and people, then, objects Miller, it must have been a contract with the ancestors of the very people who had been deprived of their property, 'a preposterous fiction', that the great body of the present inhabitants of Ireland were English and Britons, the ancient Irish being a mere handful. The English response, for instance by Atwood, was that the Irish were conquered and that the English title to govern rested on this.[47]

Since Molyneux was referring to the original compact between Henry II and the Irish people and all the subsequent construction of the Irish Parliament, this raises directly the question of the status of the Irish Parliament and therefore, particularly, the terms and circumstances of the Union of 1801. In the course of the eighteenth century the landed elite of Ireland did try, following Molyneux, to place their relationship with England on a contractual footing. Miller argues that such contractarianism in Ireland had to remain unrealistic because of the historical colonial situation. In Ulster Protestant, public banding was a response to the threat of public disorder posed by the presence of Catholics:

> The public band was the *ad hoc* community defined by that role and while the community was not a claimant to sovereignty, banding did have the character of a primeval social contract ... The community's essence was that its members could *trust* one another, and no one else. It stood uneasily between those who could never be trusted (the Catholics) and a sovereign power which might be trusted only within limits. The sovereign power – in the 17th century the king, in the 18th century the Westminster regime – should be compelled to agree to very explicit terms.[48]

This raises an immensely complex contradiction because the whole Home Rule movement, to which the Ulster Unionists opposed themselves, did not rest upon an exclusively colonial view of Irish identity. In the *Repeal of the Union* debate in the Dublin Corporation in 1843, O'Connell based his argument for repeal of the Union, *inter alia*, upon the incompetence of the Irish Parliament to surrender an independence which had been irrevocably guaranteed to it by the constitutional settlement of 1782, itself the culmination of Molyneux's own contractarian argument. O'Connell's argument was, further, that the Union 'was no contract or bargain, that it was carried by the grossest corruption and bribery, added to force, fraud and terror'.[49] He insisted that the right to an Irish Parliament, the right of representation of freemen, extended to the Irish precisely as the Anglo-Saxon dominion extended. It was part of the constitutional law of British dependencies to have a local Parliament.[50] The terms in which O'Connell described the Declaratory Act (whereby the English King in Parliament disclaimed forever any right to interfere with the independence of the Irish Parliament) were as 'a solemn treaty between the two nations entered into, concluded and ratified'.[51] In other words, undoing a conquest is not part of the constitutional or international law justification for a Home Rule Parliament which O'Connell gives here. So it is not enough for the Protestant Ulster community to appeal to an argument of consent to resist Home Rule, as part of a British constitutional tradition. They would have to go further and use an argument about national political identity, that the Ulster Protestant should be treated as separate from the rest of the Irish people, whether Catholic or Protestant, that is, that there is no continuity of identity between the Ulster Protestant community and the perhaps Protestant nation of Ireland of the eighteenth century.

In his review of the development of nineteenth-century political ideas Miller draws a firm dichotomy between national identity and contractarianism. The former is supposed to hold that nations are 'natural', attaching to a particular territory and not traceable to an original contract.[52] Indeed the British 'national' view of the 1688 Constitution was as a slowly evolving body of law and convention, whereas Ulster Protestant contractarianism viewed it as a once-and-for-all transaction. After Catholic Emancipation the heart could be said to be gone from this Constitution[53] and yet the English could still be loyal to the Monarch as symbolically the source of the national consensus expressed in the decisions of national institutions. However, the distinctive element of identification is to be seen as an alternative to the contractarian perspective.[54]

Miller's notion of identity is that a people consists of a 'community of *predictability by introspection*' in which one can anticipate the behaviour of others by putting oneself in their place. A consciousness of kind, of familiarity and of trust allows the diffuse support for a democratic state conterminous with such a people, because one assumes it will respect those who are 'like itself'.[55] In this sense the Ulster Protestant was neither British nor Irish, identifying himself more as a proconsul than as a citizen in Ireland. Whatever the principle of equal citizenship implied in the Act of Union, the Protestants adhered to a contractarian vision of 1688.[56] Miller builds on this by arguing that the Catholic demand for a restoration of the Irish Parliament was tied to the land question with which an industrialised North could not identify.[57] Protestant tenant farmers in turn laid claim to something they considered the Crown had granted their ancestors in the seventeenth century, while Catholics made a claim to what they believed the Crown had taken away from their ancestors.[58] At the same time the Protestant community developed an individualist-conversionist experience which it based on 'a freedom of the soul deriving from the saving truth of the Bible, long rejected by Catholicism…'.[59]

This was a development parallel to Catholic nationalism. Yet while the latter had an ostensibly secular apocalyptic vision that Protestants would realise a place for themselves in the history of their Irish Nation, the Protestants harboured a continued fear that the Catholic majority, hostile to the faith of the Bible, would attempt to crush it.[60] In my view it is certainly possible to see, in the late nineteenth century, the two political traditions changing their labels to a form recognisable today. The Protestants remain 'threatened' by the Catholic majority, while the Catholics readapt, although only slightly, O'Connell's concept of the continuity of the Irish Nation.

This is why the Protestant reaction to the Home Rule movement is not to be seen as equivalent to a modern nationalist movement. There is no measure of group identification involved. Miller notes the Ulster Liberal sense of betrayal by Gladstone's conversion to home rule is in exactly the terms of a contractual basis to imperialism, which represents the main framework of the legal argument used in 1912 that has already been mentioned. So

> When the Ulster settlements were made, there was an implied compact that they who crossed the Irish sea on what was believed to be a great colonising and civilising mission should not in themselves, nor in their descendants, be abandoned to those who regarded them as intruders and as enemies.[61]

It is remarkable how far Miller is able to contrast this perspective with that of dominant English/British nationalism. So by 1912, the removal of the House of Lords' veto decisively modified the doctrine of Parliamentary sovereignty, with no system of entrenched rights and no way that Parliament could bind its successors. The only guarantee of a citizen's rights is 'his sense of co-nationality with the whole people who constitute the polity ... a testimony to the self-perceived homogeneity of the people of that island'.[62] So the Protestant resistance to home rule could not be suppressed by the argument that it was 'British national' behaviour to submit to the will of Parliament.[63] Loyalty and allegiance would overrule any feeling of nationality which would tear Protestant and Unionist people away from their attachment to the Crown.[64] Another way of putting this might be the following: 'The rise of Ulster Unionism coincided roughly with the period in which it was just possible to believe in the viability of a group of self-conscious communities autonomous with respect to their internal affairs but acknowledging a common sovereignty which was more than symbolic.'[65]

This should have argued for the evolution of the Ulster Protestant community towards a form of dominion status as had happened with the rest of the 'white' empire. The difficulty, as already sharply pointed out by Hamilton, is that the 'natives' were still there. It became immediately apparent, with the irruption of violence after 1969, that the territorial fragmentation of the Province was very advanced and only being completed.[66] The Northern Ireland state could not implement equal rights and citizenship except under coercion from Westminster and the 1971 internment confirmed that Stormont was only capable of dealing with the Catholics as enemies not as citizens.[67]

The clear logic of this argument is, in my view, for repartition. The only constraint is the imagined cost, a massive bloodbath or equally massive population transfers. None the less, the outcome would produce a 'solution' (Miller's inverted commas). Miller says:

> It is important to recognise that this 'doomsday' scenario would very probably produce a 'solution' – namely, the emergence of a new, smaller, all-Protestant state in the North and the incorporation of the rest of Northern Ireland into the Republic. Each state would quickly come to enjoy support from its ethnically homogeneous population to legitimate its monopoly of force within its new *de facto* boundaries. The killing would stop.[68]

How Could the Ulster Protestant Population Exercise a Right of Self-Determination?

A Reconstruction of Colonial Experience

This analysis points in the direction not simply of repartition but of emphasis on the importance of an evolution of the political cultural identity of the Protestant community in Northern Ireland. It does not trace the root cause of the violence to the IRA campaign of violence, nor to the 'apocalyptic' (Miller's inverted commas) nature of Irish nationalism. Both of these retain a millennial belief in the coming to consciousness of Irishness by the Protestant community. However, these myths are only possible as projections upon the vacuum of a Protestant identity which has nothing positive to counter them.

If one takes as a starting point that the Protestant community is colonial in origin and continues to be colonial in mentality, this does not argue automatically for their expulsion from the island. It is virtually unheard of, and unprecedented, for a colonial community to be expelled to the imperial metropolis. What is expected of it is that it should evolve into some form of autonomous community. This is 'complicated', to put it mildly, by the physical presence of the 'natives' in their midst. But a challenge to political evolution is in fact encouraged by the Irish variant of nationalism. Ironically, this is precisely because of the supposedly 'imperialist' character of Irish nationalism. A purely historical nationalism which had been anxious to reclaim territory would threaten the Protestants with expulsion. However, anxieties about the Algerian analogy have only been extensively developed in Protestant political literature.[69]

Precisely because of its roots in theories of cultural nationalism, Irish nationalism challenges, if unintentionally, the Protestant community to demonstrate its own distinctly different approaches to social and political organisation, based upon its own particular historical memory.[70] This challenge is already within the parameters of the New Ireland Forum arguments which accept that there are two cultures and two traditions in Ireland. However, what I am suggesting here is that the challenge must go much further, to the point of establishing the imaginative structures necessary for an Ulster Protestant statehood. By this I do not mean that, for some reason, the Protestant community must choose political independence, but rather that the challenge of Irish cultural nationalism requires the Protestant community to put together *for itself, not for a united Ireland* an alternative vision of its own political society which is not simply the parameters of a colonialist defence-mechanism against Irish nationalism. The negative political void which the Ulster Protestant community represents is a destabilising factor in the province. Once it is clear precisely what its own political identity amounts to there will be no sense in the 'imperialist' pretensions of either constitutional or violent Irish nationalism. In this view it is of course possible that there would be cooperative relations between the Protestant community and the rest of Ireland. However, they would be at most peripheral to the essentially independent, autonomous identity of that community.

The difficulty, tied itself to the problem of repartition, is to disentangle that Protestant identity from a purely negative projection of its own *vis-à-vis* what I will call the Irish nation, a perspective which is clearly time-warped. It is this *negativity* which is preventing the evolution of the Protestant community. There are two primary barriers to the development of Protestant political culture highlighted by Todd in her *Two Traditions in Unionist Political Culture*. They are rooted in themes which this chapter has already highlighted, a closed-off view of the rest of the population of the island and a commitment to an empire which has disappeared. The deconstruction of these *negative* elements does not have to mean the disappearance of Protestant social and political culture. Indeed there are already numerous indications of the shape it could eventually take.

Todd identifies the predominant Ulster Loyalist tradition as rooted in a religious rather than nationalist imagination. The children of Israel are beset by enemies. Their Bibilical texts refer to lands as foreign, appropriated from the Canaanites, etc., and gained only at the cost of continued uncertainty about the place of the people. The Protestants are predestined to continue the struggle against the darkness of Catholicism.[71] Paisley goes so far as to identify the Catholic Church with the IRA and Smyth regards the Irish Republic as a sick country, not a civilised or Christian nation in Europe.[72]

Central to this way of thinking is that it is a closed system, self-referential and unwilling to make *gradations* between good and evil. So criticism of the Security Forces, such as the UDR, amounts to support for the IRA.[73] The reason for such a dichotomy lies in the fact that the status quo, as understood by Ulster Loyalism, means dominance. Territory is maintained through marching, and the purity of Protestantism is maintained through the construction of walls. A binary system of opposites excludes betrayal, compromise, despoilation, etc. Dominance is the means to retain identity.[74] As such it is a very obvious explanation of and support for a colonial situation.

Ulster British ideology is a late nineteenth-century phenomenon. It involves identification with the modernising bonds of citizenship and loyalty which unite every British person across the Empire.[75] A Northern Ireland Government statement in the 1950s confirmed this reasoning. Partition is not based on geography, race or language differences, but on fundamental beliefs about pluralism and liberty, about the freedom of the individual to think without submitting to authority, in other words, about modernity.[76] This is not attachment to England as such but to the great family of nations with a tradition of moral leadership, democratic majority rule, in contrast to obscurantist, backward-looking, agrarian republicanism. The Northern Ireland conflict is seen as a microcosm of the conflict between freedom, modernity and totalitarianism.[77]

Todd traces distinctive Ulster features of this imperial Britishness, in particular a reliance upon first principles of liberty and conscience rather than a more pragmatic English deference to tradition, custom and practices of social interaction.[78] This ideology is equally unable to cope with real diversity. It has no image of Catholicism or the Ulster Loyalism just described. Instead the *Other* is seen as negative, intolerant, backward-looking and, above all, parochial.[79] The prejudice against the 'natives' shows itself also in the blanket treatment of the IRA as evil and in an unwillingness to admit that there is significant discrimination against Catholics. Todd locates this blindness in the fact that criticism challenges the personal integrity of the Ulster British. This prejudice is especially marked with respect to the ambitions of Irish nationalism. There is no sympathy for the Gaelic language or Irish historical experience. Southern politics are devious and nationalist irredentism is deeply resented as interference in the North.[80]

If an autonomous Ulster Protestant community is to be developed it has to be in terms of positive aspects of the Ulster traditions which do not depend upon a dominance of the Catholic minority within Ulster for their authenticity. It should be possible to construct an original conception of 'Protestant democracy' which does not necessarily exclude religion from politics, but which does not have to be sectarian. It may still be a political philosophy unacceptable to Catholics, but the option open in that case is repartition. There is a battle to be fought within historical Ulster Protestantism which is not a matter of pretending that at a certain time, for instance the 1790s, a more enlightened form of Protestantism might have existed. That religious faith is at present a vital force. So the stakes have to be made out in its own terms, which are those of political theology.

In his major study *God Save Ulster*, Bruce points to a strong tendency for popular Calvinism, with a particular doctrine of the elect, to slide into a form of racism, an inward-looking moralism which supposes that it is pointless to attempt to convert the heathen.[81] At the same time Bruce raises the challenge that any notion of identity, including nationalism, rests upon a shared history and traditions which must exclude. What we are depends upon our definition of what we are not.[82] Calvinist theologians have always argued that only God knows who are the elect.[83] So this religious tradition does not at all require exclusivenesss or sectarianism. In Ireland its historical opposition to nationalism, an alternative identity view, does not make it for all time an 'oppositional' ideology.

Bruce argues that Free Presbyterianism in Northern Ireland still adheres to the Westminster Confession of Faith of 1643.[84] The opposition of the General Assembly of the Presbyterian Church in Ireland in the 1989 General Assembly to participation in the new Ecumenical Church organisation which includes Catholics, shows a widespread pull for such religious fundamentalism. In this context such a term simply means a return to the literal meaning of beliefs contained in what were once regarded as basic texts, whatever the pressures for rationalist secularisation. This is bound to bring 'non-conformist' Protestantism into conflict about the nature of church organisation in so far as concerns Catholicism and must mean opposition to any political society which gives a place to that Church, as does the Irish Republic. However, none of this prevents the construction of an autonomous political culture to support such Calvinism, which does not have built into its identity structure hostility to Catholicism. The simple heuristic device to explore how this might develop is to explore a Calvinist political culture which does not in practice have to be concerned with a significant Catholic presence.

Protestant political culture does not have to be more liberal-rationalist than its Catholic neighbour. It is not committed to the obsession with increased efficiency and procedural rationality which has made it impossible to look to 'the end of man'.[85] Indeed Bruce concludes by arguing that, beyond evangelical Protestantism, no secure identity is available to the Ulster Protestant. Their British identity is a British imperial one threatened by the policies of contemporary British governments.[86] He goes so far as to say that socialism is unpopular with them because it appears to be atheistic:[87] 'Unionism is about avoiding becoming a subordinate minority in a Catholic state. Avoiding becoming a Catholic means remaining a Protestant.'[88] If they see their future as either the preservation of Ulster or subordination to a Roman Catholic theocracy, the question remains how to (re)construct an Ulster political culture. In my view Bruce points as sharply as Miller to repartition in these concluding remarks:

> there is no Northern Ireland 'problem'. The word 'problem' suggests that there is a 'solution': some outcome which will please almost everybody more than it displeases almost everybody. Conflict is a more accurate term for Protestant/Catholic relationships in Northern Ireland. Conflicts have outcomes, not solutions. Somebody wins and somebody loses.[89]

At least two Field Day Pamphlets have begun to explore the possibility of a post-colonial Ulster Protestant political culture. In *The Whole Protestant Community: The Making of a Historical Myth*, Terence Brown stresses the importance of Protestant revulsion against 'forces of atavistic racial nationalism' represented by the sectarian violence of Scullabogue and Wexford in 1798, which was seen to develop a mythology glorifying violence. He takes this from recent work by Ulster Presbyterians attempting to rethink their cultural heritage.[90] A tradition of constitutional independence from the British Parliament gave way to a realpolitik which submerged a tradition of democratic independence. The difficulty is to translate the democratic egalitarianism of church organisation and theological debate into a political consciousness. Brown puts it in these words:

> For political life is conducted with a rarely challenged homogeneous ideological monolith ... If the Presbyterian respect for dissent, individual conscience and personal commitment were to be translated into the political dimension one could at least expect a toughening and sharpening in Northern Irish political discourse.[91]

This need not lead to much in the way of mutual understanding between the two communities. Dunlop points to a Presbyterian preference for rigorous, precise political thinking. It should result in definite proposals and clear statements as to where is the bottom line. Language has to be interpreted in its own terms and cannot be taken as pointing to something beyond itself. This is quite sharply opposed to a Catholic tradition where there is a place for a symbolic function for language, a space for reading between the lines – or leaving them open. The latter encourages recourse to so-called 'Framework Documents', which are intended to be inclusive and developmental, but which leave Presbyterians feeling they have more latitude on their hands than they can reasonably handle.[92] Dunlop concludes:

> Presbyterians like the words to be precise. Generally, they try to get the language right first and then build the relationships. If they can't agree on the words, then the relationships suffer, even disintegrate. Others may have a different way of approaching this. For them, relationships come first and words are then found which meet the perceived needs of the hour to keep the relationship intact.[93]

Brown also draws a severe caveat against wishful thinking. In particular the revivalist movement within Ulster Presbyterianism since 1859 rests upon an excitement of religious ecstasy which is irrational. Repeated revivals show recourse to emotional outlets which combine extremes of individualism with the gratification of mass movements. Although the Presbyterian tradition did not found the Orange Order, revivalism itself has sociological roots in a 'process of modernisation which has created a class of deracinated, lonely, frightened people prey for the exotic emotional appeal of a millenialist eschatology. Neither is supportive of a sense of Northern Protestant identity as characterised by a resolute, stable attachment to civic virtue.'[94]

It is possible to draw out of the colonial tradition and this religious extremism a common trend of the positive as well as the negative. A culture has combined resistance and dissent in 'strange parts' to produce an ethos of 'essential homelessness, dependency, anxiety, obdurate fanatacising, sacrifices in the name of liberty, villainous political opportunism, moments of idealistic aspiration'.[95] This is a culture utterly opposed to the organic, historical political culture of the Anglican, eighteenth-century English constitutional Blackstone and his Irish counterpart, Edmund Burke. The evangelical ethos is perhaps well summarised in the concluding remarks of Brown. He speaks of its intimations of profound insecurity, a 'hunger for the absolute assurance historical existence cannot secure for him and of the liberating dawn it perhaps could'.[96]

What is to be explored here is a combination of extreme libertarianism with an emotionalism/irrationalism which is based on an acute sense of a lack of a formal, local historical sense of tradition which grounds English political culture. The libertarianism is extreme in the sense that Ulster Protestant political culture is able to regard the suspension of the established state and political authority as a virtual inevitability, given its lack of correspondence with trustworthy political ideals and commitments. The emotionalism/ irrationalism may be seen to rest on the sense of not belonging in one's historical material surroundings, and therefore in need of some form of 'invisible', empirically undemonstrable basis for their continued existence.

In *Watchmen in Sion, the Protestant Idea of Liberty*, Marianne Elliot also observes an apparent combination of antiquated bigotry with libertarianism, which treats religion, not nationality, as a badge of identity.[97] Despite its colonial position since 1647 and the failure to unite Protestantism in the Westminster Assembly, Presbyterianism has taken on itself a sense of persecuted purity and righteousness. The Westminster Confession is 'illiberal' in its opposition to a 'detestable indifferencey and neutrality' in the 'common cause of religion, liberty and the peace of the kingdom'.[98] She stresses the radicalism in the Confession's focus upon direct communion between God and man. Radicalism was not only compatible with but integral to anti-Catholicism. In particular they never accepted what is the peculiarly English Anglican compromise of the sovereignty of the King in Parliament.[99] They retained the sense of a fundamental law, ordained by God, to which they would, presumably, have access through direct communion. Contrary to Blackstonian/Burkean historical traditionalism, the Ulster Presbyterian ethos was to create among themselves representative institutions, not dependent upon an established, prior, political, social order.[100]

Here it is possible to see a direct link between religious fundamentalism and an ahistoric political contractarianism. Elliot points to the Scottish universities as the leaders in this particular secularisation of a religious tradition. In this political theory contractarianism was virtually unilateral, in favour of the governed against the governors, as, in the view of Francis Hutcheson, government was a trust: 'the obligations are one-sided and the government can be rejected when that trust is seen to have been betrayed'. While Hutcheson was liberal in religious matters, his theory precedes doctrines of popular sovereignty and democracy and so cannot fill the gap of the essential political referent in the Ulster Protestant colonial situation.[101] This remains a contradiction which, in my view, is compensated by a resort to a suprarational notion of divinely legitimated ahistorical identity. At the same time this 'unilateral contractarianism' was never mediated by the English eighteenth-century settlement of the King in Parliament, where authority was conterminous with the political nation.[102] Indeed, one can easily see in this unilateralism a pre-modern conviction that government might have historically grounded rights, but that these could be suspended, even for very long periods, when their exercise interfered with the fundamental rights of the people. This still left open how the people were to constitute themselves in actively permanent political organisation.

Strands of Evangelical, Libertarian Constitutionalism

I propose to illustrate how two thinkers, one Scottish, the other Ulster Scots, might be drawn upon to develop more fully the pecular brand of 'irrationalist libertarianism' which has certain roots in Northern Ireland, the rudiments of a 'Protestant, Libertarian' Constitution. Samuel Rutherford was a key Scottish ideologue in the Westminster Assembly in 1643. His work, *Lex Rex* can be understood as a dramatic counterpoint to the all-encompassing, interpretative framework constructed by Hobbes and which provided the political epistemology for the doctrine of parliamentary sovereignty. Written in 1644, its starting point is that there is a moral-political order instituted by God which each individual is free and indeed bound to follow as his reason and conscience dictate. He does not deny that governmental authority has some independent status but it is easily undone by his general political theory.

The distinctive Presbyterian starting point is that one should not insist that elements of a political society have to be reduced, the one into the other, to ensure the indivisibility of sovereignty. As sovereignty is in God, not in the King or the people, the 'discernment' of unity in political organisation is not, somehow cognately, a mark of its legitimacy. Rutherford can say that the King is not simply a delegate of the people, whose every act may be judged as to whether it is good or bad. The King, in the executive power of laws is sovereign above the people. He may be called to account only in acts of injustice 'so tyrannous, that they be inconsistent with the habitual fiduciary repose and trust put upon him'.[103] This is to oppose the idea that power cannot be strong unless it is unlimited. It is weakness to say that the power to do good must include the power to do evil. Instead there may be strength in limited power in the king, sufficient for all acts of just government, and the adequate end of the same, which is the safety of the people.[104]

With whom and under what circumstances does the authority to resist reside? Rutherford insists that justified rebellion does not mean a dissolution of all political society. Nature makes a man, even a private man, his own judge, when he has no judge to give him justice. Where there is unjust violence against the people, Parliament and inferior judges are no less heads than the king.[105] The *rule of right* for Rutherford is the will of God. His understanding of this notion is religious:

> Things are just and good, because God willeth them and God does not will things, because they are good and just; but the

> creature, be he king or any never so eminent, do will things, because they are good and just ... If therefore, it be so ... that the king's will maketh not a just law to make an unjust and bloody sense ... No rational man can create, by any act of power never so transcendent or boundless, a sense to a law contrary to the law.[106]

It is this confidence in the clarity, as well as the compelling character, of the law of God which allows and indeed requires a remarkable measure of autonomous judgement about the law. In this Rutherford does not treat the people as sovereign. In this sense he might be regarded as pre-modern, but it seems safer simply to say that for him, the people owe their identity to their obedience to the will of God, just as much as the King, as the governmental authority.[107] By the law of nature the people are to care for their own souls and so must, in their way, defend true religion. The reason is, finally, that 'everyone standeth obliged to God for himself'.[108]

Such a fundamental, individual, religious perspective has very stark institutional implications. Rather than conceiving of an overarching positive legal order drawn up by constituent fathers and binding on future generations, with a very limited, if any, right of dissent, Rutherford provides a framework within which the members of the body politic are related to one another in a virtually horizontal perspective. Each may invoke objective, supra-individualistic standards to which all are bound to submit. This is no more threatening than the prospect that God has not shown the way to good political society. The outcome is an ultra-democratic process of perpetual mutual criticism, where each may expect in turn to criticise and to be criticised. None are above and beyond the spectrum of political judgement. So the question whether a covenant between the King and the people can be binding, since there is no one standing above either to coerce them, receives this reply from Rutherford:

> The consequence is not needful ... no more than it is necessary that there should be a king and superior ruler above the king of Israel and the king of Judah, who should compel each one to do a duty to his fellow-king; for the king and the people are each of them above and below others in divers respects: the people, because they create the man king, they are so above the king, and have a virtual power to compel him to do his duty; and the king, as king, hath an authoritative power above the people, because royalty is formally in him, and originally and virtually only in the people, therefore may he compel them to their duty ... and therefore there is no need of an earthly ruler higher than both to compel both.[109]

The radical anti-formalism of this theory of law and the state does not place final authority anywhere. Rutherford does not claim that the people are more virtuous than the King. He rejects the very idea of a search for an authority free from error, as a remnant of notions of papal infallibility. No political/legal order need look for such perfection. There is no need to construct abstract principles which have a conclusive appeal. Rutherford says he is not arguing that the people are infallible where the King is not. It is simply, in concrete practical terms, more likely that the one will destroy the many than the converse.[110] When it is asked who should punish an exorbitant Parliament and people, who may bother, the answer is 'All is true; God must remedy that only.'[111]

The question whether the law must have a sole, supreme and final interpreter is, for Rutherford, not unlike the question whether the Romish Church have a sole and peremptory power of exponing laws and the word of God. Rutherford instead sees no difficulty that the fundamental law should be the *salus populi*, and that the natural conscience of all men is the last rule on earth for exponing of laws. He adds 'I see no inconvenience, to say, that the law itself is *norma et regula judicandi*, the rule and directory to square the judge.'[112]

To employ modern language, the search for a fundamental positive norm to ground and render certain the whole legal system is to respond to a false problem. Rutherford concludes on a clear note of evangelical libertarianism. When the 'popish prelate' (his imaginary protagonist) raises the objection: 'But if the law be doubtful, as all human, all civil, all municipal laws may endure great dispute – the peremptory person exponing the law must be the supreme judge. This cannot be the people, therefore it must be the king', Rutherford is firmly convinced that this is simply an unnecessary solution to an unreal question. For one, 'the Scriptures in all fundamentals are clear and expone themselves and this is true of all laws of men in their fundamentals, which are the law of nature and of nations'.[113]

Rutherford's legal polity is a call for a dramatic tension between egalitarian/participatory democracy and quasi-judicial government, always anxious to ensure a close correspondence with objective moral/legal standards. On the one hand there is no doctrine of popular sovereignty which simply says that what the majority want must prevail. On the other hand there could be no particular quasi-judicial authority which might claim a special, permanently institutionalised authority over the rest of society. The interchange between the institution and the wider society would have to be continuous as would be dispute over the evident principles of Scripture and the law of nature. What would be virtually unique about such a political/legal authority is its very high level of tolerance and uncertainty in favour of a generalised quest for the standards to govern society most in accord with the consciences of the members of the community as a whole.[114]

Radical Liberal Constitutionalism

It may seem strange to present Francis Hutcheson in the context of 'evangelical libertarianism'. Elliot remarks how he expounded the doctrine of religious toleration 'which was to become part of the platform of New Light presbyterianism'.[115] Indeed a remarkable feature of *A System of Moral Philosophy* is that from Chapter IX in Book III it develops a catalogue of human rights which go beyond any contract of government. So Hutcheson says of freedom of opinion 'as men must assent according to the evidence that appears to them, and cannot command their own assent in opposition to it, this right is plainly inalienable: it cannot be a matter of contract'.[116] Although he considers there should be in principle a right of the magistrate to suppress atheism, attempts at suppression only encourage the offender, which leads Hutcheson to suggest that 'where there is no manifest danger of the spreading of such opinions, to let them alone to the commonsense of mankind' would be most prudent.[117] As for external religious practices themselves, there is no hope that mankind would ever agree on such matters, so 'persecution on these accounts must be the greatest folly and cruelty'.

It is a highly contentious question how far Ulster Protestantism represents a sharper regard for personal liberties than the Irish Republic. It can only be investigated in a truly scientific way after a thorough investigation of the human rights jurisprudence of the Irish courts in contrast to those within the UK jurisdiction. In *Liberty and Authority in Ireland*, another Field Day Pamphlet, R.L. McCartney develops this issue as central to the Irish crisis. He distinguishes a liberal unionism from that of the 'planter's God': 'The fundamentals of fear, suspicion and triumphalism still inform irrationalist Unionism to the present day.'[118] He identifies the dilemma of liberal Unionism in that it wishes to defend the civil liberties of the Northern Irish Catholic minority against the opposition of a non-Catholic ascendancy in Northern Ireland, while at the same time rejecting Catholic aspirations to Irish unity.[119]

He identifies irrational Unionism as a dominant force in Ulster in the sense that a devolved Ulster Parliament cannot be relied upon to guarantee civil liberties to the entire population of the Province.[120] So, in McCartney's view it is only the United Kingdom as a whole which guarantees the necessary civil liberties.[121] There is nothing to choose between what the Irish Republic, dominated by Catholicism and Gaelic nationalism, and an Ulster, dominated by irrational Unionism, would produce. He asks is it surprising that there should be 'such unanimity between conservative Protestant and Catholic theology as to the role of the state as the moral guardian of the people?'[122]

In my view where this analysis is defective is in its separation of the role of the state in the protection of civil liberties from the role of the state in facilitating the exercise of positive political rights, above all participation in government. In rejecting nationalist solutions to the question of social identity McCartney leaves out of his account how a satisfactory social identity is to be constituted. He relies, in what is undoubtedly a civic-liberal perspective, upon the UK state to resolve the identity crisis of the Ulster population by efffectively taking upon itself the government of the Province indefinitely. This cannot resolve the crisis as long as a majority of both nationalists and Unionists wish to find a way of expressing their socio-political identity.

The difficulty of simple identification with the UK state is clearer in the work of Aughey who develops McCartney's thesis in *Under Siege*. In stating the case for integration Aughey argues not only that the UK state has a proven record of guaranteeing plurality, but also that 'Unionism has little to do with the idea of national identity and everything to do with the idea of the state'.[123] Following McCartney, he says that the idea of freedom under the law is the principle of this state. It is this which is 'an inclusive principle and has nothing to do with the simplicities and exclusiveness of nationhood ... The maturity of the British state ... lies in the philosophy of right, in the doctrine of liberty, which lies at its heart.'[124]

This argument rests upon Aughey's firm conviction that the state does not imply any form of identity at all, that 'it has developed an autonomous principle of unity, that is one located in the very structure of the state rather than something lying outside or beyond it'. For Aughey the modern state 'has transcended its dependence on extrinsic legitimations such as race, nation or religion, and is grounded in the political universals of right and the rule of law'.[125]

There are apparently Hegelian traces in Aughey's analysis. He begins his case for integration with an argument, according to Berki, that idealism is born of 'the endeavour to comprehend political reality in *unitary* terms, in a series of straightforward and precise propositions' (original emphasis). The essence of idealism is to understand the world as simple. This is philosophically inadequate because it leads to dualism. Yet it is politically fundamental because of the quality of commitment of the one-sidedness of idealism. Aughey proceeds to make a fundamental distinction which underlies his rejection of theories of nationalism in favour of the rule of law as the basis for political identity. He follows Berki's differentiation 'in political thought between a "nostalgic" or conservative, vision which focuses upon a set of past experiences as the inspiration for present action, and an "imaginative", or radical vision, which focuses upon an idea, a creative engagement to achieve that which has not yet been'.[126]

While this project is very lucidly stated, it is questionable whether it can be equated with the British state as it is understood by the people of the 'mainland'. Aughey argues that if the autonomous principle of the modern state is taken to be right (in the Hegelian sense) then the relevant political concept is 'neither religion nor national identity but citizenship'. He then proceeds to claim that the UK is a state 'which, being multi-national and multi-ethnic, *can* be understood in terms of citizenship and not substantive identity'.[127] There follows a statement which Todd has identified as the form of British Commonwealth to which Ulster liberal Unionists continue to give adherence:

> And it is significant that the character of the British state has always been associated with the idea of law, common and statute. (In passing, it may be said that the apparently archaic unionist celebration of the Crown is as near as one can get to a theory of the British state.) The imperial notion of *'civus Britannicus sum'* has transformed itself into the democratic ideal of different nations, different religions and different colours, all equal citizens under one government. It is to this notion that intelligent unionism, which embraces both Protestants and Catholics, owes allegiance. It was from this notion that the Republic of Ireland seceded to construct a state on the principle of national unity.[128]

This is not the same as the British/English state founded in the central concept of Parliamentary sovereignty, which is rooted in the English Reformation and which has received theoretical expression in the works of Hooker, Hobbes, Blackstone, Burke and, finally, Dicey. The latter rests upon an all-inclusive notion of English national identity in which transcendent notions of law or human rights – which might be effectively and externally entrenched – are quite alien.[129] Aughey's is perhaps a fine ideal but its fundamental characteristic is loyalty to something beyond the political communities of mainland Britain and this is why I believe that it is McCartney and Aughey who themselves point back to the necessity for the construction of an Ulster political identity which enjoys the special characteristic of not being based on notions of tradition and historical national identity – hence the special relevance and force of Hutcheson and his development of a doctrine of *civic polity*.

Whatever modernist, chronological argument might be made about the ahistorical character of contractarian theory, and hence its indifference to tradition-based notions of social identity, it is clear that Hutcheson speaks McCartney's and Aughey's language when he focuses the problem of politics on a dichotomy between the rule of law and individual despotism. Civil government means what is necessary and conducive to the prosperity of the whole body united.[130] The root of civil government is the rule of law: 'as it is plain, from the general principles of morality, that the pleasures or interests of one, or of a few, must always be subordinated to the more extensive interests of great numbers ... the subject professes to convey powers only as they are conceived useful to the whole body'.

The notion of civility is directly tied to those of equality and non-discrimination. If each is obliged to perform laborious duties for the benefit of the whole, each one shares in the advantages of like services performed by others.[131] Hutcheson stresses how he sees his task: 'we are inquiring into the just and wise motives to enter into civil polity, and the ways it can be justly constituted; and not into points of history about facts'.[132]

There follow innumerable similarities with Rutherford's thinking and which distinguish this Ulster-Scot from Blackstone and Burke. So the end of civil power is quite distinct from the parental. Nor has God by supranational revelation named governors and specially appointed the quantity of power to be committed to them. Not only is there no place for a Divine Right of Kings, Hutcheson will not even give a place to tradition or acquired rights. Where a form of government does not guarantee the interests of the people, no amount of past acquiescence will prove the justice of the powers assumed.[133] Indeed Hutcheson goes so far as to say that whatever contracts of government are concluded the people remain the arbiters of their interest and can revoke these powers as they see fit. This is what Elliot finds so distinctive about Hutcheson in comparison to Locke and indeed, as seen above, it brings him close again to Rutherford. So Hutcheson says:

> if the majority of a rash multitude have consented to a pernicious plan; and afterwards find its destructive tendency; as they now see that they erred in the essential subject of the contract; taking that plan to tend to their good, which they find has the most oppressive tendency; they certainly have a just exception against the contract, and are free from its obligation.[134]

It is such a distrust of freedom itself as actually exercised which leads Hutcheson to devise schemes of qualified voting and proportional representation.[135] He favours the maintenance of agrarian laws which will ensure that property does not become so concentrated as to threaten liberty[136] and he recommends smaller states rather than larger ones, as there is then greater room for men of finer genius and capacity to exert their abilities 'and improve them by exercise in the service of mankind ... Accordingly we find that all virtues and ingenious arts flourished more in the little states of Greece than in any of the great Empires.'[137]

So Hutcheson's notion of *civic polity*, an active, participatory one, could not be farther removed from the ideal of *Civis Britannicus*. His ideal was the small republic where each could observe the other and be observed: 'The safest popular assembly in a mixed form is that of deputies or representatives proportionally and fairly elected for a certain term', to reflect the number of people and wealth in a district.[138] A Senate of a few elected for character and eminent ability should propose the laws, but:

> they in turn should continue only for a limited term, changing by rotation and not all at once ... The like reasons shew the advantages of making all magistracies annual, or, if that term be too short for some great designs, of limiting them at least to a certain small number of years ... And where such laws have obtained for any considerable time, there will be considerable numbers of men of distinguished abilities and experience for the several offices civil and military.[139]

In my view this is an institutional framework which ensures that each person has the maximum opportunity to offer his own interpretation of what the public good requires, with the minimum of institutionalisation of established authority. There must be traces of Rutherford in the following:

> The rights of governors, magistrates, or clergy are no otherwise sacred than those of other men ... God has not by any revelation determined the forms of government ... His law requires that government should be settled ... But the form of polity, and the degrees of power to be committed, are left to human prudence.[140]

There is the same confidence as with Rutherford that individual human judgement must be allowed to determine, in extremities, when the public good is violated. There is a right of resistance not only when the limits of a written constitution are overrun:

> But in all governments, even the most absolute, the natural end of the trust is acknowledged on all sides to be the prosperity and safety of the whole body. When therefore the power is perverted from this end ... the subjects must have a right of resistance ... all conveyance of absolute power ... with a preclusion of a right of resistance ... must be a deed originally invalid, as founded in an error about what is most essential in such transactions, the tendency of such power to the general good.

> This supposes no court or assembly superior to the king in monarchies ... or to the popular assembly in democracies ... It only supposes that the supreme civil magistrates or rulers are subject to the laws of God and Nature, and are bound by some contract, express or tacit ... and that since all civil power is granted and received avowedly for the public good, he who employs it for a contrary purpose, by this perfidity on his part, frees the other party from all obligation ... A Right of resistance against injuries imports no civil superiority, nay it is consistent with the lowest subjection.[141]

Such is precisely the view of Rutherford, that there is no need for an institutionalised, impartial third party to judge the merits of a dispute between the governors and the governed. Instead there are objective standards afforded by the law of God and Nature. It is not even a matter of pointing to an original written contract or constitution. Each person has to be the judge himself of the wrong done by a flagrant violation of such standards set by God and Nature. In a small political community which has already set itself the safeguards which Hutcheson recommends, in my view, this added *permanent threat* of resistance need only serve to restrain the exercise of power. It adds to principles of proportional representation, rotation of offices, qualified and representative majorities, etc., the guarantee that in the final analysis there are no permanent hierarchies, that everything is open to continued dispute and contestation in the light of the law of God and Nature.

Indeed Hutcheson's dismissal of the need for a *Grundnorm*, the rejection of the call for an 'impartial arbitrator/spectator' is in virtually the same terms as Rutherford's. There is inevitably the difficult question of the degree of injustice required to merit resistance. It might be thought that neither party can be an impartial judge in its own cause, 'but the ruler can have the worse pretensions to judge, as the point questioned is whether he has forfeited his power or not, and to be sure he never will give a judgement against himself'. Impartial arbitration would not be useless, but the people themselves have the best pretensions of a right to decide the question as civil power is constituted in their interest and who can best judge such a matter than 'these persons themselves who have entrusted him'.[142]

Ulster Protestant political culture is based very starkly on a material consensus about the goals of political life: the maintenance of autonomy apart from the rest of Ireland, combined with a complete unwillingness to accept any political authority which appears to falter or fail in attaining this objective. What better outline of the balance of the governed and governors, of the relation of material to formal principles could one hope to find than the concluding remarks of Hutcheson on the general principles of civil government and the right of resistance. He goes so far as to say that:

> if upon any trial the people find that the plan of power they constituted avowedly for their own good is really dangerous to them, they have a right to alter it. It must be strange effrontery in any governor ... to hold them to a contract which he knows they entered into upon this expectation and express design that it should tend to the general good, for which also he expressly undertook, when it is found to have a contrary tendency.[143]

The simplest way to give institutional expression to this perspective is to allow a very wide power of appeal to referendum or constitutional judicial review, or a combination of both.

The very tone of Hutcheson's political philosophy must surely capture the mood of a province which appears supremely beleaguered in the face of its rulers. He recognises that a people may become suspicious of their rulers without just cause. Yet even where the ruler is persuaded that there is no just cause to distrust him, he must still find some way to persuade the people if he is to retain power.[144] The reason is that nothing can justify what will occasion a general permanent suspicion and distrust.[145] It is often objected that such doctrines must cause continual seditions. Yet for Hutcheson '[T]here is no hope of making a peaceful world or country, by means of such tenets as the unlimited powers of governors, and the unlawfulness of all resistance.' There is such love of ease, tolerance of any kind of governor, fondness for ancient custom and of the advantages hoped for under the present administration, that it is seldom practicable 'to get sufficient numbers to concur in any violent efforts for that purpose' against established government, however unjust. Mankind has been generally 'too tame and tractable'.[146] Has any classical political theorist given a more blistering defence of political equality against the confusion usually attributable to 'designing princes' and servile ecclesiastics who drive out the natural notions of polity:

> No great wonder this, that millions thus look upon themselves as a piece of property to one of their fellows as silly and worthless as the meanest of them, when the like arts of superstition have made millions, nay the very artificers themselves, fall down before the block or stone they had set up, or adore monkeys, cats, and crocodiles, as the sovereign disposers of their fortunes.[147]

Hutcheson concludes quite succinctly that the Greek and Roman understanding of democracy is of such a form of the supreme power where 'the people in a body had the command, or had their turns in commanding and obeying'.[148]

CHAPTER 6

Irreconcilable Identities: The Aftermath of Conquest

The theme of this book is, inevitably, leading to the conclusion that the Northern Ireland problem has to be seen in the context of a conquest of Ireland. The so-called Protestant or Unionist community is the remnant of a colonial settler society installed on the island for the purpose of maintaining a firm British hold on the island. The so-called Catholic or nationalist/republican community is the remnant of the *native* inhabitants of Ireland, that is, the island as a whole. They are, no more than the Protestants, people who have been there since time immemorial – since many have come into the North-east since the first influx of Protestants in the seventeenth century.

This reasoning leads to a questioning of the concept of *Northern Ireland* as such. The territorial entity has no historical legitimacy in the history of either part of the population of Northern Ireland. The Protestants/Unionists were not in favour of partition. They identify themselves as a part of the greater British nation. The Catholics are Irish and claim no special identity, e.g. as successors to an ancient Ulster community. The only specific feature of Northern Ireland is that it locates the two communities in contiguity with one another. Therefore political solutions to the Irish problem which begin from the premise that the so-called *two parts of Ireland* have to come together and agree, *or* stay apart from each other, etc. are misconceived historically and ethnically.

One has to pierce the veil of the administrative unit which is called Northern Ireland. This will entail an extended discussion of the drafting and implementation of the Anglo-Irish Treaty, which will form the subject-matter of Chapter 7. To maintain that the Northern Ireland problem is part of a conquest is not to deny the legitimacy of the Ulster Protestant and Unionist position on the ground that they threatened force to remain outside a Home Rule Parliament in 1912. In terms of international law, if their presence in Ulster was legitimate in 1912, then it was legitimate for them to threaten force to remain there in the political mode which they preferred. If the nationalist/republican community wish to contest this repeated and clearly stated Protestant/Unionist wish, then they have to recognise that the logic of their position is coercive, that they cannot simply expect to prevail because of what they conceive of as the rightness of their own position.

However, the retention of a very large nationalist/republican minority within Northern Ireland is another matter. It is very much an integral part of the colonial history of the island that the minority finds itself in this position. The next chapter will offer an extended account of the circumstances in which the British state – still very much in its imperial mode – coerced a substantial minority of the Irish nation to remain within the boundaries of the United Kingdom. While the general objective of this treaty may have been desirable in formal democratic terms – it proposed to separate two political communities, one of which did not wish to be a partner of the other – this objective was not achieved because the terms of the Treaty, in particular Article 12, continued the main features of the original pattern of the conquest of the island. The boundary was drawn having regard to the strategic and economic interests of the majority of Northern Ireland and with the usual coercion of a smaller community by a much more powerful one, which has marked the history of the two islands.

This history has left two distinct societies within Northern Ireland charged with the task of cohabitation. The logic of an understanding of Irish identity as torn around the question of whether Ireland was ever conquered is that the task is an unreasonable imposition upon both so-called communities. Their actual relationship with one another can only be a function of the history of the British conquest or attempted assimilation and incorporation of Ireland into the United Kingdom. That is to say, the relationship is structurally antagonistic. International law can assist, it is claimed in this study, with a historical description of what has happened. However, it does not have effective mechanisms for the peaceful resolution of conflicts. Whatever description one might give to the Ulster Protestant and Unionist community, it does not provide an automatic solution to the conflict in Ulster, given that the very *rationale* of conquest is that it is a successful employment of coercion. It is only to be overcome, in the absence of a change of heart of the conquerors, in the event of a successful coercive response. To speak of a pathway to a voluntary reunification of Ireland in the face of an obvious lack of such a change of heart is simply not a political position. To hope that a change in the balance of population will bring about a favourable democratic majority is to ignore the fact that problems of identity, particularly ones induced by a history of conquest and subjugation, precede the option of democratic resolution. Given that the so-called nationalist/republican community in Northern Ireland is merely a part of an Irish nation of the island as a whole, it makes little difference to the presence or absence of a legitimation foundation to the Unionist presence in Ireland, whether this minority is a more or less large part of the overall Irish nation. The Protestant and Unionist community remains much the same size and as irreconciled as ever to being part of an Irish nation.

The detail of argument about partition and the subsequent fate of the so-called minority community in Northern Ireland will be the subject of Chapter 7. However, this chapter will attempt to explain the rationale which underlies the next. From an international law perspective, the question of the conquest of Ireland can be taken to be largely concluded, if not answered,* by the terms of the 1921 Treaty, except for the issue of the minority in Northern Ireland. Britain insisted upon a treaty settlement which was very close to the so-called Constitution of 1782. Admittedly, the old Irish Parliament was dominated by an English Executive. However, if that Parliament had been allowed to develop organically, as had other dominions of the Empire it would have come to resemble the 1921 Treaty. The gradual democratisation of British imperial institutions in the course of the nineteenth century would have led to a full extension of the franchise to include the entire Catholic population. The Irish Executive would, inevitably, given the representative and responsible nature of British Parliamentary institutions, have gradually come from and been answerable to the Irish Parliament.

Therefore, the assumption of this study is that the decision of the Irish state, after 1921, to transform itself, gradually into a full-blown republican constitution based upon theories of abstract natural rights of nations and of the rights of cultural self-determination of peoples, is not directly a matter of concern to the question whether Ireland was conquered. This question is concluded at the point where Britain effectively relinquishes sovereignty over the Irish nation, given that the British treated effectively with the majority which existed in the Free State in 1922, granting them dominion status. Consequently the development of the Irish Free State to a republic may be regarded as an internal matter within the Irish state, a matter of how it chose to shape and develop its own form of government.†

So the relevance of these developments to our study is confined to the following. From an international law perspective the question of the rights of the so-called minority in Northern Ireland remains

* There is the issue of whether Ireland became completely independent by virtue of achieving dominion status. This could affect the question whether it might conclude, in a final binding way, the 1925 Boundary Agreement (see Chapter 7, especially the postscript).

† Republicanism as a form of government is separate from the issue of whether complete independence in international law is achieved (see Chapter 7, especially the postscript).

open, in a manner which will be explored in more detail in Chapter 7. In summary the argument will be, there, that this aspect of the Treaty was achieved with a substantial measure of deceit and coercion and, above all, in violation of the wishes of the minority and in disregard of the principle of democratic self-determination, which was the primary ostensible justification given for the partition in favour of the so-called majority in Northern Ireland.

The republican and cultural Nationalist arguments for an Irish state were given expression in Ireland after independence and concern the exercise of independence. However, to the extent that the minority in Northern Ireland belongs to the same political community as the Irish Republic, the political developments in the latter are relevant to, albeit not absolutely determinative of, the perspectives of the former. Hence, post-independence developments in the self-conception of the Irish state will, therefore, be considered here primarily from the perspective that they ensure an ever-widening distance in perspective between the majority in Northern Ireland and the Irish nation. As such these perspectives will be considered as part of the argument that the logic of Irish history, a history of colonialism and conquest, favours, above all, a reconsideration of the terms of the Partition.

Arguments Concerning the Two Traditions

Introduction

The conflict in the North of Ireland has numerous aspects, but one fundamental feature is the rejection by a large section of the Northern majority of the legitimacy of the Irish Republic as a nation-state. This is seen to rest upon an exclusivist cultural identity which was used to justify the major part of Ireland breaking away by force from the remainder of the United Kingdom after the 1918 General Elections. The Irish state is seen by numerous Northerners as rooted in a romantic nationalism for which Southern Anglo-Irish figures bear a very large responsibility.[1] A mystical and regressive nationalism thereby led to the founding of a state incompatible with the political liberalism which has been central to the British/UK state since the Glorious Revolution of 1688. Northerners expressed determination to use force to resist incorporation in this state in the years after 1912 and continue to do so. At the same time the Irish Republic continues to claim, as a matter of legal right, that the Irish Nation extends the full length of the island of Ireland, and that it has full legal title to the entire island.

The terms of this conflict present, perhaps, from a Southern Irish perspective, an impressive case-study of the force of the claim to a right to cultural self-determination effectively implemented in very large part, but now the subject of intense internal critique, as what appears to be a final push to complete its implementation is under way. The resistance to this push takes many forms, but one of the most important is an impassioned resistance to the idea that a state should base its legitimacy upon any notion of cultural politics. The project of national cultural identity is rejected as inherently exclusivist, necessarily backward-looking and as fundamentally incompatible with the guarantee of civil liberties which is central to the heritage of the liberal state.

In my view there are at least two issues which arise very sharply in this extremely bitter confrontation. The first is the internal critique which has developed in the Republic of Ireland about the viability of a state legitimacy founded upon cultural nationalism. Both modernist and post-modernist objections have arisen concerning the cultural identity of Gaelic-Catholic Ireland. This identity is interpreted as unable to grapple with the complexities of a dominant global cosmopolitan individualism, perhaps leaving the cultural nationalist with no clearer project than that of jamming the air-waves to prevent the inflow of commercial broadcasting. This might not matter so much if it were not for the fact that the Irish independence struggle was being continued with arguments which include a large measure of cultural nationalism.

At the same time the liberal critique of Irish nationalism can also be subject to an internal or immanent critique. It has come to be seen that all universalist and abstract political theories are grounded, in fact, in particular historical traditions. Whatever the apparent openness of liberal theories of the state, in the context of international discourse, it is not difficult to unravel assumptions of superiority on the part of particular 'liberal' nation-states towards other national communities, rooted in the view that they, 'the liberals' represent a more 'advanced' form of 'universal' culture which should, therefore, be universally adopted. In other words the liberal/cultural-nationalist dichotomy conceals a struggle between competing visions of the nature of international society. In this context it is usually the weaker national communities which resort to collectivist language to defend themselves from what they see as 'imperialist' pretensions to cultural hegemony.

My own proferred resolution of this conflict is to recognise a right of cultural self-determination upon all states – as well as those nations which are not yet and may wish to become states. This is to identify liberal political societies in terms which they may not care to accept. However, I would superimpose upon each such national entity an obligation to engage in both an immanent critique of its own traditions and a dynamic hermeneutic of those traditions which they most fear. The juxtaposition of abstractly formulated equal rights to cultural self-determination is in grave danger of misrepresenting the relations between the different traditions as static. The origin of this legal language is in fact one of extreme tension and the essence of a new international cultural order is one which recognises the need for a legal hermeneutic which modifies the hegemonic in favour of the dialogic.[2] It is hard to imagine any aspect of international legal relations which would not be radically implicated by such a development.

Arguments for Cultural Self-Determination and the Irish State

Article 1 of the Irish Constitution of 1937 reads very much as the UN Covenants on Human Rights in its declaration on self-determination: 'the Irish nation hereby affirms its inalienable, indefensible and sovereign right to choose its own form of Government, to determine its relations with other nations and *to develop its political, economic and cultural life in accordance with its own genius and traditions* [emphasis added]'.[3]

In the last election held while Ireland was a part of the United Kingdom, Sinn Fein issued the following justification for an independent state in its election manifesto, for which it received a large majority of seats in Ireland as a whole, and a substantial majority of votes in what is now the Irish Republic. It said it would appeal to the Paris Peace Conference.

> At that Conference the future of the nations of the world will be settled on the principle of government by consent of the governed. Ireland's claim to the application of that principle in her favour is ... based *on our unbroken tradition of nationhood, on a unity in a national name which has never been challenged, on our possession of a distinct national culture and social order* [emphasis added], on the moral courage and dignity of our people in the face of alien aggression, on the fact that in nearly every generation, and five times within the past 120 years our people have challenged in arms the right of England to rule this country.[4]

The assumption of the conclusion of Chapter 4 was that this perspective did not prevail in the drafting and acceptance by the Irish Free State of the Treaty of 1921. However, from the time de Valera and his 'Republicans' assumed office in 1932, the Manifesto was taken up again and led to the terms of the Constitution of 1937.[5] What is central to the concerns of this chapter is not this perspective as an Irish response to the conquest. In legal terms, except for the question of the minority in Northern Ireland, the conquest came to an end with the agreement of the representatives of the Irish state in 1922. Instead the issue here is purely one of cultural hermeneutics, to understand how different concepts of cultural identity and political legitimacy divide the 'Two Traditions' in Ireland.

In a recent critical but sympathetic study *The Dynamics of Cultural Nationalism,* John Hutchinson explains precisely how and in what form a cultural nationalist movement led to the foundation of the Irish state. He does this precisely in terms of an attempt to modify the terms of the existing international normative order. Cultural nationalism evolved as an intellectual movement in the course of the nineteenth century and particularly at the turn of the century in Ireland, as a means to establish a position within world culture which avoids the pressure coming from an over-dominant immediate neighbour, in this case the English-speaking world.

Hutchinson warns against the immediately dismissive response of the liberal. 'Cultural nationalism reacts *both* against traditional ethnography *and* universalist rational belief systems. It perceives the world in polycentric terms as naturally divided into unique peoples' (emphasis added).[6] There are several interacting and contradictory pressures to be unravelled in this context. First, cultural nationalism rests itself on modernising premises: the construction of a secular intelligentsia responding to the erosion of traditional identities by modernisation.[7] Historical memory is to serve not as a refuge of regression but a source of inspiration for a regenerated national community.[8] It is precisely the anti-traditional impulse to differentiation, whether in matters of profession, sexuality or religion, which spurns the otherworldy sense of the traditional in favour of the continuously mobile community.[9] The nation to which return is to be made is not seen as having objective characteristics, such as language or race. It is a matter for secular intellectuals to evoke a symbolic politics to challenge established social identities by recourse to the evocation of particular community memories.[10]

Cultural nationalism arises in the context of a struggle to overcome the backward-pulling tendencies of a decaying traditionalism. However, it attempts to do so not by recourse to an assimilationist cosmopolitanism – which it regards as a spurious cover for another concealed form of cultural nationalism – but, through an inner reform of the traditional order, a change which is rooted in principles of equality and social mobility. Far from being isolationist, cultural nationalism presents its nationalism as a progressive culture in active contact with other nationalities, but opposed to the assimilationism of pretended universal models of development, for the simple reason that each nation has its own evolutionary path to follow.[11] It is the function of secular intellectuals to insist that a progressive evolutionary view of history requires recognition of the uniqueness of peoples in their different stages on the evolutionary ladder. It is at the same time central to such a project that cultural renovation should be facilitated by a sensitive *self-directed* assimilation of the most advanced scientific-technical experience of other national cultures.[12]

The international context of the rise of cultural nationalism in Ireland appears to have made it inevitable, thereby affording some empirical foundation for the historicist view of evolution. It was late nineteenth-century Britain which experienced a general disillusion with universalist liberal values. There was a general quest for more integrative sources of social solidarity. In Hutchinson's view, it was the English search for a more exclusive community which provoked the Irish into Gaelic revivalism. It was the British state which presented itself as an imperial supporter of an Anglo-Saxon Protestant mission in the world. As such it was far from an agent of universalist vision dedicated to dissolving cultural inequalities.[13] Gaelic nationalism, from the 1890s, rested upon an intelligentsia largely outside academia, which relied upon a Europe-wide Celtic scholarship to recover a forgotten tradition. This was not a reversion to receeding contemporary 'peasant' values, but an attempt by rising, although politically and administratively excluded, educated strata of the towns to oppose British cultural imperialism with a new high culture based upon authentic native values. The linchpin of the reliance upon international scholarship was to be able to argue that it was English culture which was provincial and the newly understood Celtic culture which afforded the most evolved and progressive vision for the future.[14]

In positive terms this cultural-social vision of a new Ireland meant an appeal to the communalist traditions of Gaelic Ireleand against the materialist individualism into which, or down to which British culture was translated/reduced.[15] This is not a matter of high-status intellectuals responding with hostility to a modernising science, but a call for a return to the glorious memory of a Celtic cooperative society in the rural community combining with a voluntary system of schools corresponding to the cultural needs of the urban classes. Above all, it was a revivalist dream of the old Gaelic political system, conceived as a decentralist polity. The crucial role for a truly independent state would be to mediate the tensions between a traditional society and the assimilationist pressures of a technically more advanced but materialist and individualist neighbour.[16]

In my view it is essential to remember the ideal self-projection of cultural nationalism in order to avoid argument at cross-purposes about the consequences of concrete attempts to implement it. The picture of Irish society which its liberal opponents reject is grim but such rejection does not go to the theoretical foundations of the project. Hence its protagonists tend to withdraw behind the conviction that they have not been understood and that, indeed, their shortcomings are merely a call to renewed effort. The most problematic dimension to cultural nationalism is the relationship between its secular prophets and the people which it has to interpret. The major apparent theoretical weakness of cultural nationalism is that it looks for a vision of the future in the past. It assumes that culture is not a cumulative historical development, that a social tradition ossifies, that it becomes alienated from itself. So it is necessary to retrace steps and retake possession of the true heritage, the true national culture of the nation – to recover the authentic essence of the people's inherent nature.[17] In other words the concept of the right to cultural self-determination of peoples has built into it a conflict between, at the very least, the *people in itself* and the *people for itself*.

Is it possible to return to the past without slipping into 'fundamentalism' both because the intellectual resources are not there to be found to respond to assimilationist modernisation, and because the grounds for political support are most likely to be in the most traditional parts of contemporary society? Without falling into a chronology of modern Irish history it might be possible to outline some difficulties which the cultural nationalist project encountered. Its leaders were responsible for the successful armed struggle for independence. Sixty-nine per cent of the post-independence elites of Ireland came through the Gaelic League, the central institution of cultural nationalism.[18] Yet to find the strongest grounds for resistance to Britain meant that one had to look to traditional sectors of society, the rural community, still partially Gaelic and steeped in a devotional Catholicism. This provides a socio-cultural explanation for a growing neo-traditionalism.[19] The social groups most attracted to cultural nationalism could very well cross the divide of the *people in itself* and the *people for itself*. Disillusioned assimilationists (usually returned emigres), depressed lower middle-class urban classes (usually excluded from higher administrative and political functions), and the core of the rural classes (tenant farmers, newly liberated peasant proprietors above all), will have as a starting point simply what actually distinguishes them in their own eyes from British society.[20]

In any case it seems common ground that post-independence Ireland quickly gave prominence to rural Catholic values, in this way to differentiate Irish society from Protestant, industrial Britain.[21] The main bones of contention with the North originate in the 1920s, especially the prohibition of divorce. The dream of a decentralised political community gave way to a state nationalism, rooted in a desire for socio-economic progress through reliance upon able administrators within the state and an isolationist population supposed somehow to develop economically apart from international society.[22]

Can the question be posed whether this fate for cultural nationalism is inevitable ? Why do its intellectual resources appear to have been exhausted since the early 1960s and how is this phenomenon connected with the apparent resurgence of the same nationalism in the North? In my view this is the fundamental theoretical question. In the 1980s an Irish intellectual who very much identifies with the shaken cultural nationalist tradition, none the less offered a critique of its disintegration. Fennell pinpoints the failure of any Irish cultural project to hold the collective imagination of the people of the Irish Republic. As a political society it has in fact reverted to the type of state organisation which cultural nationalism was supposed to replace. It is constructed around a centralised national administration which is substantially the same as the British state it took over. This is responsible for administering an open economy, fully integrated into the European Community. It is individualist and takes its consumerist mores from London and New York. It is dominated by a pseudo-metropolis, Dublin, which is merely an imitative replica of the other cities.

This has enormous implications for the relationship of the Irish Republic with the rest of the Irish nation, the large nationalist minority in the North. Consistent with his view of the Irish nation as a cultural entity he draws its boundary where it meets with the Protestant Loyalist/British in the North. However, the Southern Irish can feel no sympathy or understanding for the 'armed struggle' of some of the nationalist minority in the North. The former have lost all sense of being bonded to one another in collective historical memories of Gaelic Catholic traditions. They have given way to a virtually complete Anglicisation, although Irish remains the official language of the country. Catholicism remains strong but it has become privatised and is not seen as a legitimate foundation for the construction of a political society. As a social force it is still considerable, which means, in fact, that there is something of a stand-off between the Church's power to win referendums on divorce (a power which recently has been modified) and abortion and its disavowal of any alternative proposals to counter the attempts of some elements of the political elites to negotiate a compromise with the North.[23]

In pure logic once a state ceases to be effectively founded upon a sense of bonding of the national collective to an historical territory, the 'nation-state' is inevitably confined to the 'national territory' in the sense of the space over which its centralised organs effectively exercise jurisdiction.[24] At the same time the same state risks a loss of the very foundations of its own existence. There is nothing more natural than that it should transfer its administrative/jurisdictional responsibilities in socio-economic and, eventually, political matters to a supranational organisation. Equally it is likely that the 'abandoned' national minority in the North looks upon the Irish Republic as a semi-state, as a failed project and considers its political representatives as not effectively competent to represent them. This is a view which might be felt well beyond that part of the nationalist community until recently committed to political violence.[25] This transition must inevitably cause an immense assymetry in the conflict between the Northern majority and what it sees as the rest of the Irish nation. It objects to a project of cultural self-determination which it considers anti-liberal at a time when it is largely defunct south of the border but very much alive among its most immediate nationalist neighbours.

The British Liberal Critique of Cultural Nationalism in Ireland

By way of introduction to the liberal critique, it is necessary to repeat the basic assumption of legal method in this study which rests not on the state as such but on a form of collective identity of peoples. It is only appropriate that a material rather than a formal definition of international personality should look to a hermeneutic and, where necessary, a deconstruction of the ideological structures which represent the typical modes of experience and practice of collective groups as such. These structures form an interrelated network, simply because they have a common historical root. It is vital to stress that the unspoken cultural assumptions and beliefs are not necessarily or simply reproduced by state action or even by elite manipulation. It is not even a matter of analysis at the level of observable political behaviour and explicit political preference. Indeed individual and even party political beliefs may appear logically incoherent. Yet, it is a matter of attempting to identify the sense of community of a group in terms which it can itself recognise.[26] Such a perspective is an inevitable consequence of the assumption that the people are prior to the state and that the latter is, indeed, no more than a contingent administrative and institutional framework which the people give themselves. The viability and effectiveness of the state, particularly of its relations with other states, is to be evaluated in terms of the people it represents.

In 1956 the Northern Ireland Government produced a statement justifying partition. It is not based on geography, race or language differences but on ideas of liberal, progressive democracy. The Northern Ireland state rested on the fundamental right of the individual to think, debate and express him or herself, independent of outside (that is, church) authority. This state is committed to the principle of government solely on the basis of majority rule and, as such, it forms part of an international tradition of liberal democracy represented by the British Commonwealth. This is not an identification with England alone but with a family of nations founded upon certain principles. Northern Ireland is a bridge between a free Europe and a free America. The conflict represents a microcosm of the conflict between freedom and modernity, on the one hand, and totalitarianism, on the other hand.[27]

In her critique of this self-presentation Todd draws special attention to the dark picture which the Ulster British draws of the Other. The view of Southern society is negative – as intolerant, backward-looking and, above all, parochial. A binary opposition is drawn between civilians and barbarians, a type of thinking which is common to colonial peoples. Traditionally Ulster liberalism is marked by an unawareness of discrimination and an aloofness from sectarian politics. There is a special horror of political violence although it is only a matter of degree removed from regarding all nationalists as disloyal to the liberal principles of the British state. The hostility to any form of interference of the Irish Republic in the North, hence the unanimous resistance to the Anglo-Irish Agreement, is rooted both in a sense of superiority towards a backward society and a feeling, parallel to this, that any empirical proof that the Ulster liberal is guilty of discrimination is an impossible affront to their identity as a liberal and, as such, has to be repressed.[28]

One of the most complete contemporary statements of a liberal position is made by Aughey in *Under Siege, Ulster Unionism and the Anglo-Irish Agreement*. He draws support from McCartney's *Liberty and Authority in Ireland*. This sophisticated argument is determined to root out obvious traces of discrimination against minorities, but the question remains whether it is 'assimilationist'. It is certainly incompatible with an explicit theory of cultural nationalism. That in itself is not a fatal criticism given the logic of the liberal position. However, the question remains whether the universalist claims of liberalism can be sustained. Aughey's starting point is that it was the Northern Irish state which assured Protestants their dominance. Now Protestants and Catholics are on an equal political footing 'so long as the principles are justice and welfare and not nationalist irredentism'.[29] Unionist elitism is to be rejected equally with an authoritarian and non-pluralist Irish state. Aughey continues his argument in these terms.

The whole idea of a politics of identity ignores the artificially constructed rather than natural character of nationality. It is not true that the natural social unit is the nation and that the nation must have or be conterminous with the state: 'Nationalist presumptions cannot accept the distinction between culture (whatever that word may imply) and political value and allegiance.'[30] This is a lucid objection to the theoretical basis of cultural nationalism. Yet to whom is Aughey referring when he insists immediately that Northern Ireland 'has consistently expressed its determination to remain within the Union'?[31] This presupposes not only that the idea of the state takes precedence over the idea of the nation but also that it has a distinct referent which can overcome the cultural divisions within Northern Ireland.

Aughey insists, 'The identity of unionism has little to do with the idea of the nation and everything to do with the idea of the state.' He carries to its logical conclusion the idea that any reference to the concrete or to the particular characteristics of a population as themselves determinative of the nature of the state contradicts the very idea of a modern state:

> the modern state has transcended its dependence on extrinsic legitimations such as race, nation or religion, and is grounded in the political universals of right and the rule of law. In so far as those within the state accept the authority of the rule of law, (justice being the impartiality of law designed for the general welfare), then there can be the fullest expression of ethnic, religious and social diversity.[32]

The relevant political concept is neither religion nor nation but citizenship. The United Kingdom is a multi-national, multi-ethnic state to be understood in terms of citizenship and not substantive identity. The British state represents the democratic ideal of different nations, different religions and different colours, all equal citizens under one government. It is to this idea that an intelligent unionism will embrace both Protestants and Catholics without trying to accommodate the demands of Protestant and Catholic elitism, that is legally enshrining the 'two traditions' (nationalism and unionism) in constitutionally guaranteed power-sharing.[33] It is easy to see how for Aughey this would be to undermine the very idea of a modern state.

The difficulty with Aughey's analysis is that it has to ignore the empirical fact that any state, whatever state, must have an historical origin. At some point people must have come together, whether by agreement or otherwise; in large measure, this is the issue which cultural nationalism addresses. This appears to me to be clear in a further stage of Aughey's argument. Having excluded as extra-political the notions of sentiment and morality he reintroduces the idea of loyalty. There is no British nation, but only British citizenship. However, he has to resort to an abstraction to cover up an historical and recurring conflict. At this stage in his argument evident contradictions arise. He addresses the question how political cohesion is achieved, the identity of the state if you like (his own phraseology), but insists that the answer cannot lie in loyalty to the nation. There is an imperative in the idea of loyalty. Loyalty is to 'the idea of the Union'. This is defined as 'the willing community of peoples united not by creed, colour or ethnicity but by recognition of the authority of that Union'.[34]

Unionism is something more than simply the means whereby a democratic will can be expressed. The reason is simply that the idea of the Union refers to the subject which is to exercise its democratic will. It is at this prior level that the question of political cohesion arises. For Aughey the answer is to be found in 'insights into unionism'. He firmly distinguishes unionism from nationalism, in so far as the latter claims to be an entire philosophy of life, while the former represents simply a theory of the state. He is aware that a nationalist such as John Hume will translate unionism into his terms and call it an ethos.[35] These points are essential because it may well be the case – it is the other side of the argument which I am resisting – that it is not rationally justifiable simply to be converting one style of argument into another, the nationalist into what purports to be the constitutionalist and vice versa. Indeed my own inclination is simply to recognise, in the Irish context, that to make such conversions and reconversions is, at the very least, undemocratic. None the less, I think that the following passages on unionism concern the issue of the cohesion of political society and what they offer is a political tradition.

So Aughey writes of 'the recognition of a common political life and of sharing a general good of civil, religious political freedom; not just a general good from which Ulster people draw material benefits, but also one to which they have contributed and thereby helped to fashion'. This is to speak of the historical construction of a political identity. Aughey is, as he puts it, concerned about 'the integrity of the state'. At the very heart of the Unionist argument at present is the conviction that Ulster Unionists have, historically, contributed to the construction of the British state. It is something of which they are a part. However much one may speak of democratic majorities, 'it is not in the gift of a government to alter the conditions of the Union'.[36] This is, in my view, true precisely because the subject of democracy must precede the manner of its exercise, just as the people must precede the state.

There is, however, an important irony in Aughey's thought which rests in his conception of the state as fundamentally Hegelian and not British. The ultimate strength in his argument may well be that he affords a challenge to both the British and the Irish states, as they conceive themselves. Perhaps this might, if allowed, show a way to spring the binary liberal/cultural nationalist opposition. Aughey draws a very unBritish distinction between a 'nostalgic' or conservative vision which focuses upon a set of past experiences as the inspiration for present action and an 'imaginative', or radical, vision, which focuses upon an idea, a creative engagement to achieve that which has not yet been. He quotes Hegel as relevant to the Irish experience in saying that the tragedy of history is not the struggle between right and wrong but the struggle between right and right.[37] The language of idealism which appeals to Aughey is quite alien to the pragmatism of English political culture. Idealism he understands to mean the endeavour to understand political reality in unitary terms, precise propositions which enable one to grasp the totality in simple terms.[38]

In my view the underlying passion of this argument is to overcome prejudice and irrational discrimination between people. The distinction between the common good and the particular good is an element of classical political analysis which can be grasped by the average person.[39] How far away this is from the reality of British political culture can be seen in Aughey's quotation from the Irish literary figure, Lawrence Sterne, 'They order these things better in France.' He then expresses the bitter sentiment: 'The appalling truth is that, if there is such a thing as a British intelligentsia, it suffers from the same disease as the political establishment; an imperviousness to novel ideas and a conceited complacency which passes for wisdom.'[40] Aughey feels much more disdain for the Irish state, but it is equally from the standpoint of a German idealist libertarianism. He quotes a Southern Protestant, Clifford, who has emigrated to the North. He sets the terms of what would be a 'real offer' of unification, that might have come out of the New Ireland Forum. The offer has, in his view, only to be imagined for one to see that it would never be made: 'that the Catholic-nationalist movement which formed the Southern state should go into voluntary liquidation, that the state should be thrown into the melting pot, and that a new liberal, multi-national, secular, welfare state should be put on offer to Unionists'.[41]

If one returns to Aughey's distinction between the nostalgic and the imaginative it may be possible to replace the spatially static, because horizontal, binary opposition between liberalism and cultural nationalism with a dialectic of opposition between the historical and the possible. The possible is always in danger of becoming the historical. Aughey remarks that it is characteristic of conservative thinking that it turns chance into necessity.[42] To my mind the conclusion of such thinking is that every political society rests inevitably on some form of cultural nationalism; that equally every such society should be the subject of an incessant critique from an idealist liberalism; that it is a question of judgement which particular societies are in need of how much such critique, but that the difference will be, in any case, only a matter of degree.

The Question of Political Violence

The presentation up till now has attempted to explain how far apart are Ulster Protestant and Unionist perspectives of Irish political identity from Irish cultural nationalist perspectives. Whether these traditions can be reconciled is speculative. What is certain is that they are not as far apart as the differences raised by the Irish Republican 'physical force' tradition. It is intended to come back to the perspectives of the minority in Northern Ireland in Chapter 7 from the point of view of their right to object to the application of the Treaty of 1921. Here, a brief account will be given of this question in terms of conflicting perspectives, or subjective attitudes. It is primarily intended to provide a context for the question whether a repartition of the two so-called communities is the optimal response to the Northern Ireland crisis. Chapter 7 will not decide that question, but merely offer to outline the legal arguments which might be used should that option be taken. So, to reiterate again, what follows is not intended as offering a justification for the use of political violence.

In *Ireland's Physical Force Tradition Today: Reflections on the Enniskillen Massacre* (1989)[43] a former DUP member, C. Smyth comments on this IRA atrocity that 'it was committed by those who have dedicated themselves to a particular vision of Ireland which can only be attained through the application of physical force'.[44] Yet he objects to the media misrepresenting IRA activity as if it were something unprecedented, somehow just happening in the present, portrayed through 'clips' of reality. Instead it has to be appreciated, in Smyth's view, that the IRA is not ' a disembodied spirit acting out of impulses impenetrable to rational thought'.[45] Smyth objects equally to the police designation of IRA activity as a crime wave. Instead it has to be recognised that it has 'a sinister political purpose'.[46] The object is to generate an atmosphere of lawlessness in which it is predictable that there will be considerable civilian casualties.[47] This will exhaust the British authorities and make them think in terms of withdrawal.

What basis in political legitimacy is there for such IRA action? Smyth would argue that it is essential to understand it as part of the nationalist political tradition. He stresses that the Irish people subsequently ratified the 1916 Rising and the Anglo-Irish War, fought in their name but without their consent.[48] Smyth also goes back to de Valera's statement in October 1917 that Sinn Fein was constitutional in the sense that Irish nationalists should act in accordance with the will of the Irish people and the moral law. It is not a matter of the Irish people aligning itself with the British constitution.[49] A parallel part of this analysis is that the Irish Premier, Haughey, with colleagues, launched the Provisional IRA in 1969,[50] adding an impossible measure of insecurity to the relations between the two states, given especially that Ireland lays claim to the Province.[51] Smyth concludes that constitutional and 'physical force' nationalism have, therefore, to be seen as 'a set of pincers or jaws, grinding opponents between upsurges of terrorist violence and periods of intense political pressure for change'. A revolution expresses itself as a war of rights and it is of 'the essence of a "war of rights" that no allowance is made for the complexity of the situation'.[52] Hence, to return to a main present Unionist concern, the Anglo-Irish Agreement was necessary – an argument which could equally be extended to the so-called 'Framework Document' – to draw support away from Sinn Fein to the SDLP.[53] If further ground is given, for example a Unionist declaration on power-sharing, this will be an invitation to the IRA to strike with decisive force.[54]

Underlying Smyth's argument is a recourse to a just war theory. For an 'armed struggle' to be justified there must be, at the very least, very widespread support in the population for the struggle. It must be, in some way, authorised. This condition is, in the nature of the case, difficult to satisfy. If one is pitting 'the people' against 'the state', this means the activity takes place outside recognised institutions. The 'people' do not have an institutional form. Indeed the identity of the Irish people is precisely what is in dispute in the conflict in the Province. It is, quite simply, questionable, to ask whether the IRA have an authorisation from the people of Northern Ireland to use force. It is obvious that they do not, and, in this sense, the use of force is undemocratic. However, the question at issue is whether Northern Ireland is a political entity.

Anyway, the most important element of Smyth's argument is, in this view, the absence of a mandate for revolt. I do not wish to dispute this point directly. I think Smyth's argument about the IRA's search for retrospective validation, as far as it goes, is correct. It is equally the case that this is how much of Anglo-Irish, British and Ulster Unionist and Protestant opinion sees the original Irish 'struggle for freedom'.

The precursor of the 1916 Rising was the Irish Republican Brotherhood. A major authority on its history is J. O'Beirne Ranelagh. He attributes to the IRB a tendency for which Sinn Fein continues to be criticised, that is pre-empting or 'hijacking' the name of the Irish – the only true Irishman is one committed to achieving complete independence from the UK by supporting revolutionary action. This tendency could only be exclusionary/ sectarian and risk violence for the Irish themselves. The 1873 Oath and Constitution of the IRB declared its Supreme Council to be the 'sole Government of the Irish Republic'. O'Beirne Ranelagh says that the origin of this particular formulation was to overcome the scruples which many Irish Catholics felt about joining secret societies, a course which their Church prohibited. How could the actual government of a country be secret and, indeed, how could it rebel against itself?[55]

The 1916 Proclamation of the Republic was in the same spirit. Perhaps fewer than a thousand men spoke 'in the name of God and of the dead generations from which she [Ireland] receives her old tradition of nationhood'. This contradicts, in O'Beirne Ranelagh's view, the fact that more Irishmen joined the Royal Irish Constabulary after 1916 than the IRA until Collins directed IRA attacks on the RIC after 1920.[56] It explains, in his view, why they killed Irishmen in the RIC and the British Army in what he calls a civil war.

Whatever the strength of this argument historically, it is relevant to the present. For instance, consider the debate about features of the 'armed struggle' at an internal Sinn Fein conference in Belfast on March 25 1990 (reported in the *Irish News*, 26 March 1990). Gerry Adams, the President, said, 'It is not within Sinn Fein's area of work to dictate to the IRA how it does or does not carry on the armed struggle.' At the same time he asked the SDLP if they really wished to be place-seekers and time-servers in a discredited British colony? There is the same uncertainty concerning the legitimacy of a nationalist position which does not amount to 'wholehearted' opposition to the British presence as in the years preceding independence for the Irish Free State in 1922. For instance, the Ulster Defence Regiment maintained that it was envisaged originally to be a cross-community force, but that the massive IRA targeting of Catholic members in the early 1970s is what has produced its polarised composition (letter to *Belfast Telegraph*, 13 March 1990, pointing to a drop from 25 per cent Catholic involvement in 1972/3, when the casualty rate was in the mid-30 per cent for Catholics to the present 3 per cent 'due to a policy which is based on genocide to discourage anyone who disagrees with their views').

None the less a limitation in O'Beirne Ranelagh's argument concerns the attempt to resolve the Northern Ireland crisis by a simple appeal to a right to democracy. Consider the following fundamental assertion:

> Most Irish people even after 1916 did not think the IRB's goals were practically possible, and found its commitment to physical force demeaning and repugnant. Constitutional procedures had worked well for the average Irish person, who had settled down to the expectation of home rule at the end of the First World War, not the achievement of full independence.[57]

It has been seen that such was not Mansergh's view, and it will be seen shortly that others also disagree. The problem attaches to any appeal to the silent or moral majority. It is Baudrillard in *The Shadow of the Silent Majorities* who encapsulates the fundamental difficulty with such a statement. In a deconstruction of the

Rousseauite Grand Subject he points to the impossibility of self-invocation on the part of the people:

> Every effort to make of it a subject (real or mythical) comes up against the striking impossibility of an autonomous self-awareness. Every effort to make of it an object, to examine and analyse it ... comes up against the inverse evidence of the impossibility ... of a comprehension of the same in terms of elements of relations of structures or whatever.[58]

The language of democratic mandate must come after the definition of the 'people' who are to decide. The history of the political culture within which one attempts to unravel definitions of 'people' in the Province is violent in the sense that one can read out of authoritative or representative texts a clear willingness to have recourse to force to vindicate the definition. Perhaps the notion of infinite regress is better than that of vicious circle. In outline the arguments are very well known. They have been recently rehearsed by R.F. Foster in *Modern Ireland*.[59] The resort to political violence in the South of Ireland was made inevitable by the successful threat of political violence in the North, supported by the Conservative Party and by some elements in the British Army.

These arguments are not presented as history. Rather they are designed to show that each side pretends to the same view of the illegitimacy of violence as the other, but attributes the spiral of violence to intransigence on the other side. If the political question is how to break out of a conflict which cannot be resolved by an appeal to the rhetoric of democratic legitimacy, this has immense implications for the definition of terrorism in the context of the Province. In *Northern Ireland, The International Perspective*, Guelke raises precisely this point about the subjecthood of political society. To treat political violence as terrorism assumes the threat of terrorism to a stable liberal democracy, where the consensus for such a liberal democracy is absent.[60] Guelke speaks of representative violence.[61] To assume that Britain is an impartial intermediary is to put the subject on the 'neutral' ground of the rule of law. There is a stress on due process and the minimum use of force. Yet this also assumes the legitimacy of Northern Ireland as a political entity.[62]

Guelke consistently stresses the priority of the subject whose identity is held to be in question. He quotes Gerry Adams in *The Politics of Irish Freedom*, that violence in Ireland has its roots in the conquest of Ireland by Britain. It is questionable whether Adams successfully avoids the issue of a mandate in the extensive quotation which follows. He denies that there is any political society in which justice and peace are possible:

> We cannot have justice and peace in Ireland because we do not have a society capable of upholding them ... By its very nature British rule cannot be just or peaceful, and while this is so, revolutionary struggle will continue to strive to overthrow it ... Violence in Ireland has its roots in the conquest of Ireland by Britain ... While the armed struggle has traditionally dominated republican strategy, in this phase it has involved and depended upon a considerable degree of political support ... If a person providing support is offended by the actions of Oglaigh na hEireann then that person will withdraw her support and it will not be possible to continue with the armed struggle as before ... The tactic of armed struggle is of primary importance because it provides a vital cutting edge. Without it the issue of Ireland would not even be an issue. So, in effect, the armed struggle becomes armed propaganda. There has not been, at least not yet, a classic development from guerilla action to mass military action registering territorial gains; instead, armed struggle has become an agent of bringing about change. That reality is understood even by middle-class professional people, people who have a stake in the 6 counties. Very many people who disagree absolutely with the IRA nevertheless see it as a very important part of the political equation. They might deplore it, dislike it, have moral objections to it, but still have the feeling that if it did not exist there would be no hope of getting change.[63]

Perhaps this difficult text goes some way to explaining what is widely accepted to be the ambivalence of large sections of the nationalist minority to the IRA campaign. How precisely does the issue of a mandate arise? That is to say, do the IRA need a mandate to act on behalf of the people or, to follow Baudrillard's fragmented view of political society, can they be seen simply to be acting against a definite authority or object, the so-called 'British presence'? This is the objective as defined by Adams.[64]

To return to Guelke's analysis, he remarks how Sinn Fein see their 'armed struggle' as justified in so far as the majority of the whole island support the principle of a united Ireland.[65] This raises, once again, precisely the point made by Smyth, that whatever the difference between nationalist and republican attitudes, the former gives tacit support to the latter. Guelke remarks how the New Ireland Forum does not accord to Protestants the right to reject the principle of a united Ireland.[66] Indeed Guelke claims that Sinn Fein simply see themselves as differing from the majority of nationalists only on a matter of opinion, that is whether Irish unity can be achieved without violence, and whether any accommodation can be reached with Protestants outside of a united Ireland.[67] The strength of their perspective rests, notes Guelke, in a matter about which there is much less difference of opinion in the nationalist minority, that Loyalists will, in any case, resist Irish unity by force and that it is Protestant distrust of the nationalist aspirations of Catholics which will prevent accommodation within Northern Ireland.[68] It is therefore really a question of the extent to which the two sides of the minority political equation work out the logic of their position in relation to the majority. Guelke notes that for Sinn Fein the alternatives are violent resistance and humiliating subordination.[69] Adams says that

> Ireland is historically, culturally and geographically one single unit ... the boundaries of which were determined by a sectarian headcount and can be maintained only by continuing sectarianism ... Its essential basis is the holding by a 'pro-British' national minority of a position of privilege over a dispossessed majority. It is important to recognise the oft-ignored truth that this utterly undemocratic system was established, is controlled by and is the responsibility of the British government.[70]

Guelke's wholesale references to Adams have the effect of questioning the simplicity of the argument that democracy and violence are diametrically opposed. Democracy supposes an agreed space in which there can be a head-count. If there is not, a group of people might say that they have been coerced into a grouping not of their choice. The historical constellations which have constructed boundaries are much more compelling a factor of political legitimacy than appeals to democracy which do not convincingly define what is the collective subject of democratic rights. None of this is to say that international law at present allows forcible changing of boundaries. It is usually assumed that Article 2(4) of the United Nations Charter excludes this. While the Charter may not apply to a paramilitary organisation or to a civil war situation, it should apply to the Irish nation as a collective entity, part of which is within the present boundaries of Northern Ireland.

Conclusion

To say that one has to 'remove the root causes' of violence, and to object to the equation of political violence with terrorism, is not to say that violence is justified. Above all it is not to say that if the goals for which violence is waged were otherwise met, this would 'solve' the problem of political violence in the Province. However, it is to deny the perspective of those, particularly Unionists and the UK authorities[71] who see the defeat of republicans as a precondition of a society in which there is the rule of law.

As Guelke puts it, this is in contradistinction to seeing order as a function of a right relationship between the two communities. None the less, once one embarks upon the latter type of analysis or investigation there are a lot of questions to ask about how identity has been constructed in the Province and about what or how much it is worth.

It is precisely because there does not seem to be any agreement or consensus within Northern Ireland about this matter at present that this study will conclude with an extensive international law examination of all the ramifications of the partition in 1921 in so far as they involve the incorporation of a substantial minority within Northern Ireland who belong to the Irish nation which is at present within the Irish Republic. This chapter has given plenty of indication that there could be movement between the two broad divisions of the population of Ireland on the question of identity. However, at the same time, the final discussion of the question of political violence shows that it is intimately tied to differing global interpretations of Irish history. These differences affect the very foundation of the Irish state. The timescale which the differences span indicate how deep they appear to remain.

Whether or how the differences might be eventually resolved, the study concludes with the legal aspects of partition. Underlying this extended consideration is another legal factor which has shaped the entire study. The differences considered in this entire study concern the construction of opposing identities, in which conquest has, certainly, in the view of most of the participants, played a decisive part. It is part of the logic of the classical international law of conquest that, while one of the contesting parties may clearly have right on its side, the anarchic nature of international society is such that only with force can it make its will prevail.

CHAPTER 7

The Question of Repartition

The question of the Irish boundary as such has not figured at all in the present controversy. Yet it does afford a very definite legal response to the conflict. The boundary was drawn in disregard of the wishes of the inhabitants and in terms which have proved to be internally flawed. A redrawing of that boundary is not a political demand being made by any party. Yet it accurately reflects the benchmark of the demands which any protagonist can make. In this sense focus on such an issue has an essentially ellucidating function. It directs attention away from historical factors to do with conquest to the actuality of two nations on the island. It recognises the dilemma that a legal title to the whole island which rests upon an acceptance of the need for consent of the Protestant majority is one *which cannot be executed* and which is therefore, ultimately, not a valid positive title to territory. It also recognises that it is perfectly legitimate for the nationalist minority within the North of Ireland to withhold allegiance from the British/Northern Irish state, *even to the point of effective withdrawal from it.*

Partition and the Irish Boundary Question: The Negotiation of Article 12 of the 1921 Agreement

Article 12 of the Anglo-Irish Treaty of 1921 provided for the opting out of the new Irish state of the Six Counties. It contained crucial provisions for the changing of the boundary. A Commission was to determine the boundary 'in accordance with the wishes of the inhabitants, as far as may be compatible with economic and geographical conditions, the boundaries between Northern Ireland and the rest of Ireland'.

The first question concerning this article is whether consent to it was induced by deceit. The question of fraud and the invalidity of treaties is covered by Article 49 of the Vienna Convention on the Law of Treaties. It covers any false statements, misrepresentations or other deceitful proceedings by which a state may be induced to give a consent to a treaty which it would not otherwise have given.[1] Under Article 44(4) the state victim is entitled to opt for invalidity of this part of the treaty, subject to the general conditions affecting separability. One view is that since there was no state practice to support the application of this concept before the Convention it constitutes some measure of progressive development of international law.[2] However it is equally recognised that it is a general principle of law which must vitiate any form of consent. As Sinclair says: 'Writers and publicists have of course long accepted the principle that fraud exercised by a negotiating state to induce the conclusion of a treaty with another state may entitle the latter to claim that its consent to the treaty has been vitiated'.[3]

It is necessary to go into the facts of this case in more detail. In the account given by Pakenham, Lloyd George assured the Irish negotiator Griffith, during the final negotiations of the 1921 Treaty, that he was going to offer Ulster two options: an all-Ireland Parliament – which they had already refused – and 'a Boundary Commission to adjust the Ulster boundary, as closely as possible in accordance with the wishes of the population. If they refused both, nevertheless he would proceed with the second.'[4] This was to mean that there would be no break by Griffith in negotiations on the Ulster question. Jones, Secretary to Lloyd George, was given the task of putting this understanding in writing, the relevant terms being 'a Boundary Commission would be directed to adjust the line by inclusion and exclusion so as to make the boundary conform as closely as possible to the wishes of the population'.[5] Griffith saw this proposal as a British tactic in engaging with the Ulster unionists. However, he was taken at the final stage of the negotiations as having accepted it as an alternative to a united Ireland.

The second major stage in negotiation on the boundary question came in negotiations between Collins and Lloyd George on Monday 5 December. A crucial one-to-one meeting, a conversation took place, a version of which was recorded by Collins. 'Concerning the question of the North-East, Mr. Lloyd George remarked that I myself had pointed out on a previous occasion that the North would be forced economically to come in.' If the Boundary Commission approached was adopted 'we would save Tyrone and Fermanagh, parts of Derry, Armagh and Down ... Mr Lloyd George expressed the view that this might be put to Craig.' Packenham does not see any extra assurances given to Collins here. Collins himself leaves the meeting with his own reassurance that Ireland would gain 'large territories' and that Ulster, reduced to an uneconomic unit, would be 'forced in' before long.[6]

However, the discussion would have been based, as far as Lloyd George was concerned, upon the understanding which Griffith had accepted on 12 and 13 November. Later in the same day he confronted Collins with this *written* understanding. It appeared that Collins had no exact knowledge of the passage of this document between Lloyd George, Jones and Griffith. However, Chamberlain at once handed Collins a copy of the document. It said, once again, 'a Boundary Commission which could be directed to adjust the line both by inclusion and exclusion so as to make the boundary conform as closely as possible to the wishes of the population'.[7] Collins' remarks recorded after the interview with Lloyd George but before the signing of the Treaty, were clearly based upon the principle of a head count.[8] All that remained was for the Irish delegation to fail to see what they were actually signing. In Packenham's words: 'In this last case, the fault, in so far as it was Irish, must rest on ... the legal intelligence of 1921.'[9]

Indeed Lloyd George told the Cabinet, at one point, that if Ulster insisted on exclusion, Sinn Fein was entitled to Tyrone and Fermanagh.[10] Yet immediately after signing the Treaty the British Prime Minister reported to Cabinet that despite what had been said to Collins the Treaty was not a threat to Ulster. Far from truncating Northern Ireland, it was suggested that she might actually gain territory.[11]

A contrary argument is that the partition was already an accepted fact at the time of the beginning of the negotiations. When Lloyd George was first confronted with the question of a coercion of the Catholic minority, he had replied that nationalists had accepted partition from 1914 and 1916 and that Sinn Fein was a successor to this.[12] However, this was at the beginning of the negotiations. In any case, Packenham notes the exchange in the following terms. Immediately after Griffith said 'if the majority of the North-East are not to be coerced they in turn must not coerce others' ... Lloyd George let slip the pregnant words 'That is fair, if applied all round, for example in North Cavan ...'[13] Another version of the same incident is that when Lloyd George had argued that the nationalists had preferred six counties to a boundary commission in 1914, Collins had relied upon the idea of a county option. Lloyd George did insist that the existing boundary be kept or a nine-county boundary, but this was on 17 October.[14] Churchill, Chamberlain and Birkenhead (the other chief British negotiators) all expressed reservations about the justice of the six-counties unit and the draft proposal of 12 and 13 November was produced.[15] The difficulty was that at the beginning of December the final draft form of Article 12 was produced, concerning the wishes of the inhabitants 'so far as may be compatible with economic and geographical conditions'.[16] However, none of this takes away from the interview between Lloyd George and Collins on 5 December and the subsequent confrontation of Collins with the 12–13 November document later in the same day.[17]

The real difficulty with the argument of deceit is in pinning it down to the overall importance of the actual terms of the treaty in the negotiations between the two sides. As Packenham puts it at the beginning of the story of the negotiation: 'Ulster indeed will come into our story less as an area or as a people than as a strange abstract factor in tactics, its importance derived from its reactions on the central conflict.'[18]

It is clear that the Irish negotiators do not confine the issue of the frontier to the wishes of the inhabitants. The Irish negotiators may well have failed to insist upon a precise definition of the Commission's functions, accepting instead a loosely worded formula, in the belief that it would be interpreted in Sinn Fein's favour. Plebiscites in specified local units, without mention of economic and geographical considerations, would have been the most exact way to assess the popular will. The European peace treaties insisted upon detailed provision for supervision of plebiscites and there could have been the possibility of arbitration in the absence of agreement. It is easy enough to speculate that the reason for this Irish laxity as to detail was attributable to confidence in the assurance that redrawing of the boundary would make the North of Ireland unviable and lead to unification of the island. However, it is precisely this which the exact wording of Article 12 is intended to prevent. In my view, Irish nationalists in both the North and in the Free State looked to Article 12 in the hope that it would provide the mechanism for the abolition of Partition.[19] So they did not address the detail of procedures necessary to *extract* the Catholic minority from the North of Ireland. *Such remains the case until the present.* At the same time, all of this is pure speculation. On the other side of the argument are the clear terms of the 13 November document and what the Irish delegation clearly expected these terms to produce.

The record is that the Irish signatories genuinely believed that the Boundary Commission would result in significant land gains for the Irish state, laying considerable claim on the 'wishes of the inhabitants' clause. In turn, the British encouraged the Irish delegation to believe that the wishes of the inhabitants would be primary, and that economic and geographical considerations would be secondary.[20] This interpretation of the British inducement is so important because the Commission was to, as will be seen, reverse the order of priority.

So, it is possible to argue that there is a certain duplicity in the Irish position as well. To reason that the remaining areas would not be economically viable[21] is to confirm that there was a definite sense in the decision, in the wording of Article 12, to tie together the wishes of the parties and the other mentioned factors of economy and geography. Nothing would be more reasonable than for the Irish side to resist a repartition, and hence population transfer, where this would have the effect to make the remaining Northern territorial unit more viable politically, because the nationalist minority had been substantially reduced. It is arguable that the failure of the Irish delegation to insist upon a closer wording of Article 12 was due to uncertainty as to how they wished to use the presence of the nationalist minority strategically in the context of assuring a united Ireland. Still, the element of British duplicity remains. It lies precisely in the fact that they were, simultaneously, assuring the North that their territorial sovereignty was secure.[22]

That duplicity can arise in this way is perhaps peculiar to the nature of international diplomacy and the manner in which treaties are concluded. Curran argues that it is very difficult to apply the notion of duplicity as a simple moral concept to a factual situation as complex as the highly charged Anglo-Irish peace negotiations. The assurances which the Irish received privately from the British negotiators – that repartition in accordance with the wishes of the inhabitants, would force a rump Northern Ireland into an all-Ireland unit – could not have been made publicly without precipitating a Tory Party revolt and wrecking the negotiations. At the same time, if the Irish delegation

> had been more astute and aggressive, they would have demanded that the boundary be redrawn in accordance with plebiscites in specified local units – without introduction of limiting factors, such as economic and geographical considerations which could nullify the popular will ... The British delegates would have found it hard to resist such a demand. After all, Sinn Fein was prepared to accept terms which did not guarantee unity and, having pledged not to coerce Ulster, it had every right to ensure that Ulster did not coerce nationalists.[23]

As noted by Sinclair, in drafting the relevant clause in the Vienna Convention, the International Law Commission warned against seeking to apply to the interpretation of the concept of fraud in international law the detailed connotations given to such an expression as fraud or *dol* in national law.[24] The difficulty is that international law does not regulate the very common incidence of a discrepancy between public and private assurances which are, presumably, an inevitable part of any intense treaty negotiating process. As Curran remarks, 'Why should they [the Irish] have accepted reports of private British assurances about boundary revision, when they rejected public British pledges on every other matter relating to the Treaty?'[25] In the last analysis Curran sees that he can only speculate. In and surrounding the Dail debates one might suppose the absence of criticism of Article 12 was due to either support of it, inability to devise a better alternative, or simply the belief that there was no solution to partition.[26]

However, the picture becomes clearer once the Irish realise that the British are not keeping to their private assurances. One can take the absence of an effective, deliberate refutation of the Irish charge of deception, coming after 1922, as a confirmation that the British government had at least agreed to a form of words which it hoped later to interpret in a way opposed to that which it had led the Irish negotiators to understand the same words. So just after the signing of the Treaty, Lloyd George was saying that Article 12 was intended to *readjust* the boundaries. The British view then emerged that the article was not intended to transfer large territories. In 1924 the British signatories announced that 'they never had any intention of interfering with the essential integrity of the Six Counties'.[27]

This led the Irish Prime Minister to make a statement in the Irish Parliament alleging fraud, precisely in the sense that it was the private assurances of the British which led, and which they must have known would lead, to the conclusion of the 1921 Treaty. That is to say, the assurances made to the Irish negotiators, whether public or private, *in any case clearly documented*, actually led them to consent and to sign. It is this dimension, the very essence of fraud, which overcomes the relevance of the public/private dichotomy peculiar to international diplomacy. So Premier Cosgrave says 'I have observed references by British politicians and British signatories to the Treaty, opinions which were carefully concealed when the negotiations, that resulted in the Treaty, were being undertaken. Had these pronouncements been made at the time there would not have been Irish signatories to the Treaty.'[28]

That is to say, the Irish negotiators were induced to conclude the Treaty by the assurances made to them that the effect of Article 12 would be to give primary importance to the wishes of the inhabitants. That assurance is incompatible with language which stresses the 'essential integrity of the Six Counties'.

Premier Cosgrave put this interpretation in the context of the general purpose of the Treaty. It was to end the coercion of Ireland and thereby

> to substitute the principle of democratic government based on the consent of the governed. No other interpretation of art. 12 could possibly accord with the general spirit of the Treaty. It was clearly intended, in the event of Northern Ireland deciding to secede from the Irish Free State, to bring relief to the Nationalist inhabitants of the Six counties.[29]

The Boundary Commission Report

The Boundary Commission Report was never published, appearing only in 1969. None the less, before considering the political and legal implications of the 1925 Boundary Agreement, it is felt worthwhile to examine closely the deliberations, of the Chairman of the Commission, as these contain clear legal interpretations of the key Article 12 of the 1921 Treaty. The most important feature of his deliberations is not simply his prioritisation of economic and geographical factors over the wishes of the populations, but rather the process whereby he reifies the existence of Northern Ireland as a historical entity, within five years of its coming into existence. This extraordinary process, set in place here for the first time, has, in fact, come to be an unquestioned way of thinking of all of the parties to the conflict in Ireland.

The view of Hand in his Introduction to the papers making up the Report of the Irish Boundary Commission, is that historians are not agreed as to whether there was a deliberate attempt at deception or whether the full legal implications of ambiguities were realised by either side at the time.[30] However, Hand does not himself engage in a detailed treatment of the undertakings made to the Irish negotiators, followed by an almost immediate reliance, within British political circles, upon a restrictive interpretation of the article.

Hand considers the expression 'so far as may be compatible with' as meaning, correctly in the view of the Commission, that where there was conflict between the wishes of the population and economic or geographical considerations, effect could not be given to the wishes of the inhabitants, for instance with respect to the people of Newry and South Down.[31] The second vital question was whether there could be large transfers of land or merely a matter of minor modifications to the existing boundaries. The Commission was to decide that the terms of the article made it necessary that Northern Ireland should remain ' the same provincial entity' and that there was consequently a scale of changes which could not be recommended. Apparently for Hand there is not a logically compelling argument here – in my view, a much more important point – and the Commission seems to have been influenced by the public battle after 1921 between restrictive and broad interpretations of the article.[32]

The Commission did not give itself the task of determining the wishes of the inhabitants in so far as compatible with economic and geographical considerations. It started with the principle of the legitimacy of the Northern Irish entity and decided that no changes in the boundary should affect the integrity of this entity. Perhaps it was pushed in this direction by the possible underlying motivation of the Irish desire for a Commission decision that would make Northern Ireland unviable. So at one point (all of what follows comes from the Chairman's Memorandum) it is said that a possible Irish call for a vote in all parts of the North, could open up the fundamental question whether the North of Ireland should exist at all, or so to reduce the size of the North of Irleand as to make its continued existence as such impossible.[33]

Why should the Chairman have put such an interpretation on the proposal to give full effect to the wishes of the inhabitants, given that it was well known that at least a million people wished to have no part of the Irish Free State? To respect the wishes of the inhabitants need never have a destructive effect on the existence of a Northern Ireland Protestant and Unionist territorial community, provided one attempts to reach a fair division of territory, having regard to the overall weight of population – at this time approximately two-thirds Protestant and Unionist. The interpretation taken separates the question of the legitimacy of the North of Ireland from that of the satisfaction of the wishes of the inhabitants, before the task of interpretation of the article is even begun. The standpoint of the Chairman is the prior legitimacy of the entity Northern Ireland, mentioned in the Government of Ireland Act 1920.

So the Chairman says that the term 'Northern Ireland' as used in Article 12 clearly means not some vague indefinite area in the North of Ireland but the Northern Ireland established and defined by the 1920 Act 'and it is the boundary between this "Northern Ireland" and "the rest of Ireland" which is to be "determined", or *in effect, as there is already an existing boundary, redetermined'*(my emphasis).[34] The Chairman has explicitly changed the terms of the article to accommodate his interpretation. The North of Ireland is now an entity separate from the wishes of its inhabitants and no expression of the wishes of these inhabitants must be allowed to undermine its integrity, an integrity established not by international treaty but by means of legislation of the UK Parliament. The Chairman reverses the order of the article, which puts the inhabitants first, and reifies the entities already mentioned. So he persists in the view that a strict application of the principle of the consent of the governed constitutes a threat to the very existence of Northern Ireland. This means there is no possibility that expression will be given to the wishes of the inhabitants, because it will virtually always be possible for the Commission to say that to give any expression to the wishes of the inhabitants will be incompatible with economic or geographical considerations. It is these which are bound to be affected by any substantial change in the boundaries of Northern Ireland. The wishes of the inhabitants are clearly to be completely subordinated to the need to maintain the integrity of the entity. This renders any interpretation of Article 12 as nugatory.

The Chairman writes in the following passage so as to leave out altogether any reference to the wishes of the inhabitants:

> What has already been said on the question of interpreting the words 'determine the boundaries between Northern Ireland and the rest of Ireland' is sufficient to show that the theory, that it

> is the duty of the Commission to start *ne novo* on a reconstruction of the map without any regard to the existing boundary, is in my opinion quite untenable. The Article does not say the Commission is to decide what areas are hereafter to constitute 'Northern Ireland' and 'the rest of Ireland', but that the Commission is to 'determine the boundaries between Northern Ireland and the rest of Ireland'. In dealing with 'Northern Ireland' and the 'rest of Ireland', the Commission is dealing not with vague geographical abstractions but with two ascertained territorial entities consisting, respectively, of 'Northern Ireland' and 'Southern Ireland', as constituted by section *one* of the Government of Ireland Act 1920.[35]

This interpretation is certainly a possible way of reading the reference to Northern Ireland in the Anglo-Irish Treaty, but it makes a choice between the principle of self-determination of peoples, and the principle of the territorial integrity of existing states. The choice has to be made quite simply because the two principles are not compatible. The Chairman of the Commission chooses that of territorial integrity. This has two effects. It separates the question of the existence of Northern Ireland from the wishes of its inhabitants. Secondly, it makes it impossible to give any effect to those wishes, which are, indeed, not mentioned in the above passage. Priority is given to economic and geographical considerations *before* one comes to consider the wishes of the inhabitants. These latter have, somehow, to justify themselves against the already existing Northern Irish entity. This they could only do if it were possible to appeal to some as yet unspecified factors. So the Commission 'must treat that boundary as holding good where no sufficent reason can be shown for altering it'.[36]

Indeed the Chairman introduces the notion of identity, by its nature an historical notion, into his deliberations. When it is a matter of examining the issue of transfer of counties (the most obvious option, given the nature of the Westminister electoral system which had delivered a decisive result in 1918), the Chairman says, none the less, that such an option 'is a question which must in my opinion be considered in relation to the identity of Northern Ireland as a whole'. Would the transfer of a country or even a part thereof 'destroy the identity of Northern Ireland as a whole, or so reduce its area and resources as to render it impossible for it to continue as a province of the United Kingdom'?[37] This is language used with respect to a political entity in existence for about five years, which as a six-county unit, had been unknown to the history and imagination of anyone on the island.

This reification of Northern Ireland as an historically established province leads immediately to an abandonment of the majoritarian principle in determining the wishes of the inhabitants. So the Chairman takes the example where there is a majority of one out of a unit of 2000 and declares it unreasonable to regard this as decisive.[38] This qualification is extremely serious because the very essence of respecting the democratic wishes of people is to respect mathematical majorities. To reply that the people whose wishes are to be respected has first to be defined is a valid point, but it has to be remembered that the Chairman has already attributed an historical identity to the North of Ireland which, in his view, justifies a very substantial modification of the democratic principle, even before one comes to consider whether its exercise is compatible with the economic and geographical factors. So he says:

> But in view of the fundamental character of the change involved in a transfer of territory from one jurisdiction to another, and of the dislocation of established conditions which must inevitably result from any such change, there is, I think, much to be said for adopting a rule that, where the case for a change of the existing boundary rests solely on the wishes of the inhabitants, and is not fortified by any economic or geographical considerations, the Commission would not be justified in making a change unless the majority in favour is substantial – i.e. represents a high proportion of the total number of inhabitants in the area concerned.[39]

Indeed the Chairman introduced as a general principle, the proposition that the more the territory which might be transferred, 'the higher the percentage of inhabitants who can be regarded as supporters of the change which should be required to justify it'.[40] The root of this exponential principle of territoriality is the prior assumption that the North of Ireland is an historically established identity. This is a superimposed interpretation which does not rest on ambiguities in Article 12 itself. It is an historical interpretation which is itself unargued in historical terms.

This criticism was made and the Chairman's response is that

> whatever the circumstances in which the Government of Ireland Act, 1920 was passed, the boundary fixed by that Act was a boundary legally fixed, and is therefore entitled to be respected as such, and the establishment of this boundary, which had already come into legal operation when the Articles of Agreement for a Treaty were signed, immediately gave rise to certain vested rights and interests which should not be lightly interfered with.[41]

Once again it has to be pointed out that the Chairman is putting this interpretation on the article before he even comes to consider the relevance of economic and geographical factors.

Further evidence of the clear bias of the Chairman is to be found in his treatment of the question of possible county transfer. The county was the unit for Parliamentary elections and the arrangements he had to consider concerned the dissolution of the union of Parliaments. While it is clear that the article did not mention counties and did leave the Commission a discretion as to how to respect the wishes of the inhabitants, it would have been consistent for the Chairman to have attached special weight to existing administrative/legal structures. These are sure to be an essential part of the growth of an identity. County and Poor Law Unions existed for rather longer than Northern Ireland as such. Yet the method of interpretation of the Chairman is now to play the wishes of the inhabitants against any notion of institutional identity which might have arisen historically, clearly with a view to restricting the possibility of territorial transfers:

> But if the Commission were to adopt a rule that the County or the Union must, on grounds of administrative convenience, be treated as indivisible, it would find itself compelled, in cases where the wishes of a majority of the inhabitants in one portion of a County or Union were in opposition to the wishes of the majority of the inhabitants of the whole County or Union, to override the wishes of the inhabitants of the particular portion concerned for the sake of administrative convenience; in other words, the Commission would be setting up a new factor, 'administrative considerations', as superior to the wishes of the inhabitants.[42]

This argument was to prove decisive to the Commission's deliberations. For instance, consider its conclusions with respect to Co. Tyrone. Catholic areas are larger than Protestant areas. However, they are in the interior of the country, with the Protestants in the borders of the county. So no easy proposal can be made for the transfer of Catholics without transferring Protestants. A study of the map shows how the Catholic area in the northern centre of Tyrone and the adjoining Catholic region in the south of Co. Londonderry cannot be separated from the southern part of Co. Tyrone and Co. Fermanagh. The Commission recognises that the claim of the nationalist inhabitants of Co. Tyrone was for the inclusion of the County as a whole in the Irish Free State.[43] This raises, in the view of the Commission, the question of Co. Fermanagh, as even the inclusion of western and central Tyrone in the Irish Free State would 'necessarily involve' the inclusion of the whole of Co. Fermanagh as well. Yet the northern portion of Co. Fermanagh which borders on Co. Tryone is predominantly Protestant. Again the argument is put by the nationalists that there is a majority of the county as a whole for inclusion in the Irish Free State.[44]

This issue is notorious. The division of Ulster in 1920 had been made on a county basis and yet two counties with Catholic majorities had been included in Northern Ireland. It is not the matter of economic or geographical factors which determined the outcome of the Commission's decision. Instead, it is its insistence that the North of Ireland has already acquired an established identity which is not to be disturbed. So the Commission decided that the removal of two entire counties would be a change on too large a scale. The answer is that 'no wholesale reconstruction of the map is contemplated by the proviso – the Commission is not to reconstitute the two territories, but to settle the boundaries between them'.

Yet no definite answer need be given on this basis, because a further principle can be applied. There are substantial Protestant populations included within these territories. The Commission has already formulated the principle that where it finds

> an area of sufficient size and population to merit separate consideration which is at present on the right side of the boundary, that is on the side where the inhabitants wish to remain, the existence of that area will in itself be a reason against making an alteration which would involve its transfer to the wrong side, and help to indicate the point beyond which alterations intended to give effect to the wishes of the inhabitants should not extend.[45]

The application of this principle means quite simply that the Protestant areas within the two counties are areas of sufficient size and population to make it unjustifiable to allow the total Catholic majorities to be used 'for the purpose of overwhelming the Protestant majority'.[46]

Returning to the rationale for a definition of a sufficient area, it is clear why the Chairman chose the unit of electoral district in preference to that of county. The Commission should, in endeavouring to give expression to the wishes of the inhabitants, seek to follow their wishes as closely as possible, hence the choice of old District Electoral Divisions as existing in 1911. These constitute 'as a unit the smallest area which can be fairly entitled, having regard to its size and situation, to be considered separately'.[47] In the general Chapter Three itself, the Commission was much more vague: 'No precise rule can be laid down as to the requirements which must be fulfilled in the case of individual areas in order to entitle the wishes of their inhabitants to prevail.'[48] Yet the Commission decided the outcome without difficulty.

Another illustration of the Commission's approach can be gauged from its treatment of the claims of Newry and South Down for inclusion in the Irish Free State. It was decided that on economic grounds it would be impossible to draw a line north of Newry. It depended on the north of the county for its market and it would be gravely disadvantaged as a port in relation to Belfast if it was politically separated. The additional areas that would have to be included to protect Newry's economic interest would entail overriding the wishes of Protestant majorities in such additional areas. That would be unjustified.[49] To separate parts of the Mourne Mountains would separate particularly Belfast from the sources of its water supply. This is open to what the Commission calls 'grave objection'. The separation would 'inevitably tend to produce anxiety and insecurity as to this vital necessity of their economic and industrial life'. The corporations of Belfast, Portadown and Banbridge would have to obtain the permission of the Oireachtas if they were to wish to carry out new works to develop their undertakings.[50]

So here, at least, the presumed wishes of the inhabitants were not to prevail over what the Commission took to be the best economic interests of *the same people*. Furthermore, where the wishes of nationalist inhabitants could be satisfied without compromising the wishes of Protestant inhabitants, but a transfer could still be a cause of anxiety to the latter, then there could be no question of a transfer. In two eventualities economic factors are taken to be incompatible with and to overrule the wishes of the nationalist population. First, they must not be allowed to act so as to prejudice their own economic interests. Second, their wishes, no matter how peacefully expressed, must not be allowed to cause any anxiety to any sector of the Protestant population. It is reasonable to assume that underlying this approach is the assumption that any repartition will disturb established patterns of economic activity and for that reason cannot be justified. The effect of such an interpretation of Article 12 can only be to make it impossible to give any effect to the wishes of the population in any circumstances where a substantial sector of the population, and therefore of urban or rural space, is being taken into account. So it is not surprising that the Commission should have been reduced to recommending minor border adjustments. Only these would not have disturbed what the Commission took to be the already firmly established identity of Northern Ireland.

This Northern Irish identity is an identity which had existed for five years. It was conceived by the Commission as a legal entity set up by an Act of the UK Parliament. The Commission saw it as no part of its function to wonder whether that identity might be set in question by the presence of a very large nationalist minority. It never saw the need to address systematically the presence of that minority. Nor did it ask whether the identity of Northern Ireland could be pierced to the point that it might be treated as consisting of a Protestant majority. In that event redrawing the boundary might have been more directly taken as a matter of deciding between the wishes of two opposing political communities.

Of course, the Commission did have to deal with the problem of territorially mixed populations, which does still require a fair solution.

It is obviously difficult to argue that the Chairman of the Boundary Commission simply adopted the view of the British Government as to how Article 12 should be interpreted. When asked to interpret the article by the Irish President Cosgrave, the British Government said that it could not authoritatively interpret an agreement to which it was only one party. However, the official record of the Northern Irish Cabinet shows that it had been assured in 1924 that the border was merely to be adjusted. This followed the view of Birkenhead, one of the primary negotiators on the British side.[51]

In the course of the autumn of 1924 the language of all four of the negotiators of the Treaty on the British side was brought to public attention and was very much for the restrictive interpretation, the rectification of the boundaries of an already existing entity. Lord Balfour published a letter of Birkenhead's, written in 1922, in which he assured his colleagues that Collins' view that large transfers of populations were involved were due to Collins having 'in a moment of excitement committed himself unguardedly to this doctrine, and that it has no foundation whatever except in his overheated imagination'. Birkenhead continued, with his usual coolness of tone, that 'the Tribunal, not being presided over by a lunatic, will take a rational view of the limits of its own jurisdiction'. This view was endorsed by Lloyd George.[52] Austen Chamberlain offered, on 2 October 1924, a more substantive interpretation of how, in his view, he and his colleagues would have wanted to counter the real intentions of the Irish negotiators (viz., possibly, to subvert the existence of an Ulster political entity through its nationalist minority). The article had been drafted so as to 'exclude such a dismemberment of Northern Ireland as would be created by cutting out whole counties or large slices of counties'.[53]

The final piece of the story may be taken to be the response of the Chairman in December 1924 to the proposal of the Irish Government for plebiscites on the basis of the Poor Law Unions. Feetham disagreed profoundly with Collins and Griffith: 'The new territory is to be "Northern Ireland" for the purpose of the Government of Ireland Act 1920, and should be capable of maintaining a Parliament and Government.'[54] This suggests that the whole process of reification of Northern Ireland is rooted in a fear for its very existence, because of an intention to use the presence of a minority to force a unification of the country.

The Boundary Agreement of 1925

It is common knowledge that when the Irish Government heard of the proposed recommendations of the Boundary Commission, it insisted on the suppression of the Boundary Commission. What is less clear is the legal significance of the Boundary Agreement which followed. It provides in its crucial first paragraph:

> 1. The powers conferred by the proviso to article 12 of the said Articles of Agreement on the Commission therein mentioned are hereby revoked, and the extent of Northern Ireland for the purposes of the Government of Ireland Act 1920, and of the said articles of agreement shall be such as was fixed by sub-Section 2 of Section 1 of that Act.

There were three parties to the agreement, including the Government of Northern Ireland. The preamble to the Agreement refers not merely to the three Governments but also to their respective peoples. None the less, the Agreement is subject to confirmation by the British and Irish Free State Parliaments.

This appears to recognise the status of Northern Ireland as equal to that of the Irish Free State. It is clear that the Agreement amounts to a recognition of partition along the lines of the Six Counties: in particular the wording 'the extent of Northern Ireland for the purposes ... of the said articles of agreement shall be such as was fixed by sub-Section 2 of that Act'. If the Irish Government had simply wished to leave matters in abeyance following the debacle of the Boundary Commission it could simply have agreed to the first part of the paragraph alone, revoking the powers of that Commission, without prejudice to its own claims, whatever they might be, to the rest of the territory. The other possible interpretation of the Irish signature is that it regarded the exact detail of the delimitation of the Northern Irish entity as secondary to the question whether it should exist at all. Yet this seems to be ruled out by the terms of the preamble treating the Northern Ireland Government *and people* as party to the Agreement.

The Irish President Cosgrave is reported as saying that the Agreement 'will remove obstacles which have ever been a source of bitter conflict between the peoples of Northern Ireland and the Irish Free State'.[55] This is an endorsement of the position of the Chairman of the Boundary Commission, that Northern Ireland is an already established entity. Indeed this is recognised as being the effect of ratification of the Agreement by the Irish Parliament. It was described by an opposition MP as a surrender of every principle of nationality and democracy. The only, and very significant, argument used in the other direction by a Government spokesman was that by not reducing the nationalist minority in the the North, they could represent a more potent force in bringing about ultimate unification.[56] This is, obviously, to continue the impression that bad faith on both sides was helping the process of the reification of Northern Ireland. However, the history of the negotiation between Premier Craig and President Cosgrave suggests, much more, ineptitude on the part of the latter in defending the interests of the nationalist minority. In debate in the Dail, Cosgrave argued that written guarantees for the minority were mere 'scraps of paper' and laid stress on the potential of joint North–South meetings. Representatives of Northern nationalists should enter the Belfast Parliament and make their case there. If they did, and did not receive justice, then it would be time enough to criticise the present Pact.[57]

It is an obvious point, taken up immediately by the anti-Treaty Irish party, under the leadership of de Valera, that the Irish government could not sign away the rights of the nationalist minority in Northern Ireland. Their argument will be that the rights of a Nation preceed those of the State and that the latter is there to defend it. However, before proceeding to the elaboration of this point, it is worth remarking the sentiments of the members of the nationalist minority at the time. These were disorganised, politically depressed and, most of all, divided between 'border nationalists' who hoped for most from the Boundary Commission, and East-Ulster nationalists more reconciled to the inevitability of some form of cooperation with the Northern Ireland 'identity'.[58]

Articles 2 and 3 of the 1937 Irish Constitution as a Response to the 1925 Agreement

In 1926 the Civil War faction under the leadership of de Valera had abstained from the Irish Parliament, while, at the same time, being a minority of the electorate. At the time de Valera said that the new Frontier Agreement with Britain was a violation of the Anglo-Irish Treaty. He said to the Government, 'We challenge them to put this agreement to the people. There is a referendum by which they can put it to the people of the 26 counties and I am certain that the people would turn down the new Treaty.' President Cosgrave had agreed in Dail debates to hold a referendum, but reversed that decision after the Bill, for the Agreement, had been passed. He said, with respect to the Bill confirming the Treaty, that it 'is necessary for the immediate preservation of the public peace and safety and that, accordingly, provisions of Article XLVII (Referendum) of the Constitution of Saorstat Eireann shall not apply to the Bill'.[59] The Parliament passed a resolution to the effect that the measure was necessary for the 'immediate preservation of the public peace and safety'.[60]

De Valera's position with respect to this Government was stated in 1929 as follows:

> You have secured a *de facto* position. Very well. There must be somebody in charge to keep order in the community, and by virtue of your *de facto* position you are the only people who are in a position to do it. But as to whether you have come by that position legitimately, I say you have not come by that position legitimately. You brought off a *coup d'etat* in the summer of 1922.[61]

This raises the whole issue of the fractured condition of Southern Irish political society following on from the Civil War. A central issue of that war was the question of the international legal status of Ireland, whether under the 1921 Treaty it was yet an independent state. The republican faction, represented by de Valera, did not consider that yet to be the case. So he declared in his first statement of Fianna Fail aims in 1926, *A National Policy*:

> Republicans admit that majority rule is an inevitable rule of order – a rule that cannot be set aside in a democracy without the gravest consequences. But in forcing acceptance of the 'Treaty', majority rule ran counter to the fundamental rights of the nation and so clash with a matter of natural right and justice. There are rights even of an individual, not to speak of a large minority in a nation, which no majority is justified in destroying.[62]

This is the *rationale* of the territorial provisions of the Irish Constitution and have been recently reaffirmed by the Irish Supreme/Constitutional Court. In the Irish Supreme Court decision in the case of *McGimpsey and McGimpsey* v. *Ireland* (1 March 1990, 314/88), the Supreme Court had to consider the impact of the Anglo-Irish Agreement on Ireland's legal claim to the North of Ireland. The Judgment of Findlay C.J., in which the rest of the Supreme Court concurred, reads, in part, as follows (at 16):

> The provision in Article 3 of the Constitution contained in the words 'and without prejudice to the right of the Parliament and Government established by this Constitution to exercise jurisdiction over the whole of that territory' is an express denial and disclaimer made to the community of nations of acquiescence to any claim that pending the reintegration of the national territory the frontier at present existing between the State and Northern Ireland is or can be accepted as conclusive of the matter or that there can be any prescriptive title thereby created and an assertion that there can be no espoppel created by the

> restriction in Article 3 on the application of the Laws of the State in Northern Ireland.

Findlay C.J cited Barrington J. There was, however, disagreement as to whether reliance on the idea of nationhood had legal or merely political implications, that is, whether the rights of nationhood could override apparently *positive* legal norms. The judgments are especially relevant because they consider the 1937 Constitution alongside the Government of Ireland Act 1920. The latter is treated as *positive law* which appears to be overruled by the natural rights of nations. So the relevant passage of Barrington J.'s judgment reads as follows:

> One of the theories held in 1937 by a substantial number of citizens was that a nation as distinct from a state had rights: the Irish people living in what is now called the Republic of Ireland and in Northern Ireland together form the Irish nation: that a nation has a right to unity of territory in some form, be it as a unitary or federal state: and that the Government of Ireland Act 1920, though legally binding was a violation of that national right to unity which was superior to positive law. This national claim to unity exists not in the legal but in the political order and is one of the rights which are envisaged in Article 2: it is expressly saved by Article 3 which states the area to which the laws enacted by the Parliament established by the Constitution apply (*McGimpsey and McGimpsey* v. *Ireland*, 13).

Findlay C.J. rejected the interpretation of Barrington's judgment which would have made of the territorial claim in Article 2 of the Constitution a mere political aspiration. He said that the expression 'in the political order' should be seen as occurring in a decision tracing the historical, political and social background to the Constitution, and seems more appropriately understood as a reference to the origin of the claim than to its nature. If any other interpretation was to be put on the judgment, he would not follow it. The effect of Articles 2 and 3, which should be read with the preamble, is as follows (*McGimpsey and McGimpsey* v. *Ireland*, 15):

> 1. The reintegration of the national territory is a constitutional imperative [c.f. Hederman J. in *Russell* v. *Fanning*].
> 2. Article 2 of the Constitution consists of a declaration of the extent of the national territory as a claim of legal right.

The preamble, to which Findlay C.J. refers, asserts, *inter alia* 'We, the people of Eire,... Gratefully remembering their [our fathers'] heroic and unremitting struggle to regain the rightful independence of our Nation,... And seeking to promote the common good ... so that ... the unity of our country [may be] restored...'

This 'people' is identified in Article 1 as the Irish Nation and the claim in Article 2 is to the national territory. That is to say, it is a claim of the Irish Nation and not the Irish State. The Nation as the constituent authority must precede the State. The 1937 Constitution asserts in its preamble and first three Articles that there is not yet a State to complete the representation of the Irish Nation.

The question remains: What precisely was the position of the de Valera government with respect to partition and the boundary question? When members of Fianna Fail called for the repudiation of the Boundary Agreement at the earliest opportunity, de Valera called for realism.[63] Yet this meant reference to the *de facto de jure* distinction already mentioned. When asked if a Fianna Fail government would recognise an accomplished fact and have friendly relations with the Northern Government, de Valera replied, 'We must recognise existing facts, but it does not follow that we must acquiesce in them.' Partition was a 'hideous mutilation'. At present they were 'powerless to undo what has been done, but Ireland must reserve her right to act as and when the opportunity presents itself'.[64] During the 1937 election and referendum campaigns, de Valera rejected the use of force in regard to the Six Counties as distasteful and as a course 'which probably would not succeed'. Instead he stressed that one-third of the Counties wanted unity, so that it was only a matter of winning another one-sixth.[65]

Hence it remains clear that there is a continuing ambiguity in the official Irish position on the border itself. Its legality is disputed, but within a context in which the Northern Irish entity as such is disputed. There is no acquiescence in the 'loss of the nationalist minority', but only in the sense that the whole includes the part. It would be open to the Irish state to modify a claim to the whole territory of Ireland in favour of a right to have the wishes of the nationalist minority respected, the expressed intention of both the parties to the 1921 Treaty.

In any event, the terms of Articles 2 and 3 of the Constitution produced a negative British response. The British Attorney General's view was that the articles were without 'legal result'.[66] The Northern Ireland Attorney General concurred, adding, that they were 'framed in words which may well create an impression that the position of Northern Ireland is something different from that for which provision has been made by the enactments of the Imperial Parliament'.[67]

In the autumn of 1938 de Valera compared the Irish problem with the Sudetenland, but rejected the idea of a new boundary commission and plebiscites. This would yield territory but only perpetuate partition. In January 1939 de Valera said that a local parliament in the north-east 'could not justify any claim to its present boundaries'. With guarantees to nationalists, it '*might* be tolerated under an All-Ireland Parliament'.[68] None the less in 1939 in a Senate debate on the Party's Northern policy, de Valera insisted that if Ireland had the strength of some continental powers, he 'would feel perfectly justified in using force to prevent the coercion of the Border nationalists', which could be taken as an admission that 'such a use of force could *shift* the border, not abolish it'.[69]

After 1945 it was noted that de Valera's attitude hardened. He appeared to realise that unity could not be achieved voluntarily and so he came to argue for a transfer of populations, an exchange between Ulster Unionists and Irish immigrants in Britain. The US Minister considered this to be 'about as practicable as expelling the New Englanders from Massachusetts'.[70]

During this period the British Foreign Office prepared a diplomatic response in terms of how there was:

> 'no argument' in favour of the south's independence that was not also an argument for Partition because 'the great majority of the predominantly Anglo-Scottish, Protestant and industrial community of Northern Ireland' had no wish to be incorporated in the Irish, Roman Catholic, and largely agricultural south. Partition, in fact, enabled both parts of Ireland 'to choose their own form of government in accordance with the terms of the Atlantic Charter and of President Truman's Twelve Fundamentals of American Foreign Policy'.[71]

This is a remarkable change from a simple insistence upon the terms of the 1921 Treaty in favour of a doctrine of self-determination of peoples. It implies a respect for the wishes of all the inhabitants of Northern Ireland, although, of course, it assumes the reification of this entity. Indeed, the latter point is clear in the restatement of the issue in 1949.

In 1949 the partition question arose again when the Irish Free State declared itself a Republic. The Northern Prime Minister, Brooke impressed upon the British the dangers of a Sudeten situation. The Irish Government might foment unrest among the nationalist minority in the North and use this as a pretext for sending troops into the North.[72] The security situation was stressed again in terms of the contribution Northern Ireland had made during the war.

So the Atlee Government went so far as to put the veto into the hands of the Northern Ireland entity. The Northern Ireland Act 1949 provided that 'in no event will Northern Ireland *or any part thereof* [my emphasis] cease to be a part of His Majesty's dominions and of the United Kingdom without the consent of the Parliament of Northern Ireland'.[73]

In an attempt to draw conclusions about the original significance of the 1937 Constitution as the representation of the dominant personality which produced it, Bowman makes the following remarks about de Valera. It is possible to see some adherence to a doctrine of natural boundaries in de Valera's perspective.[74] None the less he reproduced a dominant Irish attitude which was to treat the exact drawing of the boundary as peripheral to its actual presence. Compared to subsequent leaders of Fianna Fail, Bowman notes de Valera's greater concern with the injustice of the boundary as actually drawn. On one occasion he said that he had no wish to coerce anyone and was willing to accept a fair referendum to determine the boundary. This was in 1938. However, at the highest point of cordiality and effectiveness in Anglo-Irish negotiations, the British Prime Minister, Chamberlain, records that de Valera never sought a readjustment of the boundary. In 1940, during negotiations on neutrality and participation in the war, the British belief was that de Valera 'would not in any way be satisfied by a suggestion that the boundary should be revised; nothing less than the whole would content him finally'.[75] Instead, de Valera took the view that his Articles 2 and 3 in the Constitution had formally disputed the South's acceptance of the boundary in 1925, just as his whole policy had been to undo the Treaty of 1921 and to subvert the Free State.[76]

The New Ireland Forum Report and the Anglo-Irish Agreement

In the New Ireland Forum Report, a consensus of Irish 'constitutional' nationalists argued, in the early 1980s, for a single unitary state, with one Parliament elected by the whole people of Ireland. This would entail unity in agreement of the two major identities and traditions in Ireland. The argument stresses the historical fact that 'up until 1922 Ireland was governed as a single unity and prior to the Act of Union in 1801 was constitutionally a separate and theoretically equal kingdom'.[77]

The origin of the present difficulties is that the 1920 constitutional arrangements by Britain resulted in the arbitrary division of the country:

> [P]rior to 1920 and during many centuries of British rule, Ireland was administered as an integral political unit. The establishment of Northern Ireland as a separate political unit was contrary to the desire of the great majority of Irish people for the political unity and sovereignty of Ireland as expressed in the last all-Ireland election of 1918.[78]

In the view of the Forum Report, since 1949 the next formal position of the British Government on the status of Northern Ireland is contained in Section 1 of the Northern Ireland Constitution Act, 1973. In substance this provision signifies that

> the only basis for constitutional change in the status of Northern Ireland within the United Kingom is a decision by the majority of the people of Northern Ireland. In practice, however, this has been extended from consent to change in the constitutional status of the North within the United Kingdom into an effective unionist veto on any political change affecting the exercise of nationalist rights and on the form of government for Northern Ireland. This fails to take account of the origin of the problem, namely the imposed division of Ireland which created an artificial majority in the North.[79]

This argument, perhaps surprisingly, continues to show the lack of clarity in the Republic concerning the significance of the relationship between the rights of the nationalist minority within Northern Ireland and the legal status of the entity of Northern Ireland as such. However, the report does assert, as the whole will include the part (that is, a claim for a United Ireland must include a claim to 'save' the nationalist minority, and, *a fortiori* a claim that the boundary's existence cannot be a legal argument for its exclusion from the Republic), that the historical circumstances of partition allow an effective unionist veto on the exercise of the right of self-determination of the nationalist minority. In this sense the Irish Republic continues to assert, *at the very least*, the right to protect *fully* the rights of its fellow-Irish in Northern Ireland. The Anglo-Irish Agreement appears to confirm the unionist veto, but can also be understood in the above sense. It affirms that 'any change in the status of Northern Ireland would only come about with the consent of a majority of the people of Northern Ireland', that 'the present wish of a majority of the people of Northern Ireland is for no change' (Article 1).

Clearly the Article contradicts the 'United Ireland' argument of the Report and appears to enshrine the deplored unionist veto. This is the Sinn Fein view as expressed in *A Pathway to Peace* by Gerry Adams. He states:

> Likewise by signing the Hillsborough Treaty the Dublin government recognised the unionist veto. It also formally relinquished its *de jure* claim to represent all Irish people, accepting instead in return for its recognition of the British presence a facility whereby it could air its views of the grievances of nationalists in the six counties.[80]

Indeed it was understood by the Irish Government as an attempt to persuade the nationalist minority to identify with the definition of Northern Ireland to the point of participating effectively in its institutions, e.g. by joining the police. In this view the problem might be understood as one of community relations. The Agreement would merely allow the Irish Republic to participate with the British so as to improve these relations.[81] Given that Britain has no interest in the continuing division of Ireland, the problem has to be one of relations between the two communities. Coughlin quotes Garret Fitzgerald, the then Irish Prime Minister: 'Our nationalist hopes and aspirations must take second place in the short term to providing a stable, peaceful society for those citizens of Europe and of both traditions in Northern Ireland, who have suffered more than any other in our Community [i.e., the EEC] in recent years.'[82]

Coughlin's interpretation seems to be that taken up by some British authorities. It would mean that a legal claim to the whole territory of Ireland, and thereby to *all and therefore part of* Northern Ireland had been abandoned in favour of a right of protection of the rights of a nationalist minority within Northern Ireland. The interpretation of the Secretary of State for Northern Ireland, Tom King, was that Fitzgerald, as an Irish Premier who had to live with Articles 2 and 3 of his Constitution 'has in fact accepted that for all practical purposes and into perpetuity, there will not be a united Ireland ... [t]hat ... the legitimacy of the unionist position based on the majority view in Northern Ireland is accepted, and ... for all practical purposes, there is no prospect of a united Ireland.'[83]

The same view was expressed by Haughey, later the Irish Premier, in the Dail debates. He said the Treaty was incompatible with Articles 2 and 3, but that an exception to the binding nature of an international agreement is where it is manifestly contrary to a rule of internal law of fundamental importance (presumably Article 46 of the Vienna Convention on the Law of Treaties). Since no government has any authority to act in conflict with Articles 2 and 3, 'no future Irish government need, unless it so wishes, be bound by the provisions of any international agreement which are incompatible with those of the Constitution ... We will certainly not be prepared to accept it [the Agreement] in its present form.'[84]

In one view Article 1 of the Treaty does recognise that the North is *de jure* part of the United Kingdom as long as the majority of the people there wish it: 'This is a repudiation in exact, appropriate legal form of the right to self-determination of the Irish people as a whole.'[85] None the less, in their commentary to the Agreement, Boyle and Hadden register a different view:

> In the drafting of this article there was a conscious effort by both sides to avoid dispute on the definition of a current status for

> Northern Ireland. As was said at the time the two states came to the negotiations with 'different title deeds'. As a result the emphasis in Article 1 is laid on the agreed conditions for any future change in the status of Northern Ireland.[86]

The authors, Boyle and Hadden, do go so far as to say that the intention was to give Irish Government recognition to the terms of the British guarantee to the unionists in the 1973 Act. The only option left to the nationalists was to win over the unionist majority to a United Ireland. Yet this remains a line of reasoning based on the supposition that the question of the rights of the nationalist minority is tied to, and indeed equated to, the legal foundation of the Northern Ireland entity. Against this the authors can state, authoritatively, that the intention of the British, in concluding the Anglo-Irish Agreement, was that they were not prepared to make concessions to have Articles 2 and 3 removed. They, for their part, intended to give as firm a guarantee to the unionists as was compatible with the continued existence of the articles.[87] So it appears to be the British negotiators' view that they did not, and did not intend to, extract any legal concession from the Irish State on its claim to the 'national territory'.

Indeed such a British perspective could be taken to mean that it recognises that the Irish state does not consider itself in any way and for any reason estopped from making a full legal claim to the 'national territory'. Indeed, Boyle and Hadden point out that, on this occasion, the British did not repeat the declaration they made at the time of the Sunningdale Conference, that Northern Ireland was an integral part of the United Kingdom. This could be taken to deprive that previous declaration of any legal rather than merely factual significance.[88]

The fundamental difficulty for the unionists is that the Agreement, however binding in international law, does not bind either of the parties if they choose jointly to alter its terms. There is no effective way in international law that the unionist community itself can be a party to the Treaty. Therefore it affords no more guarantee to the unionists that they will remain within the United Kingdom than might depend on the continuing state of mutual understanding between the British and Irish governments.[89]

Judicial opinion is even more decisive that the Anglo-Irish Agreement does not compromise the claims of the Irish state to Northern Ireland. In *McGimpsey and McGimpsey* v. *Ireland* Barrington confirmed the view that, unlike 1973, now neither the British nor the Irish were committing themselves to a legal view of the status of Northern Ireland:

> It appears to me that in Article 1 of the Agreement the two Governments merely recognise the situation on the ground in

> Northern Ireland (para./b), form a political judgement about the likely course of future events (para./a), and state what their policy will be should events evolve in a particular way (para./c).(*McGimpsey and McGimpsey* v. *Ireland (1990) SCt. 314/88*)

Indeed, Boyle and Hadden go so far as to say that the form of the wording in Article 1.2, notably the use of *would* for *could* and the careful avoidance of any explicit statement as to what the constitutional status of Northern Ireland is, suggests that both governments thought Articles 2 and 3 amounted to a legal claim which they wished, at all costs, to avoid contradicting.[90]

In the Supreme Court, in *McGimpsey and McGimpsey* v. *Ireland* the judgment of Barrington J. quoted above was simply followed (*McGimpsey and McGimpsey* v. *Ireland, 1990 18*). The Supreme Court said that such was the only reasonable interpretation of Article 1, especially when taken in conjunction with Article 2/b, which is a denial of derogation of sovereignty. The Supreme Court goes on to consider the guarantee to the unionist majority as an acceptance that the concept of change in the *de facto* status of Northern Ireland would require the consent of the majority. Given Ireland's acceptance of general international law and a duty to undertake peaceful settlement of disputes under Article 29 of its Constitution, the signing of the agreement is no renunciation of legal right, but merely a 'realistic recognition of the *de facto* situation in Northern Ireland'.

Indeed another interpretation[91] is that the Agreement serves to state that, from a British perspective, Northern Ireland is definitely not an integral part of the United Kingom. The latter does not, any more than any other modern state, freely recognise that any part of its territory may secede at will from the state. Yet that is the effect of the Anglo-Irish Agreement. This position parallels the one taken by Britain with respect to the Falkand Islands and Gibraltar. It shows clearly that Britain regards the Northern Ireland question as a piece of unresolved colonial history. Consistently with the other cases, Britain remains firmly determined to protect the wishes of its citizens, subjects, or whatever, who remain within its jurisdiction, while it is itself indifferent to the question of historical territorial title. This might well explain why, unlike Ulster Unionists, who refer frequently to the 1925 Boundary Agreement,[92] the British Government seems no more interested in holding the Irish Government strictly to the 1925 Agreement, than the Irish are inclined to call for its rectification so as to ensure a more *bona fide* implementation of Article 12 of the 1921 Treaty.

Conclusion

It might be argued that the Irish Government should see the present British position, which has been held in one form or another since after World War II, as a return to the spirit of the undertakings which British negotiators gave to their Irish counterparts in November–December 1921. The primary British policy is to have respect for the wishes of the inhabitants of Northern Ireland. Britain itself retains no interest in the future of Northern Ireland as an entity. This, understandably, concerns Ulster Protestants and Unionists. The Irish Government gives formal approval to respect for the wishes of the population of Northern Ireland, but it is always with a view to bringing an end to the Northern Ireland entity by, eventually, obtaining a majority for this course. It has been very cogently argued that however careful the Irish state may have been at preserving its legal position, as a matter of the political history of the state, it has never been serious in engaging itself in a policy which it thought, realistically, could bring about Irish unity.[93] If this is true it is all the more reason why the Irish Government should recognise, in accordance with modern principles of the democratic, self-determination of peoples, that its rights have their basis only in so far as the Irish state is the legitimate and full representative of the Irish nation, which extends to include the the nationalist minority within the Northern Ireland entity *and no further.*

Postscript

The 'Independence' of the Irish State and the International Legal Status of the 1921 and 1925 Agreements

In international law the question might be posed whether the Irish Free State of the 1920s was fully independent in international law. This is relevant to the question of the continued legal significance of the 1921 Peace Treaty and the 1925 Boundary Agreement. In terms of the interests of the nationalist minority the arguments of republicans questioning the full international legal capacity of the Irish Free State have a double-edged quality. To say that the Boundary Agreement is not one the Irish Free State was competent to conclude – which is my view – could bring with it the argument that it was not competent to conclude the 1921 Treaty either, with the result that no useful reversion can be made to Article 12 of that Treaty. However, in my view the ground of validity of the earlier Treaty and its Article 12 was that it endeavoured, and was supposed by the parties, to give a fair expression of the principle of the democratic self-determination of peoples. The 1925 Agreement is a clear violation of this principle. It is so questionable primarily on this ground. None the less, it is appropriate to give a reasonably full account of the arguments with respect to the international legal personality of the Irish Free State. This discussion will help to illustrate the somewhat twilight international legal capacity of Ireland at the time, given Britain's own attitude. However, what follows cannot dispose of the fact that in the final analysis the Irish government appears to have freely concluded the 1925 agreement.

I consider that legally, Britain committed itself firmly to the position that in 1921 it was its intention to bring into existence on the island of Ireland a state which did not enjoy full independence in international law. Hence, from its perspective, the 1925 Agreement, although it was registered as a Treaty with the League of Nations, did not represent a legal act between two independent nation-states. It was part of evolving Anglo-Irish relations in which Britain still remained, in its own view of itself, the guiding hand. Full independence came later. After the Statute of Westminster (1931), Ireland had, in the British view, legislative sovereignty. After the so-called Treaty Ports agreements of 1938 Ireland was effectively sovereign in international relations, able to maintain its neutrality in wartime.*

The republican anti-Treaty party, led by de Valera, might well put their objection to the 1921 Treaty that it failed to ensure the independent international legal personality of Ireland. It is common ground that, with the Treaty, the Free State, enjoying 'dominion status', had won control over foreign affairs,[94] but it had not won recognition from Britain that the Free State's affairs with it were 'foreign'. The question was, in anti-Treaty and later, present Sinn Fein terms, whether the Dail, elected in the Sinn Fein mandate of 1918, and having already declared the full independence of Ireland, could be said to be incompetent to modify this independence by signing the Treaty.

So the 1918 election manifesto asserts that Sinn Fein is committed to the establishment of a constituent assembly comprising persons chosen by Irish constituencies as the supreme national authority. It asserts, further, the right of a nation to sovereign independence, resting upon immutable natural law, which cannot be made the subject of compromise, concluding, *inter alia*, 'that only a freely-elected government in a free Ireland has power to decide for Ireland the question of peace and war'.[95] The 1919 Declaration of Independence of the Dail elected with the Sinn Fein Manifesto, reads, in part,

* It has already been argued in Chapter 6 that republicanism as a form of government is not determinative of either question.

> And Whereas the Irish people is resolved to secure and maintain its complete independence ...
>
> Now, therefore, we, the elected Representatives of the ancient Irish people in National Parliament assembled, do, in the name of the Irish nation, ratify the establishment of the Irish Republic ...
>
> We ordain that the elected Representatives of the Irish people alone have power to make laws binding on the people of Ireland.[96]

In the Treaty debate the republican argument was that ratification meant disestablishment of the Republic. So Childers put the question that ratification of the Treaty was an abandonment of independence. Apart from the retention of military naval bases in Ireland, which would compromise the independence of the country in time of war, Childers could stress that the Treaty depended for its interpretation upon a British Act of Parliament. So Irish sovereignty must stem from the same source, rather than from the people of Ireland.[97] Stack pointed out how the notion of dominion status may suit peoples who have sprung from England, but not a country which has been conquered. It was not acceptable for Ireland to treat its status as a concession from England.[98] Mellows makes the point equally precisely, that the delegates (to the London negotiations) had no right to surrender the Irish Republic of which they were the plenipotentiaries: 'They had no power to agree to anything inconsistent with the existence of the Republic ... [t]he only sure foundation upon which any government or republic can exist ... is because the people gave a mandate for that Republic to be declared.'[99]

The question of continuity of the state is succinctly set out by de Valera in the course of the Civil War. 'The setting aside of the Republic in the Treaty *means an abandonment of the national sovereignty and the partition of the country* [emphasis added].' Civil war means armed opposition to the decision of the majority of the people. Given the weight of forces against republicans such a course was futile. So the solution was to revise the Treaty. This could be done by 'ignoring England. Acting in Ireland as if there was no such person as the English King, no Governor-General, no Treaty, no oath of Allegiance.'[100]

The substance of such a view is that the existing situation is merely *de facto* and without prejudice to the *de jure* rights of sovereignty of the Irish people. In terms of the Irish electorate of the 1920s there was majority support for the pro-Treaty position, but this merely proves that there was acceptance, democratically in Southern Ireland, that the relations between the Irish Free State and Britain should remain, as Britain wished, relations which were less than those between two completely independent states, viz. foreign relations.

It is essential to consider at length how Britain itself viewed the 1921 Treaty as a legal instrument. This has a special importance, as well, because the question of the boundary is anchored in a provision of a UK statute, the 1920 Government of Ireland Act. To the extent that Britain itself takes the view that it has not in fact concluded an international treaty, but merely, by internal legislative enactment, altered the status of regions of HM's territories which could in future be altered again at HM's pleasure through Her Sovereign Parliament, there would be no possibility of holding the Irish Free State as estopped in international law from disputing any aspect of the operation of the 1921 Treaty. So it is Britain which, by its refusal to recognise a Republic based on the sovereignty of the Irish people in 1921–25, makes it possible for the Irish state emerging from the 1937 Constitution to allege that there is no continuity with the Irish Free State.

So Churchill, as Colonial Secretary, made comments on the Treaty debates of 1922 which are very apposite to the question of Ireland's international legal personality. He denied the view that an Irish Republic was set up by the Irish people and that this Irish Republic can only be converted to an Irish Free State by a decision of the Irish people: 'We do not recognize the Irish Republic.' An election would disestablish the Republic, but his comment is 'These matters do not affect us in our procedure in any way.'[101]

There was a strongly-held British view in the 1920s and 1930s that Irish questions were still a matter of British constitutional law and that the only issue which could arise would be the desirability of changing legislation of the Imperial Parliament. A very prominent constitutional law commentarist, Keith, in a 1931 edition of *An Introduction to British Constitutional Law* has observed of the negotiation of the Treaty: 'the assertion of Imperial supremacy, made in 1766 as a challenge to the repudiation of that supremacy by the American colonies, was renewed in 1922 in respect of the Irish Free State'.[102]

In any case dominion status necessarily implied, in the dominant view, a right of appeal to the Privy Council. As Harrison points out, the corollary to this was that the Privy Council would have the sole ultimate authority to decide just what the Treaty did or did not amount to.[103] He records that at the vital Imperial Conference of 1931 the British intention had been to exclude the Irish Free State from the benefits of the forthcoming Statute of Westminister of 1931, bowing only to the pressure from the other Dominions.[104]

The constitutional position, from the British perspective is set out in *Moore* v. *The Attorney General of the Irish Free State* in 1935.

The Judicial Committee stated that the Constituent Act and the Constitution of the Irish Free State derived their validity from the Act of the Imperial Parliament, the Irish Free State Constitution Act 1922. This affirmed the legislative supremacy of the Imperial Parliament. In this sense the Treaty precluded the Irish Free State from exercising certain powers. However, the situation after 1931 is 'that the Statute of Westminister gave the Irish Free State a power under which they could abrogate the Treaty'. [105]

In other words, in the 1920s, in the view of the British state, the Irish Free State was a creature of British constitutional law and, in respect of any matter defined in the 1921 Treaty, a body subordinate to the Imperial Parliament.

In Harrison's view this is not a tenable interpretation of the historical and diplomatic reality of the conclusion of the Treaty and its implementation into legislation, even when seen from the British perspective. In presenting the legislation in the Commons the Attorney General said it was not for the House to deliberate whether the Constitution was good or bad, but whether it was 'going to carry out the pledge which has been given to the Irish people to enact the Constitution so long as it complies with the Treaty'.[106] In the Lords, Haldane gave an independent judgement that the Treaty was a Treaty of Peace between warring parties. A Treaty on the field of battle is sacred, which is why it does not come to Parliament. Britain had the choice of conquering Ireland or making peace. It chose the latter course. So, in effect, Harrison is making the very clear point that the language of Parliamentary sovereignty merely represents the dualist English view of the relationship between international law and municipal law. It would then say nothing about the British view of the international legal status of Ireland. This is particularly clear in the following passage of Haldane's speech, treating international affairs as very much a matter of the Royal Prerogative and not the concern of Parliament:

> the Articles of Agreement did not come before Parliament. You do not make a truce, you do not make the terms of Armistices, you do not even make the treaties which embody them, in Parliament. The Government must be responsible for them, for better or for worse. That is always so when you are dealing with war.[107]

In this view there is no question but that the Irish people are recognised as independent and capable of concluding an agreement on the basis of equality with the British state. The Treaty is the outcome of a conflict in which there was certainly a very large measure of coercion.

The issue of the struggle was none the less precisely the status to be accorded to the Irish people. Lloyd George took the view that a Republic was incompatible with Britain's security.[108] Allegiance to the Crown and participation in the Empire continued to be central demands of the British negotiators.[109] This included the element of military/naval bases. Birkenhead pointed out in negotiations that such an element in the proposed agreement was bound to compromise Irish neutrality in a conflict.[110] On the crucial question of allegiance to the Crown, Lloyd George, in the final stages of the negotiations, presented the Irish delegates with a choice, the Empire or war. With no alternative of reporting back to Dublin they had to sign at once or face war within three days. This is affirmed by one of the Irish negotiators present. He confirmed that the duress referred to the issue 'whether we should stand behind our proposals for external association, face war and maintain the Republic, or whether we should accept inclusion in the British Empire and take peace'.[111]

So the acceptance of the international law character of the Treaty and the special status of the legislation to implement it are not conclusive of the international legal status of the Irish state. Indeed, quite to the contrary, they demonstrate that the outcome of coerced negotiations was that Ireland accepted rather less than independent status. According to the international law applicable to the conclusion of treaties the manner of conclusion of the Treaty was still legal, although only just, since the consensus against coercion began to grow from the conclusion of the Kellogg–Briand Pact of 1928. At the very least it has to be said that the distinction between an independent Republic or external association and allegiance to the Crown, with incorporation in the British Empire mattered enough to the British to threaten war to achieve it. So it seems hardly possible for them to say that the State of the 1937 Constitution is the same as the Irish Free State which came out of the Treaty. The difference had to do precisely with the extent to which the Treaty amounted to a full recognition of the right to self-determination of the Irish people.

So this is the context in which one might recollect de Valera's determination simply to ignore the terms of the Treaty which are offensive to that national right. It is another matter whether that is how one can describe the external conduct of his government from 1932 and whether that is how he understood the issue of partition. However, it is clearly the intention of the Constitution of 1937 with respect to its territorial Articles 2 and 3, as has already been seen and understood, even acutely, by all parties.

My own conclusion is that it is perfectly clear from the terms of Articles 1 and 2 of the 1921 Treaty that the intention of the Britsh was to anchor the identity of the Irish Free State within the constitutional law of the Commonwealth. It is accorded identical status to Canada (Article 2). The Irish Parliament is to make laws for the 'peace, order and good government of Ireland' (Article 1), clearly a reference to internal affairs. With respect to the oath of allegiance to the Crown it is in a modified form. Faith and allegiance are sworn to the Constitution of the Irish Free State. There follow the words '... I will be faithful to H.M. George V, his heirs and successors by law, in virtue of the common citizenship of Ireland with Great Britain and her adherence to and membership of the group of nations forming the British Commonwealth of Nations.' So the Treaty does not accord and was not intended to accord full international legal personality to the Irish Free State.[112] Certainly until the Imperial Conference of 1930 it did not have it.

What the Irish state undertook after 1932 to achieve full nationhood has to be understood as an attempt to achieve full national self-determination, both with respect to the question of its continued status within the British Empire and with respect to the partition of the country. The means which it might employ to achieve this end have to be judged in terms of evolving international legal standards.

In other words, while the Treaty concluded in 1921 might have been valid in terms of the international law of the time, whether it continues to be valid depends upon the continuing evolution of international legal standards. The same applies to the Boundary Agreement of 1925. It cannot be said that Britain accorded no international legal recognition to the Irish Free State, or that the Agreement is entirely coerced. None the less, the Agreement was concluded at a time when the Irish nation, however defined (that is, with respect to the identity of the Protestant community in the North) had not achieved full independence. Its attempts to achieve it were still the subject of, at the very least, considerable pressure from Britain, including the North of Ireland. As has been noted the Boundary Agreement was ratified and enacted in the Irish Free State in terms that there was an emergency which precluded the holding of a referendum to consult the wishes of the electorate of that state. While the 1925 Agreement is certainly evidence of how the Irish Free State Government saw the question of partition it cannot be taken as conclusive of the legal expression of Irish self-determination. This is not simply because the Irish state has, since 1937, consistently opposed the implications of the 1925 Treaty by taking a different view of the nature of the legal identity of the Irish state, but also because, until 1931 at least, and probably until the Chamberlain–de Valera negotiations of 1937–38, Britain did not recognise Ireland as a fully independent state.

Notes

1 The General International Law Framework and its Applicability to Ireland

1. This is the standard concept of the state as a political authority in English jurisprudence: see John Austin, *The Province of Jurisprudence Determined etc.* with an introduction by H.L.A. Hart, Weidenfeld and Nicolson, London, 1955 at p. 194: 'If a *determinate* human superior, *not* in the habit of obedience to a like superior, receive *habitual* obedience from the *bulk* of a given society, that determinate superior is sovereign in that society, and the society (including the superior) is a society political and independent.'
2. Henry Wheaton, *Elements of International Law* 8th edition, edited by R.H. Dana, Wheaton, Sampson Low, Son and Co., London 1866, para. 22: 'The habitual obedience of the members of any political society to a superior authority must have once existed in order to constitute a sovereign State.'
3. Ibid., para. 165: 'The title of almost all the nations of Europe to the territory now possessed by them, in that quarter of the world, was originally derived from conquest, which has been subsequently confirmed by long possession and international compacts, to which all the European States have successively become parties ...'.
4. Matthew M. McMahon, *Conquest and Modern International Law, The Legal Limitations on the Acquisition of Territory by Conquest*, Catholic University of America Press, Washington, DC, 1940, p. 58, referring to English, French, German and US writers on international law (doctrine).
5. Ibid., pp. 40–3.
6. Ibid, pp. 43–4, cited by McMahon.
7. Wheaton, *The Elements of International Law*, para. 165.
8. McMahon, *Conquest and Modern International Law*, p. 47. It is obvious that McMahon's book, published by The Catholic University of America proves to be very sympathetic to the ethos of the just war tradition, going back to the canonists of the Middle Ages. At the same time his arguments have been adopted by the Max Planck Encyclopedia in its entry on conquest.
9. Istvan Bibo, *A Study of Self-determination, Concord among the Major Powers, and Political Arbitration*, John Wiley & Sons, New York, 1976, with an Introduction by B. Crick, pp. 1–2.
10. The position was reiterated most authoritatively by the International Court of Justice in the *Case Concerning the Frontier Dispute* (Burkina Faso and the Republic of Mali), Reports of the ICJ (1986), p. 554 especially para. 20; see also The Conference on Yugoslavia's

Arbitration Commission, in its Opinion No. 2 (11 January 1992), vol. 92, *International Law Reports*, (1994), pp. 167–8.

11. Bibo, *The Paralysis of International Institutions*, John Wiley, New York, 1976, p. 36.
12. Ibid., p. 5.
13. See Anthony Carty, *The Decay of International Law*, Manchester University Press, Manchester, 1986, at p. 115:

    the present style of academic,i.e. reflective as distinct from official, legal argument is quite sterile. That is to say, to test official argument against the traditional criteria of general customary law is the surest way to reach no understanding of the issues involved. Official (i.e. state or governmental) argument is, inevitably, confined to one-sided assertions of legal principle which it is thought are likely to appeal, along with many other 'non-legal' factors, either to a domestic audience or to particular allied powers.'

14. For instance, the United Nations General Assembly Resolution A/Res./47/135 3 Feb. 1993, *Declaration on the Rights of Persons Belonging to National or Ethnic, Religious and Linguistic Minorities* 32 ILM (912) 1993 speaks in article 1 of a state duty to protect minorities, that is, the legal structure of this minorities protection regime begins with the existing state system. In article 2 minorities are defined as covering national, ethnic, religious and linguistic categories, but they are not defined any further in relation to one another or to majorities within the existing states; see also *The Report of the CSCE Meeting of Experts on National Minorities* 30 ILM (1692) 1991, to the same effect. The starting point is a virtually ahistorical assertion that human rights (individual human rights) are the basis of the protection of persons belonging to national minorities (at p. 1695), but there is recognition that minority issues are a matter of international concern and that border regions may require permanent mixed commissions and international agreements (at pp. 1698–9).
15. The first judicial decision in which this principle was definitely formulated was 'Lotus' Case of the SS, Permanent Court of International Justice [1927] ser. A, No. 10, at p.28.
16. Meaning that states should adopt a certain stance towards governments which are not at all representative, see further T.M. Franck, 'The Emerging Right of Democratic Governance' vol. 86, *American Journal of Interntional Law*, Jan. 1992, p. 46 and J. Crawford, 'Democracy and International Law', vol. 64, *British Yearbook of International Law* (1993), p. 113.
17. Wheaton, *Elements of International Law*, para. 165.
18. For instance, a very large part of the jurisprudence on the 'law of territory' is cited by Crawford in a chapter on 'native communities': J. Crawford, *The Creation of States in International Law*, Oxford University Press, Oxford, 1979, Ch. 6 esp. pp. 176–85; see also R.Y. Jennings, *The Acquisition of Territory in International Law*, Manchester University Press, Manchester, 1963, which reproduces as an appendix, *the* leading case, the Palmas Island Case

(Netherlands, US), United Nations Reports of International Arbitration Awards, vol. II, p. 829 (1928). The latter was an arbitration between the Netherlands and the United States concerning the limits of the latter's 'winnings' from its war of 1899 against Spain in the Pacific. The so-called law delimits the activities of the colonial powers among themselves.

19. [1905] 2 K.B. 391.
20. I. Brownlie, *Principles of Public International Law,* 3rd edition, Oxford University Press, Oxford, 1979, pp. 47–8.
21. McMahon, *Conquest and Modern International Law,* p. 59.
22. M.F. Lindley, *The Acquisition and Government of Backward Territory in International Law, (Being a Treatise of the Law and Practice Relating to Colonial Expansion)*, London, 1926 (reprinted Negro University Press, New York, 1969), at p. 13.
23. Ibid., p. 14 citing Samuel Pufendorf, *Of the Law of Nature and Nations,* translated by Basil Kennet, Oxford, 1710.
24. Ibid.
25. Ibid., p. 15.
26. Ibid., referring to Gentilis and Seldon, writing in 1588 and 1618. After all, the terms of grant by the Spanish kings to Hernando Cortes, with respect to Mexico, and Francisco Pizarro, for Peru, concerned, in the latter case specifically, a right of discovery and conquest, Ibid., at p. 28. These declarations are of themselves not of decisive international law significance, given the virtual consensus of legal doctrine in the other direction. However, English/British pursuit of colonial power might reasonably be more concerned by the material power of its rivals than by the divisions of conscience of their legal elites.
27. Ibid., pp. 14–15.
28. Ibid., pp. 18–19.
29. Ibid., p. 29, quoting the 4th edition of Story's *Commentaries on the Constitution of the United States* by Thomas M. Cooley, Boston, 1873, para. 152.
30. Ibid., p. 30 quoting from James Kent, *The Commentaries on American Law* 14th edition by John M. Gould, Boston, 1896.
31. See the reference to these English arguments by Breandan O Buachalla in his Foreword to the 1987 Reprint of *The History of Ireland* (in Irish, with a bilingual edition) by Geoffrey Keating (1633–36), Irish Texts Society, London, Dublin, at p. 5: 'The Elizabethan intellectual rationalisation for both Reformation and conquest of Ireland rested on one simple premise: the Irish were primitive barbarians, bereft of either civility or religion.'
32. Ibid., p. 4: 'Keating's immediate purpose, in writing FFE [Foras Feasa ar Eirinn] (The History), was to answer the "falsehoods" concerning Ireland and her inhabitants which were being propagated in the writings of Cambrensis and his latter-day followers, Stanihurst, Spenser, Camden, Davies and others.' Cambrensis was the chronicler of the Norman invasion.
33. See, for instance Brownlie, *Principles of Public International Law* pp. 4–12 and literature cited therein.

34. Ibid., p. 25.
35. Giraldus Cambrensis, *Expugnatio Hibernica The Conquest of Ireland*, edited with translation and historical notes by A.B. Scott and F.X. Martin, Royal Irish Academy, Dublin, 1978.
36. Sir John Davies, *A Discovery of the True Causes Why Ireland Was Never Entirely Subdued* (1612) edited with an Introduction by James P. Meyers, The Catholic University of America Press, Indiana, 1988.
37. In particular, W.L. Renwick (ed.), *A View of the Present State of Ireland*, Oxford University Press, Oxford, 1970.
38. See *Spenser and Ireland, An Interdisciplinary Perspective*, Patricia Coughlan (ed.), Cork University Press, Cork, 1989, p. 11.
39. see Michelle O Riordan, *The Gaelic Mind and the Collapse of the Gaelic World*, Cork University Press, Cork, 1990, esp. the Introduction, pp. 1–20 for an extensive discussion of the place of the poet in Irish society until the eighteenth century and his or her use as a source of authoritative evidence of Irish attitudes.
40. The school of literary criticism, known as the 'new historicism', endeavours to see the everyday production of consciousness as one which does not allow a distinction to be drawn between 'high' and 'low' culture, or between an aesthetic sphere and an everyday historical-political sphere. A perspective of culture in action calls for a 'thick description' of an event and its rereading in such a way that analysis of tiny particulars reveals the motive forces controlling a whole society: see, in particular *The New Historicism*, ed. H. Aram Veeser, Routledge, London, 1989 and *New Historical Literary Study, Essays on Reproducing Texts, Representing History*, eds Jeffrey N. Cox and Larry J. Reynolds, Princeton University Press, Princeton, 1993.
41. A central source of materials has to be the debate on historical revisionism in Ireland. This is where the debate on the extent and consequences of the conquest is most explicitly discussed at present: see, for instance, Ciaran Brady (ed.) *Interpreting Irish History, The Debate on Historical Revisionism*, Irish Academic Press, Dublin, 1994.
42. Here, legally recognisable evidence is most easily produced: for instance, see the survey of the post-1690 situation in Martin Stephen Flaherty, 'The Empire Strikes Back: Annesley *v.* Sherlock and the Triumph of Imperial Parliamentary Supremacy', in the *Columbia Law Review*, vol. 87 (1987), p. 593. The assertion of supremacy of the British Parliament over the Irish was not only based on the right of conquest, but meant a reassertion of a stronger will in the years between 1717 and 1720.
43. Here primary weight will be placed on contemporary commentators such as Keating.
44. For instance his *Phases of Irish History* (Dublin, 1919), reprinted Kennikat Press, Port Washington, NY, London, 1970.
45. See for instance, Frank Longford, *Peace by Ordeal, the Negotiation of the Anglo-Irish Treaty 1921*, (1935), Pimlico, London, 1992 and Nicholas Mansergh, *The Unresolved Question, The Anglo-Irish*

Settlement and its Undoing (1912–72), Yale University Press, New Haven, 1991.

46. This view is expounded most lucidly by J.C. Beckett, in *The Anglo-Irish Tradition*, Blackwell, Belfast, 1976. Such is an example of contemporary Anglo-Irish imagination. It has been refined by R.F. Foster, in *Modern Ireland 1600–1972*, Penguin, London, 1988.
47. *The Case of Ireland Stated* reprinted with an introduction by J.G. Simms, The Cadenus Press, Dublin, 1977.
48. '*North* 'Inner Emigré or "Artful Voyeur"' in *The Art of Seamus Heaney* edited by Tony Curtis, Seren, Mid-Glamorgan, 3rd edition, 1994.
49. For a more recent production see Philip Robinson, *The Plantation of Ulster, British Settlement in an Irish Landscape 1600–1670*, The Ulster Historical Foundation, Belfast, 1994.
50. See A.T.Q. Stewart, *The Narrow Ground, Patterns of Ulster History*, Pretani Press, Belfast, 1986, which also argues for historical discontinuity with respect to the population of the 'six' counties, and hence the limited operational value of the concept of conquest.
51. Consider such pregnant titles as Sarah Nelson, *Ulster's Uncertain Defenders, Loyalists and the Northern Ireland Conflict*, Appletree Press, Belfast 1984; Arthur Aughey, *Under Siege, Ulster Unionism and the Anglo-Irish Agreement*, Blackstaff, Belfast, 1989, and John Dunlop, *A Precarious Belonging, Presbyterians and the Conflict in Ireland*, Blackstaff, Belfast, 1995. These works are written from a context of conquest, but not from a perspective of an established conqueror. A most graphic account of the religious culture which can accompany the Ulster Protestant predicament is afforded by Tom Paulin in his chapter 'Paisley's Progress', on Ian Paisley in his *Ireland and the English Crisis*, Bloodaxe Books, Newcastle upon Tyne, 1984, p. 155. See also, Steve Bruce, *God Save Ulster, The Religion and Politics of Paisleyism*, Oxford University Press, Oxford, 1989.
52. This is most evident in the bitterness of the exchanges at present within the revisionist historical debate and within literary criticism concerning the nature of Irish literature. I take this material as the clearest possible evidence that the deep wounds of Irish history have not healed.
53. The most graphic popular version of this argument is perhaps Finton O'Toole's *Black Hole, Green Card, The Disappearance of Ireland*, New Island Books, Dublin, 1994; however, Thomas C. Hofheinz's *Joyce and the Invention of Irish History, Finnegan's Wake in Context*, Cambridge University Press, Cambridge, 1995 draws a firm line around the influence of the Egyptian *Book of the Dead* in the construction of *Finnegan's Wake*, esp. at p. 138: 'The historical consciousness from which Joyce derived the primary terms of his experience was that of Ireland, a country seemingly condemned to a perpetually schizophrenic identity after seven hundred years of implacable and rapacious colonial rule.'
54. See for instance how Geoffrey Beattie quotes the Scottish poet Edwin Muir in *We Are the People, Journeys through the Heart of Protestant*

Ulster, Mandarin, London, 1992, after a section entitled 'The road to nowhere', pp. 185–98, at p. 198 'The Combat': 'And now, while the trees stand watching still / The unequal battle rages there / And the killing beast that cannot kill / Swells and swells in his fury till / You well might think it was despair.'

2 Legal Title by Conquest: Norman, English and British Perspectives

1. Sean Cronin, *Irish Nationalism, A History of its Roots and Ideology*, Pluto Press, London, 1980, p. 107.
2. J.C. Beckett, *The Anglo-Irish Tradition*, Blackwell, Belfast, 1976, pp. 17–18.
3. Cronin, *Irish Nationalism*, p. 100.
4. Ibid.
5. Eoin MacNeill, *Phases of Irish History* (Dublin, 1919), Kennikat Press, Port Washington, NY, London, 1970, p. 2.
6. Ibid., pp. 26–7.
7. Ibid., pp. 63–4.
8. Ibid., p. 73.
9. Ibid., p. 83.
10. Ibid., p. 97.
11. Ibid., pp. 226–7.
12. Ibid., p. 240.
13. Ibid., pp. 246–7.
14. 'Medieval Ireland 1169–1534', F.X. Martin in *A New History of Ireland*, ed. Art Cosgrave, Oxford University Press, Oxford, 1987, p. 58.
15. Ibid., p. 60.
16. Ibid., pp. 57–60.
17. Ibid., p. 57.
18. Geraldus Cambrensis, *Expugnatio Hibernica The Conquest of Ireland* edited with translation and historical notes by A.B. Scott and F.X. Martin, Royal Irish Academy, Dublin, 1978, pp. 145–7.
19. Ibid.
20. Frederick H. Russell, *The Just War in the Middle Ages*, Cambridge University Press, Cambridge, 1974, p. 56.
21. Ibid., p. 58.
22. Ibid., p. 60.
23. Ibid., p. 23.
24. Ibid., p. 28.
25. Ibid., p. 36.
26. Ibid., p. 116.
27. Ibid., p. 73.
28. Ibid., pp. 114–15.
29. Ibid., pp. 122–3.
30. Geraldus, *The Conquest of Ireland*, p. 143.
31. Eoin MacNeill, *Phases of Irish History* (Dublin, 1919), Kennikat Press, Port Washington, NY, London, 1970, p. 286.

32. Ibid., p. 287.
33. Ibid., p. 307.
34. Marie Therese Flanagan, *Irish Society, Anglo-Norman Settlers, Angevin Kingship, Interactions in Ireland in the late 12th Century*, Clarendon Press, Oxford, 1989, pp. 277–9.
35. Cosgrave (ed.), *New History of Ireland*, pp. 88–9.
36. MacNeill, *Phases of Irish History*, pp. 311–12.
37. Cosgrave (ed.), *New History of Ireland*, pp. 267–8.
38. Ibid., pp. 273, 275.
39. Ibid., p. 283.
40. Geraldus, *The Conquest of Ireland*, pp. 231 et seq.
41. Ibid., p. 191.
42. Ibid., pp. 237–41.
43. Ibid., p. 233.
44. Ibid.
45. Flanagan, *Irish Society, Anglo-Norman Settlers*, pp. 234–5, 246.
46. Ibid., p. 272.
47. Geraldus, *The Conquest of Ireland*, pp. 23, 29.
48. Ibid., p. 25.
49. Ibid., p. 31.
50. Ibid., pp. 40–1.
51. Ibid., pp. 44–5.
52. Ibid., p. 49.
53. Ibid., p. 63.
54. Ibid., p. 89.
55. Ibid., p. 99.
56. Ibid., p. 95.
57. Ibid., p. 135.
58. Ibid., p. 139.
59. Ibid., pp. 143–4; see also p. 149: an odd list of titles, for example, the Irish as Basques, quoted by Henry VIII in 1541.
60. Cosgrave (ed.), *A New History of Ireland*, p. 323.
61. Geraldus, *The Conquest of Ireland*, pp. 182–3.
62. Ibid., p. 241.
63. Ibid., p. 253 et seq., again an odd collection, including the papal privileges.
64. Ibid., pp. 249–51.
65. Ibid., p. 251.
66. Sir John Davies, *A Discovery of the True Causes Why Ireland was Never entirely Subdued* (1612), The Catholic University of America Press, Indiana, 1988, p. 47.
67. Ibid., p. 25.
68. Ibid., pp. 43–4. The death of Salisbury, Davies' immediate patron drove him to finish his tract quickly, dedicating it to the primary source of patronage, the King himself, 'the ultimate source of Irish policy'.
69. *History and the Irish Question*, reproduced in Brady (ed.), *Interpreting Irish History*, Irish Academic Press, Dublin, 1994, at pp. 123–4.
70. See, for instance, Anthony Pagden, *The Fall of Natural Man, The American Indian and the Origins of Comparative Ethnology*, Cambridge

University Press, Cambridge, which denies any effective critical dimension to Vitoria and treats him as ethnocentric. For Pagden, the real action is, in any case, elsewhere – see *Hernan Cortes Letters From Mexico* translated and edited by Anthony Pagden, with an introduction by J.H. Elliott, Yale University Press, New Haven, London, 1986.

71. Davies, *A Discovery*, p. 71.
72. Ibid., pp. 75–6.
73. Ibid., p. 76.
74. Ibid., pp. 74–5 and p. 192.
75. Ibid., p. 74.
76. Ibid., pp. 70–1.
77. Ibid., pp. 78–9.
78. Ibid., p. 109.
79. Ibid., p. 123.
80. Ibid., pp. 124 *et seq.*
81. Ibid., p. 133.
82. Ibid., p. 138.
83. Ibid., pp. 140–2. Davies concludes 'whereas, if he had cast all the English out of his protection and held them as aliens and enemies to the Crown, the Normans, perhaps, might have spent as much time in the conquest of England as the English have spent in the conquest of Ireland'; again, at pp. 150–1 for a full statement of the exterminatory logic of a discriminatory policy, which bedevilled English policy in Ireland, and which it seems, in this text, Davies is most anxious to discourage James from following.
84. Ibid., pp. 165–71.
85. Ibid., p. 217.
86. Ibid., p. 198. See also p. 197.
87. J.G. Swift MacNeill, *The Constitutional and Parliamentary History of Ireland Until the Union*, Talbot and Fischer Unwin, Dublin/London, 1917, p. 3.
88. Ibid., at pp. 3–4 , citation from Ball's *Irish Legislative Systems*, p. 23 and Coke's *Reports*, 'Calvin's Case', Part VII.
89. Ibid., pp. 4–5.
90. Ibid., p. 8, citing Ball's *Legislative Systems*, pp. 25–7.
91. Ibid.
92. Ibid., p. 9.
93. Ibid., pp. 9–11.
94. Ibid., p. 12.
94. Flaherty, 'The Empire Strikes Back: Annesley *v.* Sherlock and the Triumph of Imperial Parliamentary Supremacy', esp. p. 617, citing the reasoning of the Irish House of Lords in Annesley *v.* Sherlock 2 Ir. Lords J. (1719) at p. 655 (supra. Ch 1 Note 42).
96. Ibid., p. 597, citing 1 W. Blackstone, *Commentaries on the Laws of England,* (1765) pp. 93–110 and Campbell *v.* Hall, 1 Cowp. 204, 98 Eng. Rep. 1045 (K.B. 1774). MacNeill also remarks of Blackstone that he maintained the right of the British Parliament to bind Ireland by its laws without any qualification or restriction, Swift

MacNeill, *The Constitutional and Parliamentary History of Ireland*, p. 14.

97. L.P. Curtis, *Anglo-Saxons and Celts: A Study of Anti-Irish Prejudice in Victorian England*, University of Bridgeport, Connecticut, 1968, p. 103 quoted in Vincent J. Cheng, *Joyce, Race and Empire*, Cambridge University Press, Cambridge, 1995, p. 24.
98. Ibid.
99. Cheng, *Joyce, Race and Empire*, p. 30, citing Curtis, p. 31.
100. Ibid., p. 20 citing Curtis.
101. Ibid., p. 30 quoting Curtis.
102. Swift MacNeill, *The Constitutional and Parliamentary History of Ireland* , pp. 319 and 395, arguing that the troop reinforcements came after the Insurrection was put down, and that the Insurrection served as a pretext for the passing of the Union.
103. Ibid., p. 319.
104. Elisabeth A. Muenger, *The British Military Dilemma in Ireland, Occupation Politics, 1886–1914*, University Press of Kansas, Lawrence, KA, 1991, pp. 2–3.
105. Ibid., p. 35, citing Nora Robertson, *Crowned Harp: Memories of the Last Years of the Crown in Ireland*, 1960, Allen Figgis, Dublin, p. 26.
106. Ibid., p. 5.
107. Ibid., pp. 34 and 36; an army officer's view was that the Irishman 'soon takes his hat off when he finds a master who is not afraid of him and who is always ready to tackle him'.
108. Nicholas Mansergh, *The Unresolved Question, The Anglo-Irish Settlement and Its Undoing, 1912–72*, Yale University Press, New Haven, London, pp. 82–3.
109. Ray Foster, *Modern Ireland, 1600–1972*, Penguin, London, 1988, p. 31 *et seq*.

3 Irish Perspectives of the Conquest and the Foundation of the Irish Claim to Self-Determination

1. A full development of this point will have to await the next chapter. However, the point is easily demonstrated from Molyneaux's *The Case of Ireland Stated* (1698), reprinted with introduction by J.G. Simms, The Cadenus Press, Dublin, 1977, pp. 34–5. In his argument that Ireland was not conquered, Molyneaux said that the English and Britains who came over to Ireland could not thereby lose their immunities and freedoms as *free-born* subjects. He concludes his argument with the words: ' Now 'tis manifest that the great Body of the present People of Ireland are the Progeny of the English and the Britains, that from time to time have come over to this Kingdom; and there remains a meer handful of the Antient Irish at this day.'
2. Ray Foster, *Modern Ireland 1600–1972*, Penguin, London, 1988, p. 43. For this Foster cites Canny, infra note 6 at pp. 101–2.
3. This is clearly stated by Keating to be his function, *The History of Ireland*, Irish Texts Society, London, Dublin, 1987, vol. 1, p. 5.

4. See also Stephen Greenblatt (ed.), *New World Encounters*, University of California Press, Berkeley, 1993, Introduction, esp. pp. xvi–xvii.
5. Brendan Bradshaw, Andrew Hadfield, Willy Maley, (eds) *Representing Ireland, Literature and the Origins of Conflict 1534–1660* Cambridge University Press, Cambridge, 1993, at p. 2.
6. Nicholas Canny, 'The Formation of the Irish Mind: Religion, Politics and Gaelic Irish Literature 1580–1750', *Past and Present*, (1982), vol. 95, p. 91 at pp. 111–12.
7. Michelle O'Riordan, *The Gaelic Mind and the Collapse of the Gaelic World*, Cork University Press, Cork, 1990. The work is the product of a doctoral dissertation done under the direction of Tom Dunne, author of *The Writer as Witness: Literature as Historical Evidence*, Cork University Press, Cork, 1987.
8. O'Riordan, *The Gaelic Mind*, pp. 7–8 and literature cited in note 23.
9. Ibid., p. 10.
10. Ibid., pp. 11–12.
11. Canny, 'The Formation of the Irish Mind', p. 93.
12. Bernadette Cunningham, 'Native Culture and Political Change in Ireland' in Ciaran Brady and Raymond Gillespie (eds), *Natives and Newcomers, The Making of Irish Colonial Society 1534–1641*, Irish Academic Press, Dublin, at p. 153.
13. Ibid., p. 150.
14. Ibid., p. 159.
15. O'Riordan, *The Gaelic Mind*, p. 36.
16. Ibid., p. 41.
17. Ibid., pp. 43–4.
18. Ibid., p. 50.
19. Ibid., p. 54.
20. Ibid., p. 67, relying as does Cunningham, supra, at p. 150 on Proinsias MacCana, 'Early Irish Ideology and the Concept of Unity' in *The Irish Mind, Exploring Intellectual Traditions* Richard Kearney (ed.), Wolfhound, Dublin, 1985, p. 56.
21. Ibid., pp. 71–2.
22. Ibid., p. 90.
23. Ibid., pp. 93, 95.
24. Ibid., p. 104.
25. Ibid., p. 105.
26. Ibid., p. 111.
27. Ibid., p. 112.
28. Ibid., pp. 113, 117–18.
29. Ibid., p. 121.
30. Ibid., pp. 125–6.
31. Ibid., p. 130.
32. Ibid., p. 134 *et seq*.
33. Ibid., p. 140.
34. Ibid., pp. 149–50. O'Riordan goes on to illustrate bardic admiration for Ormond's lord, Elizabeth I, at p. 152 *et seq*.
35. Ibid., pp. 168–9, 176–8, 212–13. In particular, at p. 212:

The imposition of 'foreign' perceptions; a foreign rationale of power which accompanied the extension of the crown's administration and its officers throughout the country, more than anything else perhaps, exposed the incomprehension of the Gaelic Irish elites of this new mentality. In this context the term 'failure' is especially misleading, while individual chiefs and poets attempted to survive in a new order and failed signally, their efforts were undertaken entirely in accordance with their own concepts of survival, of values and loyalties, Gaelic aristocratic society and all its trappings failed because it wore away under the pressure exerted by a more robust society.

36. Brendon Bradshaw, 'Nationalism and Historical Scholarship in Modern Ireland' reproduced in *Interpreting Irish History, The Debate on Historical Revisionism*, Ciaran Brady (ed.), Irish Academic Press, Dublin, 1994, at p. 191.
37. O'Riordan, *The Gaelic Mind*, especially pp. 236 and 255.
38. Brendon Bradshaw, 'Geoffrey Keating: Apologist of Irish Ireland' in Bradshaw, Hadfield & Maley (eds), *Representing Ireland*, p. 166.
39. See also Cunningham, Native Culture and Political Change at p. 167 and Canny, The Formation of the Irish Mind, at p. 101.
40. Bernadette Cunningham, '17th Century Interpretations of the Past: the Case of Geoffrey Keating' vol. XXV, *Irish Historical Studies* (*IHS*) (No.98) Nov. 1986, p. 116 at 121, and also, p. 126 for references to immediate Old English uses of Keating in the seventeenth century.
41. Ibid., p. 125, citing Edmund Spenser.
42. Canny, The Formation of the Irish Mind, p. 101.
43. Keating, *History of Ireland*, vol. I, pp. 3–9.
44. Bradshaw, 'Geoffrey Keating: Apologist of Irish Ireland', p. 167.
45. Ibid., p. 169.
46. Ibid., p. 171.
47. Ibid., pp. 173–4, quoting Keating, *The History of Ireland*, vol. II, pp. 13, 31–5.
48. Ibid., pp. 174–5, citing Keating, *The History of Ireland*, vol. II, pp. 290–1, 346–7 and vol. III, pp. 348–50, and 350–7.
49. Ibid., esp. Keating, *The History of Ireland*, vol. III, pp. 348–9.
50. Ibid., p. 178, *The History of Ireland*, vol. III, pp. 342–5.
51. Ibid., p. 183. Bradshaw remarks, in a reference by way of comment, that the distinction between Christian and pagan conquest may have been inspired by the Spanish debate about the justice of conquest in the Americas, as between the argument of Sepulveda that infidels might be legitimately conquered and enslaved and that of Vitoria and Las Casas, that even infidels hold legitimate dominion based on natural justice, Ibid., pp. 189--90.
52. Bradshaw describes the argument as 'imaginative, if highly anachronistic' at p. 170, commenting on Keating's *The History of Ireland*, vol. II, pp. 131–3, 325–37 and vol. III, pp. 7–15.
53. Ibid., p. 183, Keating, *The History of Ireland* I, pp. 34–7.
54. Ibid., pp. 185–6.
55. Keating, *The History of Ireland*, vol. I, p. 5.

56. Ciaran Brady, 'The Decline of the Irish Kingdom' in *Conquest and Coalescence The Shaping of the State in Early Modern Europe*, Mark Greengrass (ed.), Arnold, London, 1991, p. 94, at pp. 102–3.
57. Ibid., p. 110 and literature cited. In particular a study of Davies himself shows how he was also implicated in this use of English law: Hans Pawlisch, *Sir John Davies and the Conquest of Ireland*, Cambridge University Press, Cambridge, 1985.
58. Ibid., pp. 111–12; also Ciaran Brady, 'The Road to the View', in Patricia Coughlan (ed.), *Spenser and Ireland: An Interdisciplinary Perspective*, Cork University Press, Cork, 1989, p. 25, at p. 43.
59. Brady, 'The Road to the View', p. 40.
60. Steven G. Ellis, *Tudor Ireland*, Longman, London, 1985, pp. 281–4, and at p. 319: 'Yet in their different ways, the 8th Earl of Kildare, St Leger and Mountjoy proved outstanding governors, while the conduct of Sussex, Grey de Wilton and Essex ought perhaps to warrant their consignment to a viceregal rogues' gallery.'
61. Patricia Coughlan, 'Ireland and Incivility in Spenser', in Coughlan (ed.), *Spenser and Ireland*, p. 46, at p. 61, quoting from Lauro Martines, *Power and Imagination, City States in Renaissance Italy*, London, 1979, p. 271.
62. Richard McCabe, 'The Fate of Irena, Spenser and Political Violence', in Coughlan (ed.), *Spenser and Ireland*, p. 109 at p. 113, citing Spenser, *A View of the Present State of Ireland* at p. 58.
63. Ibid., p. 113, citing Spenser, *A View*, p. 161.
64. Ibid., p. 114 and quoting from Spenser, *A View*, p. 95, language identical in its metaphors to that of Sir John Davies.
65. Ibid., p. 119.
66. Ibid., p. 120.
67. The metaphor of looseness was crucial because the Irish were seen as restless, unsettled people, virtually nomads unable to engage in serious agriculture or the construction of urban life, see also Coughlan, 'Ireland and Incivility' pp. 48–52.
68. Spenser, *A View* , pp. 95–6, following McCabe, 'The Fate of Irena ...' at p. 121.
69. Ibid., p. 104, following McCabe, p. 122.
70. Coughlan, 'Ireland and Incivility in Spenser', p. 70.
71. Keating, *The History of Ireland*, vol. I, p. 3.
72. Ibid., pp. 5–7.
73. Ibid., p. 9. Keating is not particularly thinking of Spenser, but one might note his remarks: 'Although there should none of them fall by the sword, nor be slain by the soldier, yet thus being kept from manurance, and their cattle from running abroad by this hard restraint, they would quickly consume themselves and devour one another', Spenser, *A View*, at p. 104, quoted by Anne Fogarty, in 'The Colonization of Language', in Coughlan, *Spenser and Ireland*, p. 90.
74. Ibid., pp. 35–7.
75. Ibid., pp. 39–41.
76. Ibid., pp. 55–7.

77. Stephen Greenblatt, *Marvelous Possessions, The Wonder of the New World*, Oxford University Press, Oxford, 1992, p. 7.
78. Ibid., pp. 59–63.
79. Sir John Davies, *A Discovery of the True Causes Why Ireland Was Never Entirely Subdued* (1612), edited with an Introduction by James P. Meyers, The Catholic University of America Press, Indiana, 1988, pp. 163–6.
80. Ibid., p. 163.
81. Keating, *The History of Ireland*, vol. I, pp. 67–71.
82. Ibid., p. 71.
83. Davies, *A Discovery* ..., pp. 162 and 171, in particular 'whereby they [the English colonies] became degenerate and metamorphosed like Nebuchadnezzar, who, although he had the face of a man, had the heart of a beast', also pp. 202 *et seq.* However, Davies's thesis was that the fair application of the common law could transform both sectors of Irish society, further, at p. 217 – absence of the law made the degenerate English Irish, while execution of the law would make the 'Irish grow civil and become English'.
84. Keating, *History of Ireland*, vol. 3, pp. 347–9.
85. Ibid., pp. 367–9, referring to Davies, *A Discovery* ..., p. 224.
86. Fergus O'Ferrall, *Catholic Emancipation, Daniel O'Connell and the Birth of Irish Democracy 1820–1830*, Gill and Macmillan, Dublin, 1985, pp. 195–6 and pp. 288–9, referring particularly to O'Connell's treatment of his Protestant opponent in the decisive County Clare by-election. The other vital incident is O'Connell's clash with the Protestant Thomas Davis, see, for instance Maurice Goldring, *Pleasant the Scholar's Life, Irish Intellectuals and the Construction of the Nation State*, Serif, London, 1993, at pp. 31–4.
87. O'Ferrall, *Catholic Emancipation* ..., p. 6. Repeal of laws could not harmonise Catholics and Protestants, because the root of the division was a struggle for mastery stretching over centuries and involving transfers of power and confiscations; p. 248, the Irish agitation could not be suppressed by legal means.
88. Ibid., p. 17, Lord Clare in Parliament at the passing of the Union, declaring that the situation in Ireland today (1800) is as it was at the Revolution, where three waves of adventurers benefited from confiscations following upon rebellions.
89. Ibid., p. 28.
90. Daniel O'Connell, *A Memoir of Ireland Native and Saxon* 1843, Kennikat Press, New York, London, 1970, p. 2, after accepting that the English dominion over Ireland began in 1172 (at p. 1).
91. Ibid., pp. 4–10.
92. Ibid., p. 25.
93. Ibid., pp. 27–32.
94. Ibid., pp. 43–8.
95. Ibid., p. 46.
96. Ibid., pp. 47–73.
97. Ibid., p. 102 *et seq.*
98. Ibid., pp. 82–4.
99. Ibid., pp. 100–1.

100. Ibid., p. 113.
101. Ibid., p. 117.
102. Davies, *A Discovery* ..., p. 109.
103. O'Connell, *A Memoir* ..., p. 122.
104. Ibid., p. 127.
105. Ibid., pp. 187–218, esp. pp. 188–96, 202–9.
106. Ibid., pp. 204–5. Davies, *A Discovery* ..., pp. 221–2: the mixing of the natives and the settlers was that they might grow up together as one nation; where the Irish were brought down from the mountains into the open country 'they might grow the milder, and bear the better and sweeter fruit'.
107. Ibid., p. 229 *et seq.*
108. Ibid., pp. 251–3.
109. Ibid., p. 289.
110. Ibid., pp. 309–15.
111. Ibid., p. 322.
112. Ibid., pp. 319–20.
113. Ibid., p. 321.
114. Ibid., pp. 47–4.
115. Ibid., pp. 123–7.

4 The Anglo-Irish Perspective: Was Ireland Really Conquered?

1. S.J. Connolly, *Religion, Law and Power, The Making of Protestant Ireland, 1660–1760,* Oxford, Clarendon, 1992, p. 105.
2. Ibid., p. 106.
3. Ibid., pp. 120–1.
4. R.F. Foster, *Modern Ireland 1600–1972,* Penguin, London, 1988, pp. 161–2.
5. Neil Longley York, *Neither Kingdom nor Nation, The Irish Quest for Constitutional Rights,* Catholic University of America Press, Indiana, 1994.
6. William Molyneux, *The Case of Ireland Stated,* reprinted with an introduction by S.G. Simms, The Cadenus Press, Dublin, 1977, pp. 30–1. He relies, thoughout this section, on Geraldus Cambrensis' *Expugnatio Hibernica The Conquest of Ireland,* edited with translation and historical notes by A.B. Scott and F.X. Martin, Royal Irish Academy, Dublin, 1978.
7. Ibid., p. 33.
8. Ibid., pp. 34–5.
9. Ibid., pp. 88–90, in particular to control navigation and the wool trade.
10. Ibid., p. 118.
11. Ibid., See, for instance, the history from pp. 63–80, through the Reformation. As for the issue of the Act in favour of Adventurers, Molyneux comments the Act was made of no force by other Acts passed by Charles in his Kingdom of Ireland. He comments that England certainly intended to legislate for Ireland, but the condition

of rebellion meant it was impossible to have an Irish parliament, while it was absolutely necessary that action be taken, which only England could do: 'But when the Storm was over, and the Kingdom quieted, we see new Measures were taken in a legal parliament of our own' at p. 86.

12. Ibid., pp. 52–3.
13. Ibid., p. 84: 'If it be concluded that the Parliament of *England* may *Bind Ireland*; it must also be Allow'd that the People of *Ireland* ought to have their *Representatives* in the Parliament of *England*. And this, I believe we should be willing enough to embrace; but this is an Happiness we can hardly hope for.'
14. Ibid., p. 83.
15. Ibid., pp. 74 and 91.
16. Ibid., pp. 116–18.
17. Ibid., p. 112.
18. Ibid., p. 91.
19. Ibid., p. 71.
20. Connolly, *Religion, Law and Power*, p. 4.
21. Ibid., pp. 103–5.
22. Linda Colley, *Britons, Forging the Nation 1707–1837*, Pimlico, London, 1992, p. 18.
23. Ibid., pp. 19–23.
24. Ibid., p. 35. See pp. 31–5.
25. Ibid., p. 43.
26. Ibid., pp. 36–43.
27. Ibid., pp. 44–8.
28. Ibid., pp. 19, 23, 53.
29. Connolly, *Religion, Law and Power*, pp. 253, 233–4.
30. Ibid., p. 260.
31. Ibid., p. 247.
32. Foster, *Modern Ireland*, p. 173.
33. Ibid., p. 175.
34. Ibid., p. 176.
35. Ibid., pp. 178–9.
36. Ibid., p. 248.
37. Ibid., pp. 251–2.
38. Ibid., p. 257.
39. *The Oxford History of Ireland* edited by R.F. Foster, Oxford University Press, Oxford, 1989, Chapter 4, 'Ascendancy and Union', by R.F. Foster, pp. 135, 141, 149–51 and especially 153–4.
40. J.G. Simms, *William Molyneux of Dublin 1656–1698*, edited by P.H. Kelly, Irish Academic Press, Dublin, 1982, p. 112. The English Parliament set up a committee to investigate the book and the House of Commons then reported that the book was dangerous because it denied the power of King and Parliament to bind the people of Ireland, and denied the dependance and subordination of Ireland upon England. The King was requested to respond to attempts, such as made by the book, to shake off dependence upon England. William responded that he would, but nothing was actually undertaken against Molyneux.

41. Ibid., p. 113.
42. Ibid., pp. 116–19.
43. T. Dunbar Ingram, *A History of the Legislative Union of Great Britain and Ireland*, Kennikat Press, 1887, New York, London 1970, p. 15.
44. Ibid., p. 21.
45. Ibid., p. 51.
46. Ibid., pp. 52–3.
47. Ibid., p. 57.
48. Ibid., p. 59.
49. Ibid., pp. 77–82, esp. p. 80.
50. Ibid., pp. 139–40.
51. Ibid., p. 146.
52. Ibid., pp. 45–8.
53. S. Rosenbaum (ed.), *Against Home Rule, The Case for the Union*, with an Introduction by Sir Edward Carson and a Preface by A. Bonar Law, Frederick Warne, London, 1912, in particular, George Cave, 'The Constitutional Question', p. 81, at p. 83.
54. Ibid. There are two chapters specifically on Ulster by the Marquis of Londonderry and Thomas Sinclair, at pp. 162 and 170.
55. Ibid., Sir Edward Carson, 'Introduction', p. 17 at p. 25.
56. L.S. Amery, 'Home Rule and the Colonial Analogy', in Rosenbaum (ed.), *Against Home Rule*, p. 128, esp. at p. 135.
57. Ibid., p. 148.
58. Cave, 'The Constitutional Question', pp. 105–6.
59. See, inter alia, A.J. Balfour, 'A Note on Home Rule', in Rosenbaum (ed.) *Against Home Rule*, p. 41 at pp. 44–5. He stresses that there is no particular Irish sense of national identity, apart from the feeling of injustice which the Irish have as a consequence of the intense religious discrimination to which they have certainly been subjected, at pp. 43–4.
60. Ibid., at p. 46; also J.R. Fisher, 'Historical Retrospect', in Rosenbaum (ed.), *Against Home Rule*, p. 47 at pp. 51–60.
61. Amery, 'Home Rule and the Colonial Analogy', esp. p. 136.
62. Sinclair, 'The Position of Ulster', in Rosenbaum (ed.), *Against Home Rule*, p. 170 at pp. 180–1.
63. Ibid., pp. 17–173. A minority is not to be measured by mere numbers. One must consider its contribution to the Constitution, to industry and public well-being, 'its association with the upbuilding of national character, by its fidelity to law and order, and by its sympathy with the world mission of the British Empire in the interests of civil and religious freedom'; and also, Londonderry, 'The Ulster Question', p. 162 at p. 165 *et seq*.
64. There are considerable differences in the style with which this phenomenon is described. Carson refers to the dangers 'involved in an unconditional surrender of the Government to the intrigues of a disloyal section of the Irish people', 'Introduction', p. 17. Carson's main concern is with the law of self-preservation of nations and what is necessary for the defence of the British Empire (Ibid., p. 18). In this context it is relevant that 'Ulster sees in Irish Nationalism a dark conspiracy, buttressed upon crime and incitement

to outrage, maintained by ignorance and pandering to superstition'(Ibid., p. 25). A. Balfour is, perhaps, more moderate. It is only confiscations and the penal laws which have created the bitter fiction that Ireland was once a nation, *A Note on Home Rule*, p. 44. However, if there was an Irish Parliament trouble would be inevitable: 'The appetite for self-assertion, inherent in every assembly, and not likely to be absent from one composed of orators so brilliantly gifted as the Irish, will take the menacing form of an international quarrel. The appeal will no longer be to precedents and statutes, but to patriotism and nationality, and the quarrel between two parliaments will become a quarrel of two peoples' (Ibid., p. 45).

65. Cave, 'The Constitutional Question', p. 81: 'Since the "new departure" initiated by Davitt and Devoy in 1878, it has been the deliberate practice of Irish Nationalists to abstain from defining the nationalist demand and to ask in general terms for "self-government", doubtless with the object of attracting the support of all who favour any change ... But such a confusion of thought, however favourable to popular agitation, is a disadvantage when the moment for legislation arrives ...'
66. Ibid., pp. 92–7. Cave quotes at length from A.V. Dicey's *A Leap in the Dark* (1911). It is not to attribute to Irishmen a special measure of original sin. Once 'you part with the executive power, all checks and "safeguards" are futile'. The experience of Canadian and Cape Government show this.
67. Earl Percy, 'The Military Disadvantage of Home Rule', in Rosenbaum (ed.), *Against Home Rule*, p. 195, at pp. 201–3; also, Carson, 'Introduction', p. 20.
68. Cave, 'The Constitutional Question', pp. 100–1, remarks how, for 200 years the Scots and the English have been united by a common constitutional bond, as well as by mutual respect and good feeling, and Scots, like Englishmen, 'have taken their part in the government of these islands'. What if there is now to be federalism or 'Home Rule all round'? Such a combination of Scots and English is to be broken up 'and Scotland to become a colony, because Ireland, unwilling to bear her share in the duties of government, desires to be reduced to that status'.
69. Carson, 'Introduction', p. 22. In the event of an international conflict Ireland's government would stock more than adequate supplies of food for itself before it allowed any to come to England: 'England's difficulty would once again become Ireland's opportunity.'
70. Even Carson is critical of the English government's handling of the famine, Ibid., at p. 24. However, A. Balfour 'A Note on Home Rule', is the most conciliatory. While denying that there is anything more to Irish identity than resentment at English and British misgovernment, at p. 44, he does go so far as to say that this cannot be described as a conquest which can be or need be undone:

    in the mind of the ordinary British Home Ruler the justification ... is historical. He pictures Ireland before the English invasion as an organised and independent State ... Personally, I believe this to be a complete misreading of history. It is not denied – at least I do not deny – that both the English and British Governments, in their dealings with Ireland have done many things that were stupid, and some things that were abominable. But among their follies or their crimes is not to be counted the destruction of any such State as I have described; for no such State existed.

If an institution is restored to Ireland it will be of English importation. This does not mean that the English are a superior race dealing with an inferior one. There is no sharp difference of race between the two. The strains of Teuton and Celt are more or less mixed on both islands.

71. Carson, 'Introduction', p. 18. It was the interest of national defence which led Pitt to undertake 'the difficult and thankless task of creating the legislative union', as necessary then as now 'for the salvation of England and the foundation of the British Empire'.
72. Fisher, 'Historical Retrospect', pp. 60–1.
73. This is the only distinction between the two countries which Balfour will allow, 'A Note on Home Rule', p. 44: 'while no sharp divisons of race exist, divisions of religion have too often taken their place; that in the constitutional struggles of the seventeenth century Ireland was not the partner but the victim of English factions'. It was the brutal consequences of these civil wars which led to the fiction that Ireland was once a nation.
74. Sinclair, 'The Position of Ulster' pp. 174–5, stressing that it is not particularly with 'their Roman Catholic neighbours, or even with their hierarchy, that Irish Protestants have to reckon; it is rather with the Vatican, the inexorable power behind them all, whose decrees necessarily over-ride all the good-will which neighbourly feeling might inspire in the Roman Catholic mind'. The *Ne Temere* decree on 'mixed marriages' shows what one can expect from a Home Rule Parliament. The whole of Catholic education, particularly of the Christian Brothers, is sectarian, at p. 177.
75. Carson, 'Introduction', pp. 26–7, making the same distinction between individual Catholics, and even the Catholic Church in Ireland, and what the Roman Catholic Church as such requires. Irish Unionists are not monsters and would like to be able to forget their points of difference with their fellow Christians, but the Church as such 'is a political, as well as a religious, institution … [I]t is by the first law of its being an intolerant and aggressive organisation.' It has established tyranny in Malta and Quebec. May we not also fear the reaction to this tyranny in France and Portugal?
76. Sinclair, 'The Position of Ulster', pp. 180–1.
77. Nicholas Mansergh, *The Commonwealth Experience*, vol. I. *The Durham Report to the Anglo-Irish Treaty*, Macmillan, London, 1969, 1982, at p. 224, and, generally, pp. 215–24.
78. Ibid., pp. 225–6. The argument of usurpation, a treaty of Union obtained through fraud and coercion, had been that of both O'Connell and Swift McNeill, see *supra*. For a detailed consideration

of Griffith's position, see Richard Davis, *Arthur Griffith and Non-Violent Sinn Fein*, Anvil Books, Dublin, 1974, esp. p. 115.

79. Davis, *Arthur Griffith*, p. 115.
80. Mansergh, *The Commonwealth Experience*, p. 227.
81. Ibid., pp. 227–8; also Davis, *Arthur Griffith*, pp. 150–1.
82. Davis, *Arthur Griffith*, pp. 231–2.
83. Ibid., pp. 150–1.
84. Ibid., p. 119.
85. Ibid., see esp. p. 115 for an exact insistence upon a comparison between 1800 and the suspension of the Hungarian Constitution of 1848. Griffith wanted the monarchy to be the foundation of a continued link between the two islands, based upon a principle of their equality under a common British monarch.
86. Ibid., p. 121.
87. Mansergh, *The Commonwealth Experience*, p. 237.
88. Ibid., p. 240. Mansergh is quoting Higgins out of the Dail Treaty debate. It is worth noting that when the delegation returned to Dublin to meet the rest of the Irish cabinet (including, of course, de Valera), Griffith denied that the Treaty had been signed under duress, although the accepted general view is that there was duress: see Frank Pakenham, *Peace by Ordeal, The Negotiation of the Anglo-Irish Treaty 1921*, with an introduction by T.P. Coogan and a preface by the author, Pimlico, London, 1935, 1972, 1992, at p. 264.

5 The Question of the Legitimacy of the 'Protestant' Presence in Ulster/Northern Ireland

1. A.T.Q. Stewart, *The Narrow Ground*, Patterns of Ulster History, Pretani Press, Belfast 1977, pp. 34–5.
2. Ibid., p. 39.
3. Ibid., pp. 39–41.
4. Ibid., pp. 115–22.
5. Ibid., pp. 121–2.
6. Michael Perceval-Maxwell, *The Scottish Migration to Ulster in the Reign of James I*, Routledge and Kegan Paul, London, 1973 (reprinted 1990), p. v.
7. Ibid., p. 2.
8. Ibid., p. 3.
9. Ibid., p. 7.
10. Ibid., p. 10.
11. Ibid., p. 11.
12. Ibid., pp. 14, 16.
13. Ibid., p. 17.
14. Ibid., p. 18.
15. Ibid., p. 29. Within the same framework of political-historical analysis as Perceval-Maxwell, Philip Robinson offers a very careful argument of historical geography to demonstrate the same thesis of the 'backwardness' of the economy of pre-Plantation Ulster, in

The Plantation of Ulster, British Settlement in an Irish Landscape, 1600–1670, Ulster Historical Foundation, Belfast, 1994, pp. 17–37.

16. Ibid., p. 47.
17. Ibid., p. 55.
18. Robinson, *The Plantation of Ulster*, esp. p. 90.
19. Maxwell, *The Scottish Migration to Ulster*, pp. 74–5.
20. Ibid., p. 81.
21. Ibid.
22. Ibid., pp. 152–3.
23. Ibid., pp. 153–4.
24. Ibid., p. 316.
25. The first and classic account of the plantation is Rev. George Hill, *An Historical Account of the Plantation in Ulster at the Commencement of the 17th Century, 1608–1620*, Belfast, 1877, reprinted, 1970, Irish University Press, Shannon. This is primarily a work of economic history, and Robinson's work is also best understood as a careful work of economic history.
26. R.F. Foster, *Modern Ireland 1600–1972*, Penguin, London, 1988, p. 78.
27. T. Sinclair, 'The Position of Ulster', in S. Rosenbaum (ed.), *Against Home Rule The Case for the Union*, Frederic Warne, London, 1912, pp. 170–1.
28. Ibid.
29. Ibid., p. 172.
30. Patrick Buckland, *Irish Unionism*, vol. 2, Ulster Unionism and the Origins of Northern Ireland, 1886–1922, Gill and Macmillan, Dublin, 1973, p. xxxi.
31. Lord Ernest William Hamilton, *The Soul of Ulster*, Hurst and Blackett, London 1917, p. 127.
32. Ibid., p. xxiv.
33. Ibid., pp. 110–12.
34. Ibid., p. 114.
35. Ibid., p. 115.
36. Ibid., p. 3.
37. Ibid., p. 120.
38. Ibid., p. 122.
39. Ibid., p. 123.
40. Ibid., p. 156.
41. Ibid., p. 157.
42. Ibid., pp. 193–4.
43. Michael Gallagher, 'Do Ulster unionists have a right of self-determination?', *Irish Political Studies*, vol. 5, 1990 (PSAI), p. 11 at p. 20 *et seq*.
44. Ibid., p. 26.
45. The conclusion of Gallagher's argument is that talk of the language of self-determination in Northern Ireland is a chimera because the geographical intermingling of the two communities would make the exercise of the right by two separate selves contingent upon major population movements, Ibid., p. 28.
46. Buckland, *Irish Unionism*, vol. 2, pp. 55–6.

47. David W. Miller, *The Queen's Rebels: Ulster loyalism in historical perspective*, Gill and Macmillan, Dublin, 1978, p. 29.
48. Ibid., p. 37.
49. *A full and revised report of the three days discussion in the corporation of Dublin on the repeal of the Union*, edited by John Levy (Dublin 1843) R.I.A. Halliday pamphlets 1873, p. 13. See also *Repeal of the Union*, House of Commons Debates, No. 14, London 1834, for another exposition by O'Connell of the views expressed here.
50. Ibid., pp. 21–2.
51. Ibid., pp. 24–5.
52. Miller, *The Queen's Rebels*, p. 44.
53. Ibid., p. 62.
54. Ibid., pp. 63–4.
55. Ibid., p. 66.
56. Ibid., pp. 66, 73.
57. Ibid., p. 76.
58. Ibid., p. 77.
59. Ibid., p. 85. For a full discussion of the question of Protestant religious identity see Flann Campbell, *The Dissenting Voice, Protestant Democracy from Plantation to Partition,* Blackstaff Press, Belfast, 1991, esp. pp. 137–44, 'The Battle of the Synods' in which the evangelical, Cooke triumphed over the liberal, Montgomery.
60. Ibid., pp. 85–6.
61. Ibid., p. 91, quoting MacKnight. The same connection between Imperial history and citizen's contractual rights is shown to be alive in contemporary Ulster Protestant and Unionist political culture in Antony Alcock, *Understanding Ulster,* Ulster Society, 1994, esp. Chapter 2, 'The Unloved, Unwanted Garrison', p. 76 *et seq*.
62. Ibid., p. 103.
63. Ibid., p. 117.
64. Ibid., p. 119.
65. Ibid., p. 118.
66. Ibid., pp. 145, 147.
67. Ibid., pp. 143, 149.
68. Ibid., p. 151.
69. A. Roberts, *Northern Ireland and the Algerian Analogy*, Atholl Press, Belfast, 1986.
70. The challenge is taken up directly in these terms by Alcock in *Understanding Ulster*, in Chapter 1, 'The Collective Memory', p. 1 *et seq*.
71. J. Todd, 'Two Traditions in Unionist Political Culture', (1987) *Irish Political Studies*, vol. 2, p. 1, at p. 6.
72. Ibid., p. 7.
73. Ibid., p. 8.
74. Ibid., pp. 9–11.
75. Ibid., p. 11.
76. Ibid., p. 13.
77. Ibid., p. 14.
78. Ibid., pp. 15–17.

79. Ibid., p. 18.
80. Ibid., pp. 18–20.
81. Steve Bruce, *God Save Ulster!, The Religion and Politics of Paisleyism*, Oxford University Press, Oxford, 1986, p. 10.
82. Ibid., p. 11.
83. Ibid., pp. 9–10.
84. Ibid., p. 221.
85. Ibid., p. 235.
86. Ibid., p. 258.
87. Ibid., p. 259.
88. Ibid., pp. 264–5.
89. Ibid., p. 265.
90. Terence Brown, *The Whole Protestant Community: The Making of a Historical Myth*, Field Day Pamphlet No. 7, Derry 1985, pp. 13–14.
91. Ibid., p. 16.
92. John Dunlop, *A Precarious Belonging, Presbyterians and the Conflict in Ireland*, Blackstaff Press, Belfast, 1995, pp. 98–9.
93. Ibid., p. 100. Of course, Dunlop's aim is to find common ground to overcome the mutually antagonistic, negative definitions which each community has of the other, and he devotes most of his energy to an internal critique of his own community.
94. Brown, *The Whole Protestant Community*, pp. 18–19; see also Campbell, *The Dissenting Voice*, pp. 260–3.
95. Ibid., p. 20.
96. Ibid., p. 23.
97. Marianne Elliot, *Watchmen in Sion, the Protestant Idea of Liberty*, Field Day Pamphlet No. 8, Derry, 1985, p. 6.
98. Ibid., p. 7.
99. Ibid., pp. 8–9.
100. Ibid., p. 11.
101. Ibid., pp. 12–13.
102. Ibid., p. 14.
103. Samuel Rutherford, *Lex Rex or The Law and the Prince – A Dispute for the Just Prerogative of King and People* (London, 1644), reprinted by Springle Publications, Harrisonburg, VA, 1982, p. 208.
104. Ibid., p. 210.
105. Ibid., p. 164.
106. Ibid., pp. 138–9.
107. Ibid., p. 55.
108. Ibid., p. 56.
109. Ibid.
110. Ibid., pp. 130–1.
111. Ibid., p. 192.
112. Ibid., p. 137.
113. Ibid., p. 117.
114. See further, Dunlop, *A Precarious Belonging*, Chapter 1, 'The Mistrust of Centralised Power', pp. 8–18, to suggest that these values are very much alive in Ulster Presbyterianism; also, Campbell, *The Dissenting Voice*, 'Epilogue: The Dilemma of Protestant Democracy in Northern Ireland, pp. 424–33. Both of these analyses insist, none

the less, on the problematic of the colonial character of Ulster as distinct from Scots Presbyterianism, its mixture of a sense of freedom and racial superiority and its complicity in the nature of the British presence in Ireland, esp. at p. 13 (quoting Lee) and p. 431 respectively.

115. See also the review of Hutcheson's significance in Terry Eagleton, *Heathcliff and the Great Hunger*, Verso, London, 1995, p. 104 *et seq.*
116. Francis Hutcheson, *A System of Moral Philosophy*, 2 vols. Special Collection, Glasgow University Library, Glasgow, 1755, p. 311. Published from the original manuscript by Hutcheson, to which is prefixed some account of the life and writings and character of the author by the Rev. William Leechman, DD.
117. Ibid., p. 314.
118. R.L. McCartney, *Liberty and Authority in Ireland*, Field Day Pamphlet No. 9, Derry, 1986, p. 22.
119. Ibid., p. 10.
120. Ibid., p. 25.
121. Ibid., pp. 25–7.
122. Ibid., p. 24.
123. Arthur Aughey, *Under Siege, Ulster Unionism and the Anglo-Irish Agreement*, Blackstaff Press, Belfast, 1989, pp. 140–1.
124. Ibid., p. 148.
125. Ibid., p. 18.
126. Ibid., pp. 132–3.
127. Ibid., p. 19.
128. Ibid.
129. See A. Carty, 'English Constitutional Law from a Post-Modern Perspective', in P. Fitzpatrick (ed.), *Dangerous Supplements*, 1991, Pluto Press (Duke U.P.), London, pp. 178–203.
130. Hutcheson, *A System of Moral Philosophy*, p. 221.
131. Ibid., p. 223.
132. Ibid., p. 225.
133. Ibid., p. 226.
134. Ibid., p. 232.
135. Ibid., p. 241.
136. Ibid., p. 248.
137. Ibid., p. 250 – the possibility of comparison with the size of an Ulster Protestant community is obvious.
138. Ibid., p. 260.
139. Ibid., pp. 261–2.
140. Ibid., pp. 268–9. The reason for the constant desire to draw comparisons between Hutcheson and Rutherford is to offer a possibility of reconciling the two traditions of unionism outlined by Todd.
141. Ibid., p. 272.
142. Ibid., pp. 272–3.
143. Ibid., p. 273.
144. Ibid., pp. 273–4.
145. Ibid., p. 275.
146. Ibid., p. 280.

147. Ibid., pp. 280–1.
148. Ibid., p. 282.

6 *Irreconcilable Identities: The Aftermath of Conquest*

1. See, for instance, R.F. Foster, *Paddy and Mr. Punch, Connections in Irish History*, Penguin, Harmondsworth, 1995, esp. Chapter 11, 'Mr Yeats and the Magic of Irish History' and Chapter 13, 'Thinking from Hand to Mouth: Anglo-Irish Literature, Gaelic Nationalism and Irish Politics in the 1890s'.
2. I develop the notion of dialogue in the framework of a legal hermeneutic in my interpretation of the Russian literary critic Bakhtin, in J.A. Carty, 'Changing Models of the International System', in W.E. Butler, *Perestroika and International Law*, Kluwer, Dordrecht, London, Nijhoff, 1990, p. 13, at pp. 24–7.
3. For instance Art. 1(i) of the 1966 United Nations Covenant on Civil and Political Rights provides: 'All peoples have the right of self-determination. By virtue of that right they freely determine their political status and freely pursue their economic, social and cultural development.'
4. A. Mitchell, P. O'Snodaigh (eds), *Irish Political Documents, 1916–49*, Dublin, Irish Academic Press, 1985, p. 48.
5. See, Deirdre McMahon, *Republicans and Imperialists, Anglo-Irish Relations in the 1930s*, Yale University Press, New Haven and London, 1984, esp. p. 214 *et seq.*
6. John Hutchinson, *The Dynamics of Cultural Nationalism: The Gaelic Revival and the Creation of the Irish Nation State*, Allen and Unwin, London, 1987, p. 197.
7. Ibid., pp. 3–4.
8. Ibid., p. 9.
9. Ibid., p. 13.
10. Ibid., pp. 19–22.
11. Ibid., pp. 33–5.
12. Ibid., p. 205.
13. Ibid., p. 241.
14. Ibid., pp. 222–3.
15. Ibid., pp. 215–19.
16. Ibid., pp. 238–9.
17. Ibid., p. 286.
18. Ibid., p. 292.
19. Ibid., pp. 287–92.
20. Ibid., pp. 231–2.
21. Ibid., pp. 309–10.
22. Ibid., p. 316.
23. D. Fennell, *The State of the Nation: Ireland since the 1960s*, Ward River Press, Dublin, 1983, and also, *Beyond Nationalism, The Struggle Against Provinciality in the Modern World*, Ward River Press, Dublin, 1985.
24. This is a reference to the claim in Articles 2 and 3 of the Irish Constitution of 1937 to the sovereignty over the whole island of

Ireland. Whether such a claim has any force in terms of an Irish right to cultural self-determination is not the same as the question whether the minority in Northern Ireland have a right to reject the authority of a six-county state. The latter issue will be considered specifically as an issue of international law in Chapter 7.

25. See, for instance, M. McKeown, *The Greening of a Nationalist*, Muolough Press, Lucan, 1986.
26. This scheme is taken from J. Todd, 'Two Traditions in Unionist Political Culture', *Irish Political Studies*, vol. 2, 1989, pp. 1–3.
27. Ibid., pp. 1–5, drawing on *Government of Northern Ireland Publications* PRONI 1726/0 1956.
28. Ibid., pp. 18–22.
29. Arthur Aughey, *Under Siege, Ulster Unionism and the Anglo-Irish Agreement*, Blackstaff Press, Belfast, 1989, p. 12.
30. Ibid., p. 16.
31. Ibid., p. 17.
32. Ibid., p. 18.
33. Ibid., p. 19.
34. Ibid., p. 24.
35. Ibid., p. 28.
36. Ibid., p. 26.
37. Ibid., p. 133.
38. Ibid., p. 132.
39. Ibid., p. 159.
40. Ibid., p. 157.
41. Ibid., p. 152.
42. Ibid., p. 133.
43. Published by the Ulster Society, Lurgan, 1989.
44. Ibid., p. 1.
45. Ibid., pp. 5–6.
46. Ibid., p. 3.
47. Ibid., p. 4.
48. Ibid., p. 6.
49. Ibid., p. 8.
50. Ibid., pp. 10–13.
51. Ibid., p. 15.
52. Ibid., p. 18.
53. Ibid., p. 28.
54. Ibid., p. 32.
55. In *The Revolution in Ireland, 1879–1923*, D. G. Boyce (ed.), London, Macmillan, 1988, see John O'Beirne Ranelagh, 'The Irish Republican Brotherhood in the Revolutionary Period, 1879–1923', p. 137, at p. 141.
56. Ibid., p. 142.
57. Ibid., p. 149.
58. See a discussion of this French text in A. Carty (ed.) *Post-Modern Law*, Edinburgh University Press, Edinburgh, 1990, at p. 83, in the Introduction.
59. R.F. Foster, *Modern Ireland 1600–1972*, Penguin, London, 1988, esp. at pp. 468–9:

if parliamentary government was being threatened in the north, there could be no logical objection to the formation of a rival force in the south ...[T]aken with the government's inept handling of threatened army insubordination some months before, the radical nationalist case against the government seemed proved.

60. Adrian Guelke, *Northern Ireland, The International Perspective*, Gill and Macmillan, Dublin, 1989, at p. 23.
61. Ibid., p. 26.
62. Ibid., p. 28.
63. Ibid., pp. 62–4, quoting from Gerry Adams, *The Politics of Irish Freedom*, Brandon, Dingle, 1986.
64. Guelke, *Northern Ireland*, p. 64.
65. Ibid., p. 59.
66. Ibid., p. 32.
67. Ibid., p. 59.
68. Ibid., pp. 59–60.
69. Ibid., p. 60.
70. Ibid., pp. 88–9.
71. Ibid., p. 33.

7 The Question of Repartition

1. I. Sinclair, *The Vienna Convention on the Law of Treaties*, 2nd edn, Manchester University Press, Manchester, 1984, p. 174.
2. Ibid., p. 16.
3. Ibid., p. 173.
4. Frank Pakenham, *Peace by Ordeal, The Negotiation of the Anglo-Irish Treaty*, (1935) Pimlico, London, 1992, p. 177.
5. Ibid., p. 178 – the stage of the negotiation being 12–13 November.
6. Ibid., pp. 221–2.
7. Ibid., pp. 236–7.
8. Ibid., p. 258.
9. Ibid., p. 254.
10. Sean Cronin, *Irish Nationalism, A History of Its Roots and Ideology*, Academy Press, Dublin, 1980; Pluto, London, 1983, pp. 135–6.
11. T.G. Fraser, *Partition in Ireland, India and Palestine: Theory and Practice*, Macmillan, London 1984, p. 61.
12. Cronin, *Irish Nationalism*, pp. 134–5; also, Mansergh, *The Unresolved Question*, p. 184 referring to an exchange between Lloyd George and Collins on 14 October, at the beginning of the negotiations.
13. Packenham, *Peace by Ordeal*, p. 130.
14. Michael Laffin, *The Partition of Ireland, 1911–1925*, Dublin Historical Association, Dundalgan Press, Dundalk, 1983, p. 81.
15. Ibid., pp. 82–6.
16. Ibid., p. 86.
17. Packenham, *Peace by Ordeal*, pp. 236–7.
18. Ibid., p. 93.

19. Jeffrey Prager, *Building Democracy in Ireland,* political order and cultural integration in a newly independent nation, Cambridge University Press, Cambridge, p. 140.
20. Ibid., p. 142.
21. Ibid., p. 143.
22. Ibid.
23. Joseph M. Curran, *The Birth of the Irish Free State 1921–1923,* University of Alabama Press, 1981, pp. 133–4.
24. Sinclair, *The Vienna Convention on the Law of Treaties,* p. 16.
25. Ibid.
26. Ibid., p. 135.
27. Prager, *Building Democracy in Ireland,* pp. 145 and 241.
28. Ibid., p. 145.
29. Ibid., p. 148.
30. *Report of the Irish Boundary Commission 1925,* Introduction by Geoffrey Hand, Irish University Press, Shannon, Ireland 1969, *Introduction,* p. xii.
31. Ibid., p. xiv.
32. Ibid.
33. Ibid., p. 34.
34. Ibid., p. 37.
35. Ibid., p. 48.
36. Ibid.
37. Ibid., p. 50.
38. Ibid., p. 52.
39. Ibid.
40. Ibid., p. 53.
41. Ibid., pp. 53–4.
42. Ibid., pp. 62–3.
43. Ibid., p. 96.
44. Ibid., p. 95.
45. Ibid.
46. Ibid., p. 98.
47. Ibid., p. 63.
48. Ibid., p. 29.
49. Ibid., p. 132.
50. Ibid., p. 133.
51. Eamon Phoenix, *Northern Nationalism, National Politics, Partition and the Catholic Minority in Northern Ireland 1890–1940,* Ulster Historical Foundation, Belfast 1994, p. 303.
52. Ibid., pp. 306–7.
53. Ibid.
54. Ibid., p. 310.
55. Arthur Mitchell and Padraig O'Snodaigh (eds), *Irish Political Documents 1916–1949,* Irish Academic Press, Blackrock, Co. Dublin, 1985, p. 169. Only the Irish Labour Party is reported as according equal status to Northern Ireland as a subordinate entity, Ibid., at p. 171.
56. Prager, *Building Democracy in Ireland,* p. 53.
57. Phoenix, *Northern Nationalism,* p. 333.

58. Ibid., generally, pp. 252–336, and esp. pp. 315 and 333–4. Phoenix queries whether even the most united and determined resistance could have made a difference, in view of Northern Irish Unionist intransigence and British determination to make an end of the issue, at p. 335. However, in a democratic political culture, people's wishes are ascertained by being asked. It was still open to the Commission to weigh those wishes against other factors.
59. Prager, *Building Democracy in Ireland*, p. 156.
60. Ibid., p. 157.
61. Deirdre McMahon, *Republicans and Imperialists, Anglo-Irish relations in the 1930s*, Yale University Press, New Haven and London, 1984, p. 15.
62. Ibid.
63. John Bowman, *De Valera and the Ulster Question 1917–1973*, Oxford University Press, Oxford, 1989, p. 97.
64. Ibid., p. 99.
65. Ibid., p. 155.
66. Ibid., p. 158.
67. Ibid.
68. Ibid., p. 187.
69. Ibid., p. 196: the latter citation being from the text of Bowman.
70. Ibid., p. 260.
71. Ibid., p. 261.
72. Ibid., p. 270.
73. Ibid., p. 271.
74. Ibid., p. 301.
75. Ibid., p. 309.
76. Ibid., p. 314.
77. *New Ireland Forum Report*, 1984, Dublin, Government Publication, 6.1.
78. Ibid., 3.1.
79. Ibid., 1984, 4.1.
80. Gerry Adams MP, *A Pathway to Peace,* The Mercier Press, Cork, p. 35.
81. Anthony Coughlin, *Fooled Again, The Anglo-Irish Agreement and After*, The Mercier Press, Cork, pp. 25–6.
82. Ibid., p. 24.
83. Ibid., p. 18.
84. Ibid., p. 27.
85. Ibid., p. 28.
86. *The Anglo-Irish Agreement, Commentary, Text, and Official Review*, Tom Hadden and Kevin Boyle (eds), Sweet and Maxwell, London, 1989, p. 26.
87. Ibid.
88. Ibid.
89. Ibid., p. 28.
90. Ibid., pp. 27–8.
91. Adrian Guelke, *Northern Ireland, The International Perspective*, Gill and Macmillan, Dublin, p. 100.

92. See, for example, the contribution of McCusker, MP in the Commons in the debate on the Anglo-Irish Agreement: see Anthony Kenny, *The Road to Hillsborough, The Shaping of the Anglo-Irish Agreement*, Pergamon Press, Oxford, p. 115.
93. Clare O'Halloran, *Partition and the Limits of Irish Nationalism, An Ideology under Stress*, Gill and Macmillan, Dublin, 1987.
94. Cronin, *Irish Nationalism*, p. 141.
95. Mitchell and O'Snodaigh (eds), *Irish Political Documents*, pp. 48–9.
96. Ibid., p. 58.
97. Cronin, *Irish Nationalism*, p. 144.
98. Ibid., p. 145.
99. Ibid., p. 147. For a very full account of the issues raised by these debates, see Vincent Delay Ryan, *Ireland Restored The New Self-Determination*, Freedom House, New York, 1991.
100. Ibid., pp. 154–5.
101. Ibid., p. 148.
102. Cited in Henry Harrison, OBE, MC, *Ireland and the British Empire 1937, Conflict or Collaboration, A Study of Anglo-Irish Differences from the International Standpoint*, Robert Hale, London, 1937, p. 139.
103. Ibid.
104. Ibid., p. 143.
105. Ibid., p. 144.
106. Ibid., p. 153.
107. Ibid., p. 154.
108. Curran, *The Birth of the Irish Free State, 1921–23*, p. 51. Of course, the issue of acceptance of the Crown and the usefulness of Ulster were connected in Lloyd George's eyes. None the less, Curran is strong in his condemnation of the ineptness of the Irish delegation's negotiation of the actual terms of Article 12, and puzzled, as are all commentators by the intensity of discussion of the Crown question compared to that of Partition. The main weight of the negotiation and the main cause of the later Civil War in Ireland were the clauses to do with Dominion Status and allegiance to the Crown. Yet, on Ulster, in his view, the record shows clearly that Lloyd George and the others had declared publicly their view that substantial parts of Ulster should be ceded to the Irish. With public statements by Irish delegates the British were under pressure to modify their statements, both publicly and privately. However, as we have seen earlier, none of this accounts for the Irish delegation not insisting on the translation of the assurances they received in the negotiations into firm terms in Article 12 – such as plebiscite by Poor Law districts, at pp. 133–5.
109. Ibid., p. 77.
110. Ibid., p. 89.
111. Cronin, *Irish Nationalism*, pp. 137, 172.
112. The British Government objected to the Irish Government registering the 1925 Treaty with the League of Nations Secretariat. According to article 18 of the League Covenant a treaty of a member of the League is only binding when registered with the Secretariat. The British Foreign Secretary, in fact the same Sir Austen Chamberlain

who negotiated the 1921 Treaty, informed the Secretariat that article 18 was applicable to neither the 1921 nor the 1925 Treaty: *League of Nations Treaty Series* vol. 44, pp. 266–268. The Irish Government wished to have it registered.

It is interesting that the academic literature makes nothing of this. See, for instance, Andreas Zimmerman, "Die Lösung der nordirischen Frage im Lichte des irischen Verfassungsrecht und Völkerrecht", *Zeitschrift für ausländisches öffentliches Recht und Völkerrecht* vol. 54, 1994, p. 182, at p. 194. See also literature cited at p. 183. Strangely, Zimmerman appears to consider the 1925 Treaty as conclusive in international law terms despite the discrepancy which he notes between the views of the two States. His article is then concerned with the issue of reunification as an Irish constitutional law question with clear parallels to Germany before unification.

Index

Index by Judith Lavender

Owners Workshop Manual
for BMW 3-Series

Martynn Randall

Models covered *(4067 - 10AQ1- 304)*

BMW 3-Series (E46) models with 4- and 6-cylinder petrol engines
316i, 318i, 320i, 323i, 325i, 328i & 330i
Saloon, Coupe & Touring

4-cyl engines: 1.8 litre (1796cc), 1.9 litre (1895cc) & 2.0 litre (1995cc), including 'Valvetronic' engines

6-cyl engines: 2.2 litre (2171cc), 2.5 litre (2494cc), 2.8 litre (2793cc) & 3.0 litre (2979cc)

Does NOT cover 1.6 litre (1596cc) petrol engine, diesel models, Compact, Convertible or M3 models
Does NOT cover new 3-Series (E90/E91/E92) range introduced during 2005

ABCDE

A book in the **Haynes Owners Workshop Manual Series**

ISBN **978 0 85733 949 2**

British Library Cataloguing in Publication Data
A catalogue record for this book is available from the British Library.

Printed in the USA

Haynes Publishing
Sparkford, Yeovil, Somerset BA22 7JJ, England

Haynes North America, Inc
861 Lawrence Drive, Newbury Park, California 91320, USA

Haynes Publishing Nordiska AB
Box 1504, 751 45 UPPSALA, Sverige

Printed using 33-ib Resolute Book 65 4.0 from Resolute Forest Products Calhoun, TN mill. Resolute is a member of World Wildlife Fund's Climate Savers programme committed to significantly reducing GHG emissions. This paper uses 50% less wood fibre than traditional offset. The Calhoun Mill is certified to the following sustainable forest management and chain of custody standards: SFI, PEFC and FSC Controlled Wood.

Contents

LIVING WITH YOUR BMW

Contents

REPAIRS & OVERHAUL

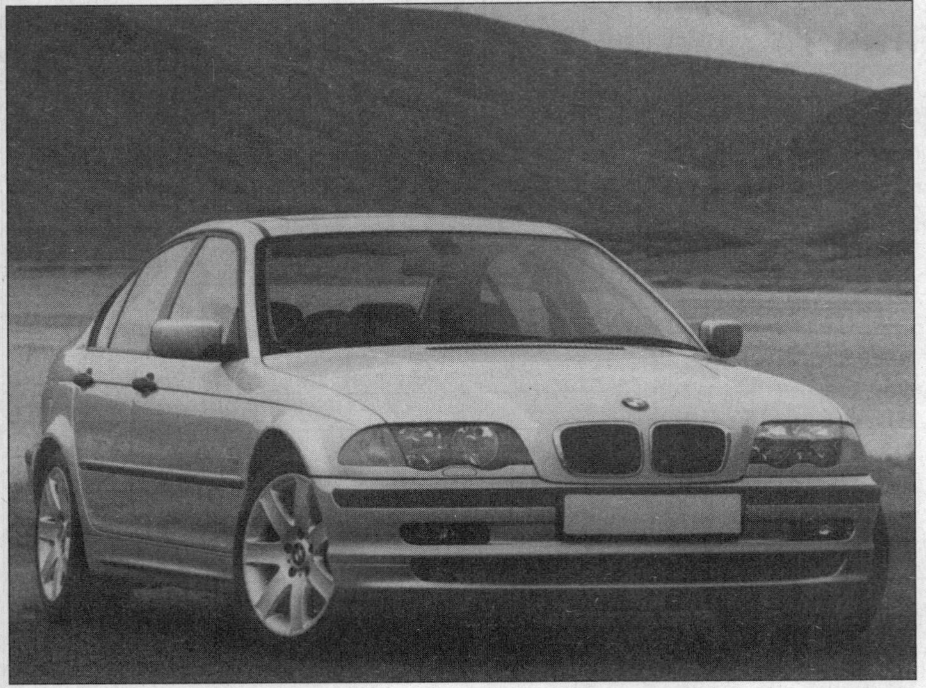

The new BMW 3 Series was introduced in September 1998 and was originally available with a choice of 1.9 litre (1895 cc), 2.5 litre (2494 cc) and 2.8 litre (2793 cc) engines. Later the engine range was extended to include 2.2 litre (2171 cc) and 3.0 litre (2979 cc) DOHC 24V engines, and in March 2001 the 2.0 litre (1995 cc) Valvetronic engine joined the range, followed by the 1.8 litre (1796 cc) version. The Coupe model was 'facelifted' in March of 2003, with redesigned bumpers, head and taillights. At first, models were only available in four-door Saloon form only, but later, a whole range of different body styles was made available.

All engines are derived from the well-proven engines which have appeared in many BMW vehicles. The engine is of four-cylinder (1.8, 1.9 and 2.0 litre engine) or six-cylinder (2.2, 2.5, 2.8 and 3.0 litre engine) overhead camshaft design, mounted longitudinally with the transmission mounted on its rear. Both manual and automatic transmissions were available.

All models have fully-independent front and rear suspension, with suspension struts and trailing arms.

A wide range of standard and optional equipment is available within the BMW 3 Series range to suit most tastes, including central locking, electric windows, air conditioning, an electric sunroof, an anti-lock braking system, a traction control system, a dynamic stability control system, and numerous airbags.

Provided that regular servicing is carried out in accordance with the manufacturer's recommendations, the BMW should prove reliable and very economical. The engine compartment is well-designed, and most of the items requiring frequent attention are easily accessible.

Your BMW 3 Series manual

The aim of this manual is to help you get the best value from your vehicle. It can do so in several ways. It can help you decide what work must be done (even should you choose to get it done by a garage). It will also provide information on routine maintenance and servicing, and give a logical course of action and diagnosis when random faults occur. However, it is hoped that you will use the manual by tackling the work yourself. On simpler jobs it may even be quicker than booking the car into a garage and going there twice, to leave and collect it. Perhaps most important, a lot of money can be saved by avoiding the costs a garage must charge to cover its labour and overheads.

The manual has drawings and descriptions to show the function of the various components so that their layout can be understood. Tasks are described and photographed in a clear step-by-step sequence.

References to the 'left' and 'right' of the vehicle are in the sense of a person in the driver's seat facing forward.

Acknowledgements

Thanks are due to Draper Tools ltd, who provided some of the workshop tools, and to all those people at Sparkford who helped in the production of this manual.

Working on your car can be dangerous. This page shows just some of the potential risks and hazards, with the aim of creating a safety-conscious attitude.

General hazards

Scalding

• Don't remove the radiator or expansion tank cap while the engine is hot.
• Engine oil, transmission fluid or power steering fluid may also be dangerously hot if the engine has recently been running.

Burning

• Beware of burns from the exhaust system and from any part of the engine. Brake discs and drums can also be extremely hot immediately after use.

Crushing

• When working under or near a raised vehicle, always supplement the jack with axle stands, or use drive-on ramps.
Never venture under a car which is only supported by a jack.
• Take care if loosening or tightening high-torque nuts when the vehicle is on stands. Initial loosening and final tightening should be done with the wheels on the ground.

Fire

• Fuel is highly flammable; fuel vapour is explosive.
• Don't let fuel spill onto a hot engine.
• Do not smoke or allow naked lights (including pilot lights) anywhere near a vehicle being worked on. Also beware of creating sparks (electrically or by use of tools).
• Fuel vapour is heavier than air, so don't work on the fuel system with the vehicle over an inspection pit.
• Another cause of fire is an electrical overload or short-circuit. Take care when repairing or modifying the vehicle wiring.
• Keep a fire extinguisher handy, of a type suitable for use on fuel and electrical fires.

Electric shock

• Ignition HT and Xenon headlight voltages can be dangerous, especially to people with heart problems or a pacemaker. Don't work on or near these systems with the engine running or the ignition switched on.

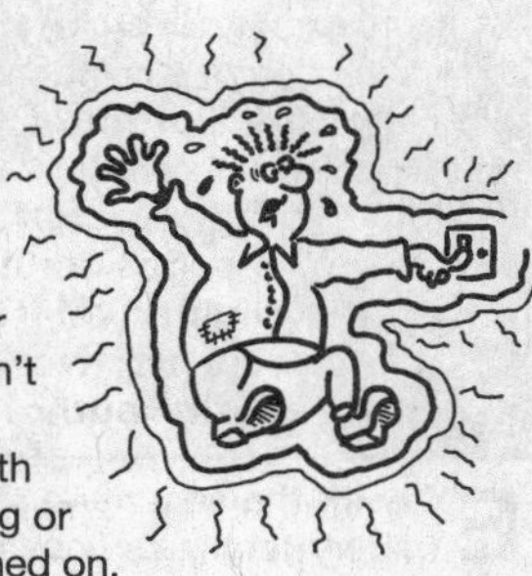

• Mains voltage is also dangerous. Make sure that any mains-operated equipment is correctly earthed. Mains power points should be protected by a residual current device (RCD) circuit breaker.

Fume or gas intoxication

• Exhaust fumes are poisonous; they can contain carbon monoxide, which is rapidly fatal if inhaled. Never run the engine in a confined space such as a garage with the doors shut.
• Fuel vapour is also poisonous, as are the vapours from some cleaning solvents and paint thinners.

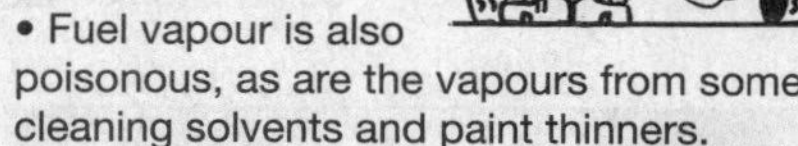

Poisonous or irritant substances

• Avoid skin contact with battery acid and with any fuel, fluid or lubricant, especially antifreeze, brake hydraulic fluid and Diesel fuel. Don't syphon them by mouth. If such a substance is swallowed or gets into the eyes, seek medical advice.
• Prolonged contact with used engine oil can cause skin cancer. Wear gloves or use a barrier cream if necessary. Change out of oil-soaked clothes and do not keep oily rags in your pocket.
• Air conditioning refrigerant forms a poisonous gas if exposed to a naked flame (including a cigarette). It can also cause skin burns on contact.

Asbestos

• Asbestos dust can cause cancer if inhaled or swallowed. Asbestos may be found in gaskets and in brake and clutch linings. When dealing with such components it is safest to assume that they contain asbestos.

Special hazards

Hydrofluoric acid

• This extremely corrosive acid is formed when certain types of synthetic rubber, found in some O-rings, oil seals, fuel hoses etc, are exposed to temperatures above 4000C. The rubber changes into a charred or sticky substance containing the acid. *Once formed, the acid remains dangerous for years. If it gets onto the skin, it may be necessary to amputate the limb concerned.*
• When dealing with a vehicle which has suffered a fire, or with components salvaged from such a vehicle, wear protective gloves and discard them after use.

The battery

• Batteries contain sulphuric acid, which attacks clothing, eyes and skin. Take care when topping-up or carrying the battery.
• The hydrogen gas given off by the battery is highly explosive. Never cause a spark or allow a naked light nearby. Be careful when connecting and disconnecting battery chargers or jump leads.

Air bags

• Air bags can cause injury if they go off accidentally. Take care when removing the steering wheel and trim panels. Special storage instructions may apply.

Diesel injection equipment

• Diesel injection pumps supply fuel at very high pressure. Take care when working on the fuel injectors and fuel pipes.

Warning: Never expose the hands, face or any other part of the body to injector spray; the fuel can penetrate the skin with potentially fatal results.

Remember...

DO

• Do use eye protection when using power tools, and when working under the vehicle.

• Do wear gloves or use barrier cream to protect your hands when necessary.

• Do get someone to check periodically that all is well when working alone on the vehicle.

• Do keep loose clothing and long hair well out of the way of moving mechanical parts.

• Do remove rings, wristwatch etc, before working on the vehicle – especially the electrical system.

• Do ensure that any lifting or jacking equipment has a safe working load rating adequate for the job.

DON'T

• Don't attempt to lift a heavy component which may be beyond your capability – get assistance.

• Don't rush to finish a job, or take unverified short cuts.

• Don't use ill-fitting tools which may slip and cause injury.

• Don't leave tools or parts lying around where someone can trip over them. Mop up oil and fuel spills at once.

• Don't allow children or pets to play in or near a vehicle being worked on.

The following pages are intended to help in dealing with common roadside emergencies and breakdowns. You will find more detailed fault finding information at the back of the manual, and repair information in the main chapters.

If your car won't start and the starter motor doesn't turn

- ☐ If it's a model with automatic transmission, make sure the selector is in P or N.
- ☐ Open the luggage compartment and make sure that the battery terminals are clean and tight.
- ☐ Switch on the headlights and try to start the engine. If the headlights go very dim when you're trying to start, the battery is probably flat. Get out of trouble by jump starting (see next page) using a friend's car.

If your car won't start even though the starter motor turns as normal

- ☐ Is there fuel in the tank?
- ☐ Is there moisture on electrical components under the bonnet? Switch off the ignition, then wipe off any obvious dampness with a dry cloth. Spray a water-repellent aerosol product (WD-40 or equivalent) on ignition and fuel system electrical connectors like those shown in the photos. Pay special attention to the ignition coil wiring connector and HT leads.

A Check that the spark plug HT leads are securely connected by pushing them onto the plugs – 4-cylinder 1895 cc models.

B Check that the HT leads are securely connected to the ignition coil – 4-cylinder 1895 cc models.

C Check that the wiring connector is securely connected to the ignition HT coil – 4-cylinder 1895 cc models.

Check that electrical connections are secure (with the ignition switched off) and spray them with a water-dispersant spray like WD-40 if you suspect a problem due to damp.

D Check the airflow meter wiring connector (where applicable) with the ignition switched off.

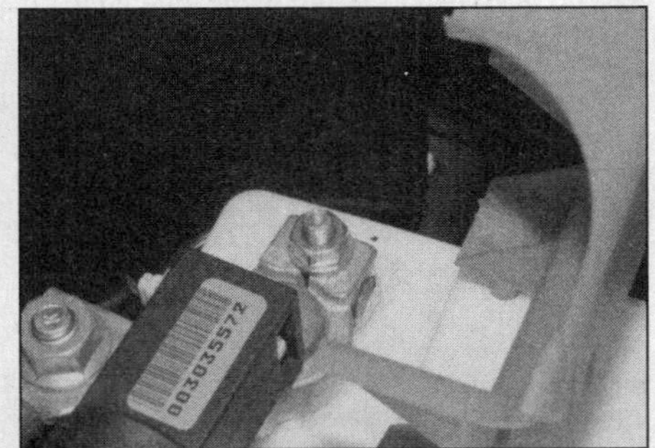

E Check the security and condition of the battery terminals (located in the luggage compartment).

Jump starting

When jump-starting a car using a booster battery, observe the following precautions:

- ✔ Before connecting the booster battery, make sure that the ignition is switched off.
- ✔ Ensure that all electrical equipment (lights, heater, wipers, etc) is switched off.
- ✔ Take note of any special precautions printed on the battery case.
- ✔ Make sure that the booster battery is the same voltage as the discharged one in the vehicle.
- ✔ If the battery is being jump-started from the battery in another vehicle, the two vehicles MUST NOT TOUCH each other.
- ✔ Make sure that the transmission is in neutral (or PARK, in the case of automatic transmission).

Jump starting will get you out of trouble, but you must correct whatever made the battery go flat in the first place. There are three possibilities:

1 The battery has been drained by repeated attempts to start, or by leaving the lights on.

2 The charging system is not working properly (alternator drivebelt slack or broken, alternator wiring fault or alternator itself faulty).

3 The battery itself is at fault (electrolyte low, or battery worn out).

1 Unclip the cover from the jump-start terminal (+) on the right-hand side of the engine compartment behind the suspension turret, and connect the red jump lead to the terminal

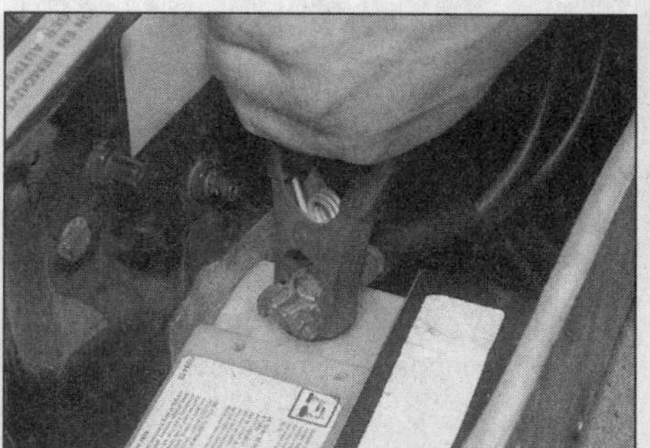

2 Connect the other end of the red lead to the positive (+) terminal of the booster battery.

3 Connect one end of the black jump lead to the negative (-) terminal of the booster battery.

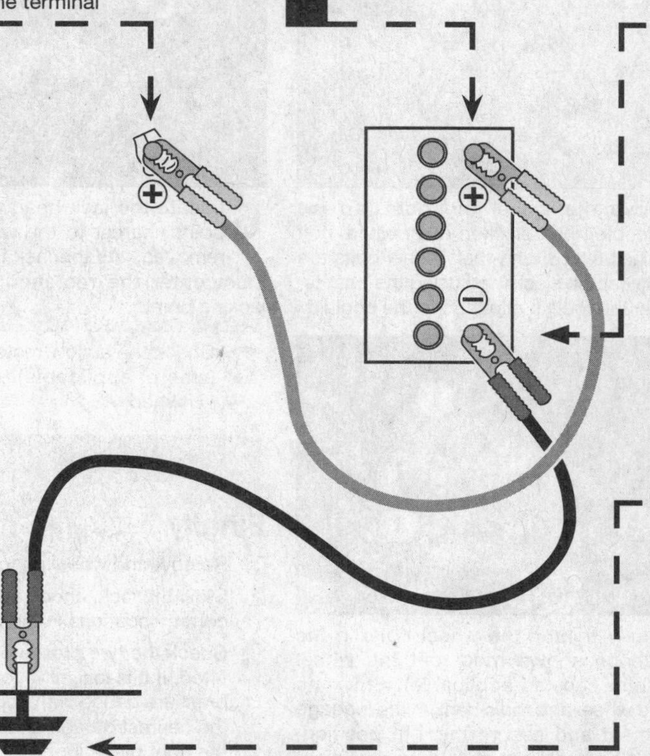

4 Connect the other end of the black jump lead to a bolt or a bracket on the engine block, well away from the battery, on the vehicle to be started. Some models are equipped with a jump start negative terminal adjacent to the master cylinder in the right-hand corner of the engine compartment

5 Make sure that the jump leads will not come into contact with the cooling fan, drivebelts or other moving parts on the engine.

6 Start the engine, then with the engine running at fast idle speed, disconnect the jump leads in the reverse order of connection. Securely refit the cover to the jump start terminal.

Wheel changing

Warning: Do not change a wheel in a situation where you risk being hit by other traffic. On busy roads, try to stop in a lay-by or a gateway. Be wary of passing traffic while changing the wheel – it is easy to become distracted by the job in hand.

Preparation

- ☐ When a puncture occurs, stop as soon as it is safe to do so.
- ☐ Park on firm level ground, if possible, and well out of the way of other traffic.
- ☐ Use hazard warning lights if necessary.
- ☐ If you have one, use a warning triangle to alert other drivers of your presence.
- ☐ Apply the handbrake and engage first or reverse gear (or Park on models with automatic transmission).
- ☐ Chock the wheel diagonally opposite the one being removed – a couple of large stones will do for this.
- ☐ If the ground is soft, use a flat piece of wood to spread the load under the jack.

Changing the wheel

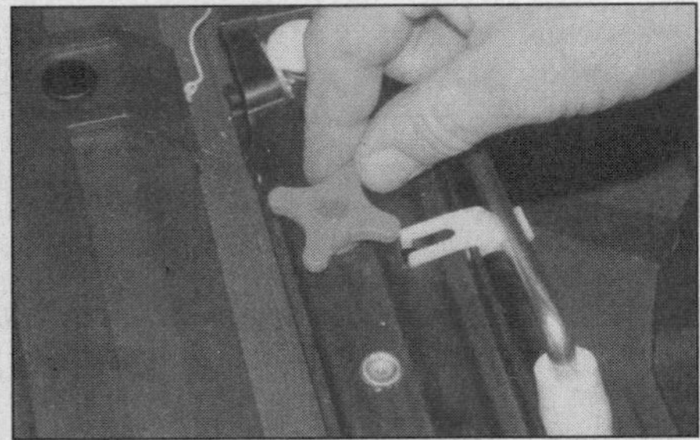

1 The spare wheel and tools are stored in the luggage compartment. Remove the cover then slacken the retaining nut and remove the jack.

2 Undo the wing nut and remove the retaining plate, and lift the spare wheel from the luggage compartment.

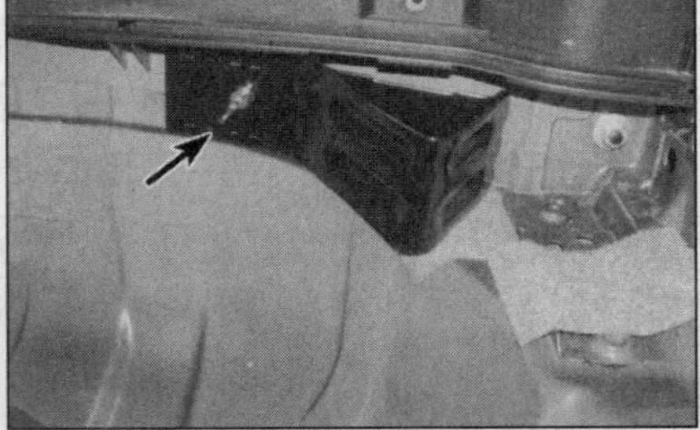

3 Undo the wing nut and remove the wheel chock from the inside of the rear panel. Place the chock behind or in front (as applicable) of the wheel diagonally opposite to the one to be removed.

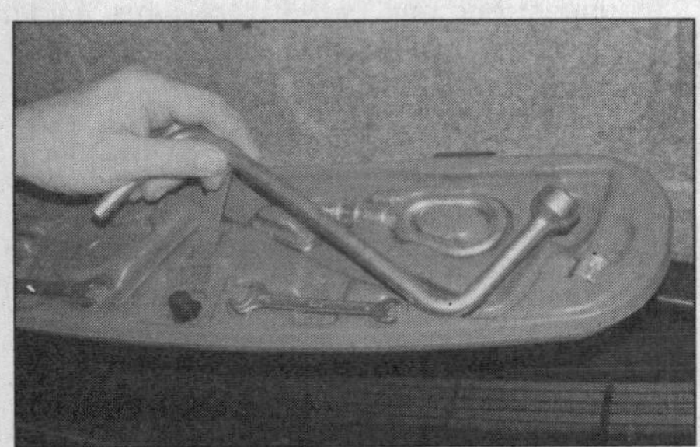

4 Remove the wheelbrace from the luggage compartment lid (Saloon and Coupe) or floor (Touring).

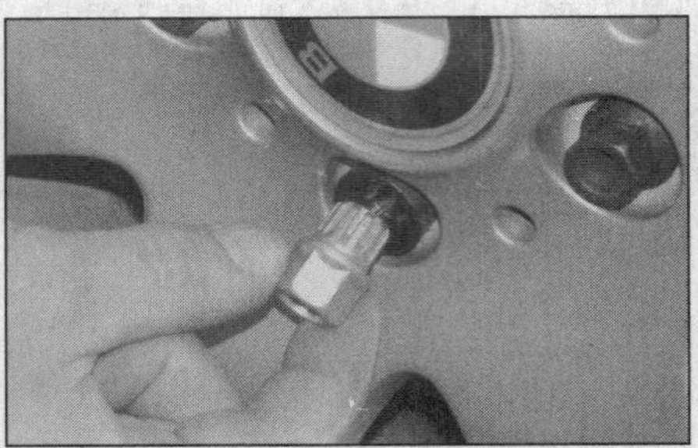

5 Remove the wheel trim/hub cap (as applicable) then slacken each wheel bolt by a half turn. If anti-theft wheel bolts are fitted, they can be slackened using the adapter supplied in the tool kit attached to the boot lid.

6 Locate the jack head under the jacking point nearest to the wheel that is to be removed. As the jack is raised, the head must enter the rectangular recess in the jacking point.

7 Make sure the jack is located on firm ground then turn the jack handle clockwise until the wheel is raised clear of the ground. Unscrew the wheel bolts and remove the wheel. Fit the spare wheel and screw in the bolts. Lightly tighten the bolts with the wheelbrace then lower the vehicle to the ground.

8 Securely tighten the wheel bolts in the sequence shown then refit the wheel trim/hub cap (as applicable). Stow the punctured wheel and tools back in the luggage compartment and secure them in position. Note that the wheel bolts should be slackened and retightened to the specified torque at the earliest possible opportunity.

Finally . . .

- ☐ Remove the wheel chocks.
- ☐ Stow the jack, chock and tools in the correct locations in the car.
- ☐ Check the tyre pressure on the wheel just fitted. If it is low, or if you don't have a pressure gauge with you, drive slowly to the nearest garage and inflate the tyre to the right pressure.
- ☐ Have the damaged tyre or wheel repaired as soon as possible.

Identifying leaks

Puddles on the garage floor or drive, or obvious wetness under the bonnet or underneath the car, suggest a leak that needs investigating. It can sometimes be difficult to decide where the leak is coming from, especially if an engine undershield is fitted. Leaking oil or fluid can also be blown rearwards by the passage of air under the car, giving a false impression of where the problem lies.

Warning: Most automotive oils and fluids are poisonous. Wash them off skin, and change out of contaminated clothing, without delay.

The smell of a fluid leaking from the car may provide a clue to what's leaking. Some fluids are distinctively coloured. It may help to remove the engine undershield, clean the car carefully and to park it over some clean paper overnight as an aid to locating the source of the leak.
Remember that some leaks may only occur while the engine is running.

Sump oil

Engine oil may leak from the drain plug...

Oil from filter

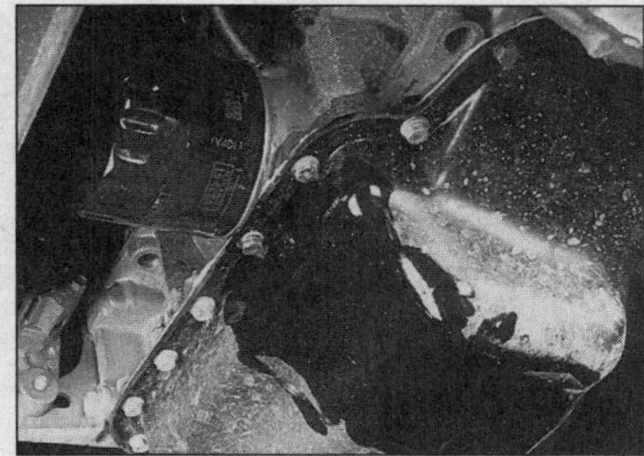

...or from the base of the oil filter.

Gearbox oil

Gearbox oil can leak from the seals at the inboard ends of the driveshafts.

Antifreeze

Leaking antifreeze often leaves a crystalline deposit like this.

Brake fluid

A leak occurring at a wheel is almost certainly brake fluid.

Power steering fluid

Power steering fluid may leak from the pipe connectors on the steering rack.

Towing

When all else fails, you may find yourself having to get a tow home – or of course you may be helping somebody else. Long-distance recovery should only be done by a garage or breakdown service. For shorter distances, DIY towing using another car is easy enough, but observe the following points:

- ☐ Use a proper tow-rope – they are not expensive. The vehicle being towed must display an ON TOW sign in its rear window.
- ☐ Only attach the tow-rope to the towing eyes provided.
- ☐ The towing eye is supplied as part of the tool kit which is fitted to the boot lid. To fit the eye, carefully prise out the access cover from the front/rear bumper (as applicable). Screw the eye into position and tighten it securely
- ☐ Always turn the ignition key to the 'on' position when the vehicle is being towed, so that the steering lock is released, and the direction indicator and brake lights work.
- ☐ Before being towed, release the handbrake and select neutral on the transmission.
- ☐ On models with automatic transmission, set the selector lever to position N. Maximum towing speed is 43 mph, and maximum distance is 90 miles.
- ☐ Note that greater-than-usual pedal pressure will be required to operate the brakes, since the vacuum servo unit is only operational with the engine running.
- ☐ On models with power steering, greater-than-usual steering effort will also be required.
- ☐ The driver of the car being towed must keep the tow-rope taut at all times to avoid snatching.
- ☐ Make sure that both drivers know the route before setting off.
- ☐ Only drive at moderate speeds and keep the distance towed to a minimum. Drive smoothly and allow plenty of time for slowing down at junctions.

Introduction

There are some very simple checks which need only take a few minutes to carry out, but which could save you a lot of inconvenience and expense.

These *Weekly checks* require no great skill or special tools, and the small amount of time they take to perform could prove to be very well spent, for example:

☐Keeping an eye on tyre condition and pressures, will not only help to stop them wearing out prematurely, but could also save your life.

☐Many breakdowns are caused by electrical problems. Battery-related faults are particularly common, and a quick check on a regular basis will often prevent the majority of these.

☐If your car develops a brake fluid leak, the first time you might know about it is when your brakes don't work properly. Checking the level regularly will give advance warning of this kind of problem.

☐If the oil or coolant levels run low, the cost of repairing any engine damage will be far greater than fixing the leak, for example.

Underbonnet check points

◀ **4-cylinder engine (2.0 litre shown)**

A *Engine oil level dipstick*
B *Engine oil filler cap*
C *Coolant expansion tank*
D *Brake and clutch fluid reservoir*
E *Screen washer fluid reservoir*

◀ **6-cylinder engine (2.5 litre shown)**

A *Engine oil level dipstick*
B *Engine oil filler cap*
C *Coolant expansion tank*
D *Brake and clutch fluid reservoir*
E *Screen washer fluid reservoir*

Engine oil level

Before you start

✔ Make sure that the car is on level ground.
✔ Check the oil level before the car is driven, or at least 5 minutes after the engine has been switched off.

If the oil is checked immediately after driving the vehicle, some of the oil will remain in the upper engine components, resulting in an inaccurate reading on the dipstick.

The correct oil

Modern engines place great demands on their oil. It is very important that the correct oil for your car is used (see *Lubricants and fluids*).

Car care

- If you have to add oil frequently, you should check whether you have any oil leaks. Place some clean paper under the car overnight, and check for stains in the morning. If there are no leaks, then the engine may be burning oil.
- Always maintain the level between the upper and lower dipstick marks (see photo 3). If the level is too low, severe engine damage may occur. Oil seal failure may result if the engine is overfilled by adding too much oil.

1 The dipstick top is often brightly coloured for easy identification (see *Underbonnet check points* for exact location). Withdraw the dipstick.

2 Using a clean rag or paper towel remove all oil from the dipstick. Insert the clean dipstick into the tube as far as it will go, then withdraw it again.

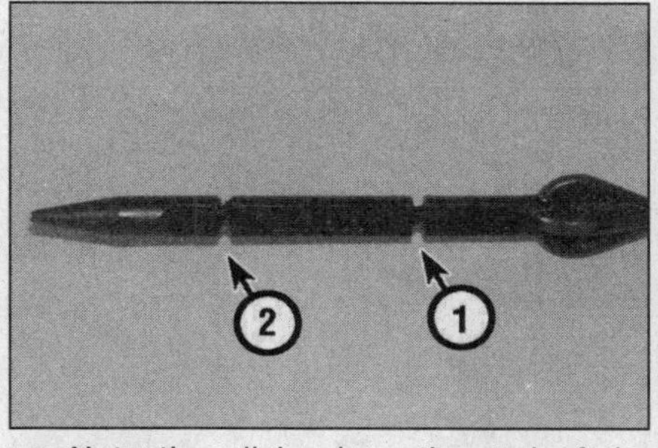

3 Note the oil level on the end of the dipstick, which should be between the upper maximum mark (1) and lower minimum mark (2). Approximately 1.0 litre of oil will raise the level from the lower mark to the upper mark.

4 Oil is added through the filler cap. Unscrew the cap and top-up the level; a funnel may help to reduce spillage. Add the oil slowly, checking the level on the dipstick often. Don't overfill (see *Car care*).

Coolant level

Warning: Do not attempt to remove the expansion tank pressure cap when the engine is hot, as there is a very great risk of scalding. Do not leave open containers of coolant about, as it is poisonous.

Car care

- With a sealed-type cooling system, adding coolant should not be necessary on a regular basis. If frequent topping-up is required, it is likely there is a leak. Check the radiator, all hoses and joint faces for signs of staining or wetness, and rectify as necessary.
- It is important that antifreeze is used in the cooling system all year round, not just during the winter months. Don't top-up with water alone, as the antifreeze will become diluted.

1 The coolant expansion tank incorporates a float device which indicates the level of coolant. When the upper end of the float protrudes no more than 20 mm above the filler neck, the level is correct. See the information adjacent to the filler cap.

2 If topping up is necessary, **wait until the engine is cold**. Slowly unscrew the expansion tank cap, to release any pressure present in the cooling system, and remove it.

3 Add a mixture of water and antifreeze to the expansion tank until the top of the coolant level indicator float protrudes no more than 20 mm above the filler neck. Refit the cap and tighten it securely.

Brake and clutch fluid level

Warning:
- ***Brake fluid can harm your eyes and damage painted surfaces, so use extreme caution when handling and pouring it.***
- ***Do not use fluid that has been standing open for some time, as it absorbs moisture from the air, which can cause a dangerous loss of braking effectiveness.***

- ***Make sure that your car is on level ground.***
- ***The fluid level in the reservoir will drop slightly as the brake pads wear down, but the fluid level must never be allowed to drop below the DANGER mark.***

Safety first!

- If the reservoir requires repeated topping-up this is an indication of a fluid leak somewhere in the system, which should be investigated immediately.
- If a leak is suspected, the car should not be driven until the braking system has been checked. Never take any risks where brakes are concerned

1 The MAX and MIN marks are indicated on the side of the reservoir. The fluid level must be kept between the marks at all times.

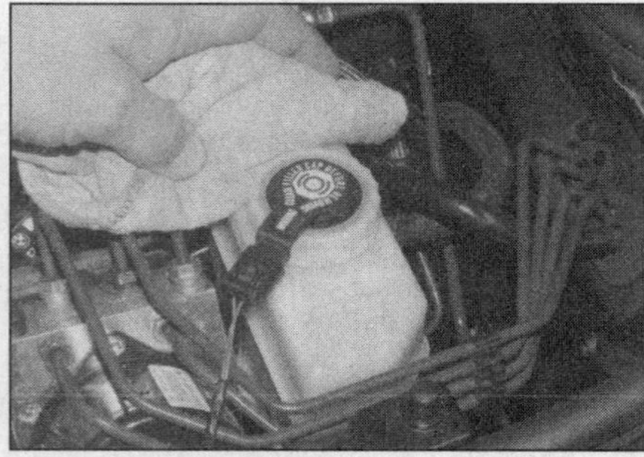

2 If topping-up is necessary, first wipe clean the area around the filler cap to prevent dirt entering the hydraulic system.

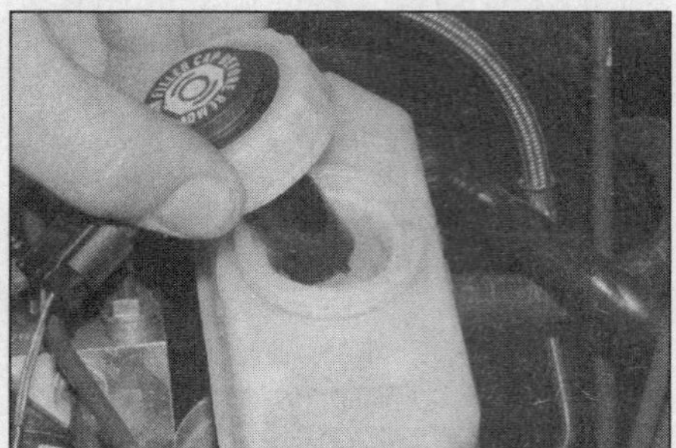

3 Unscrew the reservoir cap and carefully lift it out of position, taking care not to damage the level switch float. Inspect the reservoir, if the fluid is dirty the hydraulic system should be drained and refilled (see Chapter 1).

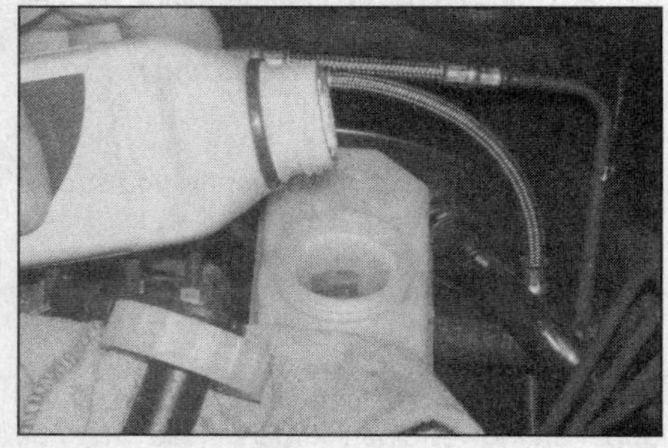

4 Carefully add fluid taking care not to spill it onto the surrounding components. Use only the specified fluid; mixing different types can cause damage to the system. After topping-up to the correct level, securely refit the cap and wipe off any spilt fluid.

Power steering fluid level

✔ Park the vehicle on level ground.
✔ Set the steering wheel straight-ahead.
✔ The engine should be turned off.

Safety first!

- The need for frequent topping-up indicates a leak, which should be investigated immediately.

1 The reservoir is located near the front of the engine compartment. Prise up the plastic rivets, and remove the air inlet hood from the front of the engine compartment (where applicable). Wipe clean the area around the reservoir filler neck and unscrew the filler cap/dipstick from the reservoir.

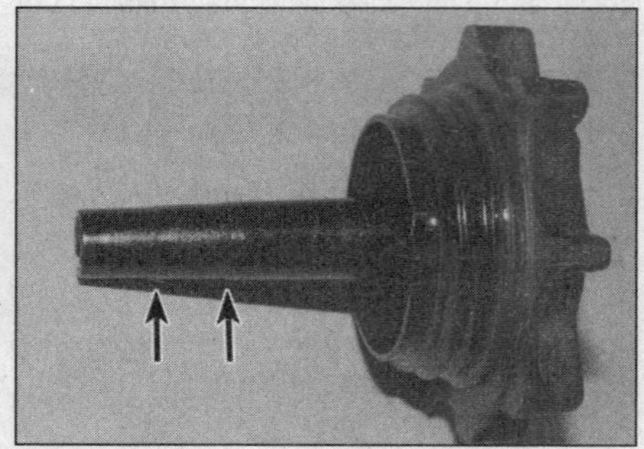

2 The fluid level should be between MIN and MAX.

3 When topping-up, use the specified type of fluid and do not overfill the reservoir. When the level is correct, securely refit the cap and switch off the engine.

Screen washer fluid level*

** On models with a headlight washer system, the screenwash is also used to clean the headlights*

● Screenwash additives not only keep the windscreen clean during bad weather, they also prevent the washer system freezing in cold weather – which is when you are likely to need it most. Don't top-up using plain water, as the screenwash will become diluted, and will freeze in cold weather.

Warning: On no account use engine coolant antifreeze in the screen washer system – this may damage the paintwork.

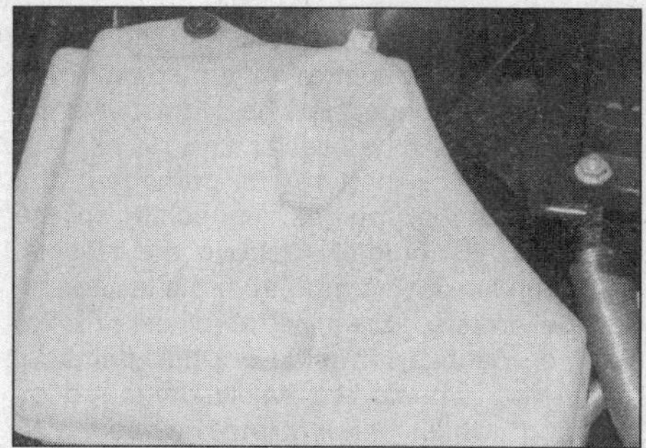

1 The screen washer fluid reservoir is located in the front right-hand corner of the engine compartment. The level is visible through the reservoir body, if topping-up is necessary, open up the cap.

2 When topping-up, add a screenwash additive in the quantities recommended by the manufacturer.

Wiper blades

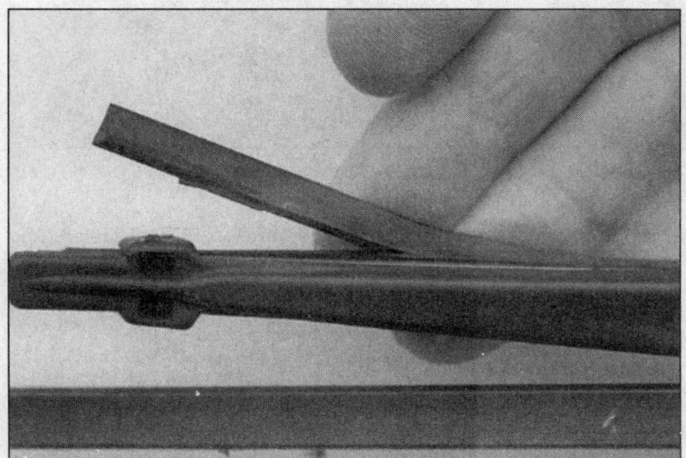

1 Check the condition of the wiper blades; if they are cracked or show any signs of deterioration, or if the glass swept area is smeared, renew them. Wiper blades should be renewed annually.

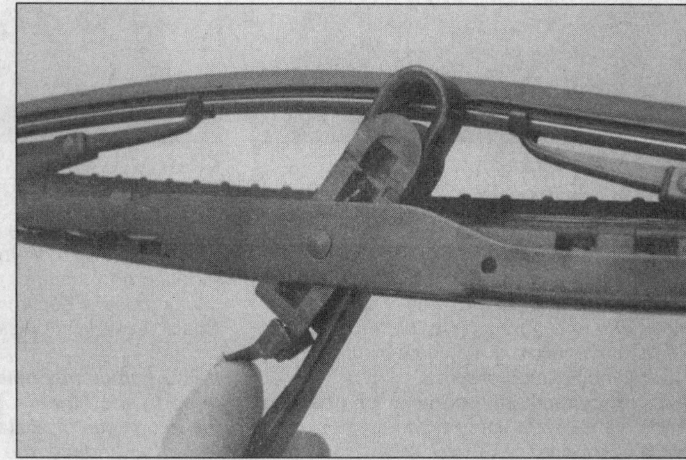

2 To remove a wiper blade, pull the arm fully away from the screen until it locks. Swivel the blade through 90°, press the locking tab with your fingers and slide the blade out of the arm's hooked end.

Tyre condition and pressure

It is very important that tyres are in good condition, and at the correct pressure - having a tyre failure at any speed is highly dangerous. Tyre wear is influenced by driving style - harsh braking and acceleration, or fast cornering, will all produce more rapid tyre wear. As a general rule, the front tyres wear out faster than the rears. Interchanging the tyres from front to rear ("rotating" the tyres) may result in more even wear. However, if this is completely effective, you may have the expense of replacing all four tyres at once!

Remove any nails or stones embedded in the tread before they penetrate the tyre to cause deflation. If removal of a nail does reveal that the tyre has been punctured, refit the nail so that its point of penetration is marked. Then immediately change the wheel, and have the tyre repaired by a tyre dealer.

Regularly check the tyres for damage in the form of cuts or bulges, especially in the sidewalls. Periodically remove the wheels, and clean any dirt or mud from the inside and outside surfaces. Examine the wheel rims for signs of rusting, corrosion or other damage. Light alloy wheels are easily damaged by "kerbing" whilst parking; steel wheels may also become dented or buckled. A new wheel is very often the only way to overcome severe damage.

New tyres should be balanced when they are fitted, but it may become necessary to re-balance them as they wear, or if the balance weights fitted to the wheel rim should fall off. Unbalanced tyres will wear more quickly, as will the steering and suspension components. Wheel imbalance is normally signified by vibration, particularly at a certain speed (typically around 50 mph). If this vibration is felt only through the steering, then it is likely that just the front wheels need balancing. If, however, the vibration is felt through the whole car, the rear wheels could be out of balance. Wheel balancing should be carried out by a tyre dealer or garage.

1 ***Tread Depth - visual check***
The original tyres have tread wear safety bands (B), which will appear when the tread depth reaches approximately 1.6 mm. The band positions are indicated by a triangular mark on the tyre sidewall (A).

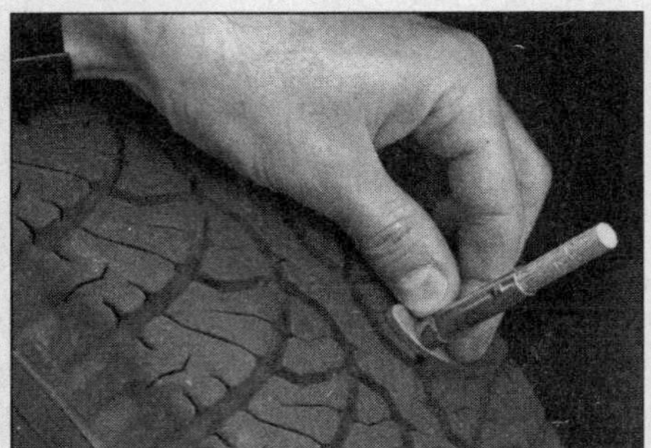

2 ***Tread Depth - manual check***
Alternatively, tread wear can be monitored with a simple, inexpensive device known as a tread depth indicator gauge.

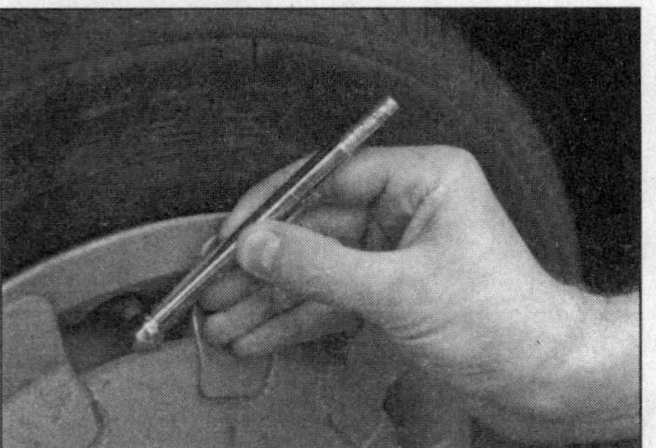

3 ***Tyre Pressure Check***
Check the tyre pressures regularly with the tyres cold. Do not adjust the tyre pressures immediately after the vehicle has been used, or an inaccurate setting will result.

Tyre tread wear patterns

Shoulder Wear

Underinflation (wear on both sides)
Under-inflation will cause overheating of the tyre, because the tyre will flex too much, and the tread will not sit correctly on the road surface. This will cause a loss of grip and excessive wear, not to mention the danger of sudden tyre failure due to heat build-up.
Check and adjust pressures
Incorrect wheel camber (wear on one side)
Repair or renew suspension parts
Hard cornering
Reduce speed!

Centre Wear

Overinflation
Over-inflation will cause rapid wear of the centre part of the tyre tread, coupled with reduced grip, harsher ride, and the danger of shock damage occurring in the tyre casing.
Check and adjust pressures

If you sometimes have to inflate your car's tyres to the higher pressures specified for maximum load or sustained high speed, don't forget to reduce the pressures to normal afterwards.

Uneven Wear

Front tyres may wear unevenly as a result of wheel misalignment. Most tyre dealers and garages can check and adjust the wheel alignment (or "tracking") for a modest charge.
Incorrect camber or castor
Repair or renew suspension parts
Malfunctioning suspension
Repair or renew suspension parts
Unbalanced wheel
Balance tyres
Incorrect toe setting
Adjust front wheel alignment
Note: *The feathered edge of the tread which typifies toe wear is best checked by feel.*

Battery

Caution: Before carrying out any work on the vehicle battery, read the precautions given in 'Safety first!' at the start of this manual.

✔ Make sure that the battery tray is in good condition, and that the clamp is tight. Corrosion on the tray, retaining clamp and the battery itself can be removed with a solution of water and baking soda, after removing the affected components from the car (see Chapter 5A). Thoroughly rinse all cleaned areas with water. Any metal parts damaged by corrosion should be covered with a zinc-based primer, then painted.

✔ Periodically (approximately every three months), check the charge condition of the battery as described in Chapter 5A.

✔ If the battery is flat, and you need to jump start your vehicle, see *Roadside Repairs*.

1 The battery is located in the right-hand rear corner of the luggage compartment. Rotate the fasteners 90° anti-clockwise, and partially remove the left-hand side luggage compartment side trim, and unclip the battery cover/first aid kit tray from the right-hand side of the luggage compartment.

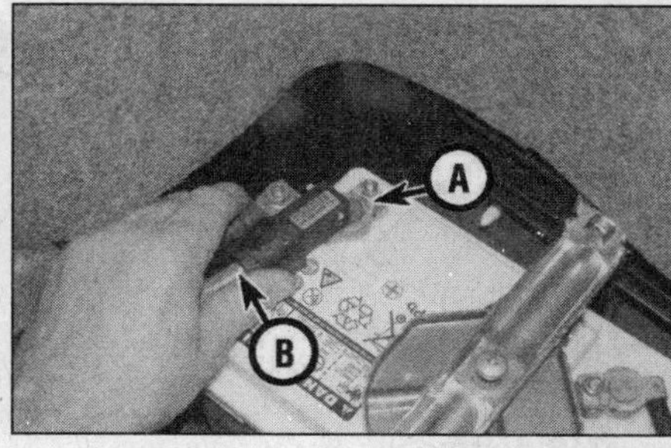

2 Check the tightness of battery clamps (A) to ensure good electrical connections. You should not be able to move them. Also check each cable (B) for cracks and frayed conductors.

Battery corrosion can be kept to a minimum by applying a layer of petroleum jelly to the clamps and terminals after they are reconnected.

3 If corrosion (white, fluffy deposits) is evident, remove the cables from the battery terminals, clean them with a small wire brush, then refit them. Automotive stores sell a tool for cleaning the battery post . . .

4 . . . as well as the battery cable clamps.

Bulbs and fuses

✔ Check all external lights and the horn. Refer to the appropriate Sections of Chapter 12 for details if any of the circuits are found to be inoperative.

✔ Visually check all accessible wiring connectors, harnesses and retaining clips for security, and for signs of chafing or damage.

If you need to check your brake lights and indicators unaided, back up to a wall or garage door and operate the lights. The reflected light should show if they are working properly.

1 If a single indicator light, brake light or headlight has failed, it is likely that a bulb has blown and will need to be renewed. Refer to Chapter 12 for details. If both brake lights have failed, it is possible that the switch has failed (see Chapter 9).

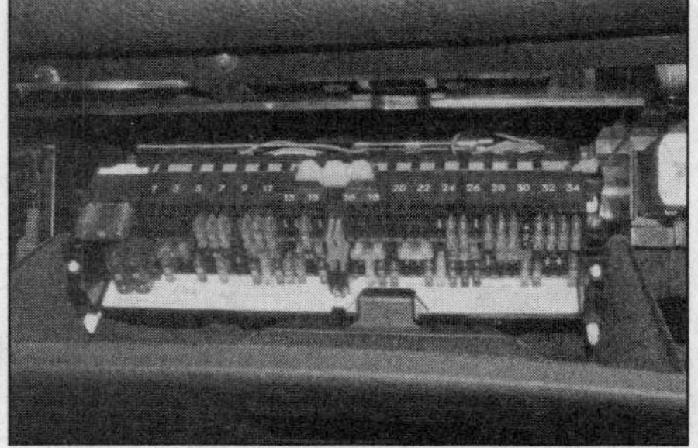

2 If more than one indicator light or tail light has failed check that a fuse has not blown or that there is a fault in the circuit (see Chapter 12). The fuses are located in the fusebox in the passenger side glovebox. Details of the circuits protected by the fuses are shown on the card in the fusebox. Open the glovebox, rotate the fasteners 90 degrees anti-clockwise and lower the fusebox cover from the roof of the glovebox.

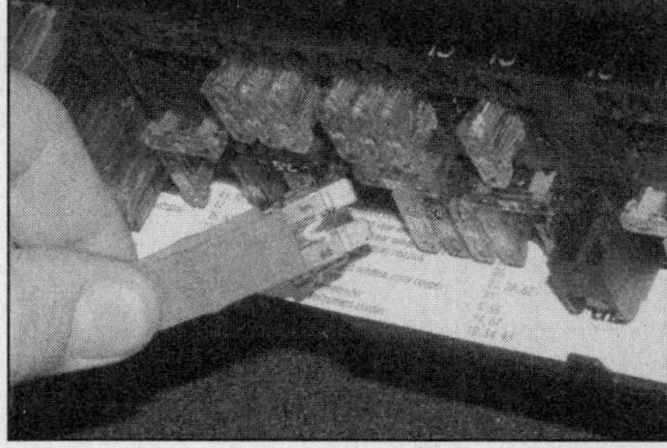

3 To renew a blown fuse, simply pull it out and fit a new fuse of the correct rating (see Chapter 12). If the fuse blows again, it is important that you find out why – a complete checking procedure is given in Chapter 12.

Lubricants and fluids

Engine	
M43TU, M52TU and M54 engines	BMW long-life oil* SAE 0W-40 or SAE 5W-30 (fully synthetic) to ACEA A3/B3, API SJ/CD, ECII
N42 engines	BMW long-life oil* SAE 0W-30 (fully synthetic) to ACEA A3, API SJ/CD, ECII
N46 engines	BMW long-life oil* SAE 5W-30 (fully synthetic) to ACEA A3, API SJ/CD, ECII
Cooling system	Long-life ethylene glycol based antifreeze*
Manual transmission	BMW Lifetime transmission oil*
Automatic transmission	BMW Life-time transmission oil*
Final drive unit	SAE 75W/90*
Braking system	Hydraulic fluid to DOT 4
Power steering	Dexron III*

** Refer to your BMW dealer for brand name and type recommendations*

Tyre pressures

The tyre pressures are given on a label affixed to the driver's door aperture

Chapter 1
Routine maintenance and servicing

Contents

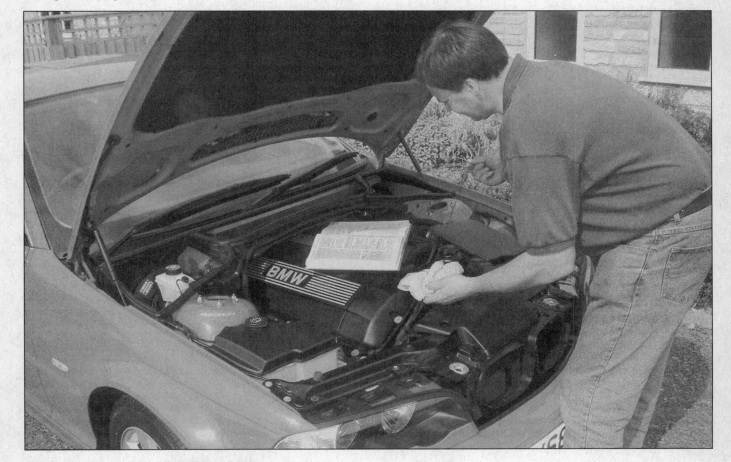

Degrees of difficulty

Easy, suitable for novice with little experience	**Fairly easy,** suitable for beginner with some experience	**Fairly difficult,** suitable for competent DIY mechanic	**Difficult,** suitable for experienced DIY mechanic	**Very difficult,** suitable for expert DIY or professional 

Lubricants and fluids

Refer to *Weekly checks* on page 0•16

Capacities

Engine oil (including filter)

4-cylinder engines:	
1796 cc (engine codes N42 B18 and N46 B18)	4.25 litres
1895 cc (engine code M43TU B19)	4.0 litres
1995 cc (engine codes N42 B20 and N46 B20)	4.25 litres
6-cylinder engines (engine codes M52TU and M54)	6.5 litres

Cooling system

4-cylinder engines:	
1796 cc (engine codes N42 B18 and N46 B18)	7.0 litres
1895 cc (engine code M43TU B19)	6.0 litres
1995 cc (engine codes N42 B20 and N46 B20)	7.0 litres
6-cylinder engines (engine codes M52TU and M54)	8.4 litres

Transmission

Manual transmission:	
5-speed	1.50 litres
6-speed	1.75 litres
Automatic transmission	3.0 litres

Final drive unit

4-cylinder models	1.1 litres
6-cylinder models	1.7 litre

Power-assisted steering

All models (approximate)	1.5 litres

Fuel tank

All models (approximate)	65 litres

Cooling system

Antifreeze mixture:	
50% antifreeze	Protection down to -30°C

Note: *Refer to antifreeze manufacturer for latest recommendations.*

Ignition system

Spark plugs:	
All engines except N46	Bosch FGR 7 DQP
N46 engines	Bosch FR7KPP332

Brakes

Brake pad friction material minimum thickness	2.0 mm
Handbrake shoe friction material minimum thickness	1.5 mm

Torque wrench settings

	Nm	lbf ft
Cylinder block coolant drain plug	25	18
Engine sump oil drain plug:		
M12 plug	25	18
M18 plug	30	22
M22 plug	60	44
Roadwheel bolts	100	74
Spark plugs:		
M12 thread	23	17
M14 thread	30	22

When the vehicle is new, it should be serviced by a dealer service department (or other workshop recognised by the vehicle manufacturer as providing the same standard of service) in order to preserve the warranty. The vehicle manufacturer may reject warranty claims if you are unable to prove that servicing has been carried out as and when specified, using only original equipment parts or parts certified to be of equivalent quality.

All E46 3-Series models are equipped with a service display in the centre of the instrument panel, which shows the type of service next due, and the distance remaining until the service is required. Once that distance is reduced to zero, the display then shows the distance since the service was due. Two types of service are specified, an 'Oil Service' and an 'Inspection Service'. For more details, refer to the Owner's Handbook supplied with the vehicle.

There are two different inspection services, Inspection I and Inspection II, these should be carried out alternately with some additional items to be included every second Inspection II. If you are unclear as to which inspection schedule was carried out last time start with Inspection II (including the additional items).

To reset the service interval display indicator on some models a BMW service tool is required (see Section 8). Aftermarket alternatives to the BMW tool are produced by several leading tool manufacturers and should be available from larger car accessory shops.

Every 250 miles or weekly

- ☐ Refer to *Weekly checks*

Oil service

- ☐ Renew the engine oil and filter (Section 3)
- ☐ Check the front brake pad thickness (Section 4)
- ☐ Check the rear brake pad thickness (Section 5)
- ☐ Check the operation of the handbrake (Section 6)
- ☐ Renew the pollen filter (Section 7)
- ☐ Reset the service interval display (Section 8)

Inspection I

Carry out all the operations listed under Oil service, along with the following:

- ☐ Check all underbonnet components and hoses for fluid leaks (Section 9)
- ☐ Check the condition of the auxiliary drivebelt(s), and adjust/renew if necessary (Section 10)
- ☐ Check the steering and suspension components for condition and security (Section 11)
- ☐ Check the exhaust system and mountings (Section 12)
- ☐ Check the condition and operation of the seat belts (Section 13)
- ☐ Lubricate all hinges and locks (Section 14)
- ☐ Check the headlight beam alignment (Section 15)
- ☐ Check the operation of the windscreen/headlight washer system(s) (as applicable) (Section 16)
- ☐ Check the engine management system (Section 17)
- ☐ Carry out a road test (Section 18)

Inspection II

Carry out all the operations listed under Inspection I, along with the following:

- ☐ Renew the spark plugs (Section 19)
- ☐ Renew the air filter element (Section 20)
- ☐ Check the condition of the driveshaft gaiters (Section 21)
- ☐ Check the condition of the handbrake shoe linings (Section 22)

Every second Inspection II

- ☐ Renew the fuel filter (Section 23)

Every 2 years

Note: *BMW specify that the following should be carried out regardless of mileage:*

- ☐ Renew the brake fluid (Section 24)

Every 4 years

Note: *BMW specify that the following should be carried out regardless of mileage:*

- ☐ Renew the coolant (Section 25)

Underbonnet view of a 2.0 litre N42 engine model

1 *Engine oil filler cap*
2 *Engine oil dipstick*
3 *Oil filter cover*
4 *Brake and clutch fluid reservoir*
5 *Air cleaner housing*
6 *Coolant expansion tank*
7 *Washer fluid reservoir*
8 *Pollen filter cover*
9 *Engine electrical box*
10 *Secondary air injection pump*
11 *Suspension strut upper mounting*

Underbonnet view of a 2.5 litre M54 engine model

1 *Engine oil filler cap*
2 *Engine oil dipstick*
3 *Oil filter cover*
4 *Brake and clutch fluid reservoir*
5 *Air cleaner housing*
6 *Coolant expansion tank*
7 *Washer fluid reservoir*
8 *Pollen filter cover*
9 *Engine electrical box*
10 *Suspension strut upper mounting*

Front underbody view (2.0 litre model shown – other models similar)

1 *Engine oil (sump) drain plug*
2 *Manual transmission drain plug*
3 *Manual transmission filler/level plug*
4 *Front exhaust pipes*
5 *Front suspension lower arm*
6 *Front brake caliper*
7 *Steering rack*
8 *Anti-roll bar*
9 *Coolant drain plug*

Rear underbody view (2.0 litre models shown – other models similar)

1 *Fuel tank*
2 *Exhaust tail box*
3 *Final drive unit*
4 *Suspension trailing arm*
5 *Suspension lower arm*
6 *Shock absorber*
7 *Driveshaft*
8 *Anti-roll bar*
9 *Carbon canister*

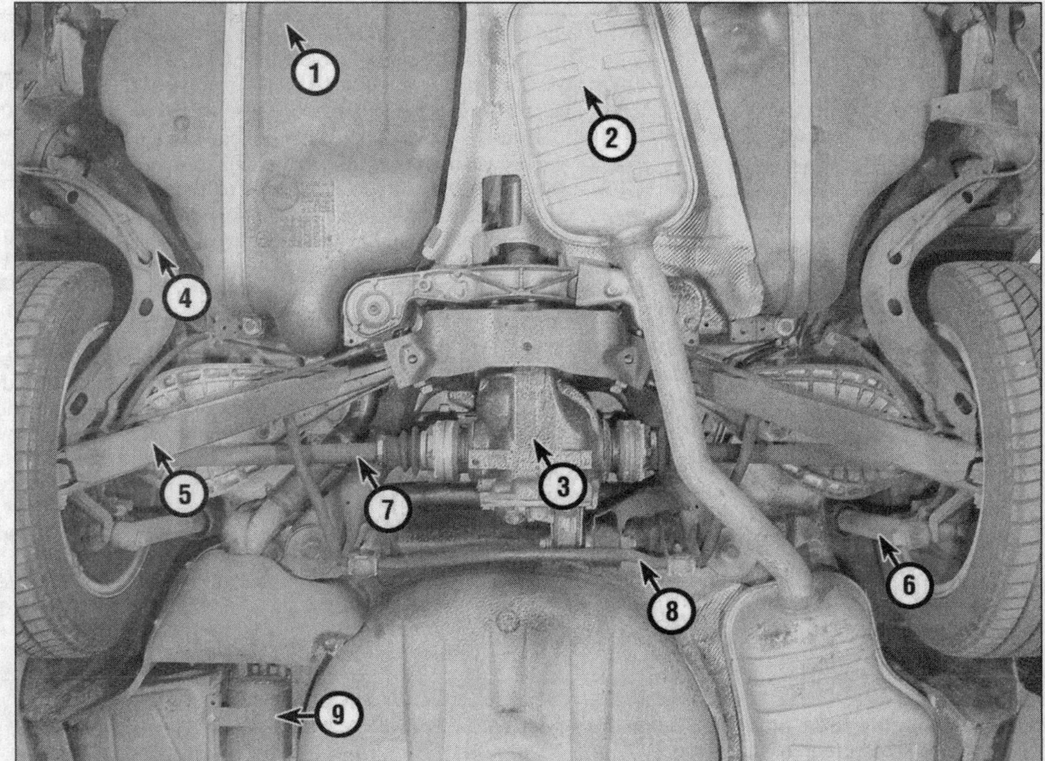

1 Introduction

1 This Chapter is designed to help the home mechanic maintain his/her vehicle for safety, economy, long life and peak performance.

2 The Chapter contains a master maintenance schedule, followed by Sections dealing specifically with each task in the schedule. Visual checks, adjustments, component renewal and other helpful items are included. Refer to the accompanying illustrations of the engine compartment and the underside of the vehicle for the locations of the various components.

3 Servicing your vehicle in accordance with the service indicator display and the following Sections will provide a planned maintenance programme, which should result in a long and reliable service life. This is a comprehensive plan, so maintaining some items but not others at the specified service intervals, will not produce the same results.

4 As you service your vehicle, you will discover that many of the procedures can – and should – be grouped together, because of the particular procedure being performed, or because of the proximity of two otherwise-unrelated components to one another. For example, if the vehicle is raised for any reason, the exhaust can be inspected at the same time as the suspension and steering components.

5 The first step in this maintenance programme is to prepare yourself before the actual work begins. Read through all the Sections relevant to the work to be carried out, then make a list and gather all the parts and tools required. If a problem is encountered, seek advice from a parts specialist, or a dealer service department.

2 Regular maintenance

1 If, from the time the vehicle is new, the routine maintenance schedule is followed closely, and frequent checks are made of fluid levels and high-wear items, as suggested throughout this manual, the engine will be kept in relatively good running condition, and the need for additional work will be minimised.

2 It is possible that there will be times when the engine is running poorly due to the lack of regular maintenance. This is even more likely if a used vehicle, which has not received regular and frequent maintenance checks, is purchased. In such cases, additional work may need to be carried out, outside of the regular maintenance intervals.

3 If engine wear is suspected, a compression test (refer to the relevant Part of Chapter 2) will provide valuable information regarding the overall performance of the main internal components. Such a test can be used as a basis to decide on the extent of the work to be carried out. If, for example, a compression test indicates serious internal engine wear, conventional maintenance as described in this Chapter will not greatly improve the performance of the engine, and may prove a waste of time and money, unless extensive overhaul work is carried out first.

4 The following series of operations are those most often required to improve the performance of a generally poor-running engine:

Primary operations

a) Clean, inspect and test the battery (See 'Weekly checks').
b) Check all the engine-related fluids (See 'Weekly checks').
c) Check the condition and tension of the auxiliary drivebelt (Section 10).
d) Renew the spark plugs (Section 19).
e) Check the condition of the air filter, and renew if necessary (Section 20).
f) Check the fuel filter (Section 23).
g) Check the condition of all hoses, and check for fluid leaks (Section 9).

5 If the above operations do not prove fully effective, carry out the following secondary operations:

Secondary operations

All items listed under *Primary operations*, plus the following:

a) Check the charging system (see Chapter 5A).
b) Check the ignition system (see Chapter 5B).
c) Check the fuel system (see Chapter 4A).

Oil service

3 Engine oil and filter renewal

1 Frequent oil and filter changes are the most important preventative maintenance work which can be undertaken by the DIY owner. As engine oil ages, it becomes diluted and contaminated, which leads to premature engine wear.

2 Before starting this procedure, gather together all the necessary tools and materials. Also make sure you have plenty of clean rags and newspapers handy, to mop-up any spills. Ideally, the engine oil should be warm, as it will drain better, and more built-up sludge will be removed with it. Take care, however, not to touch the exhaust or any other hot parts of the engine when working under the car. To avoid any possibility of scalding, and to protect yourself from possible skin irritants and other harmful contaminants in used engine oils, it is advisable to wear gloves. Access to the underside of the car will be improved if it can be raised on a lift, driven onto ramps, or jacked up and supported on axle stands (see *Jacking and vehicle support*). Whichever method is chosen, make sure the car remains level, or if it is at an angle, so that the drain plug is at the lowest point. Where necessary remove the splash guard from under the engine. On vehicles equipped with front reinforcement plate between the front suspension lower control arms, access to the sump plug is via a removable flap in the plate **(see illustration)**.

3.2 Access to the sump plug is via a flap in the reinforcement plate

3.5a Screw-fit oil filter cover

3 Working in the engine compartment, locate the oil filter housing on the left-hand side of the engine, in front of the inlet manifold.

4 Place a wad of rag around the bottom of the housing to absorb any spilt oil.

5 Using a special oil filter removal tool or socket, unscrew and remove the cover, and lift the filter cartridge out. It is possible to unscrew the cover using a strap wench **(see illustrations)**. The oil will drain from the housing back into the sump as the cover is removed.

6 Recover the O-rings from the cover.

7 Using a clean rag, wipe the mating faces of the housing and cover.

8 Fit new O-rings to the cover **(see illustration)**.

9 Lower the new filter cartridge into the housing.

10 Smear a little clean engine oil on the O-rings, refit the cover and tighten it to 25 Nm (18 lbf ft) if using the special filter removal tool, or securely if using a strap wrench.

11 Working under the car, slacken the sump drain plug about half a turn **(see illustration 3.2)**. Position the draining container under the drain plug, then remove the plug completely. If possible, try to keep the plug pressed into the sump while unscrewing it by hand the last couple of turns.

12 Recover the drain plug sealing ring.

13 Allow some time for the old oil to drain, noting that it may be necessary to reposition the container as the oil flow slows to a trickle.

14 After all the oil has drained, wipe off the drain plug with a clean rag. Check the sealing washer condition, and renew it if necessary. Clean the area around the drain plug opening, then refit and tighten the plug **(see illustration)**.

15 Remove the old oil and all tools from under the car, then lower the car to the ground (if applicable).

16 Remove the dipstick then unscrew the oil filler cap from the cylinder head cover. Fill the engine, using the correct grade and type of oil (see *Weekly checks*). An oil can spout or funnel may help to reduce spillage. Pour in half the specified quantity of oil first, then wait a few minutes for the oil to fall to the sump. Continue adding oil a small quantity at a time until the level is up to the lower mark on the dipstick. Finally, bring the level up to the upper mark on the dipstick. Insert the dipstick, and refit the filler cap.

17 Start the engine and run it for a few minutes; check for leaks around the oil filter seal and the sump drain plug. Note that there may be a delay of a few seconds before the oil pressure warning light goes out when the engine is first started, as the oil circulates through the engine oil galleries and the new oil filter, before the pressure builds-up.

18 Switch off the engine, and wait a few minutes for the oil to settle in the sump once more. With the new oil circulated and the filter completely full, recheck the level on the dipstick, and add more oil as necessary.

19 Dispose of the used filter and engine oil safely, with reference to *General repair procedures* in the *Reference* section of this manual.

4 Front brake pad check

1 Firmly apply the handbrake, then jack up the front of the car and support it securely on axle stands (see *Jacking and vehicle support*). Remove the front roadwheels.

2 For a comprehensive check, the brake pads should be removed and cleaned. The operation of the caliper can then also be checked, and the condition of the brake disc itself can be fully examined on both sides. Refer to Chapter 9 for further information.

3 If any pad's friction material is worn to the specified thickness or less, *all four pads must be renewed as a set.*

3.5b Use an oil filter removal tool . . .

3.5c . . . or a strap wrench

3.8 Fit new O-rings (arrowed) to the screw-on cover

3.14 Check the condition of the sump drain plug washer

5 Rear brake pad check

1 Chock the front wheels, then jack up the rear of the car and support it on axle stands (see *Jacking and vehicle support*). Remove the rear roadwheels.

2 For a quick check, the thickness of friction material remaining on each brake pad can be measured through the top of the caliper body. If any pad's friction material is worn to the specified thickness or less, all four pads must be renewed as a set.

3 For a comprehensive check, the brake pads should be removed and cleaned. This will permit the operation of the caliper to be checked, and the condition of the brake disc itself to be fully examined on both sides. Refer to Chapter 9 for further information.

6 Handbrake check

Check and, if necessary, adjust the handbrake as described in Chapter 9. Check that the handbrake cables are free to move easily and lubricate all exposed linkages/cable pivots.

7 Pollen filter renewal

1 Working at the rear of the engine compartment, rotate the three retaining clips 90° anti-clockwise and pull the filter cover out to the front **(see illustrations)**.

2 Pull the filter element up and to the front,

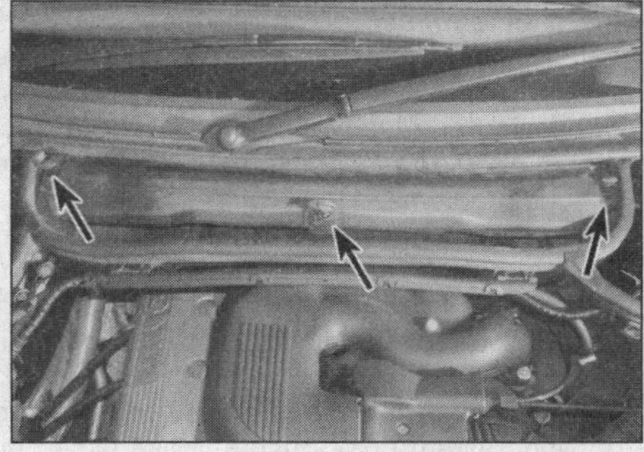

7.1a Rotate the three clips (arrowed) anti-clockwise . . .

7.1b . . . and remove the filter cover

7.2 Remove the pollen filter from the housing

and manoeuvre it from the housing **(see illustration)**.

3 Install the new filter element into the housing, ensuring that it's fitted the correct way up.

4 Refit the filter cover, and secure it in place with the retaining clips.

8 Resetting the service interval display

1 BMW E46 3-Series models are equipped with a circular diagnostic socket under the bonnet, or a 16-pin diagnostic socket in the driver's footwell. The service interval display resetting procedure depends on which socket it fitted. Proceed under the relevant heading.

Engine diagnostic socket

Note: *The following is for use with the special BMW service tool and adapter. If an aftermarket tool is being used, refer to the instructions supplied by its manufacturer.*

2 Turn the ignition off, unscrew the cap, then plug BMW service interval resetting tool 62 1 110 and into the engine compartment diagnostic socket **(see illustration)**.

3 Ensure that all electrical items are switched off then turn on the ignition switch. **Note:** *Do not start the engine.*

4 To reset an Oil Service, press and hold the yellow button; the green light will illuminate. After about 3 seconds the yellow light will illuminate for about 12 seconds, and then go out.

5 To reset an Inspection Service, press and hold the red Inspection button; the green (function check) light will illuminate. After about 3 seconds the red lamp should also light, remain on for about 12 seconds, and then go out. Release the Inspection button and the green (function check) light will go out.

6 If the clock (annual service) symbol was illuminated at the same time as the oil service or inspection indicator, wait 20 seconds then repeat the operation in paragraph 4.

7 Turn off the ignition switch and disconnect the resetting tool and adapter from the diagnostic connector.

8 Turn the ignition switch on and check that the Service Interval Display has been reset.

Driver's footwell socket

9 With the ignition switched off, press and hold the trip reset button.

8.2 Unscrew the cap of the engine diagnostic socket (arrowed)

10 Turn the ignition key to position I. After 5 seconds the words OIL SERVICE or INSPECTION are shown together with the message 'reset' or 're'.

11 Release the button, then press and hold it until the message 'reset' or 're' starts to flash.

12 Release the button, and wait for the flashing sequence to stop.

13 Press and hold the button again for 5 seconds. The time-based inspection is now displayed together with the message 'reset' or 're'.

14 Release the button, then press and hold it. After 5 seconds the message 'reset' or 're' begins to flash.

15 Release the button, then press and release it again. The new service interval is displayed.

16 Press and release the button. The message END SIA is now displayed. Switch off the ignition.

Inspection I

9 Hose and fluid leak check

1 Visually inspect the engine joint faces, gaskets and seals for any signs of water or oil leaks. Pay particular attention to the areas around the camshaft cover, cylinder head, oil filter and sump joint faces. Bear in mind that, over a period of time, some very slight seepage from these areas is to be expected – what you are really looking for is any indication of a serious leak **(see Haynes Hint)**. Should a leak be found, renew the offending gasket or oil seal by referring to the appropriate Chapters in this manual.

A leak in the cooling system will usually show up as white- or antifreeze-coloured deposits on the area adjoining the leak.

2 Also check the security and condition of all the engine-related pipes and hoses. Ensure that all cable-ties or securing clips are in place and in good condition. Clips which are broken or missing can lead to chafing of the hoses, pipes or wiring, which could cause more serious problems in the future.

3 Carefully check the radiator hoses and heater hoses along their entire length. Renew any hose which is cracked, swollen or deteriorated. Cracks will show up better if the hose is squeezed. Pay close attention to the hose clips that secure the hoses to the cooling system components. Hose clips can pinch and puncture hoses, resulting in cooling system leaks.

4 Inspect all the cooling system components (hoses, joint faces, etc) for leaks **(see Haynes Hint)**. Where any problems of this nature are found on system components, renew the component or gasket with reference to Chapter 3.

5 Where applicable, inspect the automatic transmission fluid cooler hoses for leaks or deterioration.

6 With the car raised, inspect the petrol tank and filler neck for punctures, cracks and other damage. The connection between the filler neck and tank is especially critical. Sometimes a rubber filler neck or connecting hose will leak due to loose retaining clamps or deteriorated rubber.

7 Carefully check all rubber hoses and metal fuel lines leading away from the petrol tank. Check for loose connections, deteriorated hoses, crimped lines, and other damage. Pay particular attention to the vent pipes and hoses, which often loop up around the filler neck and can become blocked or crimped. Follow the lines to the front of the car, carefully inspecting them all the way. Renew damaged sections as necessary.

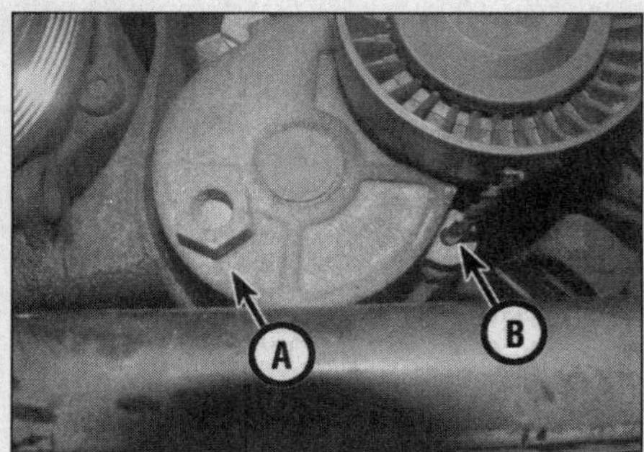

10.6 Rotate the tensioner arm with a socket on the hexagonal section (A), and lock it in place with a 4 mm drill bit (B)

8 Closely inspect the metal brake pipes which run along the car underbody. If they show signs of excessive corrosion or damage they must be renewed.

9 From within the engine compartment, check the security of all fuel hose attachments and pipe unions, and inspect the fuel hoses and vacuum hoses for kinks, chafing and deterioration.

10 Check the condition of the power steering fluid hoses and pipes.

10 Auxiliary drivebelt(s) check and renewal

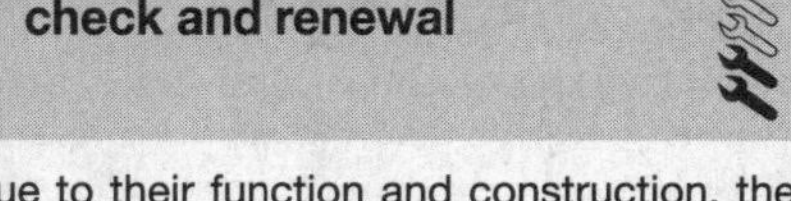

1 Due to their function and construction, the belts are prone to failure after a period of time, and should be inspected periodically to prevent problems.

2 The number of belts used on a particular car depends on the accessories fitted. Drivebelts are used to drive the coolant pump, alternator, power steering pump and air conditioning compressor.

3 To improve access for belt inspection, if desired, remove the viscous cooling fan and cowl (where fitted) as described in Chapter 3.

4 With the engine stopped, using your fingers (and an electric torch if necessary), move along the belts, checking for cracks and separation of the belt plies. Also check for fraying and glazing, which gives the belt a shiny appearance. Both sides of the belts should be inspected, which means the belt will have to be twisted to check the underside. If necessary turn the engine using a spanner or socket on the crankshaft pulley bolt to that the whole of the belt can be inspected.

M43TU 4-cylinder engine

Air conditioning compressor

5 Access is most easily obtained from under the car. If desired, jack up the front of the car and support securely on axle stands (see *Jacking and vehicle support*). Undo the bolts and remove the engine undershield.

6 Using a socket or spanner on the hexagon section, rotate the tensioner arm fully clockwise to relieve the tension, and slide the belt from the pulleys. Insert a 4 mm drill bit to lock the arm in place **(see illustration)**.

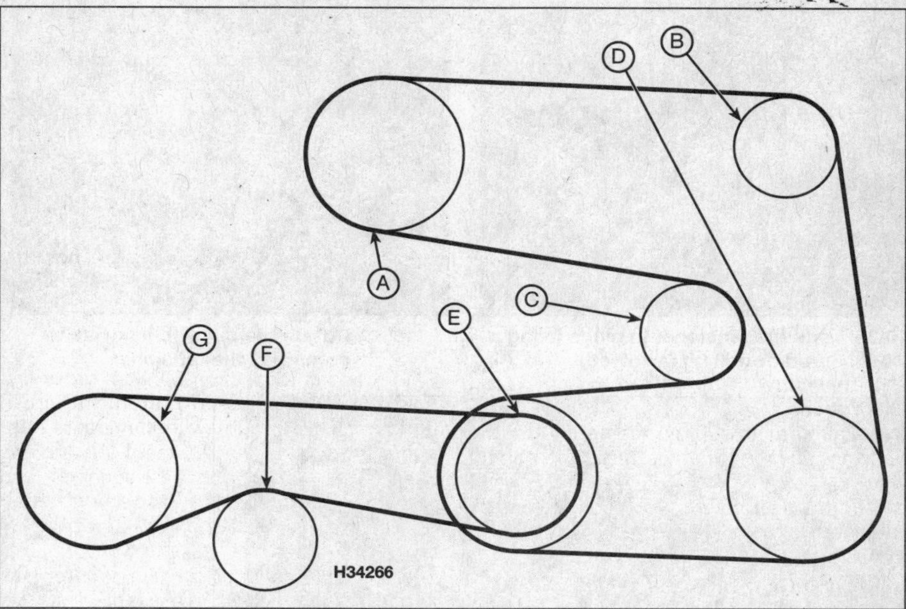

10.7 Drivebelt routing – M43TU engine

A Coolant pump
B Alternator
C Tensioner
D Power steering pump
E Crankshaft
F Tensioner
G Air conditioning compressor

7 Fit the drivebelt round the pulleys, hold the arm in place using a socket or spanner on the hexagon section, then withdraw the drill bit and allow the tensioner to rotate, and tension the belt **(see illustration)**.

8 Where applicable, refit the engine undershield and lower the car to the ground.

Coolant pump/alternator/power steering pump (hydraulic tensioner)

9 Where applicable, remove the air conditioning compressor drivebelt as described previously in this Section.

10 If the drivebelt is to be re-used, mark the running direction of the belt before removal.

11 To improve access, remove the viscous cooling fan and shroud (where fitted) as described in Chapter 3.

12 Make a careful note of the routing of the drivebelt before removal.

13 Using a spanner engaged with the lug on the tensioner, compress the tensioner piston (anti-clockwise), and slide the drivebelt from the pulleys.

14 Release the tensioner once the drivebelt has been removed.

15 If the original belt is being refitted, observe the running direction mark made before removal.

16 Again, compress the tensioner, and engage the belt with the pulleys, ensuring that it is routed as noted before removal. Make sure that the belt engages correctly with the grooves in the pulleys.

17 Refit the viscous cooling fan and shroud with reference to Chapter 3 (where applicable).

18 Where applicable, refit the air conditioning compressor drivebelt as described previously in this Section.

Coolant pump/alternator/power steering pump (mechanical tensioner)

19 Where applicable, remove the air conditioning compressor drivebelt as described previously in this Section.

20 If the drivebelt is to be re-used, mark the running direction of the belt before removal.

21 To improve access, remove the viscous cooling fan and shroud (where fitted) as described in Chapter 3.

22 Make a careful note of the routing of the drivebelt before removal.

23 Where fitted, prise the cover from the centre of the tensioner pulley.

24 Engage a hexagon key or socket and extension bar with the pulley bolt, then rotate the pulley arm (anti-clockwise) to compress the tensioner, and slide the drivebelt from the pulleys **(see illustration)**.

10.24 Rotate the tensioner anti-clockwise and remove the belt

10.25 Lock the tensioner in place using a rod or drill bit (arrowed)

10.33 Rotate the pulley clockwise to compress the tensioner

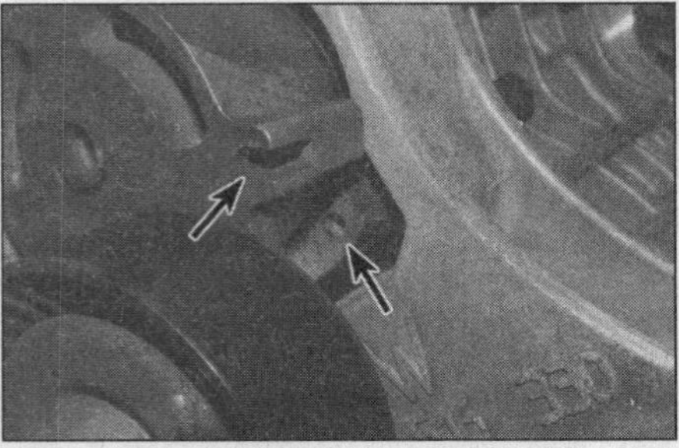

10.34 Rotate the tensioner pulley until the two holes (arrowed) align and lock it in position with a rod/drill

10.36 Note the drivebelt routing

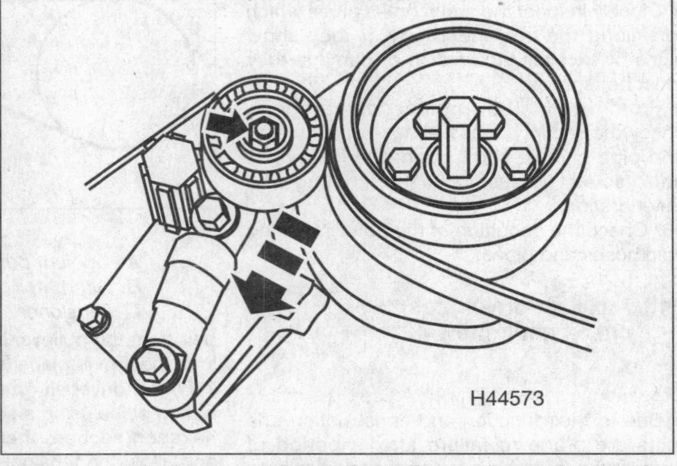

10.40 Insert the hexagon bit into the pulley centre, and rotate the tensioner clockwise (arrowed)

25 If desired, to aid refitting, the tensioner can be compressed fully and locked in position using a metal rod or drill bit engaged with the holes in the tensioner and backplate – note that the tensioner has a powerful spring, so a strong rod will be required **(see illustration)**.

26 If the original belt is being refitted, observe the running direction mark made before removal.

27 If the tensioner has not been locked in position, compress the tensioner, and engage the belt with the pulleys, ensuring that it is routed as noted before removal **(see illustration 10.7)**. Make sure that the belt engages correctly with the grooves in the pulleys.

28 Where applicable, compress the tensioner until the locking rod can be removed, then withdraw the rod and release the tensioner.

29 Refit the viscous cooling fan and shroud with reference to Chapter 3 (where applicable).

30 Where applicable, refit the air conditioning compressor drivebelt as described previously in this Section.

N42 and N46 4-cylinder engines

31 Open the bonnet. Prise up the centre pin, and remove the expanding rivets, securing the air inlet cowling at the front of the engine compartment. Pull the cowling from the air filter housing and washer reservoir, and manoeuvre it from the engine compartment.

32 If the drivebelt is to be re-used, mark the running direction of the belt before removal.

33 Using a spanner or socket, rotate the tensioner pulley (clockwise) to compress the tensioner, and slide the drivebelt from the pulleys **(see illustration)**.

34 If desired, to aid refitting, the tensioner can be compressed fully and locked in position using a metal rod engaged with the holes in the tensioner and backplate – note that the tensioner has a powerful spring, so a strong rod will be required **(see illustration)**.

35 If the original belt is being refitted, observe the running direction mark made before removal.

10.41 Rotate the pulley arm clockwise

36 If the tensioner has not been locked in position, compress the tensioner, and engage the belt with the pulleys, ensuring that it is routed as noted before removal **(see illustration)**. Make sure that the belt engages correctly with the grooves in the pulleys.

37 Where applicable, compress the tensioner until the locking rod can be removed, then withdraw the rod and release the tensioner.

38 Refit the air inlet cowling.

6-cylinder engines

Air conditioning compressor

39 Access is most easily obtained from under the car. If desired, jack up the front of the car and support securely on (see *Jacking and vehicle support*). Undo the bolts and remove the engine undershield.

40 On models with a hydraulic tensioner, prise the cover from the centre of the tensioner pulley. Engage a hexagon bit and extension bar with the tensioner bolt, and lever the tensioner clockwise **(see illustration)**. Slide the belt from the pulleys.

41 On models with a mechanical tensioner, using a spanner on the hexagon section of the pulley arm, rotate the tensioner clockwise, and remove the belt from the pulleys **(see illustration)**.

42 On all models, lever the tensioner until

the drivebelt can be fitted around the pulleys, then release the tensioner. Ensure that the belt is engaged with the grooves in the pulleys.
43 Refit the pulley cover (where applicable) and lower the car to the ground.

Coolant pump/alternator/ power steering pump

44 Where applicable, remove the air conditioning compressor drivebelt as described previously in this Section.
45 If the drivebelt is to be re-used, mark the running direction of the belt before removal.
46 To improve access, remove the viscous cooling fan and shroud (where fitted) as described in Chapter 3.
47 Make a careful note of the routing of the drivebelt before removal.
48 Using a spanner on the hexagonal section of the pulley arm, rotate the tensioner clockwise, and remove the belt from the pulleys **(see illustration)**.
49 If the original belt is being refitted, observe the running direction mark made before removal.
50 Compress the tensioner, and engage the belt with the pulleys, ensuring that it is routed as noted before removal. Make sure that the belt engages correctly with the grooves in the pulleys **(see illustration)**.
51 Where applicable, refit the viscous cooling fan and shroud with reference to Chapter 3.
52 Where applicable, refit the air conditioning compressor drivebelt as described previously in this Section.

11 Steering and suspension check

Front suspension and steering

1 Raise the front of the car, and securely support it on axle stands (see *Jacking and vehicle support*).
2 Visually inspect the balljoint dust covers and the steering rack-and-pinion gaiters for splits, chafing or deterioration. Any wear of these components will cause loss of lubricant, then dirt and water entry, resulting in rapid deterioration of the balljoints or steering gear.
3 Check the power steering fluid hoses for chafing or deterioration, and the pipe and hose unions for fluid leaks. Also check for signs of fluid leakage under pressure from the steering gear rubber gaiters, which would indicate failed fluid seals within the steering gear.
4 Grasp the roadwheel at the 12 o'clock and 6 o'clock positions, and try to rock it **(see illustration)**. Very slight free play may be felt, but if the movement is appreciable, further investigation is necessary to determine the source. Continue rocking the wheel while an assistant depresses the footbrake. If the movement is now eliminated or significantly reduced, it is likely that the hub bearings are at fault. If the free play is still evident with the footbrake depressed, then there is wear in the suspension joints or mountings.

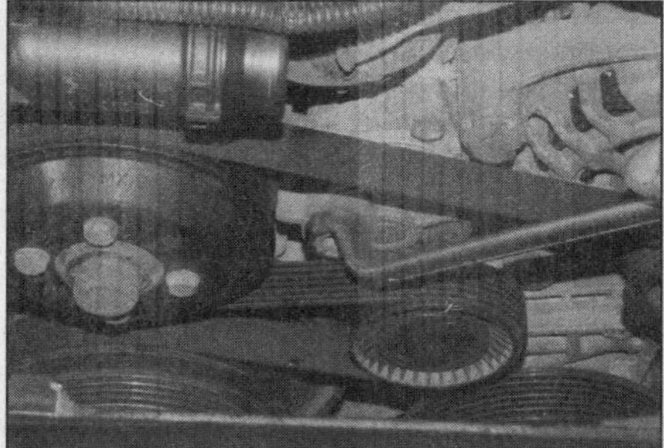

10.48 Rotate the tensioner clockwise and remove the belt

5 Now grasp the wheel at the 9 o'clock and 3 o'clock positions, and try to rock it as before. Any movement felt now may again be caused by wear in the hub bearings or the steering track rod balljoints. If the inner or outer balljoint is worn, the visual movement will be obvious.
6 Using a large screwdriver or flat bar, check for wear in the suspension mounting bushes by levering between the relevant suspension component and its attachment point. Some movement is to be expected as the mountings are made of rubber, but excessive wear should be obvious. Also check the condition of any visible rubber bushes, looking for splits, cracks or contamination of the rubber.
7 With the car standing on its wheels, have an assistant turn the steering wheel back-and-forth about an eighth of a turn each way. There should be very little, if any, lost movement between the steering wheel and roadwheels. If this is not the case, closely observe the joints and mountings previously described, but in addition, check the steering column universal joints for wear, and the rack-and-pinion steering gear itself.

Strut/shock absorber

8 Check for any signs of fluid leakage around the suspension strut/shock absorber body, or from the rubber gaiter around the piston rod. Should any fluid be noticed, the suspension strut/shock absorber is defective internally, and should be renewed. **Note:** *Suspension struts/shock absorbers should always be renewed in pairs on the same axle.*
9 The efficiency of the suspension strut/shock absorber may be checked by bouncing the car at each corner. Generally speaking, the body will return to its normal position and stop after being depressed. If it rises and returns on a rebound, the suspension strut/shock absorber is probably suspect. Examine also the suspension strut/shock absorber upper and lower mountings for any signs of wear.

11.4 Check for wear in the hub bearings by grasping the wheel and trying to rock it

10.50 Auxiliary drivebelts routing

12 Exhaust system check

1 With the engine cold (at least an hour after the car has been driven), check the complete exhaust system from the engine to the end of the tailpipe. The exhaust system is most easily checked with the car raised on a hoist, or suitably supported on axle stands, so that the exhaust components are readily visible and accessible.
2 Check the exhaust pipes and connections for evidence of leaks, severe corrosion and damage. Make sure that all brackets and mountings are in good condition, and that all relevant nuts and bolts are tight **(see illustration)**. Leakage at any of the joints or in other parts of the system will usually show up as a black sooty stain in the vicinity of the leak.
3 Rattles and other noises can often be traced to the exhaust system, especially the brackets and mountings. Try to move the pipes and silencers. If the components are able to come into contact with the body or suspension parts, secure the system with new

12.2 Check the condition of the exhaust mountings

16.1 Use a fine pin or length of wire to adjust the washer jet aim

mountings. Otherwise separate the joints (if possible) and twist the pipes as necessary to provide additional clearance.

13 Seat belt check

1 Carefully examine the seat belt webbing for cuts or any signs of serious fraying or deterioration. If the seat belt is of the retractable type, pull the belt all the way out, and examine the full extent of the webbing.

2 Fasten and unfasten the belt, ensuring that the locking mechanism holds securely and releases properly when intended. If the belt is of the retractable type, check also that the retracting mechanism operates correctly when the belt is released.

3 Check the security of all seat belt mountings and attachments which are accessible, without removing any trim or other components, from inside the car.

14 Hinge and lock lubrication

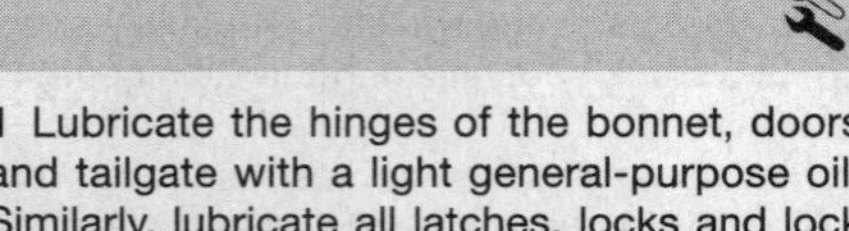

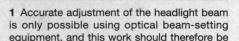

1 Lubricate the hinges of the bonnet, doors and tailgate with a light general-purpose oil. Similarly, lubricate all latches, locks and lock strikers. At the same time, check the security and operation of all the locks, adjusting them if necessary (see Chapter 11).

2 Lightly lubricate the bonnet release mechanism and cable with a suitable grease.

15 Headlight beam alignment check

1 Accurate adjustment of the headlight beam is only possible using optical beam-setting equipment, and this work should therefore be carried out by a BMW dealer or service station with the necessary facilities.

2 Basic adjustments can be carried out in an emergency, and further details are given in Chapter 12.

16 Windscreen/headlight washer system(s) check

1 Check that each of the washer jet nozzles are clear and that each nozzle provides a strong jet of washer fluid. The jets should be aimed to spray at a point slightly above the centre of the screen/headlight. On the windscreen washer nozzles where there are two jets, aim one of the jets slightly above the centre of the screen and aim the other just below to ensure complete coverage of the screen. If necessary, adjust the jets using a pin or length of fine, stiff wire **(see illustration)**. Take great care not to damage the water channels in the jets.

2 Adjustment of the headlight washer jets requires the use of BMW special tool 00 9 100.

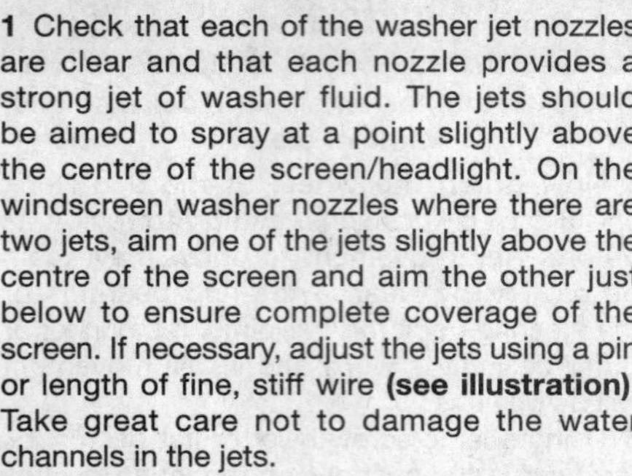

17 Engine management system check

1 This check is part of the manufacturer's maintenance schedule, and involves testing the engine management system using special dedicated test equipment. Such testing will allow the test equipment to read any fault codes stored in the electronic control unit memory.

2 Unless a fault is suspected, this test is not essential, although it should be noted that it is recommended by the manufacturers.

3 If access to suitable test equipment is not possible, make a thorough check of all ignition, fuel and emission control system components, hoses, and wiring, for security and obvious signs of damage. Further details of the fuel system, emission control system and ignition system can be found in Chapters 4 and 5.

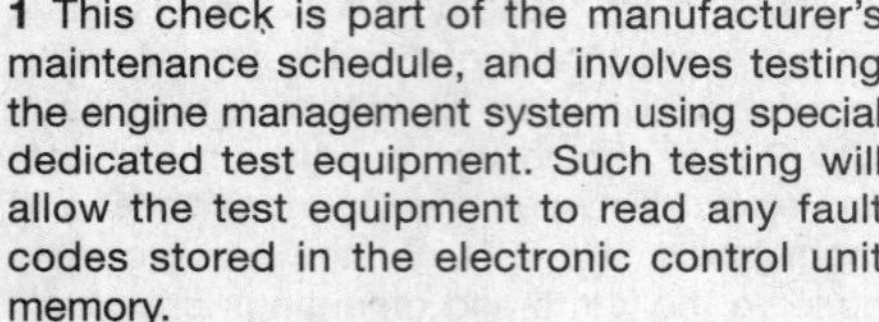

18 Road test

Instruments and electrical equipment

1 Check the operation of all instruments and electrical equipment.

2 Make sure that all instruments read correctly, and switch on all electrical equipment in turn, to check that it functions properly.

Steering and suspension

3 Check for any abnormalities in the steering, suspension, handling or road 'feel'.

4 Drive the car, and check that there are no unusual vibrations or noises.

5 Check that the steering feels positive, with no excessive 'sloppiness', or roughness, and check for any suspension noises when cornering and driving over bumps.

Drivetrain

6 Check the performance of the engine, clutch (where applicable), gearbox/transmission and driveshafts.

7 Listen for any unusual noises from the engine, clutch and gearbox/transmission.

8 Make sure that the engine runs smoothly when idling, and that there is no hesitation when accelerating.

9 Check that, where applicable, the clutch action is smooth and progressive, that the drive is taken up smoothly, and that the pedal travel is not excessive. Also listen for any noises when the clutch pedal is depressed.

10 On manual gearbox models, check that all gears can be engaged smoothly without noise, and that the gear lever action is smooth and not abnormally vague or 'notchy'.

11 On automatic transmission models, make sure that all gearchanges occur smoothly, without snatching, and without an increase in engine speed between changes. Check that all the gear positions can be selected with the car at rest. If any problems are found, they should be referred to a BMW dealer or suitably-equipped specialist.

Braking system

12 Make sure that the car does not pull to one side when braking, and that the wheels do not lock when braking hard.

13 Check that there is no vibration through the steering when braking.

14 Check that the handbrake operates correctly without excessive movement of the lever, and that it holds the car stationary on a slope.

15 Test the operation of the brake servo unit as follows. With the engine off, depress the footbrake four or five times to exhaust the vacuum. Hold the brake pedal depressed, then start the engine. As the engine starts, there should be a noticeable 'give' in the brake pedal as vacuum builds-up. Allow the engine to run for at least two minutes, and then switch it off. If the brake pedal is depressed now, it should be possible to detect a hiss from the servo as the pedal is depressed. After about four or five applications, no further hissing should be heard, and the pedal should feel much harder.

Inspection II

19 Spark plug renewal

General

1 The correct functioning of the spark plugs is vital for the correct running and efficiency of the engine. It is essential that the plugs fitted are appropriate for the engine (the suitable type is specified at the beginning of this Chapter). If this type is used, and the engine is in good condition, the spark plugs should not need attention between scheduled renewal intervals. Spark plug cleaning is rarely necessary, and should not be attempted unless specialised equipment is available, as damage can easily be caused to the firing ends.

M43TU 4-cylinder engine

2 The spark plugs are located in the right-hand side of the cylinder head.

3 To improve access, if desired, unscrew the ignition coil from the body, and move it to one side (refer to Chapter 5B if necessary).

4 If the marks on the original-equipment spark plug (HT) leads cannot be seen, mark the leads 1 to 4, corresponding to the cylinder the lead serves (No 1 cylinder is at the timing chain end of the engine). Pull the leads from the plugs by gripping the end fitting, not the lead, otherwise the lead connection may be fractured **(see illustration)**.

5 It is advisable to remove the dirt from the spark plug recesses, using a clean brush, vacuum cleaner or compressed air before removing the plugs to prevent dirt dropping into the cylinders.

6 Unscrew the plugs using a spark plug spanner, suitable box spanner, or a deep socket and extension bar **(see illustration)**. Keep the socket aligned with the spark plug – if it is forcibly moved to one side, the ceramic insulator may be broken off. As each plug is removed, examine it as follows.

7 Examination of the spark plugs will give a good indication of the condition of the engine. If the insulator nose of the spark plug is clean and white, with no deposits, this is indicative of a weak mixture or too hot a plug (a hot plug transfers heat away from the electrode slowly, a cold plug transfers heat away quickly).

8 If the tip and insulator nose are covered with hard black-looking deposits, then this is indicative that the mixture is too rich. Should the plug be black and oily, then it is likely that the engine is fairly worn, as well as the mixture being too rich.

9 If the insulator nose is covered with light tan to greyish-brown deposits, then the mixture is correct, and it is likely that the engine is in good condition.

10 When buying new spark plugs, it is important to obtain the correct plugs for your specific engine (see Specifications).

11 If the spark plugs are of the multi-electrode type, the gap between the centre electrode and the earth electrodes cannot be adjusted. However, if single electrode plugs are being fitted, the gap between the earth and centre electrode must be correct. If it is too large or too small, the size of the spark and its efficiency will be seriously impaired. The gap should be set to the value given by the spark plug manufacturer **(see illustration)**.

12 To set the gap on single electrode plugs, measure it with a feeler blade, then bend the outer plug electrode until the correct gap is achieved **(see illustration)**. The centre electrode should never be bent, as this may crack the insulator and cause plug failure, if nothing worse. If using feeler blades, the gap is correct when the appropriate-size blade is a firm sliding fit.

13 Special spark plug electrode gap adjusting tools are available from most motor accessory shops, or from some spark plug manufacturers.

14 Before fitting the spark plugs, check that the threaded connector sleeves (on top of the plug) are tight, and that the plug exterior surfaces and threads are clean. It is very often difficult to insert spark plugs into their holes without cross-threading them. To avoid this possibility, fit a short length of hose over the end of the spark plug **(see Haynes Hint)**.

15 Remove the rubber hose (if used), and tighten the plug to the specified torque (see Specifications) using the spark plug socket and a torque wrench. Fit the remaining plugs in the same way.

16 Connect the HT leads in the correct order and, where applicable, refit the ignition coil.

19.4 Pull the HT cap from the spark plug

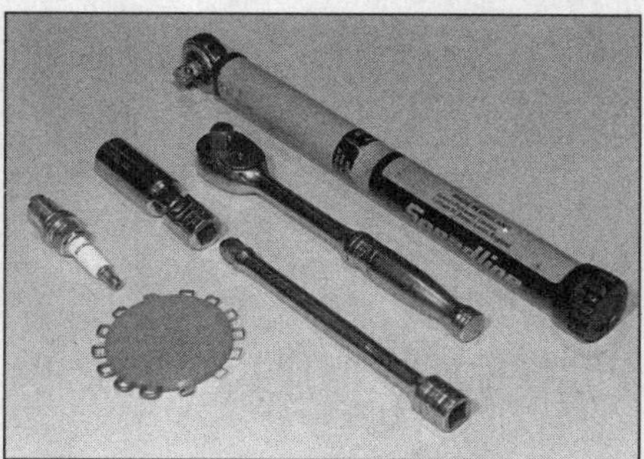

19.6 Tools required for spark plug removal, gap adjustment, and refitting

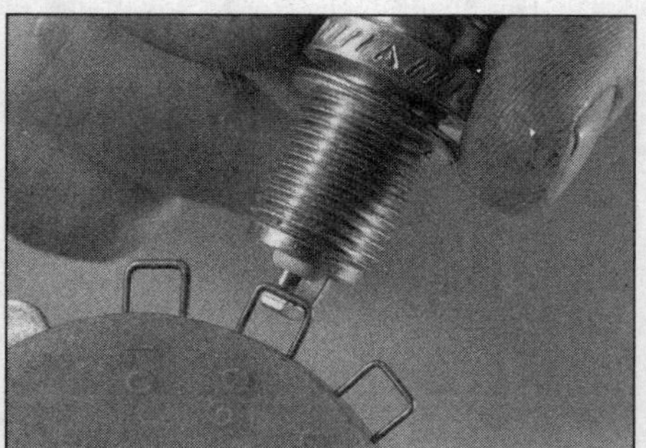

19.11 Measuring the spark plug gap with a wire gauge

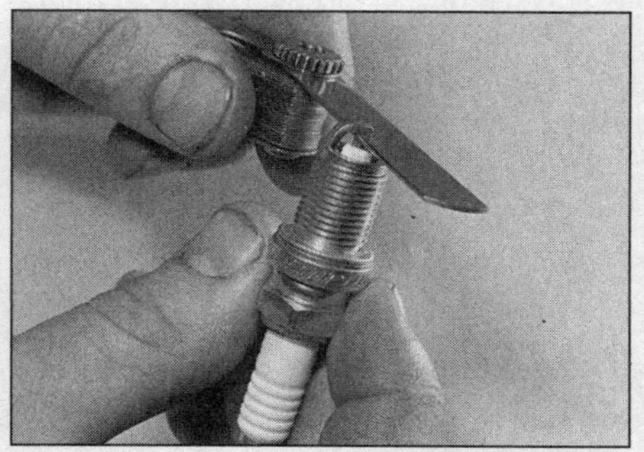

19.12 Measuring the spark plug gap with a feeler gauge

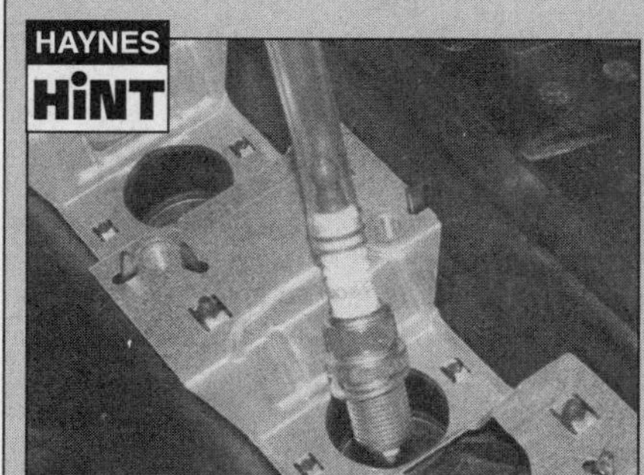

It is often difficult to insert spark plugs into their holes without cross-threading them. To avoid this possibility, fit a short length of 8 mm internal diameter rubber/plastic hose over the end of the spark plug. The flexible hose acts as a universal joint to help align the plug with the plug hole. Should the plug begin to cross-thread, then hose will slip on the spark plug, preventing thread damage to the cylinder head.

20.2 Release the four air filter cover retaining clips

N42 and N46 4-cylinder engines

17 The spark plugs are fitted under the ignition coils in the right-hand side of the cylinder head.
18 Remove the ignition coils as described in Chapter 5B.
19 Proceed as described in Paragraphs 5 to 15.
20 Refit the ignition coils as described in Chapter 5B.

6-cylinder engines

21 The spark plugs are fitted under the ignition coils in the centre of the cylinder head.
22 Remove the ignition coils (Chapter 5B).
23 It is advisable to remove any dirt from the spark plug recesses, using a clean brush, vacuum cleaner or compressed air before removing the plugs to prevent dirt dropping into the cylinders.
24 Unscrew the plugs using a spark plug

20.3 Note the rubber seal is at the top of the filter

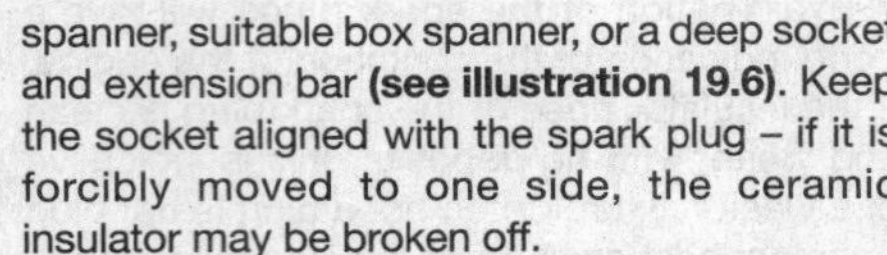

spanner, suitable box spanner, or a deep socket and extension bar **(see illustration 19.6)**. Keep the socket aligned with the spark plug – if it is forcibly moved to one side, the ceramic insulator may be broken off.
25 Proceed as described in paragraphs 7 to 15.
26 Refit the ignition coils (see Chapter 5B).

20 Air filter element renewal

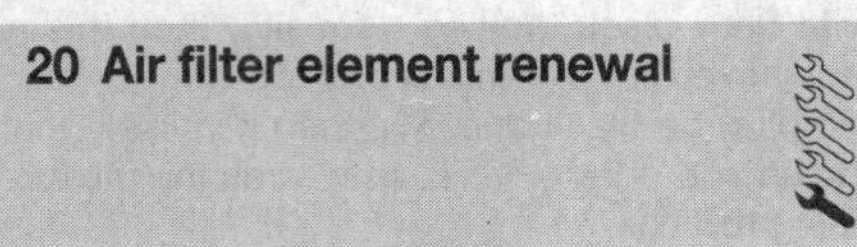

M43TU 4-cylinder engine

1 The air cleaner assembly is located at the front left-hand corner of the engine compartment.
2 Release the four securing clips, and lift off the air cleaner cover **(see illustration)**.
3 Lift out the filter element **(see illustration)**.
4 Wipe out the air cleaner housing and the cover.
5 Lay the new filter element in position, then refit the cover and secure with the clips.

N42 and N46 4-cylinder engines

6 Open the bonnet. Prise up the centre pin, and remove the expanding rivets, securing the air inlet cowling at the front of the engine compartment. Pull the cowling from the air filter housing and washer reservoir, and manoeuvre it from the engine compartment.
7 Undo the two bolts, lift up the front edge of the engine acoustic cover, and remove it **(see illustration)**.
8 Disconnect the vacuum hose from the air inlet hose (N42 engine only), slacken the hose clamp, undo the two mounting bolts, and lift the air filter housing up approximately 5 cm **(see illustration)**. Disconnect the wiring plug and remove the housing from the engine compartment.
9 Slacken the clamp, prise off the retaining clip, and disconnect the inlet hose and resonance chamber from the mass air flow sensor.
10 Turn the air filter housing over, unscrew the bolts and remove the cover **(see illustration)**.
11 Undo the two retaining nuts and remove the mass air flow sensor from the air filter housing **(see illustration)**.
12 Slide the air filter element from the housing.
13 Clean the air filter housing, removing all debris.
14 Slide the new filter element into place, ensuring the locating lugs engage correctly with the housing **(see illustration)**.
15 The remainder of refitting is a reversal of removal.

6-cylinder engines

16 The air cleaner assembly is located at the front left-hand corner of the engine compartment. On models with the M54 engine, prise up the centre pins, lever up the three plastic rivets and remove the air inlet hood from the bonnet slam panel **(see illustration)**.
17 On all models, release the securing clips, and slide the filter element tray up from the housing **(see illustration)**.

20.7 Undo the two acoustic cover bolts (arrowed)

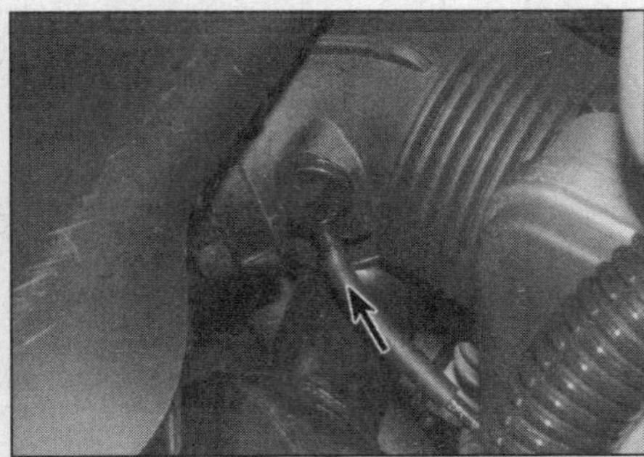

20.8 Disconnect the vacuum hose from the inlet hose (arrowed) – N42 engines only

20.10 Undo the bolts and remove the cover

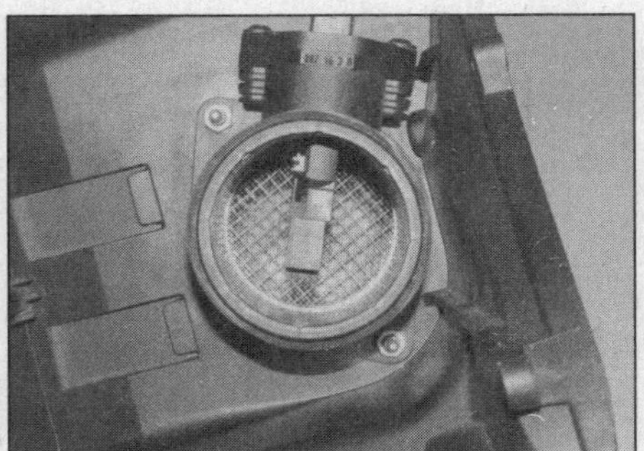

20.11 Undo the nuts and remove the mass air flow sensor

20.14 Ensure the locating lugs engage correctly

20.16 Prise up the centre pins, lever up the expansion rivets and remove the air inlet hood – M54 engine

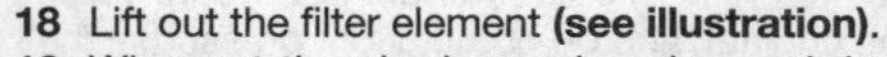

18 Lift out the filter element **(see illustration)**.
19 Wipe out the air cleaner housing and the tray.
20 Lay the new filter element in position, then slide the tray into the housing until it locks in position.
21 Secure the retaining clips, and where applicable, refit the air inlet hood.

21 Driveshaft gaiter check

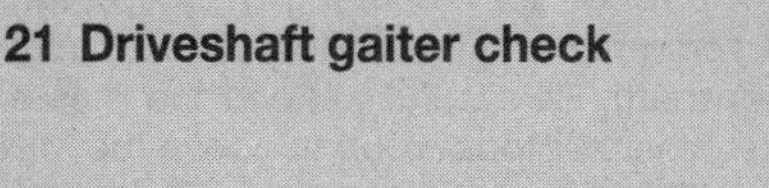

1 With the car raised and securely supported on stands, slowly rotate the rear roadwheel. Inspect the condition of the outer constant velocity (CV) joint rubber gaiters, squeezing the gaiters to open out the folds **(see illustration)**. Check for signs of cracking, splits or deterioration of the rubber, which may allow the grease to escape, and lead to water and grit entry into the joint. Also check the security and condition of the retaining clips. Repeat these checks on the inner CV joints. If any damage is found, the gaiters should be renewed (see Chapter 8).
2 At the same time, check the general condition of the CV joints themselves by first holding the driveshaft and attempting to rotate the wheel. Repeat this check by holding the inner joint and attempting to rotate the driveshaft. Any appreciable movement indicates wear in the joints, wear in the driveshaft splines, or a loose driveshaft retaining nut.

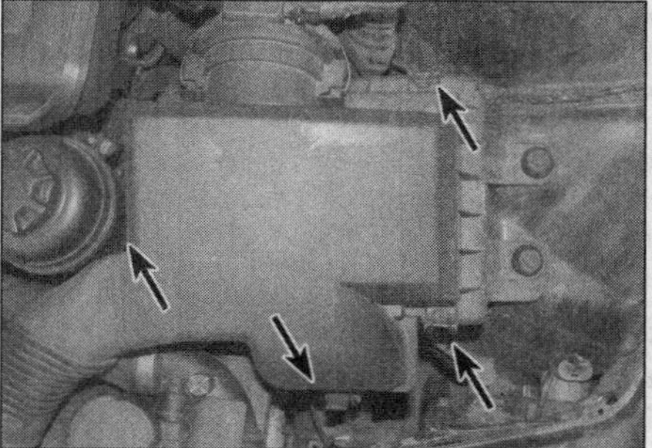

20.17 Release the retaining clips (arrowed) – M52TU engine

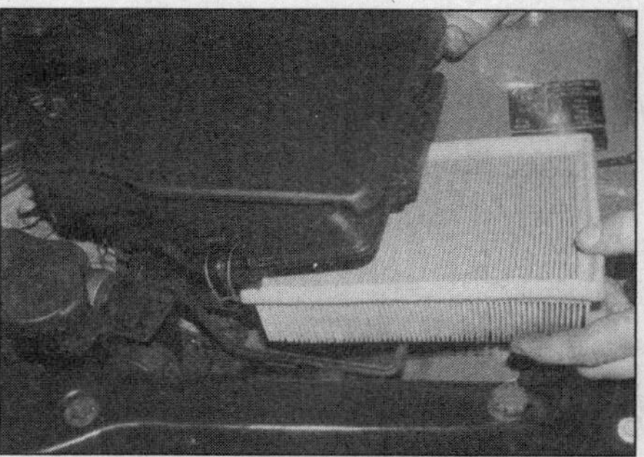

20.18 Lift out the filter element

21.1 Check the condition of the driveshaft gaiters

22 Handbrake shoe check

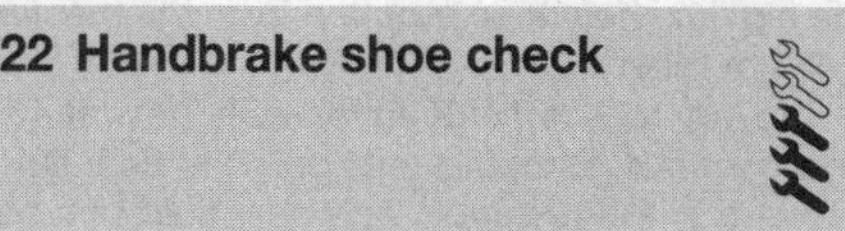

Referring to Chapter 9, remove the rear brake discs and inspect the handbrake shoes for signs of wear or contamination. Renew the shoes if necessary.

Every second Inspection II

23 Fuel filter renewal

4-cylinder engines

1 Depressurise the fuel system as described in Chapter 4A.
2 The fuel filter is located under the car **(see illustration)**.
3 Jack up the car and support on axle stands (see *Jacking and vehicle support*). Where fitted, undo the bolts and remove the transmission undershield.
4 If possible, clamp the fuel feed and return hoses to minimise fuel loss when the hoses are disconnected. On N42 and N46 engine models, note that the fuel return hose is also connected to the fuel filter at the rear and, as the fuel pressure regulator is integral with the filter, the vacuum hose from the inlet manifold is connected to the front of the filter.
5 Place a container under the filter to catch escaping fuel. Note their fitted locations, then slacken the hose clips, and disconnect the fuel hoses from the filter **(see illustrations)**.

23.2 The fuel filter is under the vehicle

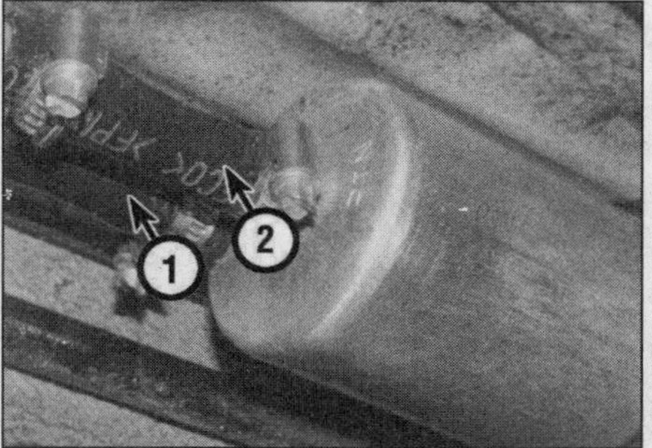

23.5a Slacken the clamps and disconnect the fuel filter hoses at the rear . . .

1 From the fuel tank
2 Fuel return (N42 and M54 engines only)

23.5b . . . and front of the filter

3 Fuel supply to injectors
4 Regulator vacuum hose (N42, N46 and M54 engines only)

23.6 Undo the clamp and remove the filter

6 Slacken the clamp nut or bolt until the filter can be slid from its mounting clamp **(see illustration)**. Note that on N42 and N46 engines, the fuel pressure regulator is integral with the filter can cannot be separated.

7 Refitting is a reversal of removal, but make sure that the flow direction arrow on the filter points in the direction of fuel flow (ie, towards the engine).

6-cylinder engines

8 Depressurise the fuel system (Chapter 4A).

9 The fuel filter is located on a bracket bolted to the left-hand chassis member adjacent to the transmission **(see illustration 23.2)**.

10 Jack up the car and support on axle stands (see *Jacking and vehicle support*). Remove the transmission undershield.

11 On models with the M54 engine, undo the bolts and remove the cover from the fuel filter/ regulator assembly.

12 On all models, note their fitted locations, and clamp the hoses to and from the fuel filter. Slacken the retaining clips and disconnect the hoses from the filter. Be prepared for fluid spillage.

13 On M54 engined models, disconnect the vacuum pipe from the regulator **(see illustration 23.5b)**.

14 On all models, slacken the filter clamp bolt or nut, and slide the filter down from under the car.

15 Refitting is a reversal of removal, but make sure that the flow direction arrow on the filter points in the direction of fuel flow (ie, towards the engine), and on completion, pressurise the fuel system with reference to Chapter 4A.

Every 2 years

24 Brake fluid renewal

Warning: Brake hydraulic fluid can harm your eyes and damage painted surfaces, so use extreme caution when handling and pouring it. Do not use fluid that has been standing open for some time, as it absorbs moisture from the air. Excess moisture can cause a dangerous loss of braking effectiveness.

1 The procedure is similar to that for the bleeding of the hydraulic system as described in Chapter 9, except that the brake fluid reservoir should be emptied using a clean poultry baster or similar before starting, and allowance should be made for the old fluid to be expelled when bleeding a section of the circuit.

2 Working as described in Chapter 9, open the first bleed screw in the sequence, and pump the brake pedal gently until nearly all the old fluid has been emptied from the master cylinder reservoir.

3 Top-up to the MAX level with new fluid, and continue pumping until only the new fluid remains in the reservoir, and new fluid can be seen emerging from the bleed screw. Tighten the screw, and top the reservoir level up to the MAX level line.

4 Work through all remaining bleed screws in the sequence until new fluid can be seen at all of them. Be careful to keep the master cylinder reservoir topped-up to above the MIN level at all times, or air may enter the system and increase the length of the task.

5 When the operation is complete, check that all bleed screws are securely tightened, and that their dust caps are refitted. Wash off all traces of spilt fluid, and recheck the master cylinder reservoir fluid level.

6 Check the operation of the brakes before taking the car on the road.

Every 4 years

25 Coolant renewal

Warning: Wait until the engine is cold before starting this procedure. Do not allow antifreeze to come in contact with your skin, or with the painted surfaces of the car. Rinse off spills immediately with plenty of water. Never leave antifreeze lying around in an open container, or in a puddle in the driveway or on the garage floor. Children and pets are attracted by its sweet smell, but antifreeze can be fatal if ingested.

Cooling system draining

1 With the engine completely cold, cover the expansion tank cap with a wad of rag, and slowly turn the cap anti-clockwise to relieve the pressure in the cooling system (a hissing sound may be heard). Wait until any pressure in the system is released, then continue to turn the cap until it can be removed.

2 Unscrew the bleed screw from the top of the hose junction above the expansion tank. Some models are equipped with a bleed screw adjacent to the oil filter cap **(see illustrations)**.

3 Undo the retaining bolts/clips and remove the undershield from beneath the engine **(see illustration)**.

4 Position a suitable container beneath the

25.2a Unscrew the bleed screw (arrowed)

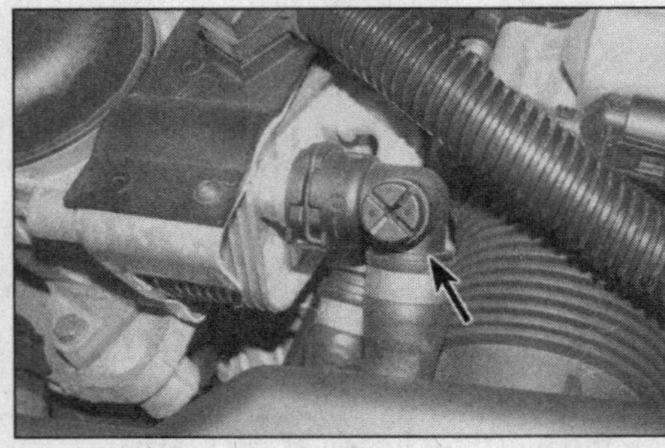
25.2b On some models, a second bleed screw is located adjacent to the oil filter cover (arrowed)

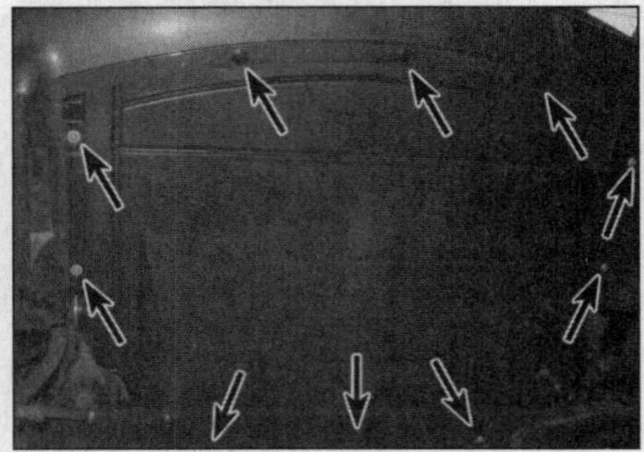
25.3 Engine undershield bolts (arrowed)

drain plugs on the base of the radiator and the expansion tank. Unscrew the drain plugs and allow the coolant to drain into the container **(see illustrations)**.

5 To fully drain the system, also unscrew the coolant drain plug from the right-hand side of the cylinder block and allow the remainder of the coolant to drain into the container. On N42 and N46 4-cylinder engines, a second block drain plug is fitted to the left-hand side of the cylinder block **(see illustrations)**.

6 If the coolant has been drained for a reason other than renewal, then provided it is clean and less than two years old, it can be re-used, though this is not recommended.

7 Once all the coolant has drained, refit the bleed screw to the hose junction. Fit a new sealing washer to the block drain plug and tighten it to the specified torque.

Cooling system flushing

8 If coolant renewal has been neglected, or if the antifreeze mixture has become diluted, then in time, the cooling system may gradually lose efficiency, as the coolant passages become restricted due to rust, scale deposits, and other sediment. The cooling system efficiency can be restored by flushing the system clean.

9 The radiator should be flushed independently of the engine, to avoid unnecessary contamination.

Radiator flushing

10 To flush the radiator, disconnect the top and bottom hoses and any other relevant hoses from the radiator, with reference to Chapter 3.

11 Insert a garden hose into the radiator top inlet. Direct a flow of clean water through the radiator, and continue flushing until clean water emerges from the radiator bottom outlet.

12 If after a reasonable period, the water still does not run clear, the radiator can be flushed with a good proprietary cooling system cleaning agent. It is important that their manufacturer's instructions are followed carefully. If the contamination is particularly bad, insert the hose in the radiator bottom outlet, and reverse-flush the radiator.

Engine flushing

13 To flush the engine, remove the thermostat as described in Chapter 3, then temporarily refit the thermostat cover.

14 With the top and bottom hoses disconnected from the radiator, insert a garden hose into the radiator top hose. Direct a clean flow of water through the engine, and continue flushing until clean water emerges from the radiator bottom hose.

15 On completion of flushing, refit the thermostat and reconnect the hoses with reference to Chapter 3.

Cooling system filling

16 Before attempting to fill the cooling system, make sure that all hoses and clips are in good condition, and that the clips are tight and the radiator and cylinder block drain plugs are securely tightened. Note that an antifreeze mixture must be used all year round, to prevent corrosion of the engine components (see following sub-Section).

17 Slacken the bleed screw(s) **(see illustration 25.2a and 25.2b)**.

18 Turn on the ignition, and set the heater control to maximum temperature, with the fan speed set to 'low'. This opens the heating valves.

19 Remove the expansion tank filler cap. Fill the system by slowly pouring the coolant into the expansion tank to prevent airlocks from forming.

20 If the coolant is being renewed, begin by pouring in a couple of litres of water, followed by the correct quantity of antifreeze, then top-up with more water.

21 As soon as coolant free from air bubbles emerges from the radiator bleed screw(s), tighten the screw(s) securely.

22 Once the level in the expansion tank starts to rise, squeeze the radiator top and bottom hoses to help expel any trapped air in the system. Once all the air is expelled, top-up the coolant level to the MAX mark and refit the expansion tank cap.

23 Start the engine and run it until it reaches normal operating temperature, then stop the engine and allow it to cool.

24 Check for leaks, particularly around disturbed components. Check the coolant level in the expansion tank, and top-up if necessary. Note that the system must be cold before an accurate level is indicated in the expansion tank. If the expansion tank cap is removed while the engine is still warm, cover the cap with a thick cloth, and unscrew the cap slowly to gradually relieve the system pressure (a hissing sound will normally be heard). Wait until any pressure remaining in the system is released, then continue to turn the cap until it can be removed.

25.4a Open the expansion tank drain plug (arrowed) . . .

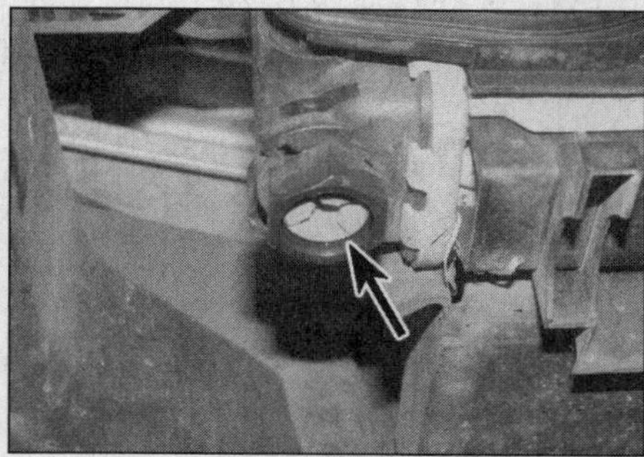

25.4b . . . and the radiator drain plug

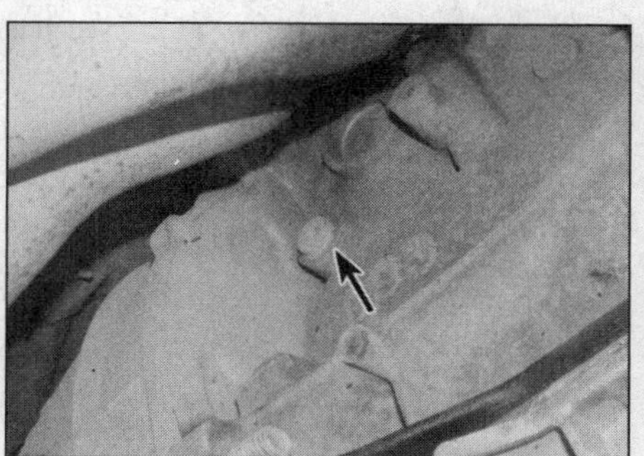

25.5a The cylinder block drain plug is located on the right-hand side (arrowed)

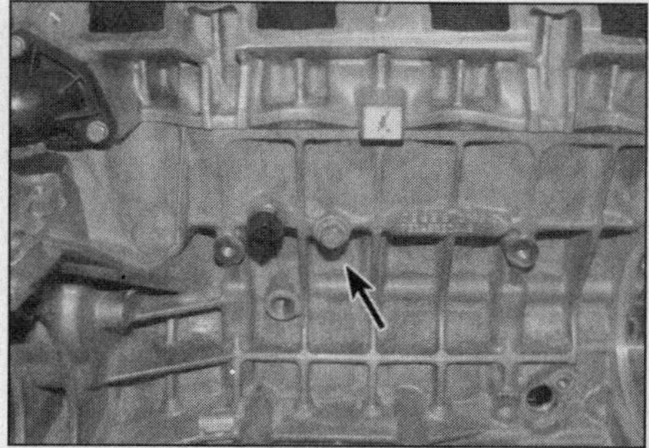

25.5b On N42 and N46 4-cylinder engines, a second engine block drain plug is located on the left-hand side (arrowed – engine removed for clarity)

Antifreeze mixture

25 The antifreeze should always be renewed at the specified intervals. This is necessary not only to maintain the antifreeze properties, but also to prevent corrosion which would otherwise occur as the corrosion inhibitors become progressively less effective.

26 Always use an ethylene-glycol based antifreeze which is suitable for use in mixed-metal cooling systems. The quantity of antifreeze and levels of protection are indicated in the Specifications.

27 Before adding antifreeze, the cooling system should be completely drained, preferably flushed, and all hoses checked for condition and security.

28 After filling with antifreeze, a label should be attached to the expansion tank, stating the type and concentration of antifreeze used, and the date installed. Any subsequent topping-up should be made with the same type and concentration of antifreeze.

29 Do not use engine antifreeze in the windscreen/tailgate washer system, as it will damage the vehicle paintwork. A screenwash additive should be added to the washer system in the quantities stated on the bottle.

Chapter 2 Part A: 4-cylinder engine in-car repair procedures

Contents

Degrees of difficulty

Easy, suitable for novice with little experience 

Fairly easy, suitable for beginner with some experience

Fairly difficult, suitable for competent DIY mechanic

Difficult, suitable for experienced DIY mechanic

Very difficult, suitable for expert DIY or professional 

Specifications

General

Engine code:		
1796 cc engine (Valvetronic)	N42 B18 and N46 B18	
1895 cc engine	M43TU B19	
1995 cc engine (Valvetronic)	N42 B20 and N46 B20	
Bore/Stroke:	**Bore**	**Stroke**
N42 engine:		
B18	84.00 mm	81.00 mm
B20	84.00 mm	90.00 mm
M43TU engine	85.00 mm	83.50 mm
N46 engine:		
B18	84.00 mm	81.00 mm
B20	84.00 mm	90.00 mm
Maximum engine power/torque	**Power**	**Torque**
N42 engine:		
B18	85 kW at 5500 rpm	175 Nm at 3750 rpm
B20	105 kW at 6000 rpm	200 Nm at 3750 rpm
M43TU engine:		
High power version	87 kW at 5500 rpm	180 Nm at 3900 rpm
Low power version	77 kW at 5300 rpm	165 Nm at 2500 rpm
N46 engine:		
B18	85 kW at 5500 rpm	180 Nm at 3750 rpm
B20	105 kW at 6000 rpm	200 Nm at 3750 rpm
Direction of engine rotation	Clockwise (viewed from front of vehicle)	
No 1 cylinder location	Timing chain end	
Firing order	1-3-4-2	
Minimum compression pressure	9.0 to 12.0 bar	
Compression ratio:		
N42 engine:		
B18	10.25 : 1	
B20	10.0 : 1	
M43TU engine	9.7 : 1	
N46 engine:		
B18	10.2 : 1	
B20	10.0 : 1	

Balancer shafts

Gear backlash:	
M43TU engine	0.06 to 0.09 mm

Camshafts

Endfloat	0.065 to 0.150 mm

Lubrication system

Minimum oil pressure at idle speed:	
N42 engine	1.0 bar
N46 engine	1.0 bar
M43TU engine	0.5 bar
Oil pump rotor clearances:	
Outer rotor-to-pump body	0.120 to 0.196 mm
Inner rotor endfloat	0.020 to 0.065 mm
Outer rotor endfloat	0.040 to 0.090 mm

Torque wrench settings

	Nm	lbf ft
Adjustment unit to camshaft (N42 and N46 engines):*		
Stage 1	20	15
Stage 2	Angle-tighten a further 90°	
Stage 3	Angle-tighten a further 90°	
Automatic transmission-to-engine bolts:		
Hexagon bolts:		
M8 bolts	24	18
M10 bolts	45	33
M12 bolts	82	61
Torx bolts:		
M8 bolts	21	15
M10 bolts	42	31
M12 bolts	72	53
Balancer shaft housing-to-cylinder block bolts:*		
Stage 1	25	18
Stage 2	Angle-tighten a further 90°	
Balancer shaft housing upper to lower section (M43TU engine):*		
Stage 1	22	16
Stage 2	Angle-tighten a further 100°	
Big-end bearing cap bolts:*		
Stage 1	20	15
Stage 2	Angle-tighten a further 70°	
Bracing shell:		
M8	22	16
M10	43	32
Camshaft bearing cap nuts:		
M6 nuts	10	7
M7 nuts	15	11
M8 nuts	20	15
Camshaft screw-in pin	20	15
Camshaft sprocket bolts:		
M6 bolts	10	7
M7 bolts	15	11
Crankshaft hub bolt:*		
N42 and N46 engines	300	221
M43TU engine	330	244
Crankshaft rear oil seal housing bolts:		
M6	10	7
M8	22	16
Crankshaft vibration damper/pulley-to-hub bolts:		
N42 and N46 engines	34	25
M43TU engine	22	16
Cylinder head bolts:*		
Stage 1	30	22
Stage 2	Angle-tighten a further 90°	
Stage 3	Angle-tighten a further 90°	
Cylinder head bolt cover plug (N42 and N46 engine)	45	33
Cylinder head cover bolts:		
M6	10	7
M7	15	11

Torque wrench settings (continued)	**Nm**	**lbf ft**
Driveplate bolts (automatic transmission)*	120	89
Eccentric shaft sensor magnetic rotor screw (N42 and N46 engine)	8	6
Front reinforcement plate/frame:*		
Stage 1	59	44
Stage 2	Angle-tighten a further 90°	
Stage 3	Angle-tighten a further 30°	
Front subframe bolts:*		
M10	45	33
M12 8.8	77	57
M12 10.9	105	77
Flywheel bolts:*		
N42 and N46 engines	130	96
M43TU engine	120	89
Lower arm bracket-to-body bolts	59	44
Main bearing cap bolts:*		
Stage 1	20	15
Stage 2:		
N42 and N46 engines	Angle-tighten a further 70°	
M43TU engine	Angle-tighten a further 50°	
Manual transmission-to-engine bolts:		
Hexagon head bolts:		
M8 bolts	25	18
M10 bolts	49	36
M12 bolts	74	55
Torx head bolts:		
M8 bolts	22	16
M10 bolts	43	32
M12 bolts	72	53
Oil pressure switch	27	20
Oil pump cover	10	7
Oil pump sprocket:		
N42 and N46 engines†	30	22
M43TU engine:		
M6	10	7
M10	25	18
Oil pump to cylinder block (M43TU engine)	23	17
Oil spray nozzle	10	7
Steering rack mounting nuts*	42	31
Sump:		
N42 and N46 engines *	30	22
M43TU engine:		
Upper section:		
M6	12	9
M8	22	16
Lower section:		
M6	12	9
M8	22	16
Sump oil drain plug:		
M12	25	18
M18	30	22
M22	60	44
Timing chain cover lower plug	45	33
Timing chain cover upper/middle plug	25	18
Timing chain cover/housing:		
M6	10	7
M7	15	11
M8	22	16
M10 nuts/bolts	47	35
Timing chain tensioner cover plug	40	30
Timing chain tensioner cylinder/piston:		
N42 and N46 engines	65	48
M43TU engine	50	37

** Do not re-use*

† Left-hand thread

1 General information

How to use this Chapter

This Part of Chapter 2 describes the repair procedures that can reasonably be carried out on the engine while it remains in the vehicle. If the engine has been removed from the vehicle and is being dismantled as described in Part C, any preliminary dismantling procedures can be ignored.

Note that, while it may be possible physically to overhaul items such as the piston/connecting rod assemblies while the engine is in the car, such tasks are not usually carried out as separate operations. Usually, several additional procedures are required (not to mention the cleaning of components and oilways); for this reason, all such tasks are classed as major overhaul procedures, and are described in Part C of this Chapter.

Part C describes the removal of the engine/transmission from the car, and the full overhaul procedures that can then be carried out.

Engine description

All 4-cylinder engines are of overhead camshaft design, mounted in-line, with the transmission bolted to the rear end. Three types of 4-cylinder engine have been fitted to the model range. The SOHC 1.9 litre M43TU engine was available from the introduction of the 3-Series model range until 1998, from 2001 the DOHC N42 engine was available in 1.8 and 2.0 litre versions, then it was replaced by the N46 engine. The N46 engine is an updated version of the earlier N42 with a few technical enhancements, resulting in meeting the EURO 4 emission levels.

On M43TU engines, a timing chain drives the single camshaft, and the valves are operated via hydraulic valve lifters and cam followers. The camshaft is supported by bearings machined directly in the cylinder head.

The N42 and N46 engines are of DOHC 16V design, and are known as Valvetronic engines. Here the duration and lift of the inlet camshaft is varied by means of an electric motor-driven eccentric shaft which effectively varies the pivot point of a lever acting between the camshaft and the rocker arm. On both these engines, the timing of both the exhaust and inlet valves is variable by means of hydraulic adjustment units on the end of each camshaft – known as VANOS units. These units vary the relationship of the timing chain and sprockets to the camshafts.

The crankshaft is supported in five main bearings of the usual shell-type. Endfloat is controlled by thrust bearing shells on No 4 or 5 main bearing (depending on model). Both engines are fitted with contra-rotating crankshaft-driven balancer shafts.

The pistons are selected to be of matching weight, and incorporate fully-floating gudgeon pins retained by circlips.

The rotor-type oil pump is located at the front of the engine, and is driven directly by the crankshaft.

Operations with engine in place

The following operations can be carried out without having to remove the engine from the vehicle:

- *a) Removal and refitting of the cylinder head.*
- *b) Removal and refitting of the chain and sprockets.*
- *c) Removal and refitting of the camshaft(s).*
- *d) Removal and refitting of the sump.*
- *e) Removal and refitting of the big-end bearings, connecting rods, and pistons.**
- *f) Removal and refitting of the oil pump.*
- *g) Renewal of the engine/transmission mountings.*
- *h) Removal and refitting of the flywheel/driveplate.*

** Although in theory it is possible to remove these components with the engine in place, for reasons of access and cleanliness it is recommended that the engine is removed.*

2 Compression test – description and interpretation

1 When engine performance is down, or if misfiring occurs which cannot be attributed to the ignition or fuel systems, a compression test can provide diagnostic clues as to the engine's condition. If the test is performed regularly, it can give warning of trouble before any other symptoms become apparent.

2 The engine must be fully warmed-up to normal operating temperature, the battery must be fully-charged, and all the spark plugs must be removed (Chapter 1). The aid of an assistant will also be required.

3 Disable the ignition and fuel injection systems by removing the DME master relay (located in the electrical box in the left-hand corner of the engine compartment), and the fuel pump fuse, located in the main fusebox in the passenger glovebox (see Chapter 12).

4 Fit a compression tester to the No 1 cylinder spark plug hole – the type of tester which screws into the plug thread is to be preferred.

5 Have the assistant fully depress the throttle pedal, and crank the engine on the starter motor. After one or two revolutions, the compression pressure should build-up to a maximum figure, and then stabilise. Record the highest reading obtained.

6 Repeat the test on the remaining cylinders, recording the pressure in each.

7 All cylinders should produce very similar pressures; a difference of more than 2 bars between any two cylinders indicates a fault. Note that the compression should build-up quickly in a healthy engine; low compression on the first stroke, followed by gradually-increasing pressure on successive strokes, indicates worn piston rings. A low compression reading on the first stroke, which does not build-up during successive strokes, indicates leaking valves or a blown head gasket (a cracked head could also be the cause). Deposits on the undersides of the valve heads can also cause low compression.

8 BMW recommended values for compression pressures are given in the Specifications.

9 If the pressure in any cylinder is low, carry out the following test to isolate the cause. Introduce a teaspoonful of clean oil into that cylinder through its spark plug hole, and repeat the test.

10 If the addition of oil temporarily improves the compression pressure, this indicates that bore or piston wear is responsible for the pressure loss. No improvement suggests that leaking or burnt valves, or a blown head gasket, may be to blame.

11 A low reading from two adjacent cylinders is almost certainly due to the head gasket having blown between them; the presence of coolant in the engine oil will confirm this.

12 If one cylinder is about 20 percent lower than the others and the engine has a slightly rough idle, a worn camshaft lobe could be the cause.

13 If the compression reading is unusually high, the combustion chambers are probably coated with carbon deposits. If this is the case, the cylinder head should be removed and decarbonised.

14 On completion of the test, refit the spark plugs (see Chapter 1), and reconnect the fuel pump relay and the DME master relay.

3 Top Dead Centre (TDC) for No 1 piston – locating

Note: *To lock the engine in the TDC position, and to check the position of the camshafts, special tools will be required. Some of these tools can be improvised – see text.*

1 Top Dead Centre (TDC) is the highest point in the cylinder that each piston reaches as it travels up-and-down when the crankshaft turns. Each piston reaches TDC at the end of the compression stroke and again at the end of the exhaust stroke, but TDC generally refers to piston position on the compression stroke. No 1 piston is at the timing chain end of the engine.

2 Positioning No 1 piston at TDC is an essential part of many procedures, such as timing chain removal and camshaft removal.

3 Proceed as follows according to engine type.

M43TU engine

4 Remove the cylinder head cover (Section 4).

5 Using a spanner or socket on the crankshaft pulley bolt, turn the crankshaft clockwise until the timing arrow on the front of the camshaft

3.5 The arrow (circled) on the camshaft sprocket must be at 90° to the gasket face

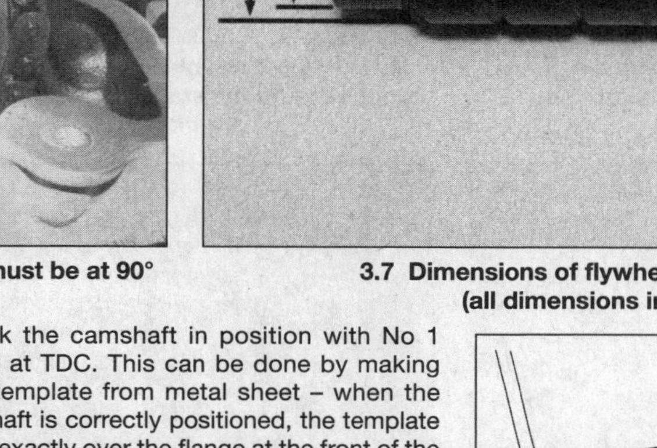

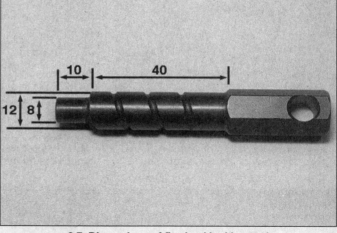

3.7 Dimensions of flywheel locking tool (all dimensions in mm)

sprocket is pointing vertically upwards (in relation to the engine block) **(see illustration)**.

6 Pull the blanking plug from the timing hole in the left-hand rear corner flange of the cylinder block.

7 To 'lock' the crankshaft in position, a special tool will be required. BMW tool 11 2 300 can be used, but an alternative can be made up by machining a length of steel rod **(see illustration)**.

8 Insert the rod through the timing hole. If necessary, turn the crankshaft slightly until the rod enters the TDC hole in the flywheel **(see illustration)**.

9 The crankshaft is now 'locked' in position with No 1 piston at TDC.

10 Note that with No 1 piston at TDC, the square flange at the front of the camshaft should be positioned with the sides of the flanges exactly at right-angles to the top surface of the cylinder head (this can be checked using a set-square), and the side of the flange with holes drilled into it uppermost.

11 For some operations it is necessary to lock the camshaft in position with No 1 piston at TDC. This can be done by making up a template from metal sheet – when the camshaft is correctly positioned, the template will fit exactly over the flange at the front of the camshaft, and rest on the upper surface of the cylinder head. Note also that with No 1 piston at TDC, the valves for No 4 cylinder will be 'rocking' – ie, the valves will be open an equal amount, and therefore the No 4 cylinder cam lobes at the rear of the camshaft will be equally inclined downwards **(see illustrations)**.

12 Do not attempt to turn the engine with the flywheel or camshaft locked in position, as engine damage may result. If the engine is to be left in the 'locked' state for a long period of time, it is a good idea to place suitable warning notices inside the vehicle, and in the engine compartment. This will reduce the possibility of the engine being cranked on the starter motor.

N42 and N46 engines

13 Remove the cylinder head cover as described in Section 4.

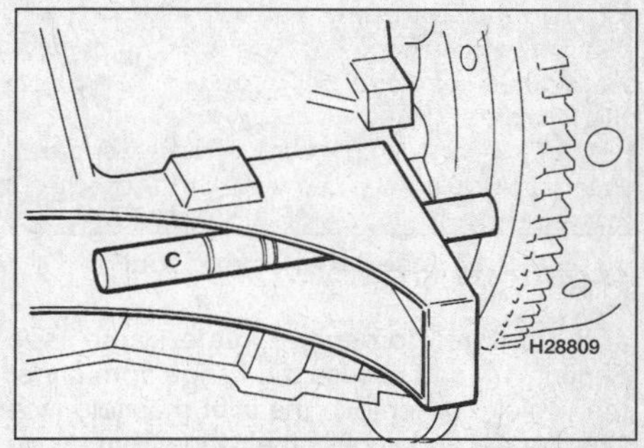

3.8 Locking tool engages with TDC hole in flywheel

14 Using a spanner or socket on the crankshaft pulley bolt, turn the crankshaft clockwise until the curved faces of the camshaft flanges are uppermost **(see illustration)**.

15 Pull the blanking plug (where fitted) from the timing hole in the left-hand rear corner flange of the cylinder block below the starter motor. Access to the flange is very limited. If necessary, remove the engine undershield

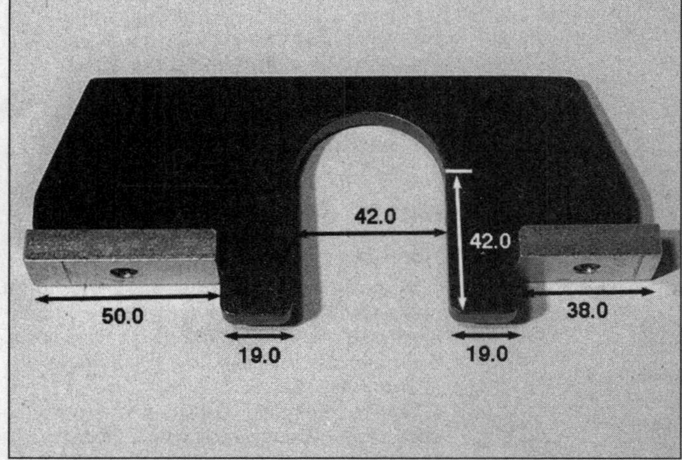

3.11a Dimensions of the camshaft locking tool (all dimensions in mm)

3.11b Camshaft locking tool in position – M43TU engine

3.14 Turn the crankshaft until the curved face (arrowed) of the camshaft flange is uppermost

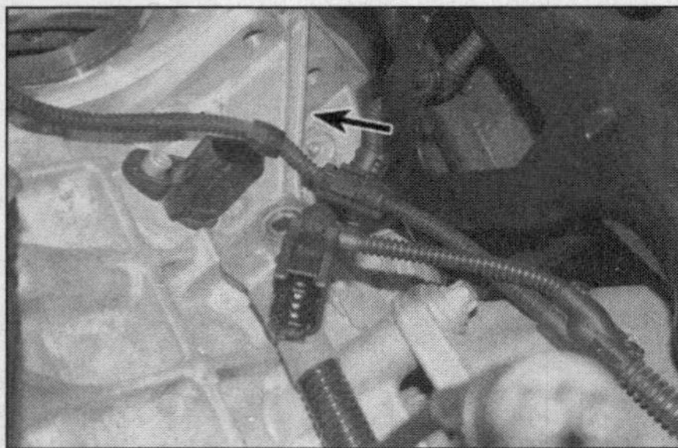
3.15 Pull out the blanking plug (where fitted) beneath the starter motor (removed for clarity)

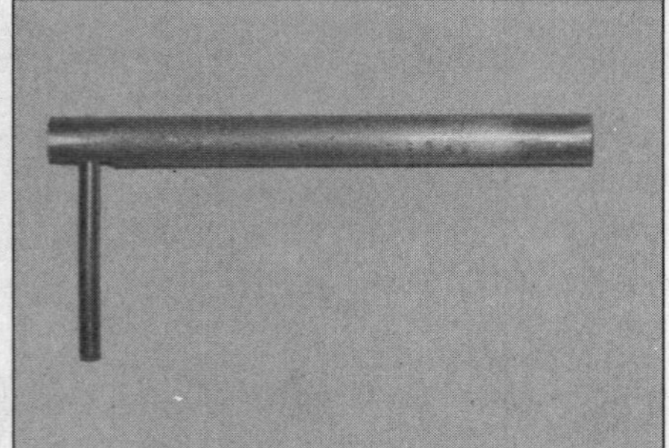
3.16 Crankshaft locking tool

3.17 Insert the locking tool

3.20a Fit the tool over the exhaust camshaft . . .

3.20b . . . then insert the inlet camshaft locking tool

and front reinforcement plate/frame (see Section 14) and access the flange from under the vehicle, or remove the inlet manifold (see Chapter 4A) and access the flange from above **(see illustration)**.

16 To 'lock' the crankshaft in position, a special tool will be required. BMW tool 11 9 190 (N42 engine) or 11 5 120 (N46 engine) can be used, but an alternative can be made up by using an 8 mm diameter rod, approximately 80 mm in length. In order to be able to extract the rod from the timing hole, we drilled into the rod at one end, and tapped in a roll-pin **(see illustration)**.

17 Insert the rod through the timing hole. If necessary, turn the crankshaft slightly until the rod enters the TDC hole in the flywheel **(see illustration)**. **Note:** *On models equipped with automatic transmission, it is possible to mistakenly insert the rod into a larger hole in the driveplate. Ensure that, when the rod is inserted, it is not possible to rotate the crankshaft at all.*

18 The crankshaft is now 'locked' in position with No 1 piston at TDC.

19 Due to the camshaft timing adjustment facility, it is necessary to check that the camshafts are in their 'initial' positions, by attempting to rotate the upper edges of the camshafts towards each other. Use a square section rod or similar to rotate the inlet camshaft, and an open-ended spanner on the hexagonal section of the exhaust camshaft. If either camshaft can be rotated, continue turning until it comes to a stop. When the camshaft(s) stop turning, or cannot be turned in the first place, they are in their 'initial' positions, and the adjustment units are locked in place.

20 In this position, it should be possible to fit BMW special tool 11 9 292 over the end of the inlet camshaft, and tool 11 9 291 over the end of the exhaust camshaft. With the camshaft correctly positioned the tools should contact the cylinder head upper surface with no air gap below them. Secure the exhaust camshaft tool in place with the retaining bolts, and tighten down the two bolts to secure the inlet camshaft tool **(see illustrations)**. Essentially, these tools hold the flat-sided ends of the camshafts at exactly 90 degrees to the cylinder head upper gasket face.

21 **Do not** attempt to turn the engine with the flywheel or camshaft locked in position, as engine damage may result. If the engine is to be left in the 'locked' state for a long period of time, it is a good idea to place suitable warning notices inside the vehicle, and in the engine compartment. This will reduce the possibility of the engine being cranked on the starter motor.

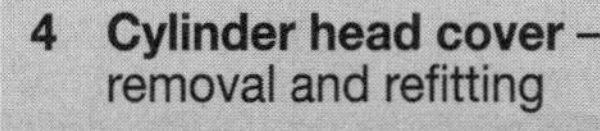

4 Cylinder head cover – removal and refitting

Note: *A new gasket and/or seals may be required on refitting – see text.*

M43TU engine

Removal

1 Working at the rear of the engine compartment, turn the fasteners 90° anti-clockwise and remove the pollen filter cover. Slide the filter from the housing. If necessary, refer to Chapter 1.

2 Release the retaining clips, and remove the cable from the ducting on the air inlet housing **(see illustration)**.

3 Undo the four bolts and pull the pollen filter housing to the front **(see illustration)**.

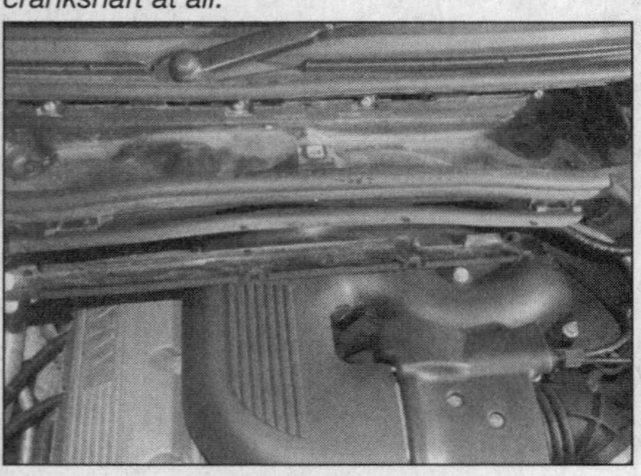
4.2 Unclip the cable ducting

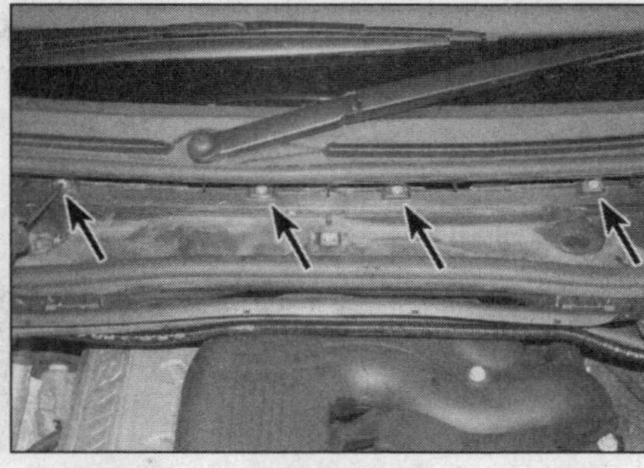
4.3 Undo the pollen filter housing bolts (arrowed)

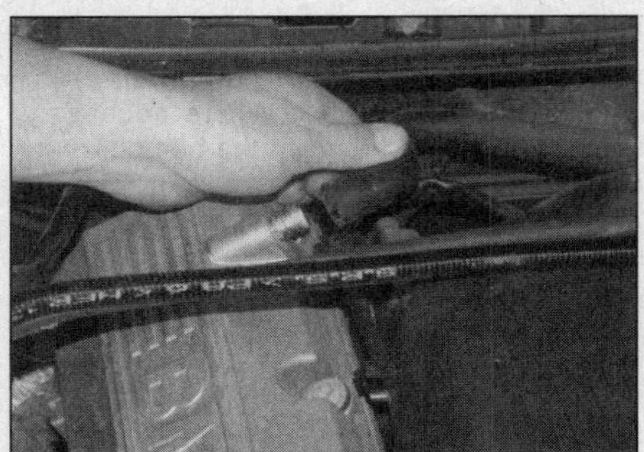

4.4 Disconnect the breather hose from the cylinder head cover

4 Disconnect the engine breather hose, then unscrew the securing bolts and lift the cover from the cylinder head. Recover the gasket **(see illustration)**.

Refitting

5 Thoroughly clean the gasket faces of the cylinder head cover and the engine.

6 Check the condition of the sealing rubbers on the cover securing bolts, and renew if necessary. Ensure that the washers and rubber seals are correctly fitted to the securing bolts **(see illustration)**.

7 Examine the cover gasket, and renew if necessary, then lay the gasket in position in the cylinder head cover.

8 Apply a little jointing compound to the cylinder head cover mating face of the joint between the upper timing chain cover and the cylinder head **(see illustration)**.

9 Position the cover on the cylinder head, ensuring that the lug on the gasket engages with the corresponding cut-out in the rear of the cylinder head.

10 Refit the cover securing bolts, and tighten to the specified torque.

N42 and N46 engines

Removal

11 Undo the two nuts, raise the front edge of the plastic cover on top of the engine, and pull it out towards the front.

12 Working at the rear of the engine compartment, turn the fasteners 90° anti-clockwise and remove the pollen filter cover. Slide the filter from the housing. If necessary, refer to Chapter 1.

4.6 Check that the rubber seals on the cylinder head cover bolts are not damaged

13 Release the retaining clips, and remove the cables/hoses from the ducting on the air inlet housing **(see illustration 4.2)**.

14 Undo the four bolts and pull the pollen filter housing to the front **(see illustration 4.3)**.

15 In the left-hand rear corner of the engine compartment, pull up the sealing strip, undo the two fasteners and pull the trim panel forwards a little **(see illustration)**.

16 Undo the two Torx bolts, and lift out the heater inlet housing **(see illustration)**.

17 Unscrew the oil filler cap, and fold it open. Align the filler cap collar marks with the marks on the filler neck **(see illustration)**. Squeeze together the unmarked sides of the collar, and pull it from the filler neck.

18 Pull the ignition coil plastic cover from the rubber retaining grommets.

19 Prise up the right-hand edge of the plastic covers over the ignition coils (above the

4.8 Apply a little sealant to the areas where the timing cover meets the cylinder head (arrowed)

spark plugs), and disconnect the coils' wiring plugs **(see illustration)**. With the wiring plugs disconnected, pull the coils from the spark plugs.

20 Disconnect the positioning motor wiring plug and eccentric shaft sensor plug, then release the ignition coil wiring harness from the clips on the cylinder head cover and lay it to one side. Note the two earth connections attached to the cylinder head cover **(see illustration)**.

21 Squeeze together the sides of the connector, and disconnect the breather hose from the cover.

22 Undo the two bolts, and remove the eccentric shaft sensor collar **(see illustration)**.

23 Undo the retaining bolts and remove the cylinder head cover **(see illustration)**. Note the length of the bolts as they are withdrawn

4.15 Remove the trim panel (arrowed) from the left-hand corner of the engine compartment

4.16 Undo the Torx bolts (one each side – arrowed) and remove the heater inlet housing

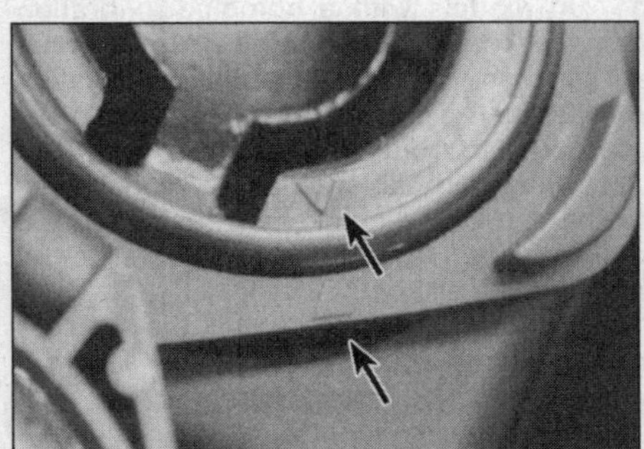

4.17 Align the cap collar marks (arrowed)

4.19 Pull up the edge of the plastic covers, and disconnect the wiring plugs

4.20 Disconnect the earth connections

4.22 Undo the bolts and remove the sensor collar

4.23 Cylinder head cover bolts

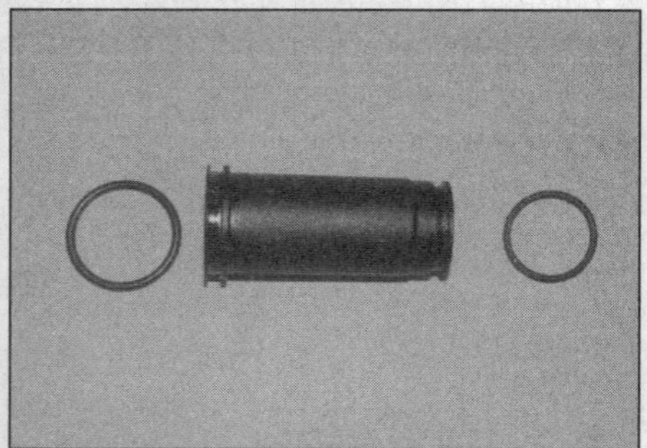

4.25 Note that the spark plug tube O-rings are not the same size

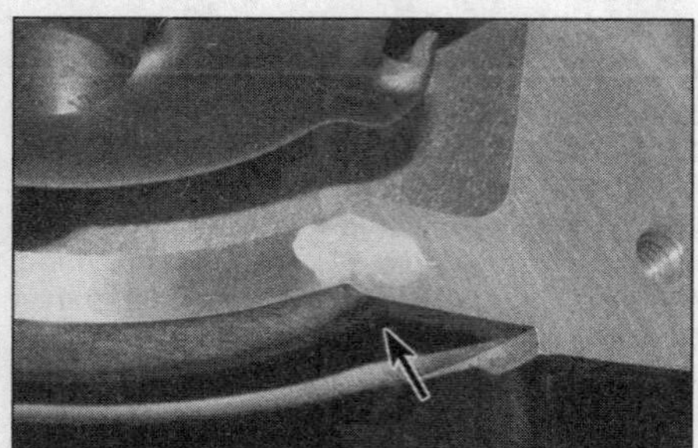

4.26 Apply sealant to the semi-circular sealing areas at the front and rear of the cylinder head (arrowed)

– some are longer than others. If the rubber seal is in good condition, it can be re-used. If not, renew it. **Note:** *At the time of writing, the gasket was only available complete with the cylinder head cover and bolts. Check with your local BMW dealer.*

24 If required, pull the spark plug sealing tubes from the cylinder head.

Refitting

25 Refit the spark plug tube O-rings, coat them with clean engine oil, and push them into place in the cylinder head **(see illustration)**.

26 Apply a thin bead of Drei Bond 1209 sealant (available from BMW dealers) to the semi-circular sealing areas on the front and rear of the cylinder head **(see illustration)**.

27 With the rubber seal in place, refit the cylinder head cover, finger-tightening the bolts at this stage.

28 Apply a little clean engine oil to the O-ring seal, and refit the camshaft sensor collar, only finger-tighten the bolts at this stage.

29 Check that the cylinder head cover seal is correctly seated all the way around, and tighten the bolts in a diagonal sequence to the specified torque.

30 Tighten the eccentric shaft sensor collar retaining bolts securely.

31 The remainder of refitting is a reversal of removal.

5 Crankshaft vibration damper/pulley and pulley hub – removal and refitting

M43TU engine

Note: *If the pulley hub is removed, a new securing bolt will be required on refitting, and a torque wrench capable of providing 330 Nm (244 lbf ft) of torque will be required.*

5.2 One-piece vibration damper/pulley and hub

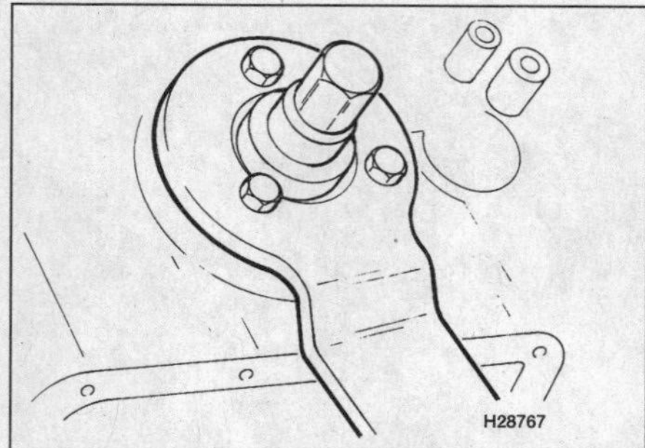

5.5 BMW special tool used to hold the hub

Removal

1 Remove the auxiliary drivebelt(s) as described in Chapter 1. Where necessary, undo the bolts and remove the belt pulley for the air conditioning compressor.

2 Some engines have a separate vibration damper/pulley which is bolted to a hub, while some engines have a one-piece combined vibration damper/pulley and hub **(see illustration)**.

3 On models with a separate vibration damper/pulley, unscrew the securing bolts, and remove the vibration damper/pulley from the hub. If necessary, counterhold the hub using a socket or spanner on the hub securing bolt.

4 On models with a combined vibration damper/pulley and hub, or if the hub is to be removed on models with a separate vibration damper/pulley, the securing bolt must be unscrewed.

Warning: The crankshaft hub securing bolt is very tight. A tool will be required to counterhold the hub as the bolt is unscrewed. Do not attempt the job using inferior or poorly-improvised tools, as injury or damage may result.

5 Make up a tool to hold the hub. A suitable tool can be fabricated using two lengths of steel bar, joined by a large pivot bolt. Bolt the holding tool to the pulley hub using the pulley-to-hub bolts. Alternatively, a tool is available from BMW dealers **(see illustration)**.

6 Using a socket and a long swing-bar, loosen the hub bolt. Note that the bolt is very tight.

7 Unscrew the hub bolt, and remove the washer. Discard the bolt, a new one must be used on refitting.

8 Withdraw the hub from the end of the crankshaft. If the hub is tight, use a puller to draw it off.

9 Recover the Woodruff key from the end of the crankshaft if it is loose.

Refitting

10 On models with a combined vibration damper/pulley and hub, or if the hub has been removed on models with a separate vibration damper/pulley, it is advisable to take the opportunity to renew the oil seal in the lower timing chain cover, with reference to Section 6.

11 On models with a combined vibration damper/pulley and hub, or if the hub has been removed on models with a separate vibration damper/pulley, proceed as follows, otherwise proceed to paragraph 17.

12 Where applicable, refit the Woodruff key to the end of the crankshaft, then align the groove in the hub with the key, and slide the hub onto the end of the crankshaft.

13 Refit the washer, noting that the shoulder on the washer must face the hub, and fit a new hub securing bolt.

14 Bolt the holding tool to the hub, as during removal, then tighten the hub bolt to the specified torque. Take care to avoid injury and/or damage.

5.20 Vibration damper/pulley bolts

15 On models with a combined vibration damper/pulley and hub, proceed to paragraph 18.

16 Where applicable, unscrew the holding tool, and refit the vibration damper/pulley, ensuring that the locating dowel on the hub engages with the corresponding hole in the damper/pulley.

17 Refit the damper/pulley securing bolts, and tighten to the specified torque. Again, counterhold the pulley if necessary when tightening the bolts.

18 Refit the auxiliary drivebelt as described in Chapter 1.

N42 and N46 engines

Note: *If the pulley hub is removed, a new securing bolt will be required on refitting, and a torque wrench capable of providing 300 Nm (221 lbf ft) of torque will be required.*

Removal

19 Remove the auxiliary drivebelt as described in Chapter 1.

20 Unscrew the three securing bolts, and remove the vibration damper/pulley from the hub. If necessary, counterhold the hub using a socket or spanner on the hub securing bolt **(see illustration)**.

21 To remove the hub, the securing bolt must be unscrewed.

Warning: If the crankshaft hub securing bolt is slackened, the timing chain/oil pump/balancer shaft sprockets will no longer be locked to the crankshaft and can rotate independently. Consequently, once the hub bolt is slackened, lock the crankshaft and camshafts in position as described in Section 3.

Warning: The crankshaft pulley hub securing bolt is very tight. A tool will be required to counterhold the hub as the bolt is unscrewed. A special tool is available from BMW. Do not attempt the job using inferior or poorly-improvised tools, as injury or damage may result.

22 Make up a tool to hold the hub. A suitable tool can be fabricated using two lengths of steel bar, joined by a large pivot bolt. Bolt the holding tool to the hub using the pulley-to-hub bolts.

23 Using a socket and a long swing-bar, loosen the hub bolt. Note that the bolt is very tight.

24 With the bolt removed, slide the hub from the end of the crankshaft. Discard the bolt, a new one must be fitted. It is advisable to take the opportunity to renew the oil seal in the lower timing chain cover, with reference to Section 18.

Refitting

25 Refitting is a reversal of removal, noting the following points:

a) *Re-adjust the position of the balancer shafts as described in Section 16.*
b) *Tighten all fasteners to the specified torque where given.*

6 Timing chain covers – removal and refitting

M43TU engine upper cover

Note: *A new gasket, a new rubber seal, and suitable sealant will be required on refitting. To aid refitting, two studs will be required to screw into the cover securing bolt holes, and a thin sheet of metal plate will be required – see text.*

Removal

1 Drain the cooling system (see Chapter 1).

2 Remove the cylinder head cover as described in Section 4.

3 Remove the camshaft position sensor from the cover, with reference to Chapter 4A if necessary.

4 Prise off the securing clips, and withdraw the wiring ducting from the front of the timing chain cover.

5 Remove the thermostat (see Chapter 3).

6 Unscrew the securing bolts, and withdraw the cover from the engine **(see illustration)**. Recover the gaskets.

7 Recover the rubber seal from the top of the lower timing chain cover.

8 In production, a one-piece gasket is fitted between the upper and lower timing chain covers and the timing chain housing. If a one-piece gasket is fitted, and the lower timing chain cover is not going to be removed, cut the top section of the gasket level with the top face of the lower timing chain cover, working from the inside outwards. A separate upper gasket is available as a spare part from BMW dealers.

Refitting

9 Commence refitting by thoroughly cleaning all gasket faces.

10 Apply sealant to the joints between the cylinder head, timing chain housing and timing chain covers **(see illustration)**.

11 Screw two long studs (or bolts with the heads cut off) into the top timing chain cover securing bolts holes.

12 Place a new upper gasket (see paragraph 8) in position on the timing chain housing. Coat the top and bottom edges of the gasket with sealant **(see illustration)**.

13 Apply sealant sparingly to the ends of the

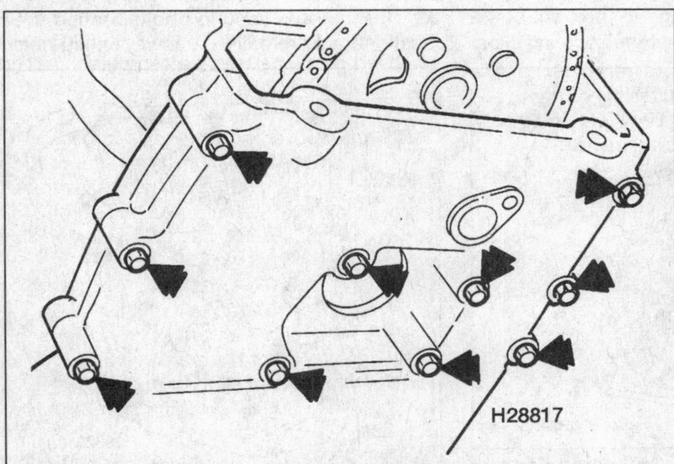

6.6 Upper timing cover bolt locations (arrowed)

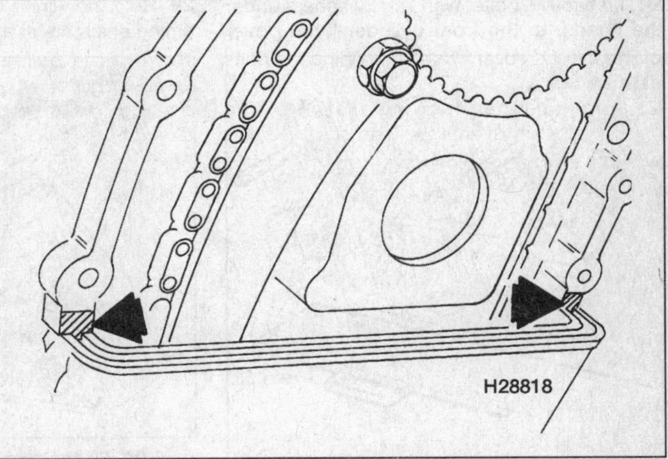

6.10 Apply sealant to the joints (arrowed) between the cylinder head, timing chain housing and timing chain covers

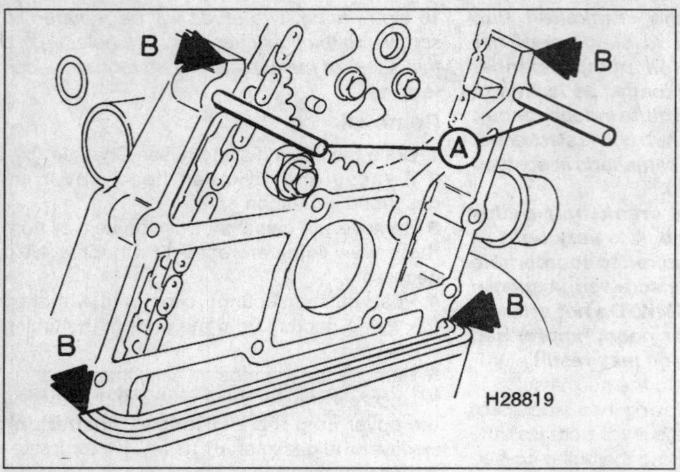

6.12 **Screw two long studs (A) into the upper securing bolts holes, and coat the top and bottom edges of the gasket (B) with sealant**

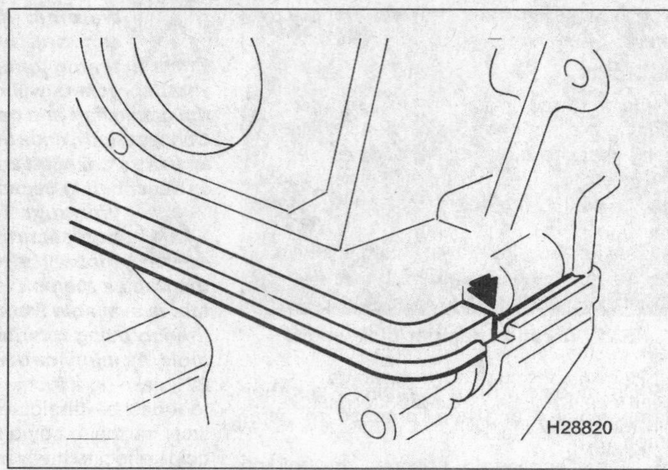

6.13 **Apply sealant to the ends of the rubber seal grooves (arrowed) in the lower timing chain cover**

rubber seal grooves in the top of the lower timing chain cover **(see illustration)**.

14 Fit a new rubber seal to the top of the lower timing chain cover, ensuring that it is correctly located in the grooves.

15 To ensure that the rubber seal seats correctly as the upper chain cover is fitted, BMW recommend the use of tool 11 2 330. This tool can be improvised using a length of very thin metal sheet (such as printer's litho plate). The sheet must be large enough to cover the whole of the rubber seal.

16 Lightly grease the upper surface of the rubber seal, and the upper and lower surfaces of the metal sheet, then lay the sheet in position on the seal **(see illustration)**.

17 Slide the upper chain cover into position over the positioning studs (see paragraph 11), then insert the four lower outer cover securing bolts, and tighten them by hand.

18 Carefully pull the metal sheet from the cover joint.

19 Lay the cylinder head cover in position, without the gasket (between the cylinder head cover and the cylinder head) fitted.

20 Fit two M6 bolts, with large washers under the heads, to the front cylinder head cover bolt locations in the cylinder head (**not** the two front-most bolt locations in the timing chain cover) **(see illustration)**.

21 Tighten the two bolts to push the upper timing chain cover down until the top face of the cover is flush with the top face of the cylinder head.

22 Tighten the previously-fitted upper timing chain cover securing bolts to the specified torque.

23 Unscrew the positioning studs from the timing chain cover, then refit the remaining cover securing bolts and tighten to the specified torque.

24 Unscrew the two M6 bolts and washers, and lift off the cylinder head cover.

25 Refit the thermostat (see Chapter 3).

26 Refit the camshaft position sensor, with reference to Chapter 4A, Section 12, if necessary.

27 Refit the cylinder head cover as described in Section 4.

28 Refill the cooling system as described in Chapter 1.

29 Refit the wiring ducting to the front of the timing chain cover and refit the securing clips.

M43TU engine lower cover

Note: *A new gasket and suitable sealant will be required on refitting.*

Removal

30 Remove the upper timing chain cover as described previously in this Section.

31 Remove the auxiliary drivebelt as described in Chapter 1.

32 The coolant pump pulley must now be removed. Counterhold the pulley by wrapping an old drivebelt around it and clamping tightly, then unscrew the securing bolts and withdraw the pulley.

33 Unscrew the crankshaft position sensor from its mounting bracket, and move it to one side, with reference to Chapter 4A, Section 12. Note that it is preferable to completely remove the sensor to avoid the possibility of damage.

34 Where applicable, release any wiring/ducting from the cover, and move clear of the working area.

35 Remove the crankshaft vibration damper/pulley and pulley hub, referring to Section 5.

36 Unscrew the securing bolts, noting their locations, and remove the lower timing chain

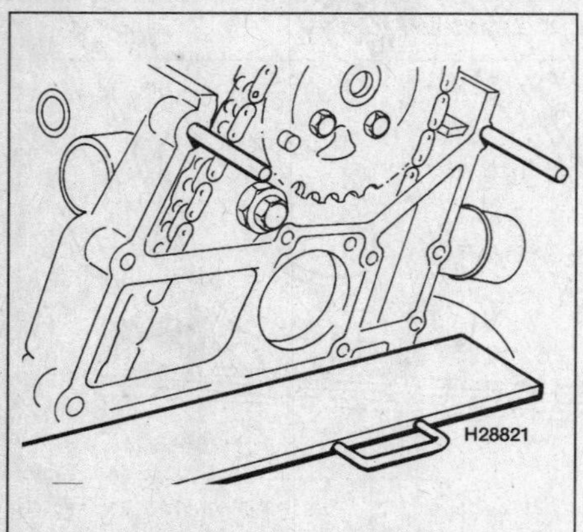

6.16 **Lay the metal sheet in position on the rubber seal**

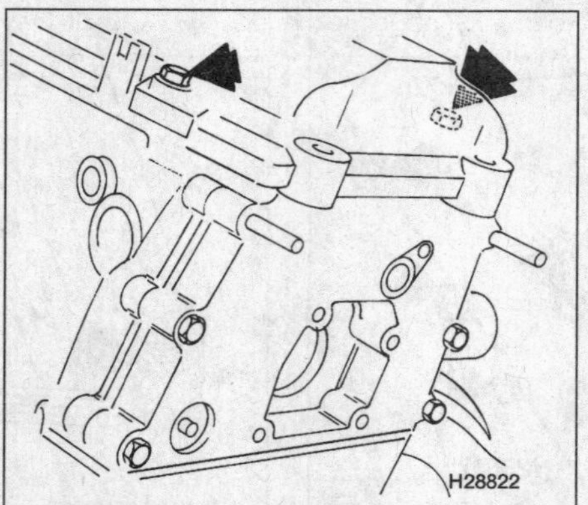

6.20 **Fit the two M6 bolts to the front cylinder head cover bolt locations in the cylinder head (arrowed)**

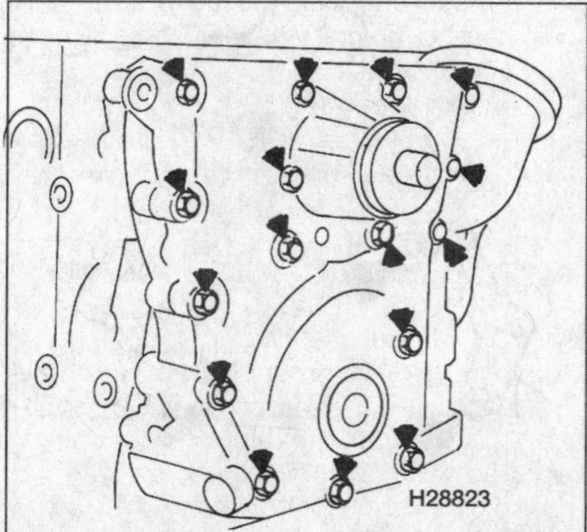

6.36 **Lower timing chain cover bolt locations (arrowed)**

cover **(see illustration)**. Recover the gasket. Refer to paragraph 8.

Refitting

37 Commence refitting by thoroughly cleaning the mating faces of the lower cover, timing chain housing and upper cover.

38 Note the fitted depth of the crankshaft front oil seal in the cover, then lever out the seal.

39 Clean the oil seal housing, then fit a new oil seal, using a large socket or tube to drive the seal into position to the previously-noted depth.

40 Check that the cover positioning dowels are in position in the timing chain housing.

41 Place a new gasket in position on the timing chain housing, using a little grease to hold the gasket in position if necessary. Note the following:

a) When refitting, a new one-piece gasket can be fitted between the upper and lower timing chain covers and the timing chain housing. Coat the top edges of the gasket with a little sealant.

b) Refit the upper timing chain cover as described previously, but if a one-piece gasket is used on refitting, ignore the references to the upper cover gasket. Similarly, if a one-piece gasket is used, there is no need to use the two positioning studs when refitting the upper timing chain cover.

42 Offer the lower cover into position, and refit the securing bolts to their original locations. Tighten the bolts to the specified torque.

43 Refit the crankshaft vibration damper/pulley and pulley hub as described in Section 5.

44 Make sure that any wiring/ducting released during removal is correctly routed and repositioned during refitting.

45 Refit the crankshaft position sensor.

46 Refit the coolant pump pulley and tighten the securing bolts.

47 Refit the auxiliary drivebelt as described in Chapter 1.

48 Refit the upper timing chain cover as described previously in this Section.

N42 and N 46 engines

49 On these engines, the cover over the timing chain is integral with the engine block.

7 Timing chain – removal, inspection and refitting

M43TU engine

Removal

1 Position No 1 piston at TDC, and lock the flywheel in position, as described in Section 3.

2 Remove the upper and lower timing chain covers, as described in Section 6.

3 Unscrew the camshaft sprocket bolts, and remove the camshaft position sensor wheel. Note its fitted position.

4 Push back the top end of the tensioner rail to relieve the tension on the chain until the camshaft sprocket can be removed **(see illustration)**. Withdraw the sprocket from the camshaft, noting which way round it is fitted, then disengage the sprocket from the chain.

5 Working at the lower end of the tensioner rail, push the end of the rail to retract the hydraulic tensioner piston until the groove in the piston is aligned with the locking pin hole in the tensioner body. Lock the tensioner in position by inserting a metal rod or drill into the locking pin hole to engage with the groove in the piston **(see illustrations)**.

6 Note the routing of the chain in relation to the chain guide and tensioner rail to aid refitting.

7 With the tensioner locked in position, slide the chain, complete with the crankshaft sprocket, from the chain housing. Recover the Woodruff key from the end of the crankshaft if it is loose.

8 If desired, the tensioner rail and the chain guide can be removed from the engine, in which case note their positions to ensure correct refitting.

Inspection

9 The chain should be renewed if the sprockets are worn or if the chain is worn (indicated by excessive lateral play between the links, and excessive noise in operation). It is wise to renew the chain in any case if the engine is dismantled for overhaul. Note that the rollers on a very badly worn chain may be slightly grooved. To avoid future problems, if there is any doubt at all about the condition of the chain, renew it.

10 Examine the teeth on the sprockets for wear. Each tooth forms an inverted V. If worn, the side of each tooth under tension will be slightly concave in shape when compared with the other side of the tooth (ie, the teeth will have a hooked appearance). If the teeth appear worn, the sprockets must be renewed. Also check the chain guide and tensioner rail contact surfaces for wear, and renew any worn components as necessary.

Refitting

11 Ensure No 1 piston is still at TDC, with the crankshaft locked in position. Check the position of the camshaft using the template (see Section 3).

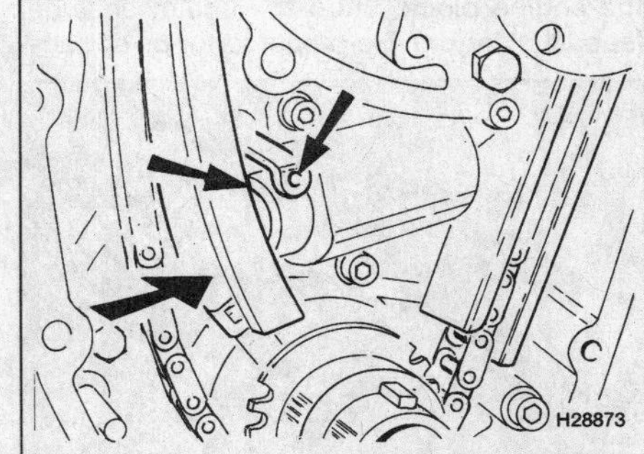

7.5a Push the end of the tensioner rail to align the tensioner piston groove with the locking pin hole in the tensioner body (arrowed)

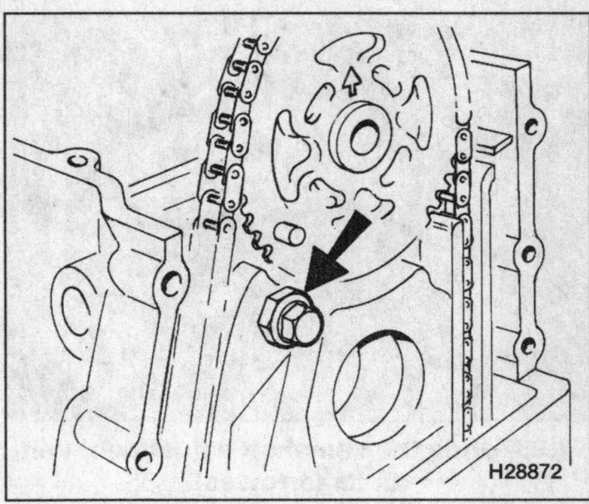

7.4 Push back the top of the tensioner rail (arrowed) to relieve the chain tension

12 Where applicable, refit the chain guide and the tensioner rail, ensuring that they are positioned correctly as noted before removal.

13 Where applicable, refit the Woodruff key to the end of the crankshaft.

14 Engage the chain with the crankshaft sprocket, then slide the chain/sprocket assembly into position, ensuring that the sprocket locates on the Woodruff key. Route the chain around the chain guide and tensioner rail as noted before removal.

15 Remove the locking pin from the chain tensioner to release the tensioner piston.

16 Push back the top end of the tensioner rail, as during removal, to allow the camshaft sprocket to be fitted. Engage the camshaft sprocket with the chain, ensuring that it is fitted the correct way round as noted before removal, and manipulate the sprocket so that the timing arrow points vertically upwards.

17 Fit the sprocket to the camshaft, aligning the bolt holes in the camshaft flange with the centres of the elongated holes in the sprocket (the camshaft should be locked in the TDC position using the template – see Section 3). Fit the sprocket securing bolts, and tighten as far as possible by hand.

18 Release the upper end of the tensioner rail, then tighten the camshaft sprocket bolts to the specified torque.

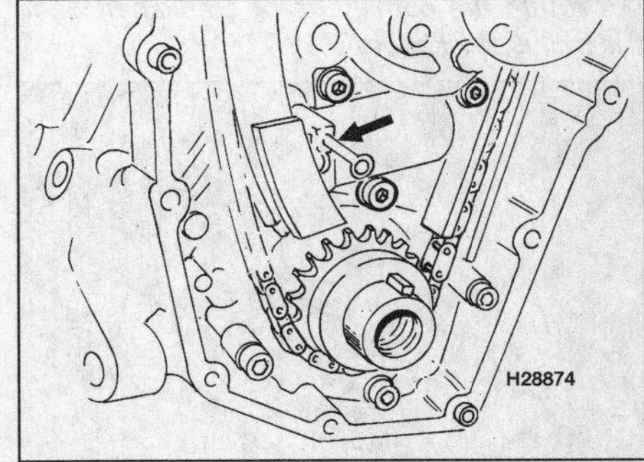

7.5b Fit a rod or drill (arrowed) to lock the tensioner in position

7.28 Undo the camshaft adjustment unit bolts (arrowed)

7.29 Undo the chain tensioner (arrowed)

7.30 Note that the camshaft adjustment units are marked EX or IN

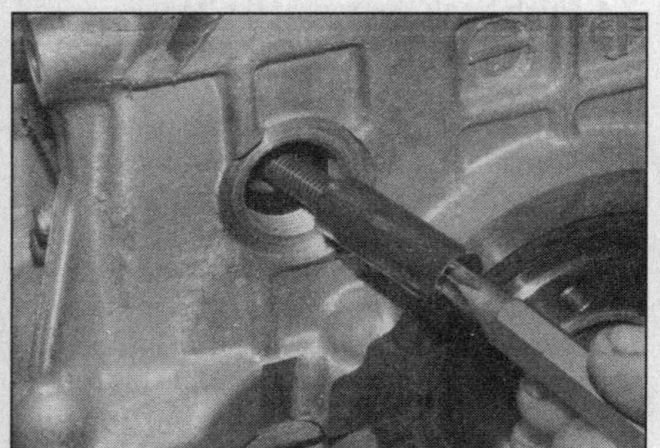
7.31 Unscrew the cover plug and undo the timing chain guide lower pin

7.33 Remove the cover plug (arrowed) and unscrew the timing chain guide upper pin

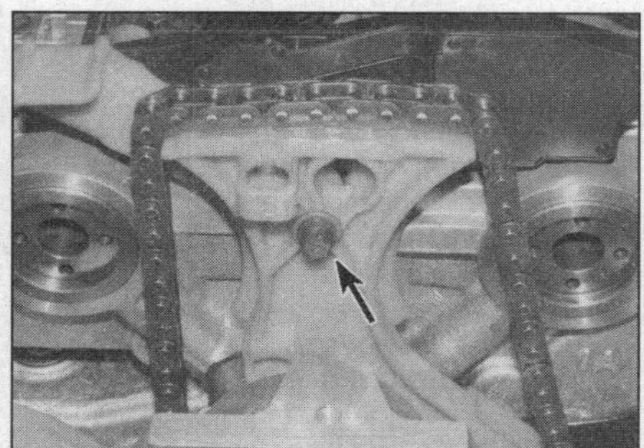
7.34 Undo the chain guide upper bolt (arrowed)

19 Remove the flywheel locking tool, and remove the template used to check the camshaft position.

20 Refit the timing chain covers as described in Section 6.

N42 and N46 engines

Removal

21 Ensure the engine is set to TDC as described in Section 3.

22 Remove the positioning motor for the eccentric shaft as described in Section 10.

23 Remove the crankshaft vibration damper/pulley and hub as described in Section 5. **Note:** *Once the hub bolt is slackened, the crankshaft is no longer locked to the timing chain/oil pump/balancer shaft sprocket. Do not rotate the camshafts or crankshaft once the bolt is slackened.*

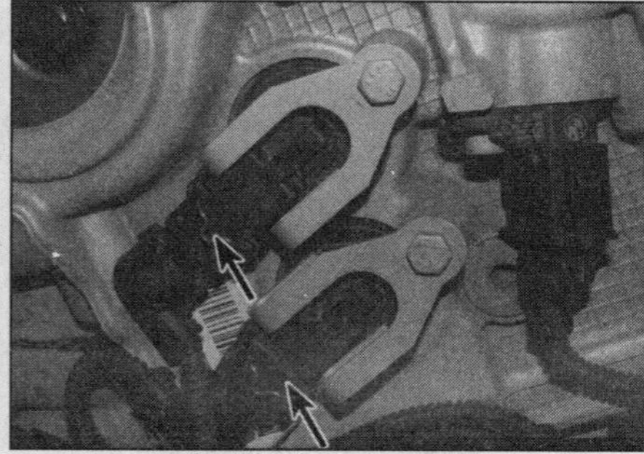
7.35a Disconnect the adjustment unit solenoids' wiring plugs (arrowed)

24 Jack up the front of the vehicle, and support it securely on axle stands (see *Jacking and vehicle support).*

25 Using an engine support beam located on the inner wings, or an engine hoist, attach lifting chains to the lifting eye at the front of the engine, and take the weight of the engine.

26 Lower the front subframe as described in Section 15. Note there is no need to detach the steering rack from the subframe, undo the steering column flexible joint pinch-bolt and separate the pinion from the column.

27 Remove the sump as described in Section 13.

28 With the camshafts locked in place as described in Section 3, slacken the exhaust and inlet camshaft adjustment unit bolts **(see illustration)**.

29 Working on the front right-hand side of the engine block, undo the chain tensioner **(see illustration)**. Be prepared for oil spillage.

7.35b Pull the solenoids from the cylinder head and discard the O-ring seals

Discard the sealing washer, a new one must be fitted. If the piston is to be re-used, holding it vertical slowly compress the piston to evacuate all the oil.

30 Completely unscrew the exhaust camshaft adjustment unit bolt, and remove the unit complete with the camshaft sensor ring and sprocket. Repeat this procedure for the inlet camshaft. Note that the units are marked EX and IN. Do not mix up the parts **(see illustration)**.

31 Using an Allen key, remove the plug to the right and above the front crankshaft oil seal, and unscrew the timing chain guide lower pin **(see illustration)**.

32 Squeeze together the lugs and disconnect the inlet camshaft position sensor wiring plug.

33 Undo the plug behind the inlet camshaft position sensor, and unscrew the upper timing chain guide upper pin **(see illustration)**.

34 Remove the chain guide upper bolt from the cylinder head **(see illustration)**.

35 At the front of the cylinder head, disconnect the inlet and exhaust camshaft adjustment units solenoids' wiring plugs **(see illustration)**. Undo the bolts and pull the solenoids from the cylinder head **(see illustration)**. Discard the O-ring seals, new ones must be fitted.

36 Remove the plug from the left-hand side of the timing chain cover, and unscrew the left-hand timing chain guide upper retaining pin **(see illustration)**.

37 Pull up on the timing chain, and remove it along with the guides and crankshaft sprocket.

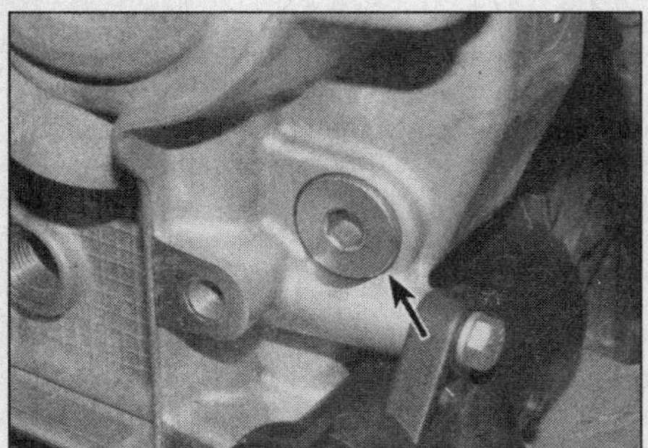

7.36 Remove the plug, and unscrew the left-hand chain guide upper retaining pin (arrowed)

7.39 Prise apart the lower edges and remove the chain from the guide (using welding rods)

7.43 Position the crankshaft sprocket in the chain, with the sprocket collar towards the crankshaft (arrowed)

38 Pull the chain down from the guides and manoeuvre the crankshaft sprocket from the chain.

39 Carefully prise apart the lower edges of the timing chain guide, and pull the chain free **(see illustration)**.

Inspection

40 The chain should be renewed if the sprockets are worn or if the chain is worn (indicated by excessive lateral play between the links, and excessive noise in operation). It is wise to renew the chain in any case if the engine is dismantled for overhaul. Note that the rollers on a very badly worn chain may be slightly grooved. To avoid future problems, if there is any doubt at all about the condition of the chain, renew it.

41 Examine the teeth on the sprockets for wear. Each tooth forms an inverted V. If worn, the side of each tooth under tension will be slightly concave in shape when compared with the other side of the tooth (ie, the teeth will have a hooked appearance). If the teeth appear worn, the sprockets must be renewed. Also check the chain guide and tensioner rail contact surfaces for wear, and renew any worn components as necessary.

Refitting

42 Carefully prise apart the lower edges of the timing chain guide, and feed the chain through **(see illustration 7.39)**.

43 Position the crankshaft sprocket in the lower loop of the chain. Note that the collar on the sprocket must face towards the crankshaft **(see illustration)**.

44 Pull the timing chain up through the guide, until the lower edge of the guide traps the sprocket in position. Hold the chain/guide/sprocket in this position.

45 Lower the assembly down through the timing chain tunnel, and install the sprocket over the end of the crankshaft.

46 Install the lower timing chain guide pin though the hole in the front of the timing cover, and tighten it securely. Using a new sealing ring, refit the cover plug and tighten it to the specified torque.

47 Install the upper timing chain guide pin through the hole in the timing cover, and tighten it securely. Using a new sealing ring, refit the cover plug and tighten it to the specified torque.

7.49a Turn the balancer shafts so the flats are aligned (wider flat on top) . . .

7.49b . . . then clamp them in place

48 Refit the crankshaft pulley hub, only finger tighten the bolt at this stage.

49 Option 1: Working underneath the vehicle, rotate the ends of the balancer shafts so that the flats of the shafts are aligned, with the wider slots at the top. Using two strips of metal and a clamp, lock the shafts in this position **(see illustrations)**.

50 Option 2: Working underneath the vehicle, rotate the ends of the balancer shafts so that the flats of the balancer weights are parallel with the crankcase mating surface, and BMW tool No. 11 5 140 can be inserted between the balancer weights and the mating surface **(see illustration)**. In the absence of the special tool, use a strip of metal.

51 Ensure that the crankshaft locking tool is still in place, and tighten the crankshaft hub bolt to 60 Nm (44 lbf ft) only. If more torque is applied to the bolt, damage may occur to the locking tool and/or the engine block.

52 Remove the strips of metal/tools locking the balancer shafts in place.

53 Refit both inlet and exhaust camshaft

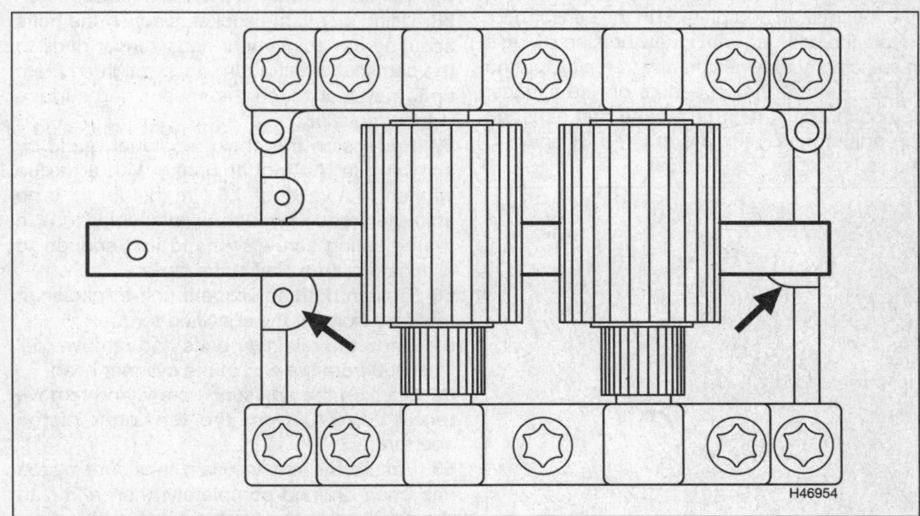

7.50 Fit the special tool between the balancer shaft weights and the machined contact points (arrowed)

7.56 Fit tool 11 9 340 into the tensioner hole

7.57a Fit tool 11 9 350 to the cylinder head

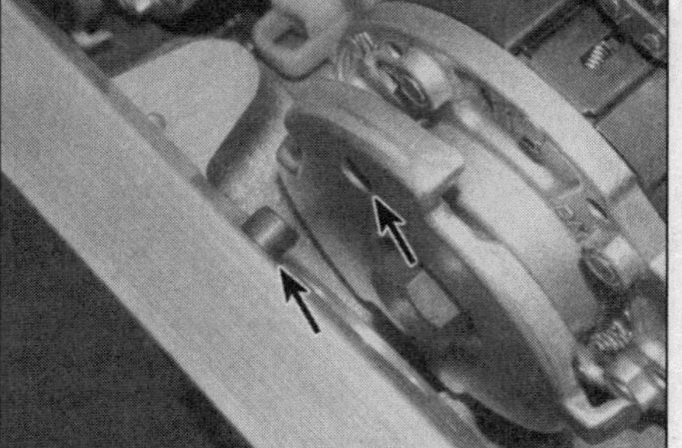
7.57b Ensure the pins of the tool engage correctly with the holes in the sensor rings (arrowed)

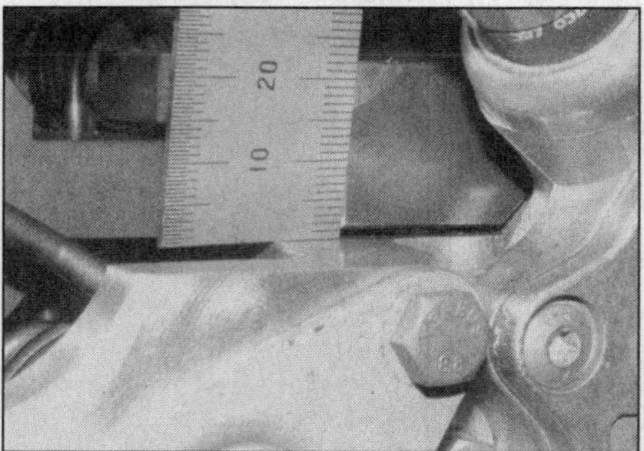
7.64 The exhaust camshaft timing is correct if the gap is less than 1.0 mm

adjuster unit solenoids to the front of the cylinder head using new O-ring seals. Tighten the retaining bolts securely, and reconnect the wiring plugs

54 Refit the timing chain upper guide upper and lower retaining bolts, and tighten them securely. Refit the sealing ring of the lower bolt cover plug, refit and tighten it to the specified torque, then reconnect the inlet camshaft position sensor wiring plug.

55 Lift the timing chain and hold it under tension. Engage the inlet camshaft adjustment unit with the chain, and position it on the end of the camshaft complete with the sensor ring. Retain the unit/ring with a new bolt, screwing it in sufficiently to eliminate any free play, but no tighter. Repeat the procedure on the exhaust camshaft adjustment unit. Note that although the adjustment units are marked IN and EX, the sensor rings are identical.

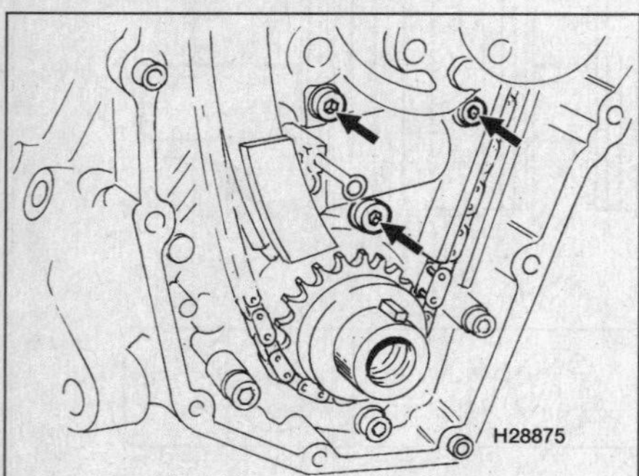

8.5 Timing chain tensioner securing bolts (arrowed)

56 Ensure that the timing chain rests correctly against the tensioner blade. Install BMW tool 11 9 340 into the tension piston hole, then turn the adjuster screw on the tool until the end of the screw just touches the tensioner rail without tensioning the chain **(see illustration)**.

57 Fit BMW tool 11 9 350 to the end of the cylinder head, ensuring that the locating pins of the tool engage correctly with the corresponding holes in the sensor ring gears **(see illustrations)**. Screw the tool to the cylinder head using the two M6 bolts supplied.

58 Using a suitable socket, slacken the bolts securing the adjustment units/sensor rings to the camshafts half a turn, then retighten them until they just touch the sensor ring surface without any play.

59 Pretension the chain tensioner guide by screwing in the tool adjusting with a torque wrench to a value of 0.6 Nm (0.4 lbf ft). If no suitable torque wrench is available, turn in the adjusting screw by hand just enough to eliminate all free play in the chain.

60 Tighten both adjustment unit-to-camshaft retaining bolts to the specified torque.

61 Undo the retaining bolts and remove tool 11 9 350 from the end of the cylinder head.

62 Slacken the adjusting screw, and remove tool 11 9 340 from the tensioner piston aperture.

63 Ensure the timing chain tensioner piston has been drained completely, then refit it to the aperture in the engine block with a new sealing ring. Tighten it to the specified torque.

64 Remove the crankshaft and camshafts locking tools, and using spanner or socket on the crankshaft hub bolt, rotate the crankshaft 720° clockwise (two turns) and check that the camshaft and crankshaft locking tools can be refitted. Note that it is permissible to have a gap of up to 1.0 mm (exhaust camshaft tool) or 0.5 mm (inlet camshaft tool) between the inlet manifold sides of the camshaft locking tools and the cylinder head upper gasket face **(see illustration)**.

65 With the timing correct, remove the locking tools, and tighten the crankshaft hub bolt to the specified torque, counterholding it using the method employed during removal.

66 The remainder of refitting is a reversal of removal.

8 Timing chain sprockets and tensioner – removal and refitting

M43TU engine

Timing chain sprockets

1 The procedure is described as part of the timing chain removal procedure in Section 7.

Timing chain tensioner

2 Position No 1 piston at TDC, and lock the flywheel in position, as described in Section 3.

3 Remove the upper and lower timing chain covers, as described in Section 6.

4 Working at the lower end of the tensioner rail, push the end of the rail to retract the hydraulic tensioner piston until the groove in the piston is aligned with the locking pin hole in the tensioner body. Lock the tensioner in position by inserting a metal rod or drill into the locking pin hole to engage with the groove in the piston.

5 Unscrew the securing bolts and remove the tensioner **(see illustration)**.

6 Do not remove the locking tool from the tensioner until after refitting. **Do not** attempt to dismantle the tensioner – a BMW special tool is required to reassemble the unit.

7 If a new tensioner is obtained, it will be supplied with a locking device to hold the piston in the locked position. In this case, **do not** remove the locking tool until the tensioner has been refitted.

8 Refitting is a reversal of removal, bearing in mind the following points.

a) Check the condition of the sealing ring, and renew if necessary.

b) Do not remove the locking tool until the tensioner has been refitted.

c) Refit the timing chain covers as described in Section 6.

N42 and N46 engines

Timing chain sprockets

9 The procedure is described as part of the timing chain removal procedure in Section 7.

Timing chain tensioner

10 The timing chain tensioner is a hydraulically-operated piston that acts upon the right-hand chain tensioner guide. Working of the right-hand front side of the cylinder block, unscrew the piston **(see illustration 7.29)**. Be prepared for fluid spillage. Discard the sealing ring, a new one must be fitted.

11 If the piston is to be refitted, hold the assembly vertically, with the hexagonal head in the palm of your hand, and slowly compress the piston against a hard, flat surface to evacuate any oil. Repeat this procedure.

12 With a new sealing ring, refit the piston and tighten it to the specified torque.

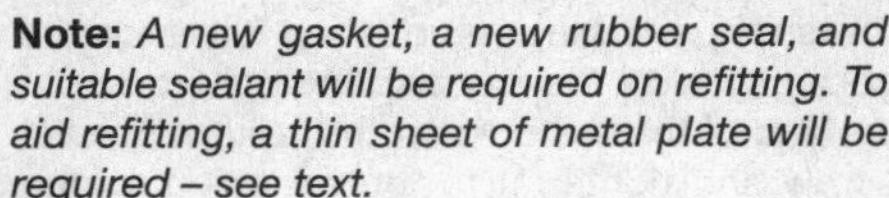

9 Timing chain housing (M43TU engine) – removal and refitting

Note: *A new gasket, a new rubber seal, and suitable sealant will be required on refitting. To aid refitting, a thin sheet of metal plate will be required – see text.*

Removal

1 Remove the timing chain, sprockets, tensioner rail and chain guide, as described in Section 7.

2 Remove the timing chain tensioner with reference to Section 8.

3 Remove the alternator as described in Chapter 5A.

4 Unscrew the alternator mounting bracket.

5 Unscrew the oil filter housing from the side of the timing chain housing. Be prepared for oil spillage, and recover the gasket and O-ring.

6 Remove the sump, referring to Section 13.

7 Unscrew the securing bolts, noting their locations, and withdraw the timing chain housing from the front of the cylinder block. Recover the gasket.

Refitting

8 Thoroughly clean the mating faces of the timing chain housing, cylinder block and cylinder head.

9 Check that the timing chain housing locating dowels are in position at the bottom of the cylinder block.

10 Apply sealant to the upper contact faces on the timing chain housing where the timing chain housing mates with the cylinder head and the timing chain cover, then fit a new rubber seal to the groove in the top of the timing chain housing **(see illustration)**.

11 Locate a new gasket over the dowels in the cylinder block.

12 To ensure that the rubber seal seats correctly as the timing chain housing is fitted, BMW use special tool 11 2 330. This tool can be improvised using a length of very thin metal sheet (such as printer's litho plate). The sheet must be large enough to cover the whole of the rubber seal.

13 Lightly grease the upper surface of the rubber seal, and the upper and lower surfaces of the metal sheet, then lay the sheet in position on the seal.

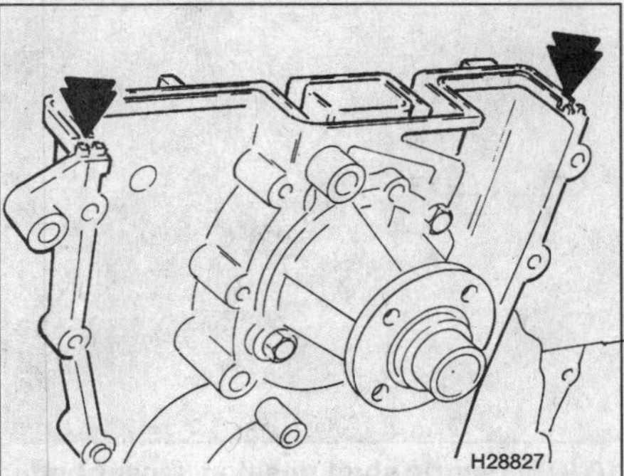

9.10 Apply sealant to the areas (arrowed) where the timing chain housing mates with the cylinder head and timing chain cover

14 Slide the timing chain housing into position over the locating dowels, then fit the securing bolts and tighten them to the specified torque **(see illustration)**.

15 Carefully pull the metal sheet from the joint between the housing and cylinder head.

16 Refit the sump as described in Section 13.

17 Refit the oil filter housing, using a new gasket and a new O-ring.

18 Refit the alternator mounting bracket, then refit the alternator, with reference to Chapter 5A.

19 Refit the timing chain tensioner with reference to Section 8.

20 Refit the timing chain guide, tensioner rail, sprockets and timing chain as described in Section 7.

10 Variable valve gear (N42 and N46 engines) – description and component renewal

Description

1 The N42 and N46 engines are equipped with a variable inlet valve operating system called Valvetronic, which is designed to improve performance and economy, whilst reducing emissions. With this system, the opening lift and duration of the inlet valves is controlled by the electronic control module, and is variable to such an extent that the traditional butterfly valve in the throttle body has been omitted. This eliminates the inlet tract 'pumping' losses associated with the throttle valve arrangement. The Valvetronic system consists of an intermediate lever between the camshaft lobe and the inlet valve rocker arm, an eccentric shaft and position sensor, a positioning motor and an electronic control module. The intermediate lever transfers the camshaft lobe lift to the rocker arm, whilst the positioning motor alters the position of the eccentric shaft, which alters the pivot point of the intermediate lever **(see illustration)**.

Component renewal

Positioning motor

2 Remove the cylinder head cover as described in Section 4.

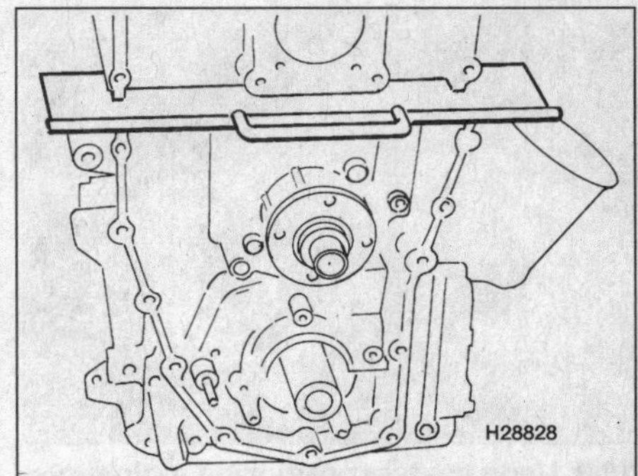

9.14 Metal sheet in place between the timing chain housing and the cylinder head

3 Unscrew the two retaining nuts **(see illustration)**.

4 Rotate the motor shaft clockwise by hand, whilst pulling the motor backwards at the same time. Discard the rubber seal, a new one must be fitted.

5 With a new seal in place, refit the motor, rotating the shaft anti-clockwise until the motor rests against the mounting bracket. Tighten the retaining nuts securely.

6 Refit the cylinder head cover as described in Section 4.

Eccentric shaft

7 Remove the inlet camshaft as described in Section 11.

8 With the camshaft removed, undo the three bolts, and remove the eccentric shaft

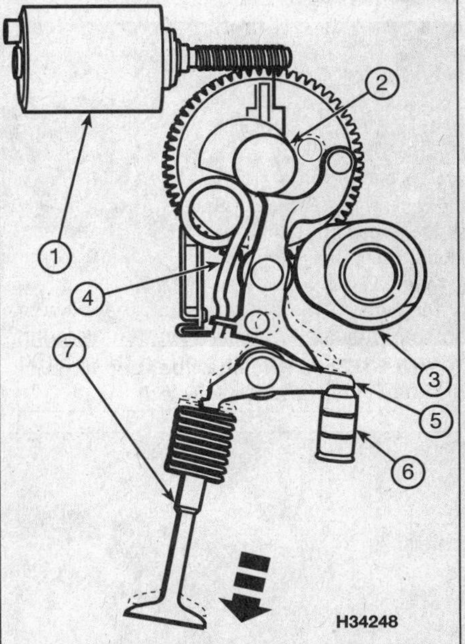

10.1 Valvetronic variable valve gear – N42 and N46 engines

1 *Positioning motor*
2 *Eccentric shaft*
3 *Camshaft*
4 *Tension spring*
5 *Rocker arm*
6 *Hydraulic compensator*
7 *Inlet valve*

10.3 Undo the two positioning motor nuts (arrowed)

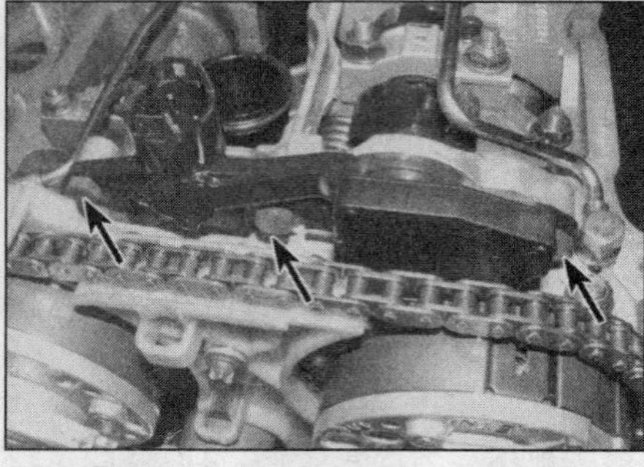

10.8 Eccentric shaft position sensor bolts (arrowed)

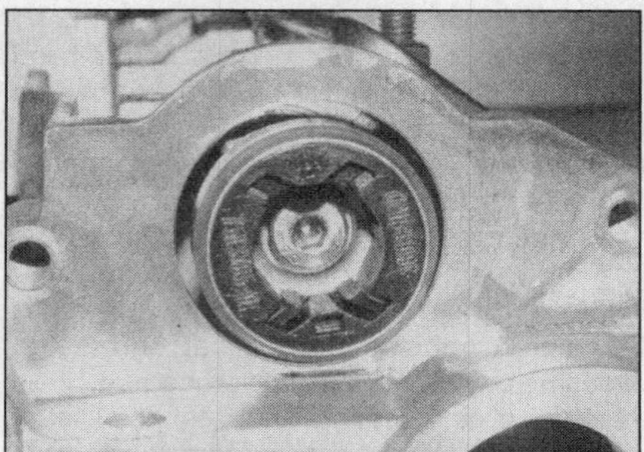

10.9 Remove the magnetic rotor from the end of the shaft

position sensor from the bearing carrier **(see illustration)**.

9 Undo the screw and remove the magnetic rotor from the end of the shaft **(see illustration)**. The rotor is very magnetic; place it in a plastic bag to prevent any magnetic swarf from attaching to it.

10 Unscrew the oil feed pipe banjo bolt, release the bearing cap retaining nuts of caps 2 and 4, and remove the oil feed pipe **(see illustration)**. Note that the caps are mark E1 to E4, with number 1 at the timing chain end

11 Release the remaining bearing caps, and lift the eccentric shaft from the bearing carrier.

12 Very carefully spread apart the shaft's needle roller bearings and remove them. Note that the bearings are very easily broken if spread too far **(see illustration)**.

13 If required, remove the bearing shells from the bearing caps.

14 To reassemble, position the new bearing shells in the bearing carrier and caps. Ensure that the locating dowels engage correctly with the corresponding oilways/locating holes, and the ends of the shells engage each other correctly **(see illustration)**.

15 Very carefully spread apart the needle roller bearings, and fit them to the bearing journals of the eccentric shaft.

16 Lubricate the needle roller bearings, and bearing shells with clean engine oil. Lay the eccentric shaft in the bearing carrier, and fit the bearing caps to their original locations. Finger-tighten the nuts retaining numbers 1 and 3 bearing caps.

17 Refit the oil feed pipe, finger-tighten the nuts retaining numbers 2 and 4 bearing caps.

18 Insert the oil feed pipe banjo bolt, and tighten it securely.

19 Ensure the bearing caps are correctly aligned, but do not finally tighten the nuts until the bearing carrier assembly is refitted to the cylinder head.

20 Refit the magnetic rotor to the end of the shaft, ensuring its locating lug engages correctly with the corresponding groove in the end of the shaft. Insert the 'anti-magnetic' screw and tighten it to the specified torque **(see illustration)**.

21 Refit the eccentric shaft position sensor, and tighten the retaining bolts securely.

22 The remainder of refitting is a reversal of removal.

Intermediate levers

23 The removal and refitting of the intermediate levers is described as part of the inlet camshaft removal procedure (see Section 11). If re-used, ensure that the levers are refitted to their original locations.

Electronic control module (ECM)

Note: *On N46 engines, the function of the Valvetronic ECM is incorporated into the engine management ECM.*

24 On left-hand drive models, remove the battery as described in Chapter 5A. Under the battery location, undo the four retaining bolts and remove the plate.

25 On right-hand drive models, the ECM is located in the left-hand corner of the engine compartment, adjacent to the electrical box. To extract the ECM from the bracket, push the base of the ECM away from the inner wing, and pull it up.

26 Disconnect the wiring plug(s), and remove the ECM **(see illustration)**.

27 Refitting is a reversal of removal. Note

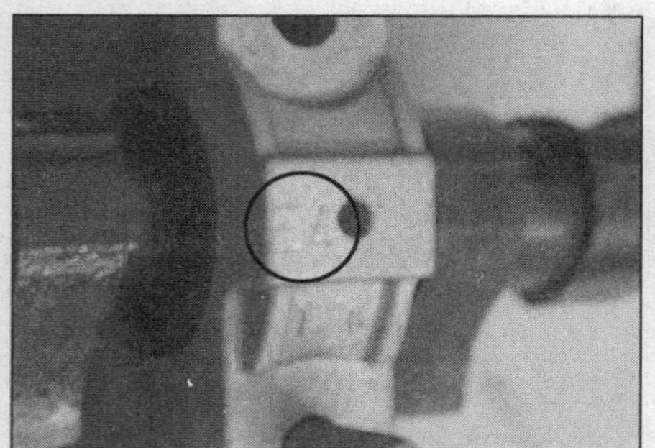

10.10 Eccentric shaft bearing caps markings (circled)

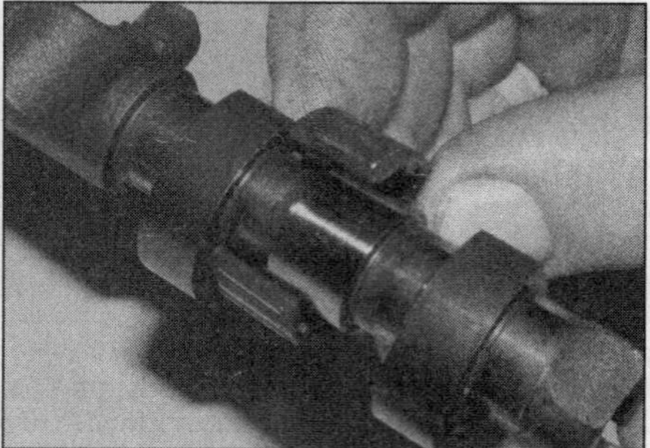

10.12 Carefully spread the bearing cage apart and remove them

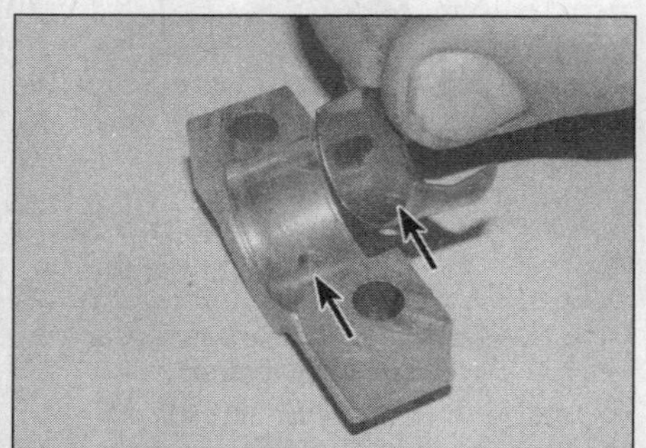

10.14 Ensure the locating dowels and holes (arrowed) engage correctly

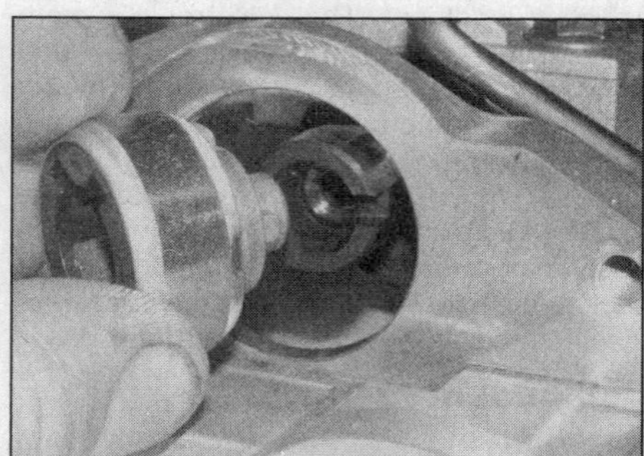

10.20 Ensure the magnetic rotor locating lugs engage correctly

10.26 Disconnect the wiring plugs and remove the ECM

that if a new ECM has been fitted, it will be necessary to code the unit using dedicated BMW test equipment (see your BMW dealer or specialist).

Eccentric shaft position sensor

28 Remove the cylinder head cover as described in Section 4.

29 Undo the three bolts and remove the sensor **(see illustration 10.8)**.

30 Refitting is a reversal of removal, tightening the sensor bolts securely.

11 Camshaft(s) and followers – removal and refitting

M43TU engine

Note: *BMW recommend that before removing the camshaft, the valves are depressed using a special tool, and the cam followers are removed. This eliminates the load on the camshaft as the bearing cap nuts are unscrewed. Provided care is taken, and the bearing cap nuts are unscrewed progressively and evenly, the procedure can be carried out without the special tool, as described in the following paragraphs. New oil spray tube securing bolt seals will be required on refitting.*

Removal

1 Remove the cylinder head cover as described in Section 4.

2 Turn the crankshaft to position No 1 piston at TDC, as described in Section 3, but do not fit the tools to lock the crankshaft and camshaft in position.

3 Turn the crankshaft through one further full revolution clockwise to bring No 4 piston to TDC on the firing stroke, then unscrew the two accessible camshaft sprocket bolts.

4 Turn the crankshaft again through one further revolution to again position No 1 piston at TDC. Fit the tools to lock the crankshaft and camshaft in position (see Section 3).

5 Unscrew the remaining two camshaft sprocket bolts which should now be accessible. Remove the camshaft position sensor rotor from the camshaft sprocket.

6 Push back the top end of the chain tensioner rail to relieve the tension on the chain until the camshaft sprocket can be removed. Withdraw the sprocket from the camshaft, noting which way round it is fitted, then disengage the sprocket from the chain. Ensure that tension is kept on the chain – tie the chain up or support it using wire, to prevent it from dropping into the timing chain housing.

7 Unscrew the securing bolts and withdraw the oil spray tube from the camshaft bearing caps **(see illustration)**. Recover the seals from the securing bolts.

8 Check the camshaft bearing caps for identification marks. The front (timing chain end) bearing cap is not marked, but the remaining caps should be marked 2 to 5 from the timing chain end of the engine **(see illustration)**. Make suitable marks if necessary.

11.7 Oil spray tube securing bolt (arrowed)

11.8 Camshaft bearing cap identification mark

9 Progressively unscrew and remove the camshaft bearing cap nuts, then remove the bearing caps.

10 Lift the camshaft from the cylinder head.

11 Prepare a compartmentalised box, filled with clean engine oil, to store the hydraulic valve lifters so that they are kept in their original fitted order. Note that the cam followers and the thrust pads must also be kept in their original order.

12 Withdraw the cam followers and the thrust pads, and store them in order so that they can be refitted to their original locations **(see illustrations)**.

13 Lift the hydraulic valve lifters from the cylinder head, and place them in the oil-filled box **(see illustrations)**.

Inspection

14 Clean all the components, including the bearing surfaces in the bearing castings and bearing caps. Examine the components carefully for wear and damage. In particular, check the bearing and cam lobe surfaces of the camshaft(s) for scoring and pitting. Examine the surfaces of the cam followers for signs wear or damage. Renew components as necessary.

Refitting

15 Lubricate the valve lifter bores in the cylinder head, then fit the valve lifters to their original locations.

16 Locate the thrust pads and the cam followers on the valves and the valve lifters in their original positions.

17 Lubricate the bearing surfaces in the cylinder head, then lay the camshaft in position so that the valves of No 1 cylinder are both open, and the valves of No 4 cylinder are 'rocking' (exhaust closing and inlet opening). Note also that the square flange at the front

11.12a Withdraw the cam followers . . .

11.12b . . . the thrust pads . . .

11.13a . . . and valve lifters

11.13b Place the valve lifters in an oil-filled box

11.22 The arrow on the camshaft must be in the 12 o'clock position in relation to the engine block

of the camshaft should be positioned with the side of the flange exactly at right-angles to the top surface of the cylinder head (this can be checked using a set-square). The position of the camshaft can be checked by fitting the template described in Section 3.

18 Lubricate the bearing surfaces in the bearing caps.

19 Fit the bearing caps to their correct locations as noted before removal, then fit the securing nuts, and tighten progressively to the specified torque.

20 Fit new seals to the oil spray tube securing bolts, then refit the spray tube and tighten the bolts.

21 Push back the top end of the chain tensioner rail, as during removal, to allow the camshaft sprocket to be fitted. Engage the camshaft sprocket with the chain, ensuring that it is fitted the correct way round as noted before removal, and manipulate the sprocket so that the timing arrow points vertically upwards.

22 Fit the sprocket to the camshaft, aligning the bolt holes in the camshaft flange with the centres of the elongated holes in the sprocket (the camshaft should be locked in the TDC position using the template – see Section 3). Refit the camshaft position sensor rotor to the sprocket with the arrow pointing vertically upwards **(see illustration)**. Fit the two upper sprocket securing bolts, and tighten as far as possible by hand.

23 Release the upper end of the tensioner rail, then tighten the two accessible camshaft sprocket bolts to the specified torque.

24 Remove the flywheel locking tool, and remove the template used to check the camshaft position.

25 Turn the crankshaft through one further full revolution clockwise to bring No 4 piston to TDC on the firing stroke, then refit and tighten the remaining two camshaft sprocket bolts.

26 Refit the cylinder head cover as described in Section 4.

N42 and N46 engines

Note: *Removal of the inlet camshaft requires access to several BMW special tools.*

Inlet camshaft removal

27 Set the engine in the TDC on No 1 cylinder position, as described in Section 3.

28 With the camshafts locked in place as described in Section 3, slacken the exhaust and inlet camshaft adjustment unit bolts **(see illustration 7.28)**.

29 Working on the front right-hand side of the engine block, undo the chain tensioner piston **(see illustration 7.29)**. Be prepared for oil spillage. Discard the sealing washer, a new one must be fitted. If the piston is to be re-used, holding it vertical slowly compress the piston to evacuate all the oil.

30 Completely unscrew the exhaust camshaft adjustment unit bolt, and remove the unit complete with the camshaft sensor ring and sprocket. Repeat this procedure for the inlet camshaft. Note that the units are marked EX and IN. Do not mix up the parts **(see illustration)**. Ensure that tension is kept on the chain – tie the chain up or support it using wire, to prevent it from dropping into the engine.

31 Remove the eccentric shaft positioning motor, as described in Section 10.

32 Squeeze together the locking tabs, and disconnect the camshaft position sensor wiring plug from the front of the timing chain cover.

33 Undo the plug behind the inlet camshaft position sensor, and unscrew the right-hand timing chain guide upper pin **(see illustration 7.33)**.

34 Remove the upper timing chain guide bolt, carefully spread apart the top of the left-hand chain guide, and release the lower part of the upper guide. Remove the upper timing chain guide **(see illustrations)**.

35 Unscrew the exhaust camshaft oil feed pipe banjo bolt, and push the pipe to the rear approximately 20 mm.

36 Remove the camshafts locking tools.

37 Using an open-ended spanner on the hexagonal section, rotate the eccentric shaft so that the torsion spring at the rear end of the shaft is under the least amount of tension **(see illustration)**.

38 Using a cable-tie or similar, pull the end of the torsion spring up and to the rear, to disengage it from the arm and roller of the eccentric shaft **(see illustration)**.

39 Rotate the eccentric shaft, so that it is in the minimum stroke position **(see illustration)**.

40 Fit BMW special tool 11 9 302 to the front

11.30 Undo the camshaft adjustment unit bolt

11.34a Remove the upper timing chain guide bolt . . .

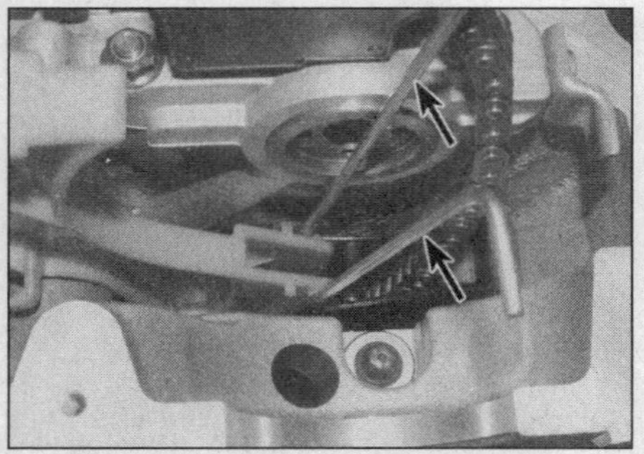

11.34b . . . and spread apart the top of the left-hand guide using two lengths of rod (arrowed) to separate the guides

11.37 Rotate the eccentric shaft so the spring (arrowed) is under the least amount of tension

11.38 Use a cable-tie (or similar) to disengage the spring from the arm (arrowed)

11.39 Turn the eccentric shaft to the minimum stroke position

11.40 Fit BMW tool 11 9 302 (arrowed) over the end of the camshaft and hold it in place with the bolt (BMW tool 11 9 303)

11.41 Secure the camshaft to the eccentric shaft using BMW tool 11 9 301 (arrowed)

11.42 Fit the BMW tools (arrowed) to the underside of the intermediate levers and the oil feed pipe

11.43 Undo the nuts (arrowed) and lift away the bearing carrier

end of the inlet camshaft and secure it in place with special tool 11 9 303. This secures the camshaft to the bearing carrier **(see illustration)**.

41 At the rear end of the camshaft, secure the eccentric shaft to the camshaft using BMW special tool 11 9 301 **(see illustration)**. Tighten the thumbwheel by hand only, to prevent the camshaft from rotating.

42 Attach BMW special tools No 11 9 310 to the oil feed pipe and the underside of all the intermediate levers to hold the levers in place **(see illustration)**.

43 The bearing carrier is retained by 13 nuts. Progressively and evenly unscrew the nuts and remove the bearing carrier **(see illustration)**.

44 Prior to removing the camshaft, the tension on the eccentric shaft-to-intermediate lever torsion springs must be relieved using BMW special tools 11 9 390 and 11 9 320 as follows. Clamp special tool 11 9 320 in a bench vice. Invert the bearing carrier assembly, and place it on the special tool **(see illustration)**.

45 Pull out the spark plug tubes from the assembly. Discard the tube O-ring seals, new ones must be fitted.

46 Position special tool 11 9 390 over the camshaft, in between the two halves of the torsion spring for No 4 cylinder. Secure it in place using the bolt provided with the tool **(see illustrations)**.

47 With the tool secured in place, ensure that the tool's jaw is located correctly at the top of the spring retaining plate, and squeeze together the jaws of the tool. Undo the plate retaining bolt, and slowly release the tool jaws to relieve the tension in the spring **(see illustrations)**.

Warning: Do not attempt to remove the torsion spring without the BMW tool. The springs are under tension and injury could result.

11.44 With BMW tool 11 9 320 (arrowed) clamped in a bench vice, invert the assembly and locate in the tool

11.46a Locate the BMW tool 11 9 390 (arrowed) in between the two halves of the spring . . .

11.46b . . . and finger-tighten the retaining bolt (arrowed)

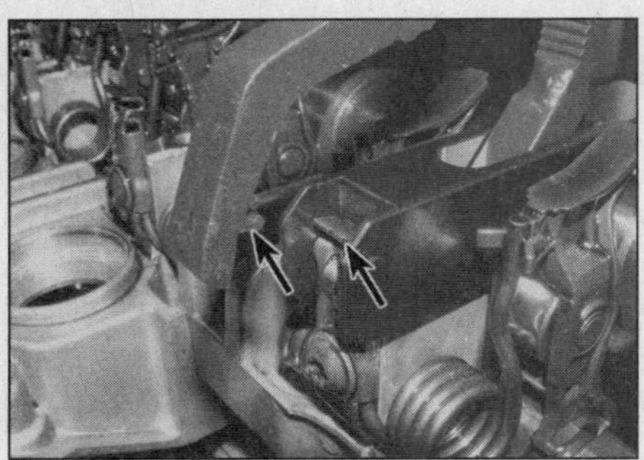
11.47a Ensure the tool jaw (arrowed) located into the top of the spring plate (arrowed)

11.47b With the tool jaws clamped, undo the spring plate retaining Torx bolt

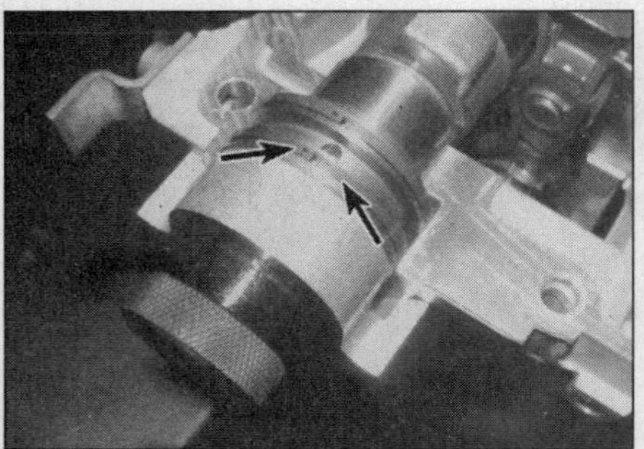
11.53 Press one end of the ring down, and the other end up (arrowed)

11.56 The curved face (arrowed) of the rear end of the camshaft must point down

48 Remove the torsion spring complete with retaining plate.

49 Remove the tool 11 9 390 and repeat the procedure on the remaining torsion springs.

50 Remove the tools securing the intermediate levers to the oil feed pipe. Remove the intermediate levers, and store in order. It is essential that, if re-used, they are refitted to their original locations.

51 Remove the tools at each end securing the camshaft. Lift out the camshaft.

52 If required, lift the rocker arms complete with hydraulic adjusters from above the inlet valves. It is essential that the rockers, if re-used, are refitted to their original positions. Separate the rockers from the adjusters. Store them in order. The hydraulic adjusters should be stored in containers and immersed in clean engine oil.

53 If required, remove the compression rings on the end of the camshaft, be pressing one end of the ring into the groove, pulling up the other ring, and unhooking it **(see illustration)**. Take care as the rings are easily broken.

Inlet camshaft inspection

54 Clean all the components, including the bearing surfaces in the bearing castings and bearing caps. Examine the components carefully for wear and damage. In particular, check the bearing and cam lobe surfaces of the camshaft(s) for scoring and pitting. Examine the surfaces of the cam followers and intermediate levers for signs wear or damage. Renew components as necessary.

Inlet camshaft refitting

55 With the bearing carrier assembly inverted, and located on BMW tool 11 9 320 clamped in a vice, lubricate the camshaft bearing surfaces with clean engine oil.

56 Lay the inlet camshaft in the bearing carrier, with the curved face of the rear end of the camshaft pointing downwards **(see illustration)**.

57 Ensure that the ends of the compression rings at the front end of the camshaft point upwards **(see illustration 11.53)**.

58 Fit tools 11 9 302 and 11 9 303 to the front, and 11 9 301 to the rear of the camshaft. With the tool fitted, the camshaft is secured to the bearing carrier and the eccentric shaft. Ensure the eccentric shaft is correctly positioned.

59 Lubricate the bearing surfaces of the intermediate levers, and insert them into place between the camshaft and eccentric shaft **(see illustrations)**.

60 Use BMW special tools No 11 9 310 around the oil feed pipe and intermediate levers to secure them in place.

61 As during dismantling, fit BMW tool 11 9 390 over the camshaft (starting at the rear end of the assembly), in between where the two halves of the torsion spring will be fitted. Install the torsion spring, ensuring the end of the spring retaining plate engages with the lower edge of the tool's jaw **(see illustration)**.

62 Carefully close the tools jaws and tension the spring. Refit the spring retaining plate bolt, and tighten it securely. Repeat this procedure on the remaining torsion springs.

63 Fit new O-ring seals to the spark plug tubes, noting that the smaller diameter seals are fitted to the base of the tubes **(see illustration 4.25)**. Coat the seals with clean engine oil, and refit them to the cylinder head.

64 Where removed, refit the rocker arms to the inlet valves, ensuring they are fitted to their original positions.

65 Refit the bearing carrier assembly to the cylinder head, and only finger-tighten the 13 retaining nuts at this stage.

66 Working from the inside outwards, evenly tighten the bearing carrier retaining nuts to 5 Nm (4 lbf ft), then working in the same pattern to 10 Nm (7 lbf ft). If the eccentric shaft had previously been removed, now is the time to finally tighten the shaft bearing caps.

67 Remove the tools securing the intermediate levers to the oil feed pipe, and the camshaft to the bearing carrier/eccentric shaft. Pull the exhaust camshaft oil feed pipe forward, insert and tighten the banjo bolt securely (note the absence of sealing washers).

68 Using an open-ended spanner, rotate the

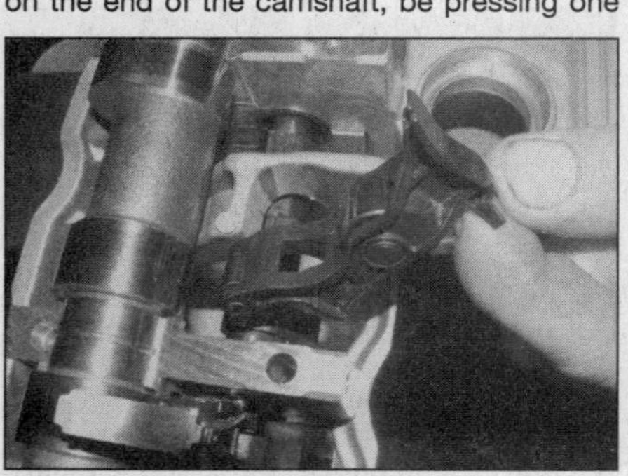
11.59a Insert the intermediate levers . . .

11.59b . . . into place

11.61 Ensure the spring retaining plate engages correctly with the tool (arrowed)

11.80 The curved side of the rear face of the camshaft must face up

11.81 The ends of the rings must be at the top

11.86 The pump drive fits into the slot in the end of the camshaft (arrowed)

eccentric shaft so that the torsion spring at the rear end of the camshaft can be pulled (using a cable-tie or strap), then fitted into the groove in the roller on the eccentric shaft arm. Rotate the eccentric shaft so that the torsion spring is now under maximum tension.

69 With reference to Section 3, refit the tools to lock the camshafts in the TDC position for No 1 cylinder.

70 The remainder of refitting is a reversal of removal.

Exhaust camshaft removal

71 Remove the bearing carrier assembly as described in Paragraphs 27 to 43 of this Section.

72 Undo the 3 bolts and remove the vacuum pump from the rear end of the exhaust camshaft (see Chapter 9). Discard the O-ring seal, a new one must be fitted.

73 Pull the exhaust camshaft oil feed pipe from the retaining clips on the bearing caps.

74 Gradually and evenly undo the bearing caps retaining nuts. Note that the caps are marked A1, A2, A3 and A4 when read from the inlet side, with A1 at the timing chain end of the engine. Remove the caps, noting that the oil feed pipe clips are located on caps Nos 1 and 4.

75 Lift the camshaft from the cylinder head. If required, remove the compression rings on the end of the camshaft, by pressing one side of the ring into the groove, pulling up the other side, and unhooking it **(see illustration 11.53)**. Take care as the rings are easily broken.

76 If required, lift the rocker arms, complete with hydraulic adjusters, from above the exhaust valves. Separate the rockers from the adjusters. Store them in order, and refit them to their original positions if re-used. The hydraulic adjusters should be stored in containers and immersed in clean engine oil.

Exhaust camshaft inspection

77 See Paragraph 54.

Exhaust camshaft refitting

78 Lubricate the camshaft bearing surfaces with clean engine oil.

79 Where removed, refit the rocker arms above the exhaust camshaft.

80 Lay the camshaft in position, with the curved side of the rear face of the camshaft pointing upwards **(see illustration)**.

81 Ensure that the ends of the compression rings at the front end of the camshaft point upwards **(see illustration)**.

82 Lubricate the bearing caps with clean engine oil, and lay the caps in place over the camshaft. Note the markings and orientation of the caps – see Paragraph 74.

83 Fit the oil feed pipe retaining clips to the Nos 1 and 4 bearing caps, then fit the nuts and tighten the nuts gradually and evenly until the underside of the caps touches the cylinder head.

84 Working from the inside out, tighten the nuts half-a-turn at a time, until the specified torque is obtained.

85 Refit the oil feed pipe to the retaining clips, and push the pipe approximately 20 mm to the rear.

86 Refit the vacuum pump with a new O-ring seal, ensuring the pump drive engages correctly with the slot in the rear of the camshaft **(see illustration)**.

87 Beginning with refitting the bearing carrier assembly, the remainder of refitting is a reversal of removal.

12 Cylinder head – removal and refitting

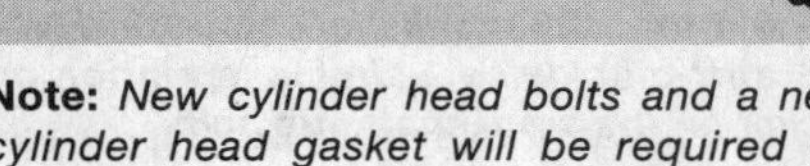

Note: *New cylinder head bolts and a new cylinder head gasket will be required on refitting.*

M43TU engine

Removal

1 Depressurise the fuel system as described in Chapter 4A, then disconnect the battery negative lead (see Chapter 5A).

2 Drain the cooling system as described in Chapter 1.

3 Remove the air cleaner assembly and the airflow sensor as described in Chapter 4A, Section 12.

4 Remove the upper and lower sections of the inlet manifold as described in Chapter 4A.

5 Disconnect the exhaust front section from the manifold as described in Chapter 4A.

6 Disconnect the coolant hose from the cylinder head.

7 Remove the upper timing chain cover as described in Section 6.

8 Remove the ignition coils as described in Chapter 5B.

9 Remove the spark plugs as described in Chapter 1.

10 If not already done, disconnect the wiring plugs from the coolant temperature sensors located in the left-hand side of the cylinder head.

11 Disconnect the heater coolant hoses at the bulkhead and heater valve.

12 Turn the crankshaft to position No 1 piston at TDC, as described in Section 3. Lock the crankshaft and camshaft in position as described.

13 Unscrew the camshaft sprocket securing bolts, remove the exhaust position sensor wheel.

14 Push back the top end of the chain tensioner rail to relieve the tension on the chain until the camshaft sprocket can be removed. Withdraw the sprocket from the camshaft, noting which way round it is fitted, then disengage the sprocket from the chain. Ensure that tension is kept on the chain – tie the chain up or support it using wire, to prevent it from dropping behind the lower timing chain cover.

15 Unscrew the bolts securing the chain tensioner rail and the chain guide to the cylinder head.

Warning: To avoid any possibility of piston-to-valve contact when refitting the cylinder head, it is necessary to ensure that none of the pistons are at TDC. Before proceeding further, remove the locking rod from the timing hole in the cylinder block, then turn the crankshaft approximately 45° anti-clockwise using a spanner or socket on the crankshaft hub bolt.

16 Make a final check to ensure that all relevant hoses and wires have been disconnected to allow cylinder head removal.

17 Progressively loosen the cylinder head bolts, working in a spiral pattern from the outside of the head inwards.

18 Remove the cylinder head bolts **(see illustration)**.

19 Release the cylinder head from the cylinder block and locating dowels by rocking it. Do not prise between the mating faces

12.18 Remove the cylinder head bolts

12.35 Cylinder head bolt tightening sequence – M43TU engine

of the cylinder head and block, as this may damage the gasket faces.

20 Ideally, two assistants will now be required to help remove the cylinder head. Have one assistant hold the timing chain up, clear of the cylinder head, making sure that tension is kept on the chain. With the aid of another assistant, lift the cylinder head from the block – take care, as the cylinder head is heavy. Support the timing chain from the cylinder block using wire.

21 Recover the cylinder head gasket, and recover the rubber seals from the top of the timing chain housing and the lower timing chain cover.

Inspection

22 Refer to Chapter 2C for details of cylinder head dismantling and reassembly.

23 The mating faces of the cylinder head and block must be perfectly clean before refitting the head. Use a scraper to remove all traces of gasket and carbon, and also clean the tops of the pistons. Take particular care with the aluminium cylinder head, as the soft metal is easily damaged. Also make sure that debris is not allowed to enter the oil and water passages. Using adhesive tape and paper, seal the water, oil and bolt holes in the cylinder block. To prevent carbon entering the gap between the pistons and bores, smear a little grease in the gap. After cleaning each piston, rotate the crankshaft so that the piston moves **down** the bore, then wipe out the grease and carbon with a cloth rag.

24 Check the block and head for nicks, deep scratches and other damage. If very slight, they may be removed from the cylinder block carefully with a file. More serious damage may be repaired by machining, but this is a specialist job.

25 If warpage of the cylinder head is suspected, use a straight-edge to check it for distortion, with reference to Chapter 2C.

26 Clean out the bolt holes in the block using a pipe cleaner or thin rag and a screwdriver. Make sure that all oil and water is removed, otherwise there is a possibility of the block being cracked by hydraulic pressure when the bolts are tightened.

27 Examine the bolt threads and the threads in the cylinder block for damage. If necessary, use the correct size tap to chase out the threads in the block.

Refitting

28 Ensure that the mating faces of the cylinder block, timing chain housing, and head are spotlessly clean, that the cylinder head bolt threads are clean and dry, and that they screw in and out of their locations.

29 Check that the cylinder head locating dowels are correctly positioned in the cylinder block.

Warning: To avoid any possibility of piston-to-valve contact when refitting the cylinder head, it is necessary to ensure that none of the pistons are at TDC. Before proceeding further, if not already done, turn the crankshaft to position No 1 piston at TDC (check that the locking rod can be engaged with the flywheel, then remove the locking rod and turn the crankshaft approximately 45° anti-clockwise using a spanner or socket on the crankshaft hub bolt.

30 Fit a new cylinder head gasket to the block, locating it over the dowels. Make sure that it is the correct way up. Note that 0.3 mm thicker-than-standard gaskets are available for use if the cylinder head has been machined (see Chapter 2C).

31 Fit new rubber seals to the top of the timing chain housing – do not fit the lower timing chain cover rubber seal at this stage.

32 If not already done, fit the template to the cylinder head to ensure that the camshaft is correctly positioned (No 1 piston at TDC) – see Section 3.

33 Lower the cylinder head into position. As the cylinder head is lowered, push the timing chain tensioner rail away from the centre of the engine to allow the cylinder head to be lowered onto the block. Ensure that the cylinder head engages with the locating dowels.

34 Fit the **new** cylinder head bolts, and tighten the bolts as far as possible by hand.

35 Tighten the bolts in the order shown **(see illustration)**, and in the stages given in the Specifications – ie, tighten all bolts in sequence to the Stage 1 torque, then tighten all bolts in sequence to the Stage 2 torque, and so on.

36 Refit and tighten the bolts securing the timing chain tensioner rail and the chain guide to the cylinder head.

37 Turn the crankshaft 45° clockwise, to position No 1 piston at TDC again, then refit the flywheel locking tool and refit the template to check the position of the camshaft, as described in Section 3.

38 Push back the top end of the chain tensioner rail, as during removal, to allow the camshaft sprocket to be fitted. Engage the camshaft sprocket with the chain, ensuring that it is fitted the correct way round as noted before removal, and manipulate the sprocket so that the timing arrow points vertically upwards.

39 Fit the sprocket to the camshaft, aligning the bolt holes in the camshaft flange with the centres of the elongated holes in the sprocket (the camshaft should be locked in the TDC position using the template – see Section 3). Refit the camshaft position sensor wheel to the sprocket, with the arrow pointing vertically upwards. Fit the sprocket securing bolts, and tighten as far as possible by hand.

40 Release the upper end of the tensioner rail, then tighten the camshaft sprocket bolts to the specified torque.

41 Remove the flywheel locking tool, and remove the template used to check the camshaft position.

42 Further refitting is a reversal of removal, bearing in mind the following points.

a) Ensure that all hoses and wires are correctly reconnected and routed as noted before removal.

b) Refit the lower and upper sections of the inlet manifold as described in Chapter 4A.

12.53 Disconnect the wiring plugs, undo the bolts and remove the solenoid valves (arrowed)

12.57 Rotate the eccentric shaft so the quadrant is on the inlet side

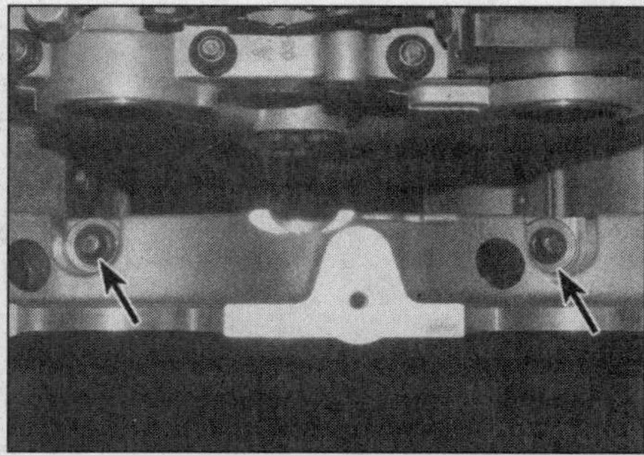

12.58 Undo the two bolts in the timing chain tunnel (arrowed)

c) Refit the air cleaner assembly and the air mass sensor with reference to Chapter 4A.
d) Reconnect the exhaust front section to the manifold, referring to Chapter 4A.
e) Refit the spark plugs as described in Chapter 1.
f) Refit the upper timing chain cover as described in Section 6.
g) On completion, refill the cooling system as described in Chapter 1, and prime the fuel system as described in Chapter 4A.

N42 and N46 engines

Removal

43 Drain the cooling system and cylinder block as described in Chapter 1.

44 Set the engine in the TDC on No 1 cylinder position, as described in Section 3.

45 With the camshafts locked in place as described in Section 3, slacken the exhaust and inlet camshaft adjustment unit bolts **(see illustration 7.28)**.

46 Working on the front right-hand side of the engine block, undo the chain tensioner piston **(see illustration 7.29)**. Be prepared for oil spillage. Discard the sealing washer, a new one must be fitted. If the piston is to be re-used, hold it vertical and slowly compress the piston to evacuate all the oil.

47 Completely unscrew the exhaust camshaft adjustment unit bolt, and remove the unit complete with the camshaft sensor ring and sprocket **(see illustration 7.30)**. Repeat this procedure for the inlet camshaft. Note that the units are marked EX and IN. Do not mix up the parts. Ensure that tension is kept on the chain – tie the chain up or support it using wire, to prevent it from dropping into the engine.

48 Remove the inlet and exhaust manifolds, as described in Chapter 4A.

49 Remove the eccentric shaft positioning motor, as described in Section 10.

50 Squeeze together the locking tabs, and disconnect the inlet camshaft position sensor wiring plug from the front of the timing chain cover.

51 Undo the plug behind the inlet camshaft position sensor, and unscrew the right-hand timing chain guide upper pin **(see illustration 7.33)**. Take care not to drop the pin into the timing cover.

52 Remove the upper timing chain guide bolt, carefully spread apart the top of the left-hand chain guide, and release the lower part of the upper guide. Remove the upper timing chain guide **(see illustrations 11.34a and 11.34b)**.

53 Working on the front of the engine, note their fitted locations, disconnect the camshaft adjustment solenoid valves' wiring plugs, undo the retaining bracket bolts, and pull the solenoid valves from the engine casing **(see illustration)**.

54 Remove the plug from the left-hand side of the timing chain cover (behind the lifting eye), and with a Torx bit, unscrew the left-hand timing chain guide upper retaining pin **(see illustration 7.36)**.

55 Remove the camshaft locking tools.

56 Disconnect all electrical connections to the cylinder head, taking note of their fitted locations, and harness routing.

57 Using an open-ended spanner on its hexagonal section, rotate the eccentric shaft so that the shaft's toothed quadrant is on the inlet side **(see illustration)**. In this position the inlet side cylinder head bolts are accessible.

58 Undo the two bolts in the timing chain tunnel securing the cylinder head to the cylinder block **(see illustration)**.

59 Unscrew the cover plug from the eccentric shaft positioning motor support bracket.

60 Working from the outside inwards, in the reverse of the tightening sequence **(see illustration 12.74)**, evenly and gradually unscrew the cylinder head bolts. Bolts in positions 7 to 10 have an M8 thread with an E10 head, whilst bolts 1 to 6 have an M10 thread with an E12 head. Note that the bolt in position 10 is shorter than the others.

61 Release the cylinder head from the cylinder block and locating dowels by rocking it. Do not prise between the mating faces of the cylinder head and block, as this may damage the gasket faces.

62 Ideally, two assistants will now be required to help remove the cylinder head. Have one assistant hold the timing chain up, clear of the cylinder head, making sure that tension is kept on the chain. With the aid of another assistant, lift the cylinder head from the block – take care, as the cylinder head is heavy. Support the timing chain from the cylinder block using wire.

63 Recover the cylinder head gasket.

Inspection

64 The mating faces of the cylinder head and block must be perfectly clean before refitting the head. Use a scraper to remove all traces of gasket and carbon, and also clean the tops of the pistons. Take particular care with the aluminium cylinder head, as the soft metal is easily damaged. Also make sure that debris is not allowed to enter the oil and water passages. Using adhesive tape and paper, seal the water, oil and bolt holes in the cylinder block. To prevent carbon entering the gap between the pistons and bores, smear a little grease in the gap. After cleaning each piston, rotate the crankshaft so that the piston moves **down** the bore, then wipe out the grease and carbon with a cloth rag.

65 Check the block and head for nicks, deep scratches and other damage. If very slight, they may be removed from the cylinder block carefully with a file. More serious damage may be repaired by machining, but this is a specialist job.

66 If warpage of the cylinder head is suspected, use a straight-edge to check it for distortion, with reference to Chapter 2C.

67 Clean out the bolt holes in the block using a pipe cleaner or thin rag and a screwdriver. Make sure that all oil and water is removed, otherwise there is a possibility of the block being cracked by hydraulic pressure when the bolts are tightened.

68 Examine the bolt threads and the threads in the cylinder block for damage. If necessary, use the correct size tap to chase out the threads in the block.

69 At the front edge of the cylinder block are located the inlet and exhaust camshaft oil supply non-return valves and rubber spacers. If the valves are heavily fouled or contaminated, prise the spacers and valves out and renew them (use a small magnet to extract the valve sleeves). Note that when correctly fitted, the top of the spacers should be slightly proud of the cylinder block gasket surface **(see illustrations)**.

Refitting

70 Ensure that the mating faces of the cylinder block, timing chain housing, and head are spotlessly clean, that the cylinder head bolt threads are clean and dry, and that they screw in and out of their locations.

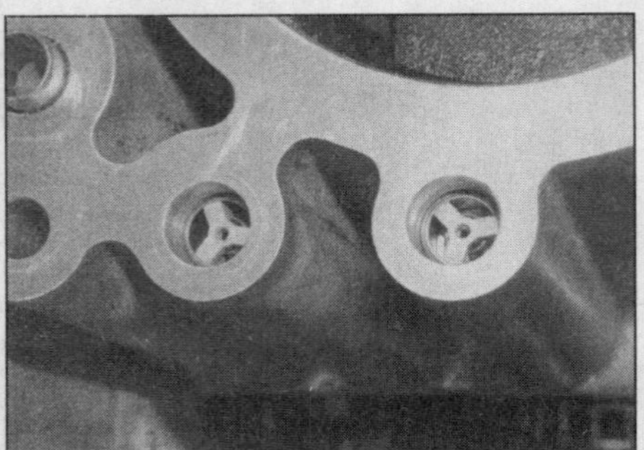
12.69a Oil supply non-return valves

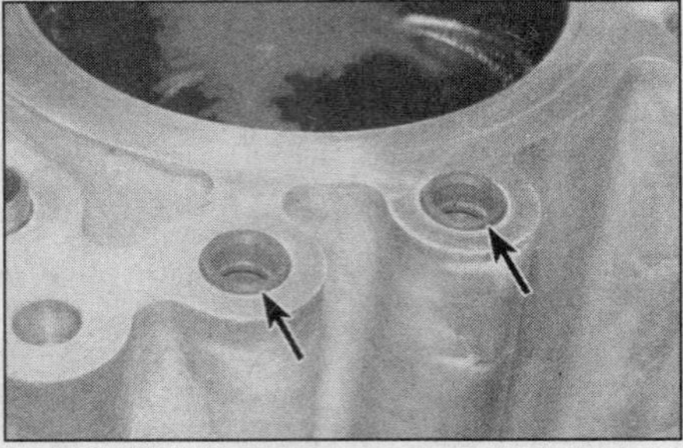
12.69b The oil non-return valve seals (arrowed) should be slightly proud of the gasket surface

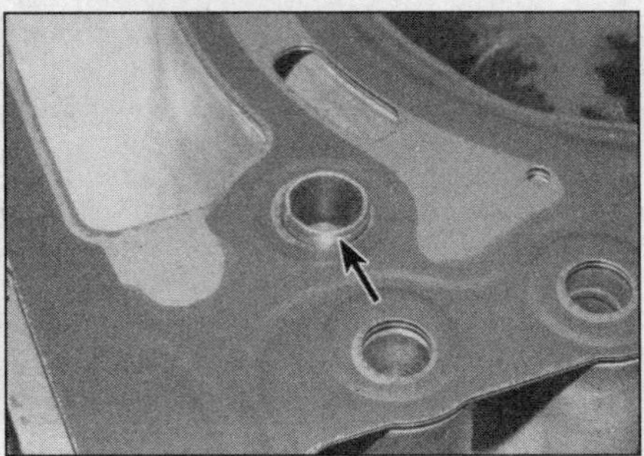
12.72 Fit the new cylinder head gasket over the dowels (arrowed)

71 Check that the cylinder head locating dowels are correctly positioned in the cylinder block.

Warning: To avoid any possibility of piston-to-valve contact when refitting the cylinder head, it is necessary to ensure that none of the pistons are at TDC. Before proceeding further, if not already done, turn the crankshaft to position No 1 piston at TDC (check that the locking rod can be engaged with the flywheel, then remove the locking rod and turn the crankshaft approximately 45° anti-clockwise using a spanner or socket on the crankshaft pulley hub bolt.

72 Fit a new cylinder head gasket to the block, locating it over the dowels **(see illustration)**. Make sure that it is the correct way up. Note that 0.3 mm thicker-than-standard gaskets are available for use if the cylinder head has been machined (see Chapter 2C).

73 With the new gasket in place, lower the cylinder head into position.

74 Apply a thin coat of clean engine oil to the new cylinder bolt threads and washer contact area, then insert the bolts and washers into their correct locations. Note that bolts in positions 1 to 6, have M10 thread and an E12 Torx head, whilst the bolts in positions 7 to 10 have an M8 thread with E10 Torx heads. The bolt in position 10 is shorter than the others. Tighten the bolts in the order shown **(see illustration)**, and in the stages given in the Specifications – ie, tighten all bolts in sequence to the Stage 1 torque, then tighten all bolts in sequence to the Stage 2 torque, and so on. Note that both M10 and M8 bolts should be tightened to the same torque.

75 Insert the two bolts in the timing chain tunnel at the front of the cylinder head, and tighten them securely.

76 With a new sealing ring fitted, refit the cover plug to the eccentric shaft positioning motor bracket, and tighten it securely.

77 Align the left-hand chain guide, and insert the upper retaining pin. Tighten the pin securely. Refit the cover plug with a new seal, and tighten it to the specified torque.

78 With an open-ended spanner on the hexagonal section, rotate the eccentric shaft to the position where the end spring is under maximum tension.

79 Refit the camshaft locking tools – see Section 3.

80 Rotate the crankshaft back to TDC, and refit the crankshaft locking tool.

81 With new O-ring seals, refit the camshaft adjustment solenoids to the front of the engine. Pulling the timing chain up and apart, insert the solenoids though the chain. Refit the solenoid retaining brackets, and tighten the bolts securely. Reconnect the solenoid wiring plugs.

82 Pull up the timing chain, and refit the upper chain guide. Carefully prise apart the top of the left-hand guide and press the upper guide to engage correctly with the locating holes **(see illustration)**.

83 Refit the upper timing chain guide upper retaining bolt, and only finger-tighten it at this stage.

84 Refit the upper timing chain guide lower bolt, and tighten both the chain guide upper and lower bolts securely. Refit the bolt cover plug to the casing and tighten it to the specified torque.

85 Refit the timing chain, sprockets and camshaft adjustment units as described in Section 7.

86 The remainder of refitting is a reversal of removal.

13 Sump – removal and refitting

M43TU engine

Removal

1 Drain the engine oil (see Chapter 1).

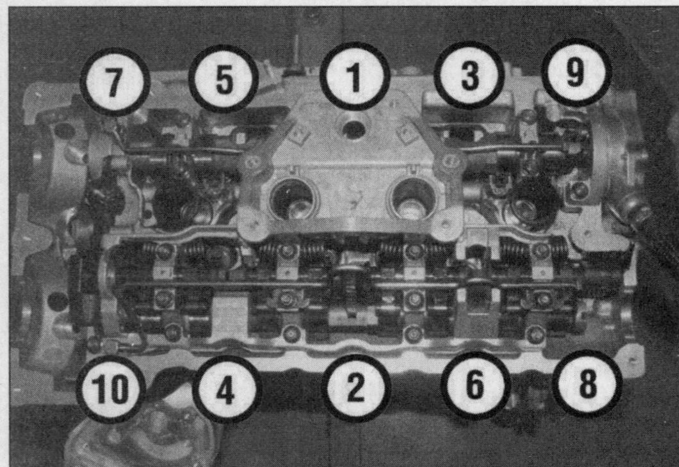

12.74 Cylinder head bolt tightening sequence – N42 and N46 engines

12.82 Press the upper guide into the locating holes in the lower guide (arrowed)

2 Lower the front subframe as described in Section 15.
3 Unscrew the bolt securing the dipstick tube to the inlet manifold, release any wiring harnesses clipped to the dipstick tube, then pull the lower end of the tube from the sump, and withdraw the dipstick tube assembly.
4 Where applicable, unclip the fuel pipes and/ or the automatic transmission fluid cooler pipes from the brackets on the sump, and move the pipes clear of the working area.
5 Working under the vehicle, disconnect the oil level sensor wiring plug, and progressively unscrew and remove all the sump securing bolts, including the two at the rear of the sump through the edge of the transmission bellhousing. The three lower transmission-to-engine bolts must also be removed, as they screw into the sump **(see illustration)**.
6 Lower the sump, and manipulate it out towards the rear of the vehicle. If necessary, lower the subframe further, using the jack, to give sufficient clearance.
7 Recover the sump gasket, and discard it. If required, undo the four bolts, and remove the baffle plate from the sump, then remove the two bolts and pull the oil pick-up pipe from place **(see illustrations)**.

Refitting

8 Commence refitting by thoroughly cleaning the mating faces of the sump and cylinder block. If removed, refit the oil pick-up pipe (with a new O-ring) and baffle plate to the sump **(see illustration)**. Use a smear of thread-locking compound on the bolt threads.
9 Lightly coat the areas where the crankshaft rear oil seal housing and the timing chain housing join the cylinder block with Drei Bond 1209 sealant (available from BMW dealers).
10 Place a new gasket in position on the sump flange. If necessary, apply more sealant (sparingly) to hold the gasket in place.
11 Offer the sump up to the cylinder block, ensuring that the gasket stays in place.
12 Refit the sump securing bolts, tightening them finger-tight only at this stage.
13 Progressively tighten the sump-to-cylinder block bolts to the specified torque.
14 Tighten the sump-to-transmission-to-engine bolts to the specified torque.
15 Check the condition of the dipstick sealing ring (at the sump end of the tube) and renew if necessary. Refit the dipstick tube and tighten the bracket securing bolt.
16 On models with automatic transmission, secure the fluid cooler lines to the sump. Similarly, where applicable, clip the fuel pipes into position.
17 Raise the front subframe using the jack, then refit the new securing bolts and tighten to the specified torque.
18 Refit the bolts securing the suspension lower control arms to the body, ensuring that the washers are in place, and tighten the bolts to the specified torque.
19 Lower the engine until the mountings are resting on the subframe, ensuring that the lugs on the engine mountings engage with the corresponding holes in the subframe. Fit the new engine mounting nuts and tighten them securely.
20 Refit the axle reinforcement plate/frame, and tighten the new bolts to the specified torque.
21 Disconnect and withdraw the engine lifting tackle and hoist.
22 Further refitting is a reversal of removal, but on completion refill the engine with oil as described in Chapter 1.

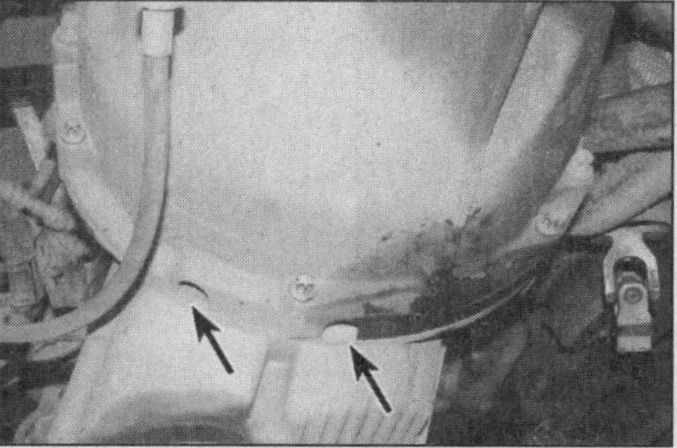
13.5 Remove the three lower transmission-to-engine bolts, as well as the two up through the casing (arrowed)

13.7b . . . then remove the oil pick-up pipe bolts (arrowed)

13.7a Undo the 4 bolts (arrowed) and remove the baffle plate . . .

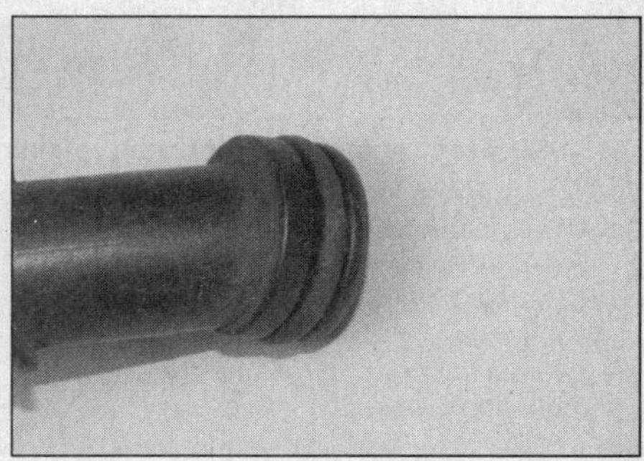
13.8 Renew the oil pick-up pipe O-ring seal

N42 and N46 engines

Removal

23 Drain the engine oil (see Chapter 1).
24 Remove the air cleaner housing as described in Chapter 4A.
25 Lower the front subframe as described in Section 15.
26 Unclip any hoses from the oil dipstick guide tube and support bracket. Unscrew the support bracket mounting bolt, and using a clockwise twisting motion, pull the guide tube from the sump. Inspect the O-ring seal and renew if necessary.
27 Disconnect the oil level sensor wiring plug.
28 Cut through the cable-tie securing the wiring harness to the transmission lower cover plate. Undo the bolts and remove the cover plate.
29 At the front of the engine, undo the two bolts and remove the auxiliary belt guide pulley (where fitted).
30 Undo the sump retaining bolts. Lower the sump, and manipulate it out towards the rear of the vehicle. If necessary, lower the subframe further, using the jack, to give sufficient clearance. Similarly, if necessary, unscrew the oil pick-up pipe to ease sump removal.
31 Recover the sump gasket, and discard it.

Refitting

32 Commence refitting by thoroughly cleaning the mating faces of the sump and cylinder block.
33 Position a new gasket on the sump **(see illustration)**.
34 Refit the sump, insert the new retaining bolts and tighten them to the specified torque.
35 The remainder of refitting is a reversal of removal, noting the following points:
a) *Tighten all fasteners to the specified torque where given.*
b) *Refill the engine with oil as described in Chapter 1.*

13.33 Position a new gasket on the sump

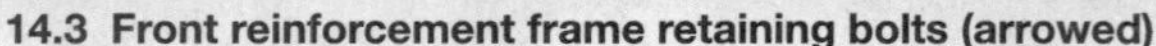
14.3 Front reinforcement frame retaining bolts (arrowed)

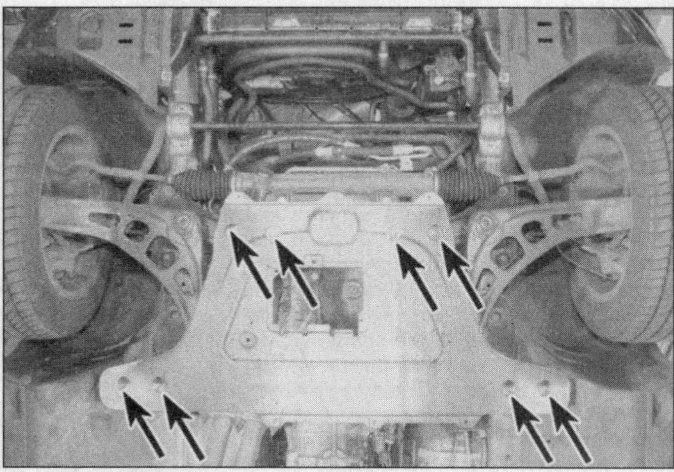
14.4 Front reinforcement plate retaining bolts (arrowed)

c) Where applicable refit the auxiliary drivebelt as described in Chapter 1.
d) Use new bolts when refitting the subframe.
e) Use new nuts when refitting the engine mounting brackets.

14 Front reinforcement plate/frame – removal and refitting

Removal

1 One of two different types of front end reinforcement may be fitted. Either a frame type (known as 'Cruciform'), or a flat plate type

2 Apply the handbrake, then jack up the front of the vehicle and support securely on axle stands (see *Jacking and vehicle support*). Undo the bolts and remove the engine undershield.

Frame type

3 Undo the 4 bolts and remove the reinforcement frame **(see illustration)**.

Plate type

4 Undo the 8 bolts and remove the plate **(see illustration)**.

Refitting

Frame type

5 Position the reinforcement under the subframe, and insert the new bolts. If the frame rests on the lower control arm mounting or bracket, a special washer must be fitted under the outer frame mountings and the vehicle body.

6 Tighten the bolts to the specified torque.

Plate type

7 From 02/2001, new 66 mm control arm bushes were fitted, and a slightly different reinforcement plate. In order to accommodate the larger bushes, the inside of the plate has two indentations. If an early model is fitted subsequently with the later, larger control arm bushes, insert appropriate-sized washers between the plate rear mounting points and the vehicle body. The control arm bushes must not contact the reinforcement plate. Position the plate, insert the new bolts (and washers where applicable), and tighten them to the specified torque.

All types

8 Refit the engine undershield, and lower the vehicle to the ground.

15 Front subframe – lowering, removal and refitting

Lowering

1 The front subframe must be lowered in order to carry out various procedures, including sump removal. Begin by removing the front reinforcement plate/frame as described in the previous Section.

2 Remove the air cleaner housing as described in Chapter 4A.

3 Position a hoist and lifting tackle over the engine compartment, and connect the lifting tackle to the front engine lifting bracket.

4 Unscrew the nuts securing the left- and right-hand engine mountings to the subframe **(see illustration)**.

5 With the steering wheel and roadwheels in the 'straight-ahead' position, engage the steering lock.

6 Remove the steering column flexible joint pinch-bolt, and separate the joint from the rack pinion **(see illustration)**.

7 Unscrew the anti-roll bar clamps bolts – see Chapter 10 if necessary.

8 Unscrew the lower control arms rear mounting bolts from the vehicle body **(see illustration)**.

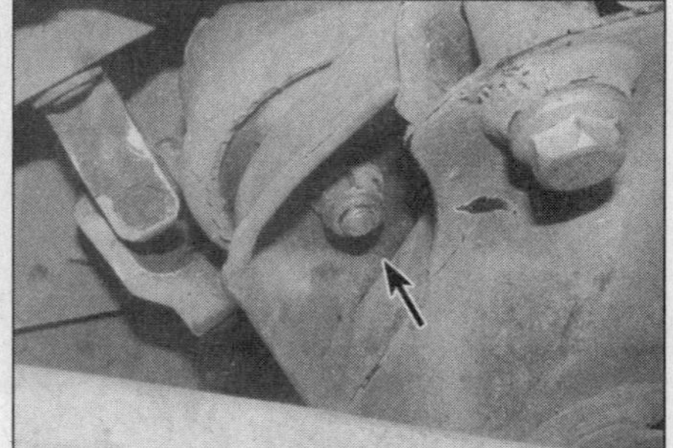
15.4 Undo the mounting-to-subframe nut (arrowed) – one each side

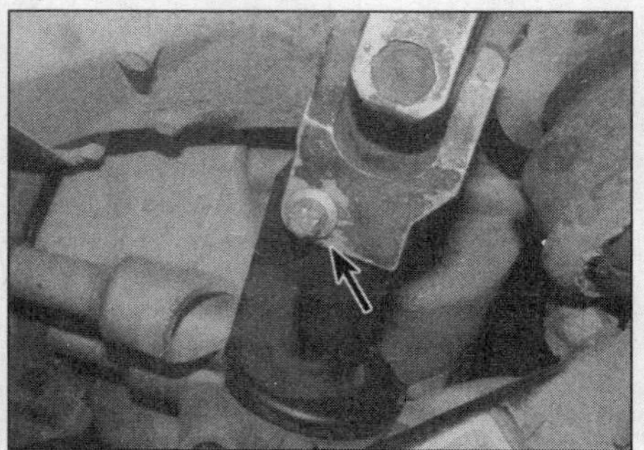
15.6 Remove the flexible joint pinch-bolt (arrowed)

15.8 Unscrew the control arm mounting bolts on each side

15.10 Undo the front subframe mounting bolts (arrowed) – two each side

9 Support the centre of the subframe, using a jack and a block of wood.

10 Unscrew the subframe securing bolts, then lower the subframe slightly using the jack **(see illustration)**.

Caution: Do not allow the power steering hoses to be stretched.

11 Refitting the subframe is a reversal of lowering, noting the following points.

a) Tighten the subframe rear mounting bolts first.

b) Use new subframe and reinforcement plate/frame mounting bolts.

c) Tighten all fasteners to the specified torque where given.

Removal

Note: *After refitting the front subframe, it is essential that the alignment of the wheels is checked by a BMW dealer or suitably-equipped specialist.*

12 Remove the air cleaner housing as described in Chapter 4A.

13 Position a hoist and lifting tackle over the engine compartment, and connect the lifting tackle to the front engine lifting bracket.

14 Unscrew the nuts securing the left- and right-hand engine mountings to the brackets on the subframe.

15 With the steering wheel and roadwheels in the 'straight-ahead' position, engage the steering lock.

16 On models equipped with xenon gas discharge headlights, undo the mounting nuts and detach the ride height sensor from the front subframe.

17 On all models, unscrew the suspension lower control arms mounting bolts, separate the balljoints and remove the control arms (see Chapter 10 if necessary).

18 Remove the two bolts securing the steering rack to the subframe **(see illustration)**. Discard the self-locking nuts, new ones must be fitted.

19 Support the centre of the subframe, using a jack and a block of wood.

20 Remove the subframe mounting bolts, and lower it to the ground **(see illustration 15.10)**.

Refitting

21 Refitting is a reversal of removal, noting the following points:

a) Refit the subframe using new mounting bolts.

b) Tighten the subframe rear mounting bolts first.

c) Tighten all fasteners to the specified torque where given.

d) Have the wheel alignment check by a BMW dealer or specialist as soon as possible.

16 Balancer shafts – information, removal and refitting

Information

1 The N42 and N46 4-cylinder engines are equipped with balancer shafts to smooth out any engine vibration. These contra-rotating shafts are driven by a chain from the crankshaft sprocket, and are integral with the oil pump. For details of the balancer shaft removal and refitting procedure, refer to the Section regarding oil pump removal.

2 M43TU 4-cylinder engines are also equipped with contra-rotating balancer shafts and housing, although they are gear-driven from the crankshaft. Unlike the N42 and N46 engines, it is possible to remove the shafts and housing separately from the oil pump. Therefore the following procedure applies only to the M43TU engine.

Removal

3 Remove the sump as described in Section 13.

4 Using a socket on the crankshaft pulley bolt, rotate the crankshaft until pistons 1 and 4 are at TDC, and the crankshaft locking tool can be inserted into the rear of the flywheel – see Section 3.

5 Working in the reverse of the tightening sequence **(see illustration 16.8)**, undo the retaining bolts, and remove the balancer shaft housing. Note that the housing is heavy. Recover the shims between the housing and cylinder block.

Refitting

6 Check the locating dowels are still in place in the cylinder block, and refit the shims over the dowels. **Note:** *If the cylinder block, crankshaft, main bearing shells or balancer shaft housing have been renewed, it will be necessary to carry out a check on the amount of backlash between the crankshaft and balancer shaft gears. If this is the case, to eliminate the possibility of damage, fit thick shims (2.25 mm) at this stage.*

16.7 The holes in the front ends of the shafts (arrowed) must be in the 6 o'clock position relative to the engine block

15.18 Remove the steering rack bolts (arrowed)

7 Rotate the balancer shafts so that the holes bored into the front ends of the shafts are in the 6 o'clock position (relative to the engine block) **(see illustration)**.

8 Locate the housing over the dowels, and insert the mounting bolts. If the backlash needs checking (see previous paragraph), use the old bolts, as the housing may need to be removed again to fit different thickness shims. If the backlash does not need checking, use new bolts. Tighten the bolts to the specified torque **(see illustration)**.

9 If the backlash needs checking (see Paragraph 6), fix the anvil of a DTI gauge against the balancer shaft gear teeth, and zero the gauge. Take a reading of the backlash, then remove the crankshaft locking tool, and rotate the crankshaft 120°, and then 240°, taking readings at these points. Add the three measurements together, then divide by three to arrive at an average backlash measurement. Compare this figure with that given in the Specifications. If the backlash needs adjusting, shims of varying thickness are available from BMW. A reduction in shim thickness of 0.03 mm will result in a backlash reduction of approximately 0.02 mm. If necessary remove the housing, insert the correct shims (must be equal thickness both sides), and refit the housing using new bolts. Tighten the bolts in the correct sequence to the specified torque.

10 Refit the sump as described in Section 13.

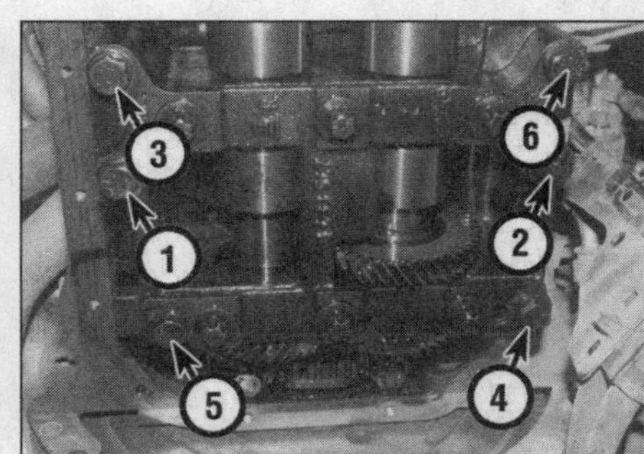

16.8 Tighten the balancer shaft housing bolts in the sequence shown

17.3a Unscrew the securing bolts . . .

17.3b . . . and remove the oil pump cover

17.4a Remove the inner . . .

17 Oil pump – removal, inspection and refitting

M43TU engines

Removal

1 The oil pump is integral with the timing chain housing.

2 Remove the timing chain housing, referring to Section 9.

Inspection

3 Unscrew the oil pump cover from the rear of the timing belt/chain housing to expose the oil pump rotors **(see illustrations)**.

4 Check the rotors for identification marks, and if necessary mark the rotors to ensure they are refitted in their original positions (mark the top faces of both rotors to ensure they are refitted the correct way up). Remove the rotors from the housing **(see illustrations)**.

5 Clean the housing and the rotors thoroughly, then refit the rotors to the housing, ensuring that they are positioned as noted before removal.

6 Using feeler blades, measure the clearance between the oil pump body and the outer rotor. Using the feeler blades and a straight-edge, measure the clearance (endfloat) between each of the rotors and the oil pump cover mating face **(see illustration)**.

7 If the clearances are not as given in the Specifications, consult a BMW dealer regarding the availability of spare parts. The rotors should always be renewed as a matched pair. It may be necessary to renew the complete rotor/ housing assembly as a unit.

8 If the clearances are within the tolerances given, remove the rotors, then pour a little engine oil into the housing. Refit the rotors and turn them to lubricate all the contact surfaces.

9 Refit the oil pump cover plate, and tighten the securing bolts to the specified torque.

10 To check the oil pressure relief valve, extract the circlip and remove the sleeve, spring and piston. As no specifications are available concerning the spring free-length, compare the spring with a new one **(see illustrations)**.

11 Reassemble the pressure relief valve using a reversal of the dismantling procedure.

Refitting

12 Refit the timing chain housing as described in Section 9.

17.4b . . . and outer rotors from the oil pump

17.6 Measure the clearance between the oil pump body and the outer rotor

17.10a Remove the pressure relief valve circlip . . .

17.10b . . . and remove the sleeve . . .

17.10c . . . spring . . .

17.10d . . . and piston

17.14 Undo the bolts and remove the oil pump pick-up tube (arrowed)

17.17 Use a length of rod to lock the tensioner blade in place

17.19 Use a length of wire to pull the sprocket from the splines

N42 and N46 engines

Removal

13 On these engines, the oil pump is integral with the balancer shaft housing. The two must not be separated or dismantled. Remove the sump as described in Section 13.

14 Unscrew the two retaining bolts, rotate the oil pick-up tube out of the oil pump, and pull it downwards **(see illustration)**. Discard the O-ring seal, a new one must be fitted.

15 Using a socket on the crankshaft pulley bolt, rotate the crankshaft to TDC (see Section 3), and lock it in place with the crankshaft locking tool.

16 Undo the oil pump sprocket retaining nut. **Note:** *This nut has a **left-hand** thread.*

17 Push the oil pump chain tensioner away from the chain, and lock it in place with a length of rod inserted through the hole in the guide **(see illustration)**.

18 Undo the bolts securing the chain lower guide to the oil pump/balancer shaft housing.

19 Using a length of wire or rod, pull the sprocket from the oil pump shaft, and disengage it from the shaft splines **(see illustration)**.

20 Have an assistant support the housing, undo the 8 bolts, and pull the housing down slightly at the rear, then manoeuvre backwards out of place **(see illustration)**. Ease the chain tensioner guide from its locating pin as the assembly is removed. No dismantling of the assembly is recommended.

21 In order to renew the oil pump drive chain, remove the timing chain as described in Section 7, Unscrew the cover plug to the right of the crankshaft, and undo the bolt securing the upper section of the oil pump drive chain tensioner/guide **(see illustration)**.

22 Slide the chain tensioner/guide down from its location and lift the chain from its location. Note that the tensioner can only be removed from the guide once the assembly has been removed.

Refitting

23 Where removed, refit the oil pump drive chain to the crankshaft, and the timing chain (see Section 7).

24 Slide the chain guide/tensioner into place and finger-tighten the retaining bolt at this stage.

25 Check that the locating dowels are still in place, and insert the balancer shaft/oil pump housing shaft into the chain sprocket, and manoeuvre it onto the locating dowels. Oil the threads and insert the new retaining bolts. Tighten the Torx socket head bolts to the specified torque, and tighten the remaining two Torx bolts at the front of the housing securely.

26 Using a length of wire or rod, pull the sprocket away from the pump and off from the shaft splines **(see illustration 17.19)**.

27 Option 1: Using two straight strips of metal, align the flat sides of the two balancer shafts, and lock them in this position using a G-clamp or similar **(see illustrations 7.49a and 7.49b)**. Note that the wider slots in the ends of the balancer shaft must be at the top (nearest the main bearing housing.

28 Option 2: Working underneath the vehicle, rotate the ends of the balancer shafts so that the flats of the balancer weights are parallel with the crankcase mating surface, and BMW tool No 11 5 140 can be inserted between the balancer weights and the mating surface **(see illustration 7.50)**. In the absence of the special tool, use a strip of metal.

29 Check that the crankshaft is still locked in the TDC position (see Section 3), and push the sprocket over the splines on the shaft. Pull out the rod locking the chain tensioner in place and check the balancer shafts still align. If they do not, or the sprocket splines do not align, pull the sprocket from the shaft, and rotate the balancer shafts 360° and try again. In some

17.20 Oil pump/balance shaft housing Torx socket head bolts (arrowed). Note the 2 bolts at the timing chain end (not shown) must be unscrewed first

17.21 Undo the cover plug and unscrew the guide screw (arrowed)

18.4 Drill some holes and screw in self-tapping screws

circumstances, it may take 7 attempts to align the sprocket and shaft.

30 With the shafts aligned and the sprocket over the splines, if not already done so, refit the bolts retaining the tensioner/guide, and tighten them securely. Refit the cover plug to the engine front casing.

31 Refit the sprocket nut, and tighten it to the specified torque. **Note:** *The nut has a* ***left-hand*** *thread.*

32 Refit the oil pump pick-up tube with a new O-ring seal. Tighten the retaining bolt securely.

33 Remove the crankshaft locking tool, and refit the sump as described in Section 13.

18 Oil seals – renewal

Crankshaft front oil seal

M43TU engines

1 Oil seal renewal is described as part of the lower timing chain cover removal and refitting procedure in Section 6.

N42 and N46 engines

2 Remove the crankshaft vibration damper/pulley as described in Section 5. Do not remove the hub.

3 Note the fitted depth of the oil seal in the cover. On the engine we examined, the outer edge of the seal was flush with the front edge of the seal bore in the cylinder block.

18.9 Inject sealant into both grooves

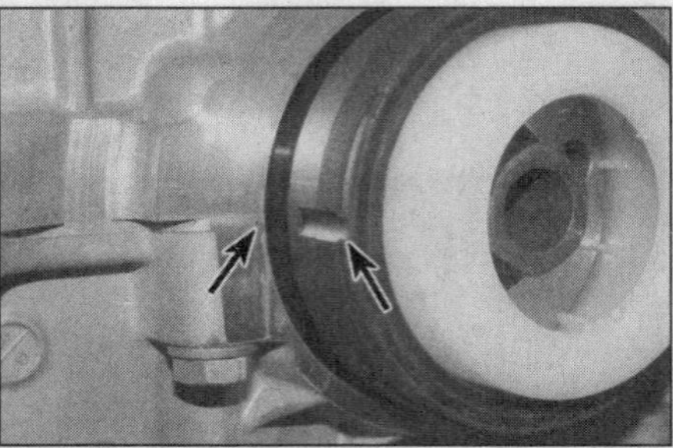

18.7a Align the two grooves in the edge of the seal with the joint in the engine casing (arrowed) . . .

4 Pull the oil seal from the cover using a hooked instrument. Alternatively, drill three small holes in the oil seal, and screw self-tapping screws into the holes, then use pliers to pull the seal out **(see illustration)**. Apply a little grease to the drill bit to catch any swarf. Take great care not to damage the pulley hub or the sealing surface of the engine block. If you are unable to pull the seal out using these methods, the crankshaft pulley hub must be removed (see Section 5), and the seal levered from place using a hammer and chisel.

5 Clean the oil seal housing and the hub sealing surface. Apply a little clean engine oil to the surface of the hub.

6 New seals are supplied with a support sleeve to aid fitment. Slide the sleeve with the oil seal fitted, over the hub.

7 Align the two grooves in the outer edge of the seal with the horizontal joint in the engine casing **(see illustration)**. Carefully drive the seal into the housing until it is at the same depth as the original, using a tubular spacer that bears evenly on the hard, outer edge of the seal **(see illustration)**.

8 Using the sealing kit available from BMW (comprising of Loctite sealing compound, primer and injector), push the integral brush into the grooves in the oil seal to coat the surfaces with primer.

9 Use the injector in the kit to fill both grooves with sealing compound **(see illustration)**. Then coat the end of the grooves with primer.

10 Refit the crankshaft vibration damper/pulley as described in Section 5.

Crankshaft rear oil seal

M43TU engines

11 Proceed as described for 6-cylinder engines in Chapter 2B, Section 14.

N42 and N46 engines

12 Remove the flywheel as described in Section 19.

13 Measure and note the fitted depth of the oil seal.

14 Drill several small holes in the oil seal, and screw in self-tapping screws. Pull the screws, complete with seal, from the housing **(see illustration 18.4)**.

18.7b . . . then drive it to the original depth using a tubular drift

15 Clean the oil seal housing and the crankshaft sealing surface. Apply a light coat of clean engine oil to the crankshaft sealing surface.

16 New seals are supplied with a support sleeve to aid fitment. Slide the sleeve, with the seal fitted, over the crankshaft.

17 Align the two grooves in the outer edge of the seal with the horizontal joint in the engine casing **(see illustration 18.7a)**. Carefully drive the seal into the housing until it is at the same depth as the original, using a tubular spacer that bears evenly on the hard, outer edge of the seal **(see illustration 18.7b)**.

18 Using the sealing kit available from BMW (comprising of Loctite sealing compound, primer and injector), push the integral brush into the grooves in the oil seal to coat the surfaces with primer.

19 Use the injector in the kit to fill both grooves with sealing compound **(see illustration 18.9)**. Then coat the end of the grooves with primer.

20 Refit the flywheel as described in Section 19.

19 Flywheel/driveplate – removal and refitting

The procedure is as described for 6-cylinder engines in Chapter 2B, Section 15.

20 Crankshaft spigot bearing – renewal

The procedure is as described for 6-cylinder engines in Chapter 2B, Section 16.

21 Engine/transmission mountings – inspection and renewal

The procedure is as described for 6-cylinder engines in Chapter 2B, Section 17.

22.2 Oil pressure switch – M43TU engine

22.7 Undo the three nuts and remove the level switch

22.12 Oil pressure switch – N42 and N46 engines

22 Oil pressure and level switches – removal and refitting

M43TU engine

Oil pressure switch

1 Unscrew the oil filter cap. Allows the oil within the filter to flow back into the sump, so reducing the amount lost during switch renewal.

2 Remove the alternator (see Chapter 5A) and mounting bracket, then disconnect the wiring plug and unscrew the switch from the base of the oil filter housing **(see illustration)**.

3 Fit the new switch, and tighten it to the specified torque.

4 Refit the alternator and mounting bracket, reconnect the wiring plug and refit the oil filter cap. Check the oil level as described in *Weekly checks*.

Oil level switch

5 Drain the engine oil as described in Chapter 1.

6 Undo the bolts and remove the engine undershield.

7 Disconnect the wiring plug, undo the three retaining nuts and remove the level switch **(see illustration)**.

8 Ensure that the sump mating surface is clean.

9 Complete with a new seal, install the oil level switch, apply a little thread locking compound and tighten the retaining nuts securely.

10 Refit the engine undershield, and replenish the engine oil as described in Chapter 1.

N42 and N46 engines

Oil pressure switch

11 The oil pressure switch is located on the left-hand side of the engine block behind the alternator. Remove the alternator as described in Chapter 5A.

12 Disconnect the wiring plug, and unscrew the switch from the engine block **(see illustration)**. Be prepared for oil spillage.

13 Refitting is a reversal of removal, using a new sealing washer, and tightening the switch to the specified torque.

Oil level switch

14 This procedure is identical to that described in Paragraphs 5 to 10.

Chapter 2 Part B:
6-cylinder engine in-car repair procedures

Contents

Degrees of difficulty

Easy, suitable for novice with little experience 

Fairly easy, suitable for beginner with some experience

Fairly difficult, suitable for competent DIY mechanic

Difficult, suitable for experienced DIY mechanic

Very difficult, suitable for expert DIY or professional 

Specifications

General

Engine code:		
2171 cc engine	M54 B22	
2494 cc engine	M52TU B25 and M54 B25	
2793 cc engine	M52TU B28	
2979 cc engine	M54 B30	
Bore/Stroke:	**Bore**	**Stroke**
M54 B22 engine	80.00 mm	72.00 mm
M52TU B25 engine	84.00 mm	75.00 mm
M54 B25 engine	84.00 mm	75.00 mm
M52TU B28	84.00 mm	84.00 mm
M54 B30 engine	84.00 mm	89.60 mm
Maximum engine power/torque:	**Power**	**Torque**
M54 B22 engine	125 kW at 6100 rpm	210 Nm at 3500 rpm
M52TU B25 engine	125 kW at 5500 rpm	245 Nm at 3500 rpm
M54 B25 engine	141 kW at 6000 rpm	245 Nm at 3500 rpm
M52TU B28 engine	142 kW at 5500 rpm	280 Nm at 3500 rpm
M54 B30 engine	170 kW at 5900 rpm	300 Nm at 3500 rpm
Direction of engine rotation	Clockwise (viewed from front of vehicle)	
No 1 cylinder location	Timing chain end	
Firing order	1-5-3-6-2-4	
Compression ratio:		
M54 B22 engine	10.8 : 1	
M52TU B25 engine	10.5 : 1	
M54 B25 engine	10.5 : 1	
M52TU B28 engine	10.2 : 1	
M54 B30 engine	10.2 : 1	
Minimum compression pressure	10.0 to 11.0 bar	

Camshafts

Endfloat	0.150 to 0.330 mm

Lubrication system

Minimum oil pressure at idle speed	0.5 bar
Regulated oil pressure	4.0 bar
Oil pump rotor clearances:	
Outer rotor to pump body	0.100 to 0.176 mm
Inner rotor endfloat	0.030 to 0.080 mm
Outer rotor endfloat	0.040 to 0.090 mm

Torque wrench settings	Nm	lbf ft
Automatic transmission-to-engine bolts:		
Hexagon bolts:		
M8 bolts	24	18
M10 bolts	45	33
M12 bolts	82	61
Torx bolts:		
M8 bolts	21	15
M10 bolts	42	31
M12 bolts	72	53
Big-end bearing cap bolts:*		
Stage 1	5	4
Stage 2	20	15
Stage 3	Angle-tighten a further 70°	
Camshaft bearing cap nuts:		
M6 nuts	10	7
M7 nuts	15	11
M8 nuts	20	15
Camshaft screw-in pin	20	15
Camshaft screw-in pin nut:		
Stage 1	5	4
Stage 2	10	7
Camshaft setscrew **(left-hand thread)**	10	7
Camshaft sprocket:		
Stage 1	5	4
Stage 2:		
Bolts	20	15
Nuts	10	7
Chain tensioner cover plug	40	30
Chain tensioner plunger cylinder	70	52
Crankshaft pulley hub bolt*	410	303
Crankshaft rear oil seal housing bolts:		
M6 bolts	10	7
M8 bolts	22	16
Crankshaft vibration damper/pulley-to-hub bolts	22	16
Cylinder head bolts:*		
Stage 1	40	30
Stage 2	Angle-tighten a further 90°	
Stage 3	Angle-tighten a further 90°	
Cylinder head cover bolts:		
M6 bolts	10	7
M7 bolts	15	11
Driveplate bolts*	120	89
Flywheel bolts*	105	77
Front crossmember bolts:*		
M10	47	35
M12	105	77
Ignition coil bolts	5	4
Main bearing cap bolts:*		
Stage 1	20	15
Stage 2	Angle-tighten a further 70°	
Manual transmission-to-engine bolts:		
Hexagon head bolts:		
M8 bolts	25	18
M10 bolts	49	36
M12 bolts	74	55
Torx head bolts:		
M8 bolts	22	16
M10 bolts	43	32
M12 bolts	72	53
Oil feed pipe to VANOS adjustment unit	32	24
Oil filter housing and pipes on crankcase:		
M8	22	16
M20	40	30
Oil pipe to camshaft bearings	10	7
Oil pressure switch:		
M52TU	35	26
M54	27	20

Torque wrench settings (continued)	Nm	lbf ft
Oil pump bolts (M8 bolts)	22	16
Oil pump cover	10	7
Oil pump sprocket nut **(left-hand thread)**:		
M6 thread	10	7
M10 x 1.00 mm thread	25	18
M10	47	35
Oil spray nozzles	10	7
Oil temperature switch:		
M52TU	35	26
M54	27	20
Reinforcement frame/plate:		
Stage 1	59	44
Stage 2	Angle-tighten a further 90°	
Stage 3	Angle-tighten a further 30°	
Sump oil drain plug:		
M12 plug	25	18
M22 plug	60	44
Sump to block:		
M6	10	7
M8	22	16
Sump lower section to upper section	10	7
Timing chain cover to crankcase:		
M6	10	7
M8	22	16
Stage 1	20	15
Stage 2	Angle-tighten a further 70°	
Upper and lower timing chain cover nuts and bolts:		
M6 nuts/bolts	10	7
M7 nuts/bolts	15	11
M8 nuts/bolts	20	15
M10 nuts/bolts	47	35
VANOS solenoid valve	30	22
VANOS oil feed pipe to oil filter housing	32	24
VANOS adjustment unit screw plugs	50	37
M6	10	7
M10	47	35
M10 x 1.0 mm	25	18

** Do not re-use*

1 General information

How to use this Chapter

This Part of Chapter 2 describes the repair procedures that can reasonably be carried out on the engine while it remains in the vehicle. If the engine has been removed from the vehicle and is being dismantled as described in Part C, any preliminary dismantling procedures can be ignored.

Note that, while it may be possible physically to overhaul items such as the piston/connecting rod assemblies while the engine is in the car, such tasks are not usually carried out as separate operations. Usually, several additional procedures are required (not to mention the cleaning of components and oilways); for this reason, all such tasks are classed as major overhaul procedures, and are described in Part C of this Chapter.

Part C describes the removal of the engine/transmission from the car, and the full overhaul procedures that can then be carried out.

Engine description

General

The M52TU and M54 engines are of 6-cylinder double overhead camshaft design, mounted in-line, with the transmission bolted to the rear end. The main differences between the two engines are that the M54 unit is equipped with fully electronic throttle control, and tuned for lower emissions.

A timing chain drives the exhaust camshaft, and the inlet camshaft is driven by a second chain from the end of the exhaust camshaft. Hydraulic cam followers are fitted between the camshafts and the valves. Each camshaft is supported by seven bearings incorporated in bearing castings fitted to the cylinder head.

The crankshaft runs in seven main bearings of the usual shell-type. Endfloat is controlled by thrust bearing shells on No 6 main bearing.

The pistons are selected to be of matching weight, and incorporate fully-floating gudgeon pins retained by circlips.

The oil pump is chain-driven from the front of the crankshaft.

Variable camshaft timing control

On all models, a variable camshaft timing control system, known as VANOS, is fitted. The VANOS system uses data supplied by the DME engine management system (see Chapter 4A), to adjust the timing of both the inlet and exhaust camshafts independently via a hydraulic control system (using engine oil as the hydraulic fluid). The camshaft timings are varied according to engine speed, retarding the timing (opening the valves later) at low and high engine speeds to improve low-speed driveability and maximum power respectively. At medium engine speeds, the camshaft timings are advanced (opening the valves earlier) to increase mid-range torque and to improve exhaust emissions.

Repairs with engine in place

The following operations can be carried out without having to remove the engine from the vehicle:

a) Removal and refitting of the cylinder head.
b) Removal and refitting of the timing chain and sprockets.
c) Removal and refitting of the camshafts.
d) Removal and refitting of the sump.
*e) Removal and refitting of the big-end bearings, connecting rods, and pistons.**

3.4 Release the securing clips and remove the cover from the inlet camshaft

f) Removal and refitting of the oil pump.
g) Renewal of the engine/transmission mountings.
h) Removal and refitting of the flywheel/driveplate.

** Although it is possible to remove these components with the engine in place, for reasons of access and cleanliness it is recommended that the engine is removed.*

2 Compression test – description and interpretation

1 When engine performance is down, or if misfiring occurs which cannot be attributed to the ignition or fuel systems, a compression test can provide diagnostic clues as to the engine's condition. If the test is performed regularly, it can give warning of trouble before any other symptoms become apparent.

2 The engine must be fully warmed-up to normal operating temperature, the battery must be fully charged, and all the spark plugs must be removed (Chapter 1). The aid of an assistant will also be required.

3 Remove the fuel pump fuse (located in the passenger compartment fusebox), and if possible, start the engine and allow it to run until the residual fuel in the system is exhausted. Failure to do so could result in damage to the catalytic converter.

4 On all models, fit a compression tester to the No 1 cylinder spark plug hole – the type of tester which screws into the plug thread is to be preferred.

3.8a With the No 1 piston at TDC, the tips of the front cam lobes face each other

3.5 Fit the BMW special tool to the VANOS oil port

5 Have the assistant hold the throttle wide open, and crank the engine on the starter motor. After one or two revolutions, the compression pressure should build-up to a maximum figure, and then stabilise. Record the highest reading obtained.

6 Repeat the test on the remaining cylinders, recording the pressure in each.

7 All cylinders should produce very similar pressures; a difference of more than 2 bars between any two cylinders indicates a fault. Note that the compression should build-up quickly in a healthy engine; low compression on the first stroke, followed by gradually-increasing pressure on successive strokes, indicates worn piston rings. A low compression reading on the first stroke, which does not build-up during successive strokes, indicates leaking valves or a blown head gasket (a cracked head could also be the cause). Deposits on the undersides of the valve heads can also cause low compression.

8 BMW minimum values for compression pressures are given in the Specifications.

9 If the pressure in any cylinder is low, carry out the following test to isolate the cause. Introduce a teaspoonful of clean oil into that cylinder through its spark plug hole, and repeat the test.

10 If the addition of oil temporarily improves the compression pressure, this indicates that bore or piston wear is responsible for the pressure loss. No improvement suggests that leaking or burnt valves, or a blown head gasket, may be to blame.

11 A low reading from two adjacent cylinders is almost certainly due to the head gasket having blown between them; the presence of coolant in the engine oil will confirm this.

12 If one cylinder is about 20 percent lower than the others and the engine has a slightly rough idle, a worn camshaft lobe could be the cause.

13 If the compression reading is unusually high, the combustion chambers are probably coated with carbon deposits. If this is the case, the cylinder head should be removed and decarbonised.

14 On completion of the test, refit the spark plugs (see Chapter 1) and refit the fuel pump fuse.

3 Top Dead Centre (TDC) for No 1 piston – locating

Note: *To lock the engine in the TDC position, reset the VANOS units, and to check the position of the camshafts, special tools will be required. These tools cannot easily be improvised. Read through the text prior to attempting the procedure.*

1 Top Dead Centre (TDC) is the highest point in the cylinder that each piston reaches as it travels up and down when the crankshaft turns. Each piston reaches TDC at the end of the compression stroke and again at the end of the exhaust stroke, but TDC generally refers to piston position on the compression stroke. No 1 piston is at the timing chain end of the engine.

2 Positioning No 1 piston at TDC is an essential part of many procedures, such as timing chain removal and camshaft removal.

3 Remove the cylinder head cover as described in Section 4.

4 Unclip the plastic cover from the inlet camshaft **(see illustration)**.

5 In order to accurately set the camshafts' positions, the VANOS units must be set as follows. Unscrew the VANOS unit oil pressure pipe from the inlet camshaft VANOS unit, and fit special BMW tool 11 3 450 to the port on the VANOS unit **(see illustration)**.

6 Using a clean cloth, cover the top of the VANOS unit as, when compressed air is applied, some oil will be sprayed out.

7 Connect a compressed air line to the union of the special tool, and apply a pressure of 2.0 to 8.0 bar. This pressure will reset the VANOS units as the engine is rotated.

8 Using a socket or spanner on the crankshaft pulley bolt, turn the engine clockwise at least two complete revolutions until the tips of the front cam lobes on the exhaust and inlet camshafts face one another. Note that the square flanges on the rear of the camshafts should be positioned with the sides of the flanges exactly at right-angles to the top surface of the cylinder head. BMW special tools 11 3 240 are available to lock the camshafts in this position. The tools slide over the square flanges of the camshafts and hold them at 90° to the cylinder head upper surface, once the two outer cylinder head cover studs have been removed. If the tools are not available, an alternative can be fabricated from steel or aluminium plate **(see illustrations)**.

9 Pull the blanking plug from the timing hole in the left-hand rear corner flange of the cylinder block (access is much improved if the starter motor is removed – see Chapter 5A).

10 To 'lock' the crankshaft in position, a special tool will now be required. BMW tool 11 2 300 can be used, but one can be made up by machining a length of steel rod **(see illustration)**.

11 Insert the rod through the timing hole. If

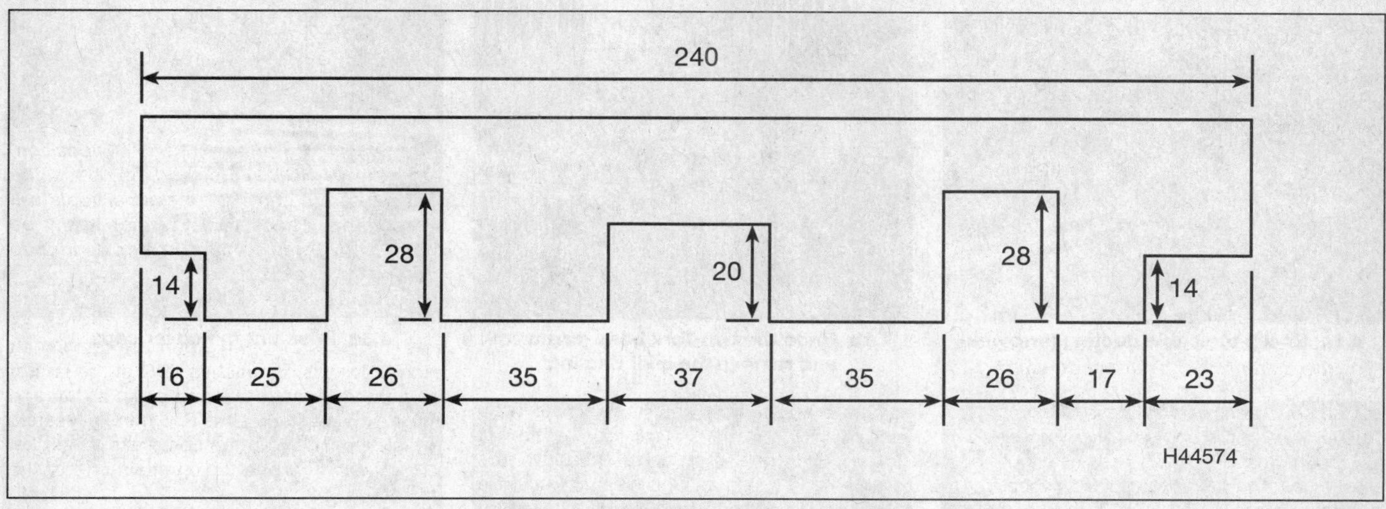

3.8b Make up a template from metal sheet
All dimensions in mm

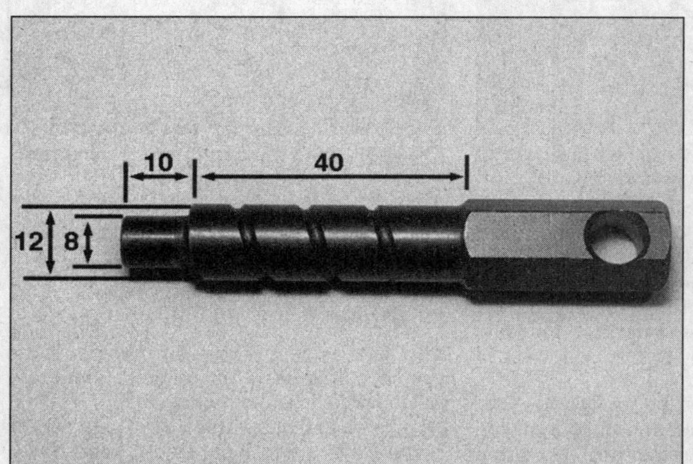

3.10 Flywheel locking tool
All dimensions in mm

3.11a Insert the rod through the timing hole . . .

necessary, turn the crankshaft slightly until the rod enters the TDC hole in the flywheel **(see illustrations)**.

12 The crankshaft is now 'locked' in position with No 1 piston at TDC. Disconnect the compressed air from the VANOS oil port.

Warning: If, for any reason, it is necessary to turn either or both of the camshafts with No 1 piston positioned at TDC, and either of the timing chain tensioners are slackened or removed (or the timing chains removed), the following precaution must be observed. Before turning the camshaft(s), the crankshaft must be turned approximately 30° anti-clockwise away from the TDC position (remove the locking rod from the TDC hole in the flywheel to do this) to prevent the possibility of piston-to-valve contact.

13 Do not attempt to turn the engine with the flywheel or camshaft(s) locked in position, as engine damage may result. If the engine is to be left in the 'locked' state for a long period of time, it is a good idea to place suitable warning notices inside the vehicle, and in the engine compartment. This will reduce the possibility of the engine being cranked on the starter motor.

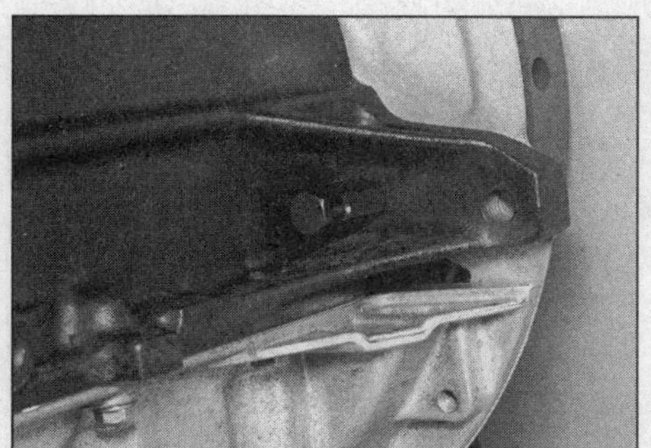
3.11b . . . until it enters the TDC hole in the flywheel – engine removed for clarity

4 Cylinder head cover – removal and refitting

Note: *New gaskets and/or seals may be required on refitting – see text.*

Removal

1 To allow sufficient clearance for the cylinder head cover to be removed, remove the heater/ventilation inlet air ducting from the rear of the engine compartment **(see illustrations)**.

a) Rotate the three fasteners 90° anti-clockwise and remove the pollen filter cover from the rear of the engine compartment. Pull the filter forward and remove it.

b) Undo the four retaining clips and thread the cable out of the ducting.

c) Unscrew the four bolts and pull the filter housing forwards and remove it.

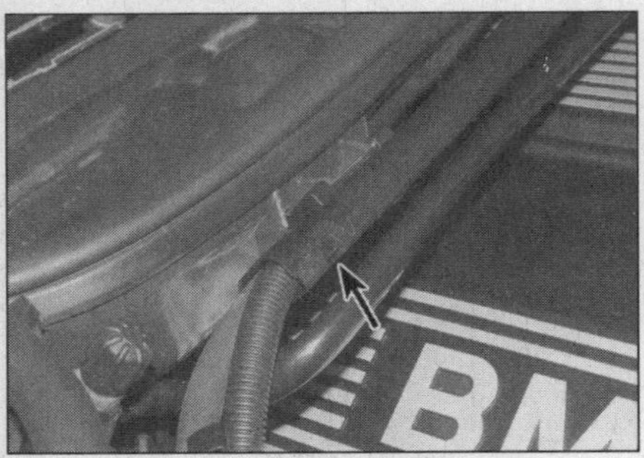
4.1a Unclip the cable ducting (arrowed)

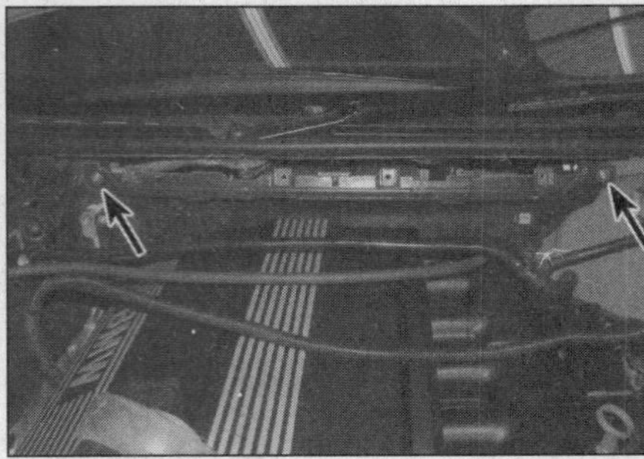
4.1b Undo the two Torx bolts (arrowed) and remove the inlet ducting

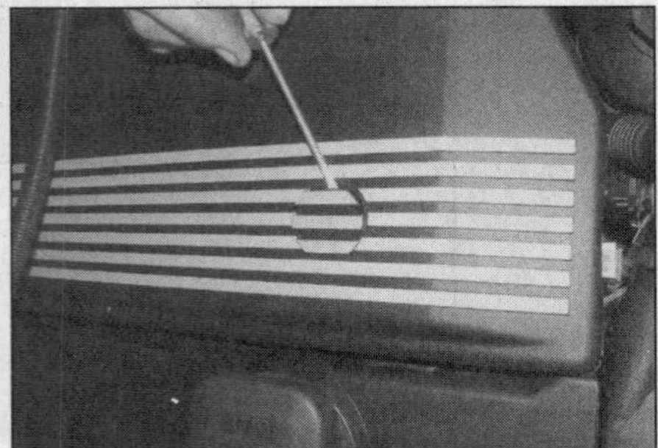
4.3a Prise out the cover caps . . .

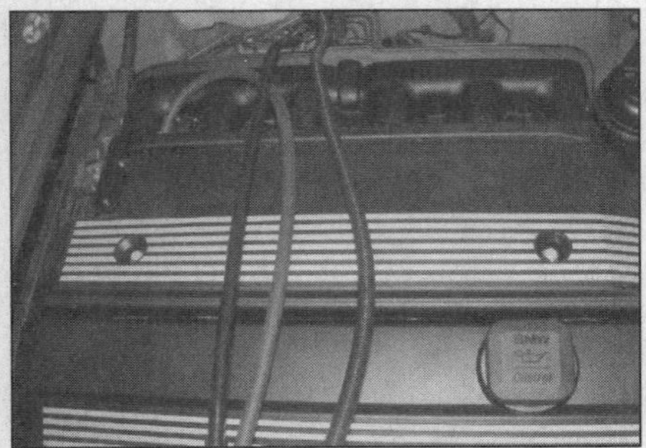
4.3b . . . and undo the bolts/nuts

4.4a Unscrew the earth strap from next to the No 1 spark plug hole (arrowed) . . .

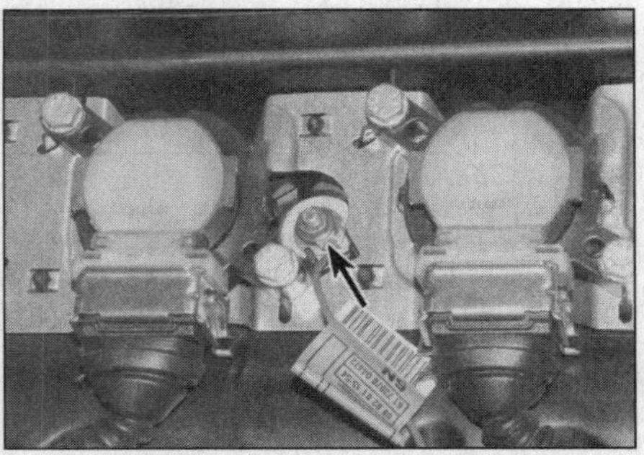
4.4b . . . and the centre of the cylinder head (arrowed)

d) *Pull up the rubber strip, rotate the two fasteners anti-clockwise, and move the dividing panel in the left-hand corner of the engine compartment forward a little.*

e) *Undo the two bolts and remove the inlet ducting upwards and out of the engine compartment.*

2 Remove the engine oil filler cap.

3 Remove the plastic covers from the fuel rail and the top of the cylinder head cover. To remove the covers, prise out the cover caps and unscrew the two securing nuts. To remove the cover from the cylinder head, lift and pull the cover forwards, then manipulate the cover over the oil filler neck **(see illustrations)**.

4 Unscrew the earth lead from cylinder head cover adjacent to the No 1 spark plug hole and, where applicable, unscrew the earth leads from the centre and rear of the cylinder head cover **(see illustrations)**.

5 Slide up the locking elements and unplug the wiring connectors from the ignition coils **(see illustration)**.

6 Release the wiring from the clips on the cylinder head cover, then move the complete ducting/wiring assembly to one side, clear of the cylinder head cover.

7 Unscrew the ignition coil securing nuts/ bolts, then carefully pull the coils from the spark plugs **(see illustration)**. Note the locations of the earth leads and the coil wiring brackets.

8 Release the securing clip and disconnect the breather hose from the side of the cylinder head cover **(see illustration)**.

9 Unclip the oxygen sensor connectors from the right-hand edge of the cylinder head cover and lay them to one side.

10 Unscrew the securing bolts/nuts (including the ones in the centre of the cover) and lift off the cylinder head cover. Note the locations of all washers, seals and gaskets, and recover any which are loose.

Refitting

11 Commence refitting by checking the condition of all seals and gaskets. Renew any which are perished or damaged.

12 Clean the gasket/sealing faces of the cylinder head and the cylinder head cover, then apply a bead of Drei Bond 1209 (available from BMW dealers and automotive parts retailers) to the area where the VANOS unit meets the cylinder head, and the corners of the semi-circular cut-out sections at the rear of the cylinder head and VANOS unit. Lay the main (outer) gasket and the spark plug hole (centre) gaskets in position on the cylinder head cover **(see illustrations)**.

13 Lay the cylinder head cover in position,

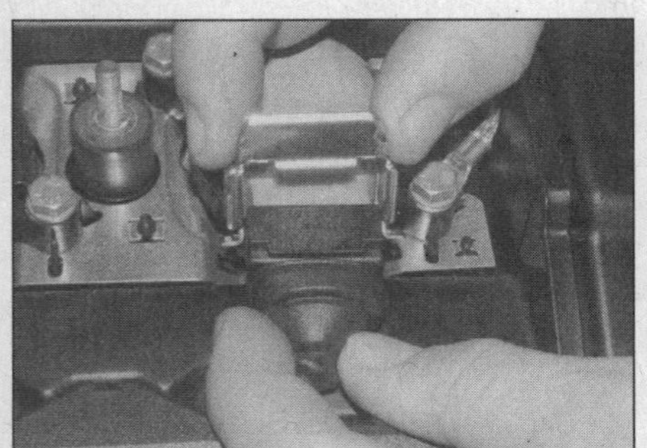
4.5 Slide up the locking elements and disconnect the coil plugs

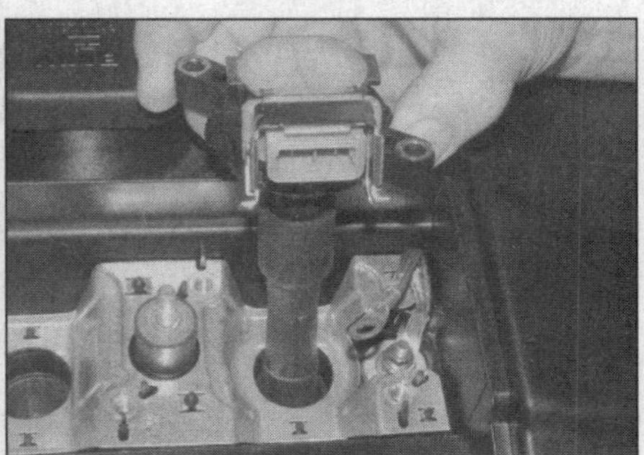
4.7 Undo the ignition coil bolts and pull them up from the spark plugs

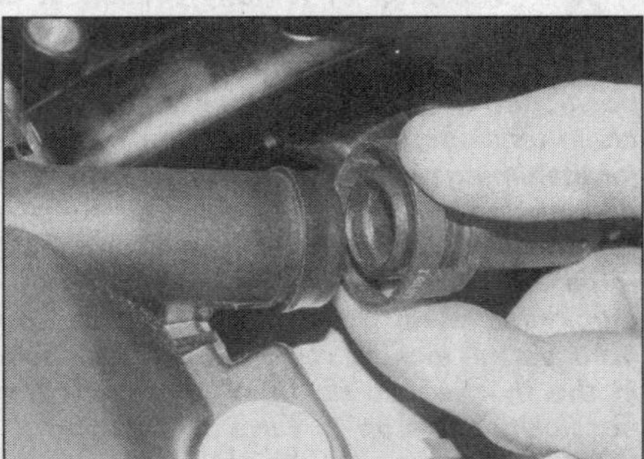
4.8 Disconnect the breather hose from the cylinder head cover

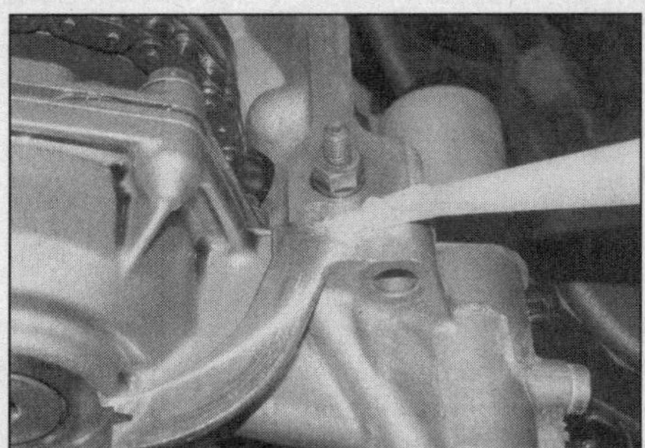

4.12a Apply sealant to the areas where the VANOS units contact the cylinder head . . .

4.12b . . . and the semi-circular cut-out sections

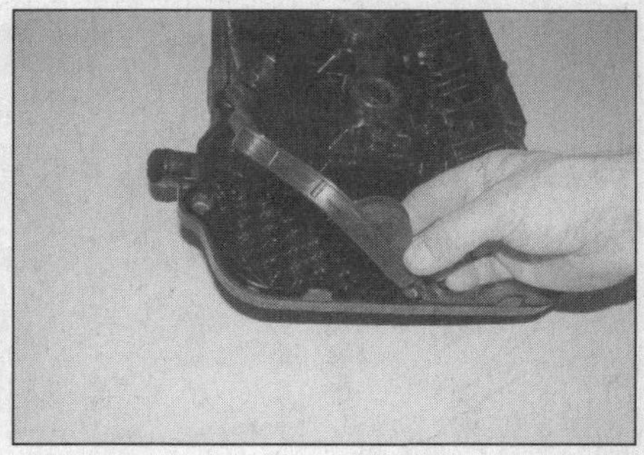

4.12c Ensure the gaskets are in position

taking care not to disturb the gaskets. Check that the tabs on the rear of the main gasket are correctly positioned in the cut-outs in the rear of the cylinder head.

14 Refit the cylinder head cover bolts/nuts, ensuring that the seals are positioned as noted during removal, then tighten the bolts progressively to the specified torque.

15 Further refitting is a reversal of the removal procedure, bearing in mind the following points.

a) Check that the ignition coil earth leads are correctly positioned as noted before removal.

b) Tighten the coil securing nuts/bolts to the specified torque.

c) Check that the rubber seals are in place when reconnecting the HT lead plugs to the coils.

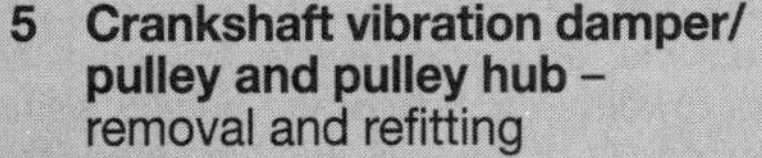

5 Crankshaft vibration damper/pulley and pulley hub – removal and refitting

Note: *If the pulley hub is removed, a new securing bolt will be required on refitting, and a torque wrench capable of providing 410 Nm (303 lbf ft) of torque will be required.*

Removal

1 Release the clips/bolts and remove the engine undershield.

2 Remove the viscous cooling fan/electric cooling fan and fan cowl assembly as described in Chapter 3.

3 Remove the auxiliary drivebelts as described in Chapter 1.

4 Two different designs of damper/pulley and hub may be fitted. On some models the pulley/damper is bolted to the hub (two piece), and on others the hub is integral with the damper/pulley (one piece).

Two piece damper/pulley and hub

5 Unscrew the securing bolts, and remove the vibration damper/pulley from the hub **(see illustration)**. If necessary, counterhold the hub using a socket or spanner on the hub securing bolt.

6 To remove the hub, the securing bolt must be unscrewed.

Warning: The crankshaft pulley hub securing bolt is very tight. A tool will be required to counterhold the hub as the bolt is unscrewed. Do not attempt the job using inferior or poorly-improvised tools, as injury or damage may result.

7 Make up a tool to hold the pulley hub. A suitable tool can be fabricated using two lengths of steel bar, joined by a large pivot bolt. Bolt the holding tool to the pulley hub using the pulley-to-hub bolts **(see illustration)**. Alternatively use special tools 11 2 150 and 11 2 410 available from BMW dealers or automotive tool specialists.

8 Using a socket and a long swing-bar, loosen the pulley hub bolt. Note that the bolt is very tight.

9 Unscrew the pulley hub bolt, and remove the washer **(see illustration)**. Discard the bolt, a new one must be used on refitting.

10 Withdraw the hub from the end of the crankshaft **(see illustration)**. If the hub is tight, use a puller to draw it off.

11 Recover the Woodruff key from the end of the crankshaft if it is loose.

One piece damper/pulley and hub

12 In order to prevent the hub from rotating whilst undoing the central bolt, BMW specify the use of tools 11 8 190 and 11 8 200, which engage in the holes between the webs of the pulley hub. In the absence of these tools, it may be possible to prevent the hub from rotating by using a strap wrench around the pulley **(see illustrations)**. The bolt is very tight, and assistance will be required.

13 Undo the hub bolt, and remove the washer. Discard the bolt, a new one must be fitted.

14 Withdraw the hub from the end of the crankshaft. If the hub is tight, use a puller to draw it off.

5.5 Undo the bolts and remove the damper/pulley from the hub

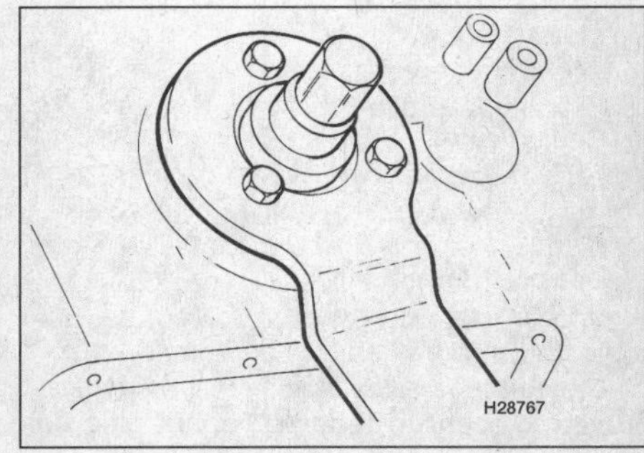

5.7 BMW special tools used to hold the crankshaft pulley hub

5.9 Unscrew the hub bolt and remove the washer . . .

5.10 . . . then withdraw the hub

5.12a Using BMW special tools to counterhold the pulley/hub . . .

5.12b . . . or use a strap wrench to hold it

15 Recover the Woodruff key from the end of the crankshaft if it is loose.

Refitting

16 If the pulley hub has been removed, it is advisable to take the opportunity to renew the oil seal in the lower timing chain cover, with reference to Section 6.
17 If the pulley hub has been removed, proceed as follows, otherwise proceed to paragraph 21 (two piece damper/pulley and hub).
18 Where applicable, refit the Woodruff key to the end of the crankshaft, then align the groove in the pulley hub with the key, and slide the hub onto the end of the crankshaft.
19 Refit the washer, noting that the shoulder on the washer must face the hub, and fit a new hub securing bolt.

Two piece damper/pulley and hub

20 Bolt the holding tool to the pulley hub, as during removal, then tighten the hub bolt to the specified torque. Take care to avoid injury and/or damage.
21 Where applicable, unscrew the holding tool, and refit the vibration damper/pulley, ensuring that the locating dowel on the hub engages with the corresponding hole in the damper/pulley.
22 Refit the damper/pulley securing bolts, and tighten to the specified torque. Again, counterhold the pulley if necessary when tightening the bolts.

One piece damper/pulley and hub

23 Counterhold the hub using the method employed during removal, and tighten the bolt to the specified torque.

All models

24 Refit the auxiliary drivebelts as described in Chapter 1.
25 Refit the viscous cooling fan and cowl as described in Chapter 3.
26 Where applicable, refit the splash guard to the engine underside.

6 Timing chain cover – removal and refitting

Note: *New timing cover gaskets and a new crankshaft front oil seal will be required on refitting. RTV sealant will be required to coat the cylinder head/cylinder block joint – see text.*

Removal

1 Drain the cooling system as described in Chapter 1.
2 Remove the cylinder head cover as described in Section 4.
3 Remove the auxiliary drivebelts as described in Chapter 1.
4 Remove the thermostat as described in Chapter 3.
5 Remove the crankshaft pulley/damper and hub as described in Section 5.
6 Remove the sump as described in Section 12.
7 Undo the two bolts and remove the auxiliary drivebelt tensioner **(see illustration)**.
8 The coolant pump pulley must now be removed. Counterhold the pulley by wrapping an old drivebelt around it and clamping tightly, then unscrew the securing bolts and withdraw the pulley.
9 Working at the top of the timing chain cover, drive out the two cover dowels. Drive out the dowels towards the rear of the engine, using a pin-punch (less than 5.0 mm diameter) **(see illustration)**.
10 It is now necessary to remove the VANOS adjustment unit (see Section 9), for access to the timing chain cover-to-cylinder head bolts.
11 Unscrew the three timing chain cover-to-cylinder head bolts, and lift the bolts from the cylinder head. Note that one of the bolts also secures the secondary timing chain guide **(see illustration)**.
12 Unscrew the timing chain cover-to-cylinder block bolts, then withdraw the cover from the front of the engine **(see illustrations)**. Recover the gaskets.

6.7 Unscrew the tensioner bolts (arrowed)

6.9 Drive the locating dowels from the timing chain cover

6.11 Remove the lower timing chain cover-to-cylinder head bolts (arrowed)

6.12a Unscrew the securing bolts (arrowed) . . .

6.12b . . . and remove the lower timing chain cover – cylinder head removed

Refitting

13 Commence refitting by levering out the oil seal from the timing chain cover.
14 Thoroughly clean the mating faces of the cover, cylinder block and cylinder head.
15 Fit a new oil seal to the timing chain cover, using a large socket or tube, or a block of wood to drive the seal into position **(see illustration)**.
16 Drive the cover dowels into position in the top of the cover so that they protrude from the rear (cylinder block mating) face of the cover by approximately 2.0 to 3.0 mm.
17 Position new gaskets on the cover, and hold them in position using a little grease.
18 Apply a little Drei Bond 1209 (available from BMW dealers and automotive parts retailers) to the cylinder head/cylinder block joint at the two points where the timing chain cover contacts the cylinder head gasket **(see illustration)**.
19 Offer the cover into position, ensuring that the gaskets stay in place. Make sure that the dowels engage with the cylinder block, and fit the cover securing bolts. Tighten the bolts finger-tight only at this stage.
20 Drive in the cover dowels until they are flush with the outer face of the cover.
21 Progressively tighten the cover securing bolts to the specified torque (do not forget the three cover-to-cylinder head bolts).
22 Refit the VANOS adjustment unit as described in Section 9.
23 Refit the crankshaft damper/pulley hub and damper/pulley as described in Section 5.
24 The remainder of refitting is a reversal of removal, bearing in mind the following points.

a) *Ensure the auxiliary drivebelt hydraulic tensioner strut is fitted correctly. The TOP/OBEN arrow must point upwards.*
b) *Refit the auxiliary drivebelts with reference to Chapter 1.*
c) *Refit the thermostat and housing with reference to Chapter 3.*
d) *Refit the cylinder head cover (Section 4).*
e) *Refit the sump as described in Section 12.*
f) *On completion, refill the cooling system and check the coolant level, as described in Chapter 1 and 'Weekly checks' respectively.*

6.15 Drive the new oil seal into position

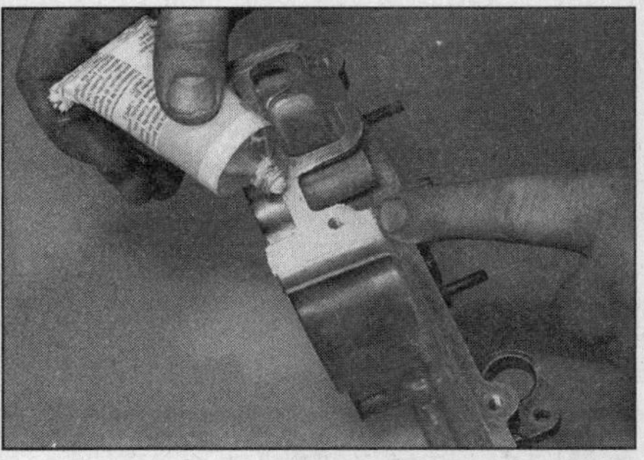

6.18 Apply sealant to the area where the lower timing chain cover contacts the cylinder head gasket

7 Timing chains – removal, inspection and refitting

Secondary chain

Removal

1 Remove the VANOS adjustment unit as described in Section 9.
2 Unscrew the timing chain tensioner plunger from the right-hand side of the engine **(see illustration)**. Discard the sealing ring, a new one must be fitted.

Warning: The chain tensioner plunger has a strong spring. Take care when unscrewing the cover plug.

3 If the tensioner is to be re-used, compress and release the tensioner plunger a few times, to evacuate any oil.
4 Press down the secondary chain tensioner plunger and lock it in place by inserting a suitable drill bit **(see illustration)**.
5 Undo the nuts and remove the camshaft position sensor gear from the exhaust camshaft sprocket, then remove the plate spring **(see illustration)**.
6 Undo the three inlet camshaft sprocket nuts and remove the corrugated washer **(see illustration)**.
7 Unscrew the three bolts from the exhaust camshaft sprocket and lift away the secondary chain together with the sprockets, friction washer and inlet camshaft splined shaft **(see illustration)**. If these items are to be re-used, store them together in order that they are refitted to their original locations.

Inspection

8 The chain should be renewed if the sprockets are worn or if the chain is worn

7.2 Unscrew the timing chain tensioner from the right-hand side of the engine

7.4 Use a drill bit (arrowed) to lock down the secondary chain tensioner

7.5 Remove the position sensor gear from the exhaust camshaft sprocket

7.6 Undo the three nuts and remove the corrugated washer from the sprocket

7.7 Remove the exhaust sprocket with the chain, friction washer, inlet sprocket and the inlet camshaft splined shaft

7.11 Fit the BMW tool into the tensioner aperture

7.12 Insert the chain and sprockets into the special tool. If the tool is not available, arrange them so there are 16 pins between the positions indicated

(indicated by excessive lateral play between the links, and excessive noise in operation). It is wise to renew the chain in any case if the engine is dismantled for overhaul. Note that the rollers on a very badly worn chain may be slightly grooved. To avoid future problems, if there is any doubt at all about the condition of the chain, renew it.

9 Examine the teeth on the sprockets for wear. Each tooth forms and inverted V. If worn, the side of each tooth under tension will be slightly concave in shape when compared with the other side of the tooth (ie, the teeth will have a hooked appearance). If the teeth appear worn the sprockets must be renewed. Also check the chain guide and tensioner contact surfaces for wear, and renew any worn components as necessary.

Refitting

10 Ensure that No 1 piston is still positioned at TDC, with the crankshaft locked in position. Check the position of the camshafts using the template.

11 Check that the primary chain and sprocket on the exhaust camshaft is still in place. Fit special tool 11 4 220 into the primary tensioner aperture, then turn the adjuster screw on the tool until the end of the screw just touches the tensioning rail **(see illustration)**.

12 In order to establish the correct relat-ionship between the two sprockets and the chain, access to BMW special tool 11 6 180 is necessary. Insert the two sprockets into the chain and lay the assembly in the special tool. In the absence of the special tool, arrange the sprockets so that there are 16 chain pins between the positions on the sprockets **(see illustration)**.

13 Fit the chain and sprockets over the end of the camshafts so that the 'master' tooth gap on the inner diameter of the inlet sprocket exactly aligns with the 'master' tooth gap on the shaft protruding from the end of the camshaft **(see illustration)**.

14 Refit the splined shaft into the end of the inlet camshaft, and insert the locking pin or 'master' spline so that it fits into the 'master' tooth gap in both the camshaft and sprocket **(see illustration)**. Push the splined shaft into the inlet sprocket until approximately 1 mm of the splines can still be seen.

15 Refit the corrugated washer onto the inlet sprocket with the FRONT marking forward. Refit the securing nuts, but only hand-tighten them at this stage.

16 Refit the bolts to the exhaust sprocket, tighten them to 5 Nm (4 lbf ft), then undo them 180°.

17 Fit the friction washer and plate spring to the exhaust sprocket. Note that the spring must be fitted with the F mark facing forward. If the mark is no longer visible, fit the spring with the convex side to the front **(see illustration)**.

18 Refit the exhaust camshaft position sensor gear with the raised section to the right-hand side of the engine and the arrow aligned with the cylinder head upper gasket face **(see illustration)**. Hand-tighten the nuts only at this stage

19 Pull out the exhaust splined shaft from the centre of the sprocket as far as it will go.

20 Compress the secondary chain tensioner plunger and remove the locking pin/drill bit.

21 Using a torque wrench, apply a torque of 0.7 Nm (0.5 lbf ft) to the adjusting screw on the special tool fitted to the primary chain tensioner aperture. In the absence of a suitable torque wrench, turn the adjusting screw by hand just

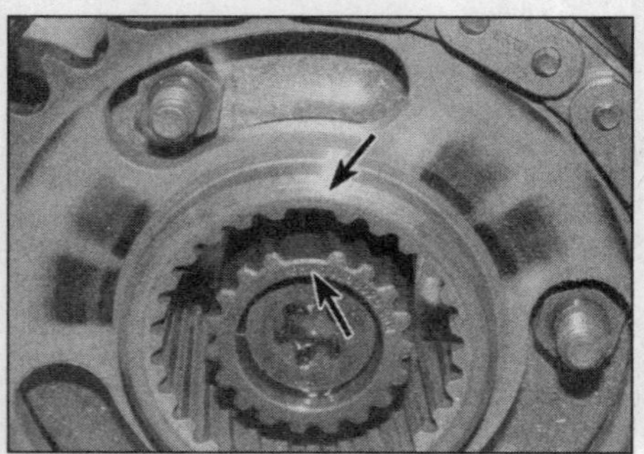
7.13 The gaps in the inlet sprocket and camshaft must align (arrowed)

7.14 Insert the splined shaft locking pin or 'master' spline into the tooth gaps

7.17 Fit the plate spring with the F at the front

7.18 Fit the sensor gear so that the arrow aligns with the upper gasket face (arrowed)

7.22 Use the special BMW tool to centre the splined shafts and sprockets

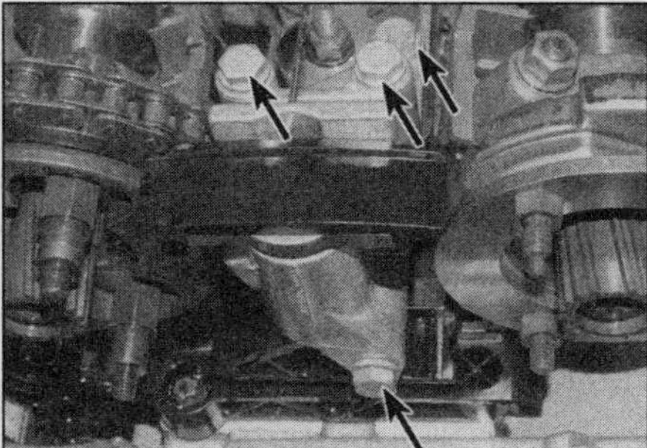

7.28 Remove the secondary chain tensioner bolts (arrowed)

7.29 Undo the three screw-in pins from the exhaust sprocket

enough to remove any play in the chain. Check that all play has been removed by attempting to turn the primary chain sprocket on the exhaust camshaft by hand.

22 To ensure that the splined shafts in the sprockets, and the sprockets themselves are correctly centred, BMW tool 11 6 150 must be fitted in place of the VANOS unit. Position the tool over the VANOS unit mounting studs (without the gasket), and evenly tighten the nuts until the tool is in full contact with the cylinder head. This tool positions the splined shafts, and holds them in place whilst the sprocket bolts/nuts are tightened **(see illustration)**. This tool is critical to the timing of the camshafts, and its use is essential.

23 Evenly and progressively tighten the sprockets nuts/bolts to the specified Stage 1 torque, beginning with the Torx bolts of the exhaust sprocket, followed by the exhaust sprocket nuts, and then the inlet sprocket nuts. Repeat the sequence tightening the bolts to the Stage 2 torque and then the nuts. With the sprockets nuts/bolts tightened and the BMW tool 11 6 150 still in place, remove the locking pin from the crankshaft, and the locking tools/template from the rear ends of the camshafts. Using a spanner or socket on the crankshaft pulley bolt, rotate the crankshaft two complete revolutions clockwise until the crankshaft locking pin can be re-inserted.

24 Check the position of the camshafts with the locking tools/template, and ensure the camshaft timing is correct. **Note:** *Due to the rubberised sprocket(s), tolerance in the VANOS unit and the splined shafts running clearance, the tool locking the inlet camshaft may misalign by up to 1.0 mm with the square flange, but the timing would still be considered correct.*

25 Remove the splined shaft/sprocket centring/positioning tool, and refit the VANOS adjustment unit as described in Section 9.

Primary chain

Removal

26 Remove the secondary timing chain as described previously in this Section.

27 Remove the splined shaft and sleeve from the centre of the exhaust camshaft sprocket.

28 Undo the four bolts and remove the secondary chain tensioner **(see illustration)**.

29 Undo the three 'screw-in' pins from the exhaust sprocket, lift the chain and remove the sprocket from the end of the camshaft **(see illustration)**. Note which way round the sprocket is fitted.

30 Remove the timing chain cover as described in Section 6.

31 Note the routing of the chain in relation to the tensioner rail and the chain guide.

32 Manipulate the tensioner rail as necessary to enable the chain to be unhooked from the crankshaft sprocket and lifted from the engine **(see illustration)**.

Warning: Once the primary timing chain has been removed, do not turn the crankshaft or the camshafts, as there is a danger of the valves hitting the pistons.

33 If desired, the tensioner rail can now be removed after removing the clip from the lower pivot **(see illustration)**.

34 Similarly, the chain guide can be removed after releasing the upper and lower retaining clips. Take care when releasing the retaining clips, as the clips are easily broken **(see illustration)**.

Refitting

35 Ensure No 1 piston is still at TDC, with the crankshaft locked in position. Check the position of the camshafts using the template.

36 Commence refitting by engaging the chain with the crankshaft sprocket.

37 Where applicable, refit the chain guide and the tensioner rail, ensuring that the chain is correctly routed in relation to the guide and tensioner rail, as noted before removal. Take care when refitting the chain guide, as the clips are easily broken.

38 Manipulate the exhaust camshaft primary chain sprocket until the timing arrow on the sprocket is aligned with the upper edge of the cylinder head, then engage the chain with the sprocket **(see illustration)**. Fit the

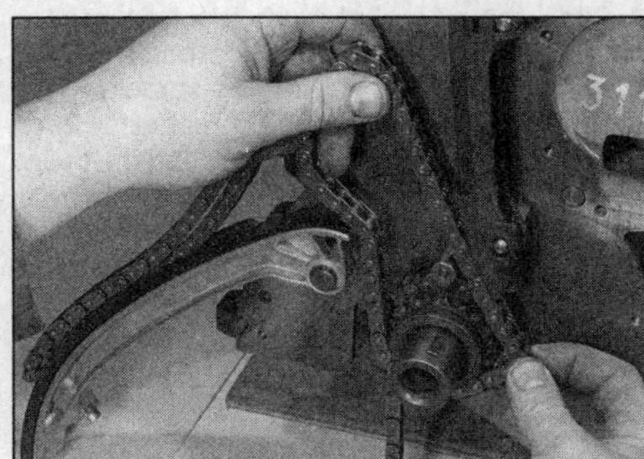

7.32 Unhook the chain from the crankshaft sprocket

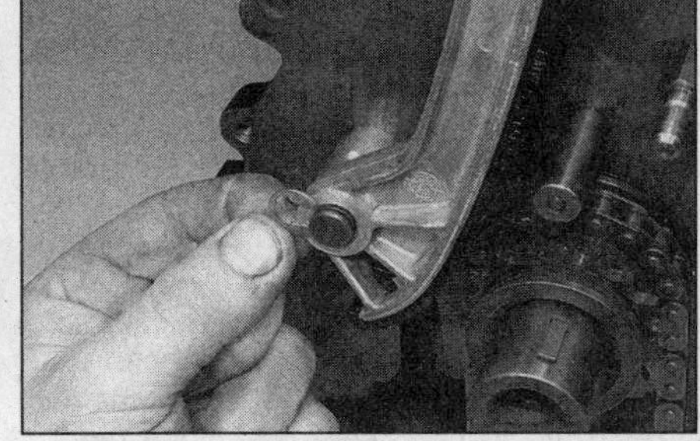

7.33 Remove the clip from the lower pivot to remove the tensioner rail – viewed with the engine removed

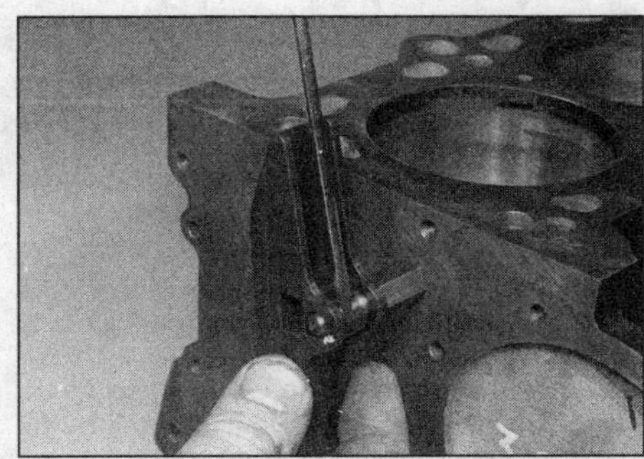

7.34 Release the retaining clips to remove the chain guide

7.38 Align the arrow on the sprocket with the upper edge of the cylinder head (arrowed)

7.43 The splined shaft 'master' spline must engage with the corresponding tooth gap in the camshaft and sleeve

sprocket to the exhaust camshaft. Ensure that the sprocket is fitted the correct way round as noted before removal, and that the timing arrow is still in alignment with the upper edge of the cylinder head.

39 Refit the timing chain cover as described in Section 6.

40 Fit special tool 11 4 220 into the tensioner aperture (see Section 9), then turn the adjuster screw on the tool until the end of the screw just touches the tensioning rail. Note that the exhaust camshaft sprocket may now have moved anti-clockwise – if necessary reposition the sprocket in the chain so that the timing arrow re-aligns with the upper surface of the cylinder head.

41 Insert the three 'screw-in' pins through the exhaust sprocket, and tighten them to the specified torque.

42 Refit the secondary timing chain tensioner and tighten the bolts securely.

43 Refit the splined shaft and sleeve to the exhaust camshaft sprocket so that the 'master' tooth gap in the sleeve aligns exactly with the corresponding tooth gap in the end of the camshaft. Note that the splined shaft incorporates a pin or 'master' spline which must engage in both tooth gaps **(see illustration)**.

44 Push the exhaust camshaft splined shaft in until the threaded holes in the camshaft sprocket are central with respect to the oval holes in the splined sleeve **(see illustration)**.

45 Refit the secondary timing chain as described in Paragraphs 10 to 25 of this Section.

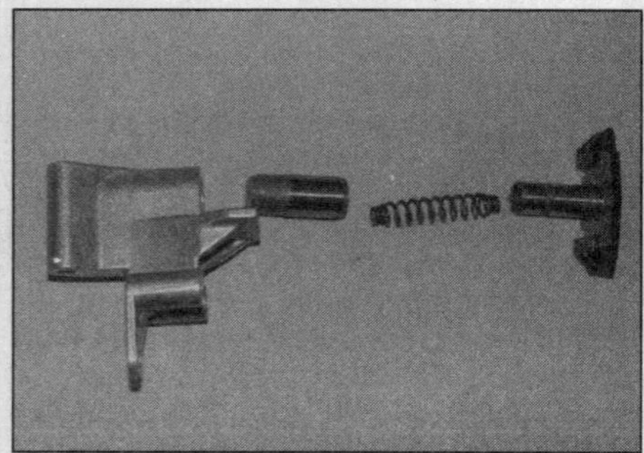

8.13 Secondary timing chain tensioner plunger, spring, and plunger housing

7.44 The holes in the sprocket must be central in the oval holes in the splined sleeve (arrowed)

8 Timing chain sprockets and tensioners – removal, inspection and refitting

Camshaft sprockets

1 Removal, inspection and refitting of the sprockets is described as part of the secondary timing chain removal and refitting procedure in Section 7.

Crankshaft sprocket

Removal

2 The sprocket is combined with the oil pump drive sprocket. On some engines, the sprocket may be a press-fit on the end of the crankshaft.

3 Remove the primary timing chain as described in Section 7.

4 Slide the sprocket from the front of the crankshaft. If the sprocket is a press-fit, use a three-legged puller to pull the sprocket from the crankshaft. Protect the threaded bore in the front of the crankshaft by refitting the pulley hub bolt, or by using a metal spacer between the puller and the end of the crankshaft. Note which way round the sprocket is fitted to ensure correct refitting.

5 Once the sprocket has been removed, recover the Woodruff key from the slot in the crankshaft if it is loose.

Inspection

6 Inspection is described with the timing chain inspection procedure in Section 7.

Refitting

7 Where applicable, refit the Woodruff key to the slot in the crankshaft.

8 Slide the sprocket into position on the crankshaft. Ensure that the sprocket is fitted the correct way round as noted before removal. If a press-fit sprocket is to be refitted, the sprocket must be heated to a temperature of 150°C. **Do not** exceed this temperature, as damage to the sprocket may result.

9 Once the sprocket has been heated to the given temperature, align the slot in the sprocket with the Woodruff key, then tap the sprocket into place with a socket or metal tube.

Warning: When the sprocket is heated, take precautions against burns – the metal will stay hot for some time.

10 Refit the primary timing chain as described in Section 7.

Secondary chain tensioner

Removal

11 Remove the secondary timing chain as described in Section 7.

12 Unscrew the securing bolts and withdraw the chain tensioner housing from the cylinder head **(see illustration 7.28)**.

13 Remove the tool locking the secondary timing chain tensioner in position, then withdraw the plunger, spring and plunger housing **(see illustration)**.

Inspection

14 Inspect the tensioner, and renew if necessary. Check the plunger and the plunger housing for wear and damage. Inspect the chain contact face of the plunger slipper for wear, and check the condition of the spring. Renew any components which are worn or damaged.

15 When refitting the plunger to the tensioner, note that the cut-out in the plunger should be positioned on the right-hand side of the engine when the assembly is refitted.

Refitting

16 Refit the chain tensioner and tighten the bolts securely.

17 Refit the tool to lock the tensioner in position.

18 Refit the secondary timing chain as described in Section 7.

Primary chain tensioner

19 Removal and refitting is described as part of the primary timing chain removal procedure in Section 7.

9 Variable valve timing system (VANOS) components – removal, inspection and refitting

VANOS adjustment unit

Removal

1 Remove the viscous cooling fan/electric cooling fan and fan cowl assembly as described in Chapter 3.

2 Remove the cylinder head cover as described in Section 4.

3 Unscrew the union bolt, and disconnect the oil feed pipe from the front of the VANOS adjustment unit **(see illustration)**. Recover the sealing rings.

4 Disconnect the exhaust camshaft position sensor and solenoid valve wiring connectors **(see illustration)**.

5 Unscrew the securing nut and bolt, and remove the engine lifting bracket from the front of the engine.

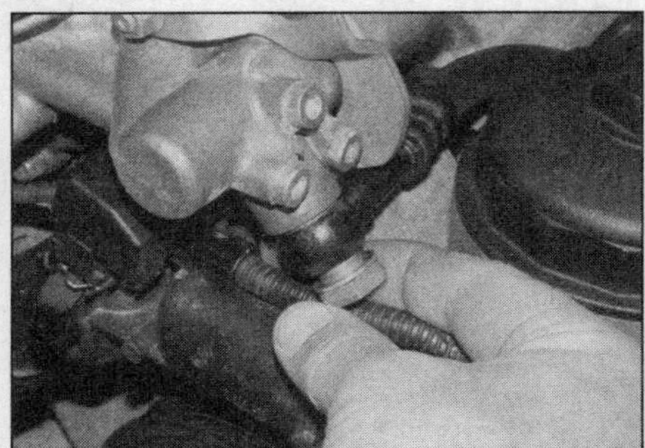

9.3 Disconnect the oil feed pipe from the VANOS unit

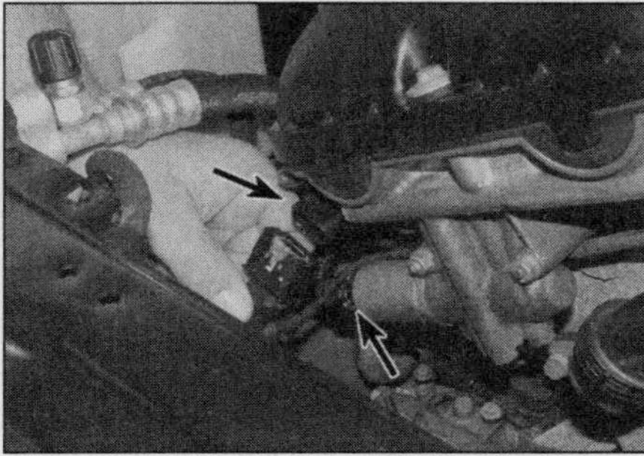

9.4 Disconnect the camshaft position sensor and the solenoid valve connectors (arrowed)

9.8 Undo the cover plugs from the VANOS unit

6 Unclip the plastic cover from the inlet camshaft.

7 Position the crankshaft and camshafts at TDC on No 1 piston, as described in Section 3.

8 Unscrew the two cover plugs from the front of the VANOS adjustment unit **(see illustration)**. Be prepared for oil spillage and discard the sealing rings, new ones must be fitted.

9 Using a pair of thin-nose pliers pull the sealing caps from the end of the camshafts **(see illustration)**.

10 Using a Torx bit, unscrew the setscrews from the end of the camshafts. Note that the setscrews are **left-hand thread (see illustration)**.

11 Undo the retaining nuts and remove the VANOS adjustment unit from the front of the engine. Recover the gasket.

12 Do not rotate the crankshaft, camshafts or move the splined shaft in the end of the camshafts with the VANOS unit removed, otherwise the pistons may come in contact with the valves.

Inspection

13 To test the operation of the VANOS adjustment unit, special equipment is required. Testing must therefore be entrusted to a BMW dealer.

Refitting

14 Ensure that the crankshaft and camshafts are still at TDC on No 1 cylinder as described in Section 3.

15 Make sure that the dowel sleeves are in position on the top VANOS adjustment unit securing studs in the cylinder head.

16 Apply a little Drei Bond 1209 sealant to the corners of the joint surfaces between the cylinder head and the VANOS adjustment unit, then fit a new gasket over the studs on the cylinder head **(see illustration)**.

17 Refit the VANOS adjustment unit and tighten the nuts to the securely.

18 Refit the setscrews into the ends of the camshafts and tighten them to the specified torque. Note that the setscrews are **left-hand thread**. Check the condition of the O-ring seals and refit the sealing caps into the ends of the camshafts.

19 The remainder of the refitting procedure is a reversal of removal, bearing in mind the following points.

a) Use new sealing rings when reconnecting the oil feed pipe to the VANOS adjustment unit.

b) Refit the cylinder head cover with reference to Section 4.

c) Refit the viscous cooling fan and cowl assembly as described in Chapter 3.

d) Ensure the crankshaft locking tool is removed prior to starting the engine.

VANOS solenoid valve

Note: *A new sealing ring will be required on refitting.*

Removal

20 Ensure that the ignition is switched off.

21 Disconnect the solenoid valve wiring connector, which is clipped to the engine wiring harness behind the oil filter assembly.

22 Using an open-ended spanner, unscrew the solenoid valve and recover the seal **(see illustration)**.

Inspection

23 Check that the solenoid plunger can be pulled freely back and forth by hand **(see illustration)**. If not, the solenoid must be renewed.

9.9 Use a pair of thin-nosed pliers to remove the sealing caps

9.10 The setscrews in the end of the camshafts have a left-hand thread

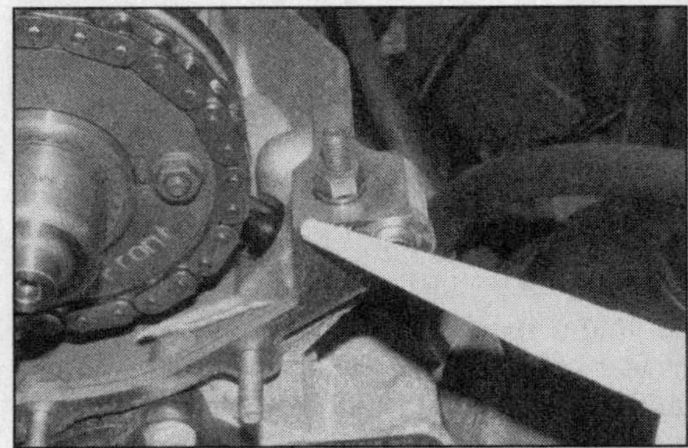

9.16 Apply a little sealant to the top of the gasket surface on each side of the cylinder head

9.22 Unscrew the VANOS solenoid valve

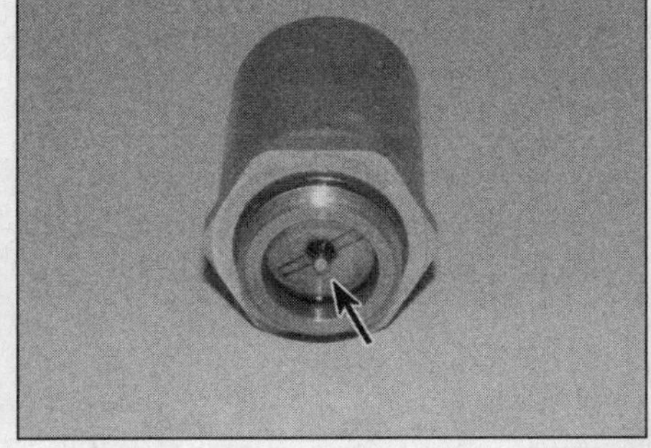

9.23 Check the solenoid plunger (arrowed) moves freely

10.7 Remove the 'screw-in' pins from the end of the camshaft

10.11 Unscrew the four camshaft cover securing studs

10.12 No 1 camshaft bearing cap is fitted with adapter sleeves

Refitting

24 Refitting is a reversal of removal, but use a new sealing ring.

10 Camshafts and followers – removal, inspection and refitting

Warning: BMW tool 11 3 260 will be required for this operation. This tool is extremely difficult to improvise due to its rugged construction and the need for accurate manufacture. Do not attempt to remove and refit the camshafts without the aid of this special tool, as expensive damage to the camshafts and/or bearings may result.

Removal

1 Remove the VANOS adjustment unit as described in Section 9.

2 Remove the secondary timing chain as described in Section 7.

3 Remove splined shaft and sleeve from the centre of the exhaust camshaft sprocket.

4 Undo the four bolts and remove the secondary chain tensioner **(see illustration 8.13)**.

5 Undo the three 'screw-in' pins from the exhaust sprocket, lift the chain and remove the sprocket from the end of the camshaft. Note which way round the sprocket is fitted.

6 Remove the crankshaft locking pin then, holding the primary timing chain under tension with your hand, carefully rotate the crankshaft 30° anti-clockwise to prevent accidental piston-to-valve contact. Use a length of wire or a cable tie through the primary timing chain and secure it to the cylinder head to prevent the chain falling down into the timing cover and/or disengaging from the crankshaft sprocket.

7 If required, undo the three 'screw-in' pins on the end of the inlet camshaft and remove the thrustwasher and camshaft sensor gear **(see illustration)**.

8 Remove the template from the camshafts.

9 Unscrew the spark plugs from the cylinder head.

10 Check the camshaft bearing caps for identification marks. The caps are numbered from the timing chain end of the engine, and the marks can normally be read from the exhaust side of the engine. The exhaust camshaft bearing caps are marked A1 to A7, and the inlet camshaft caps are marked E1 to E7.

11 Unscrew the four camshaft cover securing studs from the centre of the cylinder head **(see illustration)**.

12 As the inlet camshaft No 1 bearing cap is fitted with adapter sleeves, unscrew the nuts and remove the cap to prevent the cap from binding whilst the camshaft is removed **(see illustration)**.

13 Assemble BMW special tool 11 3 260, and mount the tool on the cylinder head by screwing the mounting bolts into the spark plug holes. Position the tool so that the plungers are located over the relevant camshaft bearing caps (ie, inlet or exhaust camshaft) **(see illustration)**.

10.13 BMW special tool fitted to the cylinder head

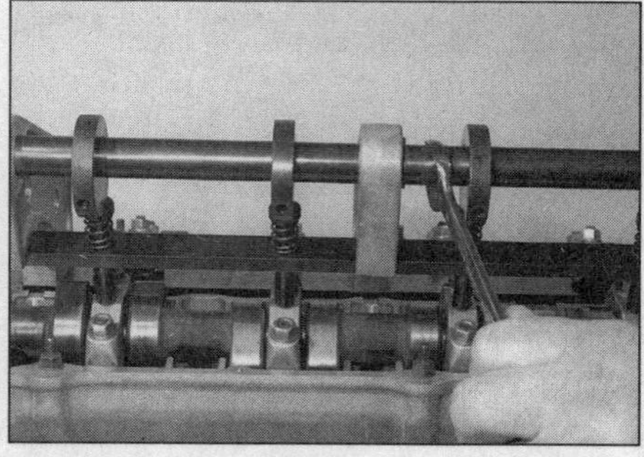

10.14 Use a spanner to turn the eccentric shaft, and apply pressure to the bearing caps

14 Apply pressure to the camshaft bearing caps by turning the eccentric shaft on the tools using a spanner **(see illustration)**.

15 Unscrew the remaining camshaft bearing cap nuts.

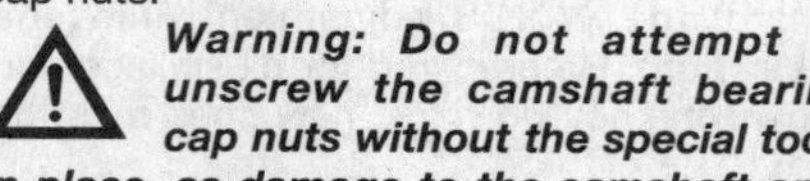

Warning: Do not attempt to unscrew the camshaft bearing cap nuts without the special tools in place, as damage to the camshaft and/or bearings may result.

16 Release the pressure on the special tool shaft, then unscrew the tool from the cylinder head.

17 Lift off the bearing caps, keeping them in order, then lift out the camshaft.

18 The camshaft bearing casting can now be lifted from the cylinder head. This should be done very slowly, as the cam followers will be released as the casting is lifted off – if the casting is lifted off awkwardly, the cam followers may fall out. Do not allow the cam followers to fall out and get mixed up, as they must be fitted to their original locations.

19 With the bearing casting removed, lift the cam followers from the cylinder head. Identify the followers for location, and store them upright in a container of clean engine oil to prevent the oil from draining from inside the followers.

20 Repeat the procedure on the remaining camshaft. Do not forget to mark the cam followers Inlet and Exhaust.

Inspection

21 Clean all the components, including the bearing surfaces in the bearing castings and bearing caps. Examine the components carefully for wear and damage. In particular, check the bearing and cam lobe surfaces of the camshaft(s) for scoring and pitting. Examine the surfaces of the cam followers for signs wear or damage. Renew components as necessary.

Refitting

22 If the camshaft lower bearing castings have been removed, check that the mating faces of the bearing castings and the cylinder head are clean, and check that the bearing casting locating dowels are in position on the studs at Nos 2 and 7 bearing locations **(see illustration)**.

23 The bearing casting(s) and cam followers must now be refitted.
24 The simplest method of refitting these components is to retain the cam followers in the bearing casting, and refit the components as an assembly.
25 Oil the bearing casting contact surfaces of the cam followers (avoid allowing oil onto the top faces of the followers at this stage), then fit each follower to its original location in the bearing casting.
26 Once all the followers have been fitted, they must be retained in the bearing casting, so that they do not fall out as the assembly is refitted to the cylinder head.
27 With the cam followers retained in the bearing casting, refit the casting to the cylinder head. Note that the exhaust side casting is marked A and the inlet side casting is marked E. When the castings are refitted, the marks should face each other at the timing chain end of the cylinder head.

Warning: The cam followers expand when not subjected to load by the camshafts, and therefore require some time before they can be compressed. If the camshaft refitting operation is carried out rapidly, there is a possibility that the 'closed' valves will be forced open by the expanded cam followers, resulting in piston-to-valve contact.

28 To minimise the possibility of piston-to-valve contact after refitting the camshaft(s) observe the delays listed in the following table before turning the crankshaft back to the TDC position:

Temperature	Delay
Room temperature (20°C)	4 minutes
10°C to 20°C	11 minutes
0°C to 10°C	30 minutes

29 First identify the camshafts to ensure that they are fitted in the correct locations. The inlet camshaft has a triangular front flange and the exhaust camshaft has a circular front flange. Ensure that the crankshaft is still positioned at 30° anti-clockwise from the TDC position.
30 Position the camshaft on the cylinder head, so that the tips of the front cam lobes on the exhaust and inlet camshafts face one another. Note also that the square flanges on the rear of the camshaft should be positioned with the sides of the flanges exactly at right-angles to the top surface of the cylinder head (this can be checked using a set-square), and the side of the flange with holes drilled into it uppermost. Feed the primary timing chain over the end of the exhaust camshaft as it is installed.
31 Place the bearing caps in position, noting that the caps carry identification marks. The exhaust camshaft caps are marked A1 to A7, and the inlet camshaft caps are marked E1 to E7. Place the bearing caps in their original locations as noted before removal.
32 Re-assemble BMW special tool 11 3 260, and refit it to the cylinder head as during removal.

Warning: Again, do not attempt to refit the camshafts without the aid of the special tools.

33 Apply pressure to the relevant bearing caps by turning the eccentric shaft on the tools using a spanner.
34 With pressure applied to the bearing caps, refit the bearing cap securing nuts, and tighten them as far as possible by hand.
35 Tighten the bearing cap nuts to the specified torque, working progressively in a diagonal sequence.
36 Once the bearing cap nuts have been tightened, unscrew the tool used to apply pressure to the bearing caps.
37 Repeat the procedure on the remaining camshaft.
38 Refit the spark plugs, and refit the camshaft cover studs to the cylinder head.
39 Refit the special tool/template used to check the position of the camshafts. If necessary, turn the camshaft(s) slightly using a spanner on the flats provided until the template can be fitted.

Warning: Note the warning in paragraph 27 before proceeding.

40 Turn the crankshaft back 30° clockwise to the TDC position, then re-engage the locking tool with the flywheel to lock the crankshaft in position.
41 Refit the camshaft sprockets and timing chains as described in Section 7.
42 Refit the VANOS adjustment unit as described in Section 9.
43 To minimise the possibility of piston-to-valve contact, after refitting the camshaft(s), observe the following delays before cranking the engine:

Temperature	Delay
Room temperature (20°C)	10 minutes
10°C to 20°C	30 minutes
0°C to 10°C	75 minutes

11 Cylinder head – removal and refitting

Note: *New cylinder head bolts and a new cylinder head gasket will be required on refitting.*

11.5 Undo the Torx bolts (arrowed) securing the secondary timing chain guide

10.22 Bearing casting location dowel (arrowed) on the cylinder head stud at No 2 bearing location

Removal

1 Drain the cooling system as described in Chapter 1.
2 Remove the inlet and exhaust manifolds as described in Chapter 4A.
3 Remove the camshafts and followers as described in Section 10.
4 Trace the wiring back from the camshaft position sensors, then disconnect the sensor connectors. Unscrew the securing bolts, and remove the sensors from the cylinder head.
5 Undo the two Torx bolts and remove the secondary timing chain guide from the cylinder head **(see illustration)**.
6 Unscrew the bolts securing the lower timing chain cover to the cylinder head.
7 Remove the thermostat as described in Chapter 3.
8 Undo the two bolts and remove the coolant pipe from the inlet side of the cylinder head. To improve access if necessary, undo the union bolt and disconnect the VANOS adjustment unit oil feed pipe from the rear of the oil filter housing **(see illustration)**. Recover the oil pipe sealing washers.
9 Disconnect wiring plugs from the temperature sensor located in the left-hand side of the cylinder head.
10 Progressively loosen the cylinder head bolts, working in the **reverse** of the tightening sequence **(see illustration 11.27)**.
11 Remove the cylinder head bolts, and recover the washers. Note that some of the washers may be captive in the cylinder head, in which case they cannot be withdrawn.
12 Release the cylinder head from the

11.8 If necessary, undo the VANOS oil feed pipe from behind the oil filter housing (arrowed)

11.24 Fit a new cylinder head gasket

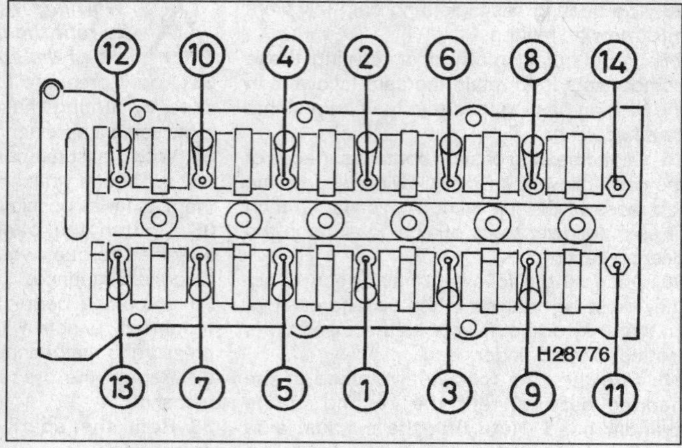

11.27 Cylinder head bolt tightening sequence

cylinder block and locating dowels by rocking it. Do not prise between the mating faces of the cylinder head and block, as this may damage the gasket faces.

13 Ideally, two assistants will now be required to help remove the cylinder head. Have one assistant hold the timing chain up, clear of the cylinder head, making sure that tension is kept on the chain. With the aid of another assistant, lift the cylinder head from the block – take care, as the cylinder head is heavy. As the cylinder head is removed, feed the timing chain through the aperture in the front of the cylinder head, and support it from the cylinder block using the wire.

14 Recover the cylinder head gasket.

Inspection

15 Refer to Chapter 2C for details of cylinder head dismantling and reassembly.

16 The mating faces of the cylinder head and block must be perfectly clean before refitting the head. Use a scraper to remove all traces of gasket and carbon, and also clean the tops of the pistons. Take particular care with the aluminium cylinder head, as the soft metal is easily damaged. Make sure that debris is not allowed to enter the oil and water passages. Using adhesive tape and paper, seal the water, oil and bolt holes in the cylinder block. To prevent carbon entering the gap between the pistons and bores, smear a little grease in the gap. After cleaning each piston, rotate the crankshaft so that the piston moves down the bore, then wipe out the grease and carbon with a cloth rag.

17 Check the block and head for nicks, deep scratches and other damage. If slight, they may be removed from the cylinder block carefully with a file. More serious damage may be repaired by machining, but this is a specialist job.

18 If warpage of the cylinder head is suspected, use a straight-edge to check it for distortion, with reference to Chapter 2C.

19 Clean out the bolt holes in the block using a pipe cleaner or thin rag and a screwdriver. Make sure that all oil and water is removed, otherwise there is a possibility of the block being cracked by hydraulic pressure when the bolts are tightened.

20 Examine the bolt threads and the threads in the cylinder block for damage. If necessary, use the correct size tap to chase out the threads in the block.

Refitting

Warning: As the camshafts have been removed from the cylinder head, note the warnings given in Section 10, regarding expanded cam followers.

21 To minimise the possibility of piston-to-valve contact after refitting the camshaft(s), observe the following delays before refitting the cylinder head.

Temperature	Delay
Room temperature (20°C)	4 minutes
10°C to 20°C	11 minutes
0°C to 10°C	30 minutes

22 Ensure that the mating faces of the cylinder block and head are spotlessly clean, that the cylinder head bolt threads are clean and dry, and that they screw in and out of their locations. Check that the cylinder head locating dowels are correctly positioned in the cylinder block.

Warning: To avoid any possibility of piston-to-valve contact when refitting the cylinder head, it is necessary to ensure that none of the pistons are at TDC. Before proceeding further, if not already done, turn the crankshaft to position No 1 piston at TDC (check that the locking rod can be engaged with the flywheel, then remove the locking rod and turn the crankshaft approximately 30° anti-clockwise using a spanner or socket on the crankshaft pulley hub bolt.

23 Apply a thin bead of Drei Bond 1209 to the area where the cylinder block meets the timing cover.

24 Fit a new cylinder head gasket to the block, locating it over the dowels. Make sure that it is the correct way up **(see illustration)**. Note that 0.3 mm thicker-than-standard gaskets are available for use if the cylinder head has been machined (see Chapter 2C).

25 Lower the cylinder head onto the block, engaging it over the dowels.

26 Apply a light coat of clean engine oil to the threads and washer contact areas then fit the new cylinder head bolts, complete with new washers, where necessary, and tighten the bolts as far as possible by hand. Ensure that the washers are correctly seated in their locations in the cylinder head. **Note:** *Do not fit washers to any bolts which are fitted to locations where there are already captive washers in the cylinder head. If a new cylinder head is fitted (without captive washers), ensure that new washers are fitted to all the bolts.*

27 Tighten the bolts in the order shown, and in the stages given in the Specifications – ie, tighten all bolts in sequence to the Stage 1 torque, then tighten all bolts in sequence to the Stage 2 torque, and so on **(see illustration)**.

28 Refit and tighten the bolts securing the lower timing chain cover to the cylinder head.

29 Refit the secondary timing chain guide to the cylinder head and tighten the Torx bolts securely.

30 Refit the camshafts and followers as described in Section 10.

31 Turn the crankshaft 30° clockwise back to the TDC position, then re-engage the locking rod with the flywheel to lock the crankshaft in position.

32 The remainder of refitting is a reverse of removal. On completion, refill the cooling system as described in Chapter 1.

12 Sump – removal and refitting

Note: *A new sump gasket and/or a new dipstick tube sealing will may be required on refitting, and suitable gasket sealant will be required.*

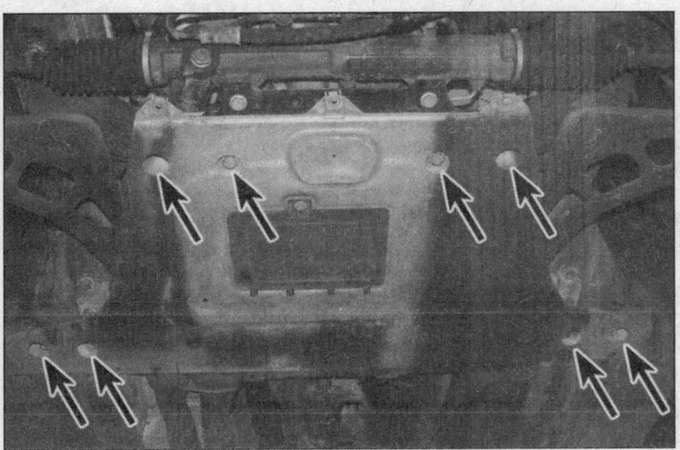

12.3 Undo the bolts (arrowed) and remove the reinforcement frame/plate from under the engine

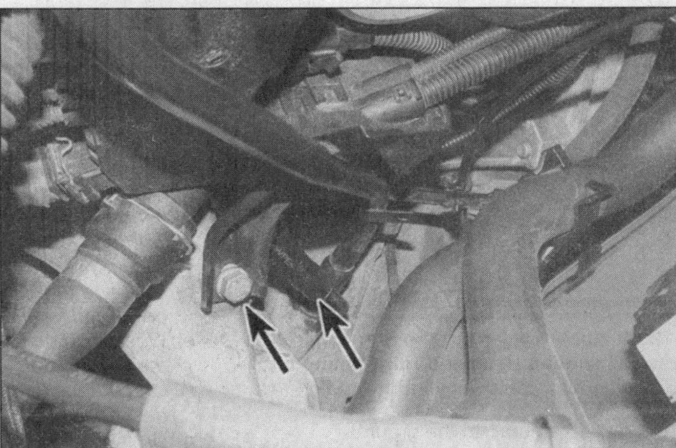

12.8 Dipstick guide tube oil return hose and mounting bracket bolt (arrowed)

Removal

1 Undo the bolts and remove the engine undershield and drain the engine oil, referring to Chapter 1.

2 Apply the handbrake, then jack up the front of the vehicle and support securely on axle stands (see *Jacking and vehicle support*).

3 Undo the bolts and remove the front reinforcement frame/plate from under the engine **(see illustration)**. Discard the bolts, new ones must be fitted.

4 Unscrew the securing bolts and/or nuts, and remove the alternator air ducting from the front of the vehicle.

5 Remove the air cleaner assembly as described in Chapter 4A.

6 In order to remove the sump, the front crossmember must be lowered and, therefore, the engine suspended. Manoeuvre an engine lifting hoist or crane into position and attach a lifting chain or sling to the 'eye' at the front of the cylinder head. Take the weight of the engine.

7 On automatic transmission models, disconnect the oil pipes from the transmission oil pan. Be prepared for fluid spillage.

8 Undo the retaining bolt and detach the oil return hose from the oil separator, and pull the dipstick guide tube and return hose from the sump **(see illustration).** Discard the O-ring seal, a new one must be fitted.

9 Ensure that the steering wheel is facing straight-ahead, and engage the steering lock. Make alignment marks between the steering column joint flange and the steering rack pinion, then undo the pinch-bolt, and pull the joint from the pinion. Whilst the column is separated from the rack it is essential that neither the steering wheel or roadwheels are moved from their positions **(see illustration).**

10 Remove the auxiliary drivebelt as described in Chapter 1.

11 Unscrew the power support bracket from the rear of the pump, then unscrew the pump mounting bracket from the alternator mounting bracket, and move the pump to one side, clear of the engine, leaving the fluid lines connected. Ensure that the pump is adequately supported, and take care not to strain the fluid lines.

12 Unscrew the nuts securing the left- and right-hand engine mountings to the subframe. Using the engine hoist or crane, raise the engine approximately 10 to 15 mm, ensuring that the rear of the cylinder head does not crush or trap the brake pipes along the engine compartment bulkhead.

13 Where applicable, unclip any pipes, hoses and/or wiring from the engine mounting brackets, and sump.

14 Undo the bolts and detach the front left- and right-hand control arm brackets from the front chassis legs **(see illustration).**

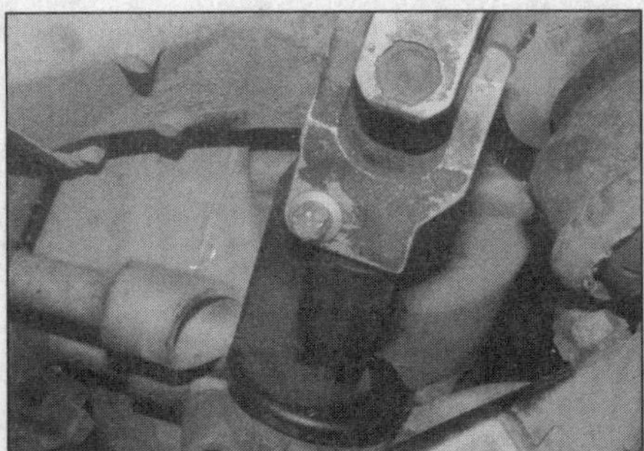

12.9 Undo the pinch-bolt and pull the joint from the pinion

12.16 Undo the chassis-to-crossmember bolts each side (arrowed)

15 Unscrew the anti-roll bar clamp bolts – see Chapter 10 if necessary.

16 Remove the crossmember-to-chassis bolts and, using a trolley jack for support, lower the crossmember, taking care not to strain the power steering hoses **(see illustration).** Where fitted, remove the rubber damping block from between the crossmember and the sump.

17 Working under the vehicle, progressively unscrew and remove all the sump securing bolts. Note that the rear sump securing bolts are accessible through the holes in the gearbox/transmission bellhousing **(see illustration).** Also note that the three lower gearbox/transmission-to-engine bolts must be removed, as they screw into the sump.

12.14 Remove the control arm-to-chassis bolts on each side

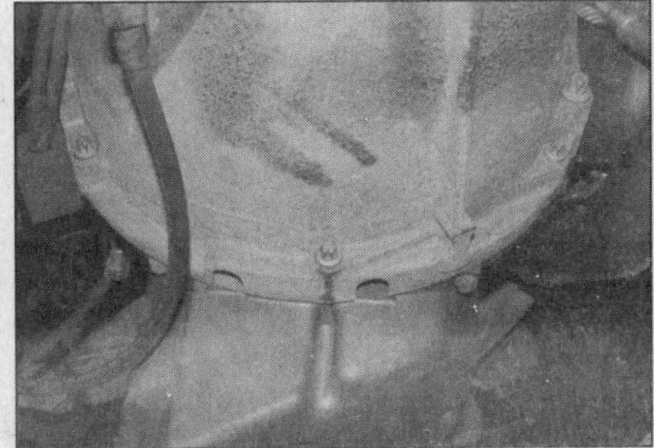

12.17 The rear sump bolts are accessible through the slots in the transmission housing

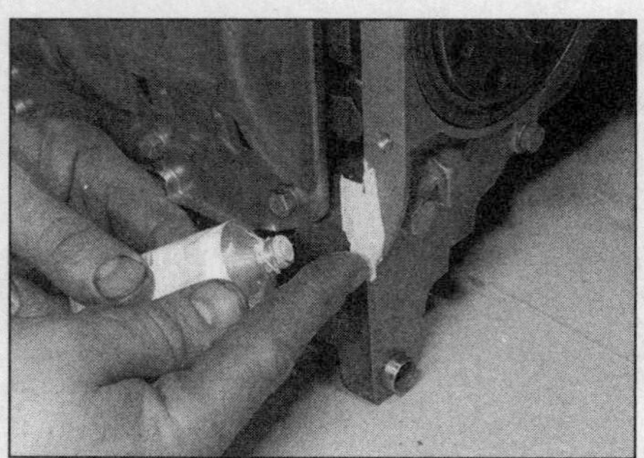

12.21 Apply sealant to the area where the rear oil seal housing and front timing chain cover join the cylinder block

18 Lower the sump to the ground.
19 Recover the sump gasket.

Refitting

20 Commence refitting by thoroughly cleaning the mating faces of the sump and cylinder block.
21 Lightly coat the areas where the crankshaft rear oil seal housing and front timing chain cover join the cylinder block with Drei Bond 1209 sealant **(see illustration)**.
22 Place the gasket in position on the sump flange.
23 Offer the sump up to the cylinder block, ensuring that the gasket stays in place, and refit the sump securing bolts, tightening them finger-tight only at this stage.
24 Progressively tighten the sump-to-cylinder block bolts to the specified torque.

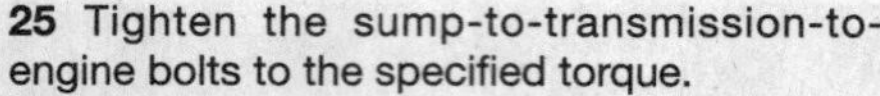

25 Tighten the sump-to-transmission-to-engine bolts to the specified torque.
26 Further refitting is a reversal of removal, noting the following points.
a) When raising the crossmember into position, make sure that no pipes, hoses and/or wiring are trapped.
b) Renew the crossmember and reinforcement frame/plate bolts.
c) Tighten the engine mounting nuts securely.
d) Refit and tension the auxiliary drivebelt as described in Chapter 1.
e) When refitting the dipstick tube, renew the O-ring seal.
f) On completion, refill the engine with oil as described in Chapter 1.
g) On automatic transmission models, check the transmission fluid level as described in Chapter 7B.

13 Oil pump and drive chain – removal, inspection and refitting

Oil pump

Note: *A new pick-up pipe O-ring, a new relief valve spring cap O-ring and a new relief valve circlip will be required on refitting.*

Removal and refitting

1 Remove the sump as described in Section 12.
2 Unscrew the nut securing the sprocket to the oil pump shaft. Note that the nut is **left-hand thread (see illustration)**.
3 Pull the sprocket and chain from the oil pump shaft.
4 On models where the pump is integral with the sump baffle plate, undo the bolts and remove the plate complete with the pump and pick-up tube.
5 On models where the pump is separate from the baffle plate, undo the two bolts securing the pick-up pipe to the baffle plate, and the bolt securing the pipe to the pump **(see illustration)**. Remove the pipe.
6 Undo the four bolts and remove the oil pump **(see illustration)**.

Inspection

7 Unscrew the cover from the front of the pump **(see illustration)**.
8 Withdraw the driveshaft/rotor and the outer rotor from the pump body.
9 Check the pump body, rotors and cover for any signs of scoring, wear or cracks. If any wear or damage is evident, fit new rotors or renew the complete pump, depending on the extent of the damage. Note that it is wise to renew the complete pump as a unit.
10 Refit the rotors to the pump body, then using feeler blades, measure the clearance between the outer rotor and the pump body. Using the feeler blades and a straight-edge, measure the clearance (endfloat) between each of the rotors and the oil pump cover mating face **(see illustrations)**. Compare the measurements with the values given in the Specifications, and if necessary renew any worn components, or renew the complete pump as a unit.

13.2 Unscrew the oil pump sprocket securing nut – it has a *left-hand thread*

13.5 Unscrew the oil pick-up pipe bolts (arrowed)

13.6 Undo the four bolts (arrowed) and remove the oil pump

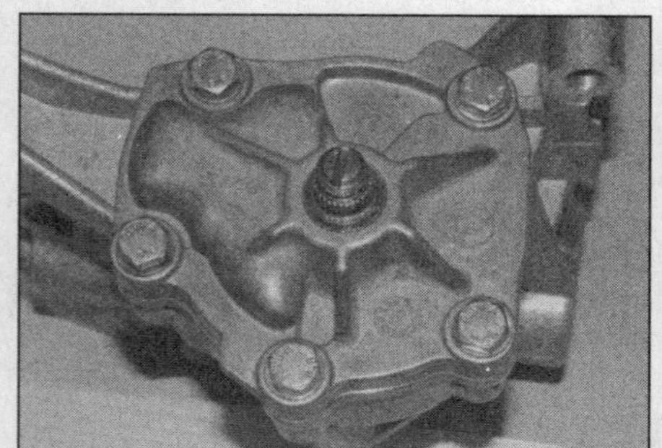

13.7 Remove the cover from the oil pump

13.10a Measure the clearance between the outer oil pump rotor and the pump body . . .

13.10b . . . and the rotor endfloat

11 To remove the pressure relief valve components, press the valve into its housing slightly, using a metal tool, then extract the circlip from the top of the housing using circlip pliers **(see illustration).**

Warning: The relief valve has a strong spring. Take care when removing the circlip.

12 Withdraw the spring cap, spring and piston from the relief valve housing **(see illustrations).**

13 Fit a new O-ring seal to the top of the relief valve spring cap, then refit the components to the housing using a reversal of the removal procedure. Take care not to damage the surface of the spring cap during fitting, and secure the components using a new O-ring.

14 Refit the rotors to the pump body, then refit the cover to the pump. Ensure that the locating dowels are in position in the pump cover. Refit and tighten the cover bolts to the specified torque.

15 The remainder of refitting is a reversal of removal, noting the following points:

a) Where applicable renew the oil pick-up tube O-ring seal.

*b) Tighten the oil pump sprocket retaining nut **(left-hand thread)** to the specified torque.*

Oil pump drive chain

Removal

16 Remove the primary timing chain as described in Section 7.

17 Withdraw the chain from the crankshaft sprocket.

Inspection

18 Proceed as described for the secondary timing chain in Section 7.

Refitting

19 Refit the chain to the crankshaft sprocket, then refit the primary timing chain as described in Section 7.

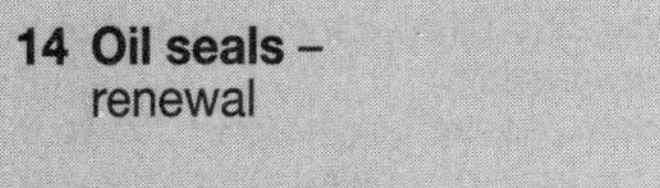

14 Oil seals – renewal

Crankshaft front oil seal

1 The procedure is described as part of the lower timing chain cover removal and refitting procedure in Section 6.

Crankshaft rear oil seal

Note: *A new oil seal housing gasket will be required on refitting.*

2 Remove the flywheel/driveplate, as described in Section 15.

3 Working at the bottom of the oil seal housing, unscrew the bolts securing the rear of the sump to the housing.

4 Unscrew the bolts securing the oil seal housing to the cylinder block.

5 If the housing is stuck to the sump gasket, run a sharp, thin blade between the housing and the sump gasket. Take care not to damage the sump gasket.

13.11 Extract the circlip . . .

13.12a . . . and withdraw the oil pressure relief valve spring cap . . .

13.12b . . . spring . . .

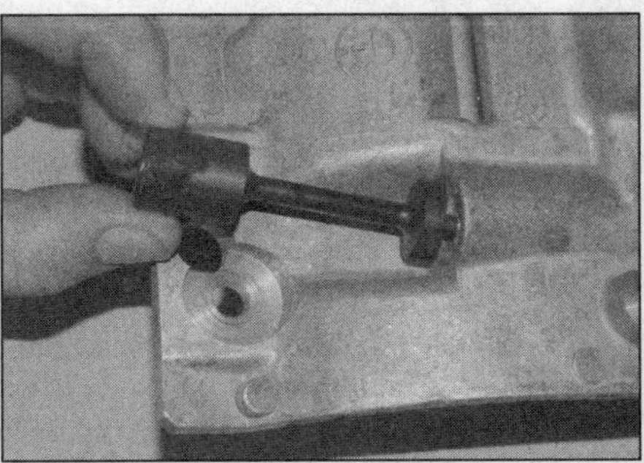

13.12c . . . and piston

6 Withdraw the housing from the cylinder block. If the housing is stuck, tap it gently using a soft-faced mallet. Do not lever between the housing and the cylinder block, as this may damage the gasket surfaces.

7 Recover the gasket.

8 Thoroughly clean all traces of old gasket and sealant from the mating faces of the oil seal housing and the cylinder block. Again, take care not to damage the sump gasket. If the sump gasket has been damaged during removal, it is advisable to fit a new one with reference to Section 12.

9 Support the oil seal housing on blocks of wood, then drive out the seal from the rear of the housing using a hammer and drift.

10 Clean the seal mating surfaces in the housing.

11 From April 1998 a new type of oil seal is fitted. This seal can be identified by the lack of tension spring. This seal must only be fitted with the aid of the seal protector (supplied with the seal). Leave the seal protector fitted into the centre of the seal at this stage. Do not touch the sealing lip with your fingers, the lip is very sensitive and must not be kinked. Carefully drive it into position in the housing, using either a large tube of the correct diameter, or a block of wood, to avoid damage to the seal **(see illustration).**

12 Ensure that the locating dowels are in position in the rear of the cylinder block, then locate a new oil seal housing gasket over the dowels.

13 Carefully offer the housing to the cylinder block, sliding the oil seal protector over the crankshaft flange, and push the seal and housing into place. Take care not to damage the oil seal lips.

14 Refit the housing-to-cylinder block and the sump-to-housing bolts, and tighten them lightly by hand.

15 Tighten the housing-to-cylinder block bolts to the specified torque, then tighten the sump-to-housing bolts to the specified torque.

16 Refit the flywheel/driveplate as described in Section 15.

Camshaft oil seals

17 No camshaft oil seals are fitted. Sealing is provided by the cylinder head cover gasket and the timing chain cover gaskets.

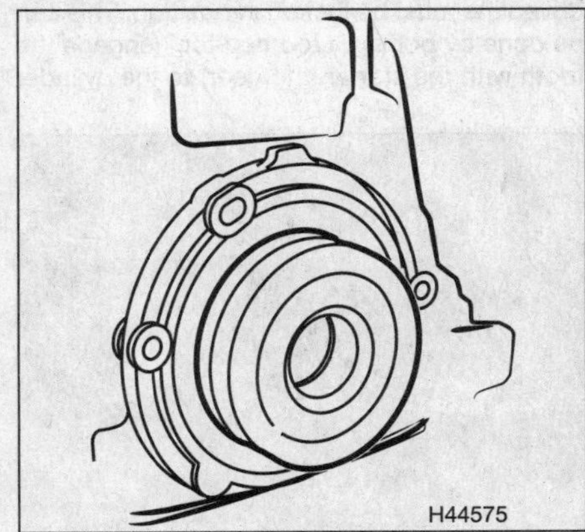

14.11 Leave the seal protector in the centre of the seal and drive it into place

15.3 Toothed tool used to lock the flywheel in position when unscrewing flywheel bolts

15.6 Ensure the engine/transmission intermediate plate is correctly located

15.7 The notch (arrowed) indicates the position of the locating hole for the dowel

15.8 If the bolt threads are not already coated in thread-locking compound, then apply some – 6-cylinder engines

15 Flywheel/driveplate – removal and refitting

Note: *New flywheel/driveplate securing bolts will be required on refitting, and thread-locking compound may be required (see text).*

Removal

1 Remove the manual gearbox as described in Chapter 7A, or the automatic transmission as described in Chapter 7B, as applicable.

2 On models with a manual gearbox, remove the clutch as described in Chapter 6.

3 In order to unscrew the bolts, the flywheel/driveplate must be locked in position. This can be done by bolting a toothed tool (engage the tooth with the starter ring gear) to the cylinder block using one of the engine-to-gearbox bolts **(see illustration)**.

4 Progressively unscrew the securing bolts, then withdraw the flywheel/driveplate from the crankshaft. Note that the flywheel/driveplate locates on dowels.

Warning: Take care as the flywheel/driveplate is heavy.

5 Recover the engine/transmission intermediate plate (where fitted), noting its orientation.

Refitting

6 Refit the engine/transmission intermediate plate (where fitted), ensuring that it is correctly located on the dowel(s) **(see illustration)**.

7 Refit the flywheel/driveplate to the end of the crankshaft, ensuring that the locating dowel engages. Note that on dual-mass flywheels, the position of the dowel is indicated by one or two notches in the flywheel adjacent to the relevant locating hole **(see illustration)**.

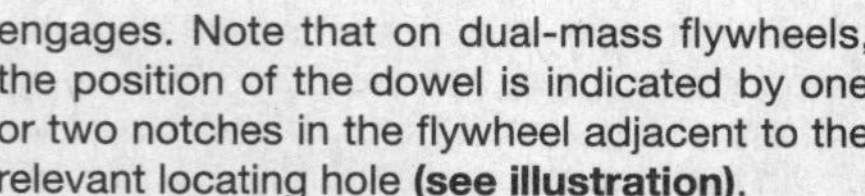

8 On 6-cylinder engines, examine the threads of the **new** securing bolts. If the threads are not already coated with thread-locking compound, then apply suitable thread-locking compound to them, then refit the bolts **(see illustration)**. On 4-cylinder engines, the new bolts are fitted without thread-locking compound.

9 Tighten the bolts progressively in a diagonal sequence to the specified torque. Counterhold the flywheel/driveplate by reversing the tool used during removal.

10 Where applicable, refit the clutch as described in Chapter 6.

11 Refit the manual gearbox or the automatic transmission, as applicable, as described in Chapter 7A or 7B respectively.

16 Crankshaft spigot bearing – renewal

1 On manual gearbox models, a ball-bearing assembly is fitted to the end of the crankshaft to support the end of the gearbox input shaft **(see illustration)**.

2 To renew the bearing, proceed as follows.

3 Remove the flywheel as described in Section 15.

4 Pack the space behind, and the centre bore, of the bearing with general-purpose grease.

5 Position a metal rod or bolt in the entrance of the bearing bore. The rod/bolt diameter should be just less than the diameter of the bearing bore.

6 Strike the end of the rod/bolt with a hammer several times **(see illustration)**. As the rod/bolt is struck, the compressed grease forces the bearing from position. Continue until the bearing is removed.

7 Thoroughly clean the bearing housing in the end of the crankshaft.

8 Tap the new bearing into position, up to the stop, using a tube or socket on the bearing outer race.

9 Refit the flywheel as described in Section 15.

16.1 Crankshaft spigot bearing (arrowed)

16.6 Use grease and a close-fitting rod to extract the spigot bearing

17 Engine/transmission mountings – inspection and renewal

Inspection

1 Two engine mountings are used, one on either side of the engine.

2 If improved access is required, raise the front of the vehicle and support it securely on axle stands (see *Jacking and vehicle support*).

3 Check the mounting rubber to see if it is cracked, hardened or separated from the metal at any point. Renew the mounting if any such damage or deterioration is evident.

17.7a Unscrew the engine mounting bracket from the cylinder block

4 Check that all the mounting fasteners are securely tightened.

5 Using a large screwdriver or a crowbar, check for wear in the mounting by carefully levering against it to check for free play. Where this is not possible, enlist the aid of an assistant to move the engine/transmission back-and-forth, or from side-to-side, while you observe the mounting. While some free play is to be expected, even from new components, excessive wear should be obvious. If excessive free play is found, check first that the fasteners are correctly secured, then renew any worn components as required.

Renewal

6 Support the engine, either using a hoist and lifting tackle connected to the engine lifting brackets (refer to *Engine – removal and refitting* in Part C of this Chapter), or by positioning a jack and interposed block of wood under the sump. Ensure that the engine is adequately supported before proceeding.

7 Unscrew the nuts securing the left- and

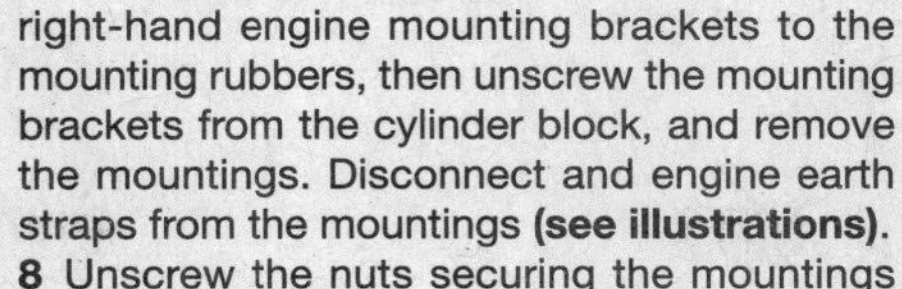

right-hand engine mounting brackets to the mounting rubbers, then unscrew the mounting brackets from the cylinder block, and remove the mountings. Disconnect and engine earth straps from the mountings **(see illustrations)**.

8 Unscrew the nuts securing the mountings to the body, then withdraw the mountings.

9 Refitting is a reversal of removai, but ensure that the metal protector plates are in position on the mountings, and securely tighten all fixings.

18 Oil pressure, level and temperature switches – removal and refitting

Oil pressure switch

1 Unscrew the oil filter cap; this allows the oil within the filter flows back into the sump, so reducing the amount lost during switch renewal.

2 Remove the air filter housing as described in Chapter 4A.

3 Disconnect the wiring plug and unscrew the switch from the base of the oil filter housing **(see illustration)**.

4 Fit the new switch, and tighten it to the specified torque.

5 Refit the air filter housing and oil filter cap. Check the oil level as described in *Weekly Checks*.

Oil level switch

6 Drain the engine oil as described in Chapter 1.

7 Undo the bolts and remove the engine undershield.

8 Disconnect the wiring plug, undo the three

17.7b An earth strap is fitted to the right-hand engine mounting bracket

retaining nuts and remove the level switch **(see illustration)**.

9 Ensure that the sump mating surface is clean.

10 Complete with a new seal, install the oil level switch and tighten the retaining nuts securely.

11 Refit the engine undershield, and replenish the engine oil as described in Chapter 1.

Oil temperature switch

12 Unscrew the oil filter cap. Allows the oil within the filter flows back into the sump, so reducing the amount lost during switch renewal.

13 Remove the air filter housing as described in Chapter 4A.

14 Disconnect the wiring plug and unscrew the switch from the base of the oil filter housing **(see illustration)**.

15 Fit the new switch, and tighten it to the specified torque.

16 Refit the air filter housing and oil filter cap. Check the oil level as described in *Weekly checks*.

18.3 Disconnect the wiring plug from the oil pressure switch (arrowed)

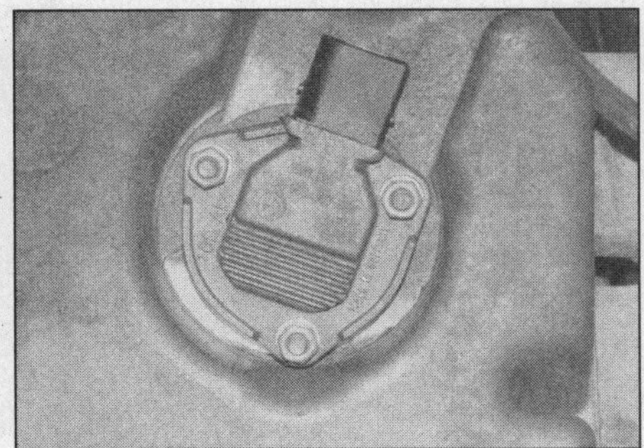

18.8 The oil level switch is retained by three nuts

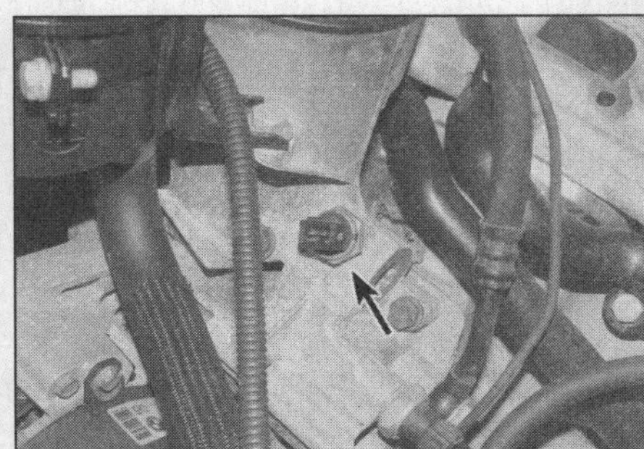

18.14 Disconnect the wiring plug from the oil temperature switch (arrowed)

Notes

Chapter 2 Part C:
General engine overhaul procedures

Contents

Degrees of difficulty

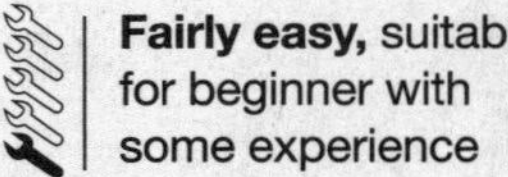

Easy, suitable for novice with little experience	**Fairly easy,** suitable for beginner with some experience	**Fairly difficult,** suitable for competent DIY mechanic	**Difficult,** suitable for experienced DIY mechanic	**Very difficult,** suitable for expert DIY or professional

Specifications

Engine codes

4-cylinder engines

1796 cc engines	N42 B18 and N46 B18
1895 cc engines	M43TU B19
1995 cc engines	N42 B20 and N46 B20

6-cylinder engines

2171 cc engines	M54 B22
2494 cc engines	M52TU B25 and M54 B25
2793 cc engines	M52TU B28
2979 cc engines	M54 B30

Cylinder head

Maximum gasket face distortion	0.050 mm
New cylinder head height:	
4-cylinder engines:	
M43TU	141.00 mm
N42 and N46	143.30 mm
6-cylinder engines	140.00 mm
Minimum cylinder head height after machining:	
4-cylinder engines:	
M43TU	140.55 mm
N42 and N46	143.00 mm
6-cylinder engines	139.70 mm

Valves

Valve head diameter:	**Inlet**	**Exhaust**
M43TU engines	41.40 mm	35.60 mm
N42 engines	31.50 mm	28.40 mm
N46 engines	32.00 mm	29.00 mm
6-cylinder engines:		
All engines except M54 2.2 litre	33.00 mm	30.50 mm
M54 2.2 litre	30.00 mm	27.00 mm
Maximum side-to-side movement of valve in guide (measured at valve head with top of valve stem flush with guide)	0.50 mm	

Cylinder block

Cylinder bore diameter:	
M43TU engines	85.00 mm (nominal)
N42 and N46 engines	84.00 mm (nominal)
M52 TU engines	84.00 mm (nominal)
M54 engines:	
All except 2.2 litre	84.00 mm (nominal)
2.2 litre	80.00 mm (nominal)
Maximum cylinder bore ovality	0.010 mm
Maximum cylinder bore taper	0.010 mm

Pistons

Piston diameter:	
M43TU engines	84.985 mm (nominal); 0.25 mm and 0.50 mm oversizes available
N42 engines	83.996 mm (nominal); 0.25 mm oversize available
N46 engines	83.996 mm (nominal; oversizes may be available
M52 TU engines	83.980 mm (nominal); 0.25 mm oversize available
M54 engines:	
All except 2.2 litre	83.995 mm (nominal); 0.25 mm oversize available
2.2 litre	79.980 mm (nominal); 0.25 mm oversize available
Piston-to-cylinder bore running clearance	0.010 to 0.047 mm
Maximum play between piston and cylinder wall	0.150 mm

Connecting rods

Maximum weight difference between two connecting rods	4.000 g

Crankshaft

Endfloat:	
All except N46 engines	0.080 to 0.163 mm
N46 engines	0.060 to 0.250 mm

Piston rings

End gaps:	
M43TU engines:	
Top compression ring	0.20 to 1.0 mm
Second compression ring	0.20 to 1.0 mm
Oil control ring	N/A
N42 and N46 engines:	
Top compression ring	0.10 to 0.30 mm
Second compression ring	0.20 to 0.40 mm
Oil control ring	0.40 to 1.40mm
M52 TU engines:	
Top compression ring	0.10 to 0.30 mm
Second compression ring	0.20 to 0.40 mm
Oil control ring	0.25 to 0.50 mm
M54 engines:	
All except 2.2 litre:	
Top compression ring	0.20 to 0.40 mm
Second compression ring	0.20 to 0.40 mm
Oil control ring	0.20 to 0.45 mm
2.2 litre:	
Top compression ring	0.10 to 0.30 mm
Second compression ring	0.20 to 0.40 mm
Oil control ring	0.25 to 0.50 mm

Torque wrench settings

4-cylinder engines	Refer to Chapter 2A Specifications
6-cylinder engines	Refer to Chapter 2B Specifications

1 General information

Included in this Part of Chapter 2 are details of removing the engine/transmission from the car and general overhaul procedures for the cylinder head, cylinder block/crankcase and all other engine internal components.

The information given ranges from advice concerning preparation for an overhaul and the purchase of new parts, to detailed step-by-step procedures covering removal, inspection, renovation and refitting of engine internal components.

After Section 5, all instructions are based on the assumption that the engine has been removed from the car. For information concerning in-car engine repair, as well as the removal and refitting of those external components necessary for full overhaul, refer to Part A or B of this Chapter as applicable and to Section 5. Ignore any preliminary dismantling operations described in Parts A or B that are no longer relevant once the engine has been removed from the car.

Apart from torque wrench settings, which are given at the beginning of Parts A and B, all specifications relating to engine overhaul are at the beginning of this Part of Chapter 2.

2 Engine overhaul – general information

1 It is not always easy to determine when, or if, an engine should be completely overhauled, as a number of factors must be considered.

2 High mileage is not necessarily an indication that an overhaul is needed, while low mileage does not preclude the need for an overhaul. Frequency of servicing is probably the most important consideration. An engine which has had regular and frequent oil and filter changes, as well as other required maintenance, should give many thousands of miles of reliable service. Conversely, a neglected engine may require an overhaul very early in its life.

3 Excessive oil consumption is an indication that piston rings, valve seals and/or valve guides are in need of attention. Make sure that oil leaks are not responsible before deciding that the rings and/or guides are worn. Perform a compression test, as described in Part A or B of this Chapter (as applicable), to determine the likely cause of the problem.

4 Check the oil pressure with a gauge fitted in place of the oil pressure switch, and compare it with that specified. If it is extremely low, the main and big-end bearings, and/or the oil pump, are probably worn out. It is a good idea to renew the oil pump whenever the engine is overhauled.

5 Loss of power, rough running, knocking or metallic engine noises, excessive valve gear noise, and high fuel consumption may also point to the need for an overhaul, especially if they are all present at the same time. If a complete service does not remedy the situation, major mechanical work is the only solution.

6 A full engine overhaul involves restoring all internal parts to the specification of a new engine. During a complete overhaul, the pistons and the piston rings are renewed, and the cylinder bores are reconditioned. New main and big-end bearings are generally fitted; if necessary, the crankshaft may be reground, to compensate for wear in the journals. The valves are also serviced as well, since they are usually in less-than-perfect condition at this point. Always pay careful attention to the condition of the oil pump when overhauling the engine, and renew it if there is any doubt as to its serviceability. The end result should be an as-new engine that will give many trouble-free miles.

7 Critical cooling system components such as the hoses, thermostat and water pump should be renewed when an engine is overhauled. The radiator should be checked carefully, to ensure that it is not clogged or leaking.

8 Before beginning the engine overhaul, read through the entire procedure, to familiarise yourself with the scope and requirements of the job. Overhauling an engine is not difficult if you follow carefully all of the instructions, have the necessary tools and equipment, and pay close attention to all specifications. It can, however, be time-consuming. Plan on the car being off the road for a minimum of two weeks, especially if parts must be taken to an engineering works for repair or reconditioning. Check on the availability of parts and make sure that any necessary special tools and equipment are obtained in advance. Most work can be done with typical hand tools, although a number of precision measuring tools are required for inspecting parts to determine if they must be renewed. Often the engineering works will handle the inspection of parts and offer advice concerning reconditioning and renewal.

9 Always wait until the engine has been completely dismantled, and until all components (especially the cylinder block/ crankcase and the crankshaft) have been inspected, before deciding what service and repair operations must be performed by an engineering works. The condition of these components will be the major factor to consider when determining whether to overhaul the original engine, or to buy a reconditioned unit. Do not, therefore, purchase parts or have overhaul work done on other components until they have been thoroughly inspected. As a general rule, time is the primary cost of an overhaul, so it does not pay to fit worn or sub-standard parts.

10 As a final note, to ensure maximum life and minimum trouble from a reconditioned engine, everything must be assembled with care, in a spotlessly-clean environment.

3 Engine removal – methods and precautions

1 If you have decided that the engine must be removed for overhaul or major repair work, several preliminary steps should be taken.

2 Locating a suitable place to work is extremely important. Adequate work space, along with storage space for the car, will be needed. If a workshop or garage is not available, at the very least, a flat, level, clean work surface is required.

3 Cleaning the engine compartment and engine/transmission before beginning the removal procedure will help keep tools clean and organised.

4 An engine hoist or A-frame will also be necessary. Make sure the equipment is rated in excess of the weight of the engine. Safety is of primary importance, considering the potential hazards involved in lifting the engine/ transmission out of the car.

5 If this is the first time you have removed an engine, an assistant should ideally be available. Advice and aid from someone more experienced would also be helpful. There are many instances when one person cannot simultaneously perform all of the operations required when lifting the engine out of the vehicle.

6 Plan the operation ahead of time. Before starting work, arrange for the hire of or obtain all of the tools and equipment you will need. Some of the equipment necessary to perform engine/transmission removal and installation safely and with relative ease (in addition to an engine hoist) is as follows: a heavy duty trolley jack, complete sets of spanners and sockets (see *Tools and working facilities*), wooden blocks, and plenty of rags and cleaning solvent for mopping-up spilled oil, coolant and fuel. If the hoist must be hired, make sure that you arrange for it in advance, and perform all of the operations possible without it beforehand. This will save you money and time.

7 Plan for the car to be out of use for quite a while. An engineering works will be required to perform some of the work which the do-it-yourselfer cannot accomplish without special equipment. These places often have a busy schedule, so it would be a good idea to consult them before removing the engine, in order to accurately estimate the amount of time required to rebuild or repair components that may need work.

8 Always be extremely careful when removing and refitting the engine/transmission. Serious injury can result from careless actions. Plan ahead and take your time, and a job of this nature, although major, can be accomplished successfully.

9 On all models, the engine is removed by first removing the transmission, then lifting the engine out from above the vehicle.

4 Engine – removal and refitting

Note: *This is an involved operation. Read through the procedure thoroughly before starting work, and ensure that adequate lifting tackle and jacking/support equipment is available. Make notes during dismantling to ensure that all wiring/hoses and brackets are correctly repositioned and routed on refitting.*

Removal

1 Remove the bonnet as described in Chapter 11.

2 Depressurise the fuel system as described in Chapter 4A, then disconnect the battery negative lead (see Chapter 5A).

3 Drain the cooling system as described in Chapter 1.

4 Drain the engine oil, referring to Chapter 1.

5 Remove the manual gearbox (Chapter 7A) or the automatic transmission (Chapter 7B), as applicable.

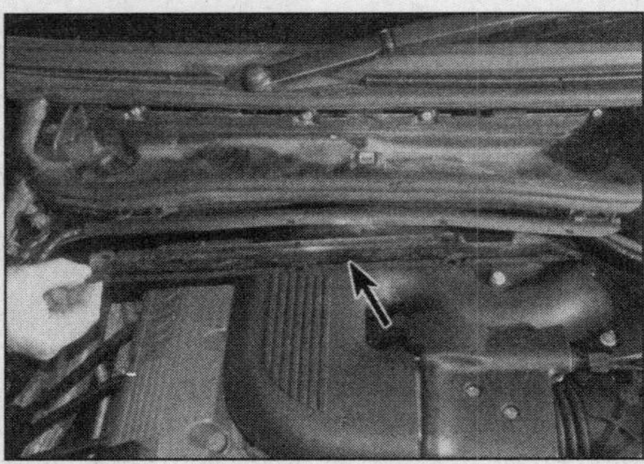
4.11a Undo the clips to release the cable ducting (arrowed)

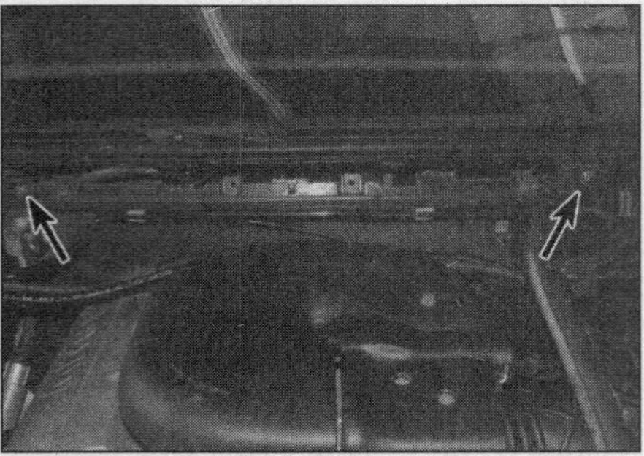
4.11b Undo the bolts (arrowed) and remove the inlet ducting

6 Unless a hoist is available which is capable of lifting the engine out over the front of the vehicle with the vehicle raised, it will now be necessary to remove the axle stands and lower the vehicle to the ground. Ensure that the engine is adequately supported during the lowering procedure.

7 To improve access and working room, temporarily support the engine from underneath the sump, using a trolley jack and interposed block of wood, then disconnect and withdraw the hoist and lifting tackle used to support the engine during transmission removal.

Warning: Ensure that the engine is securely and safely supported by the jack before disconnecting the lifting tackle.

8 Remove the radiator (see Chapter 3).

9 On the M43TU engine, remove the ignition coils as described in Chapter 5B, and the secondary air injection pump as described in Chapter 4B.

10 Remove the air cleaner/airflow meter assembly as described in Chapter 4A.

11 If not already done, remove the heater/ventilation inlet air ducting from the rear of the engine compartment as follows **(see illustrations)**.

a) Rotate the three fasteners 90° anti-clockwise and remove the pollen filter cover from the rear of the engine compartment. Pull the filter forward and remove it.
b) Undo the four retaining clips and thread the cable out of the ducting.
c) Unscrew the four bolts and pull the filter housing forwards and remove it.
d) Pull up the rubber strip, rotate the two fasteners anti-clockwise, and move the dividing panel in the left-hand corner of the engine compartment forward a little.
e) Undo the two bolts and remove the inlet ducting upwards and out of the engine compartment.

12 On 4-cylinder models, slacken the power steering pump pulley bolts, then remove the auxiliary drivebelt with reference to Chapter 1.

13 Unscrew the power steering reservoir, and move the reservoir to one side, leaving the fluid lines connected **(see illustration)**.

14 Unscrew the air conditioning compressor from the engine where applicable, release the pipes from the retaining clips, and support the compressor clear of the working area, as described in Chapter 3.

Warning: Do not disconnect the refrigerant lines – refer to Chapter 3 for precautions to be taken.

15 Unscrew the power steering pump as described in Chapter 10, and move it to one side, leaving the fluid lines connected. If necessary, release the power steering flexible hose from the steering rack mounting to allow the pump and reservoir to be moved from the work area.

16 Unscrew the earth lead(s) from the engine mounting bracket(s).

17 If not already done so, remove the inlet manifold as described in Chapter 4A.

18 On N42 and N46 engines, squeeze together the sides of the locking collar and disconnect the hose from the secondary air injection valve on the right-hand side of the cylinder head. Undo the nuts and remove the valve from the cylinder head.

4.13 The power steering fluid reservoir is retaining by two nuts

4.25 Attach the lifting tackle to the front and rear lifting eyes

19 On all engines, note their fitted positions, then disconnect all engine coolant/vacuum hoses. Note the hose routing to aid refitting.

20 To reduce the risk of damage during engine removal, remove the oil dipstick guide tube. Discard the O-ring seal, a new one must be fitted.

21 Note their fitted positions, then unplug all electrical connectors from the engine. Note also the harness routing and bracket fitment to aid refitting.

22 Unscrew the securing bolts, and release any clips (noting their locations) and release the wiring harness/wiring ducting assembly from the engine. Move the assembly to one side, clear of the engine. On N42 and N46 engines we found it necessary to undo the three mounting bolts and remove the alternator to allow the engine harness to be removed.

23 Check that all relevant wiring has been disconnected from the engine to enable engine removal.

24 Make a final check to ensure that all relevant hoses, pipes and wiring have been disconnected from the engine and moved clear to allow the engine to be lifted out.

25 Reposition the lifting tackle and hoist to support the engine both from the lifting eye at the rear left-hand corner of the cylinder block, and from the lifting bracket at the front of the cylinder head **(see illustration)**. Raise the hoist to just take the weight of the engine.

26 Unscrew the nuts securing the left- and right-hand engine mounting brackets to the mounting rubbers, then unscrew the mounting brackets from the cylinder block, and remove the mountings. On N42 and N46 engines we found it impossible to access all the bolts securing the right-hand engine mounting bracket to the cylinder block from above. Consequently, we left the bracket attached and separated it from the mounting rubber, but still completely removed the left-hand bracket.

27 With the aid of an assistant, raise the hoist, and lift the engine from the engine compartment.

Refitting

28 Refitting is a reversal of removal, bearing in mind the following points.

a) Tighten all fixings to the specified torque where given.
b) Ensure that all wiring, hoses and brackets are positioned and routed as noted before removal.
c) Refit the auxiliary drivebelt with reference to Chapter 1.
d) Refit the lower and upper sections of the inlet manifold as described in Chapter 4A.
e) Refit the radiator, referring to Chapter 3.
f) Refit the manual gearbox or automatic transmission as described in Chapter 7A or 7B respectively.
g) On completion, refill the engine with oil, and refill the cooling system as described in Chapter 1.

5 Engine overhaul – dismantling sequence

1 It is much easier to dismantle and work on the engine if it is mounted on a portable engine stand. These stands can often be hired from a tool hire shop. Before the engine is mounted on a stand, the flywheel/driveplate should be removed, so that the stand bolts can be tightened into the end of the cylinder block/crankcase.

2 If a stand is not available, it is possible to dismantle the engine with it blocked up on a sturdy workbench, or on the floor. Be extra careful not to tip or drop the engine when working without a stand.

3 If you are going to obtain a reconditioned engine, all the external components must be removed first, to be transferred to the new engine (just as they will if you are doing a complete engine overhaul yourself). These components include the following:

- *a) Ancillary unit mounting brackets (oil filter, starter, alternator, power steering pump, etc).*
- *b) Thermostat and housing (Chapter 3).*
- *c) Dipstick tube.*
- *d) All electrical switches and sensors.*
- *e) Inlet and exhaust manifolds – where applicable (Chapter 4A).*
- *f) Ignition coils and spark plugs – as applicable (Chapters 5B and 1).*
- *g) Flywheel/driveplate (Part B of this Chapter).*

Note: *When removing the external components from the engine, pay close attention to details that may be helpful or important during refitting. Note the fitted position of gaskets, seals, spacers, pins, washers, bolts, and other small items.*

4 If you are obtaining a 'short' engine (which consists of the engine cylinder block/crankcase, crankshaft, pistons and connecting rods all assembled), then the cylinder head, sump, oil pump, and timing chain will have to be removed also.

5 If you are planning a complete overhaul, the engine can be dismantled, and the internal components removed, in the order given below, referring to Part A or B of this Chapter unless otherwise stated.

- *a) Inlet and exhaust manifolds – where applicable (Chapter 4A).*
- *b) Timing chains, sprockets and tensioner(s).*
- *c) Cylinder head.*
- *d) Flywheel/driveplate.*
- *e) Sump.*
- *f) Oil pump.*
- *g) Piston/connecting rod assemblies (Section 9).*
- *h) Crankshaft (Section 10).*

6 Before beginning the dismantling and overhaul procedures, make sure that you have all of the correct tools necessary. Refer to *Tools and working facilities* for further information.

6.3a Compress the valve springs using a spring compressor tool

6 Cylinder head – dismantling

Note: *New and reconditioned cylinder heads are available from the manufacturer, and from engine overhaul specialists. Be aware that some specialist tools are required for the dismantling and inspection procedures, and new components may not be readily available. It may therefore be more practical and economical for the home mechanic to purchase a reconditioned head, rather than dismantle, inspect and recondition the original head. A valve spring compressor tool will be required for this operation.*

4-cylinder engines

1 Remove the cylinder head as described in Part A of this Chapter.

2 Remove the camshafts, cam followers/rocker arms and hydraulic adjusters as described in Part A of this Chapter.

3 Using a valve spring compressor, compress the spring(s) on each valve in turn until the split collets can be removed. Note that M43TU engines were fitted with two springs per valve up to 09/97. Release the compressor, and lift off the spring retainer, springs and spring seats. Using a pair of pliers, carefully extract the valve stem oil seal from the top of the guide **(see illustrations)**.

4 If, when the valve spring compressor is screwed down, the spring retainer refuses to free and expose the split collets, gently tap the top of the tool, directly over the retainer, with a light hammer. This will free the retainer.

5 Withdraw the valve through the combustion chamber.

6 It is essential that each valve is stored together with its collets, retainer, springs, and spring seats. The valves should also be kept in their correct sequence, unless they are so badly worn that they are to be renewed. If they are going to be kept and used again, place each valve assembly in a labelled polythene bag or similar small container **(see illustration)**. Note that No 1 valve is nearest to the timing chain end of the engine.

6-cylinder engines

7 Remove the cylinder head as described in Part B of this Chapter.

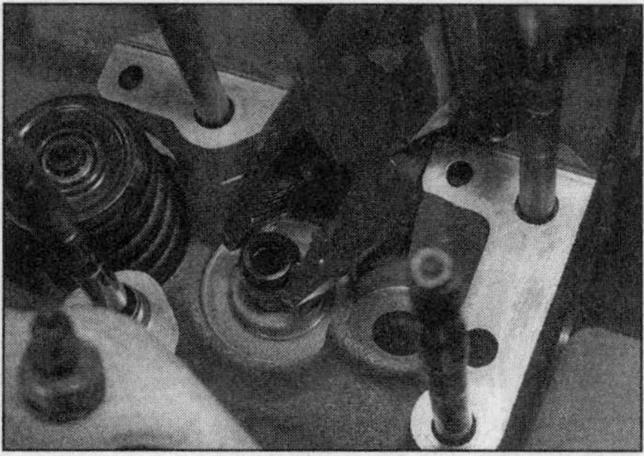

6.3b Remove the valve stem oil seals

8 Remove the camshafts, cam followers and camshaft bearing castings as described in Part B of this Chapter.

9 Proceed as described in paragraphs 3 to 6, noting that 6-cylinder engines have single valve springs.

7 Cylinder head and valves – cleaning and inspection

1 Thorough cleaning of the cylinder head and valve components, followed by a detailed inspection, will enable you to decide how much valve service work must be carried out during the engine overhaul. **Note:** *If the engine has been severely overheated, it is best to assume that the cylinder head is warped – check carefully for signs of this.*

Cleaning

2 Scrape away all traces of old gasket material from the cylinder head.

3 Scrape away the carbon from the combustion chambers and ports, then wash the cylinder head thoroughly with paraffin or a suitable solvent.

4 Scrape off any heavy carbon deposits that may have formed on the valves, then use a power-operated wire brush to remove deposits from the valve heads and stems.

Inspection

Note: *Be sure to perform all the following inspection procedures before concluding that the services of a machine shop or engine*

6.6 Place each valve and its associated components in a labelled polythene bag

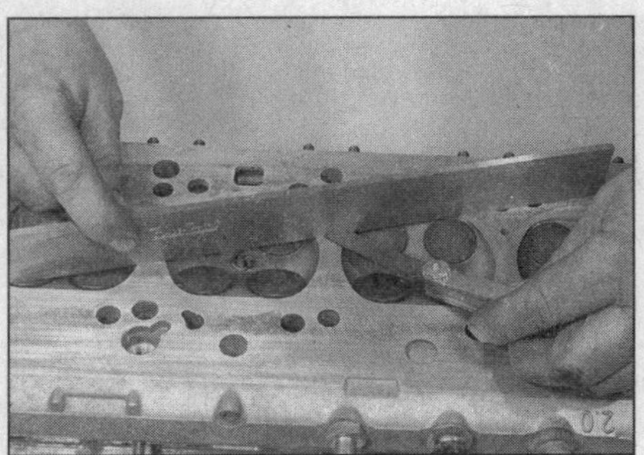

7.6 Check the cylinder head gasket face for distortion

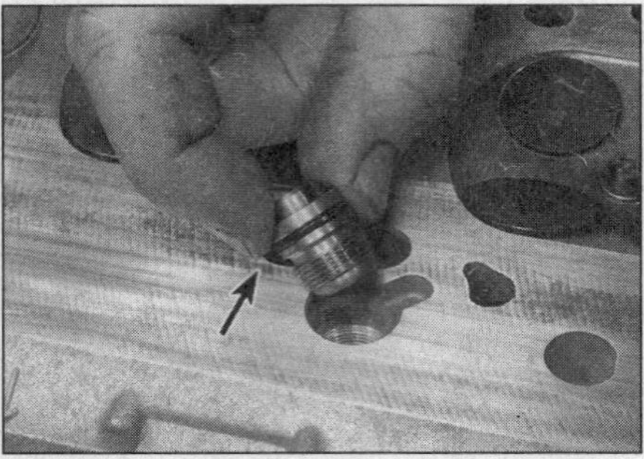

7.9 Fit a new O-ring (arrowed) to the cylinder head oil pressure check valve

overhaul specialist are required. Make a list of all items that require attention.

Cylinder head

5 Inspect the head very carefully for cracks, evidence of coolant leakage, and other damage. If cracks are found, a new cylinder head should be obtained.

6 Use a straight-edge and feeler blade to check that the cylinder head gasket surface is not distorted **(see illustration)**. If it is, it may be possible to have it machined, provided that the cylinder head is not reduced to less than the specified height. **Note:** *If 0.3 mm is machined off the cylinder head, a 0.3 mm thicker cylinder head gasket must be fitted when the engine is reassembled. This is necessary in order to maintain the correct dimensions between the valve heads, valve guides and cylinder head gasket face.*

7 Examine the valve seats in each of the combustion chambers. If they are severely pitted, cracked, or burned, they will need to be renewed or recut by an engine overhaul specialist. If they are only slightly pitted, this can be removed by grinding-in the valve heads and seats with fine valve-grinding compound, as described later in this Section.

8 Check the valve guides for wear by inserting the relevant valve, and checking for side-to-side motion of the valve. A very small amount of movement is acceptable. If the movement seems excessive, renew the valve. Separate valve guides are not available, although different grades (sizes) of valves (stems) are.

9 On 6-cylinder engines, unscrew the oil pressure check valve from the bottom of the cylinder head. Check that the valve can be blown through from bottom-to-top, but not from top-to-bottom. Thoroughly clean the valve and fit a new O-ring, then refit the valve to the cylinder head and tighten securely **(see illustration)**.

10 Examine the bearing surfaces in the cylinder head or bearing castings (as applicable) and the bearing caps for signs of wear or damage.

11 On N42, N46 and all 6-cylinder engines, check the camshaft bearing casting mating faces on the cylinder head for distortion. Use a straight-edge and feeler blade to check that the cylinder head faces are not distorted. If the distortion is outside the specified limit, the cylinder head and bearing castings must be renewed.

Valves

Warning: The exhaust valves fitted to some engines are filled with sodium to improve their heat transfer. Sodium is a highly reactive metal, which will ignite or explode spontaneously on contact with water (including water vapour in the air). These valves must NOT be disposed of as ordinary scrap. Seek advice from a BMW dealer or your local authority when disposing of the valves.

12 Examine the head of each valve for pitting, burning, cracks, and general wear. Check the valve stem for scoring and wear ridges. Rotate the valve, and check for any obvious indication that it is bent. Look for pits or excessive wear on the tip of each valve stem. Renew any valve that shows any such signs of wear or damage.

13 If the valve appears satisfactory at this stage, measure the valve stem diameter at several points using a micrometer **(see illustration)**. Any significant difference in the readings obtained indicates wear of the valve stem. Should any of these conditions be apparent, the valve(s) must be renewed.

14 If the valves are in satisfactory condition, they should be ground (lapped) into their respective seats, to ensure a smooth, gas-tight seal. If the seat is only lightly pitted, or if it has been recut, fine grinding compound *only* should be used to produce the required finish. Coarse valve-grinding compound should *not* be used, unless a seat is badly burned or deeply pitted. If this is the case, the cylinder head and valves should be inspected by an expert, to decide whether seat recutting, or even the renewal of the valve or seat insert (where possible) is required.

15 Valve grinding is carried out as follows. Place the cylinder head upside-down on a bench.

16 Smear a trace of (the appropriate grade of) valve-grinding compound on the seat face, and press a suction grinding tool onto the valve head **(see illustration)**. With a semi-rotary action, grind the valve head to its seat, lifting the valve occasionally to redistribute the grinding compound. A light spring placed under the valve head will greatly ease this operation.

17 If coarse grinding compound is being used, work only until a dull, matt even surface is produced on both the valve seat and the valve, then wipe off the used compound, and repeat the process with fine compound. When a smooth unbroken ring of light grey matt finish is produced on both the valve and seat, the grinding operation is complete. *Do not* grind-in the valves any further than absolutely necessary, or the seat will be prematurely sunk into the cylinder head.

18 When all the valves have been ground-in, carefully wash off *all* traces of grinding compound using paraffin or a suitable solvent, before reassembling the cylinder head.

Valve components

19 Examine the valve springs for signs of damage and discoloration. No minimum free length is specified by BMW, so the only way of judging valve spring wear is by comparison with a new component.

20 Stand each spring on a flat surface, and check it for squareness. If any of the springs are damaged, distorted or have lost their tension, obtain a complete new set of springs. It is normal to renew the valve springs as a matter of course if a major overhaul is being carried out.

21 Renew the valve stem oil seals regardless of their apparent condition.

Cam followers/valve lifters

22 Examine the contact surfaces for wear or scoring. If excessive wear is evident, the component(s) should be renewed.

7.13 Measure the valve stem diameter

7.16 Grinding-in a valve

8 Cylinder head – reassembly

Note: *New valve stem oil seals should be fitted, and a valve spring compressor tool will be required for this operation.*

M43TU engines

1 Proceed as described in Paragraphs 4 to 9.
2 Refit the hydraulic valve lifters, cam followers and camshafts (see Part A of this Chapter).
3 Refit the cylinder head as described in Part A of this Chapter.

N42, N46 and 6-cylinder engines

4 Lubricate the stems of the valves, and insert the valves into their original locations **(see illustration)**. If new valves are being fitted, insert them into the locations to which they have been ground.
5 Working on the first valve, dip the new valve stem seal in fresh engine oil. New seals are normally supplied with protective sleeves which should be fitted to the tops of the valve stems to prevent the collet grooves from damaging the oil seals. If no sleeves are supplied, wind a little thin tape round the top of the valve stems to protect the seals. Carefully locate the seal over the valve and onto the guide. Take care not to damage the seal as it is passed over the valve stem. Use a suitable socket or metal tube to press the seal firmly onto the guide **(see illustrations)**.
6 Refit the spring seat(s) **(see illustrations)**.
7 Locate the valve spring(s) on top of the seat(s), then refit the spring retainer **(see illustrations)**. Where the spring diameter is different at each end, the larger diameter end of the valve spring fits against the seat on the cylinder head.
8 Compress the valve spring(s), and locate the split collets in the recess in the valve stem. Release the compressor, then repeat the procedure on the remaining valves.
9 With all the valves installed, support the cylinder head on blocks of wood and, using a hammer and interposed block of wood, tap the end of each valve stem to settle the components.
10 Refit the camshaft bearing castings, cam followers and camshafts as described in Part B of this Chapter.
11 Refit the cylinder head as described in Part B of this Chapter.

9 Piston/connecting rod assembly – removal

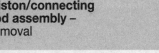

Warning: On engines with oil spray jets fitted to the cylinder block, take care not to damage the jets as the piston/connecting rod assemblies are removed. BMW recommend that the spray jet alignment is checked using a BMW tool after removing and refitting the piston/connecting rod assemblies.

1 On 4-cylinder engines, remove the cylinder head, sump and balancer shaft housing as described in Part A of this Chapter.
2 On 6-cylinder engines, remove the cylinder head, sump and oil pump as described in Part B of this Chapter.

8.4 Lubricate the valve stem

8.5a Fit the protective sleeve to the valve stem . . .

8.5b . . . then fit the oil seal using a socket

8.6a Fit the outer . . .

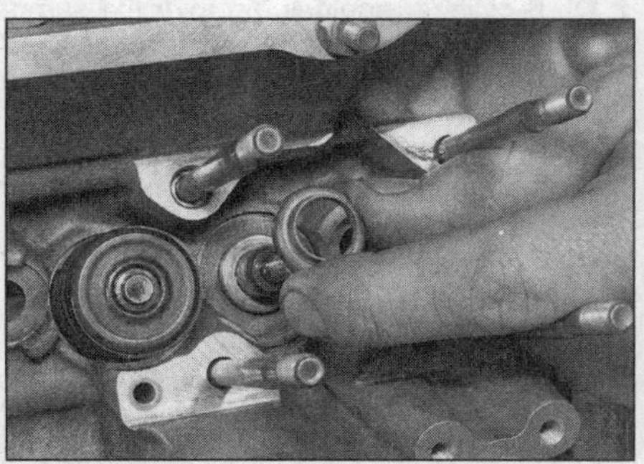

8.6b . . . and inner spring seats

8.7a Fit the inner . . .

8.7b . . . and the outer valve springs . . .

8.7c . . . followed by the spring retainer

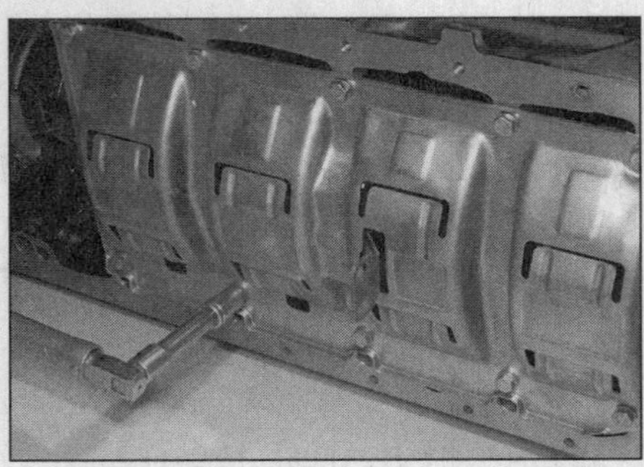
9.3 Unscrew the oil baffle plate from the cylinder block (6-cylinder engine)

9.5 Big-end bearing cap marks

9.7 Remove the big-end bearing cap

3 Where applicable, unscrew the oil baffle from the bottom of the cylinder block **(see illustration)**.

4 If there is a pronounced wear ridge at the top of any bore, it may be necessary to remove it with a scraper or ridge reamer, to avoid piston damage during removal. Such a ridge indicates excessive wear of the cylinder bore.

5 Check the connecting rods and big-end caps for identification marks. Both rods and caps should be marked with the cylinder number. Note that No 1 cylinder is at the timing chain end of the engine. If no marks are present, using a hammer and centre-punch, paint or similar, mark each connecting rod and big-end bearing cap with its respective cylinder number on the flat machined surface provided **(see illustration)**.

6 Turn the crankshaft to bring pistons 1 and 4 (4-cylinder engines), or 1 and 6 (6-cylinder engines), as applicable, to BDC (bottom dead centre).

7 Unscrew the bolts from No 1 piston big-end bearing cap. Take off the cap, and recover the bottom half bearing shell **(see illustration)**. If the bearing shells are to be re-used, tape the cap and the shell together.

8 Using a hammer handle, push the piston up through the bore, and remove it from the top of the cylinder block. Recover the bearing shell, and tape it to the connecting rod for safe-keeping. Take care not to damage the oil spray jets.

9 Loosely refit the big-end cap to the connecting rod, and secure with the bolts – this will help to keep the components in their correct order.

10 Remove No 4 piston assembly (4-cylinder engines), or No 6 piston assembly (6-cylinder engines), as applicable, in the same way.

11 Turn the crankshaft as necessary to bring the remaining pistons to BDC, and remove them in the same way.

10 Crankshaft – removal

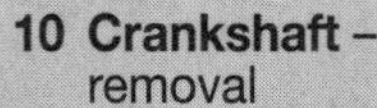

1 On 4-cylinder engines, remove the sump, timing chain, balancer shaft housing, timing chain housing (M43TU engine only), and the flywheel/driveplate as described in Part A of this Chapter. On N42 and N46 engines, remove the crankshaft vibration damper/ pulley hub as described in Chapter 2A.

2 On 6-cylinder engines, remove the sump, the primary timing chain, and the flywheel/ driveplate, as described in Part B of this Chapter.

3 Remove the pistons and connecting rods, as described in Section 9. If no work is to be done on the pistons and connecting rods, there is no need to remove the cylinder head, or to push the pistons out of the cylinder bores. The pistons should just be pushed far enough up the bores so that they are positioned clear of the crankshaft journals.

Warning: If the pistons are pushed up the bores, and the cylinder head is still fitted, take care not to force the pistons into the open valves.

4 Check the crankshaft endfloat as described in Section 13, then proceed as follows.

5 On all except N42 and N46 engines, slacken and remove the retaining bolts, and remove the oil seal carrier from the rear (flywheel/ driveplate) end of the cylinder block, along with its gasket **(see illustration)**.

6 On 6-cylinder engines, if not already done, remove the oil pump drive chain and, if necessary, remove the crankshaft sprocket with reference to Part B of this Chapter.

7 On M43TU engines, the main bearing caps should be numbered 1 to 5 from the timing chain end of the engine. Caps 1 to 3 are numbered, cap No 4 has shoulders machined into the end faces, and cap No 5 is unmarked. If the bearing caps are not marked, mark them using a centre-punch.

8 On 6-cylinder engines, the main bearing caps should be numbered 1 to 7 on the exhaust side of the engine, starting from the timing chain end of the engine **(see illustration)**. If not, mark them using a centre-punch.

9 On all except N42 and N46 engines, slacken and remove the main bearing cap retaining bolts, and lift off each bearing cap **(see illustration)**. Recover the lower bearing shells, and tape them to their respective caps for safe-keeping.

10 On N42 and N46 engines, the bearing shells are fitted into a 'crankcase lower half'. Slacken and remove the retaining bolts, and lift away the lower crankcase.

11 On 4-cylinder engines, note that the lower thrust bearing shell, which controls crankshaft endfloat, may be fitted to No 4 or No 5 main

10.5 Remove the oil seal carrier from the rear of the cylinder block

10.8 Main bearing cap identification number (6-cylinder engines)

10.9 Lift off the main bearing caps

bearing saddle. The correct location can be identified by the machined area for the thrust bearings to locate.

12 On 6-cylinder engines, note that the lower thrust bearing shell, which controls crankshaft endfloat, is fitted to No 6 main bearing cap. Also note the oil pick-up tube support bracket, which is secured by the No 5 main bearing cap bolts.

13 Lift out the crankshaft. Take care as the crankshaft is heavy.

14 Recover the upper bearing shells from the cylinder block **(see illustration)**, and tape them to their respective caps for safe-keeping. Again, note the location of the upper thrust bearing shell.

10.14 Lift the upper main bearing shells from the cylinder block

11 Cylinder block/crankcase – cleaning and inspection

Warning: On engines with oil spray jets fitted to the cylinder block, take care not to damage the jets as the piston/connecting rod assemblies are removed. BMW recommend that the spray jet alignment is checked using a BMW tool after removing and refitting the piston/connecting rod assemblies.

Cleaning

1 Remove all external components and electrical switches/sensors from the block. For complete cleaning, the core plugs should ideally be removed. Drill a small hole in the plugs, then insert a self-tapping screw into the hole. Pull out the plugs by pulling on the screw with a pair of grips, or by using a slide hammer.

2 Where applicable, pull/unscrew the piston oil jet spray tubes from the bearing locations in the cylinder block. The tubes are fitted to Nos 2 to 5 bearing locations on 4-cylinder engines, and Nos 2 to 7 bearing locations on 6-cylinder engines **(see illustration)**.

3 On M43TU engines, where applicable, remove the oil pressure check valve(s) from the top face of the cylinder block. A screw-in type check valve may be fitted or, on later engines, a calibrated jet may be fitted, with a rubber-lined spacer sleeve above **(see illustrations)**. On N42 and N46 engines, two check valves are fitted at the front of the cylinder block gasket surface – simply pull the spacer and valve from the hole **(see illustration)**.

4 Scrape all traces of gasket from the cylinder block/crankcase, taking care not to damage the gasket/sealing surfaces.

5 Remove all oil gallery plugs (where fitted). The plugs are usually very tight – they may have to be drilled out, and the holes retapped. Use new plugs when the engine is reassembled.

6 If any of the castings are extremely dirty, all should be steam-cleaned.

7 After the castings are returned, clean all oil holes and oil galleries one more time. Flush all internal passages with warm water until the water runs clear. Dry thoroughly, and apply a light film of oil to all mating surfaces, to prevent rusting. Also oil the cylinder bores. If you have access to compressed air, use it to speed up the drying process, and to blow out all the oil holes and galleries.

Warning: Wear eye protection when using compressed air.

8 If the castings are not very dirty, you can do an adequate cleaning job with hot (as hot as you can stand), soapy water and a stiff brush. Take plenty of time, and do a thorough job. Regardless of the cleaning method used, be sure to clean all oil holes and galleries very thoroughly, and to dry all components well. Protect the cylinder bores as described above, to prevent rusting.

9 All threaded holes must be clean, to ensure accurate torque readings during reassembly. To clean the threads, run the correct-size tap into each of the holes to remove rust, corrosion, thread sealant or sludge, and to restore damaged threads **(see illustration)**. If possible, use compressed air to clear the holes of debris produced by this operation.

10 Ensure that all threaded holes in the cylinder block are dry.

11 After coating the mating surfaces of the new core plugs with suitable sealant, fit them to the cylinder block. Make sure that they are driven in straight and seated correctly, or leakage could result.

12 Apply suitable sealant to the new oil gallery plugs, and insert them into the holes in the block. Tighten them securely.

13 Where applicable, thoroughly clean the oil pressure check valve/calibrated jet (see paragraph 3), then refit the components as follows.

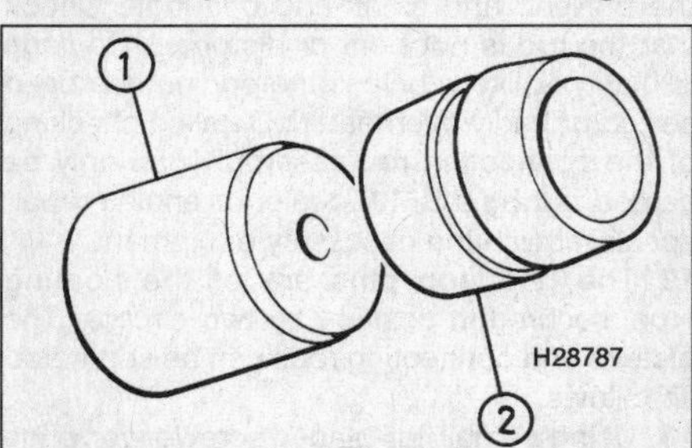

11.3b Oil pressure calibrated jet components (later engines)

1 Jet *2 Spacing sleeve*

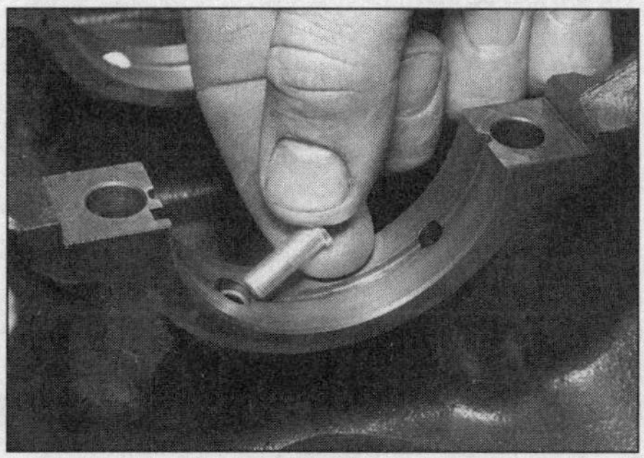

11.2 Remove the piston oil spray jet tubes from the main bearing locations

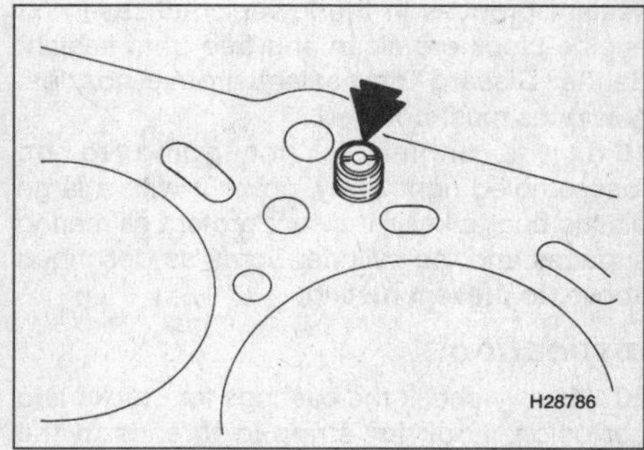

11.3a Oil pressure check valve location in the cylinder block (early engines)

11.3c Simply pull out the valves with a small magnet

11.9 Clean the cylinder block threaded holes using a suitable tap

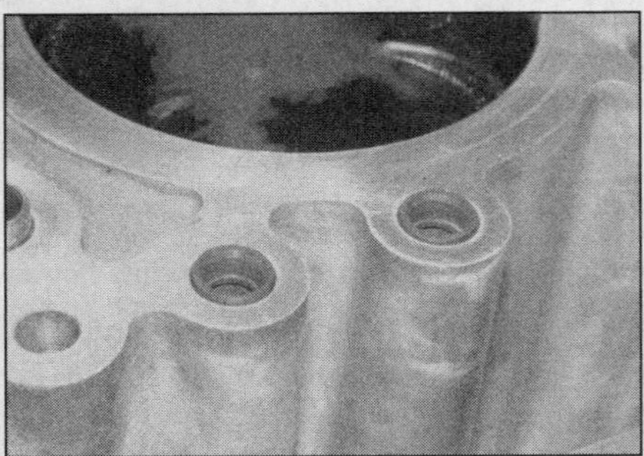

11.16 When fitted, the tubular spacers should be slightly proud of the cylinder block gasket surface

14 If a screw-in type check valve is fitted, check that the valve can be blown through from bottom-to-top, but not from top-to-bottom. Thoroughly clean the valve, and where applicable, fit a new O-ring, then refit the valve and tighten securely.

15 If a calibrated jet is fitted, refit the jet, ensuring that it is fitted the correct way up, with the stepped collar at the bottom, then refit the spacer sleeve.

Warning: If the calibrated jet is fitted incorrectly, it may starve the oil supply to the head.

16 On N42 and N46 engines, fit the check valves and spacers to the cylinder block gasket surface **(see illustration)**.

17 Where applicable, thoroughly clean the piston oil spray tubes which fit in the bearing locations in the cylinder block, then refit the tubes **(see illustration)**.

18 On N42 and N46 engines, ensure the sealant grooves in the lower crankcase and engine block are clean and free from sealant debris. Discard the sealant groove nozzles, new ones must be fitted.

19 If the engine is not going to be reassembled right away, cover it with a large plastic bag to keep it clean; protect all mating surfaces and the cylinder bores as described above, to prevent rusting.

Inspection

20 Visually check the castings for cracks and corrosion. Look for stripped threads in the threaded holes. If there has been any history of internal water leakage, it may be worthwhile having an engine overhaul specialist check the cylinder block/crankcase with special equipment. If defects are found, have them repaired if possible, or renew the assembly.

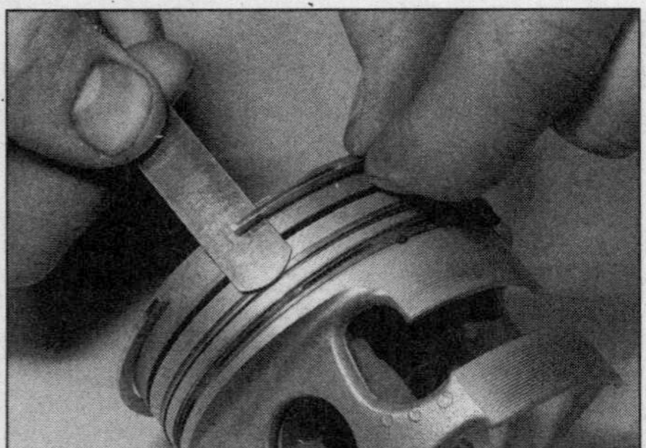

12.2 Remove the piston rings with the aid of a feeler gauge

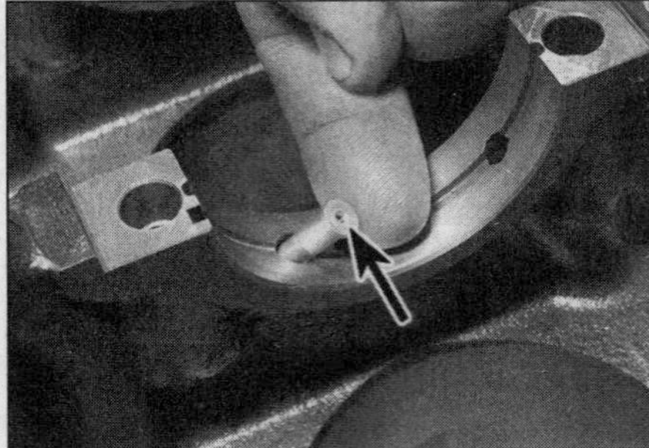

11.17 Clean the holes (arrowed) in the oil spray tubes

21 Check each cylinder bore for scuffing and scoring. Check for signs of a wear ridge at the top of the cylinder, indicating that the bore is excessively worn.

22 Have the bores of the engine block measured by a BMW dealer or automotive engineering workshop. Then if the bore wear exceeds the permitted tolerances, or if the bore walls are badly scuffed or scored, then the cylinders must be rebored. Have the work carried out by a BMW dealer or automotive engineering workshop, who will also be able to supply suitable oversize pistons and rings.

12 Piston/connecting rod assembly – inspection

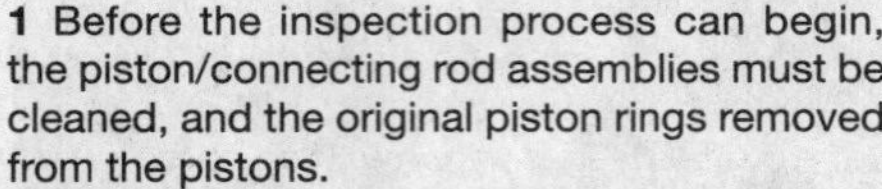

1 Before the inspection process can begin, the piston/connecting rod assemblies must be cleaned, and the original piston rings removed from the pistons.

2 Carefully expand the old rings over the top of the pistons. The use of two or three old feeler blades will be helpful in preventing the rings dropping into empty grooves **(see illustration)**. Be careful not to scratch the piston with the ends of the ring. The rings are brittle, and will snap if they are spread too far. They are also very sharp – protect your hands and fingers. Note that the third ring incorporates an expander. Always remove the rings from the top of the piston. Keep each set of rings with its piston if the old rings are to be re-used. Note which way up each ring is fitted.

3 Scrape away all traces of carbon from the top of the piston. A hand-held wire brush (or a piece of fine emery cloth) can be used, once the majority of the deposits have been scraped away.

4 Remove the carbon from the ring grooves in the piston, using an old ring. Break the ring in half to do this. Be careful to remove only the carbon deposits – do not remove any metal, and do not nick or scratch the sides of the ring grooves.

5 Once the deposits have been removed, clean the piston/connecting rod assembly with paraffin or a suitable solvent, and dry thoroughly. Make sure that the oil return holes in the ring grooves are clear.

6 If the pistons and cylinder bores are not damaged or worn excessively, and if the cylinder block does not need to be rebored, the original pistons can be refitted. Measure the piston diameters, and check that they are within limits for the corresponding bore diameters. If the piston-to-bore clearance is excessive, the block will have to be rebored, and new pistons and rings fitted. Normal piston wear shows up as even vertical wear on the piston thrust surfaces, and slight looseness of the top ring in its groove. New piston rings should always be used when the engine is reassembled.

7 Carefully inspect each piston for cracks around the skirt, around the gudgeon pin holes, and at the piston ring 'lands' (between the ring grooves).

8 Look for scoring and scuffing on the piston skirt, holes in the piston crown, and burned areas at the edge of the crown. If the skirt is scored or scuffed, the engine may have been suffering from overheating, and/or abnormal combustion which caused excessively high operating temperatures. The cooling and lubrication systems should be checked thoroughly. Scorch marks on the sides of the pistons show that blow-by has occurred. A hole in the piston crown, or burned areas at the edge of the piston crown, indicates that abnormal combustion (pre-ignition, knocking, or detonation) has been occurring. If any of the above problems exist, the causes must be investigated and corrected, or the damage will occur again. The causes may include incorrect ignition timing, inlet air leaks, or incorrect air/fuel mixture.

9 Corrosion of the piston, in the form of pitting, indicates that coolant has been leaking into the combustion chamber and/or the crankcase. Again, the cause must be corrected, or the problem may persist in the rebuilt engine.

10 New pistons can be purchased from a BMW dealer.

11 Examine each connecting rod carefully for signs of damage, such as cracks around the big-end and small-end bearings. Check that the rod is not bent or distorted. Damage is highly unlikely, unless the engine has been seized or badly overheated. Detailed checking of the connecting rod assembly can only be carried out by a BMW dealer or engine repair specialist with the necessary equipment.

12 The gudgeon pins are of the floating type, secured in position by two circlips. The pistons and connecting rods can be separated as follows.

13 Using a small flat-bladed screwdriver, prise out the circlips, and push out the gudgeon pin **(see illustrations)**. Hand pressure should be sufficient to remove the pin. Identify the piston and rod to ensure correct reassembly.

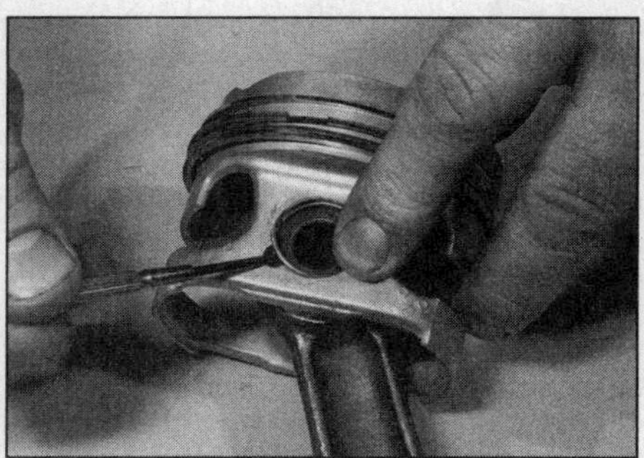

12.13a Prise out the circlips . . .

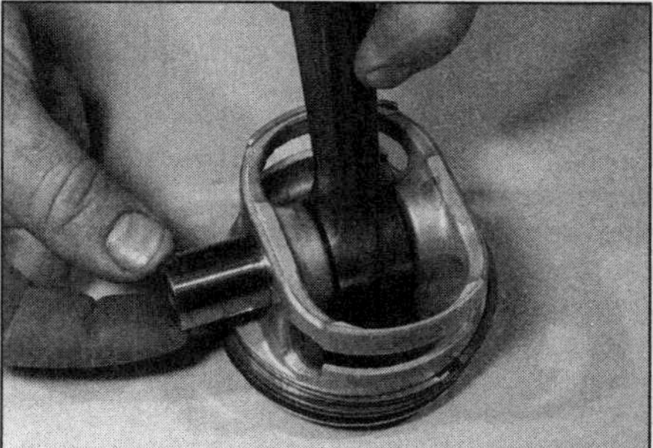

12.13b . . . and remove the gudgeon pins from the pistons

Discard the circlips – new ones must be used on refitting. Note that BMW recommend that gudgeon pins must not be renewed separately – they are matched to their respective pistons.

14 Examine the gudgeon pin and connecting rod small-end bearing for signs of wear or damage. It should be possible to push the gudgeon pin through the connecting rod by hand, without noticeable play. Wear can only be cured by renewing both the pin and piston.

15 The connecting rods themselves should not be in need of renewal, unless seizure or some other major mechanical failure has occurred. Check the alignment of the connecting rods visually, and if the rods are not straight, take them to an engine overhaul specialist for a more detailed check.

16 Examine all components, and obtain any new parts from your BMW dealer. If new pistons are purchased, they will be supplied complete with gudgeon pins and circlips. Circlips can also be purchased individually.

17 Position the piston in relation to the connecting rod, so that when the assembly is refitted to the engine, the identifying cylinder numbers on the connecting rod and big-end cap are positioned on the exhaust manifold side of the engine, and the installation direction arrow on the piston crown points towards the timing chain end of the engine **(see illustrations)**.

18 Apply a smear of clean engine oil to the gudgeon pin. Slide it into the piston and through the connecting rod small-end. Check that the piston pivots freely on the rod, then secure the gudgeon pin in position with two new circlips. Ensure that each circlip is correctly located in its groove in the piston.

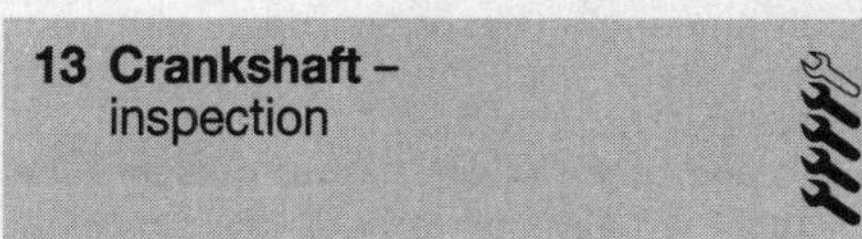

13 Crankshaft – inspection

Checking endfloat

1 If the crankshaft endfloat is to be checked, this must be done when the crankshaft is still installed in the cylinder block/crankcase, but is free to move.

2 Check the endfloat using a dial gauge in contact with the end of the crankshaft. Push the crankshaft fully one way, and then zero the gauge. Push the crankshaft fully the other way, and check the endfloat. The result can be compared with the specified amount, and will give an indication as to whether new thrust bearing shells are required **(see illustration)**.

3 If a dial gauge is not available, feeler blades can be used. First push the crankshaft fully towards the flywheel end of the engine, then use feeler blades to measure the gap between the web of No 4 or 5 crankpin and the thrust bearing shell on 4-cylinder engines, or between No 6 crankpin and the thrust bearing shell on 6-cylinder engines **(see illustration)**.

Inspection

4 Clean the crankshaft using paraffin or a suitable solvent, and dry it, preferably with compressed air if available. Be sure to clean the oil holes with a pipe cleaner or

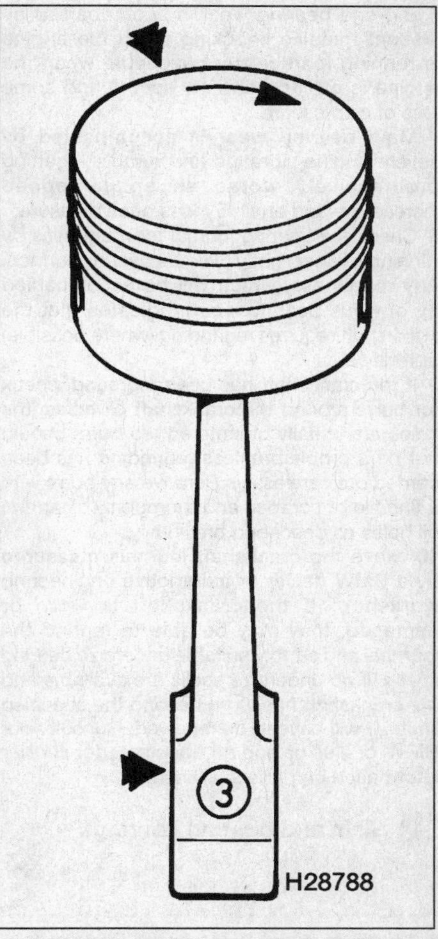

12.17a The cylinder number markings should be on the exhaust manifold side of the engine, and the arrow on the piston crown should point towards the timing chain end of the engine

similar probe, to ensure that they are not obstructed.

Warning: Wear eye protection when using compressed air.

5 Check the main and big-end bearing journals for uneven wear, scoring, pitting and cracking.

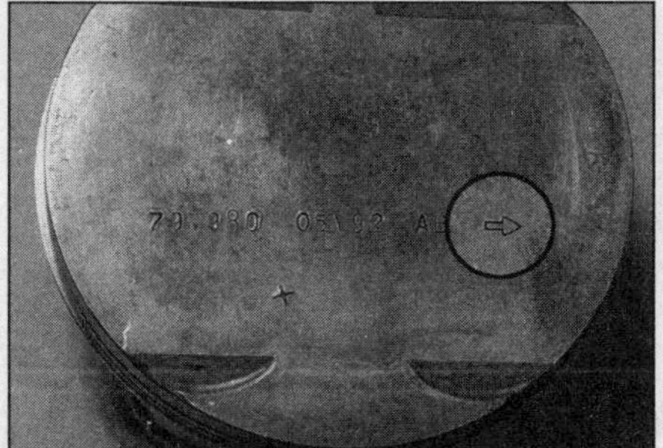

12.17b Installation direction arrow on 6-cylinder engine piston crown

13.2 Measuring the crankshaft endfloat using a dial gauge . . .

13.3 . . . or feeler gauges

6 Big-end bearing wear is accompanied by distinct metallic knocking when the engine is running (particularly noticeable when the engine is pulling from low speed) and some loss of oil pressure.

7 Main bearing wear is accompanied by severe engine vibration and rumble – getting progressively worse as engine speed increases – and again by loss of oil pressure.

8 Check the bearing journal for roughness by running a finger lightly over the bearing surface. Any roughness (which will be accompanied by obvious bearing wear) indicates that the crankshaft requires regrinding (where possible) or renewal.

9 If the crankshaft has been reground, check for burrs around the crankshaft oil holes (the holes are usually chamfered, so burrs should not be a problem unless regrinding has been carried out carelessly). Remove any burrs with a fine file or scraper, and thoroughly clean the oil holes as described previously.

10 Have the crankshaft journals measured by a BMW dealer or automotive engineering workshop. If the crankshaft is worn or damaged, they may be able to regrind the journals and supply suitable undersize bearing shells. If no undersize shells are available and the crankshaft has worn beyond the specified limits, it will have to be renewed. Consult your BMW dealer or engine specialist for further information on parts availability.

14 Main and big-end bearings – inspection

1 Even though the main and big-end bearings should be renewed during the engine overhaul, the old bearings should be retained for close examination, as they may reveal valuable information about the condition of the engine.

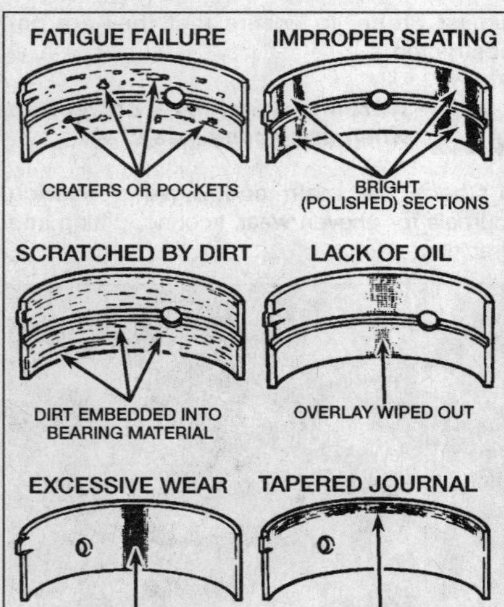

14.2 Typical bearing failures

The bearing shells are graded by thickness, the grade of each shell being indicated by the colour code marked on it.

2 Bearing failure can occur due to lack of lubrication, the presence of dirt or other foreign particles, overloading the engine, or corrosion **(see illustration)**. Regardless of the cause of bearing failure, the cause must be corrected (where applicable) before the engine is reassembled, to prevent it from happening again.

3 When examining the bearing shells, remove them from the cylinder block/crankcase, the connecting rods and the connecting rod big-end bearing caps. Lay them out on a clean surface in the same general position as their location in the engine. This will enable you to match any bearing problems with the corresponding crankshaft journal. *Do not* touch any shell's bearing surface with your fingers while checking it, or the delicate surface may be scratched.

4 Dirt and other foreign matter gets into the engine in a variety of ways. It may be left in the engine during assembly, or it may pass through filters or the crankcase ventilation system. It may get into the oil, and from there into the bearings. Metal chips from machining operations and normal engine wear are often present. Abrasives are sometimes left in engine components after reconditioning, especially when parts are not thoroughly cleaned using the proper cleaning methods. Whatever the source, these foreign objects often end up embedded in the soft bearing material, and are easily recognised. Large particles will not embed in the bearing, and will score or gouge the bearing and journal. The best prevention for this cause of bearing failure is to clean all parts thoroughly, and keep everything spotlessly-clean during engine assembly. Frequent and regular engine oil and filter changes are also recommended.

5 Lack of lubrication (or lubrication breakdown) has a number of interrelated causes. Excessive heat (which thins the oil), overloading (which squeezes the oil from the bearing face) and oil leakage (from excessive bearing clearances, worn oil pump or high engine speeds) all contribute to lubrication breakdown. Blocked oil passages, which usually are the result of misaligned oil holes in a bearing shell, will also oil-starve a bearing, and destroy it. When lack of lubrication is the cause of bearing failure, the bearing material is wiped or extruded from the steel backing of the bearing. Temperatures may increase to the point where the steel backing turns blue from overheating.

6 Driving habits can have a definite effect on bearing life. Full-throttle, low-speed operation (labouring the engine) puts very high loads on bearings, tending to squeeze out the oil film. These loads cause the bearings to flex, which produces fine cracks in the bearing face (fatigue failure). Eventually, the bearing material will loosen in pieces, and tear away from the steel backing.

7 Short-distance driving leads to corrosion of bearings, because insufficient engine heat is produced to drive off the condensed water and corrosive gases. These products collect in the engine oil, forming acid and sludge. As the oil is carried to the engine bearings, the acid attacks and corrodes the bearing material.

8 Incorrect bearing installation during engine assembly will lead to bearing failure as well. Tight-fitting bearings leave insufficient bearing running clearance, and will result in oil starvation. Dirt or foreign particles trapped behind a bearing shell result in high spots on the bearing, which lead to failure.

9 *Do not* touch any shell's bearing surface with your fingers during reassembly; there is a risk of scratching the delicate surface, or of depositing particles of dirt on it.

10 As mentioned at the beginning of this Section, the bearing shells should be renewed as a matter of course during engine overhaul; to do otherwise is false economy.

15 Engine overhaul – reassembly sequence

1 Before reassembly begins, ensure that all new parts have been obtained, and that all necessary tools are available. Read through the entire procedure to familiarise yourself with the work involved, and to ensure that all items necessary for reassembly of the engine are at hand. In addition to all normal tools and materials, thread-locking compound will be needed. A suitable tube of Drei Bond 1209 sealant (available from BMW dealers) will also be required.

2 In order to save time and avoid problems, engine reassembly can be carried out in the following order, referring to Part A or B of this Chapter unless otherwise stated:

a) Crankshaft (Section 17).
b) Piston/connecting rod assemblies (Section 18).
c) Oil pump/balancer shaft housing.
d) Sump.
e) Flywheel/driveplate.
f) Cylinder head.
g) Timing chain, tensioner and sprockets.
h) Engine external components.

3 At this stage, all engine components should be absolutely clean and dry, with all faults repaired. The components should be laid out (or in individual containers) on a completely clean work surface.

16 Piston rings – refitting

1 Before fitting new piston rings, the ring end gaps must be checked as follows.

2 Lay out the piston/connecting rod assemblies and the new piston ring sets, so that the ring sets will be matched with the

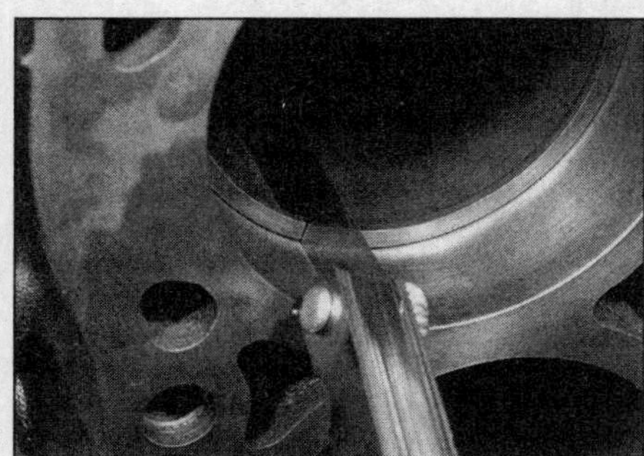

16.5 Measure the piston ring end gaps

same piston and cylinder during the end gap measurement and subsequent engine reassembly.

3 Insert the top ring into the first cylinder, and push it down the bore using the top of the piston. This will ensure that the ring remains square with the cylinder walls. Position the ring near the bottom of the cylinder bore, at the lower limit of ring travel. The top and second compression rings are different. The second ring is easily identified by the step on its lower surface, and by the fact that its outer face is tapered.

4 Measure the end gap using feeler blades.

5 Repeat the procedure with the ring at the top of the cylinder bore, at the upper limit of its travel **(see illustration)**, and compare the measurements with the figures given in the Specifications.

6 If the gap is too small (unlikely if genuine BMW parts are used), it must be enlarged, or the ring ends may contact each other during engine operation, causing serious damage. Ideally, new piston rings providing the correct end gap should be fitted. As a last resort, the end gap can be increased by filing the ring ends very carefully with a fine file. Mount the file in a vice equipped with soft jaws, slip the ring over the file with the ends contacting the file face, and slowly move the ring to remove material from the ends. Take care, as piston rings are sharp, and are easily broken.

7 With new piston rings, it is unlikely that the end gap will be too large. If the gaps are too large, check that you have the correct rings for your engine and for the particular cylinder bore size.

8 Repeat the checking procedure for each ring in the first cylinder, and then for the rings in the remaining cylinders. Remember to keep rings, pistons and cylinders matched up.

9 Once the ring end gaps have been checked and if necessary corrected, the rings can be fitted to the pistons.

10 Fit the piston rings using the same technique as for removal. Fit the bottom (oil control) ring first, and work up. When fitting a three-piece oil control ring, first insert the expander, then fit the lower rail with its gap positioned 120° from the expander gap, then fit the upper rail with its gap positioned 120° from the lower rail. When fitting a two-piece oil control ring, first insert the expander, then

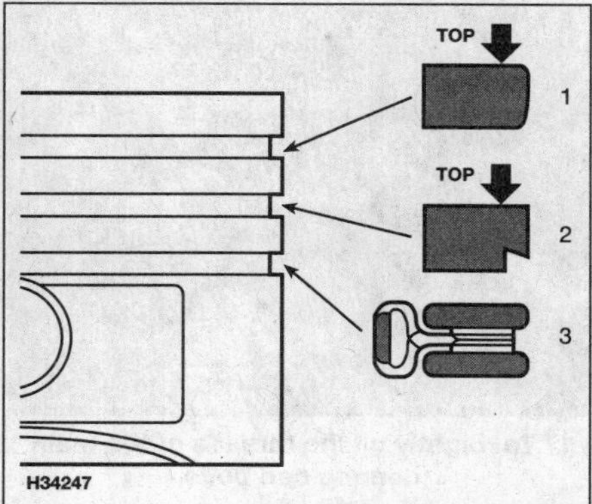

16.10a 4-cylinder engine piston rings

1 Top compression ring
2 2nd compression ring
3 Three-part oil control ring

fit the control ring with its gap positioned 180° from the expander gap. Ensure that the second compression ring is fitted the correct way up, with its identification mark (either a dot of paint or the word TOP stamped on the ring surface) at the top, and the stepped surface at the bottom **(see illustrations)**. Arrange the gaps of the top and second compression rings 120° either side of the oil control ring gap, but make sure that none of the ring's gaps are positioned over the gudgeon pin hole. **Note:** *Always follow any instructions supplied with the new piston ring sets – different manufacturers may specify different procedures. Do not mix up the top and second compression rings, as they have different cross-sections.*

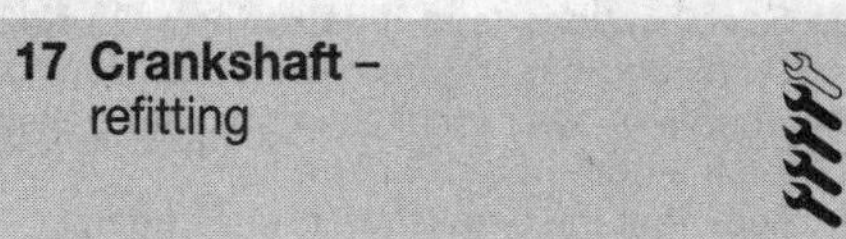

17 Crankshaft – refitting

Selection of bearing shells

1 Have the crankshaft inspected and measured by a BMW dealer or automotive engineering workshop. They will be able to carry out any regrinding/repairs, and supply suitable main and big-end bearing shells.

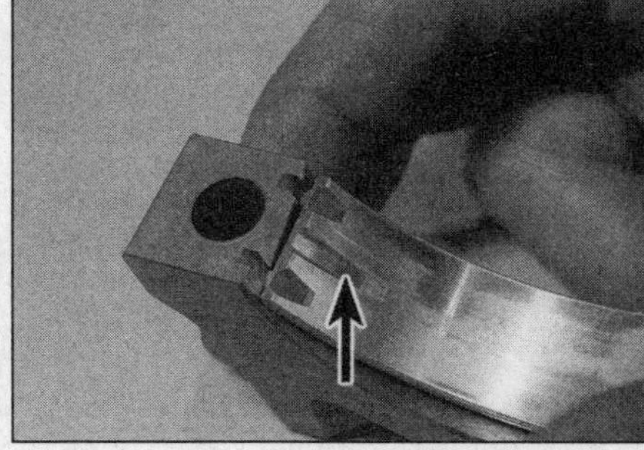

17.4a The lower bearing shells have short tapered oil grooves (arrowed)

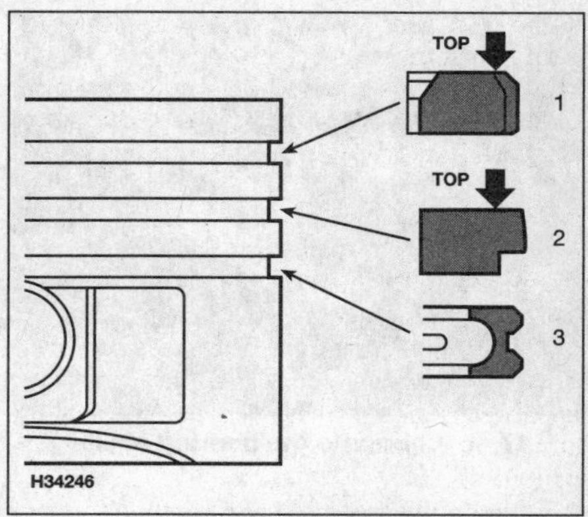

16.10b 6-cylinder engine piston rings

1 Top compression ring
2 2nd compression ring
3 Two-part oil control ring

Crankshaft refitting

Note: *New main bearing cap/lower crankcase bolts must be used when refitting the crankshaft.*

2 Where applicable, ensure that the oil spray jets are fitted to the bearing locations in the cylinder block.

3 Clean the backs of the bearing shells, and the bearing locations in both the cylinder block/crankcase and the main bearing caps/ lower crankcase.

4 Press the bearing shells into their locations, ensuring that the tab on each shell engages in the notch in the cylinder block/crankcase or bearing cap/lower crankcase. Take care not to touch any shell's bearing surface with your fingers. Note that the upper bearing shells have an oil groove running along the full length of the bearing surface, whereas the lower shells have a short, tapered oil groove at each end. The thrust bearing shells fit in No 4 or No 5 bearing location on 4-cylinder engines, or No 6 bearing location on 6-cylinder engines **(see illustrations)**. Ensure that all traces of protective grease are cleaned off using paraffin. Wipe dry the shells with a lint-free cloth. Liberally lubricate each bearing shell in the cylinder block/crankcase and cap/ lower crankcase with clean engine oil **(see illustration)**.

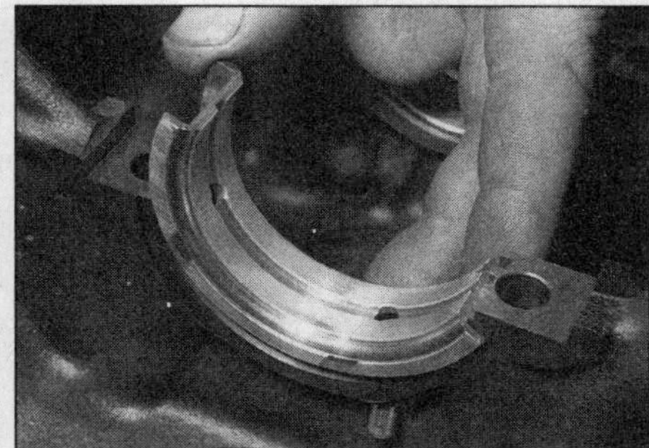

17.4b The thrust bearing shell is fitted to No 6 bearing location on 6-cylinder engines

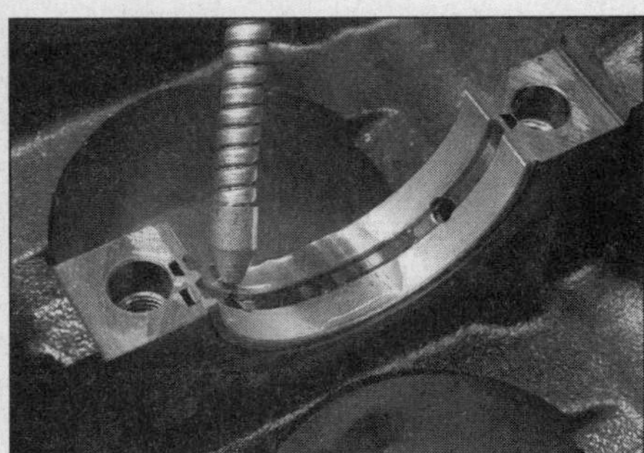

17.4c Lubricate the bearing shells

17.7a Lightly oil the threads of the main bearing cap bolts

17.7b On 6-cylinder engines, ensure the oil pick-up tube support bracket is in position on the No 5 main bearing cap bolts

17.8 Tighten the main bearing cap bolts to the specified torque

5 Lower the crankshaft into position so that Nos 1 and 4 cylinder crankpins (4-cylinder engines), or Nos 1 and 6 cylinder crankpins (6-cylinder engines), as applicable, will be at BDC, ready for fitting No 1 piston. Check the crankshaft endfloat as described in Section 13.

6 Lubricate the lower bearing shells in the main bearing caps with clean engine oil. Make sure that the locating lugs on the shells engage with the corresponding recesses in the caps.

7 Fit the main bearing caps to their correct locations, ensuring that they are fitted the correct way round (the bearing shell tab recesses in the block and caps must be on the same side). On N42 and N46 engines, check the locating dowels are in place and refit the lower crankcase. Thoroughly clean the new main bearing bolts, and lightly oil the threads, then insert the bolts, tightening them only loosely at this stage. On 6-cylinder engines, ensure that the oil pick-up tube support bracket is correctly in position on the No 5 main bearing cap bolts **(see illustrations)**.

8 Tighten the main bearing cap bolts to the specified torque, in the two stages given in the Specifications **(see illustration)**. On N42 and N46 engines tighten the inner row of main bearing/lower crankcase bolts first, then tighten the outer rows of bolts.

9 Check that the crankshaft rotates freely.

M43TU and 6-cylinder engines

10 Fit a new crankshaft rear oil seal to the oil seal carrier, then refit the oil seal carrier using a new gasket, as described in Part A or B of this Chapter, as applicable.

11 Where applicable, on 6-cylinder engines, refit the crankshaft sprocket and the oil pump drive chain, as described in Part B of this Chapter.

N42 and N46 engines

12 Refit the oil pump/balancer shaft drive chain, and crankshaft vibration damper/pulley hub as described in Chapter 2A.

13 Press new front and rear crankshaft oil seals into place as described in Chapter 2A. Ensure the grooves in the seals align with the lower crankcase-to-block joint.

14 Obtain an 'Injection Gasket Service Kit' from a BMW dealer. This kit includes Loctite primer. Use the integral brush to coat the inside of the grooves/joint with primer.

15 Drive the new 'nozzles' into the holes on each side of the lower crankcase/block joint. A BMW tool 11 9 360 is available for this task, or use a suitably-shaped punch/drift **(see illustration)**.

16 Using the injector supplied, force the sealing compound through the nozzle, until it can be seen to emerge from the grooves in the front and rear crankshaft oil seals **(see illustration)**. Repeat this procedure on the other side.

17 Again, using the integral brush, coat the surface of the sealing compound at the seals with primer to bind the sealant.

All engines

18 Refit the piston/connecting rod assemblies as described in Section 18.

19 On 4-cylinder engines, refit the flywheel/driveplate, the timing chain/housing, baffle plate (where applicable) and the sump, as described in Part A of this Chapter.

20 On 6-cylinder engines, refit the flywheel/driveplate, the primary timing chain, and the sump, as described in Part B of this Chapter.

17.15 Drive the new nozzles into place

17.16 Force the sealing compound through the nozzles until it emerges from the grooves alongside the crankshaft oil seals

18 Piston/connecting rod assembly – refitting

Warning: On engines with oil spray jets fitted to the cylinder block, take care not to damage the jets as the piston/connecting rod assemblies are removed. BMW recommend that the spray jet alignment is checked using a BMW tool after removing and refitting the piston/connecting rod assemblies.

Selection of bearing shells

1 There are a number of sizes of big-end bearing shell produced by BMW; a standard size for use with the standard crankshaft, and undersizes for use once the crankshaft journals have been reground.

2 Have the crankshaft inspected and measured by a BMW dealer or automotive engineering workshop. They will be able to carry out any regrinding/repairs, and supply suitable main and big-end bearing shells.

Piston/connecting rod refitting

Note: *New big-end cap bolts must be used when finally refitting the piston/connecting rod*

assemblies. A piston ring compressor tool will be required for this operation.

3 Note that the following procedure assumes that the main bearing caps are in place (see Section 17).

4 Press the bearing shells into their locations, ensuring that the tab on each shell engages in the notch in the connecting rod and cap. Take care not to touch any shell's bearing surface with your fingers. Ensure that all traces of the protective grease are cleaned off using paraffin. Wipe dry the shells and connecting rods with a lint-free cloth.

5 Lubricate the cylinder bores, the pistons, and piston rings, then lay out each piston/connecting rod assembly in its respective position.

6 Start with assembly No 1. Make sure that the piston rings are still spaced as described in Section 16, then clamp them in position with a piston ring compressor.

7 Insert the piston/connecting rod assembly into the top of cylinder No 1. Ensure that the arrow on the piston crown points towards the timing chain end of the engine, and that the identifying marks on the connecting rods and big-end caps are positioned as noted before removal. Using a block of wood or hammer handle against the piston crown, tap the assembly into the cylinder until the piston crown is flush with the top of the cylinder **(see illustrations)**.

8 Ensure that the bearing shell is still correctly installed. Liberally lubricate the crankpin and both bearing shells. Taking care not to mark the cylinder bores, pull the piston/connecting rod assembly down the bore and onto the crankpin. Refit the big-end bearing cap. Note that the bearing shell locating tabs must abut each other.

9 Fit new bearing cap securing bolts, then tighten the bolts evenly and progressively to the Stage 1 torque setting. Once both bolts have been tightened to the Stage 1 setting, angle-tighten them through the specified Stage 2 angle, using a socket and extension bar. It is recommended that an angle-measuring gauge is used during this stage of the tightening, to ensure accuracy. If a gauge is not available, use a dab of white paint to make alignment marks between the bolt and bearing cap prior to tightening; the marks can then be used to check that the bolt has been rotated sufficiently during tightening.

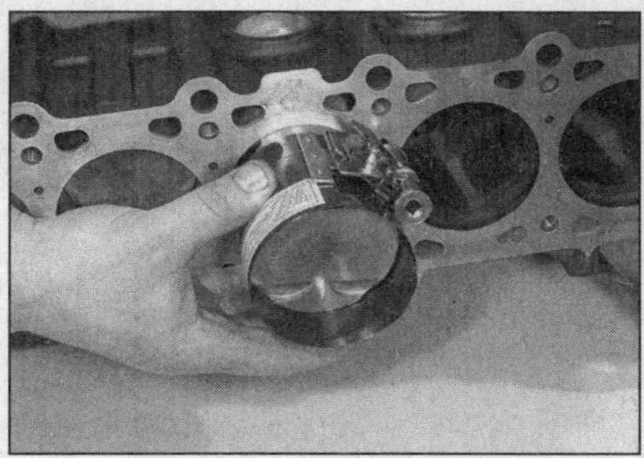

18.7a Insert the piston/connecting rod assembly into the cylinder bore . . .

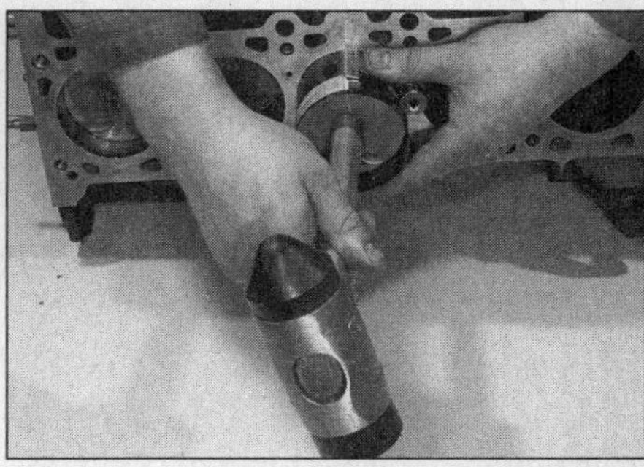

18.7b . . . then lightly tap the assembly into the cylinder

10 Once the bearing cap bolts have been correctly tightened, rotate the crankshaft. Check that it turns freely; some stiffness is to be expected if new components have been fitted, but there should be no signs of binding or tight spots.

11 Refit the remaining piston/connecting rod assemblies in the same way.

12 Where applicable, refit the oil baffle to the bottom of the cylinder block.

13 On 4-cylinder engines, refit the cylinder head, balancer shaft housing/oil pump, and sump as described in Part A of this Chapter.

14 On 6-cylinder engines, refit the cylinder head, oil pump and sump as described in Part B of this Chapter.

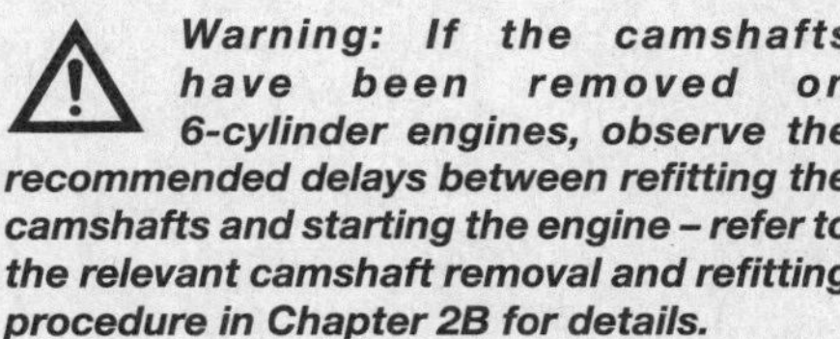

19 Engine – initial start-up after overhaul

Warning: If the camshafts have been removed on 6-cylinder engines, observe the recommended delays between refitting the camshafts and starting the engine – refer to the relevant camshaft removal and refitting procedure in Chapter 2B for details.

1 With the engine refitted in the vehicle, double-check the engine oil and coolant levels. Make a final check that everything has been reconnected, and that there are no tools or rags left in the engine compartment.

2 Disable the ignition and fuel injection systems by removing the engine management relay (located in the engine electrical box), and the fuel pump fuse (located in the main fusebox – see Chapter 12), then turn the engine on the starter motor until the oil pressure warning light goes out.

3 Refit the relays (and ensure that the fuel pump fuse is fitted), and switch on the ignition to prime the fuel system.

4 Start the engine, noting that this may take a little longer than usual, due to the fuel system components having been disturbed.

Caution: When first starting the engine after overhaul, if there is a rattling noise from the valvegear, this is probably due to the hydraulic valve lifters partially draining. If the rattling persists, do not run the engine above 2000 rpm until the rattling stops.

5 While the engine is idling, check for fuel, water and oil leaks. Don't be alarmed if there are some odd smells and smoke from parts getting hot and burning off oil deposits.

6 Assuming all is well, keep the engine idling until hot water is felt circulating through the top hose, then switch off the engine.

7 After a few minutes, recheck the oil and coolant levels as described in *Weekly checks*, and top-up as necessary.

8 If new pistons, rings or crankshaft bearings have been fitted, the engine must be treated as new, and run-in for the first 500 miles. Do not operate the engine at full-throttle, or allow it to labour at low engine speeds in any gear. It is recommended that the oil and filter are changed at the end of this period.

Chapter 3
Cooling, heating and ventilation systems

Contents

Degrees of difficulty

Easy, suitable for novice with little experience 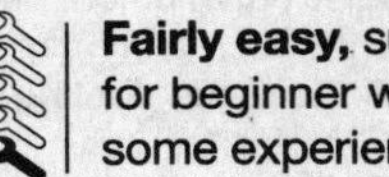	**Fairly easy,** suitable for beginner with some experience	**Fairly difficult,** suitable for competent DIY mechanic	**Difficult,** suitable for experienced DIY mechanic	**Very difficult,** suitable for expert DIY or professional 

Specifications

Engine codes

4-cylinder engines

1796 cc engines	N42 B18 and N46 B18
1895 cc engines	M43TU B19
1995 cc engines	N42 B20 and N46 B20

6-cylinder engines

2171 cc engines	M54 B22
2494 cc engines	M52TU B25 and M54 B25
2793 cc engines	M52TU B28
2979 cc engines	M54 B30

General

Expansion tank cap opening pressure	2.0 ± 0.2 bar

Thermostat

Opening temperatures:	
4-cylinder engines:	
M43TU	105°C
N42	103°C (nominal)
N46	Not available
6-cylinder engines	97°C

Torque wrench settings

Torque wrench settings	Nm	lbf ft
Coolant pump nuts/bolts (all except N42 and N46 engines):		
M6 nuts/bolts	10	7
M8 nuts/bolts	22	16
Coolant pump to power steering pump (N42 and N46 engines)	32	24
Cooling fan viscous coupling to coolant pump (**left-hand thread**)	40	30
Thermal switch to radiator	15	11
Thermostat cover bolts	10	7

2.3a Prise up the wire locking clip . . .

2.3b . . . and pull the hose from the fitting

1 General information and precautions

The cooling system is of pressurised type, comprising of a pump, an aluminium crossflow radiator, cooling fan, and a thermostat. The system functions as follows. Cold coolant from the radiator passes through the hose to the coolant pump where it is pumped around the cylinder block and head passages. After cooling the cylinder bores, combustion surfaces and valve seats, the coolant reaches the underside of the thermostat, which is initially closed. The coolant passes through the heater and is returned through the cylinder block to the coolant pump.

When the engine is cold the coolant circulates only through the cylinder block, cylinder head, expansion tank and heater. When the coolant reaches a predetermined temperature, the thermostat opens and the coolant passes through to the radiator. On some models, the thermostat opening and closing is controlled by the engine management ECM by a heating element within the wax capsule of the thermostat. This allows fine control of the engine running temperature, resulting in less emissions, and better fuel consumption. As the coolant circulates through the radiator it is cooled by the inrush of air when the car is in forward motion. Airflow is supplemented by the action of the cooling fan. Upon reaching the radiator, the coolant is now cooled and the cycle is repeated.

Two different fan configurations are used, depending on model. On M54 and 4-cylinder engines the fan is electrically-operated, and mounted on the engine side of the radiator. On M52TU engines a belt-driven cooling fan is fitted. The belt is driven by the crankshaft pulley via a viscous fluid coupling. The viscous coupling varies the fan speed, according to the engine temperature. At low temperatures, the coupling provides very little resistance between the fan and pump pulley so only a slight amount of drive is transmitted to the cooling fan. As the temperature of the coupling increases, so does its internal resistance therefore increasing the drive to the cooling fan. On these engines an additional electrically-operated cooling fan is fitted on the bumper side of the radiator.

Refer to Section 11 for information on the air conditioning system.

Warning: Do not attempt to remove the expansion tank filler cap or disturb any part of the cooling system while the engine is hot, as there is a high risk of scalding. If the expansion tank filler cap must be removed before the engine and radiator have fully cooled (even though this is not recommended) the pressure in the cooling system must first be relieved. Cover the cap with a thick layer of cloth, to avoid scalding, and slowly unscrew the filler cap until a hissing sound can be heard. When the hissing has stopped, indicating that the pressure has reduced, slowly unscrew the filler cap until it can be removed; if more hissing sounds are heard, wait until they have stopped before unscrewing the cap completely. At all times keep well away from the filler cap opening.

- ***Do not allow antifreeze to come into contact with skin or painted surfaces of the vehicle. Rinse off spills immediately with plenty of water. Never leave antifreeze lying around in an open container or in a puddle in the driveway or on the garage floor. Children and pets are attracted by its sweet smell. Antifreeze can be fatal if ingested.***
- ***Refer to Section 11 for precautions to be observed when working on models equipped with air conditioning.***

2 Cooling system hoses – disconnection and renewal

Note: *Refer to the warnings given in Section 1 of this Chapter before proceeding.*

1 If the checks described in Chapter 1 reveal a faulty hose, it must be renewed as follows.

2 First drain the cooling system (see Chapter 1). If the coolant is not due for renewal, it may be re-used if it is collected in a clean container.

3 To disconnect a hose, prise up the wire retaining clip and pull the hose from its fitting **(see illustrations)**. Some hoses may be secured using traditional hose clips. To disconnect these hoses, release its retaining clips, then move them along the hose, clear of the relevant inlet/outlet union. Carefully work the hose free. While the hoses can be removed with relative ease when new, or when hot, do not attempt to disconnect any part of the system while it is still hot.

4 Note that the radiator inlet and outlet unions are fragile; do not use excessive force when attempting to remove the hoses. If a hose proves to be difficult to remove, try to release it by rotating the hose ends before attempting to free it.

5 To refit a hose, simply push the end over the fitting until the retaining clip engages and lock the hose in place. Pull the hose to make sure its locked in place. When fitting a hose with traditional hose clips, first slide the clips onto the hose, then work the hose into position. If clamp type clips were originally fitted, it is a good idea to use screw-type clips when refitting the hose. If the hose is stiff, use a little soapy water as a lubricant, or soften the hose by soaking it in hot water. Work the hose into position, checking that it is correctly routed, then slide each clip along the hose until it passes over the flared end of the relevant inlet/outlet union, before securing it in position with the retaining clip.

6 Refill the cooling system with reference to Chapter 1.

7 Check thoroughly for leaks as soon as possible after disturbing any part of the cooling system.

3 Radiator – removal, inspection and refitting

Removal

1 Disconnect the battery negative lead (see Chapter 5A).

2 Drain the cooling system as described in Chapter 1.

3 Remove the air filter housing as described in Chapter 4A.

6-cylinder models

4 Remove the cooling fan and viscous coupling (Section 5), or electric cooling fan (Section 6) as applicable. Some models are equipped with an electric cooling fan behind the radiator, whilst others are equipped with the viscous coupling and fan behind the radiator; there is no need to remove the fan on the bumper side.

5 Prise out the locking wire clips and disconnect the upper coolant hose from the radiator and expansion tank **(see illustration)**.

6 Prise out the locking wire clip and disconnect the hose from the expansion tank **(see illustration)**.

4-cylinder models

7 Remove the electric cooling fan and shroud as described in Section 6.

3.5 Disconnect the upper coolant hose from the radiator and expansion tank

3.6 Disconnect the hose from the expansion tank – 6 cylinder models

3.8 Disconnect the hose junction from the radiator and expansion tank

8 Prise out the locking wire clips and disconnect the upper coolant hose junction from the radiator and expansion tank **(see illustration)**.

All models

9 Prise out the locking wire clip and disconnect the lower hose from the radiator.

10 Reach underneath the coolant expansion tank and disconnect the wiring from the coolant level sensor. Pull out the retaining clip from the base of the expansion tank **(see illustration)**.

11 Disconnect the hose from the base of the expansion tank or left-hand side of the radiator depending on model **(see illustration)**. Pull the expansion tank up from the radiator and remove it.

12 Depending on the model, the radiator is retained by one or two bolts and one expanding plastic rivet in the upper corners of the radiator. Undo the bolt(s)/lever up the centre pin and prise out the rivet, then lift the radiator upwards and out of the engine compartment **(see illustrations)**.

Inspection

13 If the radiator has been removed due to suspected blockage, reverse flush it as described in Chapter 1.

14 Clean dirt and debris from the radiator fins, using an airline (in which case, wear eye protection) or a soft brush. Be careful, as the fins are easily damaged, and are sharp.

15 If necessary, a radiator specialist can perform a 'flow test' on the radiator, to establish whether an internal blockage exists.

16 A leaking radiator must be referred to a specialist for permanent repair. Do not attempt to weld or solder a leaking radiator, as damage may result.

17 Inspect the radiator lower mounting rubbers for signs of damage or deterioration and renew if necessary.

Refitting

18 Refitting is the reverse of removal, noting the following points.

a) Ensure that the lower mounting rubbers are correctly located in the body then lower the radiator into position, engage it with the mountings and secure it in position with the retaining bolts/clip ***(see illustration)****.*

b) Ensure that the fan cowl is correctly located with the lugs on the radiator and secure it in position with the clips.

d) Reconnect the hoses and ensure the retaining clips engage securely.

e) Check the condition of the O-ring seals in the end of the radiator fittings. Renew any that are defective.

f) On completion, reconnect the battery and refill the cooling system (see Chapter 1).

4 Thermostat – removal and refitting

Note: *A new thermostat sealing ring and (where fitted) housing gasket/seal will be required on refitting.*

Removal

1 Disconnect the battery negative lead (see Chapter 5A).

3.10 Disconnect the level sensor wiring plug, and pull out the expansion tank retaining clip (arrowed)

3.11 Prise out the locking wire clip and disconnect the hose from the base of the expansion tank

3.12a Torx bolt (arrowed) in the upper right-hand corner of the radiator . . .

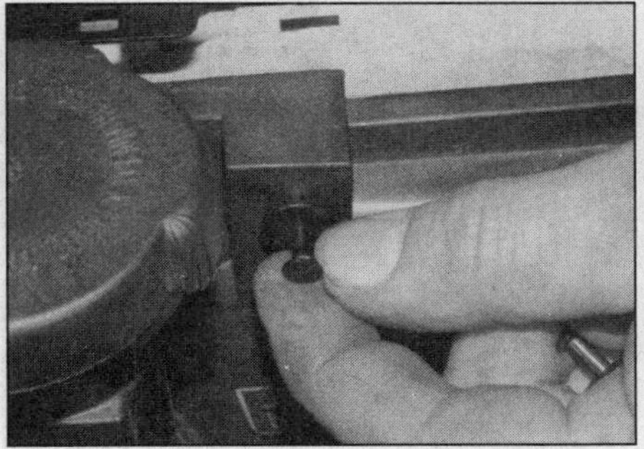
3.12b . . . and a plastic expansion rivet in the left-hand corner

3.18 The radiator must sit in the V in the mounting (arrowed)

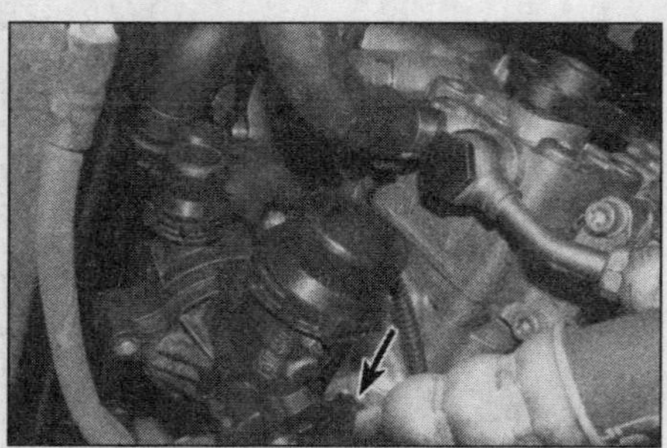
4.3 Disconnect the lower hose from the thermostat housing, then unplug the wiring connector (arrowed)

4.4 Undo the Torx bolts and remove the thermostat cover

4.7 Undo the retaining bolts and remove the thermostat housing

4.8 Renew the thermostat housing O-ring seal

2 Drain the cooling system as described in Chapter 1.

N42 and N46 engines

3 Pull out the wire locking clip and disconnect the lower hose from the thermostat housing **(see illustration)**. Where applicable, disconnect the thermostat wiring plug.

4 Undo the retaining Torx bolts, and remove the thermostat cover (complete with thermostat) downwards **(see illustration).** Note that the thermostat is integral with the cover, and can only be renewed as a complete assembly. Discard the O-ring seal, a new one must be fitted.

M43TU and 6-cylinder engines

5 Where applicable, to improve access to the thermostat housing, remove the cooling fan and coupling as described in Section 5.

6 Prise out the locking wire clips and disconnect the coolant hose(s) from the thermostat housing on the front of the cylinder head/timing chain cover (as applicable). On models with an electrically-heated thermostat, disconnect the wiring plug.

7 Slacken and remove the retaining bolts and remove the thermostat housing **(see illustration)**. Recover the housing gasket/seal (where fitted). On 6-cylinder engines, it will be necessary to unscrew the engine lifting bracket to allow the housing to be removed.

8 Note that the thermostat is integral with the housing. Recover the sealing ring **(see illustration)**.

Refitting

9 Refitting is a reversal of removal, bearing in mind the following points.

a) Renew the thermostat cover O-ring seal.
b) Tighten the thermostat cover bolts to the specified torque.
c) On 6-cylinder engines, refit the cooling fan as described in Section 5.
d) On completion refill the cooling system as described in Chapter 1.

5.4a Slacken the cooling fan coupling using the special open-ended spanner . . .

5.4b . . . and remove the cooling fan

5 Cooling fan and viscous coupling – removal and refitting

Note: *A special 32 mm narrow open-ended spanner will be required to remove the fan and viscous coupling assembly.*

Removal

1 Remove the expansion rivets and remove the plastic cover from above the radiator.

2 Disconnect the auxiliary cooling ducts from the shroud and remove them from the engine compartment.

3 Release the fan shroud upper retaining clips by pulling out their centre pins then lift the shroud upwards and out of position. **Note:** *It may be necessary to remove the fan to enable the shroud to be removed.*

4 Using the special open-ended spanner unscrew the viscous coupling from the coolant pump and remove the cooling fan **(see illustrations). Note:** *The viscous coupling has a **left-hand thread.*** If necessary use a strip of metal bolted to the drive pulley to counterhold the nut.

5 If necessary, slacken and remove the retaining bolts and separate the cooling fan from the coupling noting which way around the fan is fitted.

Refitting

6 Where necessary, refit the fan to the viscous coupling and securely tighten its retaining bolts. Make sure the fan is fitted the correct way around. **Note:** *If the fan is fitted the wrong way around the efficiency of the cooling system will be significantly reduced.*

7 Refit the fan and shroud. Screw the fan onto the coolant pump and tighten it to the specified torque. Engage the fan shroud with the lugs on the radiator and secure it in position with the retaining clips.

8 Reconnect the auxiliary cooling ducts (where fitted) to the shroud then refit the plastic cover to the bonnet crossmember and securely tighten its retaining bolts.

6 Electric cooling fan and shroud – removal and refitting

Removal

Primary cooling fan

1 Prise out the expansion rivets, and remove the air intake hood from the centre of the bonnet slam panel **(see illustration)**. Where fitted, undo the two bolts, lift the plastic engine cover and pull it forward to remove it. On N42 engines, remove the air cleaner housing as described in Chapter 4A.

2 Jack up the front of the vehicle, and support

it securely on axle stands (see *Jacking and vehicle support*). Undo the bolts and remove the engine undershield at the front.

3 Where fitted, lever up the centre pin, prise out the expansion rivet, and remove the secondary air injection filter assembly from the shroud. Release the air injection inlet hose from the retaining clips on the shroud.

4 Note their fitted locations, then unclip and disconnect any electrical connectors from the fan/shroud **(see illustration)**.

5 Where applicable, unclip the hoses from the clips on the lower part of the shroud. Where plastic expansion rivets are fitted, lever up the centre pin, then prise the entire rivet from place.

6 Remove the bolt in the upper right-hand corner of the fan shroud, and the expanding rivet in the upper left-hand corner **(see illustrations)**.

7 Lift the fan upwards and out of the engine compartment. Take care not to damage the radiator whilst manoeuvring the fan shroud assembly.

8 Undo the three bolts and remove the fan motor from the shroud **(see illustration)**. **Note:** *Do not lift the assembly by the fan blades or the balance of the fan may be disturbed, resulting in excessive noise whilst the fan is in use.*

9 If required, undo the four bolts and remove the timer unit from the shroud **(see illustration)**.

Auxiliary cooling fan

10 Prise out the expansion rivets, and remove the air intake hood from the centre of the bonnet slam panel **(see illustration)**.

11 Remove the front bumper as described in Chapter 11.

12 Unclip and disconnect the fan motor wiring plug.

13 Prise out the four expansion rivets, and remove the fan shroud.

14 Remove the four bolts and withdraw the fan and motor.

Refitting

15 Refitting is a reversal of removal, ensuring the lugs on the lower edge of the shroud engage in the corresponding slots in the radiator edge.

7 Cooling system electrical switches – testing, removal and refitting

Radiator outlet switch

Testing

1 Testing of the switch should be entrusted to a BMW dealer.

Removal

2 The switch is located in the radiator lower hose. The engine and radiator should be cold before removing the switch.

3 Disconnect the battery negative lead (see Chapter 5A).

4 Either drain the cooling system to below the level of the switch (as described in Chapter 1), or have ready a suitable plug which can be used to plug the switch aperture in the radiator whilst the switch is removed. If a plug is used, take great care not to damage the radiator, and do not use anything which will allow foreign matter to enter the radiator.

5 Disconnect the wiring plug from the switch **(see illustration)**.

6 Release the retaining clip, and remove the switch. Recover the sealing ring.

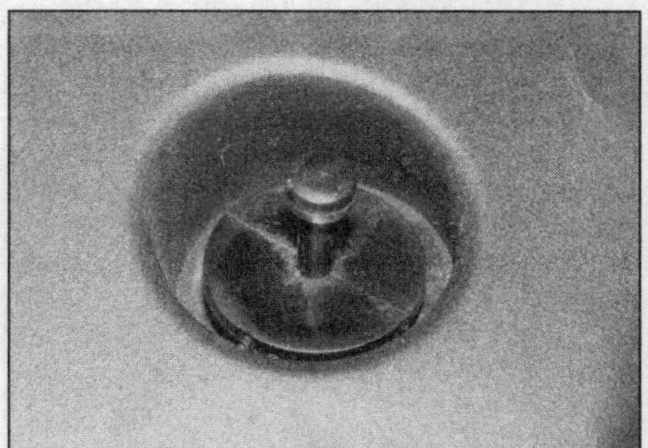

6.1 Prise up the centre pin, then remove the expansion rivet

6.4 Undo the connectors from the shroud (arrowed)

6.6a Remove the bolt in the right-hand corner (arrowed) . . .

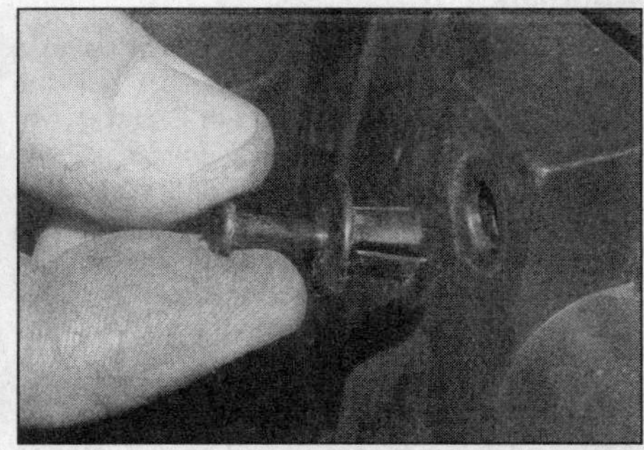

6.6b . . . and the plastic expanding rivet in the left-hand corner

6.8 The fan motor is secured by three bolts (arrowed)

6.9 Undo the four bolts and remove the timer unit

6.10 Prise out the expansion rivets and remove the intake hood

7.5 The radiator outlet thermostatic switch is located in the lower hose

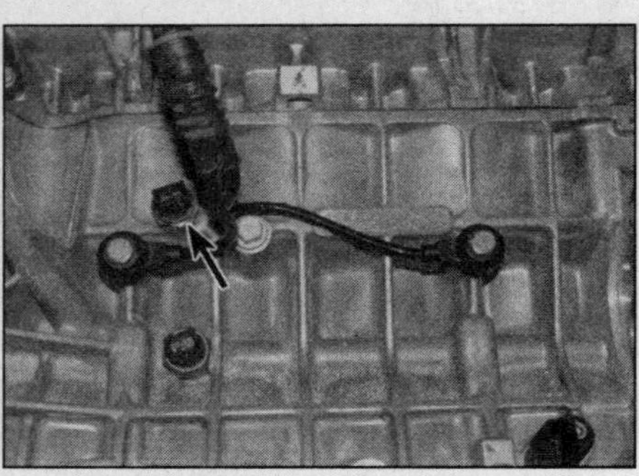

7.11 Engine coolant temperature sensor (arrowed – engine removed for clarity)

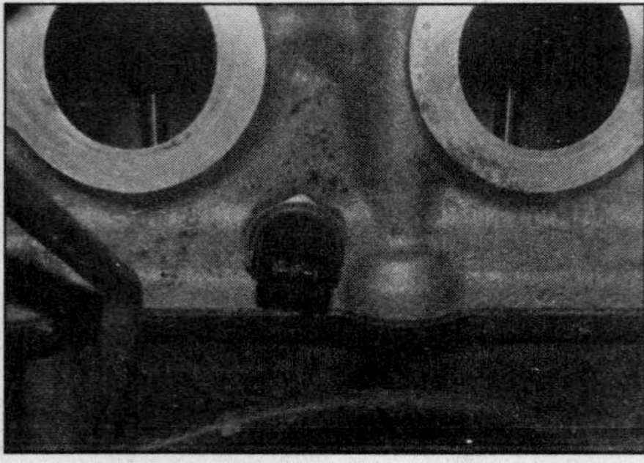

7.15 Coolant temperature sensor (shown with the inlet manifold removed)

Refitting

7 Refitting is a reversal of removal using a new sealing washer. On completion, refill the cooling system as described in Chapter 1 or top-up as described in *Weekly checks*.

8 Start the engine and run it until it reaches normal operating temperature, then continue to run the engine and check that the cooling fan cuts in and functions correctly.

Coolant temperature sensor

Testing

9 Testing of the sensor should be entrusted to a BMW dealer.

Removal – N42 and N46 engines

10 Either partially drain the cooling system to just below the level of the sensor (as described in Chapter 1), or have ready a suitable plug which can be used to plug the sensor aperture whilst it is removed. If a plug is used, take great care not to damage the sensor unit aperture, and do not use anything which will allow foreign matter to enter the cooling system.

11 The sensor is located on the left-hand side of the cylinder block below the inlet manifold **(see illustration)**. To access the sensor, remove the alternator as described in Chapter 5A.

12 Disconnect the wiring plug, and unscrew the sensor from the cylinder block. Recover the sealing ring.

Removal – M43TU and 6-cylinder engines

13 Either partially drain the cooling system to just below the level of the sensor (as described in Chapter 1), or have ready a suitable plug which can be used to plug the sensor aperture whilst it is removed. If a plug is used, take great care not to damage the sensor unit aperture, and do not use anything which will allow foreign matter to enter the cooling system.

8.2 Slacken the two bolts securing the power steering pump to the coolant pump (arrowed)

8.4 Disconnect the three hoses from the thermostat housing (arrowed)

8.6 Renew the coolant pump-to-block connecting piece O-rings (arrowed)

8.8 Undo the bolts to separate the halves of the coolant pump

14 The sensor is screwed into the left-hand side of the cylinder head, under the inlet manifold.

15 Disconnect the wiring from the sensor. Unscrew the sensor unit from the cylinder head and recover its sealing washer **(see illustration)**.

Refitting

16 Fit a new sealing washer to the sensor unit and refit the sensor, tightening it securely.

17 Reconnect the wiring connector then refill the cooling system as described in Chapter 1 or top-up as described in *Weekly checks*.

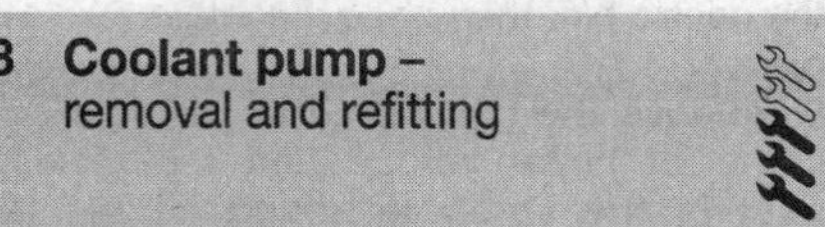

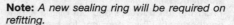

8 Coolant pump – removal and refitting

Note: *A new sealing ring will be required on refitting.*

Removal

1 Drain the cooling system as described in Chapter 1.

N42 and N46 engines

2 Slacken the power steering pump pulley bolts, and remove the auxiliary drivebelt as described in Chapter 1. Note that the coolant pump is bolted to the power steering pump, and both items must be removed together. Slacken the two bolts securing the power steering pump to the coolant pump **(see illustration)**.

3 Jack up the front of the vehicle, and support it securely on axle stands (see *Jacking and vehicle support*). Undo the bolts and remove the engine undershield.

4 Prise up the locking wire clips and disconnect the three hoses from the thermostat housing **(see illustration)**. Note that the power steering pump hoses remain connected.

5 Undo the four bolts and separate the power steering pump from the engine block. Unscrew the bolt and remove the bracket supporting power steering pipes at the front of the engine block.

6 Remove the two coolant pump-to-power steering pump bolts previously slackened, and remove the coolant pump. Discard the pump-to-block connecting piece O-rings, new ones must be fitted **(see illustration)**.

7 If necessary, the coolant pump can be separated from the thermostat housing by removing the housing cover (complete with thermostat), and unscrewing the four bolts securing the housing to the pump body.

8 The coolant pump can be opened for seal renewal by removing the 6 bolts and separating the two halves of the pump. Discard the rubber seal, a new one must be fitted **(see illustration)**.

M43TU and 6-cylinder engines

9 On 6-cylinder models, remove the cooling fan and coupling as described in Section 5.

10 Slacken the coolant pump pulley bolts then remove the auxiliary drivebelt as described in Chapter 1.

11 Unscrew the retaining bolts and remove the pulley from the pump, noting which way around it is fitted **(see illustration)**.

12 Slacken and remove the pump retaining bolts/nuts (as applicable) and withdraw the pump. If the pump is a tight fit, screw two M6 bolts into the jacking holes on either side of the pump and use the bolts to draw the pump out of position **(see illustration)**.

13 Recover the sealing ring from the rear of the pump **(see illustration)**.

Refitting

N42 and N46 engines

14 If the two halves of the pump have been separated, renew the rubber seal, reassemble the two halves, and tighten the 6 bolts securely.

15 If removed, refit the thermostat housing and cover, using new O-ring seals. Tighten the bolts securely.

16 Renew the pump-to-engine block connecting piece O-rings, and lubricate them with anti-seize compound. Fit the connecting piece to the pump.

17 Smear the pump drive lugs with grease, and align them with the corresponding lugs of the power steering pump.

18 Fit the coolant pump to the power steering pump, finger-tightening the bolts only at this stage.

19 Refit the power steering pump to the engine block, ensuring that the coolant pump connecting piece engages correctly with the corresponding hole in the block. Tighten the power steering pump mounting bolts securely.

20 Tighten the coolant pump-to-power steering pump bolts to the specified torque.

21 The reminder of refitting is a reversal of removal.

M43TU and 6-cylinder engines

22 Fit the new sealing ring to the rear of the pump and lubricate it with a smear of grease to ease installation.

8.11 Undo the coolant pump pulley bolts

23 Locate the pump in position and refit the retaining bolts/nuts. Tighten the bolts/nuts evenly and progressively to the specified torque, making sure the pump is drawn squarely into position.

24 Refit the pulley to the pump, making sure it is the correct way around, and screw in its retaining bolts.

25 Refit the auxiliary drivebelt as described in Chapter 1 then securely tighten the pulley bolts.

26 Refit the cooling fan assembly (where applicable) as described in Section 5.

27 Refill the cooling system as described in Chapter 1.

9 Heating and ventilation system – general information

1 The heating/ventilation system consists of a four-speed blower motor, face-level vents in the centre and at each end of the facia, and air ducts to the front and rear footwells.

2 The control unit is located in the facia, and the controls operate flap valves to deflect and mix the air flowing through the various parts of the heating/ventilation system. The flap valves are contained in the air distribution housing, which acts as a central distribution unit, passing air to the various ducts and vents.

3 Cold air enters the system through the grille at the rear of the engine compartment. A pollen filter is fitted to the inlet to filter out dust, spores and soot from the incoming air.

4 The airflow, which can be boosted by the blower, then flows through the various ducts, according to the settings of the controls. Stale air is expelled through ducts at the rear of the vehicle. If warm air is required, the cold air is passed through the heater matrix, which is heated by the engine coolant.

5 If necessary, the outside air supply can be closed off, allowing the air inside the vehicle to be recirculated. This can be useful to prevent unpleasant odours entering from outside the vehicle, but should only be used briefly, as the recirculated air inside the vehicle will soon deteriorate.

6 Certain models are fitted with heated front seats. The heat is produced by electrically-heated mats in the seat and backrest cushions (see Chapter 12). The temperature is regulated automatically by a thermostat, and can be set at one of three levels, controlled by switches on the facia.

10 Heater/ventilation components – removal and refitting

Without air conditioning

Heater/ventilation control unit

1 Disconnect the battery negative lead (see Chapter 5A).

2 Remove the audio unit as described in Chapter 12.

3 Pull off the control knobs from each of the heater controls.

4 Slacken and remove the retaining bolts and unclip the front panel from the heater control unit **(see illustration)**.

8.12 If the coolant pump is a tight fit, draw the pump out of position using two jacking bolts (arrowed)

8.13 Recover the sealing ring from the rear of the coolant pump

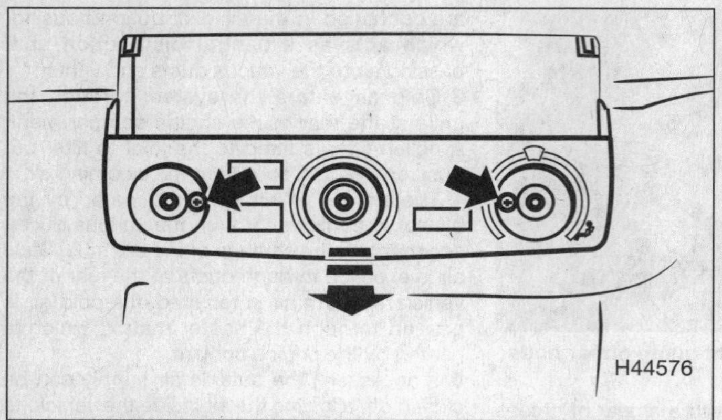

10.4 **Remove the bolts (arrowed) and unclip the front panel**

10.5 Undo the four bolts (1)

5 Undo the four bolts securing the aperture frame, release the control panel retaining clips, push the panel inwards, and remove the frame from the facia **(see illustration)**.

6 Disconnect the wiring connector(s) then unclip the control cables and release each cable from the control unit. Note each cables correct fitted location and routing; to avoid confusion on refitting, label each cable as it is disconnected.

7 Refitting is reversal of removal. Ensure that the control cables are correctly routed and reconnected to the control panel, as noted before removal. Clip the outer cables in position and check the operation of each knob/lever before refitting the storage compartment to the centre console.

Heater/ventilation control cables

8 Remove the heater/ventilation control unit from the facia as described above in paragraphs 1 to 6, detaching the relevant cable from the control unit.

9 On right-hand drive models, undo the retaining bolts then unclip the driver's side lower facia panel and remove it from the vehicle. On left-hand drive models, remove the glovebox as described in Chapter 11, Section 27.

10 Follow the run of the cable behind the facia, taking note of its routing, and disconnect the cable from the air distribution housing.

11 Fit the new cable by reversing the removal procedure, ensuring that it is correctly routed and free from kinks and obstructions. Check the operation of the control knob then refit the control unit as described previously in this Section.

Heater matrix

12 Working in the engine compartment, remove the heater/ventilation inlet air ducting from the rear of the engine compartment as follows.

a) *Rotate the three fasteners 90° anti-clockwise and remove the pollen filter cover from the rear of the engine compartment. Pull the filter forward and remove it.*
b) *Undo the retaining clips and thread the cable out of the ducting* ***(see illustration).***
c) *Unscrew the four bolts and pull the filter housing forwards and remove it.*
d) *Undo the two bolts and remove the inlet ducting upwards and out of the engine compartment* ***(see illustration).***
e) *Where necessary, pull up the weatherstrip, unto the two fasteners and pull out the dividing panel from the left-hand side of the engine compartment* ***(see illustration).***

13 Unscrew the expansion tank cap (referring to the **Warning** note in Section 1) to release any pressure present in the cooling system then securely refit the cap.

14 Clamp both heater hoses as close to the bulkhead as possible to minimise coolant loss. Alternatively, drain the cooling system as described in Chapter 1.

15 Slacken the both clamps and disconnect the heater hoses at the bulkhead **(see illustration)**.

16 Remove the facia as described in Chapter 11.

17 Withdraw the temperature sensor from the heater distribution box. Release the wiring harness from the retaining clips **(see illustration)**.

18 Pull away the passenger side air duct from the heater box, undo the bolt and remove the heater pipe bracket from the heater box **(see illustration)**.

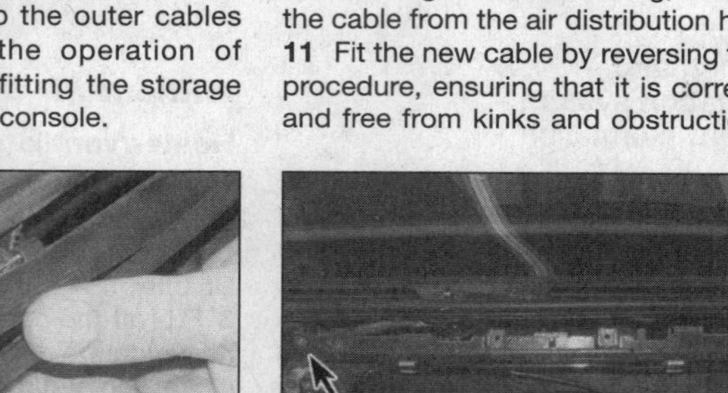

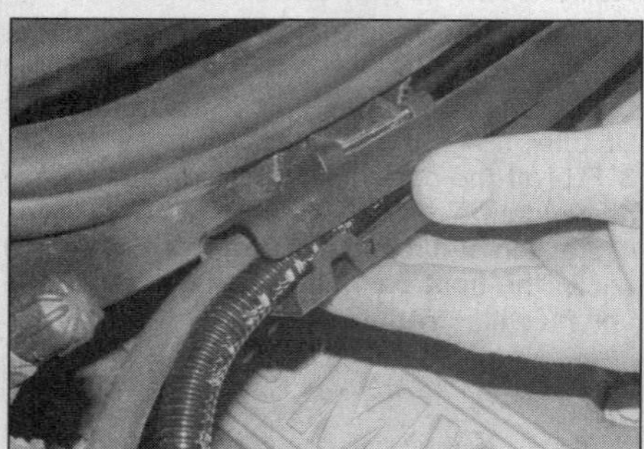

10.12a Unclip the cable ducting

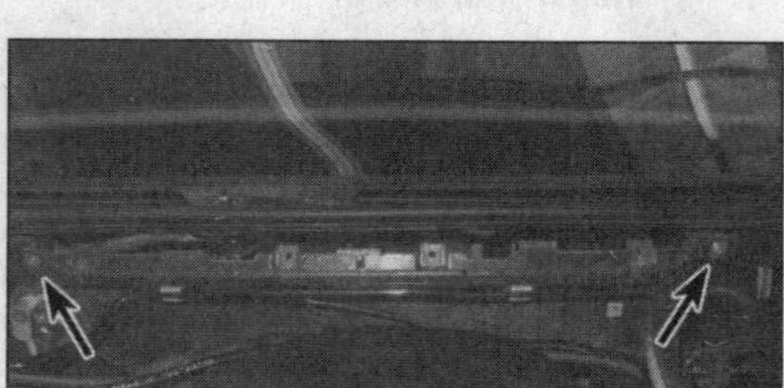

10.12b Undo the two Torx bolts (arrowed) and remove the inlet ducting

10.12c Undo the two fasteners (arrowed) and remove the dividing panel

10.15 Slacken the clamps and disconnect the heater hoses from the bulkhead

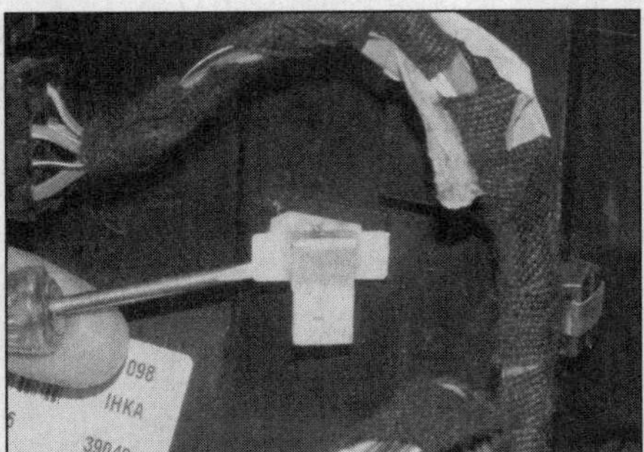

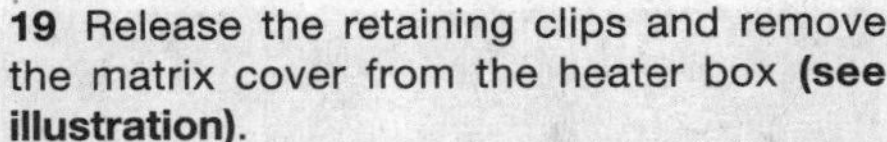

10.17 Withdraw the temperature sensor from the heater box

19 Release the retaining clips and remove the matrix cover from the heater box **(see illustration)**.

20 Remove the pipe retainers, lift the heater pipes and manoeuvre the matrix from the heater box **(see illustration)**. Recover the sealing rings from the heater pipes. **Note:** *Keep the matrix unions uppermost as the matrix is removed to prevent coolant spillage.* Mop-up any spilt coolant immediately and wipe the affected area with a damp cloth to prevent staining.

21 Refitting is the reverse of removal, using new sealing rings. On completion, refill the cooling system as described in Chapter 1.

Heater blower motor

22 Disconnect the battery negative terminal (see Chapter 5A). Remove the engine compartment heater inlet as described in Paragraph 12.

23 On 6-cylinder engines, prise out the plastic cap, undo the retaining nuts/bolts and remove the plastic covers from the top of the engine to provide space to withdraw the heater blower motor.

24 On all models, pull the rubber seal away, undo the four bolts and remove the blower motor cover.

25 Undo the retaining bolts and lower the blower motor. Disconnect the motor wiring plug as the unit is withdrawn.

26 Refitting is a reversal of the removal procedure making sure the motor is correctly clipped into the housing and the housing covers are securely refitted.

Heater blower motor resistor

27 Remove the engine compartment heater inlet as described in Paragraph 12.

28 Pull the rubber seal away, undo the four bolts and remove the blower motor cover.

29 Undo the retaining bolt, disconnect the wiring plug, then lever out the resistor.

30 Refitting is the reverse of removal.

Heater matrix coolant valve

31 The coolant valve is mounted onto the left-hand inner wing. Note that some models are fitted with an auxiliary pump adjacent to the valve **(see illustration)**. Unscrew the expansion tank cap (referring to the **Warning** note in Section 1) to release any pressure

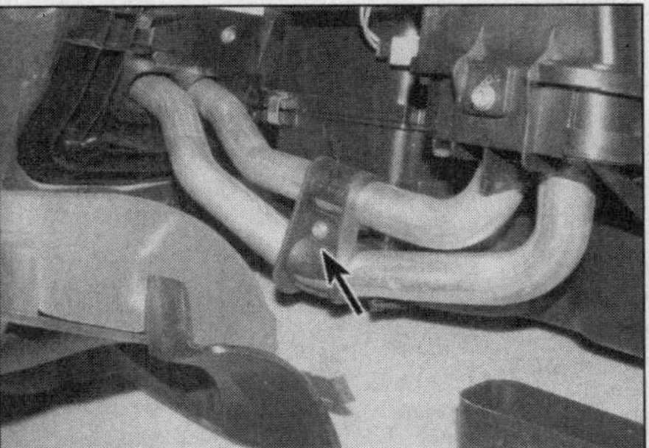

10.18 Heater pipe bracket retaining bolt (arrowed)

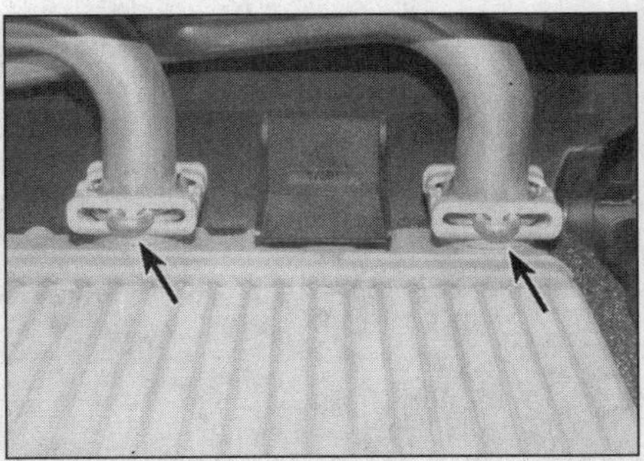

10.20 Remove the heater pipe retainers (arrowed)

present in the cooling system then securely refit the cap.

32 Remove the air cleaner housing as described in Chapter 4A.

33 Clamp both heater hoses as close to the coolant valve as possible to minimise coolant loss.

34 Disconnect the valve wiring connector(s).

35 Slacken the retaining clips and disconnect the hoses from the valve then unclip the valve and remove it from the engine compartment.

36 Refitting is the reverse of removal.

With air conditioning

Heater control unit

37 Give the gear lever knob a sharp tug straight up, and remove it from the lever (manual transmission models), or remove the selector lever (automatic transmission models – see Chapter 7B).

38 Prise up and remove the gear/selector

10.39 Withdraw the storage box from the facia

10.19 Release the clip and remove the matrix cover

10.31 Heater valve and auxiliary pump

lever surround trim. Note their fitted locations, and disconnect and wiring plugs as the trim is removed.

39 Open the storage compartment lid below the heater controls. Carefully prise out the lower edge of the compartment, starting at the corner, and withdraw it from the facia **(see illustration)**. If you are removing the glasses storage compartment, press the roof of the compartment up slightly, pull it approximately 2 mm to the rear, then press the left- and right-hand side of the lid downwards slightly, then pull it from the facia.

40 Undo the four bolts and remove the storage compartment carrier from the facia **(see illustration)**. Note their fitted positions, and disconnect and wiring plugs as the unit is withdrawn.

41 Carefully remove the control panel from the facia by pushing from below **(see illustration)**.

10.40 Undo the bolts (arrowed) and remove the carrier frame

10.41 Pull the heater control unit from the facia

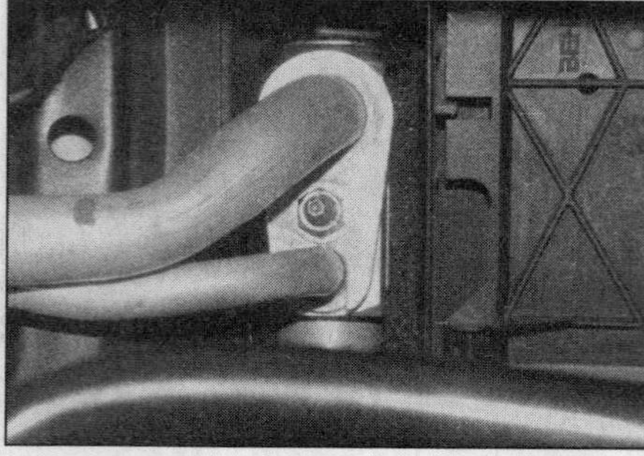
10.50 Disconnect the double pipe coupling

10.59 Lift the spindle lever to remove the flap

10.60 Undo the bolt, release the clips (arrowed) and remove the heater motor cover

10.61a Undo the two bolts (arrowed) at the right-hand side . . .

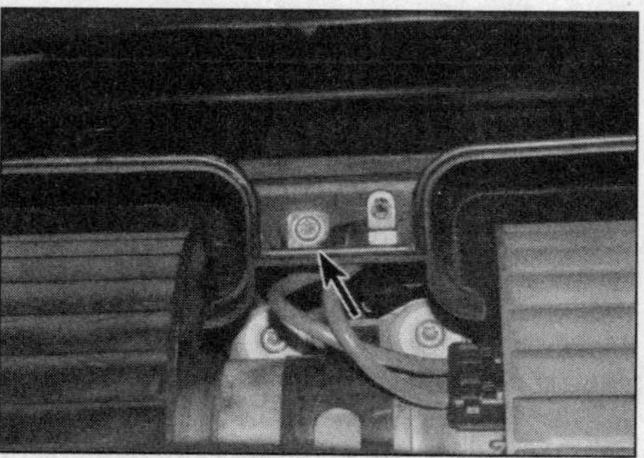
10.61b . . . and one bolt in the centre (arrowed)

42 Note their fitted locations, unlock the lever and disconnect the wiring plugs.

43 Refitting is a reversal of removal.

Heater matrix

44 Have the air conditioning system refrigerant discharged by a BMW dealer or suitably-equipped specialist.

45 Remove the facia as described in Chapter 11.

46 Remove the heater/ventilation air inlet ducting as described in Paragraph 12.

47 Clamp both heater hoses as close to the bulkhead as possible to minimise coolant loss. Alternatively, drain the cooling system as described in Chapter 1.

48 Slacken the both clamps and disconnect the heater hoses at the bulkhead.

49 Undo the bolts securing the air conditioning pipes at the engine compartment bulkhead. Discard the pipe seals, new ones must be fitted.

50 Undo the bolt securing the air conditioning double pipe coupling to the bulkhead and position the pipe to one side **(see illustration)**. Discard the sealing rings, new ones must be fitted.

51 Remove the four bolts on the engine compartment bulkhead **(see illustrations 12.7a and 12.7b)**.

52 Remove the steering column as described in Chapter 10.

53 Unscrew any brackets securing the heater box, and disconnect any wiring plugs, having noted their locations and harness routing. Remove the heater box from the vehicle.

54 Be prepared for coolant spillage and position a suitable container beneath the union on the end of the matrix.

55 Proceed as described in Paragraphs 17 to 20.

56 Refitting is the reverse of removal, using new sealing rings. On completion, refill the cooling system as described in Chapter 1, and have the air conditioning refrigerant recharged by a BMW dealer or specialist.

Heater blower motor

57 Remove the heater inlet housing as described in Paragraph 12. On models with a 6-cylinder engine and/or left-hand drive, remove the cylinder head cover as described in the relevant Part of Chapter 2.

58 Peel away the rubber sealing strip from the housing opening.

59 Pull up the right-hand flap spindle lever, and remove the flap **(see illustration)**.

60 Undo the single bolt, release the two retaining clips and remove the heater motor front cover **(see illustration)**.

61 Undo the three bolts and remove the right-hand cover from the motor **(see illustrations)**.

62 Disconnect the motor wiring plug and, using a spiked-tool, push the retaining clip down and release the motor **(see illustration)**. Manoeuvre the motor out through the passenger side of the opening.

63 Refitting is a reversal of removal. Ensure that the locating lug in the motor housing engages correctly with the rectangular hole in the motor casing **(see illustration)**.

Heater blower motor resistor

64 Refer to the information given in Section 12 regarding Blower limit switch.

Heater matrix coolant valve

65 Refer to the information given in Paragraphs 31 to 36.

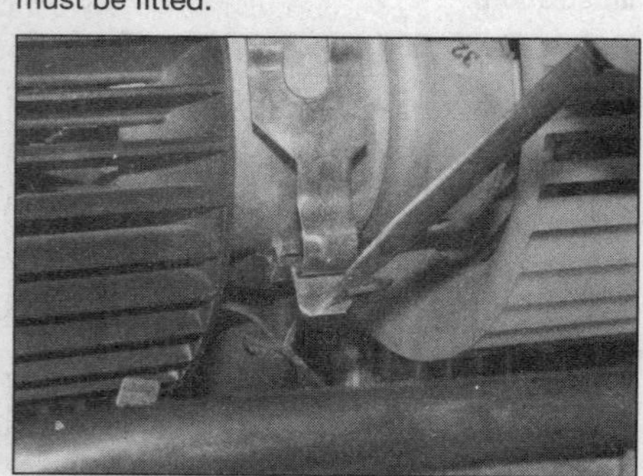
10.62 Push down the retaining clip to release the motor

10.63 Ensure the lug (arrowed) engages with the corresponding hole in the motor casing

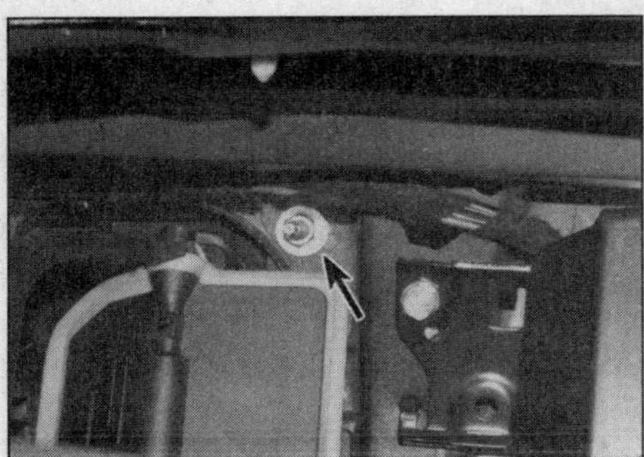
12.7a The heater is secured by two bolts at the top (one each side – arrowed) . . .

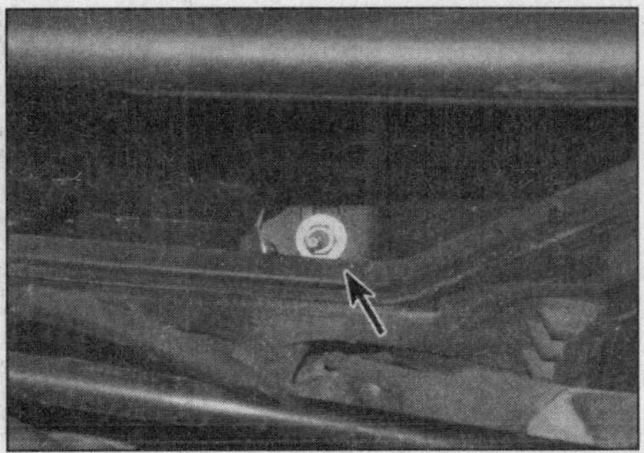
12.7b . . . and two at the bottom (one each side – arrowed) of the heater motor aperture

12.9 Disconnect the temperature sensor wiring plug (arrowed)

11 Air conditioning system – general information and precautions

General information

1 An air conditioning system is available on all models. It enables the temperature of incoming air to be lowered, and dehumidifies the air, which makes for rapid demisting and increased comfort.

2 The cooling side of the system works in the same way as a domestic refrigerator. Refrigerant gas is drawn into a belt-driven compressor and passes into a condenser mounted in front of the radiator, where it loses heat and becomes liquid. The liquid passes through an expansion valve to an evaporator, where it changes from liquid under high pressure to gas under low pressure. This change is accompanied by a drop in temperature, which cools the evaporator. The refrigerant returns to the compressor and the cycle begins again.

3 Air blown through the evaporator passes to the air distribution unit, where it is mixed with hot air blown through the heater matrix to achieve the desired temperature in the passenger compartment.

4 The heating side of the system works in the same way as on models without air conditioning (see Section 9).

5 The operation of the system is controlled by an electronic control unit, with a self-diagnosis system. Any problems with the system should be referred to a BMW dealer or suitably-equipped specialist.

Precautions

6 When an air conditioning system is fitted, it is necessary to observe special precautions whenever dealing with any part of the system, its associated components and any items which require disconnection of the system. If for any reason the system must be disconnected, entrust this task to your BMW dealer or a suitably-equipped specialist.

Warning: The refrigerant is potentially dangerous and should only be handled by qualified persons. If it is splashed onto the skin it can cause frostbite. It is not itself poisonous, but in the presence of a naked flame (including a cigarette) it forms a poisonous gas. Uncontrolled discharging of the refrigerant is dangerous and potentially damaging to the environment.

Warning: Do not operate the air conditioning system if it is known to be short of refrigerant, as this may damage the compressor.

12 Air conditioning system components – removal and refitting

Warning: Do not attempt to open the refrigerant circuit. Refer to the precautions given in Section 11.

Evaporator

Removal

1 Have the air conditioning refrigerant discharged by a BMW dealer or suitably-equipped specialist.

2 Remove the heater matrix as described in Section 10.

3 Remove the steering column as described in Chapter 10.

4 Working in the engine compartment, remove the heater/ventilation inlet air ducting from the rear of the engine compartment as follows.

a) *Rotate the three fasteners 90° anti-clockwise and remove the pollen filter cover from the rear of the engine compartment. Pull the filter forward and remove it.*
b) *Undo the four retaining clips and thread the cable out of the ducting* **(see illustration 10.12a)**.
c) *Unscrew the four bolts and pull the filter housing forwards and remove it.*
d) *Undo the two bolts and remove the inlet ducting upwards and out of the engine compartment* **(see illustration 10.12b)**. *Where necessary, pull up the weatherstrip, unto the two fasteners and pull out the dividing panel from the left-hand side of the engine compartment.*

5 Release the wiring harness(es) from any retaining clips (noting their fitted locations) securing it to the facia crossbeam. Undo the relevant bolts/nuts and remove the crossbeam from the vehicle.

6 Undo the fasteners, and disconnect the air conditioning pipes from the engine compartment bulkhead. Discard the O-ring seals, new ones must be fitted.

7 Undo the bolts securing the heater housing to the engine compartment bulkhead **(see illustrations)**.

8 Remove the air conditioning blower limit switch as described in this Section.

9 Disconnect the wiring plug and remove the temperature sensor from the evaporator housing **(see illustration)**.

10 Unclip the linkage from the servo motor, disconnect any wiring plugs and release any wiring harnesses from the retaining clips, having noted their fitted locations.

11 Release the retaining clips, remove the lower part of the evaporator housing, and remove the evaporator. **Note:** *Take care not to damage any of the evaporator cooling fins. If necessary straighten any that are bent.*

12 Refitting is a reversal of removal. Have the refrigerant recharged by a BMW dealer or specialist, and top-up the coolant level as described in *Weekly checks*.

Expansion valve

13 Have the air conditioning refrigerant discharged by a BMW dealer or suitably-equipped specialist.

14 Working in the engine compartment, remove the heater/ventilation inlet air ducting from the rear of the engine compartment as follows.

a) *Rotate the three fasteners 90° anti-clockwise and remove the pollen filter cover from the rear of the engine compartment. Pull the filter forward and remove it.*
b) *Undo the four retaining clips and thread the cable out of the ducting* **(see illustration 10.12a)**.
c) *Unscrew the four bolts and pull the filter housing forwards and remove it.*
d) *Pull up the rubber strip, rotate the two fasteners anti-clockwise, and move the dividing panel in the left-hand corner of the engine compartment forward a little.*
e) *Undo the two bolts and remove the inlet ducting upwards and out of the engine compartment* **(see illustration 10.12b)**.

12.22 Undo the bolts and disconnect the couplings

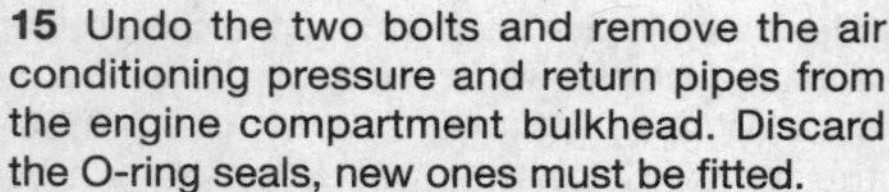

12.24 Undo the clamp bolts (arrowed)

12.30 Disconnect the compressor wiring plug

15 Undo the two bolts and remove the air conditioning pressure and return pipes from the engine compartment bulkhead. Discard the O-ring seals, new ones must be fitted.

16 Lift the locking mechanism and remove the recirculating air flap **(see illustration 10.59)**.

17 Undo the nut and move the twin pipe coupling to one side **(see illustration 10.50)**.

18 Undo the two bolts and remove the expansion valve. Discard the O-ring seals, new ones must be fitted.

19 Refitting is a reversal of removal. Have the refrigerant recharged by a BMW dealer or specialist, and top-up the coolant level as described in *Weekly checks*.

Receiver/drier

20 The receiver/drier should be renewed when:

a) *There is dirt in the air conditioning system.*
b) *The compressor has been renewed.*
c) *The condenser or evaporator has been renewed.*
d) *A leak has emptied the air conditioning system.*
e) *The air conditioning system has been opened for more than 24 hours.*

21 Have the air conditioning refrigerant discharged by a BMW dealer or suitably-equipped specialist.

22 The receiver/drier is located in the right-hand corner of the engine compartment. Undo the retaining bolts, and lift the pipes and coupling from the top of the unit **(see illustration)**. Discard the O-ring seals, new ones must be fitted. **Note:** *If the drier is to be left unconnected for more than one hour, plug the openings.*

23 Remove the right-hand front wheel arch liner as described in Chapter 11, Section 23.

24 Undo the clamp bolts and lower the receiver/drier from the clamp **(see illustration)**.

Compressor

25 Have the air conditioning refrigerant discharged by a BMW dealer or suitably-equipped specialist.

26 Firmly apply the handbrake, then jack up the front of the car and support it on axle stands. Undo the bolts and remove the engine undershield.

27 Remove the auxiliary drivebelt as described in Chapter 1.

28 On N42 and N46 engines, remove the air cleaner housing as described in Chapter 4A.

29 On 6-cylinder engines, undo the two retaining bolts, and move the windscreen washer reservoir to one side.

30 On all models, disconnect the compressor wiring plug **(see illustration)**.

31 Undo the two bolts and disconnect the air conditioning pipes from the compressor **(see illustration)**. Discard the O-ring seals, new ones must be fitted.

32 Working underneath the vehicle, undo the three mounting bolts, and remove the compressor.

33 Refitting is a reversal of removal, noting the following points:

a) *Prior to refitting the compressor, it is essential that the correct amount of refrigerant oil is added – refer to your dealer for the correct amount and specification.*
b) *Always use new seals when reconnecting the refrigerant pipes.*
c) *Upon completion, have the refrigerant recharged by a BMW dealer or specialist.*

Pressure sensor

34 The pressure sensor is fitted to the top of the receiver/drier. Have the air conditioning refrigerant discharged by a BMW dealer or suitably-equipped specialist.

35 Disconnect the sensor wiring plug, and unscrew the sensor.

36 Refitting is a reversal of removal, tighten the sensor securely, and have the refrigerant recharged by a BMW dealer or specialist.

Condenser

37 Have the air conditioning refrigerant discharged by a BMW dealer or suitably-equipped specialist.

38 The condenser is located in front of the radiator. Remove the radiator as described in Section 3.

39 Undo the two bolts and disconnect the refrigerant pipes from the condenser **(see illustration)**. Discard the O-ring seals, new ones must be fitted.

40 Undo the two plastic bolts securing the condenser through the crosspanel. Lift the condenser up and disengage it from the mounting bracket **(see illustrations)**.

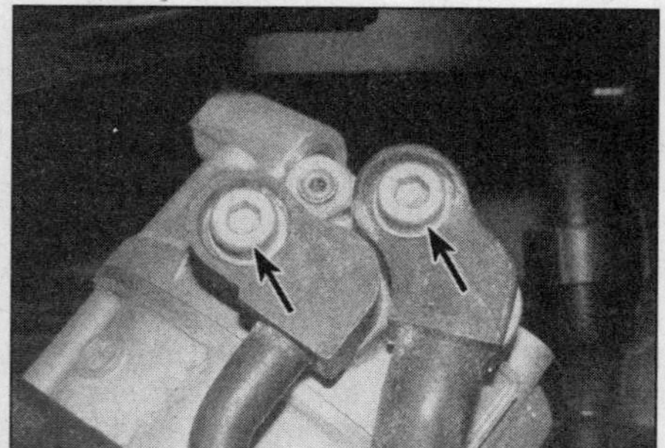

12.31 To disconnect the compressor pipes, undo the bolts (arrowed)

12.39 Undo the bolts and disconnect the refrigerant pipes

12.40a Undo the two plastic bolts . . .

12.40b . . . release the clips and lift out the condenser

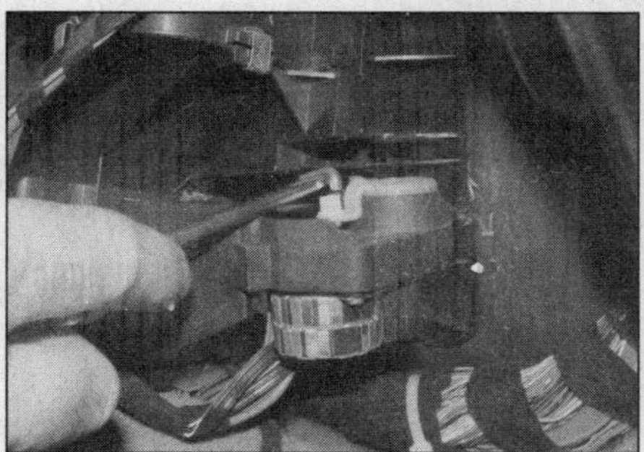

12.43 Disconnect the linkage arm from the servo motor

12.44 Remove the blower limit switch bolts (arrowed)

41 Refitting is a reversal of removal, noting the following points:

a) *Prior to refitting the condenser it is essential that the correct amount of refrigerant oil is added – refer to your dealer for the correct amount and specification.*
b) *Always use new seals when reconnecting the refrigerant pipes.*
c) *Upon completion, have the refrigerant recharged by a BMW dealer or specialist.*

Blower limit switch

42 Unclip the right-hand footwell air duct from the heater housing.

43 Carefully prise the linkage arm from the servo motor. Undo the two bolts (one above, one below) and remove the bracket and servo motor **(see illustration)**.

44 Disconnect the wiring plug, undo the two retaining bolts, push back the retaining clip and remove the blower limit switch **(see illustration)**.

45 Refitting is a reversal of removal.

Chapter 4 Part A:
Fuel and exhaust systems

Contents

Degrees of difficulty

Easy, suitable for novice with little experience 	**Fairly easy,** suitable for beginner with some experience	**Fairly difficult,** suitable for competent DIY mechanic	**Difficult,** suitable for experienced DIY mechanic	**Very difficult,** suitable for expert DIY or professional 

Specifications

Engine codes

4-cylinder engines

1796 cc engines	N42 B18 and N46 B18
1895 cc engines	M43TU B19
1995 cc engines	N42 B20 and N46 B20

6-cylinder engines

2171 cc engines	M54 B22
2494 cc engines	M52TU B25 and M54 B25
2793 cc engines	M52TU B28
2979 cc engines	M54 B30

System type

N42 and N46 engines	DME (Digital Motor Electronics) ME9 engine management
M43TU engine	DME (Digital Motor Electronics) BMS46 engine management
M52TU engine	DME (Digital Motor Electronics) MS42 engine management
M54 engine	DME (Digital Motor Electronics) MS43 engine management

Fuel system data

Fuel pump type	Electric, immersed in tank
Fuel pressure regulator rating	3.0 ± 0.06 bar
Specified idle speed:	
N42 engine	700 ± 50 rpm (not adjustable – controlled by ECM)
N46 engine	No information availabe
M43TU engine	800 ± 50 rpm (not adjustable – controlled by ECM)
M52TU engine	750 ± 50 rpm (not adjustable – controlled by ECM)
M54 engine	No information available
Specified idle mixture CO content	Not adjustable – controlled by ECM

Torque wrench settings

	Nm	lbf ft
Camshaft position sensor bolt	7	5
Coolant temperature sensor	13	10
Crankshaft position sensor bolt	10	7
Exhaust manifold nuts:*		
M6 nuts	10	7
M7 nuts	20	15
M8 nuts	22	16
Front axle reinforcement plate bolts:*		
Stage 1	59	44
Stage 2	Angle-tighten a further 90°	
Fuel rail-to-inlet manifold bolts	10	7
Fuel tank mounting bolts	23	17
Fuel tank retaining strap bolts	8	6
Inlet manifold nuts:		
M6 nuts	10	7
M7 nuts	15	11
M8 nuts	22	16

** Do not re-use*

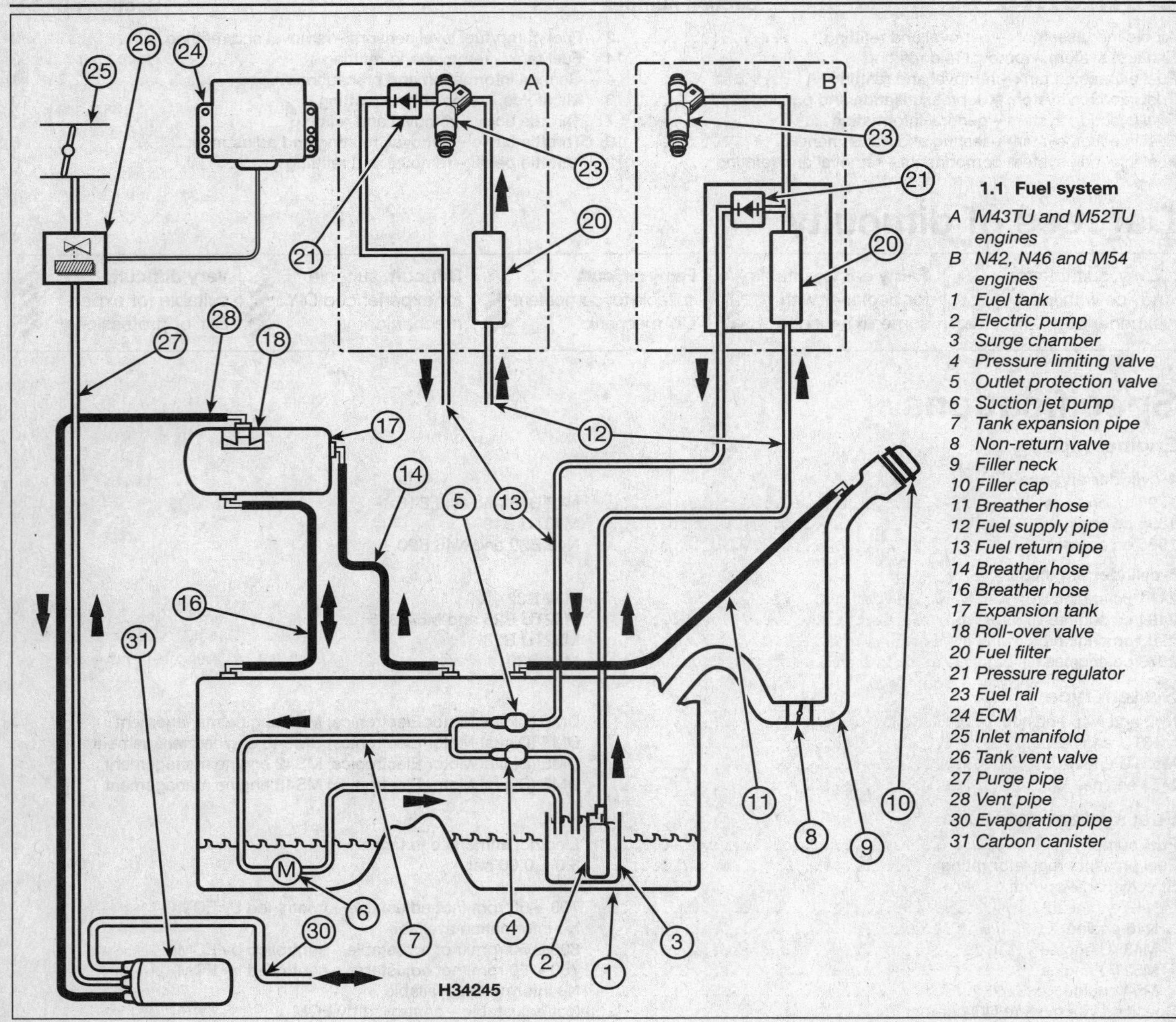

1.1 Fuel system

A M43TU and M52TU engines
B N42, N46 and M54 engines
1 Fuel tank
2 Electric pump
3 Surge chamber
4 Pressure limiting valve
5 Outlet protection valve
6 Suction jet pump
7 Tank expansion pipe
8 Non-return valve
9 Filler neck
10 Filler cap
11 Breather hose
12 Fuel supply pipe
13 Fuel return pipe
14 Breather hose
16 Breather hose
17 Expansion tank
18 Roll-over valve
20 Fuel filter
21 Pressure regulator
23 Fuel rail
24 ECM
25 Inlet manifold
26 Tank vent valve
27 Purge pipe
28 Vent pipe
30 Evaporation pipe
31 Carbon canister

1 General information and precautions

The fuel supply system consists of a fuel tank (which is mounted under the rear of the vehicle, with an electric fuel pump immersed in it), a fuel filter, fuel feed and return lines. The fuel pump supplies fuel to the fuel rail, which acts as a reservoir for the four fuel injectors which inject fuel into the inlet tracts. The fuel filter incorporated in the feed line from the pump to the fuel rail ensures that the fuel supplied to the injectors is clean. On M43TU and M52TU engines a fuel pressure regulator is fitted to the fuel injection rail, where the fuel then returns to the tank. On N42, N46 and M54 engines the pressure regulator is incorporated into the fuel filter assembly **(see illustration)**.

Refer to Section 7 for further information on the operation of the fuel injection system, and to Section 14 for information on the exhaust.

Warning: Many of the procedures in this Chapter required the disconnection of fuel lines and connections, which may result in some fuel spillage. Before carrying out any operation on the fuel system, refer to the precautions given in 'Safety first!', and follow then implicitly. Petrol is a highly dangerous and volatile liquid, and the precautions necessary when handling it cannot be overstressed.

Warning: Residual pressure will remain in the fuel lines long after the vehicle was last used. When disconnecting any fuel line, first depressurise the fuel system as described in Section 8.

2 Air cleaner assembly – removal and refitting

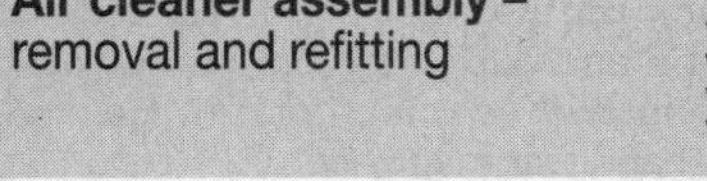

Removal

N42 and N46 engines

1 Lever out the expansion rivets, lift the air inlet hood approximately 5 cm, and pull it from the air cleaner housing and windscreen washer reservoir. Remove it from the vehicle.

2.2 Undo the two nuts (arrowed) and pull the cover forward

2 Undo the two nuts, and pull the front edge of the plastic cover on the top of the engine forward and remove it **(see illustration)**.

3 Release the inlet hose clamp from the throttle body, disconnect the vacuum hose (N42 engines only), and undo the two bolts securing the housing to the inner wing **(see illustration)**.

4 Lift the housing up and out, disconnecting the wiring plug and the hose from the throttle body as the housing is removed.

M43TU engines

5 Disconnect the wiring plug, squeeze together the sides of the retaining collar and disconnect the fuel tank vent hose from the vent valve on the side of the air cleaner housing **(see illustration)**.

6 Rotate the vent valve 90° anti-clockwise whilst pulling it up, and remove it from the bracket on the housing.

7 Where fitted, undo the nut and bolt, then remove the cruise control actuator from the left-hand inner wing.

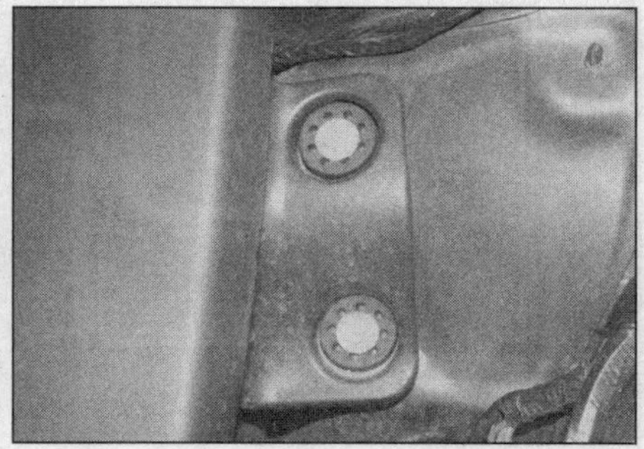

2.3 Undo the air filter housing bolts

8 Release the housing-to-airflow meter retaining clips, undo the retaining bolt, unclip the air inlet neck, and remove the air cleaner housing from the engine compartment **(see illustrations)**. Recover the sealing ring.

M52TU and M54 engines

9 Release the engine wiring harness from the retaining bracket on the air cleaner housing.

10 Release the two clips and disconnect the inlet hose from the top section of the housing.

11 Unscrew the two retaining bolts and remove the air cleaner housing from the engine compartment, disengaging it from the inlet ducting as it is withdrawn **(see illustration)**.

Refitting

12 Refitting is a reversal of removal, but ensure that the lower mounting engages with the plastic lug on the body **(see illustration)**,

2.5 Squeeze together the sides of the locking collar and disconnect the hose from the vent valve

2.8a Undo the retaining bolt (arrowed) . . .

2.8b . . . and remove the air cleaner housing

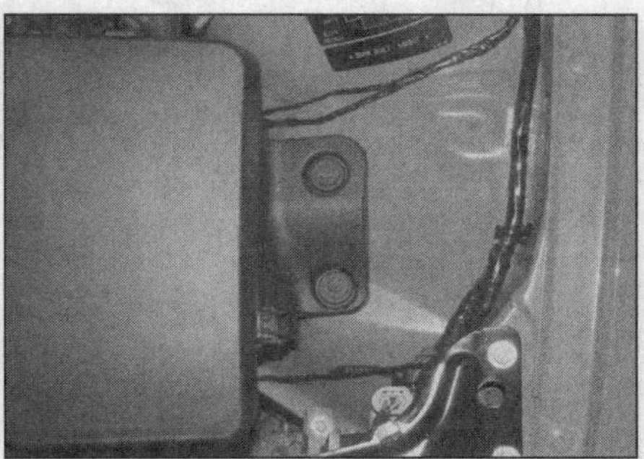

2.11 Air cleaner housing bolts – 6-cylinder models

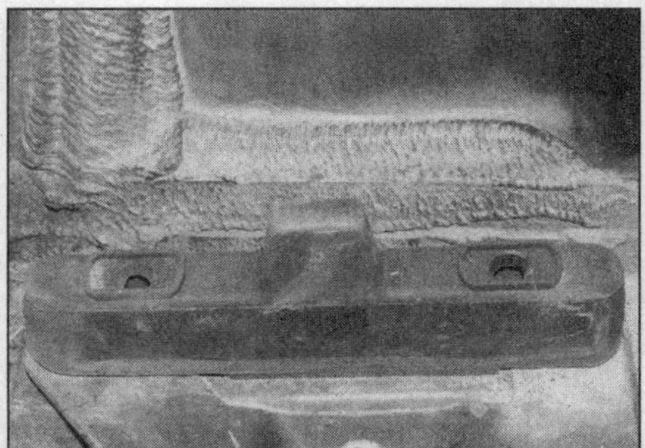

2.12 The air cleaner housing is located on a plastic mounting bolted to the inner wing

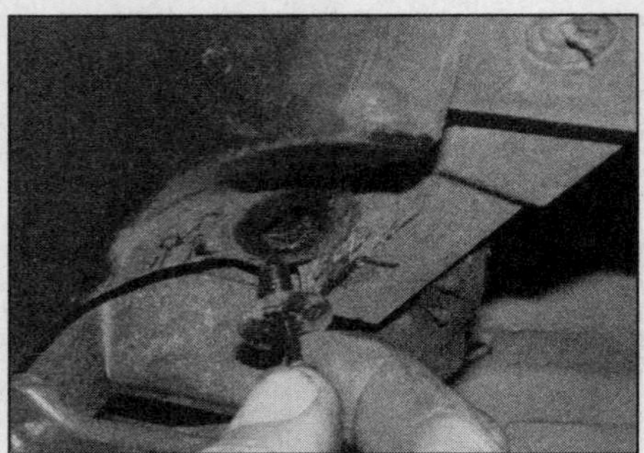

3.6a Prise up the centre pins, remove the rivets . . .

3.6b . . . and remove the trim panels from either side of the fuel tank

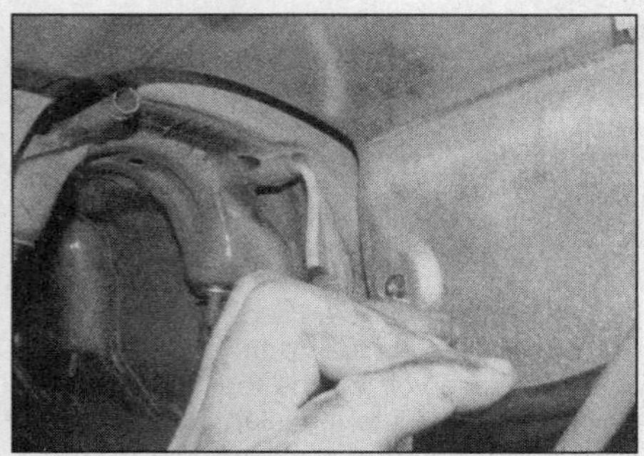

3.7 Pull the handbrake cables from the guide tubes

and where a rubber seal is fitted between the inlet hose and the housing, apply a little acid-free grease to the seal to ease refitting.

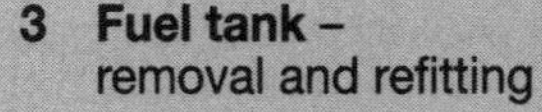

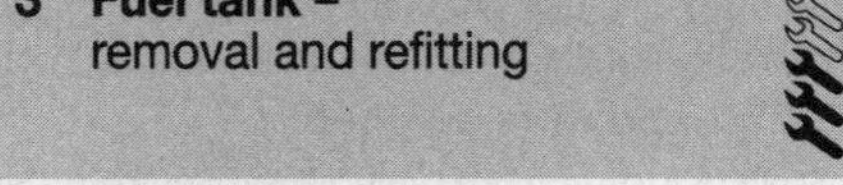

3 Fuel tank – removal and refitting

Removal

1 Disconnect the battery negative lead as described in Chapter 5A.

2 Before removing the fuel tank, all fuel should be drained from the tank. Since a fuel tank drain plug is not provided, it is preferable to carry out the removal operation when the tank is nearly empty.

3 Jack up the rear of the vehicle, and support it securely on axle stands (see *Jacking and vehicle support*).

4 Detach the handbrake cables from the handbrake lever as described in Chapter 9.

5 Remove the propeller shaft as described in Chapter 8.

6 Working under the vehicle, prise up the centre pins and remove the plastic expansion rivets, then remove the trim panel from under the left-hand side of the tank and the sill trim **(see illustrations)**. Repeat this procedure on the right-hand side of the tank.

7 Pull the handbrake cables from the guide tubes **(see illustration)**.

8 Mark them to aid refitment, then release the clips and disconnect the fuel supply and return hoses **(see illustration)**. Be prepared for fuel spillage, and clamp or plug the open ends of the hoses and pipes to prevent dirt entry and further fuel spillage.

9 Slacken the hose clip, then disconnect the fuel filler hose from the tank neck **(see illustration)**.

10 Support the fuel tank using a trolley jack and an interposed block of wood.

11 Undo the retaining bolt in the centre, rear of the tank, and the bolts securing the tank retaining straps **(see illustration)**.

12 Lower the tank slightly, note their fitted positions then disconnect the wiring plug(s).

13 Release the clamp and disconnect the breather hose from the tank **(see illustration)**. Lower the tank, and manoeuvre it from under the vehicle.

Refitting

14 Refitting is a reversal of removal. Note that once the tank is refitted, at least 5 litres of fuel must be added to allow the fuel system to function correctly.

4 Fuel expansion tank – removal and refitting

Removal

1 Jack up the right-hand rear side of the vehicle and support it on axle stands (see *Jacking and vehicle support*). Remove the right-hand rear roadwheel.

2 Undo the plastic nuts/bolts/expansion rivets and remove the right-hand rear wheel arch liner as described in Chapter 11, Section 23.

3 Undo the retaining nut, disconnect the lower hose, and pull the bottom of the tank forward **(see illustration)**.

4 Note their fitted positions, then release the clips and disconnect the remaining two

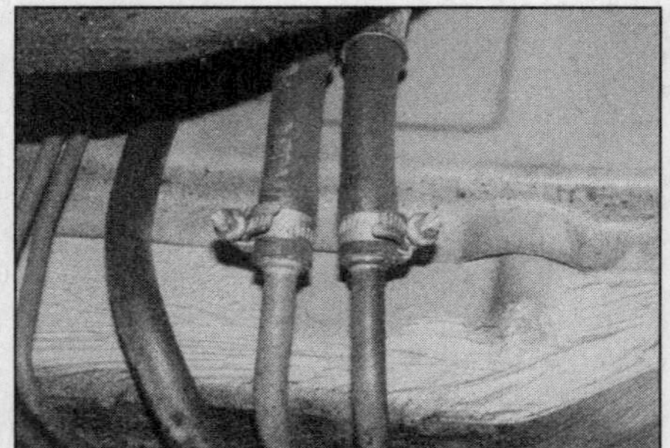

3.8 Disconnect the fuel supply and return hoses

3.9 Slacken the clamp and disconnect the fuel filler hose

3.11 Remove the fuel tank centre bolt

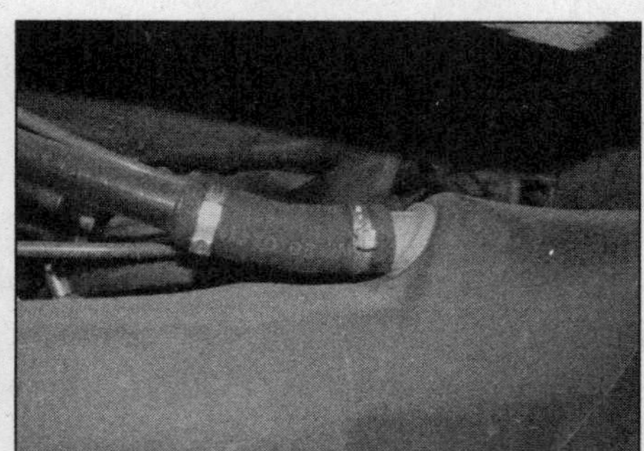

3.13 Disconnect the tank breather pipe

4.3 Undo the expansion tank retaining nut (arrowed)

5.1 Undo the bolts and remove the cover

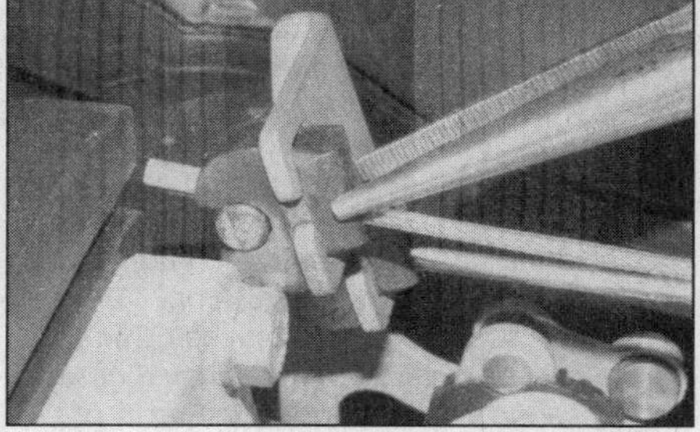

5.2 Squeeze together the sides of the grommet and push it out from the throttle lever

5.3 Pull the outer cable, then the grommet, from the supporting bracket

breather hoses from the tank. Remove the tank.

Refitting

5 Refitting is a reversal of removal.

5 Throttle cable – removal, refitting and adjustment

Removal

1 Undo the two bolts, and remove the plastic cover from the top of the throttle body **(see illustration)**.

2 Use a pair of pliers to squeeze together the sides of the end fitting grommet, slide the grommet from the throttle lever and feed the cable through the slot in the lever **(see illustration)**.

3 Pull the cable outer and the rubber grommet from the supporting bracket **(see illustration)**.

4 Working inside the vehicle, release the retaining clips/bolts, and withdraw the driver's side lower facia panel (see Chapter 11).

5 Disengage the inner throttle cable from the top of the throttle operating lever **(see illustration)**.

6 Working under the facia, squeeze together the two retaining clips, and push the cable outer end fitting from the mounting in the bulkhead **(see illustration)**.

7 Note the correct routing, then free the cable from any retaining clips/grommets and manoeuvre it from the engine compartment.

Refitting

8 Refitting is a reversal of removal, ensuring that the cable is routed as before. Carry out the adjustment procedure as follows.

Adjustment

9 In order to accurately adjust the throttle cable, access to specialised BMW diagnostic equipment is required to establish the throttle potentiometer position expressed as a percentage. However, the basic position for manual transmission models can be established as follows, providing the setting is checked by a BMW dealer or suitably-equipped specialist afterwards. **Note:** *On automatic transmission models, have the cable adjusted by a BMW dealer or suitably-equipped specialist.*

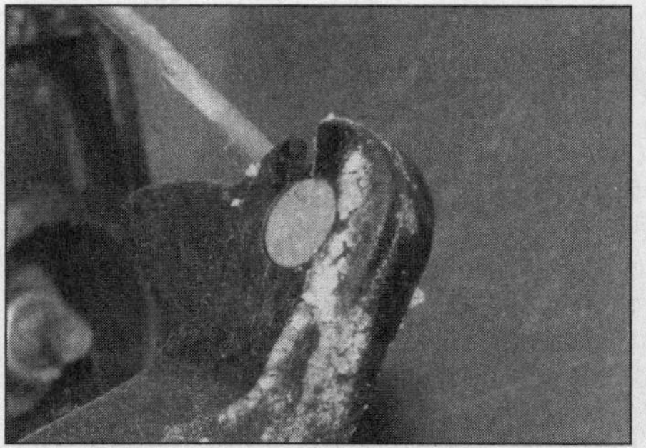

5.5 Disengage the throttle cable nipple from the lever

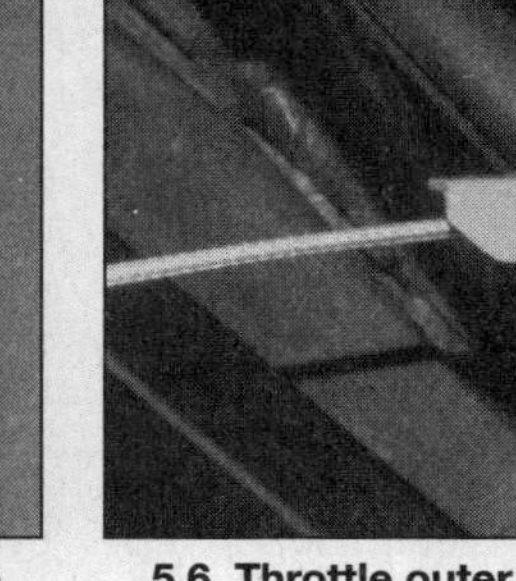

5.6 Throttle outer cable retaining clips (arrowed)

10 Check that the accelerator pedal and throttle quadrant are in the idle position.

11 Rotate the knurled cable adjustment sleeve on the outer cable to eliminate free play in the cable.

12 Screw the sleeve a quarter of a turn to allow a little free play in the cable.

13 Have an assistant fully depress the accelerator pedal, and check that there is still 0.5 mm of free play at the throttle valve in the throttle body.

14 If necessary, turn the pedal full-throttle stop (screwed into the floor) to give the correct amount of free play. On some models, it will be necessary to slacken a locknut before the stop can be adjusted.

6 Throttle pedal – removal and refitting

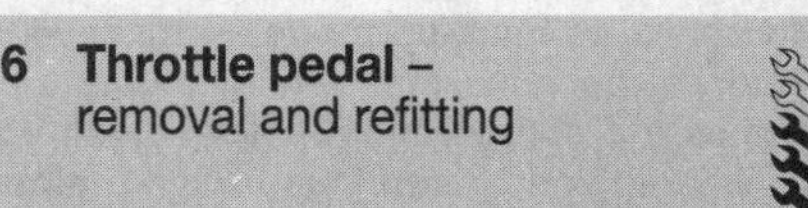

Warning: Once the throttle pedal has been removed, it MUST be renewed. Removal will damage the pedal retaining clips, and if the original pedal is refitted, it could work loose, causing an accident.

Models with throttle cable

1 Press down on the carpet under the pedal, then bend back the lower pedal retaining clips, and lever the pedal upwards to release it from the floor **(see illustration)**. Manoeuvre the pedal and free it from the throttle cable operating lever. Discard the pedal – a new one must used on refitting.

2 Engage the new pedal with the throttle cable operating lever.

3 Push the pedal down to engage the lower retaining clips with the floor plate. Ensure that the clips snap securely into place.

4 Check the throttle cable adjustment as described in Section 5.

Models with electronic throttle

5 Using a flat-bladed screwdriver, depress the retaining clip and slide the pedal assembly towards the centre of the cabin **(see illustration)**. Disconnect the wiring plug as the assembly is withdrawn.

6 To fit, reconnect the wiring plug and slide the assembly into the mounting, ensuring that it is correctly located. When correctly located, two 'clicks' should be heard as the clips engage,

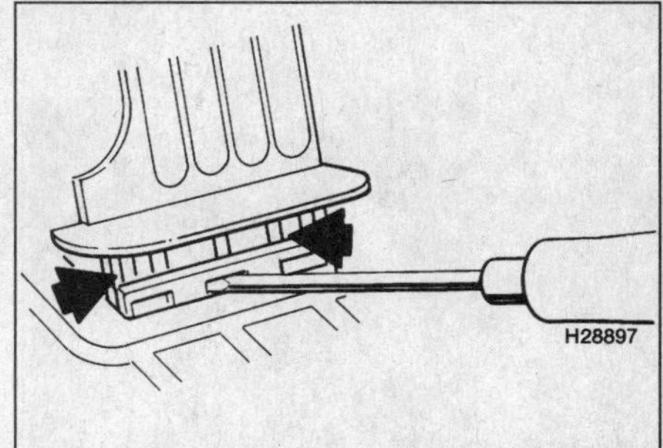

6.1 Release the throttle pedal from the floor

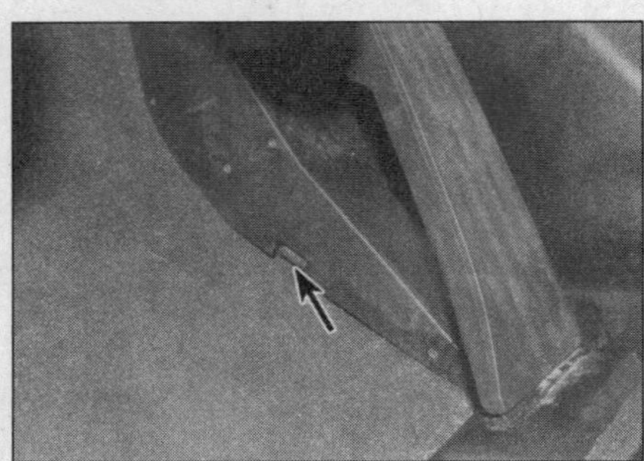
6.5 Depress the clip (arrowed), and slide the pedal assembly towards the centre of the cabin

and the right-hand side of the assembly is flush with the side of the mounting.

7 Fuel injection system – general information

1 An integrated engine management system known as DME (Digital Motor Electronics) is fitted to all models, and the system controls all fuel injection and ignition system functions using a central ECM (Electronic Control Module).

2 On all models, the system incorporates a closed-loop catalytic converter and an evaporative emission control system, and complies with the very latest emission control standards. Refer to Chapter 5B for information on the ignition side of the system; the fuel side of the system operates as follows.

3 The fuel pump (which is immersed in the fuel tank) supplies fuel from the tank to the fuel rail, via a filter. Fuel pressure is controlled by the pressure regulator in the fuel rail on M43TU and M52TU engines, and integral with the fuel filter on N42, N46 and M54 engines. When the optimum operating pressure of the fuel system is exceeded, the regulator allows excess fuel to return to the tank.

4 The electrical control system consists of the ECM, along with the following sensors:

a) *Hot film air mass meter – informs the ECM of the quantity and temperature of air entering the engine.*
b) *Throttle position sensor (M43TU engine) – informs the ECM of the throttle position, and the rate of throttle opening/closing.*
c) *Coolant temperature sensor(s) – informs the ECM of engine temperature.*
d) *Crankshaft position sensor – informs the ECM of the crankshaft position and speed of rotation.*
e) *Camshaft position sensor(s) – informs the ECM of the camshaft(s) position.*
f) *Oxygen sensor(s) – informs the ECM of the oxygen content of the exhaust gases (explained in greater detail in Part B of this Chapter).*
g) *Vehicle speed sensor – informs the ECM of the vehicle's roadspeed.*
h) *Inlet air temperature sensor – informs the ECM of the temperature of the air entering the engine (M52TU and M54 engines).*
i) *Oil temperature – informs the ECM of the engine oil temperature.*

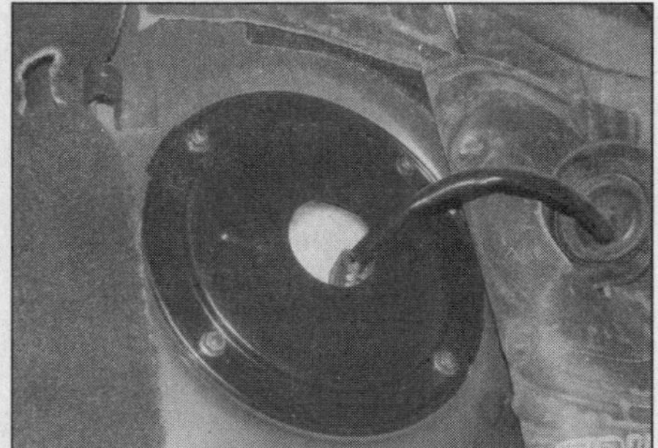
9.5 Undo the four nuts and remove the access cover

5 All the above signals are analysed by the ECM which selects the fuelling response appropriate to those values. The ECM controls the fuel injectors (varying the pulse width – the length of time the injectors are held open – to provide a richer or weaker mixture, as appropriate). The mixture is constantly varied by the ECM to provide the best setting for cranking, starting (with a hot or cold engine), warm-up, idle, cruising and acceleration.

6 The ECM also has full control over the engine idle speed, via an auxiliary air valve which bypasses the throttle valve. When the throttle valve is closed, the ECM controls the opening of the valve, which in turn regulates the amount of air entering the manifold, and so controls the idle speed.

7 The ECM controls the exhaust and evaporative emission control systems, which are described in Part B of this Chapter.

8 On all engines, a Differential Air Inlet System (DISA) is fitted. Variable length inlet tracts incorporated in the inlet manifold are operated by a butterfly valve according to engine speed and load. This improves the engine's torque at low and medium engine speeds. The butterfly valve is operated by a vacuum actuator fitted under the manifold.

9 If there is an abnormality in any of the readings obtained from the sensors, the ECM enters its back-up mode. In this event, it ignores the abnormal sensor signal and assumes a preprogrammed value which will allow the engine to continue running (albeit at reduced efficiency). If the ECM enters this back-up mode, the relevant fault code will be stored in the ECM memory.

10 If a fault is suspected, the vehicle should be taken to a BMW dealer at the earliest opportunity. A complete test of the engine management system can then be carried out, using a special electronic diagnostic test unit which is simply plugged into the system's diagnostic connector. The 16-pin OBD socket is located under the facia on the driver's side, whilst the BMW diagnostic socket (not fitted to all models) is located in the right-hand corner of the engine compartment or under the facia on the driver's side **(see illustrations 10.2a and 10.2b)**.

8 Fuel injection system – depressurisation and priming

Depressurisation

1 Remove the fuel pump fuse from the fusebox. The fuse is located in the main fusebox in the passenger glovebox, and the exact location is given on the fusebox cover (see Chapter 12).

2 Start the engine, and wait for it to stall. Switch off the ignition.

3 Remove the fuel filler cap.

4 The fuel system is now depressurised. **Note:** *Place a wad of rag around fuel lines before disconnecting, to prevent any residual fuel from spilling onto the engine.*

5 Disconnect the battery negative lead before working on any part of the fuel system (see Chapter 5A).

Priming

6 Refit the fuel pump fuse, then switch on the ignition and wait for a few seconds for the fuel pump to run, building-up fuel pressure. Switch off the ignition unless the engine is to be started.

9 Fuel pump/fuel level sensors – removal and refitting

Removal

1 There are two level sensors fitted to the fuel tank – one in the left-hand side of the tank, and one in the right-hand side. The pump is integral with the right-hand side sensor, and at the time of writing can only be renewed as a complete unit.

Right-hand sensor/fuel pump

2 Before removing the fuel level sensor/pump, all fuel should be drained from the tank. Since a fuel tank drain plug is not provided, it is preferable to carry out the removal operation when the tank is nearly empty.

3 Remove the rear bench seat as described in Chapter 11.

4 Unclip the rubber wiring grommet, and fold back the rubber matting to expose the access cover.

5 Undo the four nuts, and remove the access cover from the floor **(see illustration)**.

6 Slide out the locking element to disconnect the wiring plug, then cut the original metal hose clamp from place using side-cutters (or similar) and disconnect the fuel hose **(see illustration)**. Be prepared for fuel spillage.

7 Unscrew the fuel pump/level sensor unit locking ring and remove it from the tank. Although a BMW tool 16 1 020 is available

9.6 Slide out the locking element (arrowed) to disconnect the plug, then snip the hose clip

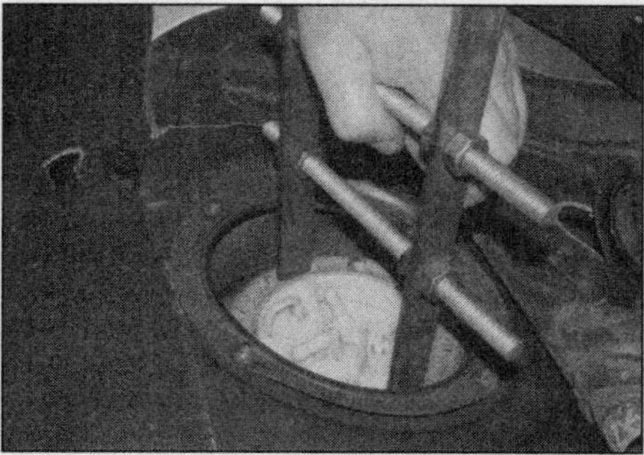

9.7 Using a home-made tool to undo the locking ring

9.8a Carefully lift the assembly from the fuel tank

9.8b Depress the clip, and remove the strainer from the base of the pump

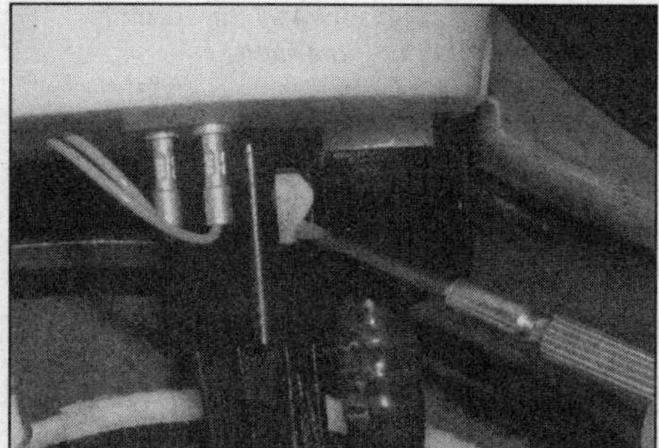

9.9 Press in the detent and disconnect the wiring plug

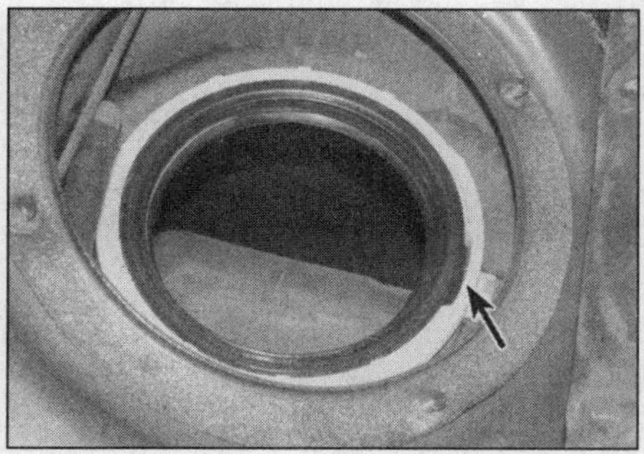

9.10 Note the slot in the fuel tank collar (arrowed)

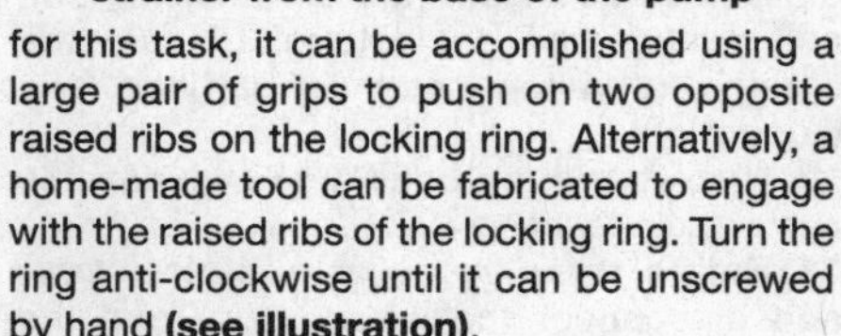

for this task, it can be accomplished using a large pair of grips to push on two opposite raised ribs on the locking ring. Alternatively, a home-made tool can be fabricated to engage with the raised ribs of the locking ring. Turn the ring anti-clockwise until it can be unscrewed by hand **(see illustration)**.

8 Carefully lift the fuel pump/level sensor unit from the tank, taking care not to bend the sensor float arm (gently push the float arm towards the unit if necessary). Recover the sealing ring. If necessary the strainer on the base of the pump can be unclipped for cleaning **(see illustrations)**, but no further dismantling is recommended.

Left-hand sensor

9 Removal of the left-hand sensor is almost identical to the right-hand sensor described previously, except that the wiring plug is clipped into place. When lifting out the sensor unit, depress the detent and disconnect the expansion tank pipe from the unit **(see illustration)**.

Refitting

10 Refitting is a reversal of removal, noting the following points:

a) Use a new sealing ring.

b) To allow the unit to pass through the aperture in the fuel tank, press the float arm against the fuel pick-up strainer.

c) When the unit is fitted, the locating lug on the unit must engage with the corresponding slot in the fuel tank collar ***(see illustration)****.*

d) Use a new hose clamp to secure the fuel hose.

10 Fuel injection system – testing and adjustment

Testing

1 If a fault appears in the fuel injection system, first ensure that all the system wiring connectors are securely connected and free of corrosion. Ensure that the fault is not due to poor maintenance; ie, check that the air cleaner filter element is clean, the spark plugs are in good condition and correctly gapped, the cylinder compression pressures are correct, and that the engine breather hoses are clear and undamaged, referring to the relevant Parts of Chapters 1, 2 and 5 for further information.

2 If these checks fail to reveal the cause of the problem, the vehicle should be taken to a BMW dealer or suitably-equipped specialist for testing. A wiring block connector is incorporated in the engine management circuit, into which a special electronic diagnostic tester can be plugged. The BMW diagnostic connector is clipped to the right-hand suspension turret on some models **(see illustration)**, whilst on others the OBD 16-pin socket is located above the pedals in the driver's footwell **(see illustration)**. The tester will locate the fault quickly and simply, alleviating the need to test all the system components individually, which is a time-consuming operation that also carries a risk of damaging the ECM.

Adjustment

3 Experienced home mechanics with a considerable amount of skill and equipment (including a tachometer and an accurately calibrated exhaust gas analyser) may be able

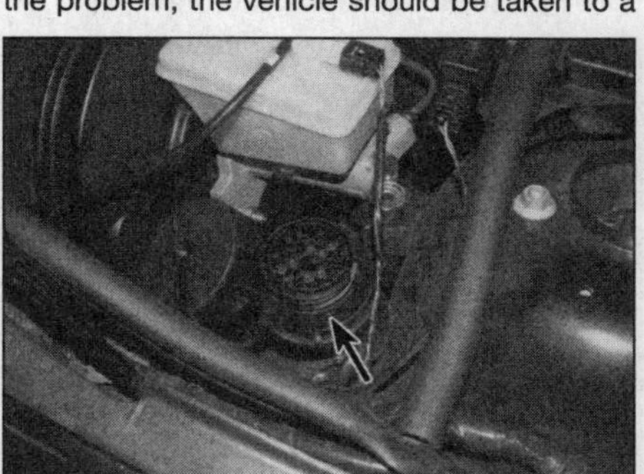

10.2a Unscrew the cap to expose the BMW diagnostic plug (arrowed)

10.2b The OBD 16-pin diagnostic socket is above the driver's pedals

11.3 Remove the support bracket bolt (arrowed)

11.6a Undo the throttle body mounting bolts (arrowed – 4th bolt hidden)

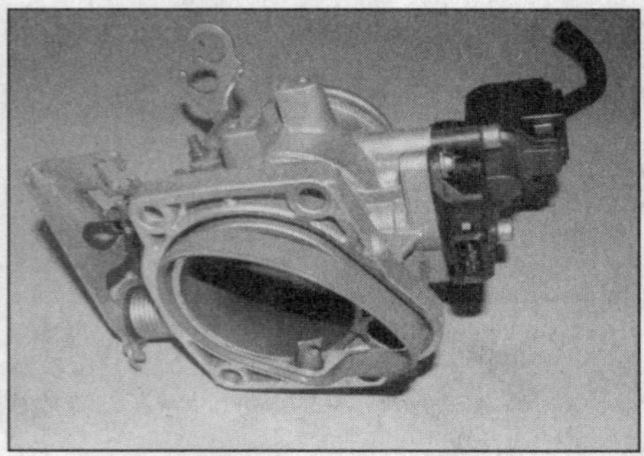
11.6b Renew the throttle body gasket

to check the exhaust CO level and the idle speed. However, if these are found to be in need of adjustment, the car must be taken to a BMW dealer or specialist for further testing.

11 Throttle body – removal and refitting

M43TU engines

Note: *New throttle body gasket will be required on refitting.*

Removal

1 Disconnect the battery negative lead (see Chapter 5A).

2 Remove the bolts, and lift the cover from the throttle body.

3 Undo the bolt securing the supporting bracket to the throttle body **(see illustration)**.

4 Disconnect the throttle position sensor and idle speed control valve wiring plugs.

5 Disconnect the throttle cable(s) from the throttle body and the cable support bracket **(see illustrations 5.2 and 5.3)**. Where applicable, disconnect the cruise control cable in the same manner.

6 Unscrew the four securing bolts, and withdraw the throttle body from the inlet manifold. Recover the gasket between the throttle body and inlet manifold **(see illustrations)**.

Refitting

7 Refitting is a reversal of removal, bearing in mind the following points.

a) Use new gasket between the throttle body and the inlet manifold.

b) Reconnect and if necessary adjust the throttle cable with reference to Section 5.

c) On completion, have a BMW dealer or specialist interrogate the engine management self-diagnosis fault memory, and delete any fault codes stored.

N42 and N46 engines

Removal

8 Remove the air cleaner housing as described in Section 2.

9 Disconnect the wiring plug, undo the four bolts and remove the throttle body **(see illustration)**.

Refitting

10 Examine the throttle body-to-inlet manifold O-ring seal. If it is good condition, it can be re-used. Refit the throttle body to the manifold, and tighten the four bolts securely.

11 Reconnect the wiring plug, and refit the air cleaner housing.

12 On completion, have a BMW dealer or specialist interrogate the engine management self-diagnosis fault memory, and delete any fault codes stored.

M52TU engines

Removal

13 Disconnect the battery negative lead as described in Chapter 5A.

14 Remove the air cleaner housing as described in Section 2.

15 Remove the mass airflow sensor and ducting as described in Section 12.

16 Disconnect the throttle cable(s) from the throttle quadrant and support bracket.

17 Release the retaining clips, and disconnect the air inlet ducting from the throttle body and the idle speed control valve.

18 Note their fitted locations, and disconnect any wiring plugs attached to the throttle body.

19 Disconnect the oil pressure and oil temperature switches wiring plugs adjacent to the oil filter housing.

20 Unclip the fuel pipes and fuel regulator vacuum hose (where fitted) from the retaining bracket on the oil dipstick guide tube.

21 Disconnect the oil return pipe from the dipstick guide tube, undo the retaining bolt and remove the guide tube. Discard the O-ring seal, a new one must be fitted **(see illustration)**.

22 Undo the three bolts/nuts securing the cable duct mounting.

23 Rotate the plug collar anti-clockwise, and disconnect the wiring plug from the throttle body (M52TU engines) or release the retaining clip and disconnect the wiring plug (M54 engines), undo the four bolts and remove the body from the inlet manifold **(see illustration)**.

Refitting

24 Examine the throttle body-to-inlet manifold O-ring seal. If it is good condition, it can be re-used. Refit the throttle body to the manifold, and tighten the four bolts securely.

25 Prior to reconnecting the throttle body wiring plug on M52TU engines, rotate the plug collar until the red locking pin is visible though the opening in the collar. Align the arrow on

11.9 Undo the throttle body mounting bolts (arrowed)

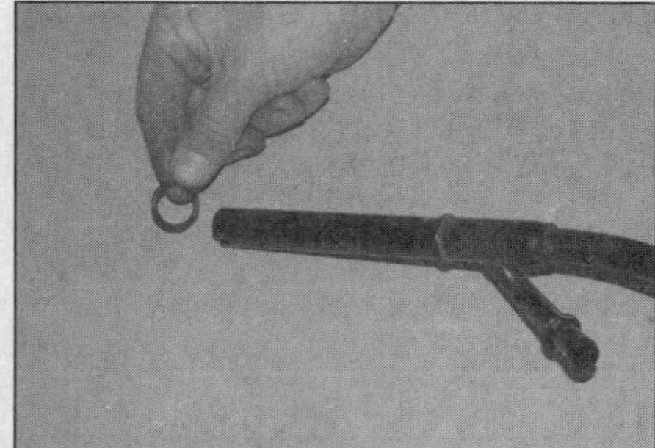
11.21 Discard the oil dipstick tube O-ring

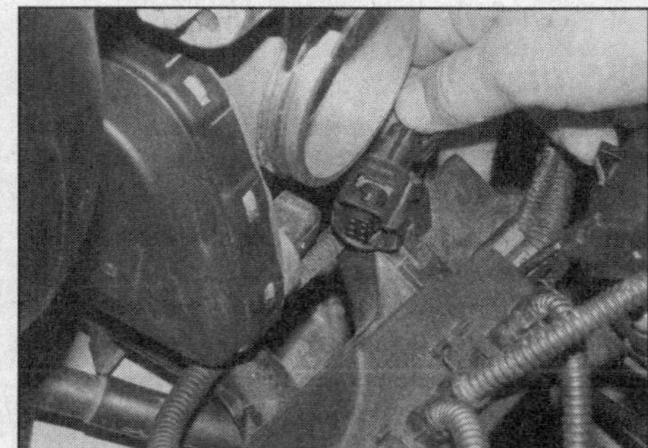
11.23 Disconnect the throttle body wiring plug (M54 engine shown)

the collar with the arrow on the throttle body terminal. Push the wiring plug on, rotating the collar clockwise until the second arrow on the collar aligns **(see illustration)**. On M54 engines, simply refit the wiring plug.

26 The remainder of refitting is a reversal of removal. Note that if a new throttle body has been fitted, the 'learnt adaption' values stored in the engine management ECM must be reset using dedicated test equipment. Have this carried out be a BMW dealer or suitably-equipped specialist.

M54 engines

Removal

27 Disconnect the battery negative lead as described in Chapter 5A.

28 Remove the air cleaner housing as described in Section 2.

29 Release the retaining clips, disconnect the wiring plug and vacuum hose, and remove air cleaner housing-to-connecting piece inlet ducting.

30 Disconnect the wiring plug, undo the two mounting Torx bolts, and remove the DISA adjustment unit from the inlet manifold **(see illustration)**.

31 Unscrew the bolt securing the suction jet tube to the inlet manifold **(see illustration)**.

32 Release the clamps, and disconnect the inlet ducting from the throttle body and idle speed control valve.

33 Disconnect the idle speed control valve wiring plug.

34 Disconnect the wiring plugs for the oil temperature and oil pressure switches adjacent to the oil filter housing.

35 Press in the retaining clip to unlock the wiring plug, and detach it from the tank venting valve **(see illustration)**.

36 Proceed as described in Paragraphs 20 to 23.

Refitting

37 Refitting is as described in Paragraphs 24 to 26.

12 Fuel injection system components – removal and refitting

Electronic control module

1 Disconnect the battery negative lead, as described in Chapter 5A. **Note:** *Disconnecting the battery will erase any fault codes stored in the ECM. It is recommended that the fault code memory of the module is interrogated using special test equipment prior to battery disconnection. Entrust this task to a BMW dealer or suitably-equipped specialist.*

2 Working in the left-hand corner of the engine compartment, undo the four bolts, and remove the cover from the electrical box **(see illustration)**.

3 Disconnect the module wiring plugs, and remove it from the box **(see illustrations)**.

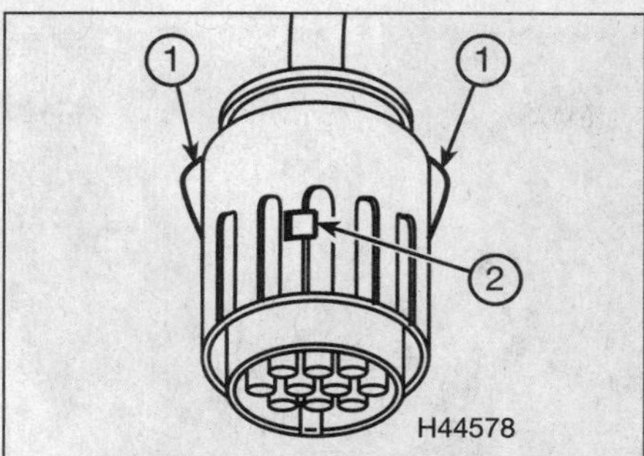

11.25 Wiring connector arrows (1) and opening (2)

11.31 Undo the bolt securing the suction jet tube (arrowed)

4 Refitting is a reversal of removal. **Note:** *If a new module has been fitted, it will need to be coded using special test equipment. Entrust this task to a BMW dealer or suitably-equipped specialist.* After reconnecting the battery, the vehicle must be driven for several miles so that the ECM can learn its basic settings. If the engine still runs erratically, the basic settings may be reinstated by an BMW dealer or specialist using special diagnostic equipment.

Fuel rail and injectors

Warning: Refer to the warning notes in Section 1 before proceeding.

5 Depressurise the fuel system as described in Section 8, then disconnect the battery negative lead (see Chapter 5A).

M43TU engines

Note: *New fuel injector O-rings should be used on refitting.*

12.3a Depress the tag . . .

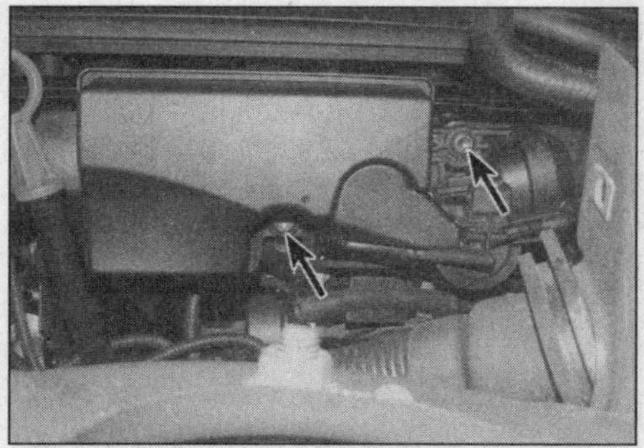

11.30 Undo the bolts (arrowed) and remove the DISA adjustment unit

11.35 Disconnect the tank vent valve wiring plug

6 Remove the upper section of the inlet manifold as described in Section 13.

7 Slacken the retaining clip and disconnect the fuel return pipe, then undo the union and disconnect the fuel supply pipe from the fuel

12.2 Undo the bolts and remove the electrical box cover

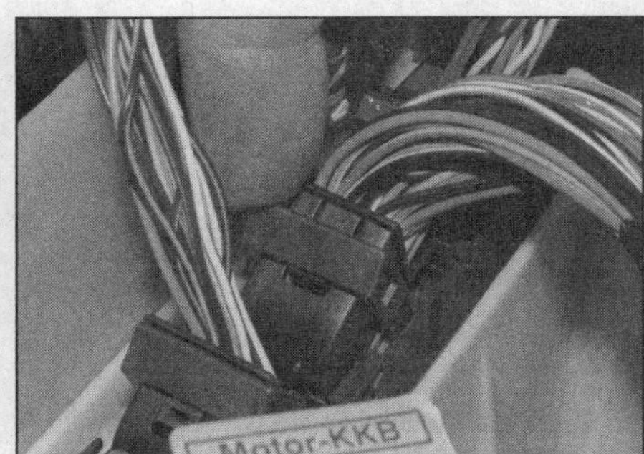

12.3b . . . and push the lever down to unlock the wiring plug

12.7a Disconnect the fuel supply and return pipes (arrowed)

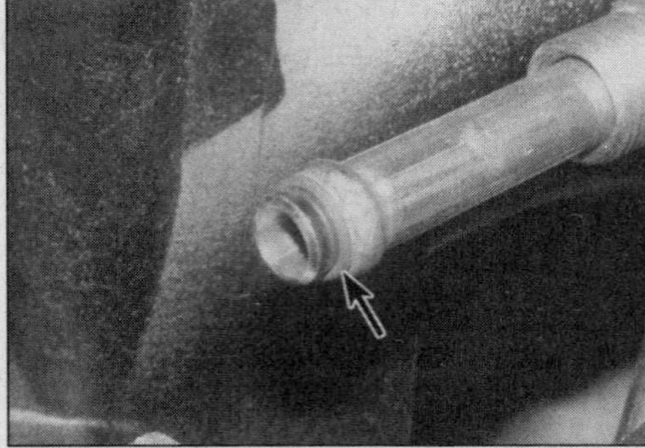
12.7b If damaged, renew the fuel supply pipe union O-ring seal (arrowed)

12.10 The fuel rail is secured by two bolts (arrowed)

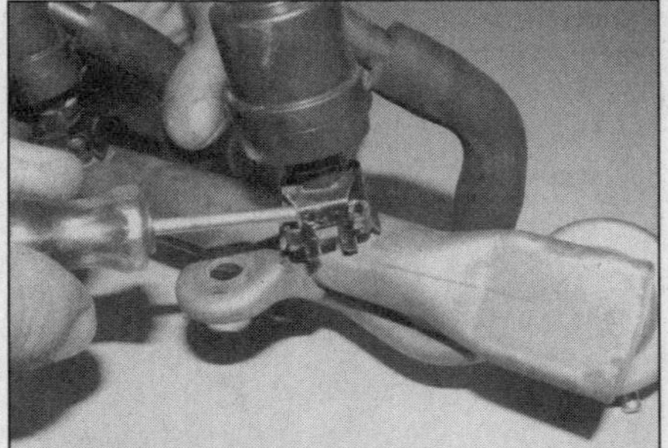
12.12 Prise out the clip and detach the injector from the fuel rail

12.13 Always renew the injector O-ring seals

rail **(see illustrations)**. Be prepared for fuel spillage, and take adequate fire precautions. Plug the open ends of the pipes and hoses to prevent dirt entry and further fuel spillage. Discard the fuel supply pipe union O-ring, a new one must be fitted.

8 Disconnect the vacuum hose from the fuel pressure regulator.

9 Disconnect the injector wiring plugs and release the wiring harness from the retaining clips.

10 Unscrew the two bolts securing the fuel rail to the inlet manifold **(see illustration)**.

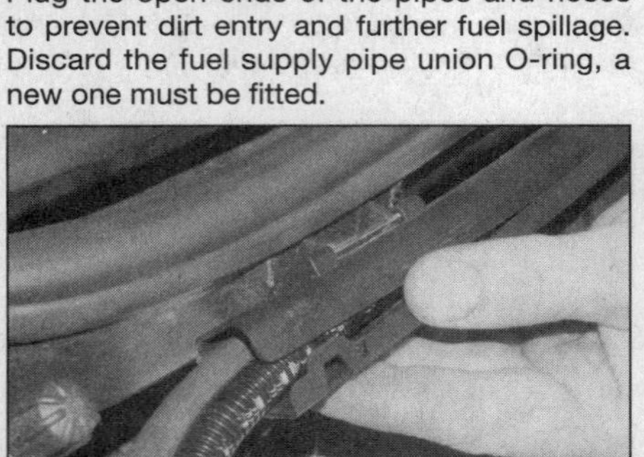
12.21 Unclip the cable ducting

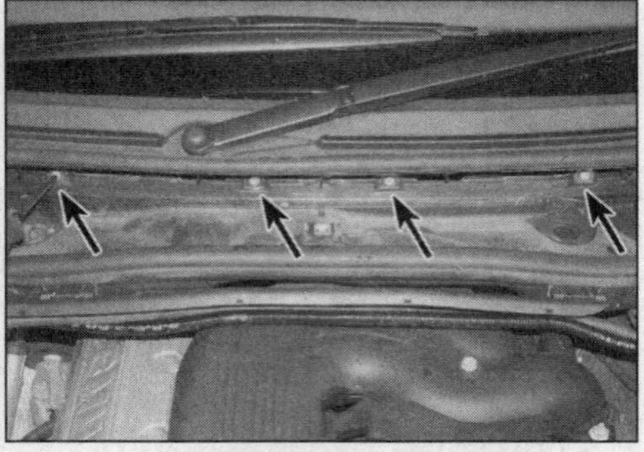
12.22 The pollen filter housing is secured by four bolts (arrowed)

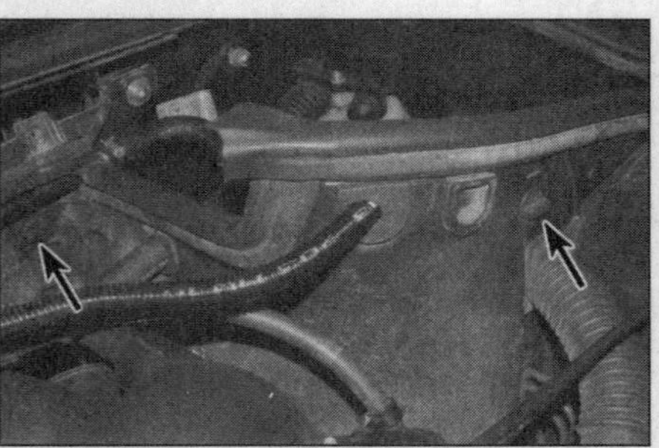
12.23 Pull up the sealing strip, undo the two fasteners (arrowed) and pull the panel forwards

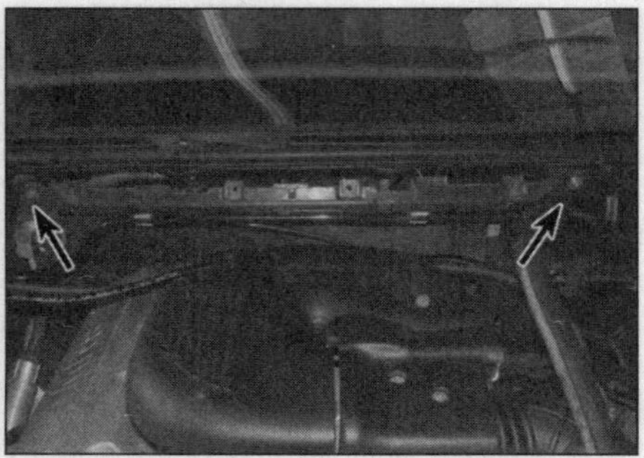
12.24 Undo the Torx bolts (arrowed) and remove the inlet housing

11 Carefully pull the fuel rail upwards to release the fuel injectors from the cylinder head, then withdraw the complete fuel rail/fuel injector assembly.

12 To remove a fuel injector from the fuel rail, proceed as follows.

a) Prise off the metal securing clip, using a screwdriver ***(see illustration)****.*

b) Pull the fuel injector from the fuel rail.

13 Before refitting, it is wise to renew all the fuel injector O-rings as a matter of course **(see illustration)**.

14 Check that the plastic washer at the bottom of each injector is positioned above the lower O-ring.

15 Lightly lubricate the fuel injector O-rings with a little petroleum jelly or SAE 90 gear oil.

16 Where applicable, refit the fuel injectors to the fuel rail, ensuring that the securing clips are correctly fitted. Note that the injectors should be positioned so that the wiring sockets are uppermost when the assembly is refitted.

17 Slide the fuel rail/fuel injector assembly into position, ensuring that the injectors engage with their bores in the inlet manifold.

18 Further refitting is a reversal of removal, but refit the upper section of the inlet manifold as described in Section 13, and pressurise the fuel system (refit the fuel pump fuse and switch on the ignition) and check for leaks before starting the engine.

N42 and N46 engines

19 Undo the two nuts, raise the front edge of the plastic cover on top of the engine, and pull it out towards the front.

20 Working at the rear of the engine compartment, turn the fasteners 90° anti-clockwise and remove the pollen filter cover. Slide the filter from the housing. If necessary, refer to Chapter 1.

21 Release the retaining clips, and remove the cable from the ducting on the air inlet housing **(see illustration)**.

22 Undo the four bolts and pull the pollen filter housing to the front **(see illustration)**.

23 In the left-hand rear corner of the engine compartment, pull up the sealing strip, undo the two fasteners and pull the trim panel forwards a little **(see illustration)**.

24 Undo the two Torx bolts, and lift out the heater inlet housing **(see illustration)**.

25 Press in the locking collar, and detach the fuel supply pipe from the fuel rail. Be prepared for fuel spillage, and take adequate fire precautions. Plug the open ends of the pipe and hose to prevent dirt entry and further fuel spillage **(see illustration).**

26 Unclip the cable, undo the two nuts securing the bracket to the cylinder head, then unscrew the two retaining bolts, and remove the fuel rail complete with injectors **(see illustration).**

27 Disconnect the injector wiring plugs, and if required, cut through the cable-ties to free the rail **(see illustration).**

28 Prise out the retaining clips and remove the injectors from the fuel rail **(see illustration).** Check the condition of the O-ring seals, and renew if necessary.

29 Lightly lubricate the fuel injector O-rings with a little petroleum jelly, or acid-free grease.

30 Refit the injectors to the fuel rail, and retain them in place with the clips pushed into the grooves.

31 Further refitting is a reversal of removal.

M52TU engines

32 Proceed as described in Paragraphs 20 to 24.

33 Prise out the plastic caps, undo the two bolts, and remove the plastic cover from the over the injectors **(see illustration 12.44).**

34 Disconnect the fuel regulator vacuum hose.

35 Disconnect the air inlet temperature sensor wiring plug, and pull the wiring rail from the fuel injectors.

36 Mark the two oxygen sensor wiring connectors to aid refitting, unplug them and release them from the retaining clips.

37 Label the fuel supply and return pipes, then disconnect the pipes at the quick-release connectors.

38 Undo the four bolts and remove the fuel rail complete with the injectors **(see illustration 12.48).**

39 To remove a fuel injector from the fuel rail, proceed as follows.

a) Prise off the metal securing clip, using a screwdriver.

b) Pull the fuel injector from the fuel rail.

40 Lightly lubricate the fuel injector O-rings with a little petroleum jelly, or acid-free grease.

41 Refit the injectors to the fuel rail, and retain them in place with the clips pushed into the grooves.

42 Further refitting is a reversal of removal.

M54 engines

43 Proceed as described in Paragraphs 20 to 24.

44 Prise out the plastic caps, undo the two bolts, and remove the plastic cover from over the injectors **(see illustration).**

45 Mark the two oxygen sensor wiring connectors to aid refitting, unplug them and release them from the retaining clips.

46 Disconnect the air inlet temperature sensor wiring plug and the VANOS solenoid wiring plug, and release the retaining clips and pull the wiring rail from the fuel injectors **(see illustrations).**

47 Disconnect the fuel supply pipe at the quick-release connector **(see illustration).**

48 Undo the four bolts and remove the fuel rail complete with the injectors **(see illustration).**

49 To remove a fuel injector from the fuel rail, proceed as follows.

a) Prise off the metal securing clip, using a screwdriver.

12.25 Depress the collar and disconnect the fuel supply hose

12.26 Undo the two bolts (arrowed) and remove the fuel rail complete with injectors

12.27 Disconnect the injector wiring plugs (arrowed)

12.28 Prise out the clip and remove the injector from the rail

12.44 Undo the bolts and remove the plastic cover from the injectors

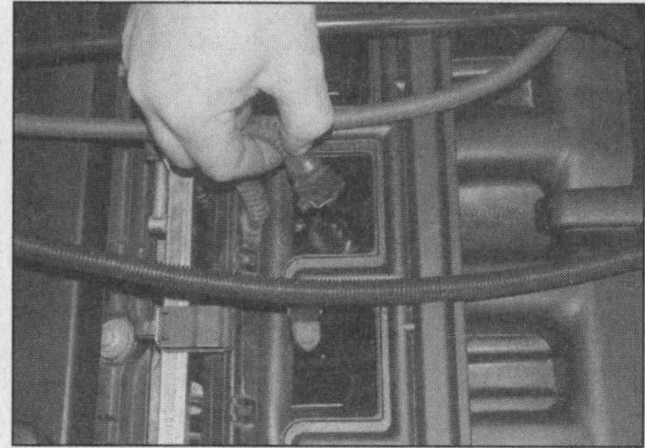

12.46a Disconnect the air inlet temperature sensor . . .

12.46b . . . and the VANOS solenoid . . .

12.46c . . . then release the wiring rail plugs clips

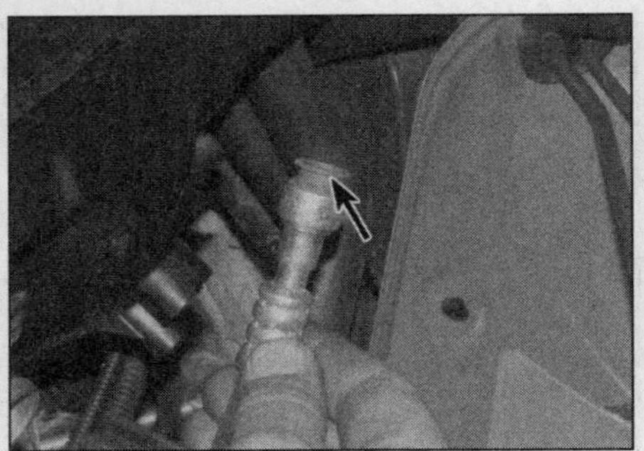

12.47 Depress the collar (arrowed) and disconnect the fuel supply hose

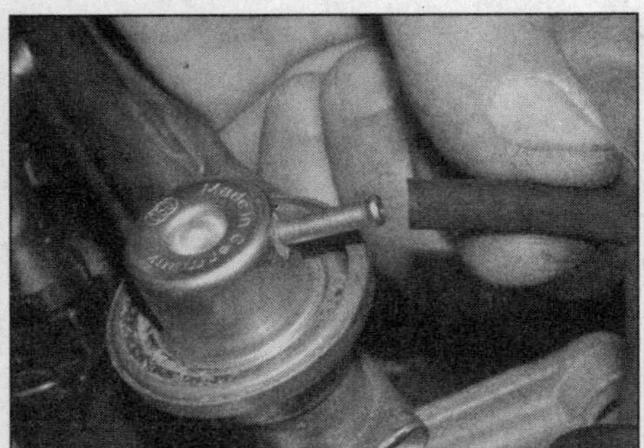

12.54 Pull the vacuum hose from the fuel pressure regulator

b) Pull the fuel injector from the fuel rail.

50 Lightly lubricate the fuel injector O-rings with a little petroleum jelly, or acid-free grease.

51 Refit the injectors to the fuel rail, and retain them in place with the clips pushed into the grooves.

52 Further refitting is a reversal of removal.

Fuel pressure regulator

Warning: Refer to the warning notes in Section 1 before proceeding.

53 Depressurise the fuel system as described in Section 8, then disconnect the battery negative lead (see Chapter 5A).

M43TU engines

Note: *New O-rings may be required on refitting.*

54 Pull the vacuum hose from the pressure regulator **(see illustration)**.

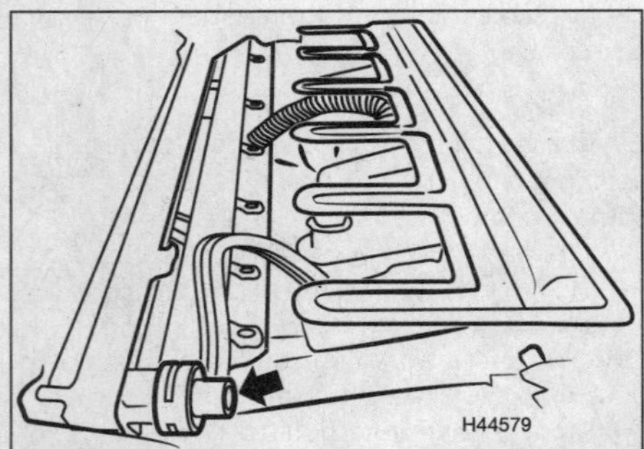

12.67 Pull the vacuum hose (arrowed) from the regulator

12.48 Undo the bolts (arrowed) and remove the fuel rail

12.61 Check the condition of the O-rings (arrowed)

55 Where applicable, to improve access, disconnect the breather hose from the front of the cylinder head cover.

56 Note the angle of the vacuum inlet on the pressure regulator, so that it can be refitted in the same position.

57 Where applicable, to give sufficient clearance to remove the pressure regulator, unscrew the engine lifting bracket from the cylinder head.

58 On models where the regulator is secured by a clamping bracket retained by a nut, unscrew the securing nut and withdraw the clamping bracket.

59 On models where the regulator is secured by a locking clip, pull out the clip.

60 Twist and pull the regulator from the fuel rail. Note that it will be difficult to pull the regulator from the fuel rail due to the tight-fitting O-rings.

61 Before refitting, check the O-rings, and renew if necessary **(see illustration)**.

12.73 Squeeze together the sides of the wiring plug and disconnect the airflow sensor

62 Refitting is a reversal of removal.

N42 and N46 engines

63 On these engines, the regulator is integral with the fuel filter assembly.

64 If defective, renew the complete filter housing.

M52TU engines

65 To allow sufficient clearance, remove the heater/ventilation inlet air ducting from the rear of the engine compartment as follows.

a) Rotate the three fasteners 90° anti-clockwise and remove the pollen filter cover from the rear of the engine compartment. Pull the filter forward and remove it.

b) Undo the four retaining clips and thread the cable out of the ducting ***(see illustration 12.21).***

c) Unscrew the four bolts and pull the filter housing forwards and remove it.

d) Undo the two bolts and remove the inlet ducting upwards and out of the engine compartment ***(see illustration 12.24).***

66 Prise up the two caps, undo the bolts and remove the plastic cover from above the fuel rail.

67 Pull the vacuum hose from the fuel regulator **(see illustration)**.

68 Remove the circlip, twist and pull the regulator from the fuel rail.

69 Before refitting, check the O-rings, and renew if necessary **(see illustration 12.61)**.

70 Refitting is a reversal of removal, bearing in mind the following points.

a) Ensure that the regulator is pushed firmly into position in the end of the fuel rail.

b) Make sure that the circlip correctly engages with the recess in the fuel rail..

c) On completion, pressurise the fuel system (refit the fuel pump fuse and switch on the ignition) and check for leaks before starting the engine.

M54 engines

71 On these engines, the regulator is integral with the fuel filter assembly. If defective, renew the complete filter housing.

Mass airflow sensor

M43TU engines

Note: *A new airflow sensor seal may be required on refitting.*

72 Disconnect the battery negative lead (see Chapter 5A).

73 Disconnect the wiring plug from the airflow sensor **(see illustration)**.

74 Loosen the hose clip, and disconnect the air ducting from the airflow sensor.

75 Release the clips, and remove the sensor from the air cleaner housing. Recover the seal.

76 Refitting is a reversal of removal, but check the condition of the seal and renew if necessary.

N42 and N46 engines

77 Remove the air cleaner housing as described in Section 2.

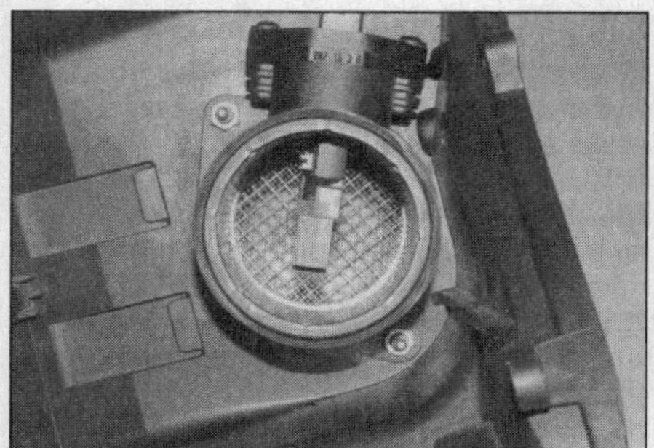

12.79 Undo the two nuts and remove the mass airflow sensor

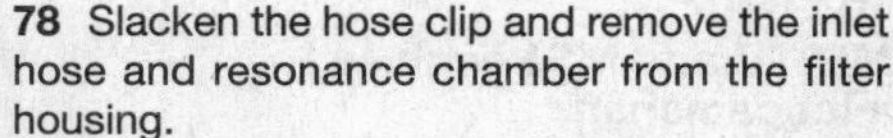

78 Slacken the hose clip and remove the inlet hose and resonance chamber from the filter housing.

79 Undo the two nuts, and remove the sensor from the filter housing **(see illustration)**.

80 Refitting is a reversal of removal.

M52TU engines

Note: *A new airflow sensor seal may be required on refitting.*

81 Ensure the ignition is turned off, and disconnect the wiring plug from the sensor **(see illustration 12.84)**.

82 Pull the vacuum hose from the inlet ducting, release the retaining clips, and remove the sensor complete with the inlet ducting. Recover the seal.

83 Refitting is a reversal of removal, but check the condition of the seal and renew if necessary.

M54 engines

Note: *A new airflow sensor seal may be required on refitting.*

84 Ensure the ignition is turned off, and disconnect the wiring plug from the sensor **(see illustration)**.

85 Release the retaining clips and detach the inlet ducting from the sensor, and the sensor from the air cleaner housing. Recover the seal.

86 Refitting is a reversal of removal, but check the condition of the seal and renew if necessary.

Throttle position sensor

M43TU engines

Note: *A new O-ring may be required on refitting.*

87 Ensure the ignition is turned off.

88 Disconnect the wiring plug from the sensor **(see illustration)**.

89 Unscrew the two securing bolts, and withdraw the sensor from the throttle body. Where applicable, recover the O-ring

90 Refitting is a reversal of removal, but where applicable, check the condition of the O-ring and renew if necessary, and ensure that the O-ring is correctly positioned. Note that adjustment of the unit is not necessary.

N42 and N46 engines

91 On these engines, although the throttle

12.84 Mass airflow sensor

body valve is not used to control engine load, it is used to provide inlet manifold vacuum for purging the carbon canister, etc. The throttle positioning motor is integral with the throttle body. Remove the throttle body as described in Section 11. The accelerator pedal position sensor is integral with the accelerator pedal. Remove the pedal as described in Section 6.

M52TU and M54 engines

92 The throttle position sensor is integral with the throttle body. Remove the throttle body as described in Section 11.

93 Refitting is a reversal of removal. Note that if a new throttle body/position sensor has been fitted, it will be necessary to clear the adaption values stored in the engine management ECM using specialist test equipment. Entrust this task to a BMW dealer or suitably-equipped specialist. Once cleared, new adaption values will be 'learnt' as the engine is started and used.

Coolant temperature sensor

M43TU engines

94 The sensor is located in the left-hand side of the cylinder head. Partially drain the cooling system as described in Chapter 1, and remove the upper section of the inlet manifold as described in Section 13.

95 Unscrew the sensor from the cylinder head.

96 Refitting is a reversal of removal. Tighten the sensor to the specified torque, and top-up the coolant as described in Chapter 1.

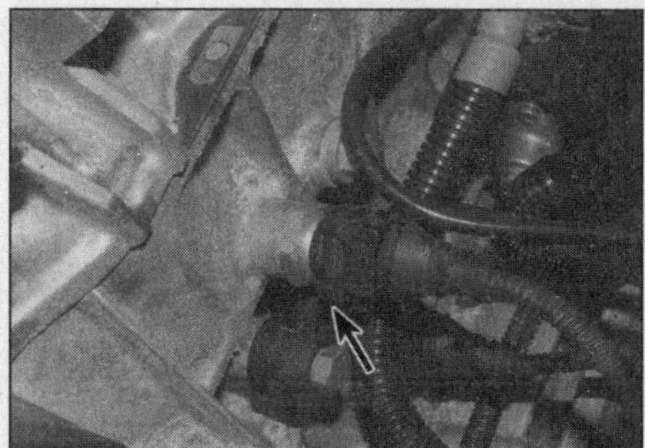

12.99 Coolant temperature sensor (arrowed – inlet manifold removed for clarity)

12.88 Throttle position sensor

N42 and N46 engines

97 The sensor is located in the left-hand side of the cylinder block. Partially drain the cooling system as described in Chapter 1.

98 Remove the alternator as described in Chapter 5A.

99 Disconnect the wiring plug and unscrew the sensor from the cylinder block **(see illustration)**.

100 Refitting is a reversal of removal. Tighten the sensor to the specified torque, and top-up the coolant as described in Chapter 1.

M52TU and M54 engines

101 The sensor is located in the left-hand side of the cylinder head under the inlet manifold. Partially drain the cooling system as described in Chapter 1, and remove the inlet manifold, as described in Section 13.

102 Disconnect the sensor wiring plug, and unscrew it from the cylinder head.

103 Refitting is a reversal of removal. Tighten the sensor to the specified torque, and top-up the coolant as described in Chapter 1.

Crankshaft position sensor

M43TU engines

104 Jack up the front of the vehicle and support it securely on axle stands (see *Jacking and vehicle support*). Undo the bolts and remove the engine undershield.

105 The sensor is located below the starter motor. Disconnect the sensor wiring plug, undo the retaining bolt and remove the sensor. Recover the seal.

106 Refitting is a reversal of removal. Check the condition of the seal and renew if necessary.

N42 and N46 engines

107 The sensor is located below the starter motor. Remove the inlet manifold as described in Section 13.

108 Disconnect the sensor wiring plug, undo the retaining bolt and remove the sensor **(see illustration)**. Recover the seal.

109 Check the condition of the sealing ring and renew if necessary. Refit the sensor and tighten the retaining bolt to the specified torque.

110 The remainder of refitting is a reversal of removal.

12.108 Crankshaft position sensor (arrowed) is located below the starter motor

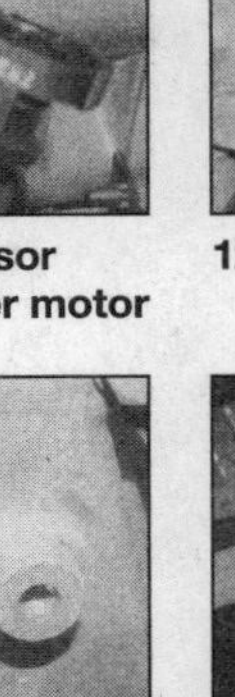

12.119 Remove the camshaft position sensor retaining bolt (arrowed)

M52TU engines

111 Proceed as described in Paragraphs 104 to 106.

M54 engines

112 Jack up the front of the vehicle and support it securely on axle stands (see *Jacking and vehicle support*). Undo the bolts and remove the engine undershield.

113 Undo the bolts and remove the reinforcement plate from between the lower control arms. Note that new bolts will be needed upon refitting.

114 The sensor is located under the starter motor. Disconnect the sensor wiring plug, undo the retaining bolt and remove the sensor. Recover the seal.

115 Refitting is a reversal of removal, but use new bolts when refitting the front axle reinforcement plate.

12.118 Undo the bolts (arrowed) and remove the secondary air injection solenoid valve

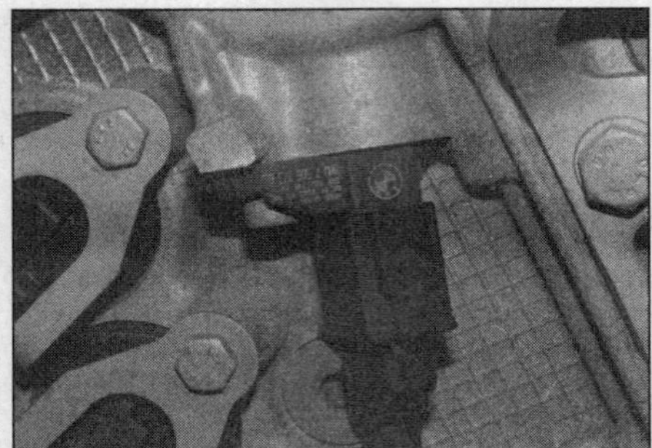

12.125 Disconnect the camshaft position sensor wiring plug

Camshaft position sensor(s)

M43TU engines

116 The sensor is located in the front of the upper timing chain cover.

117 Ensure the ignition is switched off, and disconnect the sensor wiring plug.

118 To improve access, unscrew the solenoid valve and bracket, then move it to one side **(see illustration)**.

119 Undo the retaining bolt and remove the sensor from the engine **(see illustration)**. Recover the seal.

120 Check the condition of the sealing ring, and renew if necessary.

121 Refit the sensor to the engine, and tighten the retaining bolt securely.

122 The remainder of refitting is a reversal of removal.

N42 and N46 engines

123 The sensors are located in the front side of the cylinder head, under their respective camshaft ends. Ensure the ignition is switched off.

124 Prise out the two expanding rivets, and remove the air inlet hood from the bonnet slam panel.

125 Squeeze together the locking lugs, and disconnect the sensor wiring plug **(see illustration)**.

126 Undo the retaining bolt and remove the sensor. Recover the seal.

127 Refitting is a reversal of removal. Check the condition of the seal and renew it if necessary.

M52TU and M54 engines – inlet camshaft

128 Ensure the ignition is turned off, and remove the air cleaner housing as described in Section 2.

129 Disconnect the wiring plug, then unscrew the VANOS solenoid valve to access the sensor **(see illustration)**.

130 Trace the wiring back from the sensor, and disconnect the wiring plug where it clips to the cable ducting behind the alternator.

131 Undo the retaining bolt and remove the sensor from the cylinder head **(see illustration)**. Recover the seal.

M52TU and M54 engines – exhaust camshaft

132 Ensure the ignition is switched off.

133 Disconnect the sensor wiring plug, undo the retaining bolt and remove the sensor **(see illustration)**. Recover the seal.

134 Refitting is a reversal of removal. Check the condition of the seal and renew it if necessary.

Oxygen sensor

135 Refer to Chapter 4B.

Idle speed control valve

M43TU engines

136 The valve is mounted on the side of the throttle body **(see illustration)**.

137 Ensure the ignition is switched off.

138 Disconnect the wiring plug from the valve.

12.129 Unscrew the VANOS solenoid

12.131 Undo the bolt and remove the camshaft position sensor

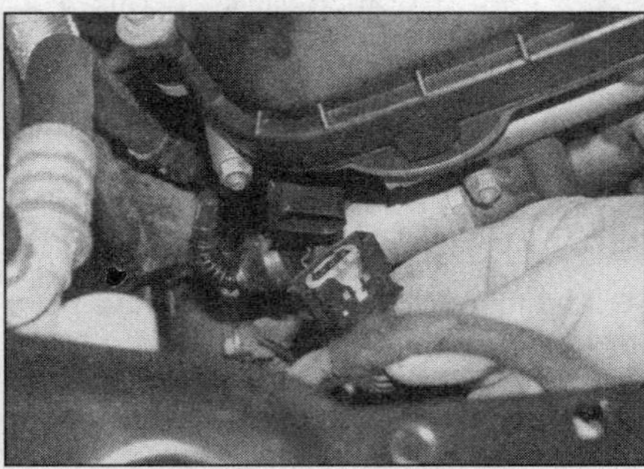

12.133 Disconnect the exhaust camshaft sensor wiring plug

139 Disconnect the vacuum hose from the valve.
140 Remove the two securing bolts, and withdraw the valve from the throttle body. Recover the seal.
141 Refitting is a reversal of removal, but clean the sealing face of the valve, and check the condition of the seal. Renew the seal if necessary.

N42 and N46 engines

142 On these engines, the idle speed is regulated by the lift and duration of the inlet valves, controlled by the engine management ECM.

M52TU and M54 engines

143 Disconnect the battery negative lead as described in Chapter 5A.
144 The idle speed control valve is located below the inlet manifold, and above the throttle body.
145 Remove the air cleaner housing as described in Section 2.
146 Pull the throttle cable outer (where fitted) from the support bracket on the throttle body.
147 Undo the two clamps and disconnect the inlet ducting from the throttle body and idle speed control valve.
148 Disconnect the wiring plugs from the idle speed control valve and the manifold resonance flap actuator solenoid valve.
149 Undo the nut securing the cable support bracket, and the two bolts securing the idle speed control valve bracket. Manoeuvre the valve from the manifold **(see illustration)**. Discard the seal between the valve and the manifold, a new one must be fitted.
150 Smear the new seal with grease and fit it to the inlet manifold. Push the idle speed control valve into place and securely tighten the bracket retaining bolts/nuts.
151 The remainder of refitting is a reversal of removal.

Fuel pump relay

152 Disconnect the battery negative lead as described in Chapter 5A.
153 Remove the passenger side glovebox, as described in Chapter 11, Section 27.
154 Insert a flat-bladed screwdriver into the slot in the end of the glovebox light and carefully prise it from place. Disconnect the wiring plug as the light is withdrawn.
155 Undo the five bolts, release the expanding rivet and remove the glovebox frame from the facia (see Chapter 11 if necessary).
156 Undo the locking levers, and disconnect the wiring plugs from the general control module **(see illustration)**.
157 Pull the fuel pump relay from the relay plate **(see illustration)**.
158 Refitting is a reversal of removal.

Main engine management relay

159 Ensure the ignition is switched off.
160 Working in the left-hand corner of the engine compartment, undo the four bolts, and remove the cover from the electrical box **(see illustration 12.2)**.

12.136 Idle speed control motor

12.149 Idle speed control motor mounting bolts (arrowed)

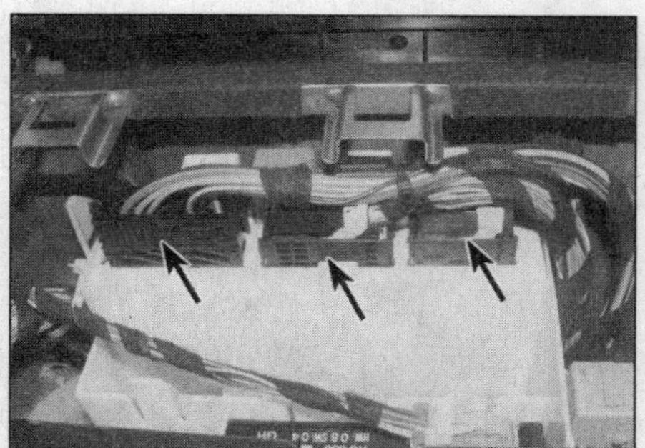

12.156 Disconnect the general control module wiring plugs (arrowed)

12.157 Fuel pump relay (arrowed)

161 Pull the relay from the relay socket **(see illustration)**.
162 Refitting is a reversal of removal.

Throttle pedal position sensor

N42 and N46 engines

163 The throttle pedal position sensor is integral with the pedal assembly. Refer to Section 6 for the removal procedure.

Inlet manifold differential pressure sensor

164 Ensure the ignition is switched off, undo the two nuts, lift the front edge, and pull the plastic engine cover to the front and remove it.
165 Disconnect the wiring plug, undo the bolts and remove the sensor from the manifold **(see illustration)**.
166 Refitting is a reversal of removal.

13 Manifolds – removal and refitting

Inlet manifold upper section

M43TU engines

Note: *A new manifold gasket and new pressure control valve seals will be required on refitting.*
1 Ensure the ignition is switched off.
2 To allow sufficient clearance, remove the heater/ventilation inlet air ducting from the rear of the engine compartment as follows.
- *a) Rotate the three fasteners 90° anti-clockwise and remove the pollen filter cover from the rear of the engine compartment. Pull the filter forward and remove it.*

12.161 Engine management relay (arrowed)

12.165 Undo the two bolts and remove the differential pressure sensor

13.5a Remove the two bolts at the front of the manifold (arrowed) . . .

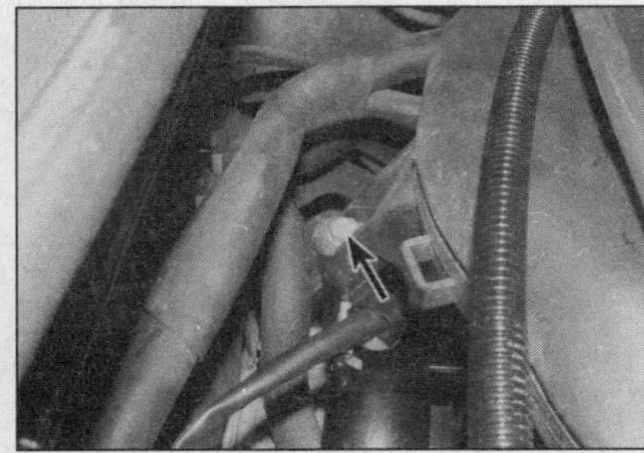

13.5b . . . and the one at the rear (arrowed)

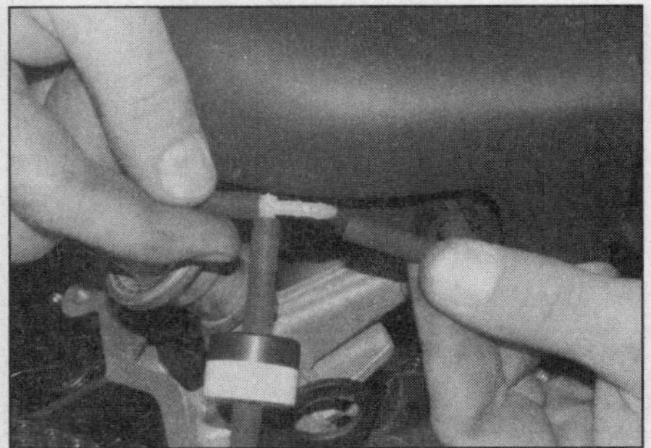

13.6 Disconnect the vacuum hose at the front of the manifold

13.9 Remove the upper section of the manifold

- *b) Undo the four retaining clips and thread the cable out of the ducting **(see illustration 12.21)**.*
- *c) Unscrew the four bolts and pull the filter housing forwards and remove it **(see illustration 12.22)**.*

3 Disconnect the throttle cable from the throttle body as described in Section 5. Where fitted, use the same procedure to disconnect the cruise control cable from the throttle body lever.

4 Release the retaining clips, and remove the inlet ducting (complete with mass airflow sensor). Disconnect the sensor wiring plug and fuel rail vacuum hose as it is withdrawn.

5 Undo the two bolts securing the support bracket to the front of the manifold, and the bolt at the rear of the manifold **(see illustrations)**. At the front support bracket, release the wiring harness from the retaining clip.

6 Disconnect the vacuum hose from the front of the manifold **(see illustration)**.

7 Disconnect the throttle position sensor and idle speed control valve wiring plugs.

8 Slacken the retaining clip and disconnect the servo vacuum hose from the manifold.

9 Undo the bolts/nuts and lift off the upper section of the manifold **(see illustration)**. Recover the seals.

10 Refitting is a reversal of removal, bearing in mind the following points.

- *a) Use a new seals when refitting the upper section of the manifold.*
- *b) Ensure that all wires and hoses are correctly routed and reconnected as noted before removal.*
- *c) Reconnect and if necessary adjust the throttle cable with reference to Section 5.*

Inlet manifold lower section

M43TU engine

11 Depressurise the fuel system as described in Section 8.

12 Remove the upper section of the manifold as described previously in this Section.

13 Drain the cooling system as described in Chapter 1.

14 Remove the fuel injectors as described in Section 12.

15 Unscrew the bolt securing the dipstick tube support bracket to the manifold.

16 Release the engine wiring harness from the lower section of the manifold.

17 Unscrew and remove the manifold support bracket **(see illustration)**.

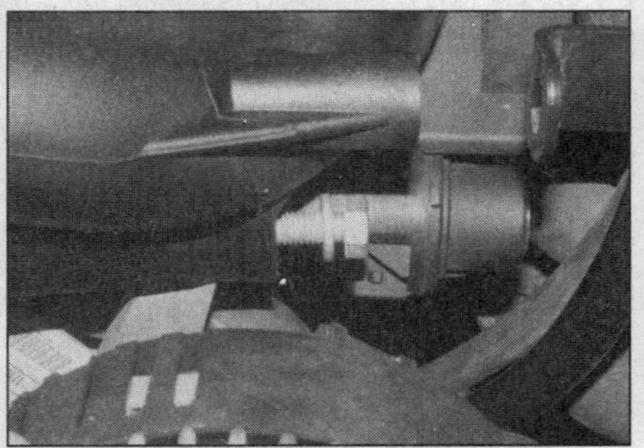

13.17 Unscrew and remove the manifold support bracket

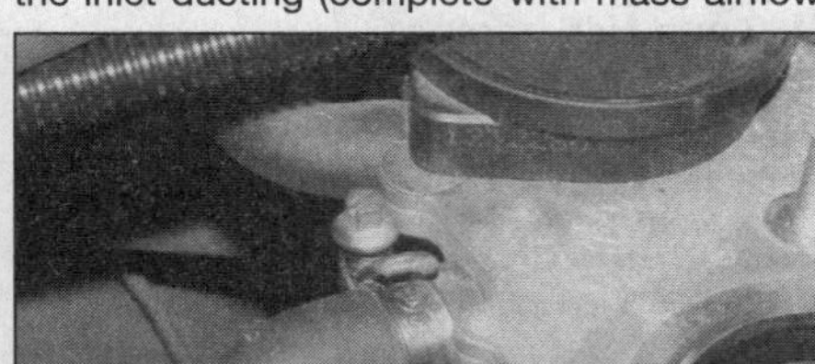

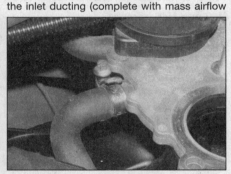

13.19 Disconnect the coolant hose from the manifold flange

18 Disconnect and release any remaining hoses and wiring looms/plugs from the manifold and sensors, noting their locations and routing to ensure correct refitting.

19 Disconnect the coolant hose from the manifold flange **(see illustration)**.

20 Unscrew the securing nuts, and lift the lower section of the manifold from the cylinder head. Recover the seals **(see illustration)**.

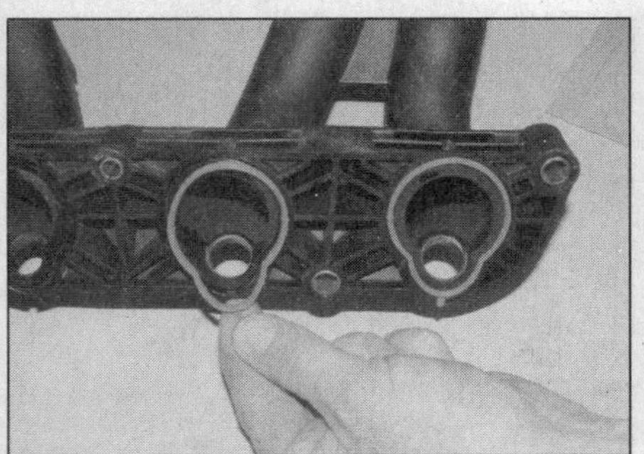

13.20 Recover the inlet manifold seals

13.21 Always renew the manifold seals

21 Refitting is a reversal of removal, bearing in mind the following points.

- *a) Use new seals when refitting the lower section of the manifold.*
- *b) Use new seals when refitting the upper section of the manifold **(see illustration)**.*
- *c) Ensure that all wiring looms/plugs and hoses are correctly routed and reconnected as noted before removal.*
- *d) Refit the fuel injectors (see Section 12).*
- *e) Refit the upper section of the manifold as described previously in this Section.*
- *f) On completion, pressurise the fuel system (refit the fuel pump fuse and switch on the ignition) and check for leaks before starting the engine.*

Inlet manifold

N42 and N46 engines

Note: *Access to the underside of the manifold is limited.*

22 Ensure the ignition is turned off, and remove the air cleaner housing as described in Section 2.

23 Remove the fuel rail and injectors as described in Section 12.

24 Rotate fasteners 90° anti-clockwise, and lift the compartment partition panel from the left-hand corner of the engine compartment. Pull the hoses/leads with the rubber grommets from the panel **(see illustration 12.23)**.

25 Note their fitted positions, then disconnect all wiring plugs from the throttle body/manifold, and release the wiring harness/cables from the retaining clips on the manifold. Unclip the battery positive lead from the oil dipstick guide tube.

26 Release the retaining clip and disconnect the fuel tank vent valve hose from the underside of the manifold.

27 Working underneath the manifold, undo the bolt securing the oil dipstick guide tube, then undo the two Torx bolts securing the support bracket to the manifold **(see illustration)**. The bolts are more easily accessed from below, except on air conditioned vehicles, where the front bolt is accessed from above.

28 Undo the bolt securing the coolant pipe support bracket to the cylinder block beneath the starter motor. This is to allow the metal coolant pipes at the rear of the manifold to move to the rear, facilitating manifold removal.

29 Disconnect the vent hose from the top of the manifold **(see illustration)**.

30 Undo the two nuts securing the oil separator to the underside of the manifold **(see illustration)**.

31 Undo the five bolts, then lift the manifold from the cylinder head **(see illustration)**. Recover the seals.

32 Check the condition of the manifold seals, and renew if necessary.

33 Refitting is a reversal of removal, noting the following points:

a) *Ensure that the oil separator locates correctly with the guide rails on the underside of the manifold.*
b) *Tighten the manifold bolts securely.*

M52TU and M54 engines

34 To allow sufficient clearance, remove the heater/ventilation inlet air ducting from the rear of the engine compartment as follows.

a) *Rotate the three fasteners 90° anti-clockwise and remove the pollen filter cover from the rear of the engine compartment. Pull the filter forward and remove it.*
b) *Undo the four retaining clips and thread the cable out of the ducting **(see illustration 12.21)**.*
c) *Unscrew the four bolts and pull the filter housing forwards and remove it.*
d) *Pull up the rubber strip, rotate the two fasteners anti-clockwise, and move the dividing panel in the left-hand corner of the engine compartment forward a little **(see illustration 12.23)**.*
e) *Undo the two bolts and remove the inlet ducting upwards and out of the engine compartment **(see illustration 12.24)**.*

13.27 Inlet manifold support bracket bolt holes (arrowed – manifold removed for clarity) and fuel tank vent valve hose (A)

13.29 Depress the clips (arrowed) and disconnect the vent hose from the top of the manifold

35 Remove the throttle body (Section 11), and fuel rail with injectors (Section 12).

36 Open the jump starting connection point on the right-hand side of the engine compartment, and disconnect the starter motor supply lead **(see illustration)**.

37 Disconnect the VANOS solenoid wiring plug at the left-hand front side of the cylinder head (if not already done).

38 Squeeze together the sides of the locking collar and disconnect the breather hose from the cylinder head cover.

39 Push in the retaining clip and disconnect the hose on the base of the tank venting valve **(see illustration)**.

40 Note their fitted positions, then release any wiring harness(s) from the retaining clips on the manifold and support bracket (under the manifold).

41 To disconnect the servo vacuum hose above the manifold, cut off the hose clamp with a pair of side-cutters, and pull the plastic tube from the rubber hose.

42 Undo the nine nuts securing the manifold to the cylinder head, and the nut securing the manifold support bracket to the cylinder block (under the manifold), and remove the manifold from the cylinder head. As the manifold is withdrawn, feed the starter motor cable through the manifold, and on M54 engines disconnect the fuel regulator

13.30 Undo the two nuts (arrowed) securing the oil separator to the manifold

13.31 Unscrew the five manifold bolts (arrowed)

13.36 Disconnect the starter motor supply lead

13.39 Push in the clip, and disconnect the hose

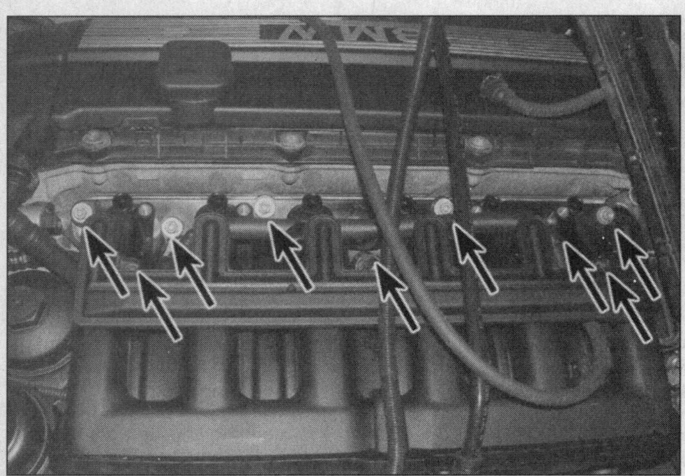

13.42a Inlet manifold nuts (arrowed)

13.42b Undo the manifold support bracket nut (arrowed)

vacuum hose **(see illustrations)**. Recover the seals.

43 Check the condition of the seals and renew if necessary.

44 Refitting is a reversal of removal.

Exhaust manifold

M43TU engines

Note: *New gaskets and new manifold securing nuts will be required on refitting.*

45 To improve access, jack up the front of the vehicle and support securely on axle stands (see *Jacking and vehicle support*). Undo the bolts and remove the engine undershield.

46 Working underneath the vehicle, unscrew the nuts securing the exhaust front section to the manifold **(see illustration)**.

47 Working at the gearbox/transmission exhaust bracket, unscrew the bolt(s) securing the two exhaust mounting clamp halves together.

48 Loosen the bolt securing the clamp halves to the bracket on the gearbox/transmission, then lower the exhaust downpipes down from the manifold studs. Recover the gasket(s).

49 Working in the engine compartment, unscrew the manifold securing nuts. Where fitted, undo the nuts and disconnect the secondary air injection pipe from the exhaust manifold.

50 Withdraw the manifold from the studs and recover the gasket(s).

51 It is possible that some of the manifold studs may be unscrewed from the cylinder head when the manifold securing nuts are unscrewed. In this event, the studs should be screwed back into the cylinder head once the manifolds have been removed, using two manifold nuts locked together.

52 Refitting is a reversal of removal, but use new gaskets and new manifold securing nuts.

N42 and N46 engines

53 Jack up the front of the vehicle and support it securely on axle stands (see *Jacking and vehicle support*). Undo the bolts and remove the engine undershield.

54 Undo the eight bolts and remove the front axle reinforcement plate from between the lower control arms (see Chapter 2A). Discard the bolts, new ones must be fitted.

55 Trace the oxygen sensors(s) wiring back and disconnect the wiring plugs. Label them to ensure they are correctly reconnected.

56 Undo the nuts/bolts and separate the exhaust system from the manifold.

57 Undo the nuts and remove the heat shield and exhaust manifold from the cylinder head **(see illustration)**. Discard the gasket. It is possible that some of the manifold studs may be unscrewed from the cylinder head when the manifold securing nuts are unscrewed. In this event, the studs should be screwed back into the cylinder head once the manifolds have been removed, using two manifold nuts locked together.

58 Refitting is a reversal of removal, but use new gaskets and new manifold securing nuts.

M52TU and M54 engines

59 To allow sufficient clearance, remove the heater/ventilation inlet air ducting from the rear of the engine compartment as follows.

a) *Rotate the three fasteners 90° anti-clockwise and remove the pollen filter cover from the rear of the engine compartment. Pull the filter forward and remove it.*

b) *Undo the four retaining clips and thread the cable out of the ducting **(see illustration 12.21)**.*

c) *Unscrew the four bolts and pull the filter housing forwards and remove it.*

d) *Pull up the rubber strip, rotate the two fasteners anti-clockwise, and move the dividing panel in the left-hand corner of the engine compartment forward a little.*

e) *Undo the two bolts and remove the inlet ducting upwards and out of the engine compartment **(see illustration 12.24)**.*

60 Jack up the front of the vehicle, and support it securely on axle stands (see

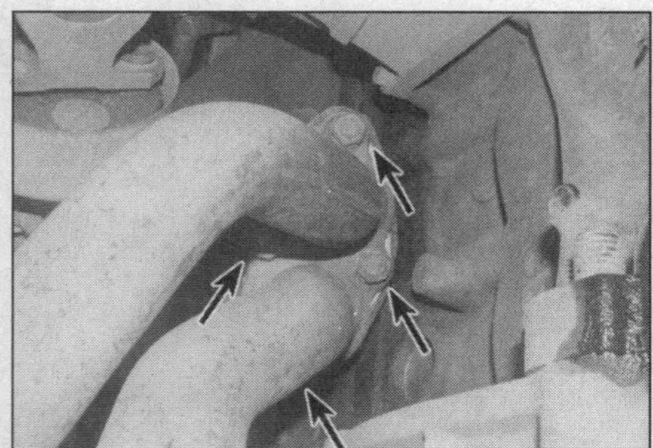

13.46 Undo the nuts (arrowed) securing the exhaust front section to the manifold

13.57 Undo the manifold and heat shield nuts

13.68 Withdrawn the front exhaust manifold from the cylinder head

14.3 Undo the exhaust front section-to-manifold nuts

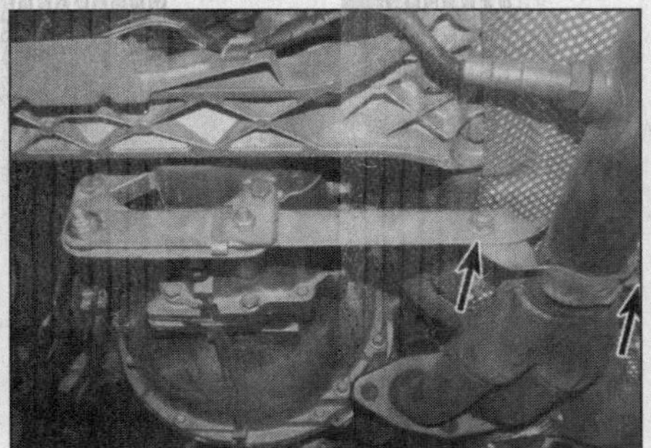

14.4 Exhaust clamp bolt and pivot bolt (arrowed)

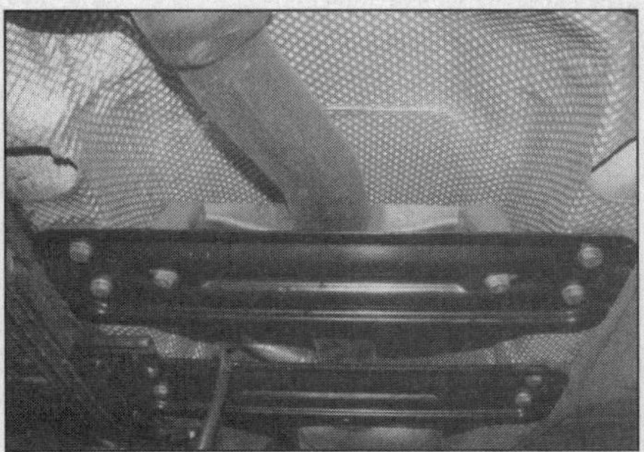

14.5 The rear reinforcement plate is secured to the exhaust by rubber mountings

Jacking and vehicle support). Undo the bolts and remove the engine undershield.

61 Undo the eight bolts are remove the front axle reinforcement plate from between the lower control arms. Discard the bolts, new ones must be fitted.

62 Attach an engine hoist to the lifting eye at the front of the cylinder head and take the weight of the engine.

63 Working underneath the vehicle, remove the right-hand engine mounting complete with support arm.

64 Prise out the plastic caps, undo the two bolts, and remove the plastic cover from the over the injectors.

65 Trace back the wiring from the oxygen sensor(s), and disconnect the wiring plugs. Label the plugs to ensure correct refitting. Unclip the cable harness from any retainers on the manifolds.

66 Undo the nuts/bolts, and separate the exhaust pipe from the manifold.

67 Using the engine hoist, raise the engine approximately 5 mm.

68 Starting with the front exhaust manifold, undo the nuts and manoeuvre the manifold from the engine compartment **(see illustration)**. Take great care not to damage the oxygen sensor fitted to the manifold. Discard the gasket.

69 Undo the nuts and remove the rear exhaust manifold. Again take great care not to damage the oxygen sensor. Discard the gasket.

70 Refitting is a reversal of removal, noting the following points:

a) *Apply some anti-seize high-temperature grease to the manifold studs.*
b) *Always renew the manifold gaskets.*
c) *Tighten the manifold nuts to the specified torque.*

14 Exhaust system – removal and refitting

Note: *New exhaust front section-to-manifold gaskets and securing nuts will be required on refitting.*

Removal

1 Jack up the vehicle and support securely on axle stands (see *Jacking and vehicle support*). Undo the bolts and remove the engine undershield.

2 On N42 and N46 engine models, trace back the oxygen sensor wiring and disconnect the plug. Free the wiring from the guide.

3 On all models, unscrew the securing nuts, and disconnect the exhaust front section from the manifold. Recover the gasket **(see illustration)**.

4 Unscrew the clamp bolt securing the two halves of the gearbox/transmission exhaust mounting bracket together, then unscrew the clamp pivot bolt, and pivot the clamp halves away from the exhaust system **(see illustration)**.

5 Undo the bolts, and remove the reinforcement plates from across the transmission tunnel. Note that the rear reinforcement plate is attached to the exhaust system by rubber mountings **(see illustration)**.

6 Slide the rear exhaust mounting rubbers from the brackets on the exhaust system.

7 Withdraw the complete exhaust system from under the vehicle.

8 To remove the heat shield, undo the nuts and bolts, then lower it to the ground.

Refitting

9 Refitting is a reversal of removal, bearing in mind the following points.

a) *Use new gaskets when reconnecting the exhaust front section to the manifold. Also use new nuts, and coat the threads of the new nuts with copper grease.*
b) *Check the position of the tailpipes in relation to the cut-out in the rear valence, and if necessary adjust the exhaust mountings to give sufficient clearance between the system and the valence.*
c) *Once the mountings have been reconnected and tightened, slacken the two nuts and bolts securing the exhaust mounting bracket to the gearbox/transmission bracket, and if necessary slide the bracket within the elongated holes to release any sideways tension on the system. Once the system is correctly positioned, tighten the nuts and bolts.*

Chapter 4 Part B:
Emission control systems

Contents

Degrees of difficulty

Easy, suitable for novice with little experience 	**Fairly easy,** suitable for beginner with some experience 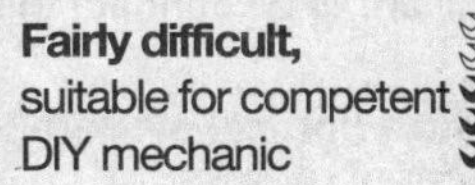	**Fairly difficult,** suitable for competent DIY mechanic	**Difficult,** suitable for experienced DIY mechanic	**Very difficult,** suitable for expert DIY or professional 

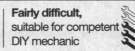

Specifications

Engine codes

4-cylinder engines

1796 cc engines	N42 B18 and N46 B18
1895 cc engines	M43TU B19
1995 cc engines	N42 B20 and N46 B20

6-cylinder engines

2171 cc engines	M54 B22
2494 cc engines	M52TU B25 and M54 B25
2793 cc engines	M52TU B28
2979 cc engines	M54 B30

Torque wrench setting

	Nm	lbf ft
Oxygen sensor to exhaust system	50	37

1 General information

1 All models have various built-in fuel system features which help to minimise emissions, including a crankcase emission control system, catalytic converter, and an evaporative emission control system. 4-cylinder and M52TU engine models are also equipped with secondary air injection to shorten the catalytic converter warm-up phase.

2 Note that leaded fuel must not be used.

Crankcase emission control

3 To reduce the emission of unburned hydrocarbons from the crankcase into the atmosphere, the engine is sealed, and the blow-by gases and oil vapour are drawn from the crankcase and the cylinder head cover through an oil separator into the inlet tract, to be burned by the engine during normal combustion.

4 Under conditions of high manifold depression (idling, deceleration) the gases will be sucked positively out of the crankcase. Under conditions of low manifold depression (acceleration, full-throttle running) the gases are forced out of the crankcase by the (relatively) higher crankcase pressure; if the engine is worn, the raised crankcase pressure (due to increased blow-by) will cause some of the flow to return under all manifold conditions.

Exhaust emission control

5 To minimise the amount of pollutants which escape into the atmosphere, all models are fitted with a catalytic converter in the exhaust system. The system is of the 'closed-loop' type; one or two oxygen (lambda) sensors in the exhaust system provides the fuel injection/ignition system ECM with constant feedback, enabling the ECM to adjust the mixture to provide the best possible conditions for the converter to operate.

6 An oxygen sensor has a built-in heating element, controlled by the ECM, to quickly bring the sensor's tip to an efficient operating temperature. The sensor's tip is sensitive to oxygen, and sends the ECM a varying voltage depending on the amount of oxygen in the exhaust gases. If the inlet air/fuel mixture is too rich, the exhaust gases are low in oxygen, so the sensor sends a low-voltage signal. The voltage rises as the mixture weakens and the amount of oxygen in the exhaust gases rises. Peak conversion efficiency of all major pollutants occurs if the inlet air/fuel mixture is maintained at the chemically-correct ratio for the complete combustion of petrol – 14.7 parts (by weight) of air to 1 part of fuel (the 'stoichiometric' ratio). The sensor output voltage alters in a large step at this point, the ECM using the signal change as a reference point, and correcting the inlet air/fuel mixture accordingly by altering the fuel injector pulse width (the length of time that the injector is open).

Evaporative emission control

7 To minimise the escape into the atmosphere of unburned hydrocarbons, an evaporative emissions control system is fitted to all models. The fuel tank filler cap is sealed, and a charcoal canister, mounted under the rear of the vehicle, collects the petrol vapours generated in the tank when the car is parked. The canister stores them until they can be cleared from the canister (under the control of the fuel injection/ignition system ECM) via the purge solenoid valve. When the valve is opened, the fuel vapours pass into the inlet tract, to be burned by the engine during normal combustion.

8 To ensure that the engine runs correctly when it is cold and/or idling, the ECM does not open the purge control valve until the engine has warmed-up and is under load; the valve solenoid is then modulated on and off, to allow the stored vapour to pass into the inlet tract.

2.3 Prise out the expansion rivet (arrowed) and remove the panel

2.4 Squeeze together the sides of the locking collars to disconnect the hoses

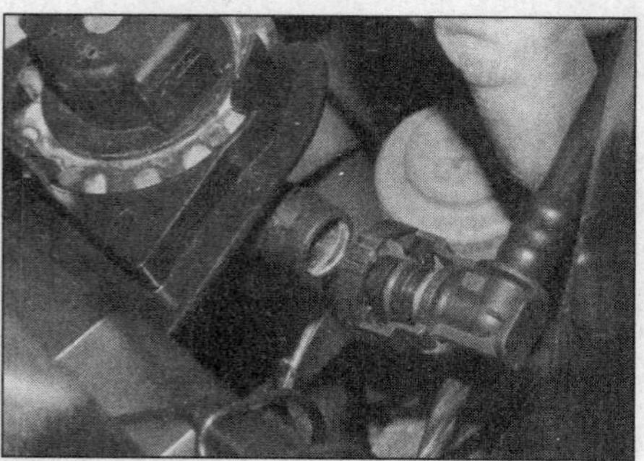
2.9 Squeeze together the sides of the locking collar to disconnect the hose

Secondary air injection

9 Some 4-cylinder and M52TU engine models are equipped with a system which is designed to shorten the amount of time the catalytic converter takes to warm-up. In order to function correctly, the catalytic converter needs to be at a temperature of at least 300°C. This temperature level is achieved by the action of the exhaust gases passing through. In order to reduce the catalyst warm-up phase, a secondary air injection pump injects fresh air just behind the exhaust valves in the exhaust manifold. This oxygen rich mixture causes an 'afterburning' effect in the exhaust, greatly increasing the gas temperature, and therefore the catalyst temperature. The system is only active during cold starts (up to 33°C coolant temperature), and only operates for approximately 2 minutes.

2 Emission control systems – component renewal

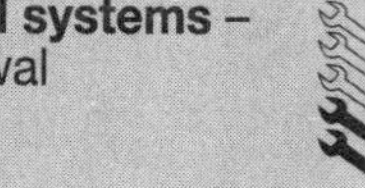

Crankcase emission control

1 The components of this system require no routine attention, other than to check that the hoses are clear and undamaged at regular intervals.

Charcoal canister renewal

2 The canister is located under the rear of the vehicle. Jack up the rear and support it securely on axle stands (see *Jacking and vehicle support*).

3 Remove the bolts/expansion rivet, and remove the plastic panel (where fitted) at the right-hand side of the spare wheel well **(see illustration)**.

4 Disconnect the hoses from the canister. If the hoses are secured by plastic locking clips, squeeze the sides of the clips to release them from the connection on the canister. Note the hose locations to ensure correct refitting **(see illustration)**.

5 Unscrew the securing bolts, and withdraw the canister/bracket assembly from the engine compartment.

6 Refitting is a reversal of removal, but ensure that the hoses are correctly reconnected as noted before removal, and make sure that the hose securing clips are correctly engaged.

Purge solenoid valve renewal

M43TU engines

7 The valve is located on a bracket, next to the air cleaner housing.

8 Ensure the ignition is switched off.

9 Squeeze together the sides of the locking collar, and disconnect the hose from the carbon canister **(see illustration)**.

10 Disconnect the wiring plug from the valve.

11 Rotate the valve 90° anti-clockwise and pull up at the same time, so that the remaining hoses can be disconnected.

12 Pull the valve from its mounting **(see illustration)**.

13 Refitting is a reversal of removal, but make sure that all hoses are correctly reconnected as noted before removal.

N42 and N46 engines

14 The valve is located under the inlet manifold. To allow sufficient clearance, remove the heater/ventilation inlet air ducting from the rear of the engine compartment as follows.

a) Rotate the three fasteners 90° anti-clockwise and remove the pollen filter cover from the rear of the engine compartment. Pull the filter forward and remove it.

b) Undo the four retaining clips and thread the cable out of the ducting ***(see illustration)****.*

c) Unscrew the four bolts and pull the filter housing forwards and remove it.

d) Undo the two bolts and remove the inlet ducting upwards and out of the engine compartment ***(see illustration)****.*

15 Pull up the sealing strip, rotate the fasteners 90° anti-clockwise, and lift the compartment partition panel from the left-hand

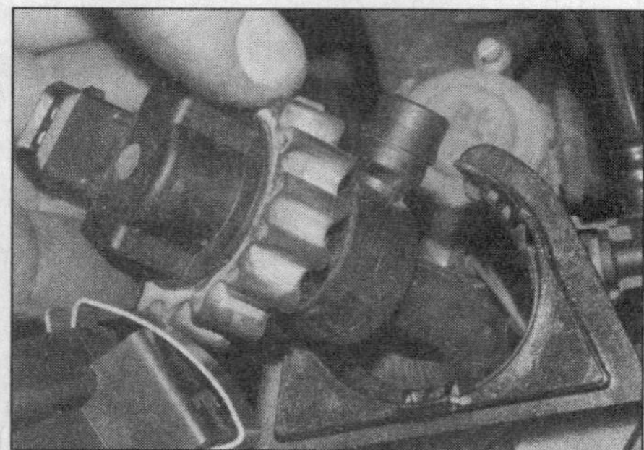
2.12 Pull the valve from its mounting

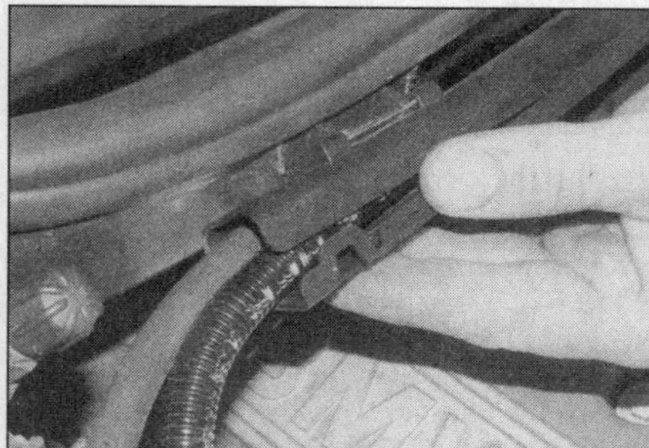
2.14a Unclip the cable ducting

2.14b Undo the two Torx bolts (arrowed) and remove the inlet housing

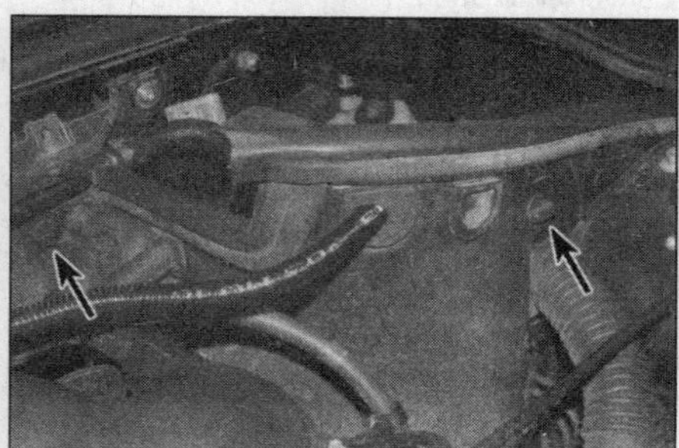
2.15 Pull up the sealing strip, undo the two fasteners (arrowed) and pull the panel forward

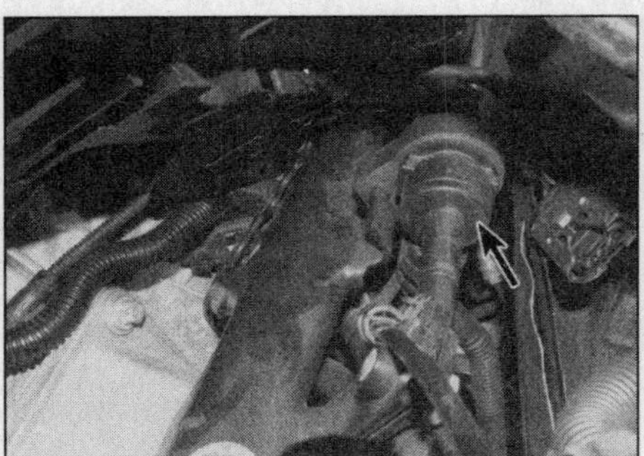
2.17 Purge solenoid valve (arrowed – manifold removed for clarity)

2.20 Disconnect the purge solenoid valve wiring plug

2.29 The oxygen sensor wiring connector is clipped into the ducting (arrowed)

corner of the engine compartment. Pull the hoses/leads with the rubber grommets from the panel **(see illustration)**.

16 Reach down, squeeze together the locking lugs, and detach the hose from the underside of the inlet manifold.

17 Disconnect the solenoid wiring plug, pull the valve/solenoid from the holder and disconnect the remaining hose **(see illustration)**.

18 Refitting is a reversal of removal.

M52TU and M54 engines

19 The valve is located under the inlet manifold. Proceed as described in Paragraph 14.

20 Reach under the manifold, and disconnect the valve wiring plug **(see illustration)**.

21 Depress the locking catch and disconnect the hose from the underside of the valve.

22 Disconnect the remaining hose and pull the valve from the rubber holder.

23 Refitting is a reversal of removal.

Catalytic converter renewal

4-cylinder engines

24 The catalytic converter is integral with the front section of the exhaust system. In order to renew the catalytic converter, it is necessary to renew the front section of the exhaust system.

6-cylinder engines

25 The catalytic converters are integral with the exhaust manifolds. In order to renew them, it is necessary to renew the manifolds.

Oxygen sensor renewal

Note: *Ensure that the exhaust system is cold before attempting to remove the oxygen sensor.*

26 The oxygen sensor(s) is screwed into the following locations.

a) *M43TU engines – in front of and after the catalytic converter.*
b) *N42 and N46 engines – in front of and after the catalytic converter.*
c) *M52TU and M54 engines – front exhaust downpipes before and after the catalytic converters.*

27 Ensure the ignition is switched off.

28 Apply the handbrake, then jack up the front of the vehicle and support securely on axle stands (see *Jacking and vehicle support*). Undo the bolts and remove the engine undershield.

4-cyinder engines

29 Trace the wiring back from the sensor to the wiring connector under the vehicle, and disconnect the connector **(see illustration)**.

6-cylinder engines

Note: *Due to the limited access, if the sensor for cylinders 4 to 6 is to be removed, the complete exhaust system must be removed.*

30 To allow sufficient clearance, remove the heater/ventilation inlet air ducting from the rear of the engine compartment as follows.

a) *Rotate the three fasteners 90° anti-clockwise and remove the pollen filter cover from the rear of the engine compartment. Pull the filter forward and remove it.*
b) *Undo the four retaining clips and thread the cable out of the ducting* ***(see illustration 2.14a)****.*
c) *Unscrew the four bolts and pull the filter housing forwards and remove it.*
d) *Pull up the rubber strip, rotate the two fasteners anti-clockwise, and move the dividing panel in the left-hand corner of the engine compartment forward a little.*
e) *Undo the two bolts and remove the inlet ducting upwards and out of the engine compartment* ***(see illustration 2.14b)****.*

31 Prise out the plastic caps, undo the two bolts, and remove the plastic cover from over the injectors.

32 Unclip the oxygen sensor cables from the retainer, and disconnect the wiring plugs. Label the connectors to ensure they are refitted to their original locations **(see illustration)**.

33 Remove the exhaust manifolds as described in Chapter 4A.

All models

34 Using an oxygen sensor removal socket, unscrew the sensor and remove it from the exhaust pipe.

35 Refitting is a reverse of the removal procedure, noting the following points:

a) *Tighten the sensor to the specified torque.*
b) *Check that the wiring is correctly routed, and in no danger of contacting the exhaust system.*
c) *Ensure that no lubricant or dirt comes into contact with the sensor probe.*
d) *Apply a smear of copper-based, high-temperature anti-seize grease to the sensor threads prior to refitting.*

Secondary air injection system

M43TU engine switching valve

36 The switching valve is located in the air secondary air injection pipe at the front of the cylinder head. Disconnect the vacuum hose from the valve.

37 Squeeze together the sides of the locking collar, and disconnect the pump-to-valve hose union. Release the retaining clips and disconnect the outlet hose from the valve. Note the fitted positions of the hoses **(see illustration)**.

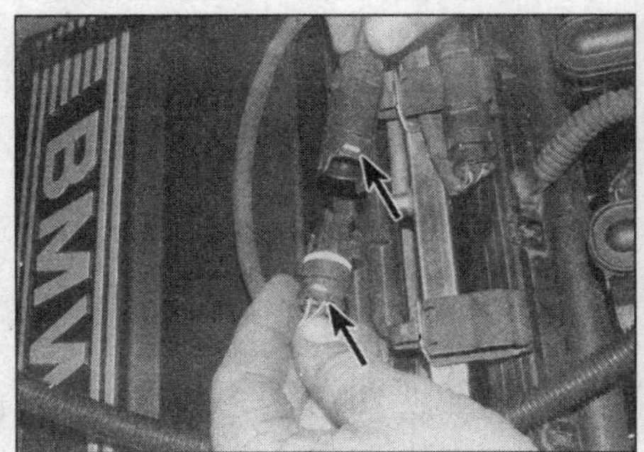

2.32 Mark or label the oxygen sensor wiring plug (arrowed)

2.37 Disconnect the inlet (A) and outlet (B) hoses from the switching valve

2.40 Note fitted locations of the valve vacuum hoses

2.44 The inlet hose simply pulls from the pump

2.48 Undo the two nuts and remove the secondary air injection valve

2.50 Squeeze together the sides of the locking collar and disconnect the hose from the secondary air injection pump

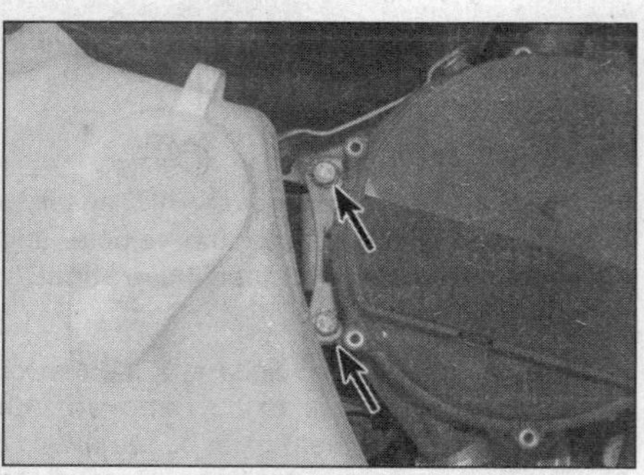
2.56 Secondary air injection pump mounting bolts (arrowed) – M52TU engine

38 Undo the three retaining bolts, and remove the valve, complete with mounting bracket, from the cylinder head.

39 Refitting is a reversal of removal.

M43TU engine diverter valve

40 The diverter valve is located on the front of the cylinder head. Disconnect the wiring plug from the valve **(see illustration)**.

41 Lift the valve from the mounting bracket, and disconnect the vacuum hoses. Note the fitted positions of the hoses.

42 Refitting is a reversal of removal.

M43TU engine air pump

43 Reach underneath the pump and disconnect the wiring plug.

44 Squeeze together the sides of the locking collar and disconnect the pump outlet hose union. The inlet hose simply pulls from its union. Note the fitted positions of the hoses **(see illustration)**.

45 Undo the three nuts, and remove the pump from its retaining bracket.

46 Refitting is a reversal of removal.

N42 engine delivery valve

47 The delivery valve is located above the exhaust manifold on the right-hand side of the cylinder head. Squeeze together the sides of the locking collar, and disconnect the pump-to-valve hose union.

48 Undo the two retaining nuts and remove the valve from the cylinder head **(see illustration)**. Recover the gaskets.

49 Refitting is the reversal of removal, tightening the retaining nuts securely.

N42 engine air pump

50 The air pump is located on a bracket bolted to the right-hand inner wing. Squeeze together the sides of the locking collar, and disconnect the pump-to-valve hose union **(see illustration)**.

51 Using a pair of side-cutters or snips, cut away the retaining clip and disconnect the pump inlet hose from the top of the pump.

52 Undo the two bolts securing the pump bracket to the inner wing bracket and remove the pump. Disconnect the pump wiring plug as the unit is withdrawn.

53 Refitting is a reversal of removal, tightening the pump bracket retaining bolts securely.

M52TU engine delivery valve

54 Proceed as described in Paragraphs 47 to 49.

M52TU engine air pump

55 The air pump is located on the right-hand inner wing. Slacken the clamp and disconnect the hose from the pump.

56 Undo the two bolts and remove the pump **(see illustration)**. Disconnect the wiring plug as the pump is removed.

57 Refitting is a reversal of removal, tightening the pump retaining bolts securely.

3 Catalytic converter – general information and precautions

The catalytic converter is a reliable and simple device, which needs no maintenance in itself, but there are some facts of which an owner should be aware, if the converter is to function properly for its full service life.

a) DO NOT use leaded petrol in a car equipped with a catalytic converter – the lead will coat the precious metals, reducing their converting efficiency, and will eventually destroy the converter.

b) Always keep the ignition and fuel systems well-maintained in accordance with the manufacturer's schedule.

c) If the engine develops a misfire, do not drive the car at all (or at least as little as possible) until the fault is cured.

d) DO NOT push- or tow-start the car – this will soak the catalytic converter in unburned fuel, causing it to overheat when the engine does start.

e) DO NOT switch off the ignition at high engine speeds.

f) DO NOT use fuel or engine oil additives – these may contain substances harmful to the catalytic converter.

g) DO NOT continue to use the car if the engine burns oil to the extent of leaving a visible trail of blue smoke.

h) Remember that the catalytic converter operates at very high temperatures. DO NOT, therefore, park the car in dry undergrowth, or over long grass or piles of dead leaves after a long run.

i) Remember that the catalytic converter is FRAGILE – do not strike it with tools during servicing work.

j) In some cases, a sulphurous smell (like that of rotten eggs) may be noticed from the exhaust. This is common to many catalytic converter-equipped cars, and once the car has covered a few thousand miles the problem should disappear.

k) The catalytic converter, used on a well-maintained and well-driven car, should last for between 50 000 and 100 000 miles – if the converter is no longer effective, it must be renewed.

Chapter 5 Part A:
Starting and charging systems

Contents

Degrees of difficulty

Easy, suitable for novice with little experience

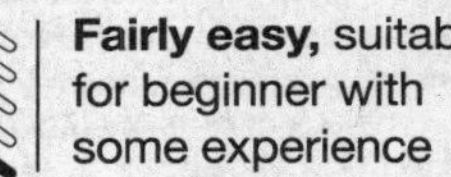

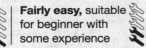

Fairly easy, suitable for beginner with some experience

Fairly difficult, suitable for competent DIY mechanic

Difficult, suitable for experienced DIY mechanic

Very difficult, suitable for expert DIY or professional

Specifications

Engine codes

4-cylinder engines

1796 cc engines	N42 B18 and N46 B18
1895 cc engines	M43TU B19
1995 cc engines	N42 B20 and N46 B20

6-cylinder engines

2171 cc engines	M54 B22
2494 cc engines	M52TU B25 and M54 B25
2793 cc engines	M52TU B28
2979 cc engines	M54 B30

System type . . . 12 volt negative earth

Alternator

Regulated voltage (at 1500 rpm engine speed with no electrical equipment switched on)	13.5 to 14.2 volts

Starter motor

Rated output	1.4 kW

Torque wrench settings

	Nm	lbf ft
Alternator to engine block (N42 and N46 engines)	21	15
Front axle reinforcement plate bolts:*		
Stage 1	59	44
Stage 2	Angle-tighten a further 90°	
Starter motor support bracket-to-engine bolts	47	35
Starter motor support bracket-to-starter motor nuts	5	4
Starter motor-to-gearbox/transmission nuts and bolts	47	35

** Do not re-use*

1.1a Earth strap fitted between the chassis and the right-hand engine mounting

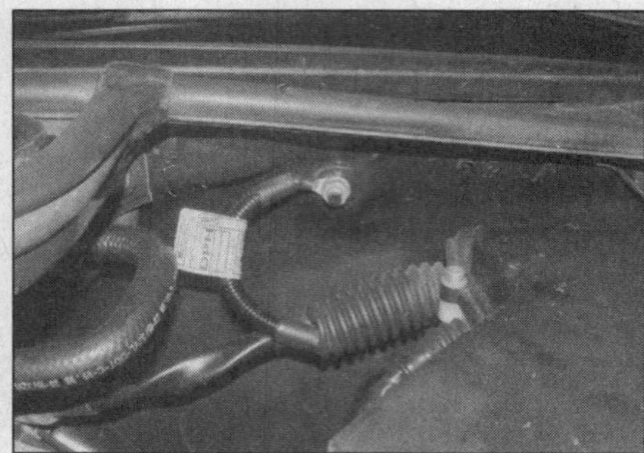

1.1b Earth connection adjacent to the electrical box in the left-hand corner of the engine compartment

1 General information and precautions

General information

The engine electrical system consists mainly of the charging and starting systems. Because of their engine-related functions, these components are covered separately from the body electrical devices such as the lights, instruments, etc (which are covered in Chapter 12). For information on the ignition system refer to Part B of this Chapter.

The electrical system is of the 12 volt negative earth type.

The battery is of the low maintenance or 'maintenance-free' (sealed for life) type and is charged by the alternator, which is belt-driven from the crankshaft pulley.

The starter motor is of the pre-engaged type incorporating an integral solenoid. On starting, the solenoid moves the drive pinion into engagement with the flywheel ring gear before the starter motor is energised. Once the engine has started, a one-way clutch prevents the motor armature being driven by the engine until the pinion disengages from the flywheel.

An earth strap is fitted between the right-hand engine mounting and the vehicle chassis, and adjacent to the electrical box in the left-hand corner of the engine compartment **(see illustrations)**.

Precautions

Further details of the various systems are given in the relevant Sections of this Chapter. While some repair procedures are given, the usual course of action is to renew the component concerned.

It is necessary to take extra care when working on the electrical system to avoid damage to semi-conductor devices (diodes and transistors), and to avoid the risk of personal injury. In addition to the precautions given in *Safety first!* at the beginning of this manual, observe the following when working on the system:

- **Always remove rings, watches, etc, before working on the electrical system.** Even with the battery disconnected, capacitive discharge could occur if a component's live terminal is earthed through a metal object. This could cause a shock or nasty burn.
- **Do not reverse the battery connections.** Components such as the alternator, electronic control units, or any other components having semi-conductor circuitry could be irreparably damaged.
- **If the engine is being started using jump leads and a slave battery, make use of the built-in jump lead connections points (see *Jump starting*, at the beginning of this manual).** This also applies when connecting a battery charger.
- **Never** disconnect the battery terminals, the alternator, any electrical wiring or any test instruments when the engine is running.
- **Do not** allow the engine to turn the alternator when the alternator is not connected.
- **Never** 'test' for alternator output by 'flashing' the output lead to earth.
- **Never** use an ohmmeter of the type incorporating a hand-cranked generator for circuit or continuity testing.
- **Always** ensure that the battery negative lead is disconnected when working on the electrical system.
- Before using electric-arc welding equipment on the car, disconnect the battery, alternator and components such as the fuel injection/ignition electronic control module to protect them from the risk of damage.
- If a radio/cassette/CD unit with a built-in security code is fitted, note the following precautions. If the power source to the unit is cut, the anti-theft system will activate. Even if the power source is immediately reconnected, the audio unit will not function until the correct security code has been entered. Therefore, if you do not know the correct security code for the unit do not disconnect the battery negative terminal of the battery or remove the radio/cassette/CD unit from the vehicle. Refer to *Audio unit anti-theft system* Section for further information.

2 Electrical fault finding – general information

Refer to Chapter 12.

3 Battery – testing and charging

Note: *The following is intended as a guide only. Always refer to the manufacturer's recommendations (often printed on a label attached to the battery) before charging a battery.*

1 All models are fitted with a maintenance-free battery in production, which should require no maintenance under normal operating conditions.

2 If the condition of the battery is suspect, remove the battery as described in Section 4, and check that the electrolyte level in each cell is up to the MAX mark on the outside of the battery case (about 5.0 mm above the tops of the plates in the cells). If necessary, the electrolyte level can be topped-up by removing the cell plugs from the top of the battery and adding distilled water (not acid).

3 An approximate check on battery condition can be made by checking the specific gravity of the electrolyte, using the following as a guide.

4 Use a hydrometer to make the check and compare the results with the following table. The temperatures quoted are ambient (air) temperatures. Note that the specific gravity readings assume an electrolyte temperature of 15°C; for every 10°C below 15°C subtract 0.007. For every 10°C above 15°C add 0.007.

	Above 25°C	Below 25°C
Fully-charged	*1.210 to 1.230*	*1.270 to 1.290*
70% charged	*1.170 to 1.190*	*1.230 to 1.250*
Discharged	*1.050 to 1.070*	*1.110 to 1.130*

5 If the battery condition is suspect, first check the specific gravity of electrolyte in each cell. A variation of 0.040 or more between any cells indicates loss of electrolyte or deterioration of the internal plates.

6 If the specific gravity variation is 0.040 or more, the battery should be renewed. If the cell variation is satisfactory but the battery is discharged, it should be charged in accordance with the manufacturer's instructions.

7 If testing the battery using a voltmeter, connect the voltmeter across the battery. A fully-charged battery should give a reading of 12.5 volts or higher. The test is only accurate if the battery has not been subjected to any kind of charge for the previous six hours. If this is not the case, switch on the headlights for 30 seconds, then wait four to five minutes before testing the battery after switching off the headlights. All other electrical circuits must be switched off, so check that the doors and tailgate are fully shut when making the test.

8 Generally speaking, if the voltage reading is less than 12.2 volts, then the battery is discharged, whilst a reading of 12.2 to 12.4 volts indicates a partially-discharged condition.

9 If the battery is to be charged with a

trickle charger, locate the recharge points in the right-hand rear corner of the engine compartment, and connect the charger leads to the connections **(see illustrations)**. If a rapid, or boost charger is used (or if in doubt as to which type of charger you have), remove the battery from the vehicle (Section 4) and charge it in accordance with its maker's instructions.

3.9a Open the plastic cover (arrowed) and connect the positive lead to the recharge point inside

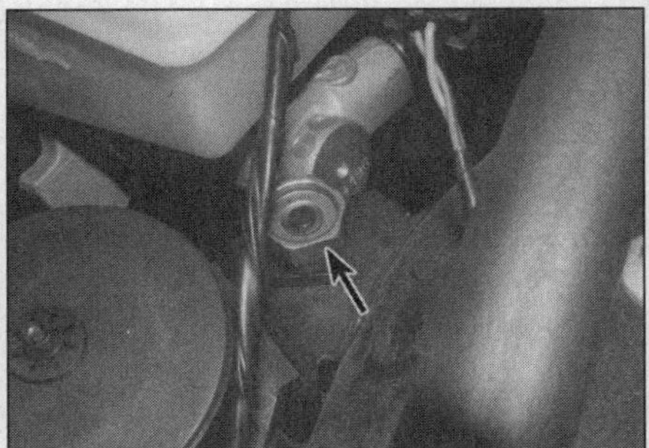

3.9b Connect the negative lead here (arrowed)

4 Battery – removal and refitting

Note: *When the battery is disconnected, any fault codes stored in the engine management ECM memory will be erased. If any faults are suspected, do not disconnect the battery until the fault codes have been read by a BMW dealer or specialist. If the vehicle is fitted with a code-protected radio, refer to 'Audio unit anti-theft system'.*

Note: *After reconnect the battery, it will be necessary to carry out the sunroof initialisation procedure as described in Section 22 of Chapter 11.*

Removal

1 The battery is located beneath a cover on the right-hand side of the luggage compartment.

2 Open the boot lid, and lift the luggage compartment floor.

3 On Saloon and Coupe models, rotate the fasteners 90° anti-clockwise, and partially remove the left-hand side luggage compartment side trim, and unclip the battery cover/first aid kit tray from the right-hand side of the luggage compartment **(see illustrations)**. On Touring models, press the button to release the trim panel below the right-hand side rear window. Undo the two nuts and remove the battery cover/storage tray above the battery **(see illustration)**.

4 Slacken the clamp nut, and disconnect the clamp from the battery negative (earth) terminal **(see illustrations)**.

5 Remove the insulation cover (where fitted) and disconnect the positive terminal lead in the same way.

6 Slacken the clamping plate bolt, then unscrew the bolts, and remove the battery retaining clamp **(see illustration)**.

7 Lift the battery from its housing, disconnect the vent hose as the battery is removed. Take care as the battery is heavy!

Refitting

8 Refitting is a reversal of removal, but smear petroleum jelly on the terminals after reconnecting the leads to combat corrosion, and always reconnect the positive lead first, and the negative lead last.

5 Charging system – testing

Note: *Refer to the warnings given in 'Safety first!' and in Section 1 of this Chapter before starting work.*

1 If the ignition warning light fails to illuminate when the ignition is switched on, first check the alternator wiring connections for security. If satisfactory, check that the warning light bulb has not blown, and that the bulbholder

4.3a Rotate the fastener anti-clockwise

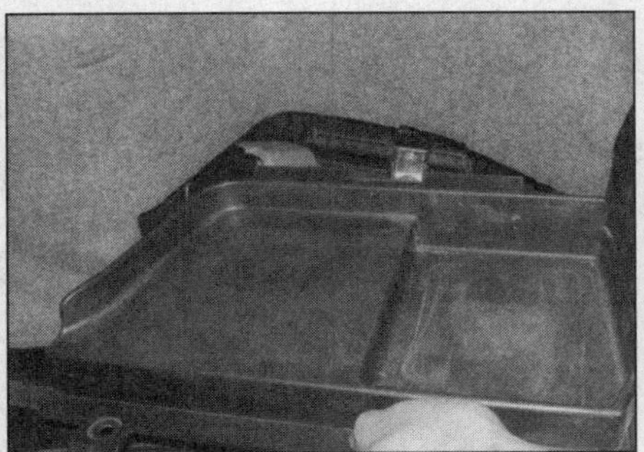

4.3b Remove the battery cover/tray

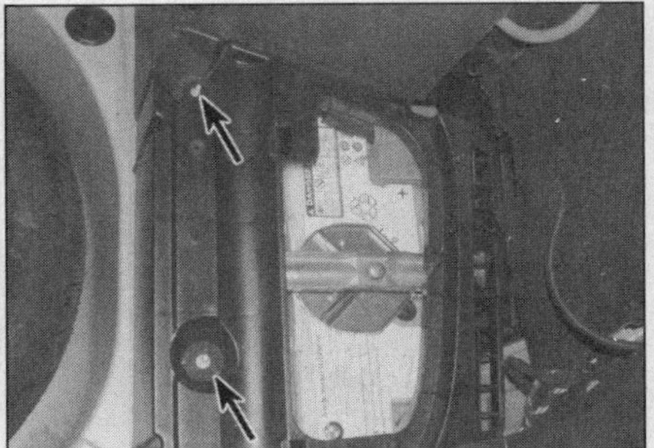

4.3c Undo the two nuts and remove the battery cover – Touring models

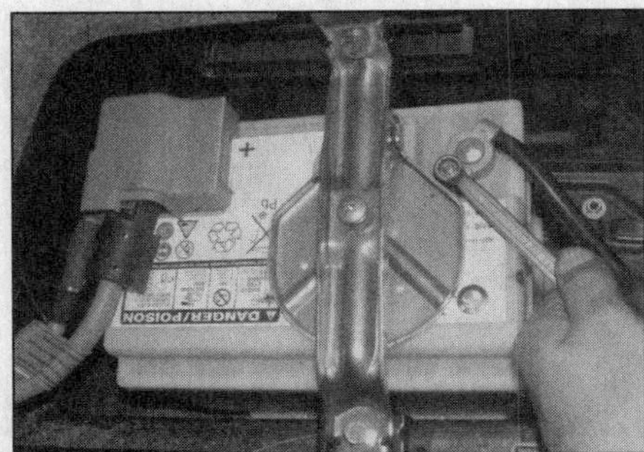

4.4a Slacken the negative terminal clamp bolt . . .

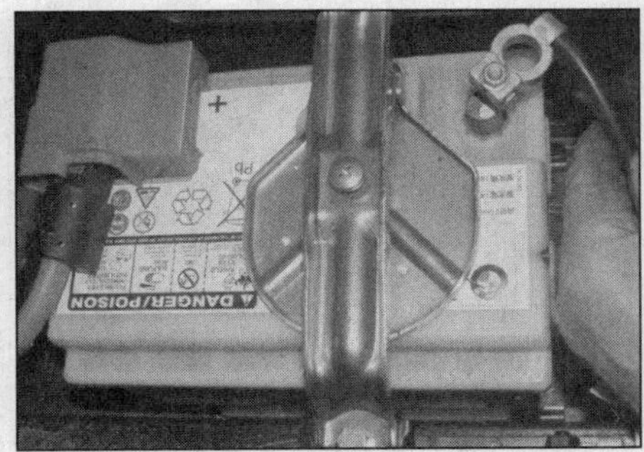

4.4b . . . and disconnect the terminal from the battery

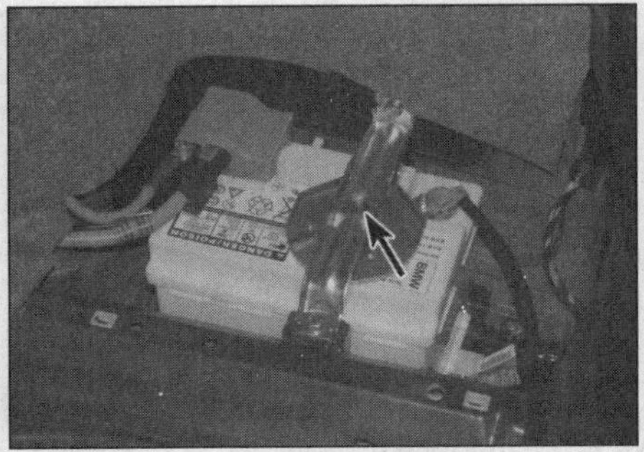

4.6 Slacken the clamping plate bolt (arrowed)

7.4 To disconnect the alternator wiring, pull back the rubber cover and unscrew the nut (arrowed) then unplug the connector (arrowed)

is secure in its location in the instrument panel. If the light still fails to illuminate, check the continuity of the warning light feed wire from the alternator to the bulbholder. If all is satisfactory, the alternator is at fault and should be renewed or taken to an auto-electrician for testing and repair.

2 If the ignition warning light illuminates when the engine is running, stop the engine and check that the drivebelt is correctly tensioned (see Chapter 1) and that the alternator connections are secure. If all is so far satisfactory, have the alternator checked by an auto-electrician for testing and repair.

3 If the alternator output is suspect even though the warning light functions correctly, the regulated voltage may be checked as follows.

4 Connect a voltmeter across the battery terminals and start the engine.

5 Increase the engine speed until the voltmeter reading remains steady; the reading should be approximately 12 to 13 volts, and no more than 14.2 volts.

6 Switch on as many electrical accessories as possible (eg, the headlights, heated rear window and heater blower), and check that the alternator maintains the regulated voltage at around 13 to 14 volts.

7 If the regulated voltage is not as stated, the fault may be due to worn alternator brushes, weak brush springs, a faulty voltage regulator, a faulty diode, a severed phase winding or worn or damaged slip-rings. The alternator should be renewed or taken to an auto-electrician for testing and repair.

6 Alternator drivebelt – removal, refitting and tensioning

Refer to the procedure given for the auxiliary drivebelt(s) in Chapter 1.

7 Alternator – removal and refitting

M43TU engines

Removal

1 Disconnect the battery negative lead (see Section 4).

2 Remove the air cleaner assembly and the mass airflow sensor as described in Chapter 4A.

7.6a Alternator upper mounting bolt (arrowed) . . .

7.6b . . . and lower mounting bolt (arrowed)

3 Remove the auxiliary drivebelt as described in Chapter 1.

4 Prise the cover(s) from the rear of the alternator, then unscrew the nut, and disconnect the wiring **(see illustration)**.

5 Where applicable, prise the cover from the centre of the drivebelt guide pulley, then unscrew the pulley for access to the upper alternator securing bolt. Note the location of the pulley to ensure correct refitting.

6 Counterhold the nuts and unscrew the upper and lower alternator securing through-bolts **(see illustrations)**.

7 Withdraw the alternator from the engine.

Refitting

8 Refitting is a reversal of removal, but ensure that the drivebelt guide pulley is correctly fitted as noted before removal, and refit the auxiliary drivebelt as described in Chapter 1. Where applicable, make sure that the lug on the drivebelt guide pulley engages with the cut-out in the alternator.

N42 and N46 engines

Removal

9 Disconnect the battery negative lead (see Section 4).

10 Remove the air cleaner housing as described in Chapter 4A.

11 Remove the alternator drivebelt as described in Chapter 1.

12 On N42 engines, at the front of the alternator, undo the bolt at the top of the cable retaining plate, and free the cables and hoses from the plate **(see illustration)**.

13 Unlock and disconnect the wiring plug, then unscrew the nut and disconnect the battery lead from the rear of the alternator **(see illustration)**.

14 Undo the two lower bolts, and manoeuvre the alternator from the engine compartment **(see illustration)**.

Refitting

15 Refitting is a reversal of removal, tightening the mounting bolts to the specified torque.

6-cylinder engines

Removal

16 Disconnect the battery negative lead (see Section 4).

7.12 Undo the bolt above the alternator at the top of the cable retaining plate (arrowed)

7.13 Undo the nut (arrowed) and disconnect the alternator wiring

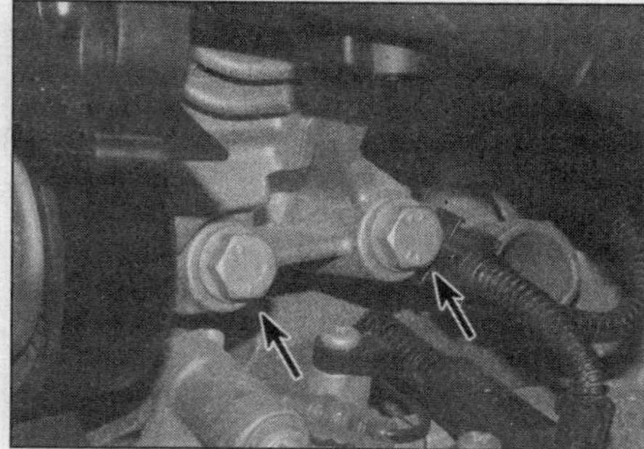

7.14 Undo the lower alternator mounting bolts (arrowed)

17 Remove the air cleaner assembly and the mass airflow sensor as described in Chapter 4A.

18 Remove the viscous cooling fan coupling as described in Chapter 3 (M52TU engines).

19 Remove the auxiliary drivebelt as described in Chapter 1.

20 Remove the power steering pump reservoir mounting bolts, and position the reservoir to one side. There is no need to disconnect the fluid hoses.

21 Reach beneath the alternator and pull the air cooling hose down and off of the alternator rear cover.

22 Pull off the cover (where fitted), then unscrew the nut and disconnect the wiring from the rear of the alternator **(see illustration)**.

23 Undo the upper and lower alternator securing bolts **(see illustration)**.

24 Withdraw the alternator from the engine.

Refitting

25 Refitting is a reversal of removal, bearing in mind the following points.

a) When refitting the tensioner idler pulley, ensure that the lug on the rear of the pulley assembly engages with the corresponding cut-out in the mounting bracket.

b) Refit the auxiliary drivebelt (see Chapter 1).

8 Alternator – testing and overhaul

If the alternator is thought to be suspect, it should be removed from the vehicle and taken to an auto-electrician for testing. Most auto-electricians will be able to supply and fit brushes at a reasonable cost. However, check on the cost of repairs before proceeding as it may prove more economical to obtain a new or exchange alternator.

9 Starting system – testing

Note: *Refer to the precautions given in 'Safety first!' and in Section 1 of this Chapter before starting work.*

1 If the starter motor fails to operate when the ignition key is turned to the appropriate position, the following possible causes may be to blame.

a) The battery is faulty.

b) The electrical connections between the switch, solenoid, battery and starter motor are somewhere failing to pass the necessary current from the battery through the starter to earth.

c) The solenoid is faulty.

d) The starter motor is mechanically or electrically defective.

2 To check the battery, switch on the headlights. If they dim after a few seconds,

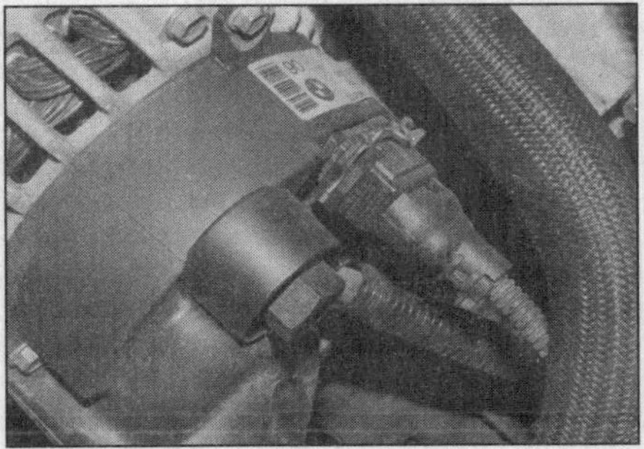

7.22 Disconnect the wiring from the rear of the alternator

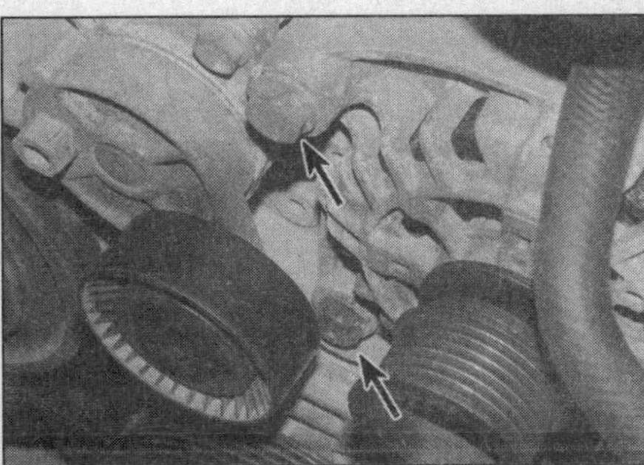

7.23 Undo the upper and lower alternator mounting bolts (arrowed)

this indicates that the battery is discharged – recharge (see Section 3) or renew the battery. If the headlights glow brightly, operate the ignition switch and observe the lights. If they dim, then this indicates that current is reaching the starter motor, therefore the fault must lie in the starter motor. If the lights continue to glow brightly (and no clicking sound can be heard from the starter motor solenoid), this indicates that there is a fault in the circuit or solenoid – see following paragraphs. If the starter motor turns slowly when operated, but the battery is in good condition, then this indicates that either the starter motor is faulty, or there is considerable resistance somewhere in the circuit.

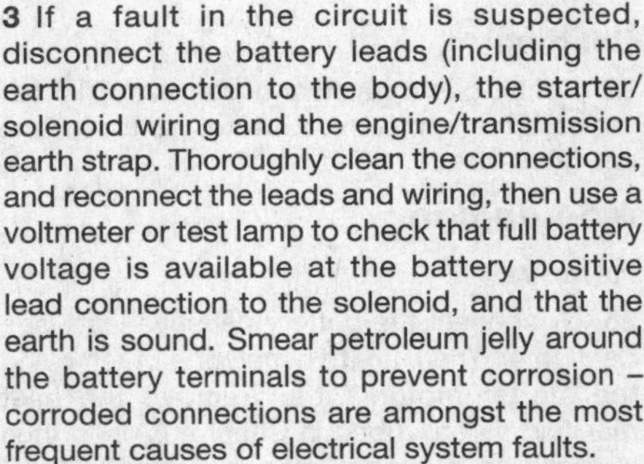

3 If a fault in the circuit is suspected, disconnect the battery leads (including the earth connection to the body), the starter/solenoid wiring and the engine/transmission earth strap. Thoroughly clean the connections, and reconnect the leads and wiring, then use a voltmeter or test lamp to check that full battery voltage is available at the battery positive lead connection to the solenoid, and that the earth is sound. Smear petroleum jelly around the battery terminals to prevent corrosion – corroded connections are amongst the most frequent causes of electrical system faults.

4 If the battery and all connections are in good condition, check the circuit by disconnecting the wire from the solenoid blade terminal. Connect a voltmeter or test lamp between the wire end and a good earth (such as the battery negative terminal), and check that the wire is live when the ignition switch is turned to the 'start' position. If it is, then the circuit is sound – if not the circuit wiring can be checked as described in Chapter 12.

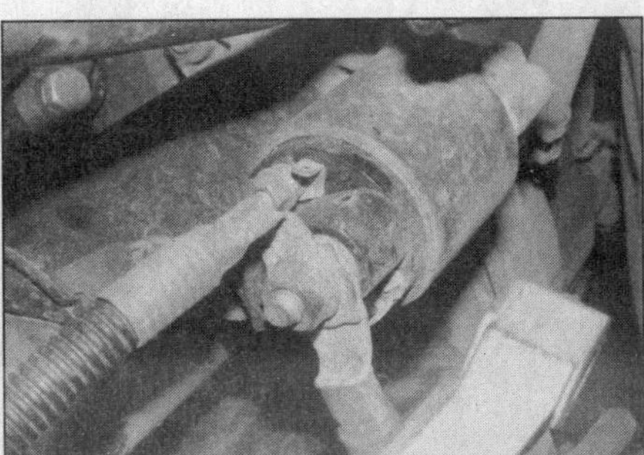

10.4 Starter motor connections – M43TU engine

5 The solenoid contacts can be checked by connecting a voltmeter or test lamp between the battery positive feed connection on the starter side of the solenoid, and earth. When the ignition switch is turned to the 'start' position, there should be a reading or lighted bulb, as applicable. If there is no reading or lighted bulb, the solenoid is faulty and should be renewed.

6 If the circuit and solenoid are proved sound, the fault must lie in the starter motor. In this event, it may be possible to have the starter motor overhauled by a specialist, but check on the cost of spares before proceeding, as it may prove more economical to obtain a new or exchange motor.

10 Starter motor – removal and refitting

M43TU engine

Removal

1 Disconnect the battery negative lead (see Section 4).

2 Apply the handbrake, then jack up the front of the vehicle and support securely on axle stands (see *Jacking and vehicle support*). Undo the bolts and remove the engine undershield.

3 To improve access, unclip the fuel hoses from the retaining clips under the starter motor, depress the tabs and disconnect the quick-release couplings. Be prepared for fuel spillage.

4 Unscrew the nuts and disconnect the wiring from the rear of the starter motor **(see illustration)**.

5 Using a socket, ratchet and long extension, undo the starter motor mounting bolts from the transmission bellhousing.

6 Pull the motor forward and manoeuvre it downwards, taking care not to damage the fuel hoses.

Refitting

7 Refitting is a reversal of removal. Tighten the starter motor mounting bolts to the specified torque.

10.10 Note their locations, then disconnect the starter motor leads – N42 and N46 engines

10.11 Starter motor mounting bolts (arrowed)

N42 and N46 engines

Removal

8 Disconnect the battery negative lead (see Section 4).

9 Remove the inlet manifold as described in Chapter 4A.

10 Note their fitted positions, then undo the nuts and disconnect the leads from the starter solenoid **(see illustration)**.

11 Undo the two Torx bolts and remove the starter motor **(see illustration)**.

Refitting

12 Refitting is a reversal of removal. Tighten the starter motor mounting bolts to the specified torque.

M52TU engine

Removal

13 Disconnect the battery negative lead (see Section 4).

14 Disconnect the mass airflow sensor wiring and the vacuum hose, release the retaining clips, and remove the air filter housing (see Chapter 4A).

15 Pull the throttle outer cable up and manoeuvre it from the retaining bracket on the throttle body. Disconnect the inner cable end from the throttle valve quadrant – refer to Chapter 4A if necessary.

16 Undo the hose clamps and detach the inlet hoses from the throttle body and idle speed control valve.

17 Apply the handbrake, then jack up the front of the vehicle and support securely on axle stands (see *Jacking and vehicle support*). Remove the engine undershield.

18 To improve access, unclip the fuel hoses from the retaining clips under the starter motor, depress the tabs and disconnect the quick-release couplings. Be prepared for fuel spillage.

19 Unscrew the nuts and disconnect the wiring from the rear of the starter motor.

20 Using a socket, ratchet and long extension, undo the starter motor mounting bolts from the transmission bellhousing.

21 Pull the motor forward and manoeuvre it downwards, taking care not to damage the fuel hoses.

Refitting

22 Refitting is a reversal of removal. Tighten the starter motor mounting bolts to the specified torque.

M54 engine

Removal

23 Disconnect the battery negative lead (see Section 4). There are two methods of removing the starter motor. Either remove the inlet manifold as described in Chapter 4A and then proceed as described from paragraph 33, or remove the starter motor from under the vehicle as described in the following paragraphs.

24 Apply the handbrake, then jack up the front of the vehicle and support securely on axle stands (see *Jacking and vehicle support*). Undo the bolts and remove the engine/transmission undershields.

25 On coupe models from 11/99, and all models from 12/00, undo the 8 bolts and remove the reinforcement plate from under the transmission. **Note:** *The vehicle must not be driven with the reinforcement plate removed, or damage may result.*

26 In order to remove the starter motor, the transmission must be lowered approximately 5 cm. Begin by removing the heater/ventilation inlet air ducting from the rear of the engine compartment as follows **(see illustrations)**.

a) Rotate the three fasteners 90° anti-clockwise and remove the pollen filter cover from the rear of the engine compartment. Pull the filter forward and remove it.
b) Undo the four retaining clips and thread the cable out of the ducting.
c) Unscrew the four bolts and pull the filter housing forwards and remove it.
d) Pull up the rubber strip, rotate the two fasteners anti-clockwise, and move the dividing panel in the left-hand corner of the engine compartment forward a little.
e) Undo the two bolts and remove the inlet ducting upwards and out of the engine compartment.

27 Remove the exhaust system as described in Chapter 4A.

28 Remove the gearchange lever or selector cable as applicable (see the relevant Part of Chapter 7).

29 Disconnect the front of the propeller shaft from the transmission and tie it to one side (see Chapter 8).

30 Support the transmission with a trolley jack and remove the crossmember from under the transmission. Lower the transmission approximately 5 cm.

31 Note their fitted positions, and disconnect the vacuum hoses from the exhaust flap vacuum tank (where fitted) located beneath the starter motor. Undo the mounting bolt and remove the vacuum tank.

32 To improve access, unclip the fuel pipe from its retaining clip, and disconnect the TDC sensor wiring plug.

33 Note their fitted positions, then undo the nuts and disconnect the wiring from the starter motor **(see illustration)**.

34 Using a socket, ratchet and long

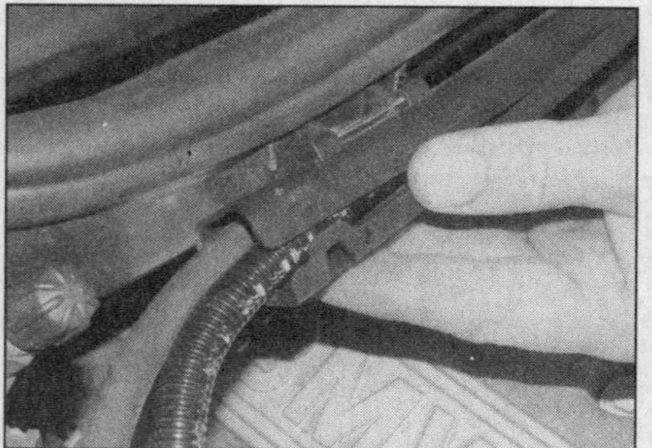
10.26a Unclip the cable ducting

10.26b Undo the two Torx bolts (arrowed) and remove the inlet housing

10.33 Disconnect the wiring from the rear of the starter motor

extension, undo the starter motor mounting bolts from the transmission bellhousing.

35 Pull the motor forward and manoeuvre it downwards.

Refitting

36 Refitting is a reversal of removal, noting the following points:

a) *Tighten all nuts/bolts to the specified torque where given.*

b) *New bolts must be used where refitting the underbody reinforcement plate.*

11 Starter motor – testing and overhaul

If the starter motor is thought to be suspect, it should be removed from the vehicle and taken to an auto-electrician for testing. Most auto-electricians will be able to supply and fit brushes at a reasonable cost. However, check on the cost of repairs before proceeding as it may prove more economical to obtain a new or exchange motor.

12 Ignition switch – removal and refitting

The ignition switch is integral with the steering column lock, and can be removed as described in Chapter 10.

Notes

Chapter 5 Part B: Ignition system

Contents

Degrees of difficulty

Easy, suitable for novice with little experience 	**Fairly easy,** suitable for beginner with some experience	**Fairly difficult,** suitable for competent DIY mechanic	**Difficult,** suitable for experienced DIY mechanic 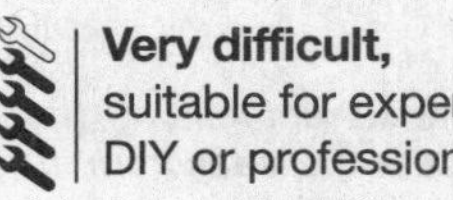	**Very difficult,** suitable for expert DIY or professional 

Specifications

Engine codes

4-cylinder engines

1796 cc engines	N42 B18 and N46 B18
1895 cc engines	M43TU B19
1995 cc engines	N42 B20 and N46 B20

6-cylinder engines

2171 cc engines	M54 B22
2494 cc engines	M52TU B25 and M54 B25
2793 cc engines	M52TU B28
2979 cc engines	M54 B30

Firing order

4-cylinder engines	1-3-4-2
6-cylinder engines	1-5-3-6-2-4

Ignition timing

Ignition timing	Electronically-controlled by DME engine management system – no adjustment possible

Torque wrench settings

Torque wrench settings	Nm	lbf ft
Knock sensor securing bolt	20	15
Spark plugs:		
M12 thread	23	17
M14 thread	30	22

1 General information and precautions

General information

The ignition system is controlled by the engine management system (see Chapter 4A), known as DME (Digital Motor Electronics). The DME system controls all ignition and fuel injection functions using a central ECM (Electronic Control Module).

The ignition timing is based on inputs provided to the ECM by various sensors supplying information on engine load, engine speed, coolant temperature and inlet air temperature (see Chapter 4A).

Some engines are fitted with knock sensors to detect 'knocking' (also known as 'pinking' or pre-ignition). The knock sensors are sensitive to vibration and detect the knocking which occurs when a cylinder starts to pre-ignite. The knock sensor provides a signal to the ECM which in turn retards the ignition advance setting until the knocking ceases.

A distributorless ignition system is used, with a separate HT coil for each cylinder, except on M43TU engines where a 'compact coil pack' is fitted to the inner wing, with HT leads to each spark plug. No distributor is used, and the coils provide the high voltage signal direct to each spark plug.

The ECM uses the inputs from the various sensors to calculate the required ignition advance and the coil charging time.

Precautions

Refer to the precautions in Chapter 5A.

Testing of ignition system components should be entrusted to a BMW dealer. Improvised testing techniques are time-consuming and run the risk of damaging the engine management ECM.

2 Ignition system – testing

1 If a fault appears in the engine management (fuel/injection) system, first ensure that the fault is not due to a poor electrical connection, or to poor maintenance, ie, check that the air cleaner filter element is clean, that the spark plugs are in good condition and correctly gapped, and that the engine breather hoses are clear and undamaged.

2 On M43TU engines, check the condition of the HT leads as follows. **Note:** *On N42, N46 and 6-cylinder engines it is not possible to check the condition of the HT leads.*

a) Make sure that the leads are numbered to

3.1 Ignition coil – M43TU engine

3.4a Release the clips to remove the plastic shielding . . .

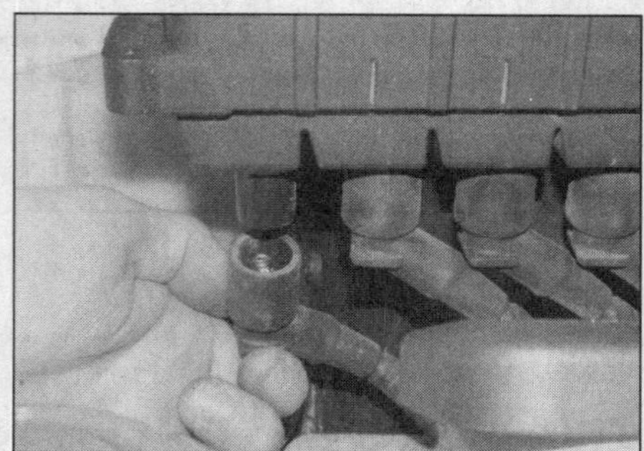
3.4b . . . and disconnect the HT leads

ensure correct refitting, then pull the end of one of the leads from the spark plug.

b) *Check inside the end fitting for corrosion, which looks like a white crusty powder.*

c) *Push the end fitting back onto the spark plug, ensuring that it is a tight fit on the plug. If not, remove the lead again, and use pliers to carefully crimp the metal connector inside the end fitting until it fits securely on the end of the spark plug.*

d) *Using a clean rag, wipe the entire length of the lead to remove any built up dirt and grease. Once the lead is clean, check for burns, cracks and other damage. Do not bend the lead excessively, nor pull the lead lengthways – the conductor inside might break.*

e) *Refit the lead securely on completion.*

f) *Check the remaining leads one at a time in the same manner.*

3 Check that the throttle cable is correctly adjusted as described in Chapter 4A.

4 If the engine is running very roughly, check the compression pressures as described in the relevant Part of Chapter 2.

5 If these checks fail to reveal the cause of the problem, then the vehicle should be taken to a BMW dealer or specialist for testing using the appropriate specialist diagnostic equipment. The ECM incorporates a self-diagnostic function which stores fault codes in the system memory (note that stored fault codes are erased if the battery is disconnected). These fault codes can be read using the appropriate BMW diagnosis equipment. Improvised testing techniques are time-consuming and run the risk of damaging the engine management ECM.

3 Ignition HT coil – removal and refitting

M43TU engines

Removal

1 Each spark plug is fed by its own coil, and the coils are combined as one unit mounted on the right-hand suspension turret in the engine compartment **(see illustration)**.

2 Ensure the ignition is switched off.

3 Turn the locking collar and disconnect the coil wiring plug.

4 Open the plastic shielding and disconnect the HT leads from the bottom of the coil unit, noting their locations to ensure correct refitting **(see illustrations)**. Note that the cylinder numbers for the respective leads are marked on the top of the coil unit. If necessary mark the leads.

5 Unscrew the securing nuts and withdraw the coil unit from the body panel.

Refitting

6 Refitting is a reversal of removal, but ensure that the HT leads are correctly reconnected.

N42 and N46 engines

Removal

7 Undo the two nuts, raise the front edge of the plastic cover on top of the engine, and pull it out towards the front.

8 Working at the rear of the engine compartment, turn the fasteners 90° anti-clockwise and remove the pollen filter cover. Slide the filter from the housing. If necessary, refer to Chapter 1.

9 Release the retaining clips, and remove the cable from the ducting on the air inlet housing **(see illustration)**.

10 Undo the four bolts and pull the pollen filter housing to the front **(see illustration)**.

11 Unscrew the oil filler cap, and fold it open. Align the filler cap collar marks with the marks on the filler neck **(see illustration)**. Squeeze together the unmarked sides of the collar, and lift it from the filler neck.

12 Pull the plastic cover from the rubber retaining grommets **(see illustration)**.

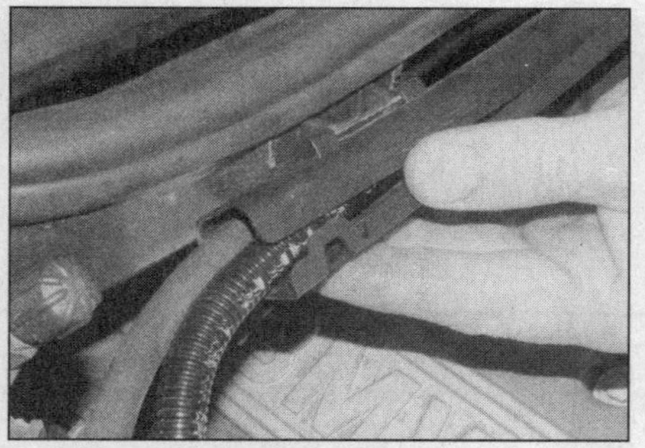
3.9 Unclip the cable ducting

3.10 Undo the four bolts (arrowed) and remove the pollen filter housing

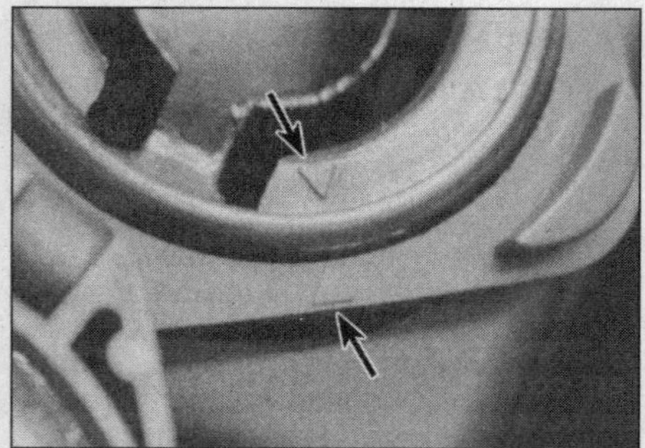
3.11 Align the oil filler cap marks (arrowed)

3.12 Pull the plastic cover from the rubber grommets

13 Prise up the right-hand edge of the plastic covers over the ignition coils (above the spark plugs), and disconnect the wiring plugs **(see illustration)**. With the wiring plugs disconnected, pull the coils from the spark plugs.

Refitting

14 Refitting is a reversal of removal, ensuring that the lug on the cylinder head engages correctly with the underside of the coil rubber seal.

6-cylinder engines

Removal

15 Each spark plug is fed by its own coil, and the coils are mounted directly on top of the spark plugs, in the cylinder head cover.

16 Ensure the ignition is switched off.

17 Remove the engine oil filler cap.

18 Remove the heater/ventilation inlet air ducting from the rear of the engine compartment as follows.

a) *Rotate the three fasteners 90° anti-clockwise and remove the pollen filter cover from the rear of the engine compartment. Pull the filter forward and remove it.*

b) *Undo the four retaining clips and thread the cable out of the ducting* ***(see illustration 3.9)****.*

c) *Unscrew the four bolts and pull the filter housing forwards and remove it.*

19 Prise up the plastic caps, undo the retaining bolts, and remove the plastic cover from above the injectors **(see illustration)**.

20 Remove the plastic cover from the top of the cylinder head cover. To remove the cover, prise out the cover plates and unscrew the two securing nuts, then lift and pull the cover forwards. Manipulate the cover over the oil filler neck **(see illustration)**.

21 Lift the securing clip, and disconnect the wiring plug from the relevant coil **(see illustration)**. If all the coils are to be removed, disconnect all the wiring connectors, then unscrew the nut securing the coil wiring earth lead to the stud on the front of the timing chain cover – the wiring harness can then be unclipped from the camshaft cover and moved to one side.

22 Unscrew the two coil securing nuts, noting the locations of any earth leads and/or brackets secured by the nuts (note that where one of the nuts also secures a metal wiring bracket, it may be necessary to unscrew the bracket securing nut from the adjacent coil, allowing the bracket to be removed to enable coil removal) **(see illustration)**. Note that the coil connectors are spring-loaded, so the top of the coil will lift as the nuts are unscrewed.

23 Pull the coil from the camshaft cover and spark plug, and withdraw it from the engine **(see illustration)**.

Refitting

24 Refitting is a reversal of removal, but ensure that any earth leads and brackets are in position as noted before removal.

3.13 Lift up the edge and disconnect the ignition coil

4 Knock sensor – removal and refitting

M43TU engines

Removal

1 Two knock sensors are fitted, screwed into the left-hand side of the cylinder block. One sensor detects knocking in Nos 1 and 2 cylinders, and the other sensor detects knocking in Nos 3 and 4 cylinders.

2 Depressurise the fuel system as described in Chapter 4A, then disconnect the battery negative lead (see Chapter 5A).

3 Remove the upper section of the inlet manifold as described in Chapter 4A.

4 Disconnect the camshaft and crankshaft position sensor wiring connectors from the wiring channel, noting their locations to ensure correct refitting.

3.19 Undo the bolts (arrowed) and remove the plastic cover from the above the injectors

5 Unscrew the two bolts securing the wiring channel to the lower section of the inlet manifold.

6 Disconnect the knock sensor wiring plug, and release it from the connector bracket.

7 The sensor for cylinders 1 and 2 is located between the oil filter and the inlet manifold, and can be removed as follows **(see illustration)**.

a) *Access to the sensor can be gained from above, between the manifold inlet tracts for cylinders 2 and 3 after disconnecting the fuel line from the fuel rail. Be prepared for fuel spillage; plug the open ends of the fuel line and fuel rail to prevent dirt ingress.*

b) *To allow clearance for the sensor to be removed, it will be necessary to slacken the bolt securing the coolant pipe to the*

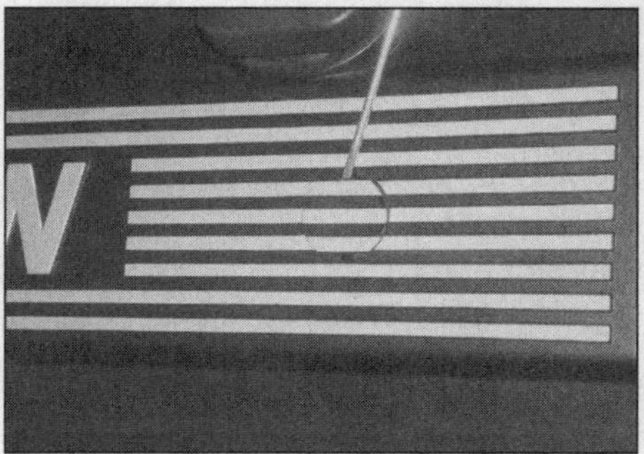

3.20 Prise up the caps, undo the nuts, and remove the cover

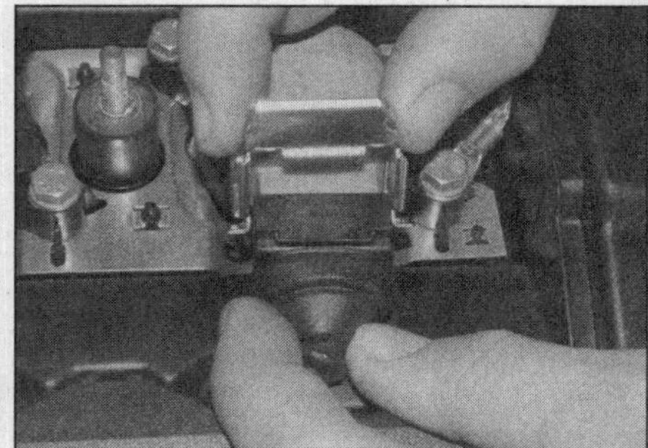

3.21 Lift the clip and disconnect the wiring plug

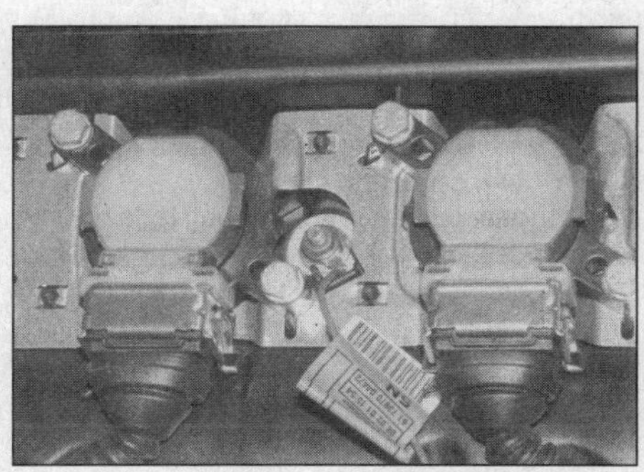

3.22 Undo the coil bolts

3.23 Pull the coil from place

4.7 Cylinders 1 and 2 knock sensor

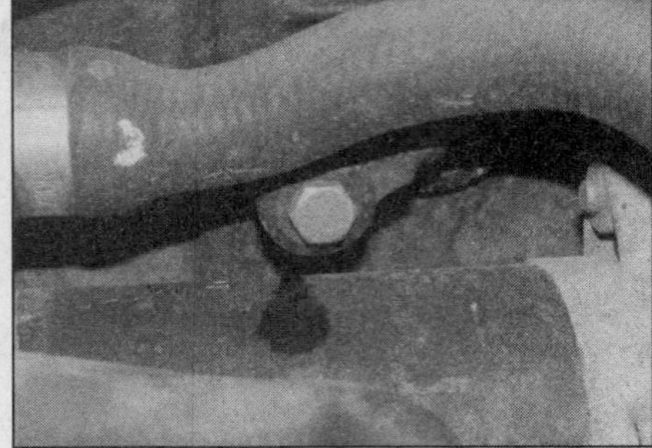
4.8 Cylinders 3 and 4 knock sensor

4.14 The rear knock sensor is obscured by the starter motor

4.16 The front knock sensor (arrowed) is adjacent to the engine coolant temperature sensor

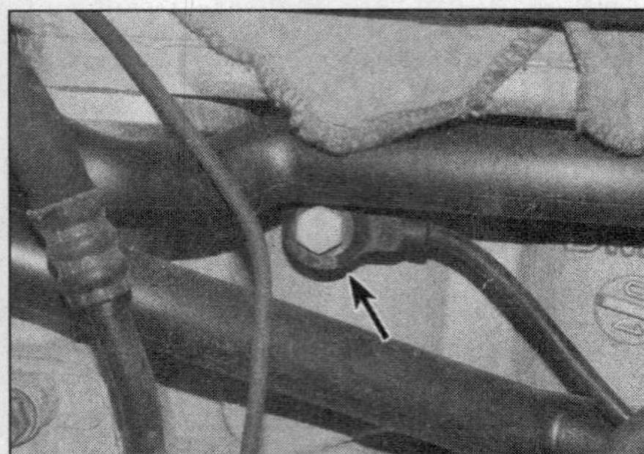
4.23 Knock sensor (arrowed)

engine, and pull the coolant pipe slightly away from the engine.

c) Unscrew the securing bolt and remove the sensor.

8 Access to the sensor for cylinders 3 and 4 is more straightforward, and the sensor can simply be unscrewed from the cylinder block **(see illustration)**.

Refitting

9 Commence refitting by cleaning the mating faces of the sensor and the cylinder block.

10 Refit the sensor and tighten the securing bolt to the specified torque.

11 Further refitting is a reversal of removal, bearing in mind the following points.

a) Ensure that all wiring connectors are correctly reconnected as noted before removal.

b) Refit the upper section of the inlet manifold as described in Chapter 4A.

c) Where applicable, on completion prime the fuel system as described in Chapter 4A.

N42 and N46 engines

Removal

12 Disconnect the battery negative lead as described in Chapter 5A.

13 Remove the inlet manifold as described in Chapter 4A.

14 Two knock sensors are fitted. The rear knock sensor is obscured by the starter motor. To access the rear sensor, undo the starter motor retaining bolts, pull the starter out from its mounting, and rotate it downwards **(see illustration)**.

15 Trace the wiring back from the sensors, and disconnect the wiring plugs.

16 Undo the bolt(s) and remove the sensor(s) **(see illustration)**.

Refitting

17 Refitting is a reversal of removal, ensuring that the sensor-to-engine block contact area is clean, and tighten the sensor bolt to the specified torque.

6-cylinder engines

Removal

18 Two knock sensors are fitted, screwed into the left-hand side of the cylinder block. One sensor detects knocking in Nos 1 to 3 cylinders, and the other sensor detects knocking in Nos 4 to 6 cylinders.

19 Disconnect the battery negative lead (see Chapter 5A).

20 Remove the inlet manifold as described in Chapter 4A.

21 Locate the sensor connector bracket which is located beneath the idle speed control valve.

Warning: If both knock sensors are to be removed, mark the wiring connectors to ensure correct refitting. Incorrect reconnection may result in engine damage.

22 Unclip the connector from the retaining clip, and disconnect the sensor wiring connector(s).

23 Unscrew the securing bolt and remove the knock sensor, noting the routing of the wiring. The sensor for cylinders 1 to 3 is located beneath the temperature sensors in the cylinder head **(see illustration)**. The sensor for cylinders 4 to 6 is located to the rear of the sensor wiring connector bracket.

Refitting

24 Commence refitting by thoroughly cleaning the mating faces of the sensor and the cylinder block.

25 Refit the sensor to the cylinder block, tightening the securing bolt to the specified torque.

26 Route the wiring as noted before removal, then reconnect the connector(s), and clip the connector to the bracket, ensuring that the connectors are positioned as noted before removal.

Warning: Ensure that the wiring connectors are correctly connected as noted before removal. If the connectors are incorrectly connected (ie, mixed up), engine damage may result.

27 Refit the inlet manifold as described in Chapter 4A.

Chapter 6
Clutch

Contents

Degrees of difficulty

Easy, suitable for novice with little experience 	**Fairly easy,** suitable for beginner with some experience	**Fairly difficult,** suitable for competent DIY mechanic	**Difficult,** suitable for experienced DIY mechanic	**Very difficult,** suitable for expert DIY or professional 

Specifications

Type .... Single dry plate with diaphragm spring, hydraulically-operated

Driveplate

Minimum lining thickness above rivet head	1.0 mm

Torque wrench settings

	Nm	lbf ft
Clutch cover-to-flywheel bolts	24	18
Clutch master cylinder bolts	22	16
Clutch slave cylinder nuts	22	16
Hydraulic pipe union bolts	20	15

1 General information

All models are fitted with a single dry plate clutch, which consists of five main components; friction disc, pressure plate, diaphragm spring, cover and release bearing.

The friction disc is free to slide along the splines of the gearbox input shaft, and is held in position between the flywheel and the pressure plate by the pressure exerted on the pressure plate by the diaphragm spring. Friction lining material is riveted to both sides of the friction disc. All models are fitted with a Self-Adjusting Clutch (SAC), which compensates for friction disc wear by altering the attitude of the diaphragm spring fingers by means of a sprung mechanism within the pressure plate cover. This ensures a consistent clutch pedal 'feel' over the life of the clutch.

The diaphragm spring is mounted on pins, and is held in place in the cover by annular fulcrum rings.

The release bearing is located on a guide sleeve at the front of the gearbox, and the bearing is free to slide on the sleeve, under the action of the release arm which pivots inside the clutch bellhousing.

The release mechanism is operated by the clutch pedal, using hydraulic pressure. The pedal acts on the hydraulic master cylinder pushrod, and a slave cylinder, mounted on the gearbox bellhousing, operates the clutch release lever via a pushrod.

When the clutch pedal is depressed, the release arm pushes the release bearing forwards, to bear against the centre of the diaphragm spring, thus pushing the centre of the diaphragm spring inwards. The diaphragm spring acts against the fulcrum rings in the cover, and so as the centre of the spring is pushed in, the outside of the spring is pushed out, so allowing the pressure plate to move backwards away from the friction disc.

When the clutch pedal is released, the diaphragm spring forces the pressure plate into contact with the friction linings on the friction disc, and simultaneously pushes the friction disc forwards on its splines, forcing it against the flywheel. The friction disc is now firmly sandwiched between the pressure plate and the flywheel, and drive is taken up.

2 Clutch assembly – removal, inspection and refitting

Warning: Dust created by clutch wear and deposited on the clutch components may contain asbestos, which is a health hazard. DO NOT blow it out with compressed air, or inhale any of it. DO NOT use petrol (or petroleum-based solvents) to clean off the dust. Brake system cleaner or methylated spirit should be used to flush the dust into a suitable receptacle. After the clutch components are wiped clean with rags, dispose of the contaminated rags and cleaner in a sealed, marked container.

Note: *If the clutch pressure plate is to be re-used, BMW tool 21 2 170 will be required to compress the diaphragm spring prior to removal of the clutch cover. Tool 21 2 142 may be required to centre the friction plate.*

Removal

1 Remove the gearbox, as described in Chapter 7A.

2.3 Use BMW tool 21 2 170 to compress the diaphragm spring

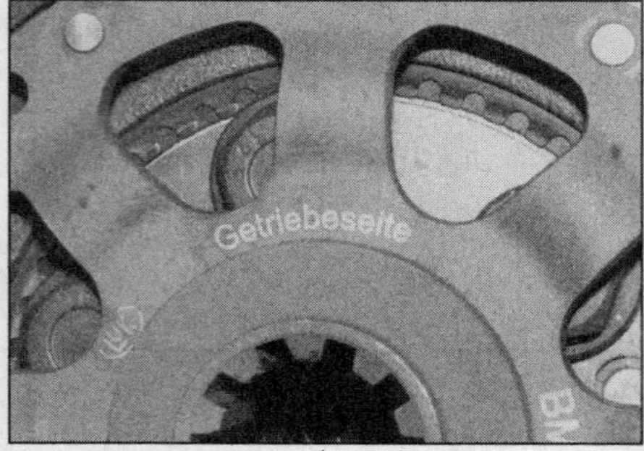

2.13a The friction disc may also be marked 'Getriebeseite' meaning 'Gearbox side'

2.13b Use BMW tool 21 2 142 (or similar) to centre the friction disc

2 If the original clutch is to be refitted, make alignment marks between the clutch cover and the flywheel, so that the clutch can be refitted in its original position.

3 If the original pressure plate is to be re-used, engage the three legs of the BMW clutch compressing tool (No 21 2 170) with the clutch cover in the area of the adjusting springs **(see illustration)**. Screw down the knurled collar to lock the legs in place, then tighten down the spindle to compress the diaphragm spring.

4 Regardless of whether the pressure plate is to be renewed, progressively unscrew the bolts securing the clutch cover to the flywheel, and where applicable recover the washers.

5 Withdraw the clutch cover from the flywheel. Be prepared to catch the clutch friction disc, which may drop out of the cover as it is withdrawn, and note which way round the friction disc is fitted – the two sides of the disc are normally marked 'Engine side' and 'Transmission side', or similar. The greater projecting side of the hub faces away from the flywheel.

Inspection

6 With the clutch assembly removed, clean off all traces of dust using a dry cloth. Although most friction discs now have asbestos-free linings, some do not, and it is wise to take suitable precautions; *asbestos dust is harmful, and must not be inhaled.*

7 Examine the linings of the friction disc for wear and loose rivets, and the disc for distortion, cracks, and worn splines. The surface of the friction linings may be highly glazed, but, as long as the friction material pattern can be clearly seen, this is satisfactory. If there is any sign of oil contamination, indicated by a continuous, or patchy, shiny black discolouration, the disc must be renewed. The source of the contamination must be traced and rectified before fitting new clutch components; typically, a leaking crankshaft rear oil seal or gearbox input shaft oil seal – or both – will be to blame (renewal procedures are given in the relevant Part of Chapter 2, and Chapter 7A respectively). The disc must also be renewed if the lining thickness has worn down to, or just above, the level of the rivet heads. Note that BMW specify a minimum friction material thickness above the heads of the rivets (see Specifications).

8 Check the machined faces of the flywheel and pressure plate. If either is grooved, or heavily scored, renewal is necessary. The pressure plate must also be renewed if any cracks are apparent, or if the diaphragm spring is damaged or its pressure suspect.

9 With the clutch removed, it is advisable to check the condition of the release bearing, as described in Section 3.

10 Check the spigot bearing in the end of the crankshaft. Make sure that it turns smoothly and quietly. If the gearbox input shaft contact face on the bearing is worn or damaged, fit a new bearing, as described in the relevant Part of Chapter 2.

Refitting

11 If new clutch components are to be fitted, ensure that all anti-corrosion preservative is cleaned from the friction material on the disc, and the contact surfaces of the pressure plate.

12 It is important to ensure that no oil or grease gets onto the friction disc linings, or the pressure plate and flywheel faces. It is advisable to refit the clutch assembly with clean hands, and to wipe down the pressure plate and flywheel faces with a clean rag before assembly begins.

13 Apply a smear of molybdenum disulphide grease to the splines of the friction disc hub, then offer the disc to the flywheel, with the greater projecting side of the hub facing away from the flywheel (most friction discs will have an 'Engine side' or Transmission side' marking which should face the flywheel or gearbox as applicable) **(see illustration)**. Using tool BMW tool 21 2 142, centre the friction disc in the flywheel. If the tool is not available, an alternative make be fabricated **(see illustration)**.

14 If the original pressure plate and cover is to be refitted, engage the legs of BMW tool 21 2 170 with the cover (if removed), and compress the diaphragm spring fingers as described in Paragraph 3. Using a screwdriver, reset the self-adjusting mechanism by pushing the adjustment ring thrust pieces fully anti-clockwise, whilst undoing the special tool spindle only enough to allow the adjustment ring to move. With the adjustment ring reset, tighten down the special tool spindle to compress the spring fingers, whilst preventing the adjustment ring thrust pieces from moving by inserting metal spacers in the gap between the thrust pieces and the cover. Note that a special tool is available from BMW to reset the adjustment ring **(see illustrations)**

2.14a Push the adjustment ring thrust pieces (arrowed) fully anti-clockwise . . .

2.14b . . . and insert metal spacers (arrowed) between the thrust pieces and the cover

2.14c A special BMW tool is available to reset the adjustment ring thrust pieces

2.15 Ensure the cover locates over the flywheel dowels

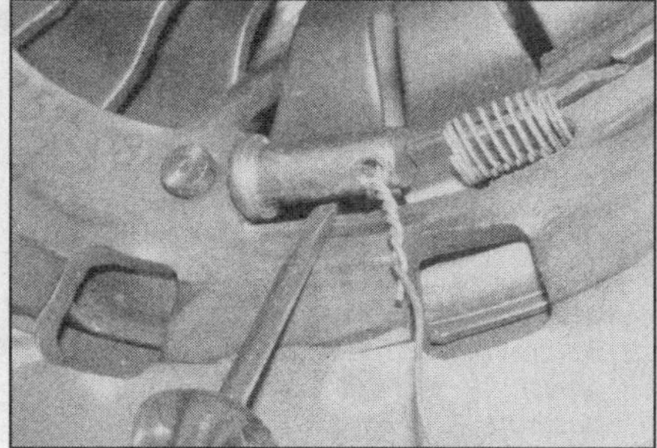

2.17 Keep all fingers away when removing the metal spacers

2.18 Thread the bolt into the end of the centring tool, and pull it out

15 Fit the clutch cover assembly, where applicable aligning the marks on the flywheel and clutch cover. Ensure that the clutch cover locates over the dowels on the flywheel **(see illustration)**. Insert the securing bolts and washers, and tighten them to the specified torque.

16 If a new pressure plate cover was fitted, insert a 14 mm Allen key into the centre of the diaphragm spring locking piece, and turn it clockwise and remove it to release the spring.

17 Where the original pressure plate cover was refitted, undo the spindle and knurled collar, then remove the compression tool from the cover. Prise out the metal spacers holding the adjustment ring thrust pieces in place **(see illustration)**.

Caution: As the last spacer is withdrawn, the adjustment ring may spring into place. Ensure all fingers are clear of the area.

18 Remove the clutch friction disc centring tool by screwing a 10 mm bolt into its end and pulling using a pair of pliers or similar **(see illustration)**.

19 Refit the gearbox as described in Chapter 7A.

3 Clutch release bearing and lever – removal, inspection and refitting

Warning: Dust created by clutch wear and deposited on the clutch components may contain asbestos, which is a health hazard. DO NOT blow it out with compressed air, or inhale any of it. DO NOT use petrol (or petroleum-based solvents) to clean off the dust. Brake system cleaner or methylated spirit should be used to flush the dust into a suitable receptacle. After the clutch components are wiped clean with rags, dispose of the contaminated rags and cleaner in a sealed, marked container.

Release bearing

Removal

1 Remove the gearbox as described in Chapter 7A.

2 Pull the bearing forwards, and slide it from the guide sleeve in the gearbox bellhousing **(see illustration)**.

Inspection

3 Spin the release bearing, and check it for excessive roughness. Hold the outer race, and attempt to move it laterally against the inner race. If any excessive movement or roughness is evident, renew the bearing. If a new clutch has been fitted, it is wise to renew the release bearing as a matter of course.

Refitting

4 Clean and then lightly apply clutch assembly grease to the release bearing contact surfaces on the release lever and guide sleeve.

5 Slide the bearing into position on the guide sleeve, ensuring that the bearing engages correctly with the release lever.

6 Refit the gearbox, referring to Chapter 7A.

Release lever

Removal

7 Remove the release bearing, as described previously in this Section.

8 Slide the release lever sideways to release it from the retaining spring clip and pivot, then pull the lever forwards from the guide sleeve **(see illustration)**.

Inspection

9 Inspect the release bearing, pivot and slave cylinder pushrod contact faces on the release lever for wear. Renew the lever if excessive wear is evident.

10 Check the release lever retaining spring clip, and renew if necessary. It is advisable to renew the clip as a matter of course.

Refitting

11 Slide the release lever into position over the guide sleeve, then push the end of the lever over the pivot, ensuring that the retaining spring clip engages correctly over the end of the release lever **(see illustration)**.

12 Refit the release bearing as described previously in this Section.

4 Hydraulic slave cylinder – removal, inspection and refitting

Warning: Hydraulic fluid is poisonous; wash off immediately and thoroughly in the case of skin contact, and seek immediate medical advice if any fluid is swallowed or gets into the eyes. Certain types of hydraulic fluid are inflammable, and may ignite when allowed into contact with hot components; when servicing any hydraulic system, it is safest to assume that the fluid is

3.2 Pull the release bearing (arrowed) from the guide sleeve

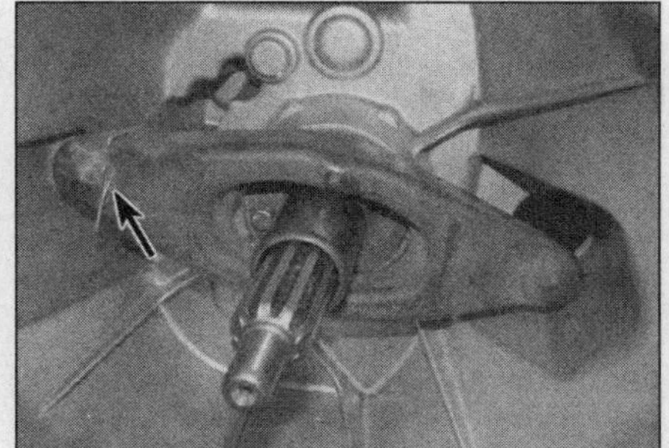

3.8 Slide the release lever sideways to disengage the retaining clip (arrowed)

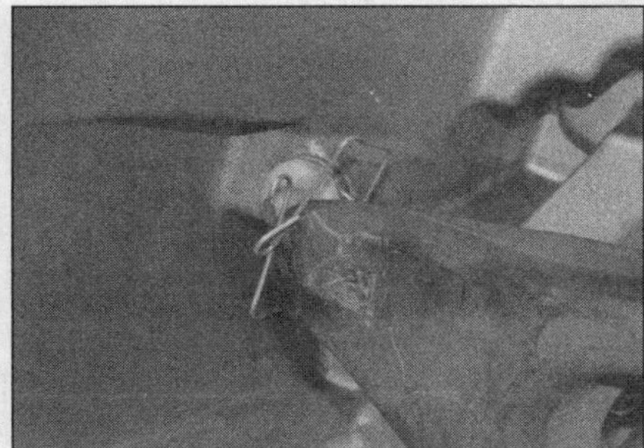

3.11 Ensure that the lever engages correctly with the retaining clip

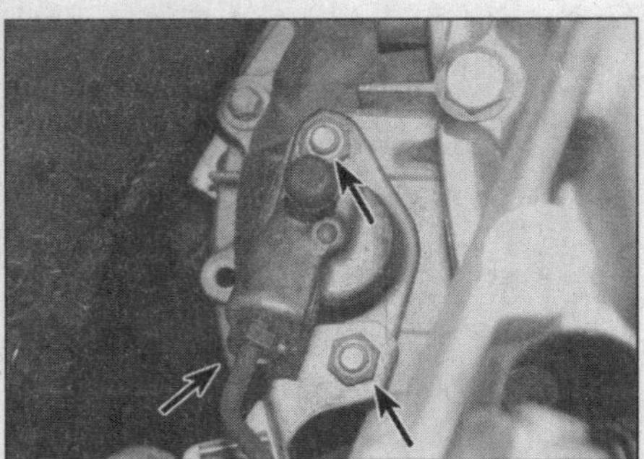

4.4 Disconnect the pipe union (arrowed) then undo the retaining nuts (arrowed)

inflammable, and to take precautions against the risk of fire as though it is petrol that is being handled. Hydraulic fluid is also an effective paint stripper, and will attack plastics; if any is spilt, it should be washed off immediately, using copious quantities of fresh water. Finally, it is hygroscopic (it absorbs moisture from the air) – old fluid may be contaminated and unfit for further use. When topping-up or renewing the fluid, always use the recommended type, and ensure that it comes from a freshly-opened sealed container.

Removal

1 Remove the brake fluid reservoir cap, and siphon out sufficient hydraulic fluid so that the fluid level is below the level of the reservoir fluid hose connection to the clutch master cylinder (the brake fluid reservoir feeds both the brake and clutch hydraulic systems). **Do not** empty the reservoir, as this will draw air into the brake hydraulic circuits.

2 To improve access, jack up the vehicle, and support it securely on axle stands (see *Jacking and vehicle support*).

3 Where applicable, remove the underbody shield for access to the gearbox bellhousing.

4 Place a container beneath the hydraulic pipe connection on the clutch slave cylinder to catch escaping hydraulic fluid. Unscrew the union nuts and disconnect the fluid pipe. Undo the nut securing the pipe bracket to the slave cylinder **(see illustration)**

5 Unscrew the remaining securing nut, and withdraw the slave cylinder from the mounting studs on the bellhousing.

Inspection

6 Inspect the slave cylinder for fluid leaks and damage, and renew if necessary. No spare parts are available for the slave cylinder, and if faulty, the complete unit must be renewed.

Refitting

7 Refitting is a reversal of removal, bearing in mind the following points.

a) Before refitting, clean and then lightly grease the end of the slave cylinder pushrod.

b) Tighten the mounting nuts to the specified torque.

c) On completion, top-up the hydraulic fluid level and bleed the clutch hydraulic circuit as described in Section 6.

5 Hydraulic master cylinder – removal, inspection and refitting

Warning: Hydraulic fluid is poisonous; wash off immediately and thoroughly in the case of skin contact, and seek immediate medical advice if any fluid is swallowed or gets into the eyes. Certain types of hydraulic fluid are inflammable, and may ignite when allowed into contact with hot components; when servicing any hydraulic system, it is safest to assume that the fluid is inflammable, and to take precautions against the risk of fire as though it is petrol that is being handled. Hydraulic fluid is also an effective paint stripper, and will attack plastics; if any is spilt, it should be washed off immediately, using copious quantities of fresh water. Finally, it is hygroscopic (it absorbs moisture from the air) – old fluid may be contaminated and unfit for further use. When topping-up or renewing the fluid, always use the recommended type, and ensure that it comes from a freshly-opened sealed container.

Removal

1 Remove the brake fluid reservoir cap, and siphon out sufficient hydraulic fluid so that the fluid level is below the level of the reservoir fluid hose connection to the clutch master cylinder (the brake fluid reservoir feeds both the brake and clutch hydraulic systems). **Do not** empty the reservoir, as this will draw air into the brake hydraulic circuits.

2 Disconnect the clutch master cylinder hose from the brake fluid reservoir. Be prepared for fluid spillage, and plug the open end of the hose to prevent dirt entry.

3 Working inside the vehicle, remove the securing bolts, and remove the driver's side lower facia trim panel (see Chapter 11).

4 Disconnect the wiring plug, and remove the clutch pedal switch by depressing the pedal, pulling out the switch red sleeve to its full extent, then squeeze together the two retaining clips and pull the switch from the bracket.

5 Squeeze together the two ends then press out the master cylinder pushrod pivot pin from the clutch pedal **(see illustration)**.

6 Unscrew the two bolts and nut securing the master cylinder to the pedal bracket in the footwell **(see illustration)**.

7 Using a small screwdriver, prise out the retaining clip and then pull the master cylinder from the hydraulic pressure pipe **(see illustration)**. Withdraw the master cylinder, and ease the fluid supply hose through the bulkhead grommet, taking care not to strain the pipe.

Inspection

8 Inspect the master cylinder for fluid leaks and damage, and renew if necessary. No spare parts are available for the master cylinder, and if faulty the complete unit must be renewed.

Refitting

9 Refitting is a reversal of removal, bearing in mind the following points.

a) Take care not to strain the master cylinder fluid pipe during refitting.

b) On completion, top-up the level in the brake fluid reservoir, then bleed the clutch hydraulic system (see Section 6).

6 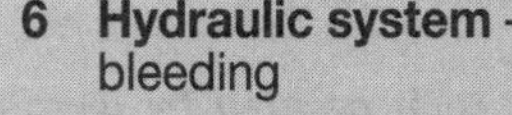

Hydraulic system – bleeding

Warning: Hydraulic fluid is poisonous; wash off immediately and thoroughly in the case of

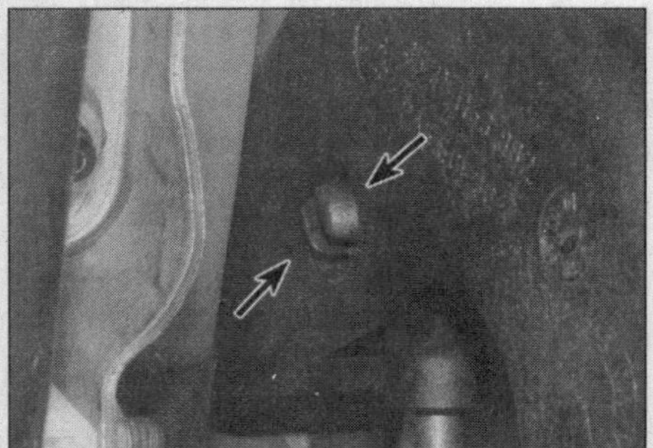

5.5 Squeeze together the ends (arrowed) and remove the pivot pin

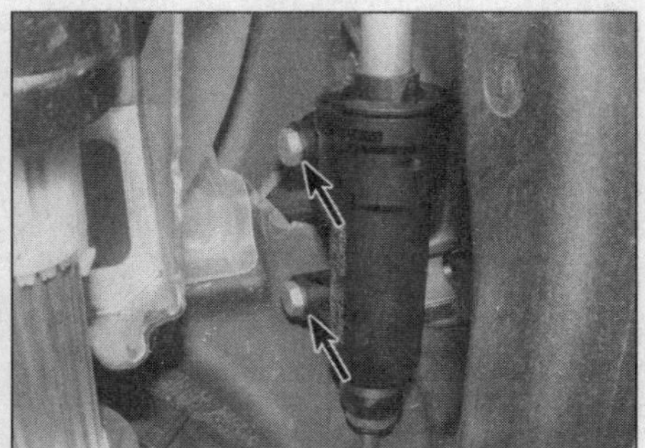

5.6 Remove the master cylinder bolts (arrowed)

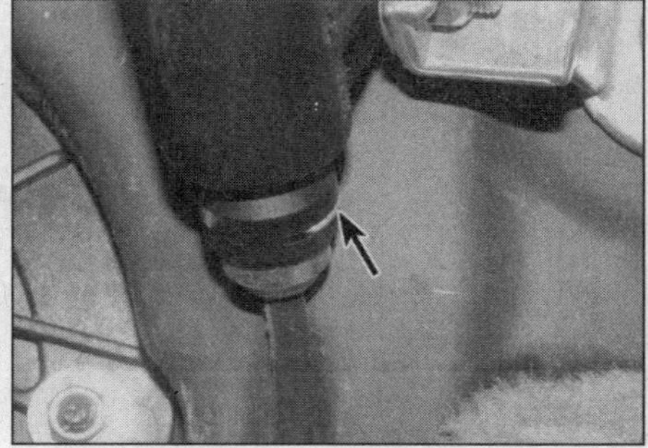

5.7 Prise out the retaining clip (arrowed)

skin contact, and seek immediate medical advice if any fluid is swallowed or gets into the eyes. Certain types of hydraulic fluid are inflammable, and may ignite when allowed into contact with hot components; when servicing any hydraulic system, it is safest to assume that the fluid is inflammable, and to take precautions against the risk of fire as though it is petrol that is being handled. Hydraulic fluid is also an effective paint stripper, and will attack plastics; if any is spilt, it should be washed off immediately, using copious quantities of fresh water. Finally, it is hygroscopic (it absorbs moisture from the air) – old fluid may be contaminated and unfit for further use. When topping-up or renewing the fluid, always use the recommended type, and ensure that it comes from a freshly-opened sealed container.

Note: *BMW recommend that pressure-bleeding equipment is used to bleed the clutch hydraulic system.*

General

1 The correct operation of any hydraulic system is only possible after removing all air from the components and circuit; this is achieved by bleeding the system.

2 During the bleeding procedure, add only clean, unused hydraulic fluid of the recommended type; never re-use fluid that has already been bled from the system. Ensure that sufficient fluid is available before starting work.

3 If there is any possibility of incorrect fluid being already in the system, the brake and clutch components and circuit must be flushed completely with uncontaminated, correct fluid, and new seals should be fitted to the various components.

4 If hydraulic fluid has been lost from the system, or air has entered because of a leak, ensure that the fault is cured before proceeding further.

5 To improve access, apply the handbrake, then jack up the front of the vehicle, and support it securely on axle stands (see *Jacking and vehicle support*).

6 Undo the bolts and remove the underbody shield for access to the gearbox bellhousing.

7 Check that the clutch hydraulic pipe(s) and hose(s) are secure, that the unions are tight, and that the bleed screw on the rear of the clutch slave cylinder (mounted under the vehicle on the lower left-hand side of the gearbox bellhousing) is closed. Clean any dirt from around the bleed screw **(see illustration)**.

8 Unscrew the brake fluid reservoir cap, and top the fluid up to the MAX level line; refit the cap loosely, and remember to maintain the fluid level at least above the MIN level line throughout the procedure, or there is a risk of further air entering the system. Note that the brake fluid reservoir feeds both the brake and clutch hydraulic systems.

9 It is recommended that pressure-bleeding equipment is used to bleed the system. Alternatively, there are a number of one-man, do-it-yourself brake bleeding kits currently available from motor accessory shops. These kits greatly simplify the bleeding operation, and also reduce the risk of expelled air and fluid being drawn back into the system. If such a kit is not available, the basic (two-man) method must be used, which is described in detail below.

10 If pressure-bleeding equipment or a one-man kit is to be used, prepare the vehicle as described previously, and follow the equipment/kit manufacturer's instructions, as the procedure may vary slightly according to the type being used; generally, they are as outlined below in the relevant sub-section.

11 Whichever method is used, the same basic process must be followed to ensure that the removal of all air from the system.

Bleeding

Basic (two-man) method

12 Collect a clean glass jar, a suitable length of plastic or rubber tubing which is a tight fit over the bleed screw, and a ring spanner to fit the screw. The help of an assistant will also be required.

13 Where applicable, remove the dust cap from the bleed screw. Fit the spanner and tube to the screw, place the other end of the tube in the jar, and pour in sufficient fluid to cover the end of the tube.

14 Ensure that the reservoir fluid level is maintained at least above the MIN level line throughout the procedure.

15 Have the assistant fully depress the clutch pedal several times to build-up pressure, then maintain it on the final downstroke.

16 While pedal pressure is maintained, unscrew the bleed screw (approximately one turn) and allow the compressed fluid and air to flow into the jar. The assistant should maintain pedal pressure, following it down to the floor if necessary, and should not release it until instructed to do so. When the flow stops, tighten the bleed screw again, have the assistant release the pedal slowly, and recheck the reservoir fluid level.

17 Repeat the steps given in paragraphs 15 and 16 until the fluid emerging from the bleed screw is free from air bubbles.

18 When no more air bubbles appear, tighten the bleed screw securely. Do not overtighten the bleed screw.

19 Temporarily disconnect the bleed tube from the bleed screw, and move the container of fluid to one side.

20 Unscrew the two securing nuts, and withdraw the slave cylinder from the bellhousing, taking care not to strain the fluid hose.

21 Reconnect the bleed tube to the bleed screw, and submerge the end of the tube in the container of fluid.

22 With the bleed screw pointing vertically upwards, unscrew the bleed screw

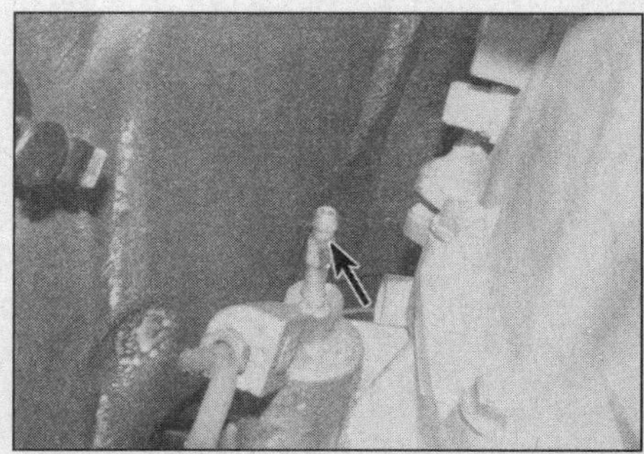

6.7 Clutch slave cylinder bleed screw (arrowed)

(approximately one turn), and slowly push the slave cylinder pushrod into the cylinder until no more air bubbles appear in the fluid.

23 Hold the pushrod in position, then tighten the bleed screw.

24 Slowly allow the pushrod to return to its rest position. Do not allow the pushrod to return quickly, as this will cause air to enter the slave cylinder.

25 Remove the tube and spanner, and refit the dust cap to the bleed screw.

26 Refit the slave cylinder to the bellhousing, and tighten the securing nuts to the specified torque.

Using a one-way valve kit

27 As their name implies, these kits consist of a length of tubing with a one-way valve fitted, to prevent expelled air and fluid being drawn back into the system; some kits include a translucent container, which can be positioned so that the air bubbles can be more easily seen flowing from the end of the tube.

28 The kit is connected to the bleed screw, which is then opened. The user returns to the driver's seat, depresses the clutch pedal with a smooth, steady stroke, and slowly releases it; this is repeated until the expelled fluid is clear of air bubbles.

29 Note that these kits simplify work so much that it is easy to forget the reservoir fluid level; ensure that this is maintained at least above the MIN level line at all times.

Using a pressure-bleeding kit

30 These kits are usually operated by the reservoir of pressurised air contained in the spare tyre. However, note that it will probably be necessary to reduce the pressure to a lower level than normal; refer to the instructions supplied with the kit.

31 By connecting a pressurised, fluid-filled container to the fluid reservoir, bleeding can be carried out simply by opening the bleed screw, and allowing the fluid to flow out until no more air bubbles can be seen in the expelled fluid.

32 This method has the advantage that the large reservoir of fluid provides an additional safeguard against air being drawn into the system during bleeding.

All methods

33 If after following the instructions given, it

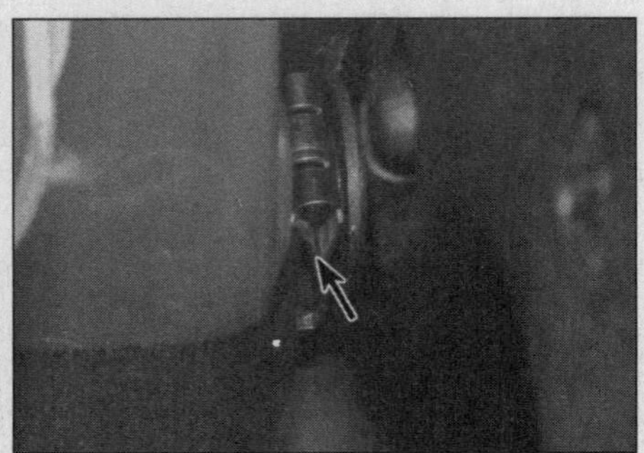

7.6 Prise off the pedal shaft clip (arrowed)

is suspected that air is still present in hydraulic system, remove the slave cylinder (Section 4) without disconnecting the hydraulic pipes, push the cylinder piston all the way in, and holding the cylinder with the bleed screw uppermost, bleed the system again. **Note:** *Steps must be taken to ensure that the slave cylinder piston is prevented from extending during the bleeding procedure. If necessary, use a metal strip and two threaded bars to fabricate a tool to hold the piston in.*

34 When bleeding is complete, and firm pedal feel is restored, wash off any spilt fluid, check that the bleed screw is tightened securely, and refit the dust cap.

35 Check the hydraulic fluid level in the reservoir, and top-up if necessary (Weekly checks).

36 Discard any hydraulic fluid that has been bled from the system; it will not be fit for re-use.

37 Check the feel of the clutch pedal. If it feels at all spongy, air must still be present in the system, and further bleeding is required. Failure to bleed satisfactorily after a reasonable repetition of the bleeding procedure may be due to worn master or slave cylinder seals.

38 On completion, where applicable refit the underbody shield and lower the vehicle to the ground.

7 Clutch pedal – removal and refitting

Note: *A new self-locking nut should be used to secure the clutch master cylinder on refitting.*

Removal

1 Working inside the vehicle, release the retaining clips/bolts, and withdraw the driver's side lower facia panel (see Chapter 11).

2 Where applicable, remove the clutch pedal switch, by depressing the pedal, pulling out the switch red sleeve to its full extent, then squeeze together the two retaining clips and pull the switch from the bracket.

3 Squeeze together the two halves of the end, then press out the master cylinder pushrod pivot pin from the clutch pedal **(see illustration 5.5).**

4 Carefully disconnect the return spring from the pedal using a pair of pliers.

5 Undo the two plastic nuts, and place the anti-theft ECM to one side.

6 Prise off the clip securing the pedal to the pivot shaft, then slide to the right, and remove the clutch pedal. Recover the pivot bushes if they are loose **(see illustration).**

Refitting

7 Before refitting the pedal to the pivot shaft, check the condition of the pivot bushes, and renew if necessary. Apply a little grease to the bushes.

8 Refitting is a reversal of removal. Ensure that the clutch switch plunger is fully extended prior to refitment.

Chapter 7 Part A:
Manual transmission

Contents

Degrees of difficulty

Easy, suitable for novice with little experience 	**Fairly easy,** suitable for beginner with some experience	**Fairly difficult,** suitable for competent DIY mechanic	**Difficult,** suitable for experienced DIY mechanic	**Very difficult,** suitable for expert DIY or professional 

Specifications

Engine codes

4-cylinder engines

1796 cc engines	N42 B18 and N46 B18
1895 cc engines	M43TU B19
1995 cc engines	N42 B20 and N46 B20

6-cylinder engines

2171 cc engines	M54 B22
2494 cc engines	M52TU B25 and M54 B25
2793 cc engines	M52TU B28
2979 cc engines	M54 B30

Lubrication

Oil capacity	Refer to Chapter 1

Torque wrench settings

Torque wrench settings	Nm	lbf ft
Gearbox crossmember-to-body bolts:		
M8 bolts	21	15
M10 bolts	42	31
Gearbox mounting-to-gearbox nuts:		
M8 nuts	21	15
M10 nuts	42	31
Gearbox-to-engine bolts:		
Hexagon head bolts:		
M8 bolts	25	18
M10 bolts	49	36
M12 bolts	74	55
Torx head bolts:		
M8 bolts	22	16
M10 bolts	43	32
M12 bolts	72	53
Oil drain plug	50	37
Oil filler/level plug	50	37
Output flange-to-output shaft nut:		
Stage 1	190	140
Stage 2	Remove nut and apply locking compound (see text)	
Stage 3	120	89
Reversing light switch	21	15

2.2 Gearbox filler plug (arrowed)

3.3 Gearbox drain plug (arrowed)

1 General information

The gearbox is a 5- or 6-speed unit, and is contained in a cast-alloy casing bolted to the rear of the engine.

Drive is transmitted from the crankshaft via the clutch to the input shaft, which has a splined extension to accept the clutch friction disc. The output shaft transmits the drive via the propeller shaft to the rear differential.

The input shaft runs in line with the output shaft. The input shaft and output shaft gears are in constant mesh with the layshaft gear cluster. Selection of gears is by sliding synchromesh hubs, which lock the appropriate output shaft gears to the output shaft.

Gear selection is via a floor-mounted lever and selector mechanism or, depending on model, switches mounted on the steering wheel. A Sports Sequential Gearbox option is available for some models, where the gearchanges can be performed sequentially using the floor-mounted lever, or the 'paddle' shift switches on the steering wheel. On models so equipped, the gearchanges can be performed automatically, with the electronic control module (ECM) controlling gearchange and clutch operation (via hydraulic controls), dictated by driving style and road conditions. A 'launch control' is available on some models, where at the press of a button, the ECM will control engine speed, clutch operation and gearchange functions, to achieve maximum acceleration – consult your owner's handbook for further details.

The selector mechanism causes the appropriate selector fork to move its respective synchro-sleeve along the shaft, to lock the gear pinion to the synchro-hub. Since the synchro-hubs are splined to the output shaft, this locks the pinion to the shaft, so that drive can be transmitted. To ensure that gearchanging can be made quickly and quietly, a synchromesh system is fitted to all forward gears, consisting of baulk rings and spring-loaded fingers, as well as the gear pinions and synchro-hubs. The synchromesh cones are formed on the mating faces of the baulk rings and gear pinions.

The transmission is filled with oil during production, and is then considered 'filled for life', with BMW making no recommendations concerning the changing of the fluid.

2 Manual gearbox oil level check

1 To improve access, jack up the vehicle and support on axle stands (see *Jacking and vehicle support*). Ensure that the car is level.

2 Unscrew the gearbox oil level/filler plug from the right-hand side of the gearbox casing **(see illustration)**.

3 The oil level should be up to the bottom of the level/filler plug hole.

4 If necessary, top-up the level, using the correct type of fluid (see *Lubricants and fluids*) until the oil overflows from the filler/level plug hole.

5 Wipe away any spilt oil, then refit the filler/level plug, and tighten to the specified torque.

6 Lower the vehicle to the ground.

3 Manual gearbox oil renewal

Note: *New gearbox oil drain plug and oil filler/level plug sealing rings may be required on refitting.*

1 The gearbox oil should be drained with the gearbox at normal operating temperature. If the car has just been driven at least 20 miles, the gearbox can be considered warm.

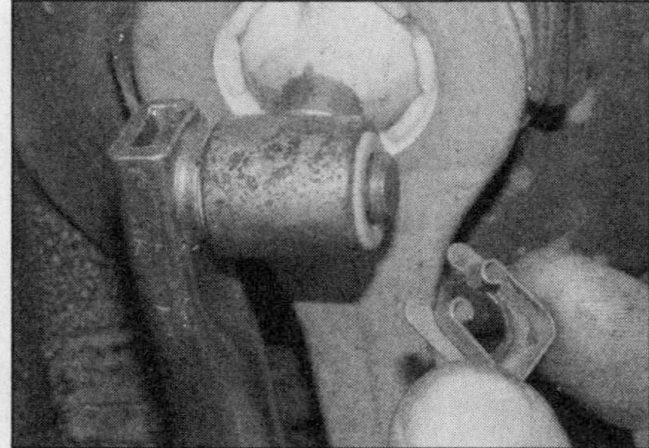

4.4 Slide the retaining clip from the selector rod pin

2 Immediately after driving the car, park it on a level surface, apply the handbrake. If desired, jack up the car and support on axle stands (see *Jacking and vehicle support*) to improve access, but make sure that the car is level. Remove the transmission undershield (where fitted).

3 Working under the car, slacken the gearbox oil drain plug about half a turn **(see illustration)**. Position a draining container under the drain plug, then remove the plug completely. If possible, try to keep the plug pressed into the gearbox while unscrewing it by hand the last couple of turns.

4 Where applicable, recover the sealing ring from the drain plug.

5 Refit the drain plug, using a new sealing ring where applicable, and tighten to the specified torque.

6 Unscrew the oil filler/level plug from the side of the gearbox, and recover the sealing ring, where applicable.

7 Fill the gearbox through the filler/level plug hole with the specified quantity and type of oil (see Specifications and *Lubricants and fluids*), until the oil overflows from the filler/level plug hole.

8 Refit the filler/level plug, using a new sealing ring where applicable, and tighten to the specified torque.

9 If applicable, lower the car to the ground.

4 Gearchange components – removal and refitting

Manual gearchange

Gear lever

Note: *A new gear lever bearing will be required on refitting.*

1 Jack up the car and support securely on axle stands (see *Jacking and vehicle support*).

2 Remove the knob from the gear lever by pulling it sharply upwards. **Note:** *Do not twist the knob or damage will result to the turning lock.*

3 Lever the gear lever gaiter from the centre console, and withdraw the gaiter over the gear lever. Where applicable, also remove the foam insulation.

4 Working under the vehicle, prise the securing clip from the end of the gear selector rod pin. Withdraw the selector rod pin from the eye on the end of the gear lever, and recover the washers **(see illustration)**.

5 It is now necessary to release the gear lever lower bearing retaining ring from the gear selector arm. A special tool is available for this purpose, but two screwdrivers, with the tips engaged in opposite slots in the bearing ring can be used instead. To unlock the bearing ring, turn it a quarter-turn anti-clockwise **(see illustration)**.

6 The bearing can now be pushed up through the housing, and the gear lever can be withdrawn from inside the vehicle.

7 If desired, the bearing can be removed from the gear lever ball by pressing it downwards. To withdraw the bearing over the lever eye, rotate the bearing until the eye passes through the slots provided in the bearing.

8 Fit a new bearing using a reversal of the removal process. Ensure that the bearing is pressed securely into position on the gear lever ball.

9 Refit the lever using a reversal of the removal process, bearing in mind the following points.

a) *Grease the contact faces of the bearing before refitting.*

b) *Lower the gear lever into position, ensuring that the arrow on the gear lever grommet points towards the front of the vehicle.*

c) *Make sure that the gear lever grommet is correctly engaged with the gear selector arm and with the opening in the vehicle floor* **(see illustration)**.

d) *When engaging the bearing with the selector arm, make sure that the arrows or tabs (as applicable) on the top of the bearing point towards the rear of the vehicle.*

e) *To lock the bearing in position in the selector arm, press down on the top of the bearing retaining tab locations until the tabs are heard to click into position.*

f) *Grease the selector rod pin before engaging it with the gear lever eye.*

Gear selector shaft eye

Note: *A new selector shaft eye securing roll-pin will be required on refitting.*

10 Jack up the car and support securely on axle stands (see *Jacking and vehicle support*).

11 Disconnect the propeller shaft from the gearbox flange, and support it clear of the gearbox using wire or string. Refer to Chapter 8 for details.

12 Prise the retaining clip from the end of the gear selector rod pin. Withdraw the selector rod pin from the selector shaft eye, and recover the washers.

13 Slide back the locking sleeve, then drive out the roll-pin securing the gear selector shaft eye to the end of the gear selector shaft **(see illustration)**.

14 Pull the gear selector shaft eye off the end of the selector shaft.

15 Refitting is a reversal of removal, bearing in mind the following points.

a) *Before refitting, check the condition of the rubber washer in the end of the selector shaft eye and renew if necessary.*

b) *Use a new roll-pin to secure the eye to the selector shaft.*

c) *Grease the selector rod pin.*

d) *Reconnect the propeller shaft to the gearbox flange as described in Chapter 8.*

Gear selector arm rear mounting

16 Jack up the car and support securely on axle stands (see *Jacking and vehicle support*).

17 Disconnect the propeller shaft from the gearbox flange, and support it clear of the gearbox using wire or string. See Chapter 8 for details.

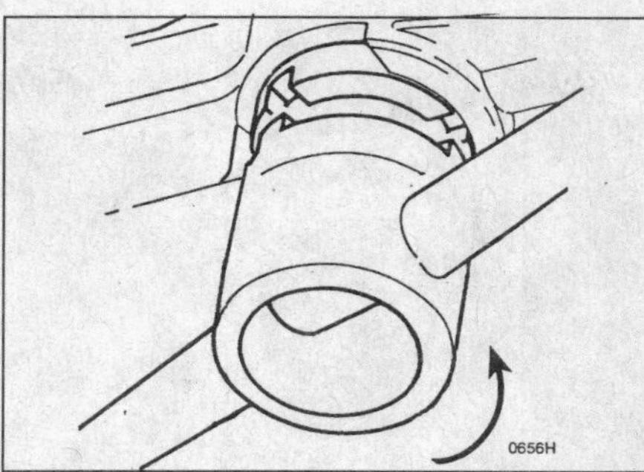

4.5 Turn the bearing ring anti-clockwise – special tool shown

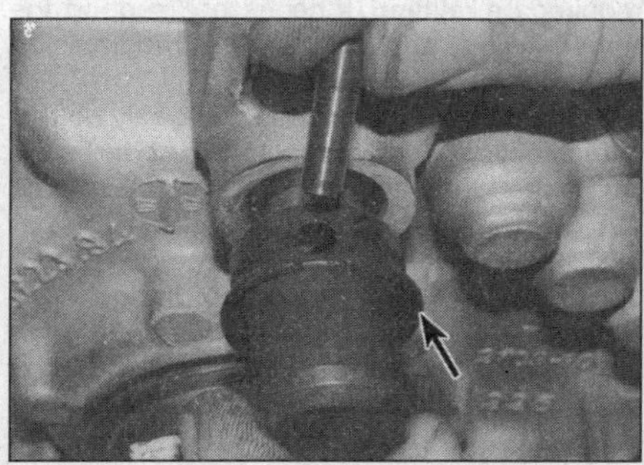

4.13 Slide back the circlip (arrowed) and drive out the pin

18 Remove the gear lever as described previously in this Section.

19 Using a screwdriver or a small pin-punch, lever the mounting sleeve from the bracket on the body **(see illustration)**.

20 Pull the mounting from the selector arm.

21 Grease the mounting, then push the mounting onto the selector arm, with the cut-out facing the rear of the vehicle, and the arrow pointing vertically upwards.

22 Clip the mounting into position in the bracket, making sure that the mounting is securely located.

23 Reconnect the propeller shaft to the gearbox flange as described in Chapter 8, then lower the vehicle to the ground.

Sequential gearchange (SSG)

24 No information was available at the time of writing.

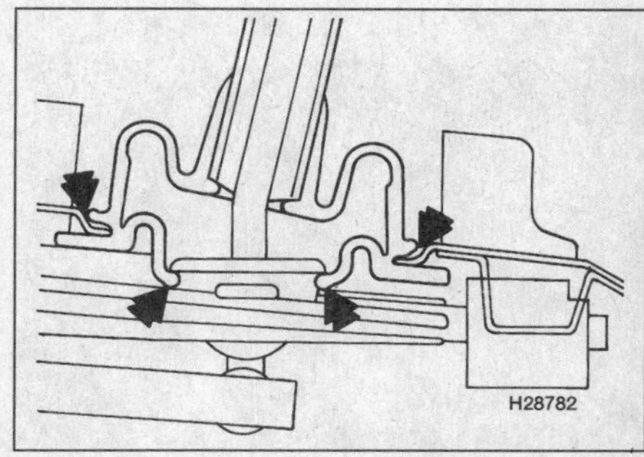

4.9 Gear lever grommet correctly engaged with the selector arm and vehicle floor

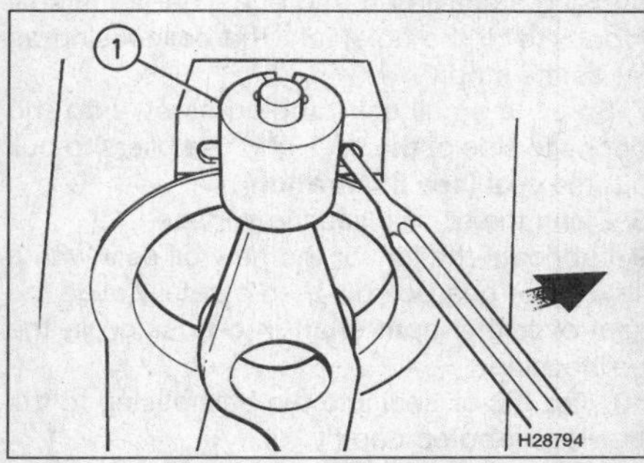

4.19 Lever the gear selector arm rear mounting sleeve (1) from the body bracket

5 Oil seals – renewal

Input shaft oil seal

1 With the gearbox removed as described in Section 7, proceed as follows.

2 Remove the clutch release bearing and lever as described in Chapter 6.

3 Unscrew the securing bolts and withdraw the clutch release bearing guide sleeve from the gearbox bellhousing **(see illustration)**.

4 Note the fitted depth of the now-exposed input shaft oil seal.

5 Drill one small hole in the oil seal (two small pilot holes should be provided at opposite points on the seal. Coat the end of the drill bit with grease to prevent any swarf from the holes entering the gearbox **(see illustration)**.

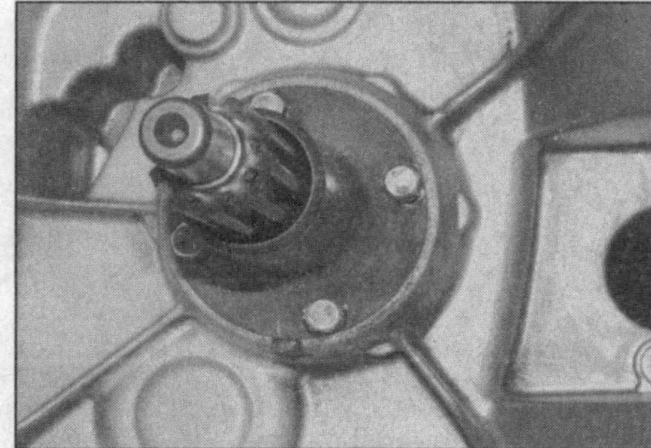

5.3 Undo the four bolts securing the clutch release bearing guide sleeve

5.5 Drill a small hole in the oil seal

5.7 Insert a self-tapping screw into the hole, and pull the seal from place with pliers

5.17 Counterhold the output flange and undo the nut using a deep socket

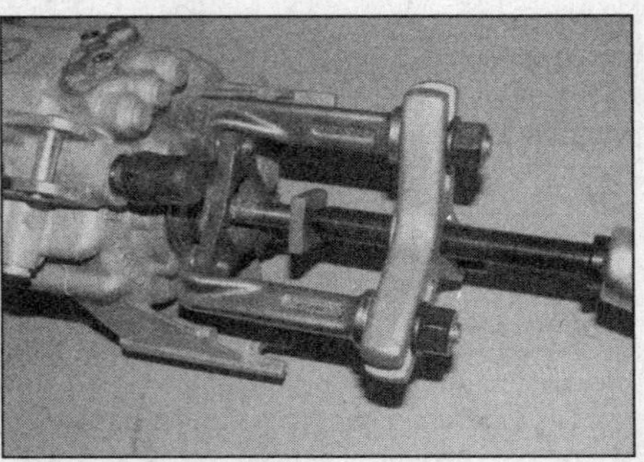

5.18 Use a three-legged puller to remove the output flange

6 Using a small drift, tap one side of the seal (opposite to the hole) into the bellhousing as far as the stop.

7 Screw a small self-tapping screw into the opposite side of the seal, and use pliers to pull out the seal **(see illustration)**.

8 Clean the oil seal seating surface.

9 Lubricate the lips of the new oil seal with a little clean gearbox oil, then carefully slide the seal over the input shaft into position in the bellhousing.

10 Tap the oil seal into the bellhousing to the previously-noted depth.

11 Refit the guide sleeve to the gearbox housing, tighten the retaining bolts securely, using a drop of locking compound on the threads of the bolts.

12 Refit the clutch release lever and bearing as described in Chapter 6.

13 Refit the gearbox as described in Section 7, then check the gearbox oil level as described in Section 2.

Output flange oil seal

Note: *Thread-locking compound will be required for the gearbox flange nut on refitting.*

14 Jack up the vehicle and support securely on axle stands (see *Jacking and vehicle support*).

15 Disconnect the propeller shaft from the gearbox flange, and support it clear of the gearbox using wire or string. See Chapter 8 for details.

16 Where applicable, prise the gearbox flange nut cover plate from the flange using a screwdriver. Discard the cover plate – it is not required on refitting. If necessary, support the transmission, and remove the transmission crossmember to improve access.

17 Counterhold the gearbox flange by bolting a forked or two-legged tool to two of the flange bolt holes, then unscrew the flange securing nut using a deep socket and extension bar **(see illustration)**.

18 Using a puller, draw the flange from the end of the gearbox output shaft **(see illustration)**. Be prepared for oil spillage.

19 Note the fitted depth of the oil seal then, using a puller (take care to avoid damage to the gearbox output shaft), pull the oil seal from the gearbox casing **(see illustration)**.

20 Clean the oil seal seating surface.

21 Lubricate the lips of the new oil seal with a little clean gearbox oil, then carefully tap the seal into the gearbox casing to the to the previously-noted depth **(see illustration)**.

22 Refit the flange to the output shaft. **Note:** *To ease refitment of the flange, immerse it in hot water for a few minutes, then install it on the shaft.*

23 Tighten the flange nut to the Stage one torque setting, then slacken and remove the nut (Stage two). Coat the threads of the flange nut with thread-locking compound, then tighten the nut to the Stage three torque as specified. Counterhold the flange as during removal.

24 If a flange nut cover plate was originally fitted, discard it. There is no need to fit a cover plate on refitting.

25 Reconnect the propeller shaft to the gearbox flange as described in Chapter 8, then check the gearbox oil level as described in Section 2, and lower the vehicle to the ground.

Gear selector shaft oil seal

Note: *A new selector shaft eye securing roll-pin will be required on refitting.*

26 Jack up the vehicle and support securely on axle stands (see *Jacking and vehicle support*).

27 Disconnect the propeller shaft from the gearbox flange, and support it clear of the gearbox using wire or string. See Chapter 8 for details. For improved access, support the transmission, and remove the transmission crossmember.

28 Slide back the locking collar, then slide out the pin securing the gear selector shaft eye to the end of the gear selector shaft.

29 Pull the gear selector shaft eye (complete with gear linkage) off the end of the selector shaft, and move the linkage clear of the selector shaft.

30 Using a small flat-bladed screwdriver, prise the selector shaft oil seal from the gearbox casing.

31 Clean the oil seal seating surface, then tap the new seal into position using a small socket or tube of the correct diameter **(see illustration)**.

32 Check the condition of the rubber washer in the end of the selector shaft eye and renew if necessary.

33 Push the selector shaft eye back onto the end of the selector shaft, then align the holes in the eye and shaft and secure the eye to the shaft using the pin.

34 Slide the locking collar into position over the roll-pin.

5.19 Carefully pull the seal from place

5.21 Tap the seal into place using a tubular spacer or socket which bears only on the hard outer edge of the seal

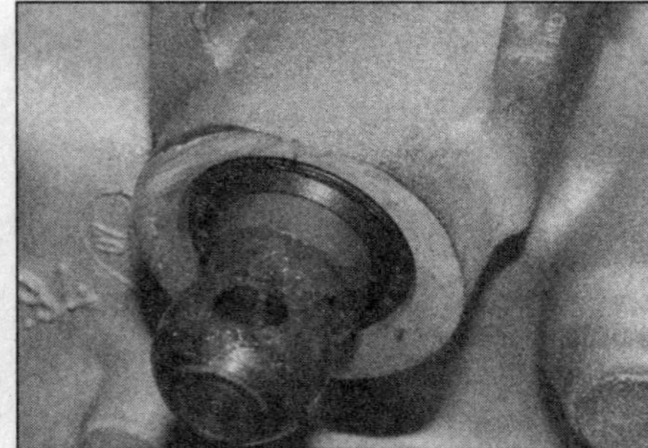

5.31 Tap the new selector shaft oil seal into position

35 Reconnect the propeller shaft to the gearbox flange as described in Chapter 8.
36 Check the gearbox oil level as described in Section 2, then lower the vehicle to the ground.

6 Reversing light switch – testing, removal and refitting

Testing

1 The reversing light circuit is controlled by a plunger-type switch screwed into the left-hand side of the Getrag gearbox casing, and the right-hand side of the ZF gearbox casing. If a fault develops in the circuit, first ensure that the circuit fuse has not blown.
2 To test the switch, disconnect the wiring connector, and use a multimeter (set to the resistance function) or a battery-and-bulb test circuit to check that there is continuity between the switch terminals only when reverse gear is selected. If this is not the case, and there are no obvious breaks or other damage to the wires, the switch is faulty, and must be renewed.

Removal

3 Jack up the vehicle and support securely on axle stands (see *Jacking and vehicle support*).
4 Disconnect the wiring connector, then unscrew the switch from the gearbox casing **(see illustration)**.

Refitting

5 Screw the switch back into position in the gearbox housing and tighten it securely. Reconnect the wiring connector, and test the operation of the circuit.
6 Lower the vehicle to the ground.

7 Manual gearbox – removal and refitting

Note: *This is an involved operation. Read through the procedure thoroughly before starting work, and ensure that adequate lifting tackle and/or jacking/support equipment is available.*

6.4 Reversing light switch (arrowed)

Removal

1 Disconnect the battery negative lead (see Chapter 5A).
2 Jack up the car and support securely on axle stands (see *Jacking and vehicle support*). Note that the car must be raised sufficiently to allow clearance for the gearbox to be removed from under the car. Undo the bolts and remove the engine/transmission undershields.
3 Remove the starter motor as described in Chapter 5A.
4 On M43TU engines, undo the nuts and remove the ignition coil from its mounting, and lay it to one side. This is to prevent any damage to the unit or HT leads as the engine is tilted to the backwards. There is no need to disconnect the HT leads.
5 Remove the propeller shaft as described in Chapter 8.
6 Working under the car, prise the retaining clip from the end of the gear selector rod pin. Withdraw the selector rod pin from the eye on the end of the gearbox selector shaft, and recover the washers. Similarly, disconnect the selector rod pin from the end of the gear lever, and withdraw the selector rod **(see illustration)**.
7 Working at the gearbox bellhousing, unscrew the nuts, and withdraw the clutch slave cylinder from the studs on the bellhousing. Support the slave cylinder clear of the working area, but do not strain the hose.
8 Note their fitted locations, then disconnect all wiring plugs, and release any wiring harnesses from the gearbox casing.
9 Remove the exhaust mounting bracket from the rear of the transmission casing.
10 Undo the securing bolts, and remove the front suspension reinforcement plate/brace.
11 On models with 6-cylinder engines, remove the heater/ventilation inlet air ducting from the rear of the engine compartment as follows **(see illustrations)**.

a) *Rotate the three fasteners 90° anti-clockwise and remove the pollen filter cover from the rear of the engine compartment. Pull the filter forward and remove it.*
b) *Undo the four retaining clips and thread the cable out of the ducting.*
c) *Unscrew the four bolts and pull the filter housing forwards and remove it.*
d) *Pull up the rubber strip, rotate the two fasteners anti-clockwise, and move the dividing panel in the left-hand corner of the engine compartment forward a little.*
e) *Undo the two bolts and remove the inlet ducting upwards and out of the engine compartment.*
f) *Remove the expanding rivets, and remove the air inlet cover from the top of the bonnet slam panel.*

12 On models with the M43TU engine, support the engine using a trolley jack under the sump, with a block of wood between the jack and sump to spread the load. Raise the jack to just touch the sump.
13 On other models, connect the lifting tackle to the engine lifting eye at the rear left-hand corner of the cylinder block (incorporated in the rear flange of the cylinder block casting).
14 Place a trolley jack under the gearbox casing, just behind the bellhousing. Use a block of wood to spread the load, then raise the jack to just take the weight of the gearbox.
15 Remove the crossmember and mountings from the rear of the transmission.
16 Using the jack(s) and engine hoist (where applicable), lower the engine and gearbox until the rear of the engine cylinder head/manifold assembly is almost touching the engine compartment bulkhead. Check that the assembly is not resting against any hoses/pipes on the bulkhead.
17 Working at the top of the gearbox, prise up the clip securing the gear selector arm pivot pin to the gearbox casing, then pull out

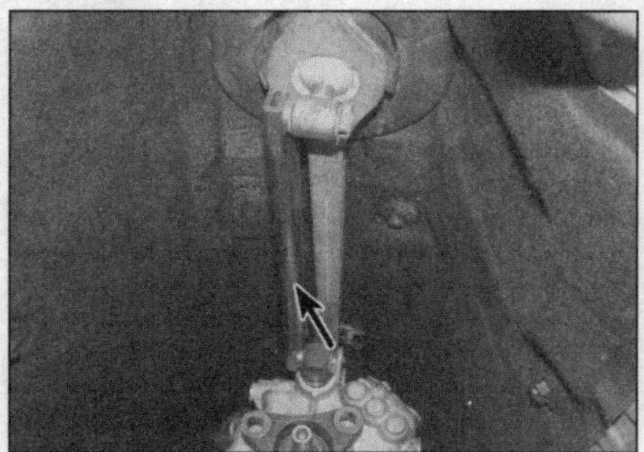

7.6 Remove the retaining clips and remove the selector rod (arrowed)

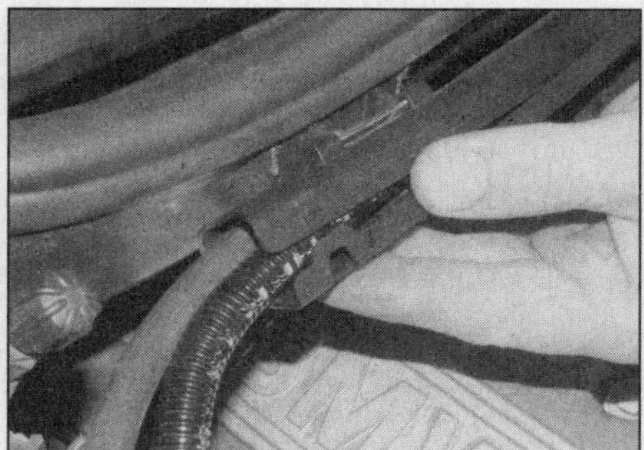

7.11a Unclip the cable ducting

7.11b Undo the two Torx bolts (arrowed) and remove the inlet housing

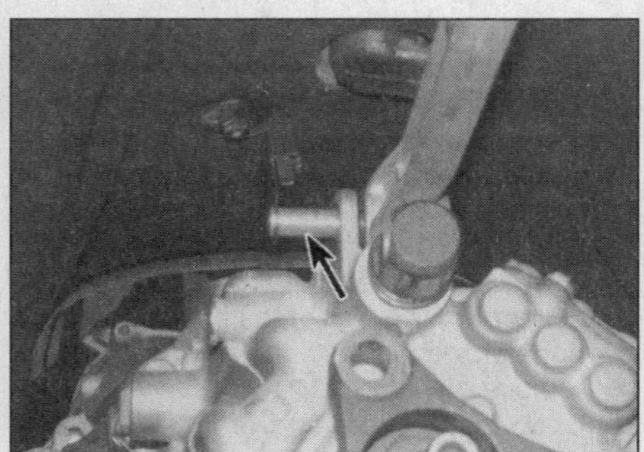

7.17 Prise up the retaining clip and slide the pivot pin out (arrowed)

the pivot pin to release the selector arm from the gearbox **(see illustration)**.

18 Where applicable, unscrew the bolt securing the engine/gearbox adapter plate to the right-hand side of the gearbox bellhousing and/or remove the flywheel lower cover plate **(see illustration)**.

19 Unscrew the engine-to-gearbox bolts, and recover the washers, then slide the gearbox rearwards to disengage the input shaft from the clutch. Take care during this operation to ensure that the weight of the gearbox is not allowed to hang on the input shaft. As the gearbox is released from the engine, check to make sure that the engine is not forced against the heater hose connections or the bulkhead.

20 Lower the gearbox and carefully withdraw it from under the car. If the gearbox is to be removed for some time, ensure that the engine is adequately supported in the engine compartment.

Refitting

21 Commence refitting by checking that the clutch friction disc is centralised as described in Chapter 6.

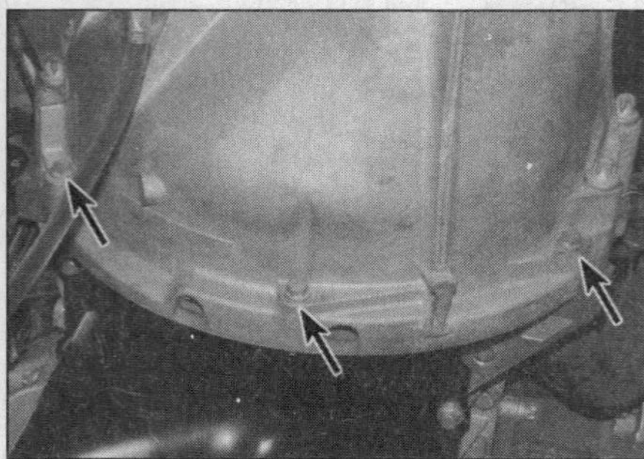

7.18 Undo the three bolts (arrowed) and remove the flywheel lower cover plate

22 Before refitting the gearbox, it is advisable to inspect and grease the clutch release bearing and lever as described in Chapter 6.

23 The remainder of the refitting procedure is a reversal of removal, bearing in mind the following points.

a) Check that the gearbox positioning dowels are securely in place at the rear of the engine.
b) Make sure that the washers are in place on the engine-to-gearbox bolts.
c) Tighten all fixings to the specified torque.
d) Lightly grease the gear selector arm pivot pin and the gear selector rod pin before refitting.
e) Reconnect the propeller shaft to the gearbox flange as described in Chapter 8.
f) Refit the starter motor as described in Chapter 5A.

8 Manual gearbox overhaul – general information

Overhauling a manual gearbox is a difficult and involved job for the DIY home mechanic. In addition to dismantling and reassembling many small parts, clearances must be precisely measured and, if necessary, changed by selecting shims and spacers. Internal gearbox components are also often difficult to obtain, and in many instances, extremely expensive. Because of this, if the gearbox develops a fault or becomes noisy, the best course of action is to have the unit overhauled by a specialist repairer, or to obtain an exchange reconditioned unit. Be aware that some gearbox repairs can be carried out with the gearbox in the car.

Nevertheless, it is not impossible for the more experienced mechanic to overhaul the gearbox, provided the special tools are available, and the job is done in a deliberate step-by-step manner, so that nothing is overlooked.

The tools necessary for an overhaul include internal and external circlip pliers, bearing pullers, a slide hammer, a set of pin punches, a dial test indicator, and possibly a hydraulic press. In addition, a large, sturdy workbench and a vice will be required.

During dismantling of the gearbox, make careful notes of how each component is fitted, to make reassembly easier and more accurate.

Before dismantling the gearbox, it will help if you have some idea what area is malfunctioning. Certain problems can be closely related to specific areas in the gearbox, which can make component examination and renewal easier. Refer to the *Fault finding* Section at the end of this manual for more information.

Chapter 7 Part B: Automatic transmission

Contents

Degrees of difficulty

Easy, suitable for novice with little experience 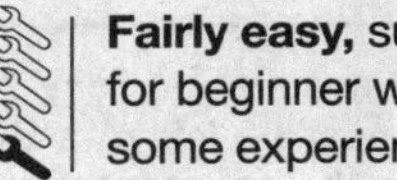	**Fairly easy,** suitable for beginner with some experience	**Fairly difficult,** suitable for competent DIY mechanic	**Difficult,** suitable for experienced DIY mechanic	**Very difficult,** suitable for expert DIY or professional 

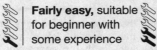

Specifications

Engine codes

4-cylinder engines

1796 cc engines	N42 B18 and N46 B18
1895 cc engines	M43TU B19
1995 cc engines	N42 B20 and N46 B20

6-cylinder engines

2171 cc engines	M54 B22
2494 cc engines	M52TU B25 and M54 B25
2793 cc engines	M52TU B28
2979 cc engines	M54 B30

Transmission fluid level

Fluid temperature	Fluid level height
20°C	3 to 15 mm
25°C	5 to 17 mm
30°C	8 to 20 mm
35°C	11 to 22 mm
40°C	13 to 25 mm
45°C	14 to 26 mm
50°C	16 to 27 mm
55°C	17 to 28 mm
60°C	19 to 29 mm
65°C	21 to 32 mm
70°C	22 to 34 mm
75°C	24 to 36 mm
80°C	26 to 38 mm
85°C	29 to 41 mm

Torque wrench settings

Torque wrench settings	Nm	lbf ft
Engine-to-transmission bolts:		
Hexagon bolts:		
M8 bolts	24	18
M10 bolts	45	33
M12 bolts	82	61
Torx bolts:		
M8 bolts	21	15
M10 bolts	42	31
M12 bolts	72	53
Engine/transmission adapter plate bolt	23	17
Output flange-to-output shaft nut:		
Stage 1	190	140
Stage 2	Remove nut and apply locking compound	
Stage 3	120	89
Torque-converter-to-driveplate bolts:		
M8 bolts	26	19
M10 bolts	49	36
Transmission crossmember-to-body bolts:		
M8 bolts	21	15
M10 bolts	42	31
Transmission mounting-to-transmission nuts:		
M8 nuts	21	15
M10 nuts	42	31
Transmission oil drain plug:		
4-speed transmission	25	18
5-speed transmission	35	26
Transmission oil filler/level plug:		
4-speed transmission	33	24
5-speed transmission	40	30

* *Use thread-locking compound*

1 General information

Depending on model, a four- or five-speed automatic transmission may be fitted, consisting of a torque converter, an epicyclic geartrain and hydraulically-operated clutches and brakes.

The torque converter provides a fluid coupling between engine and transmission, acting as a clutch, and also provides a degree of torque multiplication when accelerating.

The epicyclic geartrain provides either of the forward or reverse gear ratio, according to which of its component parts are held stationary or allowed to turn. The components of the geartrain are held or released by brakes and clutches which are activated by a hydraulic control unit. A fluid pump within the transmission provides the necessary hydraulic pressure to operate the brakes and clutches.

Driver control of the transmission is by a seven-position selector lever, and a four-position switch. The transmission has a 'drive' position, and a 'hold' facility on the first three gear ratios (four-speed transmission) or gear ratios 2 to 4 (five-speed transmissions). The 'drive' position (D) provides automatic changing throughout the range of all forward gear ratios, and is the position selected for normal driving. An automatic kickdown facility shifts the transmission down a gear if the accelerator pedal is fully depressed. The 'hold' facility is very similar, but limits the number of gear ratios available – ie, when the selector lever is in the 3 position, only the first three ratios can be selected; in the 2 position, only the first two can be selected, and so on. The lower ratio 'hold' is useful when travelling down steep gradients, or for preventing unwanted selection of top gear on twisty roads. Three driving programs are provided for selection by the switch; 'Economy', 'Sport', and 'Manual' (four-speed transmission) or 'Winter' (five-speed transmission).

Certain models are available with Steptronic gearchange where the driver is able to induce gearchanges with a simple movement of the lever – forward to change up, and back to change down.

Due to the complexity of the automatic transmission, any repair or overhaul work must be left to a BMW dealer or specialist with the necessary special equipment for fault diagnosis and repair. The contents of the following Sections are therefore confined to supplying general information, and any service information and instructions that can be used by the owner.

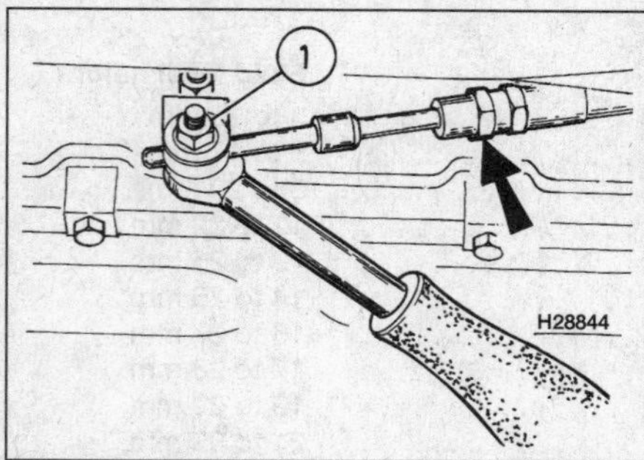

2.2 Counterhold the clamp bolt, and slacken the selector cable securing nut (1)
Cable-to-bracket securing nut arrowed

2 Gear selector lever – removal and refitting

Removal

1 Jack up the car and support securely on axle stands (see *Jacking and vehicle support*). Ensure the selector lever is in position P.

2 Working underneath the vehicle, slacken the selector cable clamping nut on the transmission lever **(see illustration)**.

3 Undo the locknut securing the selector outer cable and remove the cable from the support bracket on the transmission.

4 Working in the passenger cabin, pull the knob from the selector lever, with a strong 'tug'. **Note:** *Do not twist the knob or damage will result to the turning lock in the lever.*

5 Carefully prise up the lever trim (complete with lever gaiter) from the centre console. Note their fitted locations, and disconnect the wiring plugs from the underside of the trim.

6 Undo the two trim retaining bolts at the rear of the selector lever aperture. Starting at the rear, lift the trim and disconnect the wiring

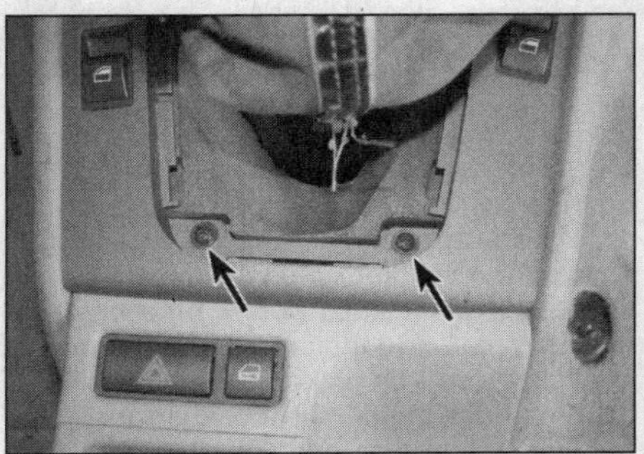

2.6 Undo the two bolts at the rear of the selector lever aperture (arrowed)

2.8 Undo the four bolts (arrowed) and remove the frame

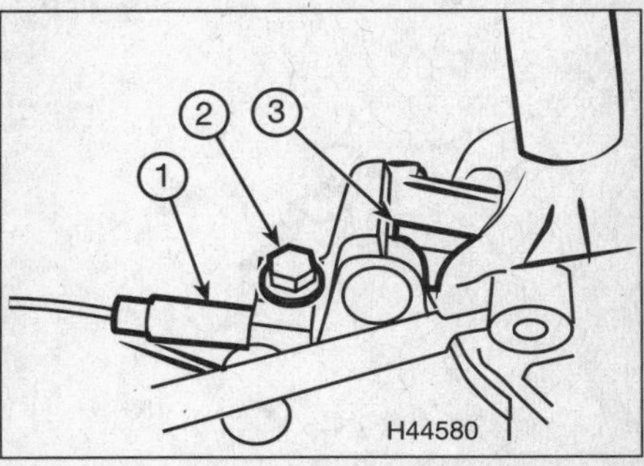

2.9 Interlock cable (1), clamping bolt (2) and interlock lever (3)

plugs from the underside of the trim – having noted their fitted locations **(see illustration)**. Remove the trim.

7 Pull out the storage tray from above the ashtray.

8 Undo the four retaining bolts, and pull the ashtray/switch frame back from the centre console. Press the switches out of the frame, and disconnect their wiring plugs – having noted their fitted positions **(see illustration)**. Remove the frame.

9 Slacken the interlock cable clamping bolt **(see illustration)**.

10 Note their fitted positions, then disconnect any wiring plugs attached to the selector lever assembly.

11 Undo the three bolts securing the lever assembly to the floor, manoeuvre the assembly up from its location, unhooking the interlock cable as it is withdrawn.

Refitting

12 Refitting is a reversal of removal, noting the following points:

a) *Prior to refitting the gear knob, push the gaiter down the lever until the locking groove in the lever is exposed.*
b) *On completion, adjust the selector cable as described in Section 3.*

3 Gear selector cable – removal, refitting and adjustment

Removal

1 Disconnect the cable from the selector lever assembly as described in Section 2.

2 To improve access, apply the handbrake, then jack up the front of the car and support securely on axle stands (see *Jacking and vehicle support*).

3 Working at the end of the cable, counterhold the clamp bolt, and loosen the securing nut. Take care not to bend the end of the cable **(see illustration 2.2)**.

4 Loosen the securing nut, and release the cable from the bracket on the transmission.

5 Slide the end of the cable from the end fitting.

6 Withdraw the cable down from under the car, noting its routing to ensure correct refitting.

Refitting

7 Refitting is a reversal of removal, bearing in mind the following points.

a) *Do not tighten the cable end securing nut and bolts until the cable has been adjusted.*
b) *Reconnect the cable to the selector lever assembly with reference to Section 2.*
c) *On completion, adjust the cable as described in the following paragraphs.*

Adjustment

8 Move the selector lever to position P.

9 If not already done, counterhold clamp bolt and loosen the clamp nut securing the cable to the end fitting (the car should be raised for access).

10 Push the operating lever on the transmission away from the cable bracket on the transmission (towards the Park position).

11 Press the end of the cable in the opposite direction (ie, towards the cable bracket), then release the cable and tighten the clamp nut (again, counterhold the bolt) **(see illustration)**.

12 Check that the cable is correctly adjusted by starting the engine, applying the brakes firmly, and moving the selector lever through all the selector positions.

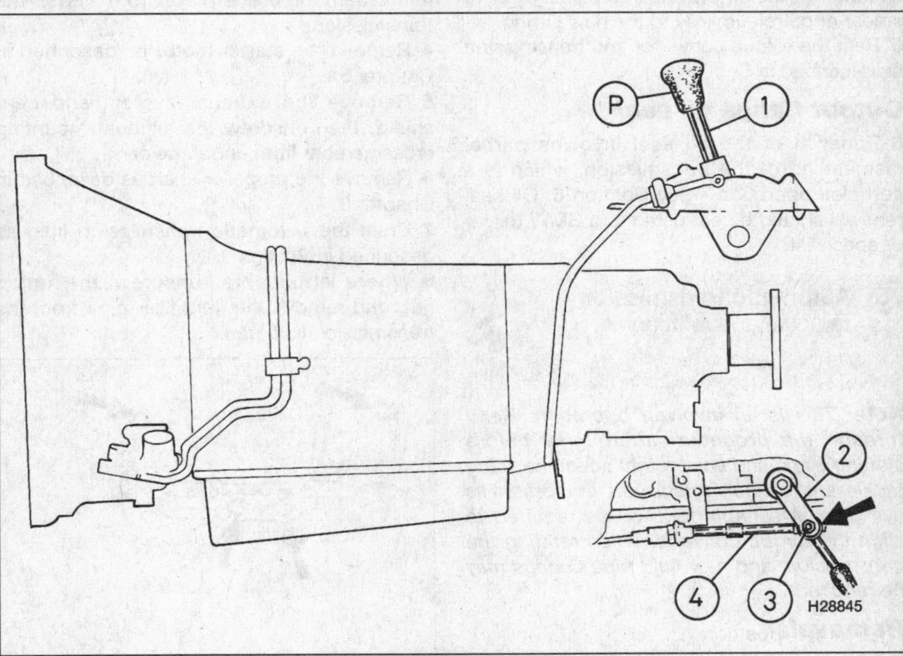

3.11 Adjusting the selector cable

P Park position
1 Selector lever
2 Operating lever
3 Clamp nut
4 Selector cable

4 Fluid seals – renewal

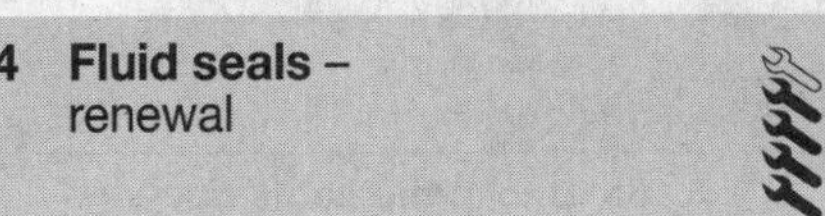

Torque converter seal

1 Remove the transmission and the torque converter as described in Section 5.

2 Using a hooked tool, prise the old oil seal from the transmission bellhousing. Alternatively, drill a small hole, then screw a

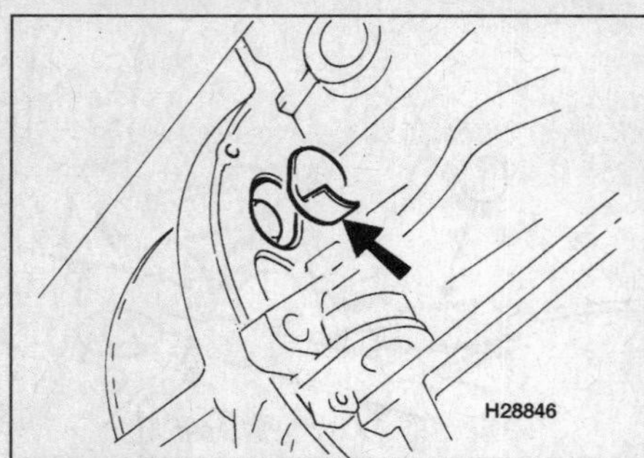

5.13a Prise the plug (arrowed) from the engine/transmission adapter plate . . .

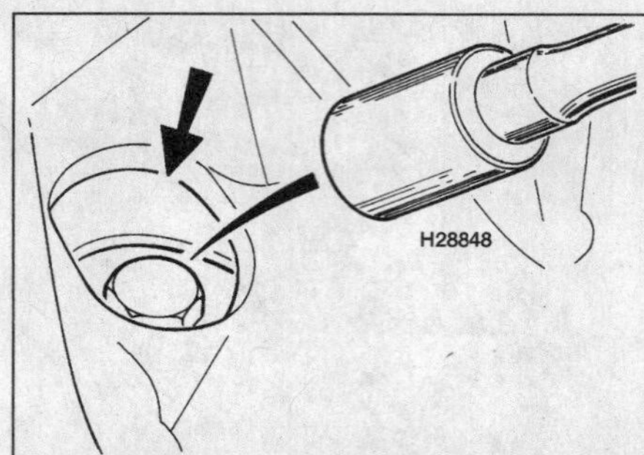

5.13b . . . or from the aperture in the crankcase

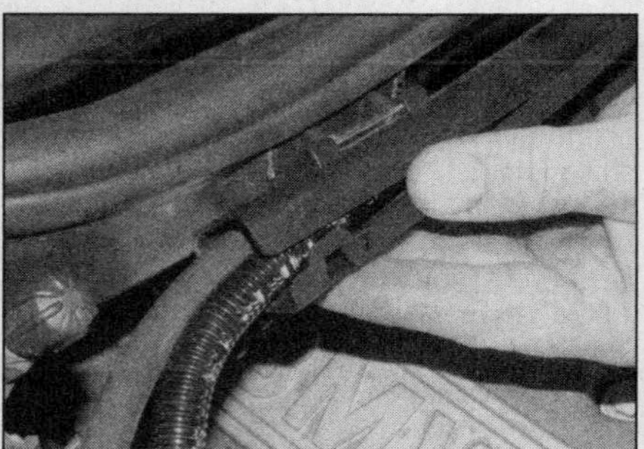
5.16a Unclip the cable ducting

5.16b Undo the two Torx bolts (arrowed) and remove the inlet housing

self-tapping screw into the seal and use pliers to pull out the seal.

3 Lubricate the lip of the new seal with clean fluid, then carefully drive it into place using a large socket or tube.

4 Remove the old O-ring seal from the input shaft, and slide a new one into place. Apply a smear of petroleum jelly to the new O-ring.

5 Refit the torque converter and transmission as described in Section 5.

Output flange oil seal

6 Renewal of the oil seal involves partial dismantling of the transmission, which is a complex operation – see Section 6. Oil seal renewal should be entrusted to a BMW dealer or specialist.

5 Automatic transmission – removal and refitting

Note: *This is an involved operation. Read through the procedure thoroughly before starting work, and ensure that adequate lifting tackle and/or jacking/support equipment is available. A suitable tool will be required to align the torque converter when refitting the transmission, and new fluid pipe O-rings may be required.*

Removal

1 Disconnect the battery negative lead – see Chapter 5A.

2 Jack up the car and support securely on axle stands (see *Jacking and vehicle support*). Note that the car must be raised sufficiently to allow clearance for the transmission to be removed from under the car. Undo the bolts and remove the engine/transmission undershield from the vehicle.

3 Undo the bolts and remove the front reinforcement brace/plate from under the transmission.

4 Remove the starter motor as described in Chapter 5A.

5 Remove the exhaust system and heat shield, then unscrew the exhaust mounting crossmember from under the car.

6 Remove the propeller shaft as described in Chapter 8.

7 Drain the automatic transmission fluid as described in Section 9.

8 Where applicable, unscrew the union nut, and remove the fluid filler pipe from the transmission fluid pan.

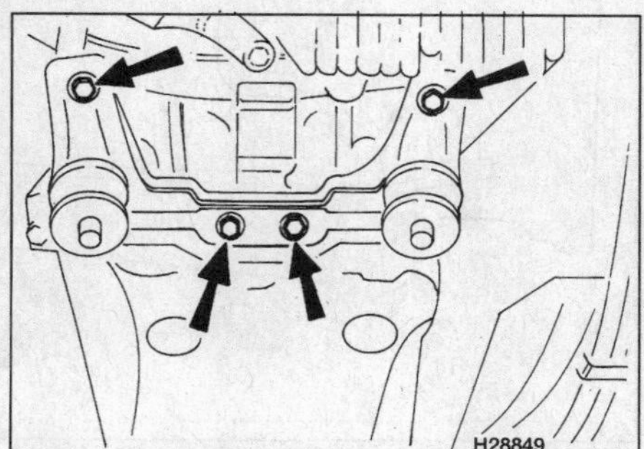

5.20 Where applicable, undo the bolts (arrowed) and remove the transmission front mounting assembly

9 Disconnect the selector cable from the transmission with reference to Section 3.

10 Note their fitted locations, then disconnect the transmission wiring harness plugs. Release the wiring harness from the brackets and clips on the transmission.

11 Where applicable, release the oxygen sensor from the bracket on the transmission.

12 Unscrew the fluid cooler pipe brackets and clamps. Undo the unions and disconnect the fluid pipes – be prepared for fluid spillage.

13 Prise the plug from the aperture in the engine/transmission adapter plate above the sump, or from the aperture in the crankcase, depending on model, for access to the torque converter securing bolts **(see illustrations)**.

14 Unscrew the three torque converter bolts, turning the crankshaft using a spanner or socket on the pulley hub bolt for access to each bolt in turn.

15 Support the transmission using a trolley jack and interposed block of wood.

Caution: The transmission is heavy, so ensure that it is adequately supported.

16 On models with 6-cylinder engines, remove the heater/ventilation inlet air ducting from the rear of the engine compartment as follows.

a) Rotate the three fasteners 90° anti-clockwise and remove the pollen filter cover from the rear of the engine compartment. Pull the filter forward and remove it.

*b) Undo the four retaining clips and thread the cable out of the ducting **(see illustration)**.*

c) Unscrew the four bolts and pull the filter housing forwards and remove it.

d) Pull up the rubber strip, rotate the two fasteners anti-clockwise, and move the dividing panel in the left-hand corner of the engine compartment forward a little.

*e) Undo the two bolts and remove the inlet ducting upwards and out of the engine compartment **(see illustration)**.*

17 On models with the M43TU engine, remove the ignition coil mounting bolts from the inner wing, and lay the coil to one side. This is to prevent damage to the coil and leads as the engine is tilted back. There is no need to disconnect the coils leads.

18 On all models with 4-cylinder engines, support the engine using a trolley jack under the sump, with a block of wood between the jack and sump to spread the load. Raise the jack to just touch the sump.

19 On models with 6-cylinder engines, connect the lifting tackle to the engine lifting eye at the rear left-hand corner of the cylinder block (incorporated in the rear flange of the cylinder block casting).

20 Where applicable, unscrew the transmission front mounting assembly **(see illustration)**.

21 Check to ensure that the engine and transmission are adequately supported then, working under the car, unscrew the nuts securing the transmission rubber mountings to the lugs on the transmission casing.

22 Remove the bolts securing the transmission crossmember to the body, then withdraw the crossmember from under the car. If necessary, bend back or unscrew the exhaust heat shield for access to the crossmember bolts.

23 Using the jack(s) and engine hoist (where applicable), lower the engine and transmission until the rear of the engine cylinder head/ manifold assembly is almost touching the engine compartment bulkhead. Check that the assembly is not resting against the heater hose connections on the bulkhead.

24 Unscrew the engine-to-transmission bolts, and recover the washers, then slide the transmission rearwards.

25 Insert a suitable metal or wooden lever through the slot in the bottom of the bellhousing to retain the torque converter. As the transmission is released from the engine, check to make sure that the engine is not forced against the heater hose connections or the bulkhead.

26 Lower the transmission and carefully withdraw it from under the car, making sure that the torque converter is held in position. If the transmission is to be removed for some time, ensure that the engine is adequately supported in the engine compartment.

27 To remove the torque converter, first remove the retaining lever.

28 Fit two long bolts to two of the torque converter securing bolt holes, and use the bolts to pull the torque converter from the transmission **(see illustration)**. Pull evenly on both bolts. Be prepared for fluid spillage.

Refitting

29 Where applicable, refit the torque converter, using the two bolts to manipulate the converter into position. Whilst applying slight pressure, turn the torque converter to ensure that the hub teeth engage with the input shaft teeth. The correct fitted depth of the torque converter is greater than 30 mm (approx) from the bellhousing face to the forward edge of the torque converter securing bolt holes.

30 Ensure that the transmission locating dowels are in position on the engine.

31 Before mating the transmission with the engine, it is essential that the torque converter is perfectly aligned with the driveplate. Once the engine and transmission have been mated, it is no longer possible to turn the torque converter to allow re-alignment.

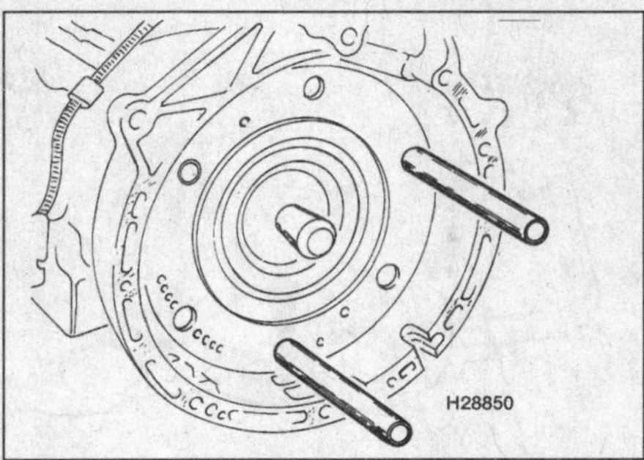

5.28 Fit two long bolts to lift out the torque converter

32 To align the driveplate with the torque converter, BMW use a special tapered tool which screws into the driveplate. It may be possible to improvise a suitable tool using an old torque converter-to-driveplate bolt with the head cut off, or a length of threaded bar – note that the end of the bolt or bar must either have a slot cut in the end, or flats machined on it to allow it to be unscrewed once the engine and transmission have been mated.

33 Turn the flywheel to align one of the torque converter-to-driveplate bolt holes with the aperture in the bottom of the sump/bellhousing (for access to the sump securing bolt), or with the aperture in the engine/transmission adapter plate (as applicable). This is essential to enable the alignment stud to be removed after the engine and transmission have been mated.

34 Screw the alignment tool into the relevant hole in the driveplate **(see illustrations)**.

35 Where applicable, remove the retaining lever from the torque converter.

36 Ensure that the transmission is adequately supported, and manoeuvre it into position under the car.

37 Turn the torque converter to align one of the torque converter-to-driveplate bolt holes with the alignment tool fitted to the driveplate, then offer the transmission into position.

38 Ensure that the alignment tool passes through the hole in the torque converter, then refit and tighten the engine-to-transmission bolts, ensuring that the washers are in place **(see illustration)**.

39 Unscrew the alignment tool from the driveplate, then refit the torque converter-to-driveplate bolt. Tighten the bolt to the specified torque.

40 Turn the crankshaft as during removal for access to the remaining two torque converter-to-driveplate bolt locations. Refit and tighten the bolts.

41 Further refitting is a reversal of removal, bearing in mind the following points.

- *a) Tighten all fixings to the specified torques, where applicable.*
- *b) Check the condition of the transmission fluid pipe O-rings and renew if necessary.*
- *c) Refit the propeller shaft (see Chapter 8).*
- *d) Refit the starter motor (see Chapter 5A).*
- *e) Reconnect and adjust the selector cable as described in Section 3.*
- *f) On completion, refill the transmission with fluid as described in Section 9.*

6 Automatic transmission overhaul – general information

In the event of a fault occurring with the transmission, it is first necessary to determine whether it is of an electrical, mechanical or hydraulic nature, and to do this special test equipment is required. It is therefore essential to have the work carried out by a BMW dealer or suitably-equipped specialist if a transmission fault is suspected.

Do not remove the transmission from the car for possible repair before professional fault diagnosis has been carried out, since most tests require the transmission to be in the car.

7 Electronic components/ sensors – removal and refitting

1 The turbine speed sensor, output speed sensor and transmission range switch are

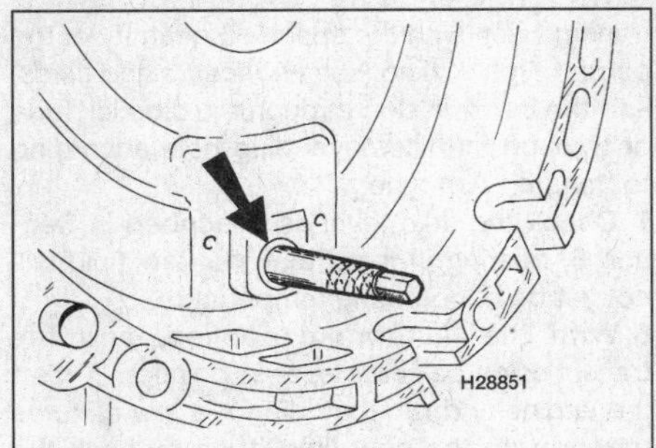

5.34a Alignment tool (arrowed) screws into the driveplate, aligned with the aperture in the bottom of the sump/bellhousing

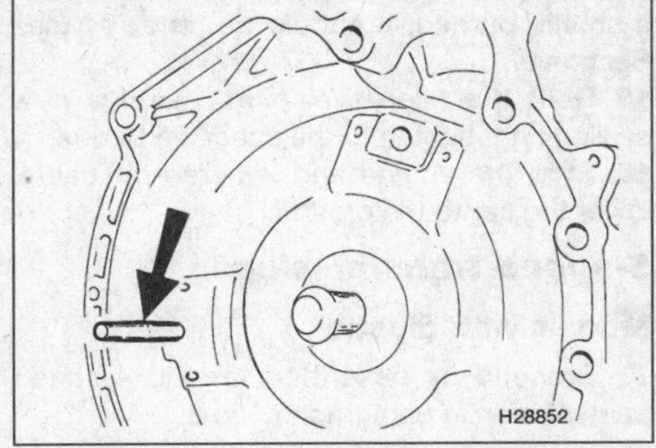

5.34b Alignment tool screws into the driveplate aligned with the aperture in the engine/transmission adapter plate (5-speed transmission)

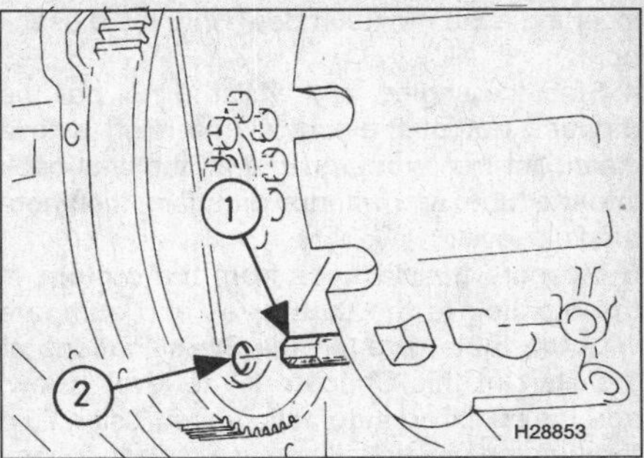

5.38 Ensure that the alignment tool (1) passes through the hole (2) in the torque converter

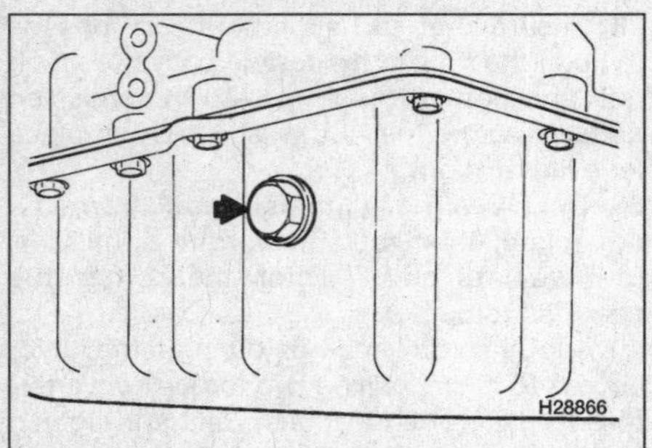

8.11 Automatic transmission oil filler/level plug

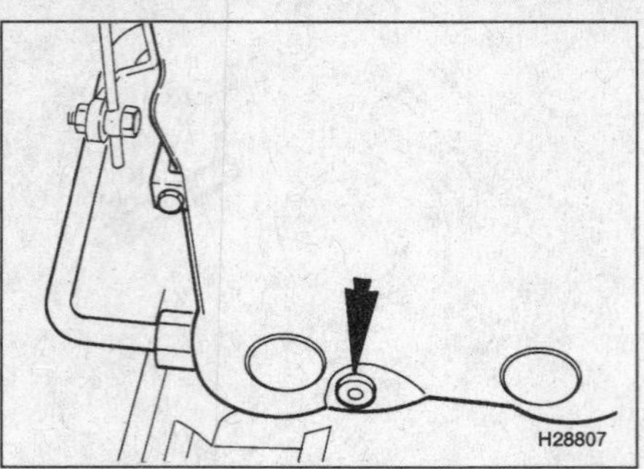

9.3a Automatic transmission oil drain plug (arrowed) – 5-speed transmission

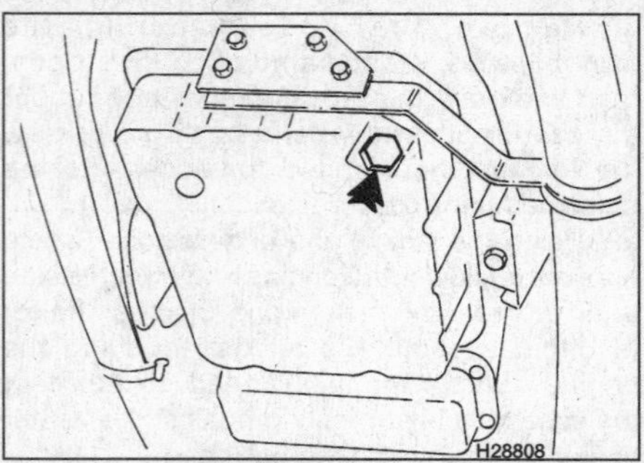

9.3b Automatic transmission oil drain plug (arrowed) – 4-speed transmission

all contained within the transmission casing. Renewal of the components involves removal and the sump and partial dismantling of the transmission, therefore this should be entrusted to a BMW dealer or suitably-equipped specialist.

2 The transmission electronic control module (ECM) is located in the 'E-box' in the left-hand corner of the engine compartment. Undo the bolts, remove the E-box lid, disconnect the wiring plug and remove the ECM.

8 Automatic transmission fluid level check

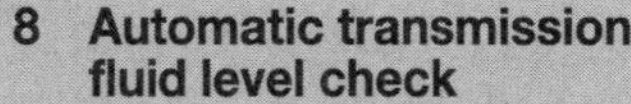

4-speed transmission

Models with dipstick

1 Park the vehicle on a level surface, apply the handbrake and start the engine. While the engine is idling, depress the brake pedal and move the selector lever through all the gear positions, beginning and ending in P.

2 The automatic transmission fluid dipstick is located in the rear left-hand corner of the engine compartment.

3 The level of the fluid within the transmission depends on its temperature. To establish this temperature BMW technicians use special diagnostic equipment plugged into the vehicle diagnostic socket in the right-hand corner of the engine compartment. However, with care the temperature of the fluid can be taken by inserting a thermometer down into the dipstick hole.

4 Start the engine, and whilst idling, pull the dipstick out of the tube, wipe it off with a clean, lint-free cloth, push it all the way back into the tube, and withdraw it again, then note the fluid level.

5 Measure the distance from the bottom of the dipstick to the fluid level, and compare with the table given in the Specifications at the start of this Chapter. If the level is low, add the specified automatic transmission fluid through the dipstick tube – use a clean funnel, preferably equipped with a fine mesh filter, to prevent spills.

Caution: Be careful not to introduce dirt into the transmission when topping-up.

6 Add just enough of the recommended fluid to fill the transmission to the proper level. Add the fluid a little at a time, and keep checking the level until it is correct.

7 On completion, stop the engine.

8 The condition of the fluid should also be checked along with the level. If the fluid is black or a dark reddish-brown colour, or if it smells burned, it should be renewed (see Section 9).

Models without dipstick

Note: *A new filler/level plug sealing ring will be required on refitting.*

9 The fluid level is checked by removing the filler/level plug from the transmission fluid pan. If desired, jack up the car and support on axle stands (see *Jacking and vehicle support*) to improve access, but make sure that the car is level.

10 While the engine is idling, depress the brake pedal and move the selector lever through all the gear positions, beginning and ending in P.

11 Working under the car, place a container under the transmission fluid pan, then unscrew the filler/level plug **(see illustration)**. Recover the sealing ring.

12 The fluid level should be up to the lower edge of the filler/level plug hole.

13 If necessary, top-up the fluid until it overflows from the plug hole.

14 The condition of the fluid should also be checked along with the level. If the fluid is black or a dark reddish-brown colour, or if it smells burned, it should be renewed (see Section 9).

15 Refit the filler/level plug, using a new sealing ring; tighten to the specified torque.

16 Stop the engine and, where applicable, lower the car to the ground.

5-speed transmission

Models with dipstick

17 Proceed as described for the 4-speed transmission in paragraphs 1 to 8.

Models without dipstick

18 On models not fitted with a dipstick, checking of the automatic transmission fluid level should be referred to a BMW dealer.

9 Automatic transmission fluid renewal

Note: *On models fitted with a 5-speed transmission without a dipstick, renewal of the transmission fluid should be entrusted to a BMW dealer, as special equipment is required to check the fluid level on completion.*

Note: *A new drain plug sealing ring will be required on refitting.*

1 The transmission fluid should be drained with the transmission at operating temperature. If the car has just been driven at least 20 miles, the transmission can be considered warm.

2 Immediately after driving the car, park it on a level surface, apply the handbrake. If desired, jack up the car and support on axle stands (see *Jacking and vehicle support*) to improve access, but make sure that the car is level.

3 Working under the car, slacken the transmission fluid pan drain plug about half a turn **(see illustrations)**. Position a draining container under the drain plug, then remove the plug completely. If possible, try to keep the plug pressed into the fluid pan while unscrewing it by hand the last couple of turns.

4 Recover the sealing ring from the drain plug.

5 Refit the drain plug, using a new sealing ring, and tighten to the specified torque.

6 With reference to Section 8, fill the transmission with the specified quantity of the correct type of fluid (see *Lubricants and fluids*) – fill the transmission through the dipstick tube or through the filler/level plug hole according to transmission type.

7 Check the fluid level as described in Section 8, bearing in mind that the new fluid will not yet be at operating temperature.

8 With the handbrake applied, and the transmission selector lever in position P, start the engine and run it at idle for a few minutes to warm up the new fluid, then recheck the fluid level as described in Section 8. Note that it may be necessary to drain off a little fluid once the new fluid has reached operating temperature.

Chapter 8
Final drive, driveshafts and propeller shaft

Contents

Degrees of difficulty

Easy, suitable for novice with little experience 

Fairly easy, suitable for beginner with some experience

Fairly difficult, suitable for competent DIY mechanic

Difficult, suitable for experienced DIY mechanic

Very difficult, suitable for expert DIY or professional 

Specifications

Final drive

Type	Unsprung, attached to rear suspension crossmember

Driveshaft

Type	Steel shafts with ball-and-cage type constant velocity joints at each end
Constant velocity joint grease capacity	80g in each joint

Propeller shaft

Type	Two-piece tubular shaft with centre bearing, centre and rear universal joint. Front joint is either rubber coupling or universal joint (depending on model)

Torque wrench settings

Note: *On some fixings different grades of bolt can be used; the grade of each bolt is stamped on the bolt head. Ensure that each bolt is tightened to the correct torque for its grade.*

Final drive unit	**Nm**	**lbf ft**
Mounting bolts:		
Front bolt	95	70
Rear bolts	174	128
Oil filler and drain plug	70	52
Propeller shaft flange retaining nut (approximate – see text):		
M20 nut	175	129
M22 nut	185	137
Vibration damper on bracket (where fitted)	77	57
Driveshaft		
Driveshaft retaining nut:		
M22 nut	200	148
M24 nut	250	185
M27 nut	300	221
Shaft-to-final drive flange bolts:		
Allen bolts:		
M10 bolts:		
Bolts with serrations under bolt head	96	71
Bolts without serrations	83	61
M12 bolts	110	81
Torx bolts:		
M8 bolts	64	47
M10 bolts:		
Plain bolts	83	61
Black bolts with serrations under bolt head	100	74
Silver bolts with serrations under bolt head	80	59
M12 bolts	135	100

Torque wrench settings (continued)

	Nm	lbf ft
Propeller shaft		
M10 bolts:		
Strength grade 8.8 (see head of bolt)	48	35
Strength grade 10.9 (see head of bolt)	64	47
M12 bolts:		
Strength grade 8.8 (see head of bolt)	81	60
Strength grade 10.9 (see head of bolt)	100	74
M14 bolts	140	103
Support bearing bracket nuts	21	15
Roadwheels		
Wheel bolts	100	74

1 General information

Power is transmitted from the transmission to the rear axle by a two-piece propeller shaft, joined behind the centre bearing by a 'slip joint' – a sliding, splined coupling. The slip joint allows slight fore-and-aft movement of the propeller shaft. The forward end of the propeller shaft is attached to the output flange of the transmission either by a flexible rubber coupling or a universal flange joint. On some models, a vibration damper is mounted between the front of the propeller shaft and coupling. The middle of the propeller shaft is supported by the centre bearing which is bolted to the vehicle body. Universal joints are located at the centre bearing and at the rear end of the propeller shaft, to compensate for movement of the transmission and differential on their mountings and for any flexing of the chassis.

The final drive assembly includes the drive pinion, the ring gear, the differential and the output flanges. The drive pinion, which drives the ring gear, is also known as the differential input shaft and is connected to the propeller shaft via an input flange. The differential is bolted to the ring gear and drives the rear wheels through a pair of output flanges bolted to driveshafts with constant velocity (CV) joints at either end. The differential allows the wheels to turn at different speeds when cornering.

The driveshafts deliver power from the final drive unit output flanges to the rear wheels. The driveshafts are equipped with constant velocity (CV) joints at each end. The inner CV joints are bolted to the differential flanges. and the outer CV joints engage the splines of the wheel hubs, and are secured by a large nut.

Major repair work on the differential assembly components (drive pinion, ring-and-pinion, and differential) requires many special tools and a high degree of expertise, and therefore should not be attempted by the home mechanic. If major repairs become necessary, we recommend that they be performed by a BMW service department or other suitably-equipped automotive engineer.

2 Final drive unit – removal and refitting

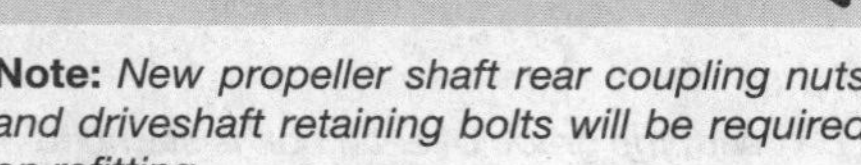

Note: *New propeller shaft rear coupling nuts and driveshaft retaining bolts will be required on refitting.*

Removal

1 Chock the front wheels. Jack up the rear of the vehicle and support it on axle stands (see *Jacking and vehicle support*). Remove both rear wheels. If necessary, drain the final drive unit as described in Section 10.

2 Using paint or a suitable marker pen, make alignment marks between the propeller shaft and final drive unit flange. Unscrew the nuts securing the propeller shaft to the final drive unit and discard them; new ones must be used on refitting.

3 Slacken and remove the retaining bolts and plates securing the right-hand driveshaft to the final drive unit flange and support the driveshaft by tying it to the vehicle underbody using a piece of wire. **Note:** *Do not allow the driveshaft to hang under its own weight as the CV joint may be damaged.* Discard the bolts, new ones should be used on refitting.

4 Disconnect the left-hand driveshaft from the final drive as described in Paragraph 3.

5 Undo the nuts/bolts and remove the heat shield panel from the left-hand end of the tension strut beneath the final drive input shaft flange.

6 Disconnect the wiring connector from the speedometer drive on the rear of the final drive unit (where fitted).

7 Slacken and remove the left- and right-hand anti-roll bar mountings (see Chapter 10).

8 Move a jack and interposed block of wood into position and raise it so that it is supporting the weight of the final drive unit.

9 Making sure the final drive unit is safely supported, slacken and remove the two bolts securing the front of the unit in position and the single bolt securing the rear of the unit in position **(see illustrations)**.

10 Carefully lower the final drive unit out of position and remove it from underneath the vehicle. Examine the final drive unit mounting rubbers for signs of wear or damage and renew if necessary.

Refitting

11 Refitting is a reversal of removal noting the following.

a) *Raise the final drive unit into position and engage it with the propeller shaft rear joint, making sure the marks made prior to removal are correctly aligned.*
b) *Tighten the final drive unit mounting bolts to the specified torque setting.*
c) *Fit the new propeller shaft joint nuts and tighten them to the specified torque.*
d) *Refit the anti-roll bar mountings (see Chapter 10).*
e) *Fit the new driveshaft joint retaining bolts and plates and tighten them to the specified torque.*
f) *On completion, refill/top-up the final drive unit with oil as described in Section 10.*

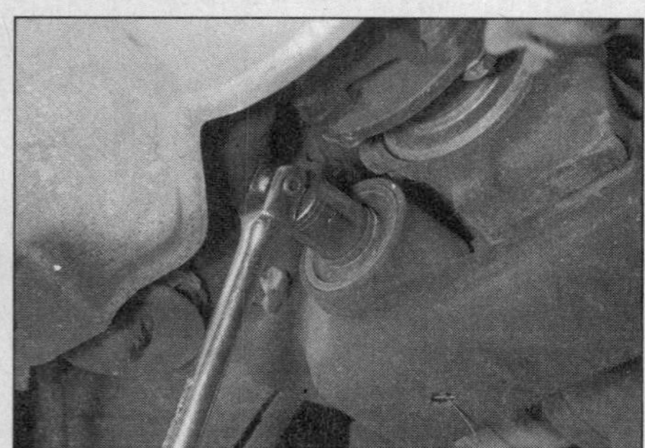

2.9a Slacken and remove the front . . .

2.9b . . . and rear final drive mounting bolts (arrowed)

3 Final drive unit oil seals – renewal

Propeller shaft flange seal

Note: *A new flange nut retaining plate will be required.*

1 Drain the final drive unit as described in Section 10.

2 Remove the final drive unit as described in Section 2 and secure the unit in a vice.

3 Remove the retaining plate and make alignment marks between the propeller flange nut, the drive flange and pinion **(see illustration)**. Discard the retaining plate, a new one must be used on refitting.

4 Hold the drive flange stationary by bolting a length of metal bar to it, then unscrew the nut noting the exact number of turns necessary to remove it.

5 Using a suitable puller, draw the drive flange from the pinion and remove the dust cover. If the dust cover shows signs of wear, renew it.

6 Lever the oil seal from the final drive casing with a screwdriver. Wipe clean the oil seal seating.

7 Smear a little oil on the sealing lip of the new oil seal, then press it squarely into the casing until flush with the outer face. If necessary the seal can be tapped into position using a metal tube which bears only on its hard outer edge.

8 Fit the dust cover and locate the drive flange on the pinion aligning the marks made on removal. Refit the flange nut, screwing it on by the exact number of turns counted on removal, so that the alignment marks align.

Warning: Do not overtighten the flange nut. If the nut is overtightened, the collapsible spacer behind the flange will be deformed necessitating its renewal. This is a complex operation requiring the final drive unit to be dismantled (see Section 1).

9 Secure the nut in position with the new retaining plate, tapping it squarely into position.

10 Refit the final drive unit as described in Section 2 and refill it with oil as described in Section 10.

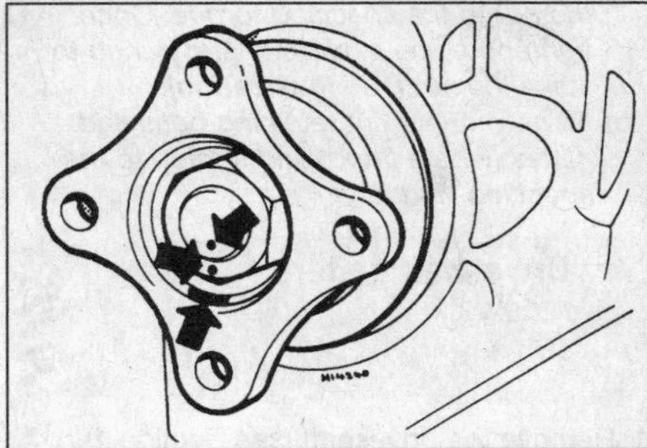

3.3 Make alignment marks (arrowed) on the flange, the pinion shaft and nut to ensure proper reassembly

Driveshaft flange seal

Note: *New driveshaft joint retaining bolts and a driveshaft flange circlip will be required.*

11 Drain the final drive unit oil as described in Section 10.

12 Slacken and remove the bolts securing the driveshaft constant velocity joint to the final drive unit and recover the retaining plates. Position the driveshaft clear of the flange and tie it to the vehicle underbody using a piece of wire. **Note:** *Do not allow the driveshaft to hang under its own weight as the CV joint may be damaged.*

13 Using a suitable lever, carefully prise the driveshaft flange out from the final drive unit taking care not to damage the dust seal or casing **(see illustration)**. Remove the flange and recover dust seal. If the dust seal shows signs of damage, renew it.

14 Carefully lever the oil seal out from the final drive unit. Wipe clean the oil seal seating.

15 With the flange removed, prise out the circlip from the end of the splined shaft **(see illustration)**.

16 Fit a new circlip, making sure its is correctly located in the splined shaft groove.

17 Smear a little final drive oil on the sealing lip of the new oil seal, then press it squarely into the casing until it reaches its stop. If necessary the seal can be tapped into position using a metal tube which bears only on its hard outer edge **(see illustration)**.

18 Fit the dust cover and insert the drive flange. Push the drive flange fully into position and check that it is securely retained by the circlip.

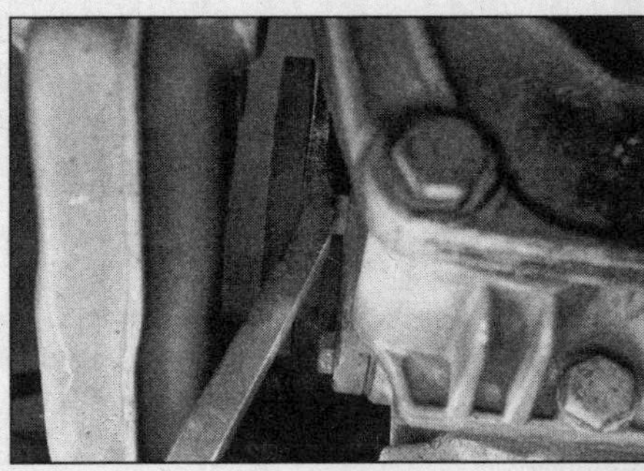

3.13 Use a suitable lever to remove the driveshaft flange from the final drive unit

19 Align the driveshaft with the flange and refit the new retaining bolts and plates, tightening them to the specified torque.

20 Refill the final drive unit with oil as described in Section 10.

4 Driveshaft – removal and refitting

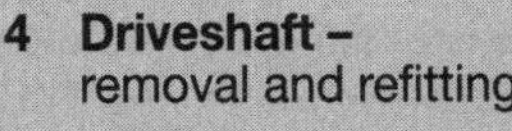

Note: *A new driveshaft retaining nut and bolts will be required on refitting.*

Removal

1 Remove the wheel trim/hub cap (as applicable) and slacken the driveshaft retaining nut with the vehicle resting on its wheels. Also slacken the wheel bolts.

2 Chock the front wheels, then jack up the rear of the vehicle and support it on axle stands (see *Jacking and vehicle support*).

3 Remove the relevant rear roadwheel.

4 If the left-hand driveshaft is to be removed, remove the exhaust system tailpipe to improve access (see Chapter 4A).

5 Slacken and remove the left- and right-hand anti-roll bar mountings and pivot the bar downwards (see Chapter 10).

6 Unscrew and remove the driveshaft nut.

7 Make alignment marks, then slacken and remove the bolts securing the driveshaft constant velocity joint to the final drive unit and recover the retaining plates (where fitted) **(see illustration)**. Position the driveshaft clear of the flange and tie it to the vehicle underbody

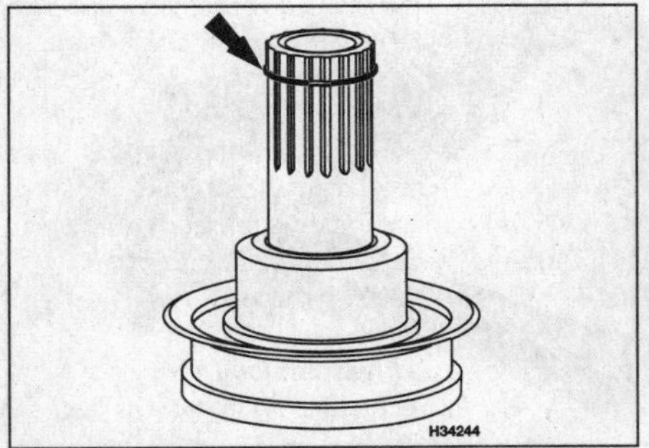

3.15 Renew the output flange circlip (arrowed)

3.17 Tap the new seal into position using a socket which bears only on the hard outer edge of the seal

4.7 Make alignment marks (arrowed) then remove the Torx bolts

4.10 When the driveshaft nut has been fully tightened, stake the nut using a punch

using a piece of wire. **Note:** *Do not allow the driveshaft to hang under its own weight as the CV joint may be damaged.*

8 Withdraw the driveshaft outer constant velocity joint from the hub assembly. The outer joint will be very tight, tap the joint out of the hub using a soft-faced mallet. If this fails to free it from the hub, the joint will have to be pressed out using a suitable tool which is bolted to the hub.

9 Remove the driveshaft from underneath the vehicle.

Refitting

10 Refitting is the reverse of removal noting the following points.

a) *Lubricate the threads of the new driveshaft nut with clean engine oil prior to fitting and tighten it to the specified torque. If necessary, wait until the vehicle is lower to the ground and then tighten the nut to the specified torque. Once tightened, use a hammer and punch to stake the nut* ***(see illustration).***

b) *Fit new inner joint retaining bolts and plates (where fitted) and tighten to the specified torque.*

5 Driveshaft gaiters – renewal

1 Remove the driveshaft (see Section 4).

2 Clean the driveshaft and mount it in a vice.

Telescopic driveshafts

3 Some models are equipped with driveshaft where the inner CV joint is mounted on a short shaft which slides into the main driveshaft body. Release the two inner joint gaiter retaining clips and slide the gaiter away from the joint.

4 Make alignment marks between the CV joint shaft and the driveshaft tube, then slide the CV joint and shaft from the driveshaft **(see illustration).**

5 Release the two outer joint gaiter retaining clips and slide both gaiters from the inner end of the shaft.

Non-telescopic driveshafts

6 Lever off the sealing cover from the end of the inner constant velocity (CV) joint **(see illustration).**

7 Release the two inner joint gaiter retaining clips and free the gaiter and dust cover from the joint **(see illustration).**

8 Scoop out excess grease and remove the inner joint circlip from the end of the driveshaft **(see illustration).**

9 Securely support the joint inner member and tap the driveshaft out of position using a hammer and suitable drift **(see illustration).** If the joint is a tight fit, a suitable puller will be required to draw off the joint. Do not dismantle the inner joint.

10 With the joint removed, slide the inner gaiter and dust cover off from the end of the driveshaft **(see illustration).**

11 Release the outer joint gaiter retaining clips then slide the gaiter along the shaft and remove it.

All driveshafts

12 Thoroughly clean the constant velocity joints using paraffin, or a suitable solvent, and dry thoroughly. Carry out a visual inspection as follows.

13 Move the inner splined driving member from side-to-side to expose each ball in turn at the top of its track. Examine the balls for cracks, flat spots or signs of surface pitting.

14 Inspect the ball tracks on the inner and outer members. If the tracks have widened, the balls will no longer be a tight fit. At the same time check the ball cage windows for wear or cracking between the windows.

15 If on inspection any of the constant velocity joint components are found to be worn or damaged, it must be renewed. The inner joint is available separately but if the outer joint is worn it will be necessary to renew the complete joint and driveshaft assembly. If

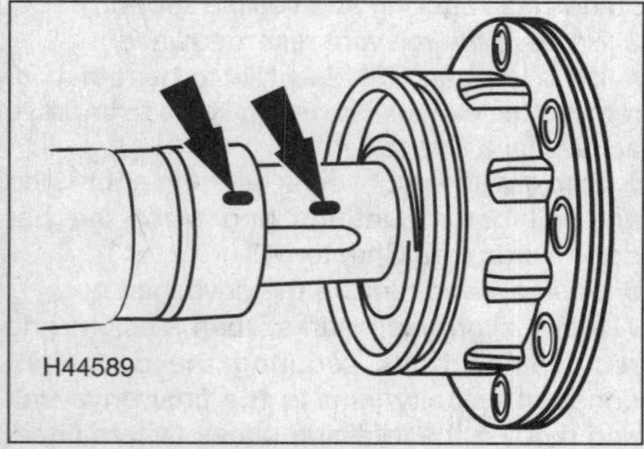

5.4 Make alignment marks (arrowed), then slide the joint from the tube

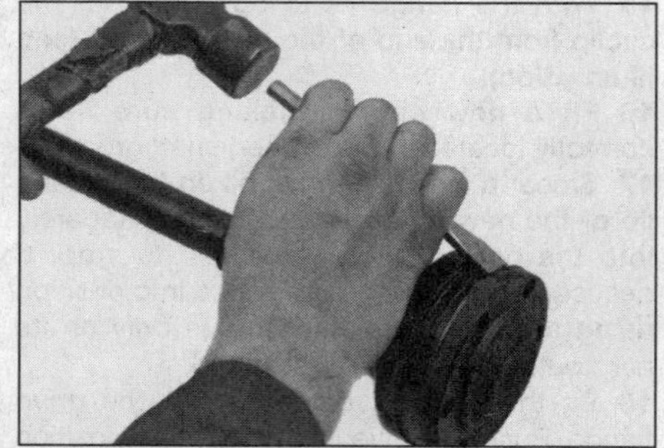

5.6 Carefully remove the sealing cover from the inner end of the joint

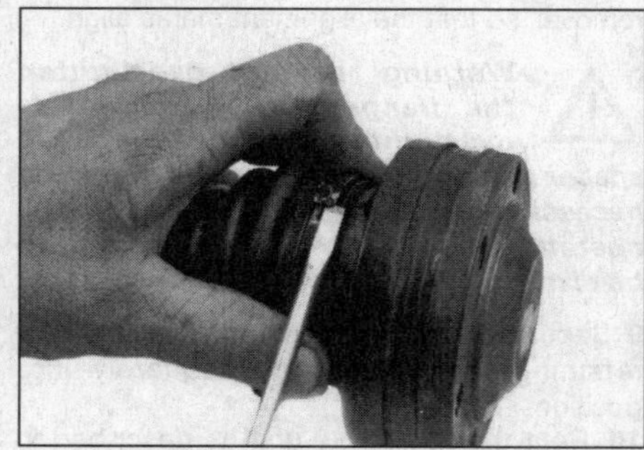

5.7 Release the gaiter retaining clips and slide the gaiter down the shaft

5.8 Remove the inner joint circlip from the driveshaft

5.9 Support the inner joint inner member then tap the driveshaft out of position . . .

5.10 . . . and slide off the gaiter

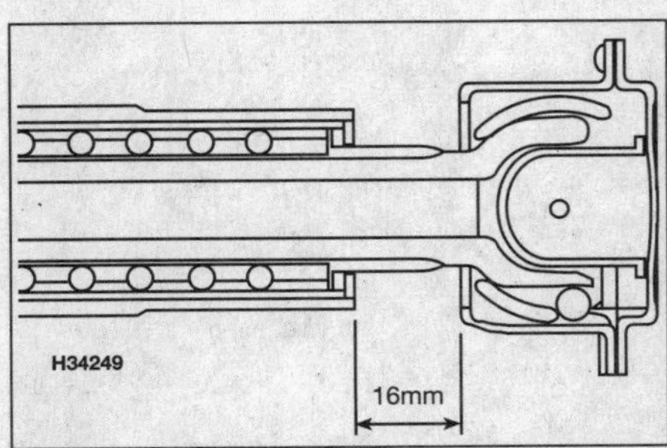

5.18 After greasing the shaft, push it in as far as it will go, then pull it out so that the gap is 16 mm (approx)

the joints are in satisfactory condition, obtain new gaiter repair kits which contain gaiters, retaining clips, an inner constant velocity joint circlip and the correct type and quantity of grease required.

Telescopic driveshafts

16 Slide the new gaiters over the inner end of the driveshaft. Note that the outer gaiter has a length of 55 mm, and the inner gaiter is 65 mm long.

17 Repack both CV joints using the grease supplied in the gaiter kits.

18 Apply grease to the splines of the inner CV joint shaft. Align the previously-made marks, and insert the CV joint shaft into the end of the driveshaft as far as it will go, then pull it back out so that the edge of the joint is the correct distance from the end of the driveshaft **(see illustration)**.

19 Ease the gaiters over the joints and ensure the gaiter lips are correctly located on the driveshaft and CV joints. Lift the outer sealing lips of the gaiters to equalise air pressure within the gaiters.

20 Position the inner joint gaiter clips so that fasteners are in line with the rivet on the flange. Secure the retaining clips in position.

21 Position the outer joint gaiter clips so that the fasteners are on the other side of the shaft from the inner clips fasteners, ie, 180° offset.

Non-telescopic driveshafts

22 Tape over the splines on the end of the driveshaft.

23 Slide the new outer gaiter onto the end of the driveshaft.

24 Pack the outer joint with the grease supplied in the gaiter kit. Work the grease well into the bearing tracks whilst twisting the joint, and fill the rubber gaiter with any excess.

25 Ease the gaiter over the joint and ensure that the gaiter lips are correctly located on both the driveshaft and constant velocity joint. Lift the outer sealing lip of the gaiter to equalise air pressure within the gaiter.

26 Fit the large metal retaining clip to the gaiter. Pull the retaining clip tight then bend it back to secure it in position and cut off any excess clip. Secure the small retaining clip using the same procedure.

5.29a Fill the inner joint with the grease supplied . . .

27 Engage the new inner gaiter with its dust cover and slide the assembly onto the driveshaft.

28 Remove the tape from the driveshaft splines and fit the inner constant velocity joint. Press the joint fully onto the shaft and secure it in position with a new circlip.

29 Work the grease supplied fully into the inner joint and fill the gaiter with any excess **(see illustrations)**.

30 Slide the inner gaiter into position and press the dust cover onto the joint, making sure the retaining bolt holes are correctly aligned. Lift the outer sealing lip of the gaiter, to equalise air pressure within the gaiter, and secure it in position with the retaining clips (see paragraph 26).

31 Apply a smear of suitable sealant (BMW recommend BMW sealing gel) and press the new sealing cover fully onto the end of the inner joint.

All driveshafts

32 Check that both constant velocity joints are free to move easily then refit the driveshaft as described in Section 4.

6 Propeller shaft – removal and refitting

Note: *New propeller shaft front and rear coupling nuts will be required on refitting.*

Removal

1 Chock the front wheels. Jack up the rear of the vehicle and support it on axle stands (see *Jacking and vehicle support*).

6.4 Slacken and remove the bolts securing the coupling to the transmission flange

5.29b . . . and work it into the bearing tracks

2 Remove the exhaust system and heat shield as described in Chapter 4A. Where necessary, unscrew the exhaust system mounting bracket(s) in order to gain the necessary clearance required to remove the propeller shaft.

3 On models where the front of the propeller shaft is bolted straight onto the transmission output flange, make alignment marks between the shaft and transmission flange then slacken and remove the retaining nuts. Discard the nuts, new ones should be used on refitting.

4 On models where a rubber coupling is fitted between the front end of the propeller shaft and transmission output flange, make alignment marks between the shaft, transmission flange and rubber coupling. Slacken and remove the nuts and bolts securing the coupling to the transmission **(see illustration)**. Discard the nuts, new ones should be used on refitting.

5 Using a large open-ended spanner, or suitable adjustable pliers, loosen the threaded sleeve nut, which is situated near the support bearing, through a couple of turns **(see illustration)**.

6 Using paint or a suitable marker pen, make alignment marks between the propeller shaft and final drive unit flange. Unscrew the nuts securing the propeller shaft to the final drive unit and discard them; new ones must be used on refitting.

7 With the aid of an assistant, support the propeller shaft then unscrew the centre support bearing bracket retaining nuts **(see**

6.5 Unscrew the large threaded sleeve a couple of turns

6.7 Unscrew the centre bearing bracket retaining nuts (arrowed)

illustration). Slide the two halves of the shaft towards each other then lower the centre of the shaft and disengage it from the transmission and final drive unit. Remove the shaft from underneath the vehicle. **Note:** *Do not separate the two halves of the shaft without first making alignment marks. If the shafts are incorrectly joined, the propeller shaft assembly may become unbalanced, leading to noise and vibration during operation.*

8 Inspect the rubber coupling (where fitted), the support bearing and shaft universal joints as described in Sections 7, 8 and 9. Inspect the transmission flange locating pin and propeller shaft bush for signs of wear or damage and renew as necessary.

Refitting

9 Apply a smear of molybdenum disulphide grease (BMW recommend Molykote Long-term 2) to the transmission pin and shaft bush and manoeuvre the shaft into position **(see illustration)**.

10 Align the marks made prior to removal, and engage the shaft with the transmission and final drive unit flanges. With the marks correctly aligned, refit the support bracket retaining nuts, tightening them lightly only at this stage.

11 Fit new retaining bolts to the rear coupling of the propeller shaft and tighten them to the specified torque.

12 On models where the propeller shaft is bolted straight onto the transmission flange, fit the new retaining nuts and tighten them to the specified torque.

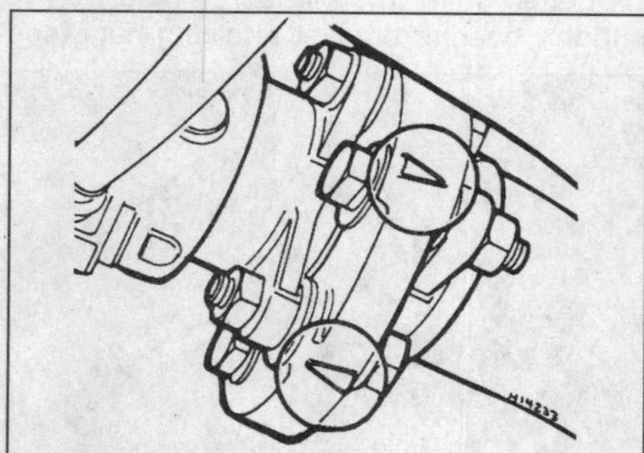
7.7 If the coupling has directional arrows, make sure the arrows are pointing towards the propeller shaft/transmission flanges and not the bolt heads

6.9 Apply molybdenum disulphide grease to the transmission pin

13 On models with a rubber coupling, insert the bolts and fit the new retaining nuts. Tighten them to the specified torque, noting that the nut/bolt should only be rotated on the flange side to avoid stressing the rubber coupling.

14 Tighten the propeller shaft threaded sleeve nut securely.

15 Loosen the centre bearing bracket nuts. Slide the bracket forwards to remove all free play, then preload the bearing by moving the bracket forwards a further 4 to 6 mm. Hold the bracket in this position and tighten its retaining nuts to the specified torque.

16 Refit the exhaust system and associated components as described in Chapter 4A.

7 Propeller shaft rubber coupling – check and renewal

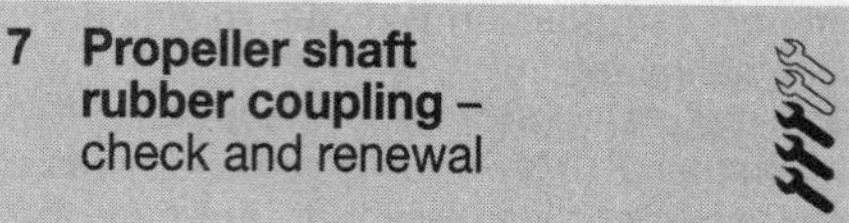

Note: *A rubber coupling is not fitted to all models. On some models, a universal joint is fitted to the front of the propeller shaft instead (see Section 9).*

Check

1 Firmly apply the handbrake, then jack up the front of the vehicle and support it on axle stands (see *Jacking and vehicle support*).

2 Closely examine the rubber coupling, linking the propeller shaft to the transmission, looking for signs of damage such as cracking or splitting or for signs of general deterioration. If necessary, renew the coupling as follows.

Renewal

Note: *New propeller shaft coupling nuts will be required.*

3 Carry out the operations described in paragraphs 1, 2, 4 and 5 of Section 6.

4 Slide the front half of the propeller shaft to the rear then disengage it from the transmission locating pin and pivot it downwards.

5 Slacken and remove the nuts securing the coupling to the shaft and remove it **(see illustration)**. If necessary, also remove the vibration damper; the damper should also be renewed if it shows signs of wear or damage.

6 Aligning the marks made on removal, fit the vibration damper (where fitted) to the propeller shaft.

7 Fit the new rubber coupling noting that

7.5 Coupling-to-propeller shaft retaining bolts (arrowed)

the arrows on the side of the coupling must point towards the propeller shaft/transmission flanges **(see illustration)**. Fit the new retaining nuts and tighten them to the specified torque.

8 Apply a smear of molybdenum disulphide grease (BMW recommend Molykote Long-term 2) to the transmission pin and shaft bush and manoeuvre the shaft into position.

9 Align the marks made prior to removal and engage the shaft with the transmission flange. With the marks correctly aligned, insert the bolts and fit the new retaining nuts. Tighten them to the specified torque, noting that the nut/bolt should only be rotated on the flange side to avoid stressing the rubber coupling.

10 Tighten the propeller shaft threaded sleeve securely.

11 Refit the exhaust system and associated components as described in Chapter 4A.

8 Propeller shaft support bearing – check and renewal

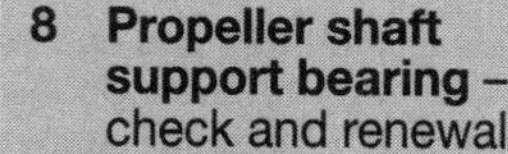

Check

1 Wear in the support bearing will lead to noise and vibration when the vehicle is driven. The bearing is best checked with the propeller shaft removed (see Section 6). To gain access to the bearing with the shaft in position, remove the exhaust system and heat shields as described in Chapter 4A.

2 Rotate the bearing and check that it turns smoothly with no sign of free play; if it's difficult to turn, or if it has a gritty feeling, renew it. Also inspect the rubber portion. If it's cracked or deteriorated, renew it.

Renewal

3 Remove the propeller shaft as described in Section 6.

4 Make alignment marks between the front and rear sections of the propeller shaft then unscrew the threaded sleeve nut and separate the two halves. Recover the sleeve nut, washer and bush noting their correct fitted locations.

5 Remove the circlip and slide off the support bearing rear dust cover.

6 Draw the support bearing off from the propeller shaft using a suitable puller then remove the front dust cover in the same way.

7 Firmly support the support bearing bracket and press out the bearing with a suitable tubular spacer.
8 Fit the new bearing to the bracket and press it into position using a tubular spacer which bears only on the bearing outer race.
9 Thoroughly clean the shaft splines and carefully press the new front dust seal onto the propeller shaft, making sure it is fitted the correct way around.
10 Press the support bearing fully onto the propeller shaft using a tubular spacer which bears only on the bearing inner race.
11 Check that the bearing is free to rotate smoothly, then fit the new rear dust seal.
12 Apply a smear of molybdenum disulphide grease (BMW recommend Molykote Long-term 2) to the splines and fit the threaded sleeve, washer and bush to the front section of the propeller shaft.
13 Align the marks made prior to separation and joint the front and rear sections of the propeller shaft.
14 Refit the propeller shaft as described in Section 6.

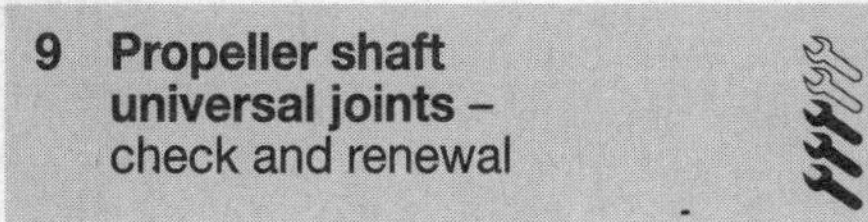

9 Propeller shaft universal joints – check and renewal

Note: *On some models a rubber coupling is fitted between the propeller shaft and transmission instead of a universal joint (see Section 7).*

Check

1 Wear in the universal joints is characterised by vibration in the transmission, noise during acceleration, and metallic squeaking and grating sounds as the bearings disintegrate. The joints can be checked with the propeller shaft still fitted noting that it will be necessary to remove the exhaust system and heat shields (see Chapter 4A) to gain access.
2 If the propeller shaft is in position on the vehicle, try to turn the propeller shaft while holding the transmission/final drive flange. Free play between the propeller shaft and the front or rear flanges indicates excessive wear.
3 If the propeller shaft is already removed, you can check the universal joints by holding the shaft in one hand and turning the yoke or flange with the other. If the axial movement is excessive, renew the propeller shaft.

Renewal

4 At the time of writing, no spare parts were available to enable renewal of the universal joints to be carried out. Therefore, if any joint shows signs of damage or wear the complete propeller shaft assembly must be renewed. Consult your BMW dealer for latest information on parts availability.
5 If renewal of the propeller shaft is necessary, it may be worthwhile seeking the advice of an automotive engineering specialist. They may be able to repair the original shaft assembly or supply a reconditioned shaft on an exchange basis.

10 Final drive unit oil renewal

1 Park the car on level ground.
2 Locate the filler/level plug in the centre of the final drive unit rear cover **(see illustration)**. Unscrew the plug and recover the sealing washer.
3 Place a suitable container beneath the final drive unit, then unscrew the drain plug from the base of the rear cover and allow the oil to drain. Recover the sealing washer.
4 Inspect the sealing washers for signs of damage and renew if necessary.

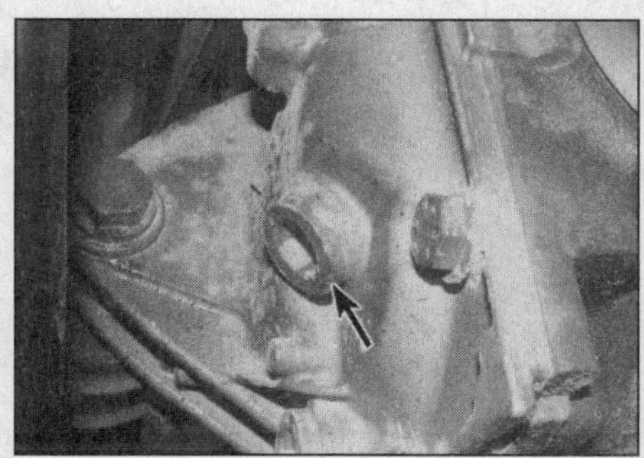

10.2 Final drive filler plug

5 When the oil has finished draining, refit the drain plug and sealing washer and tighten it to the specified torque.
6 Refill the final drive unit through the filler/level plug hole with the exact amount of the specified type of oil (see Chapter 1 and *Lubricants and fluids*); this should bring the oil level up to the base of the filler/level plug hole. If the correct amount was poured into the transmission and a large amount flows out on checking the level, refit the filler/level plug and take the car on a short journey so that the new oil is distributed fully around the final drive components.
7 On return, park on level ground and allow the car to stand for a few minutes. Unscrew the filler/level plug again. The oil level should reach the lower edge of the filler/level hole. To ensure a true level is established, wait until the initial trickle stops, then add oil as necessary until a trickle of new oil can be seen emerging. The level will be correct when the flow ceases; use only good-quality oil of the specified type.
8 When the level is correct, refit the filler/level plug and sealing washer and tighten it to the specified torque.

Chapter 9
Braking system

Contents

Degrees of difficulty

Easy, suitable for novice with little experience	**Fairly easy,** suitable for beginner with some experience	**Fairly difficult,** suitable for competent DIY mechanic	**Difficult,** suitable for experienced DIY mechanic	**Very difficult,** suitable for expert DIY or professional

Specifications

Engine codes

4-cylinder engines

1796 cc engines	N42 B18 and N46 B18
1895 cc engines	M43TU B19
1995 cc engines	N42 B20 and N46 B20

6-cylinder engines

2171 cc engines	M54 B22
2494 cc engines	M52TU B25 and M54 B25
2793 cc engines	M52TU B28
2979 cc engines	M54 B30

Front brakes

Disc diameter:	
328 and 330 models	300 mm
All other models	286 mm
Disc thickness:	
New	22.0 mm
Minimum (stamped on disc)	20.4 mm
Maximum disc run-out	0.2 mm
Brake pad friction material minimum thickness	2.0 mm

Rear brakes

Disc diameter:	
Solid disc	280 mm
Ventilated disc	294 mm
Disc thickness:	
New:	
Solid disc	10.0 mm
Ventilated disc	19.0 mm
Minimum:	
Solid disc	8.4 mm
Ventilated disc	17.4
Maximum disc run-out	0.2 mm
Brake pad friction material minimum thickness	2.0 mm

Handbrake

Handbrake drum diameter	160 mm
Handbrake shoe friction material minimum thickness	1.5 mm

Torque wrench settings	Nm	lbf ft
ABS pressure sensors to master cylinder	19	14
ABS wheel sensor retaining bolts	8	6
Brake disc retaining screw	16	12
Brake hose unions:		
M10 thread	17	13
M12 thread	19	14
Front brake caliper:		
Guide pins	35	26
Mounting bracket bolts	110	81
Master cylinder mounting nuts*	26	19
Rear brake caliper:		
Guide pins	35	26
Mounting bracket bolts	67	49
Roadwheel bolts	100	74
Servo unit mounting nuts*	22	16

** Do not re-use*

1 General information

The braking system is of the servo-assisted, dual-circuit hydraulic type. Under normal circumstances, both circuits operate in unison. However, if there is hydraulic failure in one circuit, full braking force will still be available at two wheels.

All models are fitted with front and rear disc brakes. ABS is fitted as standard to most models, and was offered as an option on other models (refer to Section 19 for further information on ABS operation). **Note:** *On models also equipped with Automatic Stability Control plus Traction (ASC+T), the ABS system also operates the traction control side of the system.*

The front disc brakes are actuated by single-piston sliding type calipers, which ensure that equal pressure is applied to each disc pad.

All models are fitted with rear disc brakes, actuated by single-piston sliding calipers, whilst a separate drum brake arrangement is fitted in the centre of the brake disc to provide a separate means of handbrake application.

Note: *When servicing any part of the system, work carefully and methodically; also observe scrupulous cleanliness when overhauling any part of the hydraulic system. Always renew components (in axle sets, where applicable) if in doubt about their condition, and use only genuine BMW parts, or at least those of known good quality. Note the warnings given in 'Safety first!' and at relevant points in this Chapter concerning the dangers of asbestos dust and hydraulic fluid.*

2 Hydraulic system – bleeding

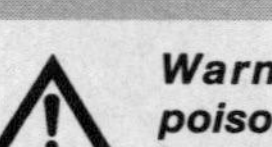

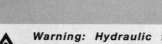

Warning: Hydraulic fluid is poisonous; wash off immediately and thoroughly in the case of skin contact, and seek immediate medical advice if any fluid is swallowed or gets into the eyes. Certain types of hydraulic fluid are flammable, and may ignite when allowed into contact with hot components; when servicing any hydraulic system, it is safest to assume that the fluid is flammable, and to take precautions against the risk of fire as though it is petrol that is being handled. Hydraulic fluid is also an effective paint stripper, and will attack plastics; if any is spilt, it should be washed off immediately, using copious quantities of fresh water. Finally, it is hygroscopic (it absorbs moisture from the air) – old fluid may be contaminated and unfit for further use. When topping-up or renewing the fluid, always use the recommended type, and ensure that it comes from a freshly-opened sealed container.

Warning: On models with ABS (with or without ASC+T), if the high-pressure hydraulic system linking the master cylinder, hydraulic unit and (where fitted) accumulator has been disturbed, then bleeding of the brakes should be entrusted to a BMW dealer or specialist. They will have access to the special service tester which is needed to operate the ABS modulator pump and bleed the high-pressure hydraulic system safely.

General

1 The correct operation of any hydraulic system is only possible after removing all air from the components and circuit; this is achieved by bleeding the system.

2 During the bleeding procedure, add only clean, unused hydraulic fluid of the recommended type; never re-use fluid that has already been bled from the system. Ensure that sufficient fluid is available before starting work.

3 If there is any possibility of incorrect fluid being already in the system, the brake components and circuit must be flushed completely with uncontaminated, correct fluid, and new seals should be fitted to the various components.

4 If hydraulic fluid has been lost from the system, or air has entered because of a leak, ensure that the fault is cured before continuing further.

5 Park the vehicle on level ground, switch off the engine and select first or reverse gear, then chock the wheels and release the handbrake.

6 Check that all pipes and hoses are secure, unions tight and bleed screws closed. Clean any dirt from around the bleed screws.

7 Unscrew the master cylinder reservoir cap, and top the master cylinder reservoir up to the MAX level line; refit the cap loosely, and remember to maintain the fluid level at least above the MIN level line throughout the procedure, or there is a risk of further air entering the system.

8 There are a number of one-man, do-it-yourself brake bleeding kits currently available from motor accessory shops. It is recommended that one of these kits is used whenever possible, as they greatly simplify the bleeding operation, and reduce the risk of expelled air and fluid being drawn back into the system. If such a kit is not available, the basic (two-man) method must be used, which is described in detail below.

9 If a kit is to be used, prepare the vehicle as described previously, and follow the kit manufacturer's instructions, as the procedure may vary slightly according to the type being used; generally, they are as outlined below in the relevant sub-section.

10 Whichever method is used, the same sequence must be followed (paragraphs 11 and 12) to ensure the removal of all air from the system.

Bleeding

Sequence

11 If the system has been only partially disconnected, and suitable precautions were taken to minimise fluid loss, it should be necessary only to bleed that part of the system.

12 If the complete system is to be bled, then it should be done working in the following sequence:

a) *Right-hand rear brake.*
b) *Left-hand rear brake.*
c) *Right-hand front brake.*
d) *Left-hand front brake.*

Warning: On models with ABS (with or without ASC+T), after bleeding, the operation of the braking system should be checked at the earliest possible opportunity by a BMW dealer or suitably-equipped specialist.

Basic (two-man) method

13 Collect a clean glass jar, a suitable length of plastic or rubber tubing which is a tight fit over the bleed screw, and a ring spanner to fit the screw. The help of an assistant will also be required.

14 Remove the dust cap from the first screw in the sequence. Fit the spanner and tube to the screw, place the other end of the tube in the jar, and pour in sufficient fluid to cover the end of the tube.

15 Ensure that the master cylinder reservoir fluid level is maintained at least above the MIN level line throughout the procedure.

16 Have the assistant fully depress the brake pedal several times to build-up pressure, then maintain it on the final downstroke.

17 While pedal pressure is maintained, unscrew the bleed screw (approximately one turn) and allow the compressed fluid and air to flow into the jar. The assistant should maintain pedal pressure, following it down to the floor if necessary, and should not release it until instructed to do so. When the flow stops, tighten the bleed screw again, have the assistant release the pedal slowly, and recheck the reservoir fluid level.

18 Repeat the steps in paragraphs 16 and 17 until the fluid emerging from the bleed screw is free from air bubbles. If the master cylinder has been drained and refilled, and air is being bled from the first screw in the sequence, allow about 5 seconds between cycles for the master cylinder passages to refill.

19 When no more air bubbles appear, tighten the bleed screw securely, remove the tube and spanner, and refit the dust cap. Do not overtighten the bleed screw.

20 Repeat the procedure on the remaining screws in the sequence, until all air is removed from the system and the brake pedal feels firm again.

Using a one-way valve kit

21 As their name implies, these kits consist of a length of tubing with a one-way valve fitted, to prevent expelled air and fluid being drawn back into the system; some kits include a translucent container, which can be positioned so that the air bubbles can be more easily seen flowing from the end of the tube **(see illustration)**.

22 The kit is connected to the bleed screw, which is then opened. The user returns to the driver's seat, depresses the brake pedal with a smooth, steady stroke, and slowly releases it; this is repeated until the expelled fluid is clear of air bubbles.

23 Note that these kits simplify work so much that it is easy to forget the master cylinder reservoir fluid level; ensure that this is maintained at least above the MIN level line at all times.

Using a pressure-bleeding kit

24 These kits are usually operated by the reservoir of pressurised air contained in the spare tyre. However, note that it will probably be necessary to reduce the pressure to a lower level than normal; refer to the instructions supplied with the kit. **Note:** *BMW specify that a pressure of 2 bar (29 psi) should not be exceeded.*

25 By connecting a pressurised, fluid-filled container to the master cylinder reservoir, bleeding can be carried out simply by opening each screw in turn (in the specified sequence), and allowing the fluid to flow out until no more air bubbles can be seen in the expelled fluid.

26 This method has the advantage that the large reservoir of fluid provides an additional safeguard against air being drawn into the system during bleeding.

27 Pressure-bleeding is particularly effective when bleeding 'difficult' systems, or when bleeding the complete system at the time of routine fluid renewal.

All methods

28 When bleeding is complete, and firm pedal feel is restored, wash off any spilt fluid, tighten the bleed screws securely, and refit their dust caps.

29 Check the hydraulic fluid level in the master cylinder reservoir, and top-up if necessary (*Weekly checks*).

30 Discard any hydraulic fluid that has been bled from the system; it will not be fit for re-use.

31 Check the feel of the brake pedal. If it feels at all spongy, air must still be present in the system, and further bleeding is required. Failure to bleed satisfactorily after a reasonable repetition of the bleeding procedure may be due to worn master cylinder seals.

3 Hydraulic pipes and hoses – renewal

Warning: On models with ABS (with or without ASC+T), under no circumstances should the hydraulic pipes/hoses linking the master cylinder, hydraulic unit and (where fitted) the accumulator be disturbed. If these unions are disturbed and air enters the high-pressure hydraulic system, bleeding of the system can only be safely carried out by a BMW dealer or suitably-equipped specialist using the special service tester.

Note: *Before starting work, refer to the warnings at the beginning of Section 2.*

1 If any pipe or hose is to be renewed, minimise fluid loss by first removing the master cylinder reservoir cap, then tightening it down onto a piece of polythene to obtain an airtight seal. Alternatively, flexible hoses can be sealed, if required, using a proprietary brake hose clamp; metal brake pipe unions can be plugged (if care is taken not to allow dirt into the system) or capped immediately they are disconnected. Place a wad of rag under any union that is to be disconnected, to catch any spilt fluid.

2 If a flexible hose is to be disconnected, unscrew the brake pipe union nut before removing the spring clip which secures the hose to its mounting bracket.

3 To unscrew the union nuts, it is preferable to obtain a brake pipe spanner of the correct size; these are available from most large motor accessory shops. Failing this, a close-fitting open-ended spanner will be required, though if the nuts are tight or corroded, their flats may be rounded-off if the spanner slips. In such a case, using self-locking pliers is often the only way to unscrew a stubborn union, but it follows that the pipe and the damaged nuts must be renewed on reassembly. Always clean a union and surrounding area before disconnecting it. If disconnecting a component with more than one union, make a careful note of the connections before disturbing any of them.

4 If a brake pipe is to be renewed, it can be obtained, cut to length and with the union nuts and end flares in place, from BMW dealers. All that is then necessary is to bend it to shape, following the line of the original, before fitting it to the car. Alternatively, most motor accessory shops can make up brake pipes from kits, but this requires very careful measurement of the original, to ensure that the new one is of the correct length. The safest answer is usually to take the original to the shop as a pattern.

5 On refitting, do not overtighten the union nuts. It is not necessary to exercise brute force to obtain a sound joint.

6 Ensure that the pipes and hoses are correctly routed, with no kinks, and that they are secured in the clips or brackets provided. After fitting, remove the polythene from the reservoir, and bleed the hydraulic system as described in Section 2. Wash off any spilt fluid, and check carefully for fluid leaks.

2.21 Bleeding a rear brake caliper using a one-way valve kit

4.2a Lever the spring away from the hub . . .

4.2b . . . then lever it out from the caliper

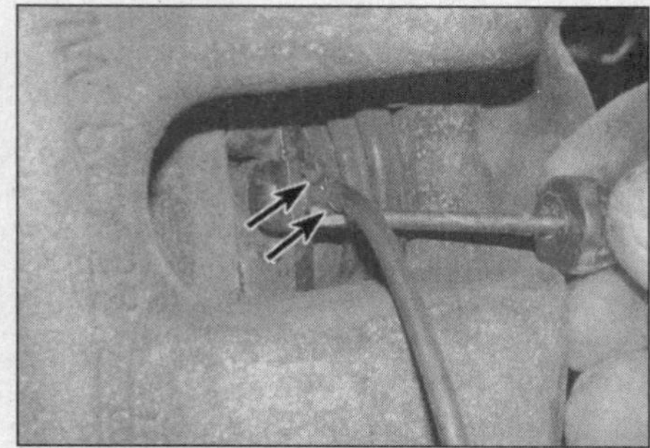

4.3a Release the clips (arrowed) . . .

4 Front brake pads – renewal

Warning: Renew both sets of front brake pads at the same time – never renew the pads on only one wheel, as uneven braking may result. Note that the dust created by wear of the pads may contain asbestos, which is a health hazard. Never blow it out with compressed air, and do not inhale any of it. An approved filtering mask should be worn when working on the brakes. DO NOT use petrol or petroleum-based solvents to clean brake parts; use brake cleaner or methylated spirit only.

1 Apply the handbrake, then jack up the front of the vehicle and support it on axle stands. Remove the front roadwheels.

2 Using a screwdriver, carefully unclip the anti-rattle spring from the side of the brake caliper, noting its correct fitted position **(see illustrations)**.

3 Slide the brake pad wear sensor from the brake pad (where fitted) and remove it from the caliper aperture **(see illustrations)**.

4 Remove the plastic plugs from the caliper guide bushes to gain access to the guide pins **(see illustration)**.

5 Slacken and remove the guide pins, noting that a suitable Allen key will be needed. Lift the caliper away from the caliper mounting bracket, and tie it to the suspension strut using a suitable piece of wire **(see illustrations)**. Do not allow the caliper to hang unsupported on the flexible brake hose.

6 Unclip the inner brake pad from the caliper piston, and withdraw the outer pad from the caliper mounting bracket **(see illustrations)**.

7 First measure the thickness of each brake pad's friction material **(see illustration)**. If either pad is worn at any point to the specified minimum thickness or less, all four pads must be renewed. Also, the pads should be

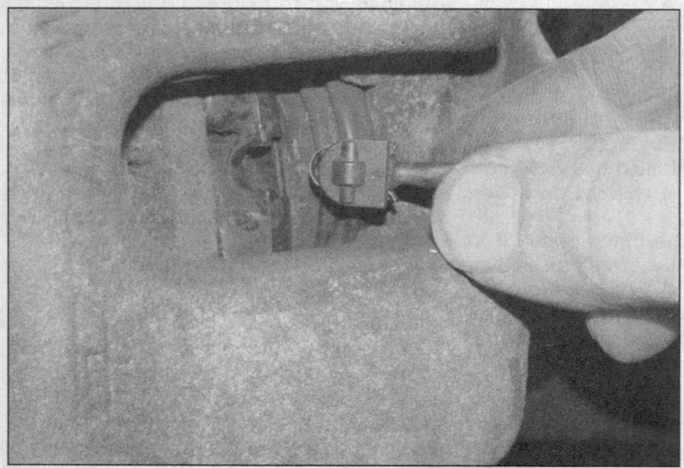

4.3b . . . and slide the wear sensor from the brake pad

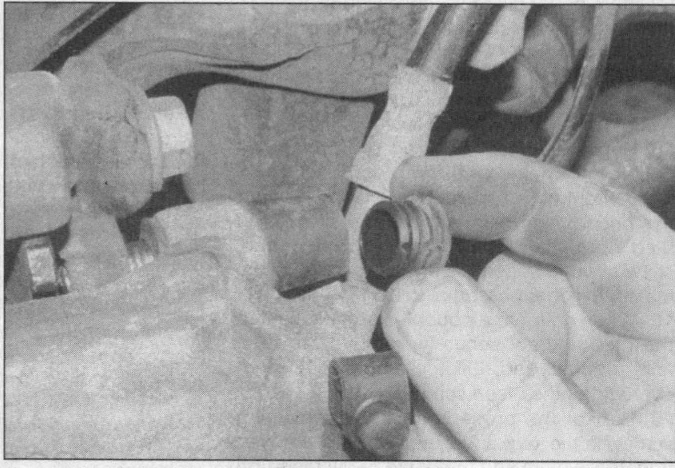

4.4 Remove the plastic plugs to access the caliper guide pins

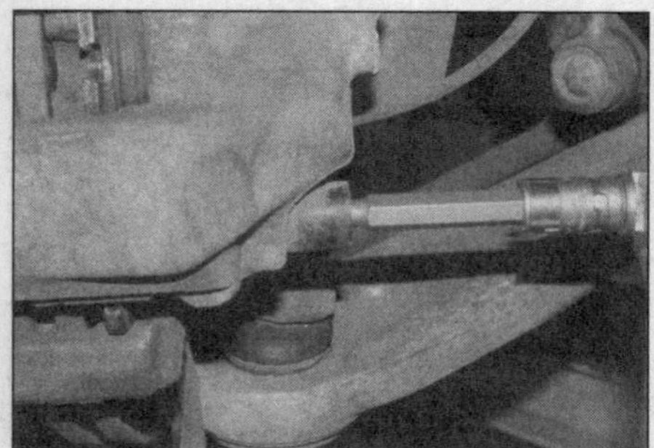

4.5a Slacken . . .

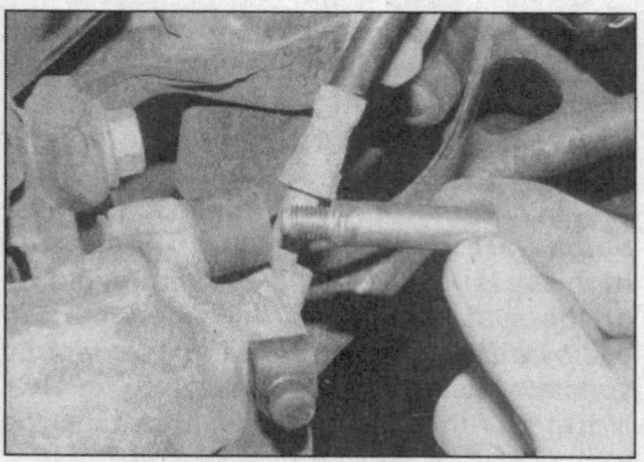

4.5b . . . and remove the caliper guide pins

4.5c Tie the caliper mounting bracket to the suspension

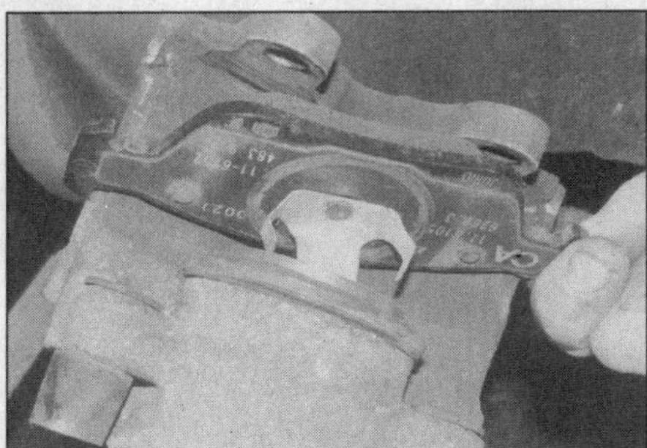
4.6a Unclip the inner pad from the caliper piston . . .

4.6b . . . and remove the outer pad from the caliper mounting bracket

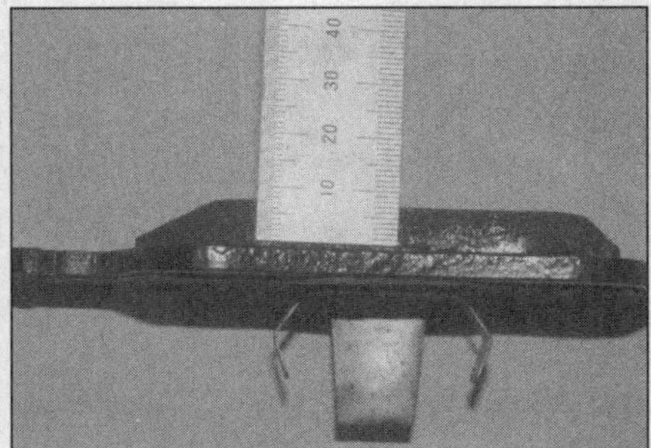
4.7 Measure the thickness of the friction material

renewed if any are fouled with oil or grease; there is no satisfactory way of degreasing friction material, once contaminated. If any of the brake pads are worn unevenly, or are fouled with oil or grease, trace and rectify the cause before reassembly.

8 If the brake pads are still serviceable, carefully clean them using a clean, fine wire brush or similar, paying particular attention to the sides and back of the metal backing. Clean out the grooves in the friction material (where applicable), and pick out any large embedded particles of dirt or debris. Carefully clean the pad locations in the caliper body/mounting bracket.

9 Prior to fitting the pads, check that the guide pins are a light, sliding fit in the caliper body bushes, with little sign of free play. Brush the dust and dirt from the caliper and piston, but *do not* inhale it, as it is a health hazard. Inspect the dust seal around the piston for damage, and the piston for evidence of fluid leaks, corrosion or damage. If attention to any of these components is necessary, refer to Section 8.

10 If new brake pads are to be fitted, the caliper piston must be pushed back into the cylinder to make room for them. Either use a piston retraction tool, a G-clamp or use suitable pieces of wood as levers. Clamp off the flexible brake hose leading to the caliper then connect a brake bleeding kit to the caliper bleed nipple. Open the bleed nipple as the piston is retracted; the surplus brake fluid will then be collected in the bleed kit vessel **(see illustration)**. Close the bleed nipple just before the caliper piston is pushed fully into the caliper. This should ensure no air enters the hydraulic system. **Note:** *The ABS unit contains hydraulic components that are very sensitive to impurities in the brake fluid. Even the smallest particles can cause the system to fail through blockage. The pad retraction method described here prevents any debris in the brake fluid expelled from the caliper from being passed back to the ABS hydraulic unit, as well as preventing any chance of damage to the master cylinder seals.*

11 Apply a smear of brake anti-squeak compound to the backing plate of each pad, and the pad backing plate contact points on the caliper bracket; do not apply excess grease, nor allow the grease to contact the friction material.

12 Fit the outer pad to the caliper mounting bracket, ensuring that its friction material is against the brake disc **(see illustration)**.

13 Clip the inner pad into the caliper piston, and manoeuvre the caliper assembly into position **(see illustration)**.

14 Install the caliper guide pins, and tighten them to the specified torque setting. Refit the plugs to the ends of the caliper guide pins.

15 Clip the pad wear sensor back into position in the outer pad, making sure its wiring is correctly routed **(see illustrations 4.3a and 4.3b)**.

16 Clip the anti-rattle spring into position in the caliper **(see illustration)**. Depress the brake pedal repeatedly, until the pads are pressed into firm contact with the brake disc, and normal (non-assisted) pedal pressure is restored.

17 Repeat the above procedure on the remaining front brake.

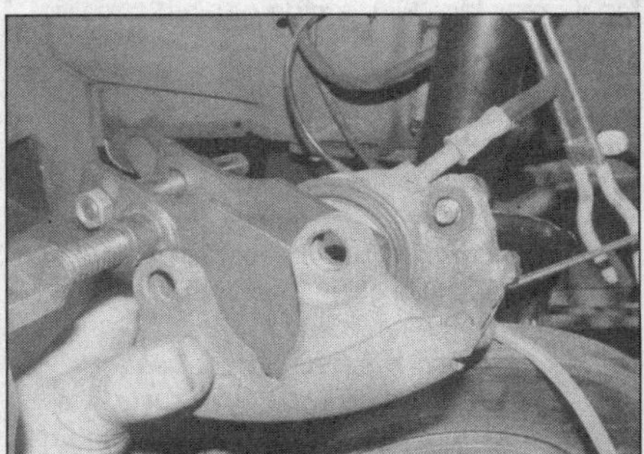
4.10 Using a piston retraction tool, with the hose clamped, and the bleed nipple open

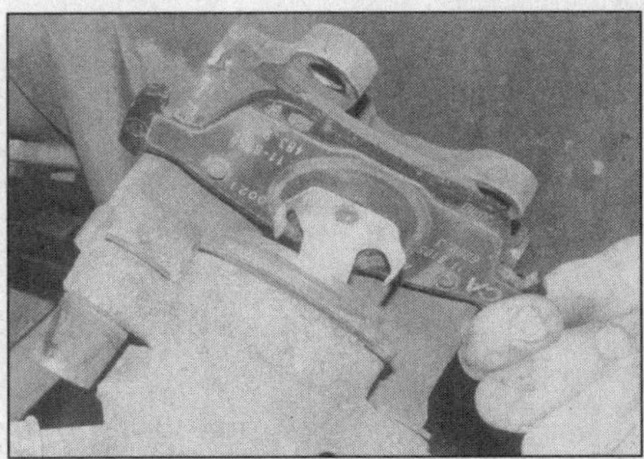
4.13 Clip the inner pad into the caliper piston

18 Refit the roadwheels, then lower the vehicle to the ground and tighten the roadwheel bolts to the specified torque setting.

5 Rear brake pads – renewal

The rear brake calipers are virtually identical to those fitted at the front. Refer to Section 4 for pad inspection and renewal details.

6 Front brake disc – inspection, removal and refitting

Note: *Before starting work, refer to the note at the beginning of Section 4 concerning the dangers of asbestos dust.*

4.12 Fit the outer pad to the caliper bracket

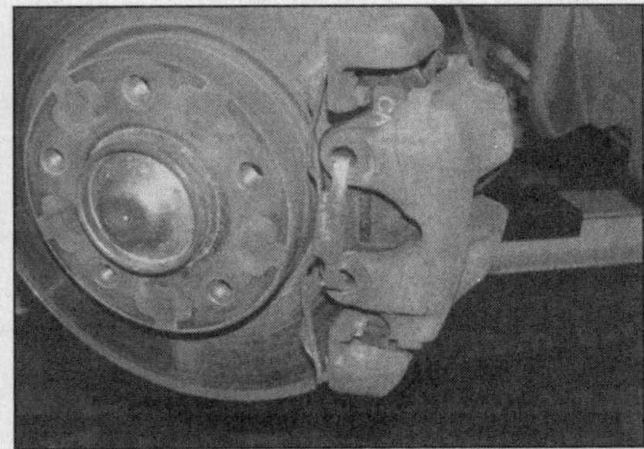
4.16 Refit the anti-rattle spring

6.3 Measure the disc thickness using a micrometer

6.7a Undo the retaining screw . . .

6.7b . . . and remove the brake disc from the hub

Note: *If either disc requires renewal, BOTH should be renewed at the same time, to ensure even and consistent braking. New brake pads should also be fitted.*

Inspection

1 Apply the handbrake, then jack up the front of the car and support it on axle stands. Remove the appropriate front roadwheel.

2 Slowly rotate the brake disc so that the full area of both sides can be checked; remove the brake pads if better access is required to the inboard surface (see Section 4). Light scoring is normal in the area swept by the brake pads, but if heavy scoring or cracks are found, the disc must be renewed.

3 It is normal to find a lip of rust and brake dust around the disc's perimeter; this can be scraped off if required. If, however, a lip has formed due to excessive wear of the brake pad swept area, then the disc's thickness must be measured using a micrometer **(see illustration)**. Take measurements at several places around the disc, at the inside and outside of the pad swept area; if the disc has worn at any point to the specified minimum thickness or less, the disc must be renewed.

4 If the disc is thought to be warped, it can be checked for run-out. Either use a dial gauge mounted on any convenient fixed point, while the disc is slowly rotated, or use feeler blades to measure (at several points all around the disc) the clearance between the disc and a fixed point, such as the caliper mounting bracket. If the measurements obtained are at the specified maximum or beyond, the disc is excessively warped, and must be renewed; however, it is worth checking first that the hub bearing is in good condition (Chapter 10). If the run-out is excessive, the disc must be renewed.

5 Check the disc for cracks, especially around the wheel bolt holes, and any other wear or damage, and renew if necessary.

Removal

6 Unscrew the two bolts securing the brake caliper mounting bracket to the hub carrier, then slide the caliper assembly off the disc. Using a piece of wire or string, tie the caliper to the front suspension coil spring, to avoid placing any strain on the hydraulic brake hose.

7 Use chalk or paint to mark the relationship of the disc to the hub, then remove the screw securing the brake disc to the hub, and remove the disc **(see illustrations)**. If it is tight, lightly tap its rear face with a hide or plastic mallet.

Refitting

8 Refitting is the reverse of the removal procedure, noting the following points:

a) Ensure that the mating surfaces of the disc and hub are clean and flat.

b) Align (if applicable) the marks made on removal, and tighten the disc retaining screw to the specified torque.

c) If a new disc has been fitted, use a suitable solvent to wipe any preservative coating from the disc before refitting the caliper.

d) Slide the caliper into position over the disc, making sure the pads pass either side of the disc. Tighten the caliper mounting bolts to the specified torque setting.

e) Refit the roadwheel, then lower the vehicle to the ground and tighten the roadwheel bolts to the specified torque. On completion, repeatedly depress the brake pedal until normal (non-assisted) pedal pressure returns.

7.3 Slide the rear caliper assembly off the disc

7.4 Undo the retaining screw and remove the rear disc

7 Rear brake disc – inspection, removal and refitting

Note: *Before starting work, refer to the note at the beginning of Section 4 concerning the dangers of asbestos dust.*

Note: *If either disc requires renewal, BOTH should be renewed at the same time, to ensure even and consistent braking. New brake pads should also be fitted.*

Inspection

1 Firmly chock the front wheels, then jack up the rear of the car and support it on axle stands. Remove the appropriate rear roadwheel. Release the handbrake.

2 Inspect the disc as described in Section 6.

Removal

3 Unscrew the two bolts securing the brake caliper mounting bracket in position, then slide the caliper assembly off the disc. Using a piece of wire or string, tie the caliper to the rear suspension coil spring, to avoid placing any strain on the hydraulic brake hose **(see illustration)**. If necessary unclip the rubber brake hose from the lower mounting bracket to provide enough slack to manoeuvre the caliper and bracket.

4 Slacken and remove the brake disc retaining screw **(see illustration)**.

5 It should now be possible to withdraw the brake disc from the stub axle by hand. If it is tight, lightly tap its rear face with a hide or plastic mallet. If the handbrake shoes are binding, first check that the handbrake is fully released, then continue as follows.

6 Referring to Section 14 for further details, fully slacken the handbrake adjustment to obtain maximum free play in the cable.

7 Insert a screwdriver through one of the

wheel bolt holes in the brake disc, and rotate the adjuster knurled wheel on the upper pivot to retract the shoes **(see illustrations 14.5a and 14.5b)**. The brake disc can then be withdrawn.

Refitting

8 If a new disc is been fitted, use a suitable solvent to wipe any preservative coating from the disc.

9 Align (if applicable) the marks made on removal, then fit the disc and tighten the retaining screw to the specified torque.

10 Slide the caliper into position over the disc, making sure the pads pass either side of the disc. Tighten the caliper bracket mounting bolts to the specified torque setting.

11 Adjust the handbrake shoes and cable as described in Section 14.

12 Refit the roadwheel, then lower the car to the ground, and tighten the roadwheel bolts to the specified torque. On completion, repeatedly depress the brake pedal until normal (non-assisted) pedal pressure returns. Recheck the handbrake adjustment.

8 Front brake caliper – removal, overhaul and refitting

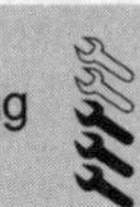

Note: *Before starting work, refer to the note at the beginning of Section 2 concerning the dangers of hydraulic fluid, and to the warning at the beginning of Section 4 concerning the dangers of asbestos dust.*

Removal

1 Apply the handbrake, then jack up the front of the vehicle and support it on axle stands. Remove the appropriate roadwheel.

2 Minimise fluid loss by using a brake hose clamp, a G-clamp or a similar tool to clamp the flexible hose.

3 Clean the area around the union, then loosen the brake hose union nut.

4 Remove the brake pads (see Section 4).

5 Unscrew the caliper from the end of the brake hose and remove it from the vehicle.

Overhaul

6 With the caliper on the bench, wipe away all traces of dust and dirt, but *avoid inhaling the dust, as it is a health hazard.*

7 Withdraw the partially-ejected piston from the caliper body, and remove the dust seal.

8 Using a small screwdriver, extract the piston hydraulic seal, taking great care not to damage the caliper bore **(see illustration)**.

9 Thoroughly clean all components, using only methylated spirit, isopropyl alcohol or clean hydraulic fluid as a cleaning medium. Never use mineral-based solvents such as petrol or paraffin, as they will attack the hydraulic system's rubber components. Dry the components immediately, using compressed air or a clean, lint-free cloth. Use compressed air to blow clear the fluid passages.

10 Check all components, and renew any that are worn or damaged. Check particularly the cylinder bore and piston; these should be renewed (note that this means the renewal of the complete body assembly) if they are scratched, worn or corroded in any way. Similarly check the condition of the guide pins and their bushes; both pins should be undamaged and (when cleaned) a reasonably tight sliding fit in the bushes. If there is any doubt about the condition of any component, renew it.

11 If the assembly is fit for further use, obtain the appropriate repair kit; the components are available from BMW dealers in various combinations. All rubber seals should be renewed as a matter of course; these should never be re-used.

12 On reassembly, ensure that all components are clean and dry.

13 Soak the piston and the new piston (fluid) seal in clean hydraulic fluid. Smear clean fluid on the cylinder bore surface.

14 Fit the new piston (fluid) seal, using only your fingers (no tools) to manipulate it into the cylinder bore groove.

15 Fit the new dust seal to the piston. Locate the rear of the seal in the recess in the caliper body, and refit the piston to the cylinder bore using a twisting motion. Ensure that the piston enters squarely into the bore, and press it fully into the bore.

Refitting

16 Screw the caliper fully onto the flexible hose union.

17 Refit the brake pads (see Section 4).

18 Securely tighten the brake pipe union nut.

19 Remove the brake hose clamp or polythene, as applicable, and bleed the hydraulic system as described in Section 2. Note that, providing the precautions described were taken to minimise brake fluid loss, it should only be necessary to bleed the relevant front brake.

20 Refit the roadwheel, then lower the vehicle to the ground and tighten the roadwheel bolts to the specified torque. On completion, check the hydraulic fluid level as described in *Weekly checks.*

9 Rear brake caliper – removal, overhaul and refitting

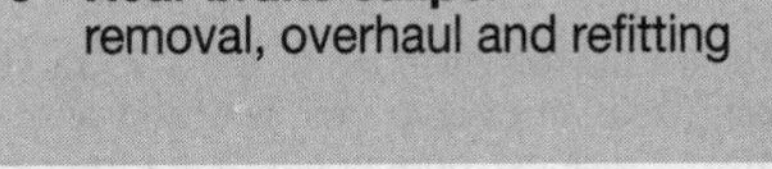

Note: *Before starting work, refer to the note at the beginning of Section 2 concerning the dangers of hydraulic fluid, and to the warning at the beginning of Section 4 concerning the dangers of asbestos dust.*

Removal

1 Chock the front wheels, then jack up the rear of the vehicle and support on axle stands. Remove the relevant rear wheel.

2 Minimise fluid loss by first removing the master cylinder reservoir cap, and then

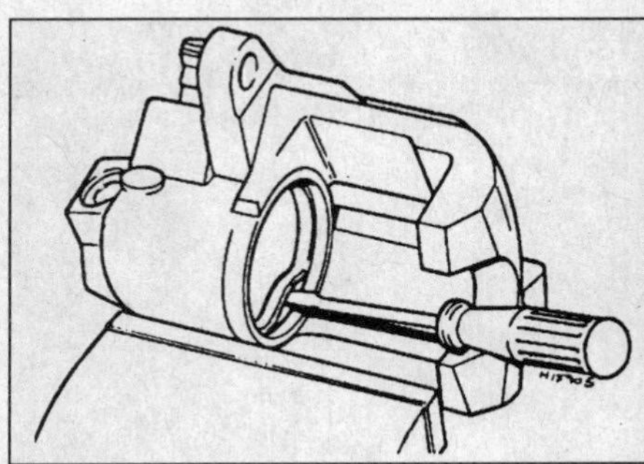

8.8 Extracting the piston seal – take care not to scratch the surface of the bore

tightening it down onto a piece of polythene, to obtain an airtight seal. Alternatively, use a brake hose clamp, a G-clamp or a similar tool to clamp the flexible hose.

3 Clean the area around the union, then loosen the brake hose union nut.

4 Remove the brake pads as described in Section 4.

5 Unscrew the caliper from the end of the flexible hose, and remove it from the vehicle.

Overhaul

6 Refer to Section 8, noting that the piston dust seal is secured in position with a circlip.

Refitting

7 Screw the caliper fully onto the flexible hose union.

8 Refit the brake pads (refer to Section 4).

9 Securely tighten the brake pipe union nut.

10 Remove the brake hose clamp or polythene, as applicable, and bleed the hydraulic system as described in Section 2. Note that, providing the precautions described were taken to minimise brake fluid loss, it should only be necessary to bleed the relevant rear brake.

11 Refit the roadwheel, then lower the vehicle to the ground and tighten the roadwheel bolts to the specified torque. On completion, check the hydraulic fluid level as described in *Weekly checks.*

10 Master cylinder – removal, overhaul and refitting

Models with ABS

1 On models fitted with ABS, although it is possible for the home mechanic to remove the master cylinder, if the hydraulic unions are disconnected from the master cylinder, air will enter the high-pressure hydraulic system linking the master cylinder and hydraulic unit. Bleeding of the high-pressure system can only be safely carried out by a BMW dealer or specialist who has access to the service tester (see Section 2). Consequently, once the master cylinder has been refitted, the vehicle **must** be taken on a trailer or transporter to a suitably-equipped BMW dealer or specialist.

10.3 Disconnect the fluid level sensor wiring plug

Removal

Note: *Before starting work, refer to the warning at the beginning of Section 2 concerning the dangers of hydraulic fluid.*

Note: *New master cylinder retaining nuts will be required on refitting.*

2 To allow sufficient clearance on LHD models, remove the heater/ventilation inlet air ducting from the rear of the engine compartment as follows.

a) Rotate the three fasteners 90° anti-clockwise and remove the pollen filter cover from the rear of the engine compartment. Pull the filter forward and remove it.

b) Undo the four retaining clips and thread the cable out of the ducting.

c) Unscrew the four bolts and pull the filter housing forwards and remove it.

d) Undo the two bolts and remove the inlet ducting upwards and out of the engine compartment.

3 Remove the master cylinder reservoir cap, and siphon the hydraulic fluid from the reservoir. **Note:** *Do not siphon the fluid by mouth, as it is poisonous; use a syringe or a hand-held vacuum pump.* Alternatively, open any convenient bleed screw in the system, and gently pump the brake pedal to expel the fluid through a plastic tube connected to the screw until the level of fluid drops below that of the reservoir (see Section 2). Disconnect the wiring connector(s) from the brake fluid reservoir **(see illustration)**.

4 Disconnect the fluid hose(s) from the side of the reservoir, and plug the hose end(s) to minimise fluid loss.

11.4 Remove the clip (arrowed) and slide out the clevis pin

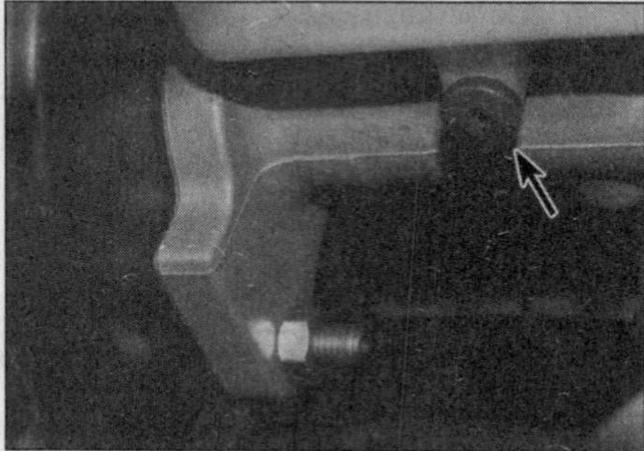

10.5 Undo the brake reservoir retaining bolt (arrowed)

5 Undo the master cylinder reservoir retaining bolt **(see illustration)**.

6 Carefully ease the fluid reservoir out from the top of the master cylinder. Recover the reservoir seals, and plug the cylinder ports to prevent dirt entry.

7 Wipe clean the area around the brake pipe unions on the side of the master cylinder, and place absorbent rags beneath the pipe unions to catch any surplus fluid. Make a note of the correct fitted positions of the unions, then unscrew the union nuts and carefully withdraw the pipes. Plug or tape over the pipe ends and master cylinder orifices to minimise the loss of brake fluid, and to prevent the entry of dirt into the system. Wash off any spilt fluid immediately with cold water.

8 Slacken and remove the two nuts and washers securing the master cylinder to the vacuum servo unit, then withdraw the unit from the engine compartment. Remove the O-ring from the rear of the master cylinder. Discard the retaining nuts, new ones should be used on refitting.

Overhaul

9 If the master cylinder is faulty, it must be renewed. Repair kits are not available from BMW dealers so the cylinder must be treated as a sealed unit. Renew the master cylinder O-ring seal and reservoir seals regardless of their apparent condition.

Refitting

10 Remove all traces of dirt from the master cylinder and servo unit mating surfaces, and fit a new O-ring to the groove on the master cylinder body.

11 Fit the master cylinder to the servo unit, ensuring that the servo unit pushrod enters the master cylinder bore centrally. Fit the new master cylinder retaining nuts and washers, and tighten them to the specified torque.

12 Wipe clean the brake pipe unions, then refit them to the master cylinder ports and tighten them securely.

13 Press the new reservoir seals firmly into the master cylinder ports, then ease the reservoir into position. Tighten the reservoir retaining bolt securely. Reconnect the fluid hose(s) to the reservoir, and reconnect the wiring connector(s).

14 Refill the master cylinder reservoir with new fluid, and bleed the complete hydraulic system as described in Section 2.

11 Brake pedal – removal and refitting

Removal

1 Disconnect the battery negative terminal.

2 Remove the brake light switch as described in Section 18.

3 Using a pair of pliers, carefully unhook the return spring from the brake pedal.

4 Slide off the retaining clip and remove the clevis pin securing the brake pedal to the servo unit pushrod **(see illustration)**.

5 Slide off the pedal pivot pin retaining clip and remove the pedal from the pivot.

6 Carefully clean and inspect all components, renewing any that are worn or damaged.

Refitting

7 Refitting is the reverse of removal. Apply a smear of multipurpose grease to the pedal pivot and clevis pin.

12 Vacuum servo unit – testing, removal and refitting

Note: *On models with ABS and Traction control (ASC+T) or Dynamic stability control (DSC), removal of the servo unit involves removal of the ABS/ASC+T and/or DSC control unit. Due to the need for special diagnostic equipment, this task should only be carried out be a BMW dealer or suitably-equipped specialist.*

Testing

1 To test the operation of the servo unit, depress the footbrake several times to exhaust the vacuum, then start the engine whilst keeping the pedal firmly depressed. As the engine starts, there should be a noticeable 'give' in the brake pedal as the vacuum builds-up. Allow the engine to run for at least two minutes, then switch it off. If the brake pedal is now depressed it should feel normal, but further applications should result in the pedal feeling firmer, with the pedal stroke decreasing with each application.

2 If the servo does not operate as described, first inspect the servo unit check valve as described in Section 13.

3 If the servo unit still fails to operate satisfactorily, the fault lies within the unit itself. Repairs to the unit are not possible – if faulty, the servo unit must be renewed.

Removal

Note: *New retaining nuts will be required on refitting.*

4 Remove the master cylinder as described in Section 10.

5 Disconnect the vacuum hose from the servo unit check valve.

6 Slacken and remove the retaining bolts securing the driver's side lower facia panel. Unclip the panel and remove it from the vehicle.

7 Referring to Section 11, unhook the brake pedal return spring, then slide off the retaining clip and remove the clevis pin securing the pedal to the servo unit pushrod **(see illustration 11.4)**.

8 Slacken and remove the servo unit retaining nuts, then return to the engine compartment and remove the servo unit from the vehicle **(see illustration)**.

Refitting

9 Refitting is the reverse of removal, noting the following points.

a) *Check the servo unit check valve sealing grommet for signs of damage or deterioration, and renew if necessary.*

b) *If a new servo unit is being installed, remove the sound insulation material from the original, and transfer it to the new one.*

c) *Ensure that the servo unit pushrod is correctly engaged with the brake pedal, then fit the new retaining nuts and tighten them to the specified torque.*

d) *Apply a smear of grease to the servo pushrod clevis pin, and secure it in position with the retaining clip.*

e) *Refit the master cylinder as described in Section 10 of this Chapter.*

f) *Refit the brake light switch as described in Section 18.*

g) *On completion, start the engine and check for air leaks at the vacuum hose-to-servo unit connection; check the operation of the braking system.*

13 Vacuum servo unit check valve – removal, testing and refitting

Removal

1 Disconnect the vacuum hose from the servo unit check valve, mounted on the servo.

2 Carefully ease the check valve out of the servo unit, taking care not to displace the grommet.

Testing

3 Examine the check valve for signs of damage, and renew if necessary.

4 The valve may be tested by blowing through it in both directions; air should flow through the valve in one direction only – when blown through from the servo unit end of the valve. Renew the valve if this is not the case.

5 Examine the servo unit rubber sealing grommet for signs of damage or deterioration, and renew as necessary.

Refitting

6 Ensure that the sealing grommet is correctly fitted to the servo unit.

7 Ease the valve into position in the servo, taking great care not to displace or damage the grommet.

12.8 Undo the servo unit retaining nuts (arrowed)

8 Reconnect the vacuum hose securely to the valve.

9 On completion, start the engine and ensure there are no air leaks at the check valve-to-servo unit connection.

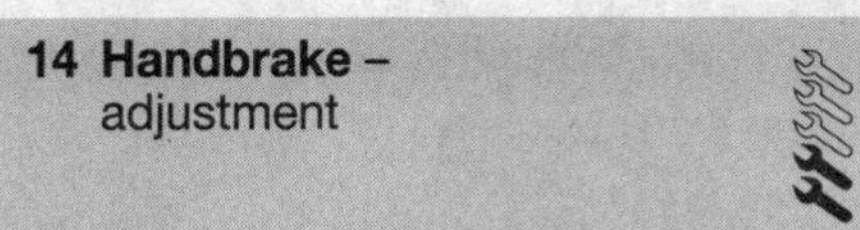

14 Handbrake – adjustment

1 Applying normal moderate pressure, pull the handbrake lever to the fully applied position, counting the number of clicks emitted from the handbrake ratchet mechanism. If adjustment is correct, there should be approximately 7 or 8 clicks before the handbrake is fully applied. If there are more than 10 clicks, adjust as follows.

2 Slacken and remove one wheel bolt from each rear wheel then chock the front wheels, jack up the rear of the vehicle and support it on axle stands.

3 Access to the handbrake cable adjusting nuts can be gained by removing the handbrake lever gaiter from the centre console **(see illustration)**. If greater access is required, the rear section of the centre console will have to be removed (Chapter 11).

4 With the handbrake fully released, undo the cable locknuts and release the adjusting nuts until all tension in the cables is released **(see illustration)**.

5 Starting on the left-hand rear wheel, fully release the handbrake and position the wheel/disc so the exposed bolt hole is positioned towards the rear at 65° from the vertical position. Make sure the handbrake lever is fully released, then insert a screwdriver in through the bolt hole and fully expand the handbrake shoes by rotating the adjuster knurled ring. When the wheel/disc can no longer be turned, back the knurled ring off by 10 teeth (catches) so that the wheel is free to rotate easily **(see illustrations)**.

6 Repeat paragraph 5 on the right-hand wheel.

7 With the handbrake set on the sixth notch of the ratchet mechanism, rotate the cable adjusting nuts equally until it is difficult to turn both rear wheels. Once this is so, fully release the handbrake lever, and check that the wheels rotate freely. Slowly apply the handbrake, and check that the brake shoes start to contact the drums when the handbrake is set to the second notch of the ratchet mechanism. Check the adjustment by applying the

14.3 Unclip the handbrake gaiter to gain access to the handbrake cable adjustment nuts (arrowed)

14.4 Slacken the handbrake cable adjusting nuts

14.5a Position one of the wheel bolt holes as shown, then insert a screwdriver through the hole . . .

14.5b . . . and rotate the adjuster knurled ring (shown with disc removed)

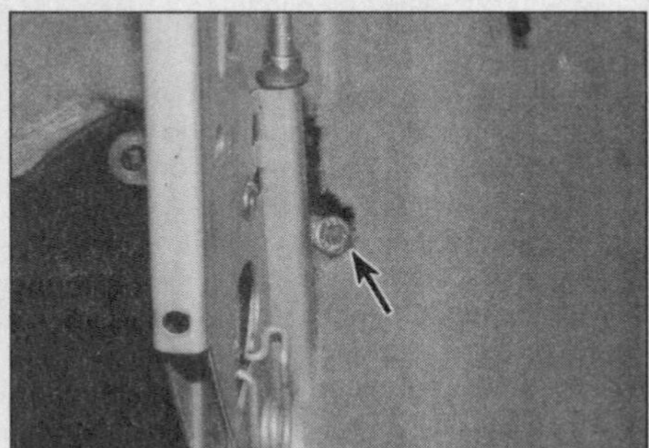

15.3 Undo the handbrake lever bracket bolt (arrowed)

16.8a Unfold the expander, then withdraw the pin (arrowed) . . .

handbrake fully, counting the clicks emitted from the handbrake ratchet and, if necessary, re-adjust.

8 Once adjustment is correct, hold the adjusting nuts and securely tighten the locknuts. Check the operation of the handbrake warning light switch, then refit the centre console section/handbrake lever gaiter (as applicable). Refit the roadwheels, then lower the vehicle to the ground and tighten the wheel bolts to the specified torque.

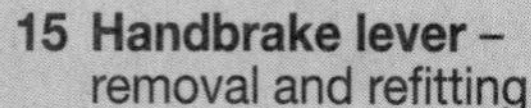

15 Handbrake lever – removal and refitting

Removal

1 Remove the rear section of the centre console and armrest (where fitted) as

17.2a Using pliers, unhook and remove the handbrake shoe front . . .

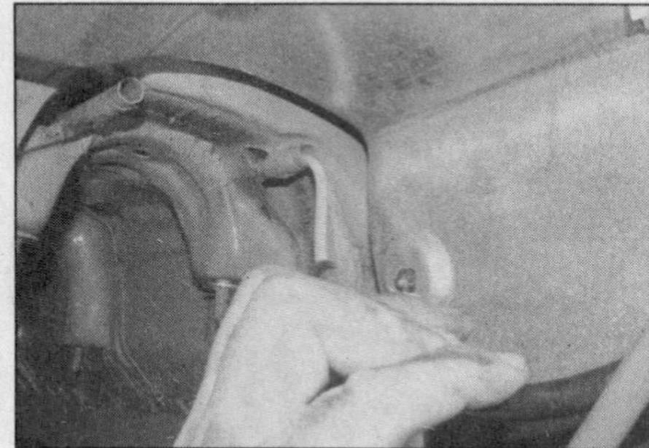

16.5 Withdraw the cable from the support guide

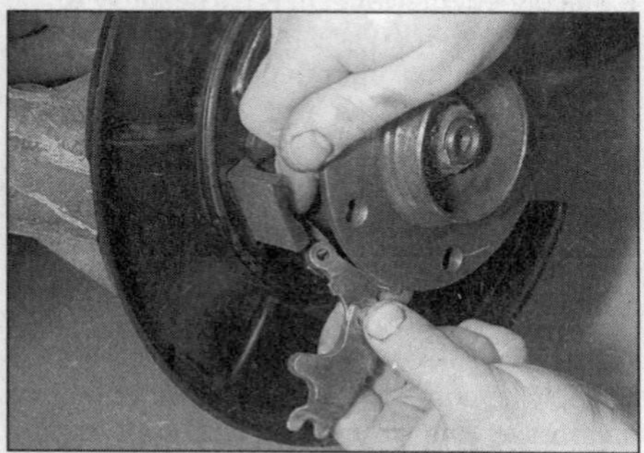

16.8b . . . and detach the expander from the end of the handbrake cable

described in Chapter 11 to gain access to the handbrake lever.

2 Slacken and remove both the handbrake cable locknuts/adjusting nuts, and detach the cables from the lever.

3 Undo the retaining bolt, and remove the lever from the vehicle **(see illustration)**.

Refitting

4 Refitting is a reversal of the removal. Prior to refitting the centre console, adjust the handbrake as described in Section 14.

16 Handbrake cables – removal and refitting

Removal

1 Remove the rear section of the centre

17.2b . . . and rear return springs

console as described in Chapter 11 to gain access to the handbrake lever. The handbrake cable consists of two sections, a right- and a left-hand section, which are connected to the lever. Each section can be removed individually.

2 Slacken and remove the relevant handbrake cable locknut and adjusting nut, and disengage the inner cable from the handbrake lever.

3 Firmly chock the front wheels, then jack up the rear of the car and support it on axle stands.

4 Referring to the relevant Part of Chapter 4, remove the exhaust system heat shield to gain access to the handbrake cables. Note that on some models (M43TU and M52TU engine codes), it may also be necessary to remove part of the exhaust system.

5 Free the front end of the outer cable from the body, and withdraw the cable from its support guide **(see illustration)**.

6 Working back along the length of the cable, noting its correct routing, and free it from all the relevant retaining clips.

7 Remove the relevant rear disc as described in Section 7.

8 Slide the cable core in the direction of the expander lock up to the stop, depress the nipple and pull out the cable core from the expander **(see illustrations)**

Refitting

9 Insert the cable into the brake carrier/guard plate, and push it in up to the stop on the cable outer sleeve.

10 Grip the sleeve of the cable end, and push it in to the expander until it snaps into place.

11 Refitting is a reversal of the removal procedure. Prior to refitting the centre console, adjust the handbrake as described in Section 14.

17 Handbrake shoes – removal and refitting

Removal

1 Remove the rear brake disc as described in Section 7, and make a note of the correct fitted position of all components.

2 Using a pair of pliers, carefully unhook and remove the handbrake shoe return springs **(see illustrations)**.

3 Release the shoe retaining pins using pliers by depressing them and rotating them through 90°, then remove the pins and springs **(see illustrations)**.

4 Remove both handbrake shoes, and recover the shoe adjuster mechanism, noting which way around it is fitted **(see illustration)**.

5 Inspect the handbrake shoes for wear or contamination, and renew if necessary. It is recommended that the return springs are renewed as a matter of course.

6 While the shoes are removed, clean and

17.3a Rotate the retainer pins through 90° . . .

inspect the condition of the shoe adjuster and expander mechanisms, renew them if they show signs of wear or damage. If all is well, apply a fresh coat of brake grease (BMW recommend Molykote Paste G) to the threads of the adjuster and sliding surfaces of the expander mechanism **(see illustration)**. Do not allow the grease to contact the shoe friction material.

Refitting

7 Prior to installation, clean the backplate, and apply a thin smear of high-temperature brake grease or anti-seize compound to all those surfaces of the backplate which bear on the shoes. Do not allow the lubricant to foul the friction material.

8 Offer up the handbrake shoes, and secure them in position with the retaining pins and springs.

9 Make sure the lower ends of the shoes are correctly engaged with the expander, then slide the adjuster mechanism into position between the upper ends of the shoes **(see illustration)**.

10 Check all components are correctly fitted, and fit the upper and lower return springs using a pair of pliers.

11 Centralise the handbrake shoes, and refit the brake disc as described in Section 7.

12 Prior to refitting the roadwheel, adjust the handbrake as described in Section 14.

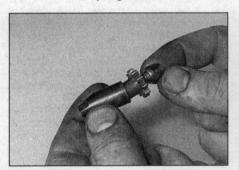

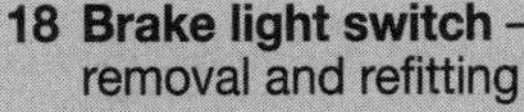

18 Brake light switch – removal and refitting

Removal

1 The brake light switch is located on the pedal bracket behind the facia.

2 Slacken and remove the retaining bolts securing the driver's side lower facia panel. Unclip the panel and remove it from the vehicle.

3 Reach up behind the facia and disconnect the wiring connector from the switch.

4 Pull the switch from the mounting. If required, depress the clips and withdraw the switch mounting from the pedal bracket **(see illustrations)**.

17.3b . . . then remove the pins and springs . . .

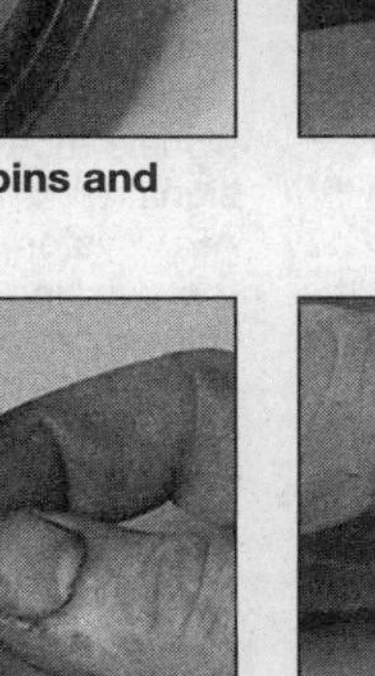

17.6 Clean the adjuster assembly and coat it with fresh brake grease

Refitting

5 Fully depress the brake pedal and hold it down, then manoeuvre the switch into position. Hold the switch fully in position, then **slowly** release the brake pedal and allow it to return to its stop. This will automatically adjust the brake light switch. **Note:** *If the pedal is released too quickly, the switch will be incorrectly adjusted.*

6 Reconnect the wiring connector, and check the operation of the brake lights. The brake lights should illuminate after the brake pedal has travelled approximately 5 mm. If the switch is not functioning correctly, it is faulty and must be renewed; no other adjustment is possible.

7 On completion, refit the driver's side lower facia panel.

17.4 . . . and handbrake shoes

17.9 Refit the adjuster assembly, making sure it is correctly engaged with both handbrake shoes

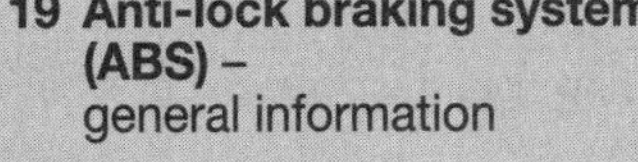

19 Anti-lock braking system (ABS) – general information

Note: *On models equipped with traction control, the ABS unit is a dual function unit, and works both the anti-lock braking system (ABS) and traction control function of the Automatic Stability Control plus Traction (ASC+T) system.*

1 ABS is fitted to most models as standard, and was available as an option on all others. The system comprises a hydraulic block which contains the hydraulic solenoid valves and the electrically-driven return pump, the four roadwheel sensors (one fitted to each wheel), and the electronic control unit (ECU).

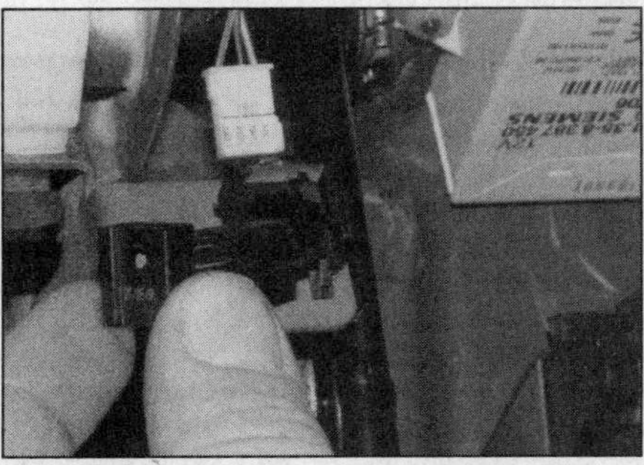

18.4a Pull the switch from the switch mounting

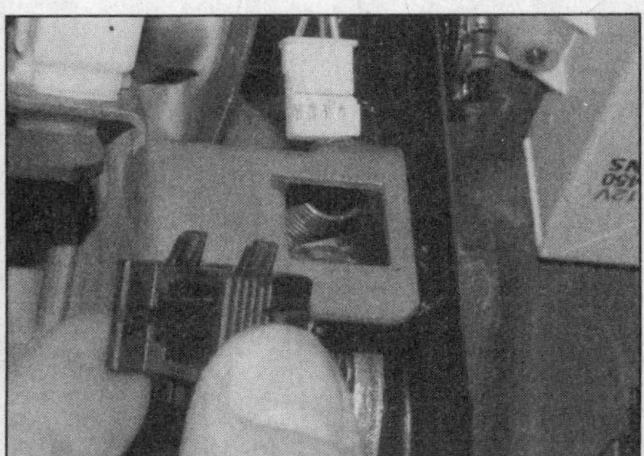

18.4b Press the retaining clips and remove the switch mounting

20.4 Unclip the lid, release and disconnect the ABS sensor wiring plug (arrowed)

The purpose of the system is to prevent the wheel(s) locking during heavy braking. This is achieved by automatic release of the brake on the relevant wheel, followed by re-application of the brake.

2 The solenoids are controlled by the ECU, which itself receives signals from the four wheel sensors (one fitted on each hub), which monitor the speed of rotation of each wheel. By comparing these signals, the ECU can determine the speed at which the vehicle is travelling. It can then use this speed to determine when a wheel is decelerating at an abnormal rate, compared to the speed of the vehicle, and therefore predicts when a wheel is about to lock. During normal operation, the system functions in the same way as a non-ABS braking system. In addition to this, the brake pedal position sensor (which is fitted to the vacuum servo unit) also informs the ECU of how hard the brake pedal is being depressed.

3 If the ECU senses that a wheel is about to lock, it operates the relevant solenoid valve in the hydraulic unit, which then isolates the brake caliper on the wheel which is about to lock from the master cylinder, effectively sealing-in the hydraulic pressure.

4 If the speed of rotation of the wheel continues to decrease at an abnormal rate, the ECU switches on the electrically-driven return pump, and pumps the hydraulic fluid back into the master cylinder, releasing pressure on the brake caliper so that the brake is released. Once the speed of rotation of the wheel returns to an acceptable rate, the pump stops and the solenoid valve opens, allowing the hydraulic master cylinder pressure to return to the caliper, which then re-applies the brake. This cycle can be carried out at up to 10 times a second.

20.5 Undo the sensor retaining bolt (arrowed)

5 The action of the solenoid valves and return pump creates pulses in the hydraulic circuit. When the ABS system is functioning, these pulses can be felt through the brake pedal.

6 The operation of the ABS system is entirely dependent on electrical signals. To prevent the system responding to any inaccurate signals, a built-in safety circuit monitors all signals received by the ECU. If an inaccurate signal or low battery voltage is detected, the ABS system is automatically shut down, and the warning light on the instrument panel is illuminated, to inform the driver that the ABS system is not operational. Normal braking should still be available, however.

7 If a fault does develop in the ABS system, the vehicle must be taken to a BMW dealer or suitably-equipped specialist for fault diagnosis and repair.

8 On models equipped with ASC+T, an accumulator is also incorporated into the hydraulic system. As well as performing the ABS function as described above, the hydraulic unit also works the traction control side of the ASC+T system. If the ECU senses that the wheels are about to lose traction under acceleration, the hydraulic unit momentarily applies the rear brakes to prevent the wheel(s) spinning. In the same way as the ABS, the vehicle must be taken to a BMW dealer or suitably-equipped specialist for testing if a fault develops in the ASC+T system.

20 Anti-lock braking system (ABS) components – removal and refitting

Hydraulic unit

1 Although it is possible for the home mechanic to remove the hydraulic unit, the unit's self-diagnosis system must be interrogated by dedicated test equipment before and after removal, and the unit must be bled by BMW service test equipment. Consequently, we recommend that removal and refitting the hydraulic unit should be entrusted to a BMW dealer or suitably-equipped specialist.

Accumulator (ASC+T models)

2 For the same reasons given in Paragraph 1, we recommend that removal and refitting of the accumulator should be entrusted to a BMW dealer or suitable-equipped specialist.

Electronic control unit (ECU)

3 In order to remove the ABS/ASC+T ECU, the hydraulic unit must first be removed, as the ECU is screwed to the side of the hydraulic unit. Consequently, we recommend that removal and refitting of the ECU is entrusted to a BMW dealer or suitably-equipped specialist.

Front wheel sensor

Removal

4 Chock the rear wheels, then firmly apply the handbrake, jack up the front of the vehicle and support on axle stands. Remove the appropriate front roadwheel. Trace the wiring back from the sensor to the connector which is situated in a protective plastic box. Unclip the lid, then free the wiring connector and disconnect it from the main harness **(see illustration)**.

5 Slacken and remove the bolt securing the sensor to the hub carrier, and remove the sensor and lead assembly from the vehicle **(see illustration)**. **Note:** *On some models, the front wheel sensors are handed, and are marked L and R. Additionally, the right-hand sensor has two green markings between the sensor and the grommet.*

Refitting

6 Prior to refitting, apply a thin coat of multipurpose grease to the sensor tip (BMW recommend the use of Staborax NBU 12/k).

7 Ensure that the sensor and hub carrier sealing faces are clean, then fit the sensor to the hub. Ensure that, where applicable, the sensor is fitted to the correct side of the vehicle (see Paragraph 5). Refit the retaining bolt and tighten it to the specified torque.

8 Ensure that the sensor wiring is correctly routed and retained by all the necessary clips, and reconnect it to its wiring connector. Refit the sensor connector into the box and securely clip the lid in position.

9 Refit the roadwheel, then lower the vehicle to the ground and tighten the roadwheel bolts to the specified torque.

Rear wheel sensor

Removal

10 Chock the front wheels, then jack up the rear of the vehicle and support it on axle stands. Remove the appropriate roadwheel.

11 Remove the sensor as described in paragraphs 4 and 5.

Refitting

12 Refit the sensor as described above in paragraphs 6 to 9.

Front reluctor rings

13 The front reluctor rings are fixed onto the rear of wheel hubs. Examine the rings for damage such as chipped or missing teeth. If renewal is necessary, the complete hub assembly must be dismantled and the bearings renewed, with reference to Chapter 10.

Rear reluctor rings

14 The rear reluctor rings are pressed onto the driveshaft outer joints. Examine the rings for signs of damage such as chipped or missing teeth, and renew as necessary. If renewal is necessary, the driveshaft assembly must be renewed (see Chapter 8).

21 Vacuum pump (N42 and N46 engines) – removal and refitting

Removal

1 On these engines a vacuum pump is necessary as, due to the Valvetronic system, very little vacuum is created in the inlet manifold for the brake servo. The vacuum pump is located on the rear of the cylinder head, and is driven by the exhaust camshaft.

2 Open the bonnet, then raise the bonnet to its fully open position, referring to Chapter 11.

3 Undo the two bolts, raise the plastic cover on top of the engine, and pull it out towards the front.

4 Working at the rear of the engine compartment, turn the fasteners 90° anti-clockwise and remove the pollen filter cover. Slide the filter from the housing. If necessary, refer to Chapter 1.

5 Release the retaining clips, and remove the cable from the ducting on the air inlet housing.

6 Undo the four bolts and pull the pollen filter housing to the front – see Chapter 1 if necessary.

7 In the left-hand rear corner of the engine compartment, pull up the sealing strip, undo the two fasteners and pull the trim panel forwards a little **(see illustration)**.

8 Undo the two Torx bolts, and lift out the heater inlet housing **(see illustration)**.

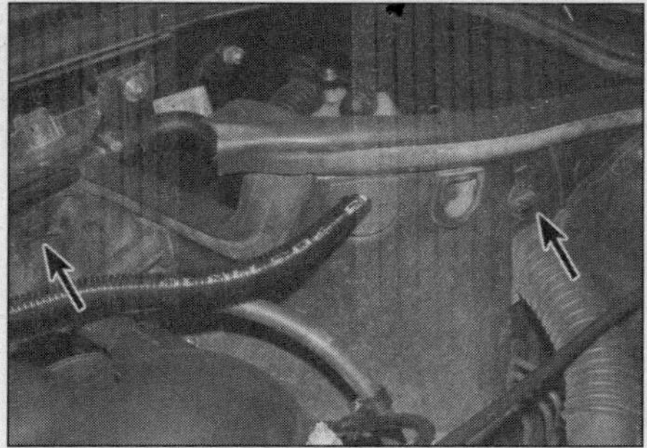

21.7 Rotate the fasteners (arrowed) 90° anti-clockwise

21.9 Undo the three bolts (arrowed) and remove the vacuum pump

9 Disconnect the vacuum hose from the pump, undo the three bolts and remove the pump **(see illustration)**. Discard the O-ring seal, a new one must be fitted.

21.8 Undo the two bolts (arrowed) and remove the inlet housing

21.10 Ensure the pump drive engages correctly with the slot in the end of the camshaft

Refitting

10 Refitting is a reversal of removal, ensuring the drive lug of the pump engages correctly with the slot in the camshaft **(see illustration)**. Tighten the pump retaining bolts securely.

Chapter 10
Suspension and steering

Contents

Degrees of difficulty

Easy, suitable for novice with little experience 	**Fairly easy,** suitable for beginner with some experience	**Fairly difficult,** suitable for competent DIY mechanic	**Difficult,** suitable for experienced DIY mechanic	**Very difficult,** suitable for expert DIY or professional 

Specifications

Engine codes

4-cylinder engines

1796 cc engines	N42 B18 and N46 B18
1895 cc engines	M43TU B19
1995 cc engines	N42 B20 and N46 B20

6-cylinder engines

2171 cc engines	M54 B22
2494 cc engines	M52TU B25 and M54 B25
2793 cc engines	M52TU B28
2979 cc engines	M54 B30

Front suspension

Type	Independent, with MacPherson struts incorporating coil springs and telescopic shock absorbers. Anti-roll bar fitted to most models

Rear suspension

Type	Independent, trailing arms located by upper and lower control arms with coil springs and shock absorbers. Anti-roll bar fitted to most models

Steering

Type	Rack-and-pinion. Power assistance standard on all models

Wheel alignment and steering angles

Vehicle must be laden to simulate front and rear passengers, and have a full fuel tank

Front wheel:	
Camber angle:	
Standard suspension	-20' ± 20'
Sports suspension	-43' ± 20'
Maximum difference between sides	30'
Castor angle:	
Standard suspension	5° 26' ± 30'
Sports suspension	3° 36' ± 30'
Maximum difference between sides	30'
Toe setting (total)	0° 14' ± 8'
Rear wheel:	
Camber angle:	
Standard suspension	-1° 30' ± 15'
Sports suspension	-2° 04' ± 15'
Maximum difference between sides	15'
Toe setting (total)	0° 16' ± 6'

Torque wrench settings

Note: *On some fixings different grades of bolt can be used; the grade of each bolt is stamped on the bolt head. Ensure that each bolt is tightened to the correct torque for its grade.*

	Nm	lbf ft
Front suspension		
Anti-roll bar connecting link nuts*	65	48
Anti-roll bar mounting clamp nuts*	22	16
Hub nut*	290	214
Lower arm balljoint nut*	65	48
Lower arm rear mounting bracket bolts	59	44
Lower arm to subframe	90	66
Reinforcement frame/plate under front subframe:*		
Stage 1	59	44
Stage 2	Angle-tighten a further 90°	
Stage 3	Angle-tighten a further 30°	
Strut mounting-to-body nuts:*		
Nuts with 18 mm diameter flange	24	18
Nuts with 21 mm diameter flange	34	25
Strut upper mounting plate/piston rod nut:		
M12 thread:		
Piston with an external hexagon end (retain with socket)	64	47
Piston with an internal hexagon end (retain with Allen key)	44	32
M14 thread	64	47
Strut-to-hub carrier bolt*	81	60
Subframe to engine crossmember:*		
M10:		
Strength grade 8.8 (see head of bolt)	42	31
Strength grade 9.8 (see head of bolt)	47	35
M12:		
Strength grade 8.8 (see head of bolt)	77	57
Strength grade 10.9 (see head of bolt)	110	81
Strength grade 12.9 (see head of bolt)	105	77
Rear suspension		
Control arm-to-subframe pivot bolts*	77	57
Shock absorber lower mounting bolt	100	74
Shock absorber piston rod nut*	14	10
Shock absorber upper mounting nuts:		
M8:		
Strength grade 8.8 (see head of bolt)	22	16
Strength grade 10.9 (see head of bolt)	30	22
Subframe:		
M12	77	57
M14	140	103
Trailing arm-to-control arm pivot bolts*	110	81
Trailing arm-to-mounting bracket pivot bolt	110	81
Trailing arm to subframe	77	57

Torque wrench settings (continued)

	Nm	lbf ft
Steering		
Lateral acceleration sensor	8	6
Power steering pump bolts	22	16
Power steering pump-to-coolant pump bolts (N42 and N46 engines)	32	24
Power steering pipe union bolts:		
M10 union bolt	12	9
M14 union bolt	35	26
M16 union bolt	40	30
M18 union bolt	45	33
Steering column universal joint clamp bolt*	22	16
Steering rack mounting nuts*	42	31
Steering wheel:		
Bolt	63	46
Nut	80	59
Track rod	100	74
Track rod balljoint:		
Retaining nut*	65	48
Locknut	14	10
Roadwheels		
Roadwheel bolts	100	74

** Do not re-use*

1 General information

Note: *The information contained in this Chapter is applicable to the standard suspension set-up. On models with M-Technic sports suspension, slight differences will be found. Refer to your BMW dealer for detail.*

The independent front suspension is of the MacPherson strut type, incorporating coil springs and integral telescopic shock absorbers. The MacPherson struts are located by transverse lower suspension arms, which use rubber inner mounting bushes, and incorporate a balljoint at the outer ends. The front hub carriers, which carry the brake calipers and the hub/disc assemblies, are bolted to the MacPherson struts, and connected to the lower arms through balljoints. A front anti-roll bar is fitted to all models. The anti-roll bar is rubber-mounted and is connected to both suspension struts/lower arms (as applicable) by connecting links.

The rear suspension is of the fully independent type consisting of trailing arms, which are linked to the rear axle carrier by upper and lower control arms. Coil springs are fitted between the upper control arms and vehicle body, and shock absorbers are connected to the vehicle body and trailing arms. A rear anti-roll bar is fitted on most models. The anti-roll bar is rubber-mounted, and is connected to the upper control arms by connecting links.

The steering column is connected to the steering rack by an intermediate shaft, which incorporates a universal joint.

The steering rack is mounted onto the front subframe, and is connected by two track rods, with balljoints at their outer ends, to the steering arms projecting forwards from the hub carriers. The track rod ends are threaded, to facilitate adjustment.

Power-assisted steering is fitted as standard to all models. The hydraulic steering system is powered by a belt-driven pump, which is driven off the crankshaft pulley.

2.3 Tap out the grease cap from the centre of the hub

2.4 Using a hammer and pointed-nosed chisel, tap out the hub nut staking

2 Front hub assembly – removal and refitting

Note: *The hub assembly should not be removed unless it is to be renewed. The hub bearing inner race is a press fit on the hub, and removal of the hub will almost certainly damaged the bearings; BMW state that the hub assembly must be renewed whenever it is removed. A new hub nut and grease cap will also be required on refitting.*

Removal

1 Remove the front brake disc (Chapter 9).

2 Undo the retaining bolt and remove the front wheel sensor (Chapter 9, Section 20).

3 Tap the grease cap out from the centre of the hub **(see illustration)**.

4 Using a hammer and suitable pointed-nosed chisel, tap up the staking securing the hub retaining nut in position, then slacken and remove the nut **(see illustration)**.

5 Attach a suitable puller to the hub assembly and draw the assembly off the hub carrier. If the bearing inner race remains on the hub, a knife-edge type puller will be required to remove it **(see illustration)**. Note that the hub bearings are not available separately – the hub must be renewed as a complete assembly.

6 If required, undo the retaining bolts and remove the disc guard from the hub carrier.

Refitting

7 Where removed, refit the disc guard to the hub carrier, and securely tighten its retaining bolts.

8 Ensure the dust cover is correctly fitted to the rear of the hub assembly, and locate the

2.5 If the hub bearing inner race remains on the stub axle, use a puller to remove it

2.8 Tap the hub assembly into position using a socket which bears only on the inner race of the new bearing

hub on the hub carrier. Tap or press the hub assembly fully onto the hub carrier shaft using a tubular spacer which bears only on the bearing inner race **(see illustration)**.

9 Screw the new hub nut onto the stub axle. Tighten the nut to the specified torque setting, and secure it in position by staking it firmly into the stub axle groove using a hammer and punch.

10 Check that the hub rotates freely, and press the new grease cap into the hub centre.

11 Refit the brake disc and ABS wheel sensor as described in Chapter 9.

3 Front hub carrier assembly – removal and refitting

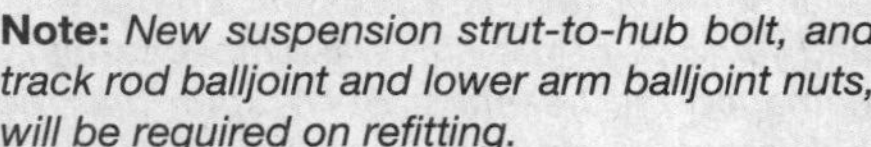

Note: *New suspension strut-to-hub bolt, and track rod balljoint and lower arm balljoint nuts, will be required on refitting.*

Removal

1 Firmly apply the handbrake, then jack up the front of the car and support it on axle stands. Remove the relevant front roadwheel.

2 If the hub carrier is to be renewed, remove the hub assembly (see Section 2).

3 If the hub carrier assembly is to be refitted, slacken and remove the two bolts securing the brake caliper mounting bracket to the carrier then slide the caliper assembly off the disc. Using a piece of wire or string, tie the caliper to the front suspension coil spring, to avoid placing any strain on the hydraulic brake hose. On models with ABS, also remove the wheel sensor (see Chapter 9, Section 20).

4 Slacken and remove the nut securing the steering rack track rod balljoint to the hub carrier, and release the balljoint tapered shank using a universal balljoint separator.

5 Unscrew the lower arm balljoint nut, and release the balljoint tapered shank from the hub carrier using a universal balljoint separator.

6 Slacken and remove the bolt securing the suspension strut to the hub carrier. Slide the hub carrier down and off from the end of the strut. To ease removal, insert a large screwdriver into the slot on the back of the hub carrier and slightly spread the hub carrier clamp **(see illustration)**. Take care to spread the carrier clamp only as much as absolutely necessary, as excessive force will cause damage.

7 Examine the hub carrier for signs of wear or damage, and renew if necessary.

Refitting

8 Prior to refitting, clean the threads of the strut-to-hub carrier bolt hole by running a tap of the correct thread size and pitch down it.

9 Engage the hub carrier with the lower arm balljoint stud, and fit the new retaining nut.

10 Locate the hub carrier correctly with the suspension strut, ensuring that the locating pin on the strut slides into the slot in the hub carrier clamp **(see illustration)**. Slide the hub carrier up until it contacts the 'stop' on the strut. Fit the new strut-to-hub carrier bolt and tighten it to the specified torque.

11 Tighten the lower arm balljoint nut to the specified torque.

12 Engage the track rod balljoint in the hub carrier, then fit a new retaining nut and tighten it to the specified torque.

13 Fit the new hub assembly (see Section 2).

14 On models where the hub was not disturbed, slide the caliper into position over the disc, making sure the pads pass either side of the disc. Lightly oil the threads of the caliper bracket mounting bolts prior to installation, and tighten them to the specified torque setting (see Chapter 9).

15 Refit the roadwheel, then lower the car to the ground and tighten the wheel bolts to the specified torque.

4 Front strut – removal, overhaul and refitting

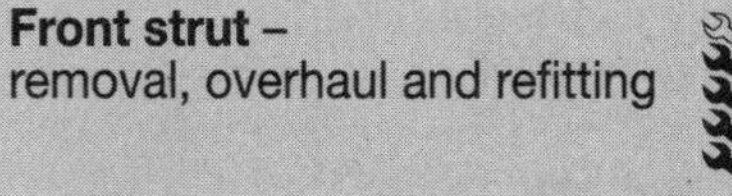

Note: *New suspension strut upper mounting nuts, and strut-to-hub carrier bolt will be required on refitting.*

Removal

1 Chock the rear wheels, apply the handbrake, then jack up the front of the car and support on axle stands. Remove the appropriate wheel.

2 To prevent the lower arm assembly hanging down whilst the strut is removed, screw a wheel bolt into the hub, then wrap a piece of wire around the bolt and tie it to the car body. This will support the weight of the hub assembly. Alternatively, support the hub assembly with a jack.

3 Unclip the brake hose and wiring harness from its clips on the base of the strut **(see illustration)**.

4 Slacken and remove the retaining nut and washer, then disconnect the anti-roll bar link from the strut. Use an open-ended spanner to counterhold the anti-roll bar link balljoint whilst undoing the nut.

5 On models fitted with a ride height sensor for headlamp range adjustment, undo the nut and remove the link bracket from the lower control arm.

6 Slacken and remove the bolt securing the suspension strut to the hub carrier. Slide the hub carrier down and off from the end of the strut. To ease removal, insert a large screwdriver into the slot on the back of the

3.6 Use a large screwdriver to gently spread the clamp

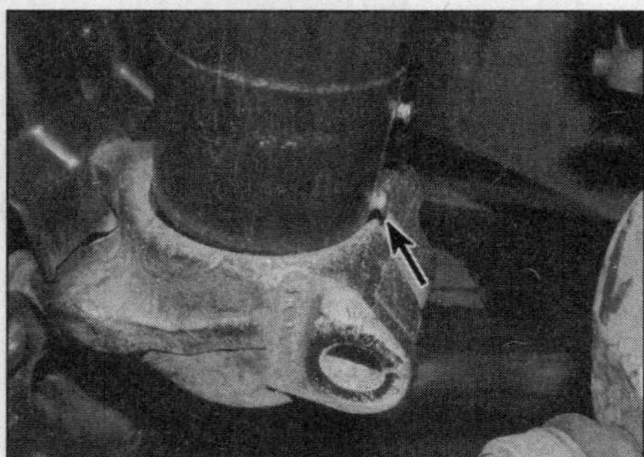

3.10 Ensure the locating pin (arrowed) slides into the slot in the clamp

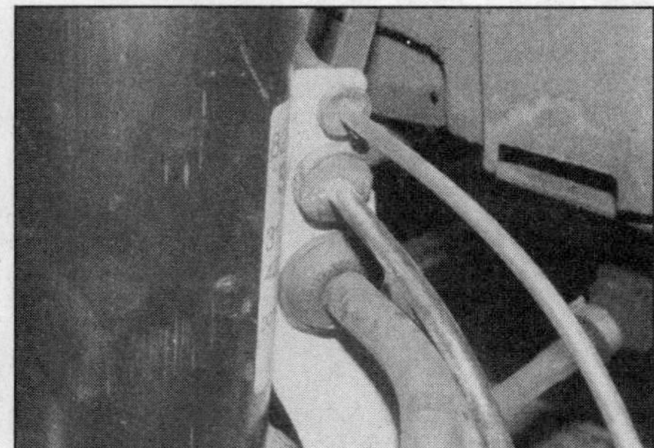

4.3 Pull the brake hose and wiring harness grommets from the bracket

hub carrier and slightly spread the hub carrier clamp **(see illustration 3.6)**. Take care to spread the carrier clamp only as much as absolutely necessary, as excessive force will cause damage.

7 From within the engine compartment, unscrew the strut upper mounting nuts, then carefully lower the strut assembly out from underneath the wing. On some models, a centring pin fixed to the strut upper mounting plate aligns with a corresponding hole in the vehicle bodywork **(see illustration)**. On models where no centring pin is fitted, make alignment marks between the mounting plate and vehicle body. It is essential that the mounting plate is fitted to its original location to preserve the strut camber angle.

Overhaul

Warning: Before attempting to dismantle the front suspension strut, a suitable tool to hold the coil spring in compression must be obtained. Adjustable coil spring compressors are readily available, and are recommended for this operation. Any attempt to dismantle the strut without such a tool is likely to result in damage or personal injury.

Note: *A new mounting plate nut will be required.*

8 With the strut removed from the car, clean away all external dirt, then mount it upright in a vice.

9 Fit the spring compressor, and compress the coil spring until all tension is relieved from the upper spring seat **(see illustration)**.

10 Remove the cap from the top of the strut to gain access to the strut upper mounting retaining nut. Slacken the nut whilst retaining the strut piston with a suitable tool **(see illustrations)**.

11 Remove the mounting nut, and lift off the mounting plate complete with thrust bearing. Remove the conical washer and flat washer, followed by the upper spring plate and upper spring seat.

12 Lift off the coil spring, followed by the bump stop, gaiter and lower spring seat.

13 With the strut assembly now completely dismantled, examine all the components for wear, damage or deformation, and check the upper mounting bearing for smoothness of operation. Renew any of the components as necessary.

14 Examine the strut for signs of fluid leakage. Check the strut piston for signs of pitting along its entire length, and check the strut body for signs of damage. While holding it in an upright position, test the operation of the strut by moving the piston through a full stroke, and then through short strokes of 50 to 100 mm. In both cases, the resistance felt should be smooth and continuous. If the resistance is jerky, or uneven, or if there is any visible sign of wear or damage to the strut, renewal is necessary.

15 If any doubt exists about the condition of the coil spring, carefully remove the spring compressors, and check the spring for distortion and signs of cracking. Renew the spring if it is damaged or distorted, or if there is any doubt as to its condition.

16 Inspect all other components for damage or deterioration, and renew any that are suspect.

17 Refit the lower spring seat, and slide the bump stop and gaiter onto the strut piston **(see illustrations)**.

18 Fit the coil spring onto the strut, making sure the rubber seat and spring are correctly located **(see illustration)**.

19 Fit the upper spring seat so that the spring end is against the seat stop **(see illustration)**.

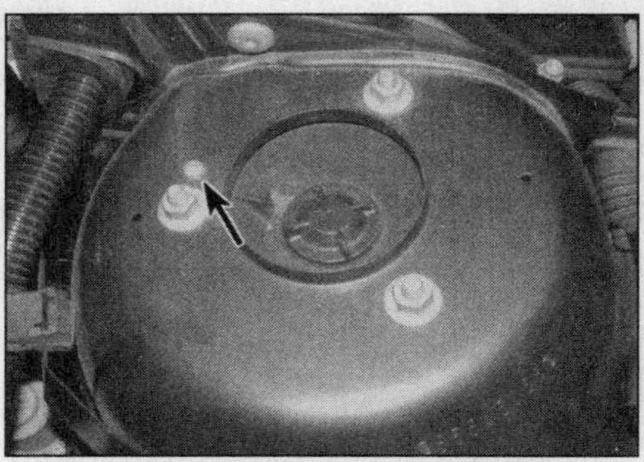

4.7 Note the centring pin (arrowed) adjacent to the strut upper mounting bolts

4.9 Fit the spring compressor

4.10a Remove the plastic cap . . .

4.10b . . . and undo the nut

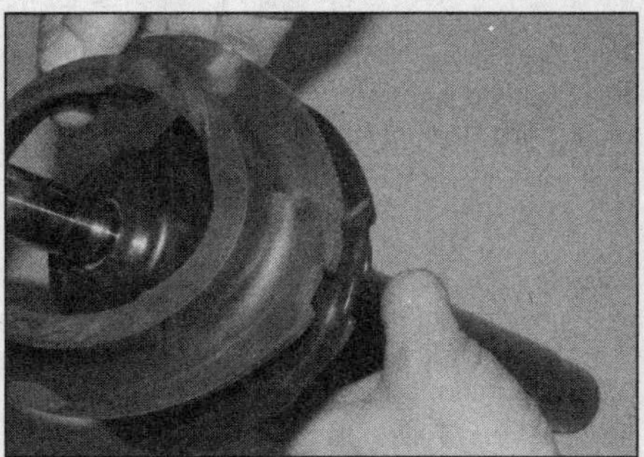

4.17a Refit the lower seat . . .

4.17b . . . followed by the gaiter and bump stop

4.18 Note the spring will only fit into the lower seat in one position

4.19 Ensure the spring end is against the seat stop (arrowed)

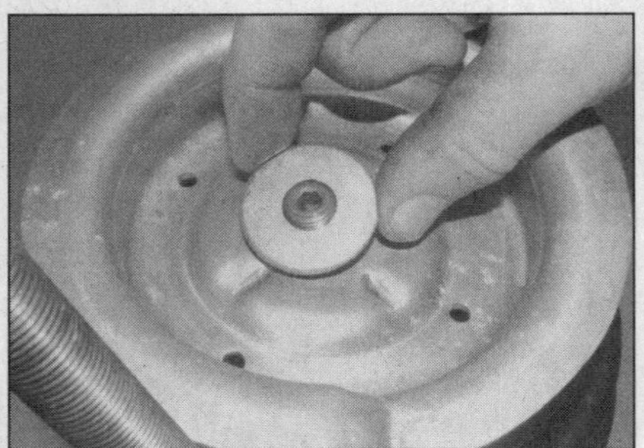
4.20a Fit the flat washer . . .

4.20b . . . followed by the conical washer, concave side up . . .

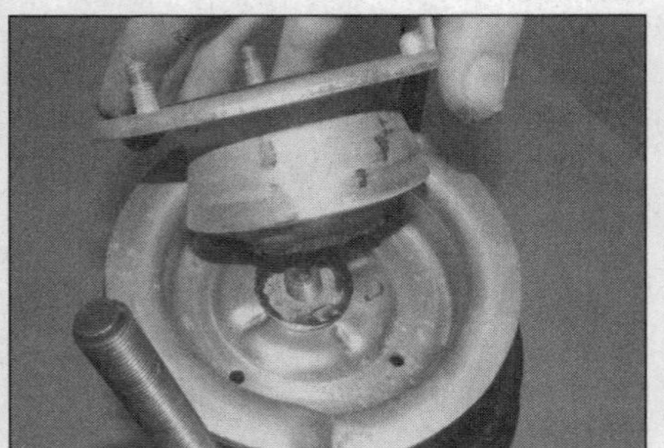
4.20c . . . then refit the upper mounting . . .

4.20d . . . and fit the new nut

20 Refit the flat washer followed by the conical washer (concave side up) and the upper mounting plate. Fit the new mounting plate nut and tighten it to the specified torque **(see illustrations)**. If the damper rod rotates whilst attempting to tighten the nut, a special 'cut-away' socket is available from BMW dealers and good tool retailers that allows an Allen key to be inserted into the top of the damper rod whilst the torque wrench is fitted.

21 Ensure the spring ends and seats are correctly located, then carefully release the compressor and remove it from the strut. Refit the cap to the top of the strut.

Refitting

22 Prior to refitting, clean the threads of the strut-to-hub carrier bolt hole by running a tap of the correct thread size and pitch down it.

23 Manoeuvre the strut assembly into position, aligning the centring pin with its corresponding hole, or previously-made marks, and fit the new upper mounting nuts.

24 Locate the hub carrier correctly with the suspension strut (see Section 3), and insert the retaining bolt. Tighten the bolt to the specified torque. Note that the wiring/hose support bracket is also retained by the bolt.

25 Tighten the strut upper mounting nuts to the specified torque.

26 Where applicable, refit the suspension height sensor link bracket to the lower control arm, and tighten the retaining nut securely.

27 Engage the anti-roll bar connecting link with the strut. Make sure the flat on the balljoint shank is correctly located against the lug on the strut, then fit the washer and new retaining nut and tighten to the specified torque.

28 Clip the hose/wiring back onto the strut, then refit the roadwheel. Lower the car to the ground and tighten the wheel bolts to the specified torque.

5 Front lower arm – removal, overhaul and refitting

Note: *New lower arm front balljoint nuts be required on refitting.*

Removal

1 Chock the rear wheels, firmly apply the handbrake, then jack up the front of the car and support on axle stands. Remove the appropriate front roadwheel.

2 Undo the bolts and remove the engine undershield.

3 Undo the bolts and remove the reinforcement cross brace, or plate from under the vehicle (see Chapter 2A).

4 On models fitted with suspension ride height sensors, undo the retaining nut and remove the sensor link bracket from the lower arm.

5 Unscrew the lower arm balljoint nut, and release the arm from the hub carrier using a universal balljoint separator **(see illustrations)**.

6 Slacken and remove the two bolts securing the lower arm rear mounting to the car body **(see illustration)**.

7 Unscrew the nut from the lower arm inner balljoint, and remove the lower arm assembly from underneath the car. Note that the balljoint may be a tight fit in the crossmember, and may need to be tapped out of position.

Overhaul

8 Thoroughly clean the lower arm and the area around the arm mountings, removing all traces of dirt and underseal if necessary, then check carefully for cracks, distortion or any other signs of wear or damage, paying particular attention to the mounting bushes and balljoint. If either bush or the balljoint requires renewal, the lower arm should be taken to a BMW dealer or suitably-equipped garage. A hydraulic press and suitable spacers are required to press the bushes out of position and install the new ones.

Refitting

9 Prior to refitting, clean the threads of the strut-to-hub carrier bolt hole by running a

5.5a Counterhold the balljoint with an Allen key whilst undoing the nut

5.5b Use a balljoint separator to release the lower arm

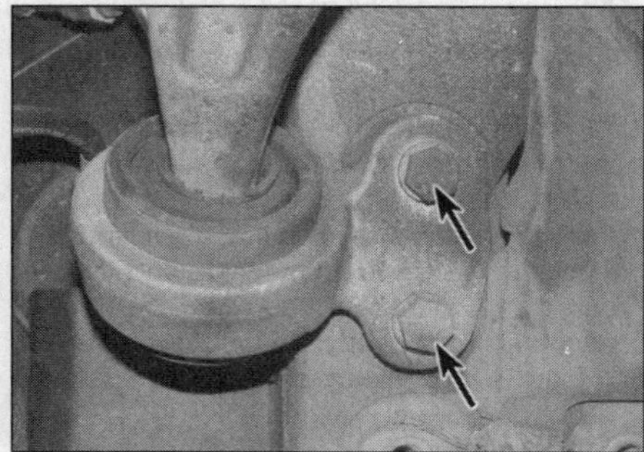
5.6 Undo the two lower arm-to-body bolts (arrowed)

tap of the correct thread size and pitch down them.

10 Ensure the balljoint studs and mounting holes are clean and dry, then offer up the lower arm.

11 Locate the inner mounting stud in the crossmember, and engage the balljoint stud with the hub carrier. If necessary, press the inner balljoint stud into position using a jack position beneath the arm.

12 Fit a new nut to the inner balljoint stud and tighten it to the specified torque.

13 Fit a new nut to the outer balljoint stud, and tighten it to the specified torque setting.

14 Refit the lower arm rear mounting bracket bolts and tighten them to the specified torque setting.

15 On models equipped with suspension ride height sensors, refit the sensor link bracket to the lower arm and tighten the retaining nut securely.

16 Refit the reinforcement cross brace or plate to the underside of the vehicle and tighten the bolts to the specified torque.

17 Refit the engine undershield.

18 Refit the roadwheel, then lower the car to the ground and tighten the wheel bolts to the specified torque.

6 Front lower arm balljoint – renewal

Front suspension lower arm balljoint renewal requires the use of a hydraulic press and several suitable spacers if it is to be carried out safely and successfully. If renewal is necessary, then the arm should be removed (Section 5) and taken to a BMW dealer or suitably-equipped workshop.

7 Front anti-roll bar – removal and refitting

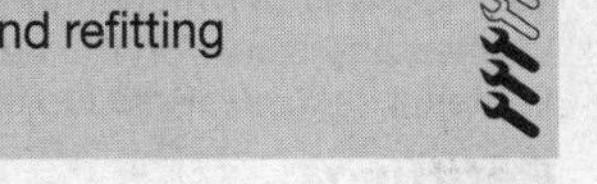

Note: *New mounting clamp nuts and connecting link nuts will be required on refitting.*

Removal

1 Chock the rear wheels, firmly apply the handbrake, then jack up the front of the car and support on axle stands. Undo the bolts and remove the engine undershield, then remove both front roadwheels.

2 Unscrew the retaining nuts, and free the connecting link from each end of the anti-roll bar using a second spanner to counterhold the balljoint stud **(see illustration)**.

3 Make alignment marks between the mounting bushes and anti-roll bar, then slacken the anti-roll bar mounting clamp retaining nuts **(see illustration)**.

4 Remove both clamps from the subframe, and manoeuvre the anti-roll bar out from underneath the car. Remove the mounting bushes from the bar.

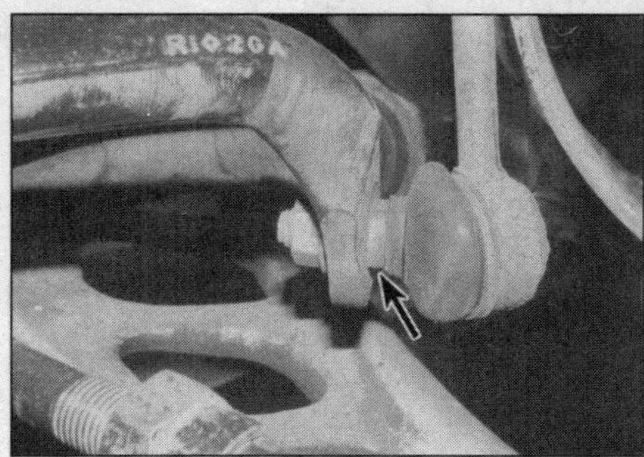

7.2 Use an open-ended spanner to counterhold the anti-roll bar link (arrowed)

5 Carefully examine the anti-roll bar components for signs of wear, damage or deterioration, paying particular attention to the mounting bushes. Renew worn components as necessary.

Refitting

6 Fit the rubber mounting bushes to the anti-roll bar, aligning them with the marks made prior to removal. Rotate each bush so that its flat surface is uppermost, and the split side on the underside.

7 Offer up the anti-roll bar, and manoeuvre it into position. Refit the mounting clamps, ensuring that their ends are correctly located in the hooks on the subframe, and fit the new retaining nuts. Ensure that the bush markings are still aligned with the marks on the bars, then tighten the mounting clamp retaining nuts to the specified torque.

8 Engage the anti-roll bar connecting links with the bar. Make sure the flats on the balljoint shank are correctly located against the lugs on the bar then fit the new retaining nuts and tighten to the specified torque.

9 Refit the roadwheels then lower the car to the ground and tighten the wheel bolts to the specified torque.

8 Front anti-roll bar connecting link – removal and refitting

Note: *New connecting link nuts will be required on refitting.*

Removal

1 Firmly apply the handbrake, then jack up the front of the car and support it on axle stands.

2 Unscrew the retaining nut, and free the connecting link from the anti-roll bar using a second spanner to counterhold the link balljoint stud.

3 Slacken and remove the nut securing the link to the suspension strut, using a second spanner to counterhold the link balljoint stud **(see illustration)**.

4 Check the connecting link balljoints for signs of wear. Check that each balljoint is free to move easily, and that the rubber gaiters are undamaged. If necessary renew the connecting link.

7.3 Undo the front anti-roll bar clamp nuts

Refitting

5 Refitting is a reverse of the removal sequence, using new nuts and tightening them to the specified torque setting.

9 Rear hub assembly – removal and refitting

Note: *The hub assembly should not be removed unless it, or the hub bearing, is to be renewed. The hub is a press fit in the bearing inner race, and removal of the hub will almost certainly damage the bearings. If the hub is to be removed, be prepared to renew the hub bearing at the same time.*

Note: *A long bolt/length of threaded bar and suitable washers will be required on refitting.*

Removal

1 Remove the relevant driveshaft as described in Chapter 8.

2 Remove the brake disc as described in Chapter 9.

3 Bolt a slide hammer to the hub surface, and use the hammer to draw the hub out from the bearing. If the bearing inner race stays attached to the hub, a puller will be required to draw it off.

4 With the hub removed, closely examine the hub bearing for signs of damage. Check that the bearing rotates freely and easily, without any sign of roughness. If the inner race remains attached to the hub, or there is any doubt about its condition, renew the bearing as described in Section 10.

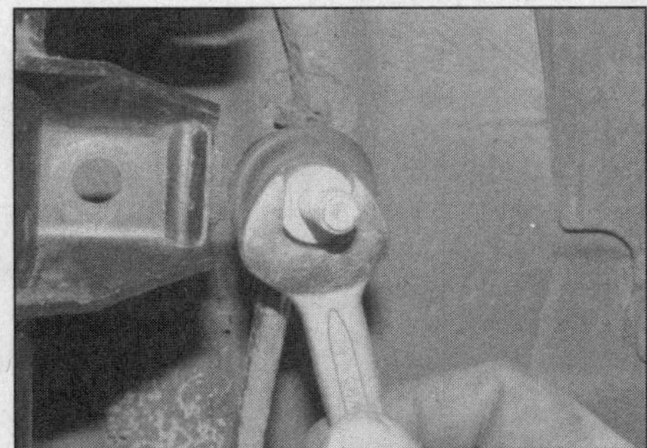

8.3 Use an open-ended spanner to counterhold the anti-roll bar link balljoint stud

11.2a Prise out the warning triangle bracket plastic rivet (arrowed)

Refitting

5 Apply a smear of oil to the hub surface, and locate it in the bearing inner race.

6 Draw the hub into position using a long bolt or threaded length of bar and two nuts. Fit a large washer to either end of the bolt/bar, so the inner one bears against the bearing inner race, and the outer one against the hub. Slowly tighten the nut(s) until the hub is pulled fully into position. **Note:** *Do not be tempted to knock the hub into position with a hammer and drift, as this will almost certainly damage the bearing.*

7 Remove the bolt/threaded bar and washers (as applicable), and check that the hub bearing rotates smoothly and easily.

8 Refit the brake disc referring to Chapter 9.

9 Refit the driveshaft referring to Chapter 8.

10 Rear hub bearings – renewal

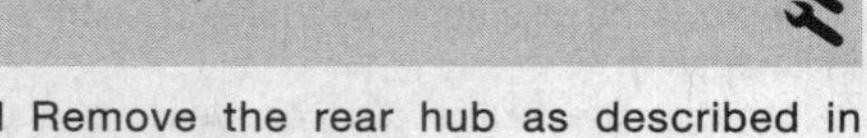

1 Remove the rear hub as described in Section 9.

2 Remove the hub bearing retaining circlip from the trailing arm.

3 Tap the hub bearing out from the trailing arm using a hammer and suitable punch.

4 Thoroughly clean the trailing arm bore, removing all traces of dirt and grease, and polish away any burrs or raised edges which might hinder reassembly. Renew the circlip if there is any doubt about its condition.

5 On reassembly, apply a light film of clean engine oil to the bearing outer race to aid installation.

11.5 Undo the lower shock absorber bolt

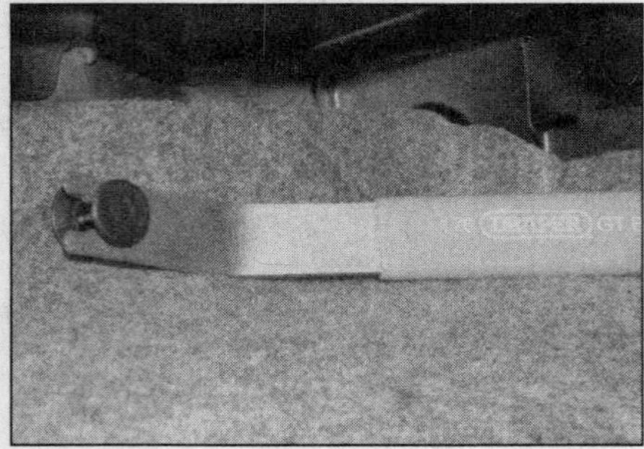

11.2b Lever up the centre pin, then prise out the plastic rivets

6 Locate the bearing in the trailing arm and tap it fully into position, ensuring that it enters the arm squarely, using a suitable tubular spacer which bears only on the bearing outer race.

7 Secure the bearing in position with the circlip, making sure it is correctly located in the trailing arm groove.

8 Fit the rear hub as described in Section 9.

11 Rear shock absorber – removal, overhaul and refitting

Note: *New shock absorber upper mounting nuts and a new mounting gasket will be required on refitting.*

Removal

1 Check the front wheels, then jack up the rear of the car and support it on axle stands. To improve access, remove the rear roadwheel.

2 On Saloon and Coupe models, lift up the luggage compartment floor panel and remove the oddments tray/battery cover. On the left-hand side, remove the warning triangle, prise out the plastic rivet, and remove the warning triangle bracket. Prise out the retaining clips securing the luggage compartment side trim cover in position, and remove the trim and insulation panel to gain access to the shock absorber upper mounting **(see illustrations)**.

3 On Touring models, remove the luggage compartment side trim panel as described in Chapter 11, Section 27.

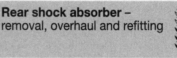

11.6 Undo the rear shock absorber upper mounting nuts (arrowed)

4 Position a jack underneath the trailing arm, and raise the jack so that it is supporting the weight of the arm. This will prevent the arm dropping when the shock absorber is unscrewed.

5 Slacken and remove the bolt securing the shock absorber to the trailing arm **(see illustration)**.

6 From within the luggage compartment, unscrew the upper mounting nuts **(see illustration)**. Lower the shock absorber out from underneath the car, and recover the gasket which is fitted between the upper mounting and body.

Overhaul

Note: *A new piston nut will be required.*

7 Remove the trim cap from the top of the shock absorber, then remove all traces of dirt. Slacken and remove the piston nut and dished washer, noting which way around it is fitted.

8 Lift off the upper mounting plate and remove the dust cover.

9 Slide the spacer and rubber stop off from the shock absorber piston.

10 Examine the shock absorber for signs of fluid leakage. Check the piston for signs of pitting along its entire length, and check the body for signs of damage. While holding it in an upright position, test the operation of the shock absorber by moving the piston through a full stroke, and then through short strokes of 50 to 100 mm. In both cases, the resistance felt should be smooth and continuous. If the resistance is jerky, or uneven, or if there is any visible sign of wear or damage, renewal is necessary.

11 Inspect all other components for signs of damage or deterioration, and renew any that are suspect.

12 Slide the rubber stop and spacer onto the strut piston, and fit the dust cover.

13 Fit the upper mounting plate and dished washer, and screw on the new piston nut and tighten it securely. Refit the trim cap.

Refitting

14 Ensure the upper mounting plate and body contact surfaces are clean and dry, and fit a new gasket to the upper mounting plate.

15 Manoeuvre the shock absorber into position, and fit the new upper mounting nuts.

16 Ensure the lower end of the shock absorber is positioned with the mounting bush spacer thrustwasher facing towards the bolt. Screw in the lower mounting bolt, tightening it by hand only at this stage.

17 Tighten the upper mounting nuts to the specified torque setting then refit the insulation panel, luggage compartment trim panel, rear light access cover and loudspeaker (as applicable).

18 Refit the roadwheel and lower the car to the ground. With the car resting on its wheels, tighten the shock absorber lower mounting bolt and roadwheel bolts to the specified torque.

12 Rear coil spring – removal and refitting

Removal

1 Chock the front wheels, then jack up the rear of the car and support it on axle stands. Remove the relevant roadwheel.

2 Referring to Chapter 8, slacken and remove the bolts and plates securing the relevant driveshaft to the final drive unit flange. Free the driveshaft and support it by tying it to the car underbody using a piece of wire. **Note:** *Do not allow the driveshaft to hang under its own weight as the CV joint may be damaged.*

3 Detach the fuel tank panel from the rear underside of the vehicle (where fitted).

4 On models equipped with suspension ride height sensors, undo the nut and detach the sensor link arm from the upper control arm.

5 Detach the rear suspension anti-roll bar (where fitted) as described in Section 16.

6 Undo the bolt and detach the brake hose bracket from the trailing arm **(see illustration)**.

7 Position a jack underneath the rear of the trailing arm, and support the weight of the arm.

8 Slacken and remove the shock absorber lower mounting bolt.

9 Slowly lower the trailing arm, keeping watch on the brake pipe/hose to ensure no excess strain is placed on them, until it is possible to withdraw the coil spring.

10 Recover the spring seats from the car body and control arm. If the car is to be left for some time, raise the trailing back up and refit the shock absorber lower mounting bolt.

11 Inspect the spring closely for signs of damage, such as cracking, and check the spring seats for signs of wear. Renew worn components as necessary.

Refitting

12 Fit the upper and lower spring seats, making sure they are correctly located on the pegs **(see illustration)**.

13 Apply a little grease to the spring ends and engage the spring with its upper seat. Note that the spring is fitted with the smaller diameter opening at the top.

14 Hold the spring in position and carefully raise the trailing arm whilst aligning the coil spring with its lower seat.

15 Raise the arm fully and refit the shock absorber lower mounting bolt, tightening it by hand only at this stage.

16 Refit the brake hose bracket to the trailing arm.

17 Refit the anti-roll bar (see Section 16).

18 Refit the panel to the fuel tank.

19 Referring to Chapter 8, connect the driveshaft to the final drive unit, then refit the retaining plates and bolts and tighten them to the specified torque.

20 Refit the roadwheel then lower the car to the ground. Tighten the wheel bolts and shock absorber lower bolt to the specified torque.

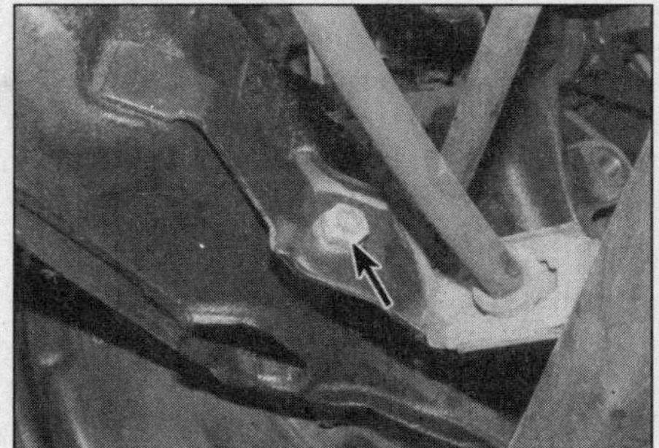

12.6 Undo the brake hose bracket bolt (arrowed)

13 Rear trailing arm – removal, overhaul and refitting

Removal

1 Chock the front wheels, then jack up the rear of the car and support it on axle stands. Remove the relevant roadwheel.

2 Remove the relevant driveshaft (see Chapter 8).

3 Unscrew the two bolts securing the brake caliper mounting bracket in position, then slide the caliper assembly off the disc. Using a piece of wire or string, tie the caliper to the rear suspension coil spring, to avoid placing any strain on the hydraulic brake hose.

4 Referring to Chapter 9, disconnect the handbrake cable from the rear wheel.

5 Remove the rear wheel ABS sensor as described in Chapter 9, Section 20.

6 Remove the rear anti-roll bar as described in Section 16.

7 Undo the retaining bolt and release the brake pipe bracket from the trailing arm.

8 Position a jack underneath the rear of the trailing arm, and support the weight of the arm.

9 Slacken and remove the shock absorber lower mounting bolt.

10 Prise out the plastic expansion rivets, and detach the trim panel adjacent to the fuel tank from the left- or right-hand rear underside of the vehicle.

11 Using paint or a suitable marker pen, make alignment marks between the lower control arm pivot bolt eccentric washer and the trailing arm. Also make alignment marks between the trailing arm front mounting bracket and the vehicle underbody **(see illustration)**. This is necessary to ensure that the rear wheel alignment and camber are correct on refitting.

12 Lower the jack and remove the coil spring.

13 Slacken and remove the nut and washer from the lower control arm pivot bolt. Withdraw the pivot bolt.

14 Slacken and remove the nut and pivot bolt securing the upper control arm to the trailing arm. Note the bolt's direction of fitting.

15 Unscrew the three bolts securing the trailing arm mounting bracket to the vehicle body and remove the trailing arm. **Note:** *Do not slacken the trailing arm pivot bush bolt unless renewal of the bush/mounting bracket is necessary.*

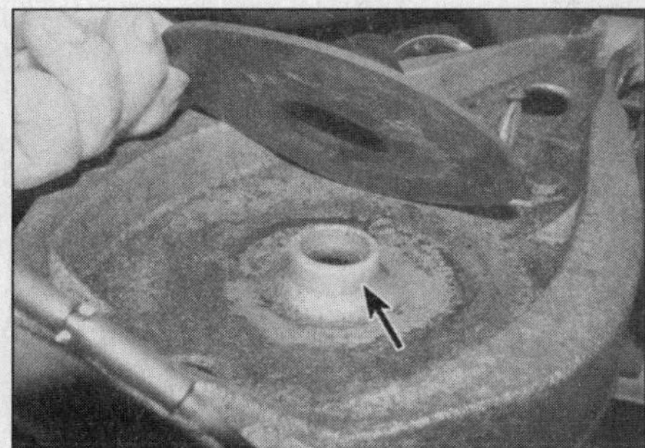

12.12 Ensure the spring seats locate over the peg (arrowed)

Overhaul

16 Slacken and remove the nut and pivot bolt and separate the front mounting bracket and trailing arm.

17 Thoroughly clean the trailing arm and the area around the arm mountings, removing all traces of dirt and underseal if necessary. Check carefully for cracks, distortion or any other signs of wear or damage, paying particular attention to the mounting bushes. If either bush requires renewal, the lower arm should be taken to a BMW dealer or suitably-equipped garage. A hydraulic press and suitable spacers are required to press the bushes out of position and install the new ones. Inspect the pivot bolts for signs of wear or damage and renew as necessary.

18 Fit the mounting bracket to trailing arm, and install the pivot bolt and nut. Position the bracket using an 8 mm rod, and tighten the pivot bolt to the specified torque **(see illustration)**.

Refitting

19 Offer up the trailing arm assembly, and refit the mounting bracket retaining bolts. Align the marks made prior to removal, then tighten the mounting bracket bolts to the specified torque.

20 Engage the upper control arm with the

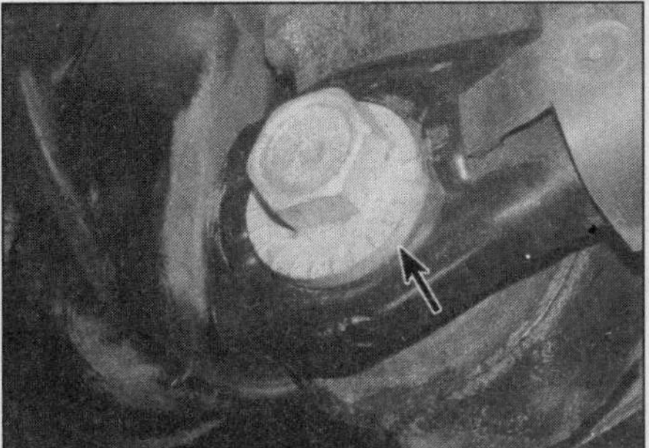

13.11 Make alignment marks between the eccentric washer (arrowed) and the trailing arm

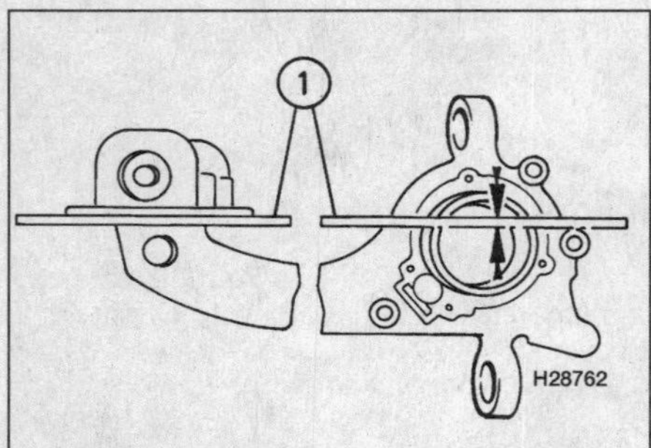

13.18 Place an 8 mm rod (1) against the mounting bracket and rest it on the trailing arm to position the mounting bracket

trailing arm and fit the pivot bolt and nut. Note that the bolt should be inserted from the rear. Tighten the bolt by hand only at this stage.

21 Refit the coil spring making sure it is correctly aligned with the spring seats, then raise the trailing arm with the jack, and fit the lower arm pivot bolt, eccentric washer and nut. Align the washer with the mark made prior to removal, then refit the shock absorber lower mounting bolt. Tighten both the pivot bolt and mounting bolt by hand only.

22 Refit the fuel tank panel to the underside of the vehicle.

23 Refit the brake pipe retaining bracket to the trailing arm, and fully tighten the bolts.

24 Refit the rear anti-roll bar as described in Section 16.

25 Referring to Chapter 9, reconnect the handbrake cable to the expander lever and refit the ABS wheel sensor. Slide the caliper into position over the disc, making sure the pads pass either side of the disc, and tighten the caliper bracket mounting bolts to the specified torque setting.

26 Refit the driveshaft as described in Chapter 8 and lower the car to the ground.

27 With the car on its wheels, rock the car to settle the disturbed components in position, then tighten the shock absorber lower mounting bolt and the upper control arm pivot bolts to the specified torque. Check that the lower arm eccentric washer is still correctly aligned with the mark, then tighten it to the specified torque. **Note:** *On completion, it is advisable to have the camber angle and wheel alignment checked and, if necessary, adjusted.*

14 Rear upper control arm – removal, overhaul and refitting

Note: *A new control arm-to-rear subframe pivot bolt and nut will be required on refitting.*

Removal

1 Remove the coil spring (see Section 12).

2 Slacken and remove the control arm-to-trailing arm pivot bolt **(see illustration)**. Note its direction of fitting.

3 Referring to Chapter 8, support the weight of the unit with a jack, and remove the final drive unit mounting bolts to allow room to withdraw the pivot bolt. Alternatively, remove the driveshaft as described in Chapter 8.

4 Slacken and remove the nut from the control arm-to-rear subframe pivot bolt. Withdraw the bolt, moving the final drive unit slightly to the rear, and remove the control arm from underneath the car **(see illustration)**. Note that on some models it may be necessary to detach the propeller shaft from the final drive unit in order to gain the clearance required to remove the pivot bolt. **Note:** *If the car is to be left for some time, refit the final drive unit mounting bolts and tighten securely.*

Overhaul

5 Thoroughly clean the control arm and the area around the arm mountings, removing all traces of dirt and underseal if necessary. Check for cracks, distortion or any other wear or damage, paying particular attention to the mounting bush. If the bush requires renewal, the arm should be taken to a BMW dealer or suitably-equipped garage. A hydraulic press and suitable spacers are required to press the bushes out of position and fit the new ones.

6 Inspect the pivot bolts for signs of wear or damage, and renew as necessary. The control arm-to-subframe bolt and nut should be renewed as a matter of course.

Refitting

7 Manoeuvre the control arm into position, and fit the new arm-to-subframe pivot bolt and nut. Tighten the nut lightly only at this stage.

8 Referring to Chapter 8, manoeuvre the final drive unit into position, and tighten its mounting bolts to the specified torque. Where necessary, reconnect the propeller shaft to the final drive unit.

9 Refit the pivot bolt and nut securing the control arm to the trailing arm, inserting it from the rear, then tighten it lightly only at this stage.

10 Refit the coil spring (see Section 12).

11 On completion, lower the car to the ground and rock the car to settle all disturbed components. With the car resting on its wheels tighten the wheel bolts, shock absorber lower mounting bolt and the control arm pivot bolts to their specified torque settings. **Note:** *On completion, it is advisable to have the camber angle and wheel alignment checked and, if necessary, adjusted.*

15 Rear lower control arm – removal, overhaul and refitting

Note: *A new control arm-to-rear subframe pivot bolt and nut will be required on refitting.*

Removal

1 Chock the front wheels, then jack up the rear of the car and support it on axle stands. To improve access, remove the rear wheel.

2 Using paint or a suitable marker pen, make alignment marks between the lower control arm pivot bolt eccentric washer and the trailing arm. This is necessary to ensure that the rear wheel alignment and camber are correct on refitting.

3 Support the trailing arm with a jack, then remove the nut and washer from the lower control arm pivot bolt. Withdraw the pivot bolt.

4 Referring to Chapter 8, support the weight of the final drive unit with a jack, and remove the unit mounting bolts. Alternatively, remove the driveshaft as described in Chapter 8.

5 Slacken and remove the pivot bolt securing the control arm to the rear subframe. Withdraw the bolt, moving the final drive unit slightly to the rear (where necessary), and remove the control arm from underneath the car. Recover the special nut from the subframe **(see illustrations)**. **Note:** *On some models it may*

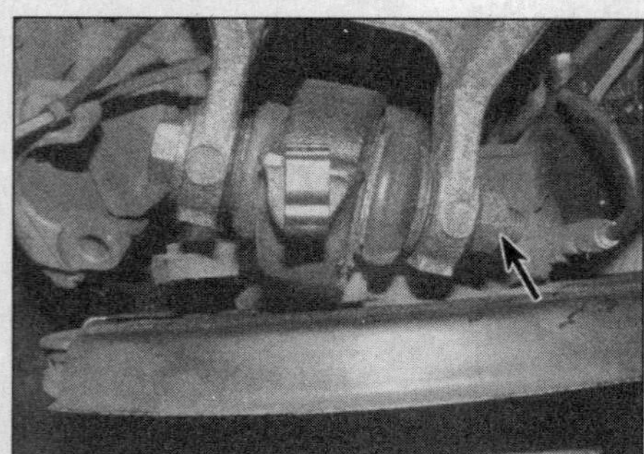

14.2 Remove the control arm-to-trailing arm bolt (arrowed)

14.4 Remove the control arm-to-subframe bolt (arrowed)

15.5a Remove the lower control arm-to-subframe bolt (arrowed)

be necessary to detach the propeller shaft from the final drive unit in order to gain the clearance required to remove the pivot bolt. If the car is to be left for some time, refit the final drive unit mounting bolts and tighten securely.

Overhaul

6 Refer to paragraphs 5 and 6 of Section 14.

Refitting

7 Locate the special nut in the subframe cut-out, and manoeuvre the control arm into position (with its welded seam uppermost). Fit the new pivot bolt, tightening it lightly only at this stage.

8 Referring to Chapter 8, manoeuvre the final drive unit into position and tighten its mounting bolts to the specified torque. Where necessary, reconnect the propeller shaft to the final drive unit.

9 Fit the lower arm-to-trailing arm pivot bolt, eccentric washer and nut. Align the washer with the mark made prior to removal and lightly tighten it.

10 Refit the roadwheel and lower the car to the ground.

11 With the car on its wheels, rock the car to settle the disturbed components in position. Check that the lower arm eccentric washer is still correctly aligned with the mark, then tighten both the control arm pivot bolts to the specified torque wrench setting. Where necessary also tighten the wheel bolts to the specified torque. **Note:** *On completion, it is advisable to have the camber angle and wheel alignment checked and, if necessary, adjusted.*

16 Rear anti-roll bar – removal and refitting

Note: *New mounting clamp nuts and connecting link nuts will be required on refitting.*

Removal

1 Chock the front wheels, then jack up the rear of the car and support it on axle stands. To improve access, remove the rear roadwheels.

2 Slacken and remove the nut and bolt securing each connecting link to the upper control arms **(see illustration)**.

3 Make alignment marks between the mounting bushes and anti-roll bar, then slacken the anti-roll bar mounting clamp retaining nuts and bolts **(see illustration)**.

4 Remove both clamps from the subframe, and manoeuvre the anti-roll bar and connecting link assembly out from underneath the car. Remove the mounting bushes and connecting links from the bar.

5 Carefully examine the anti-roll bar components for signs of wear, damage or deterioration, paying particular attention to the mounting bushes. Renew any worn components as necessary.

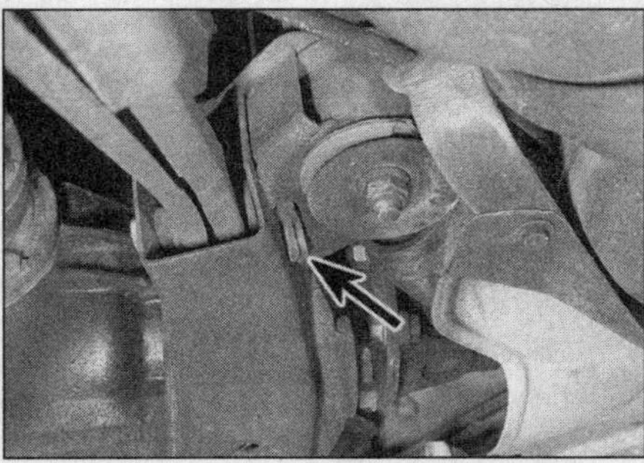

15.5b Recover the special nut (arrowed) from the subframe

Refitting

6 Fit the rubber mounting bushes to the anti-roll bar, aligning them with the marks made prior to removal. Rotate each bush so that its flat surface is facing forwards.

7 Offer up the anti-roll bar, and manoeuvre it into position. Locate the connecting links in the upper control arms, and fit the new retaining nuts and tighten securely.

8 Refit the mounting clamps, ensuring that their ends are correctly located in the hooks on the subframe, and fit the bolts and new retaining nuts. Ensure that the bush markings are still aligned with the marks on the bars, then securely tighten the mounting clamp retaining nuts.

9 Refit the roadwheels then lower the car to the ground and tighten the wheel bolts to the specified torque.

17 Steering wheel – removal and refitting

Removal

1 Remove the airbag unit from the centre of the steering wheel, referring to Chapter 12, Section 25.

2 Set the front wheels in the straight-ahead position, and set the steering lock by removing the ignition key.

3 Slacken and remove the steering wheel retaining bolt/nut. Disconnect the steering wheel wiring plug(s) **(see illustration)**.

4 Mark the steering wheel and steering column shaft in relation to each other, then lift the steering wheel off the column splines. If it is tight, tap it up near the centre, using the palm of your hand, or twist it from side-to-side, whilst pulling upwards to release it from the shaft splines **(see illustration)**. The airbag contact unit will automatically be locked in position as the wheel is removed; do not attempt to rotate it whilst the wheel is removed.

5 Inspect the horn contact ring/indicator cancelling cam for signs of wear or damage, and renew as necessary.

Refitting

6 Refitting is the reverse of removal, noting the following points.

a) *If the contact unit has been rotated with the wheel removed, centralise it by*

16.2 Undo the nut and bolt securing the anti-roll bar link

16.3 Slacken the rear anti-roll bar clamp nut (arrowed)

17.3 Disconnect the wiring plugs and unscrew the steering wheel

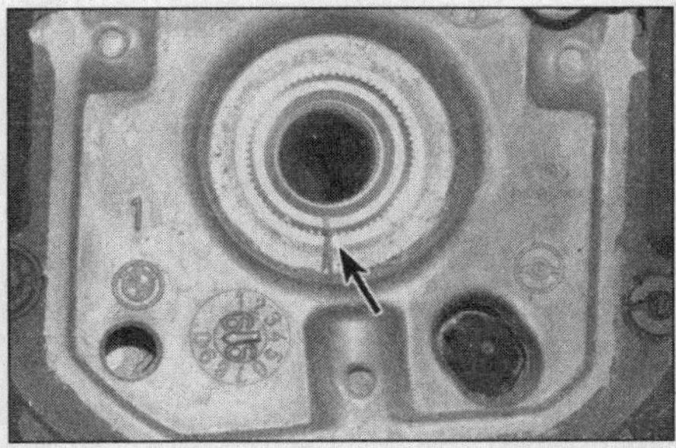

17.4 Make alignment marks between the steering wheel and the column shaft (arrowed)

18.6 Disconnect the wiring plug from the ignition switch

18.8a Undo the column retaining bolt (1) and shear-bolt (2) . . .

18.8b . . . followed by the lower mounting nuts

pressing down on the contact unit and rotating its centre fully anti-clockwise. From this position, rotate the centre back through three complete rotations in a clockwise direction.

b) Prior to refitting, ensure the indicator switch stalk is in the central (OFF) position. Failure to do so could lead to the steering wheel lug breaking the switch tab.

c) Coat the steering wheel horn contact ring with a smear of petroleum jelly and refit the wheel, making sure the contact unit wiring is correctly routed.

d) Engage the wheel with the column splines, aligning the marks made on removal, and tighten the steering wheel retaining bolt/nut to the specified torque.

e) Refit the airbag unit (see Chapter 12).

18 Steering column – removal, inspection and refitting

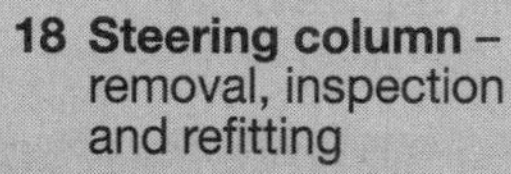

Note: *New steering column shear-bolts, and an intermediate shaft clamp bolt/nut, will be required on refitting.*

Removal

1 Disconnect the battery negative terminal (see Chapter 5A).

2 Remove the steering wheel as described in Section 17.

3 Remove the steering column combination switches (refer to Chapter 12, Section 4).

4 Working in the engine compartment, using paint or a suitable marker pen, make alignment marks between the lower end of the steering column and the intermediate shaft upper joint.

5 Slacken and remove the nut and clamp bolt, and disengage the shaft from the column.

6 Disconnect the wiring connectors from the ignition switch and free the harness from its retaining clips on the column **(see illustration)**.

7 Release the retaining clip and detach the interlock cable (where fitted) from the steering column **(see illustration 19.6)**.

8 The steering column is secured in position with two nuts, one bolt and one shear-bolt. The shear-bolt can be extracted using a hammer and suitable chisel to tap the bolt head around until it can be unscrewed by hand. Alternatively, drill a hole in the centre of the bolt head and extract it using a bolt/stud extractor (sometimes called an 'Easy-out'). Unscrew the remaining mounting bolt/nuts **(see illustrations)**.

9 Pull the column upwards and away from the bulkhead, and slide off the rubber mounting, mounting seat, washer and fixing ring off from the column lower end. Remove the collars and rubber mountings from the column mountings.

Inspection

10 The steering column incorporates a telescopic safety feature. In the event of a front-end crash, the shaft collapses and prevents the steering wheel injuring the driver. Before refitting the steering column, examine the column and mountings for damage and deformation, and renew as necessary.

11 Check the steering shaft for signs of free play in the column bushes. If any damage or wear is found on the steering column bushes, the column should be overhauled. Overhaul of the column is a complex task requiring several special tools, and should be entrusted to a BMW dealer.

Refitting

12 Ensure the mounting rubbers are in position, and fit the collars to the rear of the mounting rubbers.

13 Slide the fixing ring, washer, mounting seat and rubber mounting onto the base of the steering column **(see illustration)**.

14 Manoeuvre the column into position and engage it with the intermediate shaft splines, aligning the marks made prior to removal **(see illustration)**.

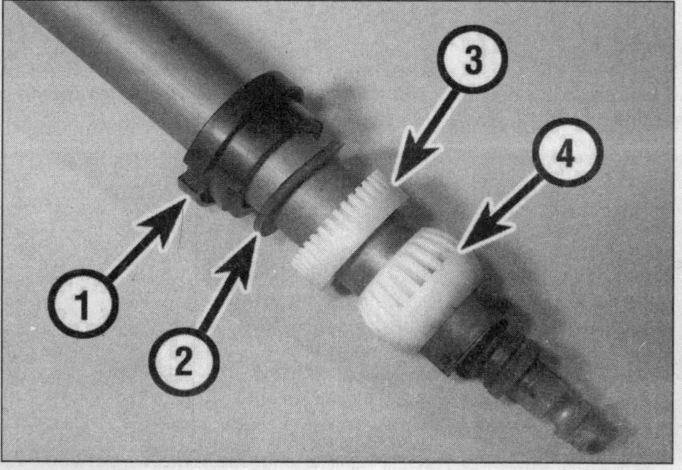

18.13 Slide the fixing ring (1), washer (2), mounting seat (3) and rubber mounting (4) onto the base of the steering column . . .

18.14 . . . and refit the column to the vehicle

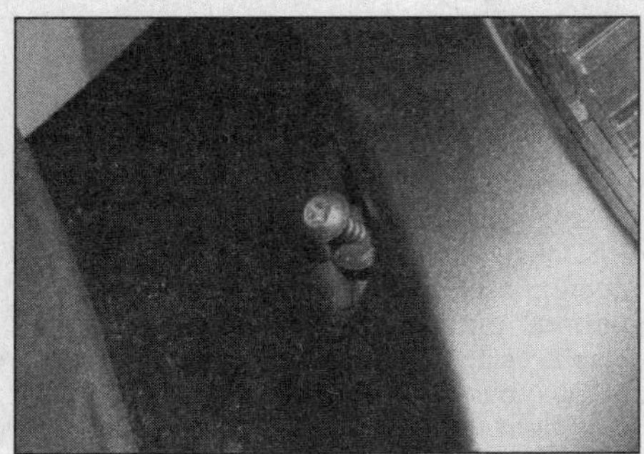

19.3 Slacken the bolt and pull it out complete with the plastic rivet

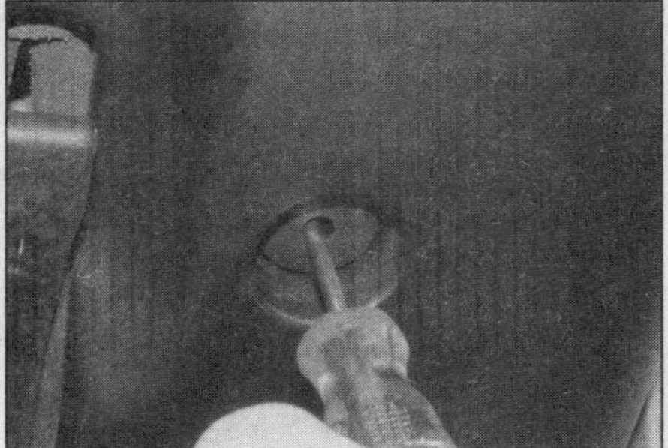

19.4 Press in the centre pins of the two expanding rivets

19.5 Carefully prise off the transponder ring

15 Locate the lower end of the column in its seat and screw in the mounting bolts and new shear-bolt; tighten them lightly only at this stage.

16 Tighten the column shear-bolt until its head breaks off. Tighten the remaining column mounting securely.

17 Reconnect the wiring connectors to the ignition switch, and secure the wiring to the column, ensuring it is correctly routed.

18 Ensure the intermediate shaft and column marks are correctly aligned, and insert the column into the shaft. Fit the new clamp bolt nut and tighten it to the specified torque.

19 Where necessary, reconnect the interlock cable to the switch and secure it in position.

20 Fit the combination switches as described in Chapter 12.

21 Refit the steering wheel as described in Section 17.

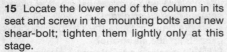

19 Ignition switch/ steering column lock – removal and refitting

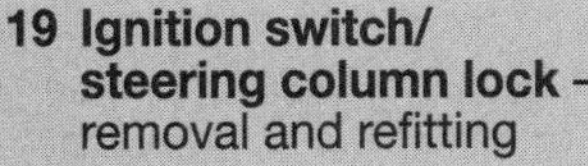

Lock assembly

1 Renewal of the lock assembly requires the steering column to be dismantled. This task requires the use of several special tools, and for this reason should be entrusted to a BMW dealer or suitably-equipped specialist.

Lock cylinder

Removal

2 Disconnect the battery negative terminal (see Chapter 5A). Insert the key into the lock and release the steering lock.

3 Slacken the retaining bolt and pull it out complete with the plastic rivet, squeeze in the sides of steering column upper shroud as shown, and remove the shroud **(see illustration)**.

4 Push in the centre pins of the two plastic expanding rivets and remove the lower steering column shroud **(see illustration)**.

5 Disconnect the wiring plug then, using two screwdrivers, carefully prise the transponder ring over the end of the ignition switch **(see illustration)**.

6 Depress the retaining clip and detach the interlock cable (where fitted) from the ignition switch **(see illustration)**.

7 Turn the ignition key to the accessory position (I), then insert a suitable rod into the hole in the cylinder. Depress the lock cylinder detent, and slide the lock cylinder out of position **(see illustrations)**.

Refitting

8 Position the lock cylinder as shown in paragraph 7 and insert the cylinder into the housing until it clicks in to position.

Ignition switch block

Removal

9 Disconnect the battery negative terminal (see Chapter 5A).

10 Remove the retaining bolt, squeeze in the sides of steering column upper shroud as shown, and remove the shroud **(see illustration 19.3)**.

11 Push in the centre pins and prise out the plastic rivets, then remove the lower steering column shroud **(see illustration 19.4)**.

12 Disconnect the wiring connector from the switch, then undo the two grub screws and remove the switch block from the lock assembly **(see illustration)**.

Refitting

13 Refitting is the reverse of removal, noting the following points:

a) Apply varnish to the switch grub screws prior to refitting, to lock them in position.

b) Reconnect the battery and check the operation of the switch prior to refitting the steering column shrouds.

19.6 Depress the retaining clip (1) and detach the interlock cable

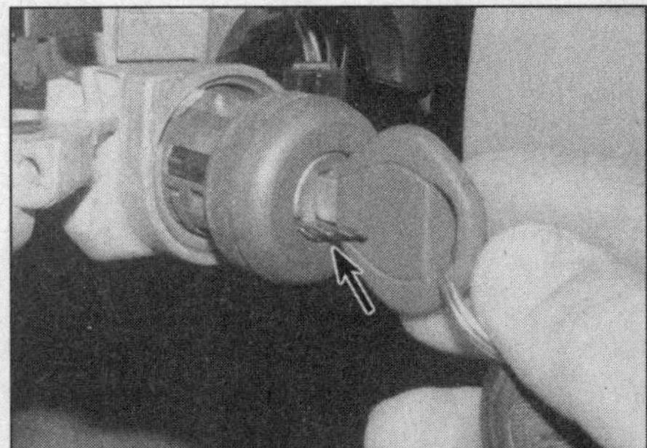

19.7a Insert a 1.2 mm (approx) into the hole in the cylinder (arrowed) . . .

19.7b . . . to depress the detent lever (arrowed – shown with lock removed)

19.12 Disconnect the wiring plug and undo the two grub screws (arrowed)

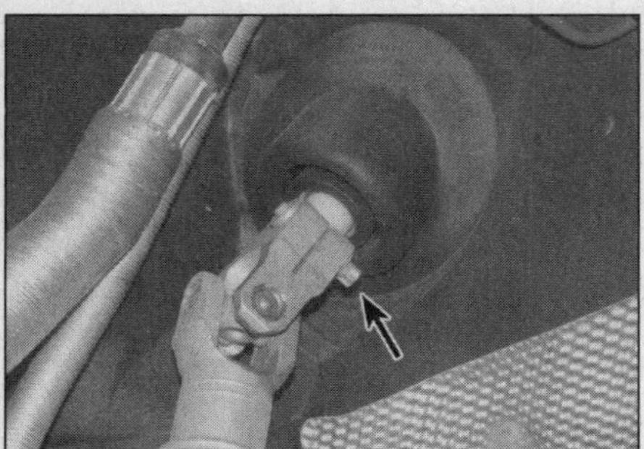

20.3 Steering column intermediate shaft upper clamp bolt (arrowed)

20 Steering column intermediate shaft – removal and refitting

Note: *New intermediate shaft clamp bolts will be required on refitting.*

Removal

1 Chock the rear wheels, firmly apply the hand-brake, then jack up the front of the car and support on axle stands. Set the front wheels in the straight-ahead position. Undo the bolts and remove the engine undershield.

2 Using paint or a suitable marker pen, make alignment marks between the intermediate shaft universal joint and the steering column, the shaft and flexible coupling, and the flexible coupling and the steering rack pinion. **Note:** *On some models an alignment mark is already provided on the pinion flange, which aligns with a mark cast into the pinion housing* ***(see illustration 21.3).***

3 Slacken and remove the clamp bolts, then slide the two halves of the shaft together and remove the shaft assembly from the car **(see illustration)**.

4 Inspect the intermediate shaft universal joint for signs of roughness in its bearings and ease of movement. Also examine the shaft rubber coupling for signs of damage or deterioration, and check that the rubber is securely bonded to the flanges. If the universal joint or rubber coupling are suspect, the complete intermediate shaft should be renewed.

Refitting

5 Check that the front wheels are still in the straight-ahead position, and that the steering wheel is correctly positioned.

6 Align the marks made on removal, and engage the intermediate shaft joint with the steering column and the coupling with the steering rack.

7 Insert the new clamp bolts, and tighten them to the specified torque setting. Lower the car to the ground.

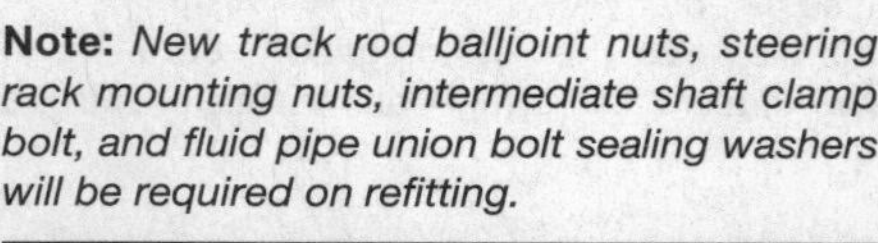

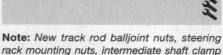

21 Steering rack assembly – removal, overhaul and refitting

Note: *New track rod balljoint nuts, steering rack mounting nuts, intermediate shaft clamp bolt, and fluid pipe union bolt sealing washers will be required on refitting.*

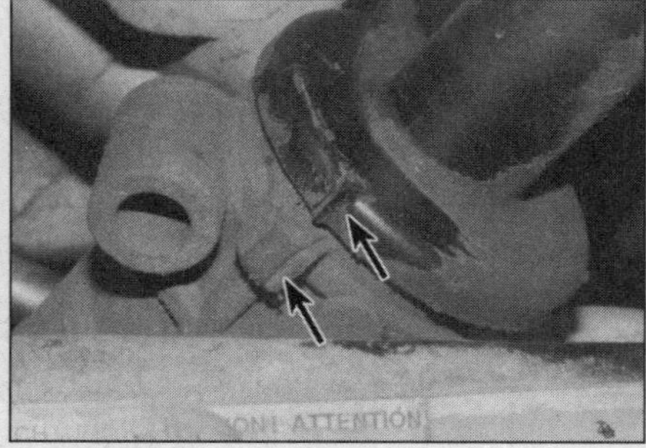

21.3 Align the mark on the pinion flange with the mark on the housing (arrowed)

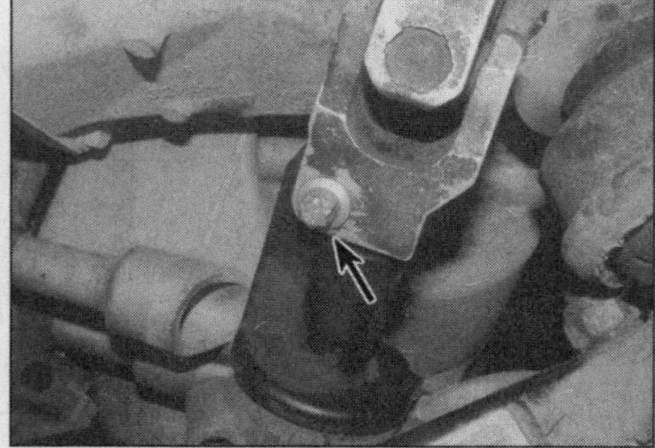

21.4 Undo the flexible coupling pinch-bolt (arrowed)

21.5 Power steering rack unions

21.6 Remove the steering rack mounting bolts (arrowed)

Removal

1 Chock the rear wheels, firmly apply the handbrake, then jack up the front of the car and support on axle stands. Remove both front roadwheels, undo the bolts and remove the engine undershield.

2 Slacken and remove the nuts securing the steering rack track rod balljoints to the hub carriers, and release the balljoint tapered shanks using a universal balljoint separator.

3 Using paint or a suitable marker pen, make alignment marks between the intermediate shaft flexible coupling and the steering rack pinion. **Note:** *On some models an alignment mark is already provided on the pinion flange, which aligns with a mark cast into the pinion housing* ***(see illustration).***

4 Slacken and remove the flexible coupling pinch-bolt **(see illustration)**.

5 Using brake hose clamps, clamp both the supply and return hoses near the power steering fluid reservoir. This will minimise fluid loss. Mark the unions to ensure they are correctly positioned on reassembly, then slacken and remove the feed and return pipe union bolts and recover the sealing washers. Be prepared for fluid spillage, and position a suitable container beneath the pipes whilst unscrewing the bolts **(see illustration)**. Plug the pipe ends and steering rack orifices, to prevent fluid leakage and to keep dirt out of the hydraulic system.

6 Slacken and remove the steering rack mounting bolts and nuts, and remove the steering rack from underneath the car **(see illustration)**.

Overhaul

7 Examine the steering rack assembly for signs of wear or damage, and check that the rack moves freely throughout the full length of its travel, with no signs of roughness or excessive free play between the steering rack pinion and rack. It is not possible to overhaul the steering rack assembly housing components; if it is faulty, the assembly must be renewed. The only components which can be renewed individually are the steering rack gaiters, the track rod balljoints and the track rods. These procedures are covered later in this Chapter.

Refitting

8 Offer up the steering rack, and insert the mounting bolts. Fit new nuts to the bolts, and tighten them to the specified torque setting.

9 Position a new sealing washer on each side of the pipe hose unions and refit the union bolts. Tighten the union bolts to the specified torque.

10 Align the marks made on removal, and connect the intermediate shaft coupling to the steering rack. Insert the new clamp bolt then tighten it to the specified torque.

11 Locate the track rod balljoints in the hub carriers, then fit the new nuts and tighten them to the specified torque.

12 Refit the roadwheels, and the engine

undershield, then lower the car to the ground and tighten the wheel bolts to the specified torque.

13 Bleed the hydraulic system as described in Section 23.

22 Power steering pump – removal and refitting

Note: *New feed pipe union bolt sealing washers will be required on refitting.*

Removal

1 Chock the rear wheels, then jack up the front of the car and support it on axle stands (see *Jacking and vehicle support*). Undo the bolts and remove the engine undershield.

2 Working as described in Chapter 1, release the drivebelt tension and unhook the drivebelt from the pump pulley, noting that on 4-cylinder engines the steering pump pulley retaining bolts should be slackened prior to releasing the tension.

3 On 4-cylinder engines, unscrew the retaining bolts and remove the pulley from the power steering pump, noting which way around it is fitted.

4 On all models, using brake hose clamps, clamp both the supply and return hoses near the power steering fluid reservoir. This will minimise fluid loss during subsequent operations.

5 Mark the unions to ensure they are correctly positioned on reassembly, then slacken and remove the feed and return pipe union bolts and recover the sealing washers. Be prepared for fluid spillage, and position a suitable container beneath the pipes whilst unscrewing the bolts. Plug the pipe ends and steering pump orifices to prevent fluid leakage and to keep dirt out of the hydraulic system.

6 On N42 and N46 engines, undo the two bolts at the front of the pump securing it to the coolant pump. Undo the four bolts securing the power steering pump to the cylinder block, and remove the pump **(see illustrations)**.

7 On all other models, slacken and remove the mounting bolts and remove the pump **(see illustration)**.

8 If the power steering pump is faulty, seek the advice of your BMW dealer as to the availability of spare parts. If spares are available, it may be possible to have the pump overhauled by a suitable specialist, or alternatively obtain an exchange unit. If not, the pump must be renewed.

Refitting

9 Where necessary, transfer the rear mounting bracket to the new pump, and securely tighten its mounting bolts.

10 Prior to refitting, ensure that the pump is primed by injecting the specified type of fluid in through the supply hose union and rotating the pump shaft.

11 Manoeuvre the pump into position and refit the pivot bolts, tightening them to the specified torque. On N42 and N46 engines, ensure the driving lugs of the pump align with those of the coolant pump, then refit the two bolts and secure the two pumps together, making sure the coolant pump connection is still engaged with the corresponding port in the engine block, then refit and tighten the pump mounting bolts **(see illustration)**. Tighten the coolant pump-to-steering pump bolts to the specified torque.

12 Position a new sealing washer on each side of the pipe hose unions and refit the union bolts. Tighten the union bolts to the specified torque.

13 Remove the hose clamps and refit the pump pulley (where applicable). Ensure the pulley is the right way around, and securely tighten its retaining bolts.

14 Refit the auxiliary drivebelt and tension it as described in Chapter 1.

15 On completion, lower the car to the ground and bleed the hydraulic system as described in Section 23.

22.6a Undo the two bolts (arrowed) securing the power steering pump to the coolant pump . . .

22.6b . . . and the four power steering pump mounting bolts (arrowed)

23 Power steering system – bleeding

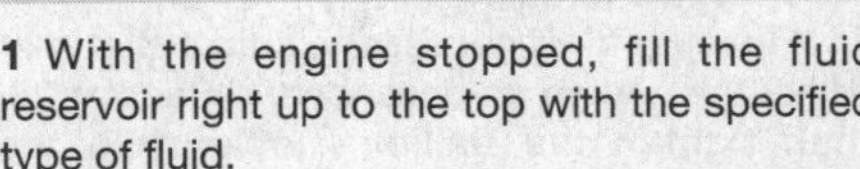

1 With the engine stopped, fill the fluid reservoir right up to the top with the specified type of fluid.

2 With the engine running, slowly move the steering from lock-to-lock twice to purge out the trapped air, then stop the engine and top-up the level in the fluid reservoir. Repeat this procedure until the fluid level in the reservoir does not drop any further.

3 If, when turning the steering, an abnormal noise is heard from the fluid lines, it indicates that there is still air in the system. Check this by turning the wheels to the straight-ahead position and switching off the engine. If the fluid level in the reservoir rises, then air is present in the system and further bleeding is necessary.

24 Steering rack rubber gaiters – renewal

1 Remove the track rod balljoint as described in Section 25. Undo the bolts and remove the engine undershield.

2 Note the correct fitted position of the gaiter on the track rod, then release the retaining clip(s) and slide the gaiter off the steering rack housing and track rod end.

3 Thoroughly clean the track rod and the steering rack housing, using fine abrasive paper to polish off any corrosion, burrs or sharp edges, which might damage the new gaiter's sealing lips on installation. Scrape off all the grease from the old gaiter, and apply it to the track rod inner balljoint. (This assumes that grease has not been lost or contaminated as a result of damage to the old gaiter. Use fresh grease if in doubt.)

22.7 Power steering pump mounting bolts – M43TU engine

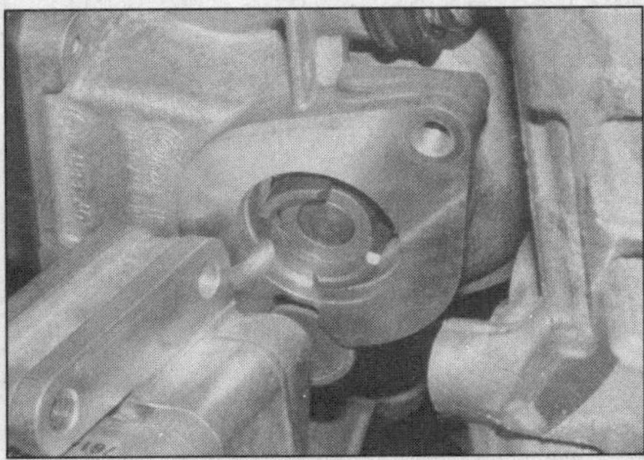

22.11 Ensure the driving lugs of the power steering pump engage with those of the coolant pump

24.4a Position the inner end of the gaiter on the rack body . . .

24.4b . . . and the outer end adjacent to the hexagon section of the track rod (arrowed)

4 Carefully slide the new gaiter onto the track rod end, and locate it on the steering rack housing. Position the outer edge of the gaiter on the track rod, as was noted prior to removal **(see illustrations)**.

5 Make sure the gaiter is not twisted, then lift the outer sealing lip of the gaiter to equalise air pressure within the gaiter. Secure the gaiter in position with the new retaining clip(s).

6 Refit the track rod balljoint as described in Section 25.

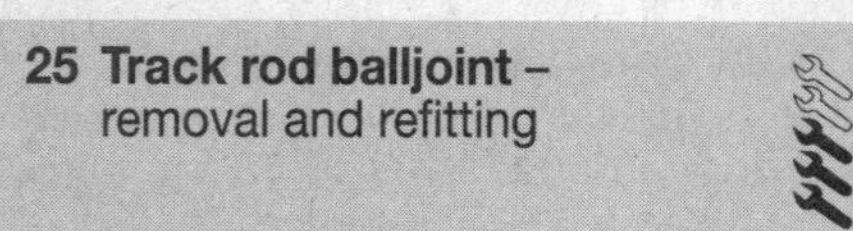

25 Track rod balljoint – removal and refitting

Note: *A new balljoint retaining nut will be required on refitting.*

Removal

1 Apply the handbrake, then jack up the front of the car and support it on axle stands. Remove the appropriate front roadwheel.

2 Make a mark on the track rod and measure the distance from the mark to the centre of the balljoint **(see illustration)**. Note this measurement down, as it will be needed to ensure the wheel alignment remains correctly set when the balljoint is installed.

3 Hold the track rod, and unscrew the balljoint locknut.

4 Slacken and remove the nut securing the track rod balljoint to the hub carrier, and release the balljoint tapered shank using a universal balljoint separator **(see illustration)**.

5 Counting the exact number of turns necessary to do so, unscrew the balljoint from the track rod end.

6 Carefully clean the balljoint and the threads. Renew the balljoint if its movement is sloppy or too stiff, if excessively worn, or if damaged in any way; carefully check the stud taper and threads. If the balljoint gaiter is damaged, the complete balljoint assembly must be renewed; it is not possible to obtain the gaiter separately.

Refitting

7 If necessary, transfer the locknut and collar to the new track rod balljoint.

8 Screw the balljoint onto the track rod by the number of turns noted on removal. This should position the balljoint at the relevant distance from the track rod mark that was noted prior to removal.

9 Refit the balljoint shank to the hub carrier, then fit a new retaining nut and tighten it to the specified torque.

10 Refit the roadwheel, then lower the car to the ground and tighten the roadwheel bolts to the specified torque.

11 Check and, if necessary, adjust the front wheel toe setting as described in Section 28, then tighten the balljoint locknut to the specified torque setting.

25.2 Make a mark on the track rod (arrowed), and measure from here to the centre of the balljoint

25.4 Use a balljoint separator to release the track rod end

26 Track rod – renewal

1 Remove the steering rack gaiter as described in Section 24.

2 Unscrew the track rod from the end of the steering rack.

3 Fit the new locking plate to the steering rack, making sure it is locating tabs are correctly seated in the steering rack grooves.

4 Screw in the track rod and tighten it to the specified torque.

5 Refit the steering gaiter as described in Section 24.

27 Dynamic Stability Control – general information and component renewal

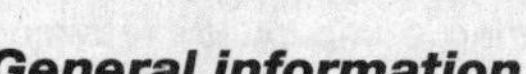

General information

1 Dynamic Stability Control (DSC) is standard on all 6-cylinder models, and available as an option on all other models. Strictly speaking, DSC includes ABS and Traction control, but this Section is concerned with Cornering Brake Control (CBC). By monitoring steering wheel movements, suspension ride heights, road speed and lateral acceleration, the system controls the pressure in the brake lines to each of the four brake calipers during braking, reducing the possibility of understeer or oversteer.

Component renewal

Steering angle sensor

2 Renewal of the steering angle sensor involves the complete dismantling of the steering column, which should be entrusted to a BMW dealer or suitably-equipped specialist. **Note:** *After renewing the steering angle sensor, the 'steering angle offset' procedure must be carrier out using dedicated BMW diagnostic equipment. Have this procedure carried out by a BMW dealer or suitably-equipped specialist.*

Front ride height sensor

3 Undo the nut securing the control rod to the sensor arm **(see illustration 12.3** in Chapter 12).

4 Remove the two retaining bolts, and withdraw the ride sensor. Disconnect the wiring plug as the sensor is removed.

5 Refitting is a reversal of removal. Have the headlight alignment check on completion.

DSC control unit

6 The DSC control unit is integral with the ABS control unit, renewal of which should be entrusted to a BMW dealer or suitably-equipped specialist – see Chapter 9, Section 20.

DSC pre-boost pump

Note: *After renewing the pre-boost pump, the brake high pressure hydraulic system needs to be bled. This necessitates the use of dedicated BMW Service equipment. Have*

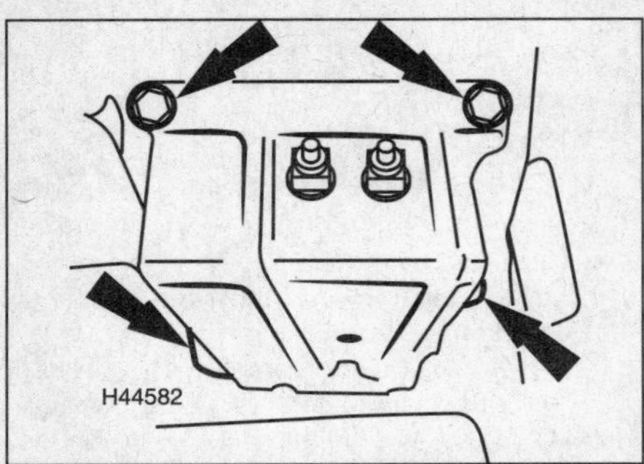

27.13 Undo the four lateral acceleration sensor bracket bolts (arrowed)

the procedure carried out by a BMW dealer or suitably-equipped specialist.

7 The DSC pre-boost pump is located under the brake master cylinder. Clamp the supply hose from the master cylinder reservoir to the pump, and disconnect the hose from the pump. Be prepared for fluid spillage.

8 Undo the union and disconnect the outlet pipe from the pump.

9 Disconnect the wiring plug from the pump and manoeuvre it from the rubber mounting.

10 Refitting is a reversal of removal. Bleed the brake hydraulic system as described in Chapter 9.

Lateral acceleration sensor

11 Remove the driver's seat as described in Chapter 11.

12 With the seat removed, lift the floor panel, and move the insulating wedge 10 cm forward to gain access to the sensor.

13 Undo the four bolts securing the sensor bracket to the body and, lifting the inner end first, remove the assembly **(see illustration)**. Disconnect the wiring plug as the unit is withdrawn. **Note:** *The sensor is extremely sensitive to vibration. Handle the unit with care.*

14 If necessary, undo the two bolts and separate the sensor from the bracket.

15 Refitting is a reversal of removal. Tighten the fasteners to the specified torque where given.

28 Wheel alignment and steering angles – general information

Definitions

1 A car's steering and suspension geometry is defined in four basic settings – all angles are expressed in degrees; the steering axis is defined as an imaginary line drawn through the axis of the suspension strut, extended where necessary to contact the ground.

2 Camber is the angle between each roadwheel and a vertical line drawn through its centre and tyre contact patch, when viewed from the front or rear of the car. Positive camber is when the roadwheels are tilted outwards from the vertical at the top; negative camber is when they are tilted inwards.

3 The front camber angle is not adjustable, and is given for reference only (see paragraph 5). The rear camber angle is adjustable and can be adjusted using a camber angle gauge.

4 Castor is the angle between the steering axis and a vertical line drawn through each roadwheel's centre and tyre contact patch, when viewed from the side of the car. Positive castor is when the steering axis is tilted so that it contacts the ground ahead of the vertical; negative castor is when it contacts the ground behind the vertical.

5 Castor is not adjustable, and is given for reference only; while it can be checked using a castor checking gauge, if the figure obtained is significantly different from that specified, the car must be taken for careful checking by a professional, as the fault can only be caused by wear or damage to the body or suspension components.

6 Toe is the difference, viewed from above, between lines drawn through the roadwheel centres and the car's centre-line. 'Toe-in' is when the roadwheels point inwards, towards each other at the front, while 'toe-out' is when they splay outwards from each other at the front.

7 The front wheel toe setting is adjusted by screwing the right-hand track rod in or out of its balljoint, to alter the effective length of the track rod assembly.

8 Rear wheel toe setting is also adjustable. The toe setting is adjusted by slackening the trailing arm mounting bracket bolts and repositioning the bracket.

Checking and adjustment

9 Due to the special measuring equipment necessary to check the settings, and the skill required to use it properly, the checking and adjustment of these settings is best left to a BMW dealer or similar expert. Note that most tyre-fitting shops now possess sophisticated checking equipment.

Chapter 11
Bodywork and fittings

Contents

Degrees of difficulty

Easy, suitable for novice with little experience 

Fairly easy, suitable for beginner with some experience

Fairly difficult, suitable for competent DIY mechanic

Difficult, suitable for experienced DIY mechanic 

Very difficult, suitable for expert DIY or professional 

Specifications

Torque wrench settings	Nm	lbf ft
Door lock retaining bolts	9	7
Door window glass and regulator fixings	9	7
Exterior mirror bolts	6	4
Rear vent window hinge bolts/screw – Coupe models	6	4
Seat belt height adjustment bracket on B-pillar	24	18
Seat belt mounting bolts	31	23
Seat belt tensioner stalk on seat rail	48	35

1 General information

The bodyshell is made of pressed-steel sections. Most components are welded together, but some use is made of structural adhesives.

The bonnet, door and some other vulnerable panels are made of zinc-coated metal, and are further protected by being coated with an anti-chip primer before being sprayed.

Extensive use is made of plastic materials, mainly in the interior, but also in exterior components. The front and rear bumpers and front grille are injection-moulded from a synthetic material that is very strong and yet light. Plastic components such as wheel arch liners are fitted to the underside of the vehicle, to improve the body's resistance to corrosion.

2 Maintenance – bodywork and underframe

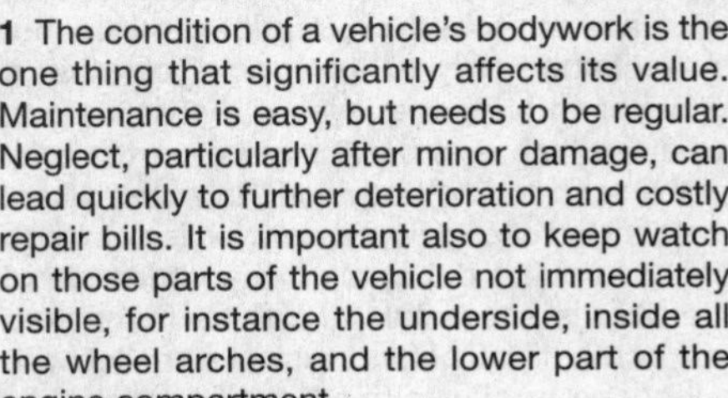

1 The condition of a vehicle's bodywork is the one thing that significantly affects its value. Maintenance is easy, but needs to be regular. Neglect, particularly after minor damage, can lead quickly to further deterioration and costly repair bills. It is important also to keep watch on those parts of the vehicle not immediately visible, for instance the underside, inside all the wheel arches, and the lower part of the engine compartment.

2 The basic maintenance routine for the bodywork is washing – preferably with a lot of water, from a hose. This will remove all the loose solids which may have stuck to the vehicle. It is important to flush these off in such a way as to prevent grit from scratching the finish. The wheel arches and underframe need washing in the same way, to remove any accumulated mud which will retain moisture and tend to encourage rust. Oddly enough, the best time to clean the underframe and wheel arches is in wet weather, when the mud is thoroughly wet and soft. In very wet weather, the underframe is usually cleaned of large accumulations automatically, and this is a good time for inspection.

3 Periodically, except on vehicles with a wax-based underbody protective coating, it is a good idea to have the whole of the underframe of the vehicle steam-cleaned, engine compartment included, so that a thorough inspection can be carried out to see what minor repairs and renovations are necessary. Steam cleaning is available at many garages, and is necessary for the removal of the accumulation of oily grime, which sometimes is allowed to become thick in certain areas. If steam-cleaning facilities are not available, there are some excellent grease solvents available which can be brush-applied; the dirt can then be simply hosed off. Note that these methods should not be used on vehicles with wax-based underbody protective coating, or the coating will be removed. Such vehicles should be inspected annually, preferably just before Winter, when the underbody should be washed down, and repair any damage to the wax coating. Ideally, a completely fresh coat should be applied. It would also be worth considering the use of such wax-based protection for injection into door panels, sills, box sections, etc, as an additional safeguard against rust damage, where such protection is not provided by the vehicle manufacturer.

4 After washing paintwork, wipe off with a chamois leather to give an unspotted clear finish. A coat of clear protective wax polish will give added protection against chemical pollutants in the air. If the paintwork sheen has dulled or oxidised, use a cleaner/polisher combination to restore the brilliance of the shine. This requires a little effort, but such dulling is usually caused because regular washing has been neglected. Care needs to be taken with metallic paintwork, as special non-abrasive cleaner/polisher is required to avoid damage to the finish. Always check that the door and ventilator opening drain holes and pipes are completely clear, so that water can be drained out. Brightwork should be treated in the same way as paintwork. Windscreens and windows can be kept clear of the smeary film which often appears, by proprietary glass cleaner. Never use any form of wax or other body or chromium polish on glass.

3 Maintenance – upholstery and carpets

Mats and carpets should be brushed or vacuum-cleaned regularly, to keep them free of grit. If they are badly stained, remove them from the vehicle for scrubbing or sponging, and make quite sure they are dry before refitting. Seats and interior trim panels can be kept clean by wiping with a damp cloth and a proprietary brand of cleaner. If they do become stained (which can be more apparent on light-coloured upholstery), use a little liquid detergent and a soft nail brush to scour the grime out of the grain of the material. Do not forget to keep the headlining clean in the same way as the upholstery. When using liquid cleaners inside the vehicle, do not over-wet the surfaces being cleaned. Excessive damp could get into the seams and padded interior, causing stains, offensive odours or even rot. If the inside of the vehicle gets wet accidentally, it is worthwhile taking some trouble to dry it out properly, particularly where carpets are involved. Do not leave oil or electric heaters inside the vehicle for this purpose.

4 Minor body damage – repair

Repairs of minor scratches

1 If the scratch is very superficial, and does not penetrate to the metal of the bodywork, repair is very simple. Lightly rub the area of the scratch with a paintwork renovator or a very fine cutting paste to remove loose paint from the scratch, and to clear the surrounding bodywork of wax polish. Rinse the area with clean water.

2 Apply touch-up paint to the scratch using a fine paint brush; continue to apply fine layers of paint until the surface of the paint in the scratch is level with the surrounding paintwork. Allow the new paint at least two weeks to harden, then blend it into the surrounding paintwork by rubbing the scratch area with a paintwork renovator or a very fine cutting paste. Finally, apply wax polish.

3 Where the scratch has penetrated right through to the metal of the bodywork, causing the metal to rust, a different repair technique is required. Remove any loose rust from the bottom of the scratch with a penknife, then apply rust-inhibiting paint to prevent the formation of rust in the future. Using a rubber or nylon applicator, fill the scratch with bodystopper paste. If required, this paste can be mixed with cellulose thinners to provide a very thin paste which is ideal for filling narrow scratches. Before the stopper-paste in the scratch hardens, wrap a piece of smooth cotton rag around the top of a finger. Dip the finger in cellulose thinners, and quickly sweep it across the surface of the stopper-paste in the scratch; this will ensure that the surface of the stopper-paste is slightly hollowed. The scratch can now be painted over as described earlier in this Section.

Repairs of dents

4 When deep denting of the vehicle's bodywork has taken place, the first task is to pull the dent out, until the affected bodywork almost attains its original shape. There is little point in trying to restore the original shape completely, as the metal in the damaged area will have stretched on impact, and cannot be reshaped fully to its original contour. It is better to bring the level of the dent up to a point which is about 3 mm below the level of the surrounding bodywork. In cases where the dent is very shallow anyway, it is not worth trying to pull it out at all. If the underside of the dent is accessible, it can be hammered out gently from behind, using a mallet with a wooden or plastic head. Whilst doing this, hold a suitable block of wood firmly against the outside of the panel, to absorb the impact from the hammer blows and thus prevent a large area of the bodywork from being 'belled-out'.

5 Should the dent be in a section of the bodywork which has a double skin, or some other factor making it inaccessible from behind, a different technique is called for. Drill several small holes through the metal inside the area – particularly in the deeper section. Then screw long self-tapping screws into the holes, just sufficiently for them to gain a good purchase in the metal. Now the dent can be pulled out by pulling on the protruding heads of the screws with a pair of pliers.

6 The next stage of the repair is the removal of the paint from the damaged area, and from an inch or so of the surrounding 'sound' bodywork. This is accomplished most easily by using a wire brush or abrasive pad on a power drill, although it can be done just as effectively by hand, using sheets of abrasive paper. To complete the preparation for filling, score the surface of the bare metal with a screwdriver or the tang of a file, or alternatively, drill small holes in the affected area. This will provide a good 'key' for the filler paste.

7 To complete the repair, see the Section on filling and respraying.

Repairs of rust holes or gashes

8 Remove all paint from the affected area, and from an inch or so of the surrounding 'sound' bodywork, using an abrasive pad or a wire brush on a power drill. If these are not available, a few sheets of abrasive paper will do the job most effectively. With the paint removed, you will be able to judge the severity of the corrosion, and therefore decide whether to renew the whole panel (if this is possible) or to repair the affected area. New body panels are not as expensive as most people think, and it is often quicker and more satisfactory to fit a new panel than to attempt to repair large areas of corrosion.

9 Remove all fittings from the affected area, except those which will act as a guide to the original shape of the damaged bodywork (eg headlamp shells etc). Then, using tin snips or a hacksaw blade, remove all loose metal and any other metal badly affected by corrosion. Hammer the edges of the hole inwards, to create a slight depression for the filler paste.

10 Wire-brush the affected area to remove the powdery rust from the surface of the remaining metal. Paint the affected area with rust-inhibiting paint; if the back of the rusted area is accessible, treat this also.

11 Before filling can take place, it will be necessary to block the hole in some way. This can be achieved with aluminium or plastic mesh, or aluminium tape.

12 Aluminium or plastic mesh, or glass-fibre matting, is probably the best material to use for a large hole. Cut a piece to the approximate size and shape of the hole to be filled, then position it in the hole so that its edges are below the level of the surrounding bodywork. It can be retained in position by several blobs of filler paste around its periphery.

13 Aluminium tape should be used for small or very narrow holes. Pull a piece off the roll, trim it to the approximate size and shape required, then pull off the backing paper (if used) and stick the tape over the hole; it can be overlapped if the thickness of one piece is insufficient. Burnish down the edges of the tape with the handle of a screwdriver or similar, to ensure that the tape is securely attached to the metal underneath.

Filling and respraying

14 Before using this Section, see the Sections on dent, deep scratch, rust holes and gash repairs.

15 Many types of bodyfiller are available, but generally speaking, those proprietary kits which contain a tin of filler paste and a tube of resin hardener are best for this type of repair which can be used directly from the tube. A wide, flexible plastic or nylon applicator will be found invaluable for imparting a smooth and well-contoured finish to the surface of the filler.

16 Mix up a little filler on a clean piece of card or board – measure the hardener carefully (follow the maker's instructions on the pack), otherwise the filler will set too rapidly or too slowly. Using the applicator, apply the filler paste to the prepared area; draw the applicator across the surface of the filler to achieve the correct contour and to level the surface. When a contour that approximates to the correct one is achieved, stop working the paste – if you carry on too long, the paste will become sticky and begin to 'pick-up' on the applicator. Continue to add thin layers of filler paste at 20-minute intervals, until the level of the filler is just proud of the surrounding bodywork.

17 Once the filler has hardened, the excess can be removed using a metal plane or file. From then on, progressively-finer grades of abrasive paper should be used, starting with a 40-grade production paper, and finishing with a 400-grade wet-and-dry paper. Always wrap the abrasive paper around a flat rubber, cork, or wooden block – otherwise the surface of the filler will not be completely flat. During the smoothing of the filler surface, the wet-and-dry paper should be periodically rinsed in water. This will ensure that a very smooth finish is imparted to the filler at the final stage.

18 At this stage, the 'dent' should be surrounded by a ring of bare metal, which in turn should be encircled by the finely 'feathered' edge of the good paintwork. Rinse the repair area with clean water, until all the dust produced by the rubbing-down operation has gone.

19 Spray the whole area with a light coat of primer – this will show up any imperfections in the surface of the filler. Repair these imperfections with fresh filler paste or bodystopper, and again smooth the surface with abrasive paper. If bodystopper is used, it can be mixed with cellulose thinners, to form a thin paste which is ideal for filling small holes. Repeat this spray-and-repair procedure until you are satisfied that the surface of the filler, and the feathered edge of the paintwork, are perfect. Clean the repair area with clean water, and allow to dry fully.

20 The repair area is now ready for final spraying. Paint spraying must be carried out in a warm, dry, windless and dust-free atmosphere. This condition can be created artificially if you have access to a large indoor working area, but if you are forced to work in the open, you will have to pick your day very carefully. If you are working indoors, dousing the floor in the work area with water will help to settle the dust which would otherwise be in the atmosphere. If the repair area is confined to one body panel, mask off the surrounding panels; this will help to minimise the effects of a slight mis-match in paint colours. Bodywork fittings (eg chrome strips, door handles etc) will also need to be masked off. Use genuine masking tape, and several thickness of newspaper, for the masking operations.

21 Before starting to spray, agitate the aerosol can thoroughly, then spray a test area (an old tin, or similar) until the technique is mastered. Cover the repair area with a thick coat of primer; the thickness should be built up using several thin layers of paint, rather than one thick one. Using 400 grade wet-and-dry paper, rub down the surface of the primer until it is smooth. While doing this, the work area should be thoroughly doused with water, and the wet-and-dry paper periodically rinsed in water. Allow to dry before spraying on more paint.

22 Spray on the top coat, again building up the thickness by using several thin layers of paint. Start spraying at the top of the repair area, and then, using a side-to-side motion, work downwards until the whole repair area and about 2 inches of the surrounding original paintwork is covered. Remove all masking material 10 to 15 minutes after spraying on the final coat of paint.

23 Allow the new paint at least two weeks to harden, then, using a paintwork renovator or a very fine cutting paste, blend the edges of the paint into the existing paintwork. Finally, apply wax polish.

Plastic components

24 With the use of more and more plastic body components by the vehicle manufacturers (eg bumpers. spoilers, and in some cases major body panels), rectification of more serious damage to such items has become a matter of either entrusting repair work to a specialist in this field, or renewing complete components. Repair of such damage by the DIY owner is not feasible, owing to the cost of the equipment and materials required for effecting such repairs. The basic technique involves making a groove along the line of the crack in the plastic, using a rotary burr in a power drill. The damaged part is then welded back together, using a hot air gun to heat up and fuse a plastic filler rod into the groove. Any excess plastic is then removed, and the area rubbed down to a smooth finish. It is important that a filler rod of the correct plastic is used, as body components can be made of different types (eg polycarbonate, ABS, polypropylene).

25 Damage of a less serious nature (abrasions, minor cracks etc) can be repaired by the DIY owner using a two-part epoxy filler repair material which can be used directly from the tube. Once mixed in equal proportions, this is used in similar fashion to the bodywork filler used on metal panels. The filler is usually cured in twenty to thirty minutes, ready for sanding and painting.

26 If the owner is renewing a complete component himself, or if he has repaired it with epoxy filler, he will be left with the problem of finding a suitable paint for finishing which is compatible with the type of plastic used. At one time, the use of a universal paint was not possible, owing to the complex range of plastics met with in body component applications. Standard paints, generally speaking, will not bond to plastic or rubber satisfactorily, but professional matched paints, to match any plastic or rubber finish, can be obtained from some dealers. However, it is now possible to obtain a plastic body parts finishing kit which consists of a pre-primer treatment, a primer and coloured top coat. Full instructions are normally supplied with a kit, but basically the method of use is to first apply the pre-primer to the component concerned, and allow it to dry for up to 30 minutes. Then the primer is applied, and left to dry for about an hour before finally applying the special-coloured top coat. The result is a correctly coloured component, where the paint will flex with the plastic or rubber, a property that standard paint does not normally posses.

5 Major body damage – repair

Where serious damage has occurred, or large areas need renewal due to neglect, it means that complete new panels will need welding-in, and this is best left to professionals. If the damage is due to impact, it will also be necessary to check completely the alignment of the bodyshell, and this can only be carried out accurately by a BMW dealer using special jigs. If the body is left misaligned, it is primarily dangerous, as the car will not handle properly, and secondly, uneven stresses will be imposed on the steering, suspension and possibly transmission, causing abnormal wear, or complete failure, particularly to such items as the tyres.

6 Front bumper – removal and refitting

Removal

1 Apply the handbrake, then jack up the front of the vehicle and support it on axle stands (see *Jacking and vehicle support*).

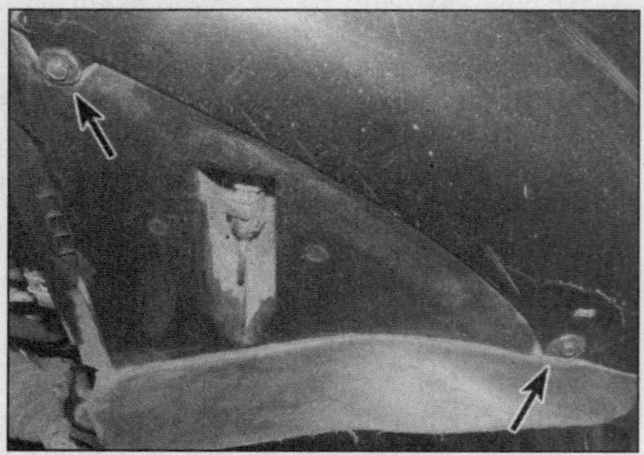
6.2 Undo the two bolts at the bumper lower edge (arrowed)

6.3 On Coupe models up to 03/2003, push the 'fins' of the trim down, release the clips and pull the foglight trims out

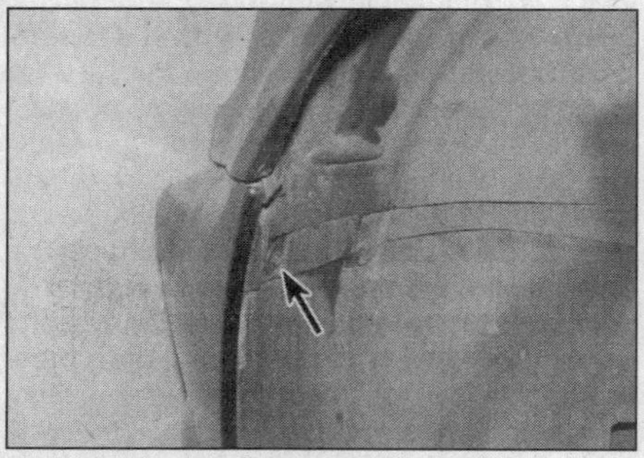

6.4 Undo the bolt (arrowed) securing the bumper to the wheel arch liner

6.5 One bolt each side secures the bumper to the impact absorber

Saloon & Touring up to 09/01 and Coupe

2 Undo the two bolts each side securing the lower edge of the bumper **(see illustration)**.

3 On Coupe models up to 03/2003, release the retaining clips and pull the foglight trims forwards away from the bumper **(see illustration)**.

4 Release the retaining bolts and detach the lower front wheel arch liner from the bumper **(see illustration)**.

5 Undo the bolt each side securing the bumper to the impact absorbers **(see illustration)**.

6 Pull the bumper forward a little, note their fitted locations, and disconnect the various wiring plugs.

7 Remove the bumper forwards and away from the vehicle.

Saloon & Touring from 10/01

8 Undo the two bolts each side securing the lower edge of the bumper.

9 Prise out the centre pins, then lever out the three expanding rivets in the front, underside of the bumper.

10 Undo the bolt each side securing the bumper to the impact absorbers.

11 Lever the wheel arch liner out from the bumper, carefully pull the bumper forward a little. Don't pull at the sides of the bumper – pull at the wheel arch.

12 Note their fitted locations, and disconnect the various wiring plugs.

13 Remove the bumper forwards and away from the vehicle.

14 Inspect the bumper mountings for signs of damage and renew if necessary.

Refitting

15 Refitting is a reverse of the removal procedure, ensuring that the bumper mounting nuts and bolts are securely tightened.

7 Rear bumper – removal and refitting

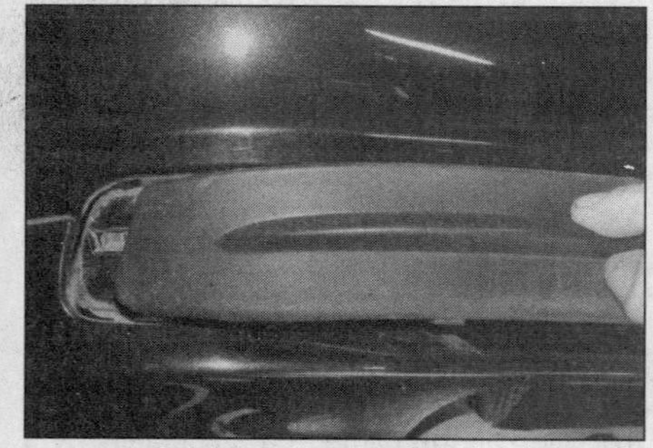

7.2 Carefully prise the plastic trim strip from the bumper

7.3 Prise out the centre pin, then remove the expanding rivet

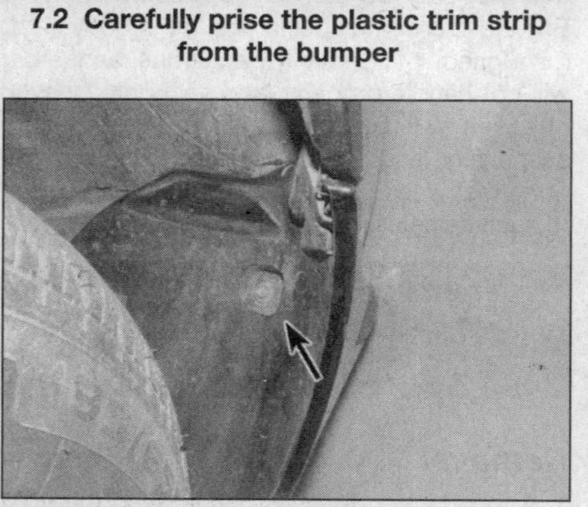
7.4 Remove the bolt (arrowed) securing the bumper to the wheel arch liner

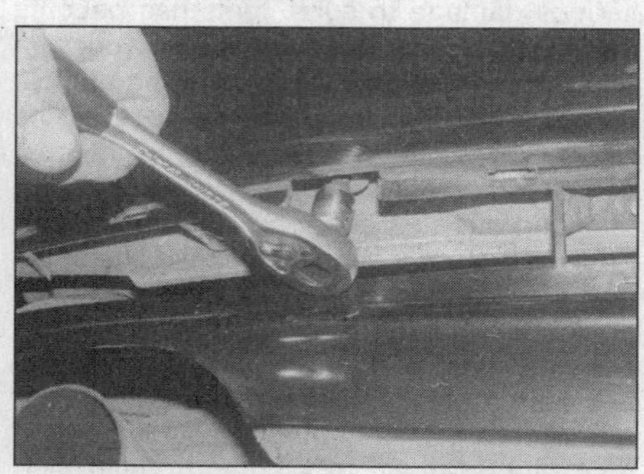
7.6a Undo the bumper mounting Torx bolts (one each side) . . .

Removal

1 To improve access, chock the front wheels, then jack up the rear of the vehicle and support it on axle stands (see *Jacking and vehicle support*).

Up to September 2001

2 Starting at the left-hand corner, carefully prise the plastic trim strip from the bumper cover **(see illustration)**. On models equipped with parking distance sensors, disconnect the wiring plugs as the panel is withdrawn.

3 Prise out the centre pin and remove the expanding rivets securing the lower edge of the wheel arch liners to the bumper ends **(see illustration)**.

4 On models up to 12/98, undo the bolt securing the wheel arch liner to the bumper **(see illustration)**.

5 On models from 12/98, release the retaining nuts, and remove the bracket each side securing the upper edge of the bumper to the wheel arch liners.

6 On all models, slacken and remove the bumper lower mounting Torx bolts, pull out the front edge of the bumper from the wheel arch, and remove the bumper from the rear of the vehicle **(see illustrations)**.

From October 2001

7 Undo the bolts (one each side) at the front lower edge of the bumper **(see illustration)**.

8 Undo the two bolts securing the bumper cover to the impact absorbers.
9 Working in the wheel arch with a flat-bladed screwdriver, carefully press the lug downwards and detach the bumper.
10 Pull the front edges of the bumper outwards and slide the bumper slightly to the rear. Disconnect any relevant wiring plugs and remove the bumper.

Refitting

11 Refitting is a reverse of the removal procedure ensuring that the bumper ends are correctly engaged with their slides. Apply locking compound to the bumper mounting bolts and tighten them securely.

8 Bonnet – removal, refitting and adjustment

Removal

1 Open the bonnet and have an assistant support it. Using a pencil or felt tip pen, mark the outline of each bonnet hinge relative to the bonnet, to use as a guide on refitting.
2 Disconnect the hose from the washer jets. On models with heated jets also disconnect the wiring connectors. Tie a length of string to the end of the wiring loom and washer hose, then pull the harness/hose from the bonnet channel. Free the harness/hose from any retaining clips. As the harness/hose is pulled from the bonnet channel, untie the string and leave it in place to aid refitment.
3 With the aid of an assistant, support the bonnet in the open position then remove the retaining clips and detach the support struts from the bonnet **(see illustration)**.
4 Slacken and remove the left and right-hand hinge-to-bonnet rear bolts and loosen the front bolts. Slide the bonnet forwards to disengage it from the hinges and remove it from the vehicle. Recover any shims which are fitted between the hinge and bonnet.
5 Inspect the bonnet hinges for signs of wear and free play at the pivots, and if necessary renew. Each hinge is secured to the body by two bolts. Mark the position of the hinge on the body then undo the retaining bolts and remove it from the vehicle. On refitting, align the new hinge with the marks and securely tighten the retaining bolts.

Refitting and adjustment

6 Fit the shims (where fitted) to the hinge and, with the aid of an assistant, engage the bonnet with the hinges. Refit the rear bolts and tighten them by hand only. Align the hinges with the marks made on removal, then tighten the retaining bolts securely. Note the earth strap attached to the base of the left-hand side hinge **(see illustration)**.
7 Close the bonnet, and check for alignment with the adjacent panels. If necessary, slacken the hinge bolts and re-align the bonnet to suit.

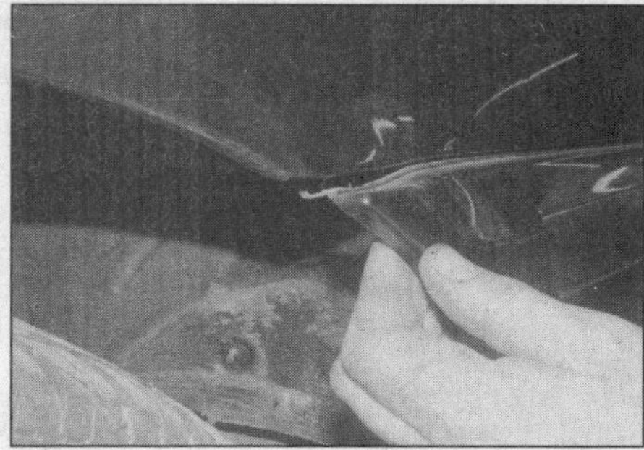

7.6b . . . and pull the front edge of the bumper away from the wheel arch

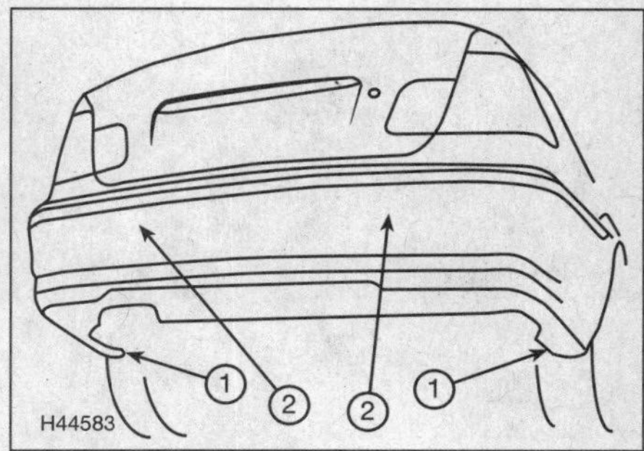

7.7 Undo the bumper lower bolts (1), and impact absorber bolts (2)

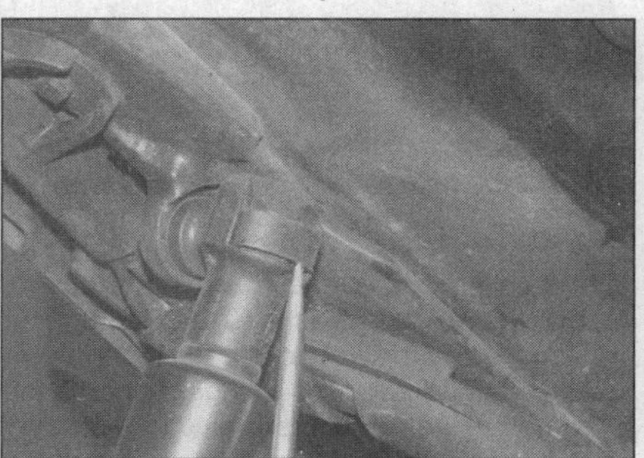

8.3 Prise out the bonnet strut clip

8.6 Bonnet hinge earth strap

Once the bonnet is correctly aligned, securely tighten the hinge bolts. Once the bonnet is correctly aligned, check that the bonnet fastens and releases satisfactorily. Tie the wiring harness/hose to the end of the string and pull them through the bonnet channel to their original positions. Reconnect the hose and wiring.

9 Bonnet release cable – removal and refitting

Removal

1 The bonnet release cable is in three sections, the main first cable from the release lever to the connection at the right-hand side inner wing (adjacent to the windscreen washer reservoir), the second from the connection to the right-hand bonnet lock, and one linking the two bonnet locks.

Release lever-to-connection cable

2 Open the driver's door, and carefully pull up the door sill trim panel.
3 Pull up the rubber weatherstrip from the door aperture adjacent to the footwell kick panel.
4 Undo the fasteners and remove the lower facia panel above the pedals. Disconnect any wiring plugs as the panel is withdrawn.
5 Undo the bolt and remove the bonnet release lever.
6 Undo the bolt and remove the footwell kick panel **(see illustration)**.
7 Separate the cable inner end fitting from the release lever.
8 Push/pull the outer release cable end fitting from the engine compartment bulkhead, and pull the cable into the engine compartment.
9 Unclip the connection housing from the inner wing. Prise open the connection housing and disconnect the inner and outer cables **(see illustration)**.

9.6 Undo the bolt (arrowed) and remove the kick panel

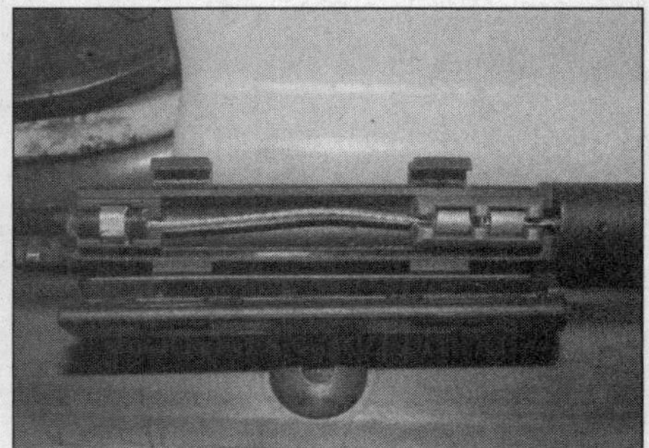

9.9 Disconnect the inner and outer cables from the connection housing

10.2 Depress the retaining clips and slide the plastic mounting covers down

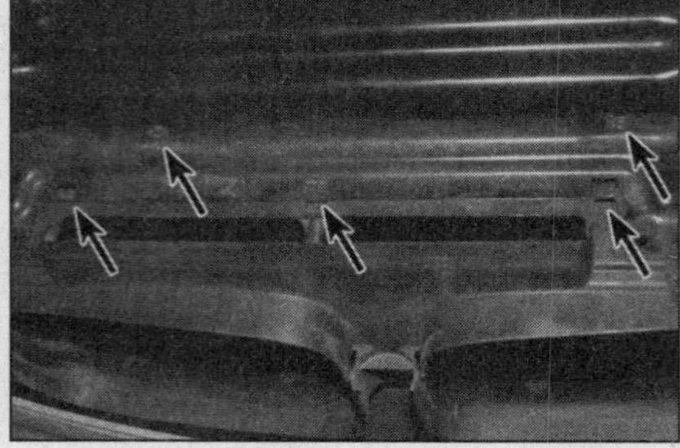
10.3 Undo the bolts, release the clips (arrowed) and slide the cover to the rear

10.4 Bonnet lock retaining bolts (arrowed)

Connection-to-bonnet lock cable

10 Unclip the connection housing from the inner wing. Prise open the housing and disconnect the inner and outer cables **(see illustration 9.9)**

11 Remove the driver's side bonnet lock as described in Section 10.

Lock linking cable

12 The linking cable is removed as part of the bonnet lock removal procedure, as described in Section 10.

Refitting

13 Refitting is the reverse of removal ensuring that the cable is correctly routed, and secured to all the relevant retaining clips. Check that the bonnet locks operate correctly before closing the bonnet.

10 Bonnet lock(s) – removal and refitting

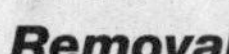

Removal

1 To gain access to the rear of the lock(s), remove the radiator described in Chapter 3.

2 On models with air conditioning, reach down under the condenser mountings, depress the retaining clips and slide the plastic mounting covers down **(see illustration)**. Carefully move the condenser backwards and down.

Caution: Do not disconnect the refrigerant pipes.

3 Undo the two bolts in the centre of the bonnet crossmember, press down the clips and remove the plastic cover to the rear **(see illustration)**.

4 Slacken and remove the lock retaining bolts then free the release outer cable(s) from the lock, then detach the inner cable(s) from the lock **(see illustration)**. Remove the lock from the vehicle.

Refitting

5 Locate the bonnet release inner cable(s) in the lock and reconnect the outer cable(s) to the lever. Seat the lock on the crossmember.

6 Align the lock with the marks made prior to removal then refit the bolts and tighten them securely.

7 Check that the locks operate smoothly when the release lever is moved, without any sign of undue resistance. Check that the bonnet fastens and releases satisfactorily.

8 Once the locks are operating correctly, refit the condenser (where applicable) and install the radiator as described in Chapter 3.

11 Door – removal, refitting and adjustment

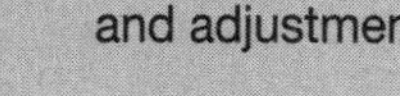

Removal

1 Disconnect the battery negative terminal (see Chapter 5A).

2 Undo the Torx bolt securing the door check link to the pillar **(see illustration)**.

3 Unscrew the hinge nuts from both the upper and lower door hinges **(see illustration)**.

4 Have an assistant support the door, undo the retaining bolt and withdraw the door wiring connector from the pillar. Pull out the locking element and unplug the connector as the door is withdrawn **(see illustrations)**. If necessary the hinge pins can be unscrewed from the hinges.

Refitting

5 Manoeuvre the door into position and reconnect the wiring plug. Push the connector into the pillar and secure it in place with the bolt.

6 Engage the hinges with the studs on the door, and tighten the nuts securely. Note that if necessary, the position of the door can be adjusted by inserting or removing shims between the hinge and the door (available from BMW dealers).

7 Align the check link with the pillar, fit and tighten the securing bolt.

11.2 Disconnect the door check strap from the pillar

11.3 Unscrew the door hinge bolts

11.4a Pull out the locking element (arrowed) and disconnect the door plug

11.4b The hinge pins (arrowed) can be unscrewed from the hinges

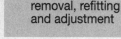

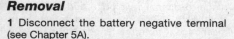

12.2 Starting at the rear, carefully prise the decorative trim from the door trim panel

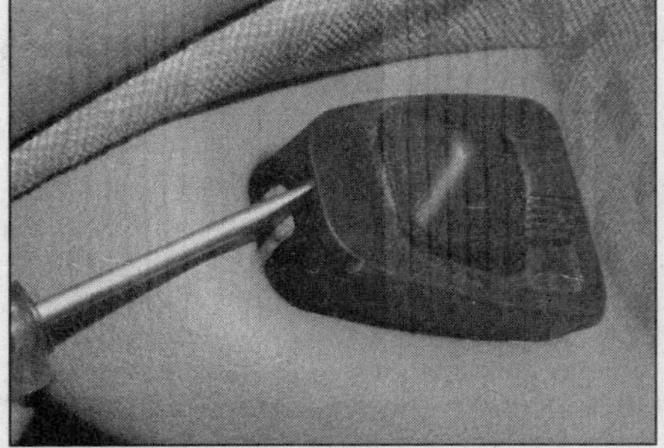
12.3a Carefully prise the mirror switch from the armrest . . .

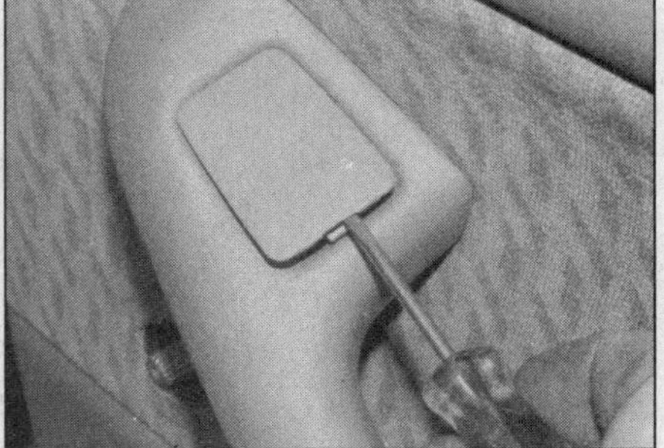
12.3b . . . or remove the plastic trim (as applicable)

Adjustment

8 Close the door and check the door alignment with surrounding body panels. If necessary, slight adjustment of the door position can be made by slackening the hinge retaining nuts and repositioning the hinge/door as necessary. Once the door is correctly positioned, securely tighten the hinge nuts. If the paint work around the hinges has been damaged, paint the affected area with a suitable touch-in brush to prevent corrosion.

12 Door inner trim panel – removal and refitting

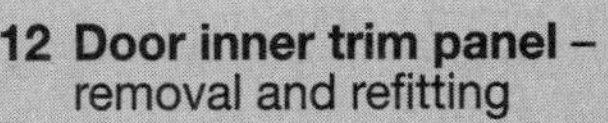

Removal – front door

1 Disconnect the battery negative terminal then open the door (see Chapter 5A).

Saloon and Touring

2 Starting at the rear of the trim, using a trim clip releasing tool or flat-bladed screwdriver, carefully prise the decorative trim from the door panel **(see illustration)**.

3 If you are removing the driver's door trim on models with electric mirrors, starting at the front edge, carefully prise the mirror switch from the armrest. Disconnect the switch wiring plugs as the switch is withdrawn. If removing the passenger's door trim, or non-electric mirror driver's door trim, prise the plastic trim out from the front of the armrest **(see illustrations)**.

4 Prise out the plastic caps from the armrest, then undo the five panel retaining bolts **(see illustrations)**. Note that the upper front panel retaining bolt is longer than the others.

Coupe

5 If you are removing the driver's door trim on models with electric mirrors. Starting at the front edge, carefully prise the mirror switch from the armrest **(see illustration 12.3a)**. Disconnect the switch wiring plugs as the switch is withdrawn.

6 In the interior door handle recess, press in the rear edge of the plastic cap, and undo the panel Torx bolt **(see illustration)**.

7 Carefully lever out the airbag emblem from the panel, and undo the retaining Torx bolt behind it **(see illustration)**.

8 Undo the three armrest securing bolts.

All models

9 Release the door trim panel clips, carefully levering between the panel and door with a flat-bladed screwdriver. Work around the outside of the panel, and when all the studs are released, ease the panel away from the top of the door, then lift it over the locking knob **(see illustrations)**.

12.4a Prise out the plastic caps . . .

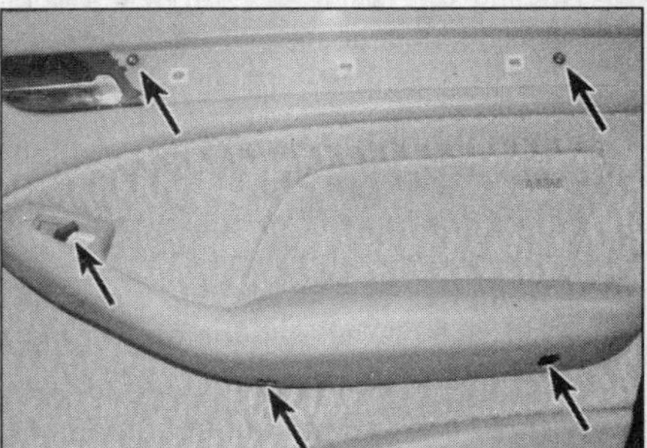
12.4b . . . and remove the five panel retaining bolts (arrowed)

12.6 Press in the rear edge of the plastic cap in the door handle recess

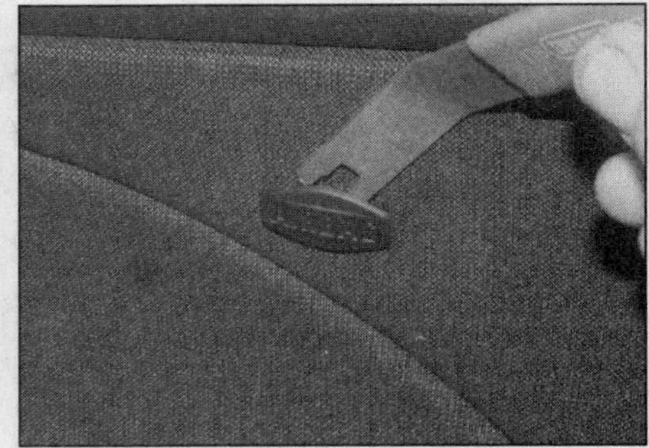
12.7 Prise out the airbag emblem, and undo the Torx bolt

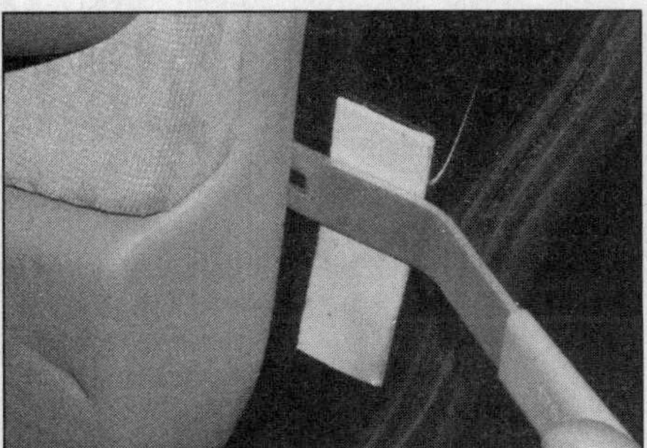
12.9a Carefully lever between the trim panel and the door to release the clips

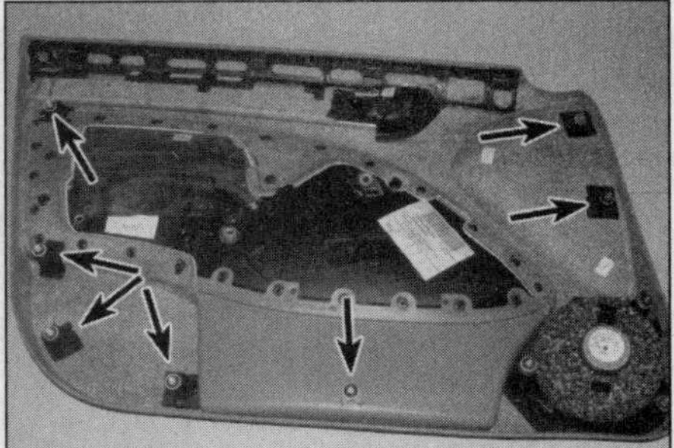
12.9b Door trim panel retaining clips (arrowed)

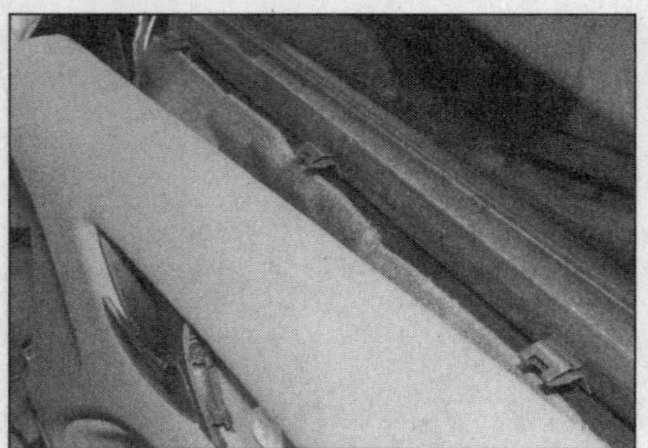
12.9c Pull the top of the trim away before lifting it over the locking knob

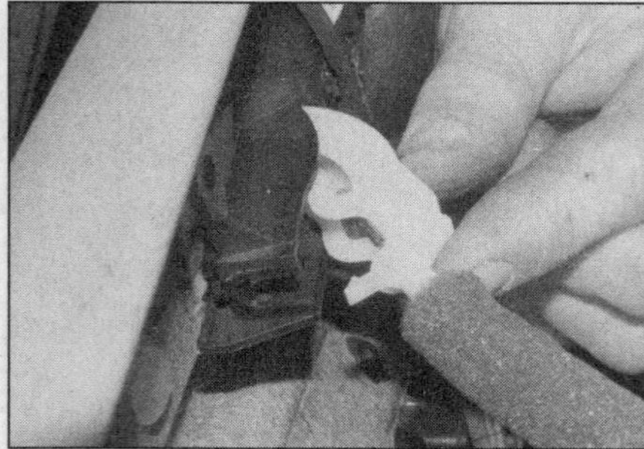
12.10 Lever out the cable lock

10 Holding the panel away from the door, pull open the inner handle, lever out the cable retaining lock, and remove the cable to the rear **(see illustration)**.

11 Disconnect the speaker wiring plugs as the panel is withdrawn.

12 Where fitted, remove the door airbag module as described in Chapter 12.

13 If required, carefully prise the sound insulation panel away from the door, using a flat-bladed tool to cut through the sealant.

Removal – rear door

14 Disconnect the battery negative terminal then open the door (see Chapter 5A).

15 Starting at the rear of the trim, using a trim clip releasing tool or flat-bladed screwdriver, carefully prise the decorative trim from the door panel **(see illustration)**.

16 On models with manual windows, carefully prise out the plastic cover from the window winder handle. Undo the retaining Torx bolt and remove the handle complete with circular bezel **(see illustrations)**. Prise the plastic trim from the front of the armrest **(see illustration 12.3b)**.

17 On models with electric windows, using a small flat-bladed screwdriver, carefully lever out the window switch from the armrest. Use a piece of cardboard under the screwdriver to prevent damage to the armrest. Disconnect the switch wiring plug as it is removed **(see illustration)**.

18 Prise out the plastic caps, then undo the five panel retaining bolts **(see illustrations)**. Note that the upper front panel retaining bolt is longer than the others.

19 Proceed as described in Paragraphs 9 to 13.

Refitting

20 Refitting of the trim panel is the reverse of removal. Before refitting, check whether any of the trim panel retaining clips were broken on removal, and renew them as necessary. Ensure that where removed, the sound insulation panel is sealed into its original location. If the sound insulation panel is damaged it must be renewed.

13 Door handle and lock components – removal and refitting

Removal

Interior door handle

1 The interior door handle is integral with the door trim, and cannot be renewed separately.

Front door lock assembly

2 Fully open the window then raise it approximately 140 mm (measured at the rear of the glass). Remove the door inner trim panel as described in Section 12. Carefully peel the plastic sound insulation panel off from the door (carefully cut through the sealant) to gain access to the lock components and continue as described under the relevant sub-heading. If the sound insulation panel is damaged on removal it must be renewed.

3 Slacken the window clamp retaining bolts **(see illustrations 14.5a and 14.5b)**, and tape or wedge the window into the fully closed position. Undo the two nuts securing the window rear support bracket, and manoeuvre it into the lower part of the door. There is no need to remove the guide rail **(see illustration 14.8)**.

4 If working on the driver's door, remove the

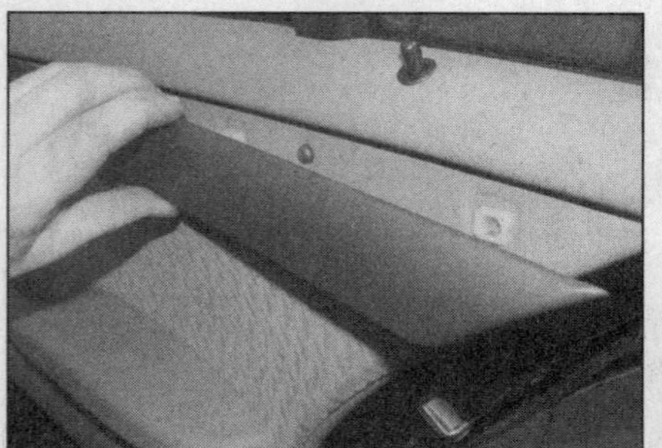
12.15 Starting at the rear, prise the trim from the door trim panel

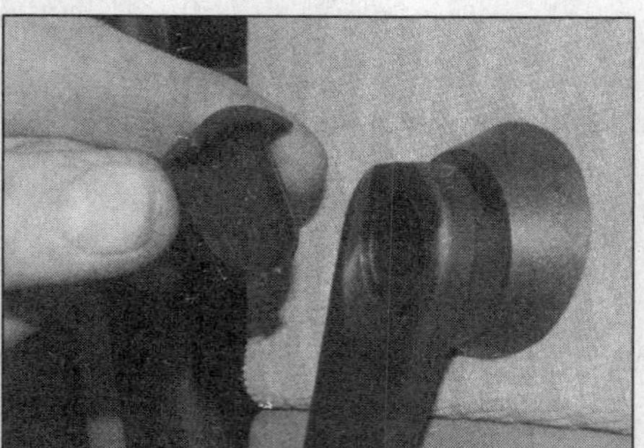
12.16a Prise the plastic cover . . .

12.16b . . . and undo the Torx bolt

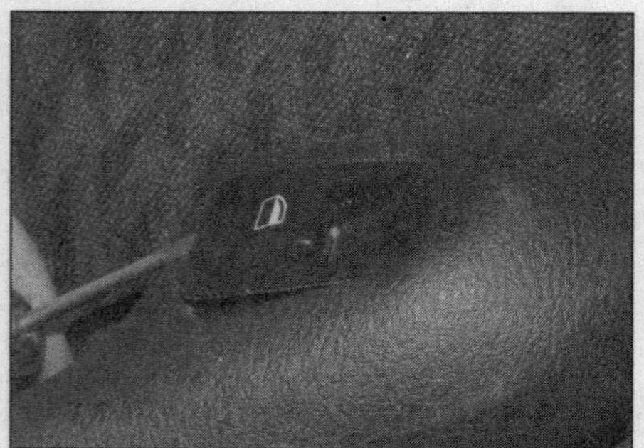
12.17 On models with rear electric windows, lever the switch from the armrest

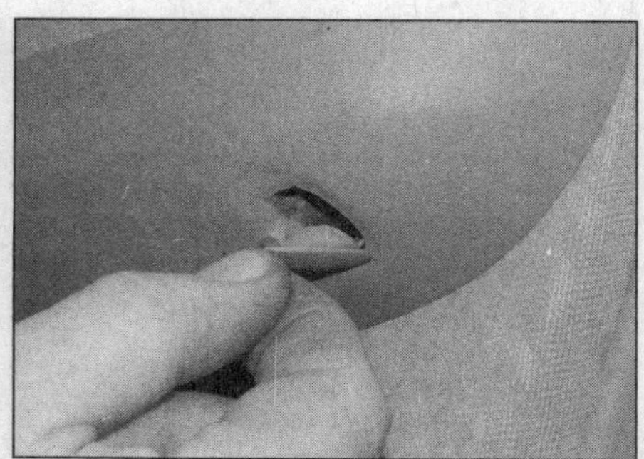
12.18a Prise out the plastic caps . . .

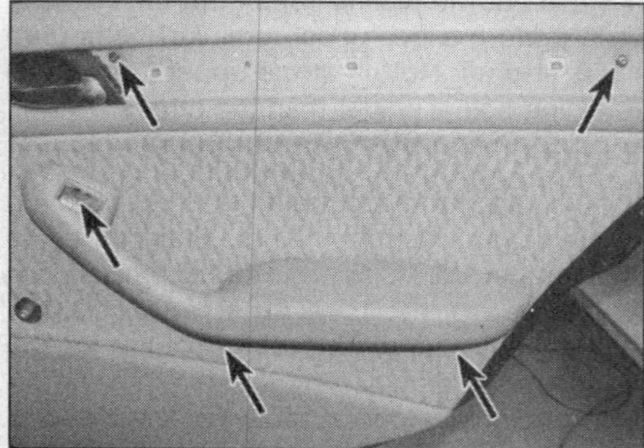
12.18b . . . and undo the five bolts (arrowed)

13.6 Prise the outer cable from the bracket and disengage the inner end from the lever

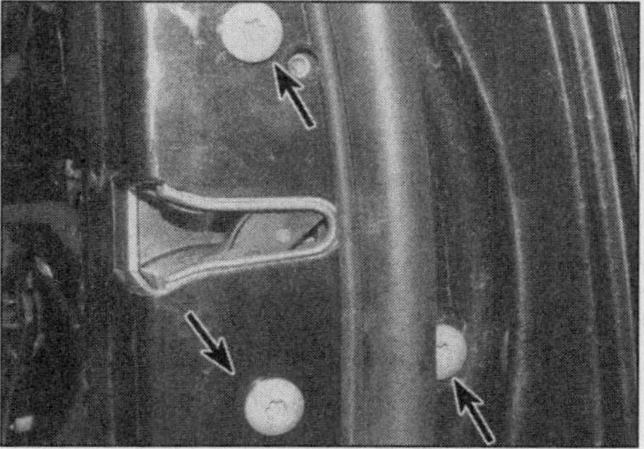
13.7 Undo the door lock retaining bolts (arrowed)

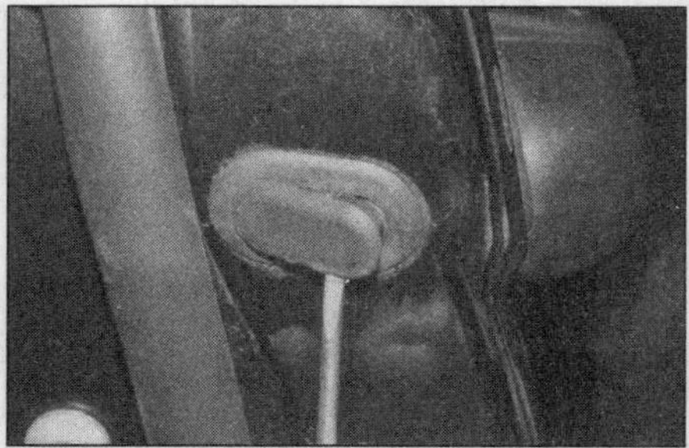
13.8a Remove the grommet to expose the handle rear cover bolt – Saloon and Touring models . . .

lock cylinder as described in Paragraphs 13 to 15.

5 Release the lock assembly wiring retaining clips and disconnect the wiring connector(s).

6 On vehicles from 09/00, prise the cable outer from the retaining bracket, and disconnect the inner end from the lever on the lock **(see illustration)**.

7 Slacken and remove the lock assembly retaining bolts then manoeuvre it behind the rear window support rail, and out from the door complete with the lock button linkage **(see illustration)**.

Front door exterior handle up to 09/00

8 If working on the driver's door, remove the lock cylinder as described in Paragraphs 13 to 15. If working on the passenger's door, prise out the grommet in the door end panel to expose the outer handle rear cover retaining bolt. On Coupe models, gently fold back the upper door rubber trim to expose the grommet. Undo the bolt with an Allen key and remove the rear cover from the outer handle **(see illustrations)**.

9 Pull the outer handle outwards and approximately 2 mm to the rear. The lock mechanism is now engaged. Press the outer handle approximately 4 mm inwards, and slide the handle to the rear and out from the door **(see illustration)**.

Front door exterior handle from 09/00

10 If working on the driver's door, remove the lock cylinder as described in Paragraphs 13 to 15. If working on the passenger's door, prise out the grommet in the door end panel to expose the outer handle rear cover retaining bolt. On Coupe models, gently fold back the upper door rubber trim to expose the grommet. Undo the bolt with an Allen key and remove the rear cover from the outer handle.

11 The lock must be placed in the 'installation position'. Pull the handle outwards and wedge it in place with a piece of wood or rag. Working through the aperture in the door end panel, turn the actuator screw anti-clockwise until it comes to a stop **(see illustration)**. Remove the piece of wood or rag.

12 Pull the rear of the handle out, and manoeuvre it from the door.

Front door lock cylinder

13 Prise out the grommet in the door end panel to expose the lock cylinder retaining bolt **(see illustration)**. On Coupe models, gently fold back the upper door rubber trim to expose the grommet.

14 Undo the retaining bolt with an Allen key, and pull the lock cylinder from the door **(see illustration)**.

15 If required, release the two retaining clips and separate the cylinder from the plastic cover **(see illustration)**.

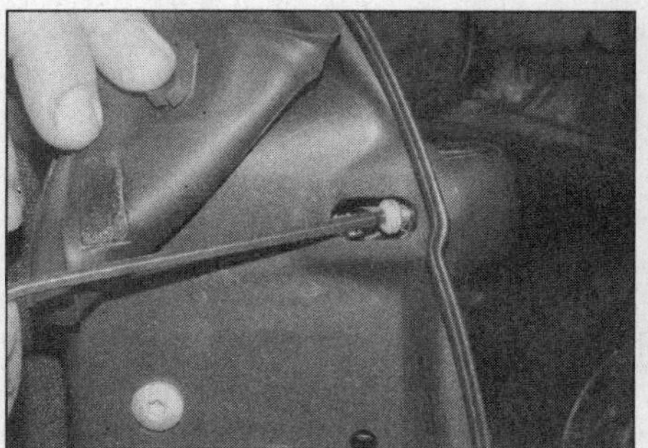
13.8b . . . and Coupe models

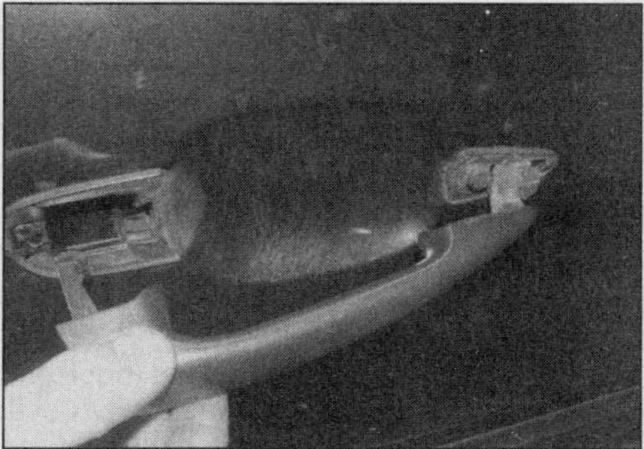
13.9 Slide the outer handle to the rear and out of the door

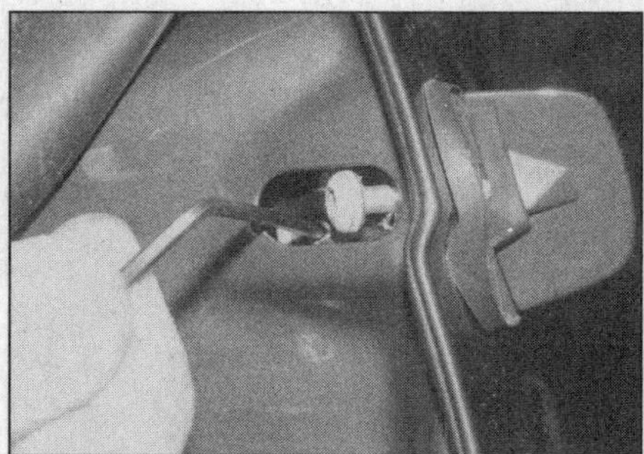
13.11 Turn the actuator screw anti-clockwise

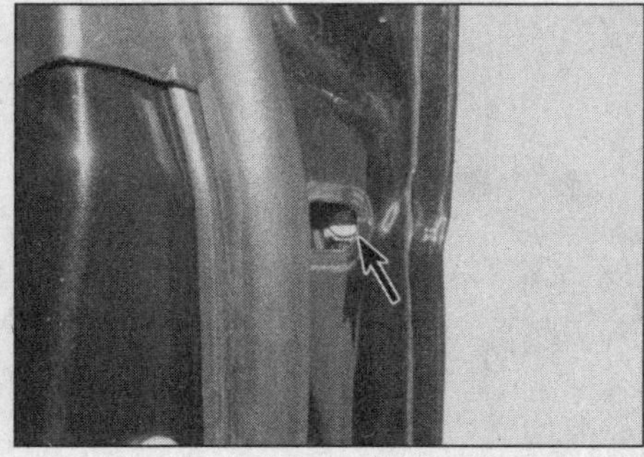
13.13 Prise out the grommet, and undo the lock cylinder retaining bolt (arrowed)

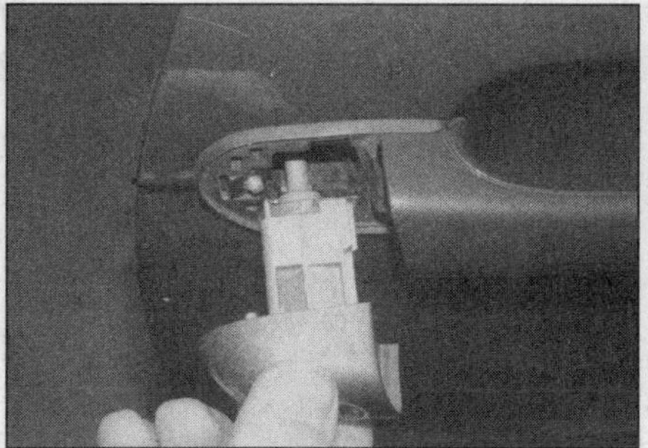
13.14 Undo the bolt and pull the lock cylinder from the door

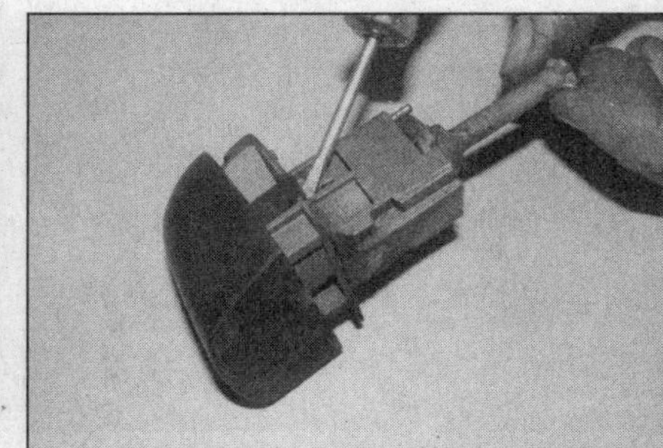
13.15 Release the retaining clips and remove the lock cylinder cover

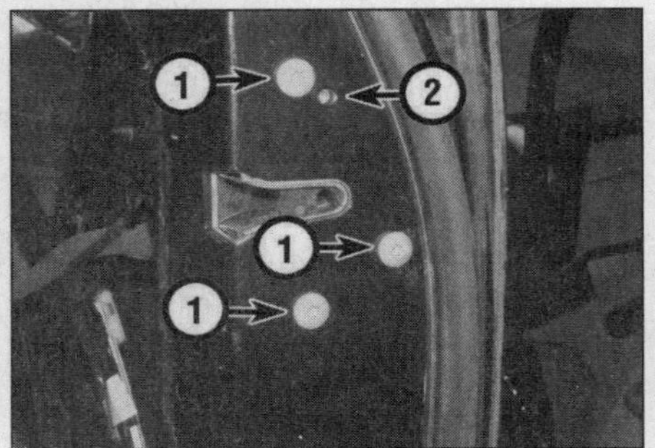

13.17 Rear door lock retaining bolts (1) and lock adjusting screw (2)

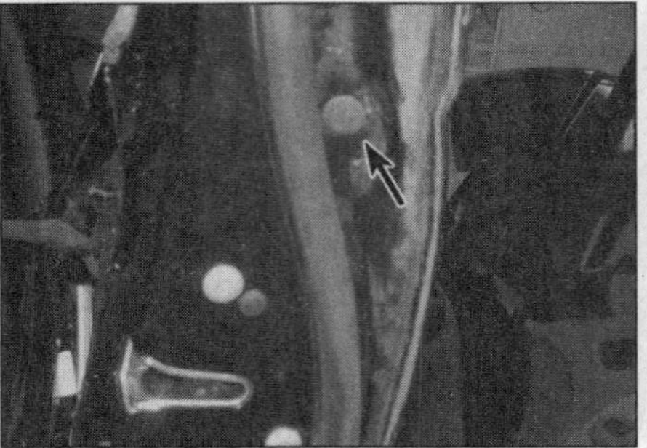
13.18a Prise out the grommet (arrowed) . . .

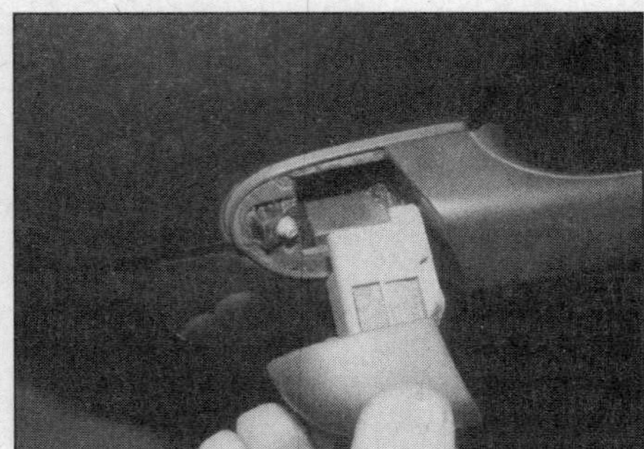
13.18b . . . undo the bolt and remove the rear handle cover

Rear door lock

16 Remove the door inner trim panel and sound insulation material as described in Section 12. Disconnect the door lock wiring plug(s).

17 Slacken and remove the lock assembly retaining bolts, then manoeuvre the lock from the door, complete with the lock button linkage **(see illustration)**.

Rear door exterior handle up to 09/00

18 Prise out the grommet in the door end panel to expose the outer handle rear cover retaining bolt. Undo the bolt with an Allen key and remove the rear cover from the outer handle **(see illustrations)**.

19 Pull the outer handle outwards and approximately 2 mm to the rear. The lock mechanism is now engaged. Press the outer handle approximately 4 mm inwards, and slide the handle to the rear and out from the door **(see illustration 13.9)**.

Rear door exterior handle from 09/00

20 Prise out the grommet in the door end panel to expose the outer handle rear cover retaining bolt. Undo the bolt with an Allen key and remove the rear cover from the outer handle.

21 The lock must be placed in the 'installation position'. Pull the handle outwards and wedge it in place with a piece of wood or rag.

22 Working through the aperture in the door end panel, turn the actuator screw anti-clockwise until it comes to a stop **(see illustration 13.11)**. Remove the piece of wood or rag.

23 Pull the rear of the handle out, and manoeuvre it from the door.

Refitting

Interior door handle

24 The interior door handle is integral with the door trim panel, and cannot be renewed separately.

Front door lock assembly

25 Remove all traces of old locking compound from the lock retaining bolts.

26 Prior to refitting the lock, slacken the lock adjustment screw. The screw has a left-hand thread on right-hand door locks, and a right-hand thread on left-hand door locks **(see illustrations)**.

27 Manoeuvre the lock assembly into position, ensuring that the lock button linkage engages correctly with the hole in the door. Make sure that the lock lever is inserted between the outer door handle support member and the outer door skin **(see illustration)**.

28 Apply fresh locking compound to the lock bolts (BMW recommend Loctite 270) then refit them and tighten them to the specified torque.

29 Reconnect the wiring connector(s) and secure the wiring in position with the relevant clips.

30 On the driver's door, refit the lock cylinder as described in Paragraphs 43 to 45.

31 On all vehicles from 09/00, reconnect the cable to the lock lever, and refit the cable outer to the retaining bracket **(see illustration)**.

32 Position the window and rear guide rail, refit the nuts and tighten them securely. Lower the window and refit it to the clamps as described in Section 14.

33 Do not close the door until the operation of the lock has been set-up and checked as follows:

*a) Prise out the small plastic cap adjacent to the lock upper retaining bolt, to access the lock adjusting bolt **(see illustrations 13.26a and 13.26b)**.*

b) On the left-hand door, tighten the adjusting screw in a clockwise direction. Tighten the driver's door lock adjusting screw anti-clockwise.

*c) Using a screwdriver 'close' the door lock by pushing in the lock lever **(see illustration)**.*

d) Using the key, unlock the door.

e) Using the outside handle, 'open' the lock.

f) If the lock fails to open, slacken the adjusting screw, then tighten it again. Recheck the lock operation.

13.26a Slacken the lock adjustment screw (arrowed) – Saloon and Touring models

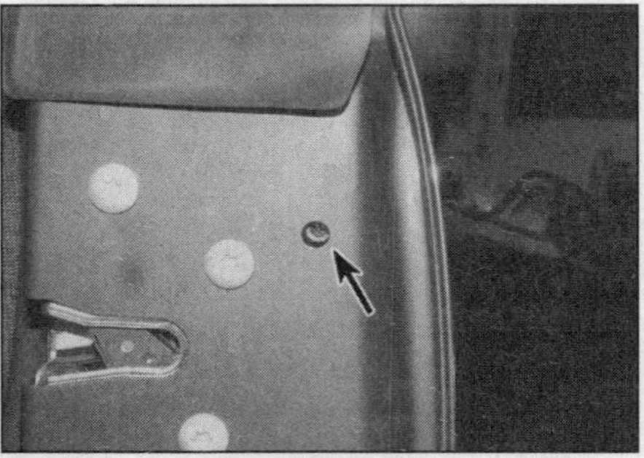
13.26b Lock adjustment screw (arrowed) – Coupe models

13.27 Ensure the lock lever (arrowed) is between the door skin and the support member

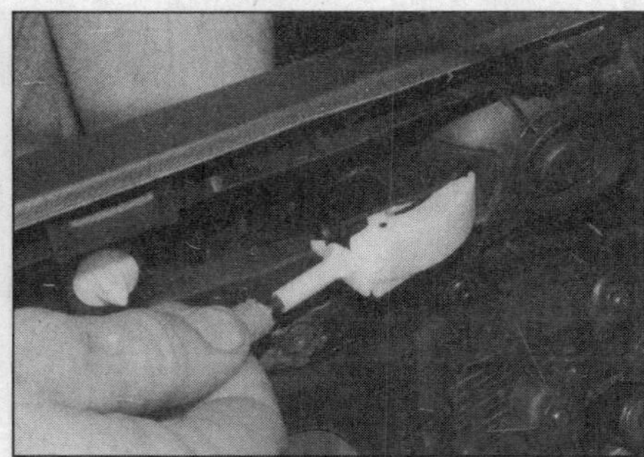
13.31 Reconnect the cable to the lock lever

*g) Do **not** close the door until you are completely satisfied that the lock is working correctly. If the door is accidentally closed, it may not be possible to open the door without cutting the door outer skin.*

h) Refit the plastic sealing cap to the door end panel.

34 Reseal the plastic sound insulation panel to the door. Refit the trim panel as described in Section 12.

Front door exterior handle up to 09/00

35 Ensure that the lock lever is positioned correctly **(see illustration 13.27)**. If not, insert a screwdriver through the aperture in the door end panel, and move the lever outwards.

36 Insert the front of the handle into the corresponding hole in the door skin, followed by the rear of the handle. Hold the handle gently again the door and push it forward until it 'clicks' into place.

37 If refitting the driver's door handle, refit the lock cylinder as described in Paragraphs 43 to 45. If refitting the passenger's handle, fit the outer handle rear cover into place, and tighten the retaining bolt securely. Refit the grommet to the door end panel.

38 Do not close the door until the operation of the lock has been set-up and checked as described in Paragraph 33. Reseal the plastic sound insulation panel to the door. Refit the trim panel as described in Section 12.

Front door exterior handle from 09/00

39 Prior to refitting the handle, the door lock must be in the 'installation position'. The distance between the lock actuator mounting and the outer door plate must not exceed 8 mm **(see illustration)**. If the distance is greater, pull the mounting outwards with a finger, until the measurement is correct.

40 Insert the front edge of the handle into the corresponding hole in the door, and then push the rear of the handle into place. Ensure the seal between the handle and door skin is not distorted. Turn the lock actuator bolt fully clockwise to release the handle lock from the installation position.

41 If refitting the driver's door handle, refit the lock cylinder as described in Paragraphs 43 to 45. If refitting the passenger's handle, fit the outer handle rear cover into place, and tighten the retaining bolt securely. Refit the grommet to the door end panel.

42 Do not close the door until the operation of the lock has been set-up and checked as described in Paragraph 33. Reseal the plastic sound insulation panel to the door. Refit the trim panel as described in Section 12.

Front door lock cylinder

43 If separated, clip the plastic cover back onto the cylinder.

44 Lubricate the outside of the lock cylinder with a suitable grease.

45 Refit the lock cylinder into the door lock, and tighten the retaining bolt securely. Refit the plastic grommet into the door end panel.

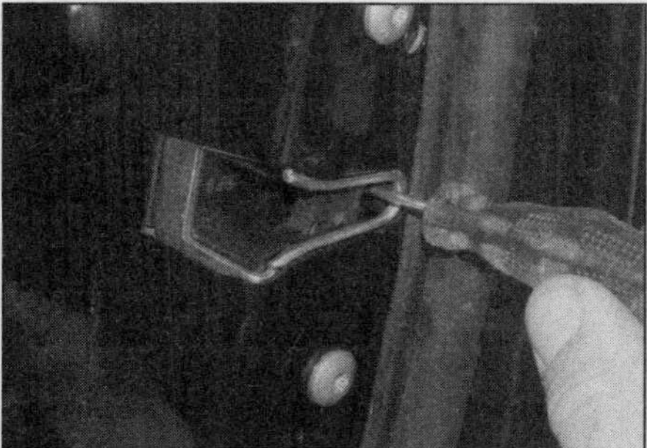

13.33 Use a screwdriver to 'close' the door lock

Before closing the door, check the lock operation as described in Paragraph 33.

Rear door lock

46 Prior to refitting, remove all traces of old locking compound from the lock retaining bolts.

47 Prior to refitting the lock, slacken the lock adjustment screw. The screw has a left-hand thread on right-hand door locks, and a right-hand thread on left-hand door locks **(see illustration)**.

48 Manoeuvre the lock assembly into position, ensuring that the lock button linkage engages correctly with the hole in the door. Make sure that the lock lever is inserted between the outer door handle support member, and the outer door skin.

49 Apply fresh locking compound to the lock bolts (BMW recommend Loctite 270) then refit them and tighten them to the specified torque. Reconnect the wiring connector(s) and secure the wiring in position with the relevant clips.

50 On all vehicles from 09/00, reconnect the cable to the lock lever, and refit the cable outer to the retaining bracket.

51 Check the operation of the lock assembly as described in Paragraph 33.

52 Reseal the plastic sound insulation panel to the door. Refit the trim panel as described in Section 12.

Rear door exterior handle up to 09/00

53 Ensure that the lock lever is positioned correctly **(see illustration)**. If not, insert a screwdriver through the aperture at the rear of the handle, and move the lever outwards.

13.47 Slacken the lock adjustment screw

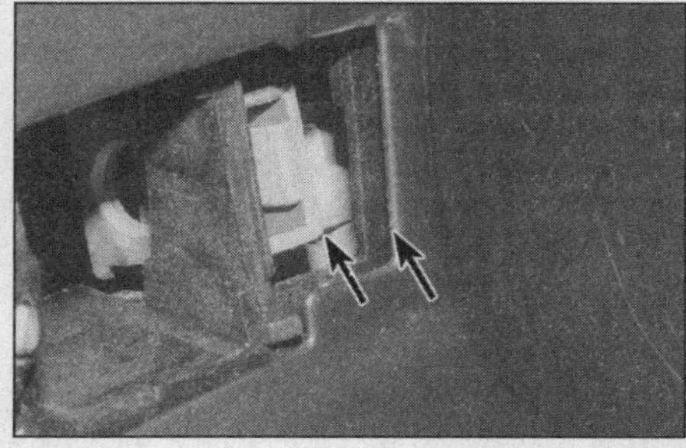

13.39 The distance between the mounting and the door plate (arrowed) must not exceed 8 mm

54 Insert the front of the handle into the corresponding hole in the door skin, followed by the rear of the handle. Hold the handle gently again the door and push it forward until it 'clicks' into place.

55 Refit the outer handle rear cover into place, and tighten the retaining bolt securely. Refit the grommet to the door end panel.

56 Do not close the door until the operation of the lock has been set-up and checked as described in Paragraph 33.

57 Reseal the plastic sound insulation panel to the door. Refit the trim panel as described in Section 12.

Rear door exterior handle from 09/00

58 Prior to refitting the handle, the door lock must be in the 'installation position'. The distance between the lock actuator mounting and the outer door plate must not exceed 8 mm **(see illustration 13.39)**. If the distance is greater, pull the mounting outwards with a finger, until the measurement is correct.

59 Insert the front edge of the handle into the corresponding hole in the door, and then push the rear of the handle into place. Ensure the seal between the handle and door skin is not distorted.

60 Refit the outer handle rear cover into place, and tighten the retaining bolt securely. Refit the grommet to the door end panel.

61 Do not close the door until the operation of the lock has been set-up and checked as described in Paragraph 33.

62 Reseal the plastic sound insulation panel to the door. Refit the trim panel as described in Section 12.

13.53 Ensure the lock lever is pulled to the outside of the door

14 Door glass and regulator (Saloon and Touring) – removal and refitting

Removal

Front door window

Note: *BMW state that each time the window is released from the fixing clamps, the plastic 'holders' in the clamps must be renewed.*

1 Fully open the window then raise it approximately 140 mm (measured at the rear of the glass).

2 On models with electric windows, disconnect the battery negative lead (see Chapter 5A).

3 Remove the inner trim panel and the sound insulation panel (Section 12).

4 Starting at the rear using a wide, flat-bladed tool, carefully lever up the window outer sealing strip from the door skin **(see illustration)**. Use a length of cardboard between the door and the tool to prevent damage to the paintwork.

5 Slacken the front and rear window clamp bolts **(see illustrations)**.

6 Lifting the rear first, remove the window from the vehicle **(see illustration)**.

Front door window regulator

7 Release the door window from the regulator clamps, as described earlier in this Section. Note that there is no need to remove the window from the door, simply use adhesive tape, or rubber wedges, to secure the window in the fully closed position.

8 Undo the bolts securing the rear window guide to the door, and lower the guide to the base of the door **(see illustration)**.

9 On models with electric windows, disconnect the window regulator wiring plugs, and release the harness from any retaining clips.

10 On all models, undo the regulator/motor mounting nuts, release any retaining clips, and lower the assembly to the base of the door. Manoeuvre the assembly from the door, rear edge first **(see illustrations)**.

11 Where applicable, undo the retaining Torx bolts and separate the motor from the regulator **(see illustrations)**.

Rear door window glass

Note: *BMW state that each time the window is released from the fixing clamps, the plastic 'holders' in the clamps must be renewed.*

12 Remove the door inner trim panel and sound insulation panel as described in Section 12.

13 Using a wide, flat-bladed tool, carefully lever up the window outer sealing strip from

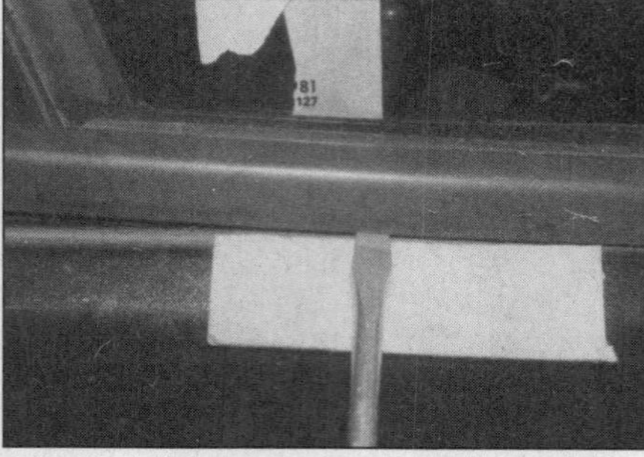

14.4 Place a strip of cardboard between the trim and the screwdriver to prevent damage

14.5a Slacken the window rear (arrowed) . . .

14.5b . . . and front (arrowed) clamp bolts

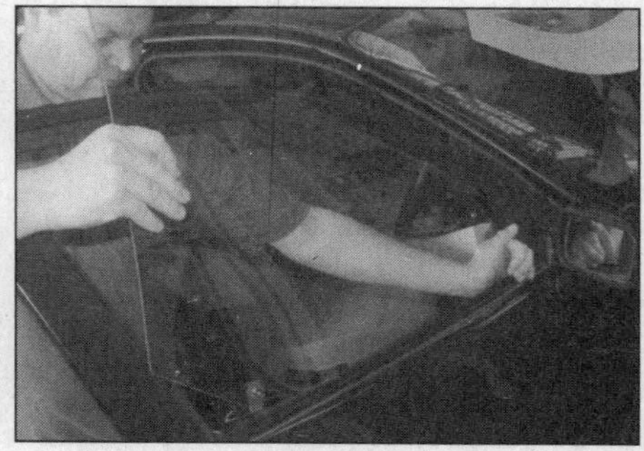

14.6 Lift the rear of the window first

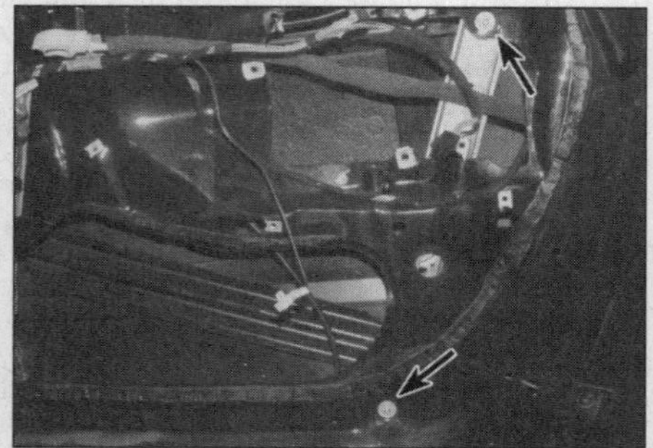

14.8 Remove the rear window guide bolts (arrowed)

14.10a Undo the regulator mounting bolts (arrowed) . . .

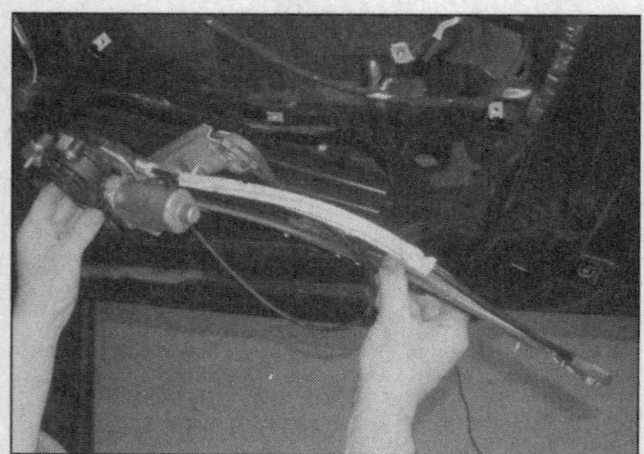

14.10b . . . and manoeuvre the assembly from the door

14.11a Undo the Torx bolts (arrowed) . . .

14.11b . . . and separate the motor from the regulator

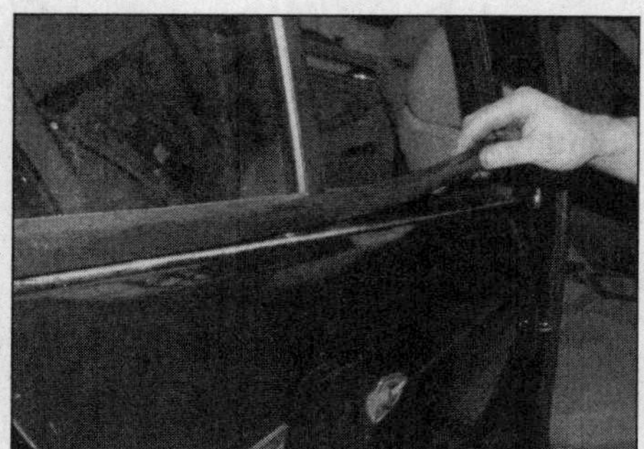

14.13 Carefully lever up the window outer sealing strip

the door skin **(see illustration)**. Use a length of cardboard between the door and the tool to prevent damage to the paintwork.

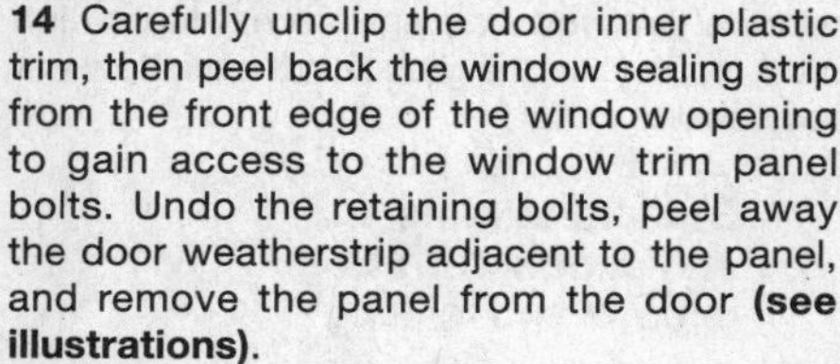

14 Carefully unclip the door inner plastic trim, then peel back the window sealing strip from the front edge of the window opening to gain access to the window trim panel bolts. Undo the retaining bolts, peel away the door weatherstrip adjacent to the panel, and remove the panel from the door **(see illustrations)**.

15 Fully lower the window, then raise it approximately 115 mm, measured at the front edge. On models with electric windows, disconnect the battery negative lead as described in Chapter 5A.

16 Slacken the window clamp bolt **(see illustration)**.

17 Manoeuvre the window out through the top of the door.

Rear door fixed window glass

18 As the rear door fixed window is bonded in place, renewal of the window should be entrusted to a BMW dealer or automotive window specialist.

Rear door window regulator

19 Remove the door inner trim panel and sound insulation panel, as described in Section 12.

20 Fully lower the window, then raise it approximately 115 mm, measured at the front edge, so that the window clamp bolt is visible. Slacken the window clamp bolt and lift the window to the top of the door frame **(see illustration 14.16)**. Secure the window in place using adhesive tape or rubber wedges **(see illustration)**.

21 On models with electric rear windows, disconnect the battery negative lead as described in Chapter 5A. Disconnect the regulator motor wiring plug **(see illustration)**, and release the harness from any retaining clips.

22 On all models, undo the regulator/motor securing bolts, release any retaining clips and lift out the lower end of the assembly, and manoeuvre it from the door **(see illustration)**.

23 Where applicable, undo the two retaining bolts, and remove the motor from the regulator **(see illustration)**.

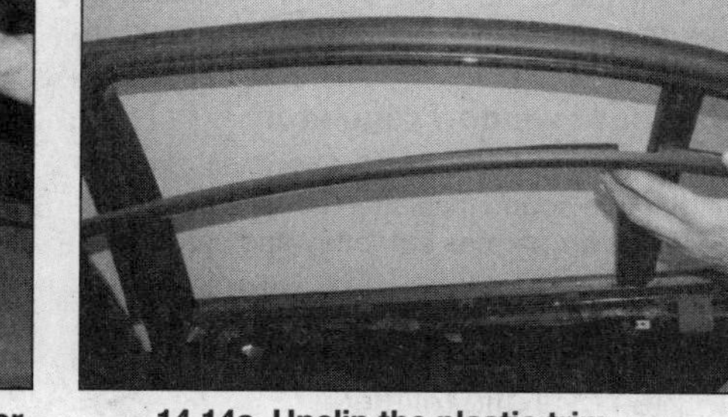

14.14a Unclip the plastic trim . . .

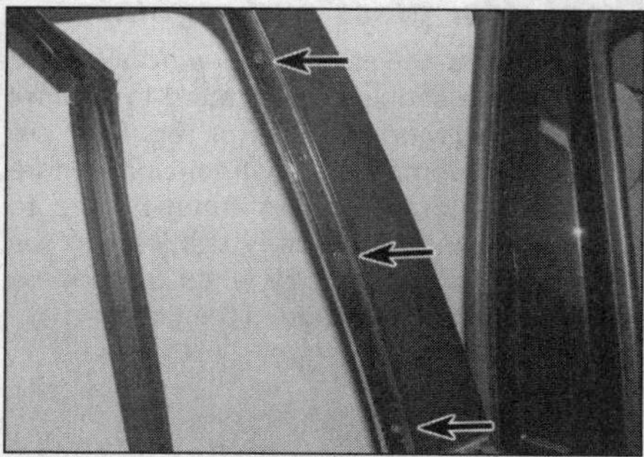

14.14c . . . undo the bolts (arrowed) and remove the trim

Rear side fixed window (Touring)

24 As the rear side fixed window is bonded in place, renewal of the window should be entrusted to a BMW dealer or automotive window specialist.

14.20 Secure the window using tape

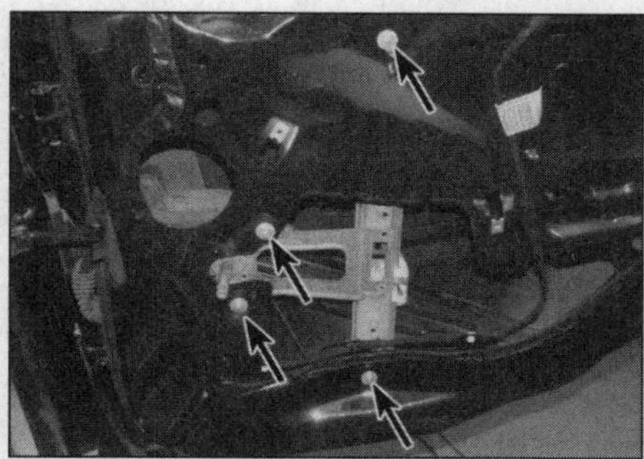

14.22 Undo the regulator mounting bolts (arrowed)

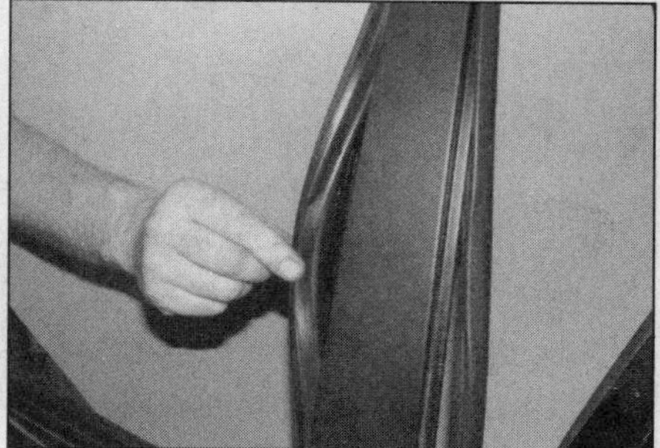

14.14b . . . peel back the sealing strips . . .

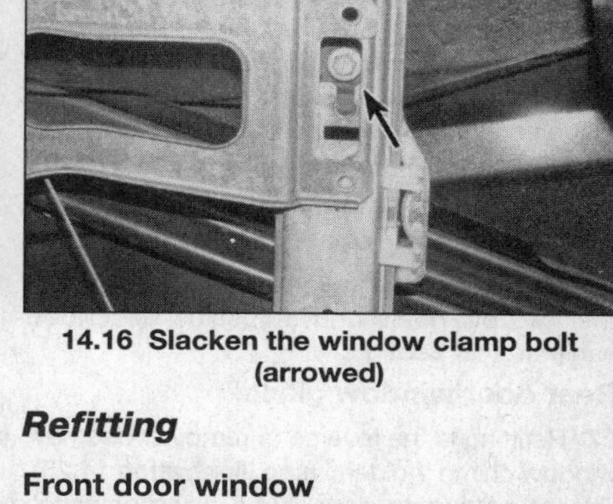

14.16 Slacken the window clamp bolt (arrowed)

Refitting

Front door window

25 Refitting is the reverse of removal. Smear the window outer sealing strip with a

14.21 Rear window regulator wiring plug (arrowed)

14.23 Rear window motor bolts (arrowed)

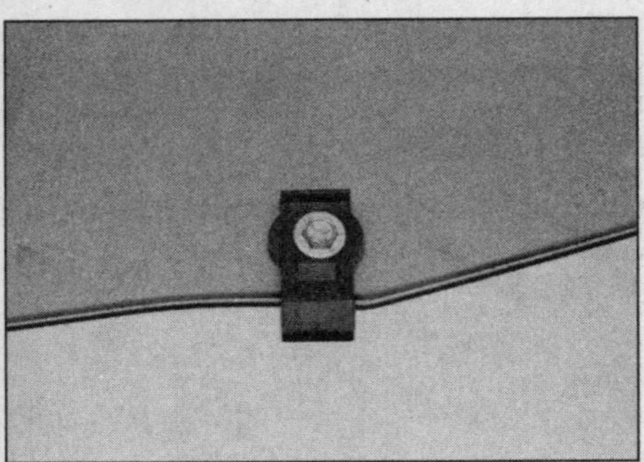

14.25 Renew the window clamp plastic holders

soapy solution (washing-up liquid). Use new window clamp 'holders' **(see illustration)**. Prior to fitting the door sound insulation panel, slacken the window rear guide securing bolts **(see illustration 14.8)**. Reconnect the battery negative lead (where applicable), and fully open the window. Tighten the rear window guide securing bolts. Operate the window and check that it moves easily and squarely in the door frame.

Front door window regulator

26 Refitting is the reverse of removal. Refit the window glass and adjust as described earlier in this Section.

Rear door window glass

27 Refitting is the reverse of removal. Use new window clamp 'holders' **(see illustration 14.25)**. Prior to refitting the door sound insulation panel, check that the window operates smoothly and easily.

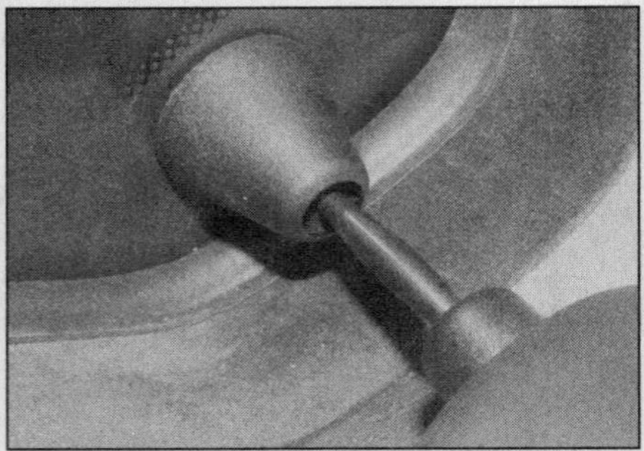

15.2 Lever the cap away from the window along the link rod

15.5 Undo the hinge retaining bolts (arrowed)

Rear door fixed window glass

28 Refitting is the reverse of removal making sure the window seal is correctly located in the door.

Rear door window regulator

29 Refitting is the reverse of removal. Prior to refitting the sound insulation panel, check that the window operates smoothly and easily.

15 Door glass, regulator and rear vent window (Coupe) – removal and refitting

Front door glass and regulator

1 Removal of the front door window glass and regulator should be entrusted to a BMW dealer. If the window glass or regulator are disturbed a complex adjustment procedure must be performed on refitting. Failure to adjust the window properly will lead to the glass contacting the body when the door is shut, resulting in breakage of the glass.

Rear vent window

Removal

2 Using a plastic wedge, carefully lever away the plastic cap over the window link rod **(see illustration)**.

3 Lever the window link rod from the mounting on the window **(see illustration)**.

4 Remove the B-pillar trim as described in Section 27.

5 Lever out the plastic caps, and undo the two hinge retaining bolts in the B-pillar **(see illustration)**.

15.3 Detach the link rod from the mounting

16.1 Undo the toolbox hinge bolts (arrowed)

6 Slide the window to the rear.

Refitting

7 Before tightening the hinge bolts, adjust the window position as follows:

a) *The distance from the rear edge of the front door window to the edge of the rear vent window sealing strip should not exceed 6 mm.*

b) *The distance from the top edge of the vent window to the rain gutter rail should be 1 mm.*

c) *The distance from the rear edge of the vent window to the rain gutter rail should be no more than 1.8 mm.*

8 The remainder of refitting is a reversal of removal, noting that the plastic cap over the window link rod has an internal lug which must locate over the groove in the window link rod socket.

16 Boot lid/tailgate and support struts – removal and refitting

Removal

Boot lid

1 Open the boot, remove the toolbox lid retaining bolt and the toolbox hinge bolts **(see illustration)**. Remove the toolbox from the boot trim panel.

2 Prise up the centre pins and remove the plastic expanding rivets, then remove the trim panel from the boot lid.

3 Support the boot lid in the open position and unclip the support struts (refer to paragraph 8).

4 Disconnect the wiring connectors from the number plate lights, luggage compartment light switch and central locking servo (as applicable) and tie a piece of string to the end of the wiring. Noting the correct routing of the wiring harness, release the harness rubber grommets from the boot lid and withdraw the wiring. When the end of the wiring appears, untie the string and leave it in position in the boot lid; it can then be used on refitting to draw the wiring into position.

5 Draw around the outline of each hinge with a

16.5 Make alignment marks around the hinges

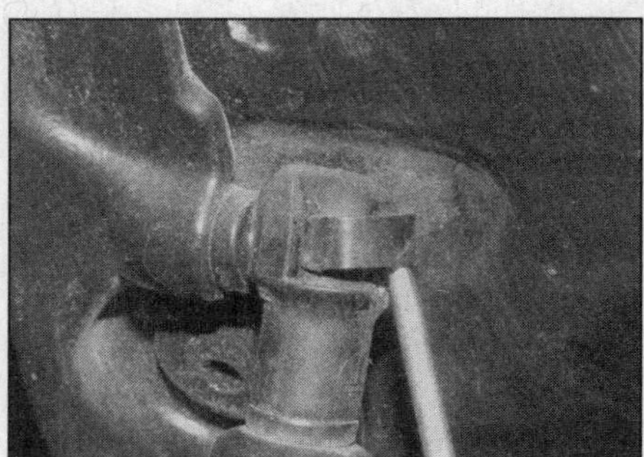

16.8 Prise out the strut retaining clip

suitable marker pen then slacken and remove the hinge retaining bolts and remove the boot lid from the vehicle **(see illustration)**.

6 Inspect the hinges for signs of wear or damage and renew if necessary; the hinges are secured to the vehicle by bolts.

Tailgate

7 Removal and refitting of the tailgate requires special BMW bodywork tools, and the experience to use them. Consequently, we recommend that this task be entrusted to a BMW dealer or suitably-equipped specialist.

Support struts

8 Support the boot lid/tailgate in the open position. Using a small flat-bladed screwdriver raise the spring clip, and pull the support strut off its upper mounting **(see illustration)**. Repeat the procedure on the lower strut mounting and remove the strut from the vehicle.

Refitting

Boot lid

9 Refitting is the reverse of removal, aligning the hinges with the marks made before removal.

10 On completion, close the boot lid and check its alignment with the surrounding panels. If necessary slight adjustment can be made by slackening the retaining bolts and repositioning the boot lid on its hinges. If the paintwork around the hinges has been damaged, paint the affected area with a suitable touch-in brush to prevent corrosion.

Support struts

11 Refitting is a reverse of the removal procedure, ensuring that the strut is securely retained by its retaining clips.

17 Boot lid/tailgate lock components – removal and refitting

Removal

Saloon & Coupe boot lid lock

1 Open the boot, remove the toolbox lid retaining bolt and the toolbox hinge bolts **(see illustration)**. Remove the toolbox from the boot trim panel.

2 Prise up the centre pins and remove the plastic expanding rivets, then remove the trim panel from the boot lid.

3 Disconnect the wiring plug, undo the two bolts and, starting at the edge adjacent to the lock, carefully pull away the cover panel from the lock **(see illustration)**.

4 Disconnect the lock wiring plug.

5 Undo the three bolts, and manoeuvre the lock from the boot lid. Lever away the actuating rod from the lock as it is withdrawn **(see illustration)**.

Saloon & Coupe boot lid lock cylinder

6 Remove the trim panel from the boot lid as described in Paragraphs 1 and 2.

7 Remove the driver's side rear light assembly as described in Chapter 12, Section 7.

8 With the light removed, undo the two retaining bolts, and remove the cover from the rear of the lock cylinder.

9 Disconnect the lock cylinder wiring plug.

10 Pull out the locking piece, then carefully pull the actuating rod from the lock cylinder arm **(see illustration)**.

11 Undo the two retaining bolts, and rotate the cylinder clockwise until the lock brackets line up with the cut-outs in the panel, then pull the lock from the panel **(see illustration)**.

Touring tailgate lock

12 Remove both D-pillar trims as described in Section 27.

13 Prise out the plastic caps, and undo the four retaining bolts from the top of the tailgate sill trim panel, then undo the two lower bolts. Manoeuvre the panel from the vehicle **(see illustration)**.

14 Using a marker pen, make alignment marks between the lock and the panel. Undo the four bolts and remove the lock **(see**

17.1 Toolbox lid hinge bolts (arrowed)

17.3 Disconnect the boot lock assembly wiring plug

17.5 Boot lid lock retaining bolts (arrowed)

17.10 Pull out the locking piece (arrowed)

17.11 Lock cylinder retaining bolts (arrowed)

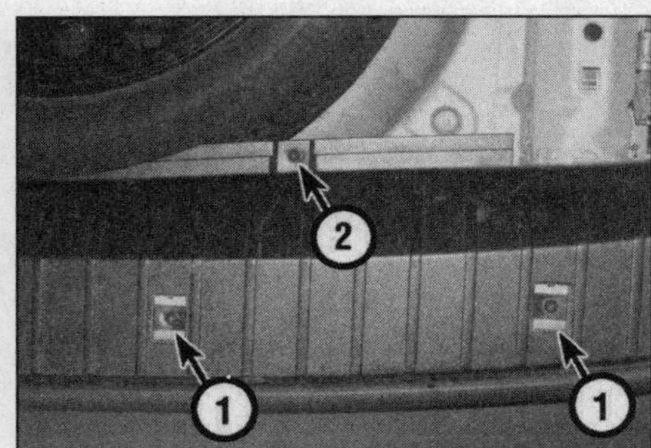

17.13 Prise out the caps and undo the upper bolts (1) and lower bolts (2)

17.14 Undo the tailgate lock retaining bolts (arrowed)

illustration). Disconnect the wiring plug as the lock is withdrawn.

15 If required, undo the two retaining bolts and remove the lock actuator from the lock.

Refitting

16 Refitting is a reversal of removal, noting the following points:

a) *Reconnect all wiring plugs, and secure the wiring harnesses using the retaining clips (where applicable).*

b) *Match up any previously-made alignment marks.*

c) *Check the operation of the locks/cylinders before refitting the trim panels.*

d) *Tighten all fasteners securely.*

18 Central locking components – removal and refitting

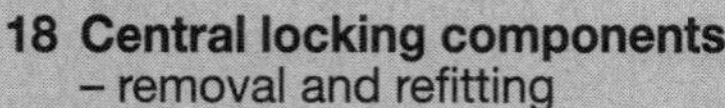

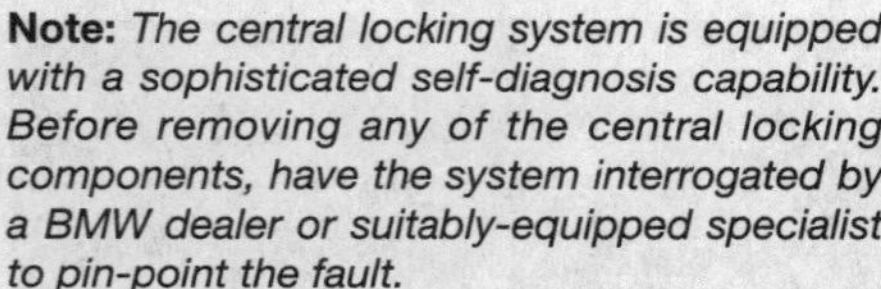

Note: *The central locking system is equipped with a sophisticated self-diagnosis capability. Before removing any of the central locking components, have the system interrogated by a BMW dealer or suitably-equipped specialist to pin-point the fault.*

Removal

Electronic control unit (ECU)

1 The central locking system is controlled by the central body electronics (ZKE V) control unit, known as the General Module (GM V), which is located behind the passenger side glovebox. To access the control unit, remove the glovebox as described in Section 27.

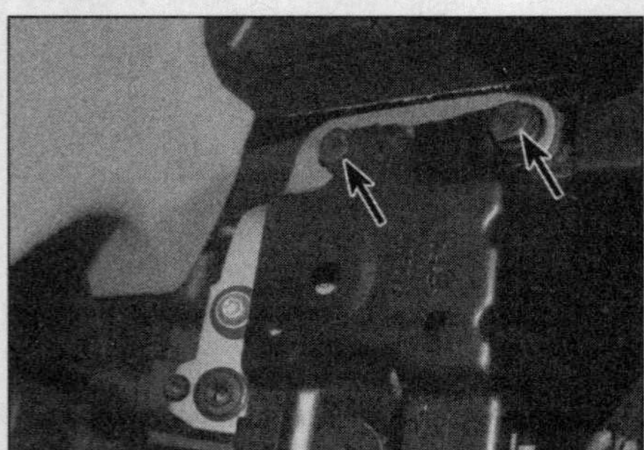

19.10 Remove the motor mounting bolts (arrowed)

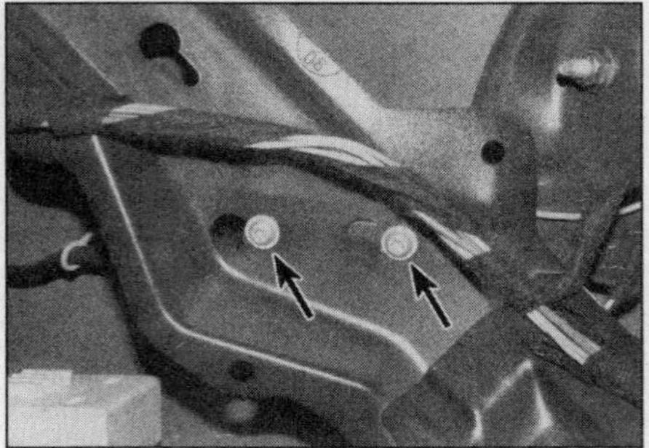

18.10 Fuel filler flap solenoid bolts (arrowed)

2 Release the retaining clips and lower the ECU out of position.

3 Release the retaining clip then disconnect the wiring connector(s) and remove the ECU from the vehicle.

Door lock actuator

4 The actuator is integral with the door lock assembly. Remove the door lock as described in Section 13.

Boot lock actuator

5 The boot lid actuator is integral with the boot lock assembly. Remove the boot lock as described in Section 17.

Tailgate lock actuator

6 Remove the tailgate lock as described in Section 17.

7 Undo the two retaining bolts and remove the actuator from the lock.

Fuel filler flap solenoid

8 Rotate the retaining clip through 90° and partially remove the right-hand luggage compartment side trim panel.

9 Lift out the first aid box plate and peel back the luggage compartment trim to reveal the solenoid.

10 Disconnect the wiring connector then slacken the retaining bolts and manoeuvre the solenoid out from the luggage compartment **(see illustration)**.

Glovebox lock solenoid

11 Remove the glovebox (see Section 27).

12 Unclip the solenoid rod from the lock and guide then undo the retaining bolts and remove the solenoid.

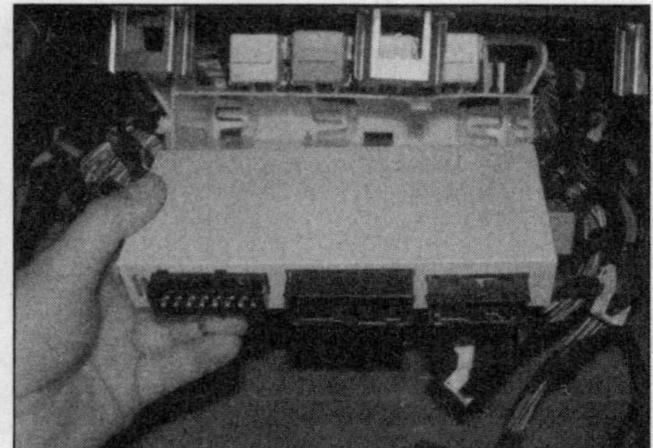

19.14 Release the clips and remove the ECU

Refitting

13 Refitting is the reverse of removal. Prior to refitting any trim panels removed for access thoroughly check the operation of the central locking system.

19 Electric window components – removal and refitting

Note: *The electric window system is equipped with a sophisticated self-diagnosis capability. Should a fault develop, before removing any of the electric window electronics, have the system interrogated by a BMW dealer or suitably-equipped specialist to pin-point the fault.*

Window switches

1 Refer to Chapter 12, Section 4.

Saloon & Touring window motors

2 Remove the window regulator as described in Section 14.

3 Slacken and remove the retaining bolts and remove the motor from the regulator.

4 On refitting, fit the motor to the regulator and securely tighten its retaining bolts.

5 Refit the regulator assembly as described in Section 14.

Coupe front window motors

6 Removal and refitting of the motors requires the regulator to be removed from the door. This task should be entrusted to a BMW dealer (see Section 15).

Coupe side window motor

7 Using a plastic wedge, carefully lever away the plastic cap over the window link rod **(see illustration 15.2)**.

8 Lever the window link rod front the mounting on the window **(see illustration 15.3)**.

9 To remove the plastic trim over the motor, press in the centre pin and remove the expanding rivet. Manoeuvre the trim over the motor link rod.

10 Undo the two mounting bolts, and remove the motor with the bracket **(see illustration)**. Disconnect the wiring plug as the motor is withdrawn.

11 If required, undo the two bolts and separate the motor from the bracket.

12 Refitting is a reversal of removal, noting that the plastic cap over the link rod has an inner lug which locates in the groove of the window link rod socket.

Electronic control unit (ECU)

13 The electric window system is controlled by the central body electronics (ZKE V) control unit, known as the General Module (GM V), which is located behind the passenger side glovebox. To access the control unit, remove the glovebox as described in Section 27.

14 Release the retaining clips and lower the ECU out of position **(see illustration)**.

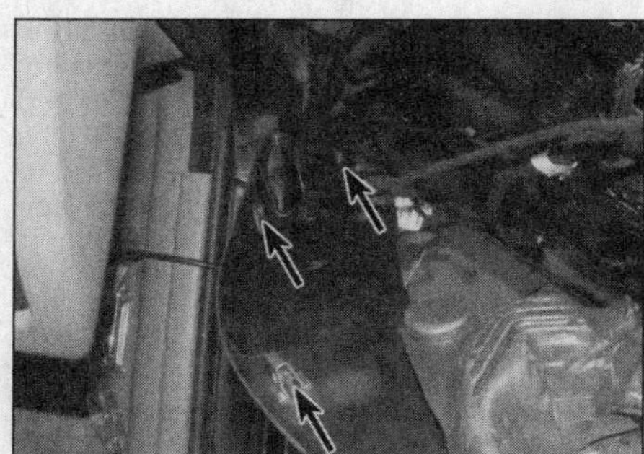
20.2a Note the clips securing the plastic trim at the front of the door edge (arrowed)

20.2b On Coupe models, lift the trim from position

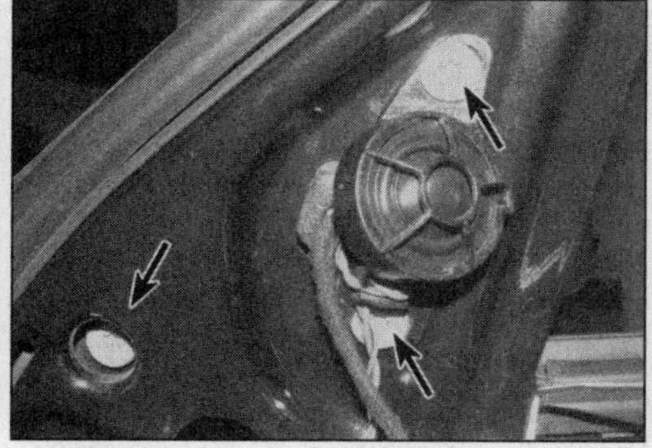
20.3 The mirror is secured by three Torx bolts (arrowed)

15 Release the retaining clip then disconnect the wiring connector(s) and remove the ECU from the vehicle.

20 Mirrors and associated components – removal and refitting

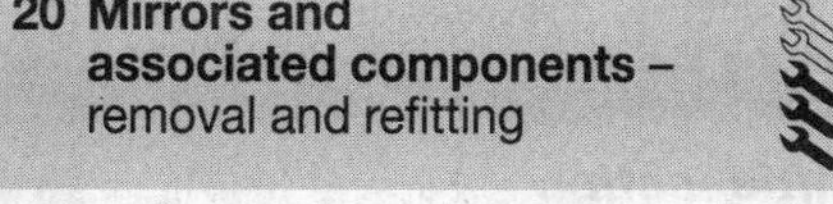

Exterior mirror assembly

1 Remove the door inner trim panel as described in Section 12.

2 Carefully pull the plastic trim away from the front inner edge of the door. On Coupe models, carefully prise away the top of the triangular plastic trim over the mirror mounting, then lift it from position **(see illustrations)**.

3 Undo the retaining Torx bolts and remove the mirror from the door. Recover the rubber seal which is fitted between the door and mirror; if the seal is damaged it must be renewed **(see illustration)**. Disconnect any wiring plugs as the mirror is withdrawn.

4 Refitting is the reverse of removal, tightening the mirror bolts to the specified torque.

Exterior mirror glass

Note: *If the mirror glass is removed when the mirror is cold the glass retaining clips are likely to break.*

5 Tilt the mirror glass fully upwards.

6 Insert a wide plastic or wooden wedge in between the base of the mirror glass and mirror housing, and carefully prise the glass from the motor **(see illustration)**. Take great care when removing the glass; do not use excessive force as the glass is easily broken.

7 Remove the glass from the mirror and, where necessary, disconnect the wiring connectors from the mirror heating element.

8 On refitting, reconnect the wiring to the glass and clip the glass onto the motor, taking great care not to break it.

Exterior mirror switch

9 Refer to Chapter 12.

Exterior mirror motor

10 Remove the mirror glass as described above.

11 Undo the three retaining bolts and pull the motor from position, lower edge first **(see illustration)**. Disconnect the wiring plug as the motor is withdrawn.

12 Refitting is the reversal of removal.

Exterior mirror housing cover

13 Remove the mirror glass as described above.

14 Release the four retaining clips and remove the mirror housing cover to the front **(see illustration)**.

15 Refitting is a reversal of removal.

Interior mirror

16 There are essentially two different types of mirror arms and mountings. One type has a plastic cover over the plug connection, and the other type has a mirror arm which splits in two to reveal the wiring plug.

Plastic cover type arm

17 Carefully lever out the plastic cover, and disconnect the mirror wiring plug (where applicable).

18 Strike the lower part of the mirror forwards with the ball of your hand to unclip the arm from the mounting.

Caution: Do not twist the arm whilst attempting removal as the clip will be damaged, and do not pull the arm to the rear as the windscreen may be damaged.

Split cover mirror arm

19 Press the two sides of the arm covers towards the mirror and pull the two sides apart. On mirrors equipped with a rain sensor, press up at the base of the covers and pull the two sides apart **(see illustrations)**.

20 Push the right-hand side of the mirror upwards and towards the front. Swivel the left-hand arm cover to the left and unclip it from the metal part of the arm.

21 Push the left-hand side of the mirror

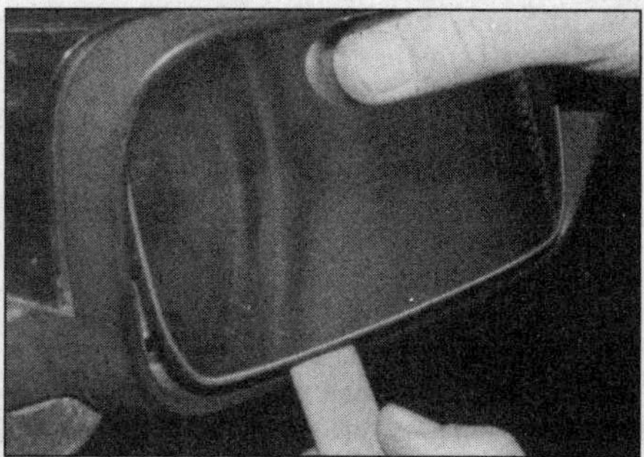
20.6 Carefully prise the mirror glass from the positioning motor

20.11 Undo the three bolt (arrowed) and pull the motor, lower edge first, from the housing

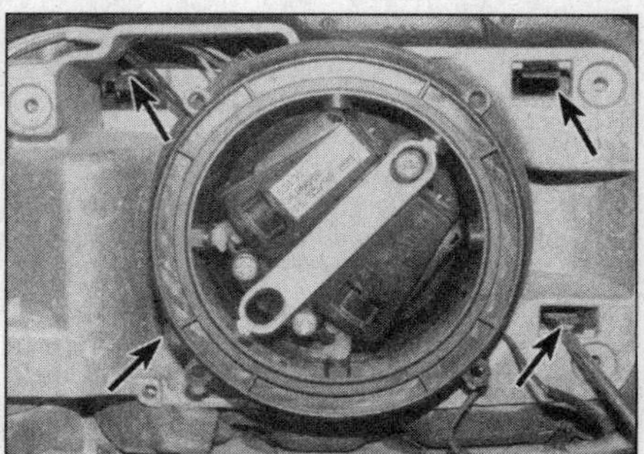
20.14 Release the retaining clips (arrowed) and remove the mirror housing cover

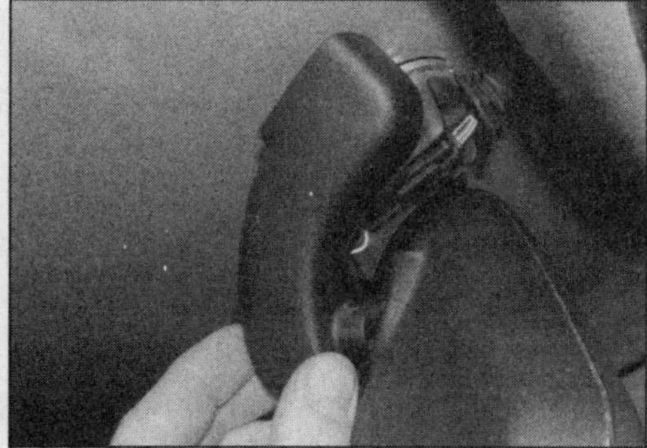
20.19a Pull the two sides of the cover apart

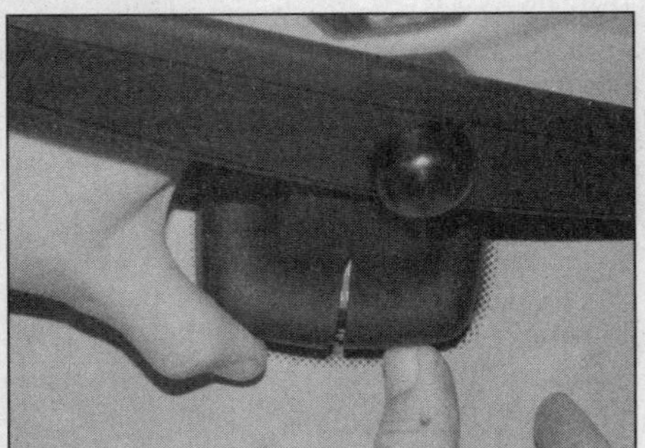
20.19b Press up at the base and pull the two sides apart

upwards and towards the front. Swivel the right-hand arm cover to the right and unclip it from the arm.

22 Disconnect the mirror wiring plug.

23 Strike the lower part of the mirror forwards with the ball of your hand to unclip the arm from the mounting.

Caution: Do not twist the arm whilst attempting removal as the clip will be damaged, and do not pull the arm to the rear as the windscreen may be damaged.

All types

24 To refit the mirrors, position the mirror arm over the mounting at an angle of 45° to the vertical on the driver's side. Push the arm to the vertical and check that it engaged correctly **(see illustration)**. Where applicable, refit the covers and reconnect the wiring plug.

21 Windscreen and rear screen/tailgate glass – general information

1 These areas of glass are secured by the tight fit of the weatherstrip in the body aperture, and are bonded in position with a special adhesive. Renewal of such fixed glass is a difficult, messy and time-consuming task, which is beyond the scope of the home mechanic. It is difficult, unless one has plenty of practice, to obtain a secure, waterproof fit. Furthermore, the task carries a high risk of breakage; this applies especially to the laminated glass windscreen. In view of this, owners are strongly advised to have this sort of work carried out by one of the many

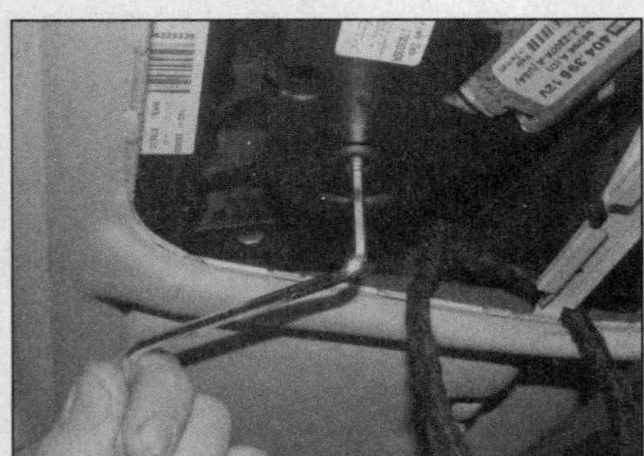
22.2 Insert the tool into the motor spindle

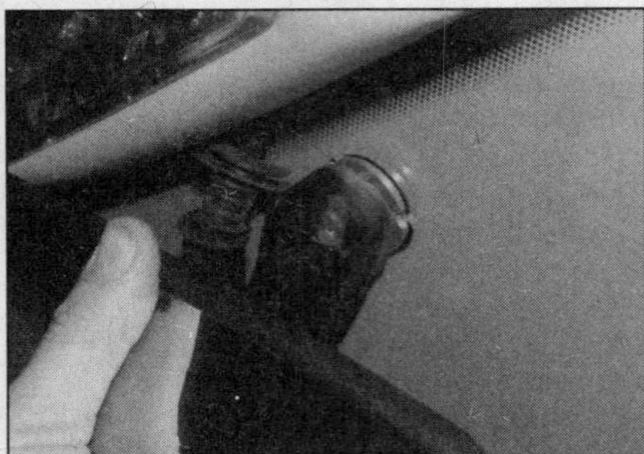
20.24 Position the mirror arm over the mounting at an angle of 45°

specialist windscreen fitters.

Touring rear screen

2 Although on these models the rear screen opens independently of the tailgate, to remove the screen the rear spoiler must be removed. This is a complex task requiring specialist bodywork tools, and experience. Any attempt to remove the spoiler without the necessary equipment is very likely to result in damage. Consequently, we recommend that this work is entrusted to a BMW dealer or suitably-equipped specialist.

22 Sunroof – general information, motor renewal and initialisation

General information

1 Due to the complexity of the sunroof mechanism, considerable expertise is needed to repair, renew or adjust the sunroof components successfully. Removal of the roof first requires the headlining to be removed, which is a complex and tedious operation, and not a task to be undertaken lightly. Therefore, any problems with the sunroof (except sunroof motor renewal) should be referred to a BMW dealer or specialist.

2 On models with an electric sunroof, if the sunroof motor fails to operate, first check the relevant fuse. If the fault cannot be traced and rectified, the sunroof can be opened and closed manually using an Allen key to turn the motor spindle (a suitable key is supplied

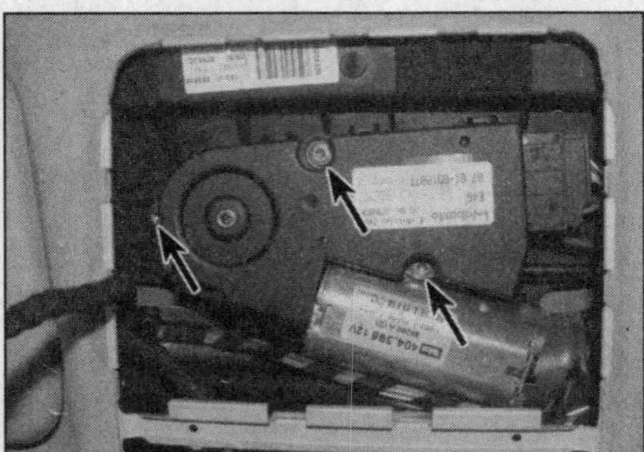
22.5 Sunroof motor bolts (arrowed)

with the vehicle tool kit). To gain access to the motor, unclip the cover from the headlining. Remove the Allen key from the tool kit and insert it into the motor spindle. Disconnect the motor wiring connector and rotate the key to move the sunroof to the required position **(see illustration)**.

Motor renewal

3 Carefully prise the interior light unit from the headlining between the sunvisors. Disconnect the wiring plug(s) as the unit is withdrawn.

4 Carefully pull the front edge of the motor panel down and remove it complete with the switch. Disconnect the wiring plug as the panel is withdrawn.

5 Undo the three retaining bolts, and pull the motor from its location. Disconnect the wiring plug as the motor is removed **(see illustration)**.

6 Refitting is a reversal of removal, but carry out the initialisation procedure as described next.

Initialisation

7 With the battery reconnected, and the ignition on, press the sunroof operating switch into the 'tilt' position and hold it there.

8 Once the sunroof has reached the 'fully-tilted' position, hold the switch in that position for approximately 20 seconds. Initialisation is complete when the sunroof briefly lifts at the rear again.

23 Body exterior fittings – removal and refitting

Wheel arch liners and body under-panels

1 The various plastic covers fitted to the underside of the vehicle are secured in position by a mixture of bolts, nuts and retaining clips, and removal will be fairly obvious on inspection. Work methodically around, removing its retaining bolts and releasing its retaining clips until the panel is free and can be removed from the underside of the vehicle. Most clips used on the vehicle are simply prised out of position. Other clips can be released by unscrewing/prising out the centre pins and then removing the clip.

2 On refitting, renew any retaining clips that may have been broken on removal, and ensure that the panel is securely retained by all the relevant clips and bolts.

Body trim strips and badges

3 The various body trim strips and badges are held in position with a special adhesive tape. Removal requires the trim/badge to be heated, to soften the adhesive, and then cut away from the surface. Due to the high risk of damage to the vehicle's paintwork during this operation, it is recommended that this task should be entrusted to a BMW dealer or suitably-equipped specialist.

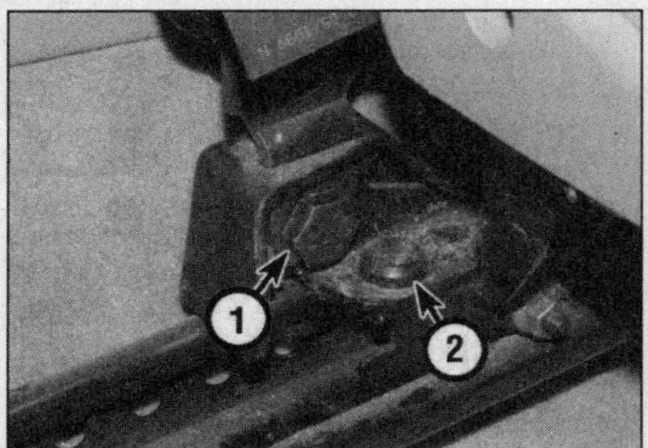

24.3 Front seat belt bolt (1) and seat rail bolt (2)

24.5 Prise the caps from the seat retaining nuts

24.7 Slide out the locking element (arrowed) and disconnect the seat wiring plug

Rear spoiler (Touring)

4 This is a complex task requiring specialist bodywork tools, and experience. Any attempt to remove the spoiler without the necessary equipment is very likely to result in damage. Consequently, we recommend that this work is entrusted to a BMW dealer or suitably-equipped specialist.

24 Seats and positioning motors – removal and refitting

Front seat removal

1 Disconnect the battery negative lead as described in Chapter 5A.

2 Slide the seat fully forwards and raise the seat cushion fully.

3 On Saloon and Touring models, undo the bolt and disconnect the seatbelt anchorage bracket from the seat rail **(see illustration)**.

4 Slacken and remove the bolts and washers securing the rear of the seat rails to the floor.

5 Slide the seat fully backwards and remove the trim caps from the seat front mounting nuts/bolts, then slacken and remove the nuts/bolts and washers **(see illustration)**.

6 Slide the seat forward so that the ends of the runners are flush with the rails.

7 Working under the front of the seat, slide out the locking element, and disconnect the seat wiring plug **(see illustration)**.

8 Lift the seat out from the vehicle.

Folding rear seat removal

Saloon and Coupe

9 Pull up on the front of the seat cushion to release the left- and right-hand retaining clips, and remove it forwards and out from the vehicle. Disconnect the seat heating wiring connectors (where applicable) as the seat is withdrawn.

10 If required, pull down the rear seat armrest (where fitted) and unscrew it from the seat back **(see illustration)**.

11 Slacken and remove the bolts securing the seat belt lower mountings to the body.

12 Fold the seat backs forward, undo the centre mounting bolt, and remove the seats **(see illustration)**.

Touring

13 Release the rear seat backrest, and fold it forward.

14 The trim panel between the seat backrest and the door aperture must be removed. Pull the top of the trim forward to release the retaining clip, and then pull the trim panel upwards to remove it **(see illustration)**. Repeat this procedure on the remaining trim panel on the other side.

15 Undo the bolts and remove the rear seat backrest centre mounting bracket **(see illustration)**.

16 Undo the two bolts securing each side's backrest outer bracket **(see illustration)**.

17 Lift the backrest assembly in the centre and disengage the outer pivots from the guides. Manoeuvre the seats from the vehicle.

Fixed rear seat removal

18 Pull down the rear seat armrest (where fitted) and unclip it from the seat back.

19 Pull up on the seat base cushion to release the left- and right-hand retaining clips and remove it from the vehicle.

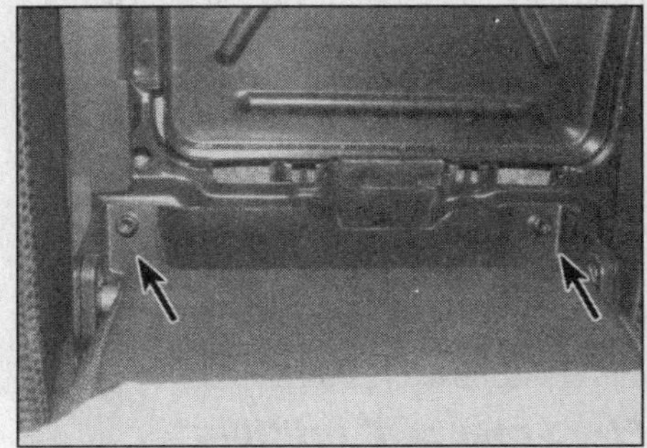
24.10 Undo the Torx bolts (arrowed) and remove the armrest from the seat back

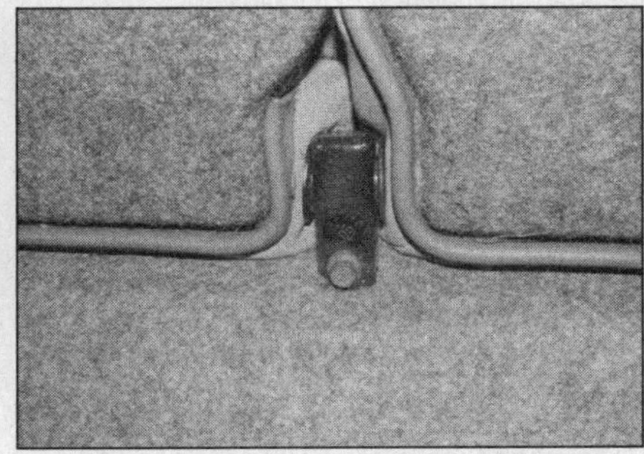
24.12 Undo the rear seat centre mounting bolt

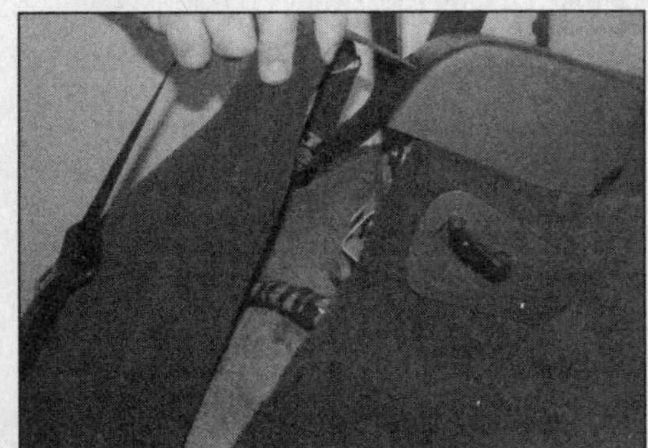
24.14 Pull the top of the trim forward to release it

24.15 Rear backrest centre mounting bracket

24.16 Rear backrest side mounting bracket

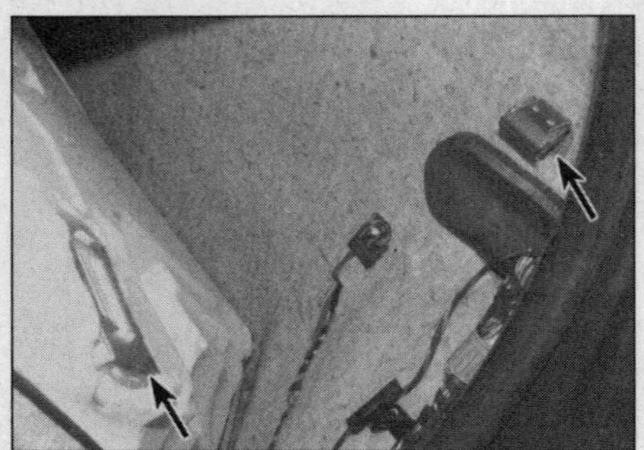

24.20 Note the clips at the top of the fixed seat back (arrowed)

24.29a Undo the two Torx bolts (arrowed) . . .

20 Unclip the top of the seat back then slide it upwards to release its lower retaining pins and remove it from the vehicle **(see illustration)**.

Front seat refitting

21 Refitting is the reverse of removal, noting the following points.

a) *On manually-adjusted seats, fit the seat retaining bolts and tighten them by hand only. Slide the seat fully forwards and then slide it back by two stops of the seat locking mechanism. Rock the seat to ensure that the seat locking mechanism is correctly engaged then tighten the mounting bolts securely.*

b) *On electrically-adjusted seats, ensure that the wiring is connected and correctly routed then tighten the seat mounting bolts securely.*

c) *On Saloon and Touring models tighten the seat belt mounting bolt to the specified torque.*

d) *Reconnect the battery negative lead as described in Chapter 5A.*

26.4 Front seat belt upper mounting bolt

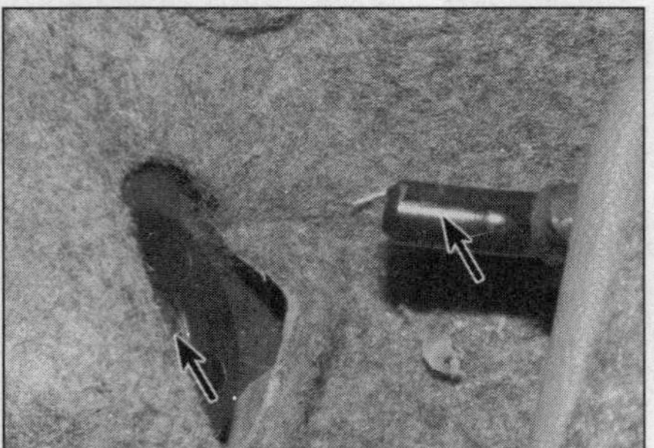

24.22 Rear seat outer locating hole and pivot (arrowed)

24.29b . . . and remove the seat positioning motor

Folding rear seat refitting

Saloon and Coupe

22 Refitting is the reverse of removal ensuring that the seat outer pivots engage correctly with the corresponding locating holes in the vehicle body **(see illustration)**. Tighten the seat belt lower mounting bolts to the specified torque setting.

Touring

23 Refitting is a reversal of removal.

24 Twist the upper retaining clip out the metal plate, and slide it into the backrest side section.

25 Locate the lower guides of the side trim panel into the corresponding brackets, and clip the upper edge into place. Refit the plastic trim at the top of the side panel.

Fixed rear seat refitting

26 Refitting is the reverse of removal, making sure the seat back lower locating pegs are correctly engaged with the body, and the seat belt buckles and lap belt are fed through the intended openings.

Front seat positioning motors

Removal

27 Remove the front seat as described previously in this Section.

28 Disconnect the wiring plug and remove it from the support bracket.

29 Undo the two Torx bolts and remove the motor from the drive gearbox **(see illustrations)**.

Refitting

30 Refitting is a reversal of removal. Tighten the motor mounting bolts securely.

25 Front seat belt tensioning mechanism – general information

1 Most models are fitted with a front seat belt tensioner system. The system is designed to instantaneously take up any slack in the seat belt in the case of a sudden frontal impact, therefore reducing the possibility of injury to the front seat occupants. Each front seat is fitted with its own system, the tensioner being situated on the inboard seat rail.

2 The seat belt tensioner is triggered by a frontal impact above a predetermined force. Lesser impacts, including impacts from behind, will not trigger the system.

3 When the system is triggered, a large spring in the tensioner mechanism retracts and locks the seat belt through a cable which acts on the inertia reel. This prevents the seat belt moving and keeps the occupant in position in the seat. Once the tensioner has been triggered, the seat belt will be permanently locked and the assembly must be renewed.

4 There is a risk of injury if the system is triggered inadvertently when working on the vehicle. If any work is to be carried out on the seat/seat belt disable the tensioner by disconnecting the battery negative lead (see Chapter 5A), and waiting at least 5 seconds before proceeding.

5 Also note the following warnings before contemplating any work on the front seat.

Warning: If the tensioner mechanism is dropped, it must be renewed, even it has suffered no apparent damage.

- ***Do not allow any solvents to come into contact with the tensioner mechanism.***
- ***Do not subject the seat to any form of shock as this could accidentally trigger the seat belt tensioner.***
- ***Check for any deformation of the seat belt stalk tensioner and anchorage brackets. Renew any that are damaged.***

26 Seat belt components – removal and refitting

Warning: Read Section 25 before proceeding.

Removal

Front seat belt – Saloon & Touring

1 Remove the front seat as described in Section 24.

2 Remove the B-pillar trim panel as described in Section 27.

3 Undo the bolts and remove the seat belt guide from the pillar.

4 Undo the bolt securing the upper seat belt mounting **(see illustration)**.

5 Unscrew the inertia reel retaining bolt and remove the seat belt from the door pillar **(see illustration)**.

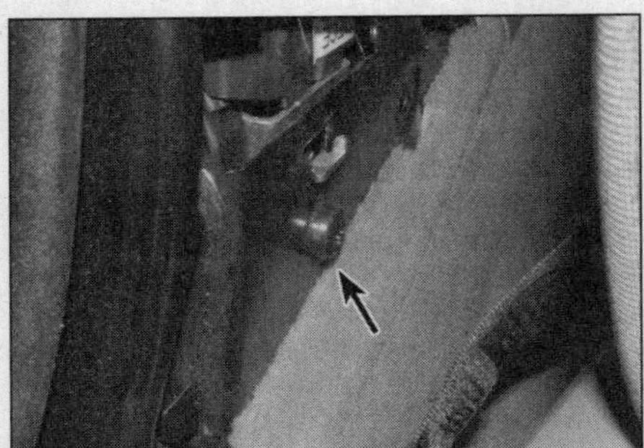

26.5 Front seat belt inertia reel mounting bolt (arrowed)

6 If necessary, undo the retaining bolts and remove the height adjustment mechanism from the door pillar.

Front seat belt – Coupe

7 Remove the front seat as described in Section 24.

8 Remove the B-pillar trim and the rear side trim panel as described in Section 27.

9 Prise off the plastic cap at the front of the seat belt lower anchorage bar, undo the securing bolt and slide the belt from the bar **(see illustration)**.

10 Undo the bolts and remove the seat belt guide from the pillar.

11 Undo the bolt securing the upper seat belt mounting.

12 Unscrew the inertia reel retaining bolt and remove the seat belt from the door pillar **(see illustration)**.

13 If necessary, undo the retaining bolts and remove the height adjustment mechanism from the door pillar.

Front seat belt stalk

14 Remove the seat as described in Section 24.

15 Release the tensioner wiring connector from the cable strap, and disconnect it **(see illustration)**.

16 Slacken and remove the stalk assembly retaining bolt and remove the assembly from the side of the seat **(see illustration)**.

Fixed rear seat side belts

17 Remove the rear seat as described in Section 24.

18 Slacken and remove the bolts and washers securing the rear seat belts to the vehicle body, and remove the centre belt and buckle.

19 Unclip the trim cover from the front of the parcel shelf and detach it from the seat belts.

20 Carefully unclip the left and right-hand trim panels from the rear pillars, disconnecting the wiring from the interior lights as the panels are removed.

21 Remove the retaining clips from the front edge of the parcel shelf and slide the shelf forwards and out of position. As the shelf is removed, disconnect the wiring connectors from the high-level brake light (where fitted).

22 Unscrew the inertia reel retaining nut and remove the seat belt(s).

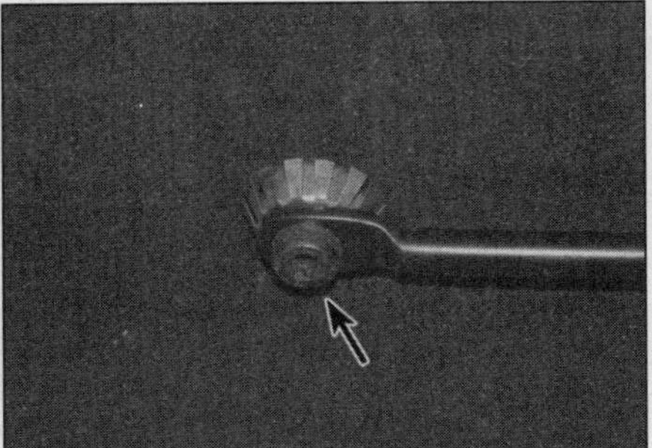

26.9 Pull of the cap and undo the anchorage bar bolt (arrowed)

Folding rear seat side belts

23 Remove the rear parcel shelf trim as described in Section 27.

24 Slacken and remove the Torx bolt securing the lower end of the belt to the body **(see illustration)**. Feed the belt through the slot in the shelf trim.

25 The inertia reel is secured by one Torx bolt **(see illustration)**. Slacken and remove the bolt and washer. On Coupe models, undo the bolt and remove the polystyrene filler piece to expose the bolt.

26 Manoeuvre the assembly from the mounting bracket and withdraw it from the vehicle.

Rear seat side belt stalk

27 Unclip the rear seat cushion and remove it from the body.

28 Slacken and remove the bolt and washer and remove the stalk from the vehicle.

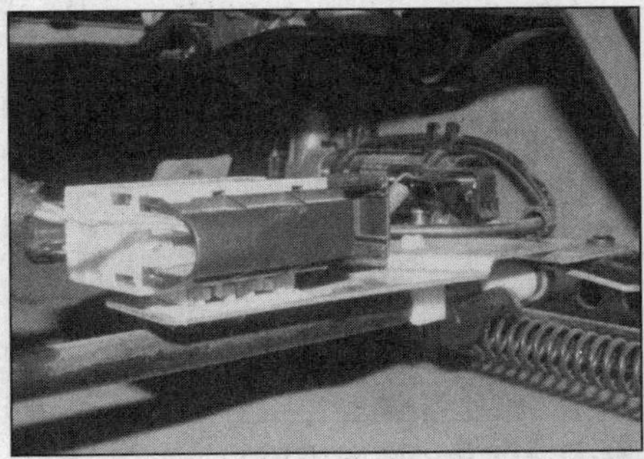

26.15 Disconnect the tensioner wiring plug

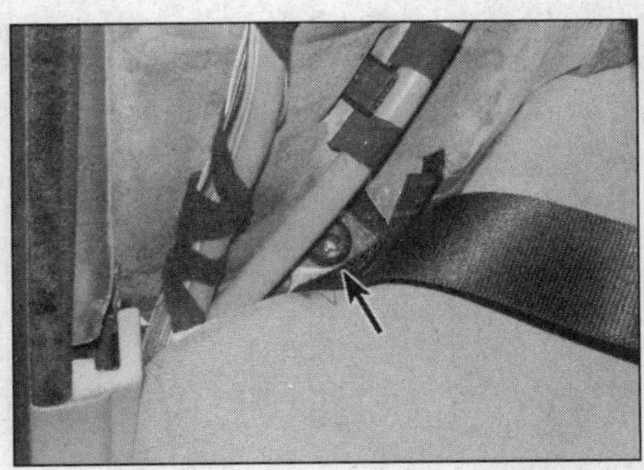

26.24 Rear lower seat belt mounting bolt (arrowed)

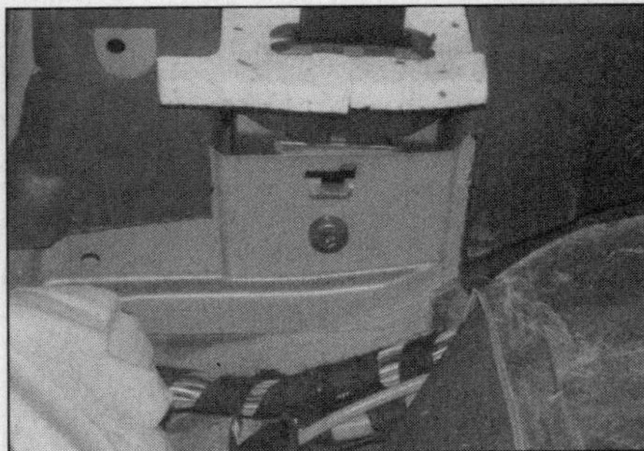

26.12 Unscrew the inertia reel retaining bolt

Rear seat centre belt and buckle

29 Unclip the rear seat cushion and remove it from the vehicle.

30 Slacken and remove the bolt securing the centre belt/buckle to the body and remove it from the vehicle.

Refitting

Front seat belt

31 Refitting is a reversal of the removal procedure, ensuring that all the seat belt mounting bolts are securely tightened, and all disturbed trim panels are securely retained by all the relevant retaining clips.

Front seat belt stalk

32 Ensure the tensioner mechanism is correctly engaged with the seat and tighten its retaining nut to the specified torque. Refit the seat as described in Section 24 and reconnect the battery negative lead.

26.16 Undo the stalk retaining bolt (arrowed)

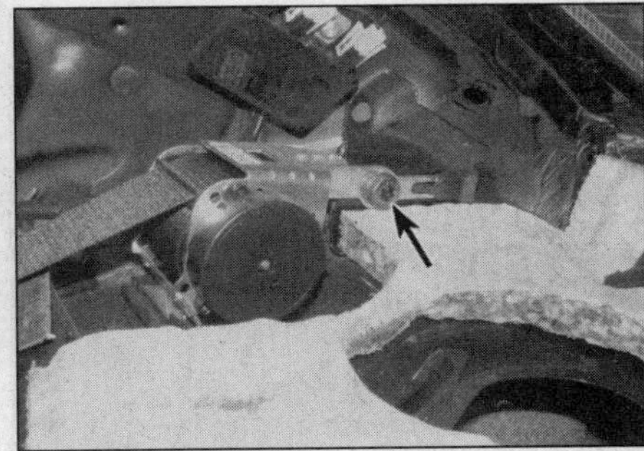

26.25 Rear seat belt inertia reel mounting bolt (arrowed)

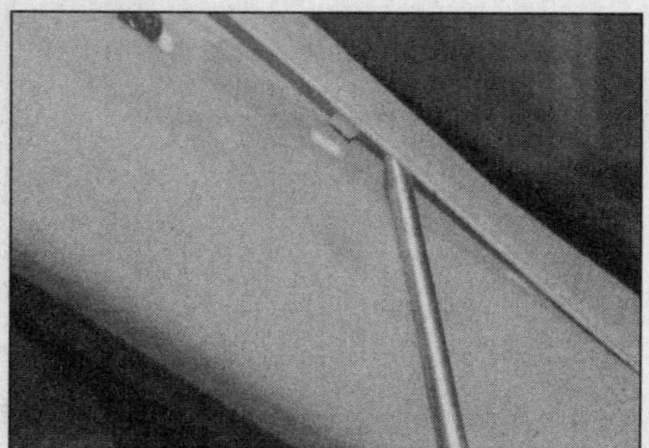

27.7 Carefully prise the insert from the A-pillar trim

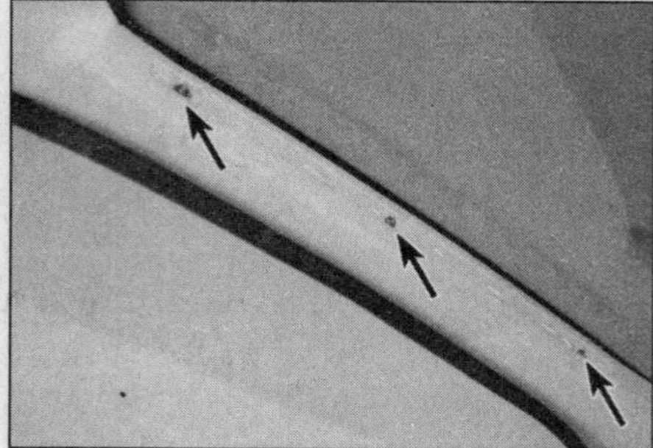

27.8 Undo the three bolts (arrowed) and remove the pillar trim

Fixed rear seat side belts

33 Refitting is the reverse of removal, ensuring that all seat belt mountings are tighten to the specified torque and all trim panels are clipped securely in position.

Folding rear seat side belts

34 Refitting is the reverse of removal, making sure the inertia reel is clipped securely in position and all seat belt mounting bolts are tightened to the torque.

Rear seat belt stalk

35 Refitting is the reverse of removal, tightening the mounting bolt to the specified torque.

Rear seat centre belt and buckle

36 Refitting is the reverse of removal, tightening the mounting bolts to the specified torque.

27 Interior trim – removal and refitting

Interior trim panels

1 The interior trim panels are secured using either bolts or various types of trim fasteners, usually studs or clips.

2 Check that there are no other panels overlapping the one to be removed; usually there is a sequence that has to be followed that will become obvious on close inspection.

3 Remove all obvious fasteners, such as bolts. If the panel will not come free, it is held by hidden clips or fasteners. These are usually situated around the edge of the panel and can be prised up to release them; note, however, that they can break quite easily so new ones should be available. The best way of releasing such clips without the correct type of tool is to use a large flat-bladed screwdriver. Note that some panels are secured by plastic expanding rivets, where the centre pin must be prised up before the rivet can be removed. Note in many cases that the adjacent sealing strip must be prised back to release a panel.

4 When removing a panel, never use excessive force or the panel may be damaged; always check carefully that all fasteners have been removed or released before attempting to withdraw a panel.

5 Refitting is the reverse of the removal procedure; secure the fasteners by pressing them firmly into place and ensure that all disturbed components are correctly secured to prevent rattles.

A-pillar trim

6 Due to the head-impact airbag fitted in the area, disconnect the battery as described in Chapter 5A.

7 Using a wooden or plastic flat-bladed lever, carefully prise out the trim insert from the A-pillar trim **(see illustration)**.

8 Undo the three retaining Torx bolts, and pull the trim to the rear, starting at the top **(see illustration)**.

9 Refitting is the reverse of the removal procedure; secure the fasteners by pressing them firmly into place and ensure that all disturbed components are correctly secured to prevent rattles.

B-pillar trim

Saloon & Touring

10 Begin by carefully prising up the front door sill trim panel from its retaining clips **(see illustration)**.

11 Starting at the base of the B-pillar trim, pull the trim in towards the centre of the cabin, and release it from the two lower retaining clips. Note how the lower part of the trim engages with the upper section of trim **(see illustration)**.

12 Undo the bolt securing the seat belt outer anchorage to the seat rail.

13 The lower edge of the upper trim is secured by two plastic expanding rivets. Prise up the centre pins, and lever out the complete rivets **(see illustration)**.

14 Feed the seat belt strap through the upper mounting, and pull the trim down and out. Note how the upper edge of the trim engages with the headlining moulding **(see illustration)**.

15 Refitting is the reverse of the removal procedure; secure the fasteners by pressing them firmly into place and ensure that all disturbed components are correctly secured to prevent rattles.

Coupe

16 Carefully prise up the front door sill trim panel from its retaining clips.

17 Pull the rubber weatherstrip from the door

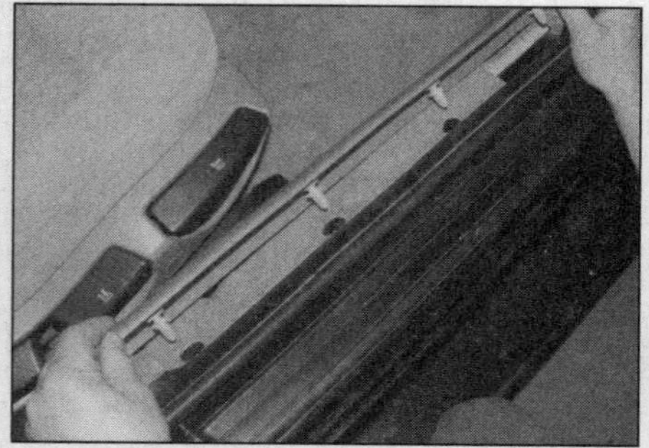

27.10 Prise up the sill trim to release the retaining clips

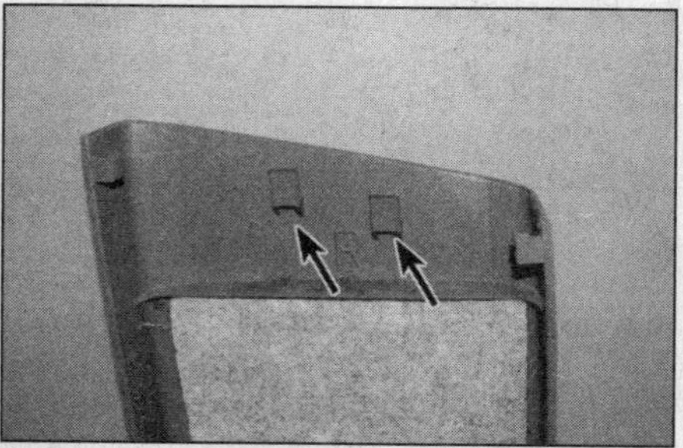

27.11 The B-pillar lower trim has two clips (arrowed) which located behind the upper trim

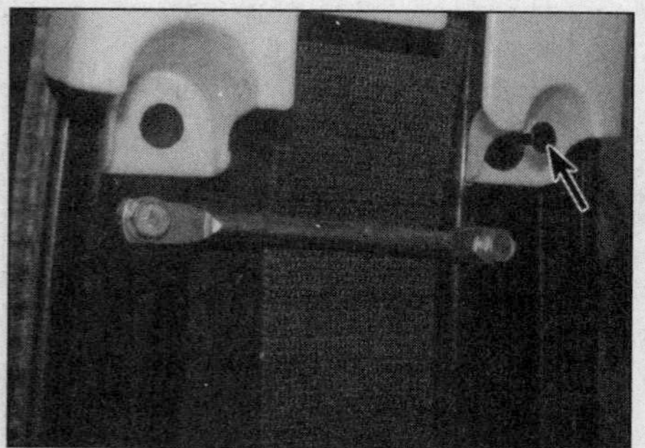

27.13 Prise out the centre pin (arrowed) then remove the plastic rivet

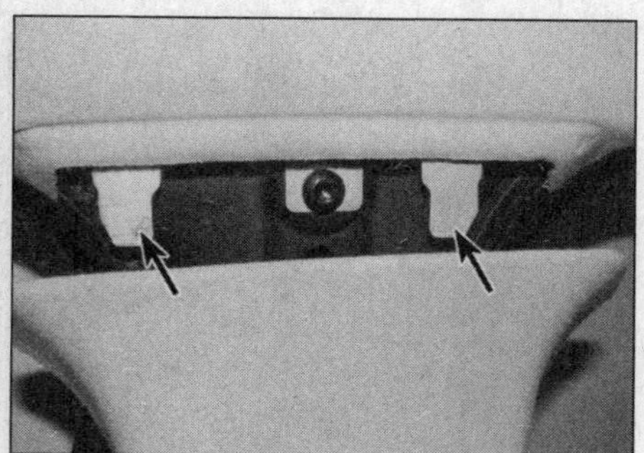

27.14 The upper edge of the B-pillar trim locates over the two lugs (arrowed)

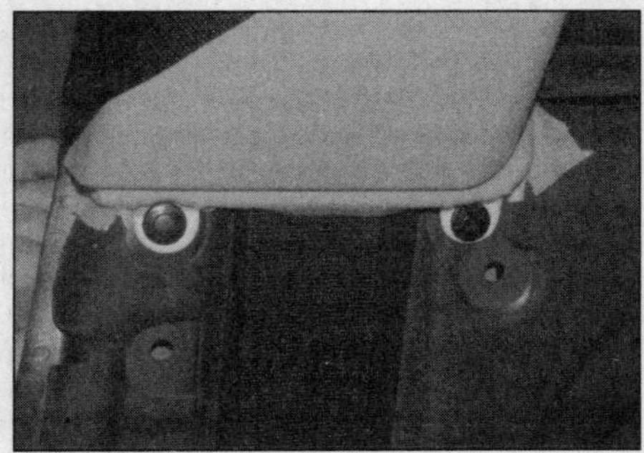

27.19a The lower edge of the B-pillar trim is secured by two expanding rivets . . .

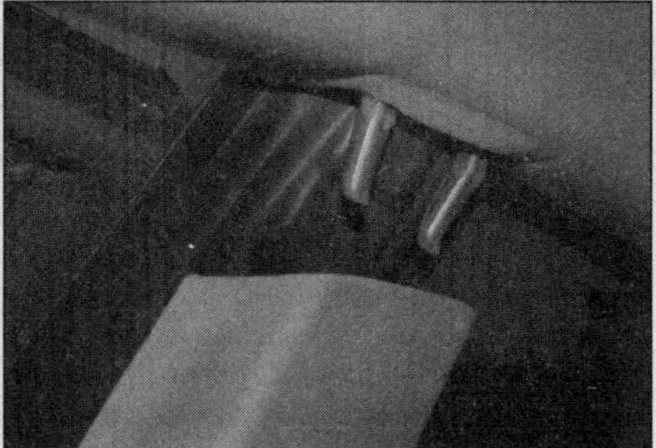

27.19b . . . and the upper edge locates with these clips

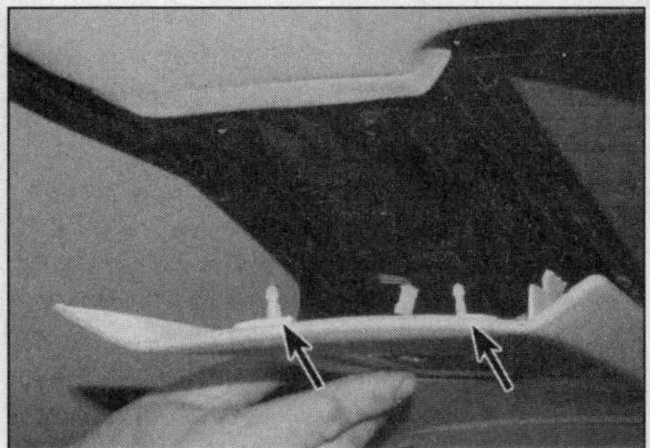

27.21 Pull the C-pillar trim at the top and release the retaining clips (arrowed)

aperture adjacent to the trim then, using a clip release tool or flat-bladed screwdriver, carefully release the front edge of the rear side panel trim from its retaining clips.

18 Prise off the plastic cap, and undo the front mounting bolt from the seat belt lower anchorage rail. Slide the belt from the rail.

19 The lower edge of the upper trim is secured by two plastic expanding rivets. Prise up the centre pins, lever out the complete rivets, and lower the trim from place **(see illustrations)**.

C-pillar trim

Saloon & Coupe

20 Prise out the outer edge of the courtesy light, and remove it from the pillar trim. Disconnect the wiring plug as the unit is withdrawn.

21 Pull the door weatherstrip away from the area adjacent to the pillar trim. Pull the top edge of the pillar trim away, releasing the two retaining clips, and then lift the trim away **(see illustration)**.

22 Refitting is the reverse of the removal procedure; secure the fasteners by pressing them firmly into place and ensure that all disturbed components are correctly secured to prevent rattles.

Touring

23 Pull the top of the pillar trim towards the centre of the cabin to release the top push-on clip **(see illustration)**.

24 With the top released, pull up the lower edge of the trim and remove it.

25 Refitting is a reversal of removal.

D-pillar trim

Touring

26 Open the tailgate, press the release button, and fold down the flap in the luggage compartment side panel.

27 The pillar trim is secured by two bolts in the centre, and two push-on clips at the top edge. Undo the bolts, pull the top of the trim to release the clips, then lift the trim away **(see illustration)**. Disconnect the luggage compartment light as the trim is removed.

28 Refitting is a reversal of removal.

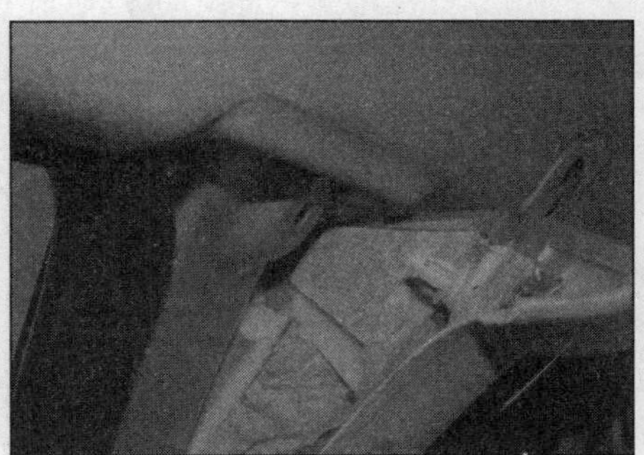

27.23 Pull the top of the trim to release the clip

Side trim panel

Coupe

Note: *On models fitted with rear side airbags, due to the proximity of the airbags, disconnect the battery as described in Chapter 5A. Wait 5 seconds before proceeding.*

29 Using a plastic wedge, carefully lever away the plastic cap over the window link rod **(see illustration 15.2)**.

30 Lever the window link rod from the mounting on the window **(see illustration 15.3)**.

31 Push the seat belt to one side, and push down the centre pin of the expanding rivet securing the plastic trim at the top of the seat side cushion **(see illustration)**. Manoeuvre the plastic trim over the hinged window link rod.

32 Remove the rear seat cushion as described in Section 24.

33 Fold the seat backrest forward and, using a screwdriver, release the retaining clip at the

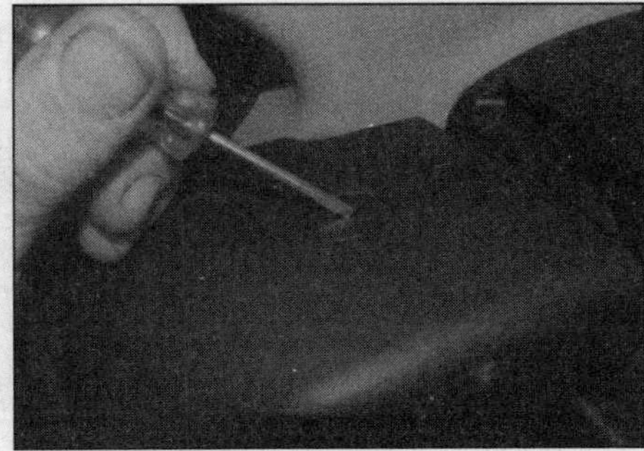

27.31 Push in the centre pin, and remove the trim

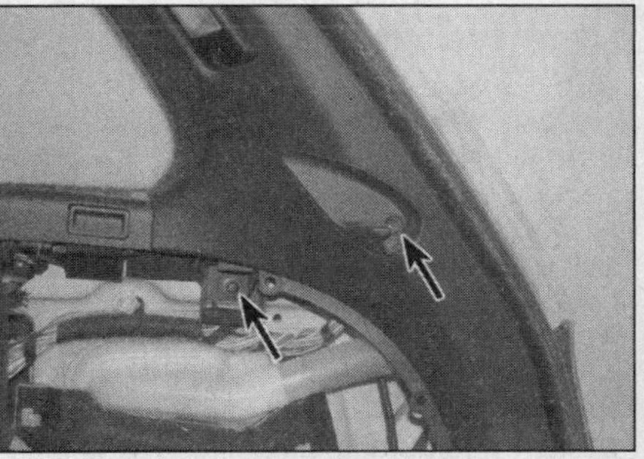

27.27 Undo the D-pillar trim bolts (arrowed)

top and pull the seat side cushion from its location **(see illustration)**. Note how the fitting at the base of the trim engages with the fitting on the wheel arch.

34 Carefully prise up the front door sill trim panel from its retaining clips, and pull the rubber weatherstrip from the door aperture adjacent to the trim panel.

35 Where applicable, carefully prise out the airbag emblem from the side panel speaker grille, undo and remove the bolt revealed. Undo the two bolts securing the armrest **(see illustration)**.

36 The side panel is now secured by 7 push-on clips around its perimeter. Using a trim removal tool or flat-bladed screwdriver, carefully release the clips, and manoeuvre the panel from the vehicle. Note their fitted locations, and disconnect and wiring plugs as the panel is withdrawn.

37 Refitting is the reverse of the removal

27.33 Release the clip (arrowed) and pull the seat side cushion forward

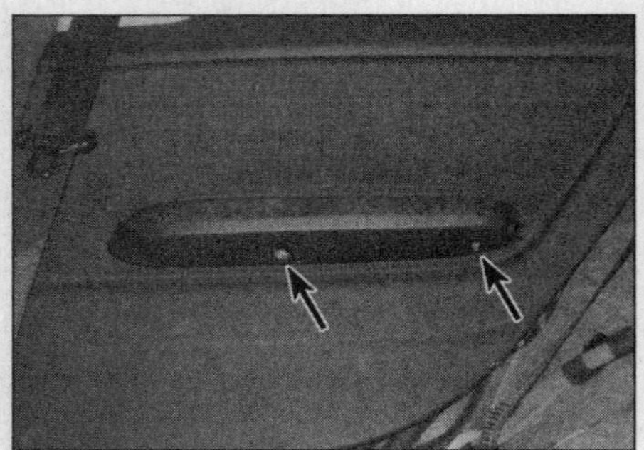
27.35 The armrest is secured by two bolts (arrowed)

27.40 Release the two clips (arrowed) and remove the trim cover

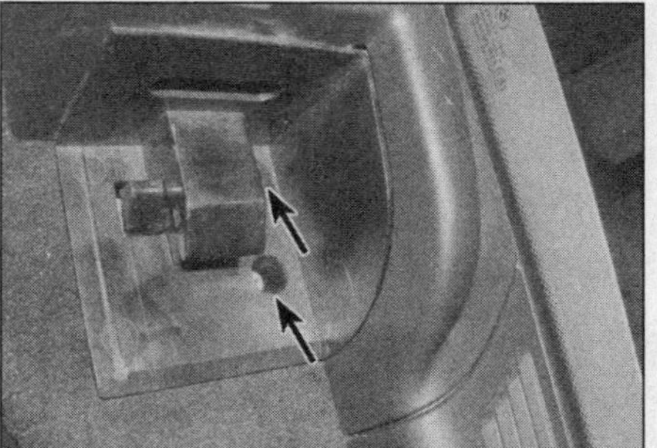
27.42 Undo the two bolts (arrowed) and remove the roller cover mounting

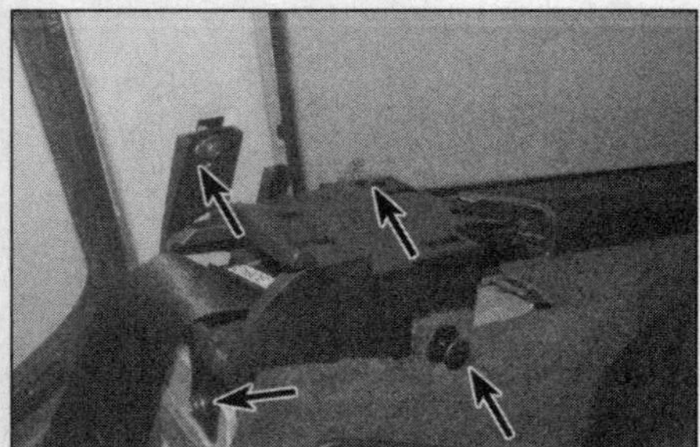
27.43 Prise out the expansion rivet, undo the bolts/nuts and remove the cover from the seat belt reel (arrowed)

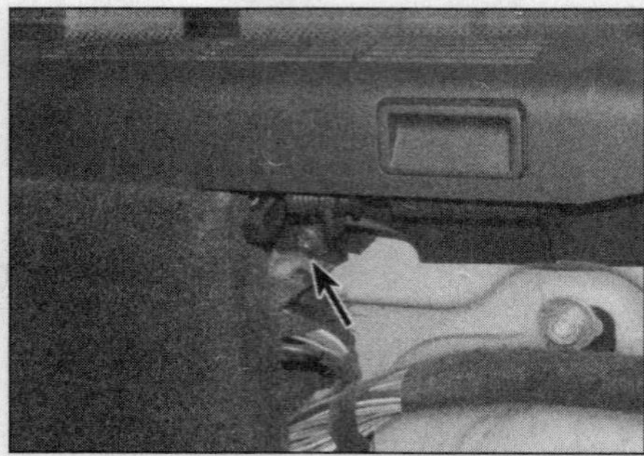
27.44 Undo the bolt (arrowed) and remove the trim

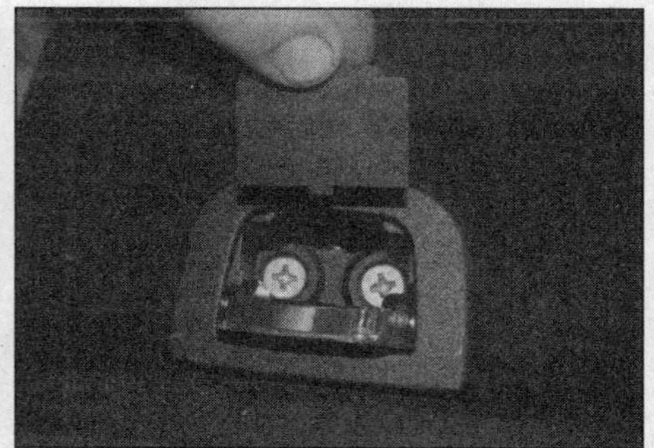
27.45 Lift the flap and undo the lashing-eye bolts

procedure; secure the fasteners by pressing them firmly into place and ensure that all disturbed components are correctly secured to prevent rattles. Note that the rear side hinged window link rod plastic cap has an internal lug which must locate over the groove in the window link rod socket.

Luggage area trim panel

Touring

38 Remove the C- and D-pillar trims as described earlier in this Section.

39 Fold the rear seat forward, unclip the top section of the side trim adjacent to the door aperture, then lift the trim upwards and remove it **(see illustration 24.14)**.

40 Release the two clips at the front edge, and remove the seat belt reel trim cover from the top of the side panel **(see illustration)**.

41 Undo the bolt securing the lower seat belt mounting.

42 Undo the two retaining bolts, and remove the luggage compartment roller cover mounting from the side panel **(see illustration)**.

43 Lever out the centre pin and prise out the expanding plastic rivet, undo the bolts/nut, then remove the cover from the seat belt reel **(see illustration)**.

44 Slacken the retaining bolt and remove the trim from the lower edge of the rear side window **(see illustration)**.

45 Lift the trim flap, undo the bolts and remove the 'lashing eye' from the side panel **(see illustration)**.

46 Carefully prise the 12V power socket from the side trim, and disconnect the wiring plugs as the socket is withdrawn.

47 Prise out the centre pin and lever out the plastic expansion rivet from the lower edge of the trim panel.

48 Lever out the mounting at the top, and remove the trim panel, feeding the power socket wiring through the hole as the panel is removed.

Glovebox

Driver's side

49 Open the glovebox, undo the two bolts and remove the glovebox **(see illustration)**. Disconnect any wiring plugs as the glovebox is removed.

Passenger side

50 Open the glovebox, and pull out the pin at the base of the retaining strap/shock absorber each side **(see illustration)**.

51 Working in the facia opening, undo the retaining bolts, and remove the glovebox complete with hinge and bracket **(see illustration)**. Disconnect and wiring plugs as the glovebox is withdrawn.

52 Refitting is the reverse of the removal procedure.

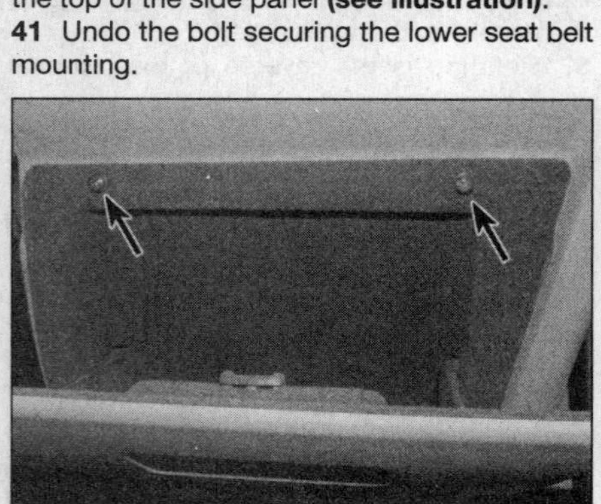
27.49 The driver's glovebox is retained by two bolts (arrowed)

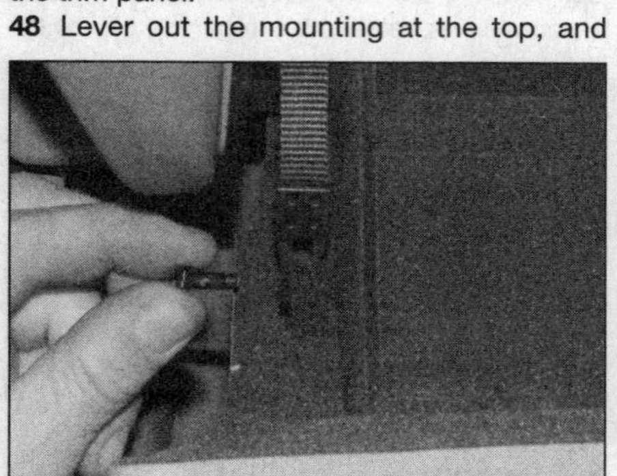
27.50 Pull out the pin at the base of the retaining strap/shock absorber each side

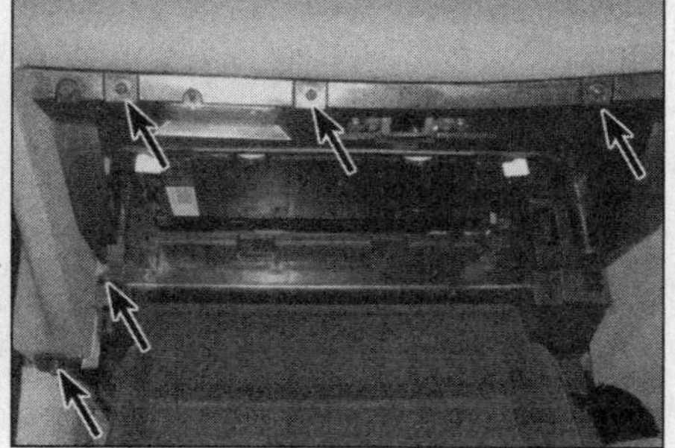
27.51 Undo the bolts (arrowed) and remove the glovebox

Glovebox lock

53 Open the glovebox lid, undo the two retaining bolts and remove the lock **(see illustration)**.

Carpets

54 The passenger compartment floor carpet is in one piece, secured at its edges by bolts or clips, usually the same fasteners used to secure the various adjoining trim panels.

55 Carpet removal and refitting is reasonably straightforward but very time-consuming because all adjoining trim panels must be removed first, as must components such as the seats, the centre console and seat belt lower anchorages.

Headlining

56 The headlining is clipped to the roof and can be withdrawn only once all fittings such as the grab handles, sunvisors, sunroof (if fitted), windscreen, rear quarter windows and related trim panels have been removed, and the door, tailgate and sunroof aperture sealing strips have been prised clear.

57 Note that headlining removal requires considerable skill and experience if it is to be carried out without damage and is therefore best entrusted to an expert.

Cup holders

58 Squeeze in the sides of the oddments tray and lift the tray, complete with the cup holders, from the centre console.

59 Refit the oddments tray first, followed by the cup holders.

Rear headrests

60 Fold the rear seats forward, or remove the rear seat back as applicable (see Section 24).

61 Pull the centre pins down, and prise out the plastic rivets, then remove the plastic trim from the front edge of the parcel shelf.

62 Lift up the front edge of the parcel shelf trim, pull out the retaining clips, and remove the rear headrest **(see illustration)**.

63 Refitting is a reversal of removal, but before refitting the shelf trim, fit the retaining clips into the rear headrest holders **(see illustration)**.

Parcel shelf

Saloon & Coupe

64 Fold the rear seats forward, or remove the rear seat back as applicable (see Section 24).

65 Pull the top of the rear seat side trim forwards releasing the retaining clips, then lift and remove it **(see illustration)**. Repeat this procedure on the remaining rear seat side trim.

66 Pull the centre pins down, and prise out the plastic rivets, then remove the plastic trim from the front edge of the parcel shelf.

27.53 The glovebox lock is retained by two bolts

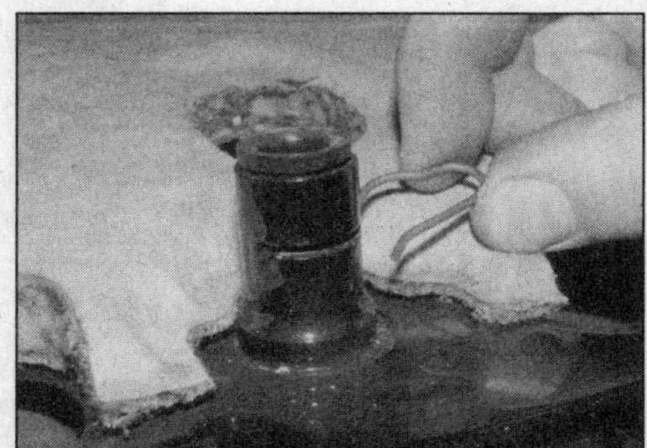

27.63 Before refitting the parcel shelf trim, insert the retaining clips into the headrest holders

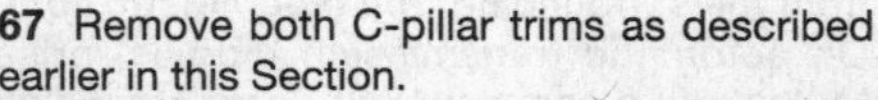

67 Remove both C-pillar trims as described earlier in this Section.

68 Lift up the front edge of the parcel shelf trim, pull out the retaining clips, and remove the rear headrests **(see illustration 27.62)**.

69 Carefully prise out the covers over the rear speakers set into the parcel shelf. Undo the bolts, disconnect the wiring plugs and remove the speakers. Lift out the fibre speaker sockets.

70 Remove the shelf trim to the front. If required, undo the Torx bolt securing the lower seat belt anchor, and feed the belt through the parcel shelf trim.

71 Refitting is a reversal of removal, but before refitting the shelf trim, fit the retaining clips into the rear headrest holders **(see illustration 27.63)**.

28.2 Press down the edge to remove the ashtray

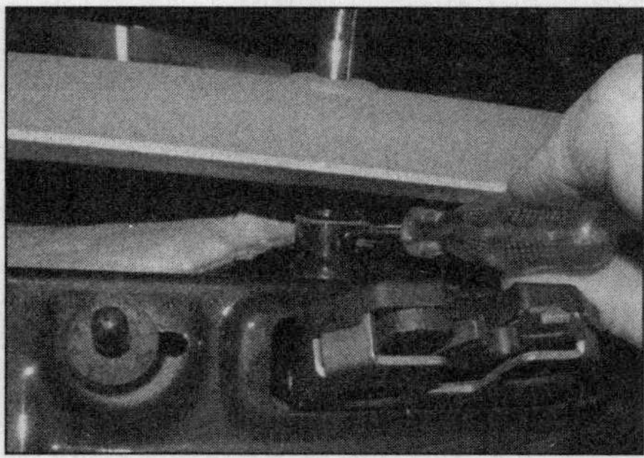

27.62 Lift up the parcel shelf edge and prise out the headrest clips

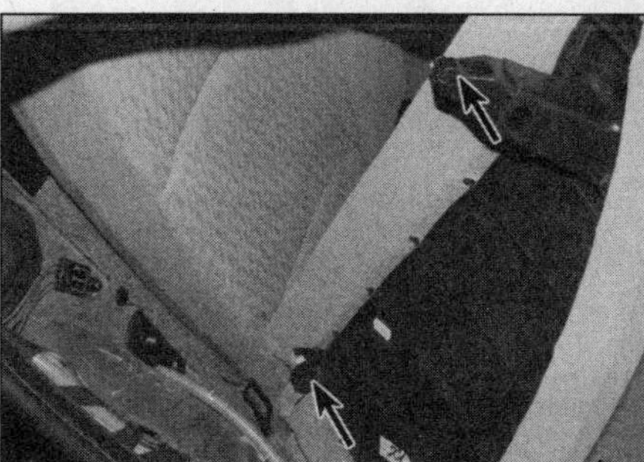

27.65 Rear seat side trim retaining clip and locating lug (arrowed)

28 Centre console – removal and refitting

Removal

1 Disconnect the battery negative terminal (see Chapter 5A).

2 Roll down the rear storage box/ashtray lid. Press down on the lid edge and lift the box/ashtray from the rear of the centre console **(see illustration)**.

3 Slacken the retaining bolts, pull the bolts out complete with the plastic expansion rivets, and remove the ashtray/storage box surround, disconnecting the illumination bulbholder as it is withdrawn **(see illustration)**.

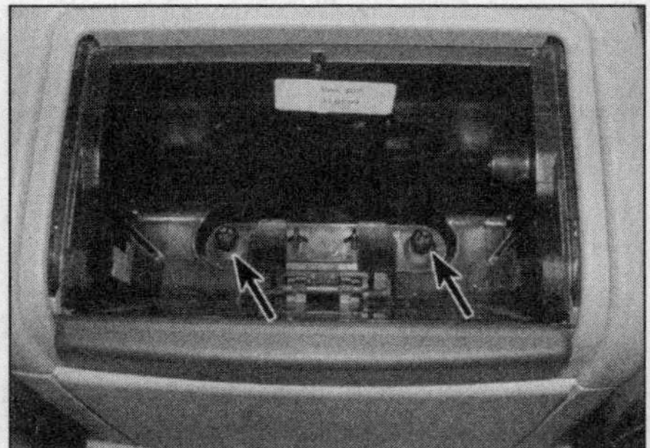

28.3 Slacken the ashtray/storage box surround bolts (arrowed)

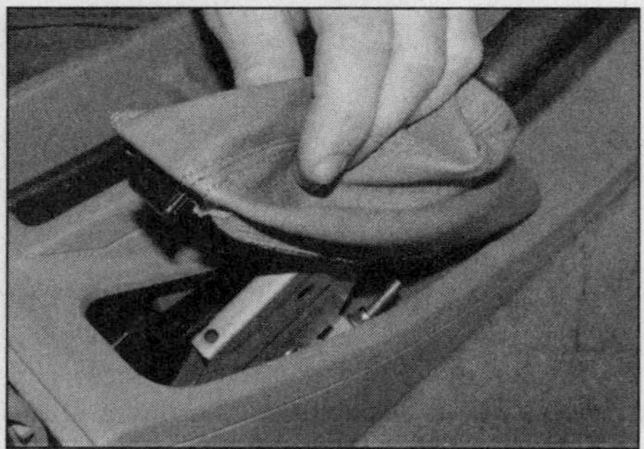

28.4 Unclip the handbrake lever gaiter

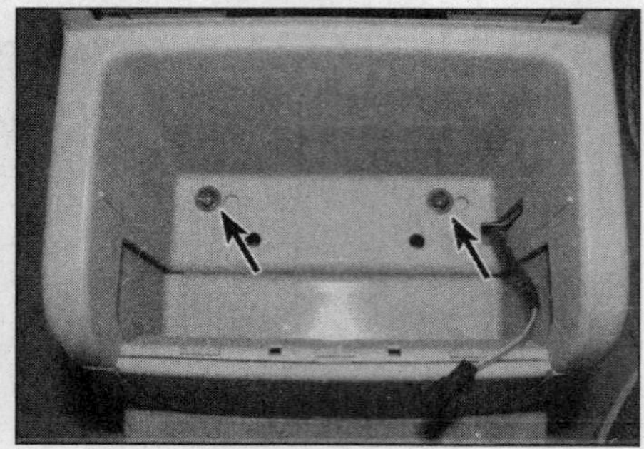

28.5 Remove the ashtray/storage box trim bolts (arrowed)

28.6 Carefully prise up the gear lever gaiter

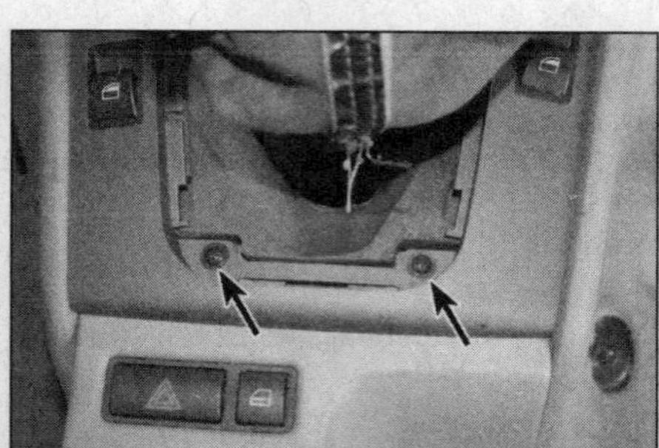

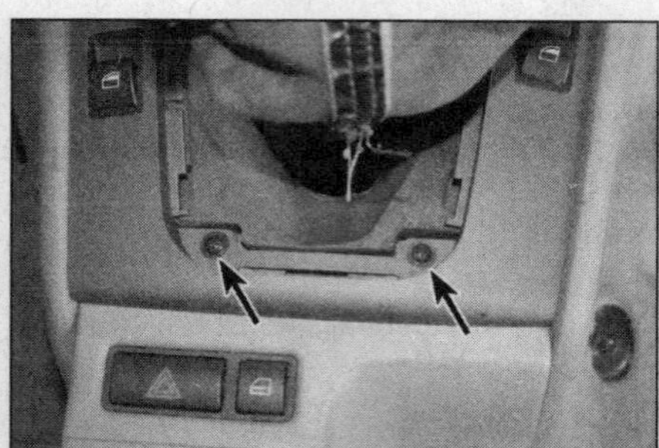

28.7 Undo the two bolts at the rear of the gear lever gaiter aperture (arrowed)

4 On all models unclip the handbrake lever gaiter from the console **(see illustration)**.

5 Undo the two bolts, then pull out the sides and remove the ashtray/storage box surround from the rear of the console **(see illustration)**.

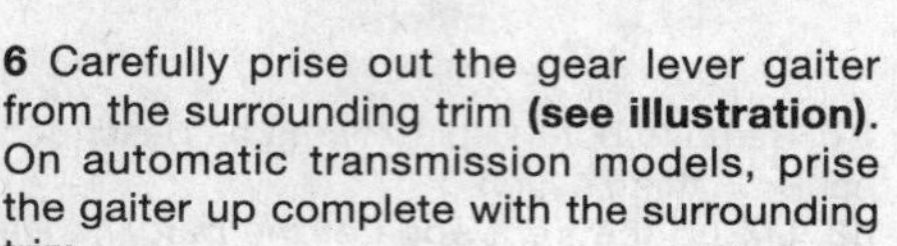

6 Carefully prise out the gear lever gaiter from the surrounding trim **(see illustration)**. On automatic transmission models, prise the gaiter up complete with the surrounding trim.

7 Undo the two bolts at the rear of the gear lever gaiter aperture, lift the gaiter surround trim, and pull the rear section of the console slightly to the rear **(see illustration)**. Note their fitted locations, then disconnect any wiring plugs as the console is withdrawn. Manoeuvre the centre console over the handbrake lever. On models with a centre armrest, lift the armrest and pull the rear of the console up and forward.

8 If required, the armrest can now be removed by unscrewing the mounting bolts and disconnecting the handbrake warning switch wiring.

Refitting

9 Manoeuvre the centre console over the handbrake lever, then over the upright armrest (where fitted). The remainder of refitting is the reverse of removal, making sure all fasteners are securely tightened.

29 Facia panel assembly – removal and refitting

Removal

1 Remove the centre console as described in Section 28.

2 Give the gear lever knob a sharp tug straight up, and remove it from the lever.

3 Remove the gear lever surround trim. Note their fitted locations, and disconnect and wiring plugs as the trim is removed.

4 Remove the steering column combination switch as described in Chapter 12, Section 4.

5 Remove the both gloveboxes as described Section 27.

6 Undo the three bolts, one expanding plastic rivet, and one plastic nut, then remove the panel from above the pedals. As the panel is removed, slide back the locking element and remove the OBD socket from the panel. Disconnect the light wiring plug at the same time **(see illustrations)**.

7 Using a wooden or plastic spatula, starting from the outside edges, carefully prise the decorative trim strips from the passenger's and driver's side of the facia, and remove the strip from the centre of the facia **(see illustrations)**.

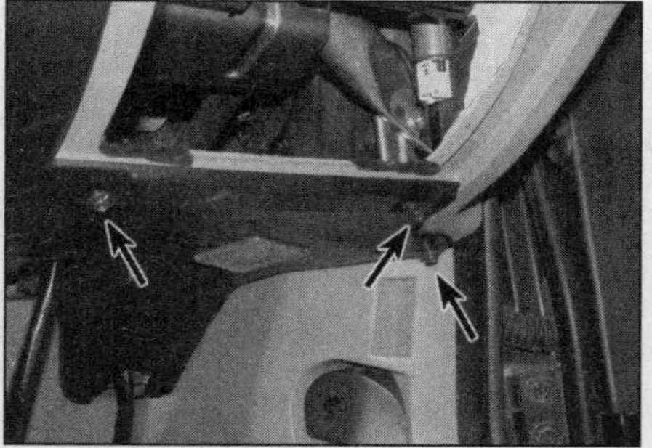

29.6a Remove the three bolts (arrowed) . . .

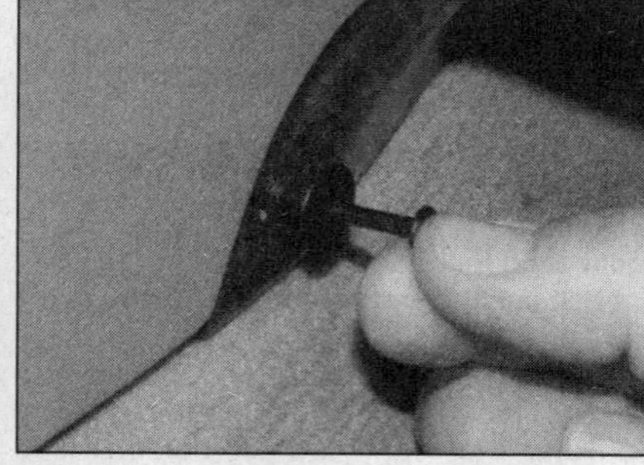

29.6b . . . and the plastic expansion rivet

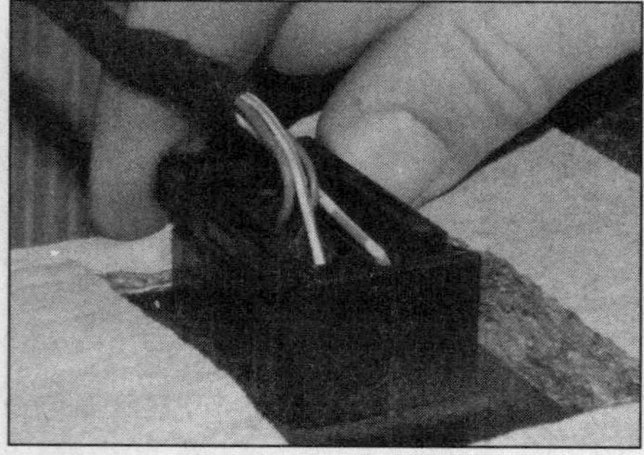

29.6c Slide back the locking element and remove the OBD socket from the panel

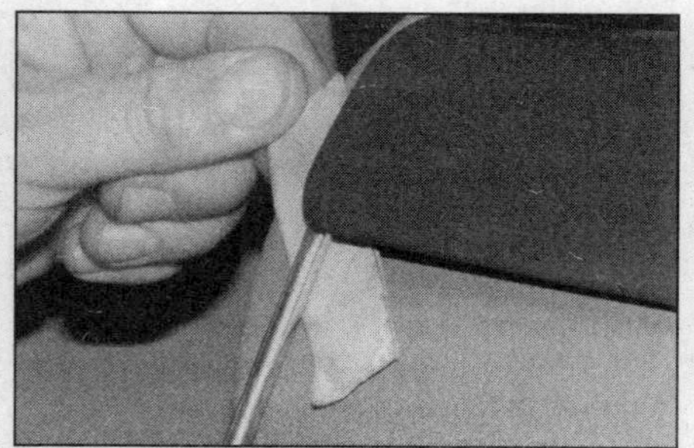

29.7a Use a piece of cardboard to protect the facia when prising up the end of the decorative strip

29.7b The decorative strips are retained by 'push-in' clips

29.7c Remove the strip from the centre of the facia

29.9 Prise out the lower edge and pull the storage compartment from the facia

29.10 Remove the four bolts (arrowed) and withdraw the storage compartment carrier

29.16 Undo the bolt in the decorative trim recess (arrowed)

29.17 Driver's side air vent bolt (arrowed)

29.19 Undo the nut at the rear of the gear lever (arrowed)

8 Remove the instrument panel assembly as described in Chapter 12.

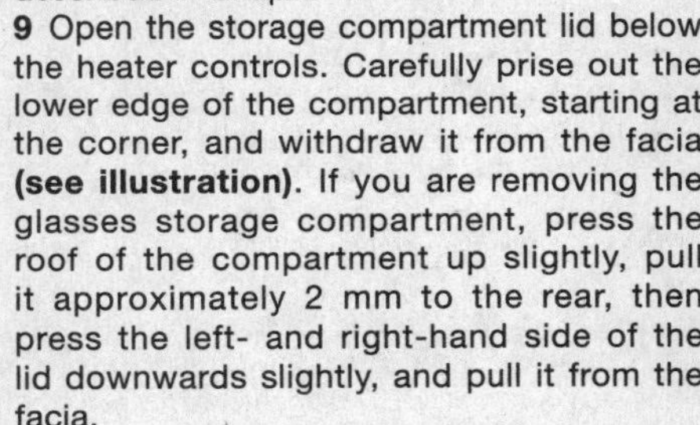

9 Open the storage compartment lid below the heater controls. Carefully prise out the lower edge of the compartment, starting at the corner, and withdraw it from the facia **(see illustration)**. If you are removing the glasses storage compartment, press the roof of the compartment up slightly, pull it approximately 2 mm to the rear, then press the left- and right-hand side of the lid downwards slightly, and pull it from the facia.

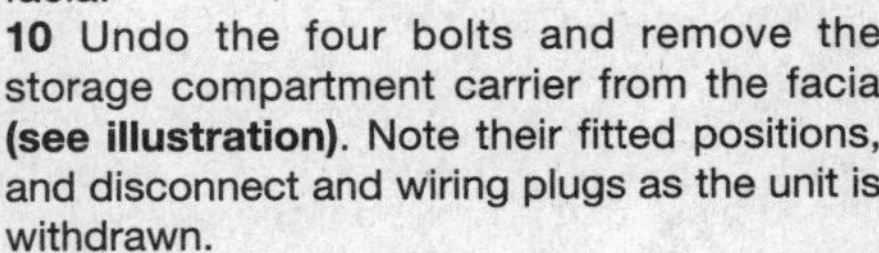

10 Undo the four bolts and remove the storage compartment carrier from the facia **(see illustration)**. Note their fitted positions, and disconnect and wiring plugs as the unit is withdrawn.

11 Remove both A-pillar trims as described in Section 27.

12 Remove the light switch from the facia as described in Chapter 12, Section 4.

13 Remove the heater control panel as described in Chapter 3.

14 Remove the audio unit from the facia as described in Chapter 12.

15 Remove the passenger airbag unit as described in Chapter 12.

16 On the passenger's side, undo the bolt in the decorative trim recess **(see illustration)**.

17 Undo the retaining bolt(s) and pull the driver's side air vent from the facia **(see illustration)**.

29.20a Undo the two nuts on the passenger side (arrowed) . . .

29.20b . . . and the two nuts on the driver's side (arrowed)

18 The passenger side end of the facia may be secured by a bolt or an expanding plastic rivet. Undo the bolt or lever out the rivet.

19 Remove the nut securing the facia to the rear of the gear lever **(see illustration)**.

20 Move the front seats as far back as possible, undo the four facia mounting nuts, and with the help of an assistant, pull the facia from the bulkhead **(see illustrations)**. Disconnect the centre air vent cable from the side of the heater box where applicable. Note their fitted locations, and disconnect any wiring plugs as the facia is withdrawn.

Refitting

21 Refitting is a reversal of the removal procedure, noting the following points:

a) Manoeuvre the facia into position and, using the labels stuck on during removal, ensure that the wiring is correctly routed and securely retained by its facia clips.

b) Clip the facia back into position, ensure the centre locating lug at the front edge of the facia engages correctly, making sure all the wiring connectors are fed through their respective apertures, then refit all the facia fasteners, and tighten them securely.

c) On completion, reconnect the battery and check that all the electrical components and switches function correctly.

Notes

Chapter 12
Body electrical systems

Contents

Degrees of difficulty

Easy, suitable for novice with little experience	**Fairly easy,** suitable for beginner with some experience	**Fairly difficult,** suitable for competent DIY mechanic	**Difficult,** suitable for experienced DIY mechanic	**Very difficult,** suitable for expert DIY or professional

Specifications

System type . . . . 12 volt negative earth

Fuses . . . . See inside fusebox lid

Bulbs	**Wattage**
Exterior lights	
Brake light	21/5
Direction indicator	21
Direction indicator side repeater	5
Front foglight	55 (HB4 type)
Front sidelight	5
Headlight (dipped and main beam)	55 (H7 type)
High-level brake light	LED
Number plate light	5
Rear foglight	21
Reversing light	21
Tail light	5

Note: *From 03/2003 Coupe models are equipped with LED tail, brake and rear indicator lights*

Interior lights	
Front courtesy lights	10
Glovebox light	5
Instrument panel:	
Illumination bulbs	3
Warning light bulbs	1.5
Luggage compartment light	10
Rear courtesy lights	5

Component location

Component	Location
Air conditioning blower relay	Behind passenger's glovebox
Air conditioning clutch relay	Behind passenger's glovebox
Airbag control module	Under carpet beneath centre console
Airbag crash sensor	Front seat crossmember under carpet
Alarm control module	Under facia on the driver's side
Automatic transmission control module	E-box in engine compartment
Engine management ECM	E-box in engine compartment
Engine management main relay	E-box in engine compartment
Foglight relay	Behind passenger's glovebox
Fuel injector relay	E-box in engine compartment
Fuel pump relay	Behind passenger's glovebox
General module (GM V)	Behind passenger's glovebox
Headlight dimmer relay	Light switch on facia
Heated rear window relay	Right-hand side of luggage compartment
Horn relay	Behind passenger's glovebox
Ignition relay	E-box in engine compartment
Instrument cluster control unit	Instrument cluster
Parking distance control module:	
Saloon and Coupe models	Right-hand side of luggage compartment
Touring models	Luggage compartment floor
Reversing light relay (automatic transmission)	E-box in engine compartment
Seat control module	Base of seat cushion
Secondary air injection pump relay	Behind passenger's glovebox
Tyre pressure control module	Behind passenger's glovebox
Windscreen washer relay	E-box in engine compartment

Note that not all models are equipped with the components listed.

Torque wrench settings

	Nm	lbf ft
Airbag system fixings:		
Door airbag retaining bolts	8	6
Driver's airbag retaining bolts	8	6
Impact sensor mounting bolts	10	7
Passenger's airbag cover straps bolts	8	6
Passenger's airbag retaining nuts	22	16
Tyre pressure transmitter Torx bolt	3.5	2.6
Wiper arm-to-wiper spindle nut	30	22

1 General information and precautions

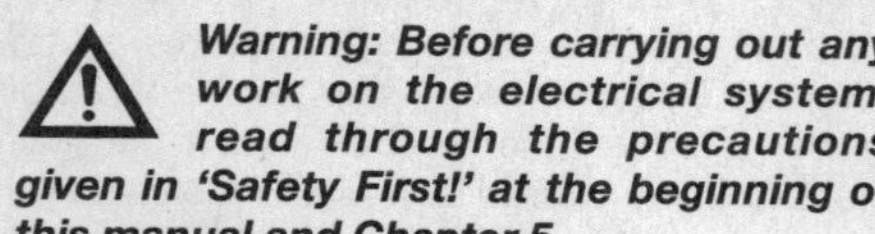

Warning: Before carrying out any work on the electrical system, read through the precautions given in 'Safety First!' at the beginning of this manual and Chapter 5.

The electrical system is of the 12 volt negative earth type. Power for the lights and all electrical accessories is supplied by a lead-acid type battery which is charged by the alternator.

This Chapter covers repair and service procedures for the various electrical components not associated with engine. Information on the battery, alternator and starter motor can be found in Chapter 5A.

It should be noted that prior to working on any component in the electrical system, the battery negative terminal should first be disconnected to prevent the possibility of electrical short circuits and/or fires (see Chapter 5A).

2 Electrical fault finding – general information

Note: *Refer to the precautions given in 'Safety first!' and in Section 1 of this Chapter before starting work. The following tests relate to testing of the main electrical circuits, and should not be used to test delicate electronic circuits (such as anti-lock braking systems), particularly where an electronic control module/unit (ECM/ECU) is used.*

Caution: The BMW 3-Series electrical system is extremely complex. Many of the ECMs are connected via a 'Databus' system, where they are able to share information from the various sensors, and communicate with each other. For instance, as the automatic gearbox approaches a gear ratio shift point, it signals the engine management ECM via the Databus. As the gearchange is made by the transmission ECM, the engine management ECM retards the ignition timing, momentarily reducing engine output to ensure a smoother transition from one gear ratio to the next. Due to the design of the Databus system, it is not advisable to backprobe the ECMs with a multimeter in the traditional manner. Instead, the electrical systems are equipped with a sophisticated self-diagnosis system which can interrogate the various ECMs to reveal stored fault codes, and help pinpoint faults. In order to access the self-diagnosis system, specialist test equipment (fault code reader/scanner) is required.

General

1 A typical electrical circuit consists of an electrical component, any switches, relays, motors, fuses, fusible links or circuit breakers related to that component, and the wiring and connectors which link the component to both the battery and the chassis. To help to pinpoint a problem in an electrical circuit, wiring diagrams are included at the end of this Chapter.

2 Before attempting to diagnose an electrical fault, first study the appropriate wiring diagram to obtain a complete understanding of the components included in the particular circuit concerned. The possible sources of a fault can be narrowed down by noting if other components related to the circuit are operating properly. If several components or circuits fail at one time, the problem is likely to be related to a shared fuse or earth connection.

3 Electrical problems usually stem from simple causes, such as loose or corroded connections, a faulty earth connection, a blown fuse, a melted fusible link, or a faulty relay (refer to Section 3 for details of testing relays). Visually inspect the condition of all fuses, wires and connections in a problem circuit before testing the components. Use the wiring diagrams to determine which terminal connections will need to be checked in order to pinpoint the trouble spot.

4 The basic tools required for electrical fault finding include a circuit tester or voltmeter (a 12 volt bulb with a set of test leads can also be used for certain tests); a self-powered test light (sometimes known as a continuity tester); an ohmmeter (to measure resistance); a battery and set of test leads; and a jumper wire, preferably with a circuit breaker or fuse incorporated, which can be used to bypass suspect wires or electrical components. Before attempting to locate a problem with test instruments, use the wiring diagram to determine where to make the connections.

5 To find the source of an intermittent wiring fault (usually due to a poor or dirty connection, or damaged wiring insulation), a 'wiggle' test can be performed on the wiring. This involves wiggling the wiring by hand to see if the fault occurs as the wiring is moved. It should be possible to narrow down the source of the fault to a particular section of wiring. This method of testing can be used in conjunction with any of the tests described in the following sub-Sections.

6 Apart from problems due to poor connections, two basic types of fault can occur in an electrical circuit – open circuit, or short circuit.

7 Open circuit faults are caused by a break somewhere in the circuit, which prevents current from flowing. An open circuit fault will prevent a component from working, but will not cause the relevant circuit fuse to blow.

8 Short circuit faults are caused by a 'short' somewhere in the circuit, which allows the current flowing in the circuit to 'escape' along an alternative route, usually to earth. Short circuit faults are normally caused by a breakdown in wiring insulation, which allows a feed wire to touch either another wire, or an earthed component such as the bodyshell. A short circuit fault will normally cause the relevant circuit fuse to blow.

Finding an open circuit

9 To check for an open circuit, connect one lead of a circuit tester or voltmeter to either the negative battery terminal or a known good earth.

10 Connect the other lead to a connector in the circuit being tested, preferably nearest to the battery or fuse.

11 Switch on the circuit, bearing in mind that some circuits are live only when the ignition switch is moved to a particular position.

12 If voltage is present (indicated either by the tester bulb lighting or a voltmeter reading, as applicable), this means that the section of the circuit between the relevant connector and the battery is problem-free.

13 Continue to check the remainder of the circuit in the same fashion.

14 When a point is reached at which no voltage is present, the problem must lie between that point and the previous test point with voltage. Most problems can be traced to a broken, corroded or loose connection.

Finding a short circuit

15 To check for a short circuit, first disconnect the load(s) from the circuit (loads are the components which draw current from a circuit, such as bulbs, motors, heating elements, etc).

16 Remove the relevant fuse from the circuit, and connect a circuit tester or voltmeter to the fuse connections.

17 Switch on the circuit, bearing in mind that some circuits are live only when the ignition switch is moved to a particular position.

18 If voltage is present (indicated either by the tester bulb lighting or a voltmeter reading, as applicable), this means that there is a short circuit.

19 If no voltage is present, but the fuse still blows with the load(s) connected, this indicates an internal fault in the load(s).

Finding an earth fault

20 The battery negative terminal is connected to 'earth' – the metal of the engine/transmission and the car body – and most systems are wired so that they only receive a positive feed, the current returning through the metal of the car body **(see illustration)**. This means that the component mounting and the body form part of that circuit. Loose or corroded mountings can therefore cause a range of electrical faults, ranging from total failure of a circuit, to a puzzling partial fault. In particular, lights may shine dimly (especially when another circuit sharing the same earth point is in operation), motors (eg, wiper motors or the radiator cooling fan motor) may run slowly, and the operation of one circuit may have an apparently unrelated effect on another. Note that on many vehicles, earth straps are used between certain components, such as the engine/transmission and the body, usually where there is no metal-to-metal contact between components due to flexible rubber mountings, etc.

21 To check whether a component is properly earthed, disconnect the battery and connect one lead of an ohmmeter to a known good earth point. Connect the other lead to the wire or earth connection being tested. The resistance reading should be zero; if not, check the connection as follows.

22 If an earth connection is thought to be faulty, dismantle the connection and clean back to bare metal both the bodyshell and the wire terminal or the component earth connection mating surface. Be careful to remove all traces of dirt and corrosion, then use a knife to trim away any paint, so that a clean metal-to-metal joint is made. On reassembly, tighten the joint fasteners securely; if a wire terminal is being refitted, use serrated washers between the terminal and the bodyshell to ensure a clean and secure connection. When the connection is remade, prevent the onset of corrosion in the future by applying a coat of petroleum jelly or silicone-based grease or by spraying on (at regular intervals) a proprietary ignition sealer or a water dispersant lubricant.

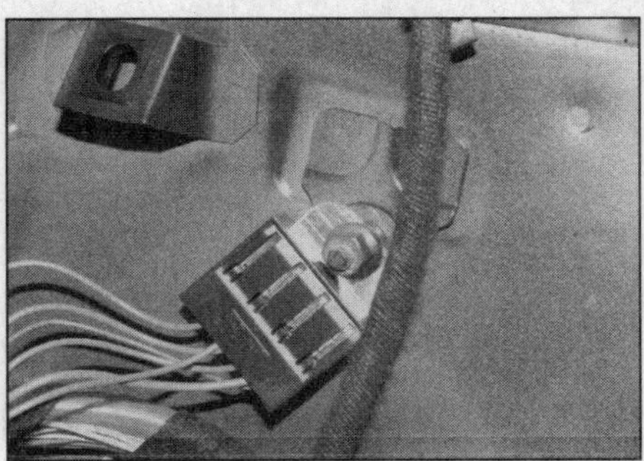

2.20 Luggage compartment earth connection

3 Fuses and relays – general information

Main fuses

1 The majority of the fuses are located behind passenger's side glovebox, whilst some others are located in the E-box located in the left-hand corner of the engine compartment.

2 To remove the main fusebox cover, open the glovebox, turn the two white quick-release fasteners and pull down the cover. The fuses in the 'E-box' are accessed once the cover retaining bolts have been removed.

3 A list of the circuits each fuse protects is given on the label attached to the inside of the main fusebox cover. A pair of tweezers for removing the fuses is also clipped to the fusebox. Note that the vertical fuses are active, and the horizontal fuses are spare. High amperage 'fusible links' are located on the top face of the fusebox, whilst the main fusible link is located adjacent to the battery in the luggage compartment **(see illustrations)**.

3.3a A list (arrowed) of the fuse allocations is included in the fusebox

3.3b The main fusible link is located in the luggage compartment

3.4 Use the tweezers provided to extract and fit the fuses

3.7 Relays behind the passenger side glovebox

4 To remove a fuse, first switch off the circuit concerned (or the ignition), then pull the fuse out of its terminals using the tweezers which are clipped to the inside of the fusebox cover **(see illustration)**. The wire within the fuse should be visible; if the fuse is blown it will be broken or melted.

5 Always renew a fuse with one of an identical rating; never use a fuse with a different rating from the original or substitute anything else. Never renew a fuse more than once without tracing the source of the trouble. The fuse rating is stamped on top of the fuse; note that the fuses are also colour-coded for easy recognition.

6 If a new fuse blows immediately, find the cause before renewing it again; a short to earth as a result of faulty insulation is most likely. Where a fuse protects more than one circuit, try to isolate the defect by switching on each circuit in turn (if possible) until the fuse blows again. Always carry a supply of spare fuses of each relevant rating on the vehicle, a spare of each rating should be clipped into the base of the fusebox.

Relays

7 The majority of relays are located behind the passenger's side glovebox **(see illustration)**, whilst other relays are located in the E-box in the left-hand corner of the engine compartment.

8 If a circuit or system controlled by a relay develops a fault and the relay is suspect, operate the system; if the relay is functioning it should be possible to hear it click as it is energised. If this is the case the fault lies with the components or wiring of the system. If the relay is not being energised then either the relay is not receiving a main supply or a switching voltage or the relay itself is faulty. Testing is by the substitution of a known good unit but be careful; while some relays are identical in appearance and in operation, others look similar but perform different functions.

9 To renew a relay first ensure that the ignition switch is off. The relay can then simply be pulled out from the socket and the new relay pressed in.

4 Switches - removal and refitting

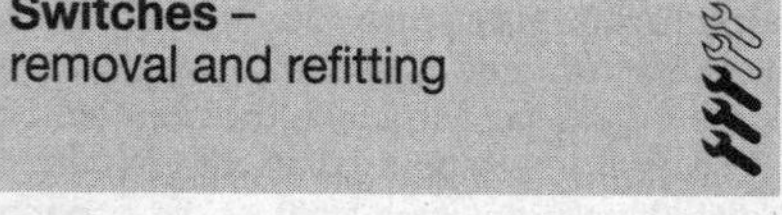

Note: *Disconnect the battery negative lead (see Chapter 5A) before removing any switch, and reconnect the lead after refitting the switch.*

Ignition switch/ steering column lock

1 Refer to Chapter 10.

Steering column switches

2 Place the steering column in the fully lowered and extended position. Remove the steering wheel as described in Chapter 10.

3 Slacken the upper column shroud retaining bolt and pull out the plastic rivet. Gently squeeze together the sides of the trim, lift the steering wheel end of the shroud first, then disengage the front end of the shroud **(see illustration)**.

4 Place the column in the highest, fully extended position. Using a small screwdriver, push in the centre pins of the two expanding rivets securing the lower shroud to the column, gently squeeze together the side of the upper shroud, and remove the lower shroud **(see illustration)**.

5 Disconnect the wiring plugs from the airbag contact unit, wiper and indicator switches.

6 Undo the four retaining bolts, and lift the switch assembly over the end of the steering column **(see illustration)**.

7 If required, the switches can be removed from the assembly by releasing the two retaining clips **(see illustration)**.

8 Refitting is a reversal of the removal procedure, ensuring that the wiring is correctly routed.

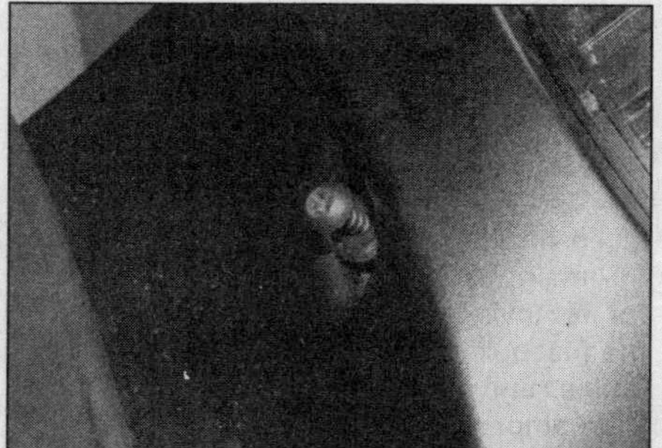
4.3 Slacken the bolt and pull it out with the plastic rivet

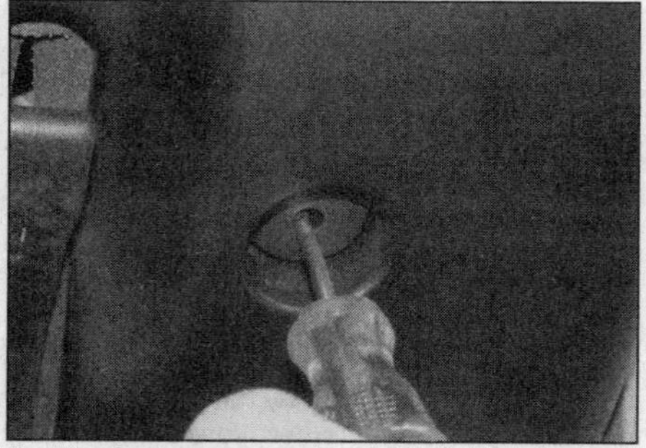
4.4 Push in the centre pins of the expanding rivets

4.6 Undo the four bolts (arrowed) and remove the switch assembly

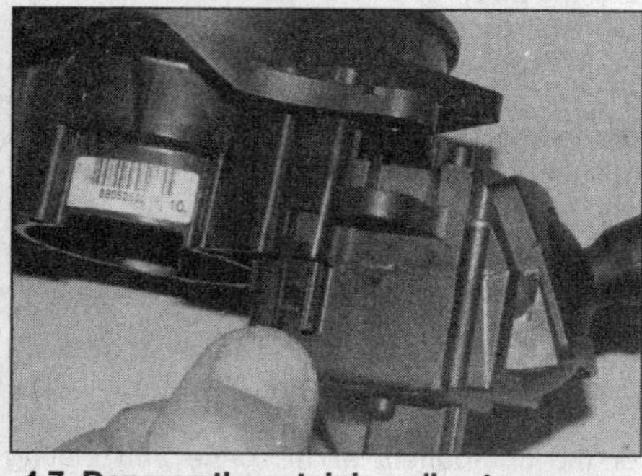
4.7 Depress the retaining clips to remove the switches

4.11a Undo the two bolts (arrowed) and remove the light switch

Lighting switch

9 Using a wooden or plastic spatula, carefully prise the decorative strip from the driver's side of the facia, above the light switch. Take care not to damage the facia panels.

10 Open the driver's side glovebox, undo the two bolts at its upper edge, and manoeuvre the glovebox from the facia. If necessary see Chapter 11, Section 27.

11 Undo the two bolts along the top edge of the light switch, lift the switch slightly, pull the top edge of the switch out and remove it from the facia. Lever over the locking catch, and disconnect the wiring plug as the switch is withdrawn **(see illustrations)**. No further dismantling of the switch is possible.

12 Refitting is the reverse of removal.

Hazard warning switch and central locking switch

13 On manual transmission models, carefully unclip the gearchange lever gaiter from the centre console and fold it back over the lever.

14 On models with automatic transmission carefully prise up the selector lever gaiter complete with plastic surrounding trim.

15 Remove the rear ashtray/storage tray, then remove the four bolts (two at the front, two at the rear) securing the centre console (see Chapter 11 if necessary), lift up the gear/selector lever surround trim.

16 Lift the front edge of the rear centre console, and press the switch(es) from place. Disconnect the wiring plugs as the switch(es) are removed **(see illustration)**.

17 Refitting is the reverse of removal.

Electric window switches

18 Unclip the gear lever/selector lever gaiter from the surrounding trim, and pull it up to expose the trim retaining bolts **(see illustration)**. Note that on automatic transmission models, the gaiter should be lifted with the adjacent trim from the centre console panel (see Chapter 7B).

19 Undo the two retaining bolts, and lift up the rear of the trim panel.

20 Press in the locking tabs and remove the switch(es) from the panel **(see illustration)**. Disconnect the wiring plug(s) as the switch is withdrawn.

21 Refitting is the reversal of removal.

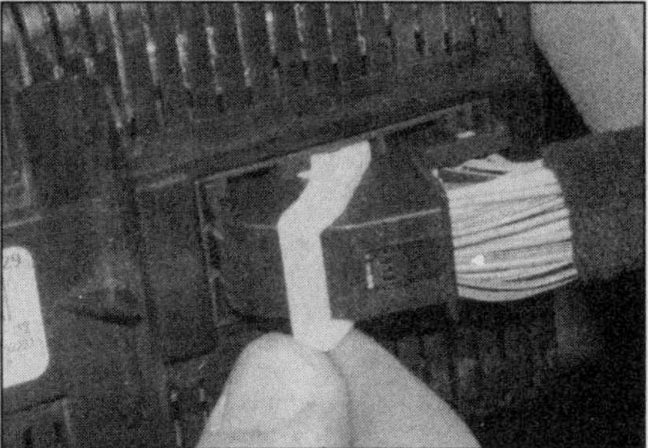

4.11b Lever over the locking catch and disconnect the wiring plug

Exterior mirror switch

22 Starting at the front edge, carefully lever the switch out from the armrest **(see illustration)**.

23 Disconnect the wiring connector and remove the switch.

24 Refitting is the reverse of removal.

Cruise control clutch switch

25 Undo the driver's side lower facia panel retaining bolts then unclip the panel and remove it from the vehicle. Note their fitted positions and disconnect any wiring plugs as the panel is withdrawn.

26 Disconnect the wiring plug from the switch.

27 Depress the clutch pedal, and pull the switch red sleeve out to its fully extended position.

28 Depress the retaining clips and slide the switch out of position **(see illustration)**.

29 Refitting is the reverse of removal.

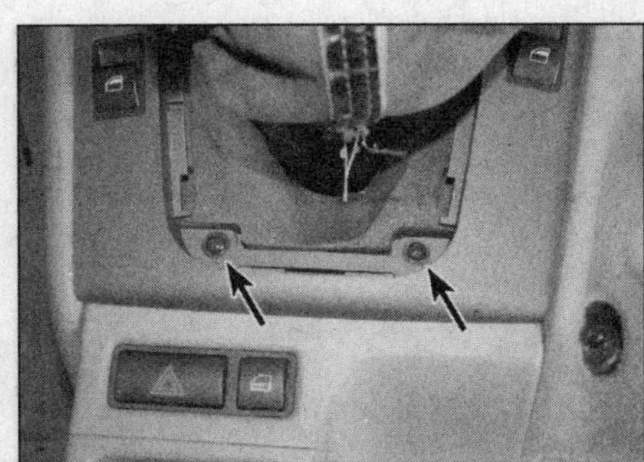

4.18 Undo the trim retaining bolts (arrowed)

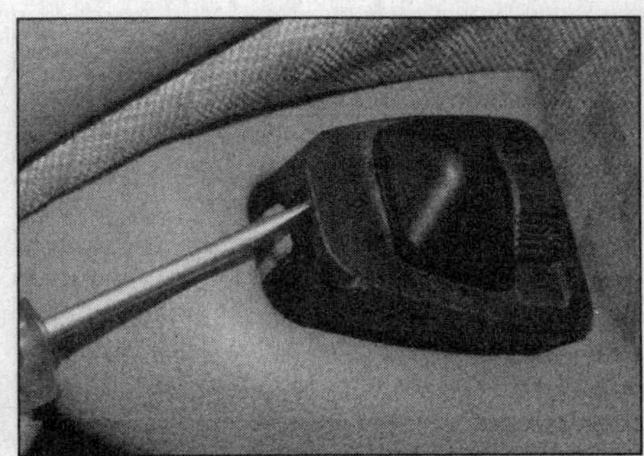

4.22 Carefully lever the mirror switch from the armrest

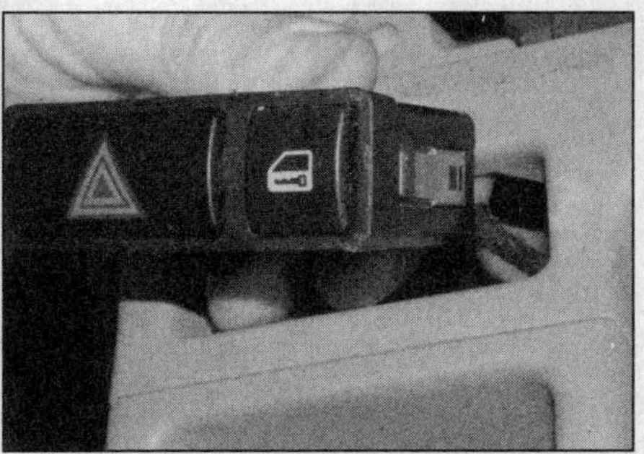

4.16 Press the hazard/central locking switch out from underneath

Heated rear window switch

Models with automatic air conditioning

30 On these models the switch is an integral part of the control unit and cannot be renewed. If the switch is faulty seek the advice of a BMW dealer.

Other models

31 On these models the switch is an integral part of the heater control panel printed circuit.

32 Remove the heater control panel as described in Chapter 3.

33 Disconnect the switch wiring plug, release the retaining clips and pull the switch from the panel.

34 Refitting is the reverse of removal. Check the operation of the switch before refitting the control panel to the facia.

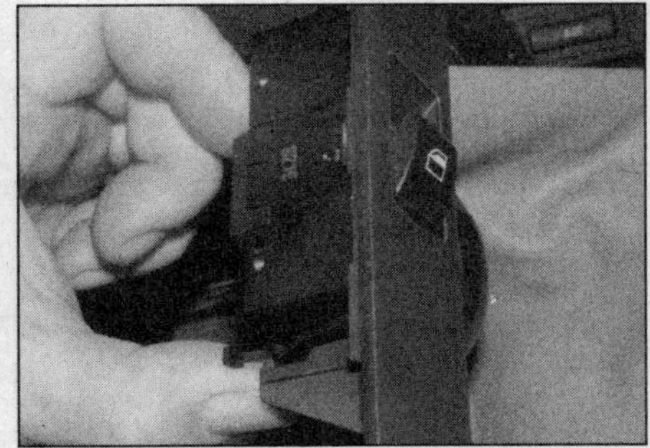

4.20 Press in the locking tabs and remove the switch

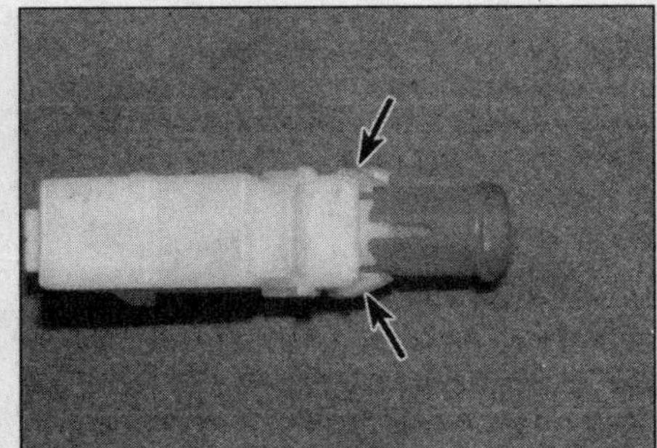

4.28 With the red sleeve fully extended, squeeze together the retaining clips (arrowed)

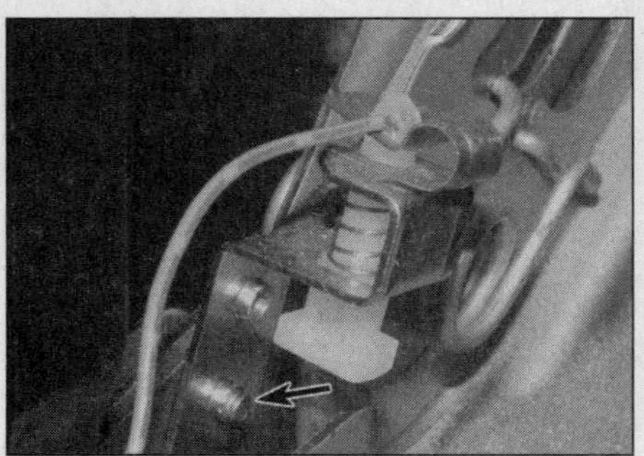

4.44 Undo the bolt (arrowed) and remove the handbrake warning switch

Heater blower motor switch

Models with automatic air conditioning

35 On these models the switch is an integral part of the control unit and cannot be renewed. If the switch is faulty seek the advice of a BMW dealer.

Other models

36 Remove the heater control panel as described in Chapter 3.

37 Undo the retaining bolts then unclip the switch from the rear of the control panel and remove it.

38 Refitting is the reverse of removal. Check the operation of the switch before refitting the control panel to the facia.

Air conditioning system switches

39 Refer to paragraphs 35 to 38.

4.49 Prise the switch from the steering wheel

Heated seat, electric sun blind and traction control switches

40 Remove the storage compartment from the centre console.

41 Disconnect the wiring connector then depress the retaining clips and slide the switch out from the panel.

42 Refitting is the reverse of removal.

Handbrake warning switch

43 Remove the rear section of the centre console as described in Chapter 11 to gain access to the handbrake lever.

44 Disconnect the wiring connector from the warning light switch then undo the bolt and remove the switch **(see illustration)**.

45 Refitting is the reverse of removal. Check the operation of the switch before refitting the centre console, the warning light should illuminate between the first and second clicks of the ratchet mechanism.

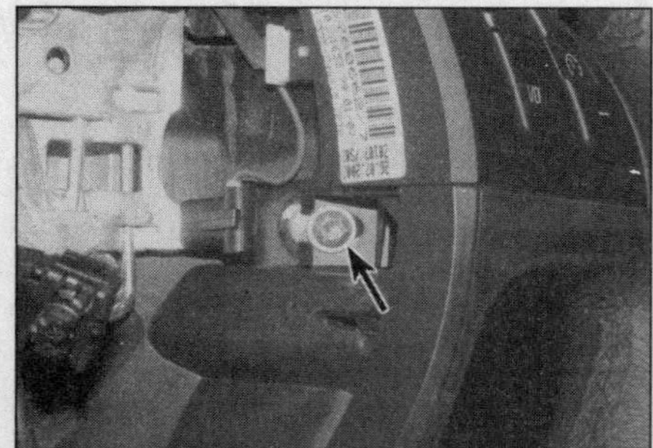

4.50a Undo the switch carrier upper bolts (arrowed) . . .

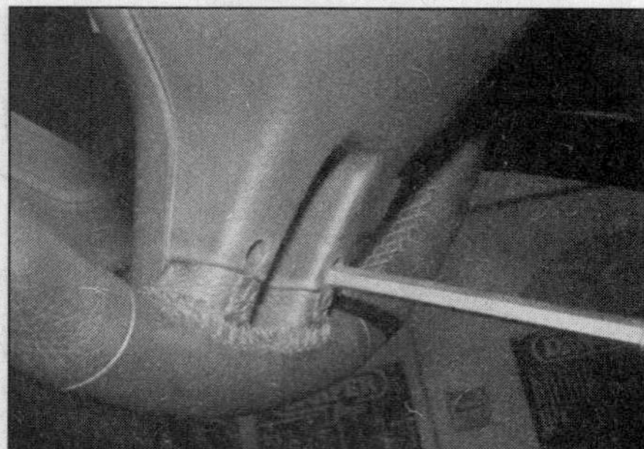

4.50b . . . and lower bolts

4.51 Press in the retaining clip and prise the switch from the panel

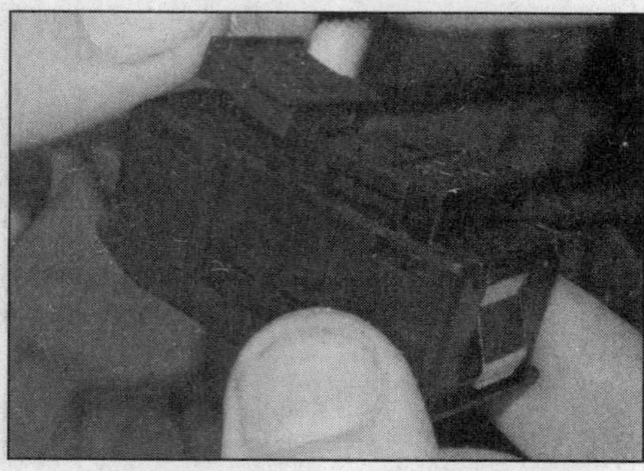

4.52 Disconnect the switch wiring plug

Brake light switch

46 Refer to Chapter 9.

Interior light switches

47 The function of the courtesy light switches is incorporated into the door/boot lid/tailgate lock assembly. To remove the relevant lock refer to Chapter 11.

Steering wheel switches

48 Two different types of steering wheels are fitted to the E46 3-Series range. Either a Multifunction steering wheel, or a Sports steering wheel. To remove the switches, remove the driver's airbag as described in Section 25, then proceed under the relevant heading.

Multifunction steering wheel

49 Carefully prise the switch from the steering wheel, and disconnect the switch wiring plugs **(see illustration)**. Note that the horn switch is integral with the airbag unit.

Sports steering wheel

50 Undo the four retaining bolts (two securing the upper section and two securing the lower section), and unclip the switch carrier panel from the steering wheel **(see illustrations)**. Disconnect the wiring plug as the panel with withdrawn.

Electric sunroof switch

51 Depress the clip at the rear of the switch, and pull the switch from the panel **(see illustration)**.

52 Disconnect the switch wiring connector then depress the retaining clips and slide the switch out of position **(see illustration)**.

53 Refitting is the reverse of removal.

5 Bulbs (exterior lights) – renewal

General

1 Whenever a bulb is renewed, note the following points.

a) *Remember that if the light has just been in use the bulb may be extremely hot.*
b) *Always check the bulb contacts and holder, ensuring that there is clean metal-to-metal contact between the bulb and its live(s) and earth. Clean off any corrosion or dirt before fitting a new bulb.*
c) *Wherever bayonet-type bulbs are fitted ensure that the live contact(s) bear firmly against the bulb contact.*
d) *Always ensure that the new bulb is of the correct rating and that it is completely clean before fitting it; this applies particularly to headlight/foglight bulbs (see below).*

Halogen headlight

All except Coupe models from 03/2003

2 Disconnect the wiring connector from the rear of the bulbholder **(see illustration)**.

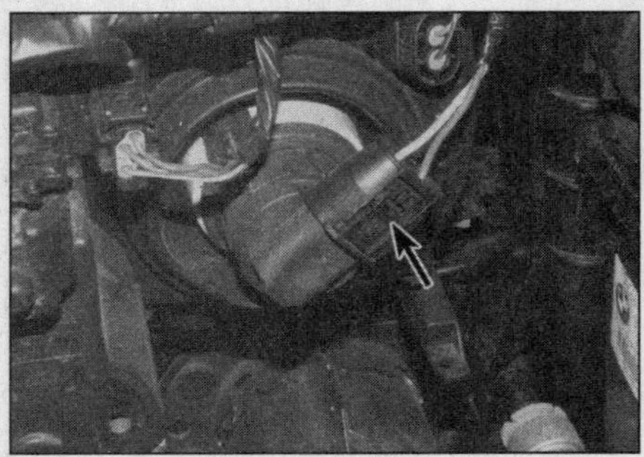

5.2 Disconnect the headlight bulb wiring plug (arrowed)

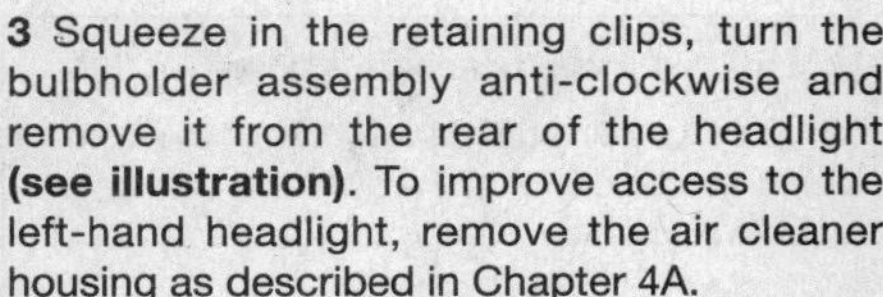

3 Squeeze in the retaining clips, turn the bulbholder assembly anti-clockwise and remove it from the rear of the headlight **(see illustration)**. To improve access to the left-hand headlight, remove the air cleaner housing as described in Chapter 4A.

4 Pull the bulb straight out from the holder **(see illustration)**.

5 When handling the new bulb, use a tissue or clean cloth to avoid touching the glass with the fingers; moisture and grease from the skin can cause blackening and rapid failure of this type of bulb. If the glass is accidentally touched, wipe it clean using methylated spirit.

6 Push the new bulb into the holder, ensuring that the bulb's contacts align with the corresponding slots in the bulbholder.

7 Refit the bulbholder to the rear of the headlight, rotating it clockwise until the retaining clips lock. Reconnect the wiring plug.

Coupe models from 03/2003

8 Rotate the plastic cap on the rear of the headlight anti-clockwise (main beam) or unclip the cover on the rear of the headlight (dipped beam) and remove it **(see illustrations)**.

9 Disconnect the wiring plug from the rear of the bulb, then release the retaining clip and pull the bulb from the reflector **(see illustrations)**.

5.3 Squeeze together the retaining clips, and rotate the bulbholder anti-clockwise

5.8a Rotate the main beam cover anti-clockwise

10 Position the new bulb in the reflector, ensuring the locating lug aligns, and secure it with the retaining clip. Reconnect the wiring plug and refit the plastic cap.

Xenon headlight

11 On models equipped with Xenon high-intensity dip beam bulbs, due to the potential high voltages involved, disconnect the battery negative lead as described in Chapter 5A. To improve access to the left-hand headlight, remove the air cleaner housing as described in Chapter 4A.

12 Pull the plastic cover from the rear of the headlight, on the dip beam (outer) side.

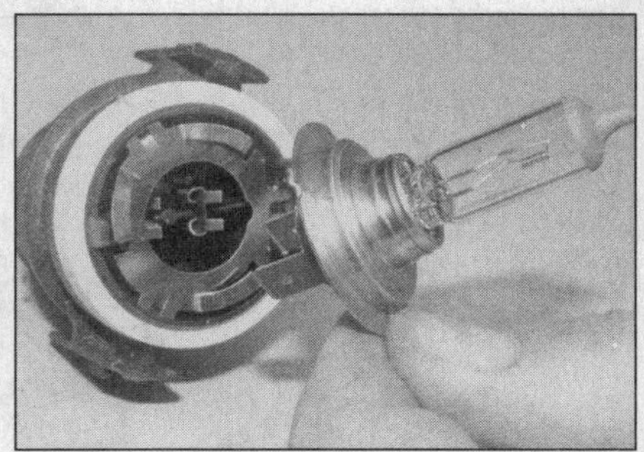

5.4 The headlight bulb is a push-fit in the bulbholder

5.8b Depress the retaining clip and remove the dipped beam cover

13 Rotate the bulb igniter unit on the rear of the bulb anti-clockwise and disconnect it **(see illustration overleaf)**.

14 Twist the bulb retaining ring anti-clockwise and remove it, with the bulb, from the headlight.

15 Fit the new bulb to the headlight, and secure it in place with the retaining ring.

16 Refit the igniter to the rear of the bulb, turning it clockwise to secure it.

17 Refit the cover to the rear of the unit. Where necessary, refit the air cleaner housing.

18 Reconnect the battery negative lead as described in Chapter 5A.

5.9a Pull the lower end of the clip (arrowed) slightly to the left, then rearwards – main beam bulb

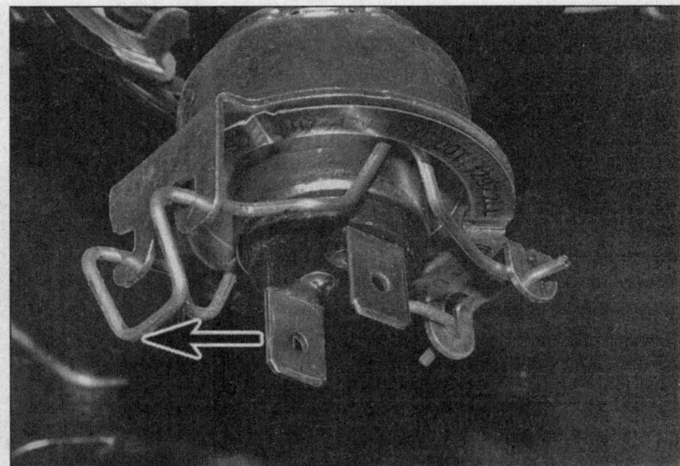

5.9b Pull the retaining clip (arrowed) slightly downwards, then rearwards – dipped beam bulb

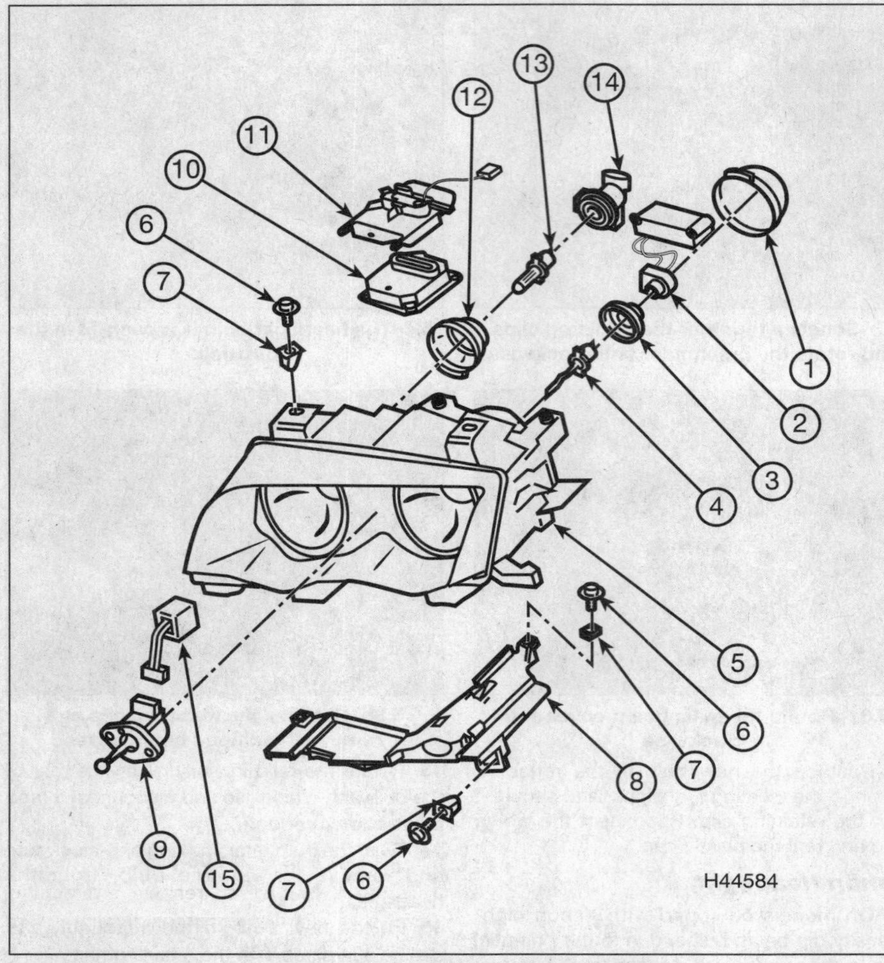

5.13 Xenon headlight

1 Dip beam cover
2 Xenon bulb igniter unit
3 Locking ring
4 Xenon bulb
5 Headlight housing
6 Bolt
7 Plastic nut
8 Headlight carrier plate
9 Headlight adjustment stepper motor
10 Xenon bulb control module
11 Bracket
12 Main beam cover
13 Main beam bulb
14 Bulb socket
15 Connector

Front sidelight

19 To improve access to the left-hand headlight on models with 6-cylinder engines, remove the air cleaner housing as described in Chapter 4A.

20 Rotate the bulbholder and withdraw it from the headlight unit. The bulb is of the capless type and is a push-fit in the holder **(see illustrations)**.

21 Refitting is the reverse of removal.

5.20a Twist the sidelight bulbholder anti-clockwise and remove it

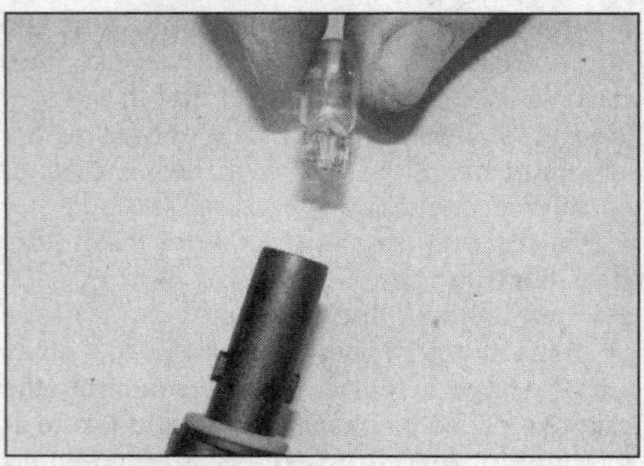
5.20b The sidelight bulb is a push-fit

Front direction indicator

All except Coupe models

22 Insert a screwdriver through the hole in the inner wing top, press down and release the light unit retaining clip. Withdraw the direction indicator light from the wing**(see illustrations)**.

23 Disconnect the wiring plug, and twist the bulbholder anti-clockwise to remove it from the light unit.

24 The bulb is a bayonet fitting in the holder. Push the bulb in slightly, then rotate it anti-clockwise and pull it from the holder **(see illustration 5.25)**.

Coupe models up to 03/2003

25 The light unit is retained by a single bolt **(see illustration)**. Disconnect the wiring plug, and twist the bulbholder anti-clockwise to remove it from the light unit. The bulb is a

5.22a Insert a screwdriver through the hole in the wing . . .

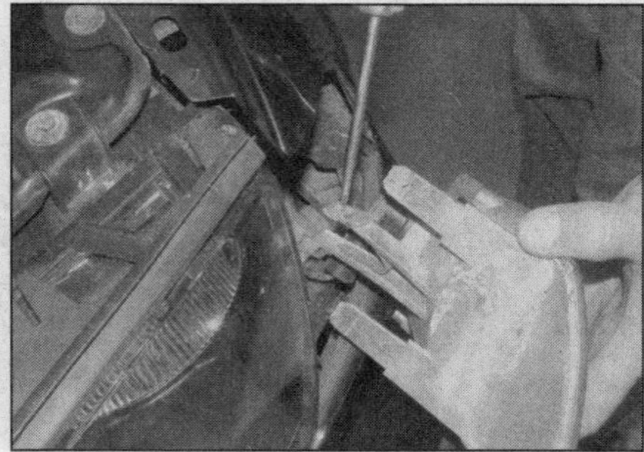
5.22b . . . to release the indicator retaining clip (except Coupe)

5.23 On Coupe models up to 03/2003, undo the bolt

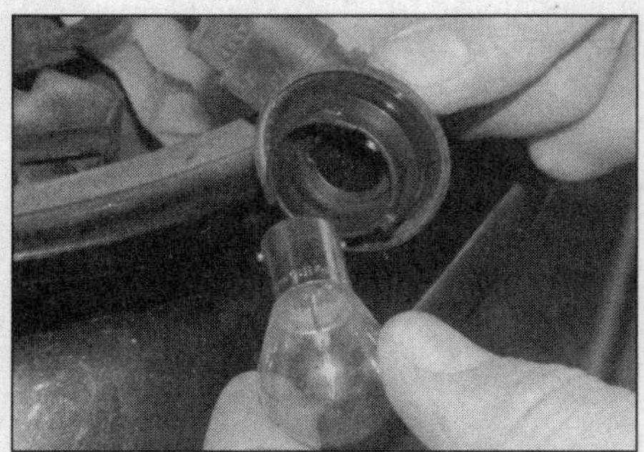
5.25 Push in and twist the bulb anti-clockwise

5.26a Rotate the bulbholder (arrowed) anti-clockwise

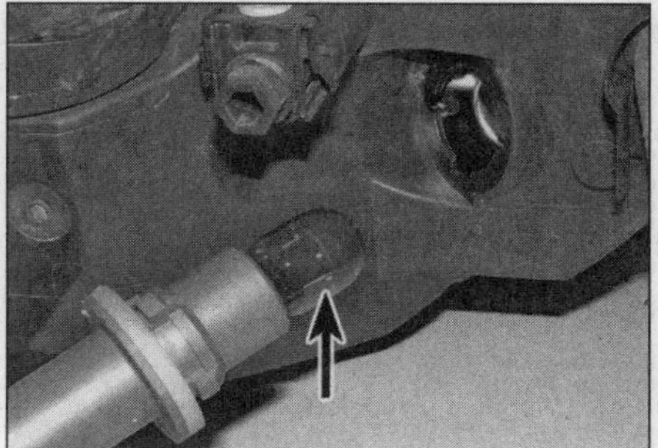
5.26b Pull the bulb (arrowed) from the holder

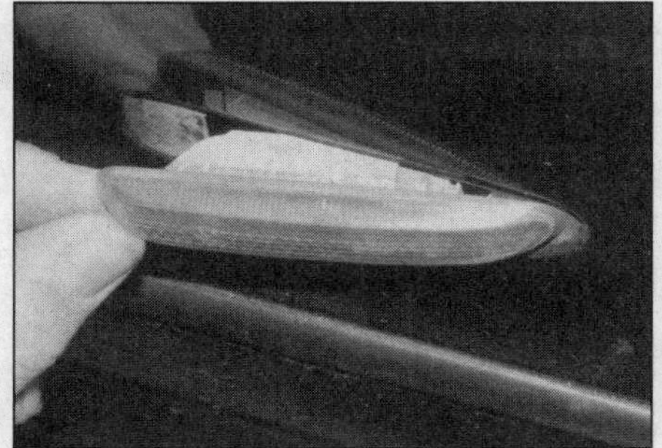
5.28 Push the repeater lens forward, and pull the rear edge out

5.29 Pull the capless bulb from the side repeater bulbholder

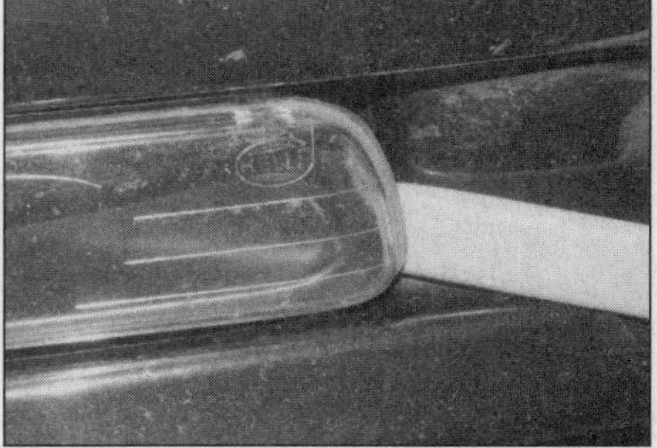
5.30 Carefully lever the foglight from the bumper

bayonet fitting in the holder. Push the bulb in slightly, then rotate it anti-clockwise and pull it from the holder **(see illustration)**.

Coupe models from 03/2003

26 Rotate the bulbholder anti-clockwise, remove it from the headlight, and pull the bulb from the holder **(see illustrations)**.

All models

27 Refitting is a reverse of the removal procedure making sure the light unit is securely retained by its retaining clip/bolt as applicable.

Side repeater

28 Using finger pressure, push the side repeater lens gently forwards. Pull out the rear edge of the lens and withdraw it from the wing **(see illustration)**.

29 Rotate the bulbholder anti-clockwise and pull it from the lens, pull the capless bulb it from the holder **(see illustration)**. Refitting is a reverse of the removal procedure.

Front foglight

Saloon and Touring models

30 Using a wooden or plastic tool, carefully lever the foglight from the bumper starting at the inside edge **(see illustration)**. Disconnect the wiring plug as the unit is withdrawn.

31 Rotate the bulbholder anti-clockwise and remove it from the light.The bulb is integral with the bulbholder **(see illustration)**.

32 Refitting is a reversal of removal. If necessary, adjust the aim of the light by rotating the adjusting screw adjacent to the lens **(see illustration)**.

Coupe models up to 03/2003

33 Lever out the catches, and remove the bumper trim from around the foglights **(see illustration)**.

34 Undo the bolts and remove the foglight, then disconnect the wiring plug as the unit is withdrawn. Rotate the bulbholder anti-clockwise, and pull the bulb from the holder.

Coupe models from 03/2003

35 Undo the 2 bolts, remove the plastic

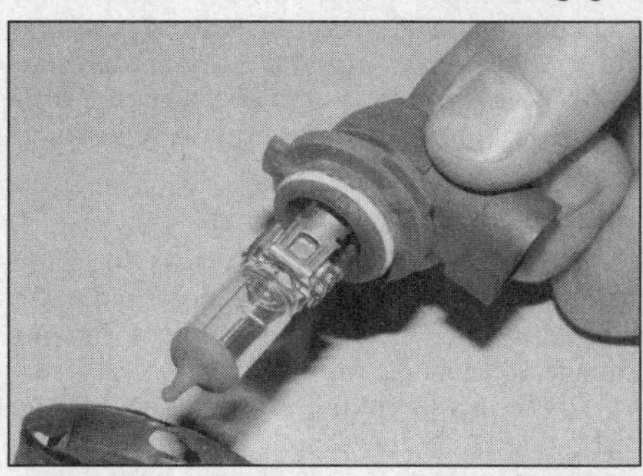
5.31 The foglight bulb is integral with the bulbholder

5.33 Release the catches and remove the foglight trim

5.32 To adjust the foglight aim, insert an Allen key (arrowed) into the aperture at the outside edge of the lens

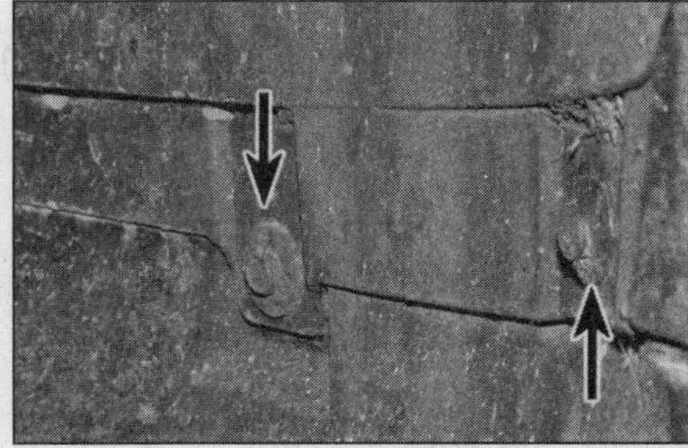
5.35a Prise out the centre pin, lever out the plastic expansion rivet, then undo the middle bolt (arrowed) . . .

5.35b . . . and the inner bolt securing the front section of the wheel arch liner

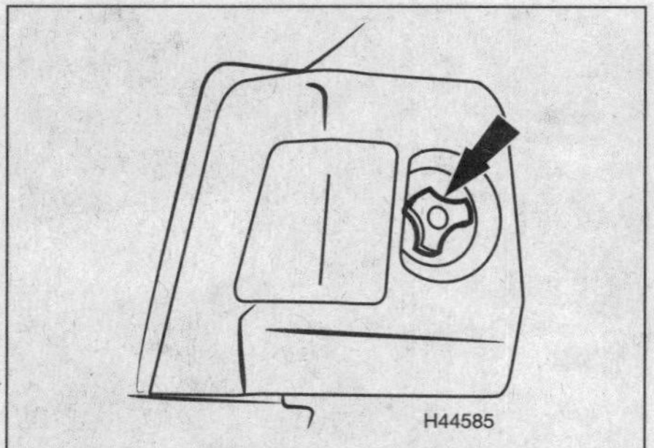

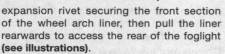

5.38b . . . or undo the fastener (arrowed – models from 10/01)

expansion rivet securing the front section of the wheel arch liner, then pull the liner rearwards to access the rear of the foglight **(see illustrations)**.

36 Disconnect the wiring plug, then rotate the bulbholder anti-clockwise and pull it from the foglight **(see illustration)**. The bulb is integral with the holder.

All models

37 Refitting is a reversal of removal. If necessary, adjust the aim of the light by rotating the adjusting screw adjacent to the lens.

Body-mounted rear lights

Saloon and Coupe models

Note: *On Coupe models from 03/2003, the body-mounted lights are non-renewable LEDs.*

38 From inside the vehicle luggage compartment, release the retaining clip (models up to 09/01 and Coupe models from 03/2003) or undo the fastener (models from 10/01) and remove the bulbholder from the rear of the light cluster **(see illustrations)**.

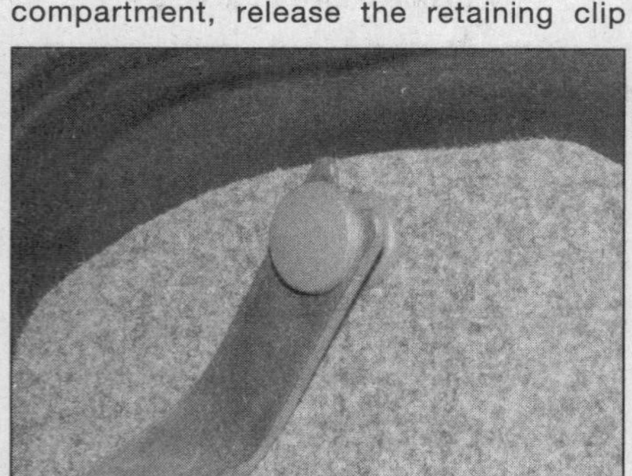

5.42 Prise out the boot lid trim retaining clips

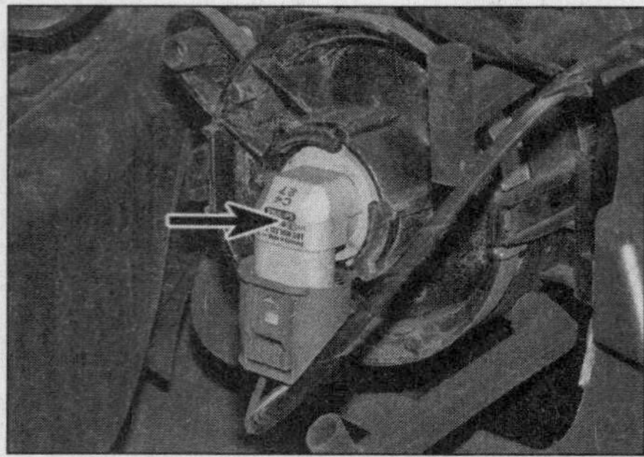

5.36 Rotate the bulbholder (arrowed) anti-clockwise

5.39 Press the bulb in, twist it anti-clockwise and remove it

39 Press the relevant bulb in slightly, twist it anti-clockwise, and remove it from the bulbholder **(see illustration). Note:** *If renewing the double element stop/tail bulb, the bayonet fitting pins are offset, and the bulb will only fit one way around.* Refitting is a reversal of removal.

Touring models

40 Fold back the flap in the luggage compartment to expose the bulbholder. To improve access to the left-hand light, remove the warning triangle from its location.

41 Release the retaining clip, and lift the bulbholder assembly slightly **(see illustration)**. Press the relevant bulb in slightly, twist it anti-clockwise, and remove it from the bulbholder. Refitting is a reversal of removal.

5.43 Release the retaining clip and remove the bulbholder

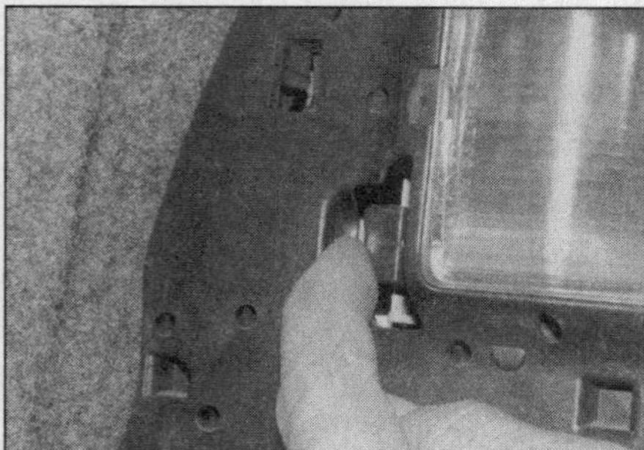

5.38a Release the retaining clip (models up to 09/01 and Coupe from 03/2003) . . .

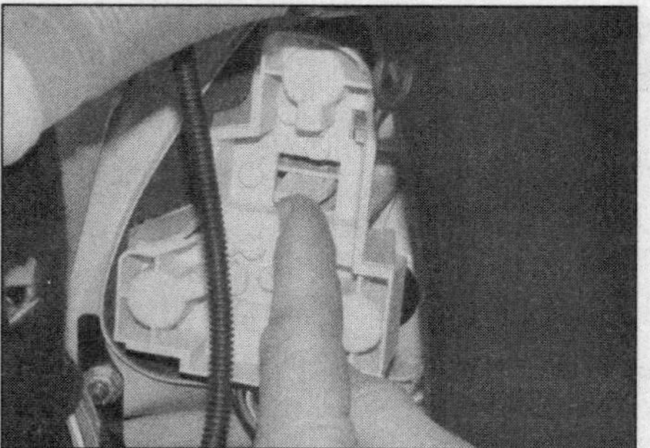

5.41 Release the clip and lift the bulbholder assembly

Boot lid-mounted rear lights

Saloon and Coupe models

42 Prise out the clips and partially release the boot lid trim panel behind the light cluster **(see illustration)**.

43 Release the retaining clip, and remove the bulbholder from the boot lid **(see illustration)**.

44 Press the relevant bulb in slightly, twist it anti-clockwise, and remove it from the bulbholder **(see illustration)**.

45 Refitting is a reversal of removal.

Tailgate-mounted rear lights

Touring models

46 Carefully prise the luggage compartment light unit from the tailgate trim panel. Disconnect the wiring plug as the unit is removed.

47 Prise up the small piece of trim at the top of the panel **(see illustration)**.

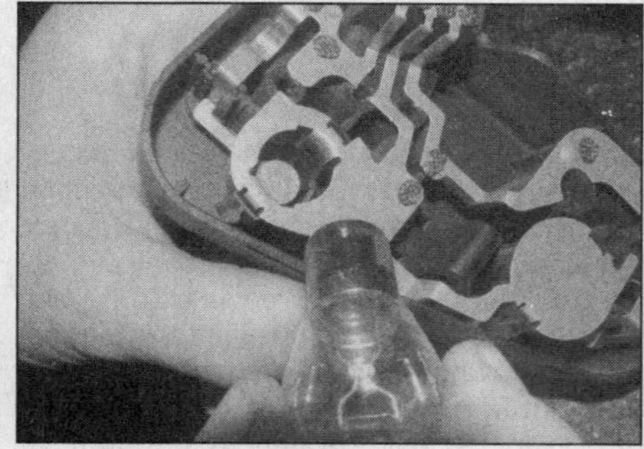

5.44 Push in the bulb, and rotate it anti-clockwise

5.47 Prise up the trim at the top of the tailgate panel

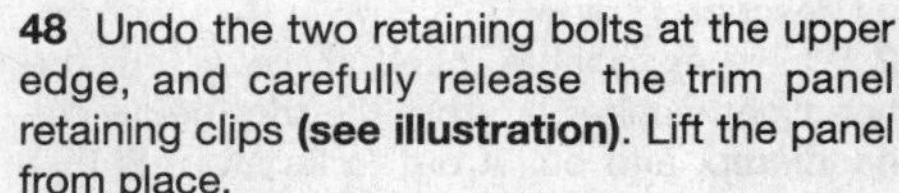

48 Undo the two retaining bolts at the upper edge, and carefully release the trim panel retaining clips **(see illustration)**. Lift the panel from place.

49 Disconnect the rear light cluster wiring plug, release the retaining clip and remove the bulbholder **(see illustration)**.

50 Press the relevant bulb in slightly, twist it anti-clockwise, and remove it from the bulbholder.

51 Refitting is a reversal of removal.

High-level brake light

Saloon and Coupe models

52 Carefully pull down the front edge, then slide the cover forward and remove it. Two types of cover may be fitted. The one-piece cover has two patches of Velcro at the front edge, whilst the split type cover has two push-in clips at the front edge.

53 Slide off the two retaining clips, and remove the light unit **(see illustration)**. Disconnect the wiring plug as the light is withdrawn. The high-level brake light is an LED strip. If a fault develops, consult your local BMW dealer or specialist.

54 Refitting is a reversal of removal, ensuring that the lugs at the rear of the cover engage correctly with the corresponding locating holes.

Touring models

55 On these models, to remove the high-level brake light, the rear spoiler must be removed. This requires special tools, and involves a complex realignment procedure. We recommend this is entrusted to your BMW dealer or specialist.

5.48 Undo the two bolts (arrowed)

5.53 Slide the retaining clips (arrowed) away from the high-level brake light

Number plate light

56 Using a small screwdriver from the inboard end, carefully prise out the light lens, and remove it from the boot lid/tailgate **(see illustration)**.

57 The bulb is of the 'festoon' type, and can be prised from the contacts.

58 Refitting is the reverse of removal, making sure the bulb is securely held in position by the contacts.

5.49 Release the bulbholder retaining clip

5.56 Prise the number plate light lens

6 Bulbs (interior lights) – renewal

General

1 Refer to Section 5, paragraph 1.

Courtesy/interior lights

2 Using a small, flat-bladed screwdriver, carefully prise light unit out of position. When removing the front central interior light or rear central interior light (Touring models) unit, prise the rear edge of the unit down and pull the light unit free. Rotate the bulbholder pull the capless bulb from the holders **(see illustrations)**.

3 Push the new bulb(s) into the holder(s), and refit them in to the light unit. Refit the light unit. Note that the front edge of the front central light unit must be fitted first, then push the rear edge into place.

Footwell light

4 Carefully lever the light lens out from the panel.

5 Prise the festoon bulb from the contacts **(see illustration)**.

6 Fit the new bulb into position and refit the lens to the light unit.

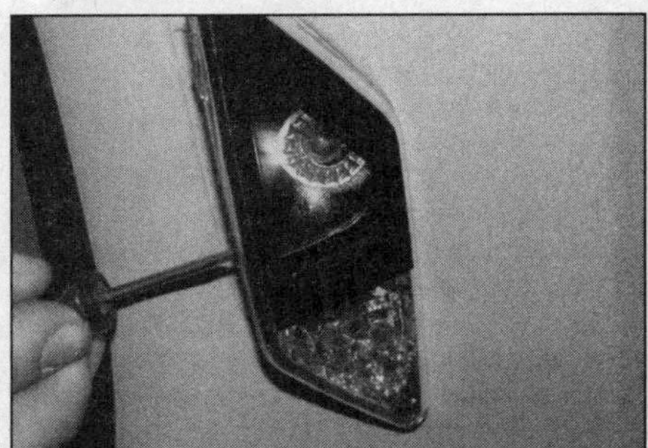

6.2a Carefully prise the courtesy light from the trim panel

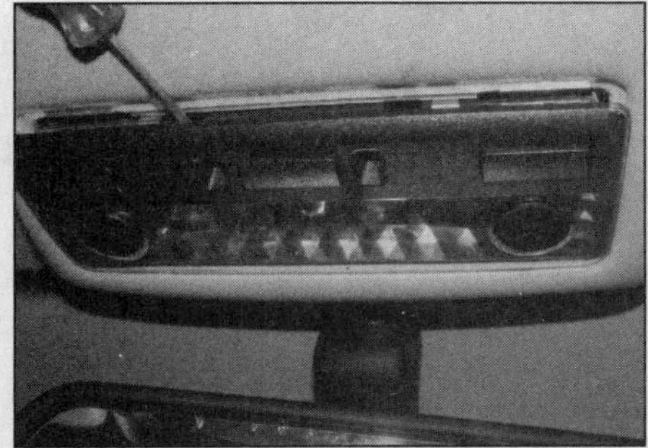

6.2b Prise the main interior light assembly from the headlining

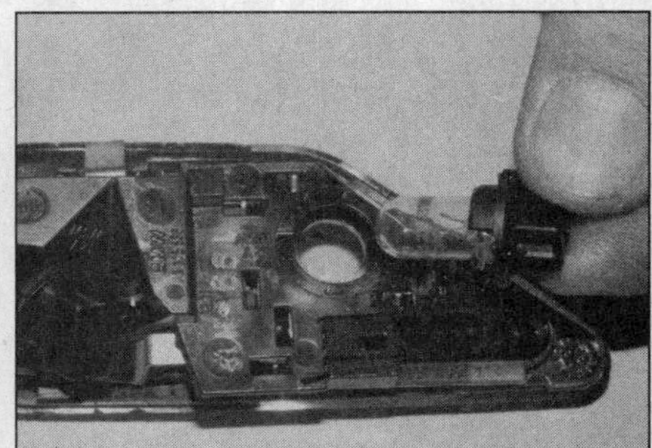

6.2c Rotate the bulbholder anti-clockwise and pull out the capless bulb

Luggage compartment light

7 Refer to paragraphs 4 to 6.

Instrument illumination/ warning lights

8 The instrument panel is illuminated by a series of LEDs which cannot be renewed.

Glovebox illumination bulb

9 Open up the glovebox. Using a small flat-bladed screwdriver, carefully prise the top of the light assembly and withdraw it. Release the bulb from its contacts.

10 Install the new bulb, ensuring it is securely held in position by the contacts, and clip the light unit back into position.

Heater control panel illumination

Models with automatic air conditioning

11 The heater control panel is illuminated by LEDs which are not serviceable. If a fault develops, have the system checked by a BMW dealer or suitably-equipped specialist.

Other models

12 Pull off the heater control panel knobs then undo the retaining bolts and unclip the faceplate from the front of the control unit.

13 Using a pair of pointed-nose pliers, rotate the bulbholder anti-clockwise and remove it from the vehicle. On some models the panel is illuminated by LEDs which are not serviceable.

14 Refitting is the reverse of removal.

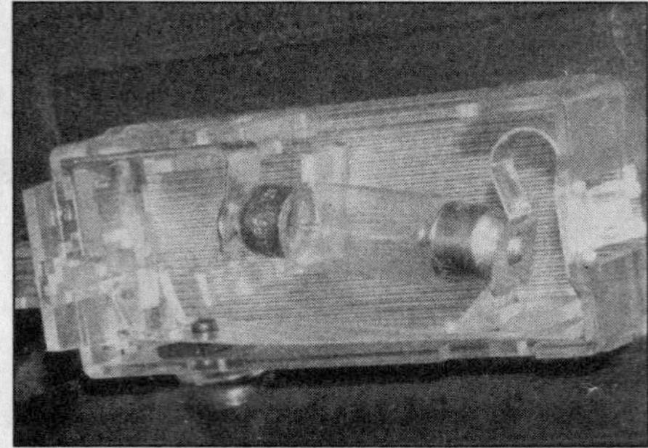

6.5 Carefully prise the festoon bulb from the contacts

Switch illumination bulbs

15 All of the switches are fitted with illuminating bulbs/LEDs; some are also fitted with a bulb/LED to show when the circuit concerned is operating. On all switches, these bulbs/LEDs are an integral part of the switch assembly and cannot be obtained separately. Bulb/LED renewal will therefore require the renewal of the complete switch assembly.

Ashtray illumination bulb

16 Prise up the gear/selector lever surround trim. Undo the two bolts at the front of the trim aperture securing the ashtray/storage compartment carrier.

17 Prise up the lower edge of the storage compartment and pull the unit from the facia. Undo the two bolts at the top of the storage compartment aperture and pull the carrier from the facia.

18 Disconnect the wiring plug, squeeze together the retaining clips and pull the bulbholder from place. The bulb is integral with the holder.

19 Refitting is a reversal of removal.

7 Exterior light units – removal and refitting

Headlight

All models except Coupe from 03/2003

1 Remove the relevant direction indicator light as described below.

2 Where applicable, carefully lever out the headlight washer jet from the trim below the headlamp, and pull it out to its stop. With a sharp tug, separate the jet from the washer tube.

3 Unclip the inboard end of the headlight trim, press the trim down slightly to release the centre retaining clips, then disengage the outboard end from the front wing **(see illustrations)**. At this point, if required, the headlight lens can be removed by releasing the retaining clips around its circumference.

4 Note their fitted positions, and disconnect all wiring plugs from the rear of the headlight.

5 Each headlight is retained by four bolts – two hexagon-head, and two Torx bolts. Slacken and remove the headlight retaining bolts **(see illustration). Note:** *As the bolts are removed, do not allow the plastic retaining clips to rotate. If necessary retain the clips with a suitable open-ended spanner.*

6 Remove the headlight unit from the vehicle.

Coupe models from 03/2003

7 Where applicable, carefully lever out the headlight washer jet from the trim below the headlamp, and pull it out to its stop. With a sharp tug, separate the jet from the washer tube.

8 The headlight is secured by 4 bolts. Slacken and remove the headlight retaining bolts, then press in the clip at the outer edge of the headlight trim, pull the headlight forwards a little and disconnect the wiring plug **(see illustrations)**. Manoeuvre the headlight from position.

7.3a Unclip the inboard . . .

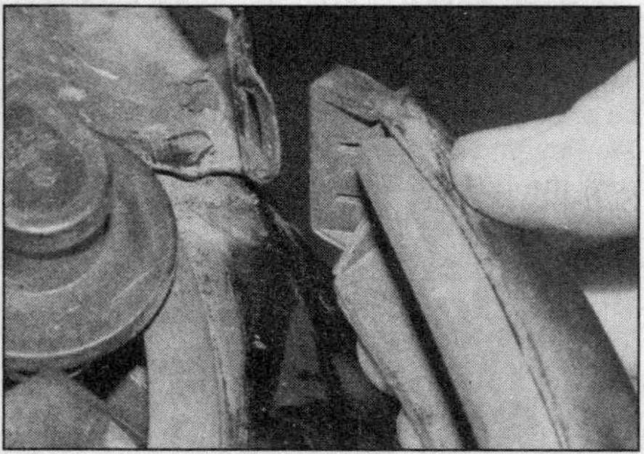

7.3b . . . and outboard end of the headlight trim

7.5 Undo the headlight retaining bolts (arrowed)

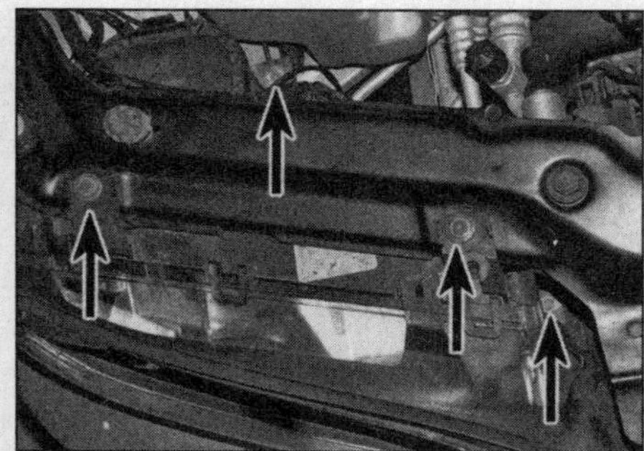

7.8a Undo the headlight retaining bolts (arrowed) . . .

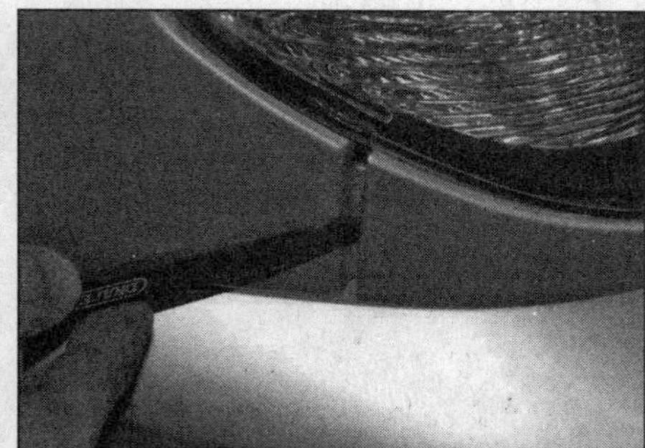

7.8b . . . press in the clip at the outer edge of the trim . . .

7.8c . . . and manoeuvre the headlight forwards

7.19 Undo the bolts (arrowed) securing the wheel arch liner to the underside of the bumper

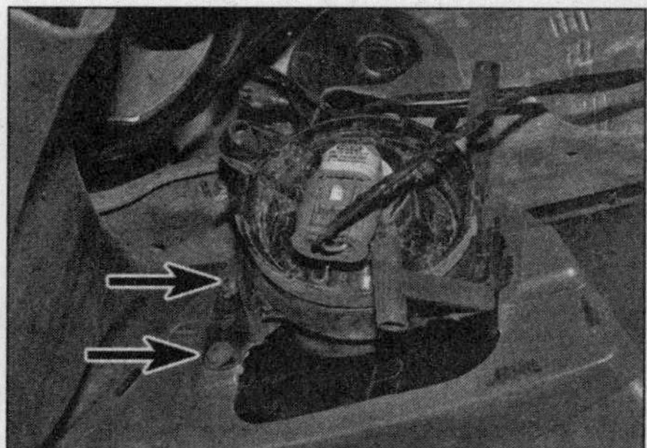

7.20 Foglight retaining bolts (arrowed) – 03/2003-on model shown

All models

9 Refitting is a direct reversal of the removal procedure. Lightly tighten the retaining bolts and check the alignment of the headlight with the bumper and bonnet. Once the light unit is correctly positioned, securely tighten the retaining bolts and check the headlight beam alignment using the information given in Section 8.

Xenon headlight control unit

10 Remove the relevant headlight as described earlier in this Section.

11 Undo the two retaining bolts, slide the control unit to the rear of the headlight remove it **(see illustration 5.10)**.

12 If required, the control unit can be separated from the mounting bracket by removing the two securing bolts.

13 Refitting is a reversal of removal.

Front direction indicator light

13 Insert a screwdriver down through the hole in the inner wing, and release the indicator light retaining clip **(see illustrations 5.22a and 5.22b)**. On Coupe models up to 03/2003, the light is secured by a single bolt **(see illustration 5.23 or 5.26 as applicable)**. On Coupe models after 03/2003, the indicator light is integral with the headlight. Slide the light forward and disconnect the wiring connector from the light unit.

14 Refitting is a reverse of the removal procedure making sure the light retaining clip engages correctly or the bolt is securely tightened.

Front indicator side repeater

15 Using finger pressure, push the side repeater lens gently forwards. Pull out the rear edge of the lens and withdraw it from the wing **(see illustration 5.28)**. Disconnect the wiring plug as the unit is withdrawn.

16 Refitting is a reverse of the removal procedure.

Front foglight

Saloon and Touring models

17 Using a wooden or plastic tool, carefully lever the foglight from the bumper **(see illustration 5.30)**. Disconnect the wiring plug as the unit is withdrawn.

18 Refitting is a reversal of removal.

Coupe models

19 On models upto 03/2003, lever out the catches, and remove the bumper trim from around the foglights **(see illustration 5.33)**. On models from 03/2003, undo the bolts, prise out the centre pin, lever the plastic expansion rivet, and remove the front, lower section of the wheel arch liner **(see illustrations 5.35a and 5.35b)**. Note the bolts on the underside of the wheel arch liner **(see illustration)**.

20 Undo the bolts and remove the foglight **(see illustration)**. Disconnect the wiring plug as the unit is withdrawn. Refitting is a reversal of removal.

Body-mounted rear lights

Saloon and Coupe models

21 From inside the vehicle luggage compartment, release the retaining clip (models up to 09/01) or undo the faster (models from 10/01) and remove the bulbholder from the rear of the light cluster **(see illustrations 5.38a and 5.38b)**.

22 Release the retaining clips and partially detach the luggage compartment side trim panel around the area of the light cluster (see Chapter 11, Section 27, if necessary).

23 Undo the three retaining nuts and remove the cluster from the wing **(see illustration)**.

24 Refitting is a reversal of removal.

Touring models

25 Fold back the flap in the luggage compartment to expose the bulbholder. To improve access to the left-hand light, remove the warning triangle from its location.

26 Release the retaining clip, and lift the bulb-holder assembly slightly **(see illustration 5.41)**.

27 Undo the three retaining nuts, and remove the light cluster **(see illustration)**.

28 Refitting is a reversal of removal.

Boot lid-mounted rear lights

Saloon and Coupe models

29 Prise out the two clips and partially release the boot lid trim panel behind the light cluster **(see illustration 5.42)**.

30 Release the retaining clip, and remove the bulbholder from the boot lid **(see illustration 5.43)**.

31 Undo the securing nut, remove the plastic retainer, and remove the light cluster **(see illustration)**. Note that the edge of the light unit wraps around the edge of the boot lid.

32 Refitting is a reversal of removal.

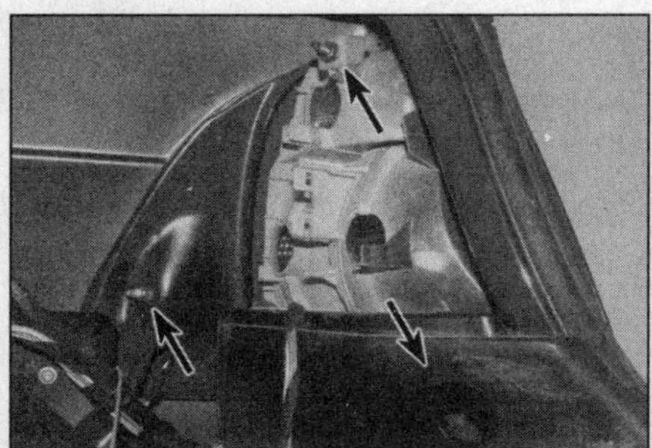

7.23 The rear light is secured by three nuts (arrowed)

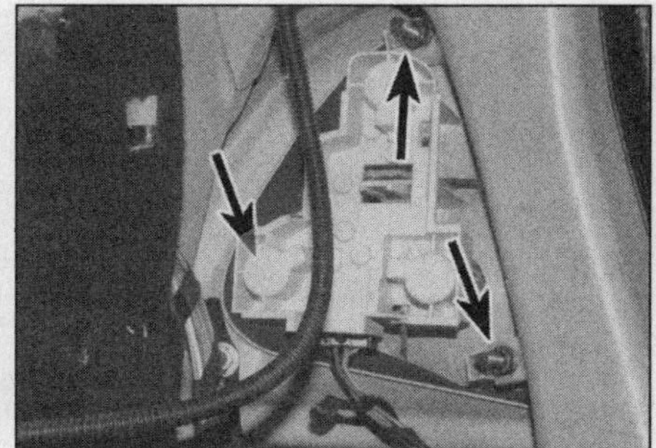

7.27 Undo the three nuts (arrowed) and remove the light unit

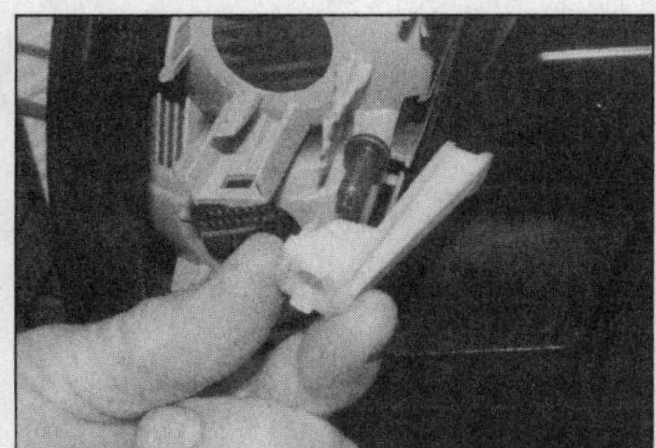

7.31 Undo the nut and remove the plastic retainer

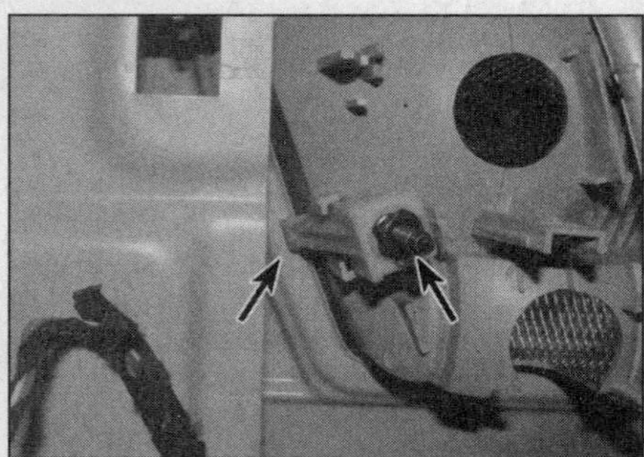
7.37 Undo the nut (arrowed) and press the lever (arrowed) towards the light cluster

7.43 Pull the 'frame' from the headlight

7.46 The headlight range control motor is retained by two bolts

Tailgate-mounted rear lights

Touring models

33 Carefully prise luggage compartment light unit from the tailgate trim panel. Disconnect the wiring plug as the unit is removed.

34 Prise up the small piece of trim at the top of the panel **(see illustration 5.47)**.

35 Undo the two retaining bolts at the upper edge, and carefully release the trim panel retaining clips **(see illustration 5.48)**. Lift the panel from place.

36 Disconnect the rear light cluster wiring plug, release the retaining clip and remove the bulbholder **(see illustration 5.49)**.

37 Slacken the securing nut, press the lock lever in the direction of the light cluster and remove it **(see illustration)**.

38 Refitting is a reversal of removal.

Number plate light

39 Using a small screwdriver, carefully prise out the light lens, and remove it from the boot lid/tailgate **(see illustration 5.56)**. Disconnect the wiring plug as the unit is withdrawn.

40 Refitting is the reverse of removal.

Headlight range control motors

41 Remove the headlight lens as described in Paragraphs 1 to 3 earlier in this Section.

42 Remove both bulbholders from the rear of the headlight as described in Section 5.

43 Carefully pull the headlight 'frame' towards the front **(see illustration)**.

44 Remove the protective rubber seals around the bulbholders from the rear of the unit.

45 Mark its original position and, counting the number of rotations, turn the central adjuster wheel clockwise (maybe 20 to 30 rotations) until the top of the insert is released from the guide slot, then the outer adjuster piece can released from the insert. Carefully disengage the range control motor rod from the socket on the rear of the insert. Manoeuvre the insert from the headlight.

46 Undo the retaining bolts, disconnect the wiring plug, and remove the range control motor **(see illustration)**.

47 When refitting the headlight insert, release the retaining clips and remove the black plastic trim from the centre of the headlight insert, then squeeze together the retaining lugs, and remove the control motor socket from the insert **(see illustrations)**. Do not refit the black plastic trim yet.

48 Locate the socket on the control motor rod, clip the outer adjuster piece onto the insert, and aligning the central adjusting piece with the corresponding slot in the headlamp shell, rotate the central adjusting wheel back to its original position. Push the insert onto the range control motor socket until its clips into place – guide the socket into place from the front of the insert **(see illustration)**. Refit the black plastic trim.

49 When completed, have the headlight beam aim checked, and if necessary adjusted.

8 Headlight beam alignment – general information

1 Accurate adjustment of the headlight beam is only possible using optical beam setting equipment and this work should therefore be carried out by a BMW dealer or suitably-equipped workshop.

2 For reference, the headlights can be adjusted by rotating the adjuster screws on the top of the headlight unit **(see illustration)**. The

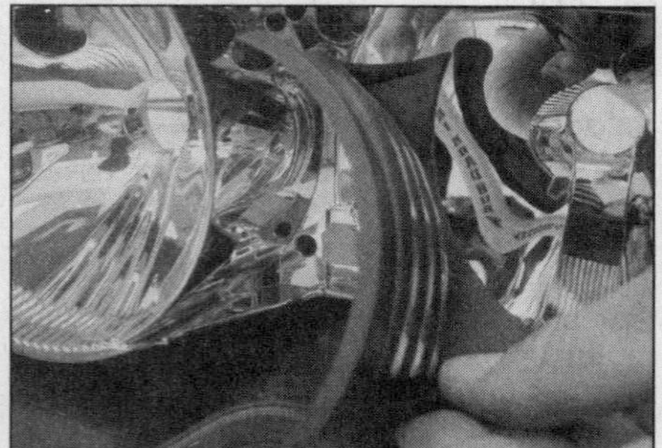
7.47a Remove the black plastic trim . . .

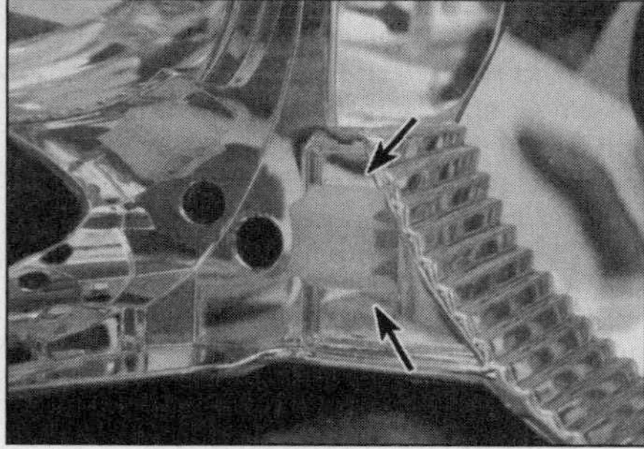
7.47b . . . then squeeze together the retaining clips (arrowed) . . .

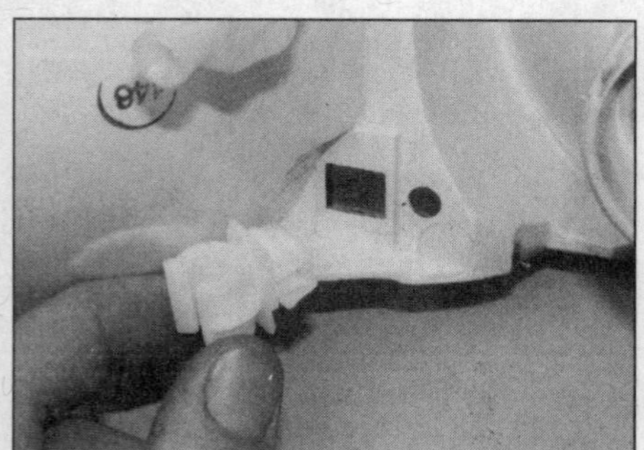
7.47c . . . and remove the control motor socket from the insert

7.48 Clip the outer adjuster piece (arrowed) onto the insert (arrowed)

8.2 Headlight beam adjustment screws (arrowed)

outer adjuster alters the horizontal position of the beam whilst the centre adjuster alters the vertical aim of the beam.

3 Some models have an electrically-operated headlight beam adjustment system which is controlled through the switch in the facia. On these models ensure that the switch is set to the off position before adjusting the headlight aim.

9 Instrument panel – removal and refitting

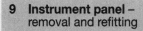

Removal

1 Disconnect the battery negative terminal (see Chapter 5A).

2 Move the steering column down as far as it will go, and extend it completely.

3 Slacken and remove the two retaining Torx bolts from the top of the instrument panel, and carefully pull the top of the panel from the facia **(see illustration)**.

4 Lift up the retaining clips then disconnect the wiring connectors and remove the instrument panel from the vehicle **(see illustration)**.

Refitting

5 Refitting is the reverse of removal, making sure the instrument panel wiring is correctly reconnected and securely held in position by any retaining clips. On completion reconnect the battery and check the operation of the panel warning lights to ensure that they are functioning correctly. **Note:** *If the instrument cluster has been renewed, the new unit must be coded to match the vehicle. This can only be carried out by a BMW dealer or suitably-equipped specialist.*

10 Instrument panel components – removal and refitting

Through its connections, via 'bus' networks with most of the systems and sensors within the vehicle, the instrument cluster is the control and information centre for the BMW 3-Series models. The 'K-bus' is connected to the supplementary restraint system, exterior and interior lights, rain sensor, heating/air conditioning, and the central body electrical system. The 'CAN-bus' (Controlled Area Network) is connected to the engine management, transmission management, and the ABS/traction control/dynamic stability control systems. The 'D-bus' is connected to the diagnostic link connector and EOBD (European On-Board Diagnostics) connector.

The speedometer displays the vehicle's roadspeed from information supplied by the ABS ECM, generated from the left-hand rear wheel speed sensor.

At the time of writing, no individual components are available for the instrument panel and therefore the panel must be treated

9.3 Remove the two bolts from the top of the instrument panel (arrowed)

9.4 Lift the retaining clips and disconnect the wiring plugs

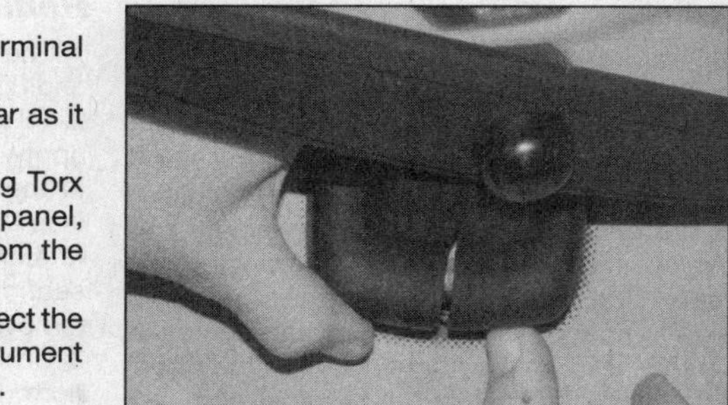

11.1 Press the two halves of the trim apart

11.3 Pull out the clip each side (arrowed) and remove the sensor

as a sealed unit. If there is a fault with one of the instruments, remove the panel as described in Section 9 and take it to your BMW dealer for testing. They have access to a special diagnostic tester which will be able to locate the fault and will then be able to advise you on the best course of action.

11 Rain sensor – removal and refitting

1 The rain sensor is incorporated into the front face of the interior mirror mounting base. Press up on the lower end of the mounting trim, and press the two halves of the mounting trim apart at the base, and release the trim retaining clips **(see illustration)**.

2 With the trim removed, disconnect the sensor wiring plug

3 Pull out the two sensor retaining clips, and pull the sensor to the rear **(see illustration)**.

4 Refitting is a reversal of removal.

12 Suspension height sensor – removal and refitting

Removal

1 Vehicles equipped with Xenon headlights are also equipped with automatic headlight adjustment. Ride sensors fitted to the front and rear suspension provide information on the suspension ride height, whilst the headlight range control motors alter the headlight beam angle as necessary. The sensors are fitted between the suspension subframes and lower arms. To access the sensors, jack the relevant end of the vehicle, and support securely on axle stands (see *Jacking and vehicle support*). Where applicable remove the engine undershield.

2 Undo the nut securing the control rod to the sensor arm, and disconnect the rod.

3 Undo the two mounting nuts and remove the sensor. Disconnect the wiring plug as the sensor is withdrawn **(see illustration)**.

Refitting

4 Refitting is a reversal of the removal procedure, ensuring all the wiring connectors are securely reconnected.

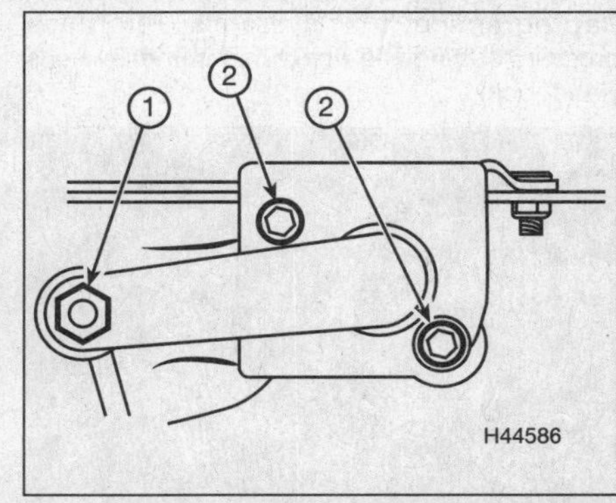

12.3 Suspension height sensor

1 Control rod nut
2 Height sensor nuts

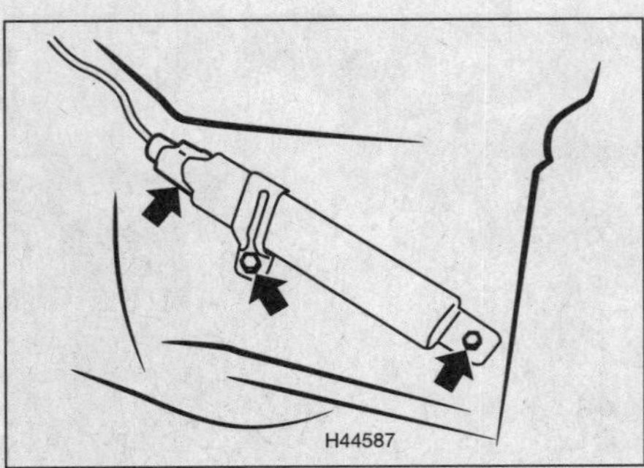

13.8 Disconnect the wiring plug, undo the two bolts, and remove the receiver

13 Tyre pressure control system (RDC) – information and component renewal

Information

1 A tyre pressure monitoring system (RDC) is available as an option on most of the 3-Series range. The system consists of a transmitter in each wheel, attached to the base of the inflation valve, a receiver behind the wheel arch liner adjacent to each wheel, and a control module behind the passenger side glovebox. A warning light in the instrument cluster alerts the driver should the tyre pressure deviate from the set pressure. Note that due to the weight of the wheel-mounted transmitter unit, it is essential that any new tyres are balanced correctly before use.

Component renewal

Control module

2 Disconnect the battery negative lead as described in Chapter 5A.
3 Remove the passenger side glovebox as described in Chapter 11, Section 27.
4 Carefully unclip the plastic panel behind the glovebox.
5 Unlock the wiring plug catch, and disconnect it. Depress the retaining clip and slide the control unit from the carrier.
6 Refitting is a reversal of removal. Reprogramme the system's reference pressure settings as described in the Owner's Handbook.

15.3 Remove the wiper spindle nut and pull/lever off the wiper arm

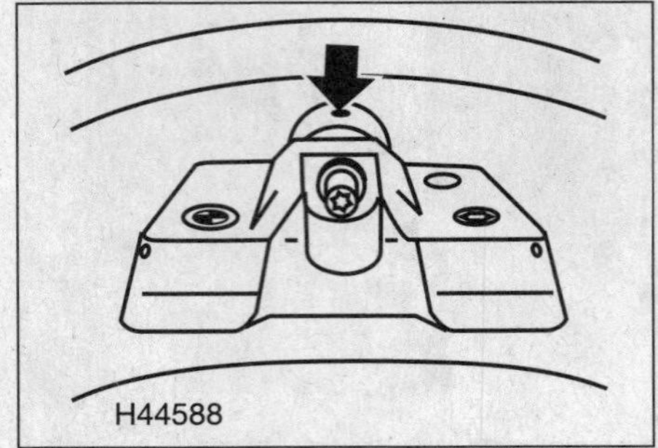

13.14 Ensure the hole in the retaining collar (arrowed) faces outwards

Receiver

7 Jack up the relevant roadwheel, and support the vehicle securely on axle stands (see *Jacking and vehicle support*). Release the retaining clips/bolts and remove the wheel arch liner.
8 Disconnect the receiver wiring plug, undo the two retaining bolts, and withdraw the unit **(see illustration)**. Note that the right-hand side front and the rear receivers are mounted on the inside of the front section of the wheel arch liner.
9 Refitting is a reversal of removal.

Transmitter

10 A transmitter is fitted to the base of each inflation valve. Have the relevant tyre removed by a suitably-equipped specialist.
11 Undo the Torx bolt and slide the transmitter from the base of the valve. Note the following precautions:

a) *Do not clean the transmitter with compressed air.*
b) *Do not clean the wheel rim (tyre removed) with high-pressure cleaning equipment.*
c) *Do not use solvent to clean the transmitter.*
d) *If tyre sealing fluid has been used, the transmitter and valve must be renewed.*
e) *It is not possible to use the valve with the transmitter removed.*

12 Insert a rod into the hole in the valve body retaining collar, unscrew the body and remove the valve.
13 Fit the new valve body (with collar) into the transmitter, only finger-tighten the Torx bolt at this stage.

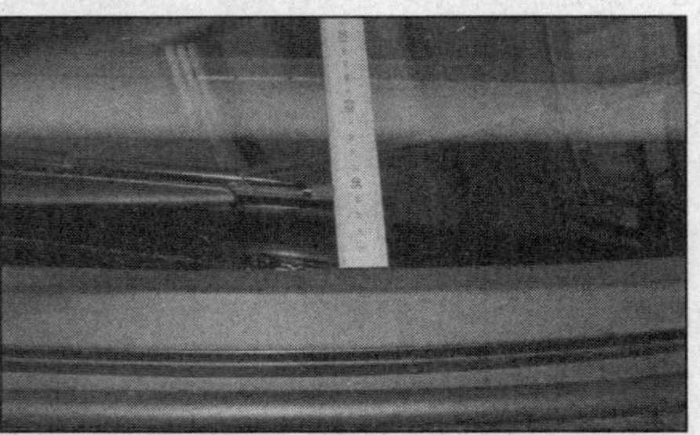

15.4 The distance from the top edge of the wiper blade to the top edge of the trim should be 44 mm on the driver's side, and 24 mm on the passenger side

14 Insert the assembly into the hole in the wheel, ensuring that the hole in the valve body retaining collar faces outwards. Tighten the valve body nut, using a rod in the hole in the collar to counterhold the nut **(see illustration)**.
15 Tighten the transmitter Torx bolt to the specified torque.
16 Have the tyre refitted.

14 Horn(s) – removal and refitting

Removal

1 The horn(s) is/are located behind the left- and right-hand ends of the front bumper.
2 To gain access to the horn(s) from below, apply the handbrake then jack up the front of the vehicle and support it on axle stands (see *Jacking and vehicle support*). Undo the retaining bolts and remove the lower front section of the wheel arch liner. Unclip and remove the brake disc cooling duct.
3 Undo the retaining nut/bolt and remove the horn, disconnecting its wiring connectors as they become accessible.

Refitting

4 Refitting is the reverse of removal.

15 Wiper arm – removal and refitting

Removal

1 Operate the wiper motor then switch it off so that the wiper arm returns to the 'at rest' position.
2 Stick a piece of masking tape along the edge of the wiper blade to use as an alignment aid on refitting.
3 Prise off the wiper arm spindle nut cover then slacken and remove the spindle nut. Lift the blade off the glass and pull the wiper arm off its spindle. If necessary the arm can be levered off the spindle using a suitable flat-bladed screwdriver or suitable puller **(see illustration)**. **Note:** *If both windscreen wiper arms are to be removed at the same time mark them for identification; the arms are not interchangeable.*

Refitting

4 Ensure that the wiper arm and spindle splines are clean and dry then refit the arm to the spindle, aligning the wiper blade with the tape fitted on removal. Note that if the knurled-tapered sleeves fitted to the arms are loose, they must be renewed. Refit the spindle nut, tightening it to the specified torque setting, and clip the nut cover back in position. If the wipers are being refitted to a new front windscreen, position the wipers arms as shown **(see illustration)**.

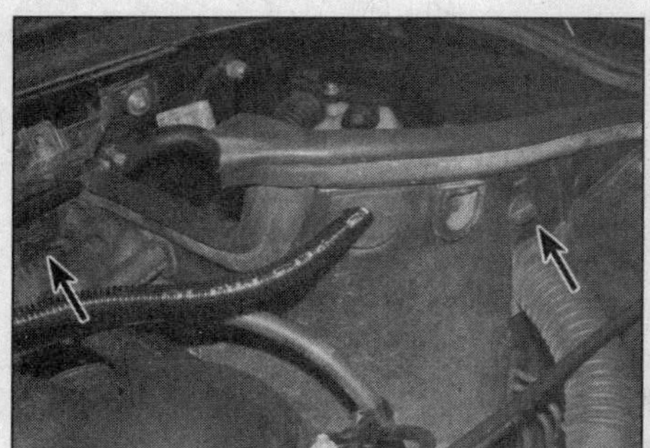

16.3a Lift the rubber strip and undo the two fasteners (arrowed)

16.3b Undo the two bolts (arrowed) and remove the inlet ducting

16.7 Undo the bolt (arrowed) securing the wiper linkage

16.9 Manoeuvre the linkage from the bulkhead

16.10 Undo the three bolts and remove the wiper motor

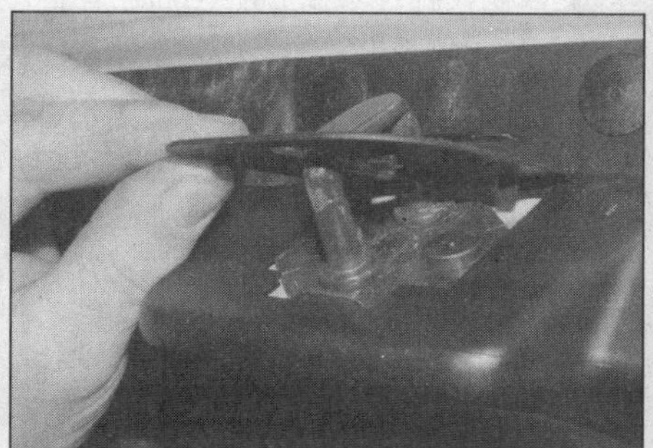

16.14 Unclip the trim around the lock striker

16 Windscreen wiper motor and linkage – removal and refitting

Removal

Front windscreen wiper motor

1 Remove the wiper arms as described in the previous Section.

2 Open the bonnet.

3 Remove the heater air inlet housing as follows **(see illustrations)**:

a) Rotate the three fasteners 90° anti-clockwise and remove the pollen filter cover from the rear of the engine compartment. Pull the filter forward and remove it.

b) Undo the four retaining clips and thread the cable out of the ducting.

c) Unscrew the four bolts and pull the filter housing forwards and remove it.

d) Pull up the rubber strip, rotate the two fasteners anti-clockwise, and move the dividing panel in the left-hand corner of the engine compartment forward a little.

e) Undo the two bolts and remove the inlet ducting upwards and out of the engine compartment.

4 Carefully pull the scuttle panel trim up, releasing it from the retaining clips.

5 Release the two retaining clips, undo the bolt and remove the front cover from the heater (see Chapter 3 if necessary).

6 Disconnect the wiper motor wiring plug.

7 Undo the bolt securing the linkage assembly to the underside of the scuttle panel **(see illustration)**.

8 Unscrew the large nuts from the wiper spindles and remove the washers.

9 Manoeuvre the motor and linkage assembly out of position **(see illustration)**. Recover the rubber grommets from the spindles, inspect them for signs of damage or deterioration, and renew if necessary.

10 If necessary, mark the relative positions of the motor shaft and crank, then prise the wiper linkage from the motor balljoint. Unscrew the retaining nut and free the crank from the motor spindle. Unscrew the motor retaining bolts and separate the motor and linkage **(see illustration)**.

Rear windscreen wiper motor

11 Open the tailgate, and carefully prise the luggage compartment light unit from the tailgate trim panel. Disconnect the wiring plug as the unit is removed.

12 Prise up the small piece of trim at the top of the panel **(see illustration 5.47)**.

13 Undo the two retaining bolts at the upper edge, and carefully release the trim panel retaining clips **(see illustration 5.48)**. Lift the panel from place.

14 Unclip the trim around the tailgate lock striker **(see illustration)**.

15 Remove the panel insert from the inner trim panel. Note how the insert engages with the trim panel **(see illustrations)**

16 Undo the seven bolts, release the four retaining clips, and remove the tailgate inner trim panel **(see illustration)**.

17 Disconnect the wiper motor wiring plugs.

18 Make alignment marks where the motor and bracket touch the tailgate to aid refitting.

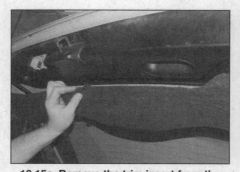

16.15a Remove the trim insert from the inner panel

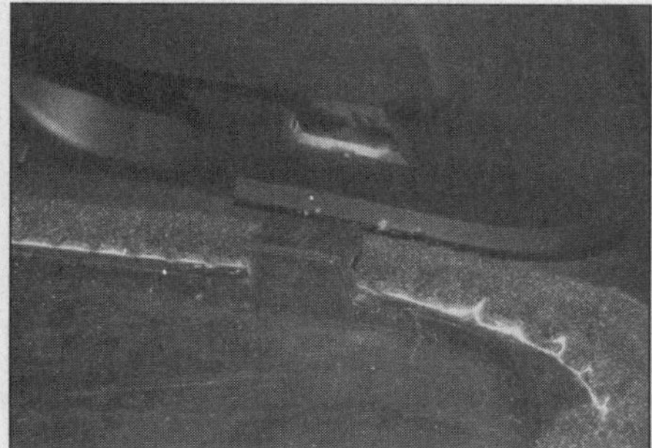

16.15b The trim insert lugs must engage correctly with the holes in the inner panel

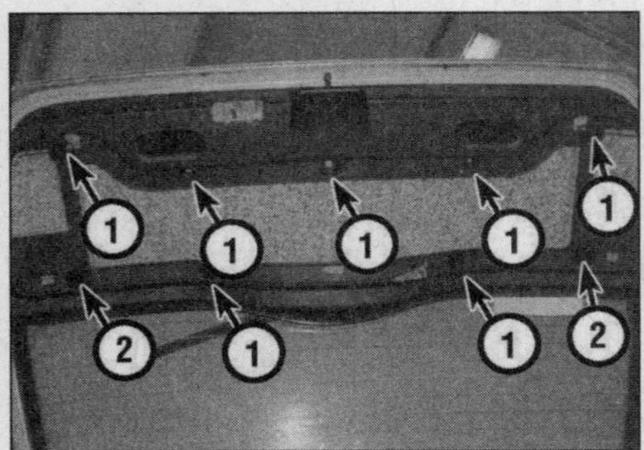

16.16 Release the bolts (1) and clips (2)

16.18a Undo the bolts (arrowed) and remove the rear wiper motor

16.18b Undo the bolts (arrowed) and remove the window lock from the wiper motor

16.20 Prise out the plastic caps and undo the two nuts (arrowed)

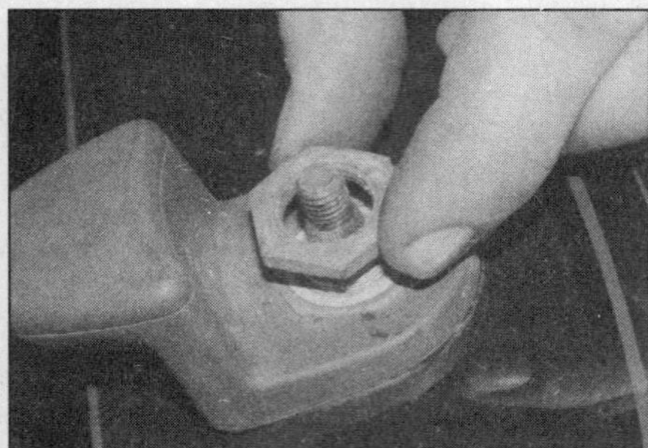
16.21 Slacken and remove the wiper spindle nut

16.22 Undo the nut (arrowed) and remove the housing complete with spindle

Undo the four bolts, and remove the wiper motor. If required, the window lock can be separated from the wiper motor by undoing the two retaining bolts **(see illustrations)**.

Rear wiper arm spindle and housing

19 Remove the rear wiper arm as described in the previous Section.

20 Open the tailgate, prise out the two plastic caps, and undo the two nuts securing the plastic cover over the spindle **(see illustration)**. Remove the cover.

21 On the outside of the windscreen, slacken and remove the wiper arm spindle nut. Recover any washers **(see illustration)**.

22 On the inside of the windscreen, undo the retaining nut, and manoeuvre the housing and spindle from position **(see illustration)**. No further dismantling is recommended.

Refitting

23 Refitting is the reverse of removal. On completion refit the wiper arms as described in Section 15.

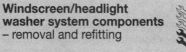

17 Windscreen/headlight washer system components – removal and refitting

Front washer system

Reservoir

1 The windscreen washer reservoir is situated in the engine compartment. On models equipped with headlight washers the reservoir also supplies the headlight washer jets via an additional pump.

2 Empty the contents of the reservoir or be prepared for fluid spillage.

3 Release the heat shield retaining clip, and disconnect the wiring connector(s) from the washer pump(s). Carefully rotate the pump(s) clockwise, and pull them up from the reservoir and position them clear. Inspect the pump sealing grommet(s) for signs of damage or deterioration and renew if necessary.

4 Disconnect the wiring connector from the reservoir level switch.

5 Slacken and remove the reservoir fastener and lift the reservoir upwards and out of position. Wash off any spilt fluid with cold water.

6 Refitting is a reversal of removal. Ensure the locating lugs on the base of the reservoir engage correctly with the corresponding slots in the inner wing. Refill the reservoir and check for leakage.

Washer pumps

7 Empty the contents of the reservoir or be prepared for fluid spillage.

8 Release the heat shield retaining clip, and disconnect the wiring connector(s) from the washer pump(s). Carefully rotate the pump(s) clockwise, and pull them up from the reservoir. Inspect the pump sealing grommet(s) for signs of damage or deterioration and renew if necessary **(see illustration)**.

9 Refitting is the reverse of removal, using a new sealing grommet if the original one shows signs of damage or deterioration. Refill the reservoir and check the pump grommet for leaks.

Reservoir level switch

10 Remove the reservoir as described earlier in this Section.

11 Rotate the level switch anti-clockwise and remove it from the reservoir **(see illustration)**.

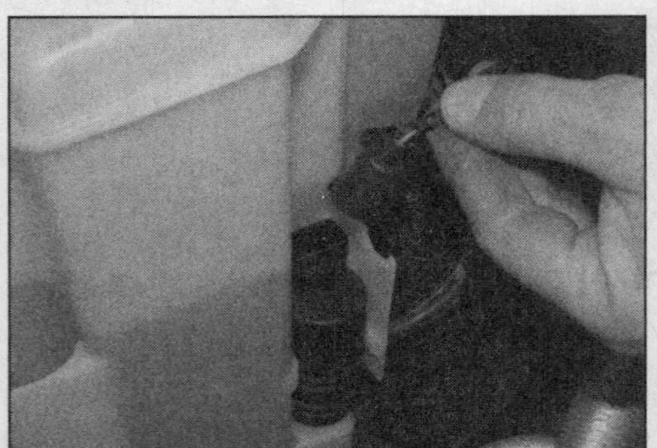
17.8 Disconnect the washer pump wiring plug and remove the heat shield

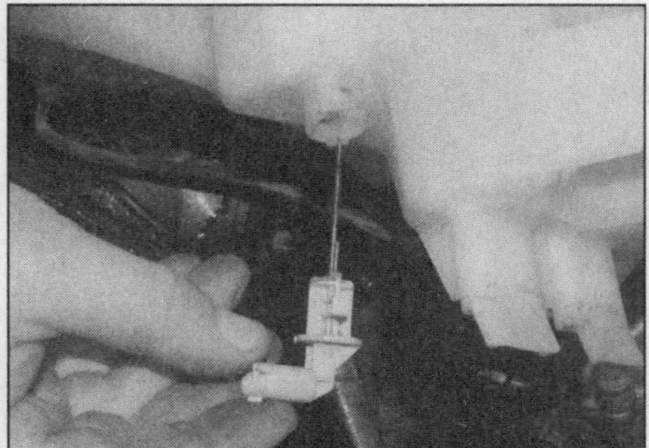
17.11 Rotate the level switch anti-clockwise and remove it from the reservoir

17.13a On some models, squeeze the retaining clips (arrowed) and pull the jet down from the bonnet . . .

17.13b . . . whilst on others, push up the rear edge the jet, and depress the clip (arrowed) at the front, then pull the jet up from the bonnet

12 Refitting is the reverse of removal, using a new sealing grommet if the original one shows signs of damage or deterioration. Refill the reservoir and check for leaks.

Windscreen washer jets

13 On early models, squeeze together the retaining clips and carefully ease the jet out from the bonnet, taking great care not to damage the paintwork. On later models disconnect the washer hose(s) and wiring plugs then, working under the bonnet, push the rear edge of the washer assembly forward and up, press in the clip at the front edge and remove the washer from the bonnet **(see illustrations)**.

14 Disconnect the washer hose(s) from the base of the jet. Where necessary, also disconnect the wiring connector from the jet.

15 On refitting early models, securely connect the jet to the hose and clip it into position in the bonnet; where necessary also reconnect the wiring connector. On later models, push the jet into place and reconnect the hose(s) and wiring plugs. Check the operation of the jet. If necessary adjust the nozzles using a pin, aiming one nozzle to a point slightly above the centre of the swept area and the other to slightly below the centre point to ensure complete coverage.

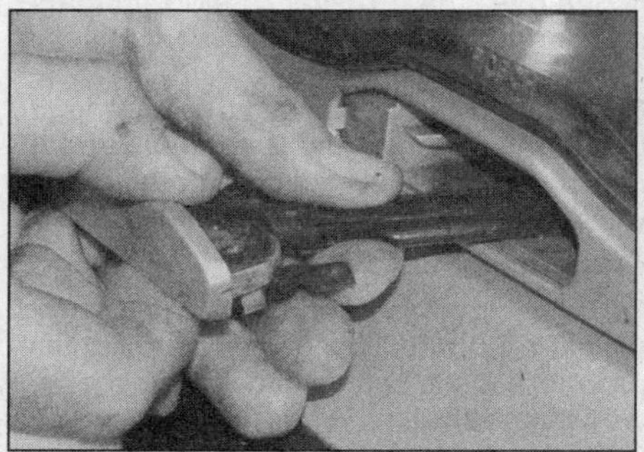

17.17 With a sharp tug, separate the washer jet from the tube

17.19 Release the retaining clips (arrowed) and separate the jet from the trim

Headlight washer jets

16 Using a wooden or plastic lever, carefully prise out the washer jet cover from below the headlight, and pull it out to its stop.

17 With a sharp tug, separate the jet assembly from the washer tube **(see illustration)**. Be prepared for fluid spillage.

18 Where applicable disconnect the jet heater wiring plug.

19 If required, the trim can be separated from the jet by releasing the retaining clips on each side of the jet **(see illustration)**.

20 On refitting, pull out the washer tube and push the jet into place. Where applicable, reconnect the wiring plug. Adjustment of the jets requires use of BMW tool 00 9 100.

Wash/wipe control module

21 The wash/wipe system is controlled by the central body electronics (ZKE V) control module, known as the General Module (GM V), which is located behind the passenger side glovebox. To access the control unit, remove the glovebox as described in Chapter 11, Section 27.

22 Disconnect the module wiring plugs. Some plugs have locking levers, and some have sliding locking elements **(see illustrations)**.

23 Release the retaining clip then remove the ECM from the vehicle **(see illustration)**.

24 Refitting is the reverse of removal.

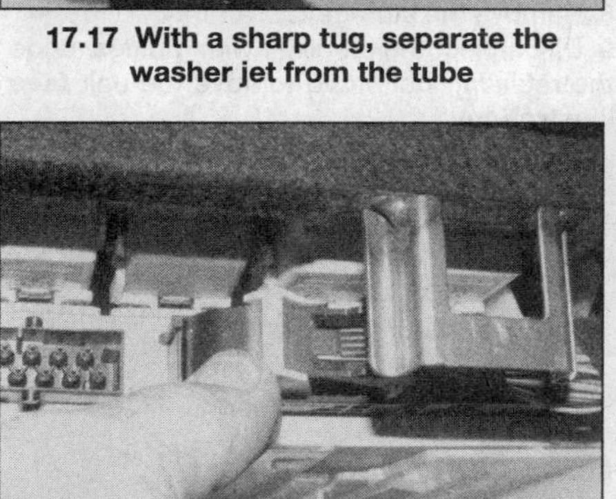

17.22a Some ECM wiring plugs have locking levers . . .

17.22b . . . whilst some have sliding locking elements

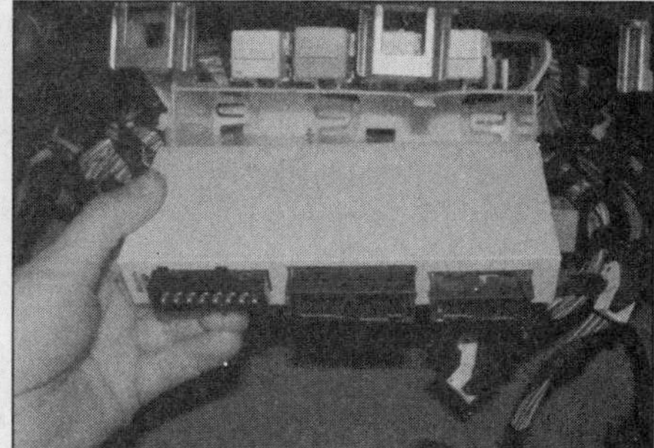

17.23 Release the retaining clip and slide the General Control Module from position

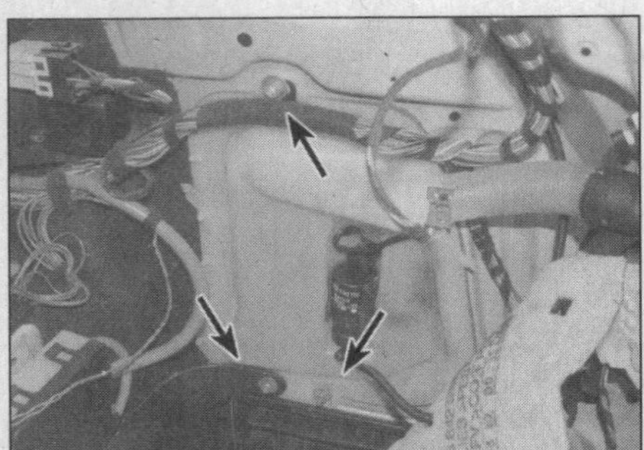
17.29 Rear washer reservoir nuts (arrowed) – Touring models

17.34 Rear washer pump – Touring models

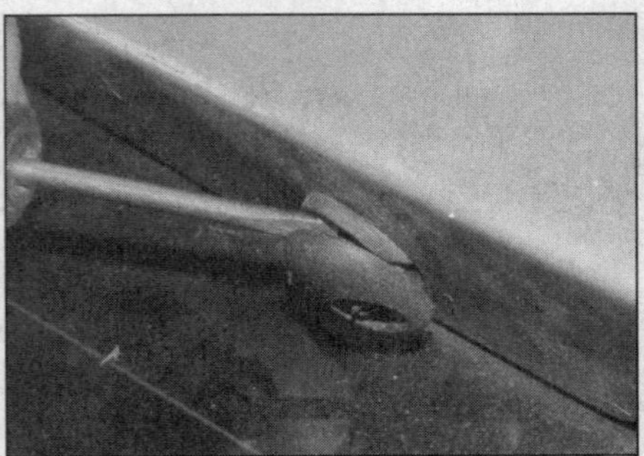
17.36 The rear washer jet is a push-fit into the tailgate

Rear screen washer system

Reservoir

25 Remove the right-hand side luggage compartment trim panel as described in Chapter 11, Section 27.
26 Empty the contents of the reservoir or be prepared for fluid spillage.
27 Disconnect the pump wiring plug.
28 Carefully detach the reservoir filler tube and pump delivery tube.
29 Remove the top mounting nut, and slacken the lower mounting nuts **(see illustration)**. Remove the reservoir.
30 Refitting is a reversal of removal.

Washer pump

31 Remove the right-hand side luggage compartment trim panel as described in Chapter 11, Section 27.
32 Empty the contents of the reservoir or be prepared for fluid spillage.
33 Disconnect the pump wiring plug.
34 Disconnect the pump delivery tube, and carefully pull the pump up and out of the reservoir **(see illustration)**.
35 Refitting is a reversal of removal.

Washer jet

36 The washer jet is a push-fit into the end of the washer tube fitting. Using a plastic or wooden lever, carefully prise the washer jet from the rubber fitting at the top of the window **(see illustration)**.
37 Refitting is a reversal of removal. Aim the jet to an area 100 mm from the top, and 320 mm from the edge of the window.

18 Audio unit – removal and refitting

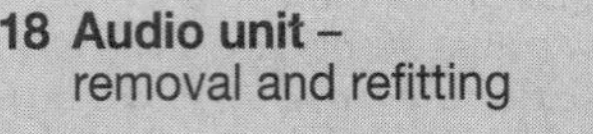

Note: *The following removal and refitting procedure is for the range of radio/cassette/CD units which BMW fit as standard equipment. Removal and refitting procedures of non-standard will differ slightly.*

18.3 Undo the two bolts (arrowed) and remove the audio unit

18.4 Slide out the locking element (arrowed) and disconnect the wiring plug

18.6 Undo the four bolts (arrowed) and remove the autochanger

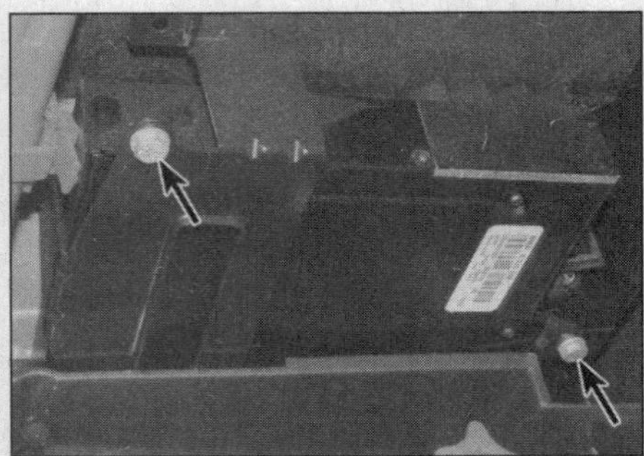
18.9 The amplifier is retained by two bolts (arrowed) – Touring model

Removal

Facia-mounted unit

1 Using a wooden or plastic lever, carefully prise away the decorative trim above the passenger side glovebox, followed by the trim above the audio unit.
2 Disconnect the battery negative lead (see Chapter 5A).
3 Undo the two bolts and pull the unit from the facia **(see illustration)**.
4 Note their fitted positions, and disconnect the wiring plugs from the rear of the unit (slide out the locking element on the main plug) **(see illustration)**.

CD autochanger

5 Remove the left-hand side luggage compartment trim panel as described in Chapter 11, Section 27.
6 Slacken the four mounting bolts, and lift the unit from position **(see illustration)**. Disconnect the wiring plugs as the unit is withdrawn.

Amplifier

7 The amplifier (where fitted) is located behind the left-hand side luggage compartment trim panel. Press the button, and remove the first aid kit trim panel.
8 Remove the storage/tool kit tray.
9 Disconnect the amplifier wiring plugs, undo the retaining bolts and remove the unit **(see illustration)**.

Refitting

10 Refitting is a reversal of removal.

19 Loudspeakers – removal and refitting

Door panel speaker(s)

1 Remove the door inner trim panel as described in Chapter 11.
2 Unscrew the three bolts and remove the speaker from the door trim **(see illustration)**.

3 Where fitted, unscrew the large retaining collar and remove the small speaker from the trim panel **(see illustration)**.
4 Refitting is the reverse of removal.

Door upper loudspeaker

5 Carefully unclip the plastic panel from the front inner edge of the door **(see illustrations)**.
6 Remove the door inner trim panel as described in Chapter 11.
7 Disconnect the speaker wiring plug, undo the two bolts and remove the speaker **(see illustration)**.
8 Refitting is a reversal of removal.

Luggage area loudspeaker

9 Remove the relevant luggage compartment side trim panel as described in Chapter 11, Section 27.
10 Undo the retaining bolts and remove the speaker, disconnect its wiring connectors as they become accessible **(see illustration)**.
11 Refitting is the reverse of removal making sure the speaker is correctly located.

Rear loudspeaker

12 Carefully prise the speaker grille out from the rear parcel shelf **(see illustration)**.
13 Undo the retaining bolts and lift the speaker. Disconnect the wiring plug as the speaker is withdrawn.
14 Refitting is the reverse of removal.

20 Radio aerial – general information

The radio aerial is built into the rear screen. In order to improve reception an amplifier is fitted to boost the signal to the radio unit. The amplifier unit is located behind the left hand rear C-pillar trim panel.

To gain access to the aerial amplifier unit, carefully remove the C-pillar trim panel as described in Chapter 11, Section 27, disconnecting the wiring from the interior light as the panel is removed. Disconnect the aerial lead and wiring then undo the retaining bolts and remove the amplifier **(see illustration)**. Refitting is the reverse of removal.

21 Cruise control system – information and component renewal

Information

1 The cruise control function is incorporated into the engine management ECM. The only renewable external components are the clutch pedal switch and the throttle actuator.

Component renewal

Clutch pedal switch

2 The trim panel above the pedals is secured by one plastic expanding rivet, two bolts, and a retaining clip. Prise out the centre pin and lever out the plastic expanding rivet, undo the two bolts, rotate the retaining clip 90° anti-clockwise and remove the panel. Note their fitted positions, and disconnect the wiring plugs as the panel is withdrawn.
3 Disconnect the switch wiring plug.
4 Depress the clutch pedal, and pull out the switch plunger to its full extent. Squeeze

19.2 The door speaker is retained by three bolts (arrowed)

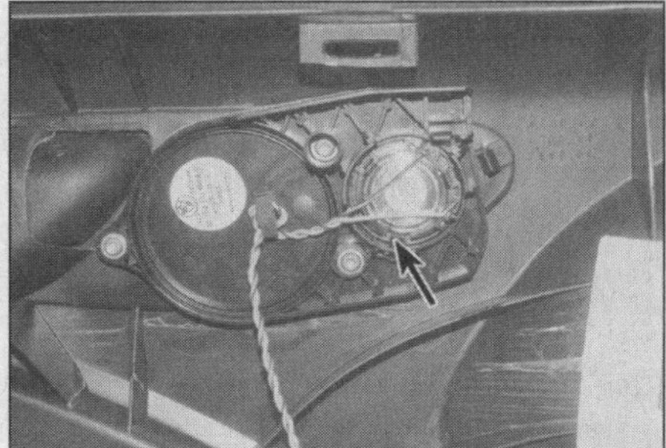
19.3 Undo the collar (arrowed) and remove the speaker

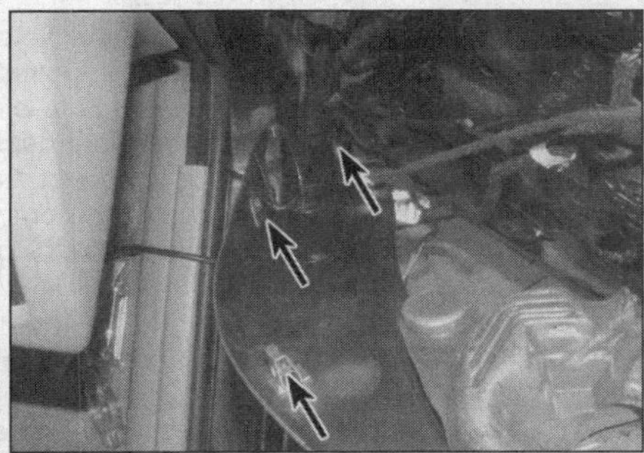
19.5a Note the clips (arrowed) retaining the plastic trim at the front edge of the door . . .

19.5b . . . and the clip at its lower edge

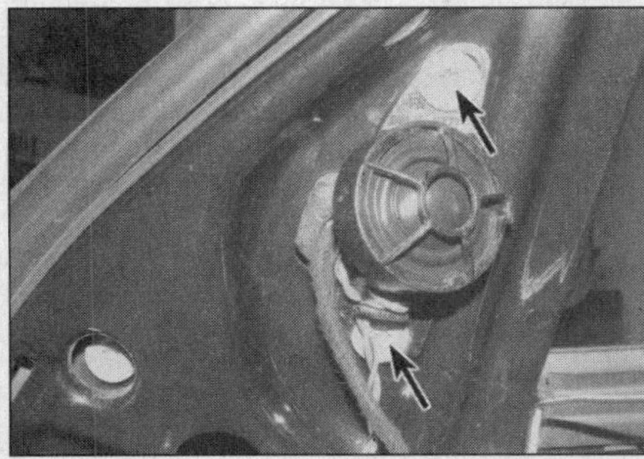
19.7 Remove the door upper loudspeaker bolts (arrowed)

19.10 Rear loudspeaker – Touring models

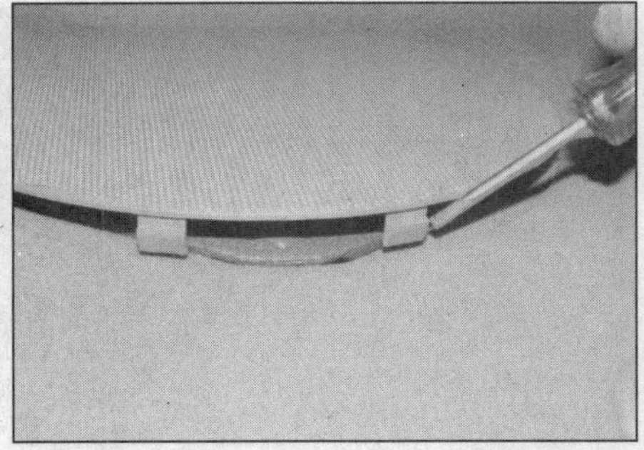
19.12 Carefully prise up the parcel shelf loudspeaker grille

20.2 Aerial signal amplifier is located behind the left-hand C-pillar trim panel

21.6a Undo the nut and bolt (arrowed) and remove the cruise control actuator

21.6b Squeeze together the sides of the grommet, and remove the cruise control cable from the throttle lever

together the retaining clips and pull the switch from the bracket.

5 Refitting is the reverse of removal, but slowly allow the pedal to return to its 'at rest' position.

Throttle actuator (M43TU engines)

6 The actuator is located on the left-hand side inner wing. Ensure the ignition is switched off, undo the nut and bolt, then remove the actuator from the inner wing. Squeeze together the sides of the grommet and separate the throttle cable from the throttle lever **(see illustrations)**.

22 Anti-theft alarm system – general information

The E46 3-Series models are equipped with a sophisticated anti-theft alarm and immobiliser system. Should a fault develop, the system's self-diagnosis facility should be interrogated using dedicated test equipment. Consult your BMW dealer or suitably-equipped specialist.

23 Heated front seat components – removal and refitting

Heater mats

On models equipped with heated front seats, a heater pad is fitted to the both the seat back and seat cushion. Renewal of either heater mat involves peeling back the upholstery, removing the old mat, sticking the new mat in position and then refitting the upholstery. Note that upholstery removal and refitting requires considerable skill and experience if it is to be carried out successfully and is therefore best entrusted to your BMW dealer or specialist. In practice, it will be very difficult for the home mechanic to carry out the job without ruining the upholstery.

Heated seat switches

Refer to Section 4.

24 Airbag system – general information and precautions

The models covered by this manual are equipped with a driver's airbag mounted in the centre of the steering wheel, a passenger's airbag located behind the facia, two head airbags located in each A-pillar/headlining, two airbags located in each front door trim panel and, on some models, behind each rear door trim. The airbag system comprises of the airbag unit(s) (complete with gas generators), impact sensors, the control unit and a warning light in the instrument panel.

The airbag system is triggered in the event of a heavy frontal or side impact above a predetermined force; depending on the point of impact. The airbag(s) is inflated within milliseconds and forms a safety cushion between the cabin occupants and the cabin interior, and therefore greatly reduces the risk of injury. The airbag then deflates almost immediately.

Every time the ignition is switched on, the airbag control unit performs a self-test. The self-test takes approximately 2 to 6 seconds and during this time the airbag warning light on the facia is illuminated. After the self-test has been completed the warning light should go out. If the warning light fails to come on, remains illuminated after the initial period, or comes on at any time when the vehicle is being driven, there is a fault in the airbag system. The vehicle must be taken to a BMW dealer or specialist for examination at the earliest possible opportunity.

Warning: Before carrying out any operations on the airbag system, disconnect the battery negative terminal, and wait for 10 seconds. This will allow the capacitors in the system to discharge. When operations are complete, make sure no one is inside the vehicle when the battery is reconnected.

- ***Note that the airbag(s) must not be subjected to temperatures in excess of 90°C. When the airbag is removed, ensure that it is stored the correct way up to prevent possible inflation (padded surface uppermost).***
- ***Do not allow any solvents or cleaning agents to contact the airbag assemblies. They must be cleaned using only a damp cloth.***
- ***The airbags and control unit are both sensitive to impact. If either is dropped or damaged they should be renewed.***
- ***Disconnect the airbag control unit wiring plug prior to using arc-welding equipment on the vehicle.***

25 Airbag system components – removal and refitting

Note: *Refer to the warnings in Section 24 before carrying out the following operations.*

1 Disconnect the battery negative terminal (see Chapter 5A), then continue as described under the relevant heading.

Driver's airbag

2 Two different types of driver's airbags may be fitted. Models from 2000 are equipped with 'Smart' airbags with two stages of inflation. Where a low speed impact is detected and airbags provide 'soft' deployment, and 'hard' deployment in high speed impacts. Thus ensuring that the airbag deployment is no greater than necessary to provide protection.

Normal airbag

3 Slacken and remove the two airbag retaining Torx T30 bolts from the rear of the steering wheel, rotating the wheel as necessary to gain access to the bolts **(see illustration)**.

4 Return the steering wheel to the straight-ahead position then carefully lift the airbag assembly away from the steering wheel. Release the locking clip and disconnect the airbag wiring plug from the steering wheel **(see illustration)**. Note that the airbag must

25.3 Rotate the steering wheel to access the two Torx bolts

25.4 Release the retaining clip (arrowed) and disconnect the airbag wiring plug

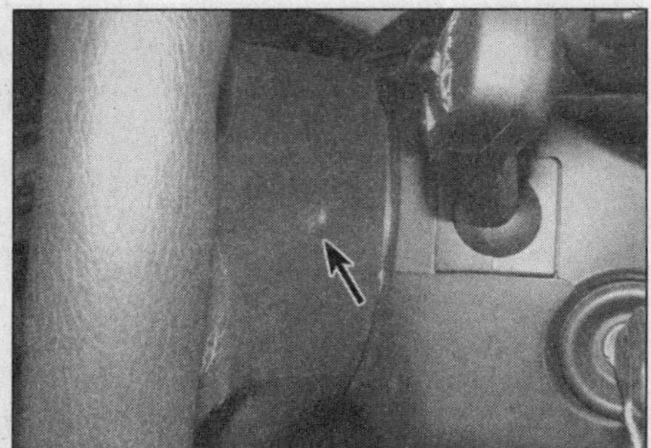

25.6a Insert a screwdriver through the hole (arrowed) in the side of the steering wheel . . .

25.6b . . . so that the screwdriver goes behind the metal plate . . .

25.6c . . . and pushes against the retaining clip (arrowed – airbag removed for clarity)

not be knocked or dropped and should be stored the correct way up with its padded surface uppermost.

5 On refitting, reconnect the wiring connector and seat the airbag unit in the steering wheel, making sure the wire does not become trapped. Fit the retaining bolts and tighten them to the specified torque setting and reconnect the battery.

Smart airbag

6 With the steering wheel in the straight-ahead position, insert a screwdriver through the hole in the rear-side of the steering wheel at 90 degrees to the steering column, to release the spring clip, and pull that side of the airbag away from the wheel **(see illustrations)**. Repeat this process on the other side of the wheel.

7 To disconnect the airbag wiring plugs, using a small flat-bladed screwdriver, lift the connector locking flap and pull the connector from position **(see illustration)**. Note that the airbag must not be knocked or dropped and should be stored the correct way up with its padded surface uppermost.

8 On refitting, reconnect the wiring plugs, and ensure that connectors are locked in place. Note that the connectors are colour-coded to ensure correct refitment. The connector plugs into the socket of the same colour. Position the airbag on the wheel and push the unit home until it locks in place. Reconnect the battery negative terminal.

Passenger airbag

9 Using a wooden or plastic level, carefully prise off the decorative strip above the passenger's glovebox.

10 Undo the two bolts and pull out the air vent on the passenger's side.

11 Carefully pull the lower edge of the airbag cover from the facia. Undo the two bolts and remove the cover **(see illustration)**. Note that after airbag deployment, a new cover must be fitted.

12 Undo the retaining nuts and remove the airbag. Press the locking tab and disconnect the wiring plug as the unit is withdrawn **(see illustrations)**.

13 Refitting is a reversal of removal. Tighten the airbag retaining bolts to the specified torque, and reconnect the battery negative terminal.

Door airbags

14 Remove the door inner trim panel as described in Chapter 11.

15 Undo the three bolts and lift the airbag from position. Pull the wiring connector from the airbag as it is removed **(see illustrations)**. Where applicable, release the wiring from any retaining clips.

16 Refitting is a reversal of removal. Tighten the airbag retaining bolts to the specified torque, and reconnect the battery negative terminal.

25.7 Lift the locking flap and disconnect the airbag wiring plug

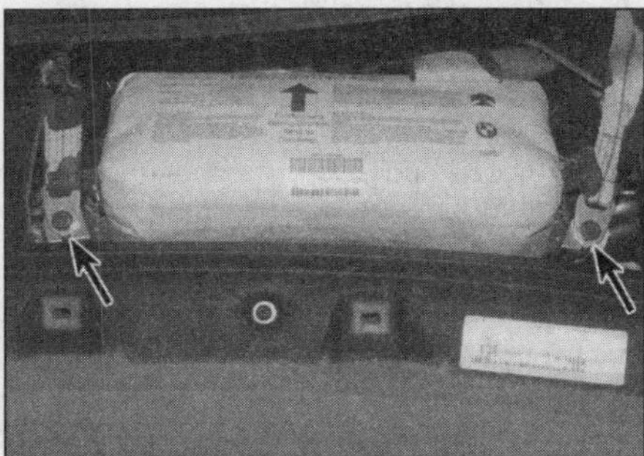

25.11 Undo the bolts (arrowed) and remove the cover

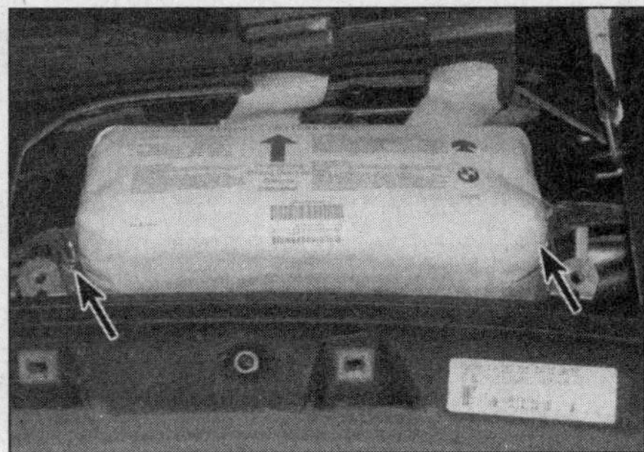

25.12a Undo the airbag nuts (arrowed)

25.12b Press the retaining clip and disconnect the airbag wiring plug

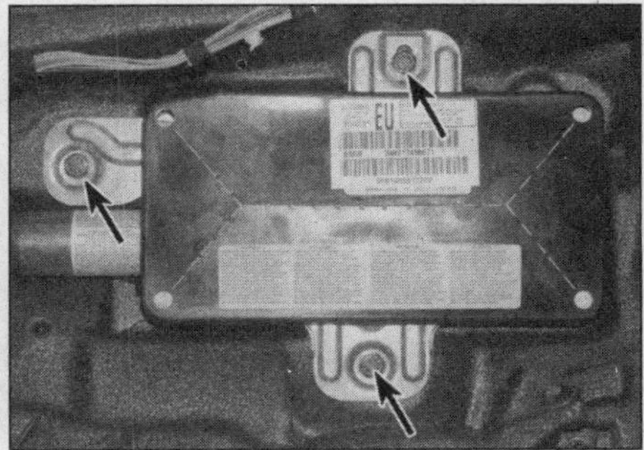

25.15a Side airbag retaining bolts (arrowed)

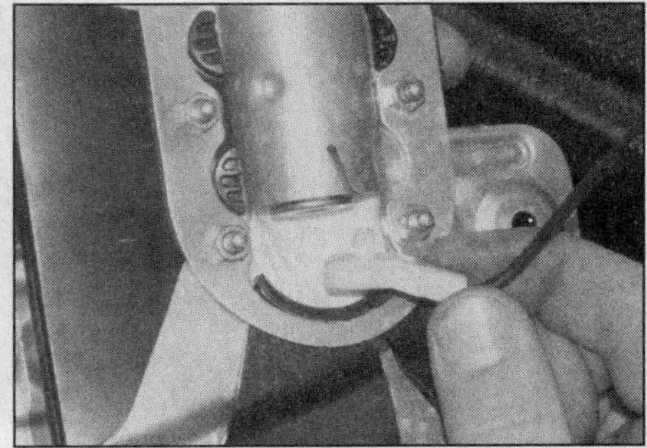

25.15b Unplug the yellow connector from the side airbag

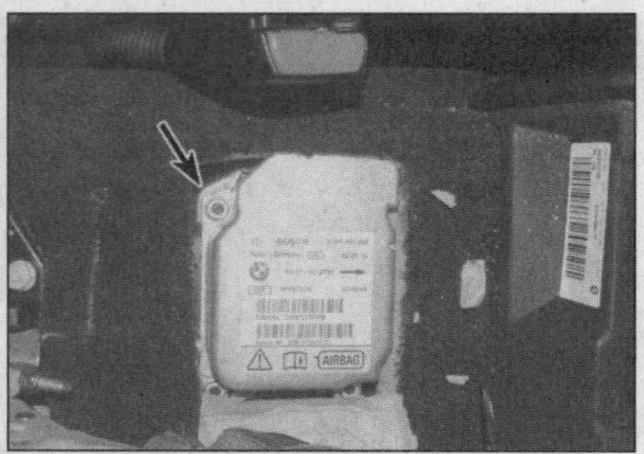

25.20a Note the earth strap (arrowed) fitted under one of the mounting nuts

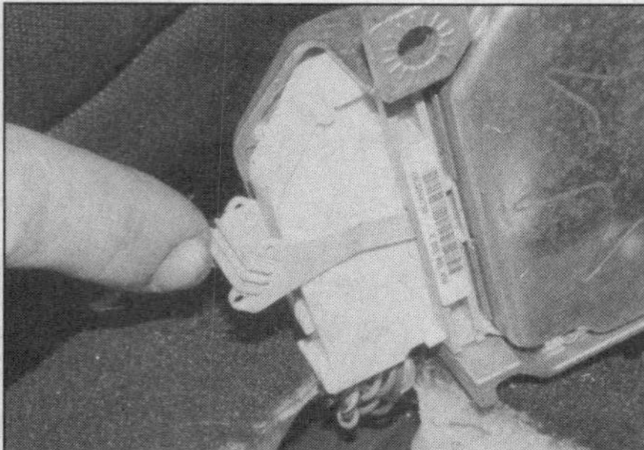

25.20b Unlock the catch and disconnect the control unit wiring plug

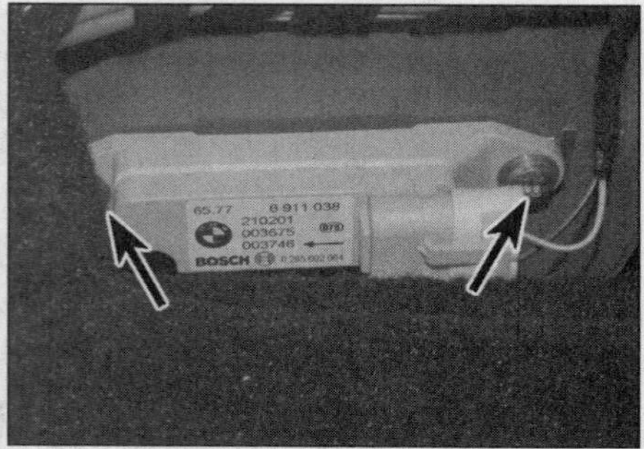

25.24 Undo the two bolts and remove the impact sensor

Head airbags

17 On each side of the passenger cabin, a Head Protection Airbag (HPS) is fitted. The airbag runs from the lower part of the windscreen pillar to above the rear door, is approximately 1.5 metres in length, and 130 mm in diameter when inflated. To remove the airbag, the entire facia and headlining must be removed. This task is outside the scope of the DIYer, and therefore we recommend that the task be entrusted to a BMW dealer or specialist.

Airbag control unit

18 Remove the rear section of the centre console as described in Chapter 11.

19 Cut the carpet in front of the handbrake lever to expose the control unit.

20 Undo the retaining nuts and lift the module. Note the earth strap fitted under one of the mounting nuts. Disconnect the wiring plug as the unit is withdrawn **(see illustrations)**.

21 Refitting is the reverse of removal. Note that the control unit must be installed with the arrow pointing towards the front of the vehicle, and that the earth strap is fitted under one of the module mounting nuts.

Impact sensor

22 There are two impact sensors, one on each side of the passenger cabin. Remove the seat as described in Chapter 11.

23 Unclip the door sill trim panel, and fold the carpet away from the side. To improve access if required, remove the floor level heater duct.

24 Undo the two retaining bolts, and remove the sensor **(see illustration)**. Disconnect the wiring plug as the sensor is withdrawn.

25 Refitting is a reversal of removal, noting that the arrow on the sensor must point towards the door sill.

26 Parking distance control (PDC) – information and component renewal

General information

1 In order to aid parking, a models in the 3-Series range can be equipped with a system that informs the driver of the distance between the rear of the vehicle and any vehicle/obstacle behind whilst reversing. The system consists of several ultrasonic sensors mounted in the rear bumper which measure the distance between themselves and the nearest object. The distance is indicated by an audible signal in the passenger cabin. The closer the object, the more frequent the signals, until at less than 30 cm the signal becomes continuous.

PDC electronic control module

Removal

2 On Saloon and Coupe models, remove the right-hand luggage compartment trim panel as described in Chapter 11, Section 27.

3 On Touring models, lift out the panel from the luggage compartment floor. Undo the wing nut and lift out the spare wheel cover. Undo the two retaining nuts and lift the rear edge of the panel between the spare wheel and the rear seats sill **(see illustration)**.

4 On all models, note their fitted positions, and disconnect the unit's wiring plugs. Undo the mounting bolts and remove the control unit **(see illustrations)**.

Refitting

5 Refitting is a reversal of removal.

Ultrasonic sensors

Removal

6 Remove the rear bumper as described in Chapter 11.

7 Disconnect the sensor wiring plugs, release the retaining clips and remove the sensors from the bumper.

Refitting

8 Refitting is the reverse of removal.

27 Wiring diagrams – general information

1 The wiring diagrams which follow only offer limited coverage of the electrical systems fitted to the E46 BMW 3-Series.

2 At the time of writing, no more wiring diagrams were available from BMW, so the inclusion of more information has not been possible.

3 Bear in mind that, while wiring diagrams offer a useful quick-reference guide to the vehicle electrical systems, it is still possible to trace faults, and to check for supplies and earths, using a simple multimeter. Refer to the general fault finding methods described in Section 2 of this Chapter (ignoring the references to wiring diagrams if one is not provided for the system concerned).

26.3 Remove the two bolts (arrowed) and lift the panel between the spare wheel and rear seats

26.4a Parking distance control module – Saloon and Coupe models

26.4b Parking distance control module – Touring models

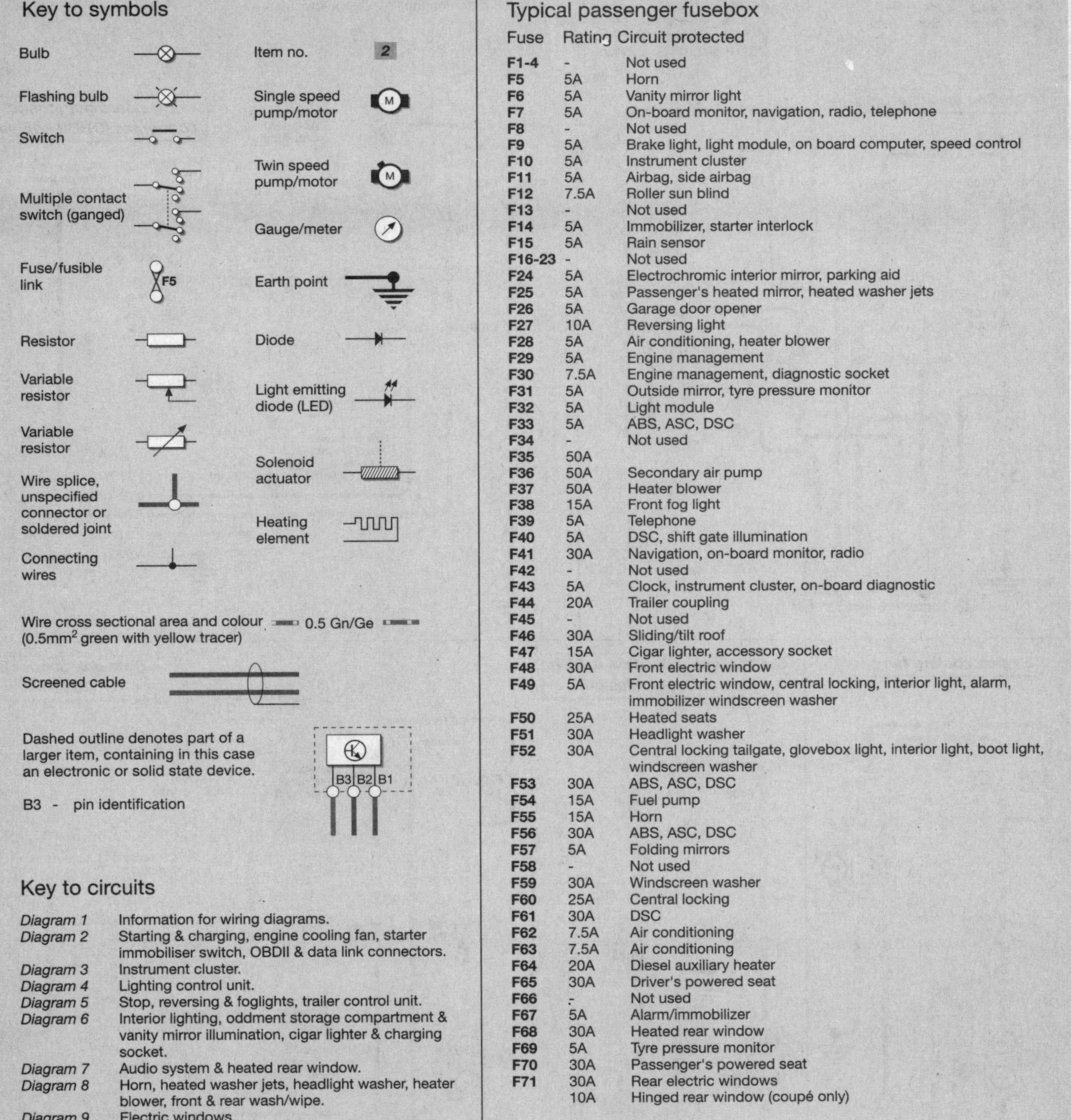

BMW 3 Series wiring diagrams

Diagram 1

Key to symbols

Key to circuits

Diagram 1 Information for wiring diagrams.
Diagram 2 Starting & charging, engine cooling fan, starter immobiliser switch, OBDII & data link connectors.
Diagram 3 Instrument cluster.
Diagram 4 Lighting control unit.
Diagram 5 Stop, reversing & foglights, trailer control unit.
Diagram 6 Interior lighting, oddment storage compartment & vanity mirror illumination, cigar lighter & charging socket.
Diagram 7 Audio system & heated rear window.
Diagram 8 Horn, heated washer jets, headlight washer, heater blower, front & rear wash/wipe.
Diagram 9 Electric windows.
Diagram 10 Central locking, electric mirrors, heated seats.
Diagram 11 ABS/ASC & tyre pressure control unit.

Typical passenger fusebox

Fuse	Rating	Circuit protected
F1-4	-	Not used
F5	5A	Horn
F6	5A	Vanity mirror light
F7	5A	On-board monitor, navigation, radio, telephone
F8	-	Not used
F9	5A	Brake light, light module, on board computer, speed control
F10	5A	Instrument cluster
F11	5A	Airbag, side airbag
F12	7.5A	Roller sun blind
F13	-	Not used
F14	5A	Immobilizer, starter interlock
F15	5A	Rain sensor
F16-23	-	Not used
F24	5A	Electrochromic interior mirror, parking aid
F25	5A	Passenger's heated mirror, heated washer jets
F26	5A	Garage door opener
F27	10A	Reversing light
F28	5A	Air conditioning, heater blower
F29	5A	Engine management
F30	7.5A	Engine management, diagnostic socket
F31	5A	Outside mirror, tyre pressure monitor
F32	5A	Light module
F33	5A	ABS, ASC, DSC
F34	-	Not used
F35	50A	
F36	50A	Secondary air pump
F37	50A	Heater blower
F38	15A	Front fog light
F39	5A	Telephone
F40	5A	DSC, shift gate illumination
F41	30A	Navigation, on-board monitor, radio
F42	-	Not used
F43	5A	Clock, instrument cluster, on-board diagnostic
F44	20A	Trailer coupling
F45	-	Not used
F46	30A	Sliding/tilt roof
F47	15A	Cigar lighter, accessory socket
F48	30A	Front electric window
F49	5A	Front electric window, central locking, interior light, alarm, immobilizer windscreen washer
F50	25A	Heated seats
F51	30A	Headlight washer
F52	30A	Central locking tailgate, glovebox light, interior light, boot light, windscreen washer
F53	30A	ABS, ASC, DSC
F54	15A	Fuel pump
F55	15A	Horn
F56	30A	ABS, ASC, DSC
F57	5A	Folding mirrors
F58	-	Not used
F59	30A	Windscreen washer
F60	25A	Central locking
F61	30A	DSC
F62	7.5A	Air conditioning
F63	7.5A	Air conditioning
F64	20A	Diesel auxiliary heater
F65	30A	Driver's powered seat
F66	-	Not used
F67	5A	Alarm/immobilizer
F68	30A	Heated rear window
F69	5A	Tyre pressure monitor
F70	30A	Passenger's powered seat
F71	30A	Rear electric windows
	10A	Hinged rear window (coupé only)

H32733

Wire colours

Bl	Blue	**Vi**	Violet
Br	Brown	**Ws**	White
Ge	Yellow	**Or**	Orange
Gr	Grey	**Rt**	Red
Gn	Green	**Sw**	Black

Key to items

1. Battery
2. Ignition switch
3. Starter motor
4. Alternator
5. Engine management control unit
6. Instrument cluster control unit
7. OBD II diagnostic connector
8. Data link connector
9. Engine cooling fan
10. Cooling fan thermal sensor
11. Starter immobilisation switch

Diagram 2

H32734

Starting and charging

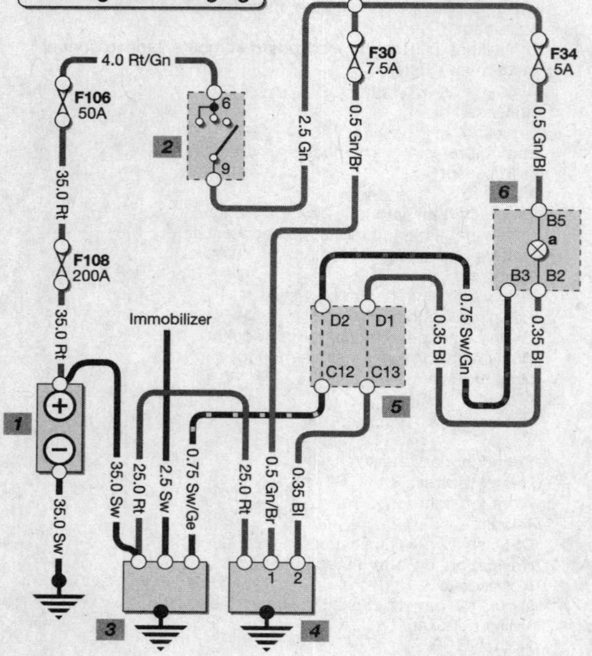

4.0 Rt/Gn
F106 50A
2
6
9
35.0 Rt
F108 200A
35.0 Rt
Immobilizer
1
35.0 Sw
35.0 Sw
25.0 Rt
2.5 Sw
0.75 Sw/Ge
25.0 Rt
0.5 Gn/Br
0.35 Bl
3
1 2
4
2.5 Gn
F30 7.5A
0.5 Gn/Br
F34 5A
0.5 Gn/Bl
6
B5
a
B3 B2
0.75 Sw/Gn
0.35 Bl
0.35 Bl
D2 D1
C12 C13
5

On-board diagnostic connector (OBDII - 16 pin)

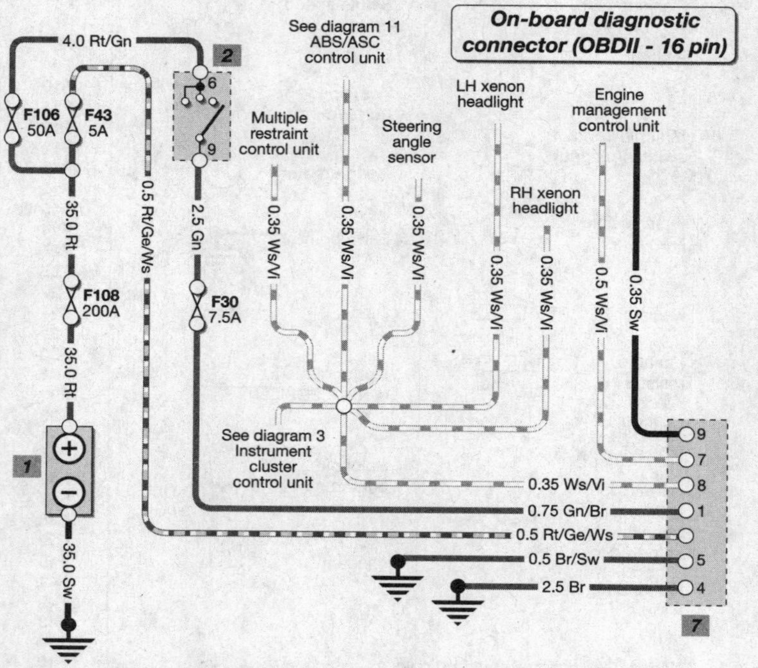

4.0 Rt/Gn
2
6
9
F106 50A
F43 5A
35.0 Rt
0.5 Rt/Ge/Ws
2.5 Gn
F108 200A
F30 7.5A
35.0 Rt
1
35.0 Sw
See diagram 11 ABS/ASC control unit
Multiple restraint control unit
Steering angle sensor
LH xenon headlight
RH xenon headlight
Engine management control unit
0.35 Ws/Vi
0.35 Ws/Vi
0.35 Ws/Vi
0.35 Ws/Vi
0.35 Ws/Vi
0.5 Ws/Vi
0.35 Sw
See diagram 3 Instrument cluster control unit
0.35 Ws/Vi
0.75 Gn/Br
0.5 Rt/Ge/Ws
0.5 Br/Sw
2.5 Br
9
7
8
1
5
4
7

Engine cooling fan

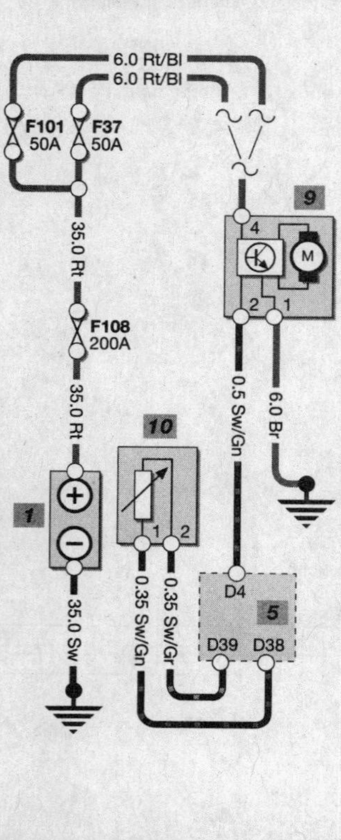

6.0 Rt/Bl
6.0 Rt/Bl
F101 50A
F37 50A
35.0 Rt
F108 200A
35.0 Rt
1
35.0 Sw
9
4
M
2 1
0.5 Sw/Gn
6.0 Br
10
1 2
0.35 Sw/Gn
0.35 Sw/Gr
D4
5
D39 D38

Starter immobilisation switch (manual transmission)

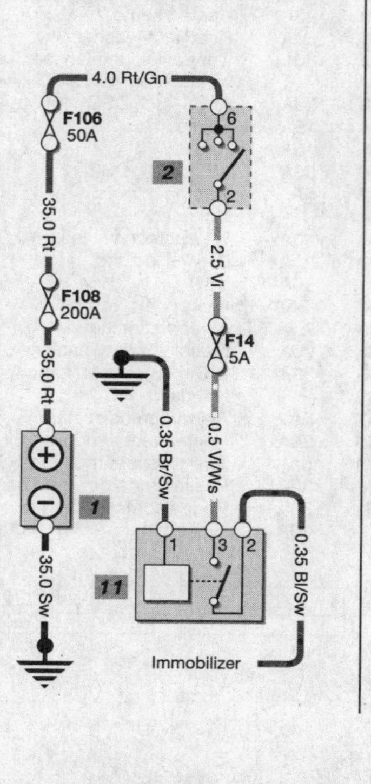

4.0 Rt/Gn
F106 50A
2
6
2
35.0 Rt
F108 200A
35.0 Rt
1
35.0 Sw
2.5 Vi
F14 5A
0.35 Br/Sw
0.5 Vi/Ws
1
3
2
11
0.35 Bl/Sw
Immobilizer

Data link connector (20 pin)

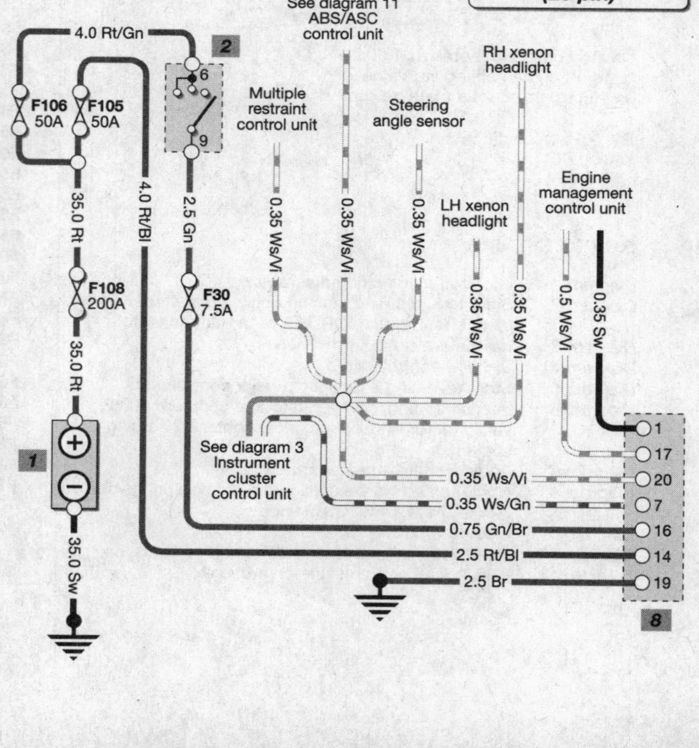

4.0 Rt/Gn
2
6
9
F106 50A
F105 50A
35.0 Rt
4.0 Rt/Bl
2.5 Gn
F108 200A
F30 7.5A
35.0 Rt
1
35.0 Sw
See diagram 11 ABS/ASC control unit
Multiple restraint control unit
Steering angle sensor
RH xenon headlight
LH xenon headlight
Engine management control unit
0.35 Ws/Vi
0.35 Ws/Vi
0.35 Ws/Vi
0.35 Ws/Vi
0.35 Ws/Vi
0.5 Ws/Vi
0.35 Sw
See diagram 3 Instrument cluster control unit
0.35 Ws/Vi
0.35 Ws/Gn
0.75 Gn/Br
2.5 Rt/Bl
2.5 Br
1
17
20
7
16
14
19
8

Wire colours

Bl	Blue	**Vi**	Violet
Br	Brown	**Ws**	White
Ge	Yellow	**Or**	Orange
Gr	Grey	**Rt**	Red
Gn	Green	**Sw**	Black

Key to items

Diagram 3

1 Battery
2 Ignition switch
5 Engine management control unit
6 Instrument cluster control unit
18 Engine management relay
21 Outside air temperature sensor
22 LH fuel level sensor
23 RH fuel level sensor
24 Seatbelt buckle switch
25 Handbrake switch
26 Brake fluid level switch
27 LH pad wear sensor
28 RH pad wear sensor
30 Oil pressure switch
31 Coolant level switch
32 Washer fluid level switch

H32735

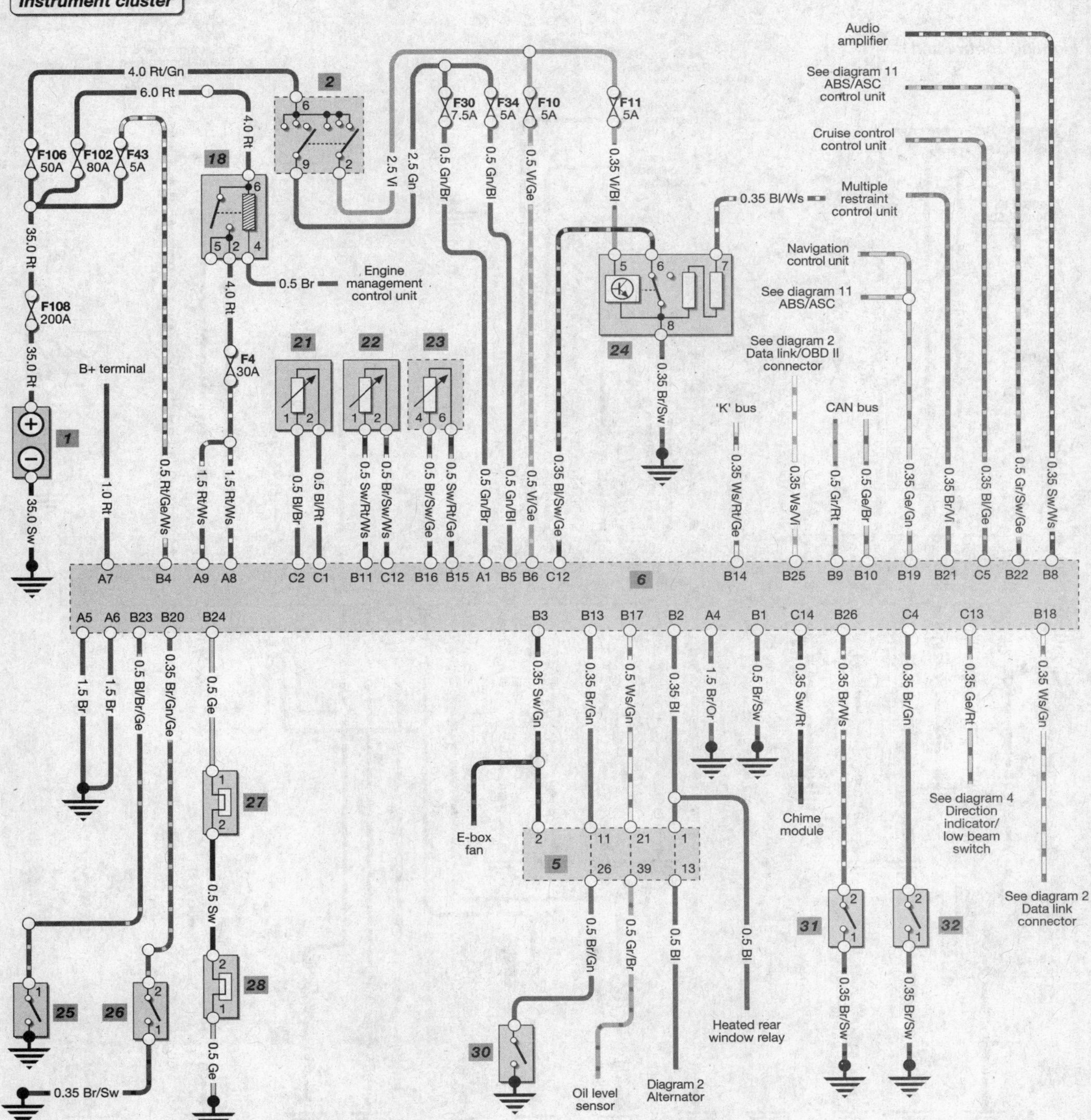

Wire colours

Bl	Blue	**Vi**	Violet
Br	Brown	**Ws**	White
Ge	Yellow	**Or**	Orange
Gr	Grey	**Rt**	Red
Gn	Green	**Sw**	Black

Key to items

Diagram 4

1 Battery
2 Ignition switch
37 Lighting control unit
38 Headlight levelling load sensor
39 LH headlight levelling motor
40 RH headlight levelling motor
41 Hazard warning/central locking switch
42 Number plate lights/tailgate release switch
43 Direction indicator/low beam switch
44 LH front parking light
45 RH front parking light
46 LH headlight low beam
47 RH headlight low beam
48 LH headlight high beam
49 RH headlight high beam
50 Front LH direction indicator
51 Front LH direction indicator side repeater
52 Front RH direction indicator
53 Front RH direction indicator side repeater
54 LH rear direction indicator
55 RH rear direction indicator
56 RH rear foglight
57 LH stop light
58 RH stop light
59 LH tail light
60 RH tail light

H32736

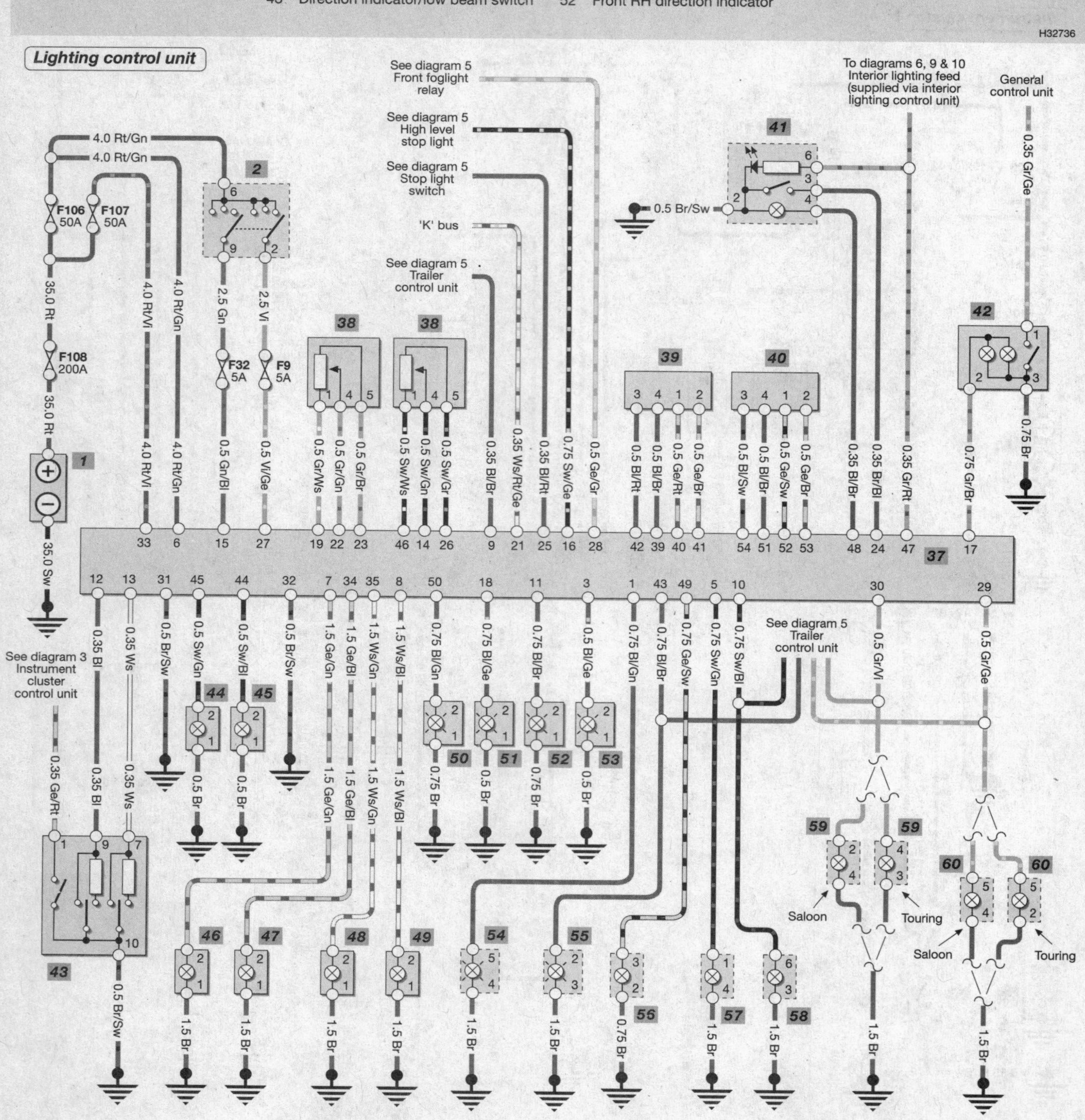

Diagram 5

Wire colours

Bl	Blue	**Vi**	Violet
Br	Brown	**Ws**	White
Ge	Yellow	**Or**	Orange
Gr	Grey	**Rt**	Red
Gn	Green	**Sw**	Black

Key to items

1	Battery	67	Reversing light relay
2	Ignition switch	68	LH reversing light
18	Engine management relay	69	RH reversing light
37	Lighting control unit	70	Reversing light switch
57	LH stop light	71	Front foglight relay
58	RH stop light	72	LH front foglight
65	Stop light switch	73	RH front foglight
66	High level stop light	74	Trailer module

H32737

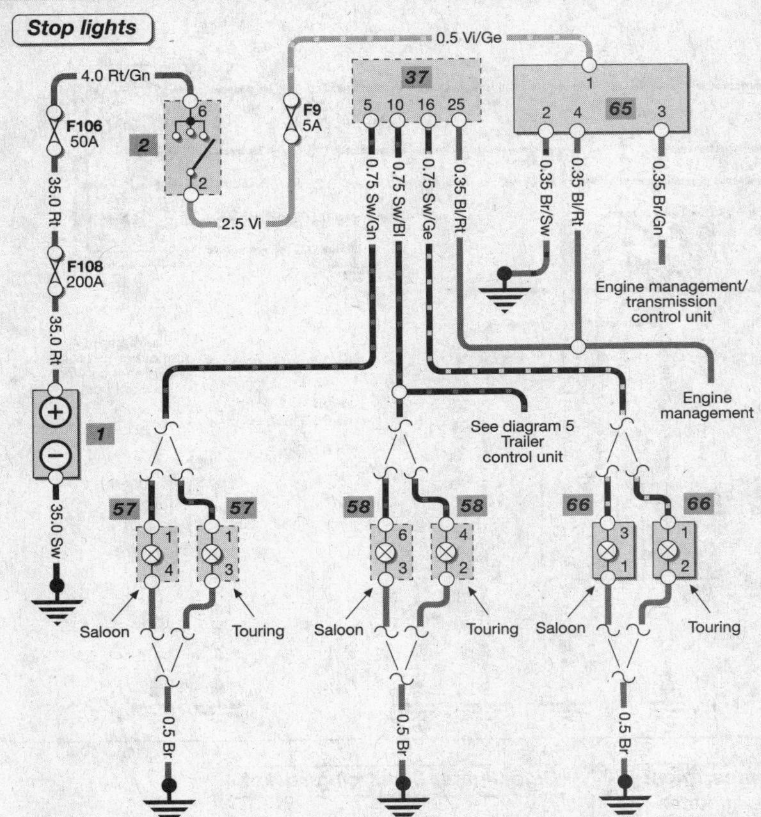

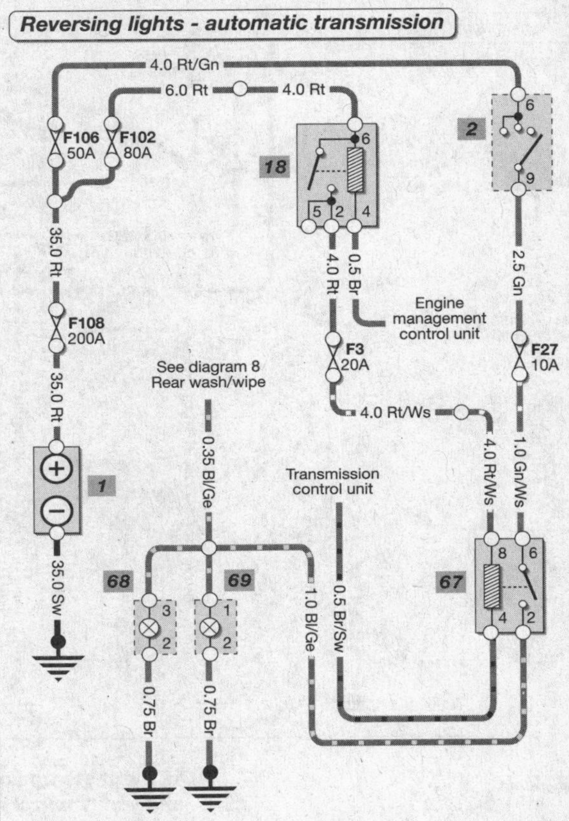

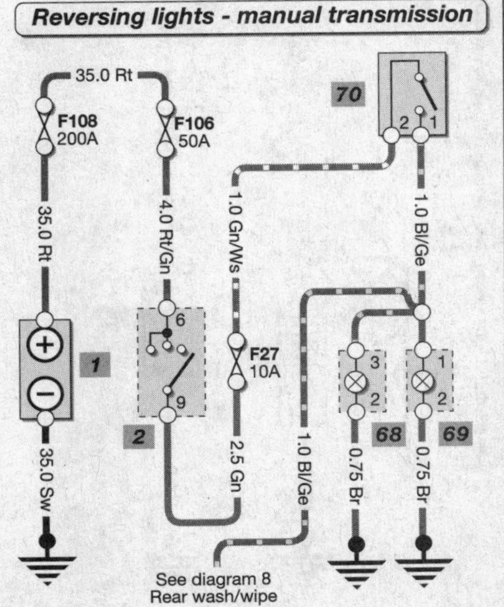

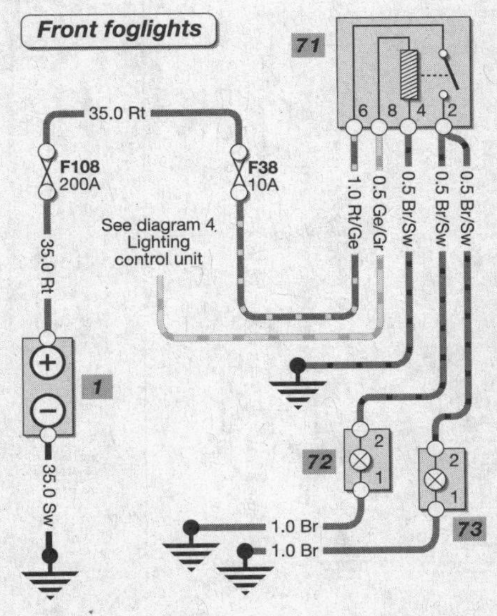

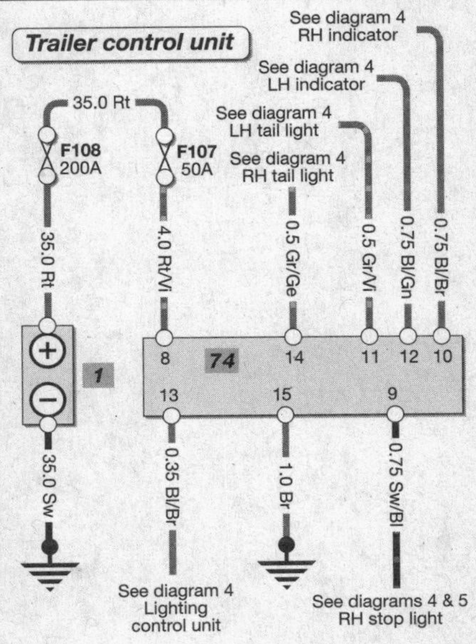

Diagram 6

Wire colours

Bl	Blue	**Vi**	Violet
Br	Brown	**Ws**	White
Ge	Yellow	**Or**	Orange
Gr	Grey	**Rt**	Red
Gn	Green	**Sw**	Black

Key to items

1 Battery
2 Ignition switch
77 General control unit
78 Interior/map reading light
79 Central locking switch
80 LH rear interior light
81 RH rear interior light
82 LH luggage compartment light
83 RH luggage compartment light
84 Glovebox light switch
85 Passenger's footwell illumination
86 Driver's footwell illumination
87 Front cigar lighter illumination
88 Rear ashtray illumination
89 LH oddment compartment light
90 RH oddment compartment light
91 Driver's vanity mirror light
92 Driver's vanity mirror light switch
93 Passenger's vanity mirror light
94 Passenger's vanity mirror light switch
95 Cigar lighter
96 Charging socket

H32738

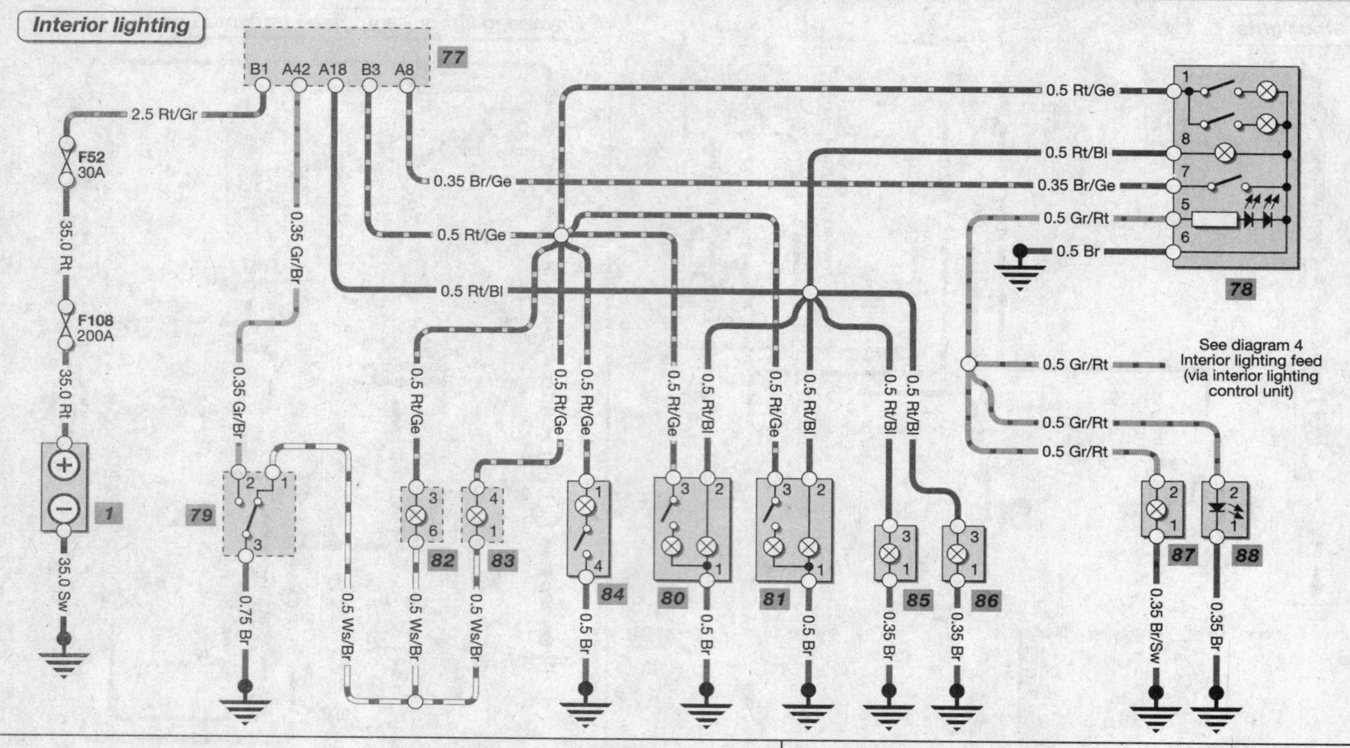

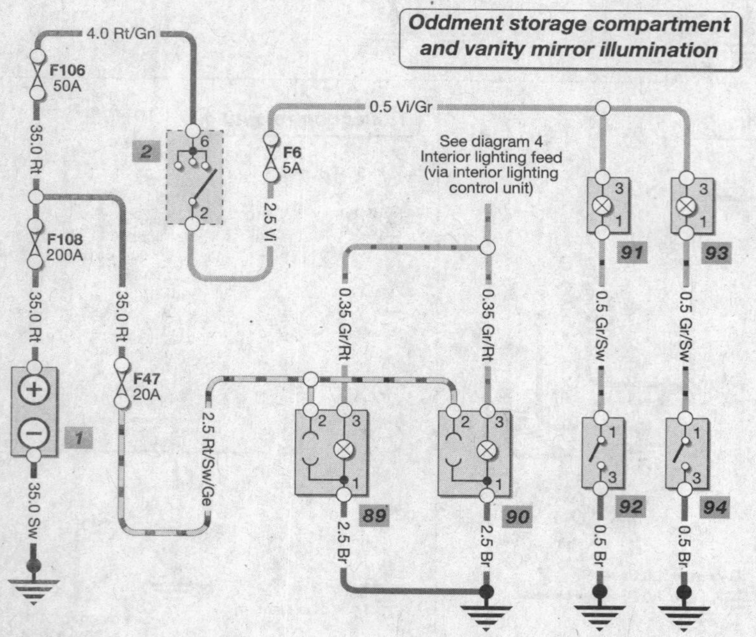

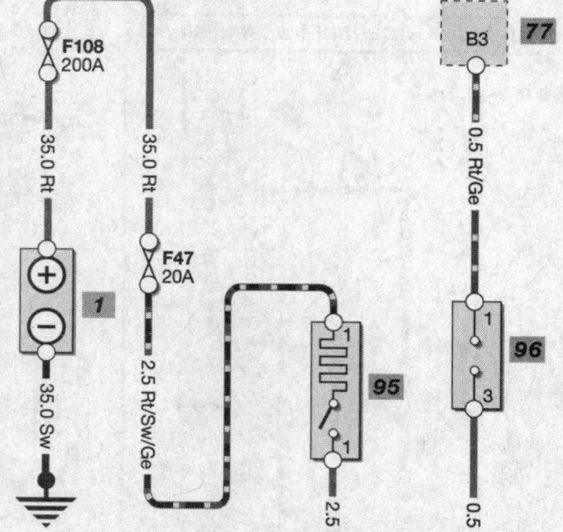

Diagram 7

Wire colours

Bl	Blue	**Vi**	Violet
Br	Brown	**Ws**	White
Ge	Yellow	**Or**	Orange
Gr	Grey	**Rt**	Red
Gn	Green	**Sw**	Black

Key to items

1 Battery
2 Ignition switch
100 Audio unit
101 On board monitor control unit
102 Antenna module
103 CD changer
104 Audio amplifier
105 LH front tweeter
106 LH front speaker
107 LH rear speaker
108 LH front mid range speaker
109 RH front tweeter
110 RH front speaker
111 RH rear speaker
112 RH front mid range speaker
113 Front bass speaker & tweeter
114 Navigation control unit
115 Heated rear window

H32739

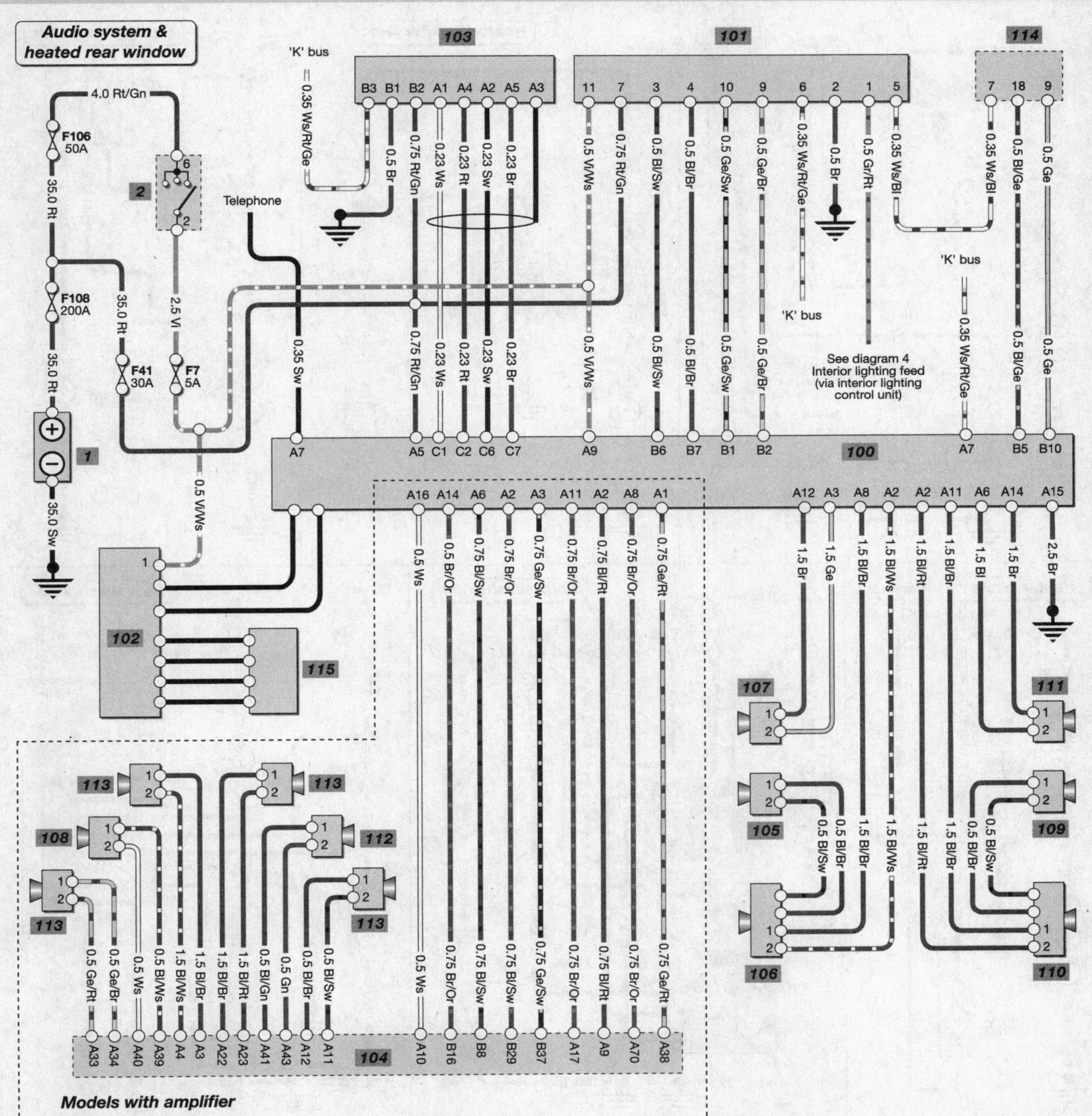

Wire colours

Bl	Blue	**Vi**	Violet
Br	Brown	**Ws**	White
Ge	Yellow	**Or**	Orange
Gr	Grey	**Rt**	Red
Gn	Green	**Sw**	Black

Key to items

1 Battery
2 Ignition switch
77 General control unit
118 Horn relay
119 Horn
120 Steering wheel clock spring
121 Horn switch
122 Heated washer jet
123 Thermal switch
124 Headlight washer relay
125 Headlight washer pump
126 Heater blower control module
127 Heater blower motor
128 Wash/wipe switch
129 Front wiper relay
130 Front wiper motor
131 Front washer pump
132 Rear wash/wipe control unit/motor
133 Tailgate open switch
134 Rear washer pump

Diagram 8

H32740

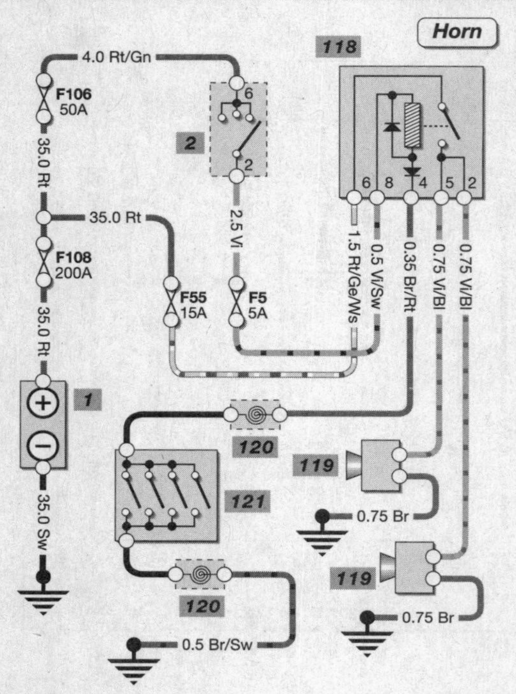

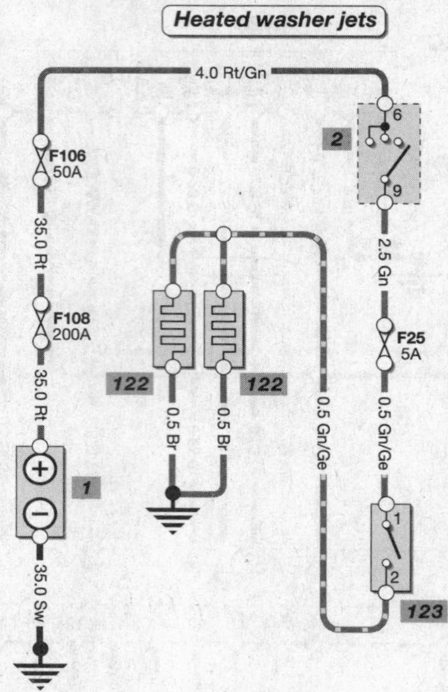

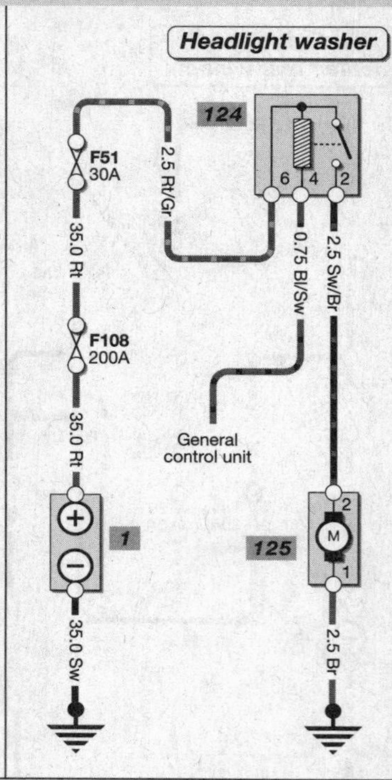

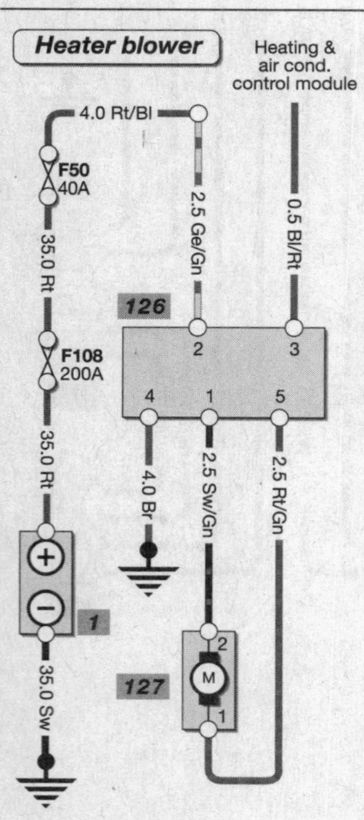

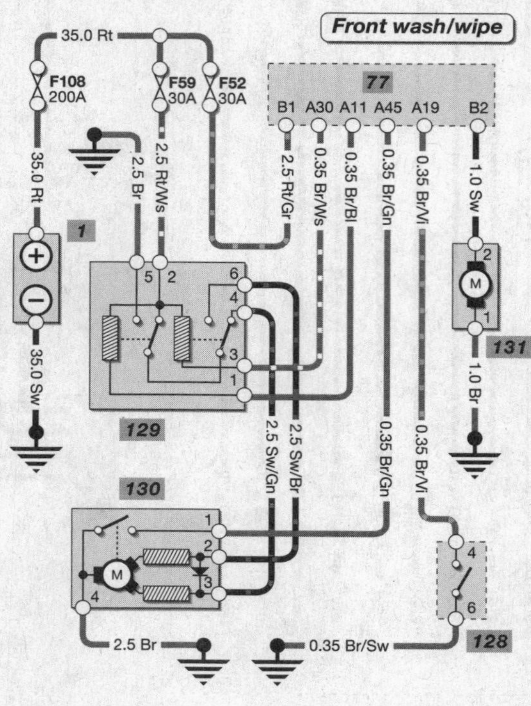

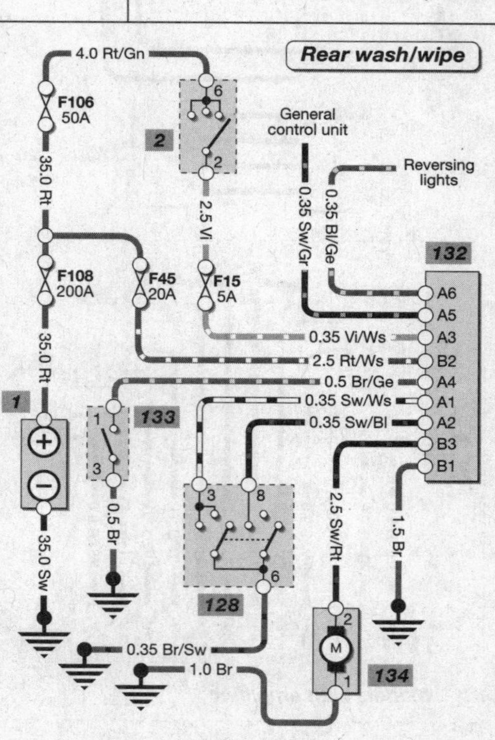

Wire colours

Bl	Blue	**Vi**	Violet
Br	Brown	**Ws**	White
Ge	Yellow	**Or**	Orange
Gr	Grey	**Rt**	Red
Gn	Green	**Sw**	Black

Key to items

1 Battery
77 General control unit
137 Driver's door switch
138 Driver's window motor
139 Driver's window jam switch
140 Passenger's door switch
141 Passenger's window motor
142 Passenger's window jam switch
143 LH rear door switch
144 LH rear window motor
145 LH rear window jam switch
146 RH rear door switch
147 RH rear window motor
148 RH rear window jam switch

Diagram 9

H32741

Electric windows

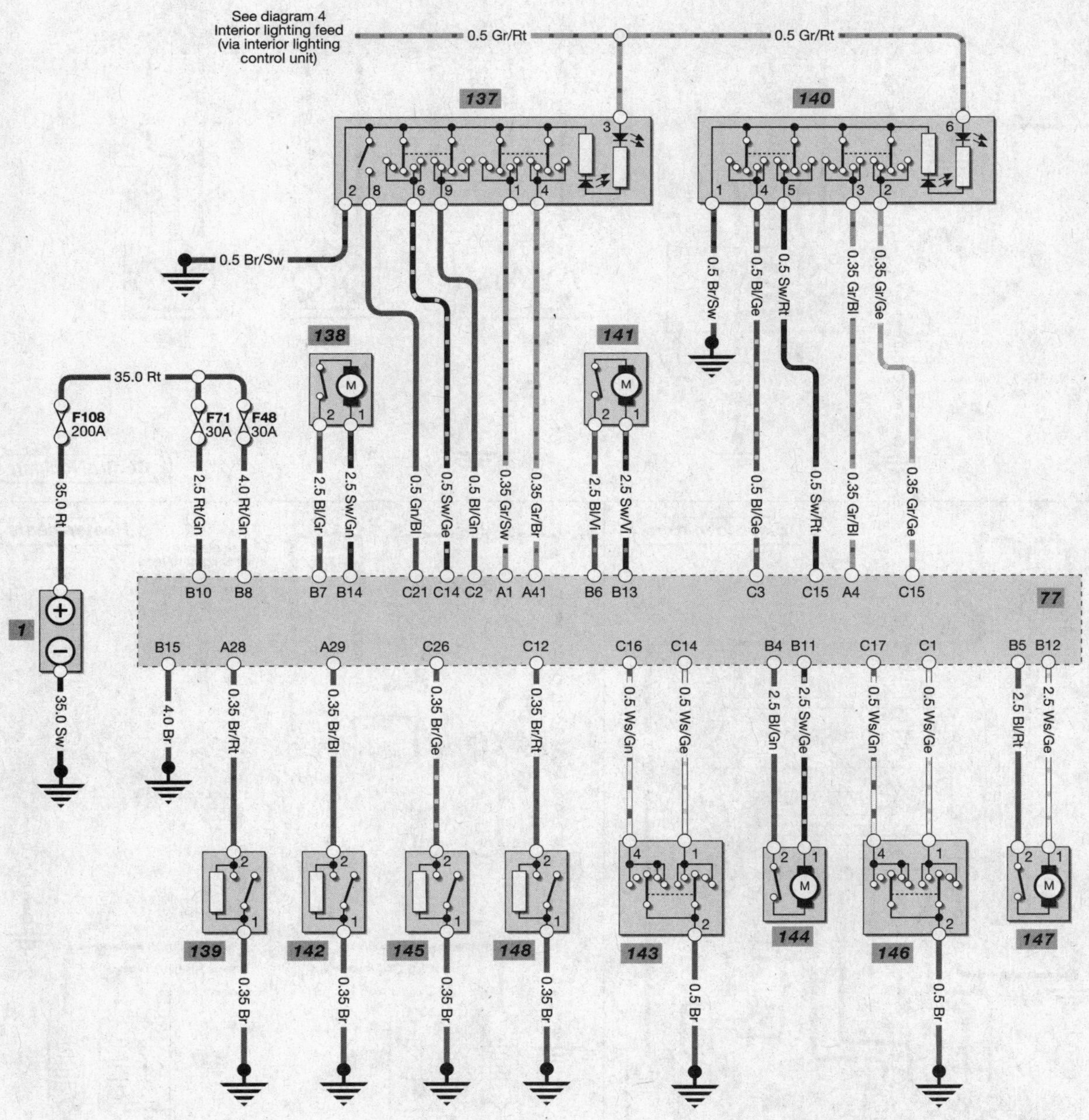

Wire colours

Bl	Blue	**Vi**	Violet
Br	Brown	**Ws**	White
Ge	Yellow	**Or**	Orange
Gr	Grey	**Rt**	Red
Gn	Green	**Sw**	Black

Key to items

1 Battery
2 Ignition switch
44 Hazard warning/central locking switch
77 General control unit
151 Driver's door lock assembly
152 Passenger's door lock assembly
153 LH rear door lock
154 RH rear door lock
155 Mirror control switch
156 Driver's mirror assembly
157 Passenger's mirror assembly
158 Switching centre control unit
159 Driver's backrest heater
160 Driver's seat heater
161 Passenger's backrest heater
162 Passenger's seat heater

Diagram 10

H32742

F60 25A
F108 200A
35.0 Rt
2.5 Rt/Sw
35.0 Sw
B9 B15 A7 A32 A32 A13 A22 A20 A20 A16 A33 A54 A25 A15 A34 A53 A14 A36 A52
77
4.0 Br
0.35 Ge/Rt
0.35 Br/Sw
0.75 Sw
0.75 Bl
0.75 Ws
0.5 Bl/Rt
0.5 Ws/Sw
0.5 Br/Gr/Ge
0.75 Br
44
1
151
152
154
153
Central locking

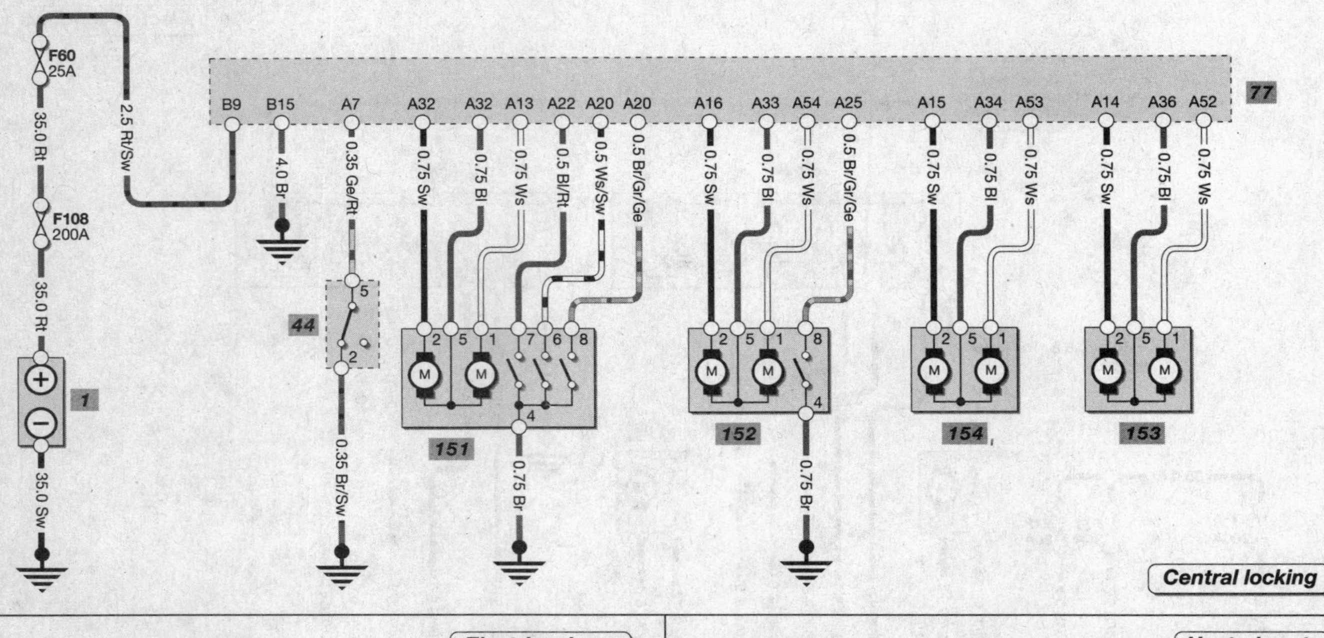

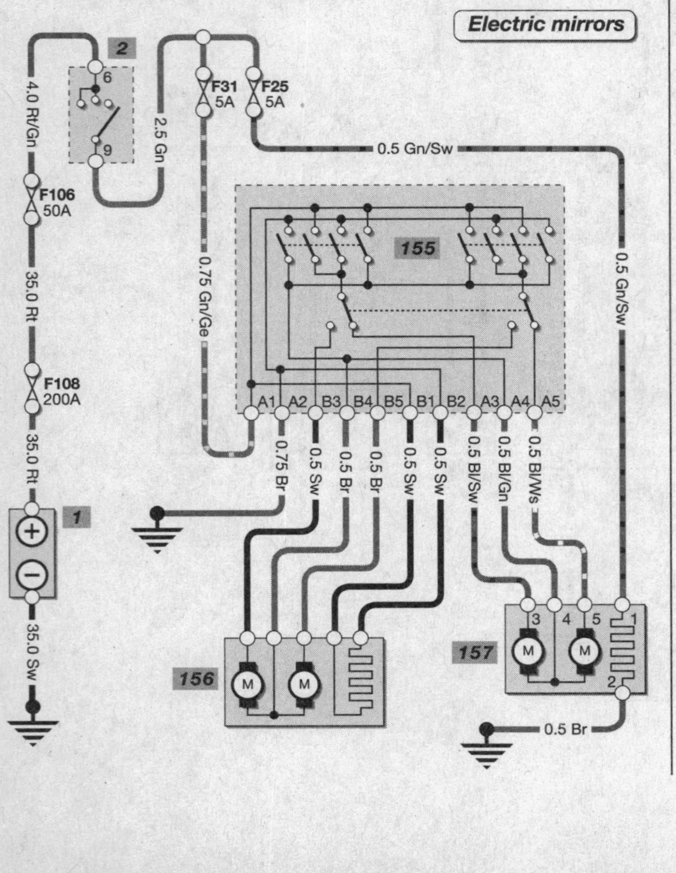

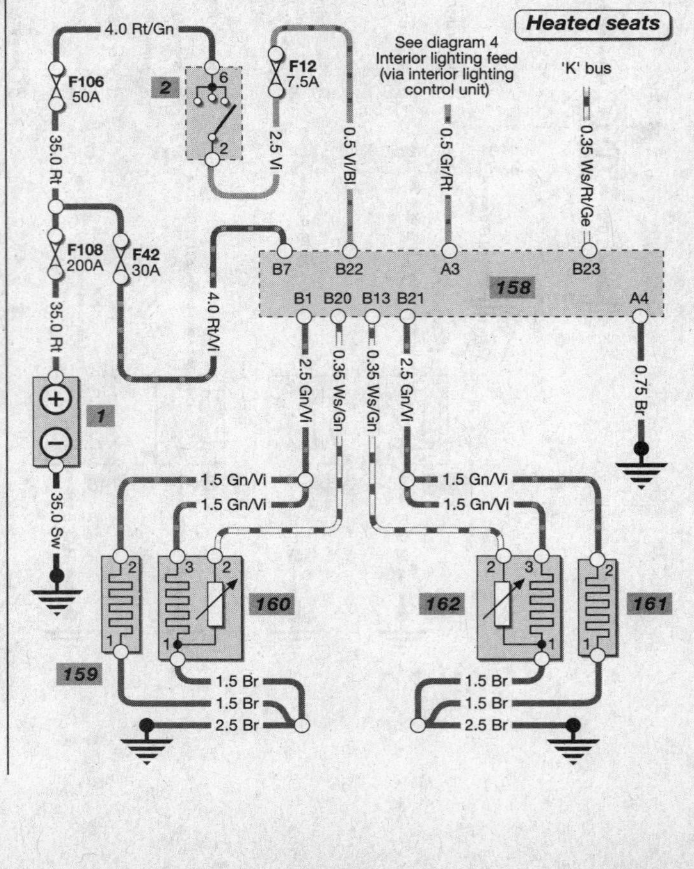

Electric mirrors
2
4.0 Rt/Gn
F106 50A
F108 200A
35.0 Rt
35.0 Sw
2.5 Gn
F31 5A
F25 5A
0.5 Gn/Sw
0.75 Gn/Ge
155
A1 A2 B3 B4 B5 B1 B2 A3 A4 A5
0.75 Br
0.5 Sw
0.5 Br
0.5 Bl/Sw
0.5 Bl/Gn
0.5 Bl/Ws
1
156
157
0.5 Br

Heated seats
4.0 Rt/Gn
F106 50A
F108 200A
F42 30A
F12 7.5A
2.5 Vi
0.5 Vi/Bl
See diagram 4 Interior lighting feed (via interior lighting control unit)
0.5 Gr/Rt
'K' bus
0.35 Ws/Rt/Ge
4.0 Rt/Vi
35.0 Rt
35.0 Sw
B7 B22 A3 B23
158
B1 B20 B13 B21 A4
2.5 Gn/Vi
0.35 Ws/Gn
0.75 Br
1.5 Gn/Vi
1.5 Br
2.5 Br
1
2
159
160
162
161

Wire colours

Bl	Blue	**Vi**	Violet
Br	Brown	**Ws**	White
Ge	Yellow	**Or**	Orange
Gr	Grey	**Rt**	Red
Gn	Green	**Sw**	Black

Key to items

1 Battery
2 Ignition switch
158 Switching centre control unit
165 ABS/ASC control unit
166 LH front wheel sensor
167 RH front wheel sensor
168 LH rear wheel sensor
169 RH rear wheel sensor
170 Tyre pressure control unit
171 LH front tyre pressure sensor
172 RH front tyre pressure sensor
173 LH rear tyre pressure sensor
174 RH rear tyre pressure sensor

Diagram 11

H32743

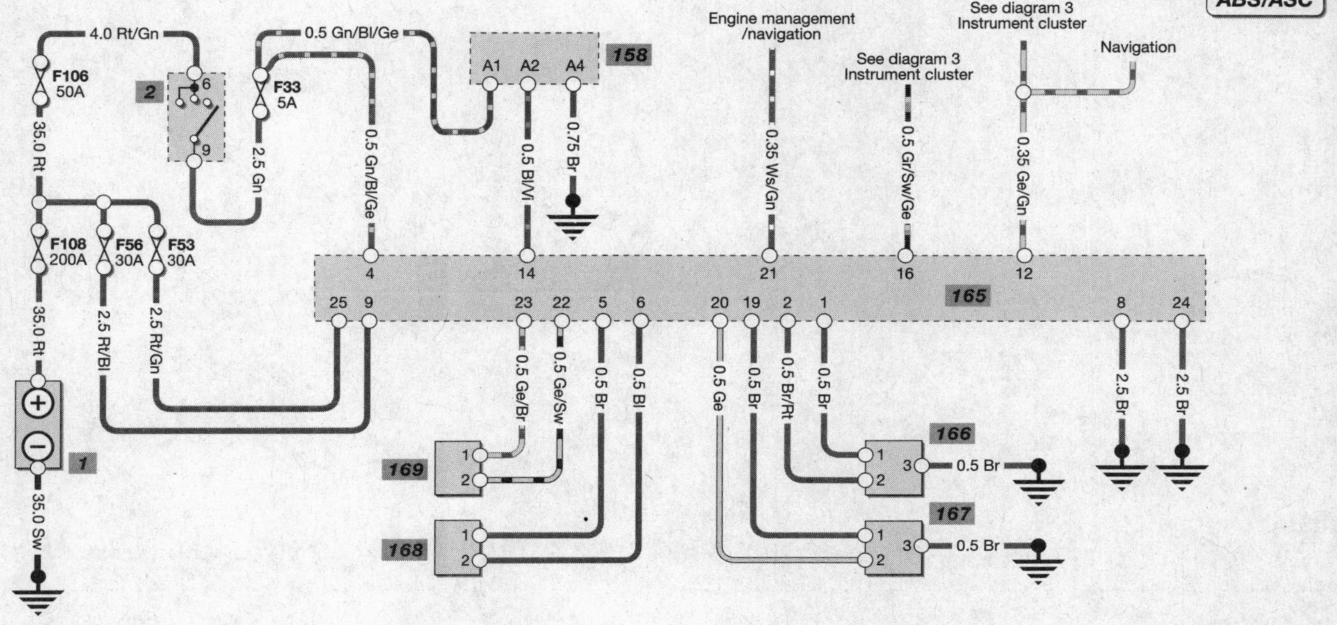

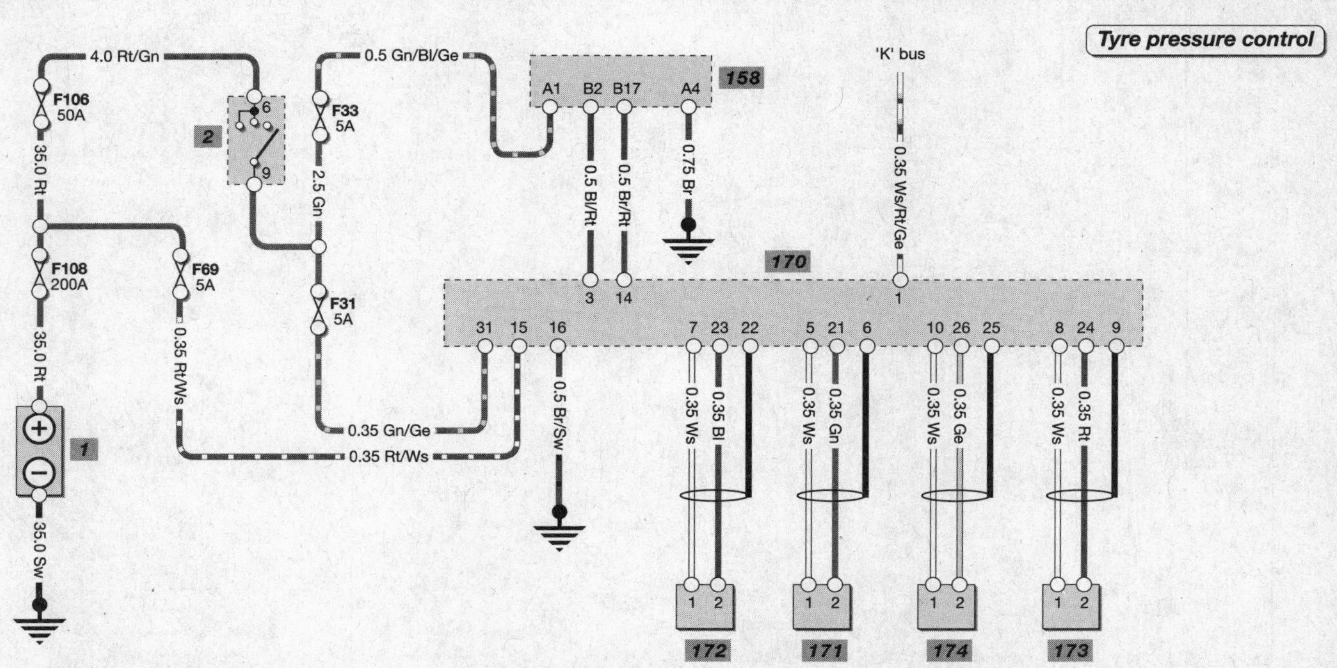

Dimensions and weights

Note: *All figures are approximate, and may vary according to model. Refer to manufacturer's data for exact figures.*

Dimensions

Overall length:	
Saloon	4471 mm
Coupe	4488 mm
Touring	4478 mm
Overall width:	
Saloon*	1739 mm
Coupe	1947 mm
Touring	1932 mm
Overall height (unladen):	
Saloon	1415 to 1434 mm
Coupe	1369 to 1387 mm
Touring	1409 to 1429 mm
Wheelbase	2725 mm

** Excluding wing mirrors*

Weights

Kerb weight:*	
Saloon	1360 to 1715 kg
Coupe	1385 to 1540 kg
Touring	1440 to 1785 kg
Maximum gross vehicle weight:*	
Saloon	1785 to 2105 kg
Coupe	1810 to 2040 kg
Touring	1905 to 2220 kg
Maximum roof rack load	75 kg
Maximum towing weight:†	
Unbraked trailer	670 to 720 kg
Braked trailer	1400 to 1700 kg

** Depending on model and specification*
† Refer to BMW dealer for exact recommendation

Conversion factors

Length (distance)

Inches (in)	x 25.4	= Millimetres (mm)	x 0.0394	= Inches (in)
Feet (ft)	x 0.305	= Metres (m)	x 3.281	= Feet (ft)
Miles	x 1.609	= Kilometres (km)	x 0.621	= Miles

Volume (capacity)

Cubic inches (cu in; in^3)	x 16.387	= Cubic centimetres (cc; cm^3)	x 0.061	= Cubic inches (cu in; in^3)
Imperial pints (Imp pt)	x 0.568	= Litres (l)	x 1.76	= Imperial pints (Imp pt)
Imperial quarts (Imp qt)	x 1.137	= Litres (l)	x 0.88	= Imperial quarts (Imp qt)
Imperial quarts (Imp qt)	x 1.201	= US quarts (US qt)	x 0.833	= Imperial quarts (Imp qt)
US quarts (US qt)	x 0.946	= Litres (l)	x 1.057	= US quarts (US qt)
Imperial gallons (Imp gal)	x 4.546	= Litres (l)	x 0.22	= Imperial gallons (Imp gal)
Imperial gallons (Imp gal)	x 1.201	= US gallons (US gal)	x 0.833	= Imperial gallons (Imp gal)
US gallons (US gal)	x 3.785	= Litres (l)	x 0.264	= US gallons (US gal)

Mass (weight)

Ounces (oz)	x 28.35	= Grams (g)	x 0.035	= Ounces (oz)
Pounds (lb)	x 0.454	= Kilograms (kg)	x 2.205	= Pounds (lb)

Force

Ounces-force (ozf; oz)	x 0.278	= Newtons (N)	x 3.6	= Ounces-force (ozf; oz)
Pounds-force (lbf; lb)	x 4.448	= Newtons (N)	x 0.225	= Pounds-force (lbf; lb)
Newtons (N)	x 0.1	= Kilograms-force (kgf; kg)	x 9.81	= Newtons (N)

Pressure

Pounds-force per square inch (psi; lbf/in^2; lb/in^2)	x 0.070	= Kilograms-force per square centimetre (kgf/cm^2; kg/cm^2)	x 14.223	= Pounds-force per square inch (psi; lbf/in^2; lb/in^2)
Pounds-force per square inch (psi; lbf/in^2; lb/in^2)	x 0.068	= Atmospheres (atm)	x 14.696	= Pounds-force per square inch (psi; lbf/in^2; lb/in^2)
Pounds-force per square inch (psi; lbf/in^2; lb/in^2)	x 0.069	= Bars	x 14.5	= Pounds-force per square inch (psi; lbf/in^2; lb/in^2)
Pounds-force per square inch (psi; lbf/in^2; lb/in^2)	x 6.895	= Kilopascals (kPa)	x 0.145	= Pounds-force per square inch (psi; lbf/in^2; lb/in^2)
Kilopascals (kPa)	x 0.01	= Kilograms-force per square centimetre (kgf/cm^2; kg/cm^2)	x 98.1	= Kilopascals (kPa)
Millibar (mbar)	x 100	= Pascals (Pa)	x 0.01	= Millibar (mbar)
Millibar (mbar)	x 0.0145	= Pounds-force per square inch (psi; lbf/in^2; lb/in^2)	x 68.947	= Millibar (mbar)
Millibar (mbar)	x 0.75	= Millimetres of mercury (mmHg)	x 1.333	= Millibar (mbar)
Millibar (mbar)	x 0.401	= Inches of water (inH_2O)	x 2.491	= Millibar (mbar)
Millimetres of mercury (mmHg)	x 0.535	= Inches of water (inH_2O)	x 1.868	= Millimetres of mercury (mmHg)
Inches of water (inH_2O)	x 0.036	= Pounds-force per square inch (psi; lbf/in^2; lb/in^2)	x 27.68	= Inches of water (inH_2O)

Torque (moment of force)

Pounds-force inches (lbf in; lb in)	x 1.152	= Kilograms-force centimetre (kgf cm; kg cm)	x 0.868	= Pounds-force inches (lbf in; lb in)
Pounds-force inches (lbf in; lb in)	x 0.113	= Newton metres (Nm)	x 8.85	= Pounds-force inches (lbf in; lb in)
Pounds-force inches (lbf in; lb in)	x 0.083	= Pounds-force feet (lbf ft; lb ft)	x 12	= Pounds-force inches (lbf in; lb in)
Pounds-force feet (lbf ft; lb ft)	x 0.138	= Kilograms-force metres (kgf m; kg m)	x 7.233	= Pounds-force feet (lbf ft; lb ft)
Pounds-force feet (lbf ft; lb ft)	x 1.356	= Newton metres (Nm)	x 0.738	= Pounds-force feet (lbf ft; lb ft)
Newton metres (Nm)	x 0.102	= Kilograms-force metres (kgf m; kg m)	x 9.804	= Newton metres (Nm)

Power

Horsepower (hp)	x 745.7	= Watts (W)	x 0.0013	= Horsepower (hp)

Velocity (speed)

Miles per hour (miles/hr; mph)	x 1.609	= Kilometres per hour (km/hr; kph)	x 0.621	= Miles per hour (miles/hr; mph)

Fuel consumption*

Miles per gallon, Imperial (mpg)	x 0.354	= Kilometres per litre (km/l)	x 2.825	= Miles per gallon, Imperial (mpg)
Miles per gallon, US (mpg)	x 0.425	= Kilometres per litre (km/l)	x 2.352	= Miles per gallon, US (mpg)

Temperature

Degrees Fahrenheit = (°C x 1.8) + 32

Degrees Celsius (Degrees Centigrade; °C) = (°F - 32) x 0.56

** It is common practice to convert from miles per gallon (mpg) to litres/100 kilometres (l/100km), where mpg x l/100 km = 282*

Spare parts are available from many sources, including maker's appointed garages, accessory shops, and motor factors. To be sure of obtaining the correct parts, it will sometimes be necessary to quote the vehicle identification number. If possible, it can also be useful to take the old parts along for positive identification. Items such as starter motors and alternators may be available under a service exchange scheme – any parts returned should be clean.

Our advice regarding spare parts is as follows.

Officially appointed garages

This is the best source of parts which are peculiar to your car, and which are not otherwise generally available (eg, badges, interior trim, certain body panels, etc). It is also the only place at which you should buy parts if the car is still under warranty.

Accessory shops

These are very good places to buy materials and components needed for the maintenance of your car (oil, air and fuel filters, light bulbs, drivebelts, greases, brake pads, touch-up paint, etc). Components of this nature sold by a reputable shop are usually of the same standard as those used by the car manufacturer.

Besides components, these shops also sell tools and general accessories, usually have convenient opening hours, charge lower prices, and can often be found close to home. Some accessory shops have parts counters where components needed for almost any repair job can be purchased or ordered.

Motor factors

Good factors will stock all the more important components which wear out comparatively quickly, and can sometimes supply individual components needed for the overhaul of a larger assembly (eg, brake seals and hydraulic parts, bearing shells, pistons, valves). They may also handle work such as cylinder block reboring, crankshaft regrinding, etc.

Engine reconditioners

These specialise in engine overhaul and can also supply components. It is recommended that the establishment is a member of the Federation of Engine Re-Manufacturers, or a similar society.

Tyre and exhaust specialists

These outlets may be independent, or members of a local or national chain. They frequently offer competitive prices when compared with a main dealer or local garage, but it will pay to obtain several quotes before making a decision. When researching prices, also ask what extras may be added – for instance fitting a new valve, balancing the wheel and tyre disposal all both commonly charged on top of the price of a new tyre.

Other sources

Beware of parts or materials obtained from market stalls, car boot sales, on-line auctions or similar outlets. Such items are not invariably sub-standard, but there is little chance of compensation if they do prove unsatisfactory. In the case of safety-critical components such as brake pads, there is the risk not only of financial loss, but also of an accident causing injury or death.

Second-hand components or assemblies obtained from a car breaker can be a good buy in some circumstances, but this sort of purchase is best made by the experienced DIY mechanic.

Vehicle identification

Modifications are a continuing and unpublicised process in vehicle manufacture, quite apart from major model changes. Spare parts manuals and lists are compiled upon a numerical basis, the individual vehicle identification numbers being essential to correct identification of the component concerned.

When ordering spare parts, always give as much information as possible. Quote the car model, year of manufacture and registration, chassis and engine numbers as appropriate.

The *Vehicle Identification Number (VIN)* plate is riveted to the left-hand suspension turret in the front corner of the engine compartment, and visible through the passenger side of the windscreen. The vehicle identification number is also stamped onto the right-hand suspension turret in the engine compartment **(see illustrations)**.

The *engine number* is stamped on the left-hand face of the cylinder block near the base of the oil level dipstick (all engines except N42 and N46), or on the front of the cylinder block adjacent to the cylinder head joint (N42 and N46 engines).

Engine codes

4-cylinder engines

1796 cc engines . . . . . . N42 B18 and N46 B18
1895 cc engines M43TU B19
1995 cc engines . . . . . . N42 B20 and N46 B20

6-cylinder engines

2171 cc engines M54 B22
2494 cc engines . . . . . . M52TU B25 and M54 B25
2793 cc engines M52TU B28
2979 cc engines M54 B30

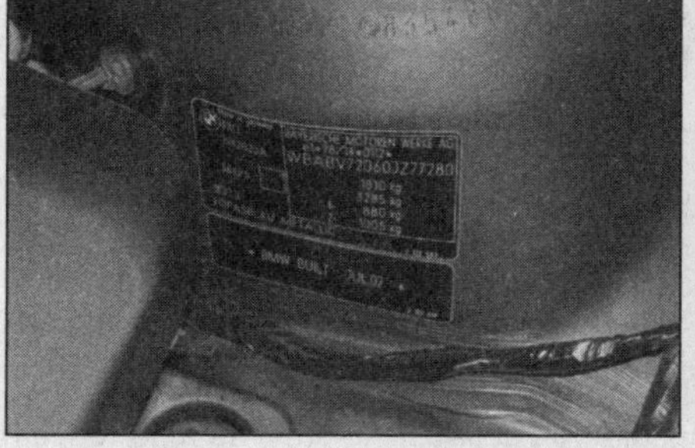

The VIN plate is riveted to the body panel in the left-hand front corner of the engine compartment

The VIN is stamped onto the right-hand suspension turret in the engine compartment

Whenever servicing, repair or overhaul work is carried out on the car or its components, observe the following procedures and instructions. This will assist in carrying out the operation efficiently and to a professional standard of workmanship.

Joint mating faces and gaskets

When separating components at their mating faces, never insert screwdrivers or similar implements into the joint between the faces in order to prise them apart. This can cause severe damage which results in oil leaks, coolant leaks, etc upon reassembly. Separation is usually achieved by tapping along the joint with a soft-faced hammer in order to break the seal. However, note that this method may not be suitable where dowels are used for component location.

Where a gasket is used between the mating faces of two components, a new one must be fitted on reassembly; fit it dry unless otherwise stated in the repair procedure. Make sure that the mating faces are clean and dry, with all traces of old gasket removed. When cleaning a joint face, use a tool which is unlikely to score or damage the face, and remove any burrs or nicks with an oilstone or fine file.

Make sure that tapped holes are cleaned with a pipe cleaner, and keep them free of jointing compound, if this is being used, unless specifically instructed otherwise.

Ensure that all orifices, channels or pipes are clear, and blow through them, preferably using compressed air.

Oil seals

Oil seals can be removed by levering them out with a wide flat-bladed screwdriver or similar implement. Alternatively, a number of self-tapping screws may be screwed into the seal, and these used as a purchase for pliers or some similar device in order to pull the seal free.

Whenever an oil seal is removed from its working location, either individually or as part of an assembly, it should be renewed.

The very fine sealing lip of the seal is easily damaged, and will not seal if the surface it contacts is not completely clean and free from scratches, nicks or grooves. If the original sealing surface of the component cannot be restored, and the manufacturer has not made provision for slight relocation of the seal relative to the sealing surface, the component should be renewed.

Protect the lips of the seal from any surface which may damage them in the course of fitting. Use tape or a conical sleeve where possible. Where indicated, lubricate the seal lips with oil before fitting and, on dual-lipped seals, fill the space between the lips with grease.

Unless otherwise stated, oil seals must be fitted with their sealing lips toward the lubricant to be sealed.

Use a tubular drift or block of wood of the appropriate size to install the seal and, if the seal housing is shouldered, drive the seal down to the shoulder. If the seal housing is unshouldered, the seal should be fitted with its face flush with the housing top face (unless otherwise instructed).

Screw threads and fastenings

Seized nuts, bolts and screws are quite a common occurrence where corrosion has set in, and the use of penetrating oil or releasing fluid will often overcome this problem if the offending item is soaked for a while before attempting to release it. The use of an impact driver may also provide a means of releasing such stubborn fastening devices, when used in conjunction with the appropriate screwdriver bit or socket. If none of these methods works, it may be necessary to resort to the careful application of heat, or the use of a hacksaw or nut splitter device. Before resorting to extreme methods, check that you are not dealing with a left-hand thread!

Studs are usually removed by locking two nuts together on the threaded part, and then using a spanner on the lower nut to unscrew the stud. Studs or bolts which have broken off below the surface of the component in which they are mounted can sometimes be removed using a stud extractor.

Always ensure that a blind tapped hole is completely free from oil, grease, water or other fluid before installing the bolt or stud. Failure to do this could cause the housing to crack due to the hydraulic action of the bolt or stud as it is screwed in.

For some screw fastenings, notably cylinder head bolts or nuts, torque wrench settings are no longer specified for the latter stages of tightening, "angle-tightening" being called up instead. Typically, a fairly low torque wrench setting will be applied to the bolts/nuts in the correct sequence, followed by one or more stages of tightening through specified angles.

When checking or retightening a nut or bolt to a specified torque setting, slacken the nut or bolt by a quarter of a turn, and then retighten to the specified setting. However, this should not be attempted where angular tightening has been used.

Locknuts, locktabs and washers

Any fastening which will rotate against a component or housing during tightening should always have a washer between it and the relevant component or housing.

Spring or split washers should always be renewed when they are used to lock a critical component such as a big-end bearing retaining bolt or nut. Locktabs which are folded over to retain a nut or bolt should always be renewed.

Self-locking nuts can be re-used in non-critical areas, providing resistance can be felt when the locking portion passes over the bolt or stud thread. However, it should be noted that self-locking stiffnuts tend to lose their effectiveness after long periods of use, and should then be renewed as a matter of course.

Split pins must always be replaced with new ones of the correct size for the hole.

When thread-locking compound is found on the threads of a fastener which is to be re-used, it should be cleaned off with a wire brush and solvent, and fresh compound applied on reassembly.

Special tools

Some repair procedures in this manual entail the use of special tools such as a press, two or three-legged pullers, spring compressors, etc. Wherever possible, suitable readily-available alternatives to the manufacturer's special tools are described, and are shown in use. In some instances, where no alternative is possible, it has been necessary to resort to the use of a manufacturer's tool, and this has been done for reasons of safety as well as the efficient completion of the repair operation. Unless you are highly-skilled and have a thorough understanding of the procedures described, never attempt to bypass the use of any special tool when the procedure described specifies its use. Not only is there a very great risk of personal injury, but expensive damage could be caused to the components involved.

Environmental considerations

When disposing of used engine oil, brake fluid, antifreeze, etc, give due consideration to any detrimental environmental effects. Do not, for instance, pour any of the above liquids down drains into the general sewage system, or onto the ground to soak away. Many local council refuse tips provide a facility for waste oil disposal, as do some garages. You can find your nearest disposal point by calling the Environment Agency on 08708 506 506 or by visiting www.oilbankline.org.uk.

Note: It is illegal and anti-social to dump oil down the drain. To find the location of your local oil recycling bank, call 08708 506 506 or visit www.oilbankline.org.uk.

Jacking and vehicle support

The jack supplied with the vehicle tool kit should only be used for changing the roadwheels – see *Wheel changing* at the front of this manual. When carrying out any other kind of work, raise the vehicle using a hydraulic (or 'trolley') jack, and always supplement the jack with axle stands positioned under the vehicle jacking points.

When using a hydraulic jack or axle stands, always position the jack head or axle stand head under the relevant rubber lifting blocks. These are situated directly underneath the vehicle jack location holes in the sill **(see illustration)**.

The jack supplied with the vehicle locates in the holes provided in the sill. Ensure that the jack head is correctly engaged before attempting to raise the vehicle.

Never work under, around, or near a raised vehicle, unless it is adequately supported in at least two places.

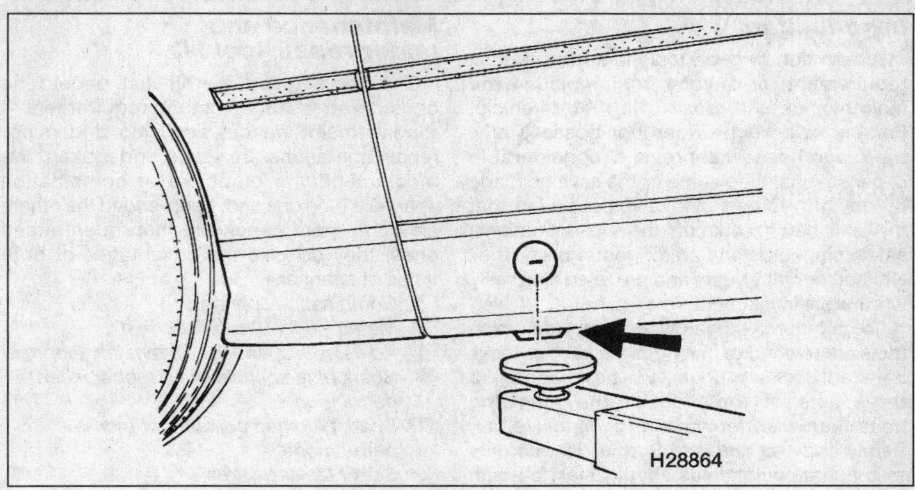

Trolley jack support point

Audio unit anti-theft system

The radio/cassette/CD player/autochanger unit fitted as standard equipment by BMW is equipped with a built-in security code, to deter thieves. If the power source to the unit is cut, the anti-theft system will activate. Even if the power source is immediately reconnected, the radio/cassette unit will not function until the correct security code has been entered. Therefore if you do not know the correct security code for the unit, **do not** disconnect the battery negative lead, or remove the radio/cassette unit from the vehicle.

The procedure for reprogramming a unit that has been disconnected from its power supply varies from model to model – consult the handbook supplied with the unit for specific details or refer to your BMW dealer.

Introduction

A selection of good tools is a fundamental requirement for anyone contemplating the maintenance and repair of a motor vehicle. For the owner who does not possess any, their purchase will prove a considerable expense, offsetting some of the savings made by doing-it-yourself. However, provided that the tools purchased meet the relevant national safety standards and are of good quality, they will last for many years and prove an extremely worthwhile investment.

To help the average owner to decide which tools are needed to carry out the various tasks detailed in this manual, we have compiled three lists of tools under the following headings: *Maintenance and minor repair*, *Repair and overhaul*, and *Special*. Newcomers to practical mechanics should start off with the *Maintenance and minor repair* tool kit, and confine themselves to the simpler jobs around the vehicle. Then, as confidence and experience grow, more difficult tasks can be undertaken, with extra tools being purchased as, and when, they are needed. In this way, a *Maintenance and minor repair* tool kit can be built up into a *Repair and overhaul* tool kit over a considerable period of time, without any major cash outlays. The experienced do-it-yourselfer will have a tool kit good enough for most repair and overhaul procedures, and will add tools from the *Special* category when it is felt that the expense is justified by the amount of use to which these tools will be put.

Maintenance and minor repair tool kit

The tools given in this list should be considered as a minimum requirement if routine maintenance, servicing and minor repair operations are to be undertaken. We recommend the purchase of combination spanners (ring one end, open-ended the other); although more expensive than open-ended ones, they do give the advantages of both types of spanner.

☐ *Combination spanners:*
Metric - 8 to 19 mm inclusive
☐ *Adjustable spanner - 35 mm jaw (approx.)*
☐ *Spark plug spanner (with rubber insert) - petrol models*
☐ *Spark plug gap adjustment tool - petrol models*
☐ *Set of feeler gauges*
☐ *Brake bleed nipple spanner*
☐ *Screwdrivers:*
Flat blade - 100 mm long x 6 mm dia
Cross blade - 100 mm long x 6 mm dia
Torx - various sizes (not all vehicles)
☐ *Combination pliers*
☐ *Hacksaw (junior)*
☐ *Tyre pump*
☐ *Tyre pressure gauge*
☐ *Oil can*
☐ *Oil filter removal tool (if applicable)*
☐ *Fine emery cloth*
☐ *Wire brush (small)*
☐ *Funnel (medium size)*
☐ *Sump drain plug key (not all vehicles)*

Repair and overhaul tool kit

These tools are virtually essential for anyone undertaking any major repairs to a motor vehicle, and are additional to those given in the *Maintenance and minor repair* list. Included in this list is a comprehensive set of sockets. Although these are expensive, they will be found invaluable as they are so versatile - particularly if various drives are included in the set. We recommend the half-inch square-drive type, as this can be used with most proprietary torque wrenches.

The tools in this list will sometimes need to be supplemented by tools from the *Special* list:

☐ *Sockets to cover range in previous list (including Torx sockets)*
☐ *Reversible ratchet drive (for use with sockets)*
☐ *Extension piece, 250 mm (for use with sockets)*
☐ *Universal joint (for use with sockets)*
☐ *Flexible handle or sliding T "breaker bar" (for use with sockets)*
☐ *Torque wrench (for use with sockets)*
☐ *Self-locking grips*
☐ *Ball pein hammer*
☐ *Soft-faced mallet (plastic or rubber)*
☐ *Screwdrivers:*
Flat blade - long & sturdy, short (chubby), and narrow (electrician's) types
Cross blade – long & sturdy, and short (chubby) types
☐ *Pliers:*
Long-nosed
Side cutters (electrician's)
Circlip (internal and external)
☐ *Cold chisel - 25 mm*
☐ *Scriber*
☐ *Scraper*
☐ *Centre-punch*
☐ *Pin punch*
☐ *Hacksaw*
☐ *Brake hose clamp*
☐ *Brake/clutch bleeding kit*
☐ *Selection of twist drills*
☐ *Steel rule/straight-edge*
☐ *Allen keys (inc. splined/Torx type)*
☐ *Selection of files*
☐ *Wire brush*
☐ *Axle stands*
☐ *Jack (strong trolley or hydraulic type)*
☐ *Light with extension lead*
☐ *Universal electrical multi-meter*

Sockets and reversible ratchet drive

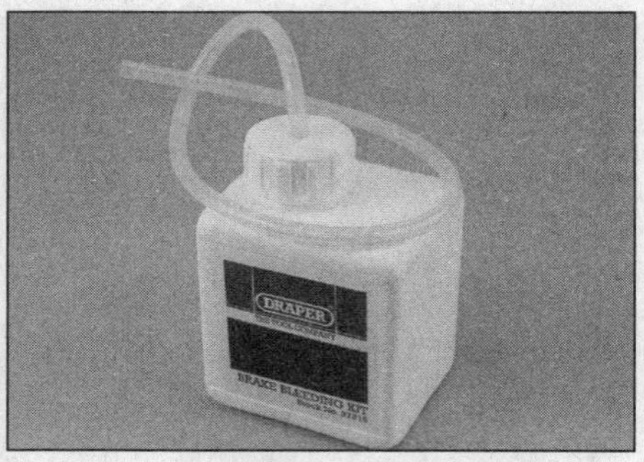

Brake bleeding kit

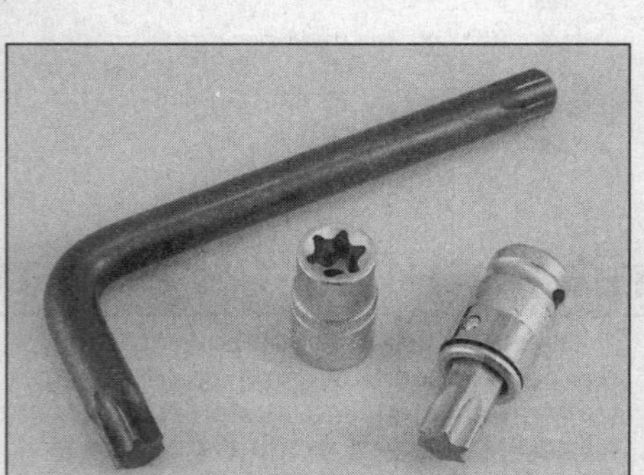
Torx key, socket and bit

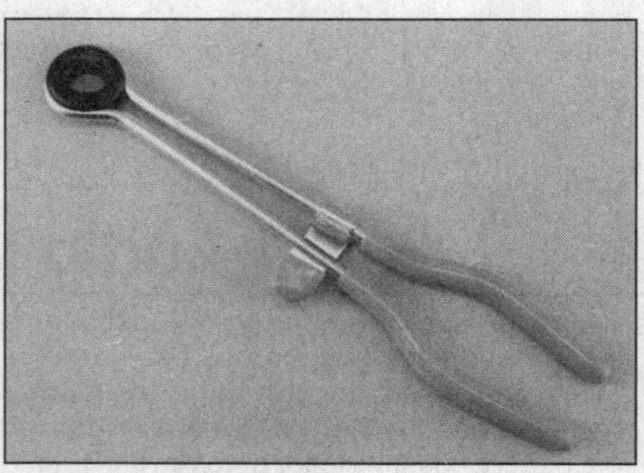
Hose clamp

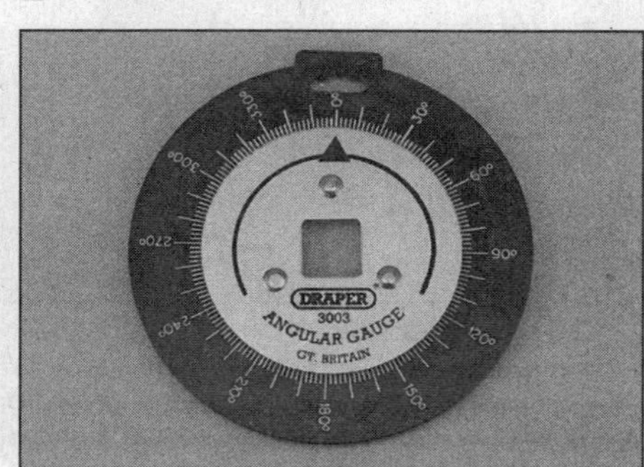

Angular-tightening gauge

Special tools

The tools in this list are those which are not used regularly, are expensive to buy, or which need to be used in accordance with their manufacturers' instructions. Unless relatively difficult mechanical jobs are undertaken frequently, it will not be economic to buy many of these tools. Where this is the case, you could consider clubbing together with friends (or joining a motorists' club) to make a joint purchase, or borrowing the tools against a deposit from a local garage or tool hire specialist.

The following list contains only those tools and instruments freely available to the public, and not those special tools produced by the vehicle manufacturer specifically for its dealer network. You will find occasional references to these manufacturers' special tools in the text of this manual. Generally, an alternative method of doing the job without the vehicle manufacturers' special tool is given. However, sometimes there is no alternative to using them. Where this is the case and the relevant tool cannot be bought or borrowed, you will have to entrust the work to a dealer.

- ☐ *Angular-tightening gauge*
- ☐ *Valve spring compressor*
- ☐ *Valve grinding tool*
- ☐ *Piston ring compressor*
- ☐ *Piston ring removal/installation tool*
- ☐ *Cylinder bore hone*
- ☐ *Balljoint separator*
- ☐ *Coil spring compressors (where applicable)*
- ☐ *Two/three-legged hub and bearing puller*
- ☐ *Impact screwdriver*
- ☐ *Micrometer and/or vernier calipers*
- ☐ *Dial gauge*
- ☐ *Tachometer*
- ☐ *Fault code reader*
- ☐ *Cylinder compression gauge*
- ☐ *Hand-operated vacuum pump and gauge*
- ☐ *Clutch plate alignment set*
- ☐ *Brake shoe steady spring cup removal tool*
- ☐ *Bush and bearing removal/installation set*
- ☐ *Stud extractors*
- ☐ *Tap and die set*
- ☐ *Lifting tackle*

Buying tools

Reputable motor accessory shops and superstores often offer excellent quality tools at discount prices, so it pays to shop around.

Remember, you don't have to buy the most expensive items on the shelf, but it is always advisable to steer clear of the very cheap tools. Beware of 'bargains' offered on market stalls, on-line or at car boot sales. There are plenty of good tools around at reasonable prices, but always aim to purchase items which meet the relevant national safety standards. If in doubt, ask the proprietor or manager of the shop for advice before making a purchase.

Care and maintenance of tools

Having purchased a reasonable tool kit, it is necessary to keep the tools in a clean and serviceable condition. After use, always wipe off any dirt, grease and metal particles using a clean, dry cloth, before putting the tools away. Never leave them lying around after they have been used. A simple tool rack on the garage or workshop wall for items such as screwdrivers and pliers is a good idea. Store all normal spanners and sockets in a metal box. Any measuring instruments, gauges, meters, etc, must be carefully stored where they cannot be damaged or become rusty.

Take a little care when tools are used. Hammer heads inevitably become marked, and screwdrivers lose the keen edge on their blades from time to time. A little timely attention with emery cloth or a file will soon restore items like this to a good finish.

Working facilities

Not to be forgotten when discussing tools is the workshop itself. If anything more than routine maintenance is to be carried out, a suitable working area becomes essential.

It is appreciated that many an owner-mechanic is forced by circumstances to remove an engine or similar item without the benefit of a garage or workshop. Having done this, any repairs should always be done under the cover of a roof.

Wherever possible, any dismantling should be done on a clean, flat workbench or table at a suitable working height.

Any workbench needs a vice; one with a jaw opening of 100 mm is suitable for most jobs. As mentioned previously, some clean dry storage space is also required for tools, as well as for any lubricants, cleaning fluids, touch-up paints etc, which become necessary.

Another item which may be required, and which has a much more general usage, is an electric drill with a chuck capacity of at least 8 mm. This, together with a good range of twist drills, is virtually essential for fitting accessories.

Last, but not least, always keep a supply of old newspapers and clean, lint-free rags available, and try to keep any working area as clean as possible.

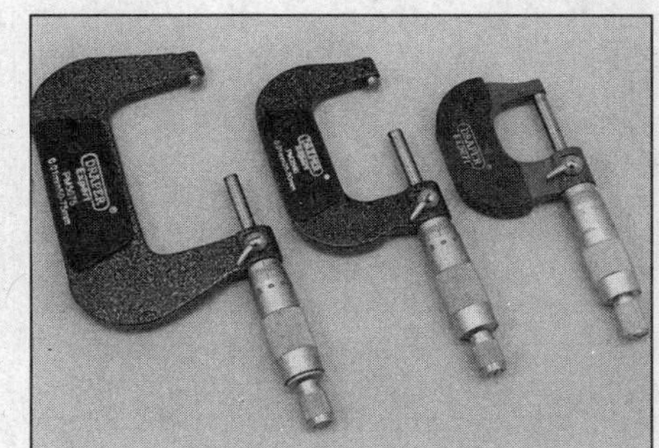

Micrometers

Dial test indicator ("dial gauge")

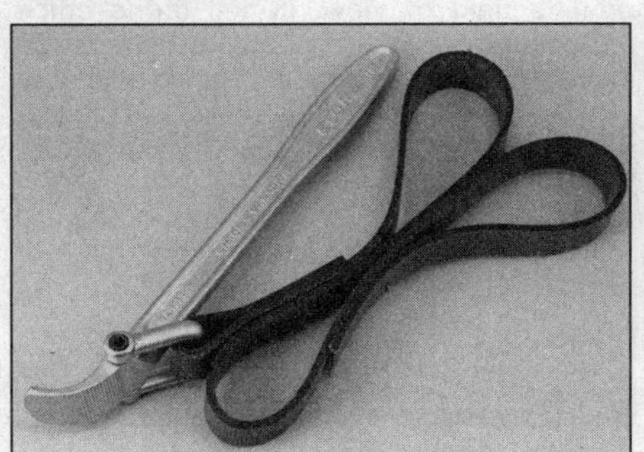

Oil filter removal tool (strap wrench type)

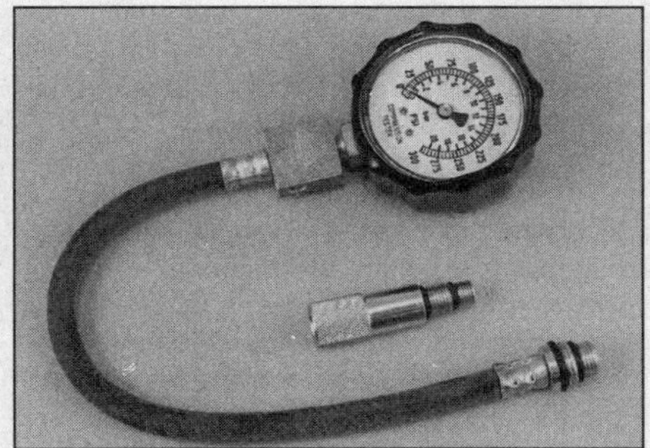

Compression tester

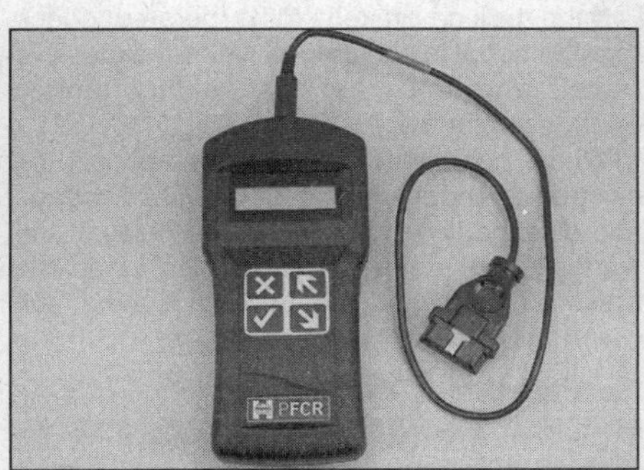

Fault code reader

This is a guide to getting your vehicle through the MOT test. Obviously it will not be possible to examine the vehicle to the same standard as the professional MOT tester. However, working through the following checks will enable you to identify any problem areas before submitting the vehicle for the test.

It has only been possible to summarise the test requirements here, based on the regulations in force at the time of printing. Test standards are becoming increasingly stringent, although there are some exemptions for older vehicles.

An assistant will be needed to help carry out some of these checks.

The checks have been sub-divided into four categories, as follows:

1 Checks carried out **FROM THE DRIVER'S SEAT**

2 Checks carried out **WITH THE VEHICLE ON THE GROUND**

3 Checks carried out **WITH THE VEHICLE RAISED AND THE WHEELS FREE TO TURN**

4 Checks carried out on **YOUR VEHICLE'S EXHAUST EMISSION SYSTEM**

1 Checks carried out FROM THE DRIVER'S SEAT

Handbrake (parking brake)

☐ Test the operation of the handbrake. Excessive travel (too many clicks) indicates incorrect brake or cable adjustment.

☐ Check that the handbrake cannot be released by tapping the lever sideways. Check the security of the lever mountings.

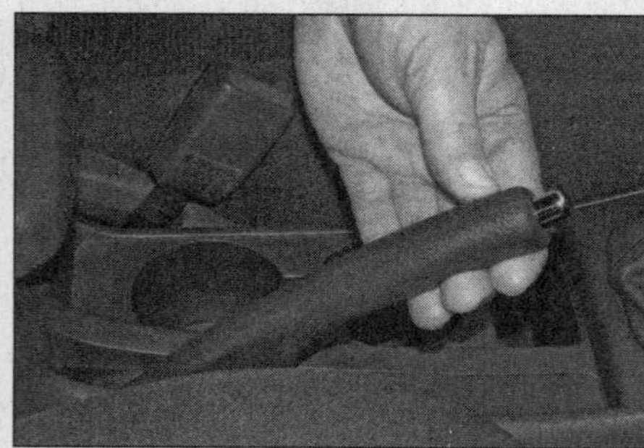

☐ If the parking brake is foot-operated, check that the pedal is secure and without excessive travel, and that the release mechanism operates correctly.

☐ Where applicable, test the operation of the electronic handbrake. The brake should engage and disengage without excessive delay. If the warning light does not extinguish when the brake is disengaged, this could indicate a fault which will need further investigation.

Footbrake

☐ Depress the brake pedal and check that it does not creep down to the floor, indicating a master cylinder fault. Release the pedal, wait a few seconds, then depress it again. If the pedal travels nearly to the floor before firm resistance is felt, brake adjustment or repair is necessary. If the pedal feels spongy, there is air in the hydraulic system which must be removed by bleeding.

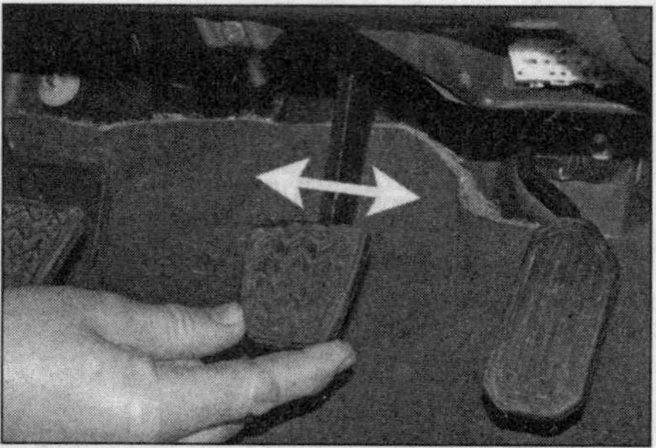

☐ Check that the brake pedal is secure and in good condition. Check also for signs of fluid leaks on the pedal, floor or carpets, which would indicate failed seals in the brake master cylinder.

☐ Check the servo unit (when applicable) by operating the brake pedal several times, then keeping the pedal depressed and starting the engine. As the engine starts, the pedal will move down slightly. If not, the vacuum hose or the servo itself may be faulty.

Steering wheel and column

☐ Examine the steering wheel for fractures or looseness of the hub, spokes or rim.

☐ Move the steering wheel from side to side and then up and down. Check that the steering wheel is not loose on the column, indicating wear or a loose retaining nut. Continue moving the steering wheel as before, but also turn it slightly from left to right.

☐ Check that the steering wheel is not loose on the column, and that there is no abnormal movement of the steering wheel, indicating wear in the column support bearings or couplings.

☐ Check that the ignition lock (where fitted) engages and disengages correctly.

☐ Steering column adjustment mechanisms (where fitted) must be able to lock the column securely in place with no play evident.

Windscreen, mirrors and sunvisor

☐ The windscreen must be free of cracks or other significant damage within the driver's field of view. (Small stone chips are acceptable.) Rear view mirrors must be secure, intact, and capable of being adjusted.

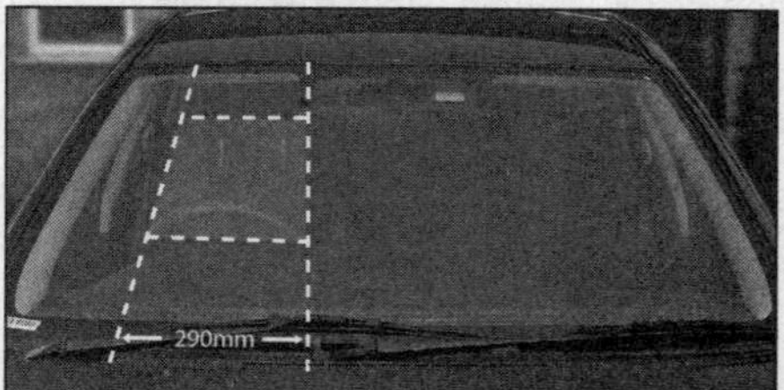

☐ The driver's sunvisor must be capable of being stored in the "up" position.

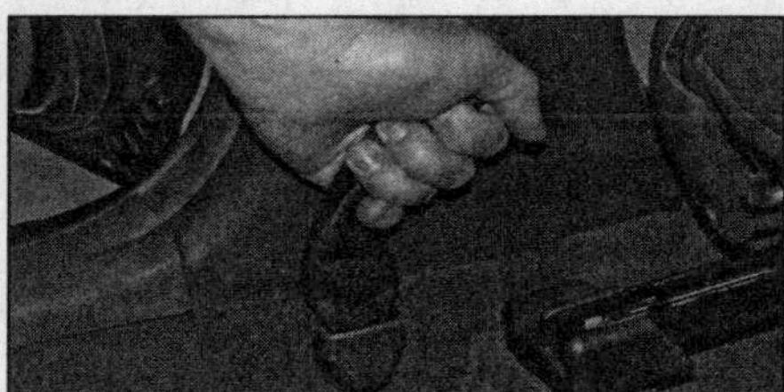

Seat belts and seats

Note: *The following checks are applicable to all seat belts, front and rear.*

☐ Examine the webbing of all the belts (including rear belts if fitted) for cuts, serious fraying or deterioration. Fasten and unfasten each belt to check the buckles. If applicable, check the retracting mechanism. Check the security of all seat belt mountings accessible from inside the vehicle, ensuring any height adjustable mountings lock securely in place.

☐ Seat belts with pre-tensioners, once activated, have a "flag" or similar showing on the seat belt stalk. This, in itself, is not a reason for test failure.

☐ The front seats themselves must be securely attached and the backrests must lock in the upright position.

Doors

☐ Both front doors must be able to be opened and closed from outside and inside, and must latch securely when closed.

Bonnet and boot/tailgate

☐ The bonnet and boot/tailgate must latch securely when closed.

2 Checks carried out WITH THE VEHICLE ON THE GROUND

Vehicle identification

☐ Number plates must be in good condition, secure and legible, with letters and numbers correctly spaced – spacing at (A) should be 33 mm and at (B) 11 mm. At the front, digits must be black on a white background and at the rear black on a yellow background. Other background designs (such as honeycomb) are not permitted.

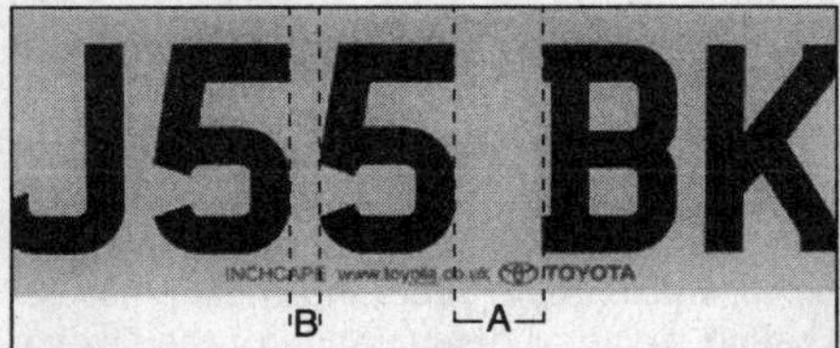

☐ The VIN plate and/or homologation plate must be permanently displayed and legible.

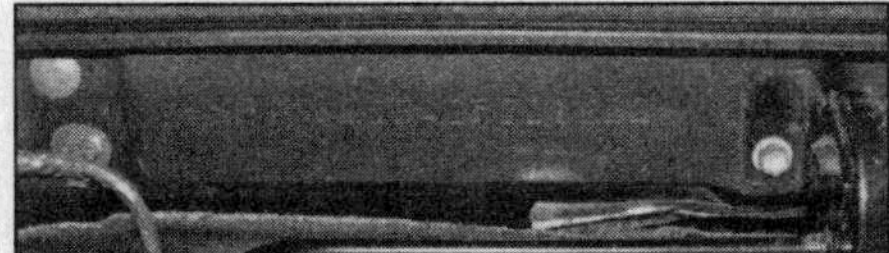

Electrical equipment

☐ Switch on the ignition and check the operation of the horn.

☐ Check the windscreen washers and wipers, examining the wiper blades; renew damaged or perished blades. Also check the operation of the stop-lights.

☐ Check the operation of the sidelights and number plate lights. The lenses and reflectors must be secure, clean and undamaged.

☐ Check the operation and alignment of the headlights. The headlight reflectors must not be tarnished and the lenses must be undamaged.

☐ Switch on the ignition and check the operation of the direction indicators (including the instrument panel tell-tale) and the hazard warning lights. Operation of the sidelights and stop-lights must not affect the indicators - if it does, the cause is usually a bad earth at the rear light cluster. Indicators should flash at a rate of between 60 and 120 times per minute – faster or slower than this could indicate a fault with the flasher unit or a bad earth at one of the light units.

☐ Check the operation of the rear foglight(s), including the warning light on the instrument panel or in the switch.

☐ The ABS warning light must illuminate in accordance with the manufacturers' design. For most vehicles, the ABS warning light should illuminate when the ignition is switched on, and (if the system is operating properly) extinguish after a few seconds. Refer to the owner's handbook.

Footbrake

☐ Examine the master cylinder, brake pipes and servo unit for leaks, loose mountings, corrosion or other damage. If ABS is fitted, this unit should also be examined for signs of leaks or corrosion.

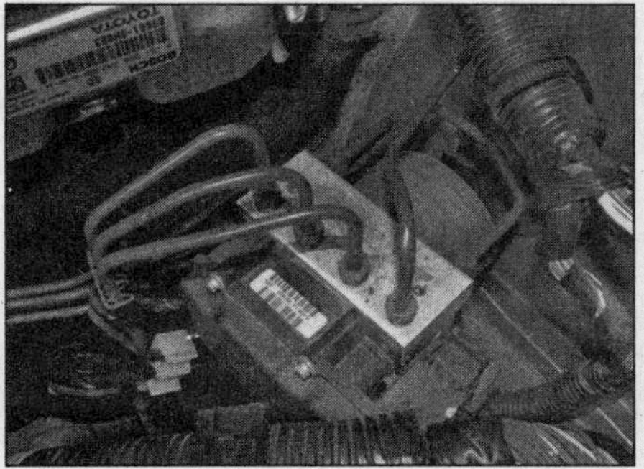

☐ The fluid reservoir must be secure and the fluid level must be between the upper (**A**) and lower (**B**) markings.

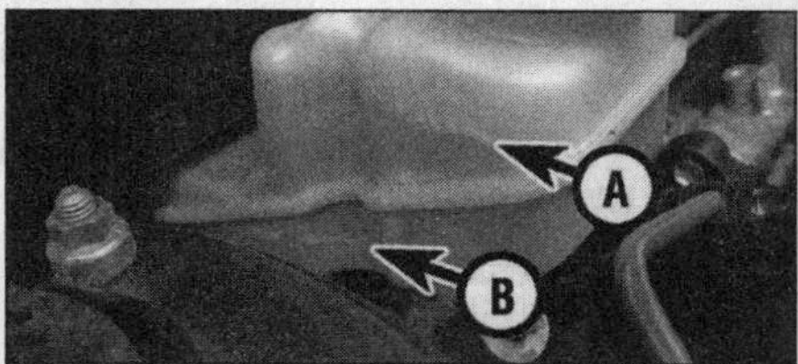

☐ Inspect both front brake flexible hoses for cracks or deterioration of the rubber. Turn the steering from lock to lock, and ensure that the hoses do not contact the wheel, tyre, or any part of the steering or suspension mechanism. With the brake pedal firmly depressed, check the hoses for bulges or leaks under pressure.

Steering and suspension

☐ Have your assistant turn the steering wheel from side to side slightly, up to the point where the steering gear just begins to transmit this movement to the roadwheels. Check for excessive free play between the steering wheel and the steering gear, indicating wear or insecurity of the steering column joints, the column-to-steering gear coupling, or the steering gear itself.

☐ Have your assistant turn the steering wheel more vigorously in each direction, so that the roadwheels just begin to turn. As this is done, examine all the steering joints, linkages, fittings and attachments. Renew any component that shows signs of wear or damage. On vehicles with power steering, check the security and condition of the steering pump, drivebelt and hoses.

☐ Check that the vehicle is standing level, and at approximately the correct ride height.

Shock absorbers

☐ Depress each corner of the vehicle in turn, then release it. The vehicle should rise and then settle in its normal position. If the vehicle continues to rise and fall, the shock absorber is defective. A shock absorber which has seized will also cause the vehicle to fail.

Exhaust system

☐Start the engine. With your assistant holding a rag over the tailpipe, check the entire system for leaks. Repair or renew leaking sections.

3 Checks carried out WITH THE VEHICLE RAISED AND THE WHEELS FREE TO TURN

Jack up the front and rear of the vehicle, and securely support it on axle stands. Position the stands clear of the suspension assemblies. Ensure that the wheels are clear of the ground and that the steering can be turned from lock to lock.

Steering mechanism

☐Have your assistant turn the steering from lock to lock. Check that the steering turns smoothly, and that no part of the steering mechanism, including a wheel or tyre, fouls any brake hose or pipe or any part of the body structure.

☐ Examine the steering rack rubber gaiters for damage or insecurity of the retaining clips. If power steering is fitted, check for signs of damage or leakage of the fluid hoses, pipes or connections. Also check for excessive stiffness or binding of the steering, a missing split pin or locking device, or severe corrosion of the body structure within 30 cm of any steering component attachment point.

Front and rear suspension and wheel bearings

☐Starting at the front right-hand side, grasp the roadwheel at the 3 o'clock and 9 o'clock positions and rock gently but firmly. Check for free play or insecurity at the wheel bearings, suspension balljoints, or suspension mount-ings, pivots and attachments.

☐Now grasp the wheel at the 12 o'clock and 6 o'clock positions and repeat the previous inspection. Spin the wheel, and check for roughness or tightness of the front wheel bearing.

☐If excess free play is suspected at a component pivot point, this can be confirmed by using a large screwdriver or similar tool and levering between the mounting and the component attachment. This will confirm whether the wear is in the pivot bush, its retaining bolt, or in the mounting itself (the bolt holes can often become elongated).

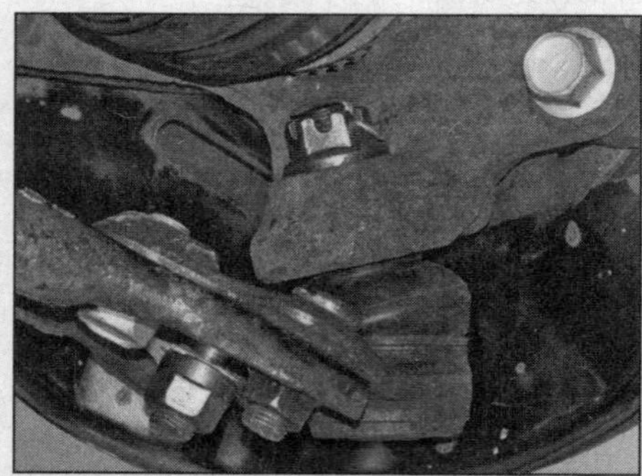

☐Carry out all the above checks at the other front wheel, and then at both rear wheels.

Springs and shock absorbers

☐Examine the suspension struts (when applicable) for serious fluid leakage, corrosion, or damage to the casing. Also check the security of the mounting points.

☐If coil springs are fitted, check that the spring ends locate in their seats, and that the spring is not corroded, cracked or broken.

☐If leaf springs are fitted, check that all leaves are intact, that the axle is securely attached to each spring, and that there is no deterioration of the spring eye mountings, bushes, and shackles.

☐The same general checks apply to vehicles fitted with other suspension types, such as torsion bars, hydraulic displacer units, etc. Ensure that all mountings and attachments are secure, that there are no signs of excessive wear, corrosion or damage, and (on hydraulic types) that there are no fluid leaks or damaged pipes.

☐Inspect the shock absorbers for signs of serious fluid leakage. Check for wear of the mounting bushes or attachments, or damage to the body of the unit.

Driveshafts (fwd vehicles only)

☐Rotate each front wheel in turn and inspect the constant velocity joint gaiters for splits or damage. Also check that each driveshaft is straight and undamaged.

Braking system

☐If possible without dismantling, check brake pad wear and disc condition. Ensure that the friction lining material has not worn excessively, (A) and that the discs are not fractured, pitted, scored or badly worn (B).

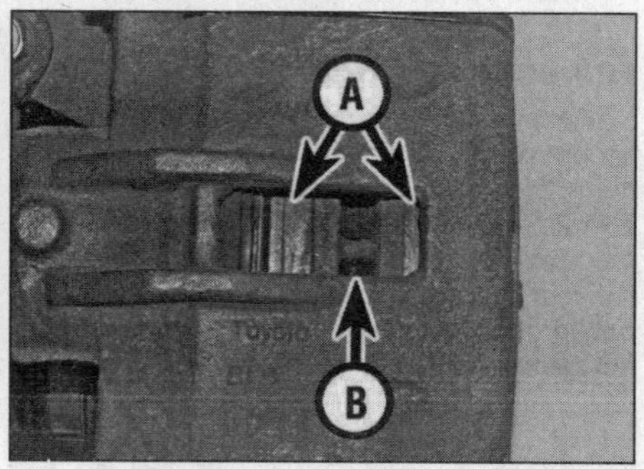

☐Examine all the rigid brake pipes underneath the vehicle, and the flexible hose(s) at the rear. Look for corrosion, chafing or insecurity of the pipes, and for signs of bulging under pressure, chafing, splits or deterioration of the flexible hoses.

☐Look for signs of fluid leaks at the brake calipers or on the brake backplates. Repair or renew leaking components.

☐Slowly spin each wheel, while your assistant depresses and releases the footbrake. Ensure that each brake is operating and does not bind when the pedal is released.

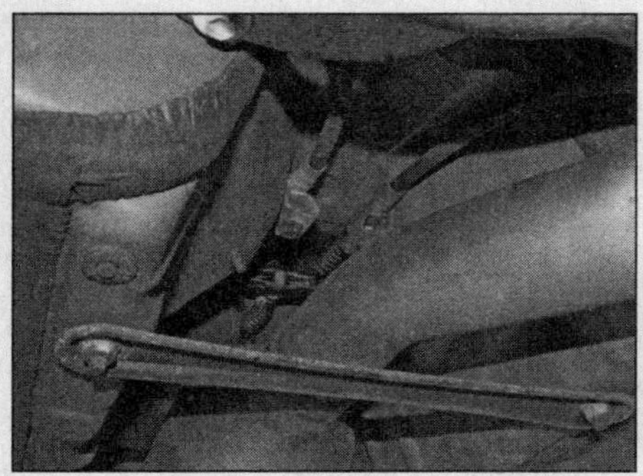

☐ Examine the handbrake mechanism, checking for frayed or broken cables, excessive corrosion, or wear or insecurity of the linkage. Check that the mechanism works on each relevant wheel, and releases fully, without binding.

☐ It is not possible to test brake efficiency without special equipment, but a road test can be carried out later to check that the vehicle pulls up in a straight line.

Fuel and exhaust systems

☐ Inspect the fuel tank (including the filler cap), fuel pipes, hoses and unions. All components must be secure and free from leaks. Locking fuel caps must lock securely and the key must be provided for the MOT test.

☐ Examine the exhaust system over its entire length, checking for any damaged, broken or missing mountings, security of the retaining clamps and rust or corrosion.

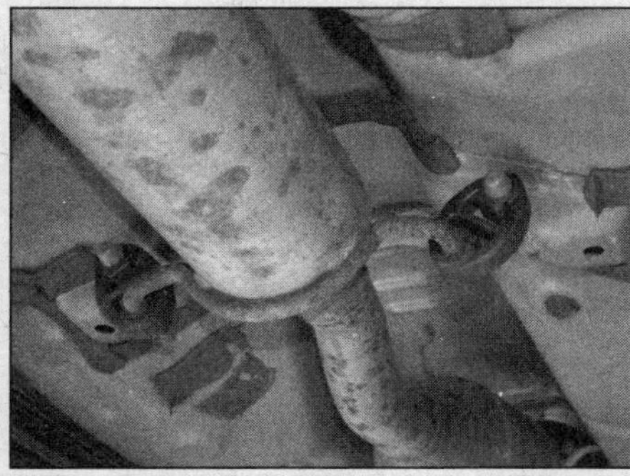

Wheels and tyres

☐ Examine the sidewalls and tread area of each tyre in turn. Check for cuts, tears, lumps, bulges, separation of the tread, and exposure of the ply or cord due to wear or damage. Check that the tyre bead is correctly seated on the wheel rim, that the valve is sound and properly seated, and that the wheel is not distorted or damaged.

☐ Check that the tyres are of the correct size for the vehicle, that they are of the same size and type on each axle, and that the pressures are correct.

☐ Check the tyre tread depth. The legal minimum at the time of writing is 1.6 mm over the central three-quarters of the tread width. Abnormal tread wear may indicate incorrect front wheel alignment or wear in steering or suspension components.

☐ If the spare wheel is fitted externally or in a separate carrier beneath the vehicle, check that mountings are secure and free of excessive corrosion.

Body corrosion

☐ Check the condition of the entire vehicle structure for signs of corrosion in load-bearing areas. (These include chassis box sections, side sills, cross-members, pillars, and all suspension, steering, braking system and seat belt mountings and anchorages.) Any corrosion which has seriously reduced the thickness of a load-bearing area (or is within 30 cm of safety-related components such as steering or suspension) is likely to cause the vehicle to fail. In this case professional repairs are likely to be needed.

☐ Damage or corrosion which causes sharp or otherwise dangerous edges to be exposed will also cause the vehicle to fail.

Towbars

☐ Check the condition of mounting points (both beneath the vehicle and within boot/hatchback areas) for signs of corrosion, ensuring that all fixings are secure and not worn or damaged. There must be no excessive play in detachable tow ball arms or quick-release mechanisms.

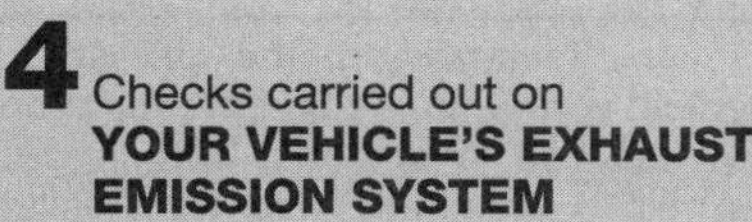

4 Checks carried out on
YOUR VEHICLE'S EXHAUST EMISSION SYSTEM

Petrol models

☐ The engine should be warmed up, and running well (ignition system in good order, air filter element clean, etc).

☐ Before testing, run the engine at around 2500 rpm for 20 seconds. Let the engine drop to idle, and watch for smoke from the exhaust. If the idle speed is too high, or if dense blue or black smoke emerges for more than 5 seconds, the vehicle will fail. Typically, blue smoke signifies oil burning (engine wear); black smoke means unburnt fuel (dirty air cleaner element, or other fuel system fault).

☐ An exhaust gas analyser for measuring carbon monoxide (CO) and hydrocarbons (HC) is now needed. If one cannot be hired or borrowed, have a local garage perform the check.

CO emissions (mixture)

☐ The MOT tester has access to the CO limits for all vehicles. The CO level is measured at idle speed, and at 'fast idle' (2500 to 3000 rpm). The following limits are given as a general guide:

At idle speed – Less than 0.5% CO
At 'fast idle' – Less than 0.3% CO
Lambda reading – 0.97 to 1.03

☐ If the CO level is too high, this may point to poor maintenance, a fuel injection system problem, faulty lambda (oxygen) sensor or catalytic converter. Try an injector cleaning treatment, and check the vehicle's ECU for fault codes.

HC emissions

☐ The MOT tester has access to HC limits for all vehicles. The HC level is measured at 'fast idle' (2500 to 3000 rpm). The following limits are given as a general guide:

At 'fast idle' – Less then 200 ppm

☐ Excessive HC emissions are typically caused by oil being burnt (worn engine), or by a blocked crankcase ventilation system ('breather'). If the engine oil is old and thin, an oil change may help. If the engine is running badly, check the vehicle's ECU for fault codes.

Diesel models

☐ The only emission test for diesel engines is measuring exhaust smoke density, using a calibrated smoke meter. The test involves accelerating the engine at least 3 times to its maximum unloaded speed.

Note: *On engines with a timing belt, it is VITAL that the belt is in good condition before the test is carried out.*

☐ With the engine warmed up, it is first purged by running at around 2500 rpm for 20 seconds. A governor check is then carried out, by slowly accelerating the engine to its maximum speed. After this, the smoke meter is connected, and the engine is accelerated quickly to maximum speed three times. If the smoke density is less than the limits given below, the vehicle will pass:

Non-turbo vehicles: 2.5m-1
Turbocharged vehicles: 3.0m-1

☐ If excess smoke is produced, try fitting a new air cleaner element, or using an injector cleaning treatment. If the engine is running badly, where applicable, check the vehicle's ECU for fault codes. Also check the vehicle's EGR system, where applicable. At high mileages, the injectors may require professional attention.

Engine

- ☐ Engine fails to rotate when attempting to start
- ☐ Engine rotates, but will not start
- ☐ Engine difficult to start when cold
- ☐ Engine difficult to start when hot
- ☐ Starter motor noisy or rough in engagement
- ☐ Starter motor turns engine slowly
- ☐ Engine starts, but stops immediately
- ☐ Engine idles erratically
- ☐ Engine misfires at idle speed
- ☐ Engine misfires throughout the driving speed range
- ☐ Engine stalls
- ☐ Engine lacks power
- ☐ Engine backfires
- ☐ Oil pressure warning light illuminated with engine running
- ☐ Engine runs-on after switching off
- ☐ Engine noises

Cooling system

- ☐ Overheating
- ☐ Overcooling
- ☐ External coolant leakage
- ☐ Internal coolant leakage
- ☐ Corrosion

Fuel and exhaust systems

- ☐ Excessive fuel consumption
- ☐ Fuel leakage and/or fuel odour
- ☐ Excessive noise or fumes from exhaust system

Clutch

- ☐ Pedal travels to floor – no pressure or very little resistance
- ☐ Clutch fails to disengage (unable to select gears)
- ☐ Clutch slips (engine speed increases, with no increase in vehicle speed)
- ☐ Judder as clutch is engaged
- ☐ Noise when depressing or releasing clutch pedal

Manual transmission

- ☐ Noisy in neutral with engine running
- ☐ Noisy in one particular gear
- ☐ Difficulty engaging gears
- ☐ Jumps out of gear
- ☐ Vibration
- ☐ Lubricant leaks

Automatic transmission

- ☐ Fluid leakage
- ☐ Transmission fluid brown, or has burned smell
- ☐ General gear selection problems
- ☐ Transmission will not downshift (kickdown) with accelerator fully depressed
- ☐ Engine will not start in any gear, or starts in gears other than Park or Neutral
- ☐ Transmission slips, shifts roughly, is noisy, or has no drive in forward or reverse gears

Differential and propeller shaft

- ☐ Vibration when accelerating and decelerating
- ☐ Low-pitched whining, increasing with road speed

Braking system

- ☐ Vehicle pulls to one side under braking
- ☐ Noise (grinding or high-pitched squeal) when brakes applied
- ☐ Excessive brake pedal travel
- ☐ Brake pedal feels spongy when depressed
- ☐ Excessive brake pedal effort required to stop vehicle
- ☐ Judder felt through brake pedal or steering wheel when braking
- ☐ Brakes binding

Suspension and steering systems

- ☐ Vehicle pulls to one side
- ☐ Wheel wobble and vibration
- ☐ Excessive pitching and/or rolling around corners, or during braking
- ☐ Wandering or general instability
- ☐ Excessively-stiff steering
- ☐ Excessive play in steering
- ☐ Lack of power assistance
- ☐ Tyre wear excessive

Electrical system

- ☐ Battery will only hold a charge for a few days
- ☐ Ignition/no-charge warning light remains illuminated with engine running
- ☐ Ignition/no-charge warning light fails to come on
- ☐ Lights inoperative
- ☐ Instrument readings inaccurate or erratic
- ☐ Horn inoperative, or unsatisfactory in operation
- ☐ Wipers inoperative, or unsatisfactory in operation
- ☐ Washers inoperative, or unsatisfactory in operation
- ☐ Electric windows inoperative, or unsatisfactory in operation
- ☐ Central locking system inoperative, or unsatisfactory in operation

Introduction

The vehicle owner who does his or her own maintenance according to the recommended service schedules should not have to use this section of the manual very often. Modern component reliability is such that, provided those items subject to wear or deterioration are inspected or renewed at the specified intervals, sudden failure is comparatively rare. Faults do not usually just happen as a result of sudden failure, but develop over a period of time. Major mechanical failures in particular are usually preceded by characteristic symptoms over hundreds or even thousands of miles. Those components which do occasionally fail without warning are often small and easily carried in the vehicle.

With any fault-finding, the first step is to decide where to begin investigations. Sometimes this is obvious, but on other occasions, a little detective work will be necessary. The owner who makes half a dozen haphazard adjustments or renewals may be successful in curing a fault (or its symptoms), but will be none the wiser if the fault recurs, and ultimately may have spent more time and money than was necessary. A calm and logical approach will be found to be more satisfactory in the long run. Always take into account any warning signs or abnormalities that may have been noticed in the period preceding the fault – power loss, high or low gauge readings, unusual smells, etc – and remember that failure of components such as fuses or spark plugs may only be pointers to some underlying fault.

The pages which follow provide an easy-reference guide to the more common problems which may occur during the operation of the vehicle. These problems and their possible causes are grouped under headings denoting various components or systems, such as Engine, Cooling system, etc. The general Chapter which deals with the problem is also shown in brackets; refer to the relevant part of that Chapter for system-specific information. Whatever the fault, certain basic principles apply. These are as follows:

Verify the fault. This is simply a matter of being sure that you know what the symptoms are before starting work. This is particularly important if you are investigating a fault for someone else, who may not have described it very accurately.

Don't overlook the obvious. For example, if the vehicle won't start, is there fuel in the tank? (Don't take anyone else's word on this particular point, and don't trust the fuel gauge either!) If an electrical fault is indicated, look for loose or broken wires before using the test gear.

Cure the disease, not the symptom. Substituting a flat battery with a fully-charged one will get you off the hard shoulder, but if the underlying cause is not attended to, the new battery will go the same way. Similarly, changing oil-fouled spark plugs for a new set will get you moving again, but remember that the reason for the fouling (if it wasn't simply an incorrect grade of plug) will have to be established and corrected.

Don't take anything for granted. Particularly, don't forget that a 'new' component may itself be defective (especially if it's been rattling around in the boot for months), and don't leave components out of a fault diagnosis sequence just because they are new or recently-fitted. When you do finally diagnose a difficult fault, you'll probably realise that all the evidence was there from the start.

Engine

Engine fails to rotate when attempting to start

- ☐ Battery terminal connections loose or corroded (*Weekly checks*)
- ☐ Battery discharged or faulty (Chapter 5A)
- ☐ Broken, loose or disconnected wiring in the starting circuit (Chapter 5A)
- ☐ Defective starter solenoid or switch (Chapter 5A)
- ☐ Defective starter motor (Chapter 5A)
- ☐ Starter pinion or flywheel ring gear teeth loose or broken (Chapter 2 or 5A)
- ☐ Engine earth strap broken or disconnected (Chapter 5A)

Engine rotates, but will not start

- ☐ Fuel tank empty
- ☐ Battery discharged (engine rotates slowly) (Chapter 5A)
- ☐ Battery terminal connections loose or corroded (*Weekly checks*)
- ☐ Air filter element dirty or clogged (Chapter 1)
- ☐ Low cylinder compressions (Chapter 2)
- ☐ Major mechanical failure (eg, broken timing chain) (Chapter 2)
- ☐ Ignition components damp or damaged (Chapter 5B)
- ☐ Fuel injection system fault (Chapter 4)
- ☐ Worn, faulty or incorrectly-gapped spark plugs (Chapter 1)
- ☐ Broken, loose or disconnected wiring in ignition circuit (Chapter 5B)

Engine difficult to start when cold

- ☐ Battery discharged (Chapter 5A)
- ☐ Battery terminal connections loose or corroded (*Weekly checks*)
- ☐ Air filter element dirty or clogged (Chapter 1)
- ☐ Worn, faulty or incorrectly-gapped spark plugs (Chapter 1)
- ☐ Low cylinder compressions (Chapter 2)
- ☐ Fuel injection system fault (Chapter 4)
- ☐ Ignition system fault (Chapter 5B)

Engine difficult to start when hot

- ☐ Battery discharged (Chapter 5A)
- ☐ Battery terminal connections loose or corroded (*Weekly checks*)
- ☐ Air filter element dirty or clogged (Chapter 1)
- ☐ Fuel injection system fault (Chapter 4)

Starter motor noisy or excessively-rough in engagement

- ☐ Starter pinion or flywheel ring gear teeth loose or broken (Chapter 2 or 5A)
- ☐ Starter motor mounting bolts loose or missing (Chapter 5A)
- ☐ Starter motor internal components worn or damaged (Chapter 5A)

Starter motor turns engine slowly

- ☐ Battery discharged (Chapter 5A)
- ☐ Battery terminal connections loose or corroded (*Weekly checks*)
- ☐ Earth strap broken or disconnected (Chapter 5A)
- ☐ Starter motor wiring loose (Chapter 5A)
- ☐ Starter motor internal fault (Chapter 5A)

Engine starts, but stops immediately

- ☐ Loose ignition system wiring (Chapter 5B)
- ☐ Dirt in fuel system (Chapter 4)
- ☐ Fuel injector fault (Chapter 4)
- ☐ Fuel pump or pressure regulator fault (Chapter 4)
- ☐ Vacuum leak at throttle body, inlet manifold or hoses (Chapters 2 and 4)

Engine idles erratically

- ☐ Air filter element clogged (Chapter 1)
- ☐ Air in fuel system (Chapter 4)
- ☐ Worn, faulty or incorrectly-gapped spark plugs (Chapter 1)
- ☐ Vacuum leak at throttle body, inlet manifold or hoses (Chapters 2 and 4)
- ☐ Uneven or low cylinder compressions (Chapter 2)
- ☐ Timing chain incorrectly fitted or tensioned (Chapter 2)
- ☐ Camshaft lobes worn (Chapter 2)
- ☐ Faulty fuel injector(s) (Chapter 4)

Engine misfires at idle speed

- ☐ Faulty fuel injector(s) (Chapter 4)
- ☐ Uneven or low cylinder compressions (Chapter 2)
- ☐ Disconnected, leaking, or perished crankcase ventilation hoses (Chapter 4)
- ☐ Vacuum leak at the throttle body, inlet manifold or associated hoses (Chapter 4)

Engine misfires throughout the driving speed range

- ☐ Fuel filter choked (Chapter 1)
- ☐ Fuel pump faulty, or delivery pressure low (Chapter 4)
- ☐ Fuel tank vent blocked, or fuel pipes restricted (Chapter 4)
- ☐ Uneven or low cylinder compressions (Chapter 2)
- ☐ Worn, faulty or incorrectly-gapped spark plugs (Chapter 1)
- ☐ Faulty spark plug HT leads (Chapter 1)

Engine stalls

- ☐ Fuel filter choked (Chapter 1)
- ☐ Blocked injector/fuel injection system fault (Chapter 4)
- ☐ Fuel pump faulty, or delivery pressure low (Chapter 4)
- ☐ Vacuum leak at the throttle body, inlet manifold or associated hoses (Chapter 4)
- ☐ Fuel tank vent blocked, or fuel pipes restricted (Chapter 4)

Engine lacks power

- ☐ Fuel filter choked (Chapter 1)
- ☐ Timing chain incorrectly fitted or tensioned (Chapter 2)
- ☐ Fuel pump faulty, or delivery pressure low (Chapter 4)
- ☐ Worn, faulty or incorrectly-gapped spark plugs (Chapter 1)
- ☐ Vacuum leak at the throttle body, inlet manifold or associated hoses (Chapter 4)
- ☐ Uneven or low cylinder compressions (Chapter 2)
- ☐ Brakes binding (Chapters 1 and 9)
- ☐ Clutch slipping (Chapter 6)
- ☐ Blocked injector/fuel injection system fault (Chapter 4)

Engine (continued)

Engine backfires

- ☐ Timing chain incorrectly fitted (Chapter 2)
- ☐ Faulty injector/fuel injection system fault (Chapter 4).

Oil pressure warning light illuminated with engine running

- ☐ Low oil level, or incorrect oil grade (*Weekly checks*)
- ☐ Faulty oil pressure sensor (Chapter 2)
- ☐ Worn engine bearings and/or oil pump (Chapter 2)
- ☐ Excessively high engine operating temperature (Chapter 3)
- ☐ Oil pressure relief valve defective (Chapter 2)
- ☐ Oil pick-up strainer clogged (Chapter 2)

Note: *Low oil pressure in a high-mileage engine at tickover is not necessarily a cause for concern. Sudden pressure loss at speed is far more significant. In any event, check the gauge or pressure sensor before condemning the engine.*

Engine runs-on after switching off

- ☐ Excessive carbon build-up in engine (Chapter 2)
- ☐ Excessively high engine operating temperature (Chapter 3)

Engine noises

Pre-ignition (pinking) or knocking during acceleration or under load

- ☐ Excessive carbon build-up in engine (Chapter 2)
- ☐ Faulty fuel injector(s) (Chapter 4)
- ☐ Ignition system fault (Chapter 5B)

Whistling or wheezing noises

- ☐ Leaking exhaust manifold gasket (Chapter 4)
- ☐ Leaking vacuum hose (Chapter 4 or 9)
- ☐ Blowing cylinder head gasket (Chapter 2)

Tapping or rattling noises

- ☐ Worn valve gear or camshaft (Chapter 2)
- ☐ Ancillary component fault (coolant pump, alternator, etc) (Chapters 3, 5, etc)

Knocking or thumping noises

- ☐ Worn big-end bearings (regular heavy knocking, perhaps less under load) (Chapter 2)
- ☐ Worn main bearings (rumbling and knocking, perhaps worsening under load) (Chapter 2)
- ☐ Piston slap (most noticeable when cold) (Chapter 2)
- ☐ Ancillary component fault (coolant pump, alternator, etc) (Chapters 3, 5, etc)

Cooling system

Overheating

- ☐ Insufficient coolant in system (*Weekly checks*)
- ☐ Thermostat faulty (Chapter 3)
- ☐ Radiator core blocked, or grille restricted (Chapter 3)
- ☐ Cooling fan or viscous coupling faulty (Chapter 3)
- ☐ Inaccurate temperature gauge sender unit (Chapter 3)
- ☐ Airlock in cooling system (Chapter 3)
- ☐ Expansion tank pressure cap faulty (Chapter 3)

Overcooling

- ☐ Thermostat faulty (Chapter 3)
- ☐ Inaccurate temperature gauge sender unit (Chapter 3)
- ☐ Viscous coupling faulty (Chapter 3)

External coolant leakage

- ☐ Deteriorated or damaged hoses or hose clips (Chapter 1)
- ☐ Radiator core or heater matrix leaking (Chapter 3)
- ☐ Pressure cap faulty (Chapter 3)
- ☐ Coolant pump internal seal leaking (Chapter 3)
- ☐ Coolant pump-to-block seal leaking (Chapter 3)
- ☐ Boiling due to overheating (Chapter 3)
- ☐ Core plug leaking (Chapter 2)

Internal coolant leakage

- ☐ Leaking cylinder head gasket (Chapter 2)
- ☐ Cracked cylinder head or cylinder block (Chapter 2)

Corrosion

- ☐ Infrequent draining and flushing (Chapter 1)
- ☐ Incorrect coolant mixture or inappropriate coolant type (Chapter 1)

Fuel and exhaust systems

Excessive fuel consumption

- ☐ Air filter element dirty or clogged (Chapter 1)
- ☐ Fuel injection system fault (Chapter 4)
- ☐ Ignition timing incorrect/ignition system fault (Chapters 1 and 5)
- ☐ Tyres under-inflated (*Weekly checks*)

Fuel leakage and/or fuel odour

- ☐ Damaged or corroded fuel tank, pipes or connections (Chapter 4)

Excessive noise or fumes from exhaust system

- ☐ Leaking exhaust system or manifold joints (Chapters 1 and 4)
- ☐ Leaking, corroded or damaged silencers or pipe (Chapters 1 and 4)
- ☐ Broken mountings causing body or suspension contact (Chapter 1)

Clutch

Pedal travels to floor – no pressure or very little resistance

- ☐ Hydraulic fluid level low/air in the hydraulic system (Chapter 6)
- ☐ Broken clutch release bearing or fork (Chapter 6)
- ☐ Broken diaphragm spring in clutch pressure plate (Chapter 6)

Clutch fails to disengage (unable to select gears)

- ☐ Clutch disc sticking on gearbox input shaft splines (Chapter 6)
- ☐ Clutch disc sticking to flywheel or pressure plate (Chapter 6)
- ☐ Faulty pressure plate assembly (Chapter 6)
- ☐ Clutch release mechanism worn or poorly assembled (Chapter 6)

Clutch slips (engine speed increases, with no increase in vehicle speed)

- ☐ Clutch disc linings excessively worn (Chapter 6)
- ☐ Clutch disc linings contaminated with oil or grease (Chapter 6)
- ☐ Faulty pressure plate or weak diaphragm spring (Chapter 6)

Judder as clutch is engaged

- ☐ Clutch disc linings contaminated with oil or grease (Chapter 6)
- ☐ Clutch disc linings excessively worn (Chapter 6)
- ☐ Faulty or distorted pressure plate or diaphragm spring (Chapter 6)
- ☐ Worn or loose engine or gearbox mountings (Chapter 2A or 2B)
- ☐ Clutch disc hub or gearbox input shaft splines worn (Chapter 6)

Noise when depressing or releasing clutch pedal

- ☐ Worn clutch release bearing (Chapter 6)
- ☐ Worn or dry clutch pedal bushes (Chapter 6)
- ☐ Faulty pressure plate assembly (Chapter 6)
- ☐ Pressure plate diaphragm spring broken (Chapter 6)
- ☐ Broken clutch disc cushioning springs (Chapter 6)

Manual transmission

Noisy in neutral with engine running

- ☐ Input shaft bearings worn (noise apparent with clutch pedal released, but not when depressed) (Chapter 7A)*
- ☐ Clutch release bearing worn (noise apparent with clutch pedal depressed, possibly less when released) (Chapter 6)

Noisy in one particular gear

- ☐ Worn, damaged or chipped gear teeth (Chapter 7A)*

Difficulty engaging gears

- ☐ Clutch fault (Chapter 6)
- ☐ Worn or damaged gearchange linkage/cable (Chapter 7A)
- ☐ Incorrectly-adjusted gearchange linkage/cable (Chapter 7A)
- ☐ Worn synchroniser units (Chapter 7A)*

Jumps out of gear

- ☐ Worn or damaged gearchange linkage/cable (Chapter 7A)
- ☐ Incorrectly-adjusted gearchange linkage/cable (Chapter 7A)
- ☐ Worn synchroniser units (Chapter 7A)*
- ☐ Worn selector forks (Chapter 7A)*

Vibration

- ☐ Lack of oil (Chapter 1)
- ☐ Worn bearings (Chapter 7A)*

Lubricant leaks

- ☐ Leaking differential output oil seal (Chapter 7A)
- ☐ Leaking housing joint (Chapter 7A)*
- ☐ Leaking input shaft oil seal (Chapter 7A)*

** Although the corrective action necessary to remedy the symptoms described is beyond the scope of the home mechanic, the above information should be helpful in isolating the cause of the condition, so that the owner can communicate clearly with a professional mechanic.*

Automatic transmission

Note: *Due to the complexity of the automatic transmission, it is difficult for the home mechanic to properly diagnose and service this unit. For problems other than the following, the vehicle should be taken to a dealer service department or automatic transmission specialist. Do not be too hasty in removing the transmission if a fault is suspected, as most of the testing is carried out with the unit still fitted.*

Fluid leakage

- ☐ Automatic transmission fluid is usually dark in colour. Fluid leaks should not be confused with engine oil, which can easily be blown onto the transmission by airflow
- ☐ To determine the source of a leak, first remove all built-up dirt and grime from the transmission housing and surrounding areas using a degreasing agent, or by steam-cleaning. Drive the vehicle at low speed, so airflow will not blow the leak far from its source. Raise and support the vehicle, and determine where the leak is coming from. The following are common areas of leakage:
  - *a) Oil pan (Chapter 1 and 7B).*
  - *b) Dipstick tube (Chapter 1 and 7B)*
  - *c) Transmission-to-fluid cooler pipes/unions (Chapter 7B)*

Transmission fluid brown, or has burned smell

- ☐ Transmission fluid level low, or fluid in need of renewal (Chapter 1)

General gear selection problems

- ☐ Chapter 7B deals with checking and adjusting the selector cable on automatic transmissions. The following are common problems which may be caused by a poorly-adjusted cable:
  - *a) Engine starting in gears other than Park or Neutral*
  - *b) Indicator panel indicating a gear other than the one actually being used*
  - *c) Vehicle moves when in Park or Neutral*
  - *d) Poor gear shift quality or erratic gear changes*
- ☐ Refer to Chapter 7B for the selector cable adjustment procedure

Transmission will not downshift (kickdown) with accelerator pedal fully depressed

- ☐ Low transmission fluid level (Chapter 1)
- ☐ Incorrect selector cable adjustment (Chapter 7B)
- ☐ Throttle position sensor fault (Chapter 4)

Engine will not start in any gear, or starts in gears other than Park or Neutral

- ☐ Incorrect selector cable adjustment (Chapter 7B)

Transmission slips, shifts roughly, is noisy, or has no drive in forward or reverse gears

- ☐ There are many probable causes for the above problems, but the home mechanic should be concerned with only one possibility – fluid level. Before taking the vehicle to a dealer or transmission specialist, check the fluid level and condition of the fluid as described in Chapter 1. Correct the fluid level as necessary, or change the fluid and filter if needed. If the problem persists, professional help will be necessary

Differential and propshaft

Vibration when accelerating or decelerating

- ☐ Worn universal joint (Chapter 8)
- ☐ Bent or distorted propeller shaft (Chapter 8)

Low-pitched whining; increasing with road speed

- ☐ Worn differential (Chapter 8)

Braking system

Note: *Before assuming that a brake problem exists, make sure that the tyres are in good condition and correctly inflated, that the front wheel alignment is correct, and that the vehicle is not loaded with weight in an unequal manner. Apart from checking the condition of all pipe and hose connections, any faults occurring on the anti-lock braking system should be referred to a BMW dealer or specialist for diagnosis.*

Vehicle pulls to one side under braking

- ☐ Worn, defective, damaged or contaminated brake pads/shoes on one side (Chapters 1 and 9)
- ☐ Seized or partially-seized brake caliper (Chapters 1 and 9)
- ☐ A mixture of brake pad lining materials fitted between sides (Chapters 1 and 9)
- ☐ Brake caliper mounting bolts loose (Chapter 9)
- ☐ Worn or damaged steering or suspension components (Chapters 1 and 10)

Noise (grinding or high-pitched squeal) when brakes applied

- ☐ Brake pad friction lining material worn down to metal backing (Chapters 1 and 9)
- ☐ Excessive corrosion of brake disc. (May be apparent after the vehicle has been standing for some time (Chapters 1 and 9)
- ☐ Foreign object (stone chipping, etc) trapped between brake disc and shield (Chapters 1 and 9)

Excessive brake pedal travel

- ☐ Faulty master cylinder (Chapter 9)
- ☐ Air in hydraulic system (Chapters 1 and 9)
- ☐ Faulty vacuum servo unit (Chapter 9)

Brake pedal feels spongy when depressed

- ☐ Air in hydraulic system (Chapters 1 and 9)
- ☐ Deteriorated flexible rubber brake hoses (Chapters 1 and 9)
- ☐ Master cylinder mounting nuts loose (Chapter 9)
- ☐ Faulty master cylinder (Chapter 9)

Excessive brake pedal effort required to stop vehicle

- ☐ Faulty vacuum servo unit (Chapter 9)
- ☐ Disconnected, damaged or insecure brake servo vacuum hose (Chapter 9)
- ☐ Primary or secondary hydraulic circuit failure (Chapter 9)
- ☐ Seized brake caliper (Chapter 9)
- ☐ Brake pads incorrectly fitted (Chapters 1 and 9)
- ☐ Incorrect grade of brake pads fitted (Chapters 1 and 9)
- ☐ Brake pads contaminated (Chapters 1 and 9)

Judder felt through brake pedal or steering wheel when braking

- ☐ Excessive run-out or distortion of discs (Chapters 1 and 9)
- ☐ Brake pad linings worn (Chapters 1 and 9)
- ☐ Brake caliper mounting bolts loose (Chapter 9)
- ☐ Wear in suspension or steering components or mountings (Chapters 1 and 10)

Brakes binding

- ☐ Seized brake caliper (Chapter 9)
- ☐ Incorrectly-adjusted handbrake mechanism (Chapter 9)
- ☐ Faulty master cylinder (Chapter 9)

Suspension and steering

Note: *Before diagnosing suspension or steering faults, be sure that the trouble is not due to incorrect tyre pressures, mixtures of tyre types, or binding brakes.*

Vehicle pulls to one side

- ☐ Defective tyre (*Weekly checks*)
- ☐ Excessive wear in suspension or steering components (Chapters 1 and 10)
- ☐ Incorrect front wheel alignment (Chapter 10)
- ☐ Accident damage to steering or suspension components (Chapter 1)

Wheel wobble and vibration

- ☐ Front roadwheels out of balance (vibration felt mainly through the steering wheel) (Chapters 1 and 10)
- ☐ Rear roadwheels out of balance (vibration felt throughout the vehicle) (Chapters 1 and 10)
- ☐ Roadwheels damaged or distorted (Chapters 1 and 10)
- ☐ Faulty or damaged tyre (*Weekly checks*)
- ☐ Worn steering or suspension joints, bushes or components (Chapters 1 and 10)
- ☐ Wheel bolts loose (Chapters 1 and 10)

Excessive pitching and/or rolling around corners, or during braking

- ☐ Defective shock absorbers (Chapters 1 and 10)
- ☐ Broken or weak spring and/or suspension component (Chapters 1 and 10)
- ☐ Worn or damaged anti-roll bar or mountings (Chapter 10)

Wandering or general instability

- ☐ Incorrect front wheel alignment (Chapter 10)
- ☐ Worn steering or suspension joints, bushes or components (Chapters 1 and 10)
- ☐ Roadwheels out of balance (Chapters 1 and 10)
- ☐ Faulty or damaged tyre (*Weekly checks*)
- ☐ Wheel bolts loose (Chapters 1 and 10)
- ☐ Defective shock absorbers (Chapters 1 and 10)
- ☐ Dynamic stability system fault (Chapter 10)

Excessively-stiff steering

- ☐ Lack of steering gear lubricant (Chapter 10)
- ☐ Seized track rod end balljoint or suspension balljoint (Chapters 1 and 10)
- ☐ Broken or incorrectly-adjusted drivebelt – power steering (Chapter 1)
- ☐ Incorrect front wheel alignment (Chapter 10)
- ☐ Steering rack or column bent or damaged (Chapter 10)

Suspension and steering (continued)

Excessive play in steering

- ☐ Worn steering column intermediate shaft universal joint (Chapter 10)
- ☐ Worn steering track rod end balljoints (Chapters 1 and 10)
- ☐ Worn rack-and-pinion steering gear (Chapter 10)
- ☐ Worn steering or suspension joints, bushes or components (Chapters 1 and 10)

Lack of power assistance

- ☐ Broken or incorrectly-adjusted auxiliary drivebelt (Chapter 1)
- ☐ Incorrect power steering fluid level (*Weekly checks*)
- ☐ Restriction in power steering fluid hoses (Chapter 1)
- ☐ Faulty power steering pump (Chapter 10)
- ☐ Faulty rack-and-pinion steering gear (Chapter 10)

Tyre wear excessive

Tyres worn on inside or outside edges

- ☐ Tyres under-inflated (wear on both edges) (*Weekly checks*)
- ☐ Incorrect camber or castor angles (wear on one edge only) (Chapter 10)
- ☐ Worn steering or suspension joints, bushes or components (Chapters 1 and 10)
- ☐ Excessively-hard cornering.
- ☐ Accident damage.

Tyre treads exhibit feathered edges

- ☐ Incorrect toe setting (Chapter 10)

Tyres worn in centre of tread

- ☐ Tyres over-inflated (*Weekly checks*)

Tyres worn on inside and outside edges

- ☐ Tyres under-inflated (*Weekly checks*)

Tyres worn unevenly

- ☐ Tyres/wheels out of balance (Chapter 1)
- ☐ Excessive wheel or tyre run-out (Chapter 1)
- ☐ Worn shock absorbers (Chapters 1 and 10)
- ☐ Faulty tyre (*Weekly checks*)

Electrical system

Note: *For problems associated with the starting system, refer to the faults listed under 'Engine' earlier in this Section.*

Battery will only hold a charge for a few days

- ☐ Battery defective internally (Chapter 5A)
- ☐ Battery terminal connections loose or corroded (*Weekly checks*)
- ☐ Auxiliary drivebelt worn or incorrectly adjusted (Chapter 1)
- ☐ Alternator not charging at correct output (Chapter 5A)
- ☐ Alternator or voltage regulator faulty (Chapter 5A)
- ☐ Short-circuit causing continual battery drain (Chapters 5A and 12)

Ignition/no-charge warning light remains illuminated with engine running

- ☐ Auxiliary drivebelt broken, worn, or incorrectly adjusted (Chapter 1)
- ☐ Alternator brushes worn, sticking, or dirty (Chapter 5A)
- ☐ Alternator brush springs weak or broken (Chapter 5A)
- ☐ Internal fault in alternator or voltage regulator (Chapter 5A)
- ☐ Broken, disconnected, or loose wiring in charging circuit (Chapter 5A)

Ignition/no-charge warning light fails to come on

- ☐ Warning light bulb blown (Chapter 12)
- ☐ Broken, disconnected, or loose wiring in warning light circuit (Chapter 12)
- ☐ Alternator faulty (Chapter 5A)

Lights inoperative

- ☐ Bulb blown (Chapter 12)
- ☐ Corrosion of bulb or bulbholder contacts (Chapter 12)
- ☐ Blown fuse (Chapter 12)
- ☐ Faulty relay (Chapter 12)
- ☐ Broken, loose, or disconnected wiring (Chapter 12)
- ☐ Faulty switch (Chapter 12)

Instrument readings inaccurate or erratic

Instrument readings increase with engine speed

- ☐ Faulty voltage regulator (Chapter 12)

Fuel or temperature gauges give no reading

- ☐ Faulty gauge sender unit (Chapters 3 and 4)
- ☐ Wiring open-circuit (Chapter 12)
- ☐ Faulty gauge (Chapter 12)

Fuel or temperature gauges give continuous maximum reading

- ☐ Faulty gauge sender unit (Chapters 3 and 4)
- ☐ Wiring short-circuit (Chapter 12)
- ☐ Faulty gauge (Chapter 12)

Horn inoperative, or unsatisfactory in operation

Horn operates all the time

- ☐ Horn push either earthed or stuck down (Chapter 12)
- ☐ Horn cable-to-horn push earthed (Chapter 12)

Horn fails to operate

- ☐ Blown fuse (Chapter 12)
- ☐ Cable or cable connections loose, broken or disconnected (Chapter 12)
- ☐ Faulty horn (Chapter 12)

Horn emits intermittent or unsatisfactory sound

- ☐ Cable connections loose (Chapter 12)
- ☐ Horn mountings loose (Chapter 12)
- ☐ Faulty horn (Chapter 12)

Windscreen wipers inoperative, or unsatisfactory in operation

Wipers fail to operate, or operate very slowly

- ☐ Wiper blades stuck to screen, or linkage seized or binding (Chapters 1 and 12)
- ☐ Blown fuse (Chapter 12)
- ☐ Cable or cable connections loose, broken or disconnected (Chapter 12)
- ☐ Faulty wiper motor (Chapter 12)

Wiper blades sweep over too large or too small an area of the glass

- ☐ Wiper arms incorrectly positioned on spindles (Chapter 1)
- ☐ Excessive wear of wiper linkage (Chapter 12)
- ☐ Wiper motor or linkage mountings loose or insecure (Chapter 12)

Wiper blades fail to clean the glass effectively

- ☐ Wiper blade rubbers worn or perished (*Weekly checks*)
- ☐ Wiper arm tension springs broken, or arm pivots seized (Chapter 12)
- ☐ Insufficient windscreen washer additive to adequately remove road film (*Weekly checks*)

Electrical system (continued)

Windscreen washers inoperative, or unsatisfactory in operation

One or more washer jets inoperative

- ☐ Blocked washer jet (Chapter 1)
- ☐ Disconnected, kinked or restricted fluid hose (Chapter 12)
- ☐ Insufficient fluid in washer reservoir (*Weekly checks*)

Washer pump fails to operate

- ☐ Broken or disconnected wiring or connections (Chapter 12)
- ☐ Blown fuse (Chapter 12)
- ☐ Faulty washer switch (Chapter 12)
- ☐ Faulty washer pump (Chapter 12)

Washer pump runs for some time before fluid is emitted from jets

- ☐ Faulty one-way valve in fluid supply hose (Chapter 12)

Electric windows inoperative, or unsatisfactory in operation

Window glass will only move in one direction

- ☐ Faulty switch (Chapter 12)

Window glass slow to move

- ☐ Regulator seized or damaged, or in need of lubrication (Chapter 11)
- ☐ Door internal components or trim fouling regulator (Chapter 11)
- ☐ Faulty motor (Chapter 11)

Window glass fails to move

- ☐ Blown fuse (Chapter 12)
- ☐ Faulty relay (Chapter 12)
- ☐ Broken or disconnected wiring or connections (Chapter 12)
- ☐ Faulty motor (Chapter 11)

Central locking system inoperative, or unsatisfactory in operation

Complete system failure

- ☐ Blown fuse (Chapter 12)
- ☐ Faulty control unit (Chapter 12)
- ☐ Broken or disconnected wiring or connections (Chapter 12)
- ☐ Faulty motor (Chapter 11)

Latch locks but will not unlock, or unlocks but will not lock

- ☐ Faulty master switch (Chapter 12)
- ☐ Broken or disconnected latch operating rods or levers (Chapter 11)
- ☐ Faulty control unit (Chapter 12)
- ☐ Faulty motor (Chapter 11)

One solenoid/motor fails to operate

- ☐ Broken or disconnected wiring or connections (Chapter 12)
- ☐ Faulty operating assembly (Chapter 11)
- ☐ Broken, binding or disconnected latch operating rods or levers (Chapter 11)
- ☐ Fault in door latch (Chapter 11)

A

ABS (Anti-lock brake system) A system, usually electronically controlled, that senses incipient wheel lockup during braking and relieves hydraulic pressure at wheels that are about to skid.

Air bag An inflatable bag hidden in the steering wheel (driver's side) or the dash or glovebox (passenger side). In a head-on collision, the bags inflate, preventing the driver and front passenger from being thrown forward into the steering wheel or windscreen.

Air cleaner A metal or plastic housing, containing a filter element, which removes dust and dirt from the air being drawn into the engine.

Air filter element The actual filter in an air cleaner system, usually manufactured from pleated paper and requiring renewal at regular intervals.

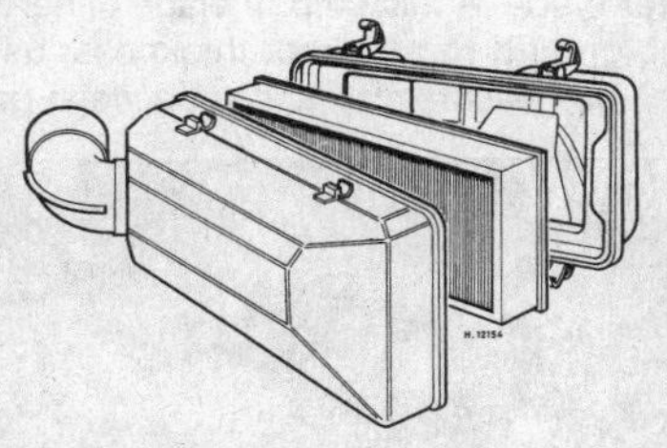

Air filter

Allen key A hexagonal wrench which fits into a recessed hexagonal hole.

Alligator clip A long-nosed spring-loaded metal clip with meshing teeth. Used to make temporary electrical connections.

Alternator A component in the electrical system which converts mechanical energy from a drivebelt into electrical energy to charge the battery and to operate the starting system, ignition system and electrical accessories.

Ampere (amp) A unit of measurement for the flow of electric current. One amp is the amount of current produced by one volt acting through a resistance of one ohm.

Anaerobic sealer A substance used to prevent bolts and screws from loosening. Anaerobic means that it does not require oxygen for activation. The Loctite brand is widely used.

Antifreeze A substance (usually ethylene glycol) mixed with water, and added to a vehicle's cooling system, to prevent freezing of the coolant in winter. Antifreeze also contains chemicals to inhibit corrosion and the formation of rust and other deposits that would tend to clog the radiator and coolant passages and reduce cooling efficiency.

Anti-seize compound A coating that reduces the risk of seizing on fasteners that are subjected to high temperatures, such as exhaust manifold bolts and nuts.

Asbestos A natural fibrous mineral with great heat resistance, commonly used in the composition of brake friction materials. Asbestos is a health hazard and the dust created by brake systems should never be inhaled or ingested.

Axle A shaft on which a wheel revolves, or which revolves with a wheel. Also, a solid beam that connects the two wheels at one end of the vehicle. An axle which also transmits power to the wheels is known as a live axle.

Axleshaft A single rotating shaft, on either side of the differential, which delivers power from the final drive assembly to the drive wheels. Also called a driveshaft or a halfshaft.

B

Ball bearing An anti-friction bearing consisting of a hardened inner and outer race with hardened steel balls between two races.

Bearing The curved surface on a shaft or in a bore, or the part assembled into either, that permits relative motion between them with minimum wear and friction.

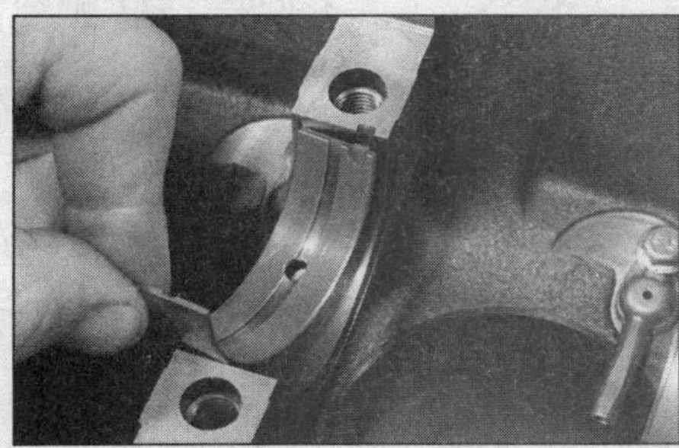

Bearing

Big-end bearing The bearing in the end of the connecting rod that's attached to the crankshaft.

Bleed nipple A valve on a brake wheel cylinder, caliper or other hydraulic component that is opened to purge the hydraulic system of air. Also called a bleed screw.

Brake bleeding Procedure for removing air from lines of a hydraulic brake system.

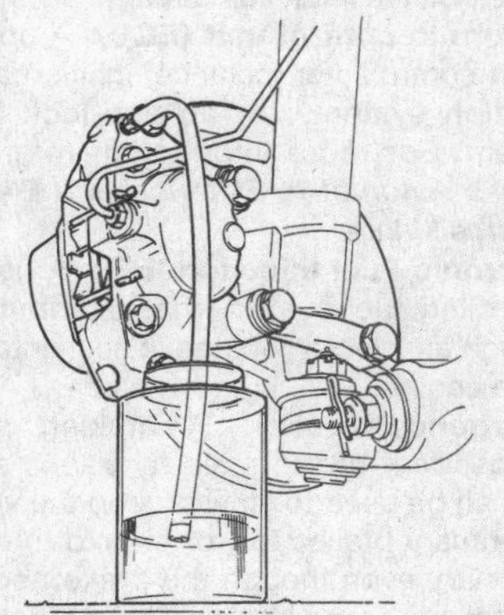

Brake bleeding

Brake disc The component of a disc brake that rotates with the wheels.

Brake drum The component of a drum brake that rotates with the wheels.

Brake linings The friction material which contacts the brake disc or drum to retard the vehicle's speed. The linings are bonded or riveted to the brake pads or shoes.

Brake pads The replaceable friction pads that pinch the brake disc when the brakes are applied. Brake pads consist of a friction material bonded or riveted to a rigid backing plate.

Brake shoe The crescent-shaped carrier to which the brake linings are mounted and which forces the lining against the rotating drum during braking.

Braking systems For more information on braking systems, consult the *Haynes Automotive Brake Manual*.

Breaker bar A long socket wrench handle providing greater leverage.

Bulkhead The insulated partition between the engine and the passenger compartment.

C

Caliper The non-rotating part of a disc-brake assembly that straddles the disc and carries the brake pads. The caliper also contains the hydraulic components that cause the pads to pinch the disc when the brakes are applied. A caliper is also a measuring tool that can be set to measure inside or outside dimensions of an object.

Camshaft A rotating shaft on which a series of cam lobes operate the valve mechanisms. The camshaft may be driven by gears, by sprockets and chain or by sprockets and a belt.

Canister A container in an evaporative emission control system; contains activated charcoal granules to trap vapours from the fuel system.

Canister

Carburettor A device which mixes fuel with air in the proper proportions to provide a desired power output from a spark ignition internal combustion engine.

Castellated Resembling the parapets along the top of a castle wall. For example, a castellated balljoint stud nut.

Castor In wheel alignment, the backward or forward tilt of the steering axis. Castor is positive when the steering axis is inclined rearward at the top.

Catalytic converter A silencer-like device in the exhaust system which converts certain pollutants in the exhaust gases into less harmful substances.

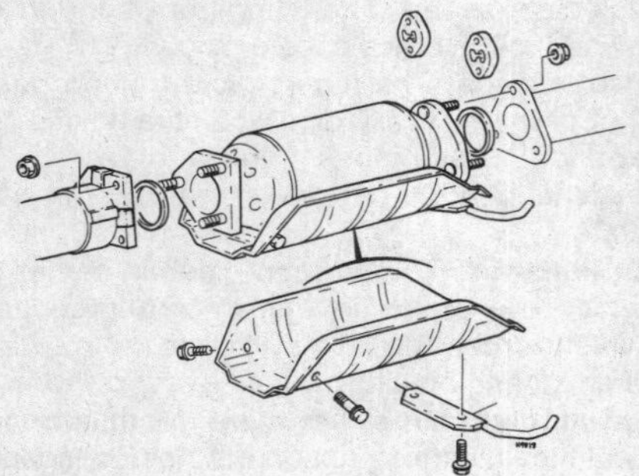

Catalytic converter

Circlip A ring-shaped clip used to prevent endwise movement of cylindrical parts and shafts. An internal circlip is installed in a groove in a housing; an external circlip fits into a groove on the outside of a cylindrical piece such as a shaft.

Clearance The amount of space between two parts. For example, between a piston and a cylinder, between a bearing and a journal, etc.

Coil spring A spiral of elastic steel found in various sizes throughout a vehicle, for example as a springing medium in the suspension and in the valve train.

Compression Reduction in volume, and increase in pressure and temperature, of a gas, caused by squeezing it into a smaller space.

Compression ratio The relationship between cylinder volume when the piston is at top dead centre and cylinder volume when the piston is at bottom dead centre.

Constant velocity (CV) joint A type of universal joint that cancels out vibrations caused by driving power being transmitted through an angle.

Core plug A disc or cup-shaped metal device inserted in a hole in a casting through which core was removed when the casting was formed. Also known as a freeze plug or expansion plug.

Crankcase The lower part of the engine block in which the crankshaft rotates.

Crankshaft The main rotating member, or shaft, running the length of the crankcase, with offset "throws" to which the connecting rods are attached.

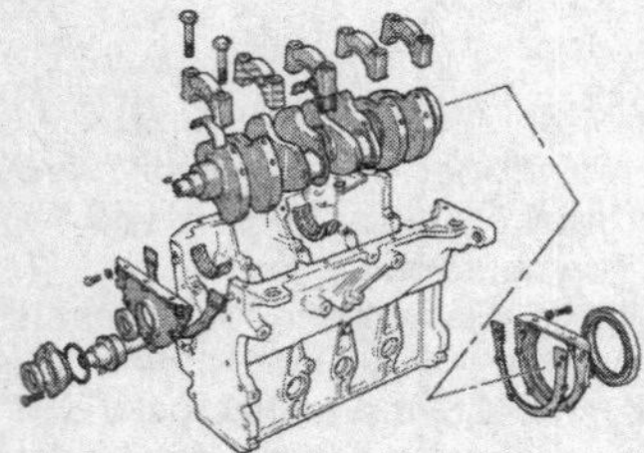

Crankshaft assembly

Crocodile clip See Alligator clip

D

Diagnostic code Code numbers obtained by accessing the diagnostic mode of an engine management computer. This code can be used to determine the area in the system where a malfunction may be located.

Disc brake A brake design incorporating a rotating disc onto which brake pads are squeezed. The resulting friction converts the energy of a moving vehicle into heat.

Double-overhead cam (DOHC) An engine that uses two overhead camshafts, usually one for the intake valves and one for the exhaust valves.

Drivebelt(s) The belt(s) used to drive accessories such as the alternator, water pump, power steering pump, air conditioning compressor, etc. off the crankshaft pulley.

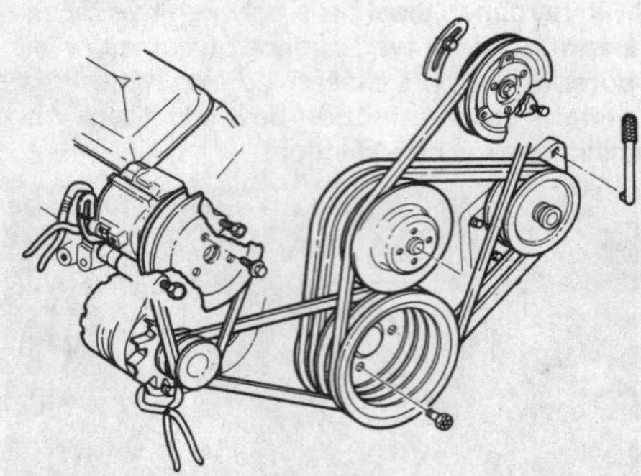

Accessory drivebelts

Driveshaft Any shaft used to transmit motion. Commonly used when referring to the axleshafts on a front wheel drive vehicle.

Drum brake A type of brake using a drum-shaped metal cylinder attached to the inner surface of the wheel. When the brake pedal is pressed, curved brake shoes with friction linings press against the inside of the drum to slow or stop the vehicle.

E

EGR valve A valve used to introduce exhaust gases into the intake air stream.

Electronic control unit (ECU) A computer which controls (for instance) ignition and fuel injection systems, or an anti-lock braking system. For more information refer to the *Haynes Automotive Electrical and Electronic Systems Manual.*

Electronic Fuel Injection (EFI) A computer controlled fuel system that distributes fuel through an injector located in each intake port of the engine.

Emergency brake A braking system, independent of the main hydraulic system, that can be used to slow or stop the vehicle if the primary brakes fail, or to hold the vehicle stationary even though the brake pedal isn't depressed. It usually consists of a hand lever that actuates either front or rear brakes mechanically through a series of cables and linkages. Also known as a handbrake or parking brake.

Endfloat The amount of lengthwise movement between two parts. As applied to a crankshaft, the distance that the crankshaft can move forward and back in the cylinder block.

Engine management system (EMS) A computer controlled system which manages the fuel injection and the ignition systems in an integrated fashion.

Exhaust manifold A part with several passages through which exhaust gases leave the engine combustion chambers and enter the exhaust pipe.

F

Fan clutch A viscous (fluid) drive coupling device which permits variable engine fan speeds in relation to engine speeds.

Feeler blade A thin strip or blade of hardened steel, ground to an exact thickness, used to check or measure clearances between parts.

Feeler blade

Firing order The order in which the engine cylinders fire, or deliver their power strokes, beginning with the number one cylinder.

Flywheel A heavy spinning wheel in which energy is absorbed and stored by means of momentum. On cars, the flywheel is attached to the crankshaft to smooth out firing impulses.

Free play The amount of travel before any action takes place. The "looseness" in a linkage, or an assembly of parts, between the initial application of force and actual movement. For example, the distance the brake pedal moves before the pistons in the master cylinder are actuated.

Fuse An electrical device which protects a circuit against accidental overload. The typical fuse contains a soft piece of metal which is calibrated to melt at a predetermined current flow (expressed as amps) and break the circuit.

Fusible link A circuit protection device consisting of a conductor surrounded by heat-resistant insulation. The conductor is smaller than the wire it protects, so it acts as the weakest link in the circuit. Unlike a blown fuse, a failed fusible link must frequently be cut from the wire for replacement.

G

Gap The distance the spark must travel in jumping from the centre electrode to the side electrode in a spark plug. Also refers to the spacing between the points in a contact breaker assembly in a conventional points-type ignition, or to the distance between the reluctor or rotor and the pickup coil in an electronic ignition.

Adjusting spark plug gap

Gasket Any thin, soft material - usually cork, cardboard, asbestos or soft metal - installed between two metal surfaces to ensure a good seal. For instance, the cylinder head gasket seals the joint between the block and the cylinder head.

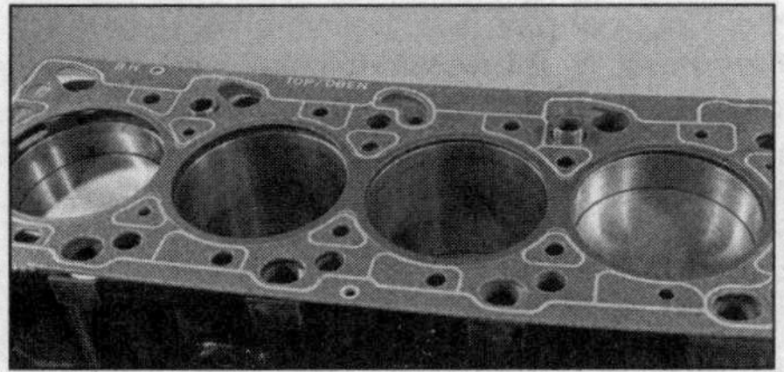

Gasket

Gauge An instrument panel display used to monitor engine conditions. A gauge with a movable pointer on a dial or a fixed scale is an analogue gauge. A gauge with a numerical readout is called a digital gauge.

H

Halfshaft A rotating shaft that transmits power from the final drive unit to a drive wheel, usually when referring to a live rear axle.

Harmonic balancer A device designed to reduce torsion or twisting vibration in the crankshaft. May be incorporated in the crankshaft pulley. Also known as a vibration damper.

Hone An abrasive tool for correcting small irregularities or differences in diameter in an engine cylinder, brake cylinder, etc.

Hydraulic tappet A tappet that utilises hydraulic pressure from the engine's lubrication system to maintain zero clearance (constant contact with both camshaft and valve stem). Automatically adjusts to variation in valve stem length. Hydraulic tappets also reduce valve noise.

I

Ignition timing The moment at which the spark plug fires, usually expressed in the number of crankshaft degrees before the piston reaches the top of its stroke.

Inlet manifold A tube or housing with passages through which flows the air-fuel mixture (carburettor vehicles and vehicles with throttle body injection) or air only (port fuel-injected vehicles) to the port openings in the cylinder head.

J

Jump start Starting the engine of a vehicle with a discharged or weak battery by attaching jump leads from the weak battery to a charged or helper battery.

L

Load Sensing Proportioning Valve (LSPV) A brake hydraulic system control valve that works like a proportioning valve, but also takes into consideration the amount of weight carried by the rear axle.

Locknut A nut used to lock an adjustment nut, or other threaded component, in place. For example, a locknut is employed to keep the adjusting nut on the rocker arm in position.

Lockwasher A form of washer designed to prevent an attaching nut from working loose.

M

MacPherson strut A type of front suspension system devised by Earle MacPherson at Ford of England. In its original form, a simple lateral link with the anti-roll bar creates the lower control arm. A long strut - an integral coil spring and shock absorber - is mounted between the body and the steering knuckle. Many modern so-called MacPherson strut systems use a conventional lower A-arm and don't rely on the anti-roll bar for location.

Multimeter An electrical test instrument with the capability to measure voltage, current and resistance.

N

NOx Oxides of Nitrogen. A common toxic pollutant emitted by petrol and diesel engines at higher temperatures.

O

Ohm The unit of electrical resistance. One volt applied to a resistance of one ohm will produce a current of one amp.

Ohmmeter An instrument for measuring electrical resistance.

O-ring A type of sealing ring made of a special rubber-like material; in use, the O-ring is compressed into a groove to provide the sealing action.

Overhead cam (ohc) engine An engine with the camshaft(s) located on top of the cylinder head(s).

Overhead valve (ohv) engine An engine with the valves located in the cylinder head, but with the camshaft located in the engine block.

Oxygen sensor A device installed in the engine exhaust manifold, which senses the oxygen content in the exhaust and converts this information into an electric current. Also called a Lambda sensor.

P

Phillips screw A type of screw head having a cross instead of a slot for a corresponding type of screwdriver.

Plastigage A thin strip of plastic thread, available in different sizes, used for measuring clearances. For example, a strip of Plastigage is laid across a bearing journal. The parts are assembled and dismantled; the width of the crushed strip indicates the clearance between journal and bearing.

Plastigage

Propeller shaft The long hollow tube with universal joints at both ends that carries power from the transmission to the differential on front-engined rear wheel drive vehicles.

Proportioning valve A hydraulic control valve which limits the amount of pressure to the rear brakes during panic stops to prevent wheel lock-up.

R

Rack-and-pinion steering A steering system with a pinion gear on the end of the steering shaft that mates with a rack (think of a geared wheel opened up and laid flat). When the steering wheel is turned, the pinion turns, moving the rack to the left or right. This movement is transmitted through the track rods to the steering arms at the wheels.

Radiator A liquid-to-air heat transfer device designed to reduce the temperature of the coolant in an internal combustion engine cooling system.

Refrigerant Any substance used as a heat transfer agent in an air-conditioning system. R-12 has been the principle refrigerant for many years; recently, however, manufacturers have begun using R-134a, a non-CFC substance that is considered less harmful to the ozone in the upper atmosphere.

Rocker arm A lever arm that rocks on a shaft or pivots on a stud. In an overhead valve engine, the rocker arm converts the upward movement of the pushrod into a downward movement to open a valve.

Rotor In a distributor, the rotating device inside the cap that connects the centre electrode and the outer terminals as it turns, distributing the high voltage from the coil secondary winding to the proper spark plug. Also, that part of an alternator which rotates inside the stator. Also, the rotating assembly of a turbocharger, including the compressor wheel, shaft and turbine wheel.

Runout The amount of wobble (in-and-out movement) of a gear or wheel as it's rotated. The amount a shaft rotates "out-of-true." The out-of-round condition of a rotating part.

S

Sealant A liquid or paste used to prevent leakage at a joint. Sometimes used in conjunction with a gasket.

Sealed beam lamp An older headlight design which integrates the reflector, lens and filaments into a hermetically-sealed one-piece unit. When a filament burns out or the lens cracks, the entire unit is simply replaced.

Serpentine drivebelt A single, long, wide accessory drivebelt that's used on some newer vehicles to drive all the accessories, instead of a series of smaller, shorter belts. Serpentine drivebelts are usually tensioned by an automatic tensioner.

Serpentine drivebelt

Shim Thin spacer, commonly used to adjust the clearance or relative positions between two parts. For example, shims inserted into or under bucket tappets control valve clearances. Clearance is adjusted by changing the thickness of the shim.

Slide hammer A special puller that screws into or hooks onto a component such as a shaft or bearing; a heavy sliding handle on the shaft bottoms against the end of the shaft to knock the component free.

Sprocket A tooth or projection on the periphery of a wheel, shaped to engage with a chain or drivebelt. Commonly used to refer to the sprocket wheel itself.

Starter inhibitor switch On vehicles with an automatic transmission, a switch that prevents starting if the vehicle is not in Neutral or Park.

Strut See MacPherson strut.

T

Tappet A cylindrical component which transmits motion from the cam to the valve stem, either directly or via a pushrod and rocker arm. Also called a cam follower.

Thermostat A heat-controlled valve that regulates the flow of coolant between the cylinder block and the radiator, so maintaining optimum engine operating temperature. A thermostat is also used in some air cleaners in which the temperature is regulated.

Thrust bearing The bearing in the clutch assembly that is moved in to the release levers by clutch pedal action to disengage the clutch. Also referred to as a release bearing.

Timing belt A toothed belt which drives the camshaft. Serious engine damage may result if it breaks in service.

Timing chain A chain which drives the camshaft.

Toe-in The amount the front wheels are closer together at the front than at the rear. On rear wheel drive vehicles, a slight amount of toe-in is usually specified to keep the front wheels running parallel on the road by offsetting other forces that tend to spread the wheels apart.

Toe-out The amount the front wheels are closer together at the rear than at the front. On front wheel drive vehicles, a slight amount of toe-out is usually specified.

Tools For full information on choosing and using tools, refer to the *Haynes Automotive Tools Manual.*

Tracer A stripe of a second colour applied to a wire insulator to distinguish that wire from another one with the same colour insulator.

Tune-up A process of accurate and careful adjustments and parts replacement to obtain the best possible engine performance.

Turbocharger A centrifugal device, driven by exhaust gases, that pressurises the intake air. Normally used to increase the power output from a given engine displacement, but can also be used primarily to reduce exhaust emissions (as on VW's "Umwelt" Diesel engine).

U

Universal joint or U-joint A double-pivoted connection for transmitting power from a driving to a driven shaft through an angle. A U-joint consists of two Y-shaped yokes and a cross-shaped member called the spider.

V

Valve A device through which the flow of liquid, gas, vacuum, or loose material in bulk may be started, stopped, or regulated by a movable part that opens, shuts, or partially obstructs one or more ports or passageways. A valve is also the movable part of such a device.

Valve clearance The clearance between the valve tip (the end of the valve stem) and the rocker arm or tappet. The valve clearance is measured when the valve is closed.

Vernier caliper A precision measuring instrument that measures inside and outside dimensions. Not quite as accurate as a micrometer, but more convenient.

Viscosity The thickness of a liquid or its resistance to flow.

Volt A unit for expressing electrical "pressure" in a circuit. One volt that will produce a current of one ampere through a resistance of one ohm.

W

Welding Various processes used to join metal items by heating the areas to be joined to a molten state and fusing them together. For more information refer to the *Haynes Automotive Welding Manual.*

Wiring diagram A drawing portraying the components and wires in a vehicle's electrical system, using standardised symbols. For more information refer to the *Haynes Automotive Electrical and Electronic Systems Manual.*

Note: *References throughout this index are in the form* **"Chapter number" • "Page number"**. *So, for example, 2C•15 refers to page 15 of Chapter 2C.*

Note: *References throughout this index are in the form* **"Chapter number" • "Page number"**. *So, for example, 2C•15 refers to page 15 of Chapter 2C.*

Note: *References throughout this index are in the form* **"Chapter number" • "Page number"**. *So, for example, 2C•15 refers to page 15 of Chapter 2C.*

Haynes Manuals – The Complete **UK Car** List

Title	Book No.
ALFA ROMEO Alfasud/Sprint (74 - 88) up to F *	0292
Alfa Romeo Alfetta (73 – 87) up to E *	0531
AUDI 80, 90 & Coupe Petrol (79 – Nov 88) up to F	0605
Audi 80, 90 & Coupe Petrol (Oct 86 – 90) D to H	1491
Audi 100 & A6 Petrol & Diesel (May 91 – May 97) H to P	3504
Audi A3 Petrol & Diesel (96 – May 03) P to 03	4253
Audi A3 Petrol & Diesel (June 03 – Mar 08) 03 to 08	4884
Audi A4 Petrol & Diesel (95 – 00) M to X	3575
Audi A4 Petrol & Diesel (01 – 04) X to 54	4609
Audi A4 Petrol & Diesel (Jan 05 – Feb 08) 54 to 57	4885
AUSTIN A35 & A40 (56 – 67) up to F *	0118
Mini (59 – 69) up to H *	0527
Mini (69 – 01) up to X	0646
Austin Healey 100/6 & 3000 (56 – 68) up to G *	0049
BEDFORD/Vauxhall Rascal & Suzuki Supercarry (86 – Oct 94) C to M	3015
BMW 1-Series 4-cyl Petrol & Diesel (04 – Aug 11) 54 to 11	4918
BMW 316, 320 & 320i (4-cyl)(75 – Feb 83) up to Y *	0276
BMW 3- & 5- Series Petrol (81 – 91) up to J	1948
BMW 3-Series Petrol (Apr 91 – 99) H to V	3210
BMW 3-Series Petrol (Sept 98 – 06) S to 56	4067
BMW 3-Series Petrol & Diesel (05 – Sept 08) 54 to 58	4782
BMW 5-Series 6-cyl Petrol (April 96 – Aug 03) N to 03	4151
BMW 5-Series Diesel (Sept 03 – 10) 53 to 10	4901
BMW 1500, 1502, 1600, 1602, 2000 & 2002 (59 – 77) up to S *	0240
CHRYSLER PT Cruiser Petrol (00-09) W to 09	4058
CITROEN 2CV, Ami & Dyane (67 – 90) up to H	0196
Citroen AX Petrol & Diesel (87- 97) D to P	3014
Citroen Berlingo & Peugeot Partner Petrol & Diesel (96 – 10) P to 60	4281
Citroen C1 Petrol (05 – 11) 05 to 11	4922
Citroen C2 Petrol & Diesel (03 – 10) 53 to 60	5635
Citroen C3 Petrol & Diesel (02 – 09) 51 to 59	4890
Citroen C4 Petrol & Diesel (04 – 10) 54 to 60	5576
Citroen C5 Petrol & Diesel (01 – 08) Y to 08	4745
Citroen C15 Van Petrol & Diesel (89 – Oct 98) F to S	3509
Citroen CX Petrol (75 – 88) up to F	0528
Citroen Saxo Petrol & Diesel (96 – 04) N to 54	3506
Citroen Xantia Petrol & Diesel (93 – 01) K to Y	3082
Citroen XM Petrol & Diesel (89 – 00) G to X	3451
Citroen Xsara Petrol & Diesel (97 – Sept 00) R to W	3751
Citroen Xsara Picasso Petrol & Diesel (00 – 02) W to 52	3944
Citroen Xsara Picasso (Mar 04 – 08) 04 to 58	4784
Citroen ZX Diesel (91 – 98) J to S	1922
Citroen ZX Petrol (91 – 98) H to S	1881
FIAT 126 (73 – 87) up to E *	0305
Fiat 500 (57 – 73) up to M *	0090
Fiat 500 & Panda (04 – 12) 53 to 61	5558
Fiat Bravo & Brava Petrol (95 – 00) N to W	3572
Fiat Cinquecento (93 – 98) K to R	3501
Fiat Grande Punto, Punto Evo & Punto Petrol (06 – 15) 55 to 15	5956
Fiat Panda (81 – 95) up to M	0793
Fiat Punto Petrol & Diesel (94 – Oct 99) L to V	3251
Fiat Punto Petrol (Oct 99 – July 03) V to 03	4066
Fiat Punto Petrol (03 – 07) 03 to 07	4746
Fiat Punto Petrol (Oct 99 – 07) V to 07	5634
Fiat X1/9 (74 – 89) up to G *	0273
FORD Anglia (59 – 68) up to G *	0001
Ford Capri II (& III) 1.6 & 2.0 (74 – 87) up to E *	0283
Ford Capri II (& III) 2.8 & 3.0 V6 (74 – 87) up to E	1309
Ford C-Max Petrol & Diesel (03 – 10) 53 to 60	4900
Ford Escort Mk I 1100 & 1300 (68 – 74) up to N *	0171
Ford Escort Mk I Mexico, RS 1600 & RS 2000 (70 – 74) up to N *	0139
Ford Escort Mk II Mexico, RS 1800 & RS 2000 (75 – 80) up to W *	0735
Ford Escort (75 – Aug 80) up to V *	0280
Ford Escort Petrol (Sept 80 – Sept 90) up to H	0686
Ford Escort & Orion Petrol (Sept 90 – 00) H to X	1737
Ford Escort & Orion Diesel (Sept 90 – 00) H to X	4081
Ford Fiesta Petrol (Feb 89 – Oct 95) F to N	1595
Ford Fiesta Petrol & Diesel (Oct 95 – Mar 02) N to 02	3397
Ford Fiesta Petrol & Diesel (Apr 02 – 08) 02 to 58	4170
Ford Fiesta Petrol & Diesel (08 – 11) 58 to 11	4907
Ford Focus Petrol & Diesel (98 – 01) S to Y	3759
Ford Focus Petrol & Diesel (Oct 01 – 05) 51 to 05	4167
Ford Focus Petrol (05 – 11) 54 to 61	4785
Ford Focus Diesel (05 – 11) 54 to 61	4807
Ford Focus Petrol & Diesel (11 – 14) 60 to 14	5632
Ford Fusion Petrol & Diesel (02 – 11) 02 to 61	5566
Ford Galaxy Petrol & Diesel (95 – Aug 00) M to W	3984
Ford Galaxy Petrol & Diesel (00 – 06) X to 06	5556
Ford Granada Petrol (Sept 77 – Feb 85) up to B *	0481
Ford Ka (96 – 08) P to 58	5567
Ford Ka Petrol (09 – 14) 58 to 14	5637
Ford Mondeo Petrol (93 – Sept 00) K to X	1923
Ford Mondeo Petrol & Diesel (Oct 00 – Jul 03) X to 03	3990
Ford Mondeo Petrol & Diesel (July 03 – 07) 03 to 56	4619
Ford Mondeo Petrol & Diesel (Apr 07 – 12) 07 to 61	5548
Ford Mondeo Diesel (93 – Sept 00) L to X	3465
Ford Transit Connect Diesel (02 – 11) 02 to 11	4903
Ford Transit Diesel (Feb 86 – 99) C to T	3019
Ford Transit Diesel (00 – Oct 06) X to 56	4775
Ford Transit Diesel (Nov 06 – 13) 56 to 63	5629
Ford 1.6 & 1.8 litre Diesel Engine (84 – 96) A to N	1172
HILLMAN Imp (63 – 76) up to R *	0022
HONDA Civic (Feb 84 – Oct 87) A to E	1226
Honda Civic (Nov 91 – 96) J to N	3199
Honda Civic Petrol (Mar 95 – 00) M to X	4050
Honda Civic Petrol & Diesel (01 – 05) X to 55	4611
Honda CR-V Petrol & Diesel (02 – 06) 51 to 56	4747
Honda Jazz (02 to 08) 51 to 58	4735
JAGUAR E-Type (61 – 72) up to L *	0140
Jaguar Mk I & II, 240 & 340 (55 – 69) up to H *	0098
Jaguar XJ6, XJ & Sovereign, Daimler Sovereign (68 – Oct 86) up to D	0242
Jaguar XJ6 & Sovereign (Oct 86 – Sept 94) D to M	3261
Jaguar XJ12, XJS & Sovereign, Daimler Double Six (72 – 88) up to F	0478
Jaguar X Type Petrol & Diesel (01 – 10) V to 60	5631
JEEP Cherokee Petrol (93 – 96) K to N	1943
LAND ROVER 90, 110 & Defender Diesel (83 – 07) up to 56	3017
Land Rover Discovery Petrol & Diesel (89 – 98) G to S	3016
Land Rover Discovery Diesel (Nov 98 – Jul 04) S to 04	4606
Land Rover Discovery Diesel (Aug 04 – Apr 09) 04 to 09	5562
Land Rover Freelander Petrol & Diesel (97 – Sept 03) R to 53	3929
Land Rover Freelander (97 – Oct 06) R to 56	5571
Land Rover Freelander Diesel (Nov 06 – 14) 56 to 64	5636
Land Rover Series II, IIA & III 4-cyl Petrol (58 – 85) up to C	0314
Land Rover Series II, IIA & III Petrol & Diesel (58 – 85) up to C	5568
MAZDA 323 (Mar 81 – Oct 89) up to G	1608
Mazda 323 (Oct 89 – 98) G to R	3455
Mazda B1600, B1800 & B2000 Pick-up Petrol (72 – 88) up to F	0267
Mazda MX-5 (89 – 05) G to 05	5565
Mazda RX-7 (79 – 85) up to C *	0460
MERCEDES-BENZ 190, 190E & 190D Petrol & Diesel (83 – 93) A to L	3450
Mercedes-Benz 200D, 240D, 240TD, 300D & 300TD 123 Series Diesel (Oct 76 – 85) up to C	1114
Mercedes-Benz 250 & 280 (68 – 72) up to L *	0346
Mercedes-Benz 250 & 280 123 Series Petrol (Oct 76 – 84) up to B *	0677
Mercedes-Benz 124 Series Petrol & Diesel (85 – Aug 93) C to K	3253
Mercedes-Benz A-Class Petrol & Diesel (98 – 04) S to 54	4748
Mercedes-Benz C-Class Petrol & Diesel (93 – Aug 00) L to W	3511
Mercedes-Benz C-Class (00 – 07) X to 07	4780
Mercedes-Benz E-Class Diesel (Jun 02 – Feb 10) 02 to 59	5710
Mercedes-Benz Sprinter Diesel (95 – Apr 06) M to 06	4902
MGA (55 – 62)	0475
MGB (62 – 80) up to W	0111
MGB 1962 to 1980 (special edition) *	4894
MG Midget & Austin-Healey Sprite (58 – 80) up to W *	0265
MINI Petrol (July 01 – 06) Y to 56	4273
MINI Petrol & Diesel (Nov 06 – 13) 56 to 13	4904
MITSUBISHI Shogun & L200 Pick-ups Petrol (83 – 94) up to M	1944
MORRIS Minor 1000 (56 – 71) up to K	0024
NISSAN Almera Petrol (95 – Feb 00) N to V	4053
Nissan Almera & Tino Petrol (Feb 00 – 07) V to 56	4612
Nissan Micra (83 – Jan 93) up to K	0931
Nissan Micra (93 – 02) K to 52	3254
Nissan Micra Petrol (03 – Oct 10) 52 to 60	4734
Nissan Primera Petrol (90 - Aug 99) H to T	1851
Nissan Qashqai Petrol & Diesel (07 – 12) 56 to 62	5610
OPEL Ascona & Manta (B-Series) (Sept 75 – 88) up to F *	0316
Opel Ascona Petrol (81 – 88)	3215
Opel Ascona Petrol (Oct 91 – Feb 98)	3156
Opel Corsa Petrol (83 – Mar 93)	3160
Opel Corsa Petrol (Mar 93 – 97)	3159
Opel Kadett Petrol (Oct 84 – Oct 91)	3196
Opel Omega & Senator Petrol (Nov 86 – 94)	3157
Opel Vectra Petrol (Oct 88 – Oct 95)	3158
PEUGEOT 106 Petrol & Diesel (91 – 04) J to 53	1882
Peugeot 107 Petrol (05 – 11) 05 to 11	4923
Peugeot 205 Petrol (83 – 97) A to P	0932

* Classic reprint

Title	Book No.
Peugeot 206 Petrol & Diesel (98 – 01) S to X	**3757**
Peugeot 206 Petrol & Diesel (02 – 09) 51 to 59	**4613**
Peugeot 207 Petrol & Diesel (06 – July 09) 06 to 09	**4787**
Peugeot 306 Petrol & Diesel (93 – 02) K to 02	**3073**
Peugeot 307 Petrol & Diesel (01 – 08) Y to 58	**4147**
Peugeot 308 Petrol & Diesel (07 – 12) 07 to 12	**5561**
Peugeot 405 Diesel (88 – 97) E to P	**3198**
Peugeot 406 Petrol & Diesel (96 – Mar 99) N to T	**3394**
Peugeot 406 Petrol & Diesel (Mar 99 – 02) T to 52	**3982**
Peugeot 407 Diesel (04 -11) 53 to 11	**5550**
PORSCHE 911 (65 – 85) up to C	**0264**
Porsche 924 & 924 Turbo (76 – 85) up to C	**0397**
RANGE ROVER V8 Petrol (70 – Oct 92) up to K	**0606**
RELIANT Robin & Kitten (73 – 83) up to A *	**0436**
RENAULT 4 (61 – 86) up to D *	**0072**
Renault 5 Petrol (Feb 85 – 96) B to N	**1219**
Renault 19 Petrol (89 – 96) F to N	**1646**
Renault Clio Petrol (91 – May 98) H to R	**1853**
Renault Clio Petrol & Diesel (May 98 – May 01) R to Y	**3906**
Renault Clio Petrol & Diesel (June 01 – 05) Y to 55	**4168**
Renault Clio Petrol & Diesel (Oct 05 – May 09) 55 to 09	**4788**
Renault Espace Petrol & Diesel (85 – 96) C to N	**3197**
Renault Laguna Petrol & Diesel (94 – 00) L to W	**3252**
Renault Laguna Petrol & Diesel (Feb 01 – May 07) X to 07	**4283**
Renault Megane & Scenic Petrol & Diesel (96 – 99) N to T	**3395**
Renault Megane & Scenic Petrol & Diesel (Apr 99 – 02) T to 52	**3916**
Renault Megane Petrol & Diesel (Oct 02 – 08) 52 to 58	**4284**
Renault Megane Petrol & Diesel (Oct 08 – 14) 58 to 64	**5955**
Renault Scenic Petrol & Diesel (Sept 03 – 06) 53 to 06	**4297**
Renault Trafic Diesel (01 – 11) Y to 11	**5551**
ROVER 216 & 416 Petrol (89 – 96) G to N	**1830**
Rover 211, 214, 216, 218 & 220 Petrol & Diesel (Dec 95 – 99) N to V	**3399**
Rover 25 & MG ZR Petrol & Diesel (Oct 99 – 06) V to 06	**4145**
Rover 414, 416 & 420 Petrol & Diesel (May 95 – 99) M to V	**3453**
Rover 45 / MG ZS Petrol & Diesel (99 – 05) V to 55	**4384**
Rover 618, 620 & 623 Petrol (93 – 97) K to P	**3257**
Rover 75 / MG ZT Petrol & Diesel (99 – 06) S to 06	**4292**
Rover 820, 825 & 827 Petrol (86 – 95) D to N	**1380**
Rover 3500 (76 – 87) up to E *	**0365**
SAAB 95 & 96 (66 – 76) up to R *	**0198**
Saab 90, 99 & 900 (79 – Oct 93) up to L	**0765**
Saab 900 (Oct 93 – 98) L to R	**3512**
Saab 9000 4-cyl (85 – 98) C to S	**1686**
Saab 9-3 Petrol & Diesel (98 – Aug 02) R to 02	**4614**
Saab 9-3 Petrol & Diesel (92 – 07) 52 to 57	**4749**
Saab 9-3 Petrol & Diesel (07-on) 57 on	**5569**
Saab 9-5 4-cyl Petrol (97 – 05) R to 55	**4156**
Saab 9-5 (Sep 05 – Jun 10) 55 to 10	**4891**
SEAT Ibiza & Cordoba Petrol & Diesel (Oct 93 – Oct 99) L to V	**3571**
Seat Ibiza & Malaga Petrol (85 – 92) B to K	**1609**
Seat Ibiza Petrol & Diesel (May 02 – Apr 08) 02 to 08	**4889**
SKODA Fabia Petrol & Diesel (00 – 06) W to 06	**4376**

Title	Book No.
Skoda Felicia Petrol & Diesel (95 – 01) M to X	**3505**
Skoda Octavia Petrol (98 – April 04) R to 04	**4285**
Skoda Octavia Diesel (May 04 – 12) 04 to 61	**5549**
SUBARU 1600 & 1800 (Nov 79 – 90) up to H *	**0995**
SUNBEAM Alpine, Rapier & H120 (68 – 74) up to N *	**0051**
SUZUKI SJ Series, Samurai & Vitara 4-cyl Petrol (82 – 97) up to P	**1942**
Suzuki Supercarry & Bedford/Vauxhall Rascal (86 – Oct 94) C to M	**3015**
TOYOTA Avensis Petrol (98 – Jan 03) R to 52	**4264**
Toyota Aygo Petrol (05 – 11) 05 to 11	**4921**
Toyota Carina E Petrol (May 92 – 97) J to P	**3256**
Toyota Corolla (Sept 83 – Sept 87) A to E	**1024**
Toyota Corolla (Sept 87 – Aug 92) E to K	**1683**
Toyota Corolla Petrol (Aug 92 – 97) K to P	**3259**
Toyota Corolla Petrol (July 97 0 Feb 02) P to 51	**4286**
Toyota Corolla Petrol & Diesel (02 – Jan 07) 51 to 56	**4791**
Toyota Hi-Ace & Hi-Lux Petrol (69 – Oct 83) up to A	**0304**
Toyota RAV4 Petrol & Diesel (94 – 06) L to 55	**4750**
Toyota Yaris Petrol (99 – 05) T to 05	**4265**
TRIUMPH GT6 & Vitesse (62 0 74) up to N *	**0112**
Triumph Herald (59 – 71) up to K *	**0010**
Triumph Spitfire (62 – 81) up to X	**0113**
Triumph Stag (70 – 78) up to T *	**0441**
Triumph TR2, TR3, TR3A, TR4 & TR4A (52 – 67) up to F *	**0028**
Triumph TR5 & TR6 (67 – 75) up to P *	**0031**
Triumph TR7 (75 – 82) up to Y *	**0322**
VAUXHALL Astra Petrol (Oct 91 – Feb 98) J to R	**1832**
Vauxhall/Opel Astra & Zafira Petrol (Feb 98 – Apr 04) R to 04	**3758**
Vauxhall/Opel Astra & Zafira Diesel (Feb 98 – Apr 04) R to 04	**3797**
Vauxhall/Opel Astra Petrol (04 – 08)	**4732**
Vauxhall/Opel Astra Diesel (04 – 08)	**4733**
Vauxhall/Opel Astra Petrol & Diesel (Dec 09 – 13) 59 to 13	**5578**
Vauxhall/Opel Calibra (90 – 98) G to S	**3502**
Vauxhall Cavalier Petrol (Oct 88 0 95) F to N	**1570**
Vauxhall/Opel Corsa Diesel (Mar 93 – Oct 00) K to X	**4087**
Vauxhall Corsa Petrol (Mar 93 – 97) K to R	**1985**
Vauxhall/Opel Corsa Petrol (Apr 97 – Oct 00) P to X	**3921**
Vauxhall/Opel Corsa Petrol & Diesel (Oct 03 – Aug 06) 53 to 06	**4617**
Vauxhall/Opel Corsa Petrol & Diesel (Sept 06 – 10) 56 to 10	**4886**
Vauxhall/Opel Corsa Petrol & Diesel (00 – Aug 06) X to 06	**5577**
Vauxhall/Opel Frontera Petrol & Diesel (91 – Sept 98) J to S	**3454**
Vauxhall/Opel Insignia Petrol & Diesel (08 – 12) 08 to 61	**5563**
Vauxhall/Opel Meriva Petrol & Diesel (03 – May 10) 03 to 10	**4893**
Vauxhall/Opel Omega Petrol (94 – 99) L to T	**3510**
Vauxhall/Opel Vectra Petrol & Diesel (95 – Feb 99) N to S	**3396**
Vauxhall/Opel Vectra Petrol & Diesel (Mar 99 – May 02) T to 02	**3930**
Vauxhall/Opel Vectra Petrol & Diesel (June 02 – Sept 05) 02 to 55	**4618**

Title	Book No.
Vauxhall/Opel Vectra Petrol & Diesel (Oct 05 – Oct 08) 55 to 58	**4887**
Vauxhall/Opel Vivaro Diesel (01 – 11) Y to 11	**5552**
Vauxhall/Opel Zafira Petrol & Diesel (05 -09) 05 to 09	**4792**
Vauxhall/Opel 1.5, 1.6 & 1.7 litre Diesel Engine (82 – 96) up to N	**1222**
VW Beetle 1200 (54 – 77) up to S	**0036**
VW Beetle 1300 & 1500 (65 – 75) up to P	**0039**
VW 1302 & 1302S (70 – 72) up to L *	**0110**
VW Beetle 1303, 1303S & GT (72 – 75) up to P	**0159**
VW Beetle Petrol & Diesel (Apr 99 – 07) T to 57	**3798**
VW Golf & Jetta Mk 1 Petrol 1.1 & 1.3 (74 – 84) up to A	**0716**
VW Golf, Jetta & Scirocco Mk 1 Petrol 1.5, 1.6 & 1.8 (74 – 84) up to A	**0726**
VW Golf & Jetta Mk 1 Diesel (78 – 84) up to A	**0451**
VW Golf & Jetta Mk 2 Petrol (Mar 84 – Feb 92) A to J	**1081**
VW Golf & Vento Petrol & Diesel (Feb 92 – Mar 98) J to R	**3097**
VW Golf & Bora Petrol & Diesel (Apr 98 – 00) R to X	**3727**
VW Golf & Bora 4-cyl Petrol & Diesel (01 – 03) X to 53	**4169**
VW Golf & Jetta Petrol & Diesel (04 – 09) 53 to 09	**4610**
VW Golf Petrol & Diesel (09 – 12) 58 to 62	**5633**
VW LT Petrol Vans & Light Trucks (76 – 87) up to E	**0637**
VW Passat 4-cyl Petrol & Diesel (May 88 – 96) E to P	**3498**
VW Passat 4-cyl Petrol & Diesel (Dec 96 – Nov 00) P to X	**3917**
VW Passat Petrol & Diesel (Dec 00 – May 05) X to 05	**4279**
VW Passat Diesel (June 05 – 10) 05 to 60	**4888**
VW Polo Petrol (Nov 90 – Aug 94) H to L	**3245**
VW Polo Hatchback Petrol & Diesel (94 – 99) M to S	**3500**
VW Polo Hatchback Petrol (00 – Jan 02) V to 51	**4150**
VW Polo Petrol & Diesel (02 – Sep 09) 51 to 59	**4608**
VW Polo Petrol & Diesel (Oct 09 – Jul 14 (59 to 14)	**5638**
VW Transporter 1600 (68 – 79) up to V	**0082**
VW Transporter 1700, 1800 & 2000 (72 – 79) up to V *	**0226**
VW Transporter (air cooled) Petrol (79 – 82) up to Y *	**0638**
VW Transporter (water cooled) Petrol (82 – 90) up to H	**3452**
VW T4 Transporter Diesel (90 – 03) H to 03	**5711**
VW T5 Transporter Diesel (July 03 – 14) 03 to 64	**5743**
VW Type 3 (63 – 73) up to M *	**0084**
VOLVO 120 & 130 Series (& P1800) (61 – 73) up to M *	**0203**
Volvo 142, 144 & 145 (66 – 74) up to N *	**0129**
Volvo 240 Series Petrol (74 – 93) up to K	**0270**
Volvo 440, 460 & 480 Petrol (87 – 97) D to P	**1691**
Volvo 740 & 760 Petrol (82 – 91) up to J	**1258**
Volvo 850 Petrol (92 – 96) J to P	**3260**
Volvo 940 Petrol (90 – 98) H to R	**3249**
Volvo S40 & V40 Petrol (96 – Mar 04) N to 04	**3569**
Volvo S40 & V50 Petrol & Diesel (Mar 04 – Jun 07) 04 to 07	**4731**
Volvo S40 & V50 Diesel (July 07 - 13) 07 to 13	**5684**
Volvo S60 Petrol & Diesel (01 – 08) X to 09	**4793**
Volvo S70, V70 & C70 Petrol (96 – 99) P to V	**3573**
Volvo V70 / S80 Petrol & Diesel (98 – 07) S to 07	**4263**
Volvo V70 Diesel (June 07 – 12) 07 to 61	**5557**
Volvo XC60 / 90 Diesel (03 – 12) 52 to 62	**5630**

* Classic reprint